WEBSTER'S DICTIONARY

Edited by
Liz Kauffman

Proofread by
Marsha Tischner

This book was not published by the original publishers of the Webster's Dictionary, or by any of their successors.

Staff

Vicki Nichols
Kathleen Flickinger
Cindy Carter
Marsha Tischner

Rules of Spelling

(1) The most common way to form the plural of a noun is to add an s (Example: girl, girls; town, towns; hall, halls).

(2) The plural of nouns which end in y following a consonant are formed by dropping the y and adding ies (Example: country, countries; baby, babies; family, families).

(3) The plural of nouns which end in y following a vowel are formed by adding an s (Example: toy, toys; boy, boys; attorney, attorneys).

In this quick reference dictionary, a double dash (--) indicates a hyphenated word, and a single dash (-) indicates syllablization.

Each entry is in bold type followed by the part of speech in italics. Sub-entries are indicated in bold type after the main definition.

Abbreviations Used In This Dictionary

abbr.	abbreviation	*L.*	Latin
adj.	adjective	*Mech.*	Mechanics
adv.	adverb	*Med.*	Medicine
Aeron.	Aeronautics	*Meteor.*	Meteorology
Aeros.	Aerospace	*Milit.*	Military
archit.	architecture	*Mus.*	Music
Astron.	Astronomy	*Myth*	Mythology
Biochem.	Biochemist	*Naut.*	Nautical
Biol.	Biology	*n.*	noun
Bot.	Botany	*Opt.*	Optics
Brit.	British	*pathol.*	Pathology
Can.	Canada	*photog.*	Photography
Chem.	Chemistry	*physiol.*	Physiology
Elect.	Electricity	*pl.*	plural
Econ.	Economist	*poet.*	Poetry
Fr.	French	*pref.*	prefix
Geol.	Geology	*pron.*	pronoun
Govt.	Government	*psychol.*	Psychologist
Gram.	Grammar	*Rom.*	Roman
Gr.	Greek	*Scot.*	Scotch
Theol.	Theology	*suff.*	suffix
Interj.	Interjection	*surg.*	surgery

A, a The first letter of the English alphabet; the highest grade, meaning excellent or best

aah *v.* to exclaim in joy

aard-vark *n.*

a burrowing African animal which resembles the anteater and feeds on ants and termites

aard-wolf *n.* hyena-like mammal feeding chiefly on carrion and insects

ab-a-ca *n.* a plant from the Philippines whose leafstalks are the source of Manila hemp.

a-back *adv.* unexpectedly; by surprise; startled; confused

abac-te-ri-al *adj.* not being caused by bacteria

ab-a-cus *n.* a frame holding parallel rods with beads used for manual computation **abacuses** n., **abaci** n.

a-baft *adv.* toward the stern of a ship

ab-a-lo-ne *n.* a member of the genus of gastropod mollusks that will cling to rocks and have a shell which is flat and lined with mother of pearl.

a-ban-don *v.* to yield utterly; to desert; to forsake; to withdraw protection, support, or help **abandonment** *n.*, **abandoner** n.

a-ban-don-ed *adj.* to be deserted; to be foresaken

a-base *v.* to lower in rank, position, prestige, or estimation; to cast down, to humble **abasement** *n.*

a-bash *v.* embarrass **abashment** n.

a-bate *v.* reduce in quantity, or value, to deduct; to make less **abatement** n., **abater** n.

ab-ba-cy *n.* a jurisdiction or an office of an abbot

ab-ba-tial *adj.* to be pertaining or related to an abbey or abbot.

ab-be *n.* a French title given to a priest.

ab-bess *n.* the femal superior of an abbey of nuns and possessing the same authority as an abbot

ab-bey *n.* monastery **abbeys** pl.

ab-bot *n.* the superior of the monastery

ab-bre-vi-ate *v.* make briefer; to shorten to reduce to a briefer form, as a word or phrase abbreviated, **abbreviating** *v.*

ab-bre-vi-a-tion *n.* shortened form of a word or phrase

ABC soil *n.* a type of soil where there are three well-defined layers.

ab-do-men *n.* the part of the human body that lies between the thorax and the pelvis and contains the stomach, spleen, liver, kidneys, bladder, pancreas, and intestines **abdominal adj.**

ab-duct *v.* carry away wrongfully by force or fraud; to kidnap; to draw aside, or away; to move apart **abductor n.**

a-beam *adv. or adj.* right angles to the keel of a ship

ab-er-rant *adj.* straying from the right course; wandering; varying from **aberrance n., aberrantly adv.**

a-bet *v.* incite **abetment n., abettor n.**

ab-hor *v.* dislike intensely **abhorrer n.**

a-bide *v.* to tolerate; to remain; to last; to conform to **abider n., abided v.**

a-bil-i-ty *n.* state of being able; competence; **-ties** *n., pl.*

ab-ject *adj.* sunk to a low condition **abjection** *n.*, **abjectly adv., -ness n.**

ab-jure *v.* renounce solemnly **abjured v.**

a-blaze *adv.* on fire, glowing

a-ble *adj.* having sufficient ability

a-ble--bodied *adj.* having a strong body **ablebodies adj.**

ab-lu-tion *n.* washing of the body as a part of religious rites **ablutionary adj.**

ab-ne-gate *v.* deny; to refuse or renounce **abnegator n., abnegation n.**

ab-nor-mal *adj.* not normal **-ity** *n.*

a-board *adv.* on board a ship, onto

a-bode *n.* temporary dwelling place

a-bol-ish *v.* put an end to, destroy

a-bom-i-na-ble *adj.* detestable; loathsome **abominably adv.**

a-bort *v.* to terminate or cause to terminate an operation or procedure before completion **aborter n.**

a-bor-tion *n.* induced termination of pregnancy before the fetus can survive **abortionist n.**

a-bound *v.* to have plenty

a-bout *adv.* approximately, all sides

a-bove *adv.* higher or greater than

ab-ra-ca-dab-ra *n.* a word believed to have magical powers, used in casting spells; nonsense, foolish talk

a-brade *v.* to wear or rub off **abrading v.**

a-breast *adv. or adj.* side by side

a-bridge *v.* to make smaller, fewer or shorter while maintaining essential contents **abridger n.**

a-broad *adv.* widely, beyond

ab-ro-gate *v.* put an end to **-ed v.**

ab-rupt *adj.* happening suddenly

ab-scess *n.* infected sore containing pus **abscessed adj.**

ab-scind *v.* to sever; to separate
ab-scond *v.* to flee from justice
ab-sent *adj.* not present absently adv.
ab-sent--mind-ed *adj.* always forgetting things; not paying attention
ab-so-lute *adj.* unconditional
ab-solve *v.* to set free from guilt
ab-sorb *v.* to take in absorbable adj.
ab-stain *v.* refrain from doing something abstainer n.
ab-ste-mi-ous *adj.* showing moderation abstemiously adv.
ab-stract *v.* summarize abstractable adj.
ab-struse *adj.* difficult to understand abstruseness n., abstrusely adv.
ab-surd *adj.* clearly unreasonable absurdness n., absurdly adv.
a-bun-dance *n.* ample supply; plenty
a-buse *v.* use in an improper or wrong way abusable adj., abuser n.
a-but *v.* to border abutted, abutting v.
a-but-ment *n.* bridge support
a-bys-mal *adj.* extension downward, inward, or inward abysmally *adv.*
a-byss *n.* deep crack or gap in the earth, great space, bottomless
a-ca-cia *n.* thorny tree or shrub
a-cad-e-my *n.* private school
acap-pel-la *adj.* singing without instrumental accompaniment
ac-cede *v.* to consent -ed v., -ing v.
ac-cel-er-ate *v.* work faster; to increase, gain acceleratingly adv.
ac-cent *n.* emphasize accentless adj.
ac-cept *v.* take what is given
ac-cept-able *adj.* satisfactory; proper, capable of being accepted
ac-cep-tance *n.* approval, being accepted or acceptable
ac-cess *n.* admission, entrance
ac-ces-si-ble *adj.* easy access or approach accessibleness n., accessibly adv.
ac-ces-sory *n.* -ies contributing
ac-ci-dent *n.* unexpected happening accidental adj., accidentally adv.
ac-claim *v.* greet with strong approval, praise acclaimer n.
ac-cli-mate *v.* become accustomed
ac-co-lade *n.* award; praise
ac-com-mo-date *v.* to give room or lodging; to adjust accommodating adj.
ac-com-pa-ni-ment *n.* something that goes well with another, unit
ac-com-pa-nist *n.* someone who plays a musical accompaniment
ac-com-pa-ny *v.* go along with
ac-com-plice *n.* companion in crime
ac-com-plish *v.* to do accomplishment *n.*
ac-cord *n.* harmony accordance *n.*
ac-cord-ing-ly *adv.* in a proper way

ac-cor-di-on *n.* musical instrument
ac-cost *v.* approach in an unfriendly manner, speak in a challenging or aggressive manner
ac-count *n.* description; record accountable *adj.*
ac-count-ing *n.* system of keeping business records or accounts
ac-cred-it *v.* give official power
ac-crete *v.* grow together
ac-crue *v.* to increase at certain times accruable adj., accrued v.
ac-cu-mu-late *v.* collect or gather
ac-cu-rate *adj.* without mistakes; careful and exact accurately adv.
ac-curs-ed *adj.* unpleasant -ness n.
ac-cu-sa-tion *n.* charge of guilty
ac-cuse *v.* find fault with; charge someone with breaking the law
ac-custom *v.* familiarize by habit accustomed adj., accustomation n.
ace *n.* playing card marked with one spot; score in tennis
ac-e-tate *n.* salt, acetic acid
a-ce-tic acid *n.* main ingredient for production of vinegar
a-cet-y-lene *n.* inflammable gas
ache *v.* have a dull, steady pain
a-chieve *v.* to succeed achievement *n.*

A-chil-les ten-don *n.*

the tendon that connects the heelbone and calf muscles
ac-id *n.* a chemical compound -ity *n.,* acidness n., acidly adv.
acid rock *n.* song lyrics suggesting drug related experiences
a-cid-u-late *v.* to become or make acid acidulated v., acidulating v.
ack-ack *n.* anti-aircraft fire or gun
ac-know-ledge *v.* to admit the truth acknowledgement n., -able adj.
ac-me *n.* the highest point
ac-ne *n.* skin disease; pimples
ac-o-lyte *n.* altar boy, assistant
ac-o-nite *n.* a poisonous plant
a-corn *n.* nut of the oak tree
a-cous-tic *adj.* having to do with sound acoustical adj., acoustically adv.
a-cous-tics *n.* study of sound
ac-quaint *v.* to make familiar acquaintance n., acquaintanceship
ac-qui-esce *v.* agree without arguing acquiesced v., acquiescing v.
ac-quire *v.* become the owner acquirement n., acquired, v.
acquired immunity *n.* immunity against

disease

ac-qui-si-tion *n.* something acquired

ac-quit *v.* rule not guilty acquital *n.*

a-cre *n.* a measurement of land, great quantity acreage *n.*

ac-rid *adj.* a sharp, bitter taste acridity *n.*, acridness n., -ly adv.

ac-ri-mo-ni-ous *adj.* bitter in speech or manner acrimoniousness n.

ac-ro-bat *n.* one skilled in gymnastic feats acrobatic *adj.*, -lly adv.

ac-ro-pho-bi-a *n.* unusual fear of being at great heights

a-cross *prep.* side to side, opposites

acrylic fiber *n.* synthetic textile fiber

act *n.* a thing done; a deed -ing *adj.*

ac-tion *n.* process of doing or acting, act of will, bringing about

ac-ti-vate *v.* put into action activation *n.*, activated v., -ing v.

ac-tive *adj.* full of action; busy, quick actively adv., activeness n.

ac-tiv-ism *n.* action to affect changes in government activistic adj.

act of God *n.* uncontrollable happening caused by nature

ac-tor *n.* performer actorish adj.

ac-tress *n.* female actor -es n.

ac-tu-al *adj.* existing in fact; real

ac-tu-ate *v.* put into mechanical motion or action actuation *n.*

a-cute *adj.* sharp and quick acutely adv., acuteness n., -er adj.

ad-age *n.* proverb, metaphorical

ad-a-mant *adj.* standing firm

a-dapt *v.* to adjust to new conditions adaption, adaptness *n.*

add *v.* join together addable adj.

ad-der *n.*

poisonous snake

ad-dict *n.* a person with a strong habit with a drug addiction *n.*

ad-di-tion *n.* adding of numbers to find the total additional *adj.*

ad-dle *v.* become or make confused

ad-dress *v.* to speak to; place where mail or goods can be delivered

ad-duce *v.* offer as proof or give as a reason adducer n., -ed v., -ing v.

ad-e-noids *n.* lymphoid tissue growths which obstructs breathing, relating to the adenoids

a-dept *adj.* highly skilled adeptly *adv.*, adeptness *n.*

ad-e-quate *adj.* sufficient -ly adv.

ad-here *v.* to stick and not come loose adhered v., adhering v.

ad-her-ent *n.* one who follows a leader adherently adv.

ad-he-sive *adj.* having a sticky surface adhesively adv., adhesiveness n.

a-dieu *n.* good-by adieus, adieux pl.

ad-in-ter-im *adj.* in the meantime

ad-ja-cent *adj.* close to or nearby

ad-jec-tive *n.* word used to describe a noun or pronoun adjectively adv.

ad-join *v.* be next to, attach or add

ad-journ *v.* close a meeting or session, to relocate adjournment *n.*

ad-judge *v.* decide by judicial procedure adjudged v., adjudging v.

ad-jure *v.* ask urgently adjuration *n.*

adjust *v.* to arrange or change adjustability *n.*, adjustable adj.

ad-just-er *n.* person who estimates damages for settlement adjustor n.

ad-lib *v.* to improvise adlibbed v.

ad-man *n.* person working in the business of advertising

ad-min-is-ter *v.* direct or manage

ad-min-is-tra-tion *n.* people who manage a school, or company administrator n., -al adj., -ist n.

ad-mi-ra-ble *adj.* worthy of being admired admirableness adv.

ad-mi-ral *n.* highest ranking naval officer, is above a vice-admiral

ad-mire *v.* regard with wonder.

ad-mis-si-ble *adj.* capable of being admitted admissibility n.

ad-mit *v.* to confess; give the right to enter or access admittance *n.*

ad-mix-ture *n.* blend; mingling

ad-mon-ish *v.* to give a person advice admonishtion *n.* admonishingly adv.

a-do *n.* fuss, excitement

a-do-be *n.* building material made from clay and straw

ad-o-les-cence *n.* between childhood and adulthood, growing up

a-dopt *v.* legally take into one's family adoption n., -ability n.

a-dor-a-ble *adj.* very likable -ness n.

a-dore *v.* to love greatly; to worship

a-dorn *v.* to add splendor or beauty, to decorate adornment *n.*

a-drift *adv.* floating freely; having no purpose, without guidance

a-droit *adj.* skillful and clever, with the hands adroitly adv.

ad-ulate *v.* give greater praise adulation *n.*, adulator n., -ed v.

a-dult *n.* person who is fully grown adulthood n., adultness n., -ly adv.

a-dul-ter-ate *v.* to make impure

a-dul-tery *n.* voluntary sexual intercourse with someone other than a spouse

ad-vance *v.* to move ahead -ment *n.*

ad-vanced *adj.* ahead in time

ad-van-tage *n.* better chance advantageous *adj.*

ad-vent *n.* the four Sundays before Christmas as a season of prayer

ad-ven-ture *n.* an exciting experience adventured v., adventuring v.

ad-verb *n.* word used to describe a verb or adjective adverbial *adj.*

ad-verse *adj.* opposed; against someone or something, opposite

ad-ver-si-ty *n.* bad luck or misfortune, a condition of suffering

ad-ver-tise *v.* draw public attention to a product advertiser *n.*

ad-vice *n.* opinion on a course of action, recommendation

ad-vis-ed-ly *adv.* deliberately

ad-vise-ment *n.* careful thought

ad-viser *n.* person who gives an opinion, one who gives advice

advocate *v.* write or speak in favor of advocated v., advocating n.

aer-ate *v.* to purify, to supply

aer-i-al *adj.* antenna for television or radio aerially adv.

aer-i-al-ist *n.* aerial acrobat

aer-o-bics *n.* strenuous exercise for the heart aerobically adv.

aer-o-nau-tics *pl., n.* science of designing aircraft aeronautical adj.

aer-o-sol *n.* liquid substance under pressurized conditions

aes-thet-ic *adj.* having a love for or judgements concerning beauty

a-far *adv.* far away, great distance

af-fa-ble *adj.* good natured; friendly

af-fair *n.* an event or happening

af-fect *v.* to move emotionally affecting adj., affectability n.

af-fec-tion *n.* fond feeling for another affectionless adj.

af-fec-tion-ate *adj.* loving and gentle affectionately adv.

af-fi-da-vit *n.* sworn written statement, has made an oath

af-fil-i-ate *v.* join or associate with common ownership affiliation n.

af-fin-i-ty *n.* natural attraction or liking, relationship by marriage

af-firm *v.* to declare positively affirmative n., affirmable adj.

af-fix *n.* to attach; to add at the end

af-flict *v.* a persistent cause of suffering or pain affliction n.

af-flu-ence *n.* wealth; abundance

af-ford *v.* be able to provide

af-fray *n.* noisy fight

af-front *v.* to confront

af-ghan *n.* a knitted or crocheted blanket of colored wool

a-fire *adv.* burning, on fire

a-float *adv.* floating on water

a-flut-ter *adj.* nervously excited

a-foot *adj.* walking, on foot

a-fore-men-tioned *adj.* mentioned before, previously

a-foul *adv.* tangled, in conflict with

a-fraid *adj.* filled with fear; reluctant, unwanting of a situation

a-fresh *adj.* to something again

aft *adv.* toward the rear of a ship

af-ter *adv. prep.* following

af-ter-math *n.* consequence

af-ter-thought *n.* idea occurring later, not thought of originally

a-gain *adv.* once more

a-gainst *prep.* in exchange for

a-gape *adv.* open-mouthed, wide

ag-ate *n.* type of quartz

age *n.* length of time a person has lived aged v., aging v.

aged *adj.* grown or become old

age-less *adj.* existing forever

a-gen-cy *n.* business that acts for others agencies n.

a-gen-da *n.* list of things to be done

a-gent *n.* one who acts as the representative of another

ag-glom-er-ate *v.* to collect

ag-gran-dize *n.* to extend, to make greater aggrandizement n.

ag-gra-vate *v.* to annoy, bothersome

ag-gre-gate *adj.* to gather together

ag-gres-sion *n.* hostile action

ag-gres-sive *adj.* pushy; offensive

a-ghast *adj.* appalled, amazement

ag-ile *adj.* ability to move easily

ag-i-tate *v.* to stir or move with violence agitation, agitator n.

a-gleam *adj.* gleaming, reflecting

ag-nos-tic *n.* disbeliever in God

a-go *adj. & adv.* in the past

a-gog *adj.* excited, interest

ag-o-nize *v.* afflict with great anguish agonized, agonizing adj.

ag-o-ny *n., pl.* -nies mental distress

a-gree *v.* to give consent agreed n. agreeable adj., agreeness n.

a-gree-ment *n.* harmony

ag-ri-cul-ture *n.* raising of livestock and crops, cultivation of soil

a-ground *adv. & adj.* stranded; beached, on or onto a shore

a-head *adv.* in advance

a-hoy *interj.* nautical greeting

aid *v.* to give help

AIDS *n.* Acquired Immune Deficiency Syndrome

ail *v.* to feel sick, pain

aim *v.* to direct a weapon; to direct purpose aimless adj., aimlessness n.

air *n.* nitrogen and oxygen mixture; a breeze airlessness n.

air conditioner *n.* equipment to control temperature indoors

air-craft *n.* a machine that flies

air-field *n.* paved runways at an airport airfields n.

air-flow *n.*

the motion of air around a body as relative to the surface of a body imersed in it

air-mail & air mail *n.* mail sent via air

air-port *n.* airplane terminal

air raid *n.* bombing attack

air-ship *n.* dirigible; lighter-than-air aircraft having propulsion

aisle *n.* passageway between rows of seats

a-jar *adv. & adj.* partially opened

a-kin *adj.* related, as in a family

al-a-bas-ter *n.* white, fine-grained gypsum alabastrine adj.

a-lac-ri-ty *n.* readiness; eagerness

a la mode *n.* pie served with ice cream, fashionable

a-larm *n.* a warning of danger; bell or buzzer of a clock alarming adv.

a-las *interj.* expressive of anxiety

a-late *or* alated *adj.* having wings

alb *n.* white robe worn by the clergy

al-ba-core *n.* large marine fish

al-ba-tross *n.*

large sea bird

al-bi-no *n.* person with abnormal whiteness of the skin and hair

al-bum *n.* a book for photographs, etc, for making a collection

al-bu-men *n.* white of an egg

al-caz-ar *n.* a spanish fortress or palace

al-co-hol *n.* intoxicating liquor

al-co-hol-ism *n.* a habit or addiction, continuous use of a drug

al-cove *n.* partly enclosed extension of a room, an arched opening

ale *n.* beverage similar to beer

a-lert *adj.* vigilant; watchful alertly adv., alertness n.

al-fal-fa *n.* plant grown for forage

al-fres-co *adv. & adj.* outside

al-ge-bra *n.* form of math

a-li-as *n., pl.* aliases assumed name

al-i-bi *n.* form of defense

a-li-en *adj.* owing allegiance to a country, differing in nature

a-light *v.* to dismount; to come down alightment n., alighting v.

a-lign *v.* to arrange in a line

a-like *adj.* similar; having close resemblance alikeness n.

al-i-mo-ny *n.* court ordered allowance for support

a-live *adj.* having life

al-ka-loid *n.* nitrogen containing organic bases obtained from plants

all *adj.* being a whole amount

al-lay *v.* to calm; to pacify -er n.

al-lege *v.* to assert; to be true

al-le-giance *n.* loyalty to one's nation, obligation, devotion

al-le-lu-ia *interj.* expressing praise to God

al-ler-gist *n.* doctor specializing in allergies

al-ler-gy *n.* -gies abnormal reaction to environmental substances

al-le-vi-ate *v.* make more bearable allevition n., alleviator n.

al-ley *n.* passageway behind buildings, narrow street alley's n.

al-li-ga-tor *n.* large amphibious reptiles having broad heads

al-lo-cate *v.* to assign allocation n.

allot *v.* to distribute or set aside. alloted v., allotting v., allotter n.

al-low *v.* to make a provision for; to permit allowable adj.

al-low-ance *n.* a regular amount of money, food, etc allowanced v.

all right *adj.* meets satisfaction; dependable, agreeable, dependable

all-round *adj.* versatile

all-star *adj.* composed entirely of star performers or participants

al-lude *n.* refer to something indirectly, to play with

al-lure *v.* to entice; to tempt allurement n., allured v., alluring v.

al-lu-sion *n.* a hint allusive adj.

al-ly *v.* unite in a close relationship or bond allied v., allying v.

al-ma ma-ter *n.* the school or university attended by a person

al-ma-nac *n.* an annual calender publication containing data

al-might-y *adj.* having absolute power, having control

al-mond *n.* oval nut

al-most adv. not quite

alms pl., n. money given to the poor

a-loft adv. toward the upper rigging of a ship, a great height, in air

a-lo-ha interj. hawaiian greeting

a-lone adj. away from other people

a-long adv. following the length or path through woods, grass, etc.

a-loof adj. distant; indifferent, at a distance aloofness n.

a-loud adv. audibly, loud mannered

alp n. high mountain, large

al-pac-a n. a mammal related to the llama, having fine woolly hair

al-pen-stock n. long staff used by mountain climbers for support

al-pha n. first letter of the Greek alphabet, something that is first

al-pha-bet n. letters arranged in order, used in writing

al-pha-bet-ize v. to arrange in alphabetical order

al-read-y adv. by this or a specified time in the past

al-so adv. likewise; in addition

al-tar n. elevated holy table

al-ter v. to change or make different

al-ter-ca-tion n. noisy quarrel

al-ter-na-tive n. choice between two or more possibilities

al-ter-na-tor n. electric generator producing alternating current

al-though conj. even though

al-tim-e-ter n. instrument for measuring altitude

al-ti-tude n. height above sea level

al-to n. low female singing voice

al-to-geth-er adv. entirely

al-tru-ism n. selfless concern for others, unconcerned

a-lu-mi-num n. silvery metallic element, used in science

a-lum-na n. a female graduate of a school or university

a-lum-nus n. a male graduate of a school or university

al-ways adv. forever; at all times

am n. first person, singular

a-mal-ga-mate v. to mix; to blend amalgation, n.

a-man-dine adj. garnished with almonds, to decorate with almonds

am-a-teur n. one who lacks expertise amateurish adj.

a-maze v. to astound amazement n.

am-bass-a-dor n. official representative of a country

am-ber n. brownish-yellow resin

am-bi-ance n. environment

am-bi-dex-trous adj. using both hands with equal facility

am-bi-ent adj. surrounding, circling

am-big-u-ous adj. uncertain; doubtful ambiguousness n.

am-bi-tion n. strong desire to succeed ambitionless adj.

am-bi-tious adj. challenging

am-ble v. move at a leisurely pace, to make comfortable ambler n.

am-bu-lance n. vehicle to transport the injured or sick to a hospital

am-bush n. surprise attack

A-me-ba also Amoeba n.

single-celled semifluid living animal

a-me-lio-rate v. to make better

a-men interj. ending of a prayer

a-me-na-ble adj. responsible -ility n.

a-mend v. to correct; to improve, make better amendment n.

a-mends pl., n. compensation for injury or sickness

a-men-i-ty n. agreeableness

a-merce v. to punish, correct

America n. United States of America, a free country

A-mer-ica-n n. a native U.S. citizen

am-e-thyst n. purple gemstone

a-mi-a-ble adj. friendly and pleasant

am-i-ca-ble adj. harmonious amicability n.

a-mid prep. to be in the middle of something, to be occupied

a-mi-go n. friend

a-miss adj. out of order or place

am-mo-nia n. colorless, pungent gas

am-mu-ni-tion n. projectiles fired from guns or other weapons

am-ne-sia n. the loss of memory

am-nes-ty n. pardon for political offenders

a-mor-al adj. neither moral nor immoral

a-mor-phous adj. something which is lacking definite form

am-or-tize v. liquidate a loan

a-mount n. sum or total quantity

am-per-age n. strength of an electric current, hot wires

am-pere n. unit of electric current

am-per-sand n. sign that represents and (&), used as an abbreviation

am-phet-a-mine n. a drug

am-phib-i-an n. an animal able to live on land and in water

am-ple adj. sufficient; abundant

am-pul n. small, sealed vial

am-pu-tate v. to remove a limb from the body, get rid of amputation n.

a-muck adv. in an uncontrolled manner,

uncontrollable

am-u-let *n.* charm worn to protect against evil, protection

a-muse *v.* entertain **amusement** *n.*

an *adj.* one sort of, others

a-nad-ro-mous *adj.* migrating up river to breed in fresh water

an-a-gram *n.* formation of a new word from another

a-nal *adj.* relating to the anus

an-al-ge-sia *n.* inability to feel pain **analgesic** *adj.*

a-nal-o-gous *adj.* similar, alikeness

a-nal-y-sis *v.* examining parts

an-a-lyze *v.* to make an analysis of

an-ar-chy *n.* state of policial disorder, absence of government

a-nat-o-mize *v.* examine in great detail, to look over carefully

a-nat-o-my *n.* structure of an organ **anatomical** *adj.*

an-ces-tor *n.* forefather

an-ces-try *n.* line of descent

an-chor *n.*

device to keep a ship from drifting, to keep in place

an-chor-age *n.* place for anchoring a ship

an-cho-vy *n.* small fish

an-cient *adj.* very old **ancientness** *n.*

and *conj.* along with; as well as; added to, to put with

an-dan-te *adv.* slow in tempo

and-i-ron *n.* heavy metal support for logs in a fireplace

an-dro-gen *n.* hormone that maintains masculine characteristics

an-ec-dote *n.* short account of a story, a long story short

a-ne-mi-a *n.* condition in which blood does not have enough red corpuscles, in hemoglobin

a-nent *prep.* regarding; concerning

an-es-thet-ic *n.* drug used during an operation to take away pain

a-new *adv.* again, to do over

an-gel *n.* an immortal being **angelic** *adj.*

an-ger *n.* feeling of extreme hostility

an-gi-na *n.* disease marked by painful choking spasms

an-gle *v.*

a shape that makes a corner

an-go-ra *n.* silky hair of the Angora rabbit; used in sweater making

an-gry *adj.* feeling of anger, hostility toward someone **angrily** *adv.*

an-guish *n.* great suffering or grief

an-gu-lar *adj.* gaunt; bony; lean

an-hy-drous *adj.* does not contain any water, without

an-i-mal *n.* any four-footed creature; beast; having four feet

an-i-mate *v.* give life or spirit to something that is still **animation** *n.*

an-i-mos-i-ty *n.* hostility

an-ise *n.* licorice-flavored herb

an-kle *n.* joint that connects the foot with the leg, support

an-klet *n.* short sock

an-nals *n.* descriptive record

an-neal *v.* treatment to make glass less brittle, not fragile

an-nex *v.* join a smaller thing to a larger one **annexation** *n.*

an-ni-hi-late *v.* destroy completely

an-ni-ver-sa-ry *n.*, *pl.* -ries date on which something happened at an earlier time in history

an-nounce *v.* to give notice, to make public **announcement** *n.*

an-nounc-er *n.* performer on radio or television who entertains

an-noy *v.* to bother **annoyance** *n.*

an-nu-al *adj.* recurring the same time each year; again

an-nu-i-ty *n.* annual payment of an income; once a year

an-nul *v.* to cancel a marriage or a law **annulment** *n.*

an-nun-ci-ate *v.* to proclaim

a-noint *v.* apply oil in a religious ceremony; to bless someone

a-non *adv.* in a short period of time

a-non-y-mous *adj.* an unknown or withheld name, agency

an-oth-er *adj.* additional

an-swer *n.* written or spoken reply

ant *n.*

small insect

an-tag-o-nize *v.* arouse hostility

ant-eat-er *n.* animal with a long snout which feeds on ants

an-te-ce-dent *adj.* event that precedes another; afterwards

an-te-lope *n.* swift-running mammal; quick-running

an-te me-rid-i-em *n.* time before noon; before 12 o'clock

an-ten-na *n.* feelers of an insect; aerial; helps in movement

an-te-ri-or *adj.* toward or at the front; a

head of

an-te-room *n.* waiting room

an-them *n.* hymn of praise

an-ther *n.* part of the flower

an-thol-o-gy *n.* collection of stories

an-thra-cite *n.* hard coal

an-thrax *n.* infectious disease found in cattle and sheep

an-thro-poid *n.* gorillas

an-thro-pol-o-gy *n.* study on the origin, and development of man

an-ti *n.* one who opposes policy or proposal; against; not for

an-ti-bi-ot-ic *n.* substance used as a germ killer; a medicine

an-ti-bod-y *n.* proteins that counteract diseases; help heal

an-tic *n.* mischievous caper or act

an-tic-i-pate *v.* to look forward; excitement anticipation *n.*

an-ti-cli-max *n.* letdown or decline

an-ti-dote *n.* substance to counteract poison -al *adj.*

an-ti-his-ta-mine *n.* a drug to relieve symptoms of allergies

an-ti-knock *n.* substance to reduce engine knock in a vehicle

an-ti-mo-ny *n.* silver-white metallic element used in medicines

an-ti-pasto *n.* appetizer

an-ti-per-spi-rant *n.* sustance to reduce perspiration and odor

an-ti-pode *n.* a direct opposite

an-tique *n.* an object that is over 100 years old

an-tiquity *n., pl.* antiquities quality of being old

an-ti--Sem-ite *n.* person hostile toward Jews; against

an-tith-e-sis *n.* direct opposition

ant-ler *n.*

horns of a deer

an-to-nym *n.* word opposite in meaning antonymous adj., -y n.

a-nus *n.* lower opening of the alimentary canal; anal

an-vil *n.* block for forming metal

anx-i-e-ty *n.* state of uncertainty

anx-ious *adj.* worried; upset

any *adj.* no matter which

any-body *pron.* anyone; any person

any-how *adv.* in any way; whatever

any-thing *pron.* any occurrence

any-time *adv.* at any time

any-way *adv.* in any manner

any-where *adv.* to any place

a-or-ta *n.* main artery from the heart

a-pace *adv.* rapid in pace; faster

a-part *adv.* separate or at a distance

a-part-heid *n.* non-white racial discrimination in South Africa

a-part-ment *n.* suite in a building

ap-a-thy *n.* lack of emotions or feelings

ape *n.* large mammal

ap-er-ture *n.* an opening

a-pex *n.* the highest point

a-pha-sia *n.* loss of the ability to express ideas; loss of expression

aphid *n.* small insects which move

aph-o-rism *n.* brief statement of truth

aph-ro-dis-i-ac *adj.* arousing the sexual desire

a-pi-ary *n.* place where bees are kept; collection of hives

a-piece *adv.* for or to each one

a-plomb *n.* poise; confident

ap-o-gee *n.* point most distant from earth; toward the outer layer

a-pol-o-get-ic *adj.* expression of apology; giving sympathy

ap-o-plex-y *n.* loss of muscular control; non-movement

a-pos-tle *n.* person sent on a mission; to accomplish something

a-pos-tro-phe *n.* mark (') of punctuation used in writing

ap-pall *v.* overcome by shock or dismay appalled v., appalling v.

ap-pa-ra-tus *n.* instrument for a specific operation or useage

ap-par-el *v.* to adorn; clothes

ap-par-ent *adj.* open to the mind; visible; open minded

ap-pa-ri-tion *n.* unusual appearance

ap-peal *n.* an earnest plea appealable adj. appealingly *adv.*

ap-pear *v.* to come into public view, in sight appearance *n.*

ap-pease *v.* to pacify; to quiet

ap-pel-late *adj.* review the decisions of the lower courts

ap-pend *v.* add an appendix

ap-pen-dec-to-my *n.* a surgical removal of the appendix

ap-pen-dix *n. Med.*

Ascending colon

Cecum

Appendix

medical term that refers to a small hollow bind or the vermiform appendix

ap-petite *n.* craving or desire for food appetitive adj.

ap-pe-tiz-er *n.* food served before a

meal for enjoyment

ap-plaud v. express approval by clapping; agreeable

ap-pli-ance n. equipment designed for a particular use

ap-pli-ca-ble adj. appropriate; suitable applicability n.

ap-pli-cant n. person applying for a job with an organization

ap-pli-ca-tion n. request or petition

ap-ply v. to put into use; useage

ap-point v. to fix or set officially appointment n.

ap-por-tion v. divide and share; divided into portions apportment n.

ap-po-site adj. pertinent

ap-prais-al n. evaluation of property

ap-praise v. estimate the value of; to set a value appraiser n.

ap-pre-ci-ate v. recognize the worth

ap-pre-hend v. anticipate with anxiety; arrest; seize; take away

ap-pre-hen-sive adj. view the future with anxiety or alarm

ap-pren-tice n. person learning a trade through on-hands training

ap-prise v. to inform; make aware

ap-proach v. to come near; in contact approachable adj.

ap-prove v. express a favorable opinion; to agree with

ap-prox-i-mate adj. almost exact -ly adv.

apron n. garment used to protect clothing; protection against

ap-ro-pos adv. by the way

apse n. polygonal projection of a church, semicircular

apt adj. appropriate aptly adv.

ap-ti-tude n. natural talent or ability

aqua n. water, greenish-blue color

aqua-naut n. scuba diver

aquar-i-um n. an artificial pond

aq-ue-ous adj. resembling water

ar-a-ble adj. land suitable for plowing; fit for cultivation

ar-bi-tra-tor n. a person chosen to decide a dispute; settlement

ar-bor n. garden shelter

ar-bor-vi-tae n. ever-green tree

arc n. Something that is curved or arched.

arch n.

the structure that spans over an open area; usually curved

ar-chae-ol-o-gy n. scientific study of ancient times archaeologist n.

arch-bishop n. a bishop of the highest rank; the highest

arch-di-o-cese n. district of an archbishop archdiocesan adj.

ar-cher-y n. art of shooting with a bow and arrow archer n.

ar-chi-tect n. person who designs and supervises construction

arch-way n. an arch over a passage

arc-tic adj. extremely cold or frigid

ar-dor n. extreme warmth or passion; to have feelings for

ar-e-a n. flat piece of ground

a-re-na n. area for public entertainment; usually a spherical shape

ar-go-sy n. fleet of ships

ar-gue v. to dispute, quarrel; to disagree on something arguement n.

ar-gyle n. knitted diamond-shaped designs in solid or outline

ar-id adj. dry; insufficient rain

a-right adv. correctly

a-rith-me-tic adj. branch of math

ark n. ship Noah built

arm n. upper limb of the human body extended outward armer n.

ar-ma-da n. fleet of warships

ar-ma-dil-lo n. burrowing nocturnal animal

ar-ma-ment n. military supplies and weapons needed for strength

ar-ma-ture n. main moving part of an electric device

arm-chair n. chair with armrests

arm-ful n. as much as the arm can hold; what can be carried

arm-hole n. an opening in a garment for the arm to go through

ar-mi-stice n. mutual agreement; truce; trusting agreement; bond

arm-let n. band worn on the upper arm made of cloth or metal

ar-moire n. large wardrobe

ar-mor n. covering to protect the body made of metal

ar-mory n. place where military equipment is stored

arm-pit n. hollow area under connection of the arm and shoulder

arm-rest n. support for the arm on a chair

arm-twist-ing n. direct pressure to achieve a desired effect

ar-my n. the land forces of a country; to defend a country

a-ro-ma n. distinctive fragrance or odor, long lasting aromatic adj.

a-round adv. to or on all sides

around-the-clock adj. lasting for a period of 24 hours; one day

arouse v. wake up from a sleep

ar-peg-gi-o n. chord produced in succession

ar-rack n. alcoholic beverage

ar-raign v. called before a court arraignment n.

ar-range v. put in correct order or sequence arrangement n.

ar-rant adj. extreme; without moderation; notoriously

ar-ras n. wall hanging of tapestry

ar-ray v. place or set in order; arrange arrayer n.

ar-rears n., pl. state of being behind, as an obligation, etc.

ar-rest n. to capture; to seize

arrest-ee n. person under arrest

ar-rest-ing adj. very impressive or striking; catching the attention of

ar-rhyth-mia n. alteration in rhythm of the heartbeat; irregular

ar-rhyth-mic adj. lacking regularity or rhythm; irregularity

ar-ri-ve v. reach or get to a destination; to make an appearance

ar-ro-gance n. overbearing manner arrogant adj., arrogantly adv.

ar-row n. weapon shot from a bow; sign to show direction

ar-row-head n. striking end of an arrow; part which does damage

ar-row-root n. starch-yielding plant

ar-rowy adj. to move swiftly

ar-se-nal n. collection of weapons; place where military equipment is stored; manufacturing of weapon

ar-se-nic n. element used to make insecticide or weed killer

ar-son n. fraudulent burning of property; destroying arsonist n.

art n. human expression of objects by painting, etc.

ar-ter-y n. blood vessel that carries blood from the heart to the body

ar-te-sian well n.

Soil
Clay or Rock
Sandstone
Rock

well that produces water without a pump; natural

art form n. form of an artistic expression

art glass n. glass designed for decorative purposes

ar-thral-gia n. pain in one or more joints arthralgic adj.

ar-thritic n. person who has arthritis; pain in joints

ar-thri-tis n. inflammation of joints

ar-thro-pod n. animal with jointed limbs and segmented body, as a spider and other insects

ar-ti-choke n. plant with an edible thistle-like head; produces fruit

ar-ti-cle n. term or clause in a contract; a paragraph or section

ar-tic-u-late adj. able to express oneself clearly; feelings

ar-ti-fact n. something made by man showing human modification artifactual adj.

ar-ti-fice n. artful or clever skill

ar-ti-fi-cial adj. not genuine; made by man artificialy adv.

ar-til-lery n. weapons, especially cannons used in wars

ar-ti-san n. a craftsman

art-ist n. a person who practices the fine arts of painting, etc.

ar-tis-tic adj. characteristic of an artist; unique in design

art-ist-ry n. ability, or quality of workmanship; artistic ability

art-less adj. crude; simple; lacking art and skill artlessly adv.

art-work n. the artistic work of an artist; expression of an artist

as adv. in the manner like; similar to; the same as

as-bes-tos n. mineral form of magnesium silicate used in fire-proofing; for putting out fires

as-cend v. to rise up from a lower level; to climb; to mount

as-cen-dant adj. rising; moving up

as-cent n. a way up; a slope

as-cer-tain v. to find out for certain; to make sure; to be correct

as-cet-icism n. practice of strict self-denial; measure of discipline

as-cot n. scarf or broad tie

as-cribe v. assign or attribute to something ascribable, v.

a-sex-u-al adj. lacking sexual reproductive organs asexuality n.

ash n. tree with a hard, elastic wood

a-shamed adj. feeling guilt, or shame; feeling unworthy; embarrassed ashamedly adv.

a-shore adv. on or to the shore

ash-tray n. container or receptacle for discarding tobacco ashes

aside adv. out of the way; to one side; off to the side

ask v. to request; to seek information; to find out about

askance adv. with suspicion or distrust

askew adv. or adj. out of line, not straight; in a different direction

a-slant *adv.* in a slanting direction

a-sleep *adv.* in a state of sleep

a-slope *adv.* in a slanting or sloping position or direction

a-so-cial *adj.* selfish, not social

as-par-a-gus *n.* a vegetable with tender shoots; edible

as-pect *n.* the situation, position, view, or appearance of something

as-peri-ty *n., pl.* -ties roughness in manner or sound

as-per-sion *v.* false charges or slander; defamation; maligning

as-phyx-i-ate *v.* to suffocate, to prevent from breathing -ion *n.*, asphyxiator *n.*

as-pic *n.* a savory jelly made from fish, meat; used to garnish meat

as-pi-rate *v.* to give pronunciation with a full breathing sound

as-pire *v.* to desire with ambition; to strive towards something that is higher

as-pi-rin *n.* medication used for the relief of pain and fever

ass *n.* a hoofed animal; a donkey

as-sail *v.* to attack violently with words or blows assailant *n.*

as-sas-sin *n.* murderer especially one that murders a politically important person either for fanatical motives or for hire

as-sas-si-nate *v.* to murder a prominent person by secret or sudden attack

as-sault *n.* a very violent physical or verbal attack on a person assaulter *n.*, assaultive *adj.*

as-say *n.* to evaluate or to assess; to try; to attempt assayer *n.*

as-sem-blage *n.* a collection of things or people; a gathering

as-sem-ble *v.* to put together the parts of something; to come together as a group assembly *n.*

as-sent *v.* to agree on something

as-sert *v.* to declare or state positively, to maintain; to defend

as-sess *v.* to fix or assign a value to something assessor *n.* assessment *n.*

as-set *n.* a value placed on goods owned by a person

as-sev-er-ate *v.* to state positively, firmly, and seriously

as-sign *v.* to designate as to duty; to give or allot; to attribute assignable *adj.*, assignor n.

as-sign-ee *n.* the person appointed to act for another

as-sim-i-late *v.* to take in, to understand; to make similar assimilation *n.*

as-sist *v.* to give support, to aid, to give help assistance, assistant *n.*

as-size *n.* a fixed or customary standard;

as-so-ci-ate *v.* to connect or join together *n.* a partner, colleague, or companion

as-so-ci-a-tion *n.* an organized body of people having a common interest; a society; as one

as-so-nance *n.* the repetition of sound in words or syllables

as-sort *v.* to distribute into groups of a classification; divide

as-sort-ed *adj.* made up of different or various kinds assortment *n.*

as-suage *v.* to quiet, pacify; to put an end to by satisfying to soothe; to lessen intensity assuagement *n.*

as-sua-sive *adj.* having a smooth, pleasant effect or quality

as-sume *v.* to take upon oneself to complete a job or duty; to take responsibility for; complete assumeable *adj.*, assumeably *adv.*

as-sump-tion *n.* an idea or statement believed to be true without proof; taken for granted

as-sure *v.* to give the feeling of confidence; to make sure

as-sured *adj.* satisfied as to the truth or certainty assuredly *adv.*

as-sur-er *n.* a person who gives assurance to someone or something

as-ter *n.*

a plant having white, bluish, purple, or pink daisy-like flowers

as-ter-isk *n.* the charac ter (*) used to indicate letters omitted or as a reference to a footnote

a-stern *adv. & adj.* toward the rear or back of an aircraft or ship

as-ter-oid *n.* one of thousands of small moving planets between Jupiter and Mars

asth-ma *n.* a respiratory disease marked by labored breathing, accompanied by wheezing asthmatic *adj.*, cally *adv.*

as though *conj.* as if

astig-ma-tism *n.* a defect of the lens of an eye resulting in blurred or imperfect images

a-stir *adj.* to be out of bed, awake; in motion; to be up and around

as to *prep.* with reference to or regard to; concerning

as-ton-ish *v.* to strike with sudden fear, wonder, or surprise

as-ton-ish-ing *adj.* causing surprise or astonishment astonishingly *adv.*

as-ton-ish-ment *n.* the state of being amazed or astonished

as-tound *v.* to fill with wonder and bewilderment astoundingly *adv.*

as-tra-khan *n.* the curly fur from a young lamb of the southeast U.S.S.R.

as-tral *adj.* resembling, or related to the stars; in resemblence

a-stray *adv.* away from a desirable or proper path; different path

a-stride *prep.* one leg on either side of something; placed or lying on both sides of; extending across or over

as-trin-gent *adj.* able to draw together or to constricting tissue astringency *n.*, astringently adv.

as-tro-dome *n.* a large stadium covered by a dome for protection

as-trol-o-gy *n.* the study of the supposed influences of the planets and stars and their movements and positions on human affairs -ical *adj.*, astrologer *n.*

as-tro-naut *n.* person who travels in a spacecraft beyond the earth's atmosphere; explores space

as-tro-nau-tics *n.* the technology and science of the construction and operation of a spacecraft -cal *adj.*

as-tro-nom-i-cal *adj.* relating to astronomy; something enormously large astronomically *adv.*

as-tron-o-my *n.* the science of the celestial bodies and their motion, magnitudes, and constitution -er *n.*

as-tute *adj.* sharp in discernment; very shrewd astutely *adv.*, astuteness *n.*

a-sun-der *adv.* separate into parts or positions apart from each other

asy-lum *n.* a refuge or institution for the care of the needy or sick

at *prep.* to indicate presence, occurrence, or condition

at-a-vism *n.* a hereditary characteristic that skips several generations atavistic *adj.*

at-el-ier *n.* an artist's workshop

a-the-ism *n.* the disbelief that God exists;

athe-ist *n.* a person who does not believe in the existence of God

a-thirst *adj.* having a strong, eager desire for something

ath-lete *n.* person who participates in the playing of sports

ath-let-ic *adj.* relating to athletes

a-thwart *adv.* opposition to the expected or right

a-tilt *adj. & adv.* inclined upward or tilted in some way

at-las *n.* a collection or book of maps for states and countries

at-mos-phere *n.* a gaseous mass that surrounds a celestial body

at-oll *n.* an island of coral that encircles a lagoon

at-om *n.*

the smallest unit of an element

atom bomb *or* atomic bomb *n.* a bomb that explodes violently

a-ton-al *adj.* marked by the deliberate avoidance of a traditional key or tonal center atonally *adv.*

a-tone *v.* to make amends

a-tone-ment *n.* amends for a wrongdoing; reconciliation

atop *adj.* on the top of something

atri-um *n.* one of the four chambers of the heart

a-tro-cious *adj.* cruel or evil

a-troc-i-ty *n., pl.* -ties the condition of being atrocious

a-tro-phy *v.* decrease in size or wasting away; progressive decline

at-tach *v.* to fasten or become fastened attachable *adj.*

at-ta-che *n.* an expert on the diplomatic staff of an embassy

at-tach-ment *n.* the state of being attached; a tie of affection or loyalty

at-tack *v.* to threaten with force or violence, to assault

at-tain *v.* to arrive at or reach a goal attainability *n.*, attainable adj.

at-tain-der *n.* the loss of civil rights that occurs following a criminal conviction or sentencing

at-tain-ment *n.* accomplishment; achievement; reached a goal

at-taint *v.* to disgrace or stain; to achieve or obtain by effort

at-tar *n.* the fragrant oil from flowers; fragrance

at-tempt *v.* to make an effort to do something

at-tend *v.* to be present; to take charge of or to look after

at-ten-dance *n.* the number of times a person attends something

at-ten-dant *n.* one who provides a service for another; caregiver

at-ten-tion *n.* observation, or mental concentration attentiveness *n.*

at-ten-u-ate *v.* to lessen the force, amount or value; to become thin attenuation *n.*, attenuated v.

at-test *v.* ive testimony or sign one's name as a witness attestation *n.*

at-tire *n.* a person's dress or clothing

worn on a daily basis

at-ti-tude *n.* a mental position; the feeling one has for oneself

at-tor-ney *n., pl.* attorneys person with legal training who is appointed by another to transact business for him

at-tract *v.* to draw by appeal

at-trib-ute *v.* explain by showing a cause

at-tune *v.* bring something into harmony

atwit-ter *adj.* excited; nervously concerned about something

au cou-rant *adj.* fully familiar or informed; aware of surroundings

auc-tion *n.* a public sale of merchandise to the highest bidder **auctioneer** *n.*, auctioned *v.*, -ing *v.*

auc-to-ri-al *adj.* having to do with an author; writer

au-da-cious *adj.* bold, daring, or fearless; insolent **audaciously** *adv.*

au-di-ble *adj.* capable of being heard and understandable

au-di-ence *n.* a group of spectators or listeners

au-di-o *adj.* relating to sound or its high-fidelity reproduction

au-dit *n.* verification or examination of financial accounts

au-di-tion *n.* trial performance given by an entertainer as to demonstrate ability

au-di-tor *n.* a person who listens or hears; one who audits accounts

au-di-to-ri-um *n.* a large room in a public building or a school that holds many people

au-di-to-ry *adj.* related to the organs or sense of hearing

aught *n.* zero (0)

aug-ment *v.* to add to or increase; to enlarge **augmentable** adj., augmentor n.

au jus *adj.* served in the juices obtained from roasting

auk *n.* sea bird living in the arctic regions and cold regions

au-ra *n., pl.* auras, aurae an emanation said to come from a person's or an animal's body

au-ral *adj.* relating to the ear or the sense of hearing

au-re-ate *adj.* of a brilliant golden color or radiance

au re-voir *interj.* used in expressing farewell to someone

au-ri-cle *n.* the two of the four upper chambers of the heart

au-ro-ra *n.* the brilliant display of moving and flashing lights in the night sky **auroral** *adj.*

aus-tere *adj.* stern in manner and appearance **austereness** n.

aus-tral *adj.* southern

au-then-tic *adj.* real; genuine; worthy of acceptance; original

au-then-ti-cate *v.* to prove that something is true or genuine **authenticity** *n.*, **authentication** n.

author *n.* a person who writes an original literary work **author** *v.*

au-thor-i-tar-i-an *adj.* blind submission and absolute, unquestioned obedience to authority

au-thor-i-ty *n., pl.* -ties group or person with power; an expert

au-thor-ize *v.* give authority; to approve; to justify **authorzation** *n.*

au-to-bi-og-ra-phy *n., pl.* -phies the life story of a person, written by that person **autobiographer** *n.*

au-toch-tho-nous *adj.* native to an area or region of land

au-toc-ra-cy *n.* government by one person who has unlimited power

au-to-di-dact *n.* a person who has taught himself to do something

au-to-graph *n.* a handwritten signature

au-to-mate *v.* to operate by automation **automatable adj**

au-to-mat-ic *adj.* operating with very little control **automatically** *adv.*

au-to-ma-tion *n.* the equipment used to acquire automation

au-top-sy *n., pl.* -sies the examination of a body after death to determine the cause of death

au-to-stra-da *n.* an expressway in Italy

au-tumn *n.* the season between summer and winter -al n.

aux-il-ia-ry *adj.* providing help or assistance to someone

auxin *n.* hormone in a plant that stimulates growth

a-vail *v.* to be of advantage or use; to use; to result in

a-vail-able *adj.* present and ready for immediate use; attainable

a-vant--garde *n.* people who invent new ideas and styles in a certain field of study

a-venge *v.* to take revenge for something

av-e-nue *n.* a street lined with trees

a-ver *v.* to state positively

av-er-age *n.* typical or usual, not being exceptional; regularly

a-verse *adj.* having a feeling of repugnance

a-ver-sion *n.* a feeling of strong dislike; the act of turning away

a-vert *v.* prevent or keep from happening; to ward off

a-vi-ary *n.* a place where birds are kept and confined

a-vi-a-tion *n.* the operation of planes and other aircraft

a-vi-a-tor *n.* pilot of an aircraft

av-id *adj.* greedy **avidly** *adv.*

av-o-ca-do *n.*

pear-shaped edible fruit from the avocado tree

av-o-ca-tion *n.* activity in addition to the regular work; a hobby

a-void *v.* to stay away from; to shun

a-vouch *v.* to guarantee

a-vow *v.* state openly on a subject

a-wake *v.* to be alert or watchful

a-ward *v.* confer as being deserved or merited

a-ware *adj.* being conscious of something; knowing of all things

a-wash *adj.* flooded; to be washed by water; to ruin by water

a-way *adv.* at a distance; apart from

awe *n.* a feeling of wonder **awe** *v.*

a-wea-ry *adj.* tired

a-weigh *adj.* hang just clear of a ship's anchor

awe-some *adj.* expressive of awe

aw-ful *adj.* very unpleasant; disagreeable **awfully** *adv.*

a-while *adv.* for a short time

a-whirl *adj.* to spin around

awk-ward *adj.* not graceful; clumsy

awl *n.* tool used to make holes in leather or in wood

awn-ing *n.* structure that serves as a shelter over a window

a-wry *adv.* in a twisted or turned position; other than upright

ax *or* **axe** *n.* tool used to split wood

ax-i-om *n.* something assumed to be true without proof

ax-is *n.*

the line around an object or body that rotates

ax-le *n.* shaft around which a wheel or pair of wheels revolve

a-yah *n.* nursemaid or maid in India

AZT *abbr.* azidothymidine; a drug that improves the symptoms of Acquired Imune Difficiency Syndrome

az-ure *n.* blue color of the sky; the unclouded sky

azurite *n.* a mineral consisting of blue basic carbonate of copper

B, b The second letter of the English alphabet

babble *v.* to chatter senselessly

babe *n.* a very young child or infant

ba-boon *n.* a species of the monkey family **baboonish** *adj.*

ba-by *n., pl.* **babies** infant, very young child **babish** *adj.*

baby grand *n.* a type of piano

bac-ca-lau-re-ate *n.* a college degree

bach-e-lor *n.* an unmarried male

ba-cil-lus *n., pl.* **bacilli** rod-like microscopic organism

back *n.* the rear part of the human body **back-less** *adj.*

back-bite *v.* gossip or speak in a nasty way **back-biter** *n.*

back-board *n.* a board that gives support

back-bone *n.* spinal column

back-er *n.* someone who gives support

back-field *n.* football players behind the line of scrimmage

back-fire *n.* explosion of ignited fuel in an engine **backfire** *v.*

back-gam-mon *n.* a board game

back-ground *n.* area behind which objects are represented

back-hand *n.* a stroke in the game of tennis

back-ing *n.* support; endorsment

back-lash *n.* violent backward movement **back-lash-er** *n.*

back-log *n.* accumulation of unfinished work

back-pack *n.* equipment to carry items on the back

back-pedal *v.* to move backward or retreat

back room *n.* a room in the rear of a building

back-side *n.* the buttocks

back-slide *v.* to lapse back into a less desirable condition

back-stage *n.* area behind the performing area in a theatre

back-stop *n.* screen to stop a ball

back-stretch *n.* side opposite the homestretch on a racecourse

back-stroke *n.* a swimming stroke

back-talk *n.* a smart or insolent reply

back-track *v.* to retrace one's previous steps or course

back-up *n.* alternative or substitute

back-ward *adv.* in a reverse order **backwardness** *n.*

back-woods *n., pl.* heavily wooded area **back-woods-man** *n.*

ba-con *n.* salted and smoked pork

bac-te-ri-cide *n.* substance that kills bacteria

bad *adj.* naughty or disobedient; inferior in quality or performance

badger *n.*

burrowing mammal *v.* harass
bad-min-ton *n.* a court game
baf-fle *v.* to perplex
bag *n.* flexible container for storing, or carrying something
ba-gel *n.* round roll with a chewy texture
bag-gage *n.* personal belongings of a traveler
bag-gy *adj.* loose **baggily** *adv.*
bag-pipe *n.* a wind instrument **bagpiper** *n.*
ba-guette *n.* a long, narrow rectangle gem
bag-worm *n.* type of moth larva
bail *n.* money given to guarantee appearance of prisoners
bail-iff *n.* officer who guards prisoners
bail-i-wick *n.* office of a bailiff
bails-man *n.* person who puts up bail for another
bait *v.* to lure
bake *v.* to cook in an oven **baker** *n.*
baker's dozen *n.* thirteen pieces
baking powder *n.* leavening agent
baking soda *n.* sodium bicarbonate
bal-a-lai-ka *n.* musical instrument
bal-ance *n.* scale for weighing of something
bal-co-ny *n.* platform projecting from the wall of a building

bald *adj.*

lacking hair on the head
bal-der-dash *n.* nonsense
bale *n.* large, bound package or bundle
ba-leen *n.* a whalebone
balk *v.* to refuse to go on **balky** *adj.*
ball *n.* round object
bal-lad *n.* folk song
bal-last *n.* heavy material for stability
ball bearing *n.* bearing to reduce friction
bal-le-ri-na *n.* a female ballet dancer
bal-let *n.* artistic expression of dance **bal-let-ic** *adj.*
bal-loon *n.* a bag inflated with gas
bal-lot *n.* slip of paper used in voting
ball-point *n.* self-inking writing pen
bal-ly-hoo *n.* exaggerated advertising
balm *n.* a fragrant soothing ointment
ba-lo-ney *n., Slang* nonsense
bal-sa *n.* wood very light in weight

bal-us-ter *n.* upright post supporting a handrail
bam-boo *n.* tall grass with hollow stems
bam-boo-zle *v.* to trick
ban *v.* to prohibit
ba-nal *adj.* trite
ba-nan-a *n.* crescent-shaped yellow fruit
band *n.* a group of musicians
band-age *n.* strip of cloth to protect an injury **bandage** *v.*
ban-dan-na *n.* brightly colored hankerchief
ban-deau *n.* narrow band worn in the hair
ban-dit *n.* a gangster or robber **banditry** *n.*
ban-do-leer *n.* a belt
ban-dy *adv.* crooked
bane *n.* cause of destruction or ruin
ban-gle *n.* a bracelet
ban-ish *v.* to drive away **banishment** *n.*
ban-jo *n.* a stringed instrument
bank *n.* land at rivers edge; establishment for saving and lending money
bank-rupt *n.* person legally insolvent
ban-ner *n.* flag
ban-nock *n.* unleavened or flat cake
ban-quet *n.* elaborate dinner or feast
ban-yan *n.* a tree
bap-tism *n.* Christian sacrament
bap-tize *v.* sprinkle with water during baptism
barb *n.* fishhook point
bar-bar-i-an *n.* uncivilized culture
bar-be-cue *n.* outdoor pit for roasting meat
bar-bell *n.* exercise bar with weights
bar-ber *n.* person who cuts and dresses hair
bard *n.* a poet
bare *adj.* exposed to view **bareness** *n.*
bare-back *adv. & adj.* ride without a saddle
bare-ly *adv.* sparsely
barf *v. Slang* to vomit
bar-gain *n.* agreement on the sale of an item
barge *n.* a flat-bottomed boat
bar-i-tone *n.* male voice between tenor and bass
bark *n.* outer covering of a tree
bar-ley *n.* type of grain for making whiskey and beer
barn *n.* a farm building
bar-na-cle *n.* fish attached to an underwater surface
ba-rom-et-er *n.* device recording atmospheric changes
ba-roque *adj.* ornate artistic style
bar-rack *n.* building for housing soldiers

bar-ra-cu-da *n.* fish with a narrow body

bar-rage *n.* discharge of missiles

bar-rel *n.* round wooden container

bar-ren *adj.* sterile

bar-rette *n.* bar used to hold hair in place

bar-ri-cade *n.* barrier

bar-ri-er *n.* structure to restrict entrance

bar-room *n.* place to purchase alcoholic beverages

bar-tend-er *n.* one who serves drinks at a bar

bar-ter *v.* to trade

ba-salt *n.* volcanic rock

base *n.* fundamental part; headquarters

base-ball *n.* game using a ball and bat

base-ment *n.* foundation of a home

bash *v.* hit with a heavy blow

bash-ful *adj.* shy

ba-sic *adj.* forming the basis

BASIC *n.* computer programming language

bas-il *n.* an herb

bas-o-lisk *n.* tropical American lizard

ba-sin *n.* a washbowl

ba-sis *n., pl.* **bases** the main part

bask *v.* relax in the warmth of the sun

bas-ket *n.* woven straw, container **basketry** *n.*

bas-ket-ball *n.* game played on a court

bass *n.*

fresh water fish

bas-si-net *n.* infant's crib

bas-soon *n.* a woodwind instrument

bas-tard *n.* an illegitimate child

baste *v.* loose stitch; moisten meat

bat *n.*

wooden stick; nocturnal flying mammal

bath *n.* the act of washing the body

bat-tal-ion *n.* a military unit

bat-ten *v.* to secure

bat-ter *v.* beat or strike continuously

bat-tery *n.* device for storing electricity

bat-tle *n.* combat between opposing forces

bawd *n.* a prostitute

bawl *v.* cry loudly

bay *n.* inlet of a body of water

bay-o-net *n.* spear-like weapon

ba-zaar *n.* a fair

be *v.* to exist; a verb to show action

beach *n.* sandy shore of a lake or river

bea-con *n.* signaling device

bead *n.* ball with a hole for threading

beak *n.* bill of a bird

beak-er *n.* widemouthed cup for drinking

beam *n.* wood or metal used in construction

bean *n.* edible seed pod

bear *n.* **bears**

large mammal *v.* to endure

beard *n.* hair growing on the chin **beardless** *adj.*

beast *n.* four-legged animal **beastly** *adj.*

beat *v.* to strike repeatedly

be-a-tif-ic *adj.* showing extreme bliss

beau *n.* sweetheart

beau-ty *n.* quality pleasing to the eye **beautifully,** *adv.*

be-cause *conj.* for a reason; since

beck *n.* a summons

be-come *v.* come to be

bed *n.* furniture for sleeping

be-dazzle *v.* confuse with bright lights

bed-bug *n.* wingless insect

bed-lam *n.* state of confusion

be-drag-gled *adj.* limp and wet; soiled

bee *n.* a stinging insect

beef *n.* cow, steer, or bull meat **beefy** *adj.*

beer *n.* an alcoholic beverage

beet *n.* red root vegetable

bee-tle *n.* an insect

be-fit *v.* be suitable

be-fore *adv.* earlier

be-friend *v.* be a friend to someone

beg *v.* ask for charity **beggar** *n.*

be-gan *v.* past tense of begin

be-get *v.* to produce

be-gin *v.* to start

be-go-nia *n.* a tropical plant

be-grudge *v.* envy someone's possessions

be-guile *v.* to delight

be-half *n.* support or interest of another

be-have *v.* function in a certain manner

be-head *v.* remove the head from the body

be-hind *adv.* at the back; slow in arriving

be-hold *v.* to look at

beige *n. or adj.* light brownish, grey color

being *n.* existence

be-lat-ed *adj.* tardy **belatedly** *adv.*

belch *v.* to expel stomach gas

bel-fry *n.* bell tower

be-lief *n.* something trusted or believed

be-lieve *v.* to accept as true or real

be-lit-tle *v.* speak in a slighting manner

bell *n.* hollow instrument that sounds when struck

bell--bot-toms *pl., n.* pants with flared legs

bel-lig-er-ent *adj.* hostile -ence *n.*

bel-low *v.* make a deep, powerful roar

bel-lows *n.* instrument that produces air

bel-ly *n.* the abdomen

be-long *n.* to be a part of

be-loved *adj.* to be dearly loved

be-low *adv.* at a lower level or place

belt *n.* band worn around the waist

belt-way *n.* a highway

be-muse *v.* to bewilder

bench *n.* long seat

bend *v.* arch; curve

beneath *adv.* below; underneath

ben-e-dict *n.* newly married bachelor

ben-e-dic-tion *n.* a blessing

ben-e-fac-tion *n.* a gift

ben-e-fice *n.* fixed capital assets

be-nef-i-cence *n.* quality of being kind

ben-e-fi-cial *adj.* helpful -ly *adv.*

ben-e-fit *n.* aid; help

be-nev-o-lence *n.* act of kindness benevolent *adj.*

be-nign *adj.* having a kind disposition

ben-i-son *n.* blessing

bent *adj.* curved

be-numb *v.* to dull

be-queath *v.* leave by a will; to hand down

be-rate *v.* scold severely

be-reave *v.* to suffer the loss of a loved one bereavement *n.*

be-ret *n.* a round, woolen cap

berg *n.* a large mass of ice; iceberg

ber-i-ber-i *n.* nervous disorder

berry *n., pl.* berries an edible fruit

ber-serk *adj.* destructively violent

berth *n.* space for a ship or boat to dock

be-seech *v.* to ask

be-side *prep.* at the side of; next to

be-siege *v.* to harass with requests

be-smear *v.* to soil

be-som *n.* broom made of twigs

be-spat-ter *v.* to soil

be-speak *v.* to indicate; foretell

best *adj.* exceeding all others in quality

bes-tial *adj.* animal-like bestially *adv.*

be-stir *v.* to rouse into action

best man *n.* attendant at a wedding

be-stow *v.* to give honor

be-stride *v.* to straddle

be-take *v.* move or to go

be-tide *v.* to happen to; to take place

be-to-ken *v.* show by a visible sign

be-tray *v.* to be disloyal or unfaithful

be-troth *v.* promise to take or give in marriage betrothal *n.*

be-trothed *n.* person engaged to be married

bet-ter *adj.* more suitable, useful

be-tween *prep.* in the middle; shared by two

be-twixt *prep.* between

bev-el *n.* angle at which one surface meets another

bev-er-age *n.* refreshing liquid to drink

bev-y *n.* a flock of birds

be-wail *v.* express regret or sorrow

be-ware *v.* cautious

be-wilder *v.* to perplex or puzzle bewilderment *n.*

be-witch *v.* fascinate completely

be-yond *prep.* outside the reach or scope of

bez-el *n.* flange or groove

be-zique *n.* card game

bi-a-ly *n.* baked roll with onions on top

bi-an-nu-al *adj.* twice a year; semiannual

bi-as *n.* diagonal line; prejudice

bib *n.* protective cloth for small children

Bi-ble *n.* book of Old and New Testaments

bib-u-lous *adj.* inclined to drink

bi-cen-ten-ni-al *adj.* every 200 years

bi-ceps *n.*

large muscle of the upper arm

bick-er *v.* to argue

bi-con-cave *adj.* bowing in on two sides

bi-cus-pid *n.* tooth with two roots

bi-cy-cle *n.* two-wheeled vehicle

bid *v.* to offer to pay a certain price

bid-dy *n.* hen

bide *v.* to wait

bi-det *n.* a basin for bathing genital and anal areas

bi-en-ni-al *adj.* every two years biennially *adv.*

bier *n.* stand on which a coffin is placed

bi-fo-cal *adj.* having two focal lengths

bi-fur-cate *v.* divide into two parts

big *adj.* very large in intensity; grownup

big-a-my *n.* married to two people at the same time bigamist *n.*

big head *adj.* conceited person

big--hearted *adj.* generous and kind

big-ot *n.* person devoted to one group

big-wig *n.* person of authority

bi-ki-ni *n.* scanty, two-piece bathing suit

bi-lat-er-al *adj.* having two sides

bile *n.* liquid that is secreted by the liver

bilge *n.* inside hull of a ship

bi-lin-gual *adj.* fluent in two languages

bil-ious *adj.* gastric distress

bilk *v.* to swindle

bill *n.* itemized fees for services rendered

bill-board *n.* sign for advertisements

bill-fold *n.* wallet

bil-liards *n.* game played on a table

bil-lion *n.* one thousand million

bil-lion-aire *n.* wealthy person

bill of lading *n.* list of merchandise shipped

bil-low *n.* large swell of water; wave
billowy *adj.*

bil-ly club *n.* wooden club for protection

billy goat *n.* male goat

bi-month-ly *adj., pl.* bimonthlies every two months

bin *n.* storage place

bi-na-ry *adj.* having two different parts

bind *v.* to bandage

bind-er *n.* a notebook

bind-er-y *n.* place where books are bound

binge *n.* a spree

bin-go *n.* a game of chance

bin-oc-u-lar *n.* device to bring objects far away into focus

bi-o-chem-is-try *n.* chemistry of biological processes

bi-o-degrad-a-ble *adj.* decomposable by natural processes

bi-ol-o-gy *n.* science of living organisms biological *adj.*

bi-o-phys-ics *n.* the physics of living organisms

bi-op-sy *n.* examination for the detection of a disease

bi-par-ti-san *adj.* support by two parties bipartisanship *n.*

bi-plane *n.* glider or airplane

birch *n.* tree with close-grained wood birch-en adj.

bird *n.* warm-blooded, egg-laying animal bird-like adj.

bird-brain *n., Slang* a person who acts silly

bird-ie *n.* stroke under par; a shuttlecock

bi-ret-ta *n.* priests cap

birth *n.* beginning of existence

birth control *n.* a technique to control or prevent the number of children born; lessening

birth-day *n.* the day a person is born; day of origin

birth-mark *n.* an unusual mark on the skin at birth

birth-rate *n.* ratio of births to a population

bis *adv.* again; encore

bis-cuit *n.* type of bread or cracker

bi-sect *v.* to divide

bi-sex-u-al *adj.* relating to or having characteristics of both sexes

bish-op *n.* Christian clergyman

bi-son *n.*

large buffalo

bisque *n.* creamy soup made from fish or of the flesh of birds

bis-sex-tile *adj.* the extra day occurring in a leap year

bis-tro *n.* bar or small nightclub

bit *n.* tiny piece

bitch *n.* a female dog; spiteful woman

bite *v.* crush with the teeth
bitingly *adv.*

bit-ter *adj.* a sharp, unpleasant taste; disagreeable taste

bit-ter-sweet *n.* root, with a bitter, then a sweet taste

bi-valve *n.* a mollusk

biv-ou-ac *n.* temporary military camp under little shelter

bi-week-ly *n.* every two weeks

bi-year-ly *n.* every two years

bi-zarre *adj.* extremely strange and odd; out of the ordinary

blab *v.* reveal a secret indiscreetly

black *adj.* very dark in color; depressing

black--and--blue *adj.* discolored skin caused by bruising

black-ball *n.* vote to prevent admission; vote against

black belt *n.* expert in karate

black-berry *n.* plant with black berries; edible fruit

black-board *n.* slate-like board written on with chalk

black box *n.* container that protects the tape recordings of airline

black eye *n.* bruise around the eye

black-head *n.* dirt that clogs the pores and creates blemishes

black-jack *n.* card game

blacklight *n.* invisible infrared light

black-mail *n.* threat of exposing a past discreditable act

black market *n.* selling illegal merchandise

black-out *n.* temporary loss of electrical power

black-smith *n.* person who shapes iron blacksmithing n.

black-top *n.* asphalt

black widow *n.* a poisonous spider
blad-der *n.* sac that holds urine
blade *n.* cutting part of a knife
blame *v.* to find fault **blameless** *n.*
blanch *v.* remove color; scald vegetables
bland *adj.* tasteless
blan-dish *v.* coax; flatter
blank *adj.* empty; confused
 blankly *adv.*
blan-ket *n.* covering used on a bed
blare *v.* loud sound
blar-ney *n.* talk that is deceptive
blast *n.* strong gust of air; sound of a horn
blast-off *n.* launching of a space ship
bla-tant *adj.* offensively loud; shameless; obvious, conspicuous
blaze *n.* a sudden burst of fire
bla-zon *v.* to make known; to announce; armorial bearings
bleach *v.* remove the color from a fabric; to make white or lighter
bleach-ers *pl., n.* tiered planks used for seating of spectators
bleak *adj.* depressing; barren; cold; harsh
bleat *n.* the cry of a sheep or goat
bleed *v.* to lose blood, as from an injury; to feel anguish or pain
bleep *n.* a signal with a quick, loud sound
blem-ish *n.* a flaw or defect
blend *v.* to mix together smoothly
bless *v.* to confer prosperity or well-being
bless-ed *adj.* Holy; enjoying happiness; bringing pleasure
bless-ing *n.* a short prayer before a meal; the act of one that blesses
blight *n.* disease of plants
blimp *n.* a large aircraft
blind *adj.* not having eyesight; unable to see; unable to discern
blind-ers *pl., n.* flaps restricting side vision
blind-fold *v.* cover the eyes with a cloth; unable to see
blink *v.* open and close the eyes quickly
blink-er *n.* a light to indicate turns
blintz *n.* hin pancake stuffed with fillings
blip *v.* erase sounds from a recording; a short crisp sound
bliss *n.* great happiness or joy
 blissful *adj.*
blis-ter *n.* swelling of skin containing a watery liquid
blithe *adj.* carefree or casual
 blitheness *n.*

blitz *n.* a sudden attack
bliz-zard *n.* a severe winter storm
bloat *v.* to swell or puff out
blob *n.* a small shapeless mass
bloc *n.* group formed for a common purpose
block *n.* solid piece of matter
 blockage *n.*
block-ade *n.* the closure of an area
blond *adj.* a golden or flaxen color
 blondish *adj.*
blonde *adj.* a person with blond hair; having light hair
blood *n.* the red fluid circulated by the heart, arteries, and capilaries
blood count *n.* the number of white and red corpuscles in a specific amount of blood
blood-hound *n.* breed of hunting dogs remarkable for senses
blood-shot *adj.* red irritation of the eyes; inflammation
blood vessel *n.* canal in which blood flows and circulates
bloom *v.* bear flowers; to flourish
 blooming *adj.*
bloom-ers *n., pl.* loose pants gathered at the knee or just below the knee
bloop-er *n.* embarrassing mistake made in public
blot *n.* a spot
blotch *n.* area of skin that is discolored; difference in shade
blouse *n.* loosely fitting shirt or top
blow *v.* move or be in motion because of a current of air
blow--by--blow *adj.* very descriptive
blow dry *v.* dry one's hair with a hair dryer; to dry completely
blow-out *n.* the sudden deflation of a tire; a bursting by pressure
blow-torch *n.* handheld tool to melt soft metals
blow-up *n.* photo enlargement
blubber *n.* fat removed from whales
blue *n.* the color of a clear sky
blue baby *n.* infant with inadequate oxygen in the blood
blue-berry *n., pl.* blueberries small, seedless berry
blue-collar *adj.* wage earners who do manual labor
blue-fish *n.* game fish of the tropical waters; various dark fishes
blue-grass *n.* folk music
blue jay *n.* a bird
blue-nose *n.* a snob
blue-print *n.* reproduction of technical drawings or plans
blue ribbon *n.* award for first place in a

contest or competition

blues *pl., n.* style of jazz music

blue spruce *n.* an evergreen tree

bluff *v.* mislead

blun-der *n.* an error or mistake

blun-der-buss *n.* gun with a flared muzzle; a blundering person

blunt *adj.* abrupt; dull

blur *v.* to smudge or smear; to become hazy

blush *v.* to turn red in the face; to feel ashamed **blushingly** *adv.*

blus-ter *n.* violent noisy wind in a storm

bo-a *n.* large nonvenomous snake

boar *n.*

wild pig

board *n.* piece of sawed lumber; area where games are played

board-walk *n.* wooden walkway along a beach

boast *v.* to brag

boat *n.* a small open craft or ship

boat-swain *n.* petty officer in charge of the rigging

bob *v.* move up and down in a quick, jerky movement

bob-bin *n.* spool that holds thread

bobby socks *pl., n.* ankle sock

bob-cat *n.* wildcat

bob-sled *n.* sled with steering controls bobsledder n.

bod-ice *n.* upper piece of a dress

bod-y *n.* main part; physical part of a person **bodily** *adv.*

body-guard *n.* person hired to protect another from harm

body-surf *v.* surf on without a surfboard bodysurfer n.

bog-gle *v.* pull away from with astonishment

bo-gus *adj.* counterfeit; worthless

bo-he-mi-an *n.* unconventional lifestyle

boil *v.* heat liquid till it bubbles

boil-er *n.* vessel used to heat water for power

bois-ter-ous *adj.* violent; undisciplined boisterously *adv.*

bold *adj.* courageous **boldly** *adv.*

bold-face *n.* style of printing type

bo-le-ro *n.* a short jacket

bo-lo-gna *n.* smoked sausage

bol-ster *n.* round pillow

bolt *n.* threaded metal pin

bomb *n.* weapon detonated upon impact; to attack with bombs

bom-bard *v.* attack with missiles or bombs **bombardment** *n.*

bom-bast *n.* very ornate speech

bomber *n.* military aircraft

bo-na fide *adj.* genuine; authentic

bo-nan-za *n.* great prosperity

bon-bon *n.* candy

bond *n.* something that fastens or binds; together

bond-age *n.* slavery

bone *n.*

calcified tissue of the skeleton

bone–dry *adj.* without water

bon-er *n., Slang* mistake or blunder

bon-fire *n.* an open outdoor fire

bo-ni-to *n.* game fish related to the tuna; medium sized

bon-kers *adj., Slang* acting crazy

bon-net *n.* a woman's hat

bon-sai *n.* a small ornamental shrub

bo-nus *n.* over and above what is expected; extra

bon voyage *n.* a farewell wish

boo *n.* expression of disapproval

boog-ie *v., Slang* dance to rock and roll music

book *n.* bound, printed literary work

book-case *n.* shelving for storing books

book-end *n.* support for holding books

book-ie *n., Slang* a bookmaker

book-ing *n.* engagement

book-keep-ing *n.* recording transactions of a business **bookeeper** *n.*

book-worm *n.* one who reads a lot

boo-mer-ang *n.* curved, missile that returns to the thrower

boon *n.* something beneficial

boon-docks *pl., n. Slang* an out-of-the-way place; country with brush

boor *n.* person with little refinement; peasant

boost *v.* lift by pushing up from below; an increase in amount

boost-er *n.* promoter

boot *n.* a protective covering for the foot usually with high tops

boot camp *n.* a military camp used for basic training

booth *n.* small compartment or area booths pl.

boot-leg *v., Slang.* sell, or transport liquor illegally

bo-rax *n.* cleaning compound

bor-der *n.* margin or edge

bore *v.* make a hole using a drill

born *adj.* brought into life or being

bor-ough *n.* self-governing town

bor-row *v.* receive money with the intentions of returning it

bos-om *n.* the female's breasts

boss *n.* supervisor bossiness *n.*

bot-a-ny *n.* science of plants
otanical *adj.*, botanist *n.*

botch *v.* ruin something by clumsiness; accidental

both *adj.* two in conjunction with one; together as one

both-er *v.* to pester bothersome *adj.*

bot-tle *n.* receptacle made of glass

bot-tle-neck *n.* narrow passage

bot-tom *n.* lowest or deepest part
bottomless *adj.*

bot-u-lism *n.* food poisoning

bough *n.* large branch of a tree

bouil-lon *n.* a clear seasoned broth made from lean meat

boul-der *n.* large round rock

boul-e-vard *n.* broad city street

bounce *v.* rebound or cause to rebound
bounced v., bouncing v.

bounc-er *n.* person who removes disorderly people

bounc-ing *adj.* lively and spirited

bound-a-ry *n.* a limit or border

bound-en *adj.* under an obligation

bound-less *adj.* without limits
boundlessly *adv.*

boun-te-ous *adj.* plentiful or generous; excess

boun-ti-ful *adj.* abundant; plentiful

bounty *n.* reward for the return of something

bou-quet *n.* cut flowers

bour-bon *n.* whiskey

bour-geois *pl.*, *n.* member of the middle class society

bout *n.* a contest

bou-tique *n.* small retail shop

bou-ton-niere *n.* flower worn in the buttonhole of a man's jacket

bo-vine *adj.* relating to an ox or cow

bow *n.* front section of a boat

bow-el *n.* digestive tract

bow-ie knife *n.* thick-bladed hunting knife which is curved cconcavely

bowl *n.* container for food or liquids

bow-leg *n.* outward curvature of the leg
bowlegged adj.

bowling alley *n.* building used for bowling

bowl over *v.* astound

box *n.* small container or chest

box-car *n.* enclosed railway car

box-er *n.* person who boxes professionally

box office *n.* where tickets are purchased for an upcoming event

boy *n.* male youth or child
boyhood *n.*

boy-cott *v.* a means of protest

bra *n.* brassiere

brace *n.* device that supports something; something with connects

brace-let *n.* ornamental band for the wrist; for show

brack-en *n.* large species of fern

brack-et *n.* support to hold a shelf

brack-ish *adj.* distasteful

brad *n.* small nail

brag *v.* assert or talk boastfully

brag-ga-do-ci-o *n.*, *pl.* cockiness or arrogant manner

brag-gart *n.* person who brags

braid *v.* interweave three or more strands;; to make by braiding

braille *n.* system of printing for the blind; reading with fingers

brain *n.* large mass of nerve tissue enclosed in the cranium brainless *adj.*

brain-storm *n.* sudden idea or inspiration; a harebrained idea

brain-wash-ing *n.* intensive indoctrination

brain wave *n.* rhythmic fluctuation between parts of the brain

braise *v.* brown meat, then simmer

brake *n.* device to stop or slow a vehicle; to decrease in speed

brake fluid *n.* liquid contained in hydraulic brake cylinders

bran *n.* husk of cereal grains

branch *n.* extension from the trunk of a tree; extension outward

brand *n.* trademark or label; mark of shame brander n.

bran-dish *v.* to wave or flourish a weapon; an aggressive manner

brand name *n.* a company's trademark

brand-new *adj.* unused

bran-dy *n.* an alcoholic liquor
brandied *adj.*

brash *adj.* unthinking; insolent; impudent

brass *n.* alloy of zinc, copper and other metals

bras-siere *n.* woman's undergarment with bust support

brat *n.* an ill-mannered child

brat-wurst *n.* fresh pork sausage

brave *adj.* having courage

bra-vo *Interj.* expressing approval

brawl *n.* noisy fight

brawn *n.* well-developed muscles

bray *v.* make a loud cry like a donkey; loudness

braze *v.* to solder

bra-zen *adj.* shameless or impudent

bra-zier *n.* person who works with brass; a utensil for holding coals

breach *n.* a break in friendly relations;

ruptered or torn condition

bread *n.* leavened food made from flour and yeast *Slang* Money

breadth *n.* distance from side to side; a comprehensive quality

breadwinner *n.* one who supports a household; a means of livelihood

break *v.* to collapse or give way

breakdown *n.* failure to function

breaker *n.* a wave

breakfast *n.* the first meal of the day

breakthrough *n.* sudden advance in technique; breaking through an obstruction

breast *n.* milk-producing glandular organs; used in breast-feeding

breast-bone *n.* the sternum

breast-stroke *n.* a swimming stroke

breathe *v.* draw air into and expel from the lungs **breathless** *adj.*

breath-tak-ing *adj.* awesome **breathtakingly** *adv.*

breech *n., pl.* breeches the buttocks

breed *v.* genetic strain of domestic animals; to produce

breeze *n.* slight gentle wind

breeze-way *n.* roofed area between two buildings

bre-vi-ar-y *n.* book of prayers and psalms for the canonical hours

brev-i-ty *n., pl.* -ties brief duration

brew *v.* to make beer

brew-er-y *n.* plant where beer is brewed and produced

bribe *v.* induce by giving a token of value

bric--a--brac *n.* collection of objects usually having a value

brick *n.* molded block of baked clay used in building

brick-lay-er *n.* person who lays bricks side by side

bride *n.* women just married

bride-groom *n.* man just married

brides-maid *n.* woman who attends a bride

bridge *n.* structure over water

bri-dle *n.* harness to guide a horse

brief *n.* concise, formal statement of a case **briefly** *adv.*

brief-case *n.* a small bag for carrying papers and books

bri-er *n.* prickly plant

brig *n.* prison on a ship; sailing ship

bri-gade *n.* military unit

bright *adj.* brilliant in color; vivid **brightness** *n.*

bril-liant *adj.* radiant; intelligent

brim *n.* edge or rim of a cup

brim-stone *n.* sulfur

brin-dle *adj.* having dark streaks or flecks; a brindled animal

brine *n.* water contained in the oceans

bring *v.* to carry to a certain place

brink *n.* upper edge of a very steep slope

bri-quette *n.* brick-shaped piece of charcoal

brisk *adj.* moving or acting quickly

bris-ket *n.* meat from the breast of an animal

bris-tle *n.* short, stiff, coarse hair

britch-es *pl., n.* trousers

brit-tle *adj.* fragile

broach *n.* tapered tool for enlarging a hole

broad *adj.* covering a wide area -ly *adv.*

broad-cast *v.* to make widely known

broad-cloth *n.* cloth with a lustrous finish

broad-mind-ed *adj.* fair

broad-side *n.* side of a ship above the water; used on one side

bro-cade *n.* silk fabric

broc-co-li *n.* green vegetable

bro-chure *n.* pamphlet

brogue *n.* strong regional accent

broil *v.* cook by direct radiant heat **broiler** *n.*

broke *adj.* completely without money; without something

bro-ken *adj.* separated violently into parts; damaged or altered

bro-ken-hearted *adj.* overcome by grief or despair

bro-mide *n.* a sedative

bron-chi-al *adj.* pertaining to the bronchi **bronchially** *adv.*

bron-co *n.* wild horse

bron-to-saur *n.* very large dinosaur

bronze *n.* alloy of tin, copper, and zinc **bronzed** *v.*, **bronzing** *v.*

brooch *n.* decorative pin

brood *n.* the young of an animal

brood-er *n.* enclosed heated area for raising young chickens

brook *n.* small fresh-water stream

broom *n.* long-handled implement for sweeping

broth *n.* liquid from cooking meats

broth-er *n.* male who shares the same parents as another

brow *n.* ridge above the eye

brow-beat *v.* bully

brown *n.* color between yellow and red in hue; medium lightness

brown bag-ging *n.* practice of bringing one's lunch to work

brown-ie *n.* chewy chocolate cake

browse *v.* look over something casually;

glance at

bruise *n.* discoloration of the skin

brunch *n.* late breakfast and an early lunch combined together

bru-net *adj.* person with dark brown hair

brush *n.* device for painting or grooming the hair

bru-tal *adj.* very harsh or cruel brutally *adv.*

bub-ble *n.* round hollow object

bu-bon-ic plague *n.* contagious fatal disease

buck *n.* male deer

buck-et *n.* vessel used to carry liquids; pail

buckle *v.* to warp

bud *n.* something not developed completely; not yet mature

bud-dy *n.* companion

budge *v.* move slightly

bud-get *n.* money for a certain purpose; financial position

buff *v.* shine

buf-fa-lo *n.* wild ox

buff-er *n.* a special tool used to polish or shine something

buf-fet *n.* a side table for serving food; counter for refreshments

buf-foon *n.* clown

bug *n.* small insect; listening device

bu-gle *n.* brass instrument without keys

build *v.* erect by uniting materials

build-ing *n.* roofed and walled structure built for permanent use

bulb *n.* light for electric lamps

bulge *n.* swelling of the surface

bulk *n.* large mass

bulk-head *n.* retaining wall on the waterfront; an upright partition

bull *n.* adult male in cattle

bull-dozer *n.* machine for moving earth; one that buldozes

bul-let *n.* projectile fired from a gun bulletproof *adj.*

bul-le-tin *n.* a public notice

bul-lion *n.* refined gold or silver

bull-pen *n.* area where pitchers warm up; a cell where prisoners are held until brought to court

bull's eye *n.* center of a target

bul-ly *n.* mean or cruel person

bul-rush *n.* tall grass

bul-wark *n.* strong support

bum *n.* one who begs from others

bum-ble-bee *n.*

large bee
bump *v.* collide with

bump-er *n.* device that absorbs shock and prevents damage

bumper--to--bumper *adj.* long line of vehicles moving very slowly

bump-kin *n.* awkward country person bumpkinly *adj.*, -ish *adj.*

bump-tious *adj.* forward; pushy

bun *n.* plain or sweet small breads; tightly rolled hair

bunch *n.* group of items

bun-co *n.* swindling scheme

bun-dle *n.* anything wrapped or held together

bundle up *v.* dress warmly

bun-ga-low *n.* one-story cottage

bun-gle *v.* act awkwardly bungling *adj.*, bungler *n.*,bunglingly *adv.*

bun-ion *n.* painful swelling of the big toe

bunk *n.* narrow bed

bunk-er *n.* tank for storing fuel on a ship bunkered *v.*, bunkering *v.*

bun-ny *n.* small rabbit

bunt *v.* tap a pitched ball with a half swing; middle part of square sail

bunt-ing *n.* hooded blanket for a baby; various stout-billed birds

buoy *n.* floating channel marker

buoy-an-cy *n.* tendency to remain afloat; ability to recover quickly

bur-den *n.* something hard to bear; a duty; something that is carried

bu-reau *n.* low chest; body of non-elected officials in government

bur-geon *v.* put forth new life

bur-glar *n.* person who steals -ize *v.*

bur-i-al *n.* act of burying

burl *n.* growth on a tree

bur-lap *n.* coarse cloth woven from hemp; lightweight material

bur-lesque *n.* theatrical entertainment burlesqued *v.*, burlesquely *adv.*

burn *v.* be destroyed by fire; consume fuel and give off heat

bur-nish *v.* to polish; make shiny

burp *n.* a belch

bur-ro *n.* a small donkey

bur-row *n.* tunnel dug in the ground by an animal for burrying

bur-si-tis *n.* inflammation of the joints

burst *adj.* explode and experience a sudden outbreak

bus *n.* large passenger vehicle

bus boy *n.* waiter's assistant; person who cleans the tables

bus-by *n.* a fur hat

bush-ing *n.* metal lining that reduces friction; electrical

busi-ness *n.* person's professional dealings or occupation; an industrial or commercial establishment; role; function

bus-y *adj.* full of activity; engaged in some form of work
busily *adv.*, **business** *n.*

but *conj.* on the contrary to; other than; if not; except for the fact

bu-tane *n.* a gas produced from petroleum, used as a fuel refrigerant and aerosol propellant

butch-er *n.* one who slaughters animals and dresses them for food
butchered *v.*, **butchering** *v.*

butt *n.* the object of ridicule; the thick large or blunt end of something. *v.* To hit with horns or the head; to place end to end

but-ter *n.* a yellow substance churned from milk

but-ter-fat *n.* the natural fat from milk that floats to the top of unpasteurized milk

but-ter-fin-gers *n.* an awkward or clumsy person

but-ter-fly *n.*

a narrow-bodied insect with four broad, colorful wings; resembles a butterfly

but-tocks *pl.*, *n.* the two round fleshy parts of the rump

but-ton *n.* a small disk that interlocks with a buttonhole

but-tress *n.* a support made of either brick or stone

bux-om *adj.* lively; full of life; happy; pleasantly plump

buy *v.* to purchase in exchange for money. *n.* Anything that is bought

buy-er *v.* a person who buys from a store or an individual

buzz *v.* to make a low vibrating sound, as a bee; to signal

buzz-er *n.* an electrical signaling device that makes a buzzing sound; the sound of a buzzer

by *prep.* up to and beyond; to go past; not later than

bye *n.* a position in which a contestant has no opponent after pairs are drawn for a tournament, and, therefore, advances to the next round

bye-bye *Slang* farewell

by-gone *adj.* gone by; past

byte *n.* in computer science, a sequence of adjacent binary digits operated on as a unit

by-word *n.* well-known proverb

C, c The third letter of the English alphabet

cab *n.* a taxicab; the compartment where a person sits to drive a large truck or machinery

ca-bal *n.* a group that conspires against a government or other public intstitution

ca-ban-a *n.* a small shelter on the beach with living facilities

cab-a-ret *n.* a restaurant that provides dancing and live entertainment

cab-bage *n.*

a plant with large, edible green leaves, eaten as a vegetable

cab-in *n.* a small house; a private room on a ship

cab-i-net *n.* a storage unit

cab-i-net-maker *n.* a person who specialized in the construction of furniture

ca-ble *n.* a very heavy rope having great strength

cable stitch *n.* a knitting stitch that produces the look of a cable

cable television *n.* a private television system which picks up signals from television stations and transmits them by cable

ca-boo-dle *n.* *Slang* the entire unit, amount, or colletion

ca-boose *n.* the last car of a train

cache *n.* a safe place

ca-dav-er *n.* a dead body

ca-det *n.* a military student

caf-e-te-ri-a *n.* a restaurant with self-service

caf-feine *n.* a stimulant **caffeinic** *adj.*

cake *n.* a sweet dessert

cal-a-mine *n.* a lotion for skin irritations

ca-lam-i-ty *n.* a misfortune
calamitously *adv.*

cal-ci-fy *v.* to become stony
calcification *n.*

cal-ci-um *n.* an element found in teeth and bones

cal-cu-late *v.* to estimate something
calculable, calculated *adj.*

cal-dron *n.* a cooking kettle

calf *n.* the offspring of a domestic cow

cal-i-co *n.* a cotton fabric used in clothing

call *v.* to call out; to telephone

cal-lus *n.* thickening of the skin

calm *adj.* an absence of motion

cal-o-rie *n.* a measurement of food energy

cam-el *n.*

a desert animal living in Africa and Asia

cam-e-o *n.* a precious gem

cam-er-a *n.* an apparatus for taking pictures

cam-i-sole *n.* a short sleeveless undergarment for women

cam-ou-flage *v.* to disguise or conseal something from view

camp *n.* a temporary lodging

cam-pus *n.* the grounds of a college

can *v.* to be physically or mentally able

ca-nal *n.* a man-made water channel

ca-nar-y *n.* a small, colorful songbird

ca-nas-ta *n.* a card game

can-cel *v.* to invalidate or annul cancelation *n.*

can-cer *n.* a malignant tumor -ous *adj.*

can-di-date *n., pl.* a person seeking an office candidacy *n.*

can-dle *n.* a wax tallow burned to produce light

cane *n.* a walking stick

ca-nine *adj.* of the dog family

can-is-ter *n.* a container to store food in

can-ker *n.* an erosive sore in the mouth which causes great discomfort

can-ni-bal *n.* a person who eats human flesh

can-non *n.* a heavy war weapon

can-ny *adj.* cautious

ca-noe *n.*

a light-weight, slender boat canoeist *n.*

can-on *n.* the laws of a church

can-o-py *n.* a cloth covering over a bed

can-tan-ker-ous *adj.* bad-tempered; ill-natured cantankerously *adv.*

can-teen *n.* a container for carrying water

can-ter *n.* movement that is slower than a gallop

can-vas *n.* a fabric used in making tents

can-vass *v.* to solicit opinions or votes; to examine very carefully

can-yon *n.* a deep, narrow gorge

cap *n.* a covering for the head

ca-pa-ble *adj.* having the ability to perform

ca-pac-i-ty *n.* the volume of something; the ability to hold

cape *n.* a covering for the shoulders

cap-il-lary *n.* small vessels that connect

cap-i-tal *n.* the seat of government

ca-pit-u-late *v.* to surrender -tor *n.*

ca-pon *n.* a young rooster

cap-size *v.* to overturn in a boat

cap-sule *n.* a gelatinous case for oral medicine

cap-tain *n.* the chief leader of a group

cap-tion *n.* a subtitle

cap-ti-vate *v.* to hold the attention of someone or thing

cap-tive *n.* a prisoner

cap-ture *v.* to take by force captuer *n.*

ca-rafe *n.* a wine bottle

car-a-mel *n.* a chewy candy

car-at *n.* a unit of weight for gems

car-a-van *n.* a group of people traveling together

car-bo-hy-drate *n.* organic compounds

car-bon *n.* a nonmetallic element carbonize *v.*, carbonic *adj*

carbon monoxide *n.* a poisonous gas

car-bun-cle *n.* an infection of the skin

car-bu-re-tor *n.* a device to mix vapor, fuel, and air

car-ci-no-ma *n.* a malignant tumor

car-di-ac *adj.* of the heart

car-di-gan *n.* a sweater with buttons down the front

car-di-ol-o-gy *n.* the study of the heart cardiologist *n.*, cardiological *adj*

card-sharp *n.* a person who cheats when playing cards

care *n.* a feeling of concern

ca-reer *n.* an occupation

care-free *adj.* free from all worries

care-ful *adj.* exercising care

ca-ress *v.* to touch gently

car-go *n.* freight

car-i-bou *n.*

large antlered deer of northern North America

car-il-lon *n.* a set of tuned bells in a tower

car-nage *n.* a massacre

car-ni-val *n.* an amusement show

car-ol *n.* a song

car-pen-ter *n.* one who works with lumber

car-pet *n.* a floor covering

car-rot *n.* an orange root vegetable

car-ry *v.* to transport from one place to another.

car-tel *n.* a group of companies organized to control prices, etc.

car-ti-lage *n.* connective tissue

car-toon *n.* a funny caricature -ist *n.*

cart-wheel *n.* a sideways handspring

cas-cade *n.* a waterfall
case *n.* a particular occurrence
cash *n.* money
cash-ew *n.* an edible nut
cash-ier *n.* an employee who handles cash
ca-si-no *n.* a public place for gambling
cask *n.* a barrel
cas-ket *n.* a coffin
cas-se-role *n.* a dish used for baking
cas-sette *n.* tape used in tape recorders
cast *v.* hurl or throw with force
castway *adj.*
cast-er *n.* a small set of swiveling rollers
cas-ti-gate *v.* to punish or criticize severely
cas-tle *n.* a fort
cast-off *adj.* to discarded or throw away
cas-trate *v.* to spay
ca-su-al *adj.* informal
ca-su-al-ty *n.* one injured or killed
cat-a-combs *n.* underground passage
cat-a-log *n.* publication listing of names and addresses
cat-a-ma-ran *n.* a pleasure boat
ca-tas-tro-phe *n.* a terrible disaster
catch *v.* to capture or seize
cat-e-go-ry *n.* a grouping of something
ca-ter *v.* to provide food
cat-er-pil-lar *n.* the larva of a moth or butterfly
cat-fish *n.* a freshwater fish
ca-the-dral *n.* a large church
cat-nap *n.* a short nap
CAT scan *n.* x-ray; using computerized axial tomography
cat-tle *n., pl.* farm animals
cau-cus *n.* the meeting of a political party
cau-li-flow-er *n.* a vegetable
caulk *v.* to seal seams against leakage
cause *v.* to produce a result
cause-way *n.* a highway through a marsh tract
cau-ter-ize *v.* to burn with a hot instrument
cau-tion *n.* a warning
cav-al-cade *n.* horse-drawn carriages
cav-al-ry *n.* army troops on horseback
cave *n.* an underground tomb or chamber
cav-i-ar *or* cav-i-are *n.* eggs of a large fish
cav-i-ty *n.* a decayed place in a tooth
cease *v.* to stop
cease-fire *v.* to stop fighting
cease-less *adj.* endless ceasely *adv.*
ce-dar *n.* an evergreen tree
ceil-ing *n.* an overhead covering of a room

cel-e-brate *v.* to observe with ceremonies celebration *n.*
cel-eb-ri-ty *n., pl.* -ies a famous person
cel-er-y *n.* a vegetable with an edible stalk
ce-les-tial *adj.* heavenly
cell *n.* smallest unit of any organism capable of independent function
cel-lar *n.* an underground area of a house
cel-lu-lite *n.* a fatty deposit
cel-lu-lose *n.* a carbohydrate
ce-ment *n.* a hard construction material
cem-e-ter-y *n.* a place for burying the dead
cen-sor *n.* a person who examines films censorship *n.*
cen-sure *n.* an expression of criticism
cen-sus *n.* the count of the population
cen-ter *n.* the equal distance from all sides
cen-tral *adj.* the center or main part centralize *v.*
cen-tu-ry *n.* a period of 100 years
ce-ram-ic *adj.* material made by firing clay
ce-re-al *n.* an edible grain; breakfast food
cer-a-bel-lum *n.* the lower part of the brain
cer-e-brum *n.* the upper part of the brain
cer-e-mo-ny *n.* a ritual
cer-tain *adj.* to be very sure -ly *adv.*
cer-tif-i-cate *n.* a document stating the truth
cer-ti-fy *v.* to declare in writing to be true
ces-sa-tion *n.* the act of stopping or ceasing
ces-sion *n.* the act of giving up rights
chafe *v.* to become sore by rubbing
chafing dish *n.* a dish for cooking food
cha-grin *n.* the feeling of disappointment
chain *n.* connecting links
chair *n.* a seat with four legs and a back
chair-man *n.* a person presiding at a meeting
cha-let *n.* a cottage
chal-ice *n.* a drinking goblet
chalk *n.* a soft mineral used for writing
chal-lah *n.* a loaf of braided bread
chal-lis *n.* a lightweight printed cloth
cham-ber *n.* a judge's office
chamber-maid *n.* maid at a hotel
champ *n.* a champion
cham-pagne *n.* a white sparkling wine
chance *n.* accidental
chan-cel *n.* an area of a church
chan-cel-lor *n.* a chief director -ship *n.*

chan-croid *n.* a lesion in the genital area

chan-de-lier *n.* a large light fixture

change *v.* to become or make different; alter

chan-nel *n.* the deepest part of a harbor, lake or river

chant *n.* a melody sung on the same note

cha-os *n.* total disorder

chap *n., Slang* a fellow

chap-el *n.* a place to worship

chap-er-on *n.* a woman who supervises younger women

chap-lain *n.* clergyman

chaps *pl., n.* leather overpants

chap-ter *n.* one division or part of a book

char-ac-ter *n.* a persons quality or trait

char-coal *n.* a material used for fuel

chard *n.* an edible white beet

charge *v.* to give full responsibility to; price

charg-er *n.* an apparatus to recharge a battery

char-i-ot *n.* a horse-drawn vehicle

char-i-ty *n.* money given to the needy

cha-ri-va-ri *n.* a playful serenade to newlyweds

charm *n.* an ability to please; ornament

chart *n.* a map

char-ter *n.* an official document

chase *v.* to run after

chasm *n.* a deep crack in the earth's surface

chaste *adj.* pure

chas-tise *v.* to reprimand

chat *v.* to converse in a friendly manner

chat-tel *n.* movable personal property

chauf-feur *n.* a person who drives someone

cheap *adj.* inexpensive; low in cost

cheapen *v.* to lessen the value

cheap-skate *n.* one who tries to avoid spending money

cheat *v.* to break the rules **cheater** *n.*

check *v.* to restrain; examine for correctness

check-book *n.* a book with blank checks

check-ers *n.* a board game

check-mate *n.* a winning chess move

ched-dar *n.* a firm, smooth cheese

cheek *n.* the fleshy part of the face

cheek-bone *n.* the facial bone below the eyes

cheerful *adj.* having good spirits

cheer-leader *n.* person who cheers at a sporting event

cheese *n.* food made from the curd of milk

cheese-cake *n.* dessert cake

chee-tah *n.* a swift-running wildcat

chef *n.* a male cook

che-mise *n.* woman's loose undergarment

chem-ist *n.* a person versed in chemistry

che-mo-ther-a-py *n.* a treatment for cancer

che-nille *n.* a soft cord used to make rugs, etc.

cher-ish *v.* to hold dear

cher-ry *n.* fruit tree bearing red fruit

cher-ub *n.* an angel resembling a child

chess *n.* game for two played on a chessboard **chessman** *n.*

chest *n.* the part of the upper body

chest-nut *n.* a tree with edible nuts

chev-ron *n.* an insignia or emblem

chew *v.* to crush or grind with the teeth

chic *adj.* fashionable

chick *n.*

a young chicken

chick-a-dee *n.* a bird

chick-en *n.* a domestic fowl

chicken pox *n.* a contagious childhood disease

chick-pea *n.* a plant with edible pea-like seeds

chic-le *n.* the juice of a tropical tree

chic-o-ry *n.* a herb used in salads

chide *v.* to scold or find fault

chief *n.* a person of highest rank; a boss

chief-tain *n.* a head of a group, or tribe

chif-fon *n.* a sheer fabric

chif-fo-nier *n.* a tall chest of drawers

chig-ger *n.* an insect

chi-gnon *n.* hair worn on the back of the neck

child *n.* a young person of either sex **childish** *adj.*

child-birth *n.* the act of giving birth

chil-i *n.* a hot pepper

chill *v.* to reduce to a lower temperature

chill-y *adj.* very cold condition

chime *n.* a set of bells tuned to a scale

chi-me-ra *n.* an absurd fantasy

chim-ney *n.* a flue for smoke to escape

chim-pan-zee *n.* an ape

chin *n.* the lower part of the face

chi-na *n.* fine porcelain from China

chin-chil-la *n.* a rodent from South America

chintz *n.* printed, glazed cotton fabric

chip-munk *n.*

striped rodent

chi-ro-prac-tic *n.* a method of therapy
chiropractor *n.*
chirp *n.* the high-pitched sound of a
bird
chis-el *n.* tool with a sharp edge to
shape
chit *n.* voucher for food or drink
chit-chat *n.* casual conversation
chiv-al-ry *n.* brave qualities of a knight
chive *n.* herb used as flavoring in cooking
chlo-rine *n.* compound used to purify
water
chock *n.* wedge placed under a wheel
choc-o-late *n.* ground cacao nuts
chocolaty *adj.*
choice *n.* select or choose
choir *n.* an organized group of singers
chok-er *n.* short necklace
cho-les-ter-ol *n.* fatty substance present
in blood cells
choose *v.* select or pick out
chop *v.* cut by making downward stroke
choppy *adj.* rough
chop-sticks *pl., n.* sticks of wood for
eating
cho-ral *adj.* sung by a choir or chorus
cho-rale *n.* hymn with a simple melody
chore *n.* a daily task
cho-re-a *n.* acute nervous disease
cho-re-og-ra-phy *n.* creation of a dance
routine in ballets
chor-is-ter *n.* a member of a choir
cho-rus *n.* a group of people singing
together
cho-sen *adj.* preferred above all others
chow *n., Slang* food
chow-der *n.* soup made with fish or
clams
Christ *n.* Jesus; The Messiah
chris-ten *v.* to baptize; give a Christian
name
Christ-mas *n.* December 25th; believed
to be the birthday of Jesus Christ by
Christians
chrome *n.* anything plated with
chromium
chron-ic *adj.* frequently recurring
chron-i-cle *n.* record of events in order
chry-san-the-mum *n.* cultivated plants
chub-by *adj.* plumb
chuck-hole *n.* hole in the street
chuck-le *v.* laugh quietly -er *n.*
chum *n.* a close friend or pal
chunk *n.* a thick piece; a lump
churl *n.* a rude person
churn *n.* container for making butter
chut-ney *n.* condiment made with fruit
ci-der *n.* juice from apples
ci-gar *n.* rolled tobacco leaves

cig-a-rette *n.* amount of tobacco rolled
in thin paper
cinch *n.* strap for holding a saddle
cin-der *n.* piece of burned wood
cin-e-ma *n.* a motion picture
cin-e-mat-o-garaph *n.* movie pro-jector
cin-e-ma-tog-ra-phy *n.* art of photo-
graphing a motion picture
cin-na-mon *n.* bark of a tree used for
spice
ci-pher *n.* zero
cir-ca *prep.* approximate
cir-cle *n.* process that ends at its starting point
cir-cuit *n.* path where electric current
flows
cir-cu-lar *adj.* moving in a circle
cir-cu-late *v.* pass from place to place
cir-cum-cise *v.* remove skin on the male
penis
cir-cum-fer-ence *n.* perimeter of a circle
cir-cum-scribe *v.* confine within boundaries
cir-cum-stance *n.* fact to consider when
making a decision
cir-cum-stan-tial *adj.* not essential
cir-cum-stan-ti-ate *adj.* provide circumstantial evidence
cir-cum-vent *v.* gain advantage
cir-cus *n.* show featuring clowns, and
trained animals
cir-rho-sis *n.* liver disease
cir-rus *n.* white, wispy cloud
cis-tern *n.* man-made tank for holding
rain water
cit-a-del *n.* fortress
cit-ta-tion *n.* official summons from a
court
cit-i-zen *n.* native or naturalized person
cit-ron *n.* fruit
cit-y *n.* place larger than a town
civ-et *n.* cat-like mammal
civ-ic *adj.* relating to or of a city
ci-vil-ian *n.* person not in active duty in
the military or police force
civ-i-li-za-tion *n.* high level development
civ-i-lize *v.* tame
claim *v.* to hold something to be true
claimable *adj.*
clair-voy-ance *n.* visualize objects hidden
from the senses
clam *n.* freshwater bivalve mollusks
clam-ber *v.* climb using both hands and
feet clamberer *n.*
clam-my *adj.* damp, cold, and sticky
clam-or *n.* loud noise or outcry
clamp *n.* device for holding things
clan *n.* group of people who are related
clan-des-tine *adj.* done in secrecy

clang v. make a loud, ringing sound

clap v. applaud

clap-board n. board covering for a house

clap-per n. part of a bell

clar-i-fy v. become or make clearer

clar-i-net n.

woodwind instrument

clash v. to collide; conflict

clasp n. hook to hold objects together

class n. group with common interest

clas-sic adj. belonging in a certain category

clause n. group of words part of a complex sentence

claus-tro-pho-bia n. fear of enclosed places

clav-i-chord n. key-board instrument

clav-i-cle n. bone that connecting breastbone and shoulder blade

claw n. sharp, curved nail on the foot of an animal

clay n. pliable earth that hardens when fired

clean adj. free from impurities

cleanse v. make pure or clean -er n.

clear adj. not cloudy; able to see easily

clearance n. distance between two objects

cleat n. metal projection to prevent slipping

cleav-er n. knife used by butchers

clef n. musical staff symbol

cler-gy n. women and men religious leaders

cler-gy-man n. member of the clergy

cler-i-cal adj. trained for office duties

clerk n. clerical worker in an office

clev-er adj. mentally quick **cleverness** n.

cli-ent n. a patron; a customer

cli-en-tele n. collection of customers

cli-mate n. weather conditions -tic adj.

cli-max n. point of greatest intensity

clinch v. to settle definitively

cling v. hold fast to; to grasp or stick

clin-ic n. medical establishment

clink v. cause a light ringing sound

clip-per n. fast sailing vessel

clique n. exclusive group of people

clob-ber v., Slang hit repeatedly

cloche n. woman's close-fitting hat

clock n.

instrument that measures time

clog v. to choke up

clone n. identical reproduction

close adj. near, as in time; nearly even

clos-et n. compartment or room for storage

clot n. thick or solid mass, as of blood

cloth n. fabric, used to cover a table

clothe v. provide clothes

cloud n. something that obscures

clout n. a heavy blow with the hand; influence

clove n. a spice

clo-ver n. herb with trifoliolate leaves

clover-leaf n. junction of highway

clown n. professional comedian -ish adj.

cloy v. make sick with too much sweetness

club n. heavy wooden stick

clump n. thick cluster

clum-sy adj. lacking coordination

clus-ter n. a group of something

clutch v. to seize and hold tightly

clut-ter n. confused mass of disorder

coach n. director of athletics, drama, etc.

co-ad-ju-tor n. assistant

coal n. mineral widely used for fuel; ember

co-a-lesce v. come together

co-ali-tion n. temporary alliance

coarse adj. lacking refinement -ness v.

coast n. land bordering the sea

coat n. outer garment

coax v. persuade by gentleness **coaxingly** adv.

cob n. male swan; a corncob

co-balt n. metallic element resembling iron and nickel

cob-ble v. make or repair shoes

co-bra n. venomous snake

cob-web n. fine thread spun into a web

co-caine n. narcotic used as a local anesthetic

coch-le-a n. spiral tube of the inner ear

cock n. adult male in the domestic fowl; the rooster

cock-a-too n. crested parrot

cock-le n. edible bivalve mollusk

cock-ney n. dialect of East End Londoners

cock-pit n. compartment where the pilot and the crew sit

cock-roach n. fast running nocturnal insect

co-co n. fruit of the coconut palm

co-coa n. powder from kernels of the cacao

co-coon n. silky, protective case spun by insect larvae

cod n. large fish of the North Atlantic

cod-dle v. to cook just below boiling point

code *n.* set of rules; set of secret words

co-ed-u-ca-tion *n.* educational system for both men and women

co-erce *v.* dominate with force

co-ex-ist *v.* exist together

cof-fee *n.* beverage prepared from ground beans

cof-fin *n.* box for burying a corpse

cog *n.* series of a teeth on the rim of a wheel

co-gent *adj.* forceful cogently *adv.*

cog-i-tate *v.* think carefully about

co-gnac *n.* fine brandy made in France

co-hab-it *v.* live as husband and wife

co-here *v.* stick or hold together

co-hort *n.* group of people united in one effort

coif *n.* hat worn under a nun's veil

coil *n.* series of connecting rings

coin *n.* piece of metal used as money

co-in-cide *v.* happen at the same time

co-in-ci-dence *n.* two events happening at the same time

coke *n.* arbonaceous fuel; cocaine

cold *adj.* having a low temperature coldness *n.*

cold–blooded *adj.* without feeling

col-ic *n.* sharp pain in the abdomen caused by muscular cramps

col-i-se-um *n.* large amphitheater

col-lab-o-rate *v.* work with another person

col-lapse *v.* fall; to give way

col-lar *n.* part of a garment around the neck

col-lar-bone *n., Anat.* the clavicle

col-late *v.* assemble in correct sequence

col-lat-er-al *adj.* security for a loan

col-league *n.* one who works in the same profession

col-lect *v.* gather or assemble

col-lege *n.* institution of higher education

col-lide *v.* come together with impact

col-lo-quy *n.* formal conference

col-lusion *n.* secret agreement

co-lon *n.* punctuation mark (:); section of the large intestine

colo-nel *n.* an officer in the armed forces colonelcy *n.*

col-o-ny *n.* group of emigrants living in a new land

col-or *n.* a hue or tint colorful *adj.*

col-or-a-tion *n.* arrangement of different colors or shades

col-or--blind *adj.* not able to distinguish colors

col-or-fast *adj.* color that will not fade

col-os-sal *adj.* large or gigantic in size

colt *n.* very young male horse -ish *adj.*

col-umn *n.* decorative, supporting pillar

col-um-nist *n.* person who writes a newspaper column

co-ma *n.* deep unciousness sleep

comb *n.* instrument for aranging the hair

com-bat *v.* oppose; to struggle

com-bi-na-tion *n.* series of numbers or letters to open locks

com-bine *v.* unite; to merge

com-bus-ti-ble *adj.* capability of burning

come *v.* arrive; to approach

com-e-dy *n.* humorous, entertaining performance

com-et *n.* celestial body orbiting the sun cometic *adj.*

com-fort *v.* console in time of grief or fear

com-fort-er *n.* heavy quilt; one who comforts

com-ic *adj.* characteristic of comedy

com-i-cal *adj.* funny

com-ma *n.* punctuation mark (,) indicating a break or series

com-mand *v.* to give orders; to dominate

com-mem-o-rate *v.* honor the memory of commemorative *adj.*

com-mence *v.* begin; start

com-mence-ment *n.* graduation ceremony

com-mend *v.* give praise -able *adj.*

com-men-su-rate *adj.* equal in duration commensurately *adv.*

com-ment *n.* statement of observation

com-merce *n.* exchanging of products

com-mer-cial *adj.* relating to a product

com-mis-er-ate *v.* feel sympathy for someone

com-mis-sary *n.* store on a military base

com-mis-sion *n.* moneys paid sales

com-mit-tee *n.* people appointed perform a task or function

com-mode *n.* movable wash-stand

com-mo-dore *n.* naval officer

com-mon *adj.* general, ordinary

common denominatior *n.* number that can be evenly divided

com-mu-ni-ca-ble *adj.* capable of being transmitted, as with a disease communicably *adv.*

com-mu-ni-cate *v.* make known

com-mu-ni-ca-tion *n.* act of transmitting ideas

com-mun-ion *n.* mutual sharing of feelings and thoughts

com-mu-nism *n.* system of government

com-mu-ni-ty *n.* group of people living in the same area

com-mute *v.* travel to one's job each day

com-pact *adj.* packed together

com-pan-ion *n.* an associate
com-pan-ion-a-ble *adj.* friendly
companionably *adv.*
com-pa-ny *n.* gathering of persons for a
social purpose
com-pa-ra-ble *adj.* capable of comparison
com-pare *v.* note the likenesses of
com-part-ment *n.* enclosed area

com-pass *n.*

instrument to deter-
mine geographic
direction
com-pas-sion *n.* sym-
pathy for someone
com-pat-i-ble *adj.* live together harmoniously
com-pa-tri-ot *n.* person of the same
country compatriotic *adj.*
com-pel *v.* urge or force action
com-pen-dium *n.* short summary
com-pen-sate *v.* make up for; to pay
com-pete *v.* to engage in a contest
com-pe-tent *adj.* having sufficient ability
com-pe-ti-tion *n.* a trial of skill or ability
competitive *adj.*
com-pet-i-tor *n.* one who competes
against another
com-pile *v.* to put together information
from other documents
com-plain-ant *n.* person filing a formal
charge
com-plaint *n.* expression of dissatisfaction, or resentment
com-plai-sance *n.* willingness to please
com-ple-ment *n.* something that adds to
com-plete *adj.* having all the necessary
parts; whole
com-plex *adj.* consisting of intricate parts
com-plex-ion *n.* natural color and texture
of the skin
com-pli-ance *n.* agreement
com-pli-cate *v.* make or become complex
com-pli-ment *n.* expression of praise
com-pli-men-ta-ry *adj.* giving a compliment
com-ply *v.* to consent
com-po-nent *n.* a constituent part
com-port *v.* conduct oneself in a certain
way
com-pose *v.* make up from elements or
parts composer *n.*
com-pos-ite *adj.* made from separate elements
com-po-si-tion *n.* artistic literary work
com-post *n.* fertilizing mixture of
vegetable matter
com-po-sure *n.* tranquillity

com-pote *n.* fruit preserved or stewed in
syrup
com-pound *n.* combination of two or
more parts compoundable *adj.*
com-pre-hend *v.* to perceive -sion *n.*
com-pre-hen-sive *adj.* large in scope
com-pres-sor *n.* a machine that for com-
pressing air
com-prise *v.* to be made up of
com-pro-mise *n.* settling of differences
comp-trol-ler *n.* person who examines
accounts
com-pute *v.* determine by the use of
math; to make calculations
com-puter *n.* electronic machine which
performs logical calculations
computerize *v.* process or store information on a computer
com-rade *n.* associate who shares one's
interest or occupation
con *v. Slang* to swindle or trick
con-cat-e-nate *v.* join, or link together
con-cave *adj.* hollowed and curved inward concavly *adv.*
con-ceal *v.* keep from sight; to hide
concealment *n.*
con-cede *v.* yield to a privilege; acknowledge as true conceded *adj.*
con-ceive *v.* become pregnant; to create
a mental image
con-cen-trate *v.* give intense thought to
something
con-cen-tra-tion *n.* state of being concentrated
con-cept *n.* generalized idea
conceptual *adj.*
con-cep-tion *n.* union of sperm and egg
con-cern *n.* sincere interest -ed *adj.*
con-cert *n.* musical performance
con-cer-to *n.* one or more solo instruments in a composition
con-ces-sion *n.* act of conceding
con-ces-sion-aire *n.* operator or holder
of a concession
conch *n.* a tropical marine mollusk
con-cil-i-ate *v.* win over or to gain a
friendship conciliation *n.*
con-cise *adj.* short and to the point
con-clave *n.* private or secret meeting to
elect a new pope
con-clude *v.* bring to an end
conclusion *n.*
con-com-i-tant *adj.* accompanying
con-cord *n.* accord; harmony
con-course *n.* open space for passage of
crowds
con-crete *n.* construction material
con-cu-pis-cence *n.* a strong sexual
desire
con-cur *v.* to agree or express approval

con-cur-rent *adj.* acting together

con-cus-sion *n.* sudden and violent jolt

con-demn *v.* to find to be wrong condemnable *adj.*

con-dense *v.* to make more compact condenser *n.*

con-di-ment *n.* relish, or sauce used to season food

con-di-tion *n.* state or existence of-something

con-di-tion-al *adj.* tentative conditionally *adv.*

con-di-tioned *adj.* prepared for a certain process or action

con-di-tion-er *n.* application that improves a substance

con-dom *n.* thin rubber sheath to cover the penis during sexual intercourse

con-do-min-i-um *n.* building in which all units are owned separately

con-done *n.* to forgive

con-dor *n.*

a very large American vulture

con-duct *v.* lead and direct a band; lead the way

con-duc-tor *n.* person who conducts a musical ensemble

con-duit *n.* pipe to pass electric wires through

cone *n.* solid body tapered evenly to a point

con-fab-u-late *v.* chat informally

con-fec-tion-er-y *n.* candy and sweets

con-fed-er-a-cy *n.* union of southern states

con-fed-er-ate *n.* ally or friend

con-fer *v.* consult with another conferment *n.*

con-fer-ence *n.* meeting for discussion

con-fess *v.* to make known or tell something

con-fet-ti *pl., n.* small pieces of paper thrown during a happy occasion

con-fide *v.* entrust a secret to another confiding *adj.*

con-fi-dence *n.* a feeling of self-assurance

con-fi-den-tial *adj.* hold as a secret confidentiality *n.*

con-fig-u-ra-tion *n.* arrangement of parts or things

con-fine *v.* keep within a certain boundary or limit confinement *n.*

con-firm *v.* establish or support the truth of something

con-fir-ma-tion *n.* act of confirming to show proof

con-fis-cate *v.* seize for public use; to officially seize confiscation *n.*

con-flict *n.* a battle; a clash -tive *adj.*

con-form *v.* similar in form or character conformably *adv.*

con-for-ma-tion *n.* the manner in which something is shaped

con-found *v.* to amaze, to confuse

con-front *v.* stand face to face with defiance confrontation *n.*

con-fuse *v.* mislead or bewilder

con-fu-sion *n.* state of being confused; disorder

con-fute *v.* prove to be invalid or false confutable *adj.*

con-geal *v.* jell; to solidify

con-gen-ial *adj.* having agreeable characteristics

con-gen-i-tal *adj.* existing from the time of birth, but not from heredity

con-gest *v.* enlarge with an excessive accumulation of blood; to clog, as with traffic congestion *n.*

con-glom-er-ate *n.* business consisting of many different companies

con-grat-u-late *v.* acknowledge an achievement with praise

con-grat-u-la-tions *pl., n.* expression of or the act of congratulating

con-gre-gate *v.* assemble together in a crowd congregator *n.*

con-gre-ga-tion *n.* group of people meeting for worship

Con-gress *n.* united States legislative body congressional *adj.*

con-gru-ent *adj.* agreeing to conform

con-jec-ture *n.* guess or conclusion based on incomplete evidence conjectural *adj.*

con-join *v.* to unite

con-ju-gate *adj.* change the form of a verb; to join in pairs -ly *adv.*

con-junct *adj.* combined

con-junc-tion *n.* act of joining; the state of being joined

con-junc-ti-va *n.* the membrane lining of the eyelids

con-junc-tive *adj.* connective

con-junc-ti-vi-tis *n. Pathol.* inflammation of the membrane that lines the eyelids

con-jure *v.* bring into the mind; to appeal or call on solemnly

con-nect *v.* join; to unite

con-nec-tion *n.* association of one person or thing to another

con-nec-tive *adj.* capable of connecting; tending to connect connectivity *n.*

con-nive *v.* ignore a known wrong, therefore implying sanction connivance *n.*

con-nois-seur *n.* a person whose expertise in an area of art or taste allows him to be a judge; an expert

con-no-ta-tion *n.* the associative meaning of a word in addition to the literal meaning

con-note *v.* imply along with the literal meaning

con-nu-bi-al *adj.* having to do with marriage or the state of marriage

con-quer *v.* subdue; to win

con-science *n.* ability to recognize right and wrong

con-sci-en-tious *adj.* honest

con-scious *adj.* aware of one's own existence and environment

con-script *n.* one who is drafted for a service or a job

con-se-crate *v.* declare something to be holy consecration *n.*

con-sec-u-tive *adj.* following in uninterrupted succession consecutively *adv.*

con-sen-sus *n.* a collective opinion

con-sent *v.* to agree; give permission

con-se-quent *adj.* following as a natural result or effect consequentially *adv.*

con-serv-a-tive *adj.* opposed to change consequentively *adv.*

con-ser-va-to-ry *n.* a school of dramatic art or music

con-serve *v.* save something from decay, loss, or depletion conservable *adj.*

con-sider *v.* seriously think about; to examine mentally

con-sid-er-a-ble *adj.* large in amount or extent; important considerably *adv.*

con-sid-er-a-tion *n.* taking into account of circumstance before forming an opinion

con-sign *v.* commit to the care of another; to deliver merchandise consignable *adj.* consignment *n.*

con-sist *v.* be made up of

con-sis-ten-cy *n.* degree of texture, viscosity, or density consistent *adj.*

con-sole *v.* give comfort to someone consolable *adj.*

con-sol-i-date *v.* combine in one or to form a union of; to form a compact mass consolidation *n.*

con-so-nant *n.* sound in speech other than a vowel consonantly *adv.*

con-sort *n.* spouse; companion or partner; agreement

con-spic-u-ous *adj.* noticeable -ly *adv.*

con-spir-a-cy *n.* plan or act of two or more persons to do an evil act

con-spire *v.* plan a wrongful act in secret conspirator *n.*

con-sta-ble *n.* peace officer

con-stant *adj.* unchanging; steady in action, purpose, and affection constancy *n.*, constantly *adv.*

con-ster-na-tion *n.* sudden confusion or amazement

con-sti-pa-tion *n.* condition of the bowels characterized by inability to empty the bowels

con-stit-u-ent *adj.* having the power to elect a representative

con-sti-tu-tion *n.* fundamental laws that govern a nation; structure or composition

con-strain *v.* restrain by physical or moral means constrained *adj.*

con-straint *n.* the threat or use of force; confinement

con-struct *v.* to create, make, or build constructor *n.*

con-struc-tion *n.* the act of constructing or building something -al *adj.*

con-struc-tive *adj.* useful; helpful; advancing, or improving constructively *adv.*, -ness *n.*

con-strue *v.* interpret; to translate

con-sul *n.* an official that resides in a foreign country

con-sult *v.* seek advice or information from; to compare views consulter *n.*

con-sume *v.* to ingest; to eat or drink; to absorb consumable *adj.*

consumer *n.* person who buys services or goods

con-sump-tion *n.* fulfillment; the act of consuming

con-sump-tive *adj.* tending to destroy or waste away

con-tact *n.* place, or junction where two or more surfaces or objects touch

con-ta-gion *n.* transmitting of a disease by contact

con-tain *v.* include or enclose

con-tain-er *n.* something that holds or carries

con-tam-i-nate *v.* pollute or make inferior

con-temn *v.* scorn or despise

con-tem-plate *v.* to ponder -ation *n.*

con-tempt *n.* viewing something as mean, vile, or worthless

con-temp-tu-ous *adj.* feeling or showing contempt

con-tend *v.* dispute; to fight; to debate; to argue

con-tent *n.* something contained within; subject matter of a book -ment *n.*

con-ten-tion *n.* competition

con-test *n.* a competition; strife; conflict contestant *n.*

con-text *n.* a sentence, or phrase

con-ti-nent *n.* one of the seven large masses of the earth

con-tin-ue *v.* maintain without interruption; to resume **continuance** *n.*

con-ti-nu-i-ty *n.* quality of being continuous

con-tin-u-ous *adj.* uninterrupted or unbroken

con-tort *v.* severely twist out of shape **contortive** *adj.*

con-tor-tion-ist *n.* an acrobat who exhibits unnatural body positions

con-tour *n.* the outline of a body, figure, or mass

con-tra-band *n.* illegal or prohibited traffic; smuggled goods

con-tra-cep-tion *n.* voluntary prevention of impregnation **-tive** *adj. or n.*

con-tract *n.* formal agreement between two or more parties

con-trac-tion *n.* a shortening of a word by using an apostrophe (')

con-trac-tile *adj.* having the power to contract

con-tra-dict *v.* express the opposite side or idea **contradiction** *n.*

con-tral-to *n., pl.* **-tos** lowest female singing voice

con-tra-puntal *adj.* relating to counterpoint

con-trast *v.* note the differences between two or more people, things, etc.

con-tra-vene *v.* be contrary; to violate

con-trib-ute *v.* give something to someone **contribution** *n.*

con-trol *v.* have the authority to regulate, direct, or dominate a situation **controlable** *adj.*

con-trol-ler *n.* the chief accounting officer of a business

con-tro-ver-sy *n.* a dispute; a debate; a quarrel **controversial** *adj.*

co-nun-drum *n.* a riddle with an answer that involves a pun

con-va-lesce *v.* grow strong after a long illness **convalescent** *adj.*

con-vene *v.* meet or assemble formally

con-ven-ience *n.* quality of being suitable

con-vent *n.* local house of a religious order, especially for nuns

con-ven-tion *n.* formal meeting; a regulatory meeting between people, or nations

con-ven-tion-al *adj.* commonplace

con-verge *v.* come to a common point

con-ver-sa-tion *n.* an informal talk

converse *v.* involve oneself in conversation with another

con-ver-sion *n.* state of changing to adopt new opinions or beliefs **conversional** *adj.*

con-vex *adj.* curved outward

con-vey *v.* transport; pass information on to someone else

con-vict *v.* prove someone guilty

con-vince *v.* persuade to believe without doubt

con-voy *n.* group of vehicles traveling together

con-vulse *v.* move or shake violently

con-vul-sion *n.* an involuntary muscular contraction

cook *v.* apply heat to food; to prepare food

cook-ie *n.* sweet, flat cake

cool *adj.* without warmth

coop *n.* enclosed area to contain chickens

co-op-er-ate *v.* work together **-tion** *n.*

co-op-er-a-tive *adj.* willing to cooperate with others

coot *n.* bird

cop *n., Informal* police officer

cope *v.* to struggle or contend with something

cop-ier *n.* machine that makes copies

co-pi-lot *n.* assistant pilot on an aircraft

co-pi-ous *n.* large in quantity; abundant

cop-per *n.* metallic element; conductor of electricity

cop-per-head *n.* venomous snake

cop-ra *n.* dried coconut meat

cop-u-late *v.* have sexual intercourse

copy *v.* reproduce an original

copy-right *n.* satutory right to distribute literary work

copy writer *n.* person who writes copy

co-quette *n.* woman who flirts

cor-al *n.* small sea creature

coral snake *n.* venomous snake

cord *n.* string or twine; an insulated wire

cor-dial *adj.* warm-hearted and sincere

cor-don *n.* circle of ships to guard an area

cor-du-roy *n.* durable ribbed cotton fabric

core *n.* innermost part of something

cork *n.* elastic bark of the oak tree

cork-screw *n.* device for removing corks from bottles

corn *n.* vegetable

corn bread *n.* bread made from crushed cornmeal

corn cob *n.* cone where kernels grow

corncrib *n.* building for storing corn

cor-ne-a *n.* membrane of the eyeball

cor-ner *n.* angle where surfaces meet

corner back *n.* the defensive halfback

corner-stone *n.* stone that forms part of

a building

cor-net *n.* brass musical instrument

corn-row *v.* braid the hair in rows

corn-starch *n.* starch made from corn used to thicken food

corn syrup *n.* sweet syrup

cor-nu-co-pi-a *n.* a curved goat's horn

co-rol-la *n.* petals of a flower

cor-ol-lary *n.* something that naturally follows or accompanies

cor-o-nar-y *adj.* relating to the arteries of the heart muscles

coronary thrombosis *n.* blockage of the coronary artery

cor-po-ral *n.* noncommissioned officer

cor-po-rate *adj.* combined into one joint body

cor-po-ra-tion *n.* group of merchants

corps *n.* branch of the armed forces

corpse *n.* dead body

cor-pu-lence *n.* excessive body fat; obesity

cor-pus-cle *n.* living cell in the blood

cor-pus delicti *n.* evidence pertaining to a crime

cor-ral *n.* enclosure for containing animals

cor-rect *v.* make free from fault or mistakes **correctable** *adj.*

cor-rel-a-tive *adj.* having a mutual relation

cor-re-spond *v.* communicate by written words **correspondence** *n.*

cor-ri-dor *n.* long hall

cor-ri-gen-dum *n.* an error accompanied by its correction

cor-ri-gi-ble *adj.* able to correct

cor-rob-o-rate *v.* support with evidence **corroboration** *n.*

cor-rode *v.* eat away **corrosion** *n.*

cor-rupt *adj.* dishonest; evil

cor-sage *n.* small bouquet of flowers

cor-sair *n.* pirate; a fast moving vessel

cor-set *n.* woman's undergarment for support

cor-tege *n.* a funeral procession

cor-tex *n.* external layer of an organ

cor-ti-sone *n.* hormone from the adrenal cortex

cor-us-cate *v.* to sparkle

cor-vette *n.* armed warship

co-ry-za *n.* acute inflammation of the respiratory system

co-sign *v.* sign a document jointly

co-sig-na-to-ry *n.* one who cosigns a document

cos-met-ic *n.* preparation to beautify the face

cos-me-tol-o-gy *n.* study of cosmetics **cosmetologist** *n.*

cos-mog-o-ny *n.* creation of the universe

cos-mo-naut *n.* a Soviet astronaut

cos-mo-pol-i-tan *adj.* being at home anywhere in the world

cos-mos *n.* orderly systematic universe

cos-set *v.* to pamper; pet

cost *n.* amount paid or charged for a purchase

cos-tive *adj.* causing constipation

cos-tume *n.* clothes worn for playing a part or dressing up in a disguise

cot *n.* small, often collapsible bed

cot-tage *n.* small house

cotter pin *n.* metal pin with flared ends

cot-ton *n.* fabric created by the weaving cotton fibers

cotton candy *n.* spun sugar

cot-ton-mouth *n.* water moccasin snake

couch *n.* piece of furniture

cou-gar *n.* mountain lion, panther, and puma

cough *v.* suddenly expel air from the lungs

could *v.* past tense of can

could-n't *contr.* could not

cou-lomb *n.* unit to measure electricity

coun-cil *n.* group of people assembled for consultation; advisory body **councilman** *n.*

coun-sel *n.* advice through consultation

coun-sel-or *n.* a lawyer

count *v.* find the total number of units; to name numbers in order

count-down *n.* counting in descending order

coun-te-nance *n.* expression of the face

coun-ter-act *v.* oppose; make ineffective

coun-ter-at-tack *n.* attack made in response to an enemy attack

coun-ter-bal-ance *n.* a weight that balances another; counterpoise

coun-ter-claim *n.* contrary claim made to offset another

coun-ter-clock-wise *adj. & adv.* opposite direction

coun-ter-es-pi-o-nage *n.* espionage aimed at thwarting enemy espionage

coun-ter-feit *v.* closely imitate or copy

coun-ter-foil *n.* stub of a check or ticket

coun-ter-man *n.* one who works at a counter

coun-ter-mand *v.* reverse a command by issuing a contrary order

coun-ter-of-fen-sive *n.* a military offensive

coun-ter-pane *n.* a covering

coun-ter-part *n.* one who complements another

coun-ter-plea *n.* plea in answer to a previous plea

coun-ter-point *n.*, *Mus.* combined melodies

coun-ter-pro-duct-ive *adj.* hinder rather than aid

coun-ter-vail *v.* counteract

coun-ter-weight *n.* an equivalent weight

count-ess *n.* wife of an earl or count

count-ing house *n.* room used for keeping books

count-less *adj.* too numerous to be counted

coun-tri-fied *adj.* rural; unsophisticated

coun-try *n.* the land of one's birth

coun-try-man *n.* a compatriot

coun-try-side *n.* rural area

coun-ty *n.* territorial division

cou-pe *n.* car with two doors

cou-ple *n.* a pair; a few

cou-plet *n.* rhyming lines of poetry

cou-pon *n.* form to obtain a discount

cour-age *n.* strength to face danger without fear **courageous** *adj.*

cou-ri-er *n.* a messenger

course *n.* a series or sequence; a series of studies

court *n.* a place where trials are conducted; area marked off for game playing

cour-te-ous *adj.* respect for others

cour-te-san *n.* prostitute

cour-te-sy *n.* courteous behavior

court-house *n.* building holding courts of law

court-yard *n.* open space enclosed by walls

cous-in *n.* child of one's uncle or aunt

cove *n.* small inlet or bay

cov-e-nant *n.* formal, binding agreement

cov-er *v.* place something on or over

cov-et *v.* to crave possessions of someone else

cov-ey *n.* small drain that runs under a road

cum-ber-some *adj.* unwieldy

cum-mer-bund *n.* group of birds

cow *n.*

mature female of cattle

cow-ard *n.* one showing great fear or timidity **cowardice** *n.*

cowl *n.* hood or long hooded cloak

cox-comb *n.* conceited foolish person

cox-swain *n.* one who steers a boat

coy *adj.* quieting or shy

coy-o-te *n.* small wolf-life animal

coz-en *v.* swindle, cheat, or deceive; win over by coaxing

co-zy *adj.* comfortable and warm; snug

crab *n.* one of numerous crustaceans

crab-by *adj.* ill-tempered and cross

crack *v.* to break without completely separating *n.* addictive form of cocaine

cra-dle *n.* small bed for infants

craft *n.* special skill or ability

crag *n.* steep, jagged rock or cliff

cram *v.* pack tightly; prepare hastily for an exam

cramp *n.* painful contraction of a muscle; abdominal pain

cran-ber-ry *n.* tree with tart red berries

crane *n.* large bird; machine for lifting heavy objects

cra-ni-um *n.* the skull

crank *n.* device to turn a shaft

crank-y *adj.* grouchy **crankiness** *n.*

cran-ny *n.* small crevice

craps *v.* gambling game with two dice

crash *v.* break noisily; collapse

crate *n.* container for shipping or storage

cra-ter *n.* depression in a volcano

cra-vat *n.* a necktie

crave *v.* desire intensely

cra-ven *adj.* lacking courage

crav-ing *n.* intense longing or desire

craw *n.* the stomach of a lower animal

crawl *v.* move on hands and knees; progress slowly

cray-on *n.* stick of wax used for coloring

craze *v.* to become insane

cra-zy *adj.* insane **craziness** *n.*

creak *v.* squeaking or grating noise

cream *n.* fatty part of milk; pale yellow-white color

crease *n.* line made by folding and pressing

cre-ate *v.* bring something into existence

cre-a-tion *n.* something created

cre-a-tive *adj.* inventive; imaginative **creativeness** *n.*

cre-a-tor *n.* God

crea-ture *n.* a living being

cre-den-za *n.* a buffet or sideboard

cred-i-ble *adj.* reasonable grounds for belief

cred-it *n.* money available in a bank; acknowledgment; college unit

cred-u-lous *adj.* gullible

creed *n.* religious belief

creek *n.* narrow stream

creel *n.* wicker basket for holding fish

creep *v.* advance at a slow pace

cre-mate *v.* reduce to ashes by burning

cre-o-sote *n.* oily liquid mixture

cre-pus-cu-lar *adj.* relating to twilight

cre-scen-do *adv.* gradually increasing in loudness

cres-cent *n.* quarter shape of the moon

cress *n.* plant with edible leaves

crest *n.* top line of a mountain or hill; ridge of a wave or roof

cre-tin-ism *n.* condition of physical stunting and mental deficiency

cre-tonne *n.* cotton or linen cloth

cre-vasse *n.* deep crack in a glacier

crev-ice *n.* narrow crack

crew *n.* group of people that work together

crew-el *n.* yarn used in embroidery

crib *n.* small baby's bed with high sides

crick-et *n.* leaping insect; a game

crime *n.* an act forbidden by law

crimp *v.* to pinch in or together

crimson *n.* deep purplish color

cringe *v.* shrink or recoil in fear

crin-kle *v.* wrinkle

crin-o-line *n.* fabric used for stiffening garments

crip-ple *n.* one who is partially disabled

cri-sis *n.* an uncertain time; turning point of a disease

crisp *adj.* brittle; brisk or cold

cri-te-ri-on *n., pl.* **criteria** rule by which something can be judged

crit-ic *n.* one who expresses an opinion

crit-i-cal *adj.* tending to criticize harshly **critically** *adv.*

crit-i-cize *v.* to find fault with

croak *n.* hoarse, raspy cry of a frog

cro-chet *n.* needlework with a hooked needle

crock *n.* earthenware pot or jar

croc-o-dile *n.*

large, tropical reptiles

cro-cus *n.* first spring plant.

crone *n.* old woman

cro-ny *n.* close friend

crook *n.* bend or curve; dishonest person

croon *v.* sing in a gentle, low voice

crop *n.* plants harvested for use or for sale

cro-quet *n.* outdoor game

cro-quette *n.* small patty of minced food

cross *n.*

an upright post with a crossbar

cross-breed *v.* breeding different species

crotch *n.* angle formed by the junction of two parts

crouch *v.* bend at the knees

croup *n.* spasmodic loud, harsh cough

crou-pi-er *n.* one who collects and pays bets at a gambling table

crou-ton *n.* piece of toasted bread

crow *n.* large, black bird

crowd *n.* large group of people together

crown *n.* head covering made of precious metal and jewels

CRT *abbr.* Cathode Ray Tube

cru-cial *adj.* extremely important

cru-ci-fy *v.* put to death on a cross

crude *adj.* lacking refinement

cruel *adj.* inflicting suffering **cruelty** *n.*

cru-et *n.* container for oil or vinegar

cruise *v.* drive or sail about for pleasure

crumb *n.* fragment of bread

crum-ble *v.* break into small pieces

crunch *v.* chew with a crackling noise

cru-sade *n.* religious journey

crush *v.* squeeze or force to damage

crust *n.* hardened exterior of bread; shell of a pie

crus-ta-cean *n.* crabs, lobsters, etc.

crutch *n.* support to or an aid for walking

crux *n.* a main or central feature

cry *v.* shed tears

crypt *n.* underground chamber or vault

cryp-tic *adj.* intended to be obscure

cryp-tog-ra-phy *n.* deciphering of messages in secret code

crys-tal *n.* glassware

crys-tal-lize *v.* to form crystals; coat with crystals

cub *n.* young of the lion, wolf, or bear

cub-by-hole *n.* small enclosed area

cube *n.* solid with six equal squares

cubic *adj.* having three dimensions

cu-bi-cle *n.* small partitioned area

cu-bit *n.* ancient unit of measurement

cud *n.* food rechewed by cattle

cud-dle *v.* caress fondly and hold close

cue *n.* signal to an actor

cuff *n.* lower part of a sleeve or pants

cui-sine *n.* style of preparing food

cull *v.* select the best

cul-mi-nate *v.* reach the highest point

cul-prit *n.* person guilty of a crime

cult *n.* system of religious worship

cul-ti-vate *v.* improve land by fertilizing and plowing

cul-ture *n.* form of civilization, beliefs, arts, and customs

cul-vert *n.* drain that runs under a road

cum-ber-some *adj.* unwieldy.

cum-mer-bund *n.* wide sash worn by men

cu-mu-lus *n.* white, fluffy cloud

cun-ning *adj.* crafty

cu-po-la *n.* rounded roof

cu-ra-tor *n.* person in charge of a museum

curb *n.* control; edge of a street

curd *n.* portion of milk for making cheese

cure *n.* recovery from a sickness

cur-few *n.* an order to be home at a certain hour

cu-ri-o *n.* unusual or rare object

cu-ri-ous *adj.* inquisitive **curiousity** *n.*

curl *v.* twist into curves

cur-rant *n.* small seedless raisin

cur-ren-cy *n.* money in circulation

cur-rent *adj.* occur in the present time

cur-ric-u-lum *n.* courses offered in a school

cur-ry *n.* spice

curse *n.* a wish for harm to come to someone or something

cursor *n.* computer screen indicator

cur-sive *n.* flowing writing

curt *adj.* abrupt; rude

cur-tail *v.* shorten

cur-tain *n.* material that covers a window

curt-sy *n.* a bow

cush-ion *n.* pillow with a soft filling

cus-pid *n.* pointed tooth

cus-pi-dor *n.* spittoon

cuss *v.* use profane language

cus-tard *n.* baked dessert milk, eggs, sugar, and flavoring

cus-to-di-an *n.* one who has the custody or care of something

cus-to-dy *n.* the act of guarding; the care and protection of a minor

customs *n.* tax one must pay on imported goods

cus-tomer *n.* person with whom a merchant or business person must deal

cut *v.* penetrate with a sharp edge, as with a knife

cute *adj.* attractive in a delightful way

cy-a-nide *n., Chem.* a poison

cyl-in-der *n.*

a long, round body that is either hollow or solid

cyn-ic *n.* one who believes that all people have selfish motives

cy-no-sure *n.* person or object that attracts admiration

cys-tic fi-bro-sis *n.* disease of the lungs and pancreas

cys-ti-tis *n.* inflammation of the bladder

cy-tol-ogy *n.* scientific study of cell formation

D, d The fourth letter of the English alphabet.

dab *v.* touch with light, short strokes

dab-ble *v.* play in a liquid with the hands

da ca-po *adv.* from the beginning

dac-tyl *n.* the fact that the three syllables have the fist one longest like the joints of the finger

dac-ty-lol-o-gy *n.* the art of communicating ideas by signs made with the fingers; sigh language

dac-ty-lous *adj.* having fingers or toes

dad *n., Informal* father

dad-dy--long-legs *n.* an insect with very long legs

daf-fo-dil *n.* a bulbous plant with yellow flowers

daft *adj.* crazy; foolish; insane **daftly** *adv.* **daftness** *n.*

dag-ger *n.* pointed, short-edged weapon

dahl-ia *n.* perennial plant having tuberous roots

dai-ly *adj.* to occur or happen every day of the week

dain-ty *adj.* delicately beautiful; having or showing refined taste **daintiness** *n.*

dai-qui-ri *n.* cocktail made with rum and lime juice

dair-y *n.* business that processes milk for resale **dairymaid** *n.* **dairyman** *n.*

dai-sy *n.* plant with yellow and white flowers

dal-ly *v.* waste time; to dawdle; to flirt **dallier** *n.,* **dalliance** *n.*

dam *n.* barrier to control water level

dam-age *n.* injury to person or property **damageable** *adj.,* **damagingly** *adv.*

dam-ask *n.* reversible fabric

damn *v.* to swear or curse at; to pronounce as bad, worthless, or a failure **damnation** *n.,* **damnableness** *n.*

damp *adj.* between dry and wet

dam-sel *n.* a maiden; a young unmarried woman

dam-son *n.* tree with an oval purple plum of the same name

dance *v.* move rhythmically to music

dan-de-lion *n.* a weed of North America; an herb; having yellow flowers

dan-dle *v.* to move a child or infant up and down on the knees or in the arms with a gentle movement

dan-druff *n.* scaly material which forms on the scalp and is shed

dan-dy *n.* elegantly dressed man; fine appearance **dandyish** *adj.*

dan-ger *n.* exposure to injury, evil, or loss; a case of danger

dan-ger-ous *adj.* unsafe **dangerously** *adv.* **dangerousness** *n.*

dan-gle *v.* hang loosely and swing to and fro **danglingly** *adv.*, **dangler** *n.*

dank *adj.* damp; wet and cold **dankness** *n.*, **dankly** *adv.*

dan-seuse *n.* female ballet dancer

dap-per *adj.* stylishly dressed

dap-ple *v.* to make variegated in color

dare *v.* have courage to take a risk or undertan an adventure; to challenge a person as to show proof of courage; **dare-devil** *n.* reckless or bold person **daredevilry** n, **daredeviltry** n.

dark *adj.* dim; to have little or no light

dark-en *v.* make dark or become dark **darkish** *adj.*, **darkly** *adv.*

dar-ling *n.* someone who is very dear; favorite person; a person tenderly loved **darlingly** *adv.*

darn *v.* mend a hole **darner** *n.*

dart *n.* pointed missile

dash *v.* to move quickly; to rush; to finish or perform a duty in haste; with sudden speed **dasher** *n.*

da-ta *pl.*, *n.* facts or firures from which conclusions may be drawn

data bank *n.* location in a computer where information is stored

date *n.* a particular point in time; the exact time at which something happens; an edible fruit **date** *v.*

date-line *n.* the date of newspaper publication; imaginary line

da-tum *n.* single piece of information **datums** pl., **data** *n.*

daub *v.* coat or smear with grease, plaster or an adhesive substance

daugh-ter *n.* female offspring of a man or woman; realtion to parent

daughter--in--law *n.* one's son's wife **daughters-in-law** pl.

daunt *v.* intimidate or discourage

dav-it *n.* small crane on the side of a ship used for boats or anchors

daw-dle *v.* waste time **daw***d***ler** n.

dawn *n.* the beginning of a new day; to begin to understand, perceive or develop; first light appearance

day *n.* period of time between dawn and night-fall; one rotation of the earth

daze *v.* stun or bewilder with a heavy blow or shock **dazedly** *adv.*

dea-con *n.* clergyman who ranks immediately below a priest

dead *adj.* without life; dormant

dead-end *n.* cannot progress

deadline *n.* time when something must be finished; the final day

dead-ly *adj.* very dangerous; likely to cause death

deaf *adj.* totally or partially unable to hear; refusing or unwilling to listen

deal *v.* pass out playing cards; to be concerned with a certain matter

deal-ing *n.*, *Slang* involved in the buying and selling of illegal drugs

dean *n.* head administrator of a college, or university **deanship** *n.*

dear *adj.* greatly cherished; loved **dearly** *adv.*, **dearness** n.

death *n.* termination; permanent cessation of all vital functions

deathly *adj.* fatal; causing death

death-trap *n.* unsafe structure

deb *n.* debutante

de-ba-cle *n.* sudden downfall or failure

de-base *v.* lower in character or value **debasement** *n.*, **debaser** *n.*

de-bate *v.* discuss or argue opposing points **debatable** *adj.*

de-bauch *v.* to corrupt **debauchment** *n.*

de-ben-ture *n.* voucher given as an acknowledgment of debt

de-bil-i-tate *v.* make feeble or weak

deb-it *n.* item recorded in an account; a sum of items entered

de-brief *v.* question or interrogate to obtain information

de-bris *n.* discarded or scattered remains or waste

debt *n.* that which someone owes as money or goods or services

debt-or *n.* person owing a debt to another, usually money, etc.

de-bug *v.* find and remove a concealed listening device; to remove errors

de-bunk *v.* expose false pretensions

de-but *n.* first public appearance; beginning of a new career; introduction

deb-u-tante *n.* young woman making her debut in society

dec-ade *n.* period of ten years; a set of ten; division of the rosary

de-ca-dence *n.* process of deterioration or decay; a period of decline

de-caf-fein-at-ed *adj.* having the caffeine removed; without

dec-a-gon *n.*, *Geom.*

a polygon with ten sides and ten angles

dec-a-gram *n.* in the metric system, weight equal to 10 grams

de-cal *n.* design or picture that is transferred by decalsomania

de-cal-co-ma-ni-a *n.* process of transferring pictures or designs to somehting

dec-a-li-ter *n.* in the metric system, measure equal to 10 liters

dec-a-logue *n.* the Ten Commandments;

a basic set of rules

dec-a-me-ter *n.* in the metric system, measure equal to 10 feet

de-camp *v.* break camp; to leave or depart suddenly **decampment** n.

de-cant-er *n.* decorative stoppered bottle for serving wine or other liquids

de-cap-i-tate *v.* cut off the head; to behead **decapitation** n.

de-cath-lon *n.* an athletic event with ten different track and field events

de-cay *v.* decline; to rot

de-cease *v.* die **decedent** *n.*

de-ceit *n.* falseness; deception

de-ceive *v.* mislead by falsehood; to lead into error; to delude

de-cel-er-ate *v.* decrease in velocity

de-cen-ni-al *adj.* happening once every 10 years; for a period of ten

de-cent *adj.* satisfactory; generous; adequate **decently** adv.

de-cen-tral-ize *v.* divide the administrative functions among local authorities

de-cep-tion *n.* act of deceiving

de-cep-tive *adj.* having the power to deceive **deceptively** adv.

de-ci-bel *n.* measurement of sound

de-cide *v.* to make up one's mind; to settle **decided** v., **deciding** v.

de-cid-ed *adj.* definite or unquestionable; determination **decidedly** adv.

de-cid-u-ous *adj.* shedding or falling off at maturity

dec-i-gram *n.* in the metric sysstem, the tenth part of a gram

dec-i-li-ter *n.* in the metric system, the tenth part of a liter

dec-i-mal *n.* proper fraction based on the number 10

decimal point *n.* period to the left of a decimal fraction

dec-i-mate *v.* destroy or kill a large proportion of something

dec-i-meter *n.* in the metric system, the tenth part of a meter

de-ci-pher *v.* to decode; to translate from code to text **decipherable** adj.

de-ci-sion *n.* a judgment or conclusion; act of deciding

de-ci-sive *adj.* ending uncertainty

deck *n.* set of playing cards; platform; resembling a ship's deck

deck hand *n.* member of a ship's crew who performs manual duties

de-claim *v.* speak loudly and rhetorically; to give speech **declamation** n.

de-clare *v.* to state formally or officially **declaration** n., **declarative** adj.

de-clas-si-fy *v.* make public

de-clen-sion *n.* sloping downward; a

decline; falling off or away

de-cline *v.* reject or refuse something **declinable** adj., **declinational** adj.

de-cliv-i-ty *n.* steep down-ward slope or surface **declivitous, declivous** adj.

de-coct *v.* extract by boiling; condense; to make concentrate **decoction** n.

de-code *v.* convert from coded message into plain language **decoder** n.

de-com-pose *v.* decay **decomposition** n.

de-com-press *v.* relieve of pressure

de-con-ges-tant *n.* agent that relieves congestion

de-con-tam-i-nate *v.* make free of contamination **decontamination** n.

de-con-trol *v.* remove all controls

de-cor *n.* style of decorating

dec-o-rate *v.* adorn with fashionable or beautiful things; dress up

dec-o-ra-tion *n.* art, process, or act of decorating; a thing or group of things which decorate; an emblem

dec-o-ra-tive *adj.* ornamental; suit-abe for decoration **decoratively** adv.

de-co-rum *n.* proper behavior

de-coy *n.* artificial animal to lure game

de-crease *v.* grow less or smaller

de-cree *n.* formal order

de-crep-it *adj.* worn out by old age

de-cry *v.* denounce

ded-i-cate *v.* commit oneself to a certain cause **deducated** v.

de-duce *v.* derive a conclusion by reasoning

de-duct *v.* subtract or take away from

deed *n.* notable achievement or feat

deem *v.* judge or consider

deep *adj.* extending far below a surface **deepness** n.

deep-en *v.* become or make deep or deeper **deepened** v., **deepening** v.

deep-freeze *v.* quick-freeze food

deep--root-ed *adj.* firmly implanted

deep-six *v., Slang* to throw overboard; toss out

deer *n., pl.* **deer**

hoofed ruminant mammal

deer fly *n.* bloodsucking flies

deer-skin *n.* deer's hide or leather made from it

de-es-ca-late *v.* decreased gradually

de-face *v.* spoil or mar the surface of something

de fac-to *adj.* actually exercising authority

de-fal-cate v. to misuse funds; to embezzle

de-fame v. to slander

de-fault v. neglect to fulfill an obligation

de-feat v. to win a victory

de-feat-ism n. accepting defeat as inevitable

def-e-cate v. discharge feces from the bowels

de-fect n. lack of perfection; a fault

de-fec-tive adj. imperfect; less than normal intelligence

de-fend v. protect

de-fend-ant n. person charged in a lawsuit; being on the devensive

de-fense n. action of defending

de-fer v. delay or postpone

de-fi-ance n. strong opposition

de-fi-cient adj. lacking a necessary element **deficiently** adv.

def-i-cit n. deficiency in amount

de-flate v. remove air; collapse

de-flect v. turn aside; swerve from a course **deflector** n.

de-flower v. rob one's virginity; to violate **deflowerer** n.

de-fog v. remove fog from

de-for-est v. to clear of trees

de-form v. distort the form of; to spoil the natural form of

de-fraud v. cheat; to swindle

de-fray v. make payment on something **defrayable** adj.

de-frost v. cause to thaw out; to remove the ice or frost from

deft adj. skillful and neat in one's actions **deftness** n.

de-funct adj. deceased

de-fuse v. remove the detonator or fuse from; to make less dangerous or harmful

de-fy v. confront or resist boldly; to dare **defier** n., **defying** n.

de-gauss v. neutralize a magnetic field **degausser** n.

de-gen-er-ate v. decline in quality or value; to become worse

de-grade v. reduce in rank; demote

de-gree n. succession of stages or steps; academic title; amount

de-horn v. remove the horns from an animal **dehorner** n.

de-hu-man-ize v. deprive of human qualities or personality

de-hu-mid-i-fy v. remove moisture from **dehumidifier** n., **dehumidification** n.

de-hy-drate v. lose moisture or water; to deprive **dehydrator** n.

de-ice v. keep free of ice **deicer** n.

de-i-fy v. glorify or idealize; raise in high regard **deified** n., **deifying** n.

deign v. to grant

de-ism n. belief in the existence of God; but not that he has control

de-ject v. lower the spirits; to dishearten; to make gloomy

de-ject-ed adj. sad; low in spirit

de ju-re adv., L. legally or rightfully

de-lay v. put off until a later time; to defer **delayer** n., **delaying** adj.

de-le n., Print mark in typesetting to delete **deled** v., **deleing** v.

de-lec-ta-ble adj. giving great pleasure **delectability** n., **delectableness** n.

de-lec-ta-tion n. enjoyment or pleasure; delight

del-e-gate n. representative for another; a deputy or agent

del-e-ga-tion n. state of being delegated **deleted** v., **deleting** v.

de-lete v. cancel; to take out by cutting or erasing **deletion** n., **deleting** n.

del-e-te-ri-ous adj. causing physical injury; harmful **deleteriously** adv.

delft n. glazed earthenware

del-i n., Slang delicatessen

de-lib-er-ate v. say or do something intentionally **deliberateness** n.

del-i-ca-cy n. select or choice food

del-i-cate adj. exquisite and fine in quality **delicately** adv.

del-i-ca-tes-sen n. specialty store

de-li-cious adj. enjoyable and pleasant to the taste **deliciously** adv.

de-li-cious n. variety of red, sweet apples **deliciously** adv.

de-light n. a giving of great joy or pleasure **delighted** adj.

de-light-ful adj. extremely pleasing

de-lim-it v. set or prescribe the limits

de-lir-i-um n. temporary mental disturbance characterized by confusion, disorder speech, and hallucinations

delirium tremens n. acute delirium resulting from use of alcohol

de-liv-er v. to hand over; assist at a birth of an offspring **delivered** v., **-ing** v.

de-liv-er-y n. act of conveying; process or act of giving birth **deliveries** pl.

del-phin-ium n. perennial plant

delta ray n. electron ejected from ionizing radiation

de-lude v. mislead the mind; to deceive

del-uge v. flood with water; to overwhelm **deluging** v., **deluged** v.

de-lu-sion n. false belief in spite of contrary evidence **delusionary** adj.

de luxe adj. elegance or luxury

delve v. search carefully for information

de-mag-net-ize v. remove the magnetic

properties demagnetiation *n.*

dem-a-gogue *n.* person who appeals to the emotions to gain power or fame

de-mand *v.* ask for in a firm tone; claim as due demander *n.*, demandable *adj.*

de-mar-cate *v.* set boundaries or limits

de-mean *v.* behave or conduct oneself in a particular manner

de-mean-or *n.* person's conduct to others

de-men-tia *n.* irreversible deterioration of the mind demential *adj.*

de-mer-it *n.* a defect

de-mesne *n.* manor house; a domain

dem-i-god *n.* mythological, semidivine being demigoddess *n.*

dem-i-john *n.* narrow-necked bottle

de-mil-i-ta-rize *v.* remove the military characteristics from

dem-i-monde *n.* class of women supported by wealthy lovers

de-mise *n.* death; a transfer of an estate by lease or will demised *v.*, -ing *v.*

dem-i-tasse *n.* small cup of very strong black coffee; the cup used to serve

dem-o *n.* demonstration to show product

de-mo-bi-lize *v.* disband; release from the military service -ation *n.*

de-moc-ra-cy *n.*, *pl.* democracies form of government by and for the people

dem-o-crat *n.* one who believes in social and political equality

de-mog-ra-phy *n.* study of the characteristics of human population

de-mol-ish *v.* tear down; to raze

dem-o-li-tion *n.* a process of demolishing something demolitionist *n.*

de-mon *n.* evil spirit; a devil

de-mon-e-tize *v.* deprive the currency of its standard value demonization *n.*

de-mo-ni-ac *adj.* like or befitting a demon demonically *adv.*

de-mon-ol-o-gy *n.* belief or study in demons

de-mon-stra-ble *adj.* obvious or apparent

dem-on-strate *v.* show or prove by evidence demonstration *n.*

de-mon-stra-tive *adj.* able to prove beyond any doubt; conclusive

de-mor-al-ize *v.* undermine the morales

de-mote *v.* reduce in rank, or grade demotion *n.*

de-mul-cent *n.* a soothing substance

de-mur *v.* take issue; to object

de-mure *adj.* reserved and modest

de-murrer *n.* plea to dismiss a lawsuit

den *n.* shelter for animals; small room

de-na-ture *v.* change the nature of

den-drol-ogy *n.* botanical study of trees

den-gue *n.*, *Pathol.* infectious tropical disease transmitted by mosquitoes

de-ni-al *n.* refusal to comply with a request or truth

den-i-grate *v.* to slander

den-im *n.* strong cotton used for jeans

de-nom-i-nate *v.* give a name to

de-nom-i-na-tion *n.* name of a group or classification

de-nom-i-na-tor *n.* the bottom half of a fraction

de-no-ta-tion *n.* meaning of or object designated by a word

de-note *v.* make known

de-noue-ment *n.* final solution of a novel

de-nounce *v.* condemn openly; accuse formally

dense *adj.* thick; slow to understand; stupid

den-si-ty *n.* state or quality of being dense

dent *n.* small surface depression

den-tal *adj.* pertaining to the teeth

dental floss *n.* a strong thread to clean between the teeth

dental hygienist *n.* dental professional who provides preventive dental care

den-ti-frice *n.* preparation for cleaning the teeth

den-tine *n.* calcified part of the tooth

den-tist *n.* licensed dental doctor

den-ti-tion *n.* number, and arrangement of teeth

den-ture *n.* set of artificial teeth

de-nude *v.* remove all covering; cause to be naked

de-nun-ci-a-tion *n.* disapproval of a person or action; an accusation

de-ny *v.* declare untrue; refuse to acknowledge

de-o-dor-ant *n.* product to prevent unpleasant odors

de-o-dor-ize *v.* destroy the odor of

de-ox-i-dize *v.* remove oxygen from

de-part *v.* leave; to go away; to deviate

de-part-ment *n.* the distinct division of something

de-part-men-tal-ize *v.* divide into organized departments

department store *n.* large retail store usually in many places

de-par-ture *n.* act of taking leave; deviation

de-pend *v.* rely on

de-pend-a-ble *adj.* trust-worthy dependability *n.*

de-pend-ence *n.* trust or reliance

de-pend-ent *adj.* needing the help of another for support

de-pict *v.* represent in a picture

de-pil-a-to-ry *n.* chemical which removes hair

de-plane *v.* disembark or leave an aircraft

de-plete *v.* exhaust, empty, or use up

de-plor-a-ble *adj.* very bad; grievous; wretched **deplorably** *adv.*

de-plore *v.* show great disapproval of something

de-ploy *v.* spread out; place or position according to plans **deployment** *n.*

de-po-lit-i-cize *v.* remove the political status or aspect from

de-po-nent *n.* a person testifing under an oath

de-pop-u-late *v.* lower the population by massacre or disease

de-port *v.* banish from a country

de-port-ment *n.* one's conduct

de-pose *v.* remove position or office

de-pos-it *v.* set something down; put money in a bank

dep-o-si-tion *n.* in law, written testimony given under oath

de-pos-i-to-ry *n.* place for safekeeping

de-pot *n.* railroad station

de-prave *v.* render bad or worse **depravity** *n.*

dep-re-cate *v.* express regret or disapproval; belittle

de-pre-ci-ate *v.* lessen in value or price

de-pre-ci-a-tion *n.* loss in value from usage

de-press *v.* make gloomy; lower the spirits

de-pres-sant *adj.* act to lower the nervous activities

de-press-ed *adj.* sad; low in spirits

de-press-ed area *n.* area with severe unemployment

de-pres-sion *n.* severe decline in business; condition of deep dejection

de-pres-sive *adj.* related to psychological depression

de-prive *v.* take something away from; to keep from using

depth *n.* distance downward; intensity of of sound; comprehension

depth charge *n.* underwater bomb

dep-u-ta-tion *n.* person acting for another or others

de-pute *v.* appoint as a deputy, an agent; delegate; to transfer

dep-u-tize *v.* to appoint as a deputy

dep-u-ty *n.* person designated act for or assist a sheriff

de-rail *v.* cause a train to run off the rails **derailment** *n.*

de-range *v.* to disturb the normal order of

der-by *n.* horse race for 3-year-olds; stiff hat with narrow brim

de-reg-u-late *v.* remove from regulation or control

der-e-lict *adj.* neglectful; remiss

der-e-lic-tion *n.* voluntary neglect

de-ride *v.* ridicule

de ri-gueur *adj.* required by manners, custom, or fashion

der-i-va-tion *n.* process of deriving

de-riv-a-tive *adj.* made from derived elements

de-rive *v.* receive or obtain from a source

der-mal *adj.* relating to or of the skin

der-ma-ti-tis *n., Pathol.* inflammation of the skin

der-ma-tol-o-gy *n.* the medical study of the skin and the diseases **dermatologist** *n.*

der-o-gate *v.* to take away from; to distract

de-rog-a-tory *adj.* effect of belittling; lessening

der-rick *n.* machine to lift heavy loads; framework of an oil well

der-ri-ere *n.* the buttocks

der-ring--do *n.* daring action or spirit

de-salt *v.* remove the salt from sea water

des-cant *v.* play or sing a varied melody

de-scend *v.* move from a higher to a lower level

de-scen-dent *n.* offspring from another individual

de-scen-dant *adj.* proceeding downward

de-scent *n.* a slope; lowering in level or status

de-scribe *v.* explain in written or spoken words **describable** *adj.*

de-scrip-tion *n.* discourse to give a mental image of something

de-scry *v.* catch sight of

des-e-crate *v.* violate something sacred **desecration** *n.*

de-seg-re-gate *v.* eliminate racial segregation in

de-sen-si-tize *v.* make less sensitive

des-ert *v.* abandon or forsake

des-ert *n.* dry, barren region

de-ser-tion *n.* act of deserting or leaving

de-serve *v.* be worthy of or entitled to

de-served *adj.* merited; earned **deservingly** *adv.*

des-ic-cant *n.* silica gel to absorb moisture

des-ic-cate *v.* preserve food by drying; dehydrate

de-sid-er-a-tum *n.* desired and necessary thing

de-sign *v.* sketch preliminary outlines; create in the mind

des-ig-nate *v.* assign a name or title to; specify

de-sign-ing *adj.* relating to the art making designs

de-sir-a-ble *adj.* attractive, or valuable desirableness *n.*

de-sire *v.* long for; to wish

de-sir-ous *adj.* have a craving or strong desire

de-sist *v.* stop doing something

desk *n.*

school and office furniture for writing

des-o-late *adj.* forlorn; forsaken desolately *adv.*

des-o-la-tion *n.* wasteland; de-serted; loneliness

de-spair *v.* lose or give up hope

des-per-a-do *n.* a dangerous, or violent criminal

des-per-ate *adj.* rash, without care; intense

des-per-a-tion *n.* state of being desperate

des-pi-ca-ble *adj.* hateful; contemptable

de-spise *v.* regard with contempt

de-spite *prep.* notwithstanding.

de-spoil *v.* rob; strip of possessions by force

de-spond *v.* lose hope, courage, or spirit

de-spon-den-cy *n.* dejection of spirits from loss hope

des-pot *n.* an absolute ruler; a tyrant

des-sert *n.* sweet food, as pastry, etc.

des-ti-na-tion *n.* goal; end of journey

des-tine *v.* determined in advance

des-ti-ny *n.* fate; predetermined course of events

des-ti-tute *adj.* impoverished; poor destitution *n.*

de-stroy *v.* ruin; to to demolish; to kill

de-stroy-er *n.* one that destroys; small maneuverable warship

de-struct *n., Aeros.* deliberate destruction of a defective missile

de-struc-ti-ble *adj.* capable of being destroyed

des-ue-tude *n.* condition or state of disuse

de-sul-fur-ize *v.* remove sulfur from

des-ul-to-ry *adj.* something occuring by chance

de-tach *v.* unfasten, or separate

de-tached *adj.* apart; separate

de-tach-ment *n.* process of separating

de-tail *n.* part considered sep-arately; task

de-tain *v.* keep from proceeding

de-tect *v.* find out; to expose or uncover, as a crime detectable *adj.*

de-tec-tive *n.* person that investigates crimes

de-tent *n.* a pawl

de-ten-tion *n.* hold in custody

de-ter *v.* prevent someone from acting by intimidation determent *n.*

de-ter-gent *n.* cleansing agent

de-te-ri-o-rate *v.* to worsen; to depreciate deterioration *n.*

de-ter-mi-nate *adj.* definitely fixed or limited; conclusive

de-ter-mine *v.* settle or decide conclusively determination *n.*

de-ter-mined *adj.* having a fixed purpose

de-ter-rent *n.* something which deters deterrently *adv.*

de-test *v.* dislike strongly detestable *adj.*

de-throne *v.* remove from the throne

det-o-nate *v.* explode suddenly violently detonation *n.*

det-o-na-tor *n.* fuse used to detonate an explosive

de-tour *n.* deviation from a direct route

de-tox-i-fy *v.* free oneself from dependence on drugs or alcohol detoxification *n.*

de-tract *v.* take away from; to divert detraction *n.*

de-train *v.* leave a railroad train detrainment *n.*

det-ri-ment *n.* damage; injury; loss detrimental *adj.*

de-tri-tus *n.* loose fragments from disintegration

deuce *n.* two

deut-sche mark *n.* standard monetary unit of Germany

de-val-u-ate *v.* reduce or lessen the value of devaluation *n.*

dev-as-tate *v.* destroy; to ruin devastation *n.*

de-vel-op *v.* expand the potentialities; to enlarge; process film

de-vel-op-er *n.* person who builds and sells homes; chemical to process film

de-vel-op-ment *n.* group of homes; improvement

de-vi-ant *adj.* stray from the norm deviantance *n.*

de-vi-ate *v.* turn away from prescribed behavior or course

de-vice *n.* something built and used for a specific purpose

dev-il *n.* spirit of evil, the ruler of Hell; Satan; wicked person

dev-il-ish *adj.* resemble or have the characteristics of a devil

dev-il-may-care *adj.* reckless

dev-il-ment *n.* reckless mischief

devil's advocate *n.* one who argues for

the sake of arguing

dev-il-try *n.* malicious mischief; cruelty or wickedness

de-vi-ous *adj.* leading away from the direct course **deviously** *adv.*

de-vise *v.* form in the mind; contrive; give real estate by will

de-vi-see *n.* person to whom a devise is made

de-vi-sor *n.* person who devises property

de-vi-tal-ize *v.* make weak

de-void *adj.* empty; lacking

de-voir *n.* act or expression of courtesy or respect

de-volve *v.* pass duty or authority on to a successor

de-vote *v.* apply oneself completely to some activity

de-vot-ed *adj.* feeling or showing loyalty **devotedly** *adv.*

dev-o-tee *n.* enthusiastic supporter

de-vo-tion *n.* strong attachment or affection **devotionly** *adv.*

de-vout *adj.* extreemely and earnestly religions; showing sincerity **devoutly** *adv.*

dew *n.* moisture condensed from the atmosphere in small drops onto cool surfaces

dew-claw *n.* rudimentary toe in some dogs and other mammals

dew-lap *n.* the loosee skin under the throat and neck of cattle and certain dogs

dex-ter-i-ty *n.* proficiency or skill in using the hands or body; cleverness; skillful

deex-ter-ous *adj.* skillful or adroit in the use of the hands

di-a-gram *n.* a sketch, plan or outline designed to demonstrate the similarity among partsof a whole

di-al *n.* graduated circular plate or face where a measurement is indicated by means of a pointer

di-a-logue *n.* conversation involving two or more persons

di-am-e-ter *n.* a straight line which passes through the center of a circle

di-a-met-ri-cal *adj.* along or relating to a diameter

dia-mond *n.* a very hard highly refractive colorless or white crystalline of carbon used as a gem

di-a-pa-son *n.* full range of a voice or an instrument

di-a-per *n.* baby's pants of absorbent material

di-aph-a-nous *adj.* transparent or translucent

di-a-phragm *n., Anat.* muscular wall be-

tween chest and abdomen; contraceptive device

di-ar-rhe-a *n.,Pathol.* disorder of the intestines

di-a-ry *n.* a daily record

di-as-tro-phism *n., Geol.* processes through which the earth's crust are formed

di-a-ther-my *n., pl.* **diathermies** *Med.* generation of heat in the body tissues

di-as-to-le *n.* rhythmnical expansion of the heart

di-a-tom *n.* various tiny planktonic algae

di-a-tom-ic *adj.* having two atoms in a molecule

di-a-ton-ic *adj., Mus.* relating to a musical scale having eight tones to an octave

di-a-tribe *n.* malicious criticism

dib-ble *n.* gardener's pointed tool for planting bulbs

dice *pl., n.*

small cubes used in a game of chance

di-chot-o-my *n., pl.* **dichotomies** division into two mutually exclusive subclasses

dick-er *v.* haggle or work towards a deal or bargain

dick-ey *n.* a woman's blouse front worn under a jacket

di-cot-y-le-don *n.* plant having two seed leaves

dic-tate *v.* speak aloud for another to record or transcribe **dictation** *n.*

dic-ta-ting ma-chine *n.* phonographic machine which records speech

dic-ta-tor *n.* person having absolute authority and supreme governmental powers **dictatorship** *n.*

dic-ta-to-ri-al *adj.* tending to dictate

dic-tion *n.* arrangement of words in speaking and writing

dic-tion-ar-y *n.* book containing words, definitions and usages

dic-tum *n.* authoritative utterance

did *v.* past tense of do

di-dac-tic *adj.* inclined to teach excessively

did-dle *v.* cheat; to swindle

did-n't *contr.* did not

die *v.* expire; to stop living

die casting *n.* process of giving an alloy or metal a desired shape

die-hard *n.* stubborn person

diel-drin *n.* highly toxic chemical used as an insecticide

di-e-lec-tric *n., Elect.* nonconductor of electricity

die-sel *n.* vehicle driven by a diesel en-

gine
diesel engine *n.* internalcombustion engine run by an air-fuel mixture
die-sink-er *n.* person who engraves metal dies
di-et *n.* regulated selection of food and drink
di-e-tet-ics *pl., n.* study of diet and regulations of a diet
di-eth-yl-bes-trol *n.* a synthetic estrogen to treat menstrual disorders
di-e-ti-tian *n.* diet planner
dif-fer *v.* have different opinions
dif-fer-ence *n.* state, or degree of being different or unlike
dif-fer-ent *adj.* not the same
dif-fer-en-tia *n.* a specific difference
dif-fer-en-tial *adj.* showing a difference or differences
dif-fer-en-ti-ate *v.* show, or distinguish the difference
dif-fi-cult *adj.* hard to do, or accomplish; hard to please
dif-fi-cul-ty *n., pl.* difficulties quality or state of being difficult
dif-fi-dent *adj.* lacking confidence in oneself; timid **diffidently** *adv.*
dif-frac-tion *n., Phys.* modification of light rays
dif-fuse *v.* spread freely in all directions; to scatter
dig *v.* break up the earth
di-gest *v.* summarize; change ingested food into usable form
di-gest-ion *n.* dissolving food in the stomach
dig-it *n.* toe or finger
dig-i-tal *adj.* expressed in digits, as for computer use
digital computer *n.* computer using data resented as digits to perform operations
dig-i-tal-is *n.* drug prepared from dried leaves of foxglove
dig-ni-fied *adj.* stately; poised
dig-ni-fy *v.* to give distinction to something
dig-ni-tary *n., pl.* dignitaries person of high rank
dig-ni-ty *n., pl.* dignities quality being excellent
di-graph *n.* pair of letters that represents a single sound
di-gress *v.* to wander
dik-dik *n.* small African antelope
dike *n.* embankment made of earth, control flood waters
di-lap-i-dat-ed *adj.* state of decay or disrepair
di-late *v.* become larger **dilateable** *adj.*

dil-a-to-ry *adj.* delaying; slow; tardy
di-lem-ma *n.* perplexing situation
dil-et-tante *n.* superficial interest in something
dil-i-gent *adj.* industrious
dill *n.* aromatic herb
di-lute *v.* reduce concentration
dim *adj.* dull
dime *n.* U. S. coin worth ten cents
di-men-sion *n.* measurable extent
di-min-ish *v.* make smaller
di-min-u-en-do *adv.* gradually lessening in volume
di-min-u-tive *adj.* very small
dim-ple *n.* depression in the skin
din *n.* loud noise
dine *v.* to eat dinner
di-nette *n.* small dining room
din-ghy *n., pl.* dinghies a small rowboat
din-ky *adj., Informal* insignificant or small; tiny **dinkier** *adv.*
din-ner *n.* last meal of the day

di-no-saur *n., Paleon.*

extinct reptiles
dinosauric adj.
dip *v.* put into a liquid momentarily
diph-the-ri-a *n., Pathol.* acute infectious disease
di-plo-ma *n.* document from school
dip-lo-mat *n.* government representative
dip-per *n.* long-handled cup
dip-so-ma-ni-a *n.* insatiable craving for alcohol
dire *adj.* dreadful or terrible
di-rect *v.* give orders
di-rec-tion *n.* act of directing; instruction
di-rect-ly *adv.* immediately; at once
di-rec-tor *n.* person who manages
di-rec-to-ry *n., pl.* directories book listing data
dirge *n.* slow mournful song
dir-i-gi-ble *n.* lighter-than-air plane
dirn-dl *n.* dress with a full skirt
dirt *n.* soil or earth
dirt-y *adj.* not clean **dirtiness** *n.*
dis-a-ble *v.* to incapacitate
dis-ad-van-tage *n.* unfavorable inferior condition
dis-a-gree *v.* vary in opinion **disagreeable** *adj.*
dis-al-low *v.* refuse to allow
dis-ap-pear *v.* vanish **disappearance** *n.*
dis-ap-point *v.* fail to satisfy
dis-ap-pro-ba-tion *n.* disapproval
dis-ap-prove *v.* refuse to approve
dis-arm *v.* make harmless

dis-ar-range v. disturb the order disarramgement n.

dis-ar-ray n. state of confusion or disorder

dis-as-sem-ble v. to take apart

dis-as-so-ci-ate v. break away or detach from an association

dis-as-ter n. event that causes distress; a suden misfortune

dis-a-vow v. disclaim or deny

dis-band v. disperse

dis-bar v. expelled from the legal profession disbarment n.

dis-be-lieve v. refuse to believe

dis-burse v. pay out money

disc or disk n., Informal phonograph record that holds information

dis-card v. to throw out

dis-cern v. understand

dis-charge v. to release

dis-ci-ple n. follower

dis-ci-pline n. train; punishment to correct poor behavior

dis-claim v. to deny interest in or assocation with

dis-close v. make known discloseure n.

dis-co n., pl. discos discotheque

dis-color v. alter or change the color of

dis-com-fit v. defeat in battle

dis-com-fort n. uneasiness; pain

dis-com-mode v. inconvenience

dis-com-pose v. disrupt composure of something

dis-con-cert v. upset

dis-con-nect v. break the connection of something

dis-con-so-late adj. unhappy

dis-con-tent n. dissatisfaction

dis-con-tin-ue v. bring to an end

dis-cord n. lacking harmony

dis-co-theque n. nightclub with

dis-count v. sell for lower price than usual or regular price

dis-coun-te-nance v. look upon with disfavor; weary

dis-cour-age v. deprived of enthusiasm or courage

dis-course n. conversation; lengthy discussion

dis-cred-it v. cast disbelief on

dis-creet adj. tactful; careful of appearances; modest

dis-crep-an-cy n., pl. discrepancies difference in facts

dis-crete adj. separate; made up of distinct parts

dis-cre-tion n. act of being discreet

dis-crim-i-nate v. distinguish between

dis-cur-sive adj. covering a wide field of subjects in a quick manner

dis-cuss v. to talk

dis-dain v. ignore; scorn

dis-ease n. sickness; illness diseased adj.

dis-em-bark v. unload

dis-em-body v. to free from the body

dis-en-chant v. free from false beliefs; disbeliefs

dis-en-gage v. to set free

dis-fig-ure v. deform appearance

dis-fran-chise v. deprive the legal right

dis-gorge v. to regurgitate; to pour out

dis-grace n. loss of honor

dis-guise v. alter appearance

dis-gust v. version

dis-har-mo-ny n. discord

dis-heart-en v. lose spirit

di-shev-el v. disarrange

dis-hon-est adj. lacking honesty

dis-hon-or n. disgrace

dis-il-lu-sion v. to disenchant

dis-in-fect v. free from infection

dis-in-gen-u-ous adj. lacking frankness

dis-in-her-it v. deprive of inheritance

dis-in-te-grate v. break into small particles; decompose

dis-in-ter-est-ed adj. unselfish, or not interested

dis-join v. to become detached

dis-like v. regard with disapproval

dis-lo-cate v. put out of place

dis-lodge v. remove from

dis-loy-al adj. untrue to obligations or duty disloyalty adj.

dis-mal adj. depressing

dis-man-tle v. to take apart

dis-may v. dishearten

dis-mem-ber v. cut into pieces

dis-miss v. to discharge

dis-mount v. get down from

dis-o-bey v. refuse or fail to obey

dis-o-blige v. act contrary to wishes

dis-or-der n. confussion

dis-or-gan-ize v. destroy or break up the unity; unorganizational

dis-own v. refuse to claim as one's own disownment n.

dis-patch v. send off on a particular destination

dis-pel v. drive or away

dis-pense v. give out

dis-perse v. scatter in various directions; to give out or distribute

dis-place v. change the position of

dis-play v. put in view

dis-please v. cause disapproval or annoyance of; to be offensive to

dis-pose v. put in place; arrange

dis-prove v. prove to be false

dis-pute v. to debate or argue

dis-qual-i-fy v. deprive of the required

conditions

dis-qui-si-tion *n.* formal inquiry

dis-re-gard *v.* to neglect

dis-re-pute *n.* state of low esteem

dis-re-spect *n.* lack of respect

dis-robe *v.* undress

dis-rupt *v.* throw into disorder

dis-sat-is-fy *v.* fail to satisfy

dis-sect *v.* cut into pieces

dis-sem-ble *v.* conceal; disguise

dis-sem-i-nate *v.* spread; distribute

dis-sen-sion *n.* difference of opinion

dis-sent *v.* differ in opinion

dis-ser-ta-tion *n.* written essay

dis-serv-ice *n.* ill turn

dis-sim-i-lar *adj.* different

dis-sim-u-late *v.* dissemble

dis-si-pate *v.* disperse or drive

dis-so-ci-ate *v.* break association

dis-solve *v.* cause to fade away

dis-so-nance *n., Mus.* lack of agreement; unagreeable

dis-suade *v.* alter the course of action; to change direction

dis-tance *n.* separation in time or space **distanced** *v.,* **distancing** *v.*

dis-tant *adj.* separate by a specified amount of time or space

dis-taste *v.* feeling aversion to

dis-tem-per *n.* contagious viral disease of dogs

dis-tend *v.* expand

dis-till *v.* extract by distillation

dis-til-late *n.* the condensed substance sep-arated by distillation

dis-tinct *adj.* clearly seen

dis-tinc-tion *n.* act of distinguishing

dis-tinc-tive *adj.* serving to give style or distinction to

dis-tin-guish *v.* to recognize as beeing different

dis-tort *v.* to twist or bend out of shape **distortion** *n.*

dis-tract *v.* to draw or divert one's attention **distractingly adv.**

dis-trait *adj.* absentminded

dis-traught *adj.* deeply agitated with doubt or anxiety

dis-trict *n.* an administrative or political section of a territory; a division of space **district** *v.*

dis-turb *v.* to destroy the tranquillity of; to unsettle mentally **disturber** *n.*

ditch *n.* trench in the earth

dive *v.* to plunge into water headfirst; to submerge

di-verge *v.* to move or extend in different directions from a common point **diverged** *v.,* **diverging** *v.*

di-veerse *adj.* unlike in characteristics; different; not similar

di-ver-si-fy *v.* to give variety to something; to engage in varied operations

di-ver-sion *n.* the act of diverting from a course or activity

di-vert *v.* to undress or strip, especially of clothing or dispossess of property

di-vide *v.* to separate into parts; to cause to be apart

di-vi-sion *n.* separation; something which divides or marks off

div-ot *n.* a square of turf or sod

diz-zy *adj.* having a whirling sensation in the head

do-cent *n.* a teacher at a college or university; conducts groups

doc-ile *adj.* easily led, taught, or managed **docility** *n.*

dock-et *n.* a brief written summary of a document

doc-tor *n.* a person trained and licensed to practive medicine

doc-tor-ate *n.* the degreee, status, or title of a doctor

doc-trine *n.* something taught as a body of principles

doc-u-ment *n.* official paper **-ation** *n.*

doc-u-men-ta-ry *adj.* relating to or based on documents

dodge *v.* avoid by moving suddenly

doe *n.* mature female deer

does-n't *contr.* does not

dog *n.* domesticated carnivorous mammal

dog-ged *adj.* stubbornly determined

dog-ma *n.* rigidly held doctrine

dog-mat-ic *adj.* marked by an authoritative assertion

dol-drums *pl., n.* a period of listlessness

dole *n.* distribution of food or money to the needy

dole-ful *adj.* filled with sadness

doll *n.* child's toy

dol-lar *n.* standard monetary unit of the U.S.

dol-men *n.* prehistoric monument

do-lor-ous *adj.* marked by grief; mournful

dol-phin *n.*

aquatic mammal

dolt *n.* stupid person

do-main *n.* territory under one government

dome *n.* round shaped roof

do-mes-tic *adj.* relating to house-hold

dom-i-cile *n.* dwelling place

dom-i-nant *adj.* prevailing

dom-i-nate *v.* rule or control

dom-i-no *n.* a small rectangular block with dots on the face

don *v.* to put on

don-key *n., pl.* **donkeys** domesticated ass

do-nor *n.* one who donates or contributes

don't *contr.* do not

doo-dle *v.* to scribble or draw aimlessly

doom *n.* an unhappy destiny

door *n.* means of entrance or exit

dope *n.* drug or narcotic

dor-mant *adj.* asleep; state of rest

dor-sal *adj., Anat.* of or relating to back

do-ry *n., pl.* **dories** small flatbottomed boat

dose *n.* measured amount of medicine take at one time

dos-si-er *n.* complete data on a person

dot *n.* small round mark

dote *v.* show excessive affection

dou-ble *adj.* twice as much

double–cross *v., Slang* to betray

doubt *v.* **doubter** *n.* uncertain of something

dough *n.* soft pastry mixture of flour and other ingredients

douse *v.* plunge into liquid or throw water on

dove *n.* any of numerous pigeons

dow-dy *adj.* not neat or tidy; old-fashioned **dowdiest** *adj.*

dow-el *n.* round wooden object that fastens two joined pieces

down *adv.* from higher to lower

down-er *n., Slang* depressant drug; a barbiturate

doz-en *n.* twelve of a kind

drab *adj.* unexciting; yellow-brown **drabness** *n.*

draft *n.* current of air; sketch or plan *Milit.* mandatory selection for service

drag *v.* pull along by force

drag-on *n.*

mythical, serpent-like monster

drain *v.* to draw off liquid gradually

drake *n.* male duck

dram *n.* small drink; a small portion

dra-ma *n.* a play recounting a serious story

drape *v.* to cover or adorn with something

dras-tic *adj.* extreme or severe

draw *v.* cause to move toward a position to sketch

draw-back *n.* undesirable feature

draw-bridge *n.* bridge that is raised or lowered

drawer *n.* one that draws pictures; a sliding receptacle in furniture

draw-ing *n.* picture; process of choosing lots

drawl *v.* to speak slowly

dray *n.* heavy cart used for hauling

dread *v.* fear greatly

dread-ful *adj.* inspiring dread; awful

dream *n.* series of thoughts or images which occur during sleep or the REM state of sleep

drea-ry *adj.* bleak and gloomy; dull **dreariness** *n.*

dredge *v.* remove sand or mud from under water **dredger** *n.*

dregs *pl., n.* sediment of a liquid

drench *v.* wet thoroughly

dress *n.* an outer garment for women and girls to put clothes on

drib-ble *v.* to slobber or drool; to bounce a ball repeatedly

drift *v.* to be carried along by a current to move about aimlessly

drill *n.* tool used in boring holes; the act of training soldiers by repeated exercise

drink *v.* to take liquid into the mouth and swallow

drip *v.* to fall in drops *n.* the sound made by falling drops

drive *v.* to propel, push, or press onward

driv-el *v.* to slobber

driz-zle *n.* fine, quiet, gentle rain

droll *adj.* whimsically comical

drom-e-dar-y *n.* one-humped camel

drone *n.* a male bee; unmanned boat or aircraft

drool *v.* to let saliva dribble from the mouth

droop *v.* to hang or bend downward

drop *n.* tiny, rounded mass of liquid; smallest unit of liquid measure

drop *v.* fall in drops; let fall

drop-sy *n., Med.* diseased condition with excessive water in the body

dross *n.* impurity forming molten metal

drought *n.* prolonged period of dryness; being without water

drove *n.* herd of cattle

drown *v.* die by suffocating in a liquid of any kind

drowse *v.* to doze

drub *v.* hit with a stick

drudge *n.* person who does menial tasks **drudgery** *n.*

drug *n.* substance for treatment of disease or illness

drum *n.*

musical percussion instrument

drunk *adj.* intoxicated with alcohol

drunk-ard *adj.* person habitually drunk

drupe *n.* one seeded fruit, as the peach

dry *adj.* free from moisture; having no rain; thirsty

dry--clean *v.* clean fabrics with chemical solvents

dry goods *n.* textile fabrics

du-al *adj.* made up or composed of two parts

dub *v.* confer knighthood upon; nickname

du-bi-ous *adj.* causing doubt; unsettled in judgment

duch-ess *n.* wife or widow of a duke

duck *n.*

swimming birds with short necks and legs

duct *n.* bodily tube or canal

duc-tile *adj.* capable of being shaped

dud *n.*, *Informal* bomb or explosive round which fails to detonate; a failure

dude *n.*, *Informal* a city person vacationing on a ranch

dudg-eon *n.* displeased, or indignant mood

due *adj.* owed; payable

dues *n.*, *pl.* fee or charge for membership

du-el *n.* premeditated combat between two people

du-et *n.* musical composition for two performers **duetted** *v.*

duke *n.* noble ranking below a prince; a nobleman of the highest hereditary rank **dukedom** *n.*

dul-cet *adj.* melodious

dul-ci-mer *n.* musical stringed instrument of trapezoidal shape played with light hammers held in hands **dulcimore** *n.*

dull *adj.* stupid; with a blunt edge or point; not exciting **dullness** *n.*

du-ly *adv.* in a proper or due manner

dumb *adj.* unable to speak; uneducated **dumbness** *n.*

dumb-bell *n.* short bar with weights

dumb-waiter *n.* small elevator used to convey food or dishes, from one floor to another

dum-dum bullet *n.* small-arms bullet designed to expand on contact

dum-found *v.* to confound with amazement

dum-my *n.* one who is stupid; hand in bridge

dump *v.* throw down or discard; dispose of garbage

dump-ling *n.* mass of dough cooked in soup or stew

dun *v.* press a debtor for payment

dunce *n.* slow-witted person

dune *n.* hill of sand drifted by the wind

dung *n.* excrement of animals; manure

dun-geon *n.* dark, underground prison chamber

du-o-de-num *n.*, *pl.* -denums first portion of the small intestine

dupe *n.* person who is easily deceived

du-pli-cate *n.* identical; exact copy of an original **duplication** *n.*

du-ra-ble *adj.* able to continue for a long period of time without deterioration **durability** *n.*

du-ra-tion *n.* period of time during which something lasts or exists

du-ress *n.* constraint by fear or force; forced restraint

dur-ing *prep.* throughout the time of; within the time of

dusk *n.* earliest part of the evening, just before darkness

dust *n.* fine, dry particles of dirt

duty *n.* something a person must do; a moral obligation

dwell *v.* to live, as an inhabitant -**er** *n.*

dwin-dle *v.* to waste away

dye *v.* fix a color in or stain materials; color with a dye

dying *adj.* coming to the end of life; about to die

dy-nam-ic *adj.* forceful; energic; productive activity or change; of or relating to energy, motion, or force -**al** *adj.*

dy-nam-ics *n.*, *Phys.* part of physics dealing with force, energy, and motion and the relationship between them

dy-na-mo *n.* machine producing electric current

dys-en-ter-y *n.* infection of the lower intestinal tract

dys-lex-i-a *n.* an impairment in one's ability to read **dyslexic** *adj.*

dys-pep-sia *n.* indigestion

dys-pro-si-um *n.* metallic element

dys-tro-phy *n.* various neuromuscular disorders, especially muscular dystrophy

E, e The fifth letter of the English alphabet.

each *adj.* everyone

each other *pron.* each of two or more in reciprocal action or relation

ea-ger *adj.* marked by enthusiastic interest **eagerness** *n.*

eager beaver *n.* one who is extremely zealous in performing his assigned duties and in volunteering for more

ea-gle *n.* large, powerful bird

eagle eye *n.* the ability to see or observe with exceptional keeness; one that observes

eagle ray *n.* any of several widely distributed large active stingrays with broad pectoral fins like wings

ea-glet *n.* young eagle

ear *n., Anat.*

hearing organ in vertebrates

earl *n.* British nobleman **earldom** *n.*

ear-ly *adj.* occurring before the usual time

earn *v.* payment for work done or services rendered **earner** *n.*

ear-nest *n.* serious intent **earnestly, earnestness** *n.*

earn-ings *pl., n.* something earned, such as a salary

earth *n.* the outer layer of the world; ground; soil; dirt

ease *n.* state of being comfortable

ea-sel *n.* frame used to support a canvas or picture

east *n.* the direction in which the sun rises **eastly** *adj. & adv.*, **eastward** *adj. & adv.*

Easter *n.* Christian festival that celebrates the resurrection of Christ

easy *adj.* little difficulty **easily** *adv.*, **easiness** *n.*

eat *v.* chew and swallow food; to erode **eater** *n.*

ebb *n.* recede of a tide towards the sea; leassening; to weaken

eb-o-ny *n., pl.* **ebonies** dark, hard, colored wood; black or very deep brown

ec-cen-tric *adj.* different or peculiar

ec-cle-si-as-ti-cal *n.* a clergyman; a person officially serving a church

ech-e-lon *n.* formation of military troops

ech-o *n., pl.* **echoes** repetition of a sound

ec-lec-tic *adj.* having components from diverse sources **eclectic** *n.*

e-clipse *n.* total or partial blocking of one celestial body by another

e-clip-tic *n., Astron.* the suns apparent path

ec-logue *n.* short pastoral poem in dialogue form

e-col-o-gy *n.* scientific study of the environment **ecologist** *n.*

ec-o-nom-ic *adj.* science relating to the necessities of life

ec-o-nom-i-cal *adj.* not wasteful **economically** *adv.*

ec-o-nom-ics *pl., n.* science which studies wealth

e-con-o-mize *v.* to manage thriftily **economizer** *n.*

e-con-o-my *n., pl.* **economies** system for the management of resources and production of goods

ec-ru *n.* light yellowish brown

ec-sta-sy *n., pl.* **ecstasies** state of intense joy or delight

ec-u-men-i-cal *adj.* worldwide; un-iversal

ec-ze-ma *n.* noncontagious skin disease marked by itching and scaly patches

ed-dy *n., pl.* **eddies** wind or water running against the main current

edge *n.* cutting side of a blade; sharpness

ed-i-ble *adj.* safe or fit for consumption

e-dict *n.* public decree

ed-i-fy *v.* improve or educate

ed-it *v.* correct for publication; to compile for an edition **editor** *n.*

e-di-tion *n.* form in which a book is published

ed-i-to-ri-al *n.* article in a newspaper or magazine **editorially** *adv.*

ed-u-cate *v.* supply with training or schooling **educator** *n.*

e-duce *v.* to call forth or bring out

eel *n., pl.* **eel** or **eels** snake-like fish

ee-rie or **ee-ry** *adj.* weird; scary; spooky **eerily** *adv.*, **eeriness** *n.*

ef-face *v.* remove or rub out

ef-fect *n.* power to produce a desired result

ef-fec-tive *adj.* producing an expected effect or result **effectiveness** *n.*

ef-fem-i-nate *adj.* having a more woman-like quality or trait

ef-fer-ent *adj., Physiol.* carrying away or outward from an organ or part **efferently** *adv.*

ef-fete *adj.* exhausted of effectiveness or force

ef-fi-ca-cious *adj.* producing an intended effect **efficaciously** *adv.*

ef-fi-cient *adj.* adequate in performance with minimum effort

ef-fi-gy *n., pl.* **effigies** image of a hated

person

ef-flo-res-cence *n.* slow process of development

ef-flu-vi-um *n., pl.* effluvivia *or* effluviums unpleasant vapor of something

ef-fort *n.* earnest attempt or achievement effortless *adj.*

ef-fron-ter-y *n., pl.* effronteries shameless; boldness; impudence

ef-ful-gent *adj.* shining brilliantly

ef-fu-sion *n.* unrestrained outpouring of feeling

egg *n.* reproductive cell of female animals

egg-beat-er *n.* tool with rotating blades used to mix food

egg-nog *n.* drink of beaten eggs, sugar, and milk or cream

egg-plant *n.* a purple, egg-shaped, edible fruit

e-go *n.* self thinking

e-go-cen-tric *adj.* thinking of oneself as the object of all experiences

e-go-ma-ni-a *n.* self obsession

e-gre-gious *adj.* remarkably bad

e-gress *n.* act of coming out; means of departing

e-gret *n.*

white wading birds

ei-der *n.* large sea duck found in northern regions

eight *n.* cardinal number which follows seven.

ei-ther *pron.* one or the other; *adv.* likewise; also

e-jac-u-late *v.* eject abruptly; to exclaim

e-ject *v.* to throw out; to expel ejection, ejector *n.*

eke out *v.* obtain with great effort

e-lab-o-rate *adj.* planned or carried out with great detail

e-lapse *v.* slip or glide away

e-las-tic *adj.* capable of easy adjustment

e-late *v.* make proud of elation *n.*

el-bow *n., Anat.* outer joint of the arm between the upper arm and forearm

elbow-room *n.* ample room to move about

eld-er *adj.* older; senior

e-lect *v.* choose or select by vote

e-lec-tric *or* e-lec-tri-cal *adj.* relating or pertaining to electricity

e-lec-tric-i-ty *n., Phys., Chem.* force that causes bodies to attract or repel each other; form of energy

e-lec-tro-cute *v.* kill by the use of electric current electrocution *n.*

e-lec-trode *n.* a conductor of electricity into or out of a battery

e-lec-tro-mag-net *n.* magnet that operates through an electric source

e-lec-tron *n., Elect.* subatomic particle with a negative electric charge

e-lec-tro-type *n.* duplicate metal plate used in printing

el-e-gance *n.* refinement in appearance

el-e-gy *n., pl.* elegies poem expressing sorrow for one who is dead elegist *n.*

el-e-ment *n.* constituent part

el-e-men-ta-ry *adj.* fundamental; essential

el-e-phant *n.*

large mammal having a long, flexible trunk

el-e-vate *v.* lift up or raise

e-lev-en *n.* cardinal number equal to ten plus one eleventh *n.*

elf *n., pl.* elves imaginary being with magical powers

e-lic-it *v.* bring or draw out

e-lide *v.* to omit; to slur over in pronunciation

e-lim-i-nate *v.* get rid of or remove

e-lite *n.* most skilled members of a group

e-lix-ir *n., Phar.* sweetened aromatic liquid of alcohol and water

elk *n.* large deer

el-lipse *n., Geom.* closed curve oval in shape

elm *n.* various valuable timber and shade trees

el-o-cu-tion *n.* art of effective public speaking

e-lope *v.* run away, especially in order to marry

el-o-quent *adj.* having the power to speak fluently

else *adj.* different; other; more

else-where *adv.* to or in another place

e-lu-ci-date *v.* make clear, clarify; to explain

e-lude *v.* to evade or avoid

e-ma-ci-ate *v.* to become extremely thin emaciation *n.*

em-a-nate *v.* to come or give forth

e-man-ci-pate *v.* liberate; to set free emancipation *n.*

e-mas-cu-late *v.* to castrate

em-balm *v.* treat a corpse with preservatives to protect from decay

em-bank v. support, protect or defend
embankment n.

em-bar-go n., pl. embargoes a restraint
on trade

em-bark v. to set out on a venture

em-bar-rass v.   feel selfconscious; to
confuse embarrassment n.

em-bas-sy n., pl. embassies headquarters
of an ambassador

em-bat-tle v. to prepare for battle

em-bed v. to enclose tightly in a surrounding mass

em-bel-lish v. to adorn; to decorate
embellishment n.

em-ber n. small piece of glowing coal

em-bez-zle v. take money or other items
fraudulently

em-bit-ter v. to create feelings of hostility embitterment n.

em-bla-zon v. decorate in bright colors

em-blem n. symbol of something; a distinctive design

em-bod-y v. give a bodily form to

em-bold-en v. to encourage; to make
bold

em-bo-lism n., Med. blockage of a
blood vessel

em-bon-point n. plumpness; stoutness

em-boss v.   shape or decorate with
raised designs

em-brace v. to clasp or hold in the arms

em-bro-cate v. moisten and rub liquid
medicine

em-broi-der v. to decorate with ornamental needlework

em-broil v. to throw into confusion
embroilment n.

em-bry-o n., pl. embryos organism in
the early development stage
embryonic adj.

em-cee n., Informal master of
ceremonies emcee v.

e-mend v. correct or remove faults
emendation n.

em-er-ald n. bright-green gemstone

e-merge v. to rise into view

e-mer-gen-cy n., pl. emergencies sudden
and unexpected situation

e-mer-i-tus adj. retired from active duty
with honor

e-met-ic adj. medicine used to induce
vomiting

em-i-grate v. to move from one country
or region emigration n.

e-mi-gre n. refugee

em-i-nent adj. high in esteem or rank
eminently adv.

em-is-sar-y n., pl. emissaries person sent
out on a mission

e-mit v. to send forth; to throw or give

out

e-mol-lient n. substance for softening of
the skin emollient adj.

e-mol-u-ment n. profit; compensation

e-mote v. to show emotion

e-mo-tion n. strong feeling of sorrow,
hate and love

em-pa-thy n., Physiol. understanding the
feelings of another person

em-pen-nage n.   rear section of an
aircraft

em-per-or n. ruler of an empire

em-pha-sis n., pl. emphases importance
attached to anything

em-pire n. nations governed by a single
supreme authority

em-pir-i-cal or em-pir-ic adj. gained
from observation or experience
empirically adv.

em-place-ment n. platform for guns or
military equipment

em-ploy v. engage the service or use of
-able adj., emoloyer, employment n.

em-ploy-ee or em-ploy-e n.   person who
works for another in return for pay

em-po-ri-um n., pl. emporiums or em-
poria large store which carries general
merchandise

em-pow-er v. to authorize; to delegate

em-press n. woman who rules an empire

emp-ty adj. containing nothing; lacking
substance

em-u-late v. strive to equal, by imitating

e-mul-sion n., Chem. mixture of small
droplets, one within the other

en-a-ble v. to make able

en-act v. to make into law; to decree
enactment n.

e-nam-el n. protective coating

en-am-or v. to inflame with love; to
charm

en-camp v. to form or stay in a camp
encampment n.

en-cap-su-late v. enclose or encase in a
capsule

en-ceph-a-li-tis n., Pathol. inflammation
of the brain

en-chain v. put in chains

en-chant v. to put under a spell
enchantment n.

en-cir-cle v. to form a circle around
encirclement n.

en-close v. to surround on all sides

en-co-mi-um n., pl. encomiums or en-
comia high praise

en-com-pass v. to surround

en-core n.   audience's demand for a
repeat performance

en-coun-ter n. unexpected meeting or
conflict

en-cour-age v. inspire with courage or hope **encouragement** n.

en-croach v. intrude upon the rights of another **encroacher, encroachment** n.

en-crust v. cover with a crust; to crust

en-cum-ber v. hinder or burden with difficulties

en-cy-clo-pe-di-a n. a book of references covering a broad range of subjects

en-cyst v. to become enclosed in a sac **encystment** n.

end n. terminal point where something is concluded

en-dan-ger v. to expose to danger **endangerment** n.

en-dear v. to make beloved or dear **endearingly** adv.

endearment n. state of being endeared

en-deav-or n. attempt to attain or do something

en-dem-ic adj. peculiar to a particular area

en-dog-e-nous adj., Biol. originating or growing from within

en-dor-phin n. painkilling hormones secreted by the brain

en-dorse v. to write one's signature on the back of a check **endorsement** n.

en-dow v. to bestow upon **endowment** n.

en-dure v. to undergo

end-wise adv. on end; lengthwise

en-e-ma n. injection of a liquid into the rectum for cleansing

en-e-my n. a hostile force

en-er-gy n., pl. **energies** vigor; growth Phys. electric power

en-er-vate v. to weaken

en-fee-ble v. to weaken **enfeeblement** n.

en-fold v. enclose; wrap in layers

en-force v. impose by force or firmness **enforceable** adj., **enforcement** n.

en-fran-chise v. to grant to give a franchise to

en-gage v. to secure or bind; pledge to marry

en-gen-der v. to exist

en-gine n. mechanical machine

en-gorge v. to swallow greedily **engorgement** n.

en-graft v., Bot. join or fasten

en-grave v. to etch into a surface

en-gross v. occupy attention

en-gulf v. enclose completely

en-hance v. make greater **-ment** n.

e-nig-ma n. anything puzzling

en-join v. to prohibit

en-joy v. feel joy or find pleasure

en-large v. make larger in size

en-list v. enroll or sign up for

en-mesh v. to entangle

en-mi-ty n., pl. **enmities** deep hatred; hostility

en-no-ble v. to confer the rank of nobility

en-nui n. boredom; weariness

e-nor-mity n., pl. **enormities** wickedness

e-nor-mous adj. very great in size **enormously** adv.

e-nough adj. adequate to satisfy demands

en-rage v. put into a rage

en-rap-ture v. to delight

en-rich v. make rich or richer

en-roll or **en-rol** v. to enter one's name on a register or record

en-sconce v. to settle securely

en-sem-ble n. group of complementary parts that are in harmony

en-shrine v. to hold saced

en-shroud v. cover with a shroud

en-sign n. identifying flag; commissioned Navy officer

en-slave v. to put in bondage **enslavement** n.

en-snare v. to catch; to trap

en-sue v. to follow as a consequence

en-sure v. to make certain of

en-tail v. necessary accompaniment or result **entailment** n.

en-tan-gle v. to complicate; to confuse **entanglement** n.

en-ter v. go into; to penetrate; to begin

en-ter-prise n. large or risky undertaking; project with risks

en-ter-tain v. to amuse; consider **entertainment** n.

en-thrall v. to fascinate; captivate **enthrallment** n.

en-thu-si-asm n. intense feeling

en-tice v. to attract by arousing desire

en-tire adj. whole; complete

en-ti-tle v. furnish with a right

en-ti-ty n., pl. **entities** something that exists alone

en-tomb v. to place in a tomb **entombment** n.

en-to-mol-o-gy n. study of insects

en-trails pl., n. internal organs of man

en-trance n. the means or place of entry

en-trance v. to fascinate

en-trap v. catch in a trap **entrapment** n.

en-treat v. to make an earnest request of

en-trench v. to fix or sit firmly **entrenchment** n.

en-tre-pre-neur n., Fr. person who undertakes business ventures

en-trust v. transfer to another for care

en-try n., pl. **entries** opening or place for entering

en-twine v. twine about or together

e-nu-mer-ate v. count off one by one

e-nun-ci-ate *v.* to pronounce with clarity; to announce

en-ve-lope *n.* paper covering for a letter

en-ven-om *v.* to make poisonous; to embitter

en-vi-a-ble *adj.* highly desirable

en-vi-ron-ment *n.* surroundings

en-vi-ron-men-tal-ist *n.* person who tries to preserve the natural environment

en-vi-rons *pl., n.* surrounding region; a place

en-vis-age *v.* form a mental image of; to visualize

en-voy *n.* messenger or agent; a diplomatic representative

en-vy *n., pl.* envies resentment for someone else's possessions

e-o-li-an *adj., Geol.* caused by or transmitted by the wind

e-on *n.* indefinite period of time

ep-au-let *or* ep-au-lette *n.* shoulder ornament on a military uniform

e-pergne *n.* centerpiece for holding flowers

e-phed-rine *n., Chem.* alkaloid used to relieve nasal congestion

e-phem-er-al *adj.* lasting a very short time

ep-ic *n.* long narrative poem

ep-i-cure *n.* a person having refined tastes

ep-i-dem-ic *adj.* something that effects many individuals

ep-i-der-mis *n., Anat.*

Epidermis
Dermis

outer nonvascular layer of the skin

ep-i-gram *n.* clever, witty observation

ep-i-lep-sy *n., Pathol.* nervous disorder with attacks of unconsciousness

ep-i-logue *or* ep-i-log *n.* short speech given by an actor to the audience at the end of a play; an appended chapter placed at the end of a novel or book, etc.

ep-i-neph-rine *or* ep-i-neph-rin *n., Biochem.* a hormone secreted by the adrenal medulla of the adrenal glands

e-piph-a-ny *n.* Christian festival held on January 6th

e-pis-co-pa-cy *n., pl.* episcopacies government of a church by bishops

e-pis-co-pal *adj.* pertaining to or governed by bishops

e-pis-co-pate *n.* term, rank, or position of a bishop

ep-i-sode *n.* a section of a poem, novel, etc., that is complete in itself

episodic *adj.*

e-pis-tle *n.* a formal letter Epistle one of the letters in the New Testament

ep-i-taph *n.* inscription, as on a tomb or gravestone

ep-i-the-li-um *n.* thin membranous tissue covering the outer bodily surface

ep-i-thet *n.* word used to characterize something

e-pit-o-me *n.* concise summary; typical example

e-pit-o-mize *v.* be a perfect example

ep-och *n.* point in time marking a new era

ep-ox-y *n., pl.* epoxies *Chem.* corrosion-resistant resin used glues and coatings

eq-ua-ble *adj.* not changing; evenly proportioned

e-qual *adj.* same quantity, or value; having the same privileges or rights

e-qual-ize *v.* become or make equal equalization *n.*

e-qua-nim-i-ty *n.* composure

e-quate *v.* consider or make equal

e-qua-tion *n.* act of being equal; mathematical statement of equality, usually shown as ($=$)

e-qua-tor *n.* imaginary circle around the earth

eq-uer-ry *n.* the officer in charge of the horses of royalty

e-ques-tri-an *n.* person who rides or performs on a horse

e-qui-an-gu-lar *adj., Geom.* having all angles equal

e-qui-dis-tant *adj.* having equal distances

e-qui-lat-er-al *adj.* having all sides equal

e-qui-lib-ri-um *n.* balance between two opposing forces; state of adjustment, or balance

e-quine *adj.* pertaining to or like a horse

e-qui-nox *n.* twice a year the sun crosses the equator and days and nights are equal in time

e-quip *v.* furnish with what is needed for any undertaking

e-qui-page *n.* carriage that is equipped with horses and attendants

e-quip-ment *n.* material provided for a special purpose

e-qui-poise *n.* a state of balance

eq-ui-ta-ble *adj.* being impartial in treatment or judgment equitableness *n.*

eq-ui-ta-tion *n.* art or act of horse riding

eq-ui-ty *n.* fairness or impartiality; value of property beyond a mortgage or liability

e-quiv-a-lent *adj.* being equal equivalence *n.*

e-quiv-o-cal *adj.* ambiguous; questionable **equivocally** *adv.*

e-quiv-o-cate *v.* use intentionally evasive or vague language **equivocation** *n.*

-er *n., suff.* person concerned with a trade; one from a certain area, as a northerner

e-ra *n.* historical period in history

e-rad-i-cate *v.* to destroy utterl

e-rase *v.* remove something written **erasable** *adj.*

er-bi-um *n., Chem.* metallic, silvery, rare-earth element

ere *prep., Poet.* prior to; before

e-rect *adj.* in a vertical position; standing up straight; upright

ere-long *adv., Archaic* before long

er-e-mite *n.* a hermit

er-go *conj. & adv.* consequently; therefore

er-got *n.* disease of cereal plants; drug used to contract involuntary muscles

er-mine *n.*

weasel with white fur

e-rode *v.* wear away gradually; to corrode

e-rog-e-nous *adj.* responsive to sexual stimulation

e-ro-sion *n.* state of being eroded

e-ro-sive *adj.* tending to erode **erosiveness** *n.*

e-rot-ic *adj.* pertaining to or promoting sexual desire

err *v.* make a mistake; to sin

er-rand *n.* trip to carry a message or perform a task

er-rant *adj.* wandering in search of adventure; straying from what is proper

er-rat-ic *adj.* lacking a fixed course; inconsistent **erratically** *adv.*

er-ra-tum *n., pl.* **errata** an error in writing or printing

er-ro-ne-ous *adj.* having or contain an error **erroneously** *adv.*

er-ror *n.* something done incorrectly; a mistake

er-satz *adj.* substitute usually inferior; artificial

erst-while *adj., Archaic* former

e-ruct *v.* to belch **eructation** *n.*

er-u-dite *adj.* scholarly

er-u-di-tion *n.* informed; great learning

e-rupt *v.* burst forth violently; explode with steam, lava, etc

er-y-sip-e-las *n.* an acute, inflammatory, skin disease resulting from streptococcus

es-ca-late *v.* intensify, increase, or enlarge

es-ca-la-tor *n.* a moving stairway

es-cal-lop *n. & v.* variation of scallop

es-ca-pade *n.* reckless behavior; a prankish trick

es-cape *v.* break free from confinement, restraint, etc.

es-cape-ment *n., Mech.* device in timepieces to control the movement of the wheel

es-cap-ism *n.* escape from unpleasant realities through day-dreams **escapist** *n. & adj.*

es-ca-role *n.* endive leaves used for salads

es-carp-ment *n.* a steep slope or drop

-escense *n., suff.* give off light in a certain way, as florescence

es-chew *v.* shun or avoid

es-cort *n.* person accompanying another to give protection

es-cri-toire *n.* a writing desk

es-crow *n.* money placed in the custody of a third party until specified conditions are met

es-cutch-eon *n.* surface with an emblem bearing a coat of arms

-ese *n. & adj., suff.* anative of; in the language or style of

e-soph-a-gus *n., pl.* **esophagi** *Anat.* membranous tube through which food passes to the stomach

es-o-ter-ic *adj.* confidential; kept secret

es-pa-drille *n.* canvas shoe

es-pal-ier *n.* framework used to train shrubs to grow a particular way

es-pe-cial *adj.* having a very special place; exceptional **especially** *adv.*

es-pi-o-nage *n.* act of spying to obtain secret intelligence

es-pla-nade *n.* flat, open stretch of land along a shoreline

es-pou-sal *n.* support or adoption of a cause

es-pouse *v.* to make something one's own; to take as a spouse

es-pres-so *n.* strong coffee brewed by steam pressure

es-prit *n.* spirit; wit; mental liveliness

es-prit de corps *n., Fr.* a group's spirit of enthusiasm to the common goals of the group

es-py *v.* catch a quick view

-esque *adj., suff.* resembling

es-quire *n.* title of courtesy or respect

-ess *n., suff.* female

es-say *n.* short composition dealing with a single topic

es-sence *n.* the most important element; being

es-sen-tial *adj.* indispensable necessary **essentially** *adv.*

-est *adj. & adv., suff.* used to form the superlative degree of adverbs and adjectives

es-tab-lish *v.* make permanent, or secure; to create or find

es-tab-lish-ment *n.* a place of residence; those of influence and status in a society

es-tate *n.* large piece of land containing a large house

es-teem *v.* regard with respect

es-ter *n., Chem.* organic compounds formed by the reaction of an acid with an alcohol

es-ti-ma-ble *adj.* worthy of respect or admiration

es-ti-mate *v.* give an approximate opinion or calculation **estimation** *n.*

es-ti-val *adj.* pertaining to or of summer

es-ti-vate *v.* pass the summer in a state of dormancy

es-trange *v.* arouse hated; disassociate or remove oneself

es-tro-gen *n., Biochem.* steroid hormones that regulate female reproductive functions

es-tu-ar-y *n., pl.* -ies wide mouth of a river where the current meets the sea

etch *v.* engrave or cut into the surface by the action of acid **etcher** *n.*

etch-ing *n.* process of engraving using a sharp instrument and acid

e-ter-nal *adj.* existing without beginning or end; unending

e-ter-ni-ty *n., pl.* externities forever; the immeasurable extent of time

eth-ane *n., Chem.* gasous hydrocarbon contained in crude petroleum

eth-a-nol *n., Chem.* the intoxicant in liquors, wines, and beers; alcohol

e-ther *n., Chem.* an anesthetic

e-the-re-al *adj.* highly refined; delicate

eth-ic *n.* the system of moral values

eth-i-cal *adj.* conforming to right principles of conduct

eth-nic *adj.* relating to or of a cultural, or racial group

eth-nog-ra-phy *n., pl.* ethnographies branch of anthropology dealing with primitive human cultures

eth-nol-o-gy *n., pl.* -gies the study of racial groups, their cultures, and origins

eth-yl-ene *n., Chem.* flammable gas used as a fuel

e-ti-ol-o-gy *n.* science and study of causes or origins

et-i-quette *n.* prescribed rules of behavior in society

-ette *n., suff.* small; female

et-y-mol-o-gy *n., pl.* -gies branch of linguistics that deals with etymologies

eu-ca-lyp-tus *n.* large, native Australian tree with aromatic leaves

Eu-cha-rist *n.* the Christian sacrament of Communion

eu-chre *n.* card game for two to four players

eu-gen-ics *n.* science of improving the physical and mental qualities of human beings

eu-lo-gize *v.* deliver a eulogy for **eulogist** *n.*

eu-lo-gy *n., pl.* eulogies a speech that honors a person or thing

eu-nuch *n.* a castrated man

eu-phe-mism *n.* substitution for a word thought to be too strong

eu-pho-ny *n., pl.* -nies agreeable sound of spoken words

eu-pho-ri-a *n.* very strong feeling of elation or well-being **euphoric** *adj.*

eu-re-ka *interj.* an expression of triumph

eu-sta-chian tube *n., Anat.* passage between the middle ear and the pharynx

eu-tha-na-sia *n.* act of putting to death painlessly a person suffering from an incurable disease

eu-then-ics *n.* study of improving the physical and mental qualities of human beings

e-vac-u-ate *v.* to leave a threatened area **evacuation** *n.*

e-vac-u-ee *n.* a person evacuated from a hazardous place

e-vade *v.* to elude; to get away from by using tricks

e-val-u-ate *v.* to determine the value of; to appraise **evaluation** *n.*

ev-a-nesce *v.* to fade away

ev-a-nes-cent *adj.* vanishing or passing quickly; fleeting

e-van-gel-i-cal *adj.* relating to the Christian gospel

e-van-gel-ism *n.* preaching and spreading of the gospel

e-van-gel-ist *n.* Protestant preacher or missionary

e-van-gel-ize *v.* to preach the gospel

e-vap-o-rate *v.* convert into vapor; remove the liquid or moisture from milk

e-va-sive *adj.* being intentionally vague **evasively** *adv.*

eve *n.* the evening before a special holiday; evening

e-ven *adj.* having a level surface; equally matched

e-ven-hand-ed *adj.* fair; impartial

evenhandedly *adv.*

eve-ning *n.* the time between sunset and bedtime

e-ven-song *n.* an evening prayer

e-vent *n.* a significant occurrence; something that takes place eventful *adj.*

e-ven-tide *n.* evening

e-ven-tu-al *adj.* expected to happen in due course of time eventually *adv.*

e-ven-tu-al-i-ty *n.* the conceivable outcome

e-ven-tu-ate *v.* to come out eventually

ev-er *adv.* at any time; throughout the entire course of time

ev-er-glade *n.* tract of low, swampy land

ev-er-green *adj.* tree with green foliage throughout the year

ev-er-last-ing *adj.* existing or lasting forever everlastingly *adv.*

ev-er-more *adv., Poet.* for and at all time to come; always

e-vert *v.* to turn inside out or outward

eve-ry *adj.* without exceptions

eve-ry-body *pron.* every person

eve-ry-day *adj.* happening every day; daily

eve-ry-one *pron.* every person

eve-ry-place *adv.* everywhere

eve-ry-thing *pron.* all things; the essential thing

eve-ry-where *adv.* in, at, or to everyplace

e-vict *v.* to put out a tenant by legal process eviction *n.*

ev-i-dence *n.* facts on which a conclusion can be based

ev-i-dent *adj.* easily seen; obvious evidently *adv.*

e-vil *adj.* morally bad or wrong; low in public esteem

e-vil-do-er *n.* person who does evil to another

e-vil--mind-ed *adj.* obsessed with evil thoughts or intentions

e-vince *v.* demonstrate or indicate clearly

e-vis-cer-ate *v.* remove the vital part of something

e-voke *v.* call or summon forth to produce a reaction

ev-o-lu-tion *n.* gradual process of development or change -ary *adj.*

e-volve *v.* develop or change gradually; developed by evolutionary processes

ewe *n.* female sheep

ew-er *n.*

wide-mouthed pitcher or jug

ex- *pref.* former

ex-ac-er-bate *v.* make more severe or worse

ex-act *adj.* accurate in every detail

ex-act-ing *adj.* making severe demands; rigorous exactingly *adv.*

ex-act-i-tude *n.* the quality of being exact

ex-ag-ger-ate *v.* represent something as being greater than it really is exaggeration *n.*

ex-alt *v.* raise in honor, rank, etc.; to praise or glorify exalted *adj.*

ex-am *n., Slang* an examination

ex-am-i-na-tion *n.* a test of skill or knowledge

ex-am-ine *v.* observe or inspect; to test by questions

ex-ample *n.* representative as a sample; one worthy of imitation

ex-as-per-ate *v.* make frustrated or angry

ex-ca-vate *v.* dig a hole or cavity

ex-ceed *v.* surpass in quantity; to go beyond the limit

ex-ceed-ing-ly *adv.* greater than

ex-cel *v.* surpass or to do better than others

ex-cel-lence *n.* quality of being superior; superior quality

ex-cel-lent *adj.* the best quality

ex-cel-si-or *n.* wood shavings to protect delicate materials

ex-cept *prep.* with the omission or exclusion of; aside from

ex-cep-tion *n.* something that is excluded or does not conform

ex-cep-tion-a-ble *adj.* open to objection exceptionably *adv.*

ex-cep-tion-al *adj.* unusual; well above average exceptionally *adv.*

ex-cerpt *n.* passage from a book, etc.

ex-cess *n.* amount beyond what is necessary

ex-ces-sive *adj.* exceeding what is necessary; extreme

ex-change *v.* return for something else; trade

ex-cheq-uer *n.* treasury of a nation

ex-cise *n.* internal tax on the sale of a commodity

ex-cise *v.* remove surgically

ex-cit-a-ble *adj.* be easily excited excitableness *n.*

ex-cite *v.* stir up strong emotion; simulate the emotions of excitant *n.*

ex-claim *v.* cry out abruptly

ex-cla-ma-tion *n.* a sudden forceful utterance

ex-clude *v.* keep out; to omit from consideration

ex-clu-sive *adj.* intended for a single source; having no duplicate -ly *adv.*

ex-com-mu-ni-cate *v.* deprive the right of

church membership -ation n.

ex-co-ri-ate v. to censure harshly

ex-cre-ment n. bodily waste

ex-cre-ta pl., n. excretions from the body such as sweat

ex-crete v. eliminate waste matter from the body

ex-cru-ci-at-ing adj. intensely painful excruciatingly adv.

ex-cul-pate v. free from wrong doing exculpation n.

ex-cur-sion n. short trip for pleasure

ex-cur-sive adj. go in one direction and then another; digressive

ex-cuse v. ask forgiveness or pardon for oneself; apologize for excuseable adj.

ex-e-cra-ble adj. extremely bad -ness n.

ex-e-crate v. to detest; abhor

ex-e-cute v. to carry out; put to death by the legal authority

ex-e-cu-tion n. act of executing a task; the death penalty

ex-e-cu-tion-er n. a person who carries out a legal execution

ex-ec-u-tive n. administrator in an organization; branch of government responsible for activating the laws of a country

ex-ec-u-tor n. person appointed to carry out the execution of a will

ex-em-plar n. something serving as a worthy model; a typical example

ex-em-pla-ry adj. worthy of imitation; commendable

ex-em-pli-fy v. show by giving examples

ex-empt v. free or excuse from an obligation or duty exemption n.

ex-er-cise n. the act of training or developing oneself

ex-ert v. put oneself through a strenuous effort exertion n.

ex-hale v. breathe out

ex-haust v. make extremely tired; drain oneself of strength

ex-haust n. discharge of waste gases; device through which waste gases are released

ex-hib-it v. display for public view

ex-hi-bi-tion-ism n. practice of drawing undue attention to oneself

ex-hil-a-rate v. to elate or refresh

ex-hort v. to urge by earnest appeal

ex-hume v. ig up and remove from a grave exhumation n.

ex-i-gen-cy n. urgency

ex-ig-u-ous adj. extremely small; scanty

ex-ile n. banishment; one who has been driven from his or her country

ex-ist v. have actual being or reality

ex-is-tence n. state of existing, or occurring

ex-is-ten-tial adj. based on experience

ex-it n. a way or passage out

ex-o-bi-ol-o-gy n. the study of extraterrestrial life

ex-o-dus n. a departure of large numbers of people

ex-on-er-ate v. free one from accusation or blame; free from responsibility

ex-or-bi-tant adj. beyond usual and proper limits

ex-or-cise v. cast out or expel an evil spirit by prayers exorcism n.

ex-o-ther-mic adj. releasing rather than absorbing heat

ex-ot-ic adj. strangely different and fascinating

ex-pand v. increase the scope, or size; develop more fully expandable adj.

ex-panse n. a wide, open stretch

ex-pan-sive adj. broad and extensive

ex-pa-ti-ate v. to talk or write at length

ex-pa-tri-ate v. to leave one's country and reside in another

ex-pect v. look forward to something as probable or certain

ex-pec-tan-cy n. state of expecting; expectation

ex-pec-tant adj. pregnant

ex-pec-ta-tion n. something that is expected and looked forward to

ex-pec-to-rant n. medicine used to promote expectoration

ex-pec-to-rate v. to spit

ex-pe-di-en-cy n. quality of being expedient

ex-pe-di-ent adj. determined by selfish interests only

ex-pe-dite v. speed up the progress of something

ex-pe-di-tion n. a journey for a definite purpose

ex-pe-di-tion-ar-y adj. sent on military service abroad

ex-pe-di-tious adj. quick; speedy

ex-pel v. drive or force out

ex-pend v. to pay out or use up

ex-pen-di-ture n. an amount spent

ex-pense n. outlay or consumption of money; funds allotted to cover incidental costs

ex-pen-sive adj. high-priced

ex-pe-ri-ence n. the knowledge or skill acquired from actual participation or training in an activity

ex-pert n. a person having great knowledge, or skill

ex-per-tise n. specialized skill in a particular area

ex-pi-ate v. to make amends for

ex-pire *v.* to come to an end; to exhale

ex-plain *v.* make understandable; to account for

ex-ple-tive *n.* an exclamation, often profane

ex-pli-cate *v.* to clear up the meaning of

ex-plic-it *adj.* plainly expressed; straightforward

ex-plode *v.* burst or blow up violently with a loud noise

ex-ploit *n.* a deed or act that is notable

ex-plore *v.* examine in a systematic way

ex-plo-sion *n.* sudden, violent release of energy

ex-po-nent *n.* person who speaks for a cause or group

ex-port *v.* send merchandise to other countries for resale

ex-pose *v.* lay open, as to ridicule; to lay bare; to reveal the identity of someone

ex-po-si-tion *n.* a statement of intent; a public exhibition

ex post facto *adj., L.* after the fact

ex-pos-tu-late *v.* try to dissuade against an action

ex-po-sure *n.* an indication of which way something faces

ex-press *v.* to formulate in words; to comunicate

ex-pres-sive *adj.* serving to indicate or express; full of expression

ex-pro-pri-ate *v.* take property from the owner for public use

ex-pul-sion *n.* act of expelling

ex-punge *v.* to delete or remove; to erase

ex-pur-gate *v.* remove objectionable material from a play, etc.

ex-qui-site *adj.* intricately beautiful in craftsmanship

ex-tant *adj.* still in existence; not destroyed; surviving

ex-tend *v.* open to full length; to prolong; offer the hand

ex-ten-sion *n.* additional time to pay a debt

ex-ten-sive *adj.* wide-spread; far-reaching

ex-tent *n.* degree to which anything is extended; the size

ex-ten-u-ate *v.* minimize the seriousness of something

ex-te-ri-or *adj.* the outside; the external layer

ex-ter-mi-nate *v.* to destroy completely

ex-ter-nal *adj.* outside; exterior

ex-tinct *adj.* no longer existing

ex-tin-guish *v.* put an end to; to make extinct **extinguishable** *adj.*

ex-tir-pate *v.* pull up by the roots

ex-tol *v.* to praise highly

ex-tort *v.* obtain money by threat, or abuse of authority **extortist** *n.*

ex-tra *adj.* over and above what is normal

ex-tract *v.* pull or draw out by force

ex-trac-tion *n.* act of extracting; one's origin or ancestry

ex-tra-cur-ric-u-lar *adj.* outside the usual duties

ex-tra-dite *v.* surrender by extradition

ex-tra-di-tion *n.* legal surrender of a criminal for trial

ex-tra-dos *n.* the upper curve of an arch

ex-tra-ga-lac-tic *adj.* coming from beyond the galaxy

ex-tra-mar-i-tal *adj.* adulterous

ex-tra-mu-ral *adj.* involving teams from different schools

ex-tra-ne-ous *adj.* coming from without **extraneously** *adv.*

ex-tra-or-di-nar-y *adj.* beyond what is usual; remarkable

ex-tra-sen-so-ry *adj.* beyond the range of normal perception

ex-tra-ter-res-tri-al *adj.* orginating outside the earth

ex-trav-a-gant *adj.* overly lavish; wasteful; unrestrained **extravagantly** *adv.*

ex-trav-a-gan-za *n.* a lavish, showy entertainment

ex-treme *adj.* going far beyond the bounds of moderation; of the highest or utmost degree **extremely** *adv.*

ex-trem-ist *n.* person who resorts to extreme measures

ex-tri-cate *v.* free from entanglement; to disengage

ex-trin-sic *adj.* outside the nature of something; external

ex-tro-vert *n.* out going person

ex-trude *v.* push or thrust out; to protrude

ex-u-ber-ant *adj.* full of high spirits **exuberance** *n.*

ex-ude *v.* to ooze or trickle forth, as sweat

ex-ult *v.* jubilant; to rejoice greatly

ex-ur-bi-a *n.* well-to-do residential area

eye *n.* an organ of sight; central area of a hurricane

eye-sight *n.* power of sight; the range of vision

eye-sore *n.* something ugly that offends the sight

eye-tooth *n.*

one of the canine teeth of the upper jaw

eye-wit-ness *n.* person who testifies to something he has seen

F, f The sixth letter of the English alphabet

fa-ba-ceous *adj.* or or relating to the legume family

Fa-bi-an *adj.* of, relating to, or in the manner of the Roman general Quintus Fabius Maximus known for his defeat of Hannibal in the Secon Punic War by the avoidance of decisive contests

fa-ble *n.* a fictitious story having a moral

fabler *n.*

fab-ric *n.* cloth produced by knitting or spinning fibers

fab-ri-cant *n.* manufacturer

fab-ri-cate *v.* make or manufacture; build **fabrication** *n.*

fab-u-lar *adj.* of, relating to, or having the form of a fable

fab-u-list *adj.* a creator or writer of fables; liar

fab-u-lous *adj.* incredible

fa-cade *n., Arch.* face or front of a building

face *n.* front surface of the head

face angle *n.* an angle formed by two edges of polyhedral angle

face card *n.* a king, queen, or jack in a deck of cards

face--cloth *n.* washcloth

face--down *adv.* with the face down

face fly *n.* European fly that is similar to the house fly, is widely established in North America, and causes great distress in livestock by clustering about the face

face--harden *v.* to harden the suface of

face--lift-ing *n.* plastic surgery for improving the facial appearance

face--off *n.* putting a puck into play by dropping it between two players

fac-er *n.* a stunning check or defeat

face--saver *n.* something that saves space

face--saving *n.* the act of preserving one's dignity

fac-et *n.* polished surface on a gemstone; aspect of a person

fa-ce-tious *adj.* humorous -ly *adv.*

fact--to--face *adj.* being within each other's sight or presence

face-up *v.* to meet without shrinking

face value *n.* apparent value of something

fa-cial *adj.* near, of, or for the face

facial index *n.* the ratio of the breadth of the face to its length times 100

facial nerve *n.* cranial nerves that supply mnnotor fibers to the muyscles of the face and jaw

fac-ile *adj.* requiring little effort

fa-cil-i-tate *v.* make easier

fa-cil-i-ty *n.* ease in performance, or doing something

fac-ing *n.* lining sewn to a garment

fac-sim-i-le *n.* an exact copy

fact *n.* something that actually occurred; piece of information

fact finder *n.* one that tries to determine the realities of a case

fac-tion *n.* self-seeking group in a government

fac-tious *adj.* creating friction; divisive

fac-ti-tious *adj.* produced by man rather than nature

fac-ti-tive *adj.* relating to a transitive verb that in some constructions requires an objective complement as well as an object

fac-tor *n.* one transacting business for another for commission

fac-tor-age *n.* the charges made by a factor for certain services

factor analysis *n.* the transformation of statistical data into linear combinations of variables that are not correlated

fac-to-ry *n.* plant where goods are manufactured

fac-to-tum *n.* employee having many duties and responsibilites

fac-tu-al *adj.* consisting of or based on facts

fac-ul-ty *n.* natural ability or power; branch of learnig or teaching

fad *n.* temporary fashion -ish *adj.*

fade *v.* lose brightness gradually

fag *v.* exhaust by hard work

fag end *n.* frayed end of a rope or cloth

fag-ot *n.* bundle of sticks, etc. used for fuel

Fahr-en-heit *adj.* temperature scale in which the freezing point of water is 32 degrees and the boiling point is 212 degrees

fa-ience *n.* earthenware decorated with a colorful opaque glaze

fail *v.* be totally ineffective; receive a grade below standard

faille *n.* ribbed material

fail--safe *adj.* a system designed to prevent equipment failure

fail-ure *n.* a breaking down in strength, or efficiency

faint *adj.* having little vigor; lacking brightness; dizzy

faint-hearted *adj.* lacking courage

fair *adj.* visually light in coloring; not stormy; exhibit of livestock, etc.

fair ball *n.* batted ball with in the foul lines

fair-way *n.* part of a golf course between the tee and the green

fair-y *n.* a tiny imaginary being

fair-y-land *n.* delightful, enchanting place

fair-y tale *n.* fictitious tale of fanciful creatures

fait ac-com-pli *n.* irreversible accomplished fact or deed

faith *n.* belief in the value, or trustworthiness of someone or something

faith-ful *adj.* true and trustworthy in obligations, etc. **faithfully** *adv.*

fake *adj.* having a misleading appearance; not genuine

fal-con *n.* bird of prey

fall *v.* drop down from a higher place; collapse

fal-la-cious *adj.* deceptive; misleading

fal-li-ble *adj.* capable of making an mistake **fallibility** *n.*

fall-ing--out *n.* fight, or quarrel

fall-ing star *n.* a meteor

fall--off *n.* a decrease in something

fal-lo-pi-an tube *n.* ducts serving as a passage for the ovum

fall-out *n.* descent of minute particles of radioactive material

fal-low *n.* unplanted plowed ground; light brown color

false *adj.* incorrect; deliberately untrue **falsely** *adv.*

false face *n.* mask used as a disguise on Halloween

false-hood *n.* act of lying; untrue statement

fal-set-to *n.* high male singing voice

fal-si-fy *v.* give an untruthful account; misrepresent

fal-ter *v.* be uncertain in action or voice **falteringly** *adv.*

fame *n.* public esteem, a good reputation **famed** *adj.*

fa-mil-iar *adj.* being well-acquainted with

fa-mil-i-ar-i-ty *n.* the knowledge of something

fa-mil-iar-ize *v.* make oneself familiar with something **familarization** *n.*

fam-i-ly *n.* a group of people connected by blood or marriage

fam-ine *n.* widespread scarcity of food

fam-ish *v.* to starve

fa-mous *adj.* well-known; renowned

fan *n.* device for putting air into motion

fa-nat-ic *n.* one moved by enthusiasm

fan-ci-er *n.* person having a special interest in something

fan-cy *n.* imagination whimsical nature

fan-cy--free *adj.* unattached

fan-fare *n.* short, loud trumpet flourish

fang *n.*

long, pointed tooth

fan-jet *n.* aircraft with turbojet engines

fan-ny *n.* *Slang* the buttocks

fan-ta-sia *n.* composition according to the composer's fancy

fan-ta-size *v.* create mental pictures

fan-tas-tic *adj.* unreal; wildly exaggerated **fantastically** *adv.*

fan-ta-sy *n.* creative imagination

far *adv.* at a considerable distance

farce *n.* theatre comedy with ludicrous situations

fare *n.* fee paid for hired transportation

fare-well *n.* goodby

far--fetched *adj.* highly improbable

far--flung *adj.* widely distributed

far-i-na-ceous *adj.* rich in, or composed of starch

farm *n.* land used for agriculture raising animals

far--off *adj.* remote

far--out *adj.* very unconventional

far-ra-go *n.* a confused mixture

far-row *n.* litter of pigs

far--sighted *adj.* seeing distance objects more clearly than nearby things

far-ther *adv.* at a more distant point

far-ther-most *adj.* most distant

far-thest *adj.* at the greatest distance

far-thing *n.* something of little worth

fas-ci-nate *v.* attract irresistibly; captivate

fas-cism *n.* one-party system of government

fashion *n.* mode or manner of dress

fast *adj.* swift; rapid

fast *v.* abstain from food

fast-back *n.* car with a downward slope roof

fast-en *v.* connect; securely fix something **fastener** *n.*

fast--food *n.* restaurant specializes in foods prepared and served quickly

fas-tid-i-ous *adj.* delicate or refined

fat *adj.* obese; plump

fat-al *adj.* causing death; inevitable **fatally** *adv.*

fa-tal-ism *n.* belief that things are predetermined by fate

fa-tal-i-ty *n.* death caused by a disaster or accident

fat cat *n.*, *Slang* powerful and wealthy person

fate *n.* predetermine events

fate-ful *adj.* governed by fate

fa-ther *n.* male parent **Father** a priest

fath-om *n.* length equal to six feet

fath-om-less *adj.* too deep to measure

fa-tigue *n.* condition of extreme tired-ness

fatigues military clothes

fat-ty *adj.* greasy

fat-u-ous *adj.* silly and foolish

fau-cet *n.* valve to draw liquids from a pipe

faugh *interj.* exclamation of contempt

fault *n.* impairment or defect

fault-find-er *n.* a petty critic

fau-vism *n.* art movement noted for flamboyant colors

faux pas *n.* a false step; a social blunder

fa-vor *n.* a helpful or considerate act

fa-vor-a-ble *adj.* expressing approval favorableness *n.*

fa-vor-ite *n.* preferred above all others favoritism *n.*

fawn *n.* a young deer; yellowish brown color

fay *n.* fairy or elf

faze *v.* to disconcert

fe-al-ty *n.* loyalty owed to a feudal lord

fear *n.* anticipation of danger

fear-less *adj.* without fear; brave

fea-si-ble *adj.* capable of being ac-complished

feast *n.* a delicious meal

feat *n.* notable achievement

feath-er *n.* protective covering of birds feathery *adj.*

feather bed *n.* feather stuffed mattress

feather-stitch *n.* an embroidery stitch

feather-weight *n.* light weight boxer

fea-ture *n.* appearance or shape of the face

feb-ri-fuge *n.* medicine used to reduce fever

feb-rile *adj.* relating to a fever

fe-ces *pl. n.* bodily waste; excrement

feck-less *adj.* weak; worthless

fe-cund *adj.* fruitful; productive

fe-cun-date *v.* make fertile

fed-er-al *adj.* agreement between two or more states

fed-er-ate *v.* unite in a federal union

fed-er-a-tion *n.* two or more states join-ing a confederacy

fe-do-ra *n.* soft hat

fed up *adj.* extremely annoyed

fee *n.* fixed charge; charge for a profes-sional service

fee-ble *adj.* very weak

feeble minded *adj.* mentally deficient

feed *v.* supply with food

feel *v.* perceive through the sense of touch

feel-ing *n.* sensation by touch

feign *v.* make a false show of; to fabri-cate feigned *adj.*

feint *n.* deceptive or misleading move-ment

fe-lic-i-tate *v.* to wish happiness felicitation *n.*

fe-lic-i-tous *adj.* most appropriate

fe-lic-i-ty *n.* great hapiness; bliss

fe-line *adj.* relating to cats

fel-low *n.* boy or man

fel-low-ship *n.* group with common in-terests

fel-ly *n.*

rim of a wooden wheel

fel-on *n.* one who has committed a felony

fel-o-ny *n.* serious crime

felt *n.* unwoven fabric

fe-male *n.* sex that produces ova

fem-i-nine *adj.* pertaining to the female sex femininity *n.*

femme fa-tale *n.* seductive, charming woman

fe-mur *n.* leg bone

fen *n.* low marshy land

fence *n.* boundary or barrier

fenc-ing *n.* sport of using a foil or saber

fend *v.* ward off

fend-er *n.* covering for the wheel of a car

fen-nel *n.* herb of the carrot family

fe-ral *adj.* not tame or domesticated

fer-de-lance *n.* snake

fer-men-ta-tion *n.* decomposition of complex organic compounds

fern *n.* flowerless, seedless plants

fe-ro-cious *adj.* extremely savage

fer-ret *n.* small, red-eyed polecat

fer-rous *adj.* containing iron

fer-rule *n.* cap at the end of a cane

fer-ry *n.* boat to transport people and vehicles

fer-tile *adj., Biol.* ability to reproduce

fer-til-ize *v.* make fertile

fer-til-iz-er *n.* manure which enriches soil

fer-ule *n.* stick to punish children

fer-vent *adj.* passionate; very hot

fer-vor *n.* great intensity

fes-cue *n.* tough perennial grass

fes-ter *v.* develop pus

fes-ti-val *n.* holiday or celebration

fes-toon *n.* garland of flowers, etc.

fet-a *n.* Greek cheese white in color

fetch *v.* go after and return with

fetch-ing *adj.* very attractive or pleasing

fete *n.* large elaborate party

fet-id *adj.* having a foul odor; stinking

fetidly *adv.*

fet-ish *n.* object having magical powers

fet-lock *n.* tuft of hair on the back of the leg of a horse

fet-ter *n.* chain to prevent escape

fe-tuc-ci-ne *n.* pasta

fe-tus *n.* unborn organism carried within the womb

feud *n.* bitter family quarrel

fe-ver *n.* abnormally high body temperature

fever blister *n.* cold sore

few *adj.* small in number

fey *adj.* acting as if under a spell

fez *n.* red felt, black-tasseled hat

fi-an-ce *n.* man engaged to be married

fi-an-cee *n.* woman engaged to be married

fi-as-co *n.* complete or total failure

fi-at *n.* positive order or decree

fib *n.* trivial lie

fi-ber *n.* piece of synthetic material

fiber-board *n.* tough building material

fiber-glass *n.* non-flammable material of spun glass

fiber optics *pl., n.* light transmitted through flexible glass rods

fib-ril-la-tion *n., Pathol.* uncoordinated contraction of the muscle of the heart

-fic *adj., suffix* causing; rendering

-fication *n., suffix* production

fib-u-la *n. Anat.*

the outer and smaller bone of the lower limb or hind leg

fi-chu *n.* scarf

fick-le *adj.* inconstant; changeable

fic-tion *n.* something created or imaginary **fictional** *adj.*

fic-ti-tious *adj.* nonexistent; imaginary **fictitiously** *adv.*

fid-dle *v.* play a violin; spend time on a fruitless activity

fiddler crab *n.* small burrowing crab

fid-dle-sticks *interj.* to express mild disgust

fi-del-i-ty *n.* faithfulness or loyalty

fidg-et *v.* move nervously or restlessly **fidgets** *pl, n.* condition of being nervous **fidgetity** *adj.*

fief *n.* feudal estate

field *n.* piece of cultivated land

field marshal *n.* army official in Europe

fiend *n.* evil spirit or demon

fierce *adj.* savage and violent

fier-y *adj.* composed of fire

fi-es-ta *n.* religious holiday or festival

fife *n.* small, shrilltoned instrument

fig *n.* tree bearing an edible fruit

fight *v.* argue or quarrel **fighting** *n.*

fight-er *n.* person who fights; airplane

fig-ment *n.* invention or fabrication

fig-u-ra-tive *adj.* containing a figure of speech **figuratively** *adv.*

fig-ure *n.* symbol that represents a number; human form or body

figure eight *n.* ice skating maneuver

figure-head *n.* person with nominal leadership

fig-u-rine *n.* molded figure; a statuette

fil-a-ment *n.* finely spun thread, or wire

fil-bert *n.* edible nut; **filch** *v.* to steal

file *n.* device for storing papers; grinding tool

fi-let *n.* filet of meat or fish

filet mi-gnon *n.* small, tender cut of beef

fil-i-al *adj.* relating to a son or daughter

fil-i-buster *n.* attempt to hinder legislative action

fil-i-gree *n.* lace-like ornamental work

fill *v.* supply fully; satisfy a need; put into **filling** *n.*

fill-er *n.* something added to increase weight or bulk

fil-lip *n.* snap of the finger

fil-ly *n.* female horse

film *n.* photosensitive paper used in photography

film-strip *n.* strip of film for projection on a screen

fil-ter *n.* device used to purify

filth *n.* dirty or foul

filth-y *adj.* covered with filth; dirty

fin *n.*

a thin membranous extension of the body of a fish, used for swimming and balance

fi-na-gle *v., Slang* get something by trickery

fi-nal *adj.* pertaining to the end; last **finally** *adv.*

fi-na-le *n.* last part; final scene in a play

fi-nal-ist *n.* person in the final round of a contest

fi-nal-ize *v.* put into final form **finalization** *n.*

fi-nance *n.* science of monetary affairs **financial** *adj.*

fin-an-cier *n.* expert in large-scale financial affairs

finch *n.* small bird

find *v.* come upon unexpectedly

find-ing *n.* something discovered

fine *adj.* superior in skill or quality; healthy **finely** *adv.*

fin-er-y n. elaborate jewels and clothes

fin-esse n. highly refined skill

fin-ger n. digits of the hand

finger bowl n. bowl of water for cleansing the fingers

finger-nail n. transparent covering of the dorsal surface of each finger

fin-i-al n. ornamental projection on a lamp shade

fin-ick-y adj. hard to please; choosy

fi-nis n. the end

fin-ish v. bring to an end; to conclude finished adj.

fi-nite adj. having bounds or limits

fink n. person who breaks a strike; unsavory person

fir n. evergreen tree

fire n. chemical reaction of burning

fire alarm n. device to alert an outbreak of fire

fire-arm n. small weapon

fire-break n. strip of land cleared to prevent a fire from spreading

fire-bug n. one who enjoys setting fire

fire-cracker n. small explosive set off to make noise

fire engine n. vehicle to carry firemen and their equipment

fire escape n. emergency exit from a building

fire extinguisher n. apparatus containing fire-extinguishing chemicals

fire fighter n. person who fights fires as an occupation

fire-proof adj. resistant to fires

fire-trap n. unsafe building

fire-works pl. n. explosives for entertainment

firm adj. solid or unyielding to pressure

fir-ma-ment n. the sky

first adj. preceding all others

first aid n. temporary medical care

first-born n. child who is born first

first class n. highest group in a classifaction

first-hand adj. directly from the original source

firth n. narrow inlet or arm of the sea

fis-cal adj. relating to the finances or treasury of a nation

fish n., pl.

cold-blooded, aquatic animal fishing n.

fish-y adj. creating doubt of suspicion

fis-sile adv. capable of being separated

fis-sion n. process of splitting into parts

fis-sure n. narrow crack in a rock

fist n. the hand closed tightly

fit v. be the proper size and shape; be in good physical condition

fitch n. hide of a polecat

fit-ful adj. capricious; restless

fit-ing adj. suitable or proper

five n. number equal to 4 + 1

fix v. make firm; mend; repair

fix-a-tion n. state of being fixed

fix-ture n. part or appendage of a house

fizz n. hissing or bubbling sound

flab n. excessive, loose body tissue

flabbergast v. overwhelm with shock; astound

flac-cid adj. lacking resilience or firmness

flac-on n. small, decorative bottle

flag n. banner of a country or nation

flag-el-lant n. whipping for sexual excitement

fla-grant adj. disgraceful; notorious

flair n. aptitude or talent for something

flak n. antiaircraft fire

flake n. thin piece peeled off a surface

flam-boy-ant adj. ornate; showy; florid

flame n. mass of burning vapor from a fire

fla-men-co n. a fiery percussive dance

flame-out n. failure of a jet aircraft engine while in flight

fla-min-go n. large, tropical wading bird

flam-ma-ble adj. capable of catching fire

flange n. collar used to strengthen or guide a wheel

flank n. fleshy part of the hip

flan-nel n. woven wool fabric

flap-per n. woman of the 1920's

flare v. blaze up with a bright light

flash v. burst into a brilliant fire or light

flash-back n. interruption of a story, for something that happened earlier

flash card n. card with numbers, letters, etc. used as a learning tool

flash-y adj. tastelessly showy; gaudy

flask n. glass container used in laboratories

flat adj. extending horizontally; prostrate or prone

flat-bed n. truck without sides

flat-car n. railroad car with no roof or sides

flat-ten v. to knock down; make flat

flat-ter v. praise extravagantly

flat-ter-y n. insincere compliments

flat-top n. aircraft carrier; short haircut

flat-u-lent adj. having gas in the intestine

flat-ware n. eating utensils

flaunt v. display showily

flau-tist n. a flutist

fla-vor n. distinctive taste of something

flavorful *adj.*

fla-vor-ing *n.* substance used to increase the flavor

flaw *n.* defect or blemish

flaw-less *adj.* without defects; perfect

flax *n.* plant that yields linseed oil

flay *v.* remove the skin of; to scold harshly

flea *n.* blood-sucking, parasitic

flea market *n.* place to sell secondhand items

fleck *n.* tiny spot

fledg-ling *n.* a young bird; immature or inexperienced person

flee *v.* run away; to move swiftly away

fleece *n.* soft wool covering a sheep

fleet *n.* number of warships

flesh *n.* soft tissue of the human body

flesh-ly *adj.* pertaining to the body; sensual; worldly

fleur-de-lis *n., pl.* **fleurs-de-lis**

heraldic emblem

flex *v.* to contract a muscle

flex-i-ble *adj.* capable of being bent; capable of adjusting to new situations; pliable

flex time *n.* system allowing employees to set their own work schedules

flick *n.* light, quick snapping movement

flick-er *v.* burn or shine unsteadily

fli-er *n.* aviator; printed advertisement of handbill

flight *n.* a scheduled airline trip

flight-y *adj.* inclined to act in a fickle fashion **flightiness** *n.*

flim-flam *n. Slang* swindle; trick; hoax

flim-sy *adj.* lacking substance; of inferior workmanship

flinch *v.* wince or pull back in pain

fling *v.* throw or toss violently; period devoted to self-indulgence

flip *v.* throw suddenly with a jerk

flip--flop *n.* sound of something flapping loosely; sudden reverse of direction

flip-pant *adj.* showing disrespect

flip-per *n.* flat limb of a seal for swimming

flip side *n.* reverse or opposite side

flirt *v.* make teasing romantic overtures **flirtation** *n.*

flit *v.* move rapidly or abruptly

flit-ter *v.* to flutter

float *n.* suspend on water; cork on a fishing line

flock *n.* group of animals

floe *n.* large, flat mass of floating ice

flog *v.* beat hard with a whip or stick

flood *n.* an overflow of water onto land

floor *n.* level base of a room

floor exercise *n.* competitive gymnastics event with tumbling maneuvers

flop *v.* fall down clumsily

flop house *n.* cheap, rundown hotel

floppy disk *n.* flexible plastic disk used to record and store computer data

flo-ra *n.* plants grown in a specific region

flo-ral *adj.* pertaining to flowers

flo-rist *n.* one who grows or sells flowers

floss *n.* embroidery thread; dental floss

flo-til-la *n.* fleet of small vessels

flot-sam *n.* debris from sunken ships

flour *n.* ground meal of wheat

flour-ish *v.* thrive; prosper and succeed

flout *v.* show open contempt for

flow *v.* move freely, as a fluid

flow-er *n.* cluster of colored petals

flub *v.* botch; to make a mess of

fluc-tu-ate *v.* shift irregularly; to change

flue *n.* pipe for escaping smoke

flu-ent *adj.* capable of flowing; facile in speech fluently *adv.*

flu-id *n.* substance, as water cap-able of flowing

fluke *n.* flat fish; stroke of good luck

flunk *v., Slang* fail an examination or course

flu-o-res-cence *n., Chem., Phys.* electromagnetic radiation

fluorescent lamp *n.* tubular electric lamp

fluor-i-date *v.* sodium compound to prevent tooth decay

flu-o-rine *n.* pale yellow, gaseous element

flu-o-ro-scope *n.* instrument used for observing the human body by means of x-rays

flur-ry *n.* sudden gust of wind; brief, light fall of snow

flush *v.* flow or rush out suddenly; become red in the face

flus-ter *v.* make nervous or confused

flute *n.* highpitched, woodwind instrument

flut-ist *n.* a flute player

flut-ter *v.* flap or wave irregularly

flux *n.* a constant flow or movement

flux-ion *n.* constant change

fly *n.*

a winged insect

flying saucer *n.* unidentified moving objects in the sky described as being saucershaped

fly-wheel *n.* rotating wheel to regulate the speed of a machine shaft

foal *n.* young horse, especially one under

a year old

foam *n.* mass of bubbles on liquid; roth **foamy** *adj.*

fob *n.* chain attached to a pocket watch

fo-cus *v.* produce a sharp clear image of; adjust a lens

fod-der *n.* coarse feed for livestock

foe *n.* enemy in war; adversary

fog *n.* vapor mass of condensed water lying close to the ground

fog-horn *n.* horn sounded to give warning in a fog

fo-gy *n.* a person with old-fashioned attitudes and ideas

foi-ble *n.* minor flaw; weakness

foil *v.* prevent from being successful; to thwart

foist *v.* pass off as valuable or genuine; force to accept by deceit

fold *v.* double or lay one part over another

fol-de-rol *n.* pretty but useless ornament

fo-li-age *n.* leaves on plants and trees

fo-li-o *n.* folder for loose papers

folk *n., pl.* **folk** *or* **folks** ethnic group of people forming a nation or tribe; a person's parents

fol-li-cle *n.* small anatomical cavity

fol-low *v.* proceed or come after; to pursue

fol-ly *n., pl.* **fillies** an instance of foolishness; costly or unprofitable undertaking

fo-ment *v.* to rouse; to incite; treat with moist heat

fond *adj.* affectionate; cherished with great affection **fondness** *n.*

fon-dant *n.* sweet soft preparation of sugar used in candies

fon-dle *v.* stroke or caress tenderly

fond-ly *adv.* in a willingly credulous manner

fon-due *n.* preparation of melted cheese and wine for dipping food into

font *n.* receptacle that holds baptismal or holy water; assortment of printing type

food *n.* substance consisting of carbohydrates and protein to sustain life

fool *n.* one lacking good sense or judgment

foot *n., pl.* **feet**

lower extremity of the leg upon which one stands; unit of measurement equal to 12 inches

foot-ball *n.* game played with an inflated ball

foot-bridge *n.* bridge for pedestrians

foot-hill *n.* hill at the foot of a mountain

foot-hold *n.* place to support the foot

foot-ing *n.* stable position for placement of the feet; a foundation

foot-locker *n.* trunk for personal belongings

foot-loose *adj.* having no ties; free to move about

foot-note *n.* note of reference below the text; a commentary

foot-path *n.* narrow path for people on foot

foot-print *n.* outline of the foot on a surface

foot-stool *n.* low stool for resting the feet

foot-work *n.* use of the feet, as in boxing

fop *n.* man concerned with his appearance **foppish** *adj.*

for *prep.* used to indicate the extent of something; behalf of someone; to be in favor of

for-age *n.* food for domestic animals; search for supplies or food **forager** *n.*

for-ay *n.* a raid to plunder

for-bear *v.* refrain from; to cease from **forbearance** *n.*

for-bid *v.* command not to do something; to prohibit by law

forbidding *adj.* very difficult; disagreeable

force *n.* energy or power; strength; intellectual influence **forceful** *adj.*

force-meat *n.* ground meat, fish, etc., used in stuffing

for-ceps *n.* forceps *pl.* instrument resembling a pair of tongs used in surgery

forc-i-ble *adj.* achieved or accomplished by force

ford *n.* shallow place in a body of water for crossing

fore *adj. & adv.* situated in, at, or toward the front; golfer's warning

fore--and--aft *adj.* from stem to stern

fore-arm *n.* part of the arm between the elbow and the wrist

fore-bear *or* **for-bear** *n.* an ancestor

fore-bode *v.* give a warning in advance; have a premonition of something evil

fore-cast *v.* estimate in advance; predict the weather

fore-cas-tle *n.* living quarters for the crew of a merchant ship

fore-close *v.* recall a mortgage in default; to exclude; to shut out

fore-fa-ther *n.* ancestor

fore-fin-ger *n.* finger next to the thumb

fore-foot *n.* front foot of an animal

fore-front *n.* very front of something; the vanguard

fore-go *v.* to precede in time, place, etc.

for-eign *adj.* outside one's native country

for-eign-er *n.* person from a different place or country; an alien

fore-knowl-edge *n.* prior knowledge of something

fore-lock *n.* lock of hair growing over the forehead

fore-man *n.* person who oversees a group of people; spokesperson for a jury

fore-most *adj. & adv.* first in rank or order

fo-ren-sic *adj.* relating to a formal debate

fore-or-dain *v.* appoint advance; predestine

fore-see *v.* know or see beforehand **foreseeable** *adj.*

fore-sight *n.* capacity of foreseeing; concern for the future **forsighted** *adj.*

for-est *n.* tract of land covered with trees **forest ranger** *n.* man in charge of protecting a public forest

fore-tell *v.* tell in advance; to predict

for-ev-er *adv.* for eternity; without end

fore-warn *v.* warn in advance

for-feit *n.* something taken away as punishment; a penalty **forfeitable** *adj.*

for-gath-er *v.* come together; to assemble

forge *n.* furnace to heat metals; a smithy *v.* give shape to; defraud

for-get *v.* lose the memory of **-ful** *adj.*

for-give *v.* pardon; to cease to feel resentment against

for-go *or* **fore-go** *v.* to give up or refrain from **forgoer** *n.*

fork *n.* eating utensil with prongs; division in a river or road

for-lorn *adj.* left in distress; hopeless; forsaken **forlornly** *adv.*

form *n.* contour of something; human body; manner determined by etiquette; fitness training; document

form *suff.* having the form or shape of; cuneiform

for-mal *adj.* adhering to convention; explicit; correct manners

for-mal-de-hyde *n.* colorless, gaseous chemical used as a disinfectant

for-mat *n.* style of a publication; basic design

for-ma-tion *n.* a given arrangement

for-ma-tive *adj.* having the power to form; pertaining to growth, or development

for-mer *adj.* previous; being the first of two persons mentioned or referred to

for-mer-ly *adv.* previously

for-mi-da-ble *adj.* extremely difficult; causing fear by size or strength **formidably** *adv.*

for-mu-la *n.* prescribed rules to be used; milk substitute for infants

for-mu-late *v.* state or express as a formula **formulation** *n.*

for-ni-ca-tion *n.* illicit sexual intercourse

for-sake *v.* abandon or renounce; to give up

for-sooth *adv.* in truth; certainly

for-swear *v.* renounce emphatically or upon oath; swear falsely; to perjure oneself

for-syth-i-a *n.* shrub with earlyblooming, bright, yellow flowers

fort *n.* fortified enclosure for defense against an enemy

forte *n.* activity one does with excellence; person's strong point

forth *adv.* out from seclusion; forward in order, place, or time

forth-with *adv.* at once; promptly

for-ti-fy *v.* provide physical strength; give courage to; enrich food with vitamins, etc.

for-ti-tude *n.* strength of mind; courage

fort-night *n.* period of two weeks

for-tress *n.* a fort

for-tu-i-tous *adj.* occurring by chance; lucky; fortunate

for-tu-nate *adj.* having good fortune

for-tune *n.* force that determines events; large amount of money

for-ty *n.* number equal to four times ten

forty winks *n., Slang* short nap

for-ward *adj.* toward a place or time in advance **forwardly** *adv.*

fos-sil *n.* remains of a past geologic age

fos-ter *v.* give parental care to; nurture

foul *adj.* spoiled or rotten; vulgar or obscene; dirty

found *v.* establish; to set up; melt metal and pour into a mold

foun-da-tion *n.* base of a building; make-up base

foun-dry *n.* place where metal is cast

fount *n.* a fountain; abundant source

foun-tain *n.* natural spring of water from the earth; artifically created spray of water

four-score *adj.* four times twenty; eighty

fourth *n.* gear in a motor vehicle

fowl *n.* bird used as food or hunted as game

fox *n.*

wild mammal; sly or crafty person

fox-hole *n.* shallow pit dug by a soldier to protect him from enemy fire fox--trot *n.* ballroom dance

fox-y *adj.* sly or crafty; sharp

foy-er *n.* lobby of a hotel, theatre, etc.; entrance hall

fra-cas *n.* noisy quarrel or disturbance

frac-tion *n.* small part of; quantity less than a whole number fractional *adj.*

frac-ture *n.* act of breaking; broken bone

frag-ile *adj.* easily broken; frail

frag-ment *n.* broken or detached part

fra-grant *adj.* having an agreeable sweet odor frangrance *n.*

frail *adj.* physically weak; fragile

frame *v.* enclosed border for a picture

frame-up *Slang* make someone appear guilty

fran-chise *n.* license to market a company's goods franchiser *n.*

fran-gi-ble *adj.* breakable; delicate frangibility *n.*

frank-furt-er *n.* smoked sausage made of beef or beef and pork

frank-in-cense *n.* aromatic gum resin used as incense

fran-tic *adj.* emotionally out of control with worry or fear frantically *adv.*

fra-ter-nal *adj.* pertaining to brothers fraterrnalism *n.*

frat-er-nize *v.* associate with others in a friendly way; mingle

frat-ri-cide *n.* killer of one's brother or sister fratricidal *adj.*

fraud *n.* deception for unlawful gain; imposter

fraud-u-lent *adj.* practicing fraud fraudulently *adv.*

fraught *adj.* accompanied by something specified

fray *n.* heated argument or dispute

fraz-zle *v., Slang* wear out; completely fatigue

freak *n.* seemingly capricious event; person with abnormalities; freak out experience hallucinations from drug use freakish *adj.*

freck-le *n.* brownish, suninduced spots on the skin

free *adj.* not imprisoned; costing nothing; under no obligation

free-bie *n.* something given or received with out charge

free-dom *n.* state of being free; independence

freeze *v.* become ice through loss of heat; set prices at a certain level

freight *n.* mode of shipping cargo; charge for shipping freight

freight-er *n.* ship for transporting cargo

fren-zy *n.* state of excitement or violent agitation

fre-quent *adj.* happening often or time after time

fres-co *n.* art of painting on moist plaster

fresh *adj.* newlymade, or obtained; not stale freshness *n.*

fresh-man *n.* first year student in college

fret *v.* anxious or irritated; ripple water fretfully *adv.*

fri-a-ble *adj.* easily crumbled; brittle friableness *n.*

fri-ar *n.* member of a Roman Catholic order

fric-as-see *n.* dish of meat or poultry in gravy

fric-tion *n.* rubbing one surface against another; a conflict or clash -al *adj.*

friend *n.* close personal companion friendship *n.*

frieze *n.* decorative band along a wall

frig-ate *n.* square-rigged warship

fright *n.* sudden alarm or fear

fright-en *v.* fill with fear; arousing fear frighteningly *adv.*

frig-id *adj.* very cold; sexually unresponsive frigidity *n.*

frill *n.* decorative ruffle; gathered border

fringe *n.* edging that consists of hanging threads, or loops

frisk *v.* skip or leap about playfully; to search someone for a concealed weapon by running the hands over the clothing quickly

frit-ter *v.* squander or waste little by little

friv-o-lous *adj.* trivial; insignificant; not serious; silly

frizz *v.* form into small, tight curls

fro *adv.* away from; back, as running to and fro

frock *n.* loosefitting robe; a robe worn by monks

frog *n.*

various small, smooth-skinned, web-footed, largely aquatic, tailless, leaping amphibians

frol-ic *n.* merriness; a playful, carefree occasion; playful

from *prep.* starting at a particular time or place; used to indicate a source; used to indicate differentiation, as knowing right from left

frond *n.* large leaf of a tropical fern, usually divided into smaller leaflets

front *n.* forward surface of an object or body; area or position located ahead

fron-tier *n.* part of an international border or the area adjacent to it; an unexplored area of knowledge or thought **frontiersman** *n.*

fron-tis-piece *n.* an illustration that usually precedes the title page of a book

frost *n.* feathery covering of minute ice crystals on a cold surface; icing on a cake **frostiness** *n.*

froth *n.* mass of bubbles on or in a liquid, resulting from agitation or fermentation; a salivary foam, as of an animal, resulting from disease

frou-frou *n.* rustling sound, as of silk; a frilly dress or decoration

frown *v.* contract the brow as in displeasure or concentration; to look on with distaste or disapproval

frow-zy *adj.* appearing unkempt

fro-zen *adj.* changed into, or made into ice; extremely cold, as a climate; immobilized or made rigid, as by fear; kept at a fixed level

fruc-tose *n.* sugar

fru-gal *adj.* economical; thrifty

fruit *n., pl.* **fruit** *or* **fruits** ripened, mature, seed-bearing part of a flowering plant, as a pod or berry; edible, fleshy plant part an apple or plum **-ful** *adj.*

fru-i-tion *n.* accomplishment of something worked for or desired; the state of bearing fruit

frump-y *adj.* unfashionable; dowdy

frus-trate *v.* keep from attaining a goal or fulfilling a desire; to thwart

fry *v.* cook in hot fat or oil, especially over direct heat; *n.* dish of any fried food

fud-dy--dud-dy *n., pl.* **fuddy-duddies** an old-fashioned person

fuel *n.* combustible matter consumed to generate energy, such as wood, coal, or oil burned to generate heat; *v.* take in or supply with fuel; to stimulate, as an argument **fueler** *n.*

fu-gi-tive *adj.* fleeing or having fled, as from arrest, pursuit, etc. *n.* One who flees or tries to escape

ful-crum *n., pl.* **fulcrums** *or* **fulcra** point on which a lever turns

ful-fill *v.* convert into actuality; to effect; to carry out; to satisfy **fulfillment** *n.*

ful-minate *v.* condemn severely; to explode

ful-some *adj.* offensively insincere

fum-ble *v.* to blunder; to mishandle a baseball or football; *n.* a fumbled ball

fume *n., often* **fumes** irritating smoke, gas, or vapor; *v.* to show or feel anger or distress

fu-mi-gate *v.* subject to fumes in order to exterminate vermin or insects **-gator** *n.*

fun *n.* enjoyment; amusement

fun-da-men-tal *adj.* basic or essential; of major significance

fu-ner-al *n.* service performed in conjunction with the burial or cremation of a dead person

fun-gus *n.* **funguses** numerous sporebearing plants including mushrooms **-gal** *adj.*

fu-nic-u-lar *n.* a cable railway along which cable cars are drawn up a mountain counterbalancing one another

funk *n.* cowardly fright or panic; fear; a state of depression

funk-y *adj., Slang* an earthy quality that is characteristic of the blues **-iness** *n.*

fun-nel *n.* coneshaped utensil for pouring liquid

fur-bish *v.* make bright by rubbing; renovate

fu-ri-ous *adj.* extremely angry; fit of rage

furl *v.* roll up and secure something

fur-lough *n.* permission to be absent from duty

fur-nace *n.* device to produce intense heat

fur-nish *v.* outfit or equip with furniture

fur-ni-ture *n.* beds, lamps, chairs and tables, etc.

fu-ror *n.* violent anger; an uproar

fur-rier *n.* dealer in furs

fur-row *n.* long, narrow trench; deep wrinkle in the skin

fur-tive *adj.* done in secret; obtained underhandedly

fu-ry *n.* uncontrolled anger; turbulence

fuse *n.* electrical safety device; device to detonate explosives

fu-see *n.* friction match; signal flare

fus-se-lage *n.* central section of an airplane

fu-sil-lade *n.* discharge of a number of firearms

fu-sion *n.* act of melting together by heat

fuss *v.* argue; bother

fussy *adj.* giving close attention to details

fu-tile *adj.* ineffectual; serving no useful purpose; hopeless

fu-til-i-ty *n.* the state or quality of being futile

fu-ture *n.* time yet to come **future** *adj.*

fu-tur-is-tic *adj.* relating to the future

fuzz *n.* small particles of fibers that may sometime collect as a ball **fuzzy** *adj.*

fyke *n.* a long net bag that is kept open with hoops

G, g The seventh letter of the English alphabet.

gab *v.*, *Slang* talk or chat idly

gab-ar-dine *n.* a firm cotton, wool, or rayon material, having a diagonal raised weave, used for suits or coats

gab-ble *v.* to speak rapidly or incoherently **gabble** *n.*

Gabriel *n.* a special messenger of God mentioned in the Bible

gad *v.* to wander about restlessly

gad-a-bout *n.*, *Slang* person who seeks excitement

gad—fly *n.* a fly that bites or annoys cattle and horses; an irritating, critical, but often constructively provocative person.

gadg-et *n.*, *Slang* small or tool for various jobs

gad-o-lin-i-um *n.* a metallic element, silvery-white in color, of the lanthanide series, symbolized by Gd

gaff *n.* sharp iron hook used for landing fish

gaf-fer *n.* an old man

gag *n.* wadded cloth, forced into the mouth to prevent speach *Slang* practical joke

ga-ga *adj. Slang* crazy; silly

gage *n.* something, as a wadded cloth, forced into or over the mouth to prevent someone from speaking or crying out; an obstacle to or any restraint of free speech, such as by censorship; *Slang* a practical joke

gag-gle *n.* flock of geese

gai-e-ty *n., pl.* **gaieties** state of being happy; cheerfulness

gain *v.* to earn or acquire possession

gain-ful *adj.* producing profits

gain-say *v.* to deny; to contradict

gait *n.* a way or manner of moving on foot; one of the foot movements in which a horse steps or runs

gai-ter *n.* a covering, as of leather or canvas, that covers the leg and extends from the knee to the instep; an old-fashioned shoe with a high top and elastic sides

gal *n.*, *Slang* a girl

ga-la *n.* festive celebration

ga-lac-tose *n.* the sugar typically occurring in lactose

gal-ax-y *n., pl.* **galaxies** *Astron.* very large cluster of stars

gale *n.*, *Meteor.* very powerful wind

ga-le-na *n.* a metallic, dull gray mineral that is the principal or of lead

gall *n.*, *Physiol.* bitter fluid secreted by the liver; bile

gal-lant *adj.* polite and attentive to women

gal-lant-ry *n.* nobility and bravery

gall-blad-der *or* **gall bladder** *n.*

Liver · Stomach · Gall bladder

small sac under the right liver that stores bile

gal-le-on *n.* large sailing ship

gal-ler-y *n., pl.* **-ries** group of spectators; building that displays works of art

gal-ley *n., pl.* **galleys** a long medieval ship ;that was propelled by sails and oars; the long tray used bvy printers to hold set type; a printer's proof made from composed type, used to detect and correct errors

gal-li-nule *n.* a wading bird with dark iridescent plumage

gal-li-um *n.* a slivery metallic element used in semiconductor technology and as a component or various low-melting alloys, symbolized by Ga

gal-li-vant *v.* roam about in search of pleasure

gal-lon *n.* liquid measurement equal to 4 quarts

gal-lop *n.* horse's gait

gal-lows *n.* framework used for execution by hanging

gall-stone *n., Pathol.* small, stony mass that forms in the gall bladder

ga-lore *adj.* in great numbers

gal-va-nism *n.* electricity produced by chemical action

gal-va-nize *v.* to protect iron or steel with rust resistant zinc

gal-va-nom-e-ter *n., Electr.* apparatus that detects electric and its strength and direction

gam-bit *n.* an opening in chess where a piece is sacrificed

gam-ble *v.* to take a chance

gam-bol *v.* frolic, skip, or leap about in play

game *n.* contest having rules; animals or birds hunted for sport or food

gam-ete *n., Biol.* mature reproductive cells

gam-in *n.* homeless child

gam-mer *n.* elderly woman

gam-ut *n.* whole range or extent of anything

gan-der *n.* male goose *Slang* quick glance

gang *n.* group of persons who work together or socialize regularly

gan-gling *adj.* tall and thin

gan-grene *n., Pathol.* the death and decay of tissue in the body

gang-ster *n.* member of a criminal gang

gap *n.* opening or wide crack

gape *v.* open the mouth wide

gar *n.* fish having a spearlike snout and elongated body

garb *n.* clothing

gar-bage *n.* food wastes; trash

gar-ble *v.* mix up or confuse

gar-den *n.* place for growing plants

gar-gan-tu-an *adj.* of enormous size

gar-ish *adj.* too showy and bright; gaudy

gar-land *n.* wreath of flowers or leaves

gar-lic *n.* plant having a strong odor, resembling an onion

gar-ment *n.* article of clothing

gar-ner *v.* gather and store

gar-net *n.* dark-red gemstone

gar-nish *v.* to add decoration

gar-ret *n.* room in an attic

gar-ri-son *n.* military post

gar-ter *n.* band worn to hold a stocking in place

gas *n., pl.* **gases** combustible mixture used as fuel; gasoline

gash *n.* long, deep cut

gas-ket *n., Mech.* seal to prevent the escape of fluid or gas

gas-o-hol *n.* fuel blended from unleaded gasoline and ethanol

gasp *v.* labored attempts to breathe

gas-tric *adj.* pertaining to the stomach

gas-tri-tis *n., Pathol.* inflammation of the stomach lining

gas-tron-o-my *n.* art of good eating

gate *n.* movable opening in a wall or fence

gath-er *v.* bring or come together into one place

gaud-y *adj.* too highly decorated for good taste

gauge *or* **gage** *n.* standard measurement

gaunt *adj.* thin in appearance

gaunt-let *or* **gant-let** *n.*

a glove to protect the hand, challenge to fight

gauze *n.* loosely-woven material used for bandages

gav-el *n.* mallet used to call for order

ga-vi-al *n.* large crocodile

gawk *v.* to gape; to stare stupidly

gawk-y *adj.* Clumsy or awkward

gay *adj.* merry; happy

gaze *v.* to look steadily at something to stare

ga-zette *n.* newspaper

gear *n., Mech.* toothed wheel

gee-zer *n., Slang* an old man

geld *v.* to castrate

gem-ol-o-gy *or* **gem-mol-o-gy** *n.* study of gems

gen-der *n.* quality of being either male or female

gene *n., Biol.* means by which hereditary characteristics are given

ge-ne-al-o-gy *n., pl.* **-ies** record or study of ones ancestry

gen-er-al-ize *v.* draw a general conclusion from facts or observations

gen-er-al-i-za-tion *n.* something arrived at by generalizing

gen-er-ate *v.* cause to be; to produce

gen-er-a-tion *n.* group of individuals born about the same time

ge-ner-ic *adj.* relating to an entire class or group; general

gen-er-ous *adj.* sharing freely; abundant

gen-e-sis *n., pl.* **-ses** act or state of originating

ge-net-ic *adj.* pertaining to the development of something

gen-ial *adj.* cheerful, pleasant and good-humored

gen-i-tal *adj.* pertaining to the reproductive organs

genitals *pl.,n.* the external sexual organs

gen-i-tive *adj., Gram.* indicating origin, source, or possession

gen-ius *n., pl.* **-ses** exceptional intellectual ability a strong, natural talent

gen-o-cide *n.* systematic extermination of a race or cultural group

gen-teel *adj.* refined or well-bred

gen-tian *n.* annual or perennial plant

Gen-tile *n.* a Christian; non-Jew

gen-tle *adj.* not harsh, mild in manner

gen-tle-man *n.* man of noble birth and social position

gen-tle-wom-an *n.* woman of noble birth and social position

gen-try *n.* people of high social standing

gen-u-flect *v.* to bend down on one knee

gen-u-ine *adj.* real; not counterfeit

ge-o-cen-tric *adj.* relating to the earth's center

ge-og-ra-phy *n., pl.* **-hies** the scientific study of the earth's features and population

ge-om-e-try *n., pl.* **ies** mathematics dealing with lines, planes, and solids

ge-o-ther-mal *adj.* relating to the internal heat of the earth

ger-i-at-rics *pl., n.* medical study that deals with diseases and hygiene of old age

germ *n.* small cell from which a new organism may develop

ger-mane *adj.* relevant to what is being considered or discussed

germ cell *n.* egg or sperm cell

ger-mi-cide *n.* agent used to destroy or disease germs

ger-mi-nate *v.* to grow, develop, or sprout

gest *n.* notable deed or feat

ges-tic-u-late *v.* make expressive gestures

ges-ture *n.* bodily motion, especially with the hands in speaking

get *v.* to receive or come into the possession of

get-up *n.* an outfit; a costume

gey-ser *n.* natural spring that ejects hot water and steam

ghast-ly *adj.* horrible; terrifying

gher-kin *n.* very small pickle

ghet-to *n.* section of a city in which members of an ethnic group lives

ghost *n.* the spirit of a dead person which is believed to appear to or haunt living persons; a spirit

gib-ber *v.* to talk or chatter incoherently or unintelligibly

gib-ber-ish *n.* meaningless speech

gib-bet *n.* a gallows *v.* To execute by hanging on a gibbet

gib-bon *n.* a slender, long-armed Asian ape

gibe *v.* to ridicule or make taunting remarks **giber** *n.*

gib-let *n., or* **giblets** the heart, liver, and gizzard of a fowl

gid-dy *adj.* affected by a reeling or whirling sensation; dizzy **giddily** *adv.,* **giddiness** *n.*

gift *n.* something that is given from one person to another

gifted *adj.* having a special ability; talented

gig *n.* a light, two-wheeled carriage drawn by one horse. *Naut.* A speedy, light rowboat

gi-gan-tic *adj.* of tremendous size; huge **gigantically** *adv.*

gig-gle *v.* to laugh in highpitched, repeated, short sounds **giggler** *n.,* **giggly** *adj.*

gig-o-lo *n.,* a man who is supported by a woman not his wife

gild *v.* to coat with a thin layer of gold; to brighten or adorn **gilded** *adj.,* **gilding,** **gilder** *n.*

gill *n., Zool.* the organ, as of fishes and various other aquatic invertebrates, used for taking oxygen from water

gilt *adj.* covered with or of the color of gold

gim-crack *n.* a cheap and useless object of little or no value

gim-let *n.* a small, sharp tool with a bar handle and a pointed, spiral tip used for boring holes

gimp *n., Slang* a person who walks with a limp; a cripple

gin *n.* an aromatic, clear, alcoholic liquor distilled from grain and flavored with juniper berries

gin-ger *n.* a tropical Asian plant with a pungent aromatic root, used in medicine and cooking

ginger ale *n.* an effervescent soft drink flavored with ginger

gin-ger-ly *adv.* doing something very cautiously

ging-ham *n.* a cotton fabric woven in solid colors and checks

gin-gi-vi-tis *n., Pathol.* inflammation of the gums

gin rummy *n.* a variety of the card game rummy

gi-raffe *n.*

the tallest of all mammals, having an extremely long neck and very long legs

gird *v.* to surround, en circle, or attach with or as if with a belt

gird-er *n.* a strong, horizontal beam, as of steel or wood

gir-dle *n.* a cord or belt worn around the waist; a supporting undergarment worn by women

girl *n.* a female child or infant; a young, unmarried woman

girth *n.* the circumference or distance around something

gis-mo *n., Slang* a part or device whose name is unknown or forgotten

gist *n.* the central or main substance

give *v.* to make a present of; to bestow; donate or contribute; to apply

giv-en *adj.* bestowed; presented

giz-zard *n.* the second stomach in birds

gla-brous *adj., Biol.* having no hair or down **glabrousness** *n.*

glacial epoch *Geol.* a portion of geological time when ice sheets covered much of the earth's surface

glad *adj.* displaying, experiencing, or affording joy and pleasure; being happy

glad-den *v.* to make glad

glade *n.* a clearing in a forest

glad-some *adj.* giving cheer

glam-or-ize *or* **glam-our-ize** *v.* to make glamorous

glam-our *or* **glam-or** *n.* alluring fascination or charm

glance *v.* to take a brief or quick look at something

gland *n.*, *Anat.* any of various body organs which excrete or secrete substances

glare *v.* to stare fiercely or angrily

glau-co-ma *n.*, *Pathol.* a disease of the eye

glau-cous *adj.* yellowish green

gleam *n.* a momentary ray or beam of light

glean *v.* to collect or gather facts by patient effort -**er** *n.*, -**ings** *pl.*, *n.*

glee *n.* joy; merriment

glen *n.* a small, secluded valley

glib *adj.* spoken easily and fluently; superficial **glibly** *adv.*, **glibness** *n.*

glide *v.* to pass or move smoothly with little or no effort **glidingly** *adv.*

glid-er *n.* one that glides; *Aeron.* an aircraft without an engine

glim-mer *n.* a faint suggestion; an indication; a dim unsteady light

glimpse *n.* a momentary look

glis-san-do *n.*, *pl.* -**di** a rapid passing from one tone to another by a continuous change of pitch

glis-ten *v.* to shine softly as reflected by light

glitch *n.* a minor mishap or malfunction

glit-ter *n.* a brilliant sparkle

gloam-ing *n.* twilight

gloat *v.* to express, feel, or observe with great malicious pleasure or selfsatisfaction **gloater** *n.*

glob *n.* a drop of something

glob-al *adj.* spherical; involving the whole world **globalize** *v.*

globe *n.* a spherical object; anything that is perfectly rounded

glob-u-lin *n.*, *Biochem.* any of a class of simple proteins found widely in blood, milk, tissue, muscle and plant seeds

gloom *n.* partial or total darkness **gloomily** *adv.*, **gloominess** *n.*

glop *n.*, *Slang* a messy mixture of food; something that is considered worthless

glo-ri-fy *v.* to worship and give glory to **glorification** *n.*

glo-ri-ous *adj.* magnificent -**ly** *adv.*

glory *n.*, *pl.* -**ies** distinguished praise or honor

gloss *n.* the sheen or luster of a polished surface

glos-sa-ry *n.*, *pl.* -**ries** a list of words and their meanings

glot-tis *n.*, *pl.* -**ises** *or* -**ides** *Anat.* the opening or cleft between the vocal cords

glow *v.* to have a bright, warm, ruddy color

glow-er *v.* to look sullenly or angrily at; to glare

glox-in-i-a *n.* a tropical South American plant

glu-cose *n.*, *Chem.* a substance less sweet than cane sugar, found as dextrose in plants and animals and obtained by hydrolysis

glut *v.* to feed or supply beyond capacity. *n.* An overabundance

glu-ten *n.* a mixture of plant proteins that is used as an adhesive **glutenous** *adj.*

glut-ton *n.* someone who eats immoderately

glyc-er-ol *n.*, *Chem.* a sweet, oily, syrupy liquid derived from fats and oils

gly-co-side *n.*, *Chem.* any of a group of carbohydrates which, when decomposed, produce glucose or other sugar

gnarl *n.* a hard, protruding knot on a tree **gnarled** *adj.*

gnash *v.* to grind or strike the teeth together

gnat *n.* a small, winged insect, specially one that bites or stings

gnaw *v.* to bite or eat away with persistence **gnawer** *n.*

gnome *n.* in folklore, a dwarf-like creature

go *v.* to proceed or pass along; to leave; pass, as of time *n.* an attempt; a try

go--ahead *n.* permission; a signal to move ahead or proceed

goal *n.* a purpose

goat-ee *n.* a short, pointed beard on a man's chin

goat-skin *n.* the skin of a goat

gob *n.* a piece or lump of something

gob-ble *v.* to eat and swallow food greedily

gob-bler *n.* a male turkey

go--be-tween *n.* a person who acts as an agent between two parties

gob-let *n.* a drinking glass

gob-lin *n.* in folklore, an ugly, grotesque creature said to be mischievous and evil

god *n.* someone considered to be extremely important or valuable

God *n.* the Supreme Being

god-less *adj.* not recognizing a god **godlessness** *n.*

god-ly *adj.* filled with love for God.

god-send *n.* something received unexpectedly that is needed or wanted

go--get-ter *n.* an enterprising, aggressive person

gog-gle *n., pl.* -gles spectacles or eyeglasses to protect the eyes

go-ing *n.* the act of moving, leaving, or departing

goi-ter *n., Pathol.* any abnormal enlargement of the thyroid gland **goitrous** *adj.*

gold *n.* a soft, yellow, metallic element that is highly ductile and resistant to oxidation

gold-en *adj.* made of or containing gold; bright yellow in color

gold-fish *n.* a reddish or brass-colored freshwater fish

gon-ad *n., Anat.* the male or female sex gland where the reproductive cells develop; an ovary or testis

gon-do-la *n.* a long, narrow, flat-bottomed boat

gong *n.* a heavy metal disk with a deep resonant tone

gon-o-coc-cus *n., pl.* -cocci the bacterium which causes gonorrhea **gonococcic** *adj.*

gon-or-rhe-a *n., Pathol.* a contagious venereal infection transmitted chiefly by sexual intercourse

goo *n.* any sticky substance

goo-ber *n., Regional* a peanut

good *adj.* having desirable or favorable qualities or characteristics; morally excellent **better, best** *adj.*

Good Book *n.* the Bible

good--by *or* **good--bye** *interj.* used to express farewell *n.* a farewell; a parting word

good--look-ing *adj.* handsome

good--na-tured *adj.* having an easygoing and pleasant disposition

good-ness *n.* the state or quality of being good

good-y *n., pl.* -ies something that is good to eat; a prissy person

goof *n., Slang* a mistake *v.* to blunder; to make a mistake

goof--off *n.* a person who shuns responsibility or work

goof-y *adj.* ridiculous; silly

gook *n., Slang* a slimy, sludgy, or dirty substance

goon *n., Slang* a thug or hoodlum hired to intimidate or injure someone

goose *n., pl.* **geese** a large water bird related to swans and ducks

go-pher *n.* a burrowing rodent with large cheek pouches

gore *v.* to stab or pierce *n.* blood that has been shed

gorge *n.* a deep, narrow ravine; deep or violent disgust **gorger** *n.*

gor-geous *adj.* beautiful; dazzling

go-ril-la *n.*

a large African jungle ape

gorse *n.* a spiny plant bearing fragrant yellow flowers

go-ry *adj.* covered or stained with blood; resembling gore

gos-hawk *n.* a large, shortwinged hawk formerly used in falconry

gos-ling *n.* a young goose

gos-pel *or* **Gos-pel** *n.* the teachings of Christ and the apostles

gos-sa-mer *n.* the fine film or strands of a spider's web floating in the air **gossamer** *adj.*

gos-sip *n.* idle, often malicious talk *v.* to spread or engage in gossip

got *v.* past tense of get

gour-mand *n.* a person who takes excessive pleasure in eating

gour-met *n.* someone who appreciates and understands fine food and drink

gout *n., Pathol.* a disease caused by a defect in metabolism and characterized by painful inflammation of the joints **gouty** *adj.*

gov-ern *v.* to guide, rule, or control by right or authority **governable** *adj.*

gov-ern-ment *n.* the authoritative administration of public policy and affairs of a nation, state or city -al *adj.*

gov-er-nor *n.* one who governs, as the elected chief executive of any state in the United States **governorship** *n.*

grab *v.* to snatch or take suddenly **grabber** *n.*, **grabby** *adj.*

gra-ben *n., Geol.* an elongated depression in the earth, caused by the downward faulting of a portion of the earth's crust

grace *n.* seemingly effortless beauty, ease, and charm of movement or form

gra-da-tion *n.* a gradual and orderly arrangement or progression according to quality, size, rank, or other value **gradational** *adj.*

grade *n.* a step or degree

gra-di-ent *n.* a slope or degree of inclination *Phys.* a rate of change in variable factors, as temperature or pressure

grad-u-al *adj.* moving or changing slowly by degrees -ly *adv.*, -ness *n.*

grad-u-ate *v.* to receive or be granted an academic diploma or degree upon completion of a course of study

grad-u-a-tion *n.* the state of graduating; a commencement ceremony

graf-fi-to *n., pl.* graffiti an inscription or drawing made on a public wall

gra-ham *n.* whole wheat flour

grail *n.* the legendary cup used by Christ at the Last Supper

grain *n.* a small, hard seed or kernel of cereal, wheat, or oats; the seeds or fruits of such plants as a group; texture; basic nature

grain alcohol *n.* ethanol

grain-y *adj.* having a granular texture **graininess** *n.*

gram *n.* a metric unit of mass and weight equal to 1/1000 kilogram and nearly equal to one cubic centimeter of water at its maximum density

gram-mar *n.* the study and description of the classes of words, their relations to each other, and their arrangement into sentences

gram molecule *n., Chem.* the quantity of a compound, expressed in grams, that is equal to the molecular weight of that compound

gran-a-ry *n., pl.* ries a building for storing threshed grain

grand *adj.* large in size, extent, or scope; magnificent

gran-deur *n.* the quality or condition of being grand

gran-dil-o-quent *adj.* speaking in or characterized by a pompous or bombastic style **grandiloquence** *n.*

gran-di-ose *adj.* impressive and grand; pretentiously pompous -ly *adv.*,

grand mal *n., Pathol.* a form of epilepsy characterized by severe convulsions and loss of consciousness

gran-ite *n.* a hard, coarsegrained igneous rock composed chiefly of quartz, mica,

and orthoclase

gran-ite-ware *n.* ironware utensils coated with hard enamel

gran-ny *or* **gran-nie** *n.* a grandmother; an old woman

gra-no-la *n.* rolled oats mixed with dried fruit and seeds

grant *v.* to allow; to consent to **granter, grantor** *n.*

gran-u-lar *adj.* composed or seeming to be composed or containing grains or granules **granularity** *n.*

gran-u-late *v.* to make or form into granules or crystals -tion *n.*

gran-ule *n.* a very small grain or particle

graph *n.* a diagram representing the relationship between sets of things

graph-ic *or* **graph-i-cal** *adj.* describing in full detail

graph-ite *n.* a soft black form of carbon having a metallic luster and slippery texture, used in lead pencils, lubricants, paints, and coatings **graphitic** *adj.*

graph-ol-o-gy *n.* the study of handwriting for the purpose of analyzing **graphologist** *n.*

grap-nel *n.* a small anchor with several flukes at the end

grap-ple *n.* an instrument with iron claws used to fasten an enemy ship alongside for boarding -er *n.*

grasp *v.* to seize and grip firmly *n.* the power to seize and hold

grasp-ing *adj.* urgently desiring material possessions; greedy **graspingly** *adv.*, **graspingness** *n.*

grass *n.* any of numerous plants having narrow leaves and jointed stems *Slang* Marijuana -iness *n.*, -y *adj.*

grass-hop-per *n.*

any of several jumping insects that has long powerful hind legs

grate *v.* to make or pulverize by rubbing against a rough or sharp surface *n.* a rasping noise -er *n.*, -ing *adj.*

grate *n.* a framework or bars placed over a window or other opening

grate-ful *adj.* thankful or appreciative for benefits or kindnesses **gratefully** *adv.*

grat-i-fy *v.* to give pleasure or satisfaction to **gratification** *n.*

grat-ing *n.* a grate

grat-is *adv. & adj.* free

grat-i-tude *n.* the state of appreciation and gratefulness

gra-tu-i-tous *adj.* given or obtained without payment; unjustified **gratuitously** *adv.*,

gra-tu-i-ty *n.*, *pl.* -ies a gift given in return for a service rendered

gra-va-men *n.*, *pl.* -mens *or* -mina in law, the part of an accusation or charge weighing most heavily against the accused

grave *n.* a burial place for a dead body *adj.* very serious or important in nature

grav-el *n.* loose rock fragments often with sand *Pathol.* the deposit of sand-like crystals that form in the kidneys

gra-vim-e-ter *n.* an implement for determining specific gravity **gravimetry** *n.*

grav-i-tate *v.* to be drawn as if by an irresistible force

grav-i-ta-tion *n.*, *Physics* the force or attraction any two bodies exert towards each other -ive *adj.*, -ally *adv.*

grav-i-ty *n.*, *pl.* -ies the gravitational force mani-fested by the tendency of material bodies to fall toward the center of the earth

gray-ling *n.*, *pl.* -ling *or* -lings any of several freshwater food and game fish with a small mouth and a large dorsal fin

gray matter *n.* the grayish-brown nerve tissue of the spinal cord and brain

graze *v.* to feed upon growing grasses or herbage

grease *n.* melted or soft animal fat *v.* to lubricate or coat with grease

great *adj.* very large in size or volume; very good or firstrate **greatly** *adv.*,

greed *n.* selfish desire to acquire more than one needs or deserves

greed-y *adj.* excessively eager to acquire or gain something

greet *v.* to address someone in a friendly way; to welcome **greeter** *n.*

greet-ing *n.* a word of salutation.

gre-gar-i-ous *adj.* habitually associating with others as in groups, flocks, or herds; sociable

grem-lin *n.* a mischievous elf

grew *v.* past tense of grow

grid *n.* an arrangement of regularly spaced bars

grid-dle *n.* a flat pan used for cooking

grief *n.* deep sadness or mental distress caused by a loss

grieve *v.* to cause, or feel sorrow

grille *or* **grill** *n.* a grating with open metalwork

grim *adj.* stern or forbidding in appearance or character; gloomy; dismal

grimly *adv.*, **grimness** *n.*

grim-ace *n.* a facial expression of pain, disgust

grime *n.* dirt, especially soot clinging to or coating a surface **griminess** *n.*, **grimy** *adj.*

grin *v.* to smile broadly

grind *v.* to reduce to fine particles; to sharpen; *n.* a person who works hard

grip *n.* a firm hold; a grasp; the ability to seize or maintain a hold

gripe *v.* to cause sharp pain or cramps in the bowels; to anger

grippe *n.* influenza **grippy** *adj.*

gris-ly *adj.* ghastly; gruesome

gris-tle *n.* cartilage of meat

grit *n.* small, rough granules; having great courage and fortitude **gritty** *adj.*

grits *pl.*, *n.* coarsely ground hominy; coarse meal

griz-zle *v.* to become gray

griz-zle bear *n.*

a large, grayish bear of western North America **grizzlies** *n.*, *pl.*, *Slang* grizzly bears

gro-cer *n.* a storekeeper who deals in various household supplies

grog-gy *adj.* dazed, weak, or not fully conscious, as from a blow -ily *adv.*

groom *n.* a person hired to tend horses; a stableman; a bridegroom

gro-tesque *adj.* incongruous or ludicrous in appearance; bizarre; outlandish

grot-to *n.*, *pl.* -toes *or* -tos a cave or cave-like structure

grouch *n.* an habitually irritable or complaining person **grouchily** *adv.*,

ground *n.* the surface of the earth

ground *v.* past tense of grind

ground hog *n.* a woodchuck

ground-less *adj.* without foundation or basis

group *n.* a collection or assemblage of people, or things

grov-el *v.* to lie or crawl face downward, as in fear; to act with abject humility

grow *v.* to increase in size, develop, and reach maturity; to expand; to increase

grub *v.* to dig up by the roots; to lead a dreary existence

grub-by *adj.* sloppy, unkempt

grudge *n.* a feeling of ill will, rancor, or deep resentment

gru-el *n.* a thin liquid made by boiling meal in water or milk

gru-el-ing *or* **gru-el-ling** *adj.* extremely

tiring gruelingly *adv.*

gruff *adj.* brusque and rough in manner; harsh in sound; hoarse
gruffly *adv.*, **gruffness** *n.*

grum-ble *v.* to complain in low, throaty sounds; to growl **grumbler** *n.*

grump-y *adj.* irritable and moody; ill tempered

grun-gy *adj.*, *Slang* dirty, run-down, or inferior in condition

grunt *n.* the deep, guttural sound of a hog

guar-an-ty *n.*, *pl.* -ies a pledge or promise to be responsible for the debt, duty, or contract of another person

guard *v.* to watch over or shield from danger or harm; to keep watch

gub-ba *v.*, *Slang* to tickle the neck area

guest *n.* one who is the recipient of hospitality from another

guf-faw *n.* a loud burst of laughter

guid-ance *n.* the act, process, or result of guiding

guide *n.* one who leads or directs another **guider** *n.*

guilt *n.* the condition of having committed a crime or wrongdoing; the feeling of responsibility for having done something wrong

gul-let *n.*, *Pathol.* the passage from the mouth to the stomach; esophagus; the throat

gul-li-ble *adj.* easily cheated

gul-ly *n.*, *pl.* -ies a ditch cut in the earth by running water

gump-tion *n.*, *Slang* boldness; initiative; enterprise

gup-py *n.*, *pl.* -ies a small, tropical freshwater fish, popular in home aquariums

gust *n.* a sudden, violent rush of wind or air; a sudden outburst
gustily *adv.*, **gusty** *adj.*

gus-ta-to-ry *adj.* of or pertaining to the sense of taste

gus-to *n.* hearty enjoyment

gut *n.* the alimentary canal or part of it *v.* to disembowel guts bowels; entrails

guts-y *n.*, *Slang* courageous

guy *n.*, *Slang* a man; a fellow

gym-na-si-um *n.*, *pl.* -ums *or* -sia a building equipped for indoor sports

gyp *v.*, *Informal* to swindle, cheat, or defraud *n.* a fraud **gypper** *n.*

gy-rate *v.* to rotate or revolve around a fixed point or axis *adj.* coiled or winding about **gyratory** *adj.*

H, h The eighth letter of the English alphabet.

ha-bil-i-ment *n.* clothing characteristic of an office, rank, or occasion

hab-it *n.* involuntary pattern of behavior acquired by frequent repetition

hab-it-a-ble *adj.* suitable for habitation

hab-i-tat *n.* the region in which an animal or plant lives or grows

hab-i-ta-tion *n.* a place of residence

hab-it--form-ing *adj.* producing physiological addiction

ha-bit-u-al *adj.* practicing by or acting according to havit; resorted to on a regular basis; regular

hack *v.* to cut with repeated irregular blows; to manage ;successfully; *n.* a tool used for hacking; taxi driver

hack-ney *n.* a horse of medium size for ordinary driving or riding

hack-neyed *adj.* trite

hack-saw *n.* a saw in a narrow frame for cutting metal

had-dock *n.* a food fish

had-n't *cont.* had not

haft *n.* a handle of a weapon or tool

hag *n.* a malicious, ugly old woman; a witch **haggish** *adj.*

hag-gard wornout, exhausted, and gaunt look, as from hunger or fatigue

hag-gle *v.* to argue or bargain on price or terms **haggler** *n.*

hag-i-og-ra-phy *n.*, *pl.* **hagiographies** biography of the lives of saints or revered persons

hai-ku *n.* an unrhymed Japanese verse form with three short lines

hail *n.* precipitation of small, hard lumps of ice and snow; a hailstone; an exclamation, greeting, acclamation

hake *n.* a marine food fish related to the cod

hal-berd *n.* a medieval weapon used in the 15th and 16th centuries

hal-cy-on *adj.* calm and tranquil; peaceful; prosperous

hale *adj.* healthy and robust; free from defect *v.* to compel to go
- **haleness** *n.*

half *n.*, *pl.* **halves** one of two equal parts into which a thing is divisible

half--wit *n.* a mentally disturbed person

hal-ite *n.* large crystal or masses of salt; salt rock

hal-i-to-sis *n.* a condition of having bad breath

hal-le-lu-jah *interj.* used to express joy, praise, or jubilation **hallelujah** *n.*

hal-low *v.* to sanctify; to make holy; to honor

hal-lu-ci-na-tion *n.* an illusion of seeing something that is nonexistent **hallucinate** *v.*

hal-lu-ci-no-gen *n.* a drug or other agent which causes hallucination **hallucinogenic** *adj.*

ha-lo *n.* a ring of colored light surrounding the head; an aura of glory

hal-o-gen *n.* any of the group of nonmentallic elements including flourine, chlorine, bromine, iodine, and astatine **halogenous** *adj.*

hal-ter *n.* a rope or strap for leading or tying an animal

halve *v.* to divide into two equal parts

hal-yard *n.* a rope for hoisting or lowering a sail, flag, or yard

ham *n.* the meat of a hog's thigh

ham-let *n.* a small rural village or town

ham-mer *n.*

a hand tool with a heavy head used to drive or strike forcefully

ham-mock *n.* a hanging bed or couch of fabric or heavy netting

ham-per *v.* to interfere with movement or progress of

ham-ster *n.* any of various rodents with large cheek pouches and a short tail

ham-string *n.* either of two tendons located at the back of the human knee

hand *n.* the part of the arm below the wrist, consisting of the palm, four fingers and a thumb

hand-gun *n.* a gun that can be held and fired with one hand

hand-i-craft *or* **hand-craft** *n.* skill and expertise in working with the hands

han-dle *v.* to touch, pick up, or hold with the hands

hand-made *adj.* made by hand or by a hand process

hand-maid *or* **hand-maid-en** *n.* a female maid or personal servant

hand-y *adj.* easy to use or reach; helpful or useful

hang *v.* to be attached to from above and unsupported from below

han-gar *n.* a building for housing aircraft

han-ger *n.* a device from which something may be hung or on which something hangs

hank *n.* a loop, coil, or piece of hair, thread, or yarn

han-ker *v.* to have a yearning or craving for something

hao-le *n.* a person who is not of the Hawaiian race, especially a Caucasian

hap-haz-ard *adj.* occurring by accident; happening by chance or at random

hap-less *adj.* unfortunate; unlucky **haplessly** *adv.*

hap-pen *v.* to occur or come to pass; to take place; to discover by chance

hap-pen-ing *n.* a spontaneous event or performance

happen-stance *n.* an event occurring by chance

hap-py *adj.* enjoying contentment and well-being; glad, joyous, satisfied or pleased **happiness** *n.*

ha-rass *v.* to disturb or annoy constantly; to torment persistently **harassment** *n.*

har-bin-ger *n.* a person that initiates or pioneers a major change

hard *adj.* difficult to perform, endure, or comprehend; solid in texture or substance **hardness** *n.*

hard copy *n.* in computer science, the printed information or data from a computer

hard disk *n.* in computer science, magnetic storage consisting of a rigid disk of aluminum coated with a magnetic recording substance; contained within a removable cartridge or mounted in the hard disk of a microcomputer

hard-en *v.* to make or become hard or harder

har-di-hood *n.* resolute courage; audacious boldness; vitality; vigor

hard-ly *adj., Slang* very little; almost certainly not. *adv.* forcefully; painfully

hard-ship *n.* a painful, difficult condition

hard-tack *n.* a hard, crackerlike biscuit made with flour and water

har-dy *adj.* bold and robust

hare *n.*

a mammal related to the rabbit but having longer ears and legs

hark *v.* to listen closely

har-le-quin *n.* a jester; a clown

har-lot *n.* a prostitute

harm *n.* emotional or physical damage or injury. *v.* to cause harm to **harmful** *adj.*

harm-less *adj.* without harm

har-mon-ic *adj.* relating to musical harmony

har-mo-ni-ous *adj.* pleasing to the ear **harmoniously** *adv.*

har-mo-ny *n., pl.* **-ies** complete agreement, as of feeling or opinion; pleasing sounds

har-ness *n.* the working gear, other than a yoke, of a horse or other draft animal **harnesser** *n.*

harp *n.* a musical instrument having a triangular upright frame with strings plucked with the fingers

har-poon *n.* a barbed spear used in hunting whales and large fish **harpoon** *v.*

harp-si-chord *n.* a piano-like instrument whose strings are plucked by using quills or leather points **-ist** *n.*

har-py *n., pl.* **harpies** a vicious woman; a predatory person

har-ri-dan *n.* a mean, hateful old woman

har-ri-er *n.* a slender, narrow-winged hawk that preys on small animals

har-row *n.* a tool with sharp teeth for breaking up and smoothing soil

har-ry *v.* to harass

harsh *adj.* disagreeable; extremely severe **harshly** *adv.*

hart *n.* a fully grown male deer after it has passed its fifth year

har-um--scar-um *adj.* reckless

har-vest *n.* the process or act of gathering a crop

hash-ish *n.* the leaves and flowering tops of the hemp plant

has-sle *n., Slang* a quarrel or argument

has-sock *n.* a firm upholstered cushion used as a footstool

haste *n.* speed; swiftness of motion or action **hasten** *v.*

hasty *adj.* rapid; swift; made or done with excessive speed **hastily** *adv.*

hat *n.* a covering for the head with a crown and brim

hatch *n.* a small opening or door, as in a ship's deck

hatch-et *n.* a small ax with a short handle

hate *v.* to feel hostility or animosity toward; to dislike intensely

haugh-ty *adj.* arrogantly proud; disdainful

haul *v.* to pull or draw with force; to move or transport

haunch *n.* the hip; the buttock and upper thigh of a human or animal

haunt *v.* to appear to or visit as a ghost or spirit; to linger in the mind **haunting** *adj.*

haut-bois *or* **haut-boy** *n.* an oboe

hau-teur *n.* a disdainful arrogance

have *v.* to hold or own, as a possession or as property **have to** need to; must

have had it suffered or endured all that one can tolerate

hav-oc *n.* mass confusion; wide-spread destruction

haw *n.* a hesitating sound made by a speaker who is groping for words

hawk *n.*

any of several predatory birds, with a short, hooked bill and strong claws for seizing small prey

haw-ser *n.* a heavy cable or rope for towing or securing a ship

hay *n.* alfalfa or grass that has been cut and dried for animal food

hay-wire *adj., Slang* broken; emotionally out of control

haz-ard *n.* a risk; chance; an accident or source of danger **hazardous** *adj.*

ha-zel-nut *n.* the edible nut of the hazel

haz-y *adj.* lacking clarity; vague **hazily** *adv.*, **haziness** *n.*

head *n.* the upper part of a human or animal body, containing the brain

head-ing *n.* a title or caption that acts as a front, beginning, or upper part of anything

head-set *n.* a pair of headphones

head-strong *adj.* not easily restrained; obstinate

heal *v.* to restore to good health; to mend **healable** *adj.*, **healer** *n.*

health *n.* the overall sound condition or function of a living organism at a particular time **healthful** *adj.*

heap *n.* a haphazard assortment of things

hear *v.* to perceive by the ear; to listen with careful attention

hear-ing *n.* one of the five senses; the range by which sound can be heard

heark-en *v.* to listen carefully

hear-say *n.* information heard from another; common talk; rumor

heart *n.*

the hollow, primary muscular organ of vertebrates which circulates blood throughout the body; the emotional center, such as in love, hate, consideration, or compassion

heart-ache *n.* emotional grief; sorrow; mental anguish

hearth *n.* the floor of a fireplace, furnace

heart-y *adj.* marked by exuberant

warmth; full of vigor; nourishing

heat *n.* a quality of being hot or warm; a degree of warmth; depth of feeling

hea-then *n.* a person or nation that does not recognize the God of Christianity, Judaism, or Islam; in the Old Testament

heave *v.* to raise or lift, especially forcibly

heav-en *n.* the sky; the region above and around the earth; the abode of God, the angels, and the blessed souls of the dead **heavenly** *adj.*

heav-y *adj.* of great weight; very thick or dense

heck-le *v.* to badger or annoy, as with questions, comments, or gibes -er *n.*

hec-tic *adj.* intensely active, rushed, or excited

he'd *conj.* he had; he would

he-don-ism *n.* the doctrine devoted to the pursuit of pleasure

heed *v.* to pay attention; to take notice of something

heft *n., Slang* weight; bulk. *v.* to gauge or estimate the weight of by lifting

heft-y *adj.* bulky; heavy; sizable

he-gem-o-ny *n.* dominance or leadership, as of one country over another

he-gi-ra *n.* a journey or departure to flee an undesirable situation

height *n.* the quality of being high; the highest or most advanced point

Heim-lich maneuver *n.* an emergency maneuver used to dislodge food from a choking person's throat; the closed fist is placed below the rib cage and pressed inward to force air from the lungs upward

hei-nous *adj.* extremely wicked; hateful or shockingly wicked

heir *n.* a person who inherits another's property or title

heist *v., Slang* to take from; to steal *n.* a robbery

hel-i-cal *adj.* of or pertaining to the shape of a helix

hel-i-cop-ter *n.*

an aircraft propelled by rotors which can take off vertically

he-li-um *n.* an extremely light, nonflammable, odorless, gaseous element, symbolized by He

hell *or* **Hell** *n.* the abode of the dead souls condemned to eternal punishment

he'll *contr.* he will

helm *n.* a wheel or steering apparatus for a ship

hel-met *n.* a protective covering for the head made of metal, leather, or plastic

helms-man *n.* one who guides a ship

help *v.* to assist or aid. *n.* Assistance; relief; one hired to help **helper** *n.,* **helpful** *adj.*

hel-ter--skel-ter *adv.* in a confused or hurried manner; in an aimless way *adj.* rushed and confused

helve *n.* a handle on a tool such as an axe or hatchet

he--man *n. Slang* a man marked by strength; a muscular man

he-ma-tol-o-gy *n.* the branch of biological science that deals with blood and blood-generating organs **hematologist** *n.*

hem-i-sphere *n.* a half sphere that is divided by a plane passing through its center

he-mo-glo-bin *n.* the respiratory pigment in the red blood cells of vertebrates containing iron and carrying oxygen to body tissues

he-mo-phil-i-a *n., Pathol.* an inherited blood disease characterized by severe, protracted, sometimes spontaneous bleeding

hem-or-rhage *n.* bleeding, especially excessive bleeding **hemorrhage** *v.*

hem-or-rhoid *n., Pathol.* a painful mass of dilated veins in swollen anal tissue

he-mo-stat *n.* an agent that stops bleeding; a clamp-like instrument for preventing or reducing bleeding

hen *n.* a mature female bird

hence-forth, hence-for-ward *adv.* from this time on

hep-a-rin *n., Biochem* a substance found especially in liver tissue having the power to slow or prevent blood clotting

her-ald *n.* a person who announces important news

her-ald-ry *n., pl.* -ries the art or science of tracing genealogies

herb-age *n.* grass or vegetation used especially for grazing

her-bar-i-um *n., pl.* **herbariums** *or* **herbaria** a collection of dried plant specimens that are scientifically arranged for study

her-bi-cide *n.* a chemical agent used to kill weeds

her-bi-vore *n.* a herbivorous animal

her-biv-o-rous *adj.* feeding chiefly on plant life or vegetables -ly *adv.*

her-cu-le-an *adj.* of unusual size, force,

or difficulty

here-af-ter *adv.* from now on; at some future time

here-by *adv.* by means or by virtue of this

he-red-i-tar-y *adj.* passing or transmitted from an ancestor to a legal heir

he-red-i-ty *n.* the genetic transmission of physical traits from parents to offspring

here-in *adv.* in or into this place

here-of *adv.* relating to or in regard to this

her-e-sy *n., pl.* **heresies** a belief in conflict with orthodox religious beliefs

here-to *adv.* to this matter, proposition, or thing

here-with *adv.* together or along with this; hereby

her-maph-ro-dite *n.* a person having both male and female reproductive organs

her-met-ic *or* **her-met-i-cal** *adj.* tightly sealed against air and liquids hermeticly *adv.*

her-mit *n.* a person who lives in seclusion, often for religious reasons

her-ni-a *n.* the protrusion of a bodily organ, as the intestine, through an abnormally weakened wall that usually surrounds it; a rupture **hernial** *adj.*

he-ro *n., pl.* **heroes** a figure in mythology and legend renowned for exceptional courage and fortitude

heroic couplet *n.* a verse consisting of two rhyming lines of iambic pentameter

her-o-in *n.* a highly addictive narcotic derivative of morphine

her-o-ine *n.* a woman of heroic character

her-o-ism *n.* heroic behavior

her-pes *n., Pathol.* a viral infection, characterized by small blisters on the skin or mucous membranes

her-pe-tol-o-gy *n.* the scientific study and treatment of reptiles and amphibians

her-ring *n.* a valuable food fish of the North Atlantic

hertz *n.* a unit of frequency equalling one cycle per second

he's *contr.* he has; he is

hes-i-tant *adj.* given to hesitating hesitancy *n.*

hes-i-tate *v.* to pause or to be slow before acting, speaking, or deciding hesitation *n.*

het-er-o-sex-u-al *adj.* of or having sexual desire to the opposite sex -ity *n.*

hew *v.* to make or shape with or as if with an axe

hex *n.* one held to bring bad luck; a jinx. *v.* to put under an evil spell; to bewitch

hex-a-gon *n.*

a polygon having six sides and six angles

hex-am-e-ter *n.* a line of verse containing six metrical feet

hi-a-tus *n.* a slight gap, break, or lapse in time from which something is missing

hi-ba-chi *n., pl.* **hibachis** a deep, portable charcoal grill used for cooking food

hi-ber-nate *v.* to pass the winter in an inactive, dormant, sleep-like state

hi-bis-cus *n.* a chiefly tropical shrub or tree

hick *n., Slang* a clumsy, unsophisticated country person

hide *v.* to put, or keep out of sight; to keep secret; to obscure from sight; *n.* the skin of an animal

hid-e-ous *adj.* physically repulsive; extremely ugly

hi-er-ar-chy *n., pl.* **hierarchies** an authoritative body or group of things or persons arranged in successive order

hi-er-o-glyph-ic *n.* a pictorial symbol representing an idea, object, or sound hieroglyphically *adv.*

high *adj.* extending upward; located at a distance above the ground

high-fa-lu-tin *adj.* pretentious or extravagant in manner or speech

high-ness *n.* the state of being high

high--pres-sure *adj., Informal* using insistent persuasive methods or tactics

high--spirited *adj.* unbroken in spirit; proud

high--strung *adj.* very nervous and excitable

hi-lar-i-ous *adj.* boisterously happy or cheerful

hill *n.* a rounded, elevation of the earth's surface, smaller than a mountain *hilly adj.*

hilt *n.* the handle of a dagger or sword to the **hilt** fully; completely; thoroughly

him *pron.* the objective case of the pronoun he

him-self *pron.* that identical male one; a form of the third person, singular masculine pronoun

hind *adj.* located at or toward the rear part; posterior

hin-der *v.* to interfere with the progress or action of

hind-most *adj.* farthest to the rear or

back
hin-drance *n.* the act of hindering or state of being hindered

hind-sight *n.* comprehension or understanding of an event after it has happened

hip *n.* the part of the human body that projects outward below the waist and thigh; the hip joint

hip *n.* the bright, red seed case of a rose

hip *adj.*, *Slang* said to be aware of or informed about current goings on

hip-pie *or* **hip-py** *n.*, *pl.* hippies a young person who adopts unconventional dress and behavior

hip-po-pot-a-mus *n.*

a large, aquatic mammal, native to Africa

hire *v.* to obtain the service of another for pay

his *adj.* the possessive case of the pronoun he

hir-sute *adj.* covered with hair

hiss *n.* a sound resembling a prolonged, sibilant sound, as that of

his-tol-o-gy *n.*, *pl.* -ies the study of the minute structures of animal and plant tissues as seen through a microscope

his-to-ri-an *n.* a person who specializes in the writing or study of history

his-tor-ic *adj.* significant or famous in history

his-to-ry *n.*, *pl.* -ries past events, especially those involving human affairs

his-tri-on-ics *pl.*, *n.* theatrical arts; feigned emotional display

hitch *v.* to fasten or tie temporarily, with a hook or knot *Slang* to unite in marriage

hith-er *adv.* to this place *adj.* situated toward this side

hith-er-to *adv.* up to now

hive *n.* a natural or man-made structure serving as a habitation for honeybees

hives *pl.*, *n.* any of various allergic conditions marked by itching welts

hoarse *adj.* having a husky, gruff, or croaking voice

hoars-en *v.* to become or make hoarse

hoar-y *adj.* ancient; aged; gray or white with age

hoax *n.* a trick or deception

hob-by *n.*, *pl.* hobbies an activity or interest undertaken for pleasure during one's leisure time

hob-gob-lin *n.* an imaginary cause of ter-

ror or dread

hob-nob *n.* to associate in a friendly manner

ho-bo *n.*, *pl.* hoboes *or* hobos a vagrant who travels aimlessly about; a tramp

hod *n.* a V-shaped trough held over the shoulder to carry loads, as bricks or mortar

hodge-podge *n.* a jumbled mixture or collection

Hodg-kin's disease *n.*, *Pathol.* a disease characterized by progressive enlargement of the lymph nodes, lymphoid tissue, and spleen, generally fatal

hoe *n.* a tool with a long handle and flat blade used for weeding

hoist *v.* to haul or raise up *n.* a machine used for raising large objects

hold *v.* to take and keep as in one's hand; to grasp

hold-ing *n.* property, as land, money, or stocks

hole *n.* a cavity or opening in a solid mass or body

ho-li-ness *n.* the state of being holy

hol-ler *v.* to shout loudly; to yell

holler *n.*

hol-low *adj.* having a cavity or space within; concaved or sunken

hol-mi-um *n.* a metallic element of the rare-earth group, symbolized by Ho

hol-o-grah *n.* a handwritten document, as a letholstered

ho-ly *adj.* regarded with or characterized by divine power

Holy Communion *n.* the Eucharist

Holy Ghost *n.* the third person of the Trinity

Holy Land *n.* palestine

Holy Spirit *n.* the Holy Ghost

hom-age *n.* great respect or honor

home *n.* the place where one resides; a place of origin

ho-me-op-a-thy *n.* a system of treating a disease with minute doses of medicines that produce the symptoms of the disease being treated

ho-me-o-sta-sis *n.*, *Biol.* a state of equilibrium that occurs between different but related functions or elements

homeostatic *adj.*

home-spun *adj.* something made, woven, or spun at home; anything that is simple and plain

home-y *or* **hom-y** *adj.* suggesting the coziness, intimacy, and comforts of home

hom-i-cide *n.* the killing of one person by another

hom-i-let-ic *n.* pertaining to the nature of

a sermon

hom-i-ly *n., pl.* **homilies** a sermon, particularly one based on a Biblical text

ho-mo-ge-ne-ous *adj.* of the same or similar nature or kind

hom-o-graph *n.* a word that is identical to another in spelling, but different from it in origin and meaning

hom-o-nym *n.* a word that has the same sound and often the same spelling as another but a different meaning and origin

hom-o-phone *n.* one of two or more words that have the same sound but different spelling, origin, and meaning

Ho-mo sa-pi-ens *n.* the scientific name for the human race

ho-mo-sex-u-al *adj.* having sexual attraction or desire for persons of the same sex **homosexuality** *n.*

hon-cho *n., pl.* **honchos** the main person in charge; the boss; the manager

hon-est *adj.* not lying, cheating, or stealing; having or giving full worth or value

honey-suck-le *n.* a shrub or vine bearing a tubular, highly fragrant flower

hon-ky--tonk *n., Slang* a cheap bar or nightclub

hon-or *n.* high regard or respect; personal integrity; reputation; privilege

hon-or-ar-y *adj.* relating to an office or title bestowed as an honor, without the customary powers, duties, or salaries

hood *n.* a covering for the head and neck; cover of an automobile engine

hood *suff.* the quality or state of; sharing a given quality or state

hood-lum *n.* a young, tough, wild, or destructive fellow

hoo-doo *n.* voodoo *Slang* one who is thought to bring bad luck

hoo-ey *n., & interj., Slang* nonsense

hoof *n., pl.* **hooves** the horny covering of the foot in various mammals; *Slang* to dance; to walk; **on the hoof** alive; not butchered

hook *n.* a curved or bent piece of metal used to catch, drag, suspend, or fasten something

hook-er *n., Slang* a prostitute

hook-worm *n.* a parasitic intestinal worm with hooked mouth parts

hook-y *n., Slang* truant **to play hooky** to be out of school without permission

hoop-la *n., Slang* noise and excitement

hoose-gow *n., Slang* a jail

hoot *n.* the loud sound or cry of an owl **hooter** *n.,* **hoot** *v.*

hoot *n., Slang* a very insignificant amount **not give a hoot** not caring

hope *v.* to want or wish for something with a feeling of confident expectation **to hope against hope** to continue hoping for something even when it may be in vain **hopeful** *adj. & n.*

horde *adj.* a large crowd

ho-ri-zon *n.* the line along which the earth and sky seem to meet

hor-mone *n., Physiol.* an internal secretion carried by the bloodstream to other parts of the body where it has a specific effect

horn *n. Mus.*

any of the various brass instruments, formerly made from animal horns; a hard, bone-like permanent projection on the heads of certain hoofed animals, as cattle, sheep, or deer

hor-net *n.* any of various wasps which are capable inflicting a severe sting

horn-swog-gle *v.* to deceive

hor-o-scope *n.* a chart or diagram of the relative positions of the planets and signs of the zodiac at a certain time, as that of a person's birth; used to predict the future

hor-ri-ble *adj.* shocking; inducing or producing horror *Informal* excessive; inordinate **horribly** *adv.*

hor-rid *adj.* horrible

hor-ri-fy *v.* to cause a feeling of horror; to dismay or shock

hor-ror *n.* the painful, strong emotion caused by extreme dread, fear, or repugnance

horse *n.*

a large, strong, hoofed quadruped mammal with a long mane and tail, used for riding and for pulling heavy objects; a device that usually has four legs, used for holding or supporting something

horse sense *n., Slang* common sense

hor-ti-cul-ture *n.* the art or science of raising and tending fruits, vegetables, flowers, or ornamental plants **horticultural** *adj.*

ho-san-na *interj.* used to praise or glorify God

ho-sier-y *n.* stockings and socks

hos-pice *n.* a lodging for travelers or the needy

hos-pi-ta-ble *adj.* treating guests with warmth and generosity; receptive

hos-pi-tal *n.* an institution where the injured or sick receive medical, surgical, and emergency care

hos-pi-tal-i-ty *n.* hospitable treatment, disposition, or reception

host *n.* one who receives or entertains guests

hos-tage *n.* a person held as security that promises will be kept or terms met by a third party

hos-tile *adj.* of or relating to an enemy; antagonistic

hos-til-i-ty *n.*, *pl.* **-ies** a very deepseated opposition or hatred; war

hour-glass *n.*

a glass instrument having two compart ments from which sand, mercury, or water flows from the top compartment to the bottom

how *adv.* in what manner or way; to what effect; in what condition or state; for what reason; with what meaning

howl *v.* to utter a loud, sustained, plaintive sound, as the wolf **howler** *n.*

hub *n.* the center of a wheel; the center of activity

hud-dle *n.* a crowd together

huff *n.* a fit of resentment or of ill temper

hug *v.* to embrace; to hold fast; to keep, cling, or stay close to

huge *adj.* of great quantity, size, or extent

hulk *n.* a heavy, bulky ship; the body of an old ship no longer fit for service

hulk-ing *adj.* unwieldy or awkward

hull *n.* the outer cover of a fruit or seed; the framework of a boat

hul-la-ba-loo *n.* a confused noise; a great uproar

hum *v.* to make a continuous low-pitched sound; to be busily active; to sing with the lips closed **hummer** *n.*

hu-man *adj.* of, relating to, or typical of man

hu-mane *adj.* to be marked by compassion, sympathy, or consideration for others

hum-ble *adj.* marked by meekness or modesty; unpretentious; lowly

hum-drum *n.*, *Slang* boring; dull

hu-mid *adj.* containing or characterized by a large amount of moisture; damp

hu-mid-i-ty *n.* a moderate amount of wetness in the air; dampness

hu-mil-i-ate *v.* to reduce one's dignity or pride to a lower position **-tion** *n.*

hu-mor *n.* something that is or has the ability to be comical or amusing

hunch *n.* a strong, intuitive feeling about a future event or result

hun-ger *n.* a strong need or desire for food

hurl *v.* to throw something with great force

hur-rah *interj.* used to express approval, pleasure, or exultation

hur-ri-cane *n.* a tropical cyclone with winds exceeding 74 miles per hour

hur-ry *v.* to move or cause to move with haste *n.* the act of hurrying

hurt *v.* to experience or inflict with physical pain; to cause physical or emotional harm to; to damage **-ful** *adj.*

hus-band *n.* a man who is married

hush *v.* to make or become quiet; to calm; to keep secret *n.* a silence

hy-dro-gen *n.* a colorless, normally odorless, highly flammable gas that is the simplest and lightest of he elements, symbolized by H

hy-dro-pho-bi-a *n.* a fear of water

hy-e-na *n.*

any of several strong carnivorous mammals of Africa and Asia, with coarse hair and very powerful jaws

hy-giene *n.* the science of the establishment and maintenance of good health and the prevention of disease

hy-men *n.* the thin membrane that partly closes the external vaginal orifice

hymn *n.* a song of praise giving thanks to God; a song of joy **hymn** *v.*

hype *v.*, *Slang* to put on; to stimulate; to promote or publicize extravagantly

hy-per-ac-tive *adj.* abnormally active

hy-per-ten-sion *n.* the condition of abnormally high blood pressure

hy-phen *n.* a punctuation mark (-) used to show connection between two or more words **hyphen** *v.*

hys-ter-ec-to-my *n.*, *pl.* **-ies** surgery on a female which partially or completely removes the uterus

hys-ter-ia *n.* a psychological condition characterized by emotional excess and or unreasonable fear

hys-ter-i-cal *adj.* emotionally out of control **hysterically** *adv.*

I, i the ninth letter of the English alphabet; the Roman numeral for one

I *pron.* the person speaking or writing *n.* the self; the ego

I *or* **i** *abbr.* island; isle

IAAF *abbr.* International Amateur Athletic Federation

i-amb *or* **i-am-bus** *n.* a metrical foot consisting of a short or unstressed syllable followed by an accented syllable

i-at-ro-gen-ic *adj.* induced inadvertently by a physician or his treatment iatrogenically *adv.*

ib *or* **ibid** *abbr., L.* ibidem, in the same place

I band *n.* a type of isotropic band that is of the striated muscle fiber

i-bex *n.*

an Old World mountain goat with long curved horns

i-bis *n.* a long-billed wading bird related to the heron and stork

ice *n.* solidly frozen water; a dessert of crushed ice which is flavored and sweetened *Informal* extreme coldness of manner *v.* to change into ice; to cool or chill; to cover with icing icily *adv.*, iciness *n.*, icy *adj.*

ice age *n., Geol.* a time of widespread glaciation

ice bag *n.* a small, flexible, waterproof bag designed to hold ice, used on parts of the body

ice-berg *n.* a thick mass of floating ice separated from a glacier

ice-boat *n.* a vehicle with runners and usually a sail, used for sailing over ice; an icebreaker

ice-bound *adj.* obstructed or covered by ice

ice-box *n.* a structure designed for holding ice in which food and other perishables are stored

ice-break-er *n.* a sturdy vessel for breaking a path through icebound waters; a pier or dock apron for deflecting floating ice from the base of a pier or bridge

ice cap *n.* an extensive perennial covering of ice and snow that covers a large area of land

ice cream *n.* a smooth mixture of milk, cream, flavoring, sweeteners, and other ingredients, beaten and frozen

ice hock-ey *n.* a version of hockey played on ice

ice-house *n.* a building where ice is stored

ice milk *n.* a food similar to ice cream but made with skim milk

ice pack *n.* a large mass of floating, compacted ice; a folded bag filled with ice and applied to sore parts of the body

ice pick *n.* a pointed tool used for breaking ice into small pieces

ice skate *n.* shoe or boot with a runner fixed to it for skating on ice ice-skate *v.*

ich-thy-ol-o-gy *n.* the zoological study of fishes ichthyologic, ichthyological *adj.*, ichthyologist *n.*

i-ci-cle *n.* hanging spike of ice formed by dripping water that freezes

ic-ing *n.* sweet preparation for coating cakes and cookies

i-con *or* **i-kon** *n.* a sacred Christian pictorial representation of Jesus Christ, the Virgin Mary, or other sacred figures

i-con-o-clast *n.* one who opposes the use of sacred images; one who attacks traditional or cherished beliefs iconoclasm *n.*, iconoclastic *adj.*

id *n., Psychol..* the unconscious part of the psyche associated with instinctual needs and drives

I'd *contr.* I had; I should; I would

i-de-a *n.* something existing in the mind; conception or thought; an opinion; a plan of action

i-de-al *n.* concept or imagined state of perfection; highly desirable; perfect; an ultimate objective; an honorable principle or motive *adj.* conforming to absolute excellence ideally *adv.*

i-de-al-ism *n.* the practice or tendency of seeing things in ideal form; pursuit of an ideal; a philosophical system believing that reality consists of ideas or perceptions idealist *n.*, idealistic *adj.*

i-de-al-ize *v.* to regard or represent as ideal idealization *n.*

i-dem *pron. & adj., L.* the same; used to indicate a previously mentioned reference

i-den-ti-cal *adj.* being the same; exactly equal or much alike; designating a twin or twins developed from the same ovum identically *adv.*

i-den-ti-fi-ca-tion *n.* the act of identifying; the state of being identified; a means of identity

i-den-ti-fy *v.* to recognize the identity of; to establish as the same or similar; to equate; to associate oneself closely with an individual or group

identifiable *adj.*

i-den-ti-ty *n., pl.* **identities** the condition or state of being a specific person or thing and recognizable as such; the condition or fact of being the same as something else

id-e-o-gram *or* **id-e-o-graph** *n.* pictorial symbol used in a writing system to represent an idea or thing, as Chinese characters; a graphic symbol, as $ or %

i-de-ol-o-gy *n., pl.* **ideologies** body of ideas that influence a person, group, culture, or political party **ideological** *adj.*

ides *pl., n.* in the ancient Roman calendar, the fifteenth day of March, May, July, and October or the thirteenth day of the other months

id-i-o-cy *n., pl.* **-cies** a condition of an idiot

id-i-om *n.* form of expression having a meaning that is not readily understood from the meaning of its component words; the dialect of people or a region; a kind of language or vocabulary **idiomatic** *adj.*, **idiomatically** *adv.*

id-i-o-syn-cra-sy *n., pl.* **-sies** peculiarity, as of behavior **idiosyncratic** *adj.*, **idiosyncratically** *adv.*

id-i-ot *n.* a mentally deficient person; an extremely foolish or stupid person **idiotic** *adj.*, **idiotically** *adv.*

i-dle *adj.* doing nothing; inactive; moving lazily; slowly; running at a slow speed or out of gear; unemployed or inactive **idleness, idler** *n.*, **idly** *adv.*

i-dol *n.* a symbol or representation of a god or deity that is worshiped; a person or thing adored

i-dol-a-try *n.* the worship of idols; blind adoration; devotion; to admire **idolater** *n.*, **idolatrous** *adj.*

i-dol-ize *v.* to admire with excessive admiration or devotion; to worship as an idol **idolization, idolizer** *n.*

i-dyll *or* **i-dyl** *n.* a poem or prose piece about country life; a scene, event, or condition of rural simplicity; a romantic interlude **idyllic** *adj.*, **idyllically** *adv.*

-ie *suff.* little; dear

if-fy *adj., Slang* marked by unknown qualities or conditions

ig-loo *n.* dome-shaped Eskimo dwelling often made of blocks of snow

ig-ne-ous *adj., Geol.* relating to fire; formed by solidification from a molten magma

ig-nite *v.* to start or set a fire; to render luminous by heat

ig-ni-tion *n.* an act or action of igniting; a process or means for igniting the fuel mixture in an engine

ig-no-ble *adj.* dishonorable in character or purpose; not of noble rank **ignobly** *adv.*

ig-no-min-i-ous *adj.* marked by or characterized by shame or disgrace; dishonorable **ignominy** *n.*

ig-no-ra-mus *n.* totally ignorant person

ig-no-rant *adj.* lacking education or knowledge; not aware; lacking comprehension **ignorance** *n.*

ig-nore *v.* to pay no attention to; to reject **ignorable** *adj.*

i-gua-na *n.*

large, dark-colored tropical American lizard

il-e-i-tis *n.* inflammation of the ileum

il-e-um *n., pl.* **ilea** the lower part of the small intestine between the jejunum and the large intestine

ilk *n.* sort; kind

ill *adj.* not healthy; sick; destructive in effect; harmful; hostile; unfriendly; not favorable; not up to standards *adv.* in an ill manner; with difficulty; scarcely *n.* evil; injury or harm; something causing suffering

I'll *contr.* I will; I shall

ill--ad-vised *adj.* done without careful thought or sufficient advice

ill--bred *adj.* ill-mannered; impolite; rude

il-le-gal *adj.* contrary to law or official rules **illegality** *n.*, **illegally** *adv.*

il-leg-i-ble *adj.* not readable; not legible **illegibly** *adv.*, **illegibility** *n.*

il-le-git-i-mate *adj.* against the law; unlawful; born out of wedlock **illegitimacy** *n.*, **illegitimately** *adv.*

ill--fat-ed *adj.* destined for misfortune; doomed; unlucky

ill--fa-vored *adj.* unattractive; objectionable; offensive; unpleasant

ill--got-ten *adj.* obtained in an illegal or dishonest way

ill--hu-mored *adj.* irritable; cross **ill-humoredly** *adv.*

il-lic-it *adj.* not permitted by custom or law; unlawful **illicitly** *adv.*

il-lit-er-ate *adj.* unable to read and write; uneducated **illiteracy, illiterate** *n.*

ill--man-nered *adj.* lacking or showing a lack of good manners; rude

ill--na-tured *adj.* disagreeable or unpleasant disposition

ill-ness *n.* sickness; a state of being in poor health

il-log-i-cal *adj.* contrary to the principles of logic; not logical **illogically** *n.*, **illogically** *adv.*

ill--tem-pered *adj.* having or showing a cross temper or disposition

il-lu-mi-nate *v.* to give light; to make clear; to provide with understanding; to decorate with pictures or designs **illumination, illuminator** *n.*

ill--use *v.* to treat cruelly or unjustly *n.* unjust treatment

il-lu-sion *n.* a misleading perception of reality; an overly optimistic idea or belief; misconception **illusive, illusory** *adj.*

il-lus-trate *v.* to explain or clarify, especially by the use of examples; to clarify by serving as an example; to provide a publication with explanatory features **illustrator** *n.*

il-lus-tra-tion *n.* the act of illustrating; an example or comparison used to illustrate

il-lus-tra-tive *adj.* serving to illustrate

il-lus-tri-ous *adj.* greatly celebrated; renowned **illustriousness** *n.*

ill will *n.* unfriendly or hostile feelings; malice

I'm *contr.* I am

im-age *n.* a representation of the form and features of someone or something; an optically formed representation of an object made by a mirror or lens; a mental picture of something imaginary *v.* to make a likeness of; to reflect; to depict vividly

im-age-ry *n.*, *pl.* -ies mental pictures; existing only in the imagination

im-ag-in-a-ble *adj.* capable of being imagined **imaginably** *adv.*

im-ag-i-nar-y *adj.* existing only in the imagination

im-ag-i-na-tion *n.* the power of forming mental images of unreal or absent objects; such power used creatively; resourcefulness **imaginative** *adj.*, **imaginatively** *adv.*

im-ag-ine *v.* to form a mental picture or idea of; to suppose; to guess

i-ma-go *n.*, *pl.* -goes *or* -gines an insect in its sexually mature adult stage

i-mam *n.* a prayer leader of Islam; rulers that claim descent from Muhammad

im-bal-ance *n.* a lack of functional balance; defective coordination

im-be-cile *n.* a mentally deficient person **imbecile, imbecilic** *adj.*, **imbecility** *n.*

im-bibe *v.* to drink; to take in **imbiber** *n.*

im-bri-cate *adj.* with edges over-lapping in a regular arrangement, as roof tiles or fish scales

im-bro-glio *n.*, *pl.* -glios a complicated situation or disagreement; a confused heap; a tangle

im-bue *v.* to saturate, as with a stain or dye

im-i-ta-ble *adj.* capable or worthy of imitation

im-i-tate *v.* to copy the actions or appearance of another; to adopt the style of; to duplicate; to appear like **imitator** *n.*

im-i-ta-tion *n.* an act of imitating; something copied from an original

im-mac-u-late *adj.* free from sin, stain, or fault; impeccably clean **immaculately** *adv.*

im-ma-nent *adj.* existing within; restricted to the mind; subjective **immanence, immanency** *n.*, **-ly** *adv.*

im-ma-te-ri-al *adj.* lacking material body or form; of no importance or relevance **immaterially** *adv.*, **immaterialness** *n.*

im-ma-ture *adj.* not fully grown; undeveloped; suggesting a lack of maturity **immaturely** *adv.*, **-ity** *n.*

im-meas-ur-a-ble *adj.* not capable of being measured **immeasurably** *adv.*

im-me-di-a-cy *n.*, *pl.* -ies the quality of being immediate; directness; something of urgent importance

im-me-di-ate *adj.* acting or happening without an intervening object, agent, or cause; directly perceived; occurring at once; close in time, location, or relation **immediately** *adv.*

im-me-mo-ri-al *adj.* beyond the limits of memory, tradition, or records

im-mense *adj.* exceptionally large **immensely** *adv.*, **immensity** *n.*

im-merse *v.* to put into a liquid; to baptize by submerging in water; to engross; to absorb **immersible** *adj.*, **immersion** *n.*

im-mi-grant *n.* one who leaves his country to settle in another

im-mi-grate *v.* to leave one country and settle in another **immigration** *n.*

im-mi-nent *adj.* about to happen **imminence** *n.*

im-mo-bile *adj.* not moving or incapable of motion **immobility** *n.*

im-mo-bi-lize *v.* to render motionless
immobilization *n.*

im-mod-er-ate *adj.* exceeding normal
bounds **immoderately** *adv.*

im-mod-est *adj.* lacking modesty; indecent; boastful
immodestly *adv.*, **immodesty** *n.*

im-mo-late *v.* to kill, as a sacrifice; to
destroy completely **immolator** *n.*

im-mor-al *adj.* not moral **immorally** *adv.*

im-mo-ral-i-ty *n.*, *pl.* **-ies** lack of
morality; an immoral act or practice

im-mor-tal *adj.* exempt from death; lasting forever, as in fame *n.* a person of
lasting fame **immortality** *n.*,
immortally *adv.*

im-mov-a-ble *adj.* not capable of moving
or being moved **immovably** *adv.*

im-mune *adj.* not affected or responsive;
resistant, as to a disease
immunity *n.*

im-mu-nize *v.* to make immune
immunization *n.*

im-mu-nol-o-gy *n.* the study of immunity
to diseases **immunologic,
immunological** *adj.*, **-ally** *adv.*

im-mu-no-sup-pres-sive *adj.* acting to
suppress a natural immune response
to an antigen

im-mure *v.* to confine by or as if by
walls; to build into a wall

im-mu-ta-ble *adj.* unchanging or unchangeable **immutability** *n.*, **-bly** *adv.*

imp *n.* a mischievous child

im-pact *n.* a collision; the impetus or
force produced by a collision; an initial, usually strong effect *v.* to pack
firmly together; to strike or affect
forcefully

im-pac-ted *adj.* wedged together at the
broken ends, as an impacted bone;
wedged inside the gum in such a way
that normal eruption is prevented, as
an impacted tooth

im-pac-tion *n.* something wedged in a
part of the body

im-pair *v.* to diminish in strength, value,
quantity, or quality **impairment** *n.*

im-pa-la *n.* large African antelope, the
male of which has slender curved
horns

im-pale *v.* to pierce with a sharp stake or
point; to kill by piercing in this fashion
impalement *n.*

im-pal-pa-ble *adj.* not perceptible to
touch; not easily distinguished
impalpability *n.*, **impalpably** *adv.*

im-part *v.* to grant; to bestow; to make
known; to communicate

im-par-tial *adj.* not partial; unbiased

impartiality *n.*, **impartially** *adv.*

im-pass-a-ble *adj.* impossible to travel
over or across

im-passe *n.* a road or passage having no
exit; a difficult situation with no apparent way out; a deadlock

im-pas-sioned *adj.* filled with passion

im-pas-sive *adj.* unemotional; showing
no emotion; expressionless
impassively *adv.*

im-pa-tient *adj.* unwilling to wait or
tolerate delay; expressing or caused by
irritation at having to wait; restlessly
eager; intolerant
impatience *n.*, **impatiently** *adv.*

im-peach *v.* to charge with misconduct in
public office before a proper court of
justice; to make an accusation against
impeachable *adj.*, **impeachment** *n.*

im-pec-ca-ble *adj.* having no flaws; perfect; not capable of sin
impeccably *adv.*

im-pe-cu-ni-ous *adj.* having no money
impecuniousness *n.*

im-ped-ance *n.* a measure of the total
opposition to the flow of an electric
current, especially in an alternating
current circuit

im-pede *v.* to obstruct or slow down the
progress of

im-ped-i-ment *n.* one that stands in the
way; something that impedes, especially an organic speech defect

im-ped-i-men-ta *pl.* *n.* things that impede or encumber, such as baggage

im-pel *v.* to spur to action; to provoke;
to drive forward; to propel **impeller** *n.*

im-pend *v.* to hover threateningly; to be
about to happen

im-pen-e-tra-ble *adj.* not capable of
being penetrated; not capable of being
seen through or understood; unfath-
omable **impenetrability** *n.*, **-bly** *adv.*

im-pen-i-tent *adj.* not sorry; unrepentant
impenitence *n.*

im-per-a-tive *adj.* expressing a command
or request; empowered to command
or control; compulsory
imperative *n.*, **imperatively** *adv.*

im-per-cep-ti-ble *adj.* not perceptible by
the mind or senses; extremely small or
slight **imperceptibly** *adv.*

im-per-fect *adj.* not perfect; of or being a
verb tense which shows an un-
completed or continuous action or
condition *n.* the imperfect tense
imperfectly *adv.*

im-per-fec-tion *n.* the quality or condition of being imperfect; a defect

im-pe-ri-al *adj.* of or relating to an empire or emperor; designating a nation or government having dependent colonies; majestic; regal *n.* a pointed beard on the lower lip or chin **imperially** *adv.*

im-pe-ri-al-ism *n.* the national policy or practice of acquiring foreign territories or establishing dominance over other nations **imperialist** *n.*, **imperialistic** *adj.*

imperial moth *n.* a large New World moth with yellow wings and brownish or purplish markings

im-per-il *v.* to put in peril; endanger

im-pe-ri-ous *adj.* commanding; domineering; urgent **imperiousness** *n.*, **imperiously** *adv.*

im-per-ish-a-ble *adj.* not perishable **imperishably** *adv.*

im-per-ma-nent *adj.* not permanent; temporary **impermanence** *n.*, -ly *adv.*

im-per-me-a-ble *adj.* not permeable **impermeability** *n.*, **impermeably** *adv.*

im-per-mis-si-ble *adj.* not permissible; not allowed

im-per-son-al *adj.* having no personal reference or connection; showing no emotion or personality -ly *adv.*

im-per-son-ate *v.* to assume the character or manner of **impersonation**, **impersonator** *n.*

im-per-ti-nent *adj.* overly bold or disrespectful; not pertinent; irrelevant **impertinence** *n.*, **impertinently** *adv.*

im-per-turb-a-ble *adj.* unshakably calm **imperturbability** *n.*, **imperturbably** *adv.*

im-per-vi-ous *adj.* incapable of being penetrated or affected **imperviously** *adv.*, **imperviousness** *n.*

im-pe-ti-go *n.* a contagious skin disease marked by pustules

im-pet-u-ous *adj.* marked by sudden action or emotion; impulsive **impetuosity** *n.*, **impetuously** *adv.*

im-pe-tus *n.* a driving force; an incitement; a stimulus; momentum

im-pi-e-ty *n.*, *pl.* -ies the quality of being impious; irreverence

im-pinge *v.* to strike or collide; to impact; to encroach **impingement** *n.*

im-pi-ous *adj.* not pious; irreverent; disrespectful **impiously** *adv.*

imp-ish *adj.* mischievous **impishly** *adv.*, **impishness** *n.*

im-pla-ca-ble *adj.* not capable of being placated or appeased **implacability** *n.*, **implacably** *adv.*

im-plant *v.* to set in firmly; to fix in the mind; to insert surgically **implant, implantation** *n.*

im-plau-si-ble *adj.* difficult to believe; unlikely **-bility** *n.*, **implausibly** *adv.*

im-ple-ment *n.* a utensil or tool *v.* to put into effect; to carry out; to furnish with implements **implementation** *n.*

im-pli-cate *v.* to involve, especially in illegal activity; to imply

im-pli-ca-tion *n.* the act of implicating or state of being implicated; the act of implying; an indirect expression; something implied

im-plic-it *adj.* contained in the nature of someone or something but not readily apparent; understood but not directly expressed; complete; absolute

im-plode *v.* to collapse or burst violently inward **implosion** *n.*

im-plore *v.* to appeal urgently to **implorer** *n.*, **imploringly** *adv.*

im-ply *v.* to involve by logical necessity; to express indirectly; to sug_est

im-po-lite *adj.* rude

im-pol-i-tic *adj.* not expedient; tactless

im-pon-der-a-ble *adj.* incapable of being weighed or evaluated precisely **imponderable** *n.*

im-port *v.* to bring in goods from a foreign country for trade or sale; to mean; to signify; to be significant *n.* something imported; meaning; significance; importance **importer** *n.*

im-por-tance *n.* the quality of being important; significance

im-por-tant *adj.* likely to determine or influence events; significant; having fame or authority **importantly** *adv.*

im-por-ta-tion *n.* the act or business of importing goods; something imported

im-por-tu-nate *adj.* persistent in pressing demands or requests -ly *adv.*

im-por-tune *v.* to press with repeated requests **importunity, importuner** *n.*

im-pose *v.* to enact or apply as compulsory; to obtrude or force oneself or a burden on another; to take unfair advantage; to palm off **imposition** *n.*

im-pos-ing *adj.* awesome; impressive **imposingly** *adv.*

im-pos-si-ble *adj.* not capable of existing or happening; unlikely to take place or be done; unacceptable; difficult to tolerate or deal with **impossibility** *n.*, **impossibly** *adv.*

im-post *n.* a tax or duty

im-pos-tor *or* **im-pos-ter** *n.* one who assumes a false identity or title for the purpose of deception

im-pos-ture *n.* deception by the assumption of a false identity

im-po-tent *adj.* without strength or vigor;

having no power; ineffectual; incapable of sexual intercourse impotence,impotency*n.*,impotently *adv.*

im-pound *v.* to confine in or as if in a pound; to seize and keep in legal custody; to hold water, as in a reservoir impoundment *n.*

im-pov-er-ish *v.* to make poor; to deprive or be deprived of natural richness or fertility impoverishment *n.*

im-prac-ti-ca-ble *adj.* incapable of being done or put into practice impracticableness, impracticability *n.*, impracticably *adv.*

im-prac-ti-cal *adj.* unwise to put into effect; unable to deal with practical or financial matters efficiently impracticality *n.*

im-pre-cise *adj.* not precise

im-preg-nate *v.* to make pregnant; to fertilize, as an ovum; to fill throughout; to saturate impregnation, -tor *n.*

im-pre-sa-ri-o *n.*, *pl.* -os a theatrical manager or producer, especially the director of an opera company

im-press *v.* to apply or produce with pressure; to stamp or mark with or as if with pressure; to fix firmly in the mind; to affect strongly and usually favorably *n.* the act of impressing; a mark made by impressing; a stamp or seal for impressing impressible *adj.*, impresser *n.*

im-pres-sion *n.* a mark or design made on a surface by pressure; an effect or feeling retained in the mind as a result of experience; an indistinct notion or recollection; a satiric or humorous imitation; the copies of a publication printed at one time

im-pres-sion-a-ble *adj.* easily influenced

im-pres-sion-ism *n.* a style of late nineteenth century painting in which the immediate appearance of scenes is depicted with unmixed primary colors applied in small strokes to simulate reflected light impressionist *n.*, impressionistic *adj.*

im-pres-sive *adj.* making a strong impression; striking impressively *adv.*, impressiveness *n.*

im-pri-ma-tur *n.* official permission to print or publish; authorization

im-print *v.* to make or impress a mark or design on a surface; to make or stamp a mark on; to fix firmly in the mind *n.* a mark or design made by imprinting; a lasting influence or effect; a publisher's name, often with the date and place of publication, printed at the bottom of a title page

im-pris-on *v.* to put in prison -ment *n.*

im-prob-a-ble *adj.* not likely to occur or be true improbability *n.*, -bly *adv.*

im-promp-tu *adj.* devised or performed without prior planning or preparation impromptu *adv.*

im-prop-er *adj.* unsuitable; indecorous; incorrect improperly *adv.*

improper fraction *n.* a fraction having a numerator larger than or the same as the denominator

im-pro-pri-e-ty *n.*, *pl.* -ies the quality or state of being improper; an improper act or remark

im-prove *v.* to make or become better; to increase something's productivity or value improvable *adj.*

im-prove-ment *n.* the act or process of improving or the condition of being improved; a change that improves

im-prov-i-dent *adj.* not providing for the future improvidence *n.*, improvidently *adv.*

im-pro-vise *v.* to make up, compose, or perform without preparation; to make from available materials improvisation, improviser, improvisator *n.*, improvisatory, improvisatorial *adj.*, -torially *adv.*

im-pru-dent *adj.* not prudent; unwise imprudence *n.*, imprudently *adv.*

im-pu-dent *adj.* marked by rude boldness or disrespect impudence *n.*, impudently *adv.*

im-pugn *v.* to attack as false; to cast doubt on

im-pulse *n.* a driving force or the motion produced by it; a sudden spontaneous urge; a motivating force; a general tendency *Physiol.* a transfer of energy from one neuron to another

im-pul-sive *adj.* acting on impulse rather than thought; resulting from impulse; uncalculated impulsively *adv.*, impulsiveness *n.*

im-pu-ni-ty *n.* exemption from punishment

im-pure *adj.* not pure; unclean; unchaste or obscene; mixed with another substance; adulterated; deriving from more than one source or style impurely *adv.*, impurity *n.*

im-pute *v.* to attribute something as a mistake, to another; to charge imputation *n.*

in *abbr.* inch

in ab-sen-tia *adv.* in the absence of

in-ac-ces-si-ble *adj.* not accessible inaccessibility *n.*, inaccessibly *adv.*

in-ac-tive *adj.* not active or inclined to be active; out of current use or service inactively *adv.*, inactivity, -ness *n.*

in-ad-e-quate *adj.* not adequate inadequacy *n.*, inadequately *adv.*

in-ad-ver-tent *adj.* unintentional; accidental; inattentive inadvertently *adv.*

in-al-ien-a-ble *adj.* not capable of being given up or transferred inalienably *adv.*, inalienability *n.*

in-ane *adj.* without sense or substance inanely *adv.*, inanity *n.*

in-an-i-mate *adj.* not having the qualities of life; not animated inanimately *adv.*, inanimateness *n.*

in-a-ni-tion *n.* exhaustion, especially from malnourishment

in-ap-pre-cia-ble *adj.* too slight to be significant inappreciably *adv.*

in-ar-tic-u-late *adj.* not uttering or forming intelligible words or syllables; unable to speak; speechless; unable to speak clearly or effectively; unexpressed inarticulately *adv.*, inarticulateness *n.*

in-as-much as *conj.* because of the fact that; since

in-au-gu-ral *adj.* of or for an inauguration

in-au-gu-rate *v.* to put into office with a formal ceremony; to begin officially inauguration, inaugurator *n.*

in--be-tween *adj.* intermediate *n.* an intermediate or intermediary in between *adv. & prep.* between

in-board *adj.* within a ship's hull; close to or near the fuselage of an aircraft

in-born *adj.* possessed at birth; natural; hereditary

in-bound *adj.* incoming

in-breed *v.* to produce by repeatedly breeding closely related individuals

inc *or* Inc *abbr.* income; increase; incorporated

in-cal-cu-la-ble *adj.* not calculable; indeterminate; unpredictable; very large

in-can-des-cent *adj.* giving off visible light when heated; shining brightly; ardently emotional or intense incandescence *n.*

incandescent lamp *n.*

a lamp in which a filament is heated to incandescence by an electric current

in-can-ta-tion *n.* a recitation of magic charms or spells; a magic formula for chanting or reciting

in-ca-pac-i-tate *v.* to render incapable; to disable; in law, to disqualify incapacitation *n.*

in-ca-pac-i-ty *n., pl.* -ies inadequate ability or strength; a defect; in law, a disqualification

in-car-cer-ate *v.* to place in jail incarceration *n.*

in-car-na-tion *n.* the act of incarnating or state of being incarnated; the embodiment of God in the human form of Jesus; one regarded as personifying a given abstract quality or idea

in-cen-di-ary *adj.* causing or capable of causing fires; of or relating to arson; tending to inflame; inflammatory incendiary *n.*

in-cense *v.* to make angry *n.* a substance, as a gum or wood, burned to produce a pleasant smell; the smoke or odor produced

in-cen-tive *n.* something inciting one to action or effort; a stimulus

in-cep-tion *n.* a beginning; an origin inceptive *adj.*

in-cer-ti-tude *n.* uncertainty; lack of confidence; instability

in-ces-sant *adj.* occurring without interruption; continuous incessantly *adv.*

in-cest *n.* sexual intercourse between persons so closely related that they are forbidden by law to marry incestuous *adj.*, incestuously *adv.*

inch *n.* a unit of measurement equal to 1/12th of a foot *v.* to move slowly

in-cho-ate *adj.* in an early stage; incipient -ly *adv.*, inchoateness *n.*

in-ci-dence *n.* the extent or rate of occurrence

in-ci-dent *n.* an event; an event that disrupts normal procedure or causes a crisis

in-ci-den-tal *adj.* occurring or likely to occur at the same time or as a result; minor; subordinate *n.* a minor attendant occurrence or condition incidentally *adv.*

in-cin-er-ate *v.* to burn up incineration *n.*

in-cin-er-a-tor *n.* one that incinerates; a furnace for burning waste

in-cip-i-ent *adj.* just beginning to appear or occur incipience *n.*, incipiently *adv.*

in-cise *v.* to make or cut into with a sharp tool; to carve into a surface; to engrave

in-ci-sion *n.* the act of incising; a cut or notch, especially a surgical cut

in-ci-sive *adj.* having or suggesting sharp

intellect; penetrating; cogent and effective; telling
incisively *adv.*, incisiveness *n.*

in-ci-sor *n.*

a cutting tooth at the front of the mouth
in-cite *v.* to provoke to action
incitement, inciter *n.*
in-clem-ent *adj.* stormy or rainy; unmerciful inclemency *n.*
in-cli-na-tion *n.* an attitude; a disposition; a tendency to act or think in a certain way; a preference; a bow or tilt; a slope
in-cline *v.* to deviate or cause to deviate from the horizontal or vertical; to slant; to dispose or be disposed; to bow or nod *n.* an inclined surface
in-clude *v.* to have as a part or member; to contain; to put into a group or total inclusion *n.*, inclusive *adj.*, -ly *adv.*
in-cog-ni-to *adv. & adj.* with one's identity hidden
in-co-her-ent *adj.* lacking order, connection, or harmony; unable to think or speak clearly or consecutively
incoherence *n.*, incoherently *adv.*
in-com-bus-ti-ble *adj.* incapable of burning incombustible *n.*
in-come *n.* money or its equivalent received in return for work or as profit from investments
income tax *n.* a tax on income earned by an individual or business
in-com-ing *adj.* coming in or soon to come in
in-com-men-su-rate *adj.* not commensurate; disproportionate; inadequate incommensurately *adv.*
in-com-mode *v.* to inconvenience; to disturb
in-com-mu-ni-ca-do *adv. & adj.* without being able to communicate with others
in-com-pa-ra-ble *adj.* incapable of being compared; without rival incomparably *adv.*
in-com-pat-i-ble *adj.* not suited for combination or association; inconsistent incompatibility *n.*, incompatibly *adv.*
in-com-pe-tent *adj.* not competent incompetence, incompetency, *n.*
in-com-plete *adj.* not complete incompletely *adv.*, incompleteness *n.*
in-con-gru-ous *adj.* not corresponding; disagreeing; made up of diverse or discordant elements; unsuited to the surrounding or setting
incongruity *n.*, incongruously *adv.*
in-con-se-quen-tial *adj.* without importance; petty inconsequentially *adv.*
in-con-sid-er-a-ble *adj.* unimportant; trivial inconsiderably *adv.*
in-con-sid-er-ate *adj.* not considerate; thoughtless inconsiderately *adv.*, inconsiderateness *n.*
in-con-sol-a-ble *adj.* not capable of being consoled inconsolably *adv.*
in-con-spic-u-ous *adj.* not readily seen or noticed inconspicuously *adv.*, inconspicuousness *n.*
in-con-stant *adj.* likely to change; unpredictable; faithless; fickle inconstancy *n.*, inconstantly *adv.*
in-con-ti-nent *adj.* not restrained; uncontrolled; unable to contain or restrain something specified; incapable of controlling the excretory functions incontinence *n.*, incontinently *adv.*
in-con-tro-vert-i-ble *adj.* unquestionable; indisputable incontrovertibly *adv.*
in-con-ven-ience *n.* the quality or state of being inconvenient; something inconvenient *v.* to cause inconvenience to; to bother
in-con-ven-ient *adj.* not convenient inconveniently *adv.*
in-cor-po-rate *v.* to combine into a unified whole; to unite; to form or cause to form a legal corporation; to give a physical form to; to embody incorporation, incorporator *n.*
in-cor-po-re-al *adj.* without material form or substance incorporeally *adv.*
in-cor-ri-gi-ble *adj.* incapable of being reformed or corrected incorrigibility, incorrigible *n.*, incorrigibly *adv.*
in-cor-rupt-i-ble *adj.* not capable of being corrupted morally; not subject to decay
incorruptibility *n.*, incorruptibly *adv.*
in-crease *v.* to make or become greater or larger; to have offspring; to reproduce *n.* the act of increasing; the amount or rate of increasing increasingly *adv.*
in-cred-i-ble *adj.* too unlikely to be believed; unbelievable; extraordinary; astonishing incredibility *n.*, incredibly *adv.*
in-cred-u-lous *adj.* skeptical; disbelieving; expressive of disbelief incredulity *n.*, incredulously *adv.*
in-cre-ment *n.* an increase; something gained or added, especially one of a series of regular additions

incremental *adj.*

in-crim-i-nate *v.* to involve in or charge with a wrongful act, as a crime incrimination *n.*, incriminatory *adj.*

in-cu-bate *v.* to warm and hatch eggs, as by bodily heat or artificial means; to maintain a bacterial culture in favorable conditions for growth incubation *n.*

in-cu-ba-tor *n.* a cabinet in which a desired temperature can be maintained, used for bacterial culture; an enclosure for maintaining a premature infant in a controlled environment; a temperature controlled enclosure for hatching eggs

in-cu-bus *n.*, *pl.* -buses *or* -bi an evil spirit believed to seize or harm sleeping persons; a nightmare; a nightmarish burden

in-cul-cate *v.* to impress on the mind by frequent repetition or instruction inculcation, inculcator *n.*

in-cul-pate *v.* to incriminate

in-cum-bent *adj.* lying or resting on something else; imposed as an obligation; obligatory; currently in office *n.* a person who is currently in office incumbency *n.*, incumbently *adv.*

in-cu-nab-u-lum *n.*, *pl.* -la a book printed before 1501

in-cur *v.* to become liable or subject to, especially because of one's own actions incurrence *n.*

in-cu-ri-ous *adj.* lacking interest; detached

in-cur-sion *n.* a sudden hostile intrusion into another's territory

in-cus *n.*, *pl.* incudes an anvil-shaped bone in the middle ear of mammals

in-debt-ed *adj.* obligated to another, as for money or a favor; beholden indebtedness *n.*

in-de-cent *adj.* morally offensive or contrary to good taste indecency *n.*, indecently *adv.*

in-de-ci-pher-a-ble *adj.* not capable of being deciphered or interpreted

in-de-ci-sion *n.* inability to make up one's mind; irresolution

in-de-ci-sive *adj.* without a clear-cut result; marked by indecision indecisively *adv.*, indecisiveness *n.*

in-dec-o-rous *adj.* lacking good taste or propriety indecorously *adv.*, indecorousness *n.*

in-deed *adv.* most certainly; without doubt; in reality; in fact *interj.* used to express surprise, irony, or disbelief

in-de-fat-i-ga-ble *adj.* tireless

indefatigably *adv.*

in-de-fin-a-ble *adj.* not capable of being defined indefinableness *n.*, indefinably *adv.*

in-def-i-nite *adj.* not decided or specified; vague; unclear; lacking fixed limits indefinitely *adv.*, -ness *n.*

in-del-i-ble *adj.* not able to be erased or washed away;permanent indelibly *adv.*

in-del-i-cate *adj.* lacking sensitivity; tactless indelicacy *n.*, indelicately *adv.*

in-dem-ni-fy *v.* to secure against hurt, loss, or damage; to make compensation for hurt, loss, or damage indemnification, indemnifier *n.*

in-dem-ni-ty *n.*, *pl.* -ties security against hurt, loss, or damage; a legal exemption from liability for damages; compensation for hurt, loss, or damage

in-dent *v.* to set in from the margin, as the first line of a paragraph; to notch the edge of; to serrate; to make a dent or depression in; to impress; to stamp *n.* an indentation

in-den-ta-tion *n.* the act of indenting or the state of being indented; an angular cut in an edge; a recess in a surface

in-den-ture *n.* a legal deed or contract; a contract obligating one party to work for another for a specified period of time *v.* to bind into the service of another

in-de-pend-ence *n.* the quality or state of being independent

in-de-pend-ent *adj.* politically self-governing; free from the control of others; not committed to a political party or faction; not relying on others, especially for financial support; providing or having enough income to enable one to live without working *n.* one who is independent, especially a candidate or voter not committed to a political party independently *adv.*

in-depth *adj.* thorough; detailed

in-de-scrib-a-ble *adj.* surpassing description; incapable of being described indescribably *adv.*

in-de-ter-mi-nate *adj.* not determined; not able to be determined; unclear or vague indeterminacy *n.*, indeterminately *adv.*

in-dex *n.*, *pl.* -dexes *or* -dices a list for aiding reference, especially an alphabetized listing in a printed work which gives the pages on which various names, places, and subjects are mentioned; something serving to guide or point out, especially a printed character calling attention to a paragraph or section; something that measures or indicates; a pointer, as in an instrument; in mathematics, a small number just above and to the left of a radical sign indicating what root is to be extracted; any number or symbol indicating an operation to be performed on a expression; a number or scale indicating change in magnitude, as of prices, relative to the magnitude at some specified point usually taken as one hundred (100) v. to provide with or enter in an index; to indicate; to adjust through

in-dex-a-tion n. the linkage of economic factors, as wages or prices, to a cost-of-living index so they rise and fall within the rate of inflation

in-dex fin-ger n.

the finger next to the thumb
in-dex of re-frac-tion n. the quotient of the speed of light in a vacuum divided by the speed of light in a medium under consideration

in-di-cate v. to point out; to show; to serve as a sign or symptom; to signify; to suggest the advisability of; to call for indication, **indicator** n.

in-dic-a-tive adj. serving to indicate; of or being a verb mood used to express actions and conditions that are objective facts n. the indicative mood; a verb in the indicative mood

in-dict v. to accuse of an offense; to charge; to make a formal accusation against by the findings of a grand jury **indictable** adj., **indictor, indictment** n.

in-dif-fer-ent adj. having no marked feeling or preference; impartial; neither good nor bad **indifference** n., **indifferently** adv.

in-dig-e-nous adj. living or occurring naturally in an area; native

in-di-gent adj. impoverished; needy **indigence** n.

in-di-ges-tion n. difficulty or discomfort in digesting food

in-dig-nant adj. marked by or filled with indignation **indignantly** adv.

in-dig-na-tion n. anger aroused by injustice, unworthiness, or unfairness

in-dig-ni-ty n., pl. -ies humiliating treatment; something that offends one's pride

in-di-go n., pl. -gos or -goes a blue dye

obtained from a plant or produced synthetically; a dark blue

in-di-go bunt-ing n. a small North American bird, the male of which has deep-blue plumage

in-di-go snake n. a non-venomous bluish-black snake found in the southern United States and northern Mexico

in-di-rect adj. not taking a direct course; not straight to the point **indirection** n., **indirectly** adv.

in-dis-creet adj. lacking discretion **indiscreetly** adv., **indiscretion** n.

in-dis-pen-sa-ble adj necessary; essential **indispensability, indispensable** n., **indispensably** adv.

in-dite v. to write; to compose; to put down in writing **inditer** n.

in-di-um n. a soft, silver-white, metallic element used for mirrors and transistor compounds, symbolized by In.

in-di-vid-u-al adj. of, for, or relating to a single human being **individually** adv.

in-di-vis-i-ble adj. not able to be divided

in-doc-tri-nate v. to instruct in a doctrine or belief; to train to accept a system of thought uncritically **indoctrination** n.

in-do-lent adj. disinclined to exert oneself; lazy **indolence** n.

in-dom-i-ta-ble adj. incapable of being subdued or defeated -**ably** adv.

in-du-bi-ta-ble adj. too evident to be doubted **indubitably** adv.

in-duce v. to move by persuasion or influence; to cause to occur; to infer by inductive reasoning **inducer** n.

in-duce-ment n. the act of inducing; something that induces

in-duct v. to place formally in office; to admit as a new member; to summon into military service **inductee** n.

in-duc-tance n. a circuit element, usually a conducting coil, in which electromagnetic induction generates electromotive force

in-duc-tion n. the act of inducting or of being inducted; reasoning in which conclusions are drawn from particular instances or facts; the generation of electromotive force in a closed circuit by a magnetic field that changes with time; the production of an electric charge in an uncharged body by bringing a charged body close to it

in-dulge v. to give in to the desires of, especially to excess; to yield to; to allow oneself a special pleasure -**ger** n.

in-dus-tri-al adj. of, relating to, or used in industry **industrially** adv.

in-dus-tri-ous *adj.* working steadily and hard; diligent
industriously *adv.*, **industriousness** *n.*

in-dus-try *n.*, *pl.* **-tries** the commercial production and sale of goods and services; a branch of manufacture and trade; industrial management as distinguished from labor; diligence

in-e-bri-ate *v.* to make drunk; to intoxicate **inebriated**,
inebriant *adj. & n.*, **inebriation** *n.*

in-ef-fa-ble *adj.* beyond expression; indescribable **ineffably** *adv.*

in-ef-fi-cient *adj.* wasteful of time, energy, or materials
inefficiency *n.*, **inefficiently** *adv.*

in-e-luc-ta-ble *adj.* not capable of being avoided or overcome **ineluctably** *adv.*

in-ept *adj.* awkward or incompetent; not suitable **ineptitude, ineptness** *n.*, **ineptly** *adv.*

in-e-qual-i-ty *n.*, *pl.* **-ies** the condition or an instance of being unequal; social or economic disparity; lack of regularity; in mathematics, an algebraic statement that a quantity is greater than or less than another quantity

in-eq-ui-ty *n.*, *pl.* **-ies** injustice; unfairness

in-ert *adj.* not able to move or act; slow to move or act; sluggish; displaying no chemical activity
inertly *adv.*, **inertness** *n.*

in-er-tia *n.* the tendency of a body to remain at rest or to stay in motion unless acted upon by an external force; resistance to motion or change
inertial *adj.*, **inertially** *adv.*

in-ev-i-ta-ble *adj.* not able to be avoided or prevented **inevitability** *n.*, **inevitably** *adv.*

in-ex-o-ra-ble *adj.* not capable of being moved by entreaty; unyielding
inexorably *adv.*

in-ex-pe-ri-ence *n.* lack of experience

in-ex-pli-ca-ble *adj.* not capable of being explained **inexplicably** *adv.*

in-ex-tre-mis *adv.* at the point of death

in-ex-tri-ca-ble *adj.* not capable of being untied or untangled; too complex to resolve **inextricably** *adv.*

in-fal-li-ble *adj.* not capable of making mistakes; not capable of failing; never wrong **infallibility** *n.*, **infallibly** *adv.*

in-fa-mous *adj.* having a very bad reputation; shocking or disgraceful
infamously *adv.*

in-fa-my *n.*, *pl.* **-ies** evil notoriety or reputation; the state of being infamous; a disgraceful, publicly known act

in-fan-cy *n.*, *pl.* **-ies** the condition or time of being an infant; an early stage of existence; in law, minority

in-fant *n.* a child in the first period of life; a very young child; in law, a minor

in-fan-ti-cide *n.* the killing of an infant

in-fan-tile *adj.* of or relating to infants or infancy; immature; childish

in-fan-tile pa-ra-ly-sis *n.* poliomyelitis

in-fan-try *n.*, *pl.* **-ies** the branch of an army made up of soldiers who are trained to fight on foot **infantryman** *n.*

in-farct *n.* an area of dead tissue caused by an insufficient supply of blood
infarcted *adj.*, **infarction** *n.*

in-fat-u-ate *v.* to arouse an extravagant or foolish love in
infatuated *adj.*, **infatuation** *n.*

in-fect *v.* to contaminate with disease-causing microorganisms; to transmit a disease to; to affect as if by contagion **infective** *adj.*

in-fec-tion *n.* invasion of a bodily part by disease-causing microorganisms; the condition resulting from such an invasion; an infectious disease

in-fe-lic-i-tous *adj.* not happy; unfortunate; not apt, as in expression
infelicity *n.*, **infelicitously** *adv.*

in-fer *v.* to conclude by reasoning; to deduce; to have as a logical consequence; to lead to as a result or conclusion **inferable** *adj.*

in-fer-ence *n.* a conclusion based on facts and premises

in-fe-ri-or *adj.* located under or below; low or lower in order, rank, or quality **inferior, inferiority** *n.*

in-fer-nal *adj.* of, like, or relating to hell; damnable; abominable **infernally** *adv.*

in-fer-no *n.* a place or condition suggestive of hell

in-fest *v.* to spread in or over so as to be harmful or offensive **infestation** *n.*

in-fi-del *n.* one who has no religion; an unbeliever in a religion, especially Christianity

in-field *n.* in baseball, the part of a playing field within the base lines
infielder *n.*

in-fil-trate *v.* to pass or cause to pass into something through pores or small openings; to pass through or enter gradually or stealthily **infiltration** *n.*

in-fi-nite *adj.* without boundaries; limitless; immeasurably great or large; in mathematics, greater in value than any specified number, however large; having measure that is infinite

infinite *n.*, infinitely *adv.*

in-fin-i-tes-i-mal *adj.* immeasurably small infinitesimally *adv.*

in-fin-i-ty *n.*, *pl.* -ies the quality or state of being infinite; unbounded space, time, or amount; an indefinitely large number

in-firm *adj.* physically weak, especially from age; feeble; not sound or valid

in-fir-ma-ry *n.*, *pl.* -ries an institution for the care of the sick or disabled

in-flame *v.* to set on fire; to arouse to strong or excessive feeling; to intensify; to produce, affect or be affected by inflammation

in-flam-ma-ble *adj.* tending to catch fire easily; easily excited

in-flam-ma-tion *n.* localized redness, swelling, heat, and pain in response to an injury or infection

in-flate *v.* to fill and expand with a gas; to increase unsoundly; to puff up; to raise prices abnormally inflatable *adj.*

in-fla-tion *n.* the act or process of inflating; a period during which there is an increase in the monetary supply, causing a continuous rise in the price of goods

in-flect *v.* to turn; to veer; to vary the tone or pitch of the voice, especially in speaking; to change the form of a word to indicate number, tense, or person inflective *adj.*, inflection *n.*

in-flex-i-ble *adj.* not flexible; rigid; not subject to change; unalterable inflexibility *n.*, inflexibly *adv.*

in-flict *v.* to cause to be suffered; to impose inflicter, inflictor, -tion *n.*

in-flo-res-cence *n.*

a characteristic arrangement of flowers on a stalk inflorescent *adj.*

in-flu-ence *n.* the power to produce effects, especially indirectly or through an intermediary; the condition of being affected; one exercising indirect power to sway or affect *v.* to exert influence over; to modify influential *adj.*

in-flu-en-za *n.* an acute, infectious viral disease marked by respiratory inflammation, fever, muscular pain, and often intestinal discomfort; the flu

in-flux *n.* a stream of people or things coming in

in-form-ant *n.* one who discloses or furnishes information which should remain secret

in-for-ma-tive *adj.* providing information; instructive

in-frac-tion *n.* a violation of a rule

in-fra-red *adj.* of, being, or using electromagnetic radiation with wave lengths longer than those of visible light and shorter than those of microwaves

in-fra-son-ic *adj.* producing or using waves or vibrations with frequencies below that of audible sound

in-fra-struc-ture *n.* an underlying base or foundation; the basic facilities needed for the functioning of a system

in-fringe *v.* to break a law; to violate; to encroach; to trespass infringement *n.*

in-fu-ri-ate *v.* to make very angry or furious; to enrage infuriatingly *adv.*, infuriation *n.*

in-fuse *v.* to introduce, instill or inculcate, as principles; to obtain a liquid extract by soaking a substance in water infusion *n.*

-ing *suff* used in forming the present participle of verbs and adjectives resembling participles; activity or action; the result or a product of an action

in-gen-ious *adj.* showing great ingenuity; to have inventive ability; clever ingeniously *adv.*, ingeniousness *n.*

in-ge-nu-i-ty *n.*, *pl.* -ies cleverness; inventive skill

in-gen-u-ous *adj.* frank and straightforward; lacking sophistication

in-gest *v.* to take or put food into the body by swallowing ingestion *n.*, ingestive *adj.*

in-gle-nook *n.* a recessed area or corner near or beside a fireplace

in-glo-ri-ous *adj.* not showing courage or honor; dishonorable ingloriously *adv.*

in-got *n.* a mass of cast metal shaped in a bar or block

in-grain *v.* to impress firmly on the mind or nature *n.* fiber or yarn that is dyed before being spun or woven

in-grained *adj.* to be worked into the inmost texture; deep-seated

in-grate *n.* a person who is ungrateful

in-gra-ti-ate *v.* to gain favor or confidence of others by deliberate effort or manipulation ingratiatingly *adv.*, ingratiation *n.*, ingratiatory *adj.*

in-grat-i-tude *n.* lack of gratitude

in-gre-di-ent *n.* an element that enters into the composition of a mixture; a part of anything

in-gress *n.* a going in or entering of a building ingression *n.*, ingressive *adj.*

in-grown *adj.* growing into the flesh;

growing abnormally within or into
in-grow-ing adj.

in-gui-nal adj., Anat. of, pertaining to, or
located in the groin

in-hab-it v. to reside in; to occupy as a
home **inhabitability, inhabiter,**
inhabitation n., **inhabitable** adj.

in-hab-i-tant n. a person who resides
permanently, as distinguished from a
visitor

in-ha-la-tion n. the act of inhaling

in-ha-la-tor n. a device that enables a
person to inhale air, anesthetics, medicated vapors, or other matter

in-hale v. to breathe or draw into the
lungs, as air or tobacco smoke; the
opposite of exhale **inhalation** n.

in-hal-er n. one that inhales; a respirator

in-here v. To be an essential or permanent feature; to belong

in-her-ent adj. forming an essential element or quality of something
inherently adv.

in-her-it v. to receive something, as
property, money, or other valuables,
by legal succession or will Biol. to
receive traits or qualities from one's
ancestors or parents **inheritable** adj.,
inheritor n.

in-her-i-tance n. the act of inheriting;
that which is inherited or to be inherited by legal transmission to a heir

in-her-i-tance tax n. a tax imposed on an
inherited estate

in-hib-it v. to restrain or hold back; to
prevent full expression
inhibitable adj., **inhibitor,**
inhibiter n., **inhibitive, inhibitory** adj.

in-hi-bi-tion n. the act of restraining,
especially a self-imposed restriction on
one's behavior; a mental or psychological restraint

in--house adj. of, relating to, or carried
on within an organization

in-hu-man adj. lacking pity, emotional
warmth, or kindness; monstrous; not
being of the ordinary human type
inhumanly adv.

in-hu-mane adj. lacking compassion or
pity; cruel **inhumanely** adv.

in-hu-man-i-ty n., pl. -ties the lack of
compassion or pity; an inhumane or
cruel act

in-im-i-cal adj. harmful opposition; hostile; malign **inimically** adv.

in-im-i-ta-ble adj. incapable of being
matched; unique **inimitably** adv.

in-iq-ui-ty n., pl. -ies the grievous violation of justice; wickedness; sinfulness
iniquitous adj.

in-i-tial adj. of or pertaining to the
beginning n. the first letter of a name
or word v. to mark or sign with initials
initially adv.

in-i-ti-ate v. to begin or start; to admit
someone to membership in an organization, fraternity, or group; to instruct in fundamentals adj. **initiated**
initiator n., **initiatory** adj.

in-i-ti-a-tive n. the ability to originate or
follow through with a plan of action;
the action of taking the first or leading
step Govt. the power or right to
propose legislative measures

in-ject v. to force a drug or fluid into the
body through a blood vessel or the
skin with a hypodermic syringe; to
throw in or introduce a comment
abruptly **injection** n.

in-junc-tion n. an authoritative command or order; in law, a court order
requiring the party to do or to refrain
from some specified action -tive adj.

in-jure v. to cause physical harm,
damage, or pain

in-ju-ri-ous adj. causing injury, damage
or hurt; slanderous; abusive
injuriously adv., **injuriousness** n.

in-ju-ry n., pl. -ies damage or harm in-
flicted or suffered

in-jus-tice n. the violation of another
person's rights; an unjust act; a wrong

ink n. any of variously colored liquids or
paste, used for writing, drawing, and
printing **inker** n.

ink-horn n. a small container to hold ink

ink-ling n. a slight suggestion or hint; a
vague idea or notion

ink-stand n. a stand or device for holding writing tools and ink

ink-well n. a small container or reservoir
for holding ink

ink-y adj. resembling ink in color; dark;
black; containing or pertaining to ink

in-laid adj. ornamented with wood,
ivory, or other materials embedded
flush with the surface

in-land adj. pertaining to or located in
the interior of a country **inlander** n.

in--law n. a relative by marriage

in-lay v. to set or embed something, as
gold or ivory, into the surface of a
decorative design

in-let n. a bay or stream that leads into
land; a passage between nearby is-
lands

in-mate n. a person who dwells in a
building with another; one confined in
a prison, asylum, or hospital

inn n. a place of lodging where a traveler

may obtain meals and/or lodging

in-nards *pl. n., Slang* the internal organs or parts of the body; the inner parts of a machine

in-nate *adj.* inborn and not acquired; having as an essential part; inherent **innately** *adv.*

in-ner *adj.* situated or occurring farther inside; relating to or of the mind or spirit

in-ner ear *n.* the part of the ear which includes the semicircular canals, vestibule, and cochlea

in-ner-most *adj.* most intimate; farthest within

in-ner tube *n.* a flexible, inflatable rubber tube placed inside a tire

in-ning *n.* in baseball, one of nine divisions of a regulation baseball game, in which each team has a turn at bat

innings *pl.* in the game of cricket, the time or period during which one side bats

inn-keep-er *n.* the proprietor or manager of an inn

in-no-cent *adj.* free from sin, evil, or moral wrong; pure; legally free from blame or guilt; not maliciously intended; lacking in experience or knowledge; naive **innocence, innocent** *n.*, **innocently** *adv.*

in-noc-u-ous *adj.* having no harmful qualities or ill effect; harmless

in-nom-i-nate bone *n., Anat.* one of the two large, irregular bones which form the sides of the pelvis

in-no-vate *v.* to introduce or begin something new **innovative** *adj.*, **innovator** *n.*

in-nu-en-do *n., pl.* -dos or -does an indirect or oblique comment, suggestion or hint

in-nu-mer-a-ble *adj.* too numerous or too much to be counted; countless

in-oc-u-late *v.* to introduce a mild form of a disease or virus to a person or animal in order to produce immunity **inoculation** *n.*

in-op-er-a-ble *adj.* unworkable; incapable of being treated or improved by surgery

in-op-er-a-tive *adj.* not working; not functioning

in-op-por-tune *adj.* inappropriate; untimely; unsuitable **inopportunely** *adv.*, **inopportuneness** *n.*

in-or-di-nate *adj.* exceeding proper or normal limits; not regulated; unrestrained **inordinately** *adv.*

in-or-gan-ic *adj.* not having or involving living organisms, their remains, or products

in-pa-tient *n.* a patient admitted to a hospital for medical treatment

in-put *n.* the amount of energy delivered to a machine; in computer science, information that is put into a data-processing system *Elect.* the voltage, current, or power that is delivered to a circuit

in-quest *n.* a legal investigation into the cause of death

in-quire *v.* to ask a question; to make an investigation **inquirer** *n.*, **inquiringly** *adv.*

in-quir-y *n., pl.* -ies the act of seeking or inquiring; a request or question for information; a very close examination; an investigation or examination of facts or evidence

in-qui-si-tion *n.* a former Roman Catholic tribunal established to seek out and punish heretics; an interrogation that violates individual rights; an investigation **inquisitor** *n.*, **inquisitorial** *adj.*

in-quis-i-tive *adj.* curious; probing; questioning **inquisitively** *adv.*, **inquisitiveness** *n.*

in-sane *adj.* afflicted with a serious mental disorder impairing a person's ability to function; the characteristic of a person who is not sane **insanely** *adv.*, **insanity** *n.*

in-san-i-tar-y *adj.* not sanitary; not hygienic and dangerous to one's health

in-scribe *v.* to write, mark, or engrave on a surface; to enter a name in a register or on a formal list; to write a short note on a card *Geom.* to enclose one figure in another so that the latter encloses the former **inscriber** *n.*

in-scru-ta-ble *adj.* difficult to interpret or understand; incomprehensible **-bility, inscrutableness** *n.*, **inscrutably** *adv.*

in-sect *n., Zool.* any of a numerous cosmopolitan class of small to minute winged invertebrate animals with 3 pairs of legs, a segmented body, and usually 2 pairs of wings

in-sec-ti-cide *n.* a substance for killing insects

in-sec-tiv-o-rous *adj.* feeding on insects

in-se-cure *adj.* troubled by anxiety and apprehension; threatened; not securely guarded; unsafe; liable to break, fail, or collapse **insecurely** *adv.*, **insecurity** *n.*

in-sem-i-nate *v.* to introduce semen into the uterus of; to make pregnant; to sow seed **insemination, inseminator** *n.*

in-sen-sate *adj.* showing a lack of humane feeling; unconscious

in-sen-si-ble *adj.* deprived of consciousness; unconscious; incapable of perceiving or feeling; unmindful; unaware **insensibility** *n.*, **insensibly** *adv.*

in-sen-ti-ent *adj.* without sensation or consciousness **insentience** *n.*

in-sep-a-ra-ble *adj.* incapable of being separated or parted **inseparability** *n.*, **inseparably** *adv.*

in-sert *v.* to put in place; to set *n.* in printing, something inserted or to be inserted **insertion** *n.*

in-set *v.* to set in; to implant; to insert

in-shore *adj.* near or moving toward the shore **inshore** *adv.*

in-side *n.* the part, surface, or space that lies within **insides** *n.* The internal parts or organs

in-sid-er *n.* one having special knowledge or access to confidential information

in-sid-i-ous *adj.* cunning or deceitful; treacherous; seductive; attractive but harmful **insidiously** *adv.*, **invidiousness** *n.*

in-sight *n.* perception into the true or hidden nature of things **insightful** *adj.*, **insightfully** *adv.*

in-sig-ni-a *n.*, *pl.* -**nia** or -**nias** a badge or emblem used to mark membership, honor, or office

in-sin-cere *adj.* not sincere; hypocritical **insincerely** *adv.*, **insincerity** *n.*

in-sin-u-ate *v.* to suggest something by giving a hint; to introduce by using ingenious and sly means **insinuating** *adv.*, **insinuation** *n.*

in-sip-id *adj.* lacking of flavor; tasteless; flat; dull; lacking interest **insipidly** *adv.*, **insipidness** *n.*

in-sist *v.* to demand or assert in a firm way; to dwell on something repeatedly, as to emphasize **insistence** *n.*, **insistent** *adj.*, **insistently** *adv.*

in-so-far *adv.* to such an extent

in-sole *n.* the fixed inside sole of a shoe or boot; a removable strip of material put inside a shoe for protection or comfort

in-sol-u-ble *adj.* incapable of being dissolved; not soluble; not capable of being solved **insolubility, insolubleness** *n.*, **insolubly** *adv.*

in-sol-vent *adj.* in law, unable to meet debts; bankrupt

in-som-ni-a *n.* the chronic inability to sleep **insomniac** *n.*

in-sou-ci-ant *adj.* lighthearted and cheerful; unconcerned; not bothered **insouciance** *n.*

in-spect *v.* to examine or look at very carefully for flaws; to examine or review officially -**ion**, **inspector** *n.*

in-spi-ra-tion *n.* the stimulation within the mind of some idea, feeling, or impulse which leads to creative action; a divine or holy presence which inspires; the act of inhaling air **inspirational** *adj.*, **inspirationally** *adv.*

in-spire *v.* to exert or guide by a divine influence; to arouse and create high emotion; to exalt; to inhale; breathe in **inspirer** *n.*, **inspiringly** *adv.*

inst *abbr.* instant; institute; institution

in-sta-bil-i-ty *n.*, *pl.* -**ties** lacking stability

in-stall *or* **in-stal** *v.* to put in position for service; to place into an office or position; to settle **installation, installer** *n.*

in-stall-ment *or* **in-stal-ment** *n.* one of several payments due in specified amounts at specified intervals

in-stance *n.* an illustrative case or example; a step in proceedings *v.* to illustrate

in-stant *n.* a very short time; a moment; a certain or specific point in time *adj.* instantaneously; immediate; urgent

in-stan-ta-ne-ous *adj.* happening with no delay; instantly; completed in a moment **instantaneously** *adv.*

in-stant-ly *adv.* immediately; at once

in-stead *adv.* in lieu of that just mentioned

in-step *n.*, *Anat.*

the arched upper part of the human foot

in-sti-gate *v.* to urge forward; to stir up; to foment; to provoke **instigation, instigator** *n.*

in-still *or* **in-stil** *v.* to introduce by gradual instruction or effort; to pour in slowly by drops **instillation, instiller** *n.*

in-stinct *n.* the complex and normal tendency or response of a given species to act in ways essential to its existence, development, and survival -**tive**, **instinctual** *adj.*, **instinctively** *adv.*

in-sti-tute *v.* to establish or set up; to find; to initiate; to set in operation; to start *n.* an organization set up to promote or further a cause; an institution for educating

in-sti-tu-tion *n.* the principle custom that forms part of a society or civilization;

an organization which performs a particular job or function, such as research, charity, or education; a place of confinement such as a prison or mental hospital **institutionalize** *v.*, **institutional** *adj.*, **institutionally** *adv.*

in-struct *v.* to impart skill or knowledge; to teach; to give orders or direction **instructive** *adj.*

in-struc-tion *n.* The act of teaching or instructing; important knowledge; a lesson; an order or direction

in-struc-tor *n.* one who instructs; a teacher; a low-rank college teacher, not having tenure **instructorship, instructress** *n.*

in-stru-ment *n.* a mechanical tool or implement; a device used to produce music; a person who is controlled by another; a dupe; in law, a formal legal document, deed, or contract

in-stru-men-tal *adj.* acting or serving as a means; pertaining to, composed for, or performed on a musical instrument **instrumentally** *adv.*

in-stru-men-tal-ist *n.* a person who plays or performs with a musical instrument

in-stru-men-tal-i-ty *n., pl.* -ies anything that serves to accomplish a purpose; means or agency

in-stru-men-ta-tion *n.* the use of instruments or work performed with instruments *Mus.* the arrangement of music for instruments

in-sub-or-di-nate *adj.* not obedient; not obeying orders **insubordinately** *adv.*, **insubordination** *n.*

in-sub-stan-tial *adj.* unreal; imaginary; not solid or firm; flimsy **insubstantiality** *n.*

in-suf-fi-cient *adj.* inadequate; not enough **insufficiently** *adv.*, **insufficiency** *n.*

in-su-lar *adj.* of or related to an island; typical or suggestive of life on an island; narrow-minded; limited in customs, opinions, and ideas **insularity** *n.*

in-su-late *v.* to isolate; to wrap or surround with nonconducting material in order to prevent the passage of heat, electricity, or sound into or out of; to protect with wrapping or insulation **insulation, insulator** *n.*

in-su-lin *n., Biochem.* the hormone released by the pancreas, essential in regulating the metabolism of sugar; a preparation of this hormone removed from the pancreas of a pig or an ox, used in the treatment of diabetes

in-sult *v.* to speak or to treat with insolence or contempt; to abuse verbally *n.* an act or remark that offends someone **insulter** *n.*, **insulting** *adj.*, **insultingly** *adv.*

in-su-per-a-ble *adj.* insurmountable; not able to be overcome **insuperability** *n.*, **insuperably** *adv.*

in-sur-ance *n.* protection against risk, loss, or ruin; the coverage an insurer guarantees to pay in the event of death, loss, or medical bills; a contract guaranteeing such protection on future specified losses in return for annual payments; any safeguard against risk or harm **insurability** *n.*, -able *adj.*

in-sure *v.* to guarantee against loss of life, property, or other types of losses; to make certain; to ensure; to buy or issue insurance **insurability** *n.*, **insurable** *adj.*

in-sured *n.* a person protected by an insurance policy

in-sur-er *n.* the person or company which insures someone against loss or damage

in-sur-mount-a-ble *adj.* incapable of being overcome **insurmountably** *adv.*

in-sur-rec-tion *n.* an open revolt against an established government **insurrectional** *adj.*, **insurrectionist** *n* **insurrectionary** *adj. & n.*,

in-sus-cep-ti-ble *adj.* immune; incapable of being infected **insusceptibility** *n.*

in-tact *adj.* remaining whole and not damaged in any way **intactness** *n.*

in-take *n.* the act of taking in or absorbing; the amount or quantity taken in or absorbed

in-tan-gi-ble *adj.* incapable of being touched; vague or indefinite to the mind **intangibility, intangibleness** *n.*, **intangibly** *adv.*

in-te-ger *n.* any of the numbers 1, 2, 3, etc., including all the positive whole numbers and all the negative numbers and zero; a whole entity

in-te-gral *adj.* being an essential and indispensable part of a whole; made up, from, or formed of parts that constitute a unity

in-te-grate *v.* to make into a whole by joining parts together; to unify; to be open to people of all races or ethnic groups **integration** *n.*, **integrative** *adj.*

in-teg-ri-ty *n.* uprightness of character; honesty; the condition, quality, or state of being complete or undivided

in-tel-lect *n.* the power of the mind to understand and to accept knowledge; the state of having a strong or brilliant mind; a person of notable intellect

in-tel-lec-tu-al *adj.* pertaining to, possessing, or showing intellect; inclined to rational or creative thought *n.* a person who pursues and enjoys matters of the intellect and of refined taste intellectuality *n.*, intellectually *adv.*

in-tel-lec-tu-al-ize *v.* to examine objectively so as not to become emotionally involved intellectualization, intellectualizer *n.*

in-tel-li-gence *n.* the capacity to perceive and comprehend meaning; information; news; the gathering of secret information, as by military or police authorities; information so collected

in-tel-li-gent *adj.* having or showing intelligence intelligently *adv.*

in-tel-li-gi-ble *adj.* having the capabilities of being understood; understanding

in-tend *v.* to have a plan or purpose in mind; to design for a particular use intended *adj.*

in-tense *adj.* extreme in strength, effect, or degree; expressing strong emotion, concentration, or strain; profound intensely *adv.*, intenseness *n.*

in-ten-si-fy *v.* to become or make more intense or acute intensification *n.*

in-ten-si-ty *n.*, *pl.* -ies the quality of being intense or acute; a great effect, concentration, or force

in-ten-sive *adj.* forceful and concentrated; marked by a full and complete application of all resources intensively *adv.*

intensive care *n.* the hospital care provided for a gravely ill patient in specially designed rooms with monitoring devices and life-support systems

in-tent *n.* a purpose, goal, aim, or design intently *adv.*, intentness *n.*

in-ten-tion *n.* a plan of action; purpose, either immediate or ultimate

in-ten-tion-al *adj.* deliberately intended or done -lity *n.*, intentionally *adv.*

in-ter *v.* to place in a grave; bury interment *n.*

inter- *pref.* mutually; with each other; together; among or between

in-ter-act *v.* to act on each other or with each other interaction *n.*, interactive *adj.*

in-ter-breed *v.* to crossbreed; to breed together two different species

in-ter-cede *v.* to argue or plead on another's behalf interceder *n.*

in-ter-cept *v.* to interrupt the path or course of; to seize or stop intercept, interception *n.*

in-ter-cep-tor *or* **in-ter-cept-er** *n.* one who or that which intercepts; a fighter plane designed for the pursuit and interception of enemy aircraft

in-ter-ces-sion *n.* an entreaty or prayer on behalf of others intercessor *n.*, intercessional, intercessory *adj.*

in-ter-change *v.* to put each in the place of another; to give and receive in return *n.* the intersection of a highway which allows traffic to enter or turn off without obstructing other traffic interchangeable *adj.*, interchanger *n.*

in-ter-col-le-gi-ate *adj.* involving or pertaining to two or more colleges

in-ter-com *n.*, *Informal* a two-way communication system, as used in different areas of a home or business

in-ter-com-mu-ni-cate *v.* to communicate with each other -tion *n.*, intercommunicative *adj.*

in-ter-con-ti-nen-tal *adj.* pertaining to or involving two or more continents

in-ter-course *n.* mutual exchange between persons or groups; communication; sexual intercourse

in-ter-dict *v.* to forbid or prohibit by official decree interdiction *n.*, interdictor *n.*, interdictory *adj.*

in-ter-est *n.* curiosity or concern about something; that which is to one's benefit; legal or financial right, claim, or share, as in a business; a charge for a loan of money, usually a percent of the amount borrowed

in-ter-est-ed *adj.* having or displaying curiosity; having a right to share in something interestedly *adv.*

in-ter-est-ing *adj.* stimulating interest, attention, or curiosity interesting *adv.* interestingness *n.*

in-ter-face *n.* a surface forming a common boundary between adjacent areas; in computer science, the software or hardware connecting one device or system to another interface *v.*, interfacial *adj.*

in-ter-fere *v.* to come between; to get in the way; to be an obstacle or obstruction interference *n.*

in-ter-ga-lac-tic *adj.* between galaxies

in-ter-im *n.* a time between events or periods *adj.* temporary.

in-te-ri-or *adj.* of, or contained in the inside; inner; away from the coast or border; inland; private; not exposed to view

in-ter-ject *v.* to go between other parts or elements; to add something between other things interjector *n.*,

interjectory *adj.*
in-ter-jec-tion *n.* a word used as an ex-clamation to express emotion, as *Oh! Heavens! Super!* **interjectional** *adj.*
in-ter-lace *v.* to join by weaving together; to intertwine; to blend
in-ter-lin-e-ar *adj.* situated or inserted between lines of a text
in-ter-lock *v.* to join closely
in-ter-loc-u-tor *n.* one who takes part in a conversation
in-ter-loc-u-to-ry *adj.* having the nature of a dialogue; in law, pronounced while a suit is pending and tem-porarily in effect
in-ter-lope *v.* to intrude or interfere in the rights of others
in-ter-lude *n.* a period of time that oc-curs in and divides some longer process; light entertainment between the acts of a show, play, or other more serious entertainment
in-ter-mar-ry *v.* to marry someone who is not a member of one's own religion, class, race, or ethnic group
intermarriage *n.*
in-ter-me-di-ar-y *n., pl.* -ies a mediator *adj.* coming between; intermediate
in-ter-me-di-ate *adj.* situated or occur-ring in the middle or between
intermediately *adv.,***intermediateness** *n.*
in-ter-min-gle *v.* to blend or become mixed together
in-ter-mis-sion *n.* a temporary interval of time between events or activities; the pause in the middle of a performance
in-ter-mit-tent *adj.* ceasing from time to time; coming at intervals
in-tern *or* **in-terne** *n.* a medical school graduate undergoing supervised prac-tical training in a hospital *v.* to con-fine, as in wartime
internment, internship *n.*
in-ter-nal *adj.* of or pertaining to the in-side; pertaining to the domestic affairs of a country; intended to be consumed by the body from the inside
in-ter-nal--com-bus-tion en-gine *n.* an engine in which fuel is burned inside the engine
in-ter-nal med-i-cine *n.* the branch of medicine that studies and treats the nonsurgical diseases
in-ter-na-tion-al *adj.* pertaining to or in-volving two or more nations
internationally *adv.*
in-ter-na-tion-al-ism *n.* the policy of cooperation among nations where politics and economics are concerned
internationalist *n.*

in-ter-nec-ine *adj.* mutually destructive to both sides; involving struggle within a group
in-tern-ee *n.* a person who is confined or interned
in-ter-nist *n.* a physician who is a specialist in internal medicine
in-ter-play *n.* action, movement, or in-fluence between or among people
interplay *v.*
in-ter-po-late *v.* to insert between other things or elements; to change some-thing by introducing additions or in-sertions **interpolation,**
interpolator *n.*
in-ter-pose *v.* to put between parts; to put in or inject a comment into a con-versation or speech; to intervene
interposer, interposition *n.*
in-ter-pret *v.* to convey the meaning of something by explaining or restating; to present the meaning of something, as in a picture; to take words spoken or written in one language and put them into another language -**able** *adj.,* **interpretation, interpreter** *n.*
in-ter-pre-ta-tive *or* **in-ter-pre-tive** *adj.* of or based on interpreting; to provide an interpretation **interpretatively** *adv.*
in-ter-ra-cial *adj.* between, among, or af-fecting different races
in-ter-reg-num *n., pl.* -nums *or* -na an in-terval between two successive reigns; a break in continuity
in-ter-re-late *v.* to have or to put into a mutual relationship
interrelation, interrelationship *n.*
in-ter-ro-gate *v.* to question formally
interrogation, interrogator *n.*
in-ter-rog-a-tive *adj.* asking or having the nature of a question *n.* a word used to ask a question **interrogatively** *adv.*
in-ter-rupt *v.* to break the continuity of something; to intervene abruptly while someone else is speaking or perform-ing **interrupter,**
interruption *n.,* **interruptive** *adj.*
in-ter-scho-las-tic *adj.* conducted be-tween or among schools
in-ter-sect *v.* to divide by cutting through or across; to form an intersection; to cross
in-ter-sec-tion *n.* a place of crossing; a place where streets or roads cross; in mathematics, the point common to two or more geometric elements
in-ter-sperse *v.* to scatter among other things **interspersion** *n.*
in-ter-state *adj.* between, involving, or among two or more states

in-ter-stel-lar *adj.* among or between the stars

in-ter-stice *n.* the small space between things **interstitial** *adj.*

in-ter-twine *v.* to unite by twisting together **intertwinement** *n.*

in-ter-ur-ban *adj.* between or among connecting urban areas

in-ter-val *n.* the time coming between two points or objects; a period of time between events or moments *Mus.* the difference in pitch between two tones

in-ter-vene *v.* to interfere or take a decisive role so as to modify or settle something; to interfere with force in a conflict **intervention** *n.*

in-ter-view *n.* a conversation conducted by a reporter to elicit information from someone; a conversation led by an employer who is trying to decide whether to hire someone **interview** *v.*, **interviewer** *n.*

in-ter-weave *v.* to weave together; to intertwine

in-tes-tate *adj.* having made no valid will; not disposed of by a will **intestacy** *n.*

in-tes-tine or **in-tes-tines** n. *Anat.*

the section of the alimentary canal from the stomach to the anus **intestinal** *adj.*, **intestinally** *adv.*

in-ti-mate *adj.* characterized by close friendship or association **intimately** *adv.*, **intimacy**, **-ness** *n.*

in-tim-i-date *v.* to make timid or fearful; to frighten; to discourage or suppress by threats or by violence **intimidation**, **intimidator** *n.*

in-to *prep.* to the inside of; to a form or condition of; to a time in the midst of

in-tol-er-a-ble *adj.* not tolerable; unbearable **intolerability**, **intolerableness** *n.*, **intolerably** *adv.*

in-tol-er-ant *adj.* not able to endure; not tolerant of the rights or beliefs of others **intolerance** *n.*, **intolerantly** *adv.*

in-to-na-tion *n.* the manner of speaking, especially the meaning and melody given to speech by changing levels of pitch

in-tone *v.* to utter or recite in a monotone; to chant **intoner** *n.*

in to *adv.*, *L.* totally

in-tox-i-cate *v.* to make drunk; to elate or excite **intoxicant**, **intoxication** *n.*

intra- *prefix* within

in-tra-cel-lu-lar *adj.* within a cell or cells

in-tra-cra-ni-al *adj.* within the skull

in-trac-ta-ble *adj.* hard to manage; difficult to cure or treat

in-tra-dos *n.*, *pl.* **-dos** or **-doses** the interior curve of an arch or vault

in-tra-mu-ral *adj.* taking place within a school, college, or institution; competition limited to a school community

in-tra-mus-cu-lar *adj.* within a muscle

in-tran-si-gent *adj.* refusing to moderate a position; uncompromising **intransigence**, **intransigency**, **intransigent** *n.*

in-tra-oc-u-lar *adj.* within the eyeball

in-tra-state *adj.* within a state

in-tra-u-ter-ine *adj.* within the uterus

in-tra-u-ter-ine de-vice *n.* a metal or plastic loop, ring, or spiral inserted into the uterus as a means of contraception

in-tra-ve-nous *adj.* within a vein **intravenously** *adv.*

in-trep-id *adj.* courageous; unshaken by fear; bold **intrepidly** *adv.*, **intrepidness** *n.*

in-tri-cate *adj.* having many perplexingly entangled parts or elements; complex; difficult to solve or understand **intricacy** *n.*, **intricately** *adv.*

in-trigue *v.* to arouse the curiosity or interest; to fascinate; to plot; to conspire; to engage in intrigues *n.* a secret or illicit love affair; a secret plot or plan **intriguer** *n.*

in-trin-sic *adj.* belonging to the true or fundamental nature of a thing; inherent **intrinsically** *adv.*

in-tro-duce *v.* to present a person face to face to another; to make acquainted; to bring into use or practice for the first time; to bring to the attention of **introducer**, **introduction** *n.*, **introductory** *adj.*

in-tro-it or **In-tro-it** *n.* a hymn or psalm sung at the beginning of a Roman Catholic Mass

in-tro-vert *n.*, *Psychol.* a person who directs his interest to himself and not to friends or social activities **introversion** *n.*, **introversive**, **introverted** *adj.*

in-trude *v.* to thrust or push oneself in; to come in without being asked or wanted

in-tu-it *v.* to understand through intuition

in-tu-i-tion *n.* the direct knowledge or

awareness of something without conscious attention or reasoning; knowledge that is acquired in this way **intuitive** adj., **intuitively** adv.

in-un-date v. to overwhelm with abundance or excess, as with work **inundation** n.

in-ure v. to become used to accepting something which is undesirable **inurement** n.

in-vade v. to enter by force with the intent to conquer or pillage; to penetrate and overrun harmfully; to violate; to encroach upon **invader** n.

in-va-lid n. a chronically sick, bedridden, or disabled person **invalid** adj. & v.

in-val-id adj. disabled by injury or disease; not valid; unsound **invalidity** n., **invalidly** adv.

in-val-i-date v. to nullify; to make invalid **invalidation, invalidator** n.

in-val-u-able adj. priceless; of great value; to be of great help or use **invaluably** adv., **invaluableness** n.

in-var-i-a-ble adj. constant and not changing **invariably** adv.

in-va-sion n. the act of invading; an entrance made with the intent of overrunning or occupying **invasive** adj.

in-veigh v. to angrily protest **inveigher** n.

in-vei-gle v. to win over by flattery **inveiglement, inveigler** n.

in-vent v. to devise or create by original effort or design **inventor** n.

in-ven-tion n. the act or process of inventing; a new process, method, or device conceived from study and testing

in-ven-tive adj. skillful at invention or contrivance; ingenious **inventively** adv., **inventiveness** n.

in-ven-to-ry n., pl. -ies a list of items with descriptions and quantities of each; the process of making such a list **inventory** v.

in-verse adj. reversed in order or sequence; inverted n. something opposite **inversely** adv.

in-ver-sion n. the act of inverting or the state of being inverted; that which is inverted

in-vert v. to turn upside down; to reverse the position, condition, or order of something **inverter** n., **invertible** adj.

in-ver-te-brate adj. lacking a backbone or spinal column **invertebrate** n.

in-vest v. to use money for the purchase of stocks or property in order to obtain profit or interest; to place in office formally; to install; to make an investment **investor** n.

in-ves-ti-gate v. to search or inquire into; to examine carefully -tive adj., **investigation, investigator** n.

in-ves-ti-ture n. the ceremony or act of investing or installing someone in a high office

in-vest-ment n. the act of investing money or capital to gain interest or income; property acquired and kept for future benefit

in-vig-o-rate v. to give strength or vitality to **invigoratingly** adv., -tion n.

in-vin-ci-ble adj. incapable of being defeated **invincibility** n., **invincibly** adv.

in-vi-o-la-ble adj. secure from profanation; safe from assault **inviolability** n., **inviolably** adv.

in-vi-o-late adj. not violated **inviolately** adv., **inviolateness** n.

in-vis-i-ble adj. not capable of being seen; not visible; not open to view; hidden **invisibility** n., **invisibly** adv.

in-vi-ta-tion n. the act of inviting; the means or words that request someone's presence or participation

in-vite v. to request the presence or participation of; to make a formal or polite request for; to provoke; to entice; to issue an invitation

in-vit-ing adj. tempting; attractive **invitingly** adv.

in-vo-ca-tion n. an appeal to a deity or other agent for inspiration, witness, or help; a prayer used at the opening of a ceremony or service

in-voice n. an itemized list of merchandise shipped or services rendered, including prices, shipping instructions, and other costs; a bill **invoice** v.

in-voke v. to call upon for aid, support, or inspiration; to conjure **invoker** n.

in-vol-un-tar-y adj. not done by choice or willingly n. Physiol. muscles which function without an individual's control **involuntariness** n.

in-volve v. to include as a part; to make a participant of; to absorb; to engross **involvement** n.

in-vul-ner-a-ble adj. to be immune to attack; impregnable; not able to be physically injured or wounded **invulnerability** n., **invulnerably** adv.

in-ward adj. situated toward the inside, center, or interior; of or existing in the mind or thoughts **inwardness** n., **inwardly** adv.

i-o-dine n. a grayish-black, corrosive, poisonous element, symbolized by I; a solution made up of iodine, alcohol, and sodium iodide or potassium iodide which is used as an antiseptic

i-on *n., Physics.* an atom or group of atoms which carries a positive or negative electric charge as a result of having lost or gained one or more electrons

i-on-ize *v.* to convert completely or partially into ions **ionization** *n.*

IOU *abbr.* I owe you

ip-so fac-to *adv., L.* by that very fact or act

IQ *abbr.* intelligence quotient

i-ras-ci-ble *adj.* easily provoked to anger; quick-tempered **irascibly** *adv.*, **irascibility, irascibleness** *n.*

i-rate *adj.* raging; angry **irately** *adv.*

ir-i-des-cent *adj.* displaying the colors of the rainbow in shifting hues and patterns **iridescence** *n.*

i-ris *n., pl.* **irises** *or* **irides**

the pigmented part of the eye which regulates the size of the pupil by contracting and expanding around it *Bot.* a plant with narrow sword-shaped leaves and large, handsome flowers, as the gladiolus and crocus

I-rish *adj.* pertaining to Ireland and its people or their language

irk *v.* to annoy or to weary

Iron Age *n.* the most recent of three early stages of human progress, following the Stone Age and the Bronze Age

i-ron-bound *adj.* bound with iron; unyielding

i-ron-clad *adj.* covered with protective iron plates; strict; unbreakable

iron curtain *n.* an impenetrable political and ideological barrier between the Soviet bloc and the rest of the world

i-ron-ic *adj.* marked by or characterized by irony **ironical** *adj.*, **ironically** *adv.*

iron lung *n.* a tank which encloses the entire body with the exception of the head and regulates the respiration of a patient by alternately increasing and decreasing air pressure

i-ron-stone *n.* a heavy, white, glazed pottery

i-ro-ny *n., pl.* **-ies** a literary device for conveying meaning by saying the direct opposite of what is really meant

ir-ra-di-ate *v.* to subject to ultraviolet light, radiation, or similar rays **irradiation, irradiator** *n.*

ir-ra-tion-al *adj.* unable to reason; contrary to reason; absurd; in mathematics, a number which is not expressible as an integer or a quotient of integers **irrationality** *n.*, **irrationally** *adv.*

ir-rec-on-cil-a-ble *adj.* not able or willing to be reconciled **irreconcilability** *n.*, **irreconcilably** *adv.*

ir-re-deem-a-ble *adj.* not capable of being recovered, bought back, or paid off; not convertible into coin

ir-re-duc-i-ble *adj.* not having the capabilities of reduction, as to a smaller amount **irreducibility** *n.*, **irreducibly** *adv.*

ir-ref-ra-ga-ble *adj.* cannot be refuted or disproved **irrefragably** *adv.*

ir-re-fut-able *adj.* cannot be disproved **irrefutability** *n.*, **irrefutably** *adv.*

ir-reg-u-lar *adj.* not according to the general rule or practice; not straight, uniform, or orderly; uneven *n.* one who is irregular **irregularity** *n.*, **irregularly** *adv.*

ir-rel-e-vant *adj.* not pertinent or related to the subject matter **-ly** *adv.*, **irrelevance, irrelevancy** *n.*

ir-re-lig-ious *adj.* lacking in religion; opposed to religion **irreligiously** *adv.*, **irreligiousness, irreligion** *n.*

ir-re-mis-si-ble *adj.* unpardonable, as for sin **irremissibility** *n.*

ir-re-mov-a-ble *adj.* not removable **irremovably** *adv.*

ir-rep-a-ra-ble *adj.* unable to be set right or repaired **irreparability** *n.*, **irreparably** *adv.*

ir-re-place-able *adj.* unable to be replaced

ir-re-press-i-ble *adj.* impossible to hold back or restrain **irrepressibility** *n.*, **irrepressibly** *adv.*

ir-re-proach-able *adj.* blameless; not meriting reproach **-ness** *n.*, **irreproachably** *adv.*

ir-re-sist-i-ble *adj.* completely fascinating; impossible to resist **irresistibility** *n.*, **irresistibly** *adv.*

ir-res-o-lute *adj.* lacking resolution; indecisive; lacking firmness of purpose **irresolutely** *adv.*, **irresoluteness** *n.*

ir-re-spec-tive *adj.* regardless of; without regard to

ir-re-spon-si-ble *adj.* lacking in responsibility; not accountable or answerable to higher authority **irresponsibility** *n.*, **irresponsibly** *adv.*

ir-re-triev-able *adj.* unable to be retrieved or recovered

ir-rev-er-ence *n.* a lack of reverence; a disrespectful action **irreverent** *adj.*, **irreverently** *adv.*

ir-re-vers-ible *adj.* impossible to reverse **irreversibility** *n.*, **irreversibly** *adv.*

ir-rev-o-ca-ble *adj.* unable or incapable of being turned in the other direction; incapable of being repealed, annulled or undone **irrevocability** *n.*, **irrevocably** *adv.*

ir-ri-gate *v.* to water the land or crops artificially, as by means of ditches or sprinklers; to refresh with water *Med.* to wash out with a medicated fluid or water **irrigation, irrigator** *n.*, **irrigational** *adj.*

ir-ri-ta-ble *adj.* easily annoyed; ill-tempered *Pathol.* to respond abnormally to stimuli **irritableness** *n.*, **irritably** *adv.*

ir-ri-ta-bil-i-ty *n.* the state or quality of being irritable

ir-ri-tate *v.* to annoy or bother; to provoke; to be sore, chafed, or inflamed **irritator, irritation** *n.*, **irritant** *adj. & n.*, **irritatingly** *adv.*

ir-rupt *v.* to burst or rush in violently; to invade **irruption** *n.*, **irruptive** *adj.*, **irruptively** *adv.*

IRS *abbr.* Internal Revenue Service.

is *v.* third person, singular, present tense of the verb to be

-ish *suffix* of or belonging to a nationality or ethnic group; characteristic of; the approximate age of; the approximate time of; somewhat

is-land *n.* a piece of land smaller than a continent, completely surrounded by water **islander** *n.*

isle *n.* a small island

ism *n., Slang* a distinctive cause, doctrine, or theory

-ism *suffix* practice; process; a manner of behavior characteristic of person or thing; a system of principles

isn't *contr.* is not

i-so-late *v.* to set apart from the others; to put by itself; to place or be placed in quarantine **isolation, isolator** *n.*

i-so-la-tion-ism *n.* a national policy of avoiding political or economic alliances or relations with other countries **isolationist** *n.*

isoln *abbr.* isolation

i-so-mer *n.* a compound having the same kinds and numbers of atoms as another compound but differing in chemical or physical properties due to the linkage or arrangement of the atoms **isomeric** *adj.*

i-sos-ce-les tri-an-gle *n.* a triangle which has two equal sides

i-so-therm *n.* a line on a map linking points that have the same temperature

i-so-tope *n.* any of two or more species of atoms of a chemical element which contain in their nuclei the same number of protons but different numbers of neutrons **isotopic** *adj.*, **-ically** *adv.*

i-so-trop-ic *adj.* having the same value in all directions **isotropy** *n.*

is-sue *n.* the act of giving out; something that is given out or published; a matter of importance to solve *Med.* a discharge as of pus or blood *v.* to come forth; to flow out; to emerge; to distribute or give out, as supplies **issuable** *adj.*, **issuer** *n.*

isth-mus *n.* a narrow strip of land which connects two larger pieces of land

it *pron.* used as a substitute for a specific noun or name when referring to places, things, or animals of unspecified sex

i-tal-ic *adj.* a style of printing type in which the letters slant to the right

i-tal-i-cize *v.* to print in italics.

-ite *suffix* a native or inhabitant of; an adherent of; a sympathizer or follower

i-tem *n.* a separately-noted unit or article included in a category or series; a short article, as in a magazine or newspaper

i-tem-ize *v.* to specify by item; to list **itemizer, itemization** *n.*

it-er-ate *v.* to state or do again; to repeat **iteration** *n.*

i-tin-er-ant *adj.* traveling from place to place; wandering

i-tin-er-ar-y *n., pl.* **-ies** a scheduled route of a trip

it'll *contr.* it will; it shall

its *adj.* the possessive case of the pronoun it

it's *contr.* it is; it has

I've *contr.* I have

i-vy *n., pl.* **-ies** a climbing plant having glossy evergreen leaves

-ization *n. suffix* the process, action, or result of doing a specified thing

-ize *suffix* to cause to become or resemble

iz-zard *n.* the letter z

J, j The tenth letter of the English alphabet.

Ja *abbr.* joint account; judge advocate

jab *v.* to poke or thrust sharply with short blows; a rapid punch **jabbingly** *adv.*

jab-ber *v.* to speak quickly or without making sense

jab-i-ru *n.* a large white bird resembling the stork

jab-ot *n.* ruffle or decoration on the front of a blouse, dress, or shirt

ja-bot-i-ca-ba *n.* a shrubby tree of the tropics

ja-cal *n.* a small hut

jack *n.* the playing card that ranks just below a queen and bears a representation of a knave; any of various tools or devices used for raising heavy objects; the male of certain animals; a man or boy; fellow; a small flag on a ship that indicates nationality

jacks *n.* game played with a set of six-pronged metal pieces and a small ball

jack-al *n.* an African or Asian dog-like, carnivorous mammal

jack-a-napes *n.* an impudent person

jack-ass *n.*

a male donkey or ass; a stupid person or one who acts in a stupid fashion

jack-boot *n.* a heavy military boot which reaches above the knee

jack-daw *n.* a glossy, black, crow-like bird

jack-et *n.* a short coat worn by men and women; an outer protective cover for a book; the skin of a cooked potato

Jack Frost *n.* a name given to frost or winter weather

jack-hammer *n.* a tool operated by air pressure, used to break pavement and to drill rock

jack--in--the--box *n.* a toy consisting of a small box from which a puppet springs up when the lid is unfastened

jack--in--the--pul-pit *n.* a common herb which grows from a turnip-shaped bulb

jack-knife *n.* a large pocketknife

jack-leg *adj.* deficient in skill; an amateur

jack--of--all--trades *n.* a person who is able to do many types of work

jack--o--lan-tern *n.* a lantern made from a hollowed out pumpkin which has

been carved to resemble a face

jack pine *n.* large pine tree

jack-pot *n.* any post, prize, or pool in which the amount won is cumulative

jack rabbit *n.*

a large American hare with long back legs and long ears

jade *n.* hard, translucent, green gemstone

jad-ed *adj.* fatigued; dulled; worn-out

jag *n.* a very sharp projection or point *Slang* a binge or spree

jag-ged *adj.* having jags or sharp notches; serrated **jaggedly** *adv.*, **jaggedness** *n.*

jag-uar *n.* large, spotted, feline mammal of tropical America with a tawny coat and black spots

jai alai *n.* game similar to handball in which players catch and throw a ball with long, curved, wicker baskets strapped to their arms

jail *n.* a place of confinement for incarceration

jail-bird *n.*, *Slang* a prisoner or ex-prisoner

jail-break *n.* prison escape using force

jail-er *n.* the officer in charge of a jail and its prisoners

ja-lop-y *n.*, *pl.* -ies *Slang* an old, rundown automobile

ja-lou-sie *n.* a window, blind, or door having adjustable horizontal slats

jam *v.* to force or wedge into a tight position *Mus.* to be a participant in a jazz session *Slang* to be in a jam *n.* a preserve of whole fruit boiled with sugar

jamb *n.* the vertical sidepiece of a door

jam-ba-lay-a *n.* a food dish made of rice, vegetables and various kinds of meats

jam-bo-ree *n.* a large, festive gathering

jam session *n.* an informal gathering of a group of jazz musicians

jan-gle *v.* to make a harsh unmusical sound *n.* a discordant sound **jangler** *n.*

jan-i-tor *n.* person who cleans and cares for a building **janitorial** *adj.*

ja-pan *n.* black varnish used for coating objects

jape *v.* to joke; to make fun of or mock by words or actions **japery** *n.*

jar *n.* deep, cylindrical vessel with a wide mouth; a harsh sound *v.* to strike against or bump into; to affect one's feelings unpleasantly

jar-di-niere *n.* decorative pot or stand

for flowers or plants

jar-gon *n.* technical or specialized vocabulary used among members of a particular profession **jargonistic** *adj.*

jas-mine *or* **jes-sa-mine** *n.* a shrub with fragrant yellow or white flowers

jas-per *n.* an opaque red, brown, or yellow variety of quartz

ja-to *n.* takeoff of an airplane which is assisted by an auxiliary rocket engine

jaun-dice *n., Pathol.* a diseased condition of the liver due to the presence of bile pigments in the blood

jaunt *n.* short journey for pleasure

jaun-ty *adj.* having a buoyantly carefree and self-confident air or matter about oneself **-ily** *adv.* **-iness** *n.*

Ja-va *n., Slang* coffee

jave-lin *n.* a light spear thrown as a weapon

jaw *n., Anat.* either of the two bony structures forming the framework of the mouth and holding the teeth

jaw-bone *n.* one of the bones of the jaw, especially the lower jaw

jaw-break-er *n.* very hard piece of candy. *Slang* A word which is hard to pronounce

jay *n.* any of various corvine birds of brilliant coloring

jay-walk *v., Slang* to cross a street carelessly, violating traffic regulations and or signals **jaywalker** *n.*

jazz *n.* kind of music which has a strong rhythmic structure with frequent syncopation and often involving ensemble and solo improvisation **-er** *n.,* **-y** *adj.*

jeal-ous *adj.* suspicious or fearful of being replaced by a rival; resentful or bitter **-ly** *adv.,* **-ness,** *n.*

jean *n.* strong, twilled cotton cloth **jeans** Pants made of denim

jeep *n.* small, military, and civilian vehicle with four-wheel drive

jeer *v.* speak or shout derisively **jeer** *n.,* **jerringly** *adv.*

Je-ho-vah *n.* God, in the Christian translations of the Old Testament

je-june *adj.* lacking in substance or nourishment; immature

je-ju-num *n., pl.* **-na** *Anat.* part of the small intestine which extends from the duodenum to the ileum

jel-ly *n. pl.* **-ies** food preparation made with pectin or gelatin and having a somewhat elastic consistency; a food made of boiled and sweetened fruit juice and used as a filler or spread; *v.* to make into jelly; to become or take the form of jelly; to become

gelatinous; to assume or cause to assume definite form

jel-lybean *n.* small candy having a hard, colored coating over a gelatinous center

jel-ly-fish *n., pl.* **fishes** any of a number of freeswimming marine animals of jelly-like substance

jeop-ard-ize *v.* to put in jeopardy; to expose to loss or danger

jeop-ard-y *n.* exposure to loss or danger

jer-bo-a *n.*

any of a type of small, nocturnal rodent of Asia and Africa with long hind legs

jer-e-mi-ad *n.* lament or prolonged complaint

jerk *v.* give a sharp twist or pull to *n.* sudden movement, as a tug or twist *Physiol.* involuntary contraction of a muscle resulting from a reflex action **jerky, jerkily** *adv.,* **jerkiness** *n.*

jer-kin *n.* close-fitting jacket, usually sleeveless

jerk-wa-ter *adj.* of little importance

jer-ry--build *v.* build flimsily and cheaply

jer-sey *n., pl.* **-seys** a soft ribbed fabric of wool, cotton, or other material; a knitted sweater, jacket, or shirt; fawn-colored, small dairy cattle which yield milk rich in butter fat

jest *n.* action or remark intended to provoke laughter; a joke; a playful mood **jester** *n.*

Jes-u-it *n.* member of the Society of Jesus, a religious order founded in 1534

Jesus *n.* founder of Christianity, son of Mary and regarded in the Christian faith as Christ the son of God, the Messiah; also referred to as Jesus Christ or Jesus of Nazareth

jet *n.*

sudden spurt or gush of liquid or gas emitted through a narrow opening; a jet airplane **jet** *adj.*

jet lag *n.* mental and physical fatigue resulting from rapid travel through several time zones

jet set *n.* international social group of wealthy individuals who travel from one fashionable place to another for pleasure **jet setter** n.

jet stream n. high-velocity wind near the troposphere, generally moving from west to east often at speeds exceeding 250 mph.; a high-speed stream of gas or other fluid expelled from a jet engine or rocket

jet-ti-son v. throw cargo overboard; to discard a useless or hampering item

jet-ty n., pl. -ies wall made of piling rocks, or other material which extends into a body of water to protect a harbor or influence the current; a pier

Jew n. descendant of the ancient Hebrew people; a person believing in Judaism

jew-el n. precious stone used for personal adornment; a person or thing of very rare excellence or value v. furnish with jewels **jewelry** n.

jew-eler or **jew-el-ler** n. person who makes or deals in jewelry

Jew's harp n. small musical instrument held between the teeth when played, consisting of a U-shaped frame with a flexible metal piece attached which is plucked with the finger to produce twanging sounds

jib n., Naut. triangular sail set on a stay extending from the head of the foremast to the bowsprit

jif-fy or **jiff** n. short time

jig n. any of a variety of fast, lively dances; the music for such a dance Mech. device used to hold and guide a tool **jig** v.

jig-ger n. small measure holding 1 1/2 oz. used for measuring liquor Naut. small sail in the stern of a sailing craft

jig-gle v. move or jerk lightly up and down n. jerky, unsteady movement

jig-saw n. saw having a slim blade set vertically, used for cutting curved or irregular lines

jigsaw puzzle n. puzzle consisting of many irregularly shaped pieces which fit together and form a picture

jilt v. discard a lover n. woman or girl who discards a lover

jim-my n., pl. -ies short crowbar, often used by a burglar v. to force open or break into with a jimmy

jim-son-weed n. tall, coarse, foul-smelling, poisonous annual weed with large, trumpet-shaped purplish or white flowers

jin-gle v. make a light clinking or ringing sound n. short, catchy song or poem, as one used for advertising

jin-go-ism n. extreme nationalism which

is marked by a belligerent foreign policy **jingoist** n., **jingoistic** adj.

jinn n., pl. **jin-ni** in the Moslem legend, a spirit with supernatural powers

jinx n., Slang person or thing thought to bring bad luck

jit-ney n. vehicle carrying passengers for a small fee

jit-ter v., Slang to be intensely nervous **jittery** adj.

jit-ter-bug n., Slang lively dance or one who performs this dance **jitterbug** v.

jit-ters n. nervousness

jive n., Slang jazz or swing music and musicians

job n. anything that is done; work that is done for a set fee; the project worked on; a position of employment

jobless adj., **joblessness** n.

job-ber n. one who buys goods in bulk from the manufacturer and sells them to retailers; a person who works by the job; a pieceworker

job-name n. Computer Science. code that is assigned to a specific job instruction in a computer program, for the operator's use

jock n., Slang male athlete in college; a person who participates in athletics

jock-ey n. person who rides a horse as a professional in a race

joc-u-lar adj. marked by joking; playful **jocularity** n., **jocularly** adv.

joc-und adj. cheerful; merry; suggestive of high spirits and lively mirthfulness **jocundity** n., **jocundly** adv.

jog n. slight movement or a slight shake; the slow steady trot of a horse; to exercise by running at a slow but steady pace **jogger** n.

jog-gle v. move or shake slightly

john n., Slang toilet; a prostitute's client

john-ny-cake n. thin bread made with cornmeal

John the Baptist n. baptizer of Jesus Christ

join v. bring or put together so as to form a unit

join-er n. person whose occupation is to build articles by joining pieces of wood

joint n.

place where two or more things or parts are joined; a point where bones are connected adj. marked by cooperation, as a joint effort

join-ture *n., Law* settlement of property arranged by a husband which is to be used for the support of his wife after his death

joist *n.* any of a number of small parallel beams set from wall to wall to support a floor

joke *n.* something said or done to cause laughter, such as a brief story with a punch line; something not taken seriously *v.* to tell or play jokes **jokingly** *adv.*

jok-er *n.* person who jokes; a playing card

jol-li-fi-ca-tion *n.* merrymaking.

jol-ly *adj.* full of good humor; merry **jollity** *n.*, **jolly** *v.*

jolt *v.* knock or shake about *n.* sudden bump or jar, as from a blow **jolty** *adj.*

jon-quil *n.* widely grown species of narcissus related to the daffodil

josh *v., Slang* make good-humored fun of someone

joss *n.* Chinese idol or image

jos-tle *v.* make one's way through a crowd by pushing, elbowing, or shoving

jot *v.* make a brief note of something *n.* tiny bit

jounce *v.* bounce; to bump; to shake **jouncey** *adj.*

jour-nal *n.* diary or personal daily record of observations and experiences; in bookkeeping, a book in which daily financial transactions are recorded

jour-nal-ese *n.* vocabulary and style of writing supposedly characteristic of most newspapers

jour-nal-ism *n.* occupation, collection, writing, editing, and publishing of newspapers and other periodicals **-ist** *n.*, **-istic** *adj.*, **journalistically** *adv.*

jour-ney *n.* trip from one place to another over a long distance

jour-ney-man *n., pl.* **-men** worker who has served an apprenticeship in a skilled trade

joust *n.* formal combat between two knights on horseback as a part of a medieval tournament

Jove *Interj.* mild expression of surprise or emphasis

jo-vi-al *adj.* good-natured; good-humored; jolly **joviality** *n.*

jowl *n.* fleshy part of the lower jaw; the cheek **jowly** *adj.*

joy *n.* strong feeling of great happiness; delight **joyfully** *adv.*, **-fulness** *n.*, **-less** *adj.*, **-lessly** *adv.*

joy-ous *adj.* joyful; causing or feeling joy **joyously** *adv.*

joy ride *Slang* ride taken for pleasure only

joy stick *Slang* control stick of an airplane or video game

ju-bi-lant *adj.* exultantly joyful or triumphant; expressing joy **jubilance** *n.*, **jubilantly** *adv.*

ju-bi-la-tion *n.* rejoicing; exultation

ju-bi-lee *n.* special anniversary of an event; any time of rejoicing

Ju-da-ism *n.* religious practices or beliefs of the Jews; a religion based on the belief in one God

judge *v., Law* public officer who passes judgment in a court *v.* decide authoritatively after deliberation

judg-ment *or* **judge-ment** *n.* ability to make a wise decision or to form an opinion; the act of judging *Law* sentence or determination of a court **judgmental** *adj.*

ju-di-ca-ture *n.* function or action of administration of justice; law, courts, or judges as a whole

ju-di-cial *adj.* pertaining to the administering of justice, to courts of law, or to judges **judicially** *adv.*

ju-di-ci-ar-y *adj.* of, or pertaining to judges, courts, or judgments *n.* department of the government which administers the law

ju-di-cious *adj.* having, showing, or exercising good sound judgement **judiciously** *adv.*, **judiciousness** *n.*

ju-do *n.* system or form of self-defense, developed from jujitsu in Japan

jug *n.* small pitcher or similar vessel for holding liquids

jug-ger-naut *n.* destructive force or object

jug-gle *v.* keep several objects continuously moving from the hand into the air; to practice fraud or deception **juggler** *n.*

jug-u-lar *adj., Anat.* of or pertaining to the region of the throat or the jugular vein

jugular vein *n., Anat.* one of the large veins on either side of the neck

juice *n.* liquid part of a vegetable, fruit, or animal *Slang* electric current

juic-er *n.* device for extracting juice from fruit

juic-y *adj.* full of; abounding with juice; full of interest; richly rewarding, especially financially

ju-jit-su *or* **ju-jut-su** *n.* Japanese system of using holds, throws, and stunning blows to subdue an opponent

juke box *n.* large, automatic, coin-operated record player equipped with push buttons for the selection of records

ju-lep *n.* mint julep

ju-li-enne *adj.* cut into thin strips *n.* clear meat soup containing vegetables chopped or cut into thin strips

jum-ble *v.* to mix in a confused mass; to throw together without order

jum-bo *n.* very large person, animal, or thing *adj.* extremely large

jump *v.* spring from the ground, floor, or other surface into the air by using a muscular effort of the legs and feet; to move in astonishment

jump-y *adj.* nervous; jittery **jumpiness** n.

jump suit *n.* one piece clothing worn by parachutes

jun-co *n.* any of various small birds of North America

junc-tion *n.* place where lines or routes meet, as roads or railways; the process of joining or the act of joining

junc-ture *n.* point where two things join; a crisis; an emergency; a point in time

jun-gle *n.* densely covered land with tropical vegetation, usually inhabited by wild animals

jun-gle rot *n.* skin disease, such as a fungus

jun-ior *adj.* younger in years or rank, used to distinguish the son from the father of the same first name; the younger of two *n.* third year of high school or college

jun-ket *n.* party, banquet, or trip -teer *n.*

junk-ie *or* **junk-y** *n., Slang* drug addict that uses heroin

ju-ry *n., pl.* -ies group of legally qualified persons summoned to serve on a judicial tribunal

just *adj.* fair and impartial in acting or judging; morally right **justly** *adv.*, **justness** *n.*

jus-tice *n.* principle of moral or ideal rightness; conformity to the law

jus-ti-fy *v.* to be just, right, or valid; to declare guiltless; to adjust or space lines to the proper length

jut *v.* extend beyond the main portion; to project

ju-ve-nile *adj.* young; youthful; not yet an adult *n.* a young person; an actor who plays youthful roles; a child's book

jux-ta-pose *v.* put side by side; to place together

K, k The eleventh letter of the English alphabet

kaa-ba *n.* building in the Great Mosque at Mecca that contains the sacred stone said to have been turned black in color, by the tears of the repentant pilgrims or by the sins of people ;who have rubbed or touched it

ka-bob *n.* small cubes of meat cooked with vegetables

ka-bu-ki *n.* traditional Japanese drama in which dances and songs are performed in a stylized fashion

Kad-dish *n.* a Jewish prayer recited by mourners after the death of a relative and during other daily prayers in the synagogue

kaf-fee-klatsch *n.* informal conversation over coffee

kaf-ir *n.* a grain sorghum that is cultivated in dry areas, having a tough leafy stalk and is used for fodder

kai-nite *n.* a mineral that is used as a fertilizer and a source of magnesium and potassium

kai-ser *n.* an Austrian ruler from 1804-1918; an emperor; the title given to German rulers between the years of 1871 and 1918

ka-ka *n.* a New Zealand parrot, having an olivebrown color

ka-ka-po *n.* a large parrot

kale *n.* a green cabbage having crinkled leaves which do not form a tight head

ka-lie-do-scope *n.* a tubular instrument rotated to make successive symmetrical designs by using mirrors reflecting the changing patterns made by pieces of loose colored glass ath the end of a tube

kame *n.* short ridge of gravel and sand that remains after glacial ice melts

kam-ik *n.* boot made of sealskin, knee-high in length and worn in the eastern arctic regions

ka-mi-ka-ze *n.* a Japanese pilot in World War II trained to make a suicidal crash; an aircraft loaded with explosives used in a suicide attack

kan-ga-roo *n., pl.* **-roo, roos**

various herbivorous marsupials, of Australia, with short forelegs, large hind limbs, capable of jumping, and a large tail

kangaroo court *n.* self-appointed, illegal court, usually marked by incompetence or dishonesty

ka-o-lin *or* **ka-o-line** *n.* fine clay used in ceramics

ka-pok *n.* silky fiber manufactured from the fruit of the silk-cotton tree and used for stuffing cushions and life preservers

ka-put *adj., Slang* destroyed or out of order

kar-a-kul *n.* any of a breed of fat-tailed sheep of central Asia having a narrow body and coarse wiry, brown fur

kar-at *n.* unit of measure for the fineness of gold

ka-ra-te *n.* Japanese art of self-defense

kar-ma *n.* over-all effect of one's behavior, held in Hinduism and Buddhism to determine one's destiny in a future existence **kar-mic** *adj.*

ka-ty-did *n.* various green insects related to grasshoppers and crickets, having specialized organs on the wings of the male that make a shrill sound when rubbed together

kay-ak *n.* watertight Eskimo boat with a light frame and covered with sealskin **kayaker** *n.*

ka-zoo *n.* toy musical instrument with a paper membrane which vibrates symathelically when a player hums into the tube

kedge *n.* small anchor *v.* pull a ship by the rope of an anchor

keel *n.* central main stem on a ship or aircraft which runs lengthwise along the center line from bow to stern, to which a frame is built upwards *v.* to capsize. *keel over.* fall over suddenly; turn upside down **-ed** *adj.* **-less** *adj.*

keel-haul *v.* drag a person under the keel of a ship as a form of punishment

keel-son *n., Naut.* structural member fastened above and parallel to the keel to give additional strength

keen *adj.* having a sharp edge or point; acutely painful or harsh; intellectually acute; strong; intense *Slang* great *n.* wailing lament especially for the dead **keenly** *adv.,* **keenness** *n.*

keep *v.* to have and hold; to not let go; to maintain, as business records; to know a secret and not divulge it; to protect and defend

keep-sake *n.* memento or souvenir

keg *n.* small barrel

keg-ler *n.* bowler

kelp *n.* any of a large brown seaweeds

kel-pie *n.* sheep dog originally bred in Australia

ken-nel *n.* shelter for or a place where dogs or cats are bred, boarded, or trained **kennel** *v.*

ke-no *n.* game of chance resembling bingo; a lottery game

kep-i *n.* French military cap having a flat, round top and a visor

ker-a-tin *n.* fibrous protein which forms the basic substance of nails, hair, horns, and hoofs **keratinous** *adj.*

ker-a-ti-tis *n.* inflammation of the cornea

ker-chief *n.* piece of cloth usually worn around the neck or on the head; scarf; a handkerchief

ker-nel *n.* grain or seed, as of corn, enclosed in a hard husk; the inner substance of a nut; the central, most important part

ker-o-sene *or* **ker-o-sine** *n.* oil distilled from petroleum or coal and used for illumination

kes-trel *n.* small falcon, with gray and brown plumage

ketch *n.* small sailing vessel with two masts

ketch-up *n.* thick, smooth sauce made from tomatoes

ket-tle *n.* pot used for cooking

ket-tle-drum *n.* musical instrument with a parchment head which can be tuned by adjusting the tension

key *n.* an instrument by which the bolt of a lock is turned *adj.* of general importance

key-board *n.* bank of keys, as on a piano, typewriter, or computer terminal *v.* to set by means of a keyed typesetting machine; to generate letters by means of a word processor **keyboarder** *n.*

key club *n.* private club that offers entertainment amd serves liquor

key-note *n., Mus.* first and harmonically fundamental tone of a scale; main principle or theme

keynote address *n.* opening speech that outlines issues for discussion

key-punch *n.* machine operated from a keyboard that uses punched holes in tapes or cards for data processing systems **keypunch** *n.,* **keypuncher** *v.*

key-stone *n.* wedge-shaped stone at the center of an arch that locks its parts together; an essential part

key-stroke *n.* stroke of a key, as of a typewriter

key-way *n.* groove for a key

kg *abbr.* kilogram

khak-i *n.* yellowish brown or olive-drab color; a sturdy cloth being khaki in color **khakis** uniform of khaki cloth

khan *n.* Asiatic title of respect; a medieval Turkish, Mongolian or Tartar ruler **khanate** *n.*

khe-dive *n.* ruler of Egypt from 1867 to 1914 governing as a viceroy of the sultan of Turkey

kibble *n.* coarsely ground grain

kib-itz *v.* Slang look on and offer meddlesome advice to others **kibitzer** *n.*

kick *n.* sudden forceful thrust with the foot

kick-stand *n.* metal rod for holding up a two-wheeled bike

kick up *n.* provoke; to stir up

kid *n.* young goat; leather made from the skin of a young goat *Slang* child; youngster *v.* mock or tease playfully to deceive for fun; to fool **kidder** *n.*

kid leather *n.* soft pliable leather made from goatskin or lambskin

kid-nap *v.* seize and hold a person; unlawfully, often for ransom **kidnapper** *n.*

kid-ney *n., pl.* **-neys**

either of two organs situated in the abdominal cavity of vertebrates whose function is to keep proper water balance in the body and to excrete wastes in the form of urine

kidney bean *n.* bean grown for its edible seeds

kidvid *n., Slang* television programming for children

kiel-ba-sa *n.* smoked Polish sausage

kill *n.* put to death; nullify; cancel; to slaughter for food

kill-deer *n., pl.* **-deer, -deers** bird characterized by a plaintive, penetrating cry

killer whale *n.* black and white carnivorous whale, found in the colder waters of the seas

kil-lick *n.* small anchor usually made from a stone

kill-joy *n.* one who spoils the enjoyment of others

kiln *n.* oven or furnace for hardening or drying a substance, especially one for firing ceramics, pottery, etc.

ki-lo *n.* kilogram

kil-o-bit *n.* in computer science, one thousand binary digits

ki-lo-cy-cle *n.* unit equal to one thousand cycles, one thousand cycles per second

kil-o-gram *n.* measurement of weight in the meteric system equal to slightly more than one third of a pound

kil-o-ton *n.* one thousand tons; an explosive power equal to that of one thousand tons of TNT

kil-o-watt *n.* unit of power equal to one thousand watts

kil-o-watt-hour *n.* unit of electric power consumption of one thousand watts throughout one hour

kilt *n.* knee-length wool skirt with deep pleats, usually of tartan, worn especially by men in the Scottish Highlands

kil-ter *n.* good condition; proper or working order

ki-mo-no *n.* loose, Japanese robe with a wide sash; a loose robe worn chiefly by women

kin *n.* one's relatives by blood

kin-der-gar-ten *n.* school or class for young children from the ages of four to six

kin-der-gart-ner *n.* child who attends kindergarten

kind-heart-ed *adj.* a sympathetic nature **-ly** *adv.* kindheartedness *n.*

kin-dle *v.* ignite; to catch fire; to stir up; to arouse; to excite, as the feelings **kindler** *n.*

kin-dling *n.* easily ignited material such as, sticks, wood chips, etc. used to start a fire

kin-dred *n.* a person's relatives by blood *adj.* having a like nature; similar **kindredness** *n.*

kin-e-mat-ics *n.* the branch of dynamics that deals with motion considered apart from force and mass **kinematical** *adj.,* **-ally** *adv.*

kin-e-scope *n.* cathoderay tube in a television set which translates received electrical into a visable picture on a screen; a film of a television on broadcast

ki-net-ic *adj.* of, or pertaining to, or produced by motion

king-bolt *n.* verticle central vehicle to the front axle

king crab *n.* large crablike crustacean common in the coastal waters of Japan, Alaska, and Siberia

king-pin *n.* foremost pin of a set arranged in order for playing bowling or tenpins; the most important or essential person

kink *n.* tight twist or knotlike curl; a sharp painful muscle cramp; a mental

quirk *v.* to form or cause to form a kink.

kink-a-jou *n.* tropical American mammal having large eyes, brown fur and a long prehensile tail

kink-y *adj.* tightly curled; sexually uninhibited **kinkily** *adv.*, **kinkiness** *n.*

ki-osk *n.* small building used as a refreshment booth or newsstand

kip *n.* untanned skin of a calf, a lamb and or an adult of any small breed

kip-per *n.* salted and smoked herring or salmon *v.* to cure by salting, smoking, or drying

kir-tle *n.* woman's long skirt

kis-met *n.* fate; appointed lot

kitch-en *n.* room in a house or building used to prepare and cook food

kite *n.* light-weight framework of wood and paper designed to fly in a steady breeze at the end of a string; any of various predatory birds of the hawk family having a long, usually forked tail

kith *or* **kin** *n.* acquaintances or family

kitsch *n.* anything that is pretentious and in poor taste

kit-ten *n.*

young cat
kit-ty--cor-nered *adj.* diagonally; cater-cornered

klep-to-ma-ni-a *n.* obsessive desire to steal or impulse to steal, especially without economic motive

klutz *n.*, *Slang* stupid or clumsy person **klutziness** *n.*, **klutzy** *adj.*

km *abbr.* kilometer

knack *n.* natural talent; aptitude

knap-sack *n.* supply or equipment bag, as of canvas or nylon, worn strapped across the shoulders

knave *n.* tricky; or dishonest person **knavish** *adj.*, **-ishness** *n.*

knead *v.* work dough into a uniform mass; to shape by or as if by kneading

knee *n.* joint in the human body which connects the calf with the thigh

knell *v.* sound a bell, especially when rung for a funeral; to toll *n.* act or instance of knelling; a signal of disaster

knick-ers *pl. n.* short loose-fitting pants gathered at the knee

knick-knack *n.* trinket; trifling article

knight *n.* medieval soldier serving a monarch; a chess piece bearing the shape of a horse's head **knighthood** *n.*, **knightly** *adj.*

knish *n.* baked or fried dough stuffed with meat, cheese, or potatoes

knit *v.*

to form by intertwining thread or yarn, by interlocking loops of a single yarn by means of needles; to fasten securely; to draw together

knitting needle *n.* long, slender, pointed rod for knitting

knob *n.* rounded protuber-ance; a lump; a rounded mountain; a rounded handle **knobed** *adj.*

knock *v.* hit or strike with a hard blow; to criticize; to collide

knock-down *adj.* designed to be easily assembled for storage or shipment

knockdown--drag--out *adj.* extremely violent or bitter

knock-er *n.* one who or that which knocks; as a metal ring for knocking on a door

knock-knee *n.* condition in which one or both knees turn inward and knock or rub together while walking **knock-kneed** *adj.*

knoll *n.* small round hill; a mound

knot-hole *n.* hole in lumber left by the falling out of a knot

knout *n.* whip or scourge for flogging criminals **knout** *v.*

know *v.* perceive directly as fact or truth; to believe to be true; to be certain of **knowable** *adj.*, **knowledge** *n.*

ko-a-la *n.*

Australian marsupial which has large hairy ears, gray fur, and feeds on eucalyptus leaves

kohl-ra-bi *n.* a variety of cabbage having a thick stem and eaten as a vegetable

kook *n.*, *Slang* crazy or eccentric person

ko-sher *adj.* conformant to eat according to Jewish dietary laws *Slang* appropriate; proper.

kow-tow *v.* show servile deference

kum-quat *n.* small, round orange fruit having a sour pulp and edible rind

ky-ack *n.* a packsack for either side of a packsaddle

ky-pho-sis *n.* the abnormal backward curve of the spine

ky-rie *n.* a short prayer that consists of the words "Lord, have mercy"

L,l The twelfth letter of the English alphabet; the Roman numeral for fifty.

lab *n.* laboratory

la-bel *n.* something that identifies or describes label *v.*

la-bi-al *adj.* pertaining to or of the labia or lips

la-bi-um *n., pl.* labia any of the four folds of the vulva

la-bor *n.* physical or manual work done for hire

lab-o-ra-to-ry *n., pl.* -ies a place equipped for conducting scientific experiments, research, or testing

labor camp *n.* a group of prisoners who have been forced into labor; a place for migrant farm workers

la-bored *adj.* bearing the marks of constraint and effort; produced with a great amount of labor; heavy

la-bo-ri-ous *adj.* toilsome; not easy; requiring much labor; diligent in service or work; industrious

la-bor-ite *n.* a person who promotes the theories, interests, and practices of a labor organization; one that belongs to a political party that is devoted mainly to labor interests

la-bret *n.* a decorative ornament worn by primitive tribes or people, usually made from a piece of wood, bone, ets. and placed through a pierced lip

la-brum *n.* the upper part of the mouth or an crustacean or insect

lab-y-rinth *n.*

a system of winding, intricate passages; a maze -thine *adj.*

lac *n.* the resinous secretion left on certain trees by the lac insect and used in making paints and varnishes and the production of red color matter

lac-er-ate *v.* to open with a jagged tear laceration *n.*

lach-ry-mal or **lac-ri-mal** *adj.* relating to or producing tears

lack *n.* the deficiency or complete absence of something

lack-a-dai-si-cal *adj.* lacking life, interest, or spirit; melancholy

lack-ey *n.* a male servant of very low status

lack-lus-ter *adj.* lacking sheen
ate *v.* to secrete or to milk
ation *n.*
e-al *adj.* of, resembling, or like milk

lac-tic acid *n.* a limpid, syrupy acid that is present in sour milk, molasses, some fruits, and wines

lac-tose *n., Biochem.* a white, odorless, crystalline sugar

la-cu-na *n., pl.* -nas, -nae a space from which something is missing

lad *n.* a boy or young man

lad-der *n.* an implement used for climbing up or down

lad-en *adj.* heavily burdened; oppressed; loaded laden *v.*

lad-ing *n.* cargo; freight

la-dle *n.*

a cup-shaped vessel with a deep bowl and a long handle ladle *v.*

la-dy *n., pl.* ladies a woman showing refinement, cultivation, and often high social position

lag *v.* to stray or fall behind; to move slowly

la-gniappe *n.* a small gift which is given to a purchaser by a storekeeper

la-goon *n.* a body of shallow water separated from the ocean by a coral reef or sandbars lagoonal *adj.*

lain *v.* past tense of lie

lais-sez--faire *n.* a policy stating that a government should exercise very little control in trade and industrial affairs

la-i-ty *n.* laymen, as distinguished from clergy

lake *n.* a large inland body of either salt or fresh water

La-maze method *n.* a method of childbirth in which the mother is prepared psychologically and physically to give birth

lamb *n.* a young sheep; the meat of a lamb used as food

lam-baste or **lambast** *v., Slang* to thrash or beat

lam-bent *adj.* lightly and playfully brilliant lambency *n.*

lame *adj.* disabled or crippled
lamely *adv.,* lameness *n.*

la-me *n.* a brocaded fabric woven with gold or silver thread

lame duck *n.* an officeholder who has been defeated but continues in office until the inauguration of his or her successor

la-ment *v.* to express sorrow

lam-i-na *n., pl.* -nae, -nas a thin scale or layer *Bot.* the blade or flat part of a leaf

lam-i-nate *v.* to form or press into thin sheets laminated *adj.*

lamp *n.* a device for generating heat or

light
lam-poon *n.* a satirical, but often humorous, attack in verse or prose

lam-prey *n.* ,*pl.* preys an eel-like fish

lance *n.* a spear-like implement used as a weapon by mounted knights or soldiers

lance corporal *n., Mil.* in the U.S. Marine Corps, an enlisted man who ranks above a private first class and below a corporal

land *n.* the solid, exposed surface of the earth as distinguished from the waters

lan-dau *n.* a four-wheeled vehicle with a closed carriage and a back seat with a collapsible top

land-er *n.* a space vehicle for landing on a celestial body

land--fill *n.* a system of trash and garbage disposal in which the waste is burned in low-lying land so as to build up the ground surface; a section built up by landfill

land grant *n.* a grant of land made by a government, especially for railroads, roads, or agricultural colleges

land-scape *n.* a view or vista of natural scenery as seen from a single point

lane *n.* a small or narrow path between walls, fences, or hedges

lan-guage *n.* the words, sounds, pronunciation and method of combining words

lan-guid *adj.* lacking in energy **languidly** *adv.*, **languidness** *n.*

lan-guish *v.* to become weak

lank *adj.* slender; lean

lan-o-lin *n.* wool grease obtained from sheep's wool and refined for use in ointments and cosmetics

lan-yard *n.* a piece of rope or line used to secure objects on ships

la-pel *n.*

the front part of a garment, especially that of a coat, that is turned back, usually a continuation of the collar

lap-in *n.* rabbit fur that is sheared and dyed

lap-is laz-u-li *n.* a semiprecious stone that is azure blue in color

lap-pet *n.* a flap or fold on a headdress or on a garment

lapse *n.* a temporary deviation or fall to a less desirable state

lar-ce-ny *n., pl.* -ies the unlawful taking of another person's property

lar-der *n.* a place, such as a pantry or room, where food is stored

large *adj.* greater than usual or average in amount or size

lar-gess *or* **lar-gesse** *n.* liberal or excessive giving to an inferior; generosity

lar-go *adv., Mus.* in a very slow, broad, and solemn manner **largo** *adj. & n.*

lar-i-at *n.* a long, light rope with a running noose at one end to catch livestock

lark *n.* a bird having a melodious ability to sing

lar-va *n., pl.* **larvae** the immature, wingless, often worm-like form of a newly hatched insect

lar-yn-gi-tis *n.* inflammation of the larynx

lar-ynx *n., pl.* **larynges** *or* **larynxes** the upper portion of the trachea which contains the vocal cords

lash *v.* to strike or move violently or suddenly

lass *n.* a young girl or woman

las-si-tude *n.* a condition of weariness; fatigue

last *adj.* following all the rest; of or relating to the final death

Last Supper *n.* the last meal eaten by Jesus Christ and his disciples, before his crucifixion

latch *n.* a device used to secure a gate or door, consisting of a bar that usually fits into a notch

latch onto to grab onto

latch-et *n.* a narrow leather strap or thong used to fasten a shoe

latch-key *n.* a key for opening an outside door

late *adj.* coming, staying, happening after the proper or usual time; having recently died -ness *n.*, -ly *adv.*

lat-er-al *adj.* relating to or of the side **laterally** *adv.*

la-tex *n.* the milky, white fluid that is produced by certain plants, such as the rubber tree

lath *n.* a thin, narrow strip of wood nailed to joists, rafters, or studding

lathe *n.* a machine for holding material while it is spun and shaped by a tool

lat-i-tude *n.* the angular distance of the earth's surface north or south of the equator

la-trine *n.* a public toilet

lat-ter *adj.* being the second of two persons or two things

laud *v.* to praise; to extol **laudable** *adj.*, **laudably** *adv.*

laugh *v.* to express amusement, satisfaction **laughable** *adj.*

laun-dry *n.*, *pl.* -ies an establishment where laundering is done professionally

lau-re-ate a person honored for his accomplishment

la-va *n.* molten rock which erupts or flows from an active volcano

lav-a-to-ry *n.*, *pl.* -ies a room with permanently installed washing and toilet facilities

lav-en-der *n.* an aromatic plant having spikes of pale violet flowers

lav-ish *adj.* generous and extravagant in giving or spending
lavisher *n.*, lavishly *adv.*

law *n.* a rule of conduct or action, recognized by custom or decreed by formal enactment, considered binding on the members of a nation, community, or group

law-ren-ci-um *n.* a short-lived radioactive element

law-suit *n.* a case or proceeding brought before a court of law for settlement

law-yer *n.* a person trained in the legal profession who acts for and advises clients or pleads in court

lax *adj.* lacking disciplinary control
laxity, laxness *n.*

lax-a-tive *n.* a medicine taken to stimulate evacuation of the bowels

lay *v.* to cause to lie; to place on a surface; past tense of lie

lay-er *n.* a single thickness, coating, or covering that lies over or under another layered *adj.*, layer *v.*

lay-ette *n.* the clothing, bedding, and equipment for a newborn child

lay-off *n.* a temporary dismissal of employees

la-zy *adj.* unwilling to work; sluggish lazily *adv.*, laziness *n.*

la-zy-bones *n.* *Slang* a lazy person

L--do-pa *n.* a drug used in treating Parkinson's disease

lea *n.*, *Poetic.* a grassy field or meadow

leach *v.* to cause a liquid to pass through a filter

lead *v.* to go ahead so as to show the way; to control the affairs or action of

lead poisoning *n.* poisoning of a person's system by the absorption of lead or any of its salts

leaf *n.*, *pl.* leaves

a flat out-growth from a plant structure or tree

leaf-let *n.* a part or a segment of a compound leaf; a small printed handbill or circular

league *n.* an association of persons, organizations, or states for common action or interest

leak *n.* an opening, as a flaw or small crack, permitting an escape or entrance of light or fluid
leakage, leakiness *n.*

lean *v.* to rest or incline the weight of the body for support leanly *adv.*, -ness *n.*

lean-ing *n.* an inclination

learn *n.* the process of acquiring knowledge learner *n.*

lease *n.* a contract for the temporary use or occupation of property or premises in exchange for payment of rent

leash *n.* a strong cord or rope for restraining a dog or other animal

least-wise *adv.*, *Slang* at least

leath-er *n.* an animal skin or hide with the hair removed

leave *v.* to go or depart from

leav-en *n.* an agent of fermentation, as yeast, used to cause batters and doughs to rise leaven *v.*

lech-er-y *n.* unrestrained indulgence in sexual activity -er *n.*, -ous *adj.*

lec-i-thin *n.* any of a group of phosphorus containing compounds found in plant and animal tissues

lec-tern *n.* a stand or tall desk, usually with a slanted top

lec-ture *n.* a speech on a specific subject

led *v.*, *p.t. & p.p.* past tense of lead

ledg-er *n.* a book in which sums of money received and paid out are recorded

lee *n.* the side of a ship sheltered from the wind

leech *n.* any of various carnivorous or bloodsucking worms

leek *n.* a culinary herb of the lily family, related to the onion

leer *n.* a sly look or sideways glance expressing desire

lee-way *n.*, *Naut.* the lateral drift of a plane or ship away from the correct course

left *adj.* pertaining to or being on the side of the body that faces north when the subject is facing east

leg-a-cy *n.*, *pl.* -ies personal property, money, and other valuables that are bequeathed by will

le-gal *adj.* of, pertaining to, or concerned with the law or lawyers -ity, -ization *n.*, legalize *v.*, legally *adv.*

le-gal-ism *n.* a strict conformity to the law, especially when stressing the letter and forms of the law rather than the spirit of justice

le-ga-tion *n.* the official diplomatic mission in a foreign country, headed by a minister

le-ga-to *adv., Music* smooth and flowing with successive notes connected **legato** *adj. & n.*

leg-end *n.* an unverifiable story handed down from the past **legendary** *adj.*

leg-horn *n.* a hat made from finely plaited wheat straw

leg-i-ble *adj.* capable of being read **legibility** *n.*, **legibly** *adv.*

le-gion *n.* any various honorary or military organizations

leg-is-late *v.* to pass or make laws

leg-is-la-tion *n.* the act or procedures of passing laws

leg-is-la-ture *n.* a body of persons officially constituted and empowered to make and change laws

leg-ume *n.* a plant of the pea or bean family

lei *n., pl.* **leis**

a wreath of flowers worn around the neck; the customary greeting of welcome in the state of Hawaii

lei-sure *n.* the time of freedom from work or duty **leisurely** *adj. & adv.*

lem-on *n.* an oval citrus fruit grown on a tree

lem-on-ade *n.* a drink made from water, lemon juice, and sugar

lend *v.* to allow the temporary use or possession of something **lender** *n.*

length *n.* the linear extent of something from end to end

length-wise *adv. & adj.* of or in the direction or dimension of length

le-ni-ent *adj.* gentle, forgiving, and mild **leniently** *adv.*

len-i-tive *adj.* having the ability to ease pain

lent *v.* past tense of lend

len-til *n.* a leguminous plant, having broad pods and containing edible seeds

leop-ard *n.*

a large member of the cat family of Africa and Asia

le-o-tard *n.* a close-fitting garment worn by dancers and acrobats

lep-er *n.* one who suffers from leprosy

lep-re-chaun *n.* a mischief elf of Irish folklore

lep-ro-sy *n., Pathol.* a chronic communicable disease characterized by nodular skin lesions and the progressive destruction of tissue **leprotic** *adj.*

les-bi-an *n.* a homosexual woman

lese maj-es-ty *or n.* an offense against a ruler or supreme power of state

le-sion *n., Pathol.* an injury; a wound

less *adj.* smaller; of smaller or lower importance or degree

-less *suffix.* without; lacking

les-see *n.* one who leases a property

les-son *n.* an instance from which something is to be or has been learned

let *v.* to give permission; to allow

le-thal *adj.* pertaining to or being able to cause death

leth-ar-gy *n., Pathol.* a state of excessive drowsiness or abnormally deep sleep; laziness **lethargic** *adj.*

let's *contr.* let us

let-ter *n.* a standard character or sign used in writing or printing to represent an alphabetical unit or speech

leu-ke-mi-a *n., Pathol.* a generally fatal disease of the blood **leukemic** *adj.*

le-vee *n.* an embankment along the shore of a body of water, built to prevent over-flowing

lev-el *n.* a relative position, rank, or height on a scale. *v.* To make or become flat or level **-er, -ness** *n.*

lever *n.* a handle that projects and is used to operate or adjust a mechanism

lev-i-tate *v.* to rise and float in the air in apparent defiance of gravity **levitation** *n.*

Le-vit-i-cus *n.* the third book of the Old Testament

lev-i-ty *n., pl.* **-ies** lack of seriousness; frivolity; lightness

lev-y *v.* to impose and collect by authority or force, as a fine or tax

lewd *adj.* preoccupied with sex; lustful **lewdness** *n.*

lex-i-cog-ra-phy *n.* the practice or profession of compiling dictionaries

lex-i-con *n.* a dictionary; a vocabulary or list of words that relate to a certain subject, occupation, or activity

li-a-bil-i-ty *n., pl.* **-ies** the condition or state of being liable

li-a-ble *adj.* legally or rightly responsible

li-ai-son *n.* a communication, as between different parts of an armed force or departments of a government

li-ar *n.* a person who tells falsehoods

li-bel *n., Law* a written statement in published form that damages a person's character or reputation

lib-er-al *adj.* characterized by generosity or lavishness in giving; abundant; ample; inclining toward opinions or policies that favor progress or reform, such as religion or politics

liberal arts *pl. n.* academic courses that include literature, philosophy, history, languages, etc.

lib-er-ate *v.* to set free, as from bondage, oppression

lib-er-ty *n., pl.* -ies the state of being free from oppression

li-bi-do *n.* one's sexual desire or impulse; the psychic energy drive that is behind all human activities

li-brar-i-an *n.* a person in charge of a library

li-brar-y *n., pl.* -ies a collection of books, pamphlets, magazines, and reference books kept for reading, reference, or borrowing

lice *n.* plural of louse

li-cense *n.* an official document that gives permission to engage in a specified activity or to perform a specified act

li-cen-ti-ate *n.* a person licensed to practice a specified profession

li-cen-tious *adj.* lacking in moral restraint; immoral

li-chen *n.* any of various flowerless plants consisting of fungi, commonly growing in flat patches on trees and rocks lichened, lichenous *adj.*

lic-it *adj.* lawful licitly *adv.*

lick *v.* to pass the tongue over or along the surface of something

lick-e-ty--split *adv.* full speed

lic-o-rice *n.* a perennial herb of Europe, the dried root of which is used to flavor medicines and candy

lid *n.* a hinged or removable cover for a container; an eyelid lidded, lidless *adj.*

lie *v.* to be in or take a horizontal recumbent position; to recline *n.* a false or untrue statement

liege *n.* a feudal lord or sovereign

lien *n.* the legal right to claim, hold, or sell the property of another to satisfy a debt or obligation

lieu *n.* place; stead in lieu of In place of

lieu-ten-ant *n.* a commissioned officer

life *n., pl.* lives the form of existence that distinguishes living organisms from dead organisms or inanimate matter in the ability to carry on metabolism, respond to stimuli, reproduce, and grow

lifer *n.* Slang a person sentenced to life in prison

life-time *n.* the period between one's birth and death

life zone *n.* a biogeographic zone

lift *v.* to raise from a lower to a higher position; to elevate; to take from; to steal

liftoff *n.* the vertical takeoff or the instant of takeoff of an aircraft or spacecraft

lig-a-ment *n.* a tough band of tissue joining bones or holding a body organ in place ligamentous *adj.*

li-gate *v.* to tie with a ligature

lig-a-ture *n.* something, as a cord, that is used to bind

light *n.* electromagnetic radiation that can be seen by the naked eye; a source of fire, such as a match lightness *n.*

light-ning *n.* the flash of light produced by a high-tension natural electric discharge into the atmosphere

lig-ne-ous *adj.* of or resembling wood; woody

lig-nite *n.* a brownish-black soft coal

lig-ro-in *n.* a volatile, flammable fraction of petroleum used as a solvent

lik-en *v.* to describe as being like; to compare

like-ness *n.* resemblance; a copy

like-wise *adv.* in a similar way

lilt *n.* a light song; a rhythmical way of speaking

lil-y *n., pl.* -ies

any of various plants bearing trumpet-shaped flowers

limb *n.* a large bough of a tree; an animal's appendage used for movement or grasping; an arm or leg

lim-ber *adj.* bending easily; pliable; moving easily; agile

lime *n.* a tropical citrus edible green fruit; calcium oxide

lime-light *n.* a focus of public attention; the center of attention

lim-er-ick *n.* a humorous verse of five lines

lim-it *n.* a boundary; a maximum or a minimum number or amount

limn *v.* to describe; to depict by drawing limner *n.*

li-mo-nite *n.* a natural iron oxide used as an ore of iron

lim-ou-sine *n.* a luxurious large vehicle; a

small bus used to carry passengers to airports and hotels

limp *v.* to walk lamely. *adj.* Lacking or having lost rigidity; not firm or strong

lim-pet *n.* any of numerous marine gastropod mollusks having a conical shell and adhering to tidal rocks

lim-pid *adj.* transparently clear limpidity *n.*, limpidly *adv.*

lin-den *n.* any of various shade trees having heart-shaped leaves

lin-e-age *n.* a direct line of descent from an ancestor

lin-e-a-ment *n.* a contour, shape, or feature of the body and especially of the the face

lin-e-ar *adj.* of, pertaining to, or resembling a line; long and narrow

lin-en *n.* thread, yarn, or fabric made of flax; household articles, such as sheets and pillow cases

ling *n.* any of various marine food fishes related to the cod

lin-ger *v.* to be slow in parting or reluctant to leave; to be slow in acting; to procrastinate linger *n.*, -ingly *adv.*

lin-ge-rie *n.* women's undergarment

lingo *n.*, *pl.* goes language that is unfamiliar; a specialized vocabulary

lin-guist *n.* one who is fluent in more than one language

lin-i-ment *n.* a liquid or semiliquid medicine applied to the skin

lin-ing *n.* a material which is used to cover an inside surface

lin-net *n.* a small Old World finch

li-no-le-um *n.* a floor covering

lin-seed *n.* the seed of flax, used in paints and varnishes

lin-tel *n.* a horizontal beam across the top of a door which supports the weight of the structure above

li-on *n.*

a large carnivorous mammal of the cat family, found in Africa and India

li-on-ize *v.* to treat someone as a celebrity

liq-ue-fy *or* liq-ui-fy *v.* to make liquid liquefaction *n.*

li-queur *n.* a sweet alcoholic beverage; a cordial

liq-ui-date *v.* to settle a debt by payment or other settlement; to close a business by settling accounts and dividing up assets; to get rid of, to kill liquidation, liquidator *n.*

liq-uor *n.* a distilled alcoholic beverage

lisle *n.* a fine, tightly twisted cotton thread

lisp *n.* a speech defect or mannerism marked by lisping

list *n.* a series of numbers or words; a tilt to one side

list-less *adj.* lacking energy or enthusiasm listlessly *adv.*

lit-a-ny *n.*, *pl.* -ies a prayer in which phrases recited by a leader are alternated with answers from a congregation

li-tchi *or* li-chee *n.* a Chinese tree, bearing edible fruit

lit-er-al *adj.* conforming to the exact meaning of a word literally *adv.*, literalistic *adj.*

lit-er-al-ism *n.* adherence to the explicit sense of a given test; literal portrayal; realism literalist *n.*

lit-er-ar-y *adj.* pertaining to literature; appropriate to or used in literature

lit-er-ate *adj.* having the ability to read and write literacy *n.*

lithe *adj.* bending easily; supple lithely *adv.*, litheness *n.*

lith-i-um *n.* a silver-white, soft metallic element symbolized by Li

li-thog-ra-phy *n.* a printing process lithograph *n. & v.*

li-thol-o-gy *n.* the microscopic study and classification of rocks -ist *n.*

lit-i-gate *v.* to conduct a legal contest by judicial process litigant, litigation *n.*

lit-to-ral *adj.* relating to or existing on a shore *n.* a shore

lit-ur-gy *n.*, *pl.* -ies a prescribed rite or body of rites for public worship

live-ly *adj.* vigorous liveableness *n.*

liv-er *n.* the large, very vascular, glandular organ of vertebrates which secretes bile

live-stock *n.* farm animals raised for human use

live wire *n.*, *Slang* an energetic person

liv-id *adj.* discolored from a bruise; very angry

liz-ard *n.*

one of various reptiles, usually with an elongated scaly body

load *n.* a mass or weight that is lifted or supported; anything, as cargo

loaf *n.*, *pl.* loaves a food, especially bread, that is shaped into a mass *v.* to spend time in idleness

loam *n.* soil that consists chiefly of sand, clay, and decayed plant matter

loan *n.* money lent with interest to be repaid; something borrowed for temporary use *v.* to lend

loath *adj.* averse

loathe *v.* to dislike intensely

loath-ing *n.* intense dislike

loath-some *adj.* arousing disgust loathsomely *adv.*, loathsomeness *n.*

lob *v.* to hit or throw in a high arc

lob-by *n., pl.* -ies a foyer, as in a hotel or theatre; a group of private persons trying to influence legislators

lobe *n.* a curved or rounded projection or division, as the fleshy lower part of the ear lobar, lobed *adj.*

lob-lol-ly *n., pl.* -ies a mudhole; mire

lo-bo *n.* the gray wolf

lo-bot-o-my *n., pl.* -mies surgical severance of nerve fibers by incision into the brain

lob-ster *n.*

any of several large, edible marine crustaceans

lob-ule *n.* a small lobe; a subdivision of a lobe

lo-cal *adj.* pertaining to, being in, or serving a particular area or place locally *adv.*

lo-cale *n.* a locality where a particular event takes place; the setting or scene, as of a novel

lo-cate *v.* to determine the place, position, or boundaries of; to look for and find locator *n.*

loch *n., Scot.* a lake

lock *n.* a device used, as on a door, to secure or fasten

lock-et *n.* a small, ornamental case for a keepsake, often a picture, worn as a pendant on a necklace

lock-jaw *n.* tetanus

lock-smith *n.* a person who makes or repairs locks

lo-co *adj., Slang* insane

lo-co-mo-tion *n.* the act of moving

lo-co-mo-tive *n.* a self-propelled vehicle that is generally electric or diesel-powered and is used for moving railroad cars

lo-cust *n.* any of numerous grasshoppers which often travel in swarms and damage vegetation

loft *n.* one of the upper, generally unpartitioned floors of an industrial building

ings

loge *n.* a small compartment, especially a box in a theatre; a small partitioned area

log-gi-a *n.* a roofed but open arcade along the front of a building; an open balcony

log-ic *n.* the science dealing with the principles of reasoning, especially of the method and validity of deductive reasoning

log-i-cal *adj.* something marked by consistency of reasoning logically *adv.*

lo-gis-tics *pl., n.* the methods of procuring, maintaining, and replacing material and personnel logistic *adj.*

lo-go-type *n.* identifying symbol for a company or publication

lo-gy *adj.* something marked by sluggishness -iness *n.*

loins the thighs and groin; the reproductive organs

loi-ter *v.* to stay for no apparent reason; to dawdle or delay loiterer *n.*

loll *v.* to move or act in a lax, lazy or indolent manner

lol-ly-gag *v., Slang* to fool around

lone *adj.* single; isolated; sole

lone-ly *adj.* being without companions loneliness *n.*

lon-er *n.* a person who avoids the company of others

long-bow *n.* a wooden bow that is approximately five to six feet in length

lon-gev-i-ty *n.* long life; long duration; seniority

lon-gi-tude *n.* the angular distance that is east and west of the prime meridian at Greenwich, England

lon-gi-tu-di-nal *adj.* of or relating to the length; relating to longitude

look *v.* to examine with the eyes; to see; to glance, gaze, or stare at

loom *v.* to come into view as an image; to seem to be threatening

loo-ny *or* **loo-ney** *adj.* loony *n.* crazy

loose *adj.* not fastened; not confined or fitting; free

loot *n.* goods, usually of significant value, taken in time of war; goods that have been stolen *v.* to plunder

lope *v.* to run with a steady gait lope, lopper *n.*

lop-sid-ed *adj.* larger or heavier on one side than on the other; tilting to one side lopsidedly *adv.*, -ness *n.*

lo-qua-cious *adj.* overly talkative loquaciously *adv.*, loquacity *n.*

Lord *n.* God. a man having dominion and power over other people

lore *n.* traditional fact; knowledge that has been gained through education or experience

lorn *n.* forlorn

lose *v.* to mislay; to fail to keep

lost *adj.* unable to find one's way

lot *n.* fate; fortune; a parcel of land having boundaries

lo-tion *n.* a liquid medicine for external use on the hands and body

lounge *v.* to move or act in a lazy, relaxed manner. *n.* A room, as in a hotel or theatre; a couch **-er** *n.*

louse *n., pl.* **lice**

a small, wingless biting or sucking insect which lives as a parasites on various animals and also on human beings.

lous-y *adj.* lice infested *Slang* mean; poor; inferior

lout *n.* an awkward, stupid person **loutish** *adj.*

love *n.* intense affection for another arising out of kinship or personal ties; a strong feeling of attraction resulting from sexual desire

lov-er *n.* a person who loves another; a sexual partner

low *adj.* not high; being below or under normal height, rank, or level; depressed

lox *n.* smoked salmon; liquid oxygen.

lu-au *n.* a traditional Hawaiian feast

lub-ber *n.* an awkward, clumsy or stupid person; an inexperienced sailor

lu-bri-cous *adj.* smooth, unstable; shifty

lu-cid *adj.* easily understood; mentally clear; rational; shining **lucidity** *n.*

Lucifer *n.* the devil; Satan

lu-cra-tive *adj.* producing profits or great wealth

lu-cre *n.* money; profit

lu-cu-brate *v.* to study or work laboriously

lu-di-crous *adj.* amusing or laughable through obvious absurdity; ridiculous

luge *n.* a small sled

lu-gu-bri-ous *adj.* mournful; dejected; especially exaggeratedly

lull *v.* to cause to rest or sleep; to cause to have a false sense of security

lul-la-by *n., pl.* **-bies** A song to lull a child to sleep

lum-ba-go *n.* painful rheumatic pain of the muscles and tendons of the lumbar region

lum-bar *adj.* part of the back and sides between the lowest ribs and the pelvis

lu-mi-nar-y *n., pl.* **-ies** a celestial body, as the sun; a notable person

lu-mi-nes-cence *n.* an emission of light without heat, as in fluorescence

lu-mi-nous *adj.* emitting or reflecting light; bathed in steady light; illuminated

lum-mox *n.* a clumsy oaf

lu-na-cy *n., pl.* **-ies** insanity

lu-nar *adj.* of, relating to, caused by the moon

lu-na-tic *n.* a crazy person

lunch-eon *n.* a lunch

lung *n.*

one of the two spongy organs that constitute the basic respiratory organ of air-breathing vertebrates

lunge *n.* a sudden forward movement

lu-pus *n.* a bacterial disease of the skin

lus-cious *adj.* very pleasant to smell or taste; appealing to the senses

lush *adj.* producing luxuriant growth or vegetation *Slang* An alcoholic **-ly** *adv.*

lust *n.* intense sexual desire; an intense longing; a craving **lustful** *adj.*

lus-ter *or* **lus-tre** *n.* a glow of reflected light; sheen; brilliance or radiance

lust-y *adj.* vigorous; healthy; robust; lively **lustily** *adv.*

lu-te-ti-um *or* **lu-te-ci-um** *n.* a silvery rare-earth metallic element symbolized by Lu

lux-u-ri-ant *adj.* growing or producing abundantly; lush; plentiful **-tly** *adv.*

lux-u-ri-ate *v.* to enjoy luxury or abundance

lymph node *n.* a roundish body of lymphoid tissue; lymph gland

lynch *v.* to execute without authority or the due process of law

lynx *n.*

a wildcat *adj.* having acute eyesight

lyre *n.* an ancient Greek stringed instrument related to the harp

ly-so-some *n.* a cellular organelle containing various hydrolytic enzymes

ly-so-zyme *n.* a basic bateriolytic protein present in human tears and saliva

M, m The thirteenth letter of the English alphabet

ma-ca-bre *adj.* suggesting death and decay **macabrly** *adv.*

mac-ad-am *n.* pavement for roads consisting of layers of compacted, broken stone, usually cemented with asphalt and tar *v.* the laying down of layers of small stones, held together with asphalt or tar

mac-a-ro-ni *n.* dried pasta made into short tubes and prepared as food

mac-a-roon *n.* small cookie

ma-caw *n.* the largest type of tropical American parrots

mace *n.* an aromatic spice made by grinding the cover of the nutmeg

mac-e-doine *n.* a jellied salad, or mixture of diced vegetables or fruits

mac-er-ate *v.* to make a solid substance soft **maceration** *n.*

ma-chet-e *n.* a large, heavy type of knife used for cutting sugarcane

mach-i-nate *v.* to plot

ma-chine *n.* device built to use energy to do work **machinery** *n.,* **machinable** *adj.,* **machined** *v.*

ma-chine lan-guage *n.* in Computer Science, the system of numbers or instructions for coding input data which can be then directly processed by a computer

ma-chin-er-y *n.* a collection of machines as a whole; the mechanism or operating parts of a machine; literary devices

ma-chin-ist *n.* the person who operates, assembles and repairs machines for others

ma-chis-mo *n.* an exaggerated sense of masculinity; a strong sense of

mach-me-ter *n.* an indicator that measures airspeed relative to the speed of sound, and then indicates the speed that an airplance using such an indiciator, can exceed without sustaining damage due to compressibility effects

ma-cho *adj.* exhibiting machismo in character; agressive

mack-er-el *n.* kind of fish that is found in the Atlantic Ocean

mack-in-tosh *n.* raincoat

mac-ra-me *n.* the craft of tying knots in a geometrical pattern

mac-ro-bi-ot-ic *adj.* being an extremely restricted diet to promote longevity; for the well-being of

ma-cron *n.* the (-) placed over a vowel to indicate a long sound

mac-ro-scop-ic *adj.* large enough to be seen by the naked eye

mad *adj.* being angry; insane **madder** adj. **madness** *n.,* **madly** *adv.*

mad-am *n.* title used to address a married woman; a polite address

made *v.* past tense of make

mad-e-moi-selle *n.* an unmarried French girl; used as a title

made--to--order *adj.* to be custommade; designed a certain way

made--up *adj.* being fabricated; invented; falsely devised

mad-house *n.* a place of confusion uproar and disorder

mad-ri-gal *n., Music* unaccompanied song **madrigalist** *n.*

mael-strom *n.* any irresistible or dangerous force; whirlpool

maes-tro *n.* a person mastering any art; a composer or conductor

mag-a-zine *n.* publication of reading marterial; explosives storehouse

ma-gen-ta *n.* a purplish red color or hue; known as fuchsine

mag-got *n.* the legless larva insects; an eccentric idea **maggoty** *adj.*

mag-ic *n.* art of illusions **magically** *adv.,* **magical** *adj.*

mag-is-trate *n.* civil officer of law **magistratically** *adv.*

mag-ma *n.* the molten rock beneath the earth's surface

mag-nan-i-mous *adj.* being forgiving; generous **-ness** *n.,* **-ly** *adv.*

mag-nate *n.* kind of business tycoon

mag-ne-sia *n.* a light, white powder used in medicine as an antacid

mag-ne-si-um *n.* a light, silvery metallic element which burns with a hot flame; the form of light

mag-net *n.*

body attracting other magnetic material **-ically** *adv.,* **-ize** *v.*

mag-net-ic *adj.* pertaining to magnetism or a magnet **magnetically** *adv.*

magnetic field *n.* the area in the neighborhood of a magnet or of an electric current, marked by the existence of a detectable magnetic force

mag-net-ite *n.* a black iron oxide in mineral form of the spinel group

mag-net-ize *v.* to have magnetic properties **magnetizable** *adj.*

mag-ne-to *n.* small alternator that uses magnets to operate

mag-nif-i-cent *adj.* beautiful **magnificence** *n.,* **magnificently** *adv.*

mag-ni-fy v. increase in size **magnification** n., **magnifiable** adj.

mag-nil-o-quent adj. speaking in a lofty manner **magniloquently** adv.

mag-ni-tude n. the greatness in size

mag-no-lia n. flowering tree

mag-num n. wine bottle holding about two quarts

mag-pie n. large, noisy bird

ma-ha-ra-ja n. a king or prince who rules an Indian state

ma-ha-ra-ni n. the wife of the maharaja; a Hindu princess

ma-hat-ma n. a title of respect

ma-hog-a-ny n., pl. **mahoganies** trees with hard wood; brownish

maid n. a young unmarried woman or girl

maid-en n. young girl

maid-en-hair n. a delicate fern with dark stems and lightgreen, feathery fronds

maid-en name n. woman's family name before marriage

mail n. printed matter **mailable** adj., **mailbox** n., **mailed** adj.

mail order n. goods which are ordered and sent by mail

maim v. to cripple or disfigure another **maimer** n.

main adj. being most important part **mainly** adv.

main-land n. the land part of a country as distinguished from an island

main-line v. to inject a drug directly into a vein; main highway

main-stream n. a main direction or line of thought or influence

main-tain v. keep in existence **maintainer** n., **maintainable** adj.

maize n. type of corn

maj-es-ty n. stateliness; one's exualted dignity **majesties** pl.

ma-jor adj. being greater in importance, rank, or dignity

ma-jor-ette n. a young woman who marches and twirls a baton in her hand usually in a parade

ma-jor-i-ty n. the state of having a greater number of something

ma-jor med-i-cal n. a type of insurance policy which one has

make v. create; cause to happen **maker** n., **makable** adj.

make--be-lieve n. something pretended; imagined; fantasy

make--up n. composition

mal-a-chite n. a green basic copper carbonate of copper

mal-a-droit adj. lacking skill **maladroitness** n., **maladroitly** adv.

mal-a-dy n., pl. **maladies** chronic disease or sickness

mal-aise n. the vague discomfort sometimes indicating the beginning of an illness

mal-a-prop-ism n. foolish misuse of a word; misapplication of a word

mal-ap-ro-pos adj. being not appropriate in style

ma-lar-i-a n., disease caused by the bite of sporozoan parasites in the red blood cells **malarious** adj.

ma-lar-key n. foolish or insincere talk

mal-con-tent adj. unhappy with surroundings; dissatisfied

mal-de-mer n. seasickness

male adj. being a man

mal-e-dic-tion n. a curse; execration; to speak evil of

mal-for-ma-tion n. a defective form of something; wrong-doing

mal-func-tion n. the failure to work

mal-ice n. the desire to harm others **maliciously** adv., **maliciousness** n.

ma-lign v. to speak evil of **malignly** adv., **maligner** n.

ma-lig-nant adj., Pathol. to be relating to tumors **malignantly** adv., -cy n.

ma-lin-ger v. pretend sickness to avoid work **malingerer** n.

mal-lard n. wild duck

mal-let n. hammer with a short handle; barrel-shaped head

mal-nour-ished adj. being underfed; lacking food; without food

mal-oc-clu-sion n. improper alignment of the teeth

mal-prac-tice n. the mistreatment by a doctor; negligent

malt n. grain **malty** adj.

mal-treat v. to treat another unkindly **maltreatment** n.

mam-mal n. the group of animals who suckle their young **mammalian** adj.

mam-mog-ra-phy n. x-ray of the breast for detection of cancer

mam-moth n. extinct form of an elephant with large, curved tusks

man n. the adult male; the human race; a human being; manhood

man-a-cle n. handcuffs

man-age v. direct or control **manageable** adj., -ability n.

man-ag-er n. one in charge of a situation **managership** n.

man-a-tee n. type of aquatic mammal with a broad round tail

man-date n. an order or command

man-da-to-ry adj. required

man-do-lin n. a musical instrument

mandolinist *n.*

mane *n.*

long and heavy hair growing on animals necks maned *adj.*

mange *n.* the skin disease of the dogs marked by the loss of hair

man-ger *n.* the box for animal feed

man-gle *v.* to disfigure or to mutilate mangled, mangling *v.*

man-grove *n.* tropical tree

man-han-dle *v.* to handle roughly manhandled *adj.*

man-hole *n.* sewer drain

ma-ni-a *n.* the desire for something

man-i-cot-ti *n.* pasta

man-i-cure *n.* the taking care of the fingernails manicurist *n.*

man-i-fest *n.* the list of cargo a vehicle carries manifestation *n.*

man-i-fold *adj.* to be having many parts, or types; having a variety

ma-nip-u-late *v.* to manage shrewdly manipulation *n.*

man-kind *n.* human race

man--made *adj.* not developed naturally; made by mankind

man-ner *n.* way in which things are done mannerless *adj.*

man-ner-ly *adj.* being well-behaved; good manners mannerliness *n.*

ma-nom-e-ter *n.* instrument to measure pressure

man-or *n.* estate manorial *adj.*

man-slaugh-ter *n., Law* the unlawful killing of another without malice

man-tel *n.* shelf over a fireplace

man-til-la *n.* light scarf

man-u-al *adj.* operated by the hand

man-u-fac-ture *v.* make a product manufacturer *n.,* -able *adj.*

ma-nure *n.* animal dung used for fertilizer on crops and grass

man-u-script *n.* a typed copy of an article, or book

man-y *adj.* indefinite number

map *n.* plane surface of a region mapper *n.,* mapped *v.,*mapping *v.*

ma-ple syr-up *n.* concentrating the sap of the sugar maple

mar *v.* deface marer *n.*

mar-a-thon *n.* the foot race of 26 miles

mar-ble *n.* the limestone marblize *v.,* marbling *n.*

march *v.* to walk with measured steps marching *n.*

mare *n.* female of the horse

mar-ga-rine *n.* kind of butter substitute

mar-gin *n.* edge of printed text marginal *adj.,* marginally *adv.*

mar-i-jua-na *n.* kind of hallucinogenic drug; a wild tobacco

ma-ri-na *n.* harbor for boats

mar-i-nade *n.* brine for soaking meat, fish, or vegetables

ma-rine *adj.* to be pertaining to the sea mariner *n.*

mar-i-o-nette *n.* puppet operated by strings

mark *n.* visible impression

mar-lin *n.* large marine game fish

ma-roon *v.* to abandon one on the shore; a dark red color

mar-riage *n.* the legal union of two people in wedlock marriageability *n.,* -able *adj.*

mar-row *n.* the tissue in bone cavities

marsh *n.* low, wet land; swamp marshy *adj.* marshiness *n.*

mar-shal *n.* military officer

marsh-mal-low *n.* kind of soft confection which is edible

mar-su-pi-al *n.* animals with external pouches such as a kangaroo

mar-ten *n.*

a weasel-like mammal of eastern North America with arboreal habits; the valuable brown fur of the marten

mar-tial arts *pl., n.* self-defense, such as karate

mar-ti-ni *n.* cocktail of gin and dry vermouth; vodka may be used

mar-tyr *n.* person who would die for a cause martyrdom *n.*

mar-zi-pan *n.* paste of almonds, sugar and egg whites made into candy shaped into various forms

mar-vel *n.* be in awe

mas-car-a *n.* the cosmetic used for coloring the eyelashes

mas-cot *n.* object to bring good luck

mas-cu-line *adj.* male sex

mash *n.* the mixture to distill alcohol; to gain the affection of

mask *n.* covering to conceal the face

mas-o-chism *n.* the sexual pleasure from pain masochistic *adj.,* masochist *n.*

ma-son *n.* brick layer

mas-quer-ade *n.* a costume party or gathering for entertainment

mass *n.* body of matter with no form; a Eucharistic celebration

mas-sa-cre *n.* savage killing of human beings **massacrer** *n.*

mas-sage *n.* rub down of one's body to relieve tension **massager** *n.*

mas-sive *adj.* of great intensity

mast *n.* pole which supports the sails of boats

mas-ter *n.* person with the control

mas-ter-piece *n.* work of art

mas-ti-cate *v.* to chew **-able adj.**

mas-to-don *n.* kind of extinct mammal which differ from mammoths

mas-tur-ba-tion *n.* ones sexual stimulation without intercourse

mat-a-dor *n.* bullfighter

match *n.* identical; piece of wood that ignites **matcher** *n.*

ma-te-ri-al-ize *v.* to take form or shape; to make material

ma-te-ri-el *n.* the equipment or the supplies used by an organization

ma-ter-nal *adj.* relating to mother **maternally** *adv.,* **maternalistic** *adj.*

math-e-mat-ics *n.* the study of form, quantity and magnitude of numbers **mathematically** *adv.,* **-cal** *adj.*

mat-i-nee *n.* afternoon movie

mat-ri-cide *n.* one who kills his mother **matricidal adj.**

ma-tric-u-late *v.* enroll into a college **matriculation** *n.*

mat-ri-mo-ny *n.* ceremony of marriage **matrimonial** *adj.*

ma-tron *n.* married woman

mat-ter *n.* the substance of anything

ma-ture *adj.* completely developed **maturity** *n.,* **maturer** adj., **-est** adj.

mat-zo *n.* flat piece of unleavened bread eaten at the Passover

maud-lin *adj.* sentimental

maul *n.* heavy hammer

maun-der *v.* talk incoherent

mau-so-le-um *n.* large tomb

mav-er-ick *n.* an unbranded calf

max-i-mum *n.* greatest possible quantity or value

may *v.* permitted or allowed

may-be *adv.* perhaps

may-on-naise *n.* the dressing used for salads and sandwiches

may-or *n.* chief magistrate of a city or town **mayoralty** *n.*

maze *n.* a complicated network of passages **mazy** *adj.*

mead *n.* alcoholic beverage

mead-ow *n.* a tract of grassland

mea-ger *adj.* thin; lean in quantity **meagerness** *n.,* **meagerly** *adv.*

mean *v.* purpose or intent; bad tempered **meanness** *n.*

me-an-der *v.* wander about **meanderingly** *adv.,* **-drous** *adj.*

mea-sles *n.* kind of contagious disease marked by red circular spots

mea-sly *adj.* very small

meas-ure *n.* the dimension of anything **measurer** *n.*

meat *n.* tissue of an animal used as food; the core of something

me-chan-ic *n.* person skilled with tools **mechanical** *adj.*

mech-a-nism *n.* the parts of a machine which help it run

med-al *n.*

an award **medalist** *n.*

med-dle *v.* to interfere in other's affairs or business **meddlesome** *adj.,* **-er** *n.*

me-di-al *adj.* being situated in the middle; between two

me-di-ate *v.* to help settle or decide a dispute **mediative adj.**

med-ic *n.* intern; corpsman

med-i-cal *adj.* the study of medicine **medically** *adv.*

med-i-cine *n.* the treatment of diseases or illness

me-di-o-cre *adj.* being common; plain **mediocrity** *n.*

med-i-tate *v.* in contemplative thought **meditator** *n.,* **meditative** *adj.*

me-di-um *n.* the middle; intermediary professing to give messages from the dead

med-ley *n.* a jumble; musical composition made up of songs

meek *adj.* to be lacking in spirit **meekness** *n.*

meet *v.* to come upon

meg-a-ton *n.* weight equal to one million tons

mel-an-chol-y *adj.* gloomy or sad **-iness** *n.* **melancholically** *adv.*

mel-a-no-ma *n.,* *pl.* **melanomas** *or* **melanomata** malignant mole

mel-io-rate *v.* to improve **meliotor** *n.,* **meliorateable** *adj.*

mel-lif-er-ous *adj.* to be producing or yielding honey

mel-o-dra-ma *n.* type of dramatic presentation **-tic** *adj.,* **-tics** *n.*

mel-on *n.* the fruit of the gourd family eaten raw as fruits

melt *v.* change from solid to liquid **melter** *n.,* **meltable** *adj.*

melt-down *n.* melting of a nuclear-reactor core

mem-ber *n.* a person belonging to a

club **membership** *n.*, **-less** *adj.*

mem-brane *n.* thin layer of skin **membranous** *adj.*

me-men-to *n.* keepsake

mem-oir *n.* an autobiography of a person; a remembrance

mem-o-ra-ble *adj.* worth remembering **memorably** *adv.*

mem-o-rize *v.* to commit to one's memory **-zation** *n.*, **-zable** *adj.*

men-ace *n.* a threatening person **menacly** *adv.*

me-nar-che *n.* beginning of the menstruation cycle

me-ni-al *adj.* requiring little skill **menially** *adv.*

men-o-pause *n.*, *Physiol.* time of final menstruation **menopausal** *adj.*

men-tal *adj.* of the mind

men-tal re-tar-da-tion *n.* a mental deficiency

men-tion *v.* refer to briefly **mentioner** *n.*, **mentionable** *adj.*

men-u *n.* the list of the food at a restaurant

mer-can-tile *adj.* to be relating to commerce

mer-ce-nar-y *n.* a greedy person **mercenarily** *adv.*

mer-cer-ize *v.* to treat cotton yarn

mer-chan-dise *n.* goods bought and sold **merchandiser** *n.*

mer-chant *n.* person who operates a retail business

mer-cu-ry *n.* the silvery liquid found in thermometers

mer-cy *n.*, *pl.* mercies kind treatment **-iless** *adj.*, **mercifully** *adv.*

mere *adj.* no more than is stated **merely** *adv.*, **merest** **adj.**

merge *v.* to unite as one **mergence** *n.*

mer-it *n.* act worthy of praise **meritedly** *adv.*, **meritless** *adj.*

mer-maid *n.* an imaginary sea creature half woman half fish

mer-ry-go-round *n.* kind of carrousel; seats in animal form

me-sa *n.* flat-topped hill

mesh *n.* open spaces in wire

mess *n.*, *pl.* messes disorderly confused heap

mes-sage *n.* the information which is sent from one person to another by word of mouth

mess-y *adj.* untidy; dirty

me-tab-o-lism *n.* chemical changes in living cells

met-a-gal-ax-y *n.* the universe

met-a-mor-pho-sis *n.* change in the structure and formation of living animals **metamorphoses** pl.

me-te-or *n.* moving particle in the solar system resembling light

me-te-or-ol-o-gy *n.* the science of weather forecasting **-al** *adj.*

meth-a-done *n.* man-made narcotic used to treat heroin addiction

meth-od *n.* the process of carrying out something

me-tic-u-lous *adj.* very precise **meticulously** *adv.*

met-ro *n.* subway system

met-ro-nome *n.* instrument designed to mark musical time **-nomic** *adj.*

me-trop-o-lis *n.* the large capital city of a state, country or region

mew *n.* hideaway

mez-za-nine *n.* the lowest balcony

mi-crobe *n.* minute living organism **microbial** *adj.*

mi-cro-com-put-er *n.* type of computer using a microprocessor

mi-cro-film *n.* film used to record reduced size printed material

mi-cro-phone *n.*

instrument which amplifies sound

mi-cro-proc-es-sor *n.* semiconductor processing unit

mi-cro-scope *n.* device to magnify small objects

mi-cro-scop-ic *adj.* very small; minute **microscopically** *adv.*

mi-cro-wave *n.* a rather short electromagnetic wave

mi-cro-wave o-ven *n.* the oven using microwaves to heat food quickly

mid-day *n.* noon

mid-dle *adj.* the center

midg-et *n.* very small person ·

mid-night *n.* 12 o'clock p.m.

mid-point *n.* near the middle

mid-riff *n.* midsection of the human torso; a section of garment

mid-ship-man *n.* person who is in training at the U.S. Naval Academy; a student

mid-term *n.* the middle of academic an term

miff *n.* a displeasure

might *n.* a force **mighty** *adj.*, **-ily** *adv.*

mi-graine *n.* kind of severe headaches **migrainous** adj.

mi-grant *n.* a person constantly moving to find work

mi-grate *v.* move from place to place **-tory** *adj.*, **migration** *n.*

mild *adj.* gentle in manner

mildness *n.*, mildly *adv.*

mile *n.* 5,280 feet

mil-i-ta-rize *v.* train for war

mi-li-tia *n.* armed forces used only in an emergency

mil-li-ner *n.* one who designs, makes, or sells women's hats

mil-lion *n.* number equal to 1,000 x 1,000; a very large number

mim-e-o-graph *n.* kind of duplicating machine which uses stencils

mim-ic *v.* imitate another person mimical *adj.*

mince *v.* to chop something into small pieces mincing *adj.*, mincer *n.*

mind *n.* organ for thought mindful *adj.*, mindfulness *n.*

mine *n.* underground excavation; personal belongings

min-er-al *n.* an inorganic crystalline

min-e-stro-ne *n.* kind of thick veg-etable soup

min-gle *v.* to mix together

min-i-a-ture *n.* copy greatly reduced in size; smaller than usual

mini-disk *n.* 5.25 inch floppy disk used for storing important data

min-i-mum *n.* least amount

min-is-ter *n.* pastor of a church ministerial *adj.*

mink *n.*

an animal with valuable fur

min-now *n.* small, fresh water fish

mi-nor *adj.* not of legal age

mi-nor-i-ty *n., pl.* minorities smaller in number of two groups

min-u-et *n.* kind of slow, stately dance; graceful

mi-nus *prep., Math.* reduced, by subtraction of numbers

min-ute *n.* 60 seconds in time; small in size; short space of time

mir-a-cle *n.* kind of supernatural event; extremely unusual

mi-rage *n.* optical illusion

mirth *n.* a merriment or a joyousness mirthfulness *n.*, mirthful *adj.*

mis-an-thrope *n.* the hatred or distrusts of mankind

mis-ap-pro-pri-ate *v.* to embezzle money misappropriation *n.*

mis-car-riage *n.* the premature birth of a fetus before it is viable

mis-cel-la-ne-ous *adj.* mixed variety of parts, etc.; many different

mis-chief *n.* a behavior causing harm or damage something

mis-con-ceive *v.* to misunderstand the meaning of something

mis-de-mean-or *n., Law* a crime less serious than a felony

mis-er *n.* person who hoards money miserly *adj.*, miserliness *n.*

mis-er-a-ble *adj.* very unhappy

mis-er-ly *n.* the state of great unhappiness; depression

mis-fire *v.* fail to explode

mis-fit *n.* one not adjusted to his environment; a poor fit

mis-for-tune *n.* bad luck

mis-giv-ing *n.* the feeling of doubt

mis-han-dle *v.* to manage inefficiently, wrong, or ignorantly

mis-hap *n.* an unfortunate accident

mish-mash *n.* jumble or hodgepodge

mis-in-ter-pret *v.* understand incorrectly misinterpreter *n.*

mis-judge *v.* make a mistake in judgment

mis-lay *v.* lose something

mis-lead *v.* to deceive misleader *n.*, misleading *adj.*

mis-no-mer *n.* an inappropriate name

mi-sog-a-my *n.* the hatred of the marriage

mis-pro-nounce *v.* to pronounce incorrectly or in an incorrect way

mi-sog-y-ny *n.* the hatred of women

Miss *n.* the title for unmarried girl

mis-sile *n.* object that shot at a target

mis-sion *n.* kind of task to be carried out to obtain a result

mis-take *n.* wrong decision

mis-tle-toe *n.* parasitic plant

mis-tress *n.* a woman in authority

mis-trust *v.* have doubt

mite *n.* very small insect

mi-ter *n.*

a joint made by cuting two pices at an angle and then fitting them together

mit-i-gate *v.* to make less painful mitigator *n.*, mitigative *adj.*

mix *v.* blend; combine; unite mixable *adj.*, mixability *n.*

mix-up *n.* state of confusion

moan *n.* dull sound of pain

moat *n.* kind of trench around a castle

mob *n.* an unruly crowd or group of people mobbish *adj.*

mode *n.* a method of doing something

mod-el *n.* clothing displayer

mod-er-ate *adj.* not excessive moderateness *n.*, moderately *adv.*

mod-ern *adj.* up-to-date

mod-ern-ize *v.* to improve on something
modernzation *n.*

mod-est *adj.* shy; reserved
modesty *n.*, **modestly** *adv.*

mod-i-fy *v.* make different in form
modifier *n.*, **modifiable** *adj.*

mod-ule *n.* a series of standardized components **modular** *adj.*

mod-us op-er-an-di *n.* the method of operating; procedure

moist *adj.* sightly wet; damp
moisten *v.*, **moistly** *adv.*

mois-ture *n.* dampness
moisturize *v.*, **moisturizer** *n.*

mo-lar *n.* the grinding tooth

mo-las-ses *n.* the light brown syrup produced from sugar

mold *n.* growth produced on damp organic matter; pattern
moldy *adj.*, **moldeer** *n.*

mole *n.* spot on the human skin

mol-e-cule *n.* smallest part retaining its identity

mo-lest *v.* to accost someone sexually
molestation *n.*

mol-li-fy *v.* make less angry
molifier *n.*, **molifiable** *adj.*

molt *v.* to cast off or shed feathers

mol-ten *adj.* transform to liquid form by heat **moltenly** *adv.*

mo-men-tous *adj.* being of a great importance

mo-men-tum *n., pl.* -ta *or* -tums increasing force; body in motion

mon-arch *n.* one who reigns an empire or kingdom; ruler

mon-as-ter-y *n., pl.* **monasteries** the place where monks work and live

mon-e-tar-y *adj.* to be relating to money
monetarily *adv.*

mon-ey *n.* the medium of exchange

mon-grel *n.* the mixed breed animal

mo-ni-tion *n.* the caution or warning about something

monk *n.* a member of a religious order
monkishness *n.*, **monkishly** *adv.*

mon-key *n., pl.* **monkeys**
member of the primates, excluding man

mon-o-cle *n.* the eyeglass used for one eye

mo-nog-a-my *n.* sexual relationship with only one person

mon-o-logue *n.* speech by one person

mon-o-ma-ni-a *n.* mental disorder

mon-o-nu-cle-o-sis *n.* kind of infectious disease

mo-nop-o-ly *n., pl.* **monopolies** the exclusive ownership

mon-o-rail *n.* train traveling on a single rail to a specific destination

mon-o-the-ism *n.* the belief there is just one God; the one and only

mon-o-tone *n.* the sounds uttered in a single unvarying tone -ic *adj.*

mo-not-o-nous *adj.* lacking variety
monotoness *n.*, **monotonously** *adv.*

mon-ox-ide *n.* oxide containing one oxygen atom per molecule

mon-soon *n.* periodic wind

mon-tage *n.* a composite picture

month-ly *adj.* being payable each month; twelve times a year

mon-u-ment *n.* the object in memory of a person **monumental** *adj.*, -ally *adv.*

mooch *v. Slang* acquire by begging

mood *n.* the temporary state of one's mind

mood-y *adj.* being gloomy
moodiness *n.*, **moodily** *adv.*

moon *n.* earth's only satellite
moony *adj.*, **mooniness** *n.*

moon-lit *adj.* lit by the moon

moor *v.* fasten with anchors

moose *n.*

very large deer

moot *v.* debate; argue

mope *v.* to be dejected

mo-ped *n.* motorbike

mor-al *adj.* referring to conduct of right or wrong

mo-rale *n.* an individual's state of mind

mor-a-to-ri-um *n.* temporary pause

mor-bid *adj.* gruesome; gloomy
morbidness *n.*, **morbidly** *adv.*

more *adj.* being of greater number or degree

more-o-ver *adv.* furthermore

mo-res *n., pl.* moral customs of a social group

morgue *n.* place to keep dead bodies until they are claimed

mo-roc-co *n.* soft leather made of goatskin tanned with sumac

mo-ron *n.* an adult with a low intelligence level **moronism** *n.*, **moronic** *adj.*, **moronity** *n.*

mor-ose *adj.* marked by gloom
morosity *n.*, **morosely** *adv.*

mor-phine *n.* a highly addictive narcotic, derived from opium

mor-sel *n.* a small quantity of food

mor-tal *adj.* to having caused death; about to cause death

mor-tar-board *n.*

an academic cap topped by a stiff, flat square; a square board with a handle, for holding mortar

mort-gage *n.* conveyance as security for the repayment of a debt

mor-ti-cian *n.* undertaker

mo-sa-ic *n.* decorative inlaid design of tile

moss *n.* small green plants

most *adj.* majority of; greatest in quantity

moth *n.* nocturnal insect

moth-er *n.* female parent

mo-tif *n.* the main element or theme of something

mo-tile *adj.* being capable of moving alone

mo-tion *n.* the act of changing position; a proposal for action

mo-tive *n.* the need or the desire to act

mo-tor *n.* the device which develops energy for motion

mound *n.* small hill of earth

mourn *v.* to express one's grief or sorrow over something

mov-ie *n.* motion picture

mow *v.* to cut down

much *adj.* being of great amount or quantity; many in number

muck *n.* moist, sticky soil

mu-cus *n.* the liquid secreted by glands in the body

muf-fle *v.* to suppress; to deaden sound; to conceal or protect

mug *n.* large drinking cup

mug-gy *adj.* being humid and being sultry **muggily** *adv.*, **-ness** n.

mull *v.* ponder; think over

multi- *prefix* multiple; two or more

mul-ti-far-i-ous *adj.* having great variety **multifariousness** n.

mul-ti-ple *adj.* to be consisting of more than one individual or part

mul-ti-ply *v.* increase in amount or number

mul-ti-tude *n.* large amount or number of something

mum *adj.* not speaking

mum-ble *v.* to speak in a confused indistinct manner

mum-my *n.*, *pl.* **mummies** body embalmed for burial **mummify** *v.*

munch *v.* chew noisily

mun-dane *adj.* relating to the world

mur-der *n.* the crime of killing a person by will

mur-mur *n.* a low sound

mus-cle *n.* bodily tissue which produces strength

mus-cu-lar *adj.* brawny

mush-room *n.*

a fungus having an embrella-shaped cap on a stalk *v.* to grow or multiply quickly

mu-sic *n.* the organized tones in sequences; melodious

mu-si-cian *n.* a performer of music

mus-lin *n.* a sheer, or coarse fabric

muss *v.* to mess up

must *v.* to be forced to

mus-tang *n.* wild horse

mus-tard *n.* from the seeds of the mustard plant

mus-ter *v.* to come or bring things together

mustn't *contr.* must not

mute *adj.* unable to speak

mu-ti-late *v.* maim or cripple

mu-ti-ny *n.*, *pl.* **mutinies** revolt against lawful authority

mutt *n.*, *Slang* a dog that is of a mixed breed

mut-ter *v.* to speak or utter in a low voice with the lips partially closed

mut-ton *n.* the flesh of a fully grown sheep used for food

mu-tu-al *adj.* having the same relationship **mutuality** *n.*

my *adj.* of myself *interj.* to express surprise, dismay, or pleasure

my-ce-li-um *n.*, *pl.* **mycelia** the mass of filaments which form the main structure of a fungus

my-col-o-gy *n.* scientific study of fungi

my-e-li-tis *n.* the inflammation of the spinal cord or the bone marrow

my-elo-ma *n.* the tumor of the bone marrow

myo-car-dio-graph *n.* recording tool which traces the action of the heart muscles

myo-car-di-um *n.* muscular layer of the heart; along the heart wall

my-o-pia *n.* a visual defect

myr-i-ad *adj.* having large, indefinite aspects

myr-mi-don *n.* loyal follower

myr-tle *n.* evergreen shrub

my-self *pron.* one identical with me

mys-ter-y *n.*, *pl.* **mysteries** something that is not understood

mys-tic *n.* person practicing or believing in mysticism **mystical** *adj.*, **-cally** *adv.*

mys-ti-fy *v.* to perplex

N, n. The fourteenth letter of the English alphabet.

nab *v.*, *Slang* to seize

na-cho *n.* a tortilla, often small and triangular in shape, topped with cheese or chili sauce and baked

nag *v.* to bother by scolding or constant complaining *n.* a worthless horse **nagger** *n.*

nai-ad *n. Gr. Mythol.* a nymph presiding over and living in springs, brooks, and fountains

nail *n.* a thin pointed piece of metal for hammering into wood and other material to hold pieces together

na-ked *adj.* without clothes on the body; nude; exposed; uncovered **nakedly** *adv.*, **nakedness** *n.*

nam-by--pam-by *adj.* weak; indecisive; lacking in substance

name *n.* a title or word by which something or someone is known *v.* to give a name **nameable** *adj.*

nape *n.* the back of the neck

nap-kin *n.* a cloth or soft paper, used at the dinner table for wiping the lips and fingers

nar-cis-sus *n.* a widely grown type of bulbous plant

nar-co-sis *n.* a deep drug induced state of stupor or unconsciousness

nar-cot-ic *n.* a drug which dulls the senses, relieves pain, and induces a deep sleep; if abused, it can become habit-forming and cause convulsions or comas

nar-rate *v.* to tell a story or give a description in detail **narration** *n.*, **narrator** *v.*

nar-row *adj.* slender or small in width **narrowly** *adj.*

narrow--mind-ed *adj.* lacking sympathy or tolerance

nar-whal *n.*

an aquatic mammal of the Arctic regions, closely related to the white whale

na-sal *adj.* of or pertaining to the nose

na-stur-tium *n.* a five-petaled garden plant usually having red, yellow, or orange flowers

nas-ty *adj.* dirty, filthy, or indecent **nastily** *adv.*, **nastiness** *n.*

na-tal *adj.* pertaining to or associated with birth

na-tion *n.* a group of people made up of one or more nationalities under one government **-al** *adj.*, **nationally** *adv.*

na-tion-al-ism *n.* devotion to or concern for one's nation

na-tion-al-i-ty *n.* the fact or condition of belonging to a nation

na-tion-al-ize *v.* to place a nation's resources and industries under the control of the state

na-tive *n.* a person born in a country or place *adj.* belonging to one by nature or birth

na-tiv-i-ty *n.* birth, circumstances, or con-ditions; the birth of Christ

nat-u-ral *adj.* produced or existing by nature; not artificial *Mus.* a note that is not sharp or flat **naturalness** *n.*, **naturally** *adv.*

natural child-birth *n.* childbirth with little stress or pain; childbirth requiring training for the mother and father and medical supervision, but without the use of drugs, anesthesia, or surgery

nat-u-ral-ize *v.* to confer the privileges and rights of full citizenship **naturalization** *n.*

na-ture *n.* the universe and its phenomena; kind, sort, or type **natured** *adj.*

naught *n.* nothing; the number 0

naugh-ty *adj.* unruly; not proper **naughtily** *adv.*, **naughtiness** *n.*

nau-se-a *n.* an upset stomach with a feeling that one needs to vomit **-ous** *adj.*

nau-ti-cal *adj.* pertaining to ships or seamanship **nautically** *adv.*

na-val *adj.* of or relating to ships

na-vel *n.* a small mark or scar on the abdomen where the umbilical cord was attached

nav-i-ga-ble *adj.* sufficiently deep and wide enough to allow ships to pass

nav-i-gate *v.* to plan the course of a ship or aircraft; to steer a course **navigation**, **navigator** *n.*

na-vy *n.* one of a nation's organizations for defense; a nation's fleet of ships; a very dark blue

Ne-an-der-thal *adj.* suggesting a caveman in behavior or appearance; primitive or crude **Neanderthal** *n.*

neap tide *n.* a tide in the minimum range which occurs twice a month

near *adv.* at, to, or within a short time or distance *adj.* closely or intimately related **nearness** *n.*

near-by *adj. & adv.* adjacent

near-sight-ed *adj.* able to see clearly at short distances only

neat *adj.* tidy and clean; free from disorder and dirt **neatly** *adv.*, **neatness** *n.*

neb-u-lous *adj.* confused or vague

nec-es-sar-y *adj.* unavoidable
necessarily *adv.*

ne-ces-si-tate *v.* to make necessary; to oblige; to require

ne-ces-si-ty *n., pl.* -ies the condition of being necessary

neck *n.* the part of the body which connects the head and trunk; a narrow part or projection, as of land, a stringed instrument, or bottle. *v.* to caress and kiss

neck-tie *n.* a narrow strip of material worn around the neck

nec-tar *n.* a good-tasting beverage; a sweet fluid in various flowers, gathered by bees to help make honey nectarous *adj.*

nee *n.* born; the surname a woman was born with

need *n.* the lack of something desirable, useful, or necessary

nee-dle *n.* a slender, pointed steel implement which contains an eye through which thread is passed

needle-point *n.* decorative stitching done on canvas

need-n't *contr.* need not

ne-far-i-ous *adj.* extremely wicked

ne-gate *v.* to nullify; to deny; to rule out negation *n.*

neg-a-tive *adj.* expressing denial or disapproval; not positive
negatively *adj.*, negativeness *n.*

neglect *v.* to ignore; to pay no attention to neglectful *adj.*

neg-li-gee *n.* a woman's loose-fitting dressing gown

neg-li-gent *adj.* to neglect what needs to be done; neglectful

ne-go-ti-ate *v.* to confer with another person to reach an agreement
negotiation, negotiator *n.*

Ne-gro *n.* a member of the Black race; a black person

ne-groid *adj.* of or relating to the Black race negroid *n.*

neigh-bor *n.* one who lives near another; fellowman

neighbor-hood *n.* a section or small region that possesses a specific quality

nei-ther *adj.* not one or the other *pron.* Not the one or the other *conj.* Not either; also not

neo *prefix* recent; new

neo-dym-i-um *n.* a metallic element of the rare-earth group, symbolized by Nd.

ne-on *n.* an inert gaseous element used in lighting fixtures, symbolized by Ne

ne-o-nate *n.* a newborn child less than a month old

ne-o-na-tol-o-gy *n.* the medical study of the first 60 days of a baby's life

neo-phyte *n.* a novice; a beginner.

ne-o-plasm *n.* a tumor tissue serving no physiologic function neoplastic *adj.*

neph-ew *n.* the son of one's sister, brother, sister-in-law, or brother-in-law

ne-phrit-ic *adj.* relating to the kidneys

nep-o-tism *n.* the act of showing favoritism to relatives or friends in the work force nepotist *n.*

nep-tu-ni-um *n.* a radioactive metallic element, symbolized by Np

nerve *n.* the bundles of fibers which convey sensation and originate motion through the body

nerv-ous *adj.* affecting the nerves or the nervous system -ly *adv.*, -ness *n.*

nervous system *n., Physiol.* the body system that coordinates, regulates, and controls the various internal functions and responses to stimuli

nest *n.* a shelter, or home built by a bird to hold its eggs and young

nest egg *n.* a supply of money accumulated or saved for future use

nes-tle *v.* to settle snugly; to lie close to nestler *n.*

net *n.* a meshed fabric made of cords, ropes, threads, or other material knotted or woven together; the profit, weight, or price which remains after all additions, subtractions, or adjustments have been made

neth-er *adj.* situated below or beneath

net-tle *n.* a plant having toothed leaves covered with stinging hairs

net-work *n.* a system of interlacing tracks, channels, or lines

neu-ral *adj.* relating to a nerve or the nervous system

neu-ral-gia *n.* pain that occurs along the course of a nerve

neu-ri-tis *n.* an inflammation of a nerve which causes pain, the loss of reflexes, and muscular decline neurotic *adj.*

neu-rol-o-gy *n.* the medical and scientific study of the nervous system and its disorders
neurological *adj.*, neurologist *n.*

neu-ron *or* neu-rone *n., Anat.*

a granular cell nerve which is the main functional unit of the nervous system

neu-ro-sis *n.* any one of various functional disorders of the mind or emo-

tions having no physical cause
neurotic *adj., n.*, neurotically *adv.*

neu-ter *adj.* neither feminine nor masculine *n.* a castrated animal

neu-tral *adj.* not supporting either side
of a debate, quarrel, or party; a color
which does not contain a decided hue
Chem. neither alkaline nor acid
neutrality *n.*, neutrally *adv.*

neu-tral-ize *v.* to make or declare neutral

neu-tron *n.* an uncharged particle in the
nucleus of an atom

nev-er *adv.* not ever

nev-er-the-less *adv.* nonetheless

new *adj.* not used before; unaccustomed;
unfamiliar

news *n., pl.* current information and happenings

news-cast *n.* a television or radio news
broadcast

news-pa-per *n.* a weekly or daily publication which contains recent news and
information

news-print *n.* an inexpensive
machinefinished paper made from
wood pulp and used chiefly for
newspapers and some paperback
books

New Testament *n.* the second part of the
Christian Bible containing the
Gospels, Acts, Epistles, and the Book
of Revelation

next *adj.* immediately following or
proceeding

nib-ble *v.* to bite a little at a time
nibble, nibbler *n.*

nice *adj.* pleasing; enjoyable
nicely *adv.*, niceness *n.*

niche *n.* a recess or alcove in a wall,
usually used for displays

nick *n.* a small chip or cut on a surface;
the final critical moment

nick-el *n.* a hard, silver, metallic element
used in alloys and symbolized by Ni; a
United States coin worth five cents

nick-el-o-de-on *n.* a movie theatre which
charged five cents for admission; a
coin-operated juke box

nick-name *n.* the familiar form of a
proper name, expressed in a shortened
form nickname *v.*

nic-o-tine *or* nicotin *n.* a poisonous
alkaloid found in tobacco and used in
insecticides and medicine

niece *n.* a daughter of one's sister or
brother or one's sister-in-law or
brother-in-law

nigh *adv.* near in relationship, time, or
space

night *n.* the time between dusk and dawn
or the hours of darkness

nightcap *n.* an alcoholic drink usually
taken before retiring for the night

night-in-gale *n.*

a songbird with
brownish plumage,
noted for the sweet, nocturnal song of
the male

night-mare *n.* a frightening and horrible
dream

nim-ble *adj.* marked by a quick, light
movement; quick-witted
nimbleness *n.*, nimbly *adv.*

nin-com-poop *n.* a silly or stupid person

nine *n.* the cardinal number that is equal
to $8+1$ nine *adj., pron.*

ni-o-bi-um *n.* a gray, metallic element
used in alloys, symbolized by Nb

nip *v.* to pinch, bite, or grab something

nip-ple *n.* the small projection of a mam-
mary gland through which milk passes

ni-tro-gen *n.* a nonmetallic gaseous element which is essential to life, symbolized by N

ni-tro-glyc-er-in *n.* a highly flammable,
explosive liquid, used to make
dynamite and, in medicine, to dilate
blood vessels

no *adv.* used to express rejection

no-bel-i-um *n.* a radioactive element,
symbolized by No

Nobel prize *n.* an award given to people
with achievements in literature,
economics, medicine, and other fields,
established by the last will and testament of Alfred Nobel

no-bil-i-ty *n., pl.* -ies the state or quality
of being noble

no-ble *adj.* morally good; superior in
character or nature -ness *n.*, -y *adv.*

no-bod-y *pron.* not anybody

noc-tur-nal *adj.* pertaining to or occurring during the night; active at night
and quiet during the daylight hours
nocturnally *adv.*

node *n.* a swollen or thickened enlargement

no-el *n.* a Christmas carol

noise *n.* a sound which is disagreeable or
loud; in computer science, unwanted
data in an electronic signal
noisy *adj.*, noisily *adv.*

no-mad *n.* a member of a group of
people who wander from place to
place nomadic *adj.*, nomadism *n.*

no-men-cla-ture *n.* the set of names used
to describe the elements of art,
science, and other fields

nom·i·nal *adj.* of or relating to something that is in name or form only **nominally** *adv.*

nom·i·nate *v.* to select a candidate for an elective office; to appoint or designate to a position nomination, -tor *n.*

nom·i·nee *n.* a person nominated for a position or office

non- *prefix* not

non·a·ge·nar·i·an *adj.* a person between the ages of 90 and 100 years

non·cha·lant *adj.* giving an effect of casual unconcern -ance *n.*, -ly *adv.*

non com·pos men·tis *adj.* mentally unbalanced; not of sound mind

non·con·form·ist *n.* a person who does not feel compelled to follow or accept his community's customs or traditions

none *pron.* not any; not one

non·sec·tar·i·an *adj.* not associated with or restricted to one religion, faction, or sect

non·sense *n.* something that seems senseless or foolish; something which is very unimportant **nonsensical** *adj.*

non seq·ui·tur *n.* an inference that does not follow as the logical result of what has preceded it

non·sex·ist *adj.* not discriminating on the basis of gender

nook *n.* a corner, recess, or secluded place

noon *n.* the middle of the day; 12:00 o'clock

noose *n.* a loop of rope secured by a slipknot, allowing it to decrease in size as the rope is pulled

nor *conj.* not either; or not

norm *n.* a rule, model, or pattern typical for a particular group

nor·mal *adj.* ordinary, average, usual; having average intelligence; standard normalcy, normality *n.*, **normally** *adv.*

north *n.* the direction to a person's left while facing east

nose *n.* the facial feature containing the nostrils; the sense of smell

nose-dive *n.* a sudden plunge as made by an aircraft

nos·tal·gia *n.* a yearning to return to the past nostalgic *adj.*

nos·tril *n.* the external openings of the nose

nos·y *or* **nos·ey** *adj.* snoopy; inquisitive; prying

not *adv.* in no manner; used to express refusal or denial

no·ta·ble *adj.* remarkable; distinguished *n.* a person or thing which is notable **notably** *adv.*

no·ta·rize *v.* to acknowledge and certify as a notary public

notary public *n.* a person who is legally authorized as a public officer to witness and certify documents

no·ta·tion *n.* a process or system of figures or symbols used in specialized fields to represent quantities, numbers, or values notational *adj.*

notch *n.* a v-shaped indentation or cut

note *n.*

a record or message in short form *Mus.* a tone or written character

not·ed *adj.* famous; well-known

noth·ing *n.* not any thing; no part or portion *adv.* in no way; not at all

no·tice *n.* an announcement; a notification *v.* to give notice; to become aware of noticeable *adj.*, -ably *adv.*

no·ti·fy *v.* to give notice of; to announce notifier, notification *n.*

no·tion *n.* an opinion; a general concept; an idea notions *pl.*, *n.* small useful articles, as thread or buttons

no·to·ri·ous *adj.* having a widely known and usually bad reputation

not·with·stand·ing *prep.* in spite of *adv.* nevertheless; anyway *conj.* although

noun *n.* a word which names a person, place, or thing

nour·ish *v.* to furnish with the nutriment and other substances needed for growth and life nourishing *adj.*, nourishment *n.*

nou·veau riche *n.* a person who has recently become rich

no·va *n.*, *pl.* -vae *or* -vas a star which flares up and fades away after a few years or months

nov·el *n.* an inventive narrative dealing with human experiences; a book

nov·el·ty *n.*, *pl.* -ies something unusual or new

nov·ice *n.* a person who is new and unfamiliar with an activity or business

now *adv.* at the present time

no·where *adv.* not in or at any place

nox·ious *adj.* harmful; obnoxious

noz·zle *n.* a projecting spout or vent of something

nu·ance *n.* a slight variation

nub *n.* a knob; a small piece or lump

nu·bile *adj.* suitable or ready for marriage

nu·cle·ar *adj.* pertaining to and resembling a nucleus

nu·cle·us *n.*, *pl.* -clei *or* -cleuses a central

element around which other elements are grouped

nude *adj.* unclothed; naked **nudity, nudist** *n.*

nudge *v.* to poke or push gently

nug-get *n.* a lump, as of precious metal

nui-sance *n.* a source of annoyance

null *adj.* invalid; having no value or consequence; having no legal value **nul-li-fy** *v.* to counteract

numb *adj.* lacking physical sensation; paralyzed or stunned **numbness** *n.*

num-ber *n.* a word or symbol which is used in counting or which indicates how many or which one in a series **number-less** *adj.* too many to be counted

nu-meral *n.* a symbol, figure, letter, word, or a group of these which represents a number

nu-mer-ous *adj.* consisting or made up of many units

nun *n.* a woman who has joined a religious group and has taken vows to give up worldly goods and never to marry

nup-tial *adj.* of or pertaining to a wedding **nuptials** *pl., n.* a wedding

nurse *n.* a person who is specially trained to care for disabled or sick persons *v.* To feed a baby from a mother's breast; to provide care to a sick or disabled person

nurs-er-y *n., pl.* -ies a room reserved for the special use of infants or small children; a business or place where trees, shrubs, and flowers are raised and sold

nur-ture *n.* the upbringing, care, or training of a child **nurture** *v.,* **nurturer** *n.*

nut *n.* a hard-shelled fruit or seed which contains an inner, often edible kernal *Slang* a person who does crazy or silly things

nu-tri-ent *n.* a substance which nourishes or promotes growth and repairs natural wastage of organic life

nu-tri-tion *n.* the process by which a living being takes in food and uses it to live and grow **nutritive, nutritional** *adj.,* **nutritionally** *adv.*

nu-tri-tious *adj.* nourishing and healthy **nutritiously** *adv.*

nuts *adj., Slang* foolish, crazy

nuz-zle *v.* to gently rub against something with the nose; to cuddle

ny-lon *n.* a strong, elastic material; yarn or fabric made from nylon **nylons** stockings made of nylon

nys-tag-mus *n.* the rapid involuntary movement of the eyeballs **-mic** *adj.*

O, o The fifteenth letter of the English alphabet.

O *n.* a word used before a name when talking to that person; an interjection

oaf *n.* a stupid or clumsy person **oafish** *adj.,* **oafishly** *adv.*

oak *n.* a large tree of durable wood bearing acorns **oaken** *adj.*

oar *n.* a long pole, flat at one end, used in rowing a boat

oar-lock *n.* a u-shaped device, on a pivot used to hold an oar during rowing.

oars-man *n.* a person who is skilled in the use of oars

oasis *n., pl.* **oases** a fertile section in the desert which contains water

oat *n.* a cultivated cereal grass whose grain or seed is used as food

oat-cake *n.* a thin, brittle cake made of oatmeal

oath *n.* a solemn promise in the name of God or on a Bible

oat-meal *n.* a cooked cereal food made from rolled oats

ob-bli-ga-to *adj.* necessary to; indispensable

ob-du-rate *adj.* stubborn **obduracy** *n.*

o-be-di-ence *n.* the havit of obeying; compliance; submission

o-be-di-ent *adj.* obeying or willing to do what one is told **obedience** *n.*

ob-e-lisk *n.* a tall, four-sided stone pillar which slopes from a pointed top

o-bese *adj.* very fat **obesity** *n.*

o-bey *v.* to carry out instructions **obeyer** *n.*

ob-fus-cate *v.* to obscure; to confuse, muddle, or bewilder

o-bi *n.* a sash that is tied over a kimono and worn by the Japanese female

o-bit *n. Slang* an obituary

o-bit-u-ar-y *n., pl.* -ies a published announcement that a person has died

ob-ject *v.* to voice disapproval *Grammar* a word in a sentence which explains who or what is acted upon

object ball *n.* in billiards the first ball struck by the cue ball.

object glass *n.* the lens or combination of lenses in a microscope or telescope, that first receives the rays from an object and forms the image through the eyepiece

ob-jec-tion *n.* a feeling of opposition or disagreement, etc.; the reason for a disagreement

ob-jec-tion-a-ble *adj.* provoking diapproval or protest; offensive or represhensible

ob-jec-tive *adj.* pertaining to or dealing

with material objects rather than mental concepts

ob-la-tion *n.* a religious offering or the act of sacrifice

ob-li-ga-tion *n.* a promise or feeling of duty; something one must do because one's conscience or law demands it

ob-lig-a-to-ry *adj.* binding legally or morally; imperative, compulsory; recording an

o-blige *v.* to constrain; to put in one's debt by a service or favor obliger *n.*, obligingly *adv.*

ob-li-gee *n.* the person to whom another is obligated or bound by a legal agreement

o-blig-ing *adj.* disposed to do favors or perform special services; willing; kind

ob-li-gor *adj.* a person who is legally bound to discharge an obligation

o-blique *adj.*

inclined; not level or straight up and down -ness, obliquity *n.*

ob-liq-ui-ty *n.* divergence from ones moral standards, an instance of mental deviation; a confusing statement

o-blit-er-ate *v.* to blot out or eliminate completely; to wipe out obliteration, obliterator *n.*, obliterative *adj.*

o-bliv-i-on *n.* the condition of being utterly forgotten

ob-liv-i-ous *adj.* not aware or conscious of what is happening; unmindful obliviously *adv.*, obliviousness *n.*

ob-long *adj.* rectangular; longer in one direction than the other oblong *n.*

ob-lo-quy *n.* abusive languange; a strongly condemnatory utterance

ob-nox-ious *adj.* very unpleasant; repugnant obnoxiousness *n.*

o-boe *n.* a double-reed, tube-shaped woodwind instrument oboist, ob-scene *adj.* indecent

ob-scene *adj.* indecent; disgusting; objectionable; tending to 9incit lust

ob-scure *adj.* remote; not clear; faint *v.* to make dim; to conceal by covering obscurely *adv.*, obscurity *n.*

ob-serve *v.* to pay attention; to watch observable, observant *adj.*, observably *adv.*, observer *n.*

ob-ser-vant *adj.* paying strict attention to something

ob-ser-va-tion *n.* the act of observing something; that which is observed; a judgment or opinion

observational *adj.* -ally *adv.*

ob-ser-va-to-ry *n., pl.* -ies a building or station furnished with instruments for studying the natural phenomenon

ob-sess *v.* to preoccupy the mind with an idea or emotion obsession *n.*

ob-so-lete *adj.* no longer in use; out-of-date obsolescence *n.*, obsolescent *adj.*

ob-sta-cle *n.* an obstruction; anything which opposes or stands in the way of

ob-ste-tri-cian *n.* a physician who specializes in the care of a woman during pregnancy and childbirth

ob-stet-rics *pl., n.* the branch of medicine which deals with pregnancy and childbirth

ob-sti-na-cy *n.* the instance, state, or quality of being obstinate

ob-sti-nate *adj.* stubbornly set to an opinion or course of action obstinacy *n.*, obstinately *adv.*

ob-strep-er-ous *adj.* noisy, unruly, or boisterous in resistance to advice or control

ob-struct *v.* to block, hinder or impede obstructor, obstruction *n.*, -tive *adj.*

ob-struc-tion-ism *n.* the deliberate interference the progress or business

ob-tain *v.* to acquire or gain possession of obtainable *adj.*, obtainer *n.*

ob-trude *v.* to thrust forward without request or warrant; to call attention to oneself

ob-tuse *adj.* lacking acuteness of feeling; insensitive; not distinct or clear to the senses, as pain or sound

ob-vert *v.* to turn in order to present a different view or surface

ob-vi-ate *v.* to counter or prevent by effective measures

ob-vi-ous *adj.* easily seen, discovered, or understood

oc-ca-sion *n.* the time an event occurs; the event itself; a celebration *v.* to bring about

oc-ca-sion-al *adj.* appearing or occurring irregularly or now and then

oc-ci-den-tal *adj.* western

oc-cip-i-tal bone *n. Anat.* the bone which forms the back of the skull

oc-cult *adj.* concealed *n.* the action or influence of supernatural agencies or secret knowledge of them occultist, occultism *n.*

oc-cult-ism *n.* study or belief in the influence or action of supernatural powers

oc-cu-pan-cy *n.* the state or act of being occupied; the act of holding in possession

oc-cu-pant *n.* a person who acquired title by occupancy

oc-cu-pa-tion *n.* a job, profession, or vocation; a foreign military force which controls an area

occupational therapy *n. Med.* the treatment of mental, nervous, or physical disabilities by means of work designed to promote recovery or readjustment

oc-cu-py *v.* to take and retain possession of; to live in occupier *n.*

oc-cur *v.* to suggest; to have something come to mind; to happen

occurrence *n.*, **-rent** *adj. and n.*

o-cean *n.* an immense body of salt water which covers 3/4 of the earth's surface

oceanic *adj.*

ocean-ar-i-um *n.* a large contained marine aquarium used for the display of fish

o-ce-an-ic *adj.* pertaining to , occurring in the ocean

ocean-front *n.* an area or building that faces the ocean

ocean-going *adj.* being capable or designed for ocean travel

o-ce-an-og-ra-phy *n.* the science of oceanic phenomena dealing with underwater research

o'clock *adv.* of, or according to the clock

oc-ta-gon *n.* a polygon with eight angles and eight sides

octagonal *adj.*, **octagonally** *adv.*

oc-tane *n.* any of several hydrocarbon compounds which occur in petroleum

oc-tave *n., Music* a tone on the eighth degree above or below another tone

oc-to-ge-nar-i-an *n.* a person between the ages of 80 and 90

oc-to-pus *n., pl.* **-es** *or* **-pi**

a cephalopod with a sac-like body and eight tentacles containing double rows of suckers

oc-u-lar *adj.* of or relating to the eye

OD *n. Slang* an overdose of a drug; one who has taken an overdose *v.* to overdose; to die from an overdose

odd *adj.* unusual; strange; singular; left over; not even **oddly** *adv.*, **oddness** *n.*

odds *pl, n.* an equalizing advantage given to a weaker opponent

ode *n.* a lyric poem usually honoring a person or event

o-dom-e-ter *n.* a device in a vehicle used to measure distance traveled **-try** *n.*

o-dor *n.* a smell; a sensation which occurs when the sense of smell is stimulated

od-ys-sey *n.* a long voyage marked by many changes of fortune; a spiritual quest

of *prep.* proceeding; composed of; relating to

off *adv.* from a position or place; no longer connected or on *adj.* canceled *prep.* away from

of-fend *v.* to make angry; to arouse resentment; to break a law **offender** *n.*

of-fense *n.* a violation of a duty, rule, or a propriety; the act of causing displeasure; the act of assaulting or attacking

of-fen-sive *adj.* disagreeable or unpleasant; causing resentment; insulting

of-fer *v.* to present for acceptance or rejection; to present as an act of worship; to make available

of-fer-ing *n.* the act of one who offers; a contribution, as money, given to the support of a church

off-hand *adv. or adj.* without preparation or premeditation

of-fice *n.* a place where business or professional duties are conducted

of-fi-cer *n.* a person who holds a title, or position of authority

of-fi-cial *adj.* something derived from proper authority *n.* one who holds a position or office; a person who referees a game such as football, basketball, or soccer

officialism *n.*, **officially** *adv.*

of-fi-ci-ate *v.* to carry out the duties and functions of a position or office

of-fi-cious *adj.* offering one's services or advice in an unduly forward manner **officiously** *adv.*, **officiousness** *n.*

off-spring *n., pl.* **-springs** the descendants of a person, plant, or animal

of-ten *adv.* frequently

oh *interj.* used to express surprise, fear, or pain

oil *n.* any of various substances, usually thick, which can be burned or easily melted; a lubricant *v.* to lubricate

oil field *n.* an area rich in petroleum; an area which has been made ready for oil production

oint-ment *n.* an oily substance used on the skin as an aid to healing or to soften the skin

o-kra *n.* a tall tropical and semitropical plant with green pods that can be either fried or cooked in soups

old *adj.* having lived or existed for a long time; of a certain age *n.* former times old-en adj. of or relating to times long past; ancient

old--fash-ioned adj. pertaining to or characteristic of former times or old customs; not modern or up-to-date

Old Glory n. the flag of the United States of America

Old Testament n. the first of two parts of the Christian Bible, containing the history of the Hebrews, the laws of Moses, the writings of the prophets, the Holy Scriptures of Judaism, and other material

Old World n. the eastern hemisphere, including Asia, Europe, and Africa

ol-fac-tory adj. pertaining to the sense of smell

oli-gar-chy pl., n. -ies a government controlled by a small group for corrupt and selfish purposes; the group exercising such control

ol-ive n.

a small oval fruit from an evergreen tree with leathery leaves and yellow flowers, valuable as a source of oil

O-lym-pic Games pl., n. international athletic competition held every four years, based on an ancient Greek festival

om-buds-man pl. n. -men a government official appointed to report and receive grievances against the government

om-e-let or om-e-lette n. a dish made from eggs and other items, such as bacon, cheese, and ham, and cooked until set

o-men n. a phenomenon which is thought of as a sign of something to come, whether good or bad

om-i-nous adj. fore-shadowed by an omen or by a presentiment of evil; threatening

o-mis-sion n. the state or act of being omitted; anything neglected or left out

o-mit v. to neglect; to leave out

om-ni-bus n. a public vehicle designed to carry a large number of people; a bus adj. covering a complete collection of objects or cases

om-nip-o-tent adj. having unlimited or infinite power or authority

om-nis-cient adj. knowing all things; having universal or complete knowledge

om-niv-or-ous adj. feeding on both vegetable and animal substances; absorbing everything omnivorously adv.

on prep. positioned upon; indicating proximity; indicating direction toward; with respect to adv. in a position of covering; forward

once adv. a single time; at any one time conj. As soon as

once-over n., Slang a swift but comprehensive glance

on-col-o-gy n. the study of tumors oncological, -gic adj., oncologist n.

one adj. single; undivided n. a single person; a unit; the first cardinal number (1). oneself pron. one's own self

one--sid-ed adj. partial to one side; unjust one-sidedness n.

on-ion n. an edible bulb plant having a pungent taste and odor

on--line adj. Computer Science controlled directly by a computer

on-ly adj. sole; for one purpose alone adv. without anyone or anything else conj. except; but

on-o-mat-o-poe-ia n. the use of a word, as buzz or hiss, which vocally imitates the sound it denotes onomatopoeic, onomatopoetic adj.

on-shore adj. moving or coming near or onto the shore onshore adv.

on-slaught n. a fierce attack

on-to prep. to a position or place; aware of

o-nus n. a burden; a responsibility or duty which is difficult or unpleasant; the blame

on-ward adv. moving forward in time or space onwards adj.

on-yx n. a gemstone; a chalcedony in layers of different colors

oo-dles pl., n., Slang a great or large quantity

ooze n. a soft deposit of slimy mud on the bottom of a body of water; muddy or marshy ground; a bog v. to flow or leak slowly; to disappear little by little

o-pal n. a translucent mineral composed of silicon, often marked with an iridescent play of colors opaline adj.

o-paque adj. not transparent; dull; obscure opacity, opaqueness n.

OPEC abbr. Organization of Petroleum Exporting Countries.

o-pen adj. having no barrier; not covered, sealed, locked, or fastened n. a contest for both amateurs and professionals v. to begin or start openness n., openly adv.

open--and--shut adj. easily settled; simple to decide

op-era n. a drama having music as a

dominant factor, an orchestral accompaniment, acting, and scenery

op-er-ate *v.* to function, act, or work effectively; to perform an operation, as surgery **operative** *adj.*

op-er-a-tion *n.* the process of operating; the system or method of operating; a series of acts to effect a certain purpose; a process; a procedure performed on the human body with surgical instruments to restore health; various mathematical or logical processes

op-er-a-tor *n.* a person who operates a machine; the owner or person in charge of a business *Slang* a shrewd person

oph-thal-mol-o-gy- *n.* a branch of medical science dealing with diseases of the eye, its structure, and functions

o-pin-ion *n.* a judgment held with confidence; a conclusion held without positive knowledge

o-pi-um *n.* a bitter, highly addictive drug; a narcotic

o-pos-sum *n., pl.* -sum *or* -sums

a nocturnal animal which hangs by its tail and carries its young in a pouch

op-po-nent *n.* an adversary; one who opposes another

op-por-tune *adj.* occurring at the right or appropriate time **opportunist** *n.,* **opportunely** *adv.*

op-por-tu-ni-ty *n., pl.* -ies a favorable position; a chance for advancement

op-pose *v.* to be in direct contention with; to resist; to be against **opposable** *adj.,* **opposition** *n.*

op-po-site *adj.* situated or placed on opposing sides **oppositeness** *n.*

op-press *v.* to worry or trouble the mind; to weigh down; to burden as if to enslave **oppression, oppressor** *n.*

op-tic *adj.* pertaining or referring to sight or the eye

op-ti-cal *adj.* pertaining to sight; constructed or designed to assist vision **optically** *adv.*

op-ti-cian *n.* a person who makes eyeglasses and other optical articles

op-ti-mism *n.* a doctrine which emphasizes that everything is for the best

op-ti-mum *n., pl.* -ma the degree or condition producing the most favorable

result *adj.* conducive to the best result

op-tion *n.* the act of choosing or the power of choice; a choice -ally *adv.*

op-tion-al *adj.* left to one's decision; elec-tive; not required

op-tom-e-try *n.* the occupation or profession of examining the eyes and prescribing corrective lenses

op-u-lence *n.* wealth in abundance; affluence

or *conj.* a word used to connect the second of two choices or possibilities, indicating uncertainty *suffix* indicating a person or thing which does something

or-a-cle *n.* a seat of worship where ancient Romans and Greeks consulted the gods for answers; a person of unquestioned wisdom **oracular** *adj.*

o-ral *adj.* spoken or uttered through the mouth; taken or administered through the mouth **orally** *adv.*

oral contraceptive *n.* a pill containing hormones, taken monthly to prevent pregnancy

or-ange *n.* a citrus fruit which is round and orange in color *adj.* Yellowish-red

o-rang-u-tan *n., pl.* -tans a large, anthropoid ape, having brownish-red hair and very long arms

o-rate *v.* to speak in an elevated manner

orb *n.* a globe or sphere

or-bit *n.* the path of a celestial body or a manmade object *v.* to revolve or move in an orbit; to circle **orbital** *adj.*

or-chard *n.* land that is devoted to the growing of fruit trees

or-ches-tra *n.* a group of musicians performing together on various instruments **orchestral** *adj.*

orchestra pit *n.* in theatres, the space reserved for musicians

or-chid *n.* a plant found the world over having three petals in various colors

or-dain *v.* to appoint as a minister, priest, or rabbi by a special ceremony; to decree

or-deal *n.* a painful or severe test of character or endurance

or-der *n.* a condition where there is a logical arrangement or disposition of things; sequence or suc-cession; method; an instruction for a person to follow; a request for certain objects *v.* to command; to demand

orderly *adj.* neat, tidy.

or-di-nance *n.* a command, rule, or order; a law issued by a municipal body

or-di-nar-y *adj.* normal; having no

exceptional quality; common; average; plain

ore *n.* a natural underground substance, as a mineral or rock, from which valuable matter is extracted

o-reg-a-no *n.* a bushy perennial herb of the mint family, used as a seasoning for food

or-gan *n.* a musical instrument of pipes, reeds, and keyboards which produces sound by means of compressed air; a part of an animal, human, or plant that performs a definite function, as the heart, a kidney, or a stamen

or-gan-dy *or* **or-gan-die** *n., pl.* -ies a translucent, stiff fabric of cotton or silk

or-gan-ic *adj.* effecting or pertaining to the organs of an animal or plant; of or relating to the process of growing plants with natural fertilizers with no chemical additives **organically** *adv.*

or-gan-i-za-tion *n.* the state of being organized or the act of organizing; a group of people united for a particular purpose **organizational** *adj.*

or-gan-ize *v.* to assemble or arrange with an orderly manner; to arrange by planning **organization** *n.*

or-gasm *n.* **Physiol.** intensive emotional excitement; the culmination of a sexual act

o-ri-ent *v.* to determine the bearings or right direction with respect to another source

Orient *n.* the countries located east of Europe **Oriental** *adj.*

or-i-fice *n.* an opening through which something may pass; a mouth

or-i-gin *n.* the cause or beginning of something; the source; a beginning place

o-rig-i-nal *adj.* belonging to the first or beginning *n.* a new idea produced by one's own imagination; the first of a kind **originality** *n.,* **originally** *adv.*

or-i-ole *n.* a songbird having brightly colored yellow and black plumage in the males

or-na-ment *n.* a decoration. *v.* To adorn or beautify **ornamental** *adj.,* **ornamentally** *adv.,* **ornamentation** *n.*

or-nate *adj.* excessively ornamental; elaborate; showy, as a style of writing

or-phan *n.* a child whose parents are deceased **orphan** *v.,* **orphanage** *n.*

or-ris *n.* any of several species having a fragrant root and used in medicine, perfumes, and cosmetics

or-tho-don-tics *n.* the branch of dentistry dealing with the correction and prevention of irregularities of the teeth

or-tho-dox *adj.* following established traditions and beliefs, especially in religion

Orthodox Judaism *n.* the branch of Jewish faith which accepts the Mosaic Laws as interpreted in the Talmud

or-tho-pe-dics *n.* the branch of surgery or manipulative treatment concerned with the disorders of the bones, joints, and muscles **orthopedist** *n.*

os-cil-late *v.* to swing back and forth with regular motion, as a pendulum **oscillation, oscillator** *n.,* **-tory** *adj.*

os-mi-um *n.* a hard, but brittle metallic element symbolized as OS

os-mo-sis *n.* the tendency of fluids separated by a semipermeable membrane to pass through it and become mixed and equal in strength **osmotic** *adj.*

os-ten-ta-tion *n.* the act of displaying pretentiously in order to excite

osteo *n. comb. form* bone; pertaining to the bones

os-te-op-a-thy *n.* a medical practice based on the theory that diseases are due chiefly to abnormalities of the body, which can be restored by manipulation of the parts by therapeutic measures

os-te-o-po-ro-sis *n.* a disorder causing gradual deterioration of bone tissue, usually occurring in older women

os-tra-cize *v.* to exile or exclude from a group; to shut out

oth-er *adj.* additional; alternate; different from what is implied or specified *pron.* a different person or thing

oth-er-wise *adv.* under different conditions of circumstances

ot-ter *n., pl.* -ter *or* -ters

web-footed aquatic mammals, related to the weasel

ouch *n. interj.* an exclamation to express sudden pain

ought *v.* used to show or express a moral duty or obligation; to be advisable or correct

ounce *n.* a unit of weight which equals 1/16 of a pound

our *adj.* of or relating to us ourselves *pron.* the possessive case of the pronoun we ourselves our own selves

oust v. to eject; to remove with force

out adv. away from the center or inside adj. away n. a means of escape prep. through; forward from

out-age n. a loss of electricity

out-break n. a sudden outburst; an occurrence

out-cast n. a person who is excluded; a homeless person

out-come n. a consequence or result

out-dated adj. old-fashioned and obsolete

out-do v. to excel in achievement

out-fit n. the equipment or tools required for a specialized purpose; the clothes a person is dressed in v. to supply

out-land-ish adj. extremely ridiculous, unusual, or strange

out-last v. to exceed; to outlive; to last longer that something else in comparison

out-law n. a person who habitually defies or breaks the law; a criminal v. to ban; prohibit; to deprive of legal protection

out-let n. an exit

out-line n. a rough draft showing the main features of something outline v.

out-look n. a person's point of view; an area offering a view of something

out-num-ber v. to go over or exceed in number

out-pa-tient n. a patient who visits a clinic or hospital for treatment but does not spend the night

out-post n. troops stationed at a distance away from the main group as a guard against attack; a frontier or outlying settlement

out-put n. production or yield during a given time

out-rage n. an extremely violent act of violence or cruelty; the violent emotion such an act engenders outrageous adj., outrage v.

out-right adj. free from reservations or complications; complete; entire

out-side n. the area beyond the boundary lines or surface; extreme adv. outdoors

out-spo-ken adj. spoken without reserve; candid outspokenly adv.

out-stand-ing adj. excellent; prominent; unsettled, as a bill owed; projecting

out-ward adj. pertaining to the outside or exterior; superficial outwards adv.

out-wit v. to trick, baffle, or outsmart with ingenuity

o-val adj. having the shape of an egg; an ellipse

o-va-ry n., pl. -ies one of the pair of female reproductive glands -rian adj.

o-va-tion n. an enthusiastic display of approval for a person or a performance; applause

ov-en n. an enclosed chamber used for baking, drying, or heating

o-ver-act v. to act in an exaggerated way

o-ver prep. above; across; upon adv. covering completely; thoroughly; again; repetition adj. higher; upper prefix excessive, as overstuffed or overcrowded

over-act v. to act in an exaggerated way

over-all adj. including or covering everything; from one side or end to another; generally n. pants with a bib and shoulder straps

over-arm adj. thrown or executed with the arms raised above the shoulders

over-bear v. to crush or bear down by superior force or weight overbearing adj.

over-board adv. over the side of a boat or ship into the water

over-cast adj. gloomy; obscured Meteor. clouds covering more than 9/10 of the sky

over-coat n. a coat worn over a suit for extra warmth

over-come v. to prevail; to conquer or defeat overcomer n.

over-con-fi-dence n. extreme or excessive confidence

over-do v. to do anything excessively; to overcook

over-dose n. to take an excessive dose of medication, especially narcotics

over-draw v. to withdraw money over the limits of one's credit

over-drive n. a gearing device in a vehicle that turns a drive shaft at a greater speed than that of the engine, therefore decreasing power output

over-due adj. past the time of return or payment

over-flow v. to flow beyond the limits of capacity; to overfill

over-hand v. to execute something with the hand above the level of the elbow or shoulder overhanded adv.

over-haul v. to make all needed repairs

over-night adj. lasting the whole night; from dusk to dawn overnight adv.

over-plus n. a surplus of something

over-ride v. to disregard; to take precedence over; to declare null and void

over-rule *v.* to put aside by virtue of higher authority

over-run *v.* to spread out; to extend or run beyond

over-seas *adv.* abroad, across the seas **overseas** *adj.*

over-see *v.* to supervise; to direct **overseer** *n.*

over-sexed *adj.* having an overactive interest in sex

over-shoe *n.* a galosh worn over a shoe for protection from snow or water

over-sight *n.* a mistake made inadvertently

over-size or oversized *adj.* larger than the average size of something

over-step *v.* to go beyond a limit or restriction

overt *adj.* open to view

over-the-counter *adj.* not traded on an organized security exchange; of or relating to drugs or medicine which can be purchased without a prescription

over-throw *v.* to remove from power by force; to bring about destruction

over-time *n.* the time worked beyond or before the specified hours

over-whelm *v.* to overcome completely; to make helpless

o-void *adj.* having the shape of an egg

ovu-late *n.* to discharge or produce eggs from an ovary

o-vum *n., pl.* ova the female reproductive cell

owe *v.* to be in debt for a certain amount; to have a moral obligation

owl *n.*

a predatory nocturnal bird, having large eyes, a short hooked bill, and long powerful claws **owlish** *adj.*

own *adj.* belonging to oneself *v.* to possess; to confess; to admit **owner** *n.*

ox-ide *n.* a compound of oxygen and another element

oxy-ac-id *n.* an acid containing oxygen

ox-y-gen *n.* a colorless, odorless, tasteless gaseous element essential to life, symbolized by O

ox-y-gen-ate *v.* to combine or treat with oxygen

oys-ter *n.* an edible marine mollusk

o-zone *n.* a pale-blue gas formed of oxygen with an odor like chlorine, formed by an electrical discharge in the air *Slang* fresh air

P p The sixteenth letter of the English alphabet.

pab-u-lom *n.* type of food such as in absorable solution

pa-ca *n.* type of large and borwn rodent that is from Central and South America having white spots

pace *n.* a person's step in walking or the length of a person's step; stride **pace** *v.*, **pacer** *n.*

pace lap *n.* the warm up lap before the start of a car race

pace-mak-er *n.* the person who sets the pace for another in a race; a type of surgically implanted electronic instrument used to stabilize or stimulate the heartbeat

pac-er *n.* one that sets

pa-chi-si *n.* another name for the game Parcheesi; ancient board game played with dice

pach-y-derm *n.* a group of animals which contains the elephant, the rhinoceros, and hippo; animals having thisk skins

pach-y-san-dra *n.* a type of species of the evergreen trailing herbs of the box family and is grown for the purpose of ground cover in areas that are shaded

pa-cif-i-ca-tion *n.* the state of something being pacified or calmed

pac-i-fi-er *n.* a person or something that will pacify another; nipple shaped device for babies to such on

pac-i-fism *n.* the policy dealing with the establishment of universal peace between all nations; opposition to violence or war as a means of settling problems or disputes

pac-i-fy *v.* to quiet or soothe anger or distress; to calm **pacification** *n.*

pack *n.* a bundle; a group or number of things tied or wrapped up

pack-age *n.* something tied up, wrapped or bound together

pack-age deal *n.* an agreement or offer that involves a number of related items, the items offered

pack-age store *n.* a retail establishment that sells alcoholic beverages only in sealed containers

pack animal *n.* an animal used to carry heavy packs

pack-board *n.* a metal fram that is usuallyt covered with canvas, used to carry goods and equipment over ones shoulder

pack-er *n.* a person who packs; one who works in an establishment that packs meat; a machine that automatically packs

pact *n.* an agreement between nations, groups, or people

pad-dy wag-on *n.*, *Slang* a police vehicle

pa-dre *n.* a title used in Spain and Italy for a priest

pa-gan *n.* a person who does not acknowledge God in any religion; a heathen **pagan** *adj.*, **paganism** *n.*

page *n.* a person hired to deliver messages or run errands; one side of the leaf of a book or letter

pag-eant *n.* an elaborate exhibition or spectacular parade for public celebration **pageantry** *n.*

pa-go-da *n.* a sacred Buddhist tower built as a memorial or shrine

paid *v.* past tense of pay

pail *n.* a cylindrical container usually having a handle

pain *n.* the unpleasant feeling resulting from injury or disease **-ful**, **-less** *adj.*

paint *n.* a mixture of colors or pigments which are spread on a surface as protection or as a decorative coating **painter**, **painting** *n.*

pair *n.*, *pl.* **pairs**, **pair** two things which are similar and used together

pa-ja-mas *pl.*, *n.* a loose fitting garment for sleeping, consisting of a jacket and pants

pal-ace *n.* the royal residence of a sovereign **palatial** *adj.*

pal-at-a-ble *adj.* pleasant to the taste

pale *n.* the pointed stake of a fence; a picket **palely** *adv.*

pal-ette *n.* a thin oval board with a hole for the thumb, on which an artist lays and mixes colors

pal-in-drome *n.* a word, number, or sentence which reads the same backward or forward

pal-i-sade *n.* a fence made of stakes for protection

pall *n.* a heavy cloth used to cover a bier or coffin

pal-la-di-um *n.* a silvery-white metallic element symbolized by Pd.

pall-bear-er *n.* a person who assists in carrying a coffin at a funeral

pal-lid *adj.* deficient in color

pal-lor *n.* lacking color; paleness

palm *n.* the inner area of the hand between the fingers and the wrist

pal-sy *n.*, *pl.* **-ies** paralysis; the loss of ability to control one's movements

pam-per *v.* to treat with extreme care

pam-phlet *n.* a brief publication which is not permanently bound

pan-a-ce-a *n.* a remedy for all diseases, difficulties, or ills

pan-cake *n.* a thin, flat cake made from batter and fried on a griddle

pan-cre-as *n.*, *Anat.* a large, irregularly shaped gland situated behind the stomach which releases digestive enzymes and produces insulin **-tic** *adj.*

pan-da *n.*

a large bear-like animal of China and Tibet

pan-de-mo-ni-um *n.* a place marked with disorder and wild confusion

pan-der or **panderer** *n.* a go-between in sexual affairs; a pimp

pan-el *n.* a flat, rectangular piece of material, often wood, which for-ms a part of a surface **panelist** *n.*

pan-ic *n.* a sudden unreasonable fear which overpowers **panicky** *adj.*

pan-nier *n.* one of a pair of large baskets which are carried on either side of an animal

pan-o-ply *n.*, *pl.* **-lies** the complete equipment of a warrior

pan-o-ram-a *n.* an unlimited or complete view in all directions

pan-sy *n.*, *pl.* **-ies** a garden plant with flowers bearing blossoms

pant *v.* to breathe in rapid or short gasps; to yearn

pan-the-ism *n.* the belief that the laws and forces of nature are all manifestations of God **pantheist** *n.*, **pantheistic** *adj.*

pan-ther *n.* a black leopard in its unspotted form

pan-to-mime *n.* communication done solely by means of facial and body gestures

pan-try *n.*, *pl.* **-ies** a closet or room for storage

pants *pl.*, *n.* trousers; underpants

pap *n.* a soft food for invalids or babies

pa-pa-cy *n.*, *pl.* **-ies** the dignity or jurisdiction of a pope

pa-per *n.* a substance made of pulp from wood and rags

papier—ma-che *n.* a material consisting of wastepaper mixed with glue or paste which can be molded when wet and becomes hard when dry

pa-poose *n.* a North American Indian child or baby

pa-pri-ka *n.* a dark red seasoning powder made by grinding red peppers

Pap test *n.* a test in which a smear of bodily secretion from the uterus, is examined for the early detection of cancer

par-a-ble *n.* a short, fictitious story which illustrates a moral lesson

par-a-chute *n.*

a folding umbrella-shaped apparatus of light fabric used to make a safe landing after a free fall from an airplane

pa-rade *n.* an organized public procession **parader** *n.*

par-a-dise *n.* a state or place of beauty, bliss or delight; heaven **paradisiac, paradisiacal** *adj.*

par-a-dox *n.* a statement which seems opposed to common sense or contradicts itself **paradoxical** *adj.*, **paradoxically** *adv.*

par-a-gon *n.* a pattern or model of excellence or perfection

par-a-graph *n.* a section of a composition dealing with a single idea, containing one or more sentences

par-a-keet *n.*

a small parrot with a long, wedge-shaped tail

par-al-lel *adj.* moving in the same direction but separated by a distance, as railroad tracks **parallel** *v.* **parallelism** *n.*

par-al-lel-o-gram *n.* a four-sided figure having parallel opposite sides which are equal

pa-ral-y-sis *n., pl.* -ses complete or partial loss of the ability to feel any sensation or to move -tic *adj. & n.*

par-a-lyze *v.* to cause to be inoperative or powerless

par-a-med-ic *n.* a person trained to give emergency medical treatment until a doctor is available

par-a-mount *adj.* superior to all others in rank, importance, and power

par-a-noi-a *n.* mental insanity marked by systematic delusions of persecution or grandeur

par-a-pher-na-lia *n.* personal effects or belongings

par-a-phrase *v.* to put something written or spoken into different words while retaining the same meaning

par-a-site *n., Biol.* an organism which lives, grows, feeds, and takes shelter in or on another organism

par-a-sol *n.* a small umbrella used as protection from the sun

par-boil *v.* to precook something in boiling water

par-cel *n.* a wrapped package; a portion of land **parcel** *v.*

parch *v.* to become very dry from intense heat

parch-ment *n.* goatskin or sheepskin prepared with a pumice stone and used as a material for writing or drawing

par-don *v.* to forgive someone for an offense **pardonable** *adj.*, **pardonably** *adv.*, **pardon** *n.*

pare *v.* to cut away or remove the outer surface gradually

par-e-go-ric *n.* a medication used to relieve stomach pains

par-ent *n.* a mother or father; a forefather; an ancestor **parenthood** *n.*, **parental** *adj.*

pa-ren-the-sis *n., pl.* -ses one of a pair of curved lines ( ) used to enclose a qualifying or explanatory remark

park *n.* a tract of land used for recreation

par-ka *n.* a cloth jacket with an attached hood

par-lia-ment *n.* the assembly which constitutes the lawmaking body of various countries

par-lor *n.* a room for entertaining visitors or guests

pa-ro-chi-al *adj.* belonging to a local parish; having to do with a parish

par-o-dy *n., pl.* -ies a composition, song, or poem which mimics another in a ridiculous way

pa-role *n.* the conditional release of a prisoner before his sentence expires **parole** *v. & adj.*

par-ox-ysm *n.* a violent attack or outburst; a spasm

par-ri-cide *n.* the crime of murdering one's parents **parricidal** *adj.*

par-rot *n.*

a brightly colored, semitropical bird

par-ry *v.* to avoid something; to turn aside **parry** *n.*

parse *v.* to identify the parts of speech in a sentence and to indicate their relationship to each other

par-si-mo-ny *n.* extreme reluctance to use one's resources or to spend money

-ious *adj.*, **parsimoniously** *adv.*

pars-ley *n.* an herb with curly leaves which is used for seasoning and garnishing

pars-nip *n.* a plant from the carrot family cultivated for its long, edible root

par-son *n.* a pastor or clergyman

parsonage *n.* the home provided by a church for its parson

part *n.* a segment, portion, or division of a whole

par-take *v.* to have a share or part; to take

par-tial *adj.* incomplete; inclined to favor one side more than the other **partiality** *n.*, **partially** *adv.*

par-tic-i-pate *v.* to join in or share; to take part

par-ti-cle *n.* a very small piece of solid matter

par-tic-u-lar *adj.* having to do with a specific person, group, thing, or category **particularly** *adv.*

part-ing *n.* a division; a separation; the place where a division or separation occurs *adj.* done, given, or said on departing

par-ti-tion *n.* a separation or division *v.* to divide

part-ner *n.* one who shares something with another

part-ner-ship *n.* two or more persons who run a business together and share in the profits and losses

par-tridge *n.*, *pl.* **partridges**

a plump or stout-bodied game bird

par-ty *n.*, *pl.* **-ies** a group of persons who gather for pleasure or entertainment

pass *v.* to proceed; to move; to transfer; to go away or come to an end

pas-sage *n.* the act of going, proceeding, or passing

pas-sen-ger *n.* one who travels in a vehicle, car, plane, or boat

pas-sion *n.* a powerful feeling; lust; sexual desire; an outburst of strong feeling

pas-sive *adj.* not working, acting, or operating; inactive **passivity** *n.*

pass-port *n.* an official permission issued to a person allowing him to travel out of this country and to return

past *adj.* having to do with or existing at a former time *n.* Before the present time

pas-tel *n.* a crayon made of ground

pigments; a drawing made with crayons of this kind

pas-teur-i-za-tion *n.* the process of killing disease-producing microorganisms by heating the liquid to a high temperature

pas-time *n.* spending spare time in a pleasant way; a diversion

pas-tor *n.* a Christian clergyman in charge of a church or congregation

pas-tor-al *adj.* referring to the duties of a pastor

past par-ti-ci-ple *n.* a participle used with reference to actions and conditions in the past

pas-try *n.* food made with dough or having a crust made of dough

pas-ture *n.* an area for grazing of domestic animals

pat *v.* to tap lightly with something flat *n.* a soft, caressing stroke

patch *n.* a piece of fabric used to repair a weakened or torn area in a garment **patchy, patchable** *adj.*

pat-ent *n.* a governmental protection assuring an inventor the exclusive right of manufacturing, using, exploiting, and selling an invention *adj.* evident **patentee, patency** *n.*, **patently** *adv.*

pa-ter-nal *adj.* relating to or characteristic of a father; inherited from a father **paternally** *adv.*, **paternalism** *n.*

path *n.* a track or course; a route; a course of action

pa-thet-ic *adj.* rousing pity, tenderness, or sympathy **pathetically** *adv.*

pa-thol-o-gy *n.* the science that deals with facts about diseases, their nature and causes **-ic, -ical** *adj.*, **-gist** *n.*

pa-thos *n.* a quality in a person that evokes sadness or pity

pa-tience *n.* the quality, state, or fact of being patient; the ability to be patient

pa-tient *adj.* demonstrating uncomplaining endurance under distress

pa-ti-o *n.* an area attached to a house, used for enjoyment and entertainment

pa-tri-arch *n.* the leader of a tribe or family who rules by paternal right; a very old and revered man **patriarchal** *adj.*

pa-tri-ot *n.* a person who loves and defends his country **patriotic** *adj.*, **patriotism** *n.*

pa-trol *n.* walking around an area for the purpose of maintaining or observing security **patrol** *v.*

pa-tron *n.* a person who fosters, protects, or supports some person, enterprise, or thing; a regular customer

patroness *n.*

pat-sy *n., pl.* **-ies** *Slang* a person who is taken advantage of

pat-tern *n.* anything designed or shaped to serve as a guide in making something else; a sample

pat-ty *n., pl.* **-ies** a small, flat piece of chopped meat

pau-per *n.* a very poor person who depends on charity

pauperism *n.*, **pauperize** *v.*

pause *v.* to linger, hesitate, or stop for a time **pause** *n.*

pave *v.* to surface with gravel, concrete, asphalt, or other material

pavement *n.* a surface that has been paved

pa-vil-ion *n.* a large, roofed structure used for shelter

paw *n.* the foot of an animal *v.* To handle clumsily or rudely

pay *v.* to give a person what is due for a debt, purchase, or work completed; to compensate

pay-ment *n.* the act of paying

pay-roll *n.* the amount of money to be paid to a list of employees

pea *n.* a round edible seed contained in a pod and grown on a vine

peace *n.* a state of physical or mental tranquillity; calm; serenity; the absence of war **peaceable**, **-ful** *adj.*

peach *n.* a round, sweet, juicy fruit

pea-cock *n.*

a male bird with brilliant blue or green plumage and a long iridescent tail

peak *n.* a projecting edge or point; the top *v.* to bring to the maximum

pea-nut *n.* a nutlike seed which ripens underground; the plant bearing this nut

pear *n.* a juicy, edible fruit which grows on a tree

peas-ant *n.* a farmhand or rustic workman; an uneducated person of the lowest class

peat *n.* the black substance formed when plants begin to decay in wet ground, as bogs **peaty** *adj.*

peb-ble *n.* a small, smooth stone

pe-can *n.* a large tree of the central and southern United States with an edible oval, thin-shelled nut

peck *v.* to strike with the beak; to eat without any appetite, taking only small bites

pec-tin *n.* a complex carbohydrate found in ripe fruits and used in making jelly **pectic** *adj.*

pe-cu-liar *adj.* odd; strange

peculiarity *n.*, **peculiarly** *adv.*

ped-al *n.* a lever usually operated by the foot

ped-dle *v.* to travel around in an attempt to sell merchandise

ped-es-tal *n.* a support or base for a statue to put on a pedestal to hold something in high respect

pe-des-tri-an *n.* a person traveling by foot

pe-di-at-rics *n.* the branch of medicine dealing with the care of children and infants **pediatric** *adj.*, **pediatrician** *n.*

ped-i-cure *n.* the cosmetic care of the toenails and feet

ped-i-gree *n.* a line of ancestors, especially of an animal of pure breed

ped-i-ment *n.* a broad, triangular architectural or decorative part above a door

pe-dom-e-ter *n.* an instrument which indicates the number of miles one has walked

pe-dun-cle *n., Biol.* a stalk-like support in some plants and animals

peek *v.* to look shyly or quickly from a place of hiding; to glance

peel *n.* the natural rind or skin of a fruit *v.* to pull or strip the skin or bark off **peeler** *n.*

peen *n.* the ball-shaped end of a hammer opposite the flat, striking surface

peep *v.* to utter a very small and weak sound, as of a young bird

peer *v.* to look searchingly

pee-vish *adj.* irritable in mood

peevishly *adv.*, **peevishness** *n.*

peg *n.* a small pin **peg** *v.*

pei-gnoir *n.* a woman's loose fitting dressing gown

pe-koe *n.* a superior black tea made from young or small leaves

pel-i-can *n.* a large, webfooted bird with a large pouch under the lower bill for the temporary storage of fish

pel-let *n.* a small round ball made from paper or wax; a small bullet

pelt *n.* the skin of an animal with the fur

pel-vis *n., pl.* **-vises** *or* **-ves** the structure of the vertebrate skeleton which rests on the lower limbs, supporting the spinal column

pen *n.* an instrument used for writing **pen** *v.*

pe-nal *adj.* of or pertaining to punishment or penalties

pen-al-ty *n., pl.* **-ties.** the legal punishment for an offense or crime

pen-ance *n.* a voluntary act to show sorrow or repentance for sin

pen-cil *n.* a writing or drawing implement made from graphite

pen-dant *or* **pen-dent** *n.* an ornament which hangs from a necklace

pend-ing *adj.* not yet decided; imminent *prep.* during; until

pen-du-lous *adj.* hanging downward so as to swing

pen-du-lum *n.* a suspended object free to swing back and forth

pen-e-trate *v.* to force a way through or into; to pierce **-ing** *adj.*, **penetration** *n.*

pen-guin *n.* a webfooted, flightless, marine bird

pen-i-cil-lin *n.* a powerful antibiotic derived from mold and used to treat certain types of bacterial infections

pen-in-su-la *n.* a piece of land projecting into water from a larger land mass

pe-nis *n., pl.* **-nises** *or* **-nes** the male sex organ

pen-i-tent *adj.* having a feeling of guilt or remorse for one's sins or misdeeds; sorry **penitence** *n.*

pen-ny *n., pl.* **-ies** a U. S. coin worth one cent ($.01)

pen-sion *n.* the amount of money a person receives regularly after retirement

pen-sive *adj.* involved in serious, quiet reflection

pen-ta-gon *n.*

any object or building having five sides and five interior angles

pent-house *n.* an apartment built on the roof of a building

pe-on *n.* a servant; a person engaged in menial work

pe-o-ny *n., pl.* **-nies** a plant with a large, fragrant red, white, or pink flower

peo-ple *n., pl.* **people** human beings

pep-per *n.* a strong, aromatic condiment *v.* to pelt or sprinkle

pep-tic *adj.* pertaining to or aiding digestion

per an-num *adv.* for, by, or in each year; annually

per-cale *n.* a closely woven cotton fabric

per--cap-i-ta *adj. & adv., Latin* of each individual

r-ceive *v.* to become aware of by the senses; to understand; to feel or observe **-able** *adj.*, **-ably** *adv.*

per-cent-age *n.* the rate per hundred; a part or proportion in relation to a whole

per-cept *n.* a mental impression of something perceived

perch *n.* a place on which birds rest or alight; any place for standing or sitting

per-cip-i-ent *adj.* having the power of perception **percipience, percipiency** *n.*

per-co-late *v.* to pass or cause to pass through a porous substance; to filter **percolation, percolator** *n.*

per-en-ni-al *adj.* lasting from year to year; perpetual **perennially** *adv.*

per-fect *adj.* having no defect or fault perfectly *adv.*, **perfectness** *n.*

per-form *v.* to execute or carry out an action **performance** *n.*

per-fume *n.* a fragrant substance which emits a pleasant scent; one distilled from flowers

per-haps *adv.* possibly; maybe; not sure

per-i-gee *n.* the point of an orbit when a satellite of the earth is closest to the earth.

per-il *n.* a source of danger; exposure to the chance of injury **perilous** *adj.*, **perilously** *adv.*

pe-ri-od *n.* an interval of time marked by certain conditions

pe-riph-er-y *n., pl.* **-ies** the outer part, boundary, or surface **peripheral** *adj.*

per-ish *v.* to ruin or spoil; to suffer an untimely or violent death

per-i-win-kle *n.* any of several edible marine snails

per-jure *v.* to give false testimony while under oath

per-ma-nent *adj.* continuing in the same state; lasting indefinitely; enduring

per-me-ate *v.* to spread through; to pervade

per-mis-sion *n.* the act of permitting something; consent

per-mit *v.* to consent to; to allow

per-ni-cious *adj.* very harmful; malicious **perniciously** *adv.*

per-ox-ide *n., Chem.* oxide containing the highest proportion of oxygen for a given series

per-pen-dic-u-lar *adj.* being at right angles to the plane of the horizon **perpendicularity** *n.*

per-pe-trate *v.* to perform; to commit; to be guilty

per-pet-u-al *adj.* lasting or continuing forever or an unlimited time **perpetually** *adv.*

per-plex *v.* to confuse or be confused; to make complicated **perplexing** *adj.*

per-se-cute *v.* to harass or annoy persistently; to oppress because of one's religion, beliefs, or race

per-se-vere *v.* to persist in any purpose or idea; to strive in spite of difficulties

per-sim-mon *n.* a tree having reddish orange, edible fruit

per-sist *v.* to continue firmly despite obstacles; to endure

per-son *n.* a human being; an individual

per-son-al *adj.* belonging to a person or persons

per-son-i-fy *v.* to think of or represent as having human qualities or life; to be a symbol of **personifier, -fication** *n.*

per-son-nel *n.* the body of people working for a business or service

per-spec-tive *n.* a painting or drawing technique in which objects seem to have depth and distance

per-spi-ra-tion *n.* the salty fluid excreted from the body by the sweat glands

per-spire *v.* to give off perspiration

per-suade *v.* to cause to convince or believe by means of reasoning or argument

per-tain *v.* to relate to; to refer to; to belong as a function, adjunct or quality

per-ti-na-cious *adj.* adhering firmly to an opinion, belief, or purpose; stubbornly persistent **pertinacity** *n.*

per-ti-nent *adj.* relating to the matter being discussed

per-turb *v.* to disturb, make anxious, or make uneasy; to cause confusion

per-vade *v.* to spread through every part of something; to permeate **pervasive** *adj.*

per-ver-sion *n.* the act of being led away from the accepted course; a deviant form of sexual behavior **perverted** *adj.*

pes-si-mism *n.* the tendency to take a gloomy view of affairs or situations and to anticipate the worst **pessimist** *n.*, **pessimistic** *adj.*

pest *n.* a person or thing which is a nuisance; an annoying person or thing; a destructive insect, plant, or animal

pes-ter *v.* to harass with persistent annoyance; to bother

pes-ti-cide *n.* a chemical substance used to destroy rodents, insects, and pests

pes-ti-lence *n.* a widespread and often fatal infectious disease

pet *n.* an animal, bird, or fish one keeps for companionship

pet-al *n., Bot.* one of the leaf-like parts of a flower

pe-tite *adj.* small in size; little

pe-ti-tion *n.* a solemn request or prayer; a formal written request addressed to a group or person in authority **petitioner** *n.*

pet-ri-fy *v.* to convert into a stony mass; to make fixed or immobilize, as in the face of danger

pe-tro-le-um *n.* an oily, thick liquid which develops naturally below the ground surface, used in products such as gasoline, fuel oil, and kerosene

pet-ty *adj.* to have little importance or value; insignificant; trivial

pe-tu-nia *n.* a widely grown tropical plant

pew *n.* a row of bench-like seats for seating people in church

pew-ter *n.* an alloy of tin with copper

pfen-nig *n., pl.* -nigs *or* -nige a small coin of Germany

phal-lus *n., pl.* -li *or* -luses a representation of the penis, often as a symbol of generative power **phallic** *adj.*

phan-tasm *n.* the creation of an imaginary image; a fantasy; a phantom

phar-ma-cy *n., pl.* -cies a drugstore

phar-ynx *n., pl.* -ynges *or* -ynxes the part of the throat located between the palate and the esophagus

phase *n.* any decisive stage in development or growth

phe-nom-e-non *n.* something that can be observed or perceived; a rare occurrence

phi-lan-der *v.* to make love without feeling or serious intentions **philanderer** *n.*

phi-lat-e-ly *n.* the collection and study of postage stamps and postmarked material **philatelist** *n.*

phil-har-mon-ic *adj.* pertaining to a symphony orchestra

phi-los-o-phy *n., pl.* -ies the logical study of the nature and source of human knowledge or human values; the set of values

pho-bi-a *n.* a compulsive fear of a specified situation or object

phone *n., Slang* a telephone *v.* to call or communicate by telephone

phon-ic *adj.* pertaining to sounds in speech; using the same symbol for each sound **phonically** *adv.*

pho-no-graph *n.* a machine which uses a needle to reproduce sound from a grooved disc or record

pho-ny *adj. Informal* counterfeit; fraudulent; not real or genuine

phos-phate *n., Chem.* a salt or phosphoric acid which contains mostly phosphorus and oxygen

phos-pho-rus *n.* a highly flammable, poisonous, nonmetallic element

pho-to *n. Slang* a photograph

pho-to-cop-y *v.* to reproduce printed material using a photographic process **photocopier, photocopy** *n.*

pho-to-graph *n.* a picture or image recorded by a camera **photography** *n.*

pho-to-syn-the-sis *n., Biochem.* the chemical process by which plants use light to change carbon dioxide and water into carbohydrates, releasing oxygen as a byproduct **photosynthesize** *v.*, **photosynthetic** *adj.*

phrase *n., Gram.* a brief or concise expression which does not contain a predicate

phre-nol-o-gy *n.* the study of or the theory that the conformation of the human skull indicates the degree of intelligence and character

phys-i-cal *adj.* relating to the human body apart from the mind or emotions

phy-si-cian *n.* a person licensed to practice medicine

phys-ics *n.* the scientific study which deals with energy, matter, motion, and related areas of science

phys-i-ol-o-gy *n., pl.* **-ies** the scientific study of living animals, plants, and their activities and functions

phys-i-o-ther-a-py *n.* the treatment of disease or physical defects by the use of heat and massage.

pi-ca *n.* a printer's type size of 12 points, equal to about 1/6 inch

pic-nic *n.* an outdoor social gathering where food is provided **picnicker** *n.*

pic-ture *n.* a visual representation on a surface, which is printed, drawn or photographed

piece *n.* an element, unit, or part of a whole

piece-meal *adv.* gradually

pier *n.* a structure extending into the water, used to secure, protect, and provide access to vessels

pierce *v.* to penetrate or make a hole in something

pi-e-ty *n., pl.* **-ties** devoutness toward God

pig *n.*

a cloven footed mammal with short legs, bristly hair, and a snout for rooting

pi-geon *n.* a bird with short legs, a sturdy body, and a small head

pig-gy-back *adv.* carried on the back and shoulders

pig-ment *n.* a material used as coloring matter, suitable for making paint

pike *n.* a long pole with a sharp, pointed steel head

pile *n.* a quantity of anything thrown in a heap

pil-fer *v.* to steal in little quantities **pilferage** *n.*

pil-grim *n.* a person who travels to a sacred place; a wanderer

pill *n.* a small tablet containing medicine which is taken by mouth **the pill** *Slang* an oral contraceptive drug taken by women

pil-lar *n.* a freestanding column which serves as a support

pil-low *n.* a cloth case filled with feathers or other soft material

pi-lot *n.* a person who is licensed to operate an aircraft

pi-men-to *n.* a sweet pepper used as a stuffing for olives or as a relish

pimp *n.* a person who arranges customers for prostitutes

pim-ple *n.* a small eruption of the skin, having an inflamed base **pimpled, pimply** *adj.*

pin *n.* a small, stiff piece of wire with a blunt head and a sharp point

pin-a-fore *n.* a sleeveless apron-like garment

pin-cer *n.* an implement having two handles and a pair of jaws working on a pivot

pinch *v.* to squeeze between a finger and thumb causing pain or discomfort

pine *n., Bot.* any of various cone-bearing evergreen trees

pine-ap-ple *n.*

a tropical American plant with spiny, curved leaves bearing a large edible fruit *Slang* a hand grenade

pink-eye *n., Pathol.* an acute, contagious conjunctivitis of the eye

pin-na-cle *n.* the highest peak

pi-noch-le *or* **pi-noc-le** *n.* a card game for two, three, or four people, played with a double deck of 48 cards

pint *n.* a liquid or dry measurement equal to half of a quart or two cups

pin-to *n., pl.* **-tos** *or* **-toes** a horse with spots

pin-worm *n.* a nematode parasite which infests the human intestines and rectum

pi-o-neer *n.* one of the first settlers of a

new region or country

pi-ous *adj.* reverently religious; devout **piously** *adv.*, **piousness** *n.*

pipe *n.* a hollow cylinder for conveying fluids

pique *n.* a feeling of resentment or irritation

pi-rate *n.* a robber of the high seas **piracy** *n.*, **piratical** *adj.*

pis-til *n.* the seed-producing female reproductive organ of a flower

pis-tol *n.* a small hand-held firearm

pis-ton *n., Mech.* a solid cylinder fitted into a larger cylinder, moving back and forth under liquid pressure

pit *n.* an artificial or manmade hole in the ground; a slight indentation in the skin

pitch *n.* a thick, sticky, dark substance which is the residue of the distillation of petroleum or coal tar

pith *n., Bot.* the sponge-like soft tissue at the center of the branch or stem of many plants

pit-i-ful *adj.* evoking or meriting pity **pitifully** *adv.*

pit-y *n., pl.* -ies. a feeling of compassion or sorrow

piv-ot *n.* a thing or person upon which development, direction, or effect depends *v.* to turn

piz-za *n.* an Italian food consisting of a doughy crust covered with tomato sauce, cheese, and other toppings and then baked

place *n.* a region; an area; a building or location used for a special purpose

place-ment *n.* the act of being placed

pla-cen-ta *n., pl.* -tas *or* -tae *Anat.* the vascular, membranous structure which supplies a fetus with nourishment before its birth

plague *n.* anything that is troublesome *Pathol.* a highly contagious and often fatal epidemic disease

plaid *n.* a rectangular wool cloth or garment, usually worn by men and women, having a crisscross or checkered design

plain *adj.* level; flat; clear; open, as in view; not rich or luxurious; not highly gifted or cultivated **plainly** *adv.*, **plainness** *n.*

plain-tiff *n.* a person who brings suit

plan *n.* a scheme or method for achieving something

plane *n.* a tool for smoothing or leveling a wood surface

plan-et *n., Astron.* a celestial body which is illuminated by light from the star around which it revolves

plank *n.* a broad piece of wood

plant *n.* a living organism belonging to the vegetable kingdom

plaque *n.* a flat piece, made from metal, porcelain, ivory, or other materials, engraved for mounting

plas-ma *n.* the clear fluid part of blood, used for transfusions

plas-tic *n.* a synthetically made material which is molded and then hardened into objects **plasticity** *n.*, **plasticize** *v.*

plastic surgery *n.* surgery dealing with the restoration or repair of deformed or destroyed parts of the body or skin

plate *n.* a shallow, flat vessel made from glass, crockery, plastic, or other material from which food is served or eaten

pla-teau *n.* an extensive level expanse of elevated land

plat-form *n.* any elevated or raised surface used by speakers; a formal declaration of principles or policy of a political party

plat-i-num *n.* a silver-white, metallic element which is corrosiveresistant, used in jewelry

pla-toon *n.* a military unit subdivision commanded by a lieutenant

plat-ter *n.* a large, oblong, shallow dish for serving food

plau-si-ble *adj.* seeming to be probable

play *v.* to amuse or entertain oneself, as in recreation; to take part in a game *n.* a dramatic presentaton

playful *adj.* lightly humorous

plea *n.* an urgent request; in law, an allegation made by either party in a law suit

plead *v.* to ask earnestly

pleas-ant *adj.* giving or promoting the feeling of pleasure -ly *adv.*

please *v.* to make happy; to give pleasure

pleas-ur-a-ble *adj.* pleasant

pleas-ure *n.* a feeling of satisfaction or enjoyment

pleat *n.* a fold in a cloth made by doubling the cloth back and fastening it down

plebe *n.* a freshman or first year student at the United States Naval Academy

pledge *n.* a solemn promise; a deposit of something as security for a loan; a promise to join a fraternity

plen-ti-ful *adj.* having great abundance

plen-ty *n.* an ample amount

pleu-ra *n., pl.* pleurae *Anat.* the membranous sac which envelops the lungs and provides a lining for the thoracic cavity

pli-a-ble *adj.* flexible

pli-ers *pl. n.* a pincers-like implement used for holding, bending, or cutting

plight *n.* a distressing circumstance, situation, or condition

plod *n.* to walk in a heavy way

plow *n.* an implement for breaking up or turning over the soil

pluck *v.* to remove by pulling out or off **plucker** *n.*

plug *n.* anything used to stop or close a hole or drain *Electr.* a two-pronged device attached to a cord and used in a jack or socket to make an electrical connection **plugger** *n.*

plum *n.* a small tree bearing an edible fruit with a smooth skin and a single hard seed

plum-age *n.* the feathers of a bird

plumb *n.* a lead weight tied to the end of a string, used to test the exact perpendicular line of something

plumb-er *n.* a person who repairs or installs plumbing in a home or business

plumb-ing *n.* the profession or trade of a plumber

plume *n.* a feather used as an ornament

plun-der *v.* to deprive of goods or property in a violent way **plunderer** *n.*

plunge *v.* to thrust or cast something, as into water

plunk *v.* to put down or place suddenly **plunker** *n.*

plu-ral *adj.* consisting of or containing more than one

plus *prep.* add the symbol (+) which indicates addition

plu-to-ni-um *n.* a radioactive metallic element symbolized by Pu.

ply *v.* to mold, bend, or shape *n.* a layer of thickness; the twisted strands of thread, yarn, or rope

pneu-mo-nia- *n.* an inflammation caused by bacteria, virus of the lungs, or irritation

pock-et *n.* a small pouch within a garment, having an open top and used for carrying items

pod *n., Bot.*

aseed vessel, as of a bean or pea *Aeron* a separate and detachable compartment in a spacecraft

po-di-a-try *n.* professional care and treatment of the feet

po-di-um *n.,pl.* -ia *or* -iums a small raised platform for an orchestra conductor or a speaker

po-em *n.* a composition in verse with language selected for its beauty and sound

po-et *n.* a person who writes poetry

po-et-ry *n.* the art of writing stories, poems, and thoughts into verse

point *n.* the sharp or tapered end of something; a mark of punctuation, as a period (.); a geometric object which does not have property or dimensions other than locaton; a degree, condition, or stage

poise *v.* to bring into or hold one's balance *n.* equilibrium; selfconfidence; the ability to stay calm in all social situations

poi-son *n.* a substance which kills, injures **poisonous** *adj.*

poke *v.* to push or prod at something with a finger or other implement

po-lar *adj.* having to do with the poles of a magnet or sphere

po-lar-ize *v.* to cause something to vibrate in an exact pattern; to break up into opposite groups -ation *n.*

pol-i-o-my-e-li-tis *n.* inflammation of the spinal cord causing paralysis; also polio

po-lice *n.* a division or department organized to maintain order. *v.* to patrol; to enforce the law

po-liceman *n.* a member of the police force **policewoman** *n.*

pol-i-cy *n., pl.* -ies any plan or principle which guides decision making

pol-ish *v.*

to make lustrous and smooth by rubbing; to become refined or elegant

po-lite *adj.* refined, mannerly, and courteous

po-lit-i-cal *adj.* concerned with or pertaining to government; involved in politics

pol-i-ti-cian *n.* a person active in governmental affairs or politics

pol-i-tics *n.* the activities and methods of a political party

poll *n.* the recording of votes in an election; a public survey on a given topic

pol-len *n.* the yellow dust-like powder which contains the male reproductive cells of a flowering plant

pol-lute *v.* to contaminate; to make unclear or impure; to dirty **pollution** *n.*

po-lo-ni-um *n.* a radioactive metallic element symbolized by PO.

pol-ter-geist *n.* a mischievous ghost or

spirit which makes much noise

pol-y-es-ter *n.* a strong lightweight synthetic resin used in fibers

pol-y-he-dron *n.* a solid bounded by polygons

pom-pa-dour *n.* a hairstyle which is puffed over the forehead

pomp-ous *adj.* a showing or appearance of dignity or importance

pond *n.* a body of still water, smaller in size than a lake

pon-der *v.* to weigh or think about very carefully; to meditate

pon-der-ous *adj.* massive; having great weight

pon-tiff *n.* a pope

po-ny *n., pl.* -ies a small horse

pool *n.* a small body of water

poor *adj.* lacking possessions and money; not satisfactory; broke; needy; destitute

pop-lar *n.* a rapid growing tree having a light, soft wood

pop-u-lar *adj.* approved of; widely liked; suited to the means of the people

pop-u-la-tion *n.* the total number of people in a given area, country, or city

por-ce-lain *n.* a hard, translucent ceramic which has been fired and glazed

porch *n.* a covered structure forming the entrance to a house

por-cu-pine *n.*

a clumsy rodent covered with long sharp quills

pore *v.* to ponder or meditate on something

pork *n.* the edible flesh of swine

por-no *n., Slang* pornography

por-nog-ra-phy *n.* pictures, films, or writing which deliberately arouse sexual excitement

por-poise *n.*

an aquatic mammal with a blunt, rounded snout

port *n.* a city or town with a harbor for loading and unloading cargo from ships; the left side of a ship; a dark-red, sweet, fortified wine

port-a-ble *adj.* capable of being moved easily

por-ter *n.* a person hired to carry baggage

port-fo-li-o *n.* a carrying case for holding papers and other items

por-tion *n.* a section or part of a whole; a share

por-tray *v.* to represent by drawing, writing, or acting

pose *v.* to place or assume a position, as for a picture

po-si-tion *n.* the manner in which something is placed; an attitude; a viewpoint; a job; employment

pos-i-tive *adj.* containing, expressing, or characterized by affirmation; very confident; absolutely certain; not negative **positively** *adv.*

pos-se *n.* a deputized group or squad

pos-ses-sion *n.* the fact or act of possessing property; the state of being possessed

pos-ses-sive *adj.* having a strong desire to possess; not wanting to share *n.* the noun or pronoun case which indicates ownership

pos-si-ble *adj.* capable of being true, happening, or being accomplished **possibility** *n.*

post *n.* an upright piece of wood or metal support; a position or employment *v.* to put up information in a public place *prefix.* after; in order; or time; behind

post-age *n.* the charge or fee for mailing something

pos-te-ri-or *adj.* located in the back *n.* the buttocks

post-mor-tem *adj.* the examination of a body after death; an autopsy

post-op-er-a-tive *adj.* following surgery

post-pone *v.* to put off; to defer to a later time

post-script *n.* a short message added at the end of a letter

pos-ture *n.* the carriag or position of the body

pot *n.* a rounded, deep container used for cooking and other domestic purposes *Slang* a large sum of money; marijuana **potful** *n.*

po-tas-si-um *n.* a silvery-white, highly reactive metallic element

po-ta-to *n., pl.* -toes a thick, edible, underground tuber plant native to America

po-tent *adj.* having great strength or physical powers; having a great influence on the mind or morals

po-ten-tial *adj.* possible, but not yet actual

pot-pour-ri *n.* a mixture of sweet-smelling dried flower petals and spices, kept in an airtight jar

pot-ter-y *n., pl.* -ies objects molded from

clay and fired by intense heat

pouch *n.* a small bag or other container for holding or carrying money, tobacco, and other small articles *Zool.* the sac-like structure in which some animals carry their young

poul-try *n.* domestic fowl as ducks and hens, which are raised for eggs or meat

pound *n., pl.* **pounds** A measure of weight equal to sixteen ounces; a public enclosure where stray animals are fed and housed *v.* to strike repeatedly or with force

pov-er-ty *n.* the condition or state of being poor and needing money

pow-der *n.* a dry substance which has been finely ground or pulverized; dust; an explosive, such as gunpowder *v.* to dust or cover

pow-er-ful *adj.* possessing energy or great force; having authority

prac-ti-cal *adj.* serving an actual use or purpose

pract-ice *n.* a custom or habit of doing something

prai-rie *n.* a wide area of level or rolling land with grass and weeds but no trees

praise *v.* to express approval; to glorify

prank *n.* a mischievous, playful action or trick

pra-seo-dym-i-um *n.* a metallic element of the rare-earth group

prawn *n.* an edible shrimp-like crustacean found in both salt and fresh water

pray *v.* to address prayers to God; to ask or request

prayer *n.* a devout request; the act of praying; a formal or set group of words used in praying

pre- *pref* earlier or prior to something; in front

preach *v.* to advocate; to proclaim; to deliver a sermon **-er, -ment** *n.,* **-y** *adj.*

pre-am-ble *n.* an introduction to something, as a law, which states the purpose and reasons for the matter which follows

pre-cau-tion *n.* a measure of caution or care taken in advance to guard against harm

pre-cede *v.* to be or go before in time, or position

prec-e-dent *n.* an instance which may serve as a rule or example in the future

pre-cept *n.* a rule, order, or commandment meant to guide one's conduct

pre-cinct *n.* an electoral district of a county, township, city, or town; an enclosure with definite boundaries

pre-cious *adj.* having great worth or value; beloved; cherished

pre-cip-i-ta-tion *n.* condensed water vapor which falls as snow, rain, sleet or hail

pre-cip-i-tous *adj.* very steep; marked with very steep cliffs

pre-cise *adj.* exact; definite; strictly following rules

pre-ci-sion *n.* exactness; the quality of being precise

pre-clude *v.* to shut out; to make impossible; to prevent

pre-co-cious *adj.* showing and developing skills and abilities very early in life

pre-con-ceive *v.* to form a notion or conception before knowing all the facts

pre-da-cious *adj.* living by preying on other animals

pred-a-tor *n.* a person who lives or gains by stealing from another person; an animal that survives by killing and eating other animals

pre-des-ti-na-tion *n.* destiny; fate; the act by which God has predestined all events

pred-i-ca-ble *adj.* capable of being predicated: to foretell

pred-i-cate *n. Gram.* the word or words which say something about the subject of a clause or sentence; the part of a sentence which contains the verb *v.* to establish

pre-dict *v.* to tell beforehand; to foretell

pre-dom-i-nant *adj.* superior in strength, authority, or number

pree-mie *n. Slang* a baby born before the expected due date

pre-empt *v.* to take or get hold of before someone else; to take the place of; to do something before someone else has a chance to do it **-ion** *n.,* **-ive** *adj.*

pre-fab-ri-cate *v.* to construct in sections beforehand

pref-ace *n.* the introduction at the beginning of a book or speech

pre-fect *n.* a high administrative official **prefecture** *n.*

pre-fer *v.* to select as being the favorite; to promote

pref-er-ence *n.* a choice; a special liking for anything over another **-ential** *adj.*

pre-fix *v.* to put at the beginning; to put before

preg-nant *adj.* carrying an unborn fetus; significant

pre-his-tor-i-cal *adj.* of or related to the period before recorded history

pre-judge v. to judge before one knows all the facts

prej-u-dice n. a biased opinion based on emotion rather than reason; bias against a group, race, or creed

pre-lim-i-nar-y adj. leading up to the main action

prel-ude n. an introductory action Music the movement at the beginning of a piece of music

pre-ma-ture adj. occurring or born before the natural or proper time prematurely adv.

pre-med-i-tate v. to plan in advance or beforehand

pre-mi-er adj. first in rank or importance premiership n.

pre-na-tal adj. existing prior to birth

pre-oc-cu-py v. to engage the mind or attention completely

prep Slang preparatory school; preparation

prep-a-ra-tion n. the process of preparing for something

pre-par-a-to-ry adj. serving as preparation

pre-pare v to make ready or qualified; to equip

pre-pay v. to pay for in advance

pre-pon-der-ate v. to have superior importance, weight, force, influence, or other qualities preponderance n.

prep-o-si-tion n., Gram. a word placed in front of a noun or pronoun to show a connection with or to something or someone

pre-pos-ter-ous adj. absurd; ridiculous; beyond all reason

prep-pie n. Slang a student attending a prep school; a young adult who behaves and dresses very traditionally

pre-rog-a-tive n. the unquestionable right belonging to a person

pres-age n. an omen or indication of something to come

pre-school adj. of or for children usually between the ages of two and five

pre-scribe v. to impose as a guide; to recommend

pre-scrip-tion n., Med. a physician's written order for medicine

pres-ence n. the state of being present; the immediate area surrounding a person or thing

pres-ent adj. now going on; not past or future Gram. denoting a tense or verb form which expresses a current state or action

pres-en-ta-tion n. a formal introduction of one person to another; to present

something as an exhibition, show, or product

pre-serv-a-tive adj. keeping something from decay or injury preservation n.

pre-serve v. to keep or save from destruction or injury

pre-side v. to have a position of authority or control; to run or control a meeting

pres-i-dent n. the chief executive officer of a government, corporation, or association presidency n., presidential adj.

press v. to act upon or exert steady pressure or force; to squeeze out or extract by pressure; to smooth by heat and pressure presser n.

pres-sure n. the act of or the state of being pressed; a constraining moral force; any burden, force, painful feeling, or influence; the depressing effect of something hard to bear

pres-tige n. importance based on past reputation and achievements

pres-to adv., Music very fast and quick; at once

pre-sume v. to take for granted; to take upon oneself without permission

pre-sump-tion n. arrogant conductor speech; something that can be logically assumed true until disproved

pre-tend v. to make believe; to act in a false way pretender n.

pre-tense n. a deceptive and false action or appearance

pre-ten-tions n. having or making claims to worth, excellence, etc.

pre-text n. a motive assumed in order to conceal the true purpose

pret-ty adj. pleasant; attractive; characterized by gracefulness; pleasing to look at

pret-zel n. a hard, cooked dough usually twisted in a knot and sprinkled with salt

pre-vail v. to succeed; to win control over something

pre-vent v. to keep something from happening; to keep from doing something

pre-ven-tive or preventative adj. protecting or serving to ward off harm, disease, or other problems

pre-view or prevue n. an advance showing or viewing to invited guests

pre-vi-ous adj. existing or occurring earlier -ly adv.

price n. the set amount of money expected or given for the sale of something

prick n. a small hole made by a sharp point

pride *n.* a sense of personal dignity; a feeling of pleasure because of something achieved **pride** *v.*

priest *n.* a clergyman in the Catholic church who serves as mediator between God and His worshipers

pri-ma-ry *adj.* first in origin, time, series, or sequence; basic

prime *adj.* first in importance, time, or rank *n.* a period of full vigor, success, or beauty

prim-i-tive *adj.* of or pertaining to the beginning or earliest time; resembling the style or manners of an earlier time

primp *v.* to dress or arrange with superfluous attention to detail

prince *n.* the son of a king; a king

prin-cess *n.* the daughter of a king

prin-ci-pal *adj.* chief; most important; owner *n.* the headmaster or chief official of a school; a sum of money invested or owed which is separate from the interest

prin-ci-ple *n.* the fundamental law or truth upon which others are based; a moral standard

print *n.* an impression or mark made with ink; the design or picture which is transferred from an engraved plate or other impression

printer *n.* a person whose occupation is printing

print-out *n. Computer Science* the output of a computer, printed on paper

pri-or *adj.* previous in order or time

pri-or-i-ty *n.* something which takes precedence; something which must be done or taken care of first

prism *n.*

a solid figure with triangular ends and rectangular sides, used to disperse light into a spectrum

pris-on *n.* a place of confinement where people are kept while waiting for a trial or while serving time for breaking the law; jail

pri-vate *adj.* secluded or removed from the public view; secret; intimate; owned or controlled by a group or person rather than by the public

priv-i-lege *n.* a special right or benefit granted to a person

priv-i-leged *adj.* to have or enjoy a given privilege

prize *n.* an award or something given to the winner of a contest

pro *n.* an argument in favor of or supporting something

prob-a-bil-i-ty *n., pl.* **-ies** the state or quality of being probable; a mathematical statement or prediction of the odds of something happening or not happening

prob-a-ble *adj.* likely to become a reality, but not certain or proved

pro-bate *n.* the act of legally proving that a will is genuine

pro-ba-tion *n.* a period used to test the qualifications and character of a new employee; the early release of lawbreakers

probe *n.* an instrument used for investigating an unknown environment; a careful investigation or examination

prob-lem *n.* a perplexing situation or question; a question presented for consideration, solution, or discussion **problematic** *adj.*

pro-ce-dure *n.* a certain pattern or way of doing something; the normal methods or forms to be followed

pro-ceed *v.* to carry on or continue an action or process

pro-ceeds *pl., n.* the profits received from a fundraising venture

proc-ess *n.* the course, steps, or methods toward a desired result *Law* any judicial request or order; in Computer Science, the sequence of operations which gives a desired result *v.* to compile, compute, or assemble; data

pro-ces-sion *n.* a group which moves along in a formal manner; a parade

pro-ces-sion-al *n.* a hymn sung during a procession *adj.* the opening of a church service

pro-ces-sor *n. Computer Science* the central unit of a computer which processes data

pro-claim *v.* to announce publicly

proc-la-ma-tion *n.* an official public declaration or announcement

pro-cras-ti-nate *v.* to put off, defer, or postpone to a later time **procrastination, procrastinator** *n.*

proc-tor *n.* a person in a university or college whose job it is to see that order is maintained during exams **proctorial** *adj.*

pro-cure *v.* to acquire; to accomplish

prod *v.* to arouse mentally; to poke with a pointed instrument *n.* a pointed implement used to prod or poke

prod-i-gal *adj.* wasteful expenditure of money, strength, or time; extravagance *n.* one who is a spendthrift or is wasteful

pro-duce *v.* to bear or bring forth by a

natural process; to manufacture; to make; to present or bring into view

producer *n.*

prod·uct *n.* something produced, manufactured, or obtained *Math.* the answer obtained by multiplying

pro·duc·tion *n.* the process or act of producing; something produced

pro·fane *adj.* manifesting disrespect toward sacred things; vulgar

pro·fess *v.* to admit or declare openly; to make an open vow

pro·fes·sion·al *adj.* having to do with a job or profession; referring to or engaging in an occupation

pro·fes·sor *n.* a faculty member of the highest rank in a college or university

pro·fi·cient *adj.* highly skilled in a field of knowledge

pro·file *n.* the outline of a person's face or figure as seen from the side; a short biographical sketch indicating the most striking characteristics

prof·it *n.* the financial return after all expenses have been accounted for *v.* to gain an advantage or a financial reward **profitable** *adj.*

pro·found *adj.* deeply held or felt

pro·fuse *adj.* extravagant; giving forth lavishly; over-flowing **profusely** *adv.*

prog·e·ny *n., pl.* -ies one's offspring, children, or descendants

prog·no·sis *n., pl.* -noses a prediction of the outcome and course a disease may take

pro·gram *n.* any prearranged plan or course; a show or performance, as one given at a scheduled time; in Computer Science, a sequence of commands which tell a computer how to perform a task or sequence of tasks

prog·ress *n.* forward motion or advancement to a higher goal; an advance; steady improvement

pro·hib·it *v.* to forbid legally; to prevent

pro·ject *n.* a plan or course of action; a proposal; a large job

pro·jec·tile *n.* anything hurled forward through the air

pro·jec·tion *n.* the act or state of being projected; the state or part that sticks out

pro·lif·er·ate *v.* to grow or produce with great speed, as cells in tissue formation

pro·logue *n.* an introductory statement at the beginning of a poem, song, or play

pro·long *v.* to extend or lengthen in time

prom·e·nade *n.* an unhurried walk for exercise or amusement; a public place

for such a walk

prom·i·nent *adj.* jutting out; widely known; held in high esteem

pro·mis·cu·ous *adj.* lacking selectivity or discrimination

prom·ise *n.* an assurance given that one will or will not do something; a pledge

pro·mote *v.* to raise to a higher rank or position; to work on behalf of

prompt *adj.* arriving on time; punctual; immediate

prone *adj.* lying flat; face down **pronely** *adv.*, **proneness** *n.*

prong *n.* a pointed, projecting part, as the end of a sharp instrument or the end of an antler

pro·noun *n., Gram.* a word which can be used in the place of a noun

pro·nounce *v.* to deliver officially; to articulate the sounds **pronunciation** *n.*

proof *n.* the establishment of a fact by evidence

prop *n.* a support to keep something upright

prop·a·gate *v.* to reproduce or multiply by natural causes; to pass on qualities or traits **propagation** *n.*

pro·pel *v.* to thrust or cause to move forward; to motivate

prop·er *adj.* appropriate; especially adapted or suited; conforming to social convention; correct

prop·er·ty *n., pl.* -ies any object of value owned or lawfully acquired, as real estate; a piece of land

proph·e·cy *n., pl.* -ies a prediction made under divine influence

proph·et *n.* one who delivers divine messages; one who foretells the future

pro·pi·ti·ate *v.* to win the goodwill of; to stop from being angry **propitiation** *n.*

pro·po·nent *n.* one who supports or advocates a cause

pro·por·tion *n.* the relation of one thing to another in size, degree, or amount **proportional, proportionate** *adj.*

pro·pose *v.* to present or put forward for consideration or action; to suggest someone for an office or position; to make an offer; to offer marriage

prop·o·si·tion *n.* a scheme or plan offered for consideration; a subject or idea to be proved or discussed

pro·pri·e·ty *n., pl.* -ies the quality or state of being proper in accordance with recognized principles or usage

pro·pul·sion *n.* the act or process of propelling

pro·rate *v.* to distribute or divide proportionately

pro-scribe v. to banish; to outlaw

prose n. ordinary language, speech, or writing which is not poetry

pros-e-cute v. to carry on *Law* to bring suit against a person; to seek enforcement for legal process prosecution n.

pros-pect n. something that has the possibility of future success; a possible customer v. to explore

pros-per v. to be successful; to achieve success prosperous adj.

pros-tate n. a small gland at the base of the male bladder

pros-ti-tute n. one who sells the body for the purpose of sexual intercourse

pros-trate adj. lying with the face down to the ground v. to overcome

prot-ac-tin-i-um n. a radioactive metallic element symbolized by Pa.

pro-tect v. to guard or shield from attack of injury; to shield protective adj.

pro-test v. to make a strong formal objection; to object to protester n.

pro-to-col n. the code and rules of diplomatic and state etiquette

pro-ton n., *Physics* a unit of positive charge equal in magnitude to an electron

pro-tract v. to extend in space

pro-trude v. to project; to thrust outward

prove v. to show with valid evidence that something is true provable adj.

prov-erb n. an old saying which illustrates a truth

pro-vide v. to supply or furnish with what is needed

pro-vi-sion n. a supply of food or needed equipment

pro-voke v. to cause to be angry; to annoy

prox-i-mate adj. immediate; direct

prox-y n., pl. proxies the authority, usually written, to act for another

prude n. a person who is very modest, especially in matters related to sex

pru-dent adj. cautious; discreet; managing very carefully

psalm n. a sacred hymn, taken from the Book of Psalms in the Old Testament

pso-ri-a-sis n., *Pathol.* a noncontagious, chronic, inflammatory skin disease characterized by reddish patches and white scales

psych v., *Slang* to prepare oneself emotionally or mentally; to outwit or outguess

psy-chi-a-try n. the branch of medicine which deals with the diagnosis and treatment of mental disorders

psy-chic adj. cannot be explained by natural or physical laws n. a person who communicates with the spirit world

psy-chol-o-gy n., pl. psychologies the science of emotions, behavior, and the mind psychological adj., psychologist n.

psy-cho-path n. a person suffering from a mental disorder characterized by aggressive antisocial behavior psychopathic adj.

pu-ber-ty n. the stage of development in which sexual reproduction can first occur pubertal, puberal adj.

pub-lic adj. pertaining to or affecting the people or community; for everyone's use

pub-li-ca-tion n. the business of publishing; any pamphlet, book, or magazine

pub-lic-i-ty n. the state of being known to the public

pub-lish v. to print and distribute a book, magazine, or any printed matter to the public publisher n.

puck n. a hard rubber disk used in playing ice hockey

pud-dle n. a small pool of water

puff n. a brief discharge of air or smoke v. to breathe in short heavy breaths

pull v. to apply force; to cause motion toward or in the same direction of

pulp n. the soft juicy part of a fruit; a soft moist mass

pul-pit n. the elevated platform lectern used in a church from which a service is conducted

pul-sate v. to beat rhythmically pulsation

pulse n., *Physiol.* the rhythmical beating of the arteries caused by the action of the heart pulse v.

pul-ver-ize v. to be reduced to dust or powder by crushing

pump-kin n. a large, edible yellow-orange fruit having a thick rind and many seeds

punc-tu-al adj. prompt; arriving on time

punc-tu-ate v. to mark words or written material with punctuation; to give or show emphasis

punc-ture v. to prick or pierce with a pointed instrument n. the act or effect of puncturing

pun-gent adj. sharp or acrid in smell or taste

pun-ish v. to subject a person to confinement or impose a penalty for a crime

pun-ish-ment n. a penalty which is imposed for breaking the law or a rule

punk *n.*, *Slang* a young, inexperienced boy *adj.* of or relating to a bizarre style of clothing; relating to punk rock bands

pup *n.*

a puppy, young dog, or the young of other animals

pupil *n.* a person who attends school and receives instruction by a teacher

pur-chase *v.* to receive by paying money as an exchange **purchaser** *n.*

pure *adj.* free from anything that damages, weakens, or contaminates

purge *v.* to make clean; to free from guilt or sin; to rid of anything undesirable

pu-ri-fy *v.* to make clean or pure **purification, purifier** *n.*

pu-ri-ty *n.* the quality of being pure; freedom from guilt or sin

pur-ple *n.* a color between red and violet

pur-port *v.* to give the appearance of intending; to imply, usually with the intent to deceive

pur-pose *n.* a desired goal; an intention

pur-sue *v.* to seek to achieve; to follow in an attempt to capture **pursuer** *n.*

pur-suit *n.* the act of pursuing an occupation

pur-vey *v.* to supply provisions as a service **purveyor** *n.*

pus *n.* a yellowish secretion formed in infected tissue which contains bacteria

pu-ta-tive *adj.* commonly supposed

pu-tre-fy *v.* to cause to decay

pyg-my *n.*, *pl.* **pygmies** a very small person or animal; a dwarf

py-lon *n.* a tower serving as a support for electrical power lines

py-or-rhe-a *n.*, *Pathol.* inflammation of the gums and sockets of the teeth

pyr-a-mid *n.*

a solid structure with a square base and triangular sides which meet at a point

pyre *n.* a pile of combustible material for burning a dead body

py-ro-ma-ni-a *n.* a compulsion to set fires

py-ro-met-al-lur-gy *n.* chemical metallurgy depending on heat action **pyrometallurgical** *adj.*

py-tho-ness *n.* a woman who practices divination **pythonic** *adj.*

Q, q the seventeenth letter of the English alphabet

qat *n.* a small plant found in Africa, the fresh leaf is chewed for a stimulating effect

qi-vi-ut *n.* yarn spun from the fine, soft hair of the musk ox

quack *n.* the harsh, croaking cry of a duck **quack** *v.*, **quackery** *n.*

quad-ran-gle *n.*, *Math* a plane figure with four sides and four angles

quad-rant *n.*

a quarter section of a circle, subtending or enclosing a central angle of 90 degrees; an instrument which is used to measure altitudes

qua-draph-o-ny *n.* the recording of sound using four transmission channels

quad-rate *adj.* being square or almost square

qua-drat-ics *n.* a branch of algebra concerned with equations

quad-ra-ture *n.* an arrangement of two celestial bodies with a separation of 90 degrees

qua-dren-ni-um *n.* a period consisting of four years

quad-ri-cen-ten-ni-al *n.* an anniversary celebrating 400 years

quad-ri-ceps *n.* the muscle located in the front of the thigh

qua-dri-ga *n.* a chariot pulled by a team of four horses

qua-drille *n.* a square dance with five or six figures exected by four couples

quad-ril-lion *n.* a thousand trillions; one followed by fifteen zeros

quad-ri-par-tite *adj.* consisting of four persons or parts

quad-ri-ple-gic *n.* a person who is paralyzed in both arms and both legs

qua-dru-ma-na *n.* a group of primates distinguished by hand-shaped fgeet

quad-ru-ped *n.* any animal having four feet

quad-ru-ple *adj.* consisting of four parts; multiplied by four

qua-dru-plet *n.* one of four infants born t the same time

qua-dru-pli-cate *n.* consisting of four identical parts

quaff *v.* to drink with abundance

quag-ga *n.* a wild ass ofr Africa related to the zebras

quag-mire *n.* an area of soft muddy land that gives away underfoot; a marsh

quail *n.*, *pl.* a small game bird

quaint *adj.* pleasing in an old-fashioned, unusual way

quake *v.* to shake or tremble voilently

qual-i-fi-ca-tion *n.* an act of qualifying; the ability, skill, or quality which makes something suitable for a given position

qual-i-fy *v.* to prove something able; restrict; limit; modify

qual-i-ty *n., pl.* , qualities a distinguishing character which makes something such as it is

qualm *n.* a sudden feeling of sickness

quan-da-ry *n.* a state of perplexity

quan-ti-ty *n.* number; amount

quan-tum *n., pl.,* quanta an amount or quantity

quar-an-tine *n.* a period of enforced isolation for a specified period of time

quar-rel *n.* an unfriendly or angry disagreement

quar-ry *n., pl.* quarries an animal hunted for food; an open pit or excavation from which limestone or other material is being extracted

quart *n.* a unit of measurement equaling four cups

quar-ter *n.* one of four equal parts into which anything may be divided; a place of lodging

quar-tet *n.* a musical composition for four voices or instruments

quartz *n.* a hard, transparent crystallized mineral

qua-sar *n.* one of the most distant and brightest bodies in the universe

quea-sy *adj.* nauseated; sick queasiness *n.*

queen *n.* the wife of a king; a woman sovereign or monarch; in chess, the most powerful piece on the board

queer *adj.* strange; unusual; different from the normal *Slang* homosexual

quell *v.* to put down with force

quench *v.* to extinguish or put out; to cool metal by thrusting into water

quer-u-lous *adj.* complaining or fretting; expressing complaints

que-ry *n.* an injury; a question

quest *n.* a search; pursuit; an expedition to find something

ques-tion *n.* an expression of inquiry which requires an answer

question mark *n.* a mark of punctuation, (?), used in writing to indicate a question

ques-tion-naire *n.* a written series of questions

quib-ble *v.* to raise trivial objection

quiche *n.* unsweetened custard baked in a pastry shell

quick *adj.* moving swiftly; occurring in a short time

quick-sand *n.* a bog of very fine, wet sand of considerable depth

quid *n.* a small portion of tobacco; a cow's cud

qui-et *adj.* silent; making very little sound; still; tranquil; calm

quill *n.*

a strong bird feather; a spine from a porcupine

quilt *n.* a bed coverlet made of two layers of cloth with a soft substance between and held in place by lines of stitching

qui-nine *n., Chem.* a very bitter, colorless, crystalline powder used in the treatment of malaria

quin-sy *n., Pathol.* a severe inflammation of the tonsils

quin-tes-sence *n.* the most essential and purest form of anything

quin-tet *n.* a musical composition written for five people

quin-tu-ple *adj.* increased five times

quire *n.* twenty-five sheets of paper removed from a complete ream of paper

quirk *n.* a sudden, sharp bend or twist; a personal mannerism

quis-ling *n.* a person who is a traitor, working against his own country from within

quit *v.* to cease; to give up; to depart; to abandon

quite *adv.* to the fullest degree; really; actually

quix-ot-ic *adj.* extravagantly romantic; impractical

quiz *v.* to question, as with an informal oral or written examination

quoin *n.* the external corner or angle of a building

quo-ta *n.* an allotment or proportional share

quo-ta-tion *n.* the exact quoting of words as a passage

quo-ta-tion mark *n.* the marks of punctuation (" ") showing a direct quote

quote *v.* to repeat exactly what someone else has previously stated

quo-tient *n., Math* the amount or number which results when one number is divided by another

R, r The eighteenth letter of the English alphabet

rab-bet *n.* a recess or groove along the edge of a piece of wood cut to fit another piece to form a joint **-ed** *v.*

rab-bi *n.* an ordained leader of Jews; the leader and teacher of a Jewish congregation **rabbinic** *adj.*

rab-bin-i-cal *adj.* to be referring or pertaining to the rabbis

rab-bit *n.*

a burrowing mammal related to but smaller than the hare

rab-ble *n.* a disorderly crowd **rabbling, rabbled** *v.*

rab-id *adj.* affected with rabies; mad; furious **rabidly** *adv.* **rabidness** *n.*

ra-bies *n.* an acute, infectious viral disease of the central nervous system, often fatal, which is transmitted by the bite of an infected animal

rac-coon *n., pl.* **-coons, -coon**

a nocturnal mammal with a black, mask-like face and a black-and-white ringed, bushy tail

race *n.* the zoological division of the human population having common origin and other physical traits, such as hair form and pigmentation; a group of people having such common characteristics or appearances; people united by a common nationality

race *n.* a contest which is judged by speed; any contest, such as a race for an elective office **raced, racer** *n.*

ra-ceme *n.* a type of plant bearing flowers along its stalk

ra-chis *n.* a type of axial structure

ra-cial *adj.* a characteristic of a race of people

rac-ism *n.* a thought or belief that one race is better than another race **racist** *n.*

rack *n.* an open framework or stand for displaying or holding something; an instrument of torture used to stretch the body; a triangular frame used to arrange the balls on a pool table *Mech.* a metal bar with teeth designed to move a cogged bar and produce a rotary or linear motion *v.* to strain, as with great effort in thinking

rack-et or **racquet** *n.* a light-weight bat-like object with netting stretched over an oval frame, used in striking a tennis ball or a shuttlecock

rack-et-eer *n.* a person who engages in acts which are illegal

rac-on-teur *n.* one who is skilled in the act of telling stories

rac-y *adj.* having a spirited or strongly marked quality; slightly improper or immodest **racily** *adv.*, **raciness** *n.*

ra-dar *n.* a system which uses radio signals to detect the presence of an object or the speed the object is traveling

ra-dar as-tron-o-my *n.* astronomy that deals with investigations of the celestial bodies of the solar system by comparing characteristics of reflected radar wave with characteristics of ones transmitted from earth

ra-dar-scope *n.* a screen or oscilloscope that serves as a visual indicator in a radar receiver

rad-dled *adj.* to be in a state of confusion; broken down; worn; lacking composure

ra-di-al *adj.* pertaining to or resembling a ray or radius; developing from a center axis

ra-di-ance *n.* the quality of being shiny; the state of being radiant; relating or emitting to radiant heat

ra-di-ant *adj.* emitting rays of heat or light; beaming with kindness or love; projecting a strong quality **-ly** *adv.*

ra-di-ant heat *n.* heat that is transmitted by radiation

ra-di-ate *v.* to move out in rays, such as heat moving through the air **-ly** *adv.*

ra-di-a-tion *n.* an act of radiating; the process or action of radiating; the process of emitting radiant energy in the form of particles or waves **radiationless** *adj.*, **radiative** *adj.*

ra-di-a-tor *n.* something which radiates

rad-i-cal *adj.* proceeding from a foundation or root; drastic; making extreme changes in views, conditions, or habits; carrying convictions or theories to their fullest application **radically** *adv.*, **radicalness** *n.*

radii *pl. of* radius

ra-di-o *n.* the technique of communicating by radio waves; the business of broadcasting programmed material to the public via radio waves **radioing, radioed** *v.*

ra-dio-ac-tive *adj.* exhibiting radioactivity **radioactively** *adv.*

ra-di-o-ac-tiv-i-ty *n., Physics* a spontaneous emission of electromagnetic radiation, as from a nuclear reaction

ra-di-o-fre-quen-cy *n.* a frequency which is above 15,000 cycles per second that is used in radio transmission

ra-di-o-gram *n.* a type of radiograph

ra-di-ol-o-gy *n.* a science which deals with rays for a radioactive substance and use for medical diagnosis **radiologist** *n.*

rad-ish *n.* the edible root of the radish plant

ra-di-um *n* a radioactive metallic element symbolized by Ra.

ra-di-us *n., pl.* **radii or raduses**

a line from the center of a circle to its surface or circumference

ra-don *n.* a heavy, colorless, radioactive gaseous element symbolized by Rn

raf-fi-a *n.* a fiber from an African palm tree used for making baskets, hats, and other woven articles

raff-ish *adj.* something that is marked by crudeness or flashy vulgarity **raffishly** *adv.,* **raffishness** *n.*

raf-fle *n.* a game of chance; a lottery in which one buys chances to win something

raft *n.* a floating structure made from logs or planks and used for water trans-portation

raft-er *n.* a timber of a roof which slopes

rag *n.* a cloth which is useless and sometimes used for cleaning purposes

rag-a-muf-fin *n.* a child who is unkempt

rag-bag *n.* a miscellaneous grouping or collection; a bag for holding scrap pieces of material

rag doll *n.* a child's doll that is usually made from scrap material and has a hand painted face

rage *n.* violent anger **raging** *adj.,* **ragingly** *adv.*

rag-ged *adj.* to be torn or ripped **raggedness** *n.,* **raggedly** *adv.*

rag-weed *n.* a type of plant whose pollen can cause hay fever

raid *n.* a sudden invasion or seizure **raider** *n.*

rail *n.* a horizontal bar of metal, wood, or other strong material supported at both ends or at intervals; the steel bars used to support a track on a railroad

rail-bird *n.* a person who sits on or near a race track rail and watches a race or workout

rail-ing *n.* a barrier of wood

rain *n.* the condensed water from atmospheric vapor, which falls to earth in the form of drops

rain-bow *n.* an arc that contains bands of colors of the spectrum and is formed opposite the sun and reflects the sun's rays, usually visible after a light rain shower

rain-coat *n.* a water-resistant or waterproof coat

rain-fall *n.* the amount of measurable precipitation

rain gauge *n.* an instrument used to measure rain fall

rain-making *n.* the act or process of producing or attempting to produce rain by the use of artificial means

raise *v.* to cause to move upward; to build; to make greater in size, price, or amount; to increase the status; to grow; as plants; to rear as children; to stir ones emotions; to obtain or collect as funds or money

rai-sin *n.* a grape dried for eating

rake *n.* a tool with a long handle at the end and a set of teeth at the other end used to gather leaves and other matter; a slope or incline, as the rake of an auditorium **rake** *v.*

ral-ly *v.* to call together for a purpose *n.* a rapid recovery, as from depression, exhaustion, or any setback; in a meeting whose purpose is to rouse or create support

ram *n.* a male sheep; an implement used to drive or crush by impact; to cram or force into place

RAM *abbr.* random access memory

ram-ble *v.* to stroll or walk without a special destination in mind; to talk without sequence of ideas **ramble** *n.,* **ramblingly** *adv.*

ram-bunc-tious *adj.* rough or boisterous **rambunctiousness** *n.*

ramp *n.* an incline which connects two different levels; movable staircase allows passengers to enter or leave an aircraft

ram-page *n.* a course of destruction or violent behavior *v.* to storm about in a rampage **rampageous** *adj.,* **rampageously** *adv.,* **rampageousness** *n.*

ram-pan-cy *n.* the state or quality of being rampant

ram-pant *adj.* exceeding or growing without control; wild in actions; standing on the hind legs and elevating both forelegs **rampantly** *adv.*

ram-rod *n.* a metal rod used to drive or plunge the charge into a muzzle-loading gun or pistol; the rod used for cleaning the barrels of a rifle or other

firearm

ram-shack-le *adj.* likely to fall apart from poor construction or maintenance

ranch *n.* a large establishment for raising cattle, sheep, or other livestock; a large farm that specializes in a certain crop or animals **rancher** *n.*

ran-cid *adj.* having a rank taste or smell

ran-dom *adj.* done or made in a way that has no specific pattern or purpose; to select from a group whose members all had an even chance of being chosen

rang *v.* past tense of ring

range *n.* an area over which anything moves; an area of activity; a tract of land over which animals such as cattle and horses graze; an extended line or row especially of mountains; an open area for shooting at a target; large cooking stove with burners and oven. *v.* to arrange in a certain order; to extend or proceed in a particular direction

range finder *n.* instrument that is used in gunnery to determine the distance of a target

rank *n.* a degree of official position or status *v.* to place in order, class, or rank *adj.* a strong and disagreeable odor, smell, or taste

ran-sack *v.* to search or plunder through every part of something

ran-som *n.* the price demanded or paid for the release of a kidnaped person; the payment for the release of a person or property detained ransom *v.*

rant *v.* to talk in a wild, loud way

ra-pa-cious *adj.* living on prey seized alive; taking by force; plundering **rapaciously** *adv.*, **rapaciousness,**

rape *n.* the crime of forcible sexual intercourse; abusive treatment **rape** *v.*, **rapist** *n.*

rap-id *adj.* having great speed; completed quickly or in a short time **rapidity, rapidness** *n.*

ra-pi-er *n.* a long, slender, straight sword with two edges

rap-ine *n.* the forcible taking of another's property

rap-port *n.* a harmonious relationship

rapt *adj.* deeply absorbed or carried away with something and not to noticing anything else; engrossed **raptness** *n.*, **raptly** *adv.*

rare *adj.* scarce; infrequent; often held in high esteem or admiration because of infrequency **rareness** *n.*

ras-cal *n.* a person full of mischief; a person who is not honest rascally *adj.*

rash *adj.* acting without consideration or caution *n.* a skin irritation or eruption caused by an allergic reaction

rasp *n.*

a file with course raised and pointed projections *v.* to scrape or rub with a course file; to utter something in a rough, grating voice **rasper** *n.*, **raspy** *adj.*

rasp-berry *n.* a small edible fruit, red or black in color and having many small seeds *Slang* contemptuous sound made by expelling air with the tongue between the lips in order to make a vibration

raspy *adj.* grating; irritable

rat *n.*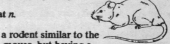

a rodent similar to the mouse, but having a longer tail *Slang* a despicable person who betrays his friends or associates

rat-a-tat *n.* a sharp tapping, or repeated knocking

ratch-et *n.* a mechanism consisting of a pawl that allows a wheel or bar to move in one direction only

ratch-et wheel *n.* a wheel with teeth that is held place with a engaging handle

rate *n.* the measure of something to a fixed unit; the degree of price or value; a fixed ratio or amount *v.* to appraise

rath-er *adv.* preferably; with more reason or justice; more accurate or precise

rat-i-fy *v.* to approve something in an official way **ratification** *n.*

rat-ing *n.* a relative evaluation or estimate of something

ra-tio *n.*, *pl.* **ratios** the relationship between two things in amount, size, degree, expressed as a proportion

ra-tion *n.* a fixed portion or share *v.* to provide or allot in rations **rationing** *n.*

ra-tion-al *adj.* having the faculty of reasoning; being of sound mind **rationality** *n.*, **-ally** *adv.* **rationalness** *n.*

rat-tan *n.* an Asian palm whose strong stems are used to make wickerworks

rat-tle *v.* to make a series of rapid, sharp noises in quick succession; to talk rapidly; chatter *n.* a baby's toy made to rattle when shaken

rat-tler *n.*, *Slang* a venomous snake which has a series of horny, modified

joints which make a rattling sound
when moved; a rattlesnake; one that
rattle

rat-tle-trap *n.* something that is rickety
or rattly

rau-cous *adj.* loud and rowdy; having a
rough hoarse sound; disorderly
raucously *adv.*, **raucousness** *n.*

rav-age *v.* to bring on heavy destruction;
devastate

rave *v.* to speak incoherently; to speak
with enthusiasm *n.* the act of raving

rav-el *v.* to separate fibers or threads; to
unravel **ravelment** *n.*

ra-ven *n.* a large bird, with shiny black
feathers *adj.* of or relating to the
glossy sheen or color of the raven

ra-vine *n.* a deep gorge with steep sides
in the earth's surface, usually created
by flowing water

rav-ish *v.* to seize and carry off; to rape
ravishment *n.*, **ravisher** *n.*

raw *adj.* uncooked; in natural condition;
not processed inexperienced; damp,
sharp, or chilly **rawly** *adv.*, **rawness** *n.*

ray *n.* a thin line of radiation or light; a
small trace or amount; one of several
lines coming from a point

ray-on *n.* a synthetic cellulose yarn; any
fabric made from such yarn

ra-zor *n.* a sharp cutting instrument used
especially for shaving

ra-zor-back *n.* a wild hog of the
southeastern United
States; the mascot of the University of
Arkansas

razz *v.*, *Slang* to heckle; to tease

raz-zle--daz-zel *n.* a state of complete
confusion

re- *prefix* again, anew or reverse action

reach *v.* to stretch out; to be able to
grasp *n.* the act of stretching out

re-act *v.* to act in response to *Chem.* to
undergo a chemical change; to experience a chemical reaction

re-ac-tor *n.* a person, object, device, or
substance which reacts to something

read *v.* to visually go over something, as
a book, and to understand its mean-
ing; to learn or be informed; to perceive something in a meaning which
may or may not actually be there

read-y *adj.* prepared for use or action;
quick or prompt; willing

re-a-gent *n* any substance which causes a
chemical reaction

re-al *adj.* something which is existing,
genuine, true, or authentic *Law*
property which is regarded as permanent or immovable

reel-to-reel *adj.* pertaining to magnetic
tape which is threaded to a take-up
reel, which moves from one reel to
another

real estate *n.* land and whatever is attached such as natural resources or
buildings

re-al-ism *n.* concern or interest with actual facts and things as they really are
realist *n.*, **-istic** *adj.*, **-stically** *adv.*

re-al-i-ty *n.*, *pl.* the fact or state of being
real or genuine; an actual situation or
event

re-al-ize *v.* to understand correctly; to
make real **realizable** *adj.*,
realization *n.*, **realizer** *n.*

re-al-ly *adv.* actually; truly; indeed

realm *n.* a scope or field of any power or
influence

ream *n.* a quantity of paper containing
500 sheets

reap *v.* to harvest a crop with a sickle or
other implement

rear *n.* the back; *adj.* of or at the rear; *v.*
to raise up on the hind legs; to raise as
an animal or child

rea-son *n.* a statement given to confirm
or justify a belief, promise, or excuse;
the ability to decide things, to obtain
ideas, to think clearly, and to make
logical and rational choices and decisions; *v.* to discuss something logically
reasoning *n.*

rea-son-a-ble *adj.* moderate; rational
reasonableness *n.*, **reasonably** *adv.*

re-a-sur-ance *n.* the act of reassuring;
reinsurance

re-bate *n.* a deduction allowed on items
sold; a discount; money which is
returned to the purchaser from the
original payment; *v.* to return part of
the payment **rebater** *n.*

re-bel *v.* to refuse allegiance; to resist
any authority; to react with violence

re-bel-lion *n.* an organized uprising to
change or overthrow an existing
authority

re-bel-lious *adj.* engaged in rebellion;
relating to a rebel or rebellion
rebelliously *adv.*, **rebelliousness** *n.*

re-birth *n.* a revival or renaissance; rein-
carnation

re-bound *v.* to spring back; to recover
from a setback or frustration; *n.* recoil

re-broad-cast *v.* to repeat or broadcast
again **rebroadcast** *n.*

re-buff *v.* to refuse abruptly; to snub
rebuff *n.*

re-build *v.* to make extensive repairs to
something; to reconstruct; remodel

re-buke *v.* to criticize something sharply; to turn back **rebuker** *n.*

re-but *v.* to try and prove someone wrong by argument or evidence **rebuttal** *n.*, **rebutable** *adj.*

re-call *v.* to order or summon to return to ask for something to be returned; so that defects can be fixed or repaired; to remember; to recollect

re-cant *v.* to formally admit that a previously held belief was wrong by making public confession

re-cap *v.* to restore an old tire; to review or summarize something

re-cede *v.* to move back; as floodwater; to withdraw from an agreement

re-ceipt *n.* the written acknowledgment of something received; *pl.*, **receipts** the amount of money received

re-ceive *v.* to take or get something; to greet customers or guests; to accept as true or correct **receiver** *n.*

re-cent *adj.* happening at a time just before the present **recently** *adv.*

re-cep-ta-cle *n.* anything which holds something; an electrical outlet designed to receive a plug

re-cep-tion *n.* the act or manner of receiving something; a formal entertainment of guests, as a wedding reception

re-cep-tion-ist *n.* an employee who greets callers and answers the telephone for a business

re-cep-tive *adj.* able to receive receptively *adv.*, **-ness, receptivity** *n.*

re-cess *n.* a break in the normal routine of something; a depression or niche in a smooth surface

re-ces-sion *n.* the act of receding; withdrawal; a period or time of reduced economic activity **-ary** *adj.*

rec-i-pe *n.* the directions and a list of ingredients for preparing food

re-cip-ro-cate *v.* to give and return mutually, one gift or favor for another

re-cite *v.* to repeat something from memory; give an account of something in detailt

reck-less *adj.* state of being careless and rash when doing something **-ness** *n.*

reck-on *v.* to calculate; to compute; to estimate; to consider; to assume

reck-on-ing *n.* the act of calculation or counting

re-claim *v.* to redeem; to reform; to recall; to change to a more desirable condition or state

rec-la-ma-tion *n.* the state of being eclaimed

re-cline *v.* to assume a prone position

rec-luse *n.* a person who chooses to live in seclusion

rec-og-ni-tion *n.* an acknowledgment which is formal

re-cog-ni-zance *n.* an amount of money which will be forfeited for a nonperformance of an obligation

rec-og-nize *v.* to experience or identify something or someone as having been known previously; to appreciative **recognizable** *adj.*, **recognizably** *adv.*

re-coil *v.* to fall back or to rebound **recoilless** *adj.*

rec-ol-lect *v.* to remember or recall to the mind **recollection** *n.*

rec-om-mend *v.* to suggest to another as desirable; advise **recommendation** *n.*, **recommedable** *adj.*

rec-om-pense *v.* to reward with something for a service

rec-on-cile *v.* to restore a friendship after an estrangement **reconcilably** *adv.*

rec-on-dite *adj.* being obscure

re-con-di-tion *v.* to return to a good condition

re-con-firm *v.* confirm something again

re-con-nais-sance *n.* an observation of territory such as that of the enemy

re-con-noi-ter *v.* to survey a region

re-con-sid-er *v.* to think about again with a view to changing a previous action or decision **reconsideration** *n.*

re-con-struct *v.* to build something again

re-con-struc-tion *n.* something which has been reconstructed or rebuilt

re-cord *v.* to write down for future use or permanent reference; to preserve sound on a tape or disk for replay; a phonograph record; *n.* information which is recorded and kept permanently

re-cord-er *n.* a person who records things such as official transactions

re-cord-ing *n.* the act of making a transcription of sounds

rec-ord play-er *n.* the machine which is used to play recordings

re-count *v.* to tell the facts; narrate or describe in detail; to count again; *n.* a second count to check the results of the first count

re-coup *v.* to be reimbursed; to recover

re-course *n.* a turning to or an appeal for help

re-cov-er *v.* to regain something which was lost; to be restored to good health; *Law* to obtain a judgment for damages

re-cov-er-y *n.* the power to regain something

rec-re-ant *adj.* cowardly; unfaithful

re-cre-ate *v.* to create again

rec-re-a-tion *n.* refreshment of body and mind; a pleasurable occupation or exercise **recreational** *adj.*

re-crim-i-nate *v.* the charging of another of the same account **recriminatory, recriminative** *adj.,* **recrimination** *n.*

re-cruit *v.* to enlist someone for military or naval purposes; to look for someone as for a service or employment **recuiter** *n.*

rec-tal *adj.* referring to the rectum of the body

rec-tan-gle *n.*

a parallelogram with all right angles **rectangular** *adj.,* **rectangularity** *n.*

rec-ti-fi-er *n.* that which rectifies something

rec-ti-fy *v.* to make correct; *Chem.* to purify by repeated distillations; *Electr.* to make an alternating current a direct current

rec-ti-lin-e-ar *adj.* made up of or indicated by straight lines; bounded by straight lines

rec-ti-tude *n.* rightness in principles and conduct; correctness

rec-to *n.* the right-hand page of a book

rec-tor *n.* a member of the clergy in charge of a parish; a priest in charge of a congregation, church, or parish; the principal or head of a school or of a college

rec-tum *n., pl.* **rectums, recta** *Anat.* the lower terminal portion of the large intestine connecting the colon and anus

re-cum-bent *adj.* lying down or reclining

re-cu-per-ate *v.* to regain strength or to regain one's health; to recover from a financial loss **recuperation** *n.,* **recuperative** *adj.*

re-cur *v.* to happen, to return, or to appear again **recurrence, recurrent** *adj.*

red *n.* having the color which resembles blood, as pigment or dye which colors red; *Slang* a communist; one who is in favor of the overthrow of an existing political order of social order; a condition indicating a loss, as in the red

re-deem *v.* to buy back; to pay off; to turn something in, as coupons or rain checks and receive something in exchange

re-demp-tion *n.* the act of redeeming; rescue; ransom; that which redeems; salvation

re-doubt *n.* a small enclosed fortification

re-doubt-a-ble *adj.* to be dreaded **redoubtably** *adv.*

re-dound *v.* to have an effect on something

re-dress *v.* to put something right

red snap-per *n.* a saltwater fish which is red in color and can be found in the Gulf of Mexico and near Florida

red tape *n.* routines which are rigid and may cause a delay in a process

re-duce *v.* to decrease; lessen in number, degree, or amount; to put into order; to lower in rank; to lose weight by dieting

re-duc-tion *n.* the state of being reduced

re-dun-dant *adj.* exceeding what is necessary; repetitive

re-du-pli-cate *v.* to repeat something **reduplication** *n.*

red-wood *n.* a tree found in California which is very tall and wide

re-ech-o *v.* to reverberate again

reed *n.* tall grass with a slender stem, which grows in wet areas; a thin tongue of wood, metal, cane, or plastic; placed in the mouthpiece of an instrument to produce sounds by vibrating **reediness** *n.,* **reedy** *adj.*

reef *n.* a chain of rocks, coral, or sand at or near the surface of the water

reef-er *n.* a jacket which is close-fitting

reek *v.* to emit vapor or smoke; to give off a strong offensive odor

reel *n.* a device which revolves on an axis and is used for winding up or letting out fishing line, rope, or other stringlike material; a lively and fast dance

re-e-lect *v.* the act of electing someone again for an office

re-em-pha-size *v.* to stress something or an idea again

re-en-list *v.* to enlist or join a group or an armed force again **reenlistment** *n.*

re-enter *v.* to enter a room or area again

re-ex-am-ine *v.* examine something or someone another time or again **reexamination** *n.*

re-fec-to-ry *n.* the place in colleges where the students dine

re-fer *v.* to direct for treatment, information, or help

ref-e-ree *n.* a person who supervises a game, making sure all the rules are followed

ref-er-ence *n.* the act of referring someone to someplace or to something

ref-er-en-dum *n.* a public vote on an item for final approval or for rejection

ref-er-ent *n.* what is referred to such as a person

re-fill *v.* to fill something with an item again

re-fine *v.* to purify by removing unwanted substances or material; to improve **refined** *adj.* **refinement** *n.*

re-fin-er-y *n.* a place or location which is used for the purpose of refining, such as sugar

re-fin-ish *v.* the act of putting a new surface onto something, such as wood

re-fit *v.* to repair something

re-flect *v.* to throw back rays of light from a surface; to give an image, as from a mirror; to ponder or think carefully about something **reflection** *n.* **reflective** *adj.*

re-flec-tor *n.* something which is able to reflect things, such as light

re-flex *adj.* turning, casting, or bending backward; *n.* an involuntary reaction of the nervous system to a stimulus

re-for-est *v.* the act of replanting a forest or wooded area with trees -ation *n.*

re-form *v.* to reconstruct, make over, or change something for the better; improve; to abandon or give up evil ways **reformer** *n.*, **reformed** *adj.*

re-for-ma-to-ry *n.* a jail-like institution for young criminals

re-fract *v.* the deflecting something, such as a ray of light **refractive** *adj.*

re-frac-tion *n.* the state of being refracted or deflected

re-frac-to-ry *adj.* unmanageable; obstinate; difficult to melt; resistant to heat; *n.* something which does not change significantly when exposed to high temperatures

re-frain *v.* to hold back

re-fresh *v.* to freshen something again

re-fresh-ment *n.* something which will refresh someone, such as a cold drink or snack

re-frig-er-ant *n.* an agent which cools something

re-frig-er-ate *v.* to chill or cool; to preserve food by chilling; to place in a refrigerator

re-frig-er-a-tor *n.* a box-like piece of equipment which chills food and other matter

re-fu-el *v.* to put fuel into something again

ref-uge *n.* shelter or protection from harm; any place one may turn for relief or help

ref-u-gee *n.* a person who flees to find safety

re-ful-gent *adj.* state of being radiant or putting off a bright light

re-fund *v.* to return or pay back; to reimburse **refundable** *adj.* **refund** *n.*

re-fur-bish *v.* to make clean; to renovate

re-fus-al *n.* the denial of something which is demanded

re-fuse *v.* to decline; to reject; to deny

ref-use *n.* rubbish; trash

re-fute *v.* to overthrow or to disprove with the use of evidence

re-gain *v.* to recover; to reach again

re-gal *adj.* of or appropriate for royalty **regally** *adv.*

re-gale *v.* to entertain or delight; to give pleasure

re-ga-li-a *n.* something which represents royalty such as a septer

re-gard *v.* to look upon closely; to consider; to have great affection for; *n.* careful attention or thought; esteem or affection; **regards** greetings of good wishes

re-gard-ful *adj.* state of being mindful

re-gard-less *adj.* state of being careless or showing no regard towards something or someone

re-gat-ta *n.* a boat race

re-gen-cy *n.*, *pl.* **regenies** the jurisdiction or office of a regent

re-gen-er-ate *v.* to reform spiritually or morally; to make or create anew; to refresh or restore

re-gent *n.* one who rules and acts as a ruler during the absence of a sovereign, or when the ruler is underage

re-gime *n.* an administration

reg-i-men *n.* government control; therapy

reg-i-ment *n.* a military unit of ground troops which is composed of several battalions **regimental** *adj.*

regimentation *n.*

re-gion *n.* an administrative, political, social, or geographical area

re-gion-al *adj.* typical or pertaining to a geographic region; limited to a particular region

reg-is-ter *n.* something which contains names or occurrences

reg-is-trar *n.* type of person who keeps a register

reg-is-tra-tion *n.* an act of recording things or names

re-gress *v.* to return to a previous state or condition **regress, regression** *n.*

re-gret *v.* to feel disappointed or distressed about; *n.* a sense of loss or expression of grief; a feeling of sorrow **regretfully, regretably** *adv.*,

regretful, regretable adj.

reg-u-lar adj. usual; normal; customary; conforming to set principles, procedures, or discipline; well-ordered; not varying **regularity** n., **regularly** adv.

reg-u-late v. to adjust to a specification or requirement **regulative, regulatory** adj., **regulator** n.

reg-u-la-tion n. a rule that is set down in order to govern an area or people

re-gur-gi-tate v. to pour something forth

re-ha-bil-i-tate v. to restore; to a former state, by education and therapy **rehabilitation** n., **rehabilitative** adj.

re-hash v. to rework or go over old material

re-hears-al n. the act of practicing for a performance **rehearse** v.

reign n. the period in time when the monarch rules over an area

re-im-burse v. to repay **reimbursement** n.

rein n. one of a pair of narrow, leather straps attached to the bit of a bridle and used to control a horse

rein-deer n. a large deer found in northern regions, both sexes having antlers

re-in-force v. to support; to strengthen with additional people or equipment **reinforcement** n.

re-in-state v. to restore something to its former position or condition **reinstatement** n.

re-it-er-ate v. to say or do something over and over again

re-ject v. to refuse; to discard as useless **reject, rejection** n.

re-joice v. to fill with joy; to be filled with joy

re-join v. to respond or to answer someone

re-join-der n. the answer to a reply made by someone to another

re-ju-ve-nate v. to restore to youthful appearance or vigor **rejuvenation** n.

re-kin-dle v. to inflame something again

re-lapse v. to fall back or revert to an earlier condition **relapse** n.

re-late v. to tell the events of; to narrate; to bring into natural association **relater** n.

re-lat-ed adj. to be in the same family; connected to each other by blood or by marriage

re-la-tion n. the relationship between people by marriage or blood lines **relational** adj.

re-la-tion-ship n. a connection by blood or family; kinship; friendship; a natural association

rel-a-tive adj. relevant; connected; considered in comparison or relationship to other; n. a member of one's family

rel-a-tiv-i-ty n. a condition or state of being relative

re-lax v. to make loose or lax; to relieve something from effort or strain; to become less formal or less reserved **relaxation** n., **relaxedly** adv.

re-lay n. a race in which a fresh team replaces another; v. to pass from one group to another

re-lease v. to set free from confinement; to unfasten; to free; to relinquish a claim on something **releaser** n.

rel-e-gate v. to banish someone or something

re-lent v. to soften in temper, attitude, or determination; to slacken **relentless** adj.

rel-e-vant adj. related to matters at hand

re-li-a-ble adj. dependable; capable of being relied upon

re-li-ance n. confidence and trust; something which is relied upon

re-li-ant adj. state of being confident or having reliance

re-lic n. something which is very old; a keepsake; an object whose cultural environment has disappeared

re-lief n. anything which decreases or lessens anxiety, pain, discomfort, or other unpleasant conditions or feelings

re-lief map n. a map which outlines the contours of the land

re-lieve v. to lessen or ease pain, anxiety, embarrassment, or other problems; to release or free from a duty by providing a replacement **reliever** n., **relievable** adj.

re-lig-ion n. an organized system of beliefs, rites, and celebrations centered on a supernatural being power; belief pursued with devotion **religious** adj.

re-lin-quish v. to release something or someone

re-lish n. pleasure; a spicy condiment taken with food to lend it flavor

re-live v. to experience something again

re-lo-cate v. to move to another area **relocation** n.

re-luc-tance n. an unwillingness

re-luc-tant adj. unwilling; not yielding

re-ly v. to trust or depend

re-main v. to continue without change; to stay after the departure of others

remainder n. something left over; *Math* the difference which remains after division or subtraction

re-mains *pl., n.* what is left after all other parts have been taken away; corpse

re-mand *n.* state of being remanded

re-mark *n.* a brief expression or comment; to take notice; to observe; to comment

re-mark-a-ble *adj.* extraordinary remarkably *adv.*

re-me-di-a-ble *adj.* being able to be remedied

rem-e-dy *n., pl.* remedies a therapy or medicine which relieves pain; something which corrects an error or fault; *v.* to cure or relieve; to rectify

re-mem-ber *v.* to bring back or recall to the mind; to retain in the mind carefully; to keep a person in one's thought; to recall a person to another as a means of greetings

re-mem-brance *n.* something which is remembered by someone

re-mind *v.* to cause or help to remember

rem-i-nisce *v.* to recall the past things which have happened

rem-i-nis-cence *n.* the practice or process of recalling the past reminiscent *adj.*

re-miss *adj.* lax in performing one's duties; negligent remissness *n.*

re-mis-sion *n.* a forgiveness; act of remitting

re-mit *v.* to send money as payment for goods; to forgive, as a crime or sin; to slacken, make less violent, or less intense remittance *n.*

rem-nant *n.* a small piece or a scrap or something

re-mod-el *v.* to reconstruct something making it like new

re-mon-strance *n.* statement of reasons against an idea or something

re-mon-strate *v.* giving strong reasons against an act or an idea

re-morse *n.* deep moral regret for past misdeeds remorseful *adj.*

re-mote *adj.* distant in time; space or relation remotely *adv.*, remoteness *n.*

re-mount *v.* to mount something again

re-mov-a-ble *adj.* being able to be removed

re-mov-al *n.* the change of a site or place

re-move *v.* to get rid of; to extract; to dismiss from office; to change one's business or residence; *n.* an act of moving removable *adj.* removal *n.*

re-moved *adj.* state of being separate from others

re-mu-ner-ate *v.* pay an equivalent for a service

ren-ais-sance *n.* a revival or rebirth; the humanistic revival of classical art, literature, and learning in Europe which occurred during the 14th through the 16th centuries

re-nal *adj.* of or relating to the kidneys

re-nas-cence *n.* a revival or a rebirth

rend *v.* to remove from with violence; to split

ren-der *v.* to give or make something available; to submit or give; to represent artistically; to liquefy or melt fat by means of heat rendering *n.*

ren-dez-vous *n.* a meeting place that has been prearranged; *v.* to meet at a particular time and place

ren-di-tion *n.* an interpretation or a translation

ren-e-gade *n.* a person who rejects one allegiance for another; an outlaw; a traitor renegade *adj.*

re-nege *v.* to fail to keep one's word

re-new *v.* to make new or nearly new by restoring; to resume renewable *adj.*, renewal *n.*

ren-net *n.* an extract taken from a calf's stomach and used to curdle milk for making cheese

re-nounce *v.* to reject something or someone

ren-o-vate *v.* to return or to restore to a good condition

re-nown *n.* the quality of being widely honored renowned *adj.*

rent *n.* the payment made for the use of another's property; *v.* to obtain occupancy in exchange for payment rental *n.*

re-nun-ci-a-tion *n.* renouncing

re-or-gan-i-za-tion *n.* the process of reorganizing something

rep. *n.*, *Slang* representative; *v.* represent

re-pair *v.* to restore to good or usable condition; to renew; refresh repairable *adj.*

re-pair-man *n.* the person who makes repairs of things that are broken

rep-a-ra-ble *adj.* being able to be corrected

rep-a-ra-tion *n.* the act of repairing something

rep-ar-tee *n.* a quick, witty response or reply

re-pa-tri-ate *v.* to go back to one's own country

re-pay *v.* to pay back money; to do something in return

re-peal *v.* to withdraw officially repeal *n.*, repealer *n.*

re-peat *v.* to utter something again; to do an action again re-peat-er *n.* something or person which repeats

re-pel *v.* to discourage; to force away; to create aversion

re-pel-lent *adj.* able to repel

re-pent *v.* to feel regret for something which has occurred; to change one's sinful way repentance *n.*, repentant *adj.*

re-per-cus-sion *n.* an unforeseen effect produced by an action repercussive *adj.* •

rep-er-toire *n.* the accomplishments or skills of a person

rep-er-to-ry *n.* a collection of things

rep-e-ti-tion *n.* the act of doing something over and over again; the act of repeating

re-place *v.* to return something to its previous place replaceable *adj.*, replacement *n.*, replacer *n.*

re-plen-ish *v.* to add to something to replace what has gone or been used

re-plete *adj.* having plenty; abounding; full

rep-li-ca *n.* a reproduction or copy of something replicate *v.*

re-ply *v.* to give an answer to either verbally or in writing reply *n.*

re-port *n.* a detailed account; usually in a formal way; *v.* to tell about; to make oneself available; to give details of reportable *adj.*, reporter *n.*

re-port card *n.* the report of the students progress

re-port-ed-ly *adv.* to be according to a report

re-pose *n.* the act of being at rest; *v.* to lie at rest reposeful *adj.*

re-pos-i-tor-y *n.* the location where things may be placed for preservation

re-pos-sess *v.* to restore ownership of something

rep-re-hend *v.* to show or express disapproval of reprehension *n.*, reprehensible *adj.*

rep-re-sent *v.* to stand for something; to serve as the official representative for

rep-re-sen-ta-tion *n.* the act of representing

rep-re-sent-a-tive *n.* a person or thing serving as an example or type; *adj.* of or relating to government by representation; typical

re-press *v.* to restrain; hold back; to remove from the conscious mind repression *n.*, repressive *adj.*

re-prieve *v.* to postpone punishment; to provide temporary relief reprievable *adj.*, reprieve *n.*, reprieve,

reprieving *v.*

rep-ri-mand *v.* to censure severely; rebuke reprimand *n.*

re-print *n.* an additional printing of a book exactly as the previous one reprint *v.*, reprinter *n.*

re-pri-sal *n.* retaliation with intent to inflict injury in return for injury received

re-proach *v.* to blame; to rebuke reproachful *adj.*

rep-ro-bate *adj.* the state of being morally depraved

re-pro-duce *v.* to produce an image or copy; *Biol.* to produce an offspring; to recreate or produce; again reproducer *n.*, reproducible *adj.*, reproduction *n.*, reproductive *adj.*

re-proof *n.* a censure

re-prove *v.* to tell or express a disapproval of something

rep-tile *n.* a cold-blooded, egg-laying vertebrate, as a snake, lizard, or turtle reptilian *n.*, *adj.*

re-pub-lic *n.* a political unit or state where representatives are elected to exercise the power

re-pub-li-can *adj.* having the character of a republic

re-pub-li-can-ism *n.* the Republican principles

Republican Party *n.* one of the two political parties in the United States

re-pu-di-ate *v.* to cast away; to refuse to pay something

re-pug-nance *n.* the state or condition of being opposed

re-pug-nant *adj.* distasteful; repulsive; offensive

re-pulse *v.* to repel or drive back; to repel or reject rudely; to disgust or be disgusted repulsion *n.*

re-pul-sive *adj.* state of causing aversion

rep-u-ta-ble *adj.* to be honorable reputability *n.*

re-put-a-tion *n.* the commonly held evaluation of a person's character

re-pute *v.* to account or to consider something

re-quest *v.* to ask for something request *n.*

re-qui-em *n.* the Roman Catholic mass for a deceased person

re-quire *v.* to demand or insist upon requirement *n.*

req-ui-site *adj.* absolutely needed; necessary

req-ui-si-tion *n.* a demand or a request

re-quit-al *n.* the act of requiting something

re-quite *v.* to reward; to repay someone

re-run *n.* a television show which is shown again

re-sale *n.* the act of selling something again

re-scind *v.* to repeal; to void rescindable *adj.*, rescission *n.*

res-cue *v.* to free from danger; *n.* an act of deliverance rescuer *n.*

re-search *n.* a scientific or scholarly investigation; to carefully seek out researcher *n.*

re-sem-ble *v.* to have similarity to something resemblance *n.*

re-sent *v.* to feel angry about resentful *adj.*, resentfully *adv.*, resentment *n.*

res-er-va-tion *n.* the act of keeping something back

re-serve *v.* to save for a special reason; to set apart; to retain; to put off; *n.* something that is saved for a future point in time; the portion of a country's fighting force kept inactive until called upon

res-er-voir *n.* a body of water stored for the future; large reserve; a supply

re-side *v.* to dwell permanently; to exist as a quality or attribute residence *n.*

res-i-due *n.* matter remaining after treatment or removal of a part; something which remains

re-sign *v.* to give up; to submit to something as being unavoidable; to quit resignation *n.*

res-in *n.* a plant substance from certain plants and trees used in varnishes and lacquers resinous *adj.*

re-sist *v.* to work against or actively oppose; to withstand resistible *adj.*

res-o-lute *adj.* coming from or characterized by determination resolutely *adv.*, resolution *n.*

re-solve *v.* to make a firm decision on something; to find a solution resolvable *adj.*, resolver *n.*, resolution *n.*

re-sort *v.* to go frequently or customarily *n.* a place, or recreation, for rest, and for a vacation

re-sound *v.* to be filled with echoing sounds; to reverberate; to ring or sound loudly resounding *adj.*, resoundingly *adv.*

re-source *n.* a source of aid or support which can be drawn upon if needed; resources one's available capital or assets resourceful *adj.*

re-spect *v.* to show consideration or esteem for; to relate to; *n.* courtesy or considerate treatment respectfully *adv.* respectful *adj.*

res-pi-ra-tion *n.* the process or act of inhaling and exhaling; the act of breathing; the process in which an animal or person takes in oxygen from the air and releases carbon dioxide respirator *n.*

res-pite *n.* a temporary postponement

re-spond *v.* to answer or reply; to act when prompted by something or someone

re-sponse *n.* a reply; the act of replying responsive *adj.*

re-spon-si-ble *adj.* trustworthy; in charge; having authority; being answerable for one's actions or the actions of others responsibility *n.*

rest *n.* a cessation of all work, activity, or motion; *Mus.* an interval of silence equal in time to a note of same value; *v.* to stop work; to place or lay restful *adj.*, restfully *adv.*

res-tau-rant *n.* a place which serves meals to the public

res-ti-tu-tion *n.* the act of restoring something to its rightful owner; compensation for injury, loss, or damage

res-tive *adj.* nervous or impatient because of a delay restively *adv.*, restiveness *n.*

re-store *v.* to bring back to a former condition; to make restitution of restoration *n.*

re-strain *v.* to hold back or be held back; to control, limit, or restrict restraint *n.*

re-strict *v.* to confine within limits restriction *n.*, restrictive *adj.*, restrictively *adv.*

re-sult *v.* to happen or exist in a particular way; *n.* the consequence of an action, course, or operation

re-sume *v.* to start again after an interruption resumption *n.*

res-u-me *n.* a summary of one's personal history, background, work, and education

re-sus-ci-ate *v.* to return to life; to revive resuscitation *n.*, resuscitator *n.*

re-tail *v.* the sale of goods or commodities to the public; *v.* to sell to the consumer retail *adj.*, retailer *n.*

re-tain *v.* to hold in one's possession; to remember; to employ someone, as for his services

re-tain-er *n.* a person or thing that

retains; a fee paid for one's services

re-tard v. to delay or slow the progress of retardant n. & adj.

re-tar-da-tion n. a condition in which mental development is slow or delayed; a condition of mental slowness

re-ten-tion n. the act or condition of being retained

ret-i-na n., pl. retinas, retinae the light sensitive membrane lining the inner eyeball connected by the optic nerve to the brain retinal adj.

re-tire v. to depart for rest; to remove oneself from the daily routine of working; Baseball to put a batter out retirement n., retired adj., retiree n.

re-trace v. to go back over

re-tract v. to draw back or to take back something that has been said retractable adj., retraction n.

re-tread v. to replace the tread of a worn tire retread n.

re-treat n. the act of withdrawing from danger; a time of study; prayer; and meditation in a quiet; isolated location retreat v.

re-trieve v. to regain; to find something and carry it back retrievable adj., retrieval n.

ret-ro-ac-tive adj. taking effect on a date prior to enactment

ret-ro-spect n. a review of things in the past retrospectively adv., retrospective adj.

re-turn v. to come back to an earlier condition; to reciprocate; n. the act of sending, bringing, or coming back returns n. a yield or profit from investments; a report on the results of an election returnable adj., returnee n. returner n.

re-un-ion n. a reuniting; the coming together of a group which has been separated for a period of time

re-veal v. to disclose or make known; to expose or bring into view

rev-eil-le n. the sounding of a bugle used to awaken soldiers in the morning

rev-el v. to take great delight in reveler n.

rev-e-la-tion n. an act of or something revealed; a manifestation of divine truth; evelation the last book in the New Testament

re-venge v. to impose injury in return for injury received revengeful adj., revenger n.

re-verse adj. turned backward in position; n. the opposite of something; a

change in fortune usually from better to worse; change or turn to the opposite direction; to transpose or exchange the positions of; Law to revoke a decision reverser n.

re-vert v. to return to a former practice or belief reversion n.

re-view v. to study or look over something again; to give a report on; n. a reexamination; a study which gives a critical estimate of something reviewer n.

re-vise v. to look over something again with the intention of improving or correcting it reviser n., revision n.

re-viv-al n. the act or condition or reviving; the return of a film or play which was formerly presented; a meeting whose purpose is religious reawakening

re-vive v. to restore, refresh, or recall; to return to consciousness or life

re-voke v. to nullify or make void by recalling revocation n.

re-volt n. to try to overthrow authority; to fill with disgust

rev-o-lu-tion n. the act or state of orbital motion around a point; the abrupt overthrow of a government; a sudden change in a system

re-volve v. to move around a central point; to spin; to rotate revolvable adj.

re-vue n. a musical show consisting of songs, dances, skits, and other similar entertainment

re-ward n. something given for a special service; v. to give a reward

R.F.D. abbr. rural free delivery

rhap-so-dy n., pl. rhapsodies an excessive display of enthusiasm

rhe-ni-um n. a metallic element symbolized by Re

rhet-o-ric n. effective expression in writing or speech; language which is not sincere

Rh fac-tor n. a substance found in the red blood cells of 85% of all humans; the presence of this factor is referred to as PH positive; the absence as PH negative

rhi-noc-er-os n.

a very large mammal with one or two upright horns on the snout

rho-di-um n. a metallic element symbolized by Rh

rhu-barb n. a garden plant with large

leaves and edible stalks used for pies

rhyme *or* **rime** *n.* a word or verse whose terminal sound corresponds with another rhyme *v.* **rhymer** *n.*

rhy-thm *n.* Music, speech, or movements which are characterized by equal or regularly alternating beats

rhythmical, rhythmic *adj.*

rhythmically *adv.*

RI *abbr.* Rhode Island

rib *n.* one of a series of curved bones enclosed in the chest of man and animals; *Slang* to tease

rib-bon *n.* a narrow band or strip of fabric, such as satin, used for trimming

rice *n.* a cereal grass grown extensively in warm climates

rich *adj.* having great wealth; of great value; satisfying and pleasing in voice, color, tone, or other qualities; extremely productive; as soil or land

rick-rack *n.* a zigzag braid used in trimming

rick-ets *n., Pathol.* a disease occurring in early childhood resulting from a lack of vitamin D and insufficient sunlight, characterized by defective bone growth and deformity

rid *v.* to make free from anything objectionable

rid-dle *v.* to perforate with numerous holes; *n.* a puzzling problem or question which requires a clever solution

ride *v.* to travel in a vehicle or on an animal; to sit on and drive, as a motorcycle

rid-er *n.* one who rides as a passenger; a clause, usually having little relevance, which is added to a document

ridge *n.* a long, narrow crest; a horizontal line formed where two sloping surfaces meet **ridge** *v.*

ridge-pole *n.* timber located at the top of a roof which is horizontal

rid-i-cule *n.* actions or words intended to make a person or thing the object of mockery **ridicule** *v.*

ri-dic-u-lous *adj.* to be causing derision or ridicule

rife *adj.* state of being abundant or abounding

rif-fle *n.* ripply water which is caused by a ridge

riff-raff *n.* the rabble; low persons in society

ri-fle *n.* a firearm having a grooved bore designed to be fired from the shoulder

ri-fling *n.* the act of putting or cutting spiral grooves in the barrel of a gun.

rift *n.* a fault; disagreement; a lack of harmony

rig *v.* to outfit with necessary equipment; *n.* the arrangement of sails, masts, and other equipment on a ship; the apparatus used for drilling water or oil wells

right *adj.* in accordance with or conformable to law, justice, or morality; proper and fitting; properly adjusted, disposed, or placed; orderly; sound in body or mind; *n.* the right side, hand, or direction; the direction opposite left; *adv.* immediately; completely; according to justice, morality, or law **rightness** *n.*

right an-gle *n., Geom.*

an angle of 90 degrees; an angle with two sides perpendicular to each other

rig-id *adj.* not bending; inflexible; severe; stern **rigidity, rigidness** *n.*

rig-or *n.* the condition of being rigid or stiff; stiffness of temper; harshness **rigorous** *adj.*, **rigorously** *adv.*

rind *n.* a tough outer layer which may be taken off or pealed off

ring *n.* a circular mark, line, or object; a small circular band worn on a finger; a group of persons acting together; especially in an illegal way; *v.* to make a clear resonant sound, as a bell when struck; *n.* the sound made by a bell

ri-ot *n.* a wild and turbulent public disturbance; *Slang* an irresistibly amusing person **riotous** *adj.*

rip *v.* to tear apart violently; to move violently or quickly; *n.* a torn place; **rip-off** *Slang* to steal

rip-cord *n.* a cord which, when pulled, releases a parachute from its pack

ripe *adj.* fully developed or aged; mature **ripeness** *n.*

rip-ple *v.* to cause to form small waves on the surface of water; to waver gently **ripple** *n.*

rise *v.* to move from a lower position to a higher one; to extend upward; to meet a challenge or demand; *n.* the act of going up or rising; an elevation in condition or rank

ris-er *n.* a person who rises

ris-i-ble *adj.* being inclined to or causing laughter

risk *n.* a chance of suffering or encountering harm or loss; danger **risky** *adj.*

rite *n.* a formal religious ceremony; any formal custom or practice

rit-u-al *n.* a prescribed method for per-

forming a religious ceremony; *adj.*
pertaining to or practiced as a rite
ritual *adj.*, **ritualism** *n.*

ri-val *n.* one who strives to compete with
another; one who equals or almost
equals another

riv-er *n.* a relatively large natural stream
of water, usually fed by another body
of water

ri-vet *n.* a metal bolt used to secure two
or more objects

RN *abbr.* Registered Nurse

roach *n.* a European freshwater fish;
cockroach; *Slang* the butt of a
marijuana cigarette

roam *v.* to travel aimlessly or without a
purpose **roamer** *n.*

roar *v.* to utter a deep prolonged sound
of excitement; to laugh loudly
roar, roarer *n.*

roast *v.* to cook meat by using dry heat
in an oven; *n.* a cut of meat.

rob *v.* to take property unlawfully from
another person **robber** *n.*, **robbery** *n.*

rob-in *n.* a large North American bird
with a black head and reddish breast

ro-bot *n.* a machine capable of performing human duties

ro-bust *adj.* full of strength and health;
rich; vigorous **robustly** *adv.*,
robustness *n.*

rock *n.* a hard naturally formed material;
Slang one who is dependable

rock-er *n.* a curved piece, usually of
wood, on which a cradle or chair
rocks

rock-et *n.*

a device propelled
with the thrust from a
gaseous combustion;
v. to move rapidly

rode *v.* past tense of ride

ro-dent *n.* a mammal, such as a rat,
mouse, or beaver having large incisors
used for gnawing

ro-de-o *n.* a public show, contest, or
demonstration of ranching skills, as
riding and roping

roe *n.* the eggs of a female fish

rogue *n.* a scoundrel or dishonest person; an innocently or playful person

roll *v.* to move in any direction by turning over and over; to sway or rock
from side to side, as a ship; to make a
deep prolonged sound as thunder; *n.* a
list of names; *Slang* a large amount of
money

roll-er *n.* a cylinder for crushing,

smoothing or rolling something; any
of a number of various cylindrical
devices

ro-mance *n.* a love affair, usually of the
young, characterized by ideals of
devotion and purity; a fictitious story
filled with extravagant adventures
romance *v.* **romancer** *n.*

Ro-man nu-mer-al *n.* the letter or letters
of the Roman system of numbering
still used in formal contexts, as: V=5,
X=10, L=50, C=100, D=500,
M=1000

romp *v.* to run, play, or frolic in a
carefree way

rood *n.* a measurement of land which
equals 1/4 acre

rook-ie *n.* an untrained person; a novice
or inexperienced person

room *n.* a section or area of a building
set off by partitions or walls; *v.* to occupy or live in a room

roast *n.* a place or perch on which birds
sleep or rest; a piece of meat which
has been or is to be roasted

root *n.*

the part of a plant
which grows in the
ground; *Math* a num-
ber which, when mul
tiplied by itself, will produce a given
quantity; *v.* to search or rummage for
something; to turn up the earth with
the snout, as a hog
rootless *adj.*, **rootless** *adj.*

root beer *n.* a type of beverage which is
made from herb and root extracts and
this if fermented in sugar and yeast

root hair *n.* a type of filament which
grows from the tip of a root

root-stock *n.* the source

rope *n.* a heavy cord of twisted fiber;
know the ropes to be familiar with all
of the conditions at hand
roping, roped *v.*

rop-y *adj.* being stringy; being like a
rope

ro-sa-ry *n.*, *pl.* -ies a string of beads for
counting prayers; a series of prayers

rose *n.* a shrub or climbing vine having
sharp prickly stems and variously
colored fragrant flowers

ro-se-ate *adj.* being rosy; optimistic;
being colored like a rose

rose-bud *n.* a bud of a rose

rose--col-ored *adj.* being pink or rosy;
cheerful

rose-mar-y *n.* a type of a green shrub

which is located in the Mediterranean region and its leaves are used for seasoning

ro-sette *n.* an ornament gathered to resemble a rose and made of silk or ribbon

rose wa-ter *n.* a fragrant product made from rose petals, steeped in water, and used in cosmetics

rose-wood *n.* a type of tropical South American tree

Rosh Ha-sha-nah *n.* the Jewish New Year

ros-in *n.* a resin which is formed as the oil of turpentine is distilled from crude turpentine

ros-ter *n.* a list of names

ros-trum *n.* the platform that a speaker gives his speach from

ros-y *adj.* being the of roses; cheerful **rosiness** *n.*

rot *v.* to decay

ro-ta-ry *adj.* turning or designed to turn; of or relating to axial rotation

ro-tate *v.* to turn on an axis; to alternate something in sequence **rotatable** *adj.*, **rotation, rotator** *n.*, **rotatory** *adj.*

ROTC *abbr.* Reserve Officer's Training Corps

ro-tis-ser-ie *n.* a rotation device with spits for roasting food

ro-tor *n.* a rotating part of a mechanical device

rot-ten *adj.* decomposed; morally corrupt; very bad

ro-tund *adj.* plump; rounded

rouge *n.* a cosmetic coloring for the cheeks

rough *adj.* having an uneven surface; violent or harsh; *n.* the part of a golf course with tall grass; *v.* to treat roughly; *adv.* in a very rude manner **roughly** *adv.*, **roughness** *n.*

rou-lette *n.* a gambling game in which players bet on which slot a small ball will land in

round *adj.* curved; circular; spherical; *v.* to become round; to surround; *adv.* throughout; prescribed duties, places, or actions **roundness** *n.*

rouse *v.* to awaken or stir up

route *n.* a course of travel; *v.* to send in a certain direction

rou-tine *n.* activities done regularly; *adj.* ordinary

rove *v.* to wander over a wide area **rover** *n.*, **roving** *adj.*

row *n.* a number of things positioned next to each other; a continuous line; *v.* to propel a boat with oars

roy-al *adj.* relating to a king or queen

roy-al-ty *n., pl.* **royalties** monarchs and or their families; a payment to someone for the use of his invention, copyright, or services

R.S.V.P. *abbr.* respondez s'il vous plait; please reply

rub *v.* to move over a surface with friction and pressure; to cause to become worn or frayed

rub-ber *n.* a resinous elastic material obtained from the coagulated and processed sap of tropical plants or produced synthetically **rubbery** *adj.*

rub-ber ce-ment *n.* a type of adhesive that is liquid and made of rubber

rub-ber-ize *v.* coat or cover something with rubber

rub-ber-neck *v.* to turn the head in order to see something

rub-ber plant *n.* type of plant that is found in East India and yields rubber

rub-ber stamp *n.* a type of rubber plate which is coated with ink and used for the purpose of leaving prints on paper or other objects

rub-bish *n.* worthless trash; nonsense **rubbishy** *adj.*

rub-ble *n.* the pieces of broken material or stones

ru-bel-la *n.* the German measles

ru-bi-cund *adj.* state of being of a red color or hue

ru-bid-i-um *n., Symbol* a silvery, highly reactive element symbolized by Rb

ru-bric *n.* a heading, title, or initial letter of a manuscript which appears in red

ru-by *n., pl.* **rubies** a deep-red precious stone

ruck-us *n., Slang* a noisy uproar, or commotion

rud-der *n., Naut.* a broad, flat, hinged device attached to the stern of a boat used for steering

rud-dy *adj.* being red in color or hue

rude *adj.* discourteous; offensively blunt

ru-di-ment *n.* a first step, element, skill, or principle; *Biol.* an undeveloped organ

rue *v.* to repent

rue-ful *adj.* to be causing sorrow or remorse

ruff *n.* a stiff collar which has pleats in it

ruf-fi-an *n.* a lawless, rowdy person

ruf-fle *n.* a pleated strip or frill; a decorative band; *v.* to disturb or destroy the smoothness

rug *n.* a heavy textile fabric used to cover a floor

rug-by *n.* a game similar to football in

which the ball is propelled toward the opponents goal by carrying or kicking

rug-ged *adj.* strong; rough; having an uneven or rough surface **ruggedness** *n.*, **ruggedly** *adv.*

ru-in *n.* total destruction; *v.* to destroy **ruination** *n.*, **ruinous** *adj.*

rule *n.* controlling power; an authoritative direction or statement which regulates the method of doing something; a standard procedure; *v.* to have control over; to make a straight line using a ruler; to be in command

rul-er *n.* a straight edge used for measuring; a person who rules as a sovereign

rul-ing *n.* a type of decision which is handed down by a judge in a trial

rum *n.* a type of liquor made from molasses and is distilled

rum-ba *n.* a type of dance which has a complex rhythm

rum-ble *v.* to make a heavy, continuous sound; *n.* a long deep rolling sound

ru-mi-nant *n.* a cud-chewing animal; as a cow, deer, sheep, or giraffe; an animal which chews something which was swallowed

ru-mi-nate *v.* to chew a cud; to ponder at length **rumination** *n.*, **ruminative** *adj.*, **ruminator** *n.*

rum-mage *v.* to look or search thoroughly by digging or turning things over; to ransack

rum-mage sale *n.* a sale of second-hand objects, conducted to make money

rum-my *n.* a card game in which each player tries to get rid of his hand in sequences of three cards or more of the same suit

ru-mor *n.* an uncertain truth which is circulated from one person to another; gossip; *v.* to speed by rumor

ru-mor-mon-ger *n.* one who aids in the spreading of rumors

rump. the fleshy hind quarter of an animal; the human buttocks

rum-ple *v.* to form into creases or folds; to wrinkle

rum-pus room *n.* a type of room which is used for parties

run *v.* to hurry busily from place to place; to move quickly in such a way that both feet leave the ground for a portion of each step; to make a rapid journey; to be a candidate seeking an office; to drain or discharge; *Law* to be effective, concurrent with; *n.* a speed faster than a walk; a streak, as of luck; the continuous extent or length of something; an outdoor area used to exercise animals; in baseball, the method of scoring a point by running the bases and returning to home plate

run-a-bout *n.* a type of boat which is open

rund-let *n.* a type of barrel which is small in size

run-down *adj.* the state of being worn down

rung *n.* a bar or board which forms a step of a ladder

run-ner *n.* the person who runs in a race

run-ner--up *n.* a contestant who finishes second in a competition

run-ning *adj.* state of moving fast or rapidly

run-off *n.* that which runs off of something

run of the mill *adj.* ordinary; not special; average

runt *n.* the smallest animal in a litter

run-through *n.* the rehearsal of a play

rup-ture *n.* a state of being broken; the act of bursting

ru-ral *adj.* pertaining to the country or country life

ru-ral-ize *v.* the act of moving to or living in the country or the rural area **ruralization** *n.*

ru-ral route *n.* a mail route which runs through the country

ruse *n.* a type of trick

rush *v.* to move quickly; to hurry; to be in a hurry

rust *n.* a substance called ferric oxide that forms on iron material, that has been exposed to moisture and oxygen

rus-tic *adj.* characteristic of country life; *n.* a simple person **rustically** *adv.*

rus-ti-cate *v.* living and staying in the country or rural area -tor, -icity *n.*

rus-tle *v.* to move making soft sounds, such as those made by leaves of a tree

rus-tler *n.* a person who steals cattle

rust-proof *adj.* being unable to rust

rust-y *adj.* to be covered by rust **rustiness** *n.*, **rustily** *adv.*

rut *n.* an indented track made by the wheels of vehicles

ru-ta-ba-ga *n.* type of vegetable which belongs to the mustard family that produces a tuber

ru-the-ni-um *n.* a metallic element symbolized by Ru

rut-ty *adj.* a state of having many ruts

rye *n.* a cultivated cereal grass whose seeds are used to make flour and whiskey

S, s The nineteenth letter of the English alphabet.

sab-a-dil-la *n.* a type of mexican plant such as of the lily family whose seeds can be used for insecticides

sab-bat *n.* the midnight assembly of the diabolists

Sab-bath *n.* seventh day of the week; set apart as the day of worship for Jews and some Christians; Sunday, the first day of the week, a day set apart as the day of worship by most Christians

sab-bat-i-cal *adj.* to be relating to the sabbath

sa-ber *n.* lightweight sword

sa-ber saw *n.* a type of light and protable electric saw

sa-bine *n.* the member of the people of the Appennines of the ancient times

sa-ble *n.* carnivorous mammal having soft, black or dark fur

sa-bot *n.* the kind of wooden shoe which is worn by the people in various European countries

sab-o-tage *n.* act of malicious destruction

sab-o-teur *n.* a person who commits sabotage

sac *n., Biol.* membranous pouch in an animal or plant, containing a liquid

sa-ca-huis-te *n.* a kind of bear grass that has long linear leaves and is used for forage

sac-cade *n.* a type of small rapid jerky movement of the eye

sac-cate *adj.* to have the form of a pouch

sac-cha-rate *n.* a tyhpe of a compound of sugar usually with a bivalent metal

sac-char-i-fy *v.* to break some compound into a simple sugar

sac-cha-rim-e-ter *n.* a kind of device which is used for the purpose of measuring the amount of sugar in a solution

sac-cha-rin *n.* white, crystalline powder used as a noncaloric sugar substitute

sac-cha-rine *adj.* pertaining to or like sugar

sac-cha-roi-dal *adj.* being of fine granular texture

sac-cha-rom-e-ter *n.* a type of hydrometer that has a special scale

sac-cu-lar *adj.* to be resembling a sac

sac-cu-late *adj.* to be formed of a series of saccular expansions

sac-cule *n.* a chamber which is the smaller of the membranous labyrinth of the ear

sac-er-do-tal *adj.* pertaining to the priesthood or to priests

sa-chem *n.* a kind of North American Indian chief

sa-chet *n.* small bag of a sweet-smelling powder used to scent clothes

sack *n.* strong bag for holding articles *Slang* dismissal from a position or job

sack-ing *n.* the material that sacks are constructed from

sack out *v.* to go or to get into bed

sack race *n.* type of race where the contestants jump inside a sack to the finish line

sacque *n.* a type of infant jacket that is short and fastens at the neck

sa-cral *adj.* pertaining to the sacrum

sac-ra-ment *n.* a formal christian rite performed in a chruch, as a baptism

sac-ra-men-tal *adj.* pertaining to the character of the sacrament

sac-ra-men-tal-ism *n.* the use of the sacramental acts or rites

sa-crar-i-um *n.* a kind of ancient Roman shrine ;which holds sacred articles

sa-cred *adj.* dedicated to worship; holy sacredly *adv.*

sa-cred mush-room *n.* a type of New World hallucinogenic fungi

sac-ri-fice *n.* practice of offering something *v.* to give up something of value for something else sacrificial *adj.*

sad *adj.* marked by sorrow; unhappy; causing sorrow sadly *adv.*, sadness *n.*

sad-dle *n.*

a seat for a rider, as on the back of a horse or bicycle; a cut of meat which includes the backbone *v.* to put a saddle on; to load down; to burden

sa-dism *n., Psychol.* condition in which sexual gratification comes from inflicting pain on others; cruelty sadist *n.*, sadistic *adj.*, -tically *adv.*

sa-fa-ri *n., pl.* safaris trip or journey; a hunting expedition in Africa

safe *adj.* secure from danger, harm, or evil; unharmed safely *adv.*, safeness *n.*

sag *v.* droop; to sink from pressure or weight sag *n.*

sa-ga *n.* long heroic story

sage *n.* person recognized for judgment and wisdom

said *v.* past tense of say

sake *n.* motive or reason for doing something

sa-la-ry *n., pl.* salaries set compensation paid on a regular basis for services rendered salaried *adj.*

sale n. exchange of goods for a price; disposal of items at reduced prices salable adj.

sa-li-ent adj. projecting beyond a line; conspicuous

sa-li-va n. tasteless fluid secreted in the mouth which aids in digestion

sal-i-vate v. to secrete saliva

sal-i-va-tion n. action or process of salivating

Salk vaccine n. vaccine used to immunize against polio

sal-low n. a European willow with broad leaves

sal-ly n., pl. sallies. sudden rush to launch an assault on something or someone

salm-on n., pl. salmons a large game fish with pinkish flesh

sal-mo-nel-la n. bacteria associated with food poison

sa-lon n. large drawing room; a business establishment pertaining to fashion

sa-loon n. place where alcoholic drinks are sold

salt n. white crystalline solid, mainly sodium chloride

sal-ta-tion n. sudden movement; dancing

salt-cel-lar n. a small personal dish used to hold salt

salt-ed adj. seasoned with salt; preserved

sal-tine n. a thin, salted cracker

salt mine n. a mine from which salt is dug

salt-y adj. tasting or containing salt saltiness n.

sal-u-tar-y adj. wholesome; healthful; beneficial

sal-u-ta-tion n. an expression; a greeting of good will salutational adj.

sa-lu-ta-to-ry n. message of welcome delivered at com-mencements

sa-lute v. to show honor n. act of respect or greeting by saluting saluter n.

sal-u-tif-er-ous adj. referring to something healthful or beneficial

salv-a-ble adj. something that may be salvaged salvability n.

salve n. medicated ointment used to soothe the pain of a burn or wound

sal-va-tion n. preservation from destruction or danger -al adj., -ism n.

salve v. to salvage, as a ship

sa-mar-i-um n. a metallic element

same adj. identical; exactly alike; similar; not changing

sam-ple n. portion which represents the whole v. to try a little; to examine

san-a-to-ri-um n., pl. sanatoriums an institution for treating chronic diseases

sanc-ti-fy v. to make holy sanctification n.

sanc-tion n. permission from a person of authority; a penalty to ensure compliance

sanc-tu-ar-y n., pl. -ies. sacred, holy place, as the part of a church, where services are held; a safe place; a refuge

san-dal n.

a shoe which is fastened to the foot by straps attached to the sole; a low shoe or slipper with an ankle strap

sane adj. having a healthy, sound mind; showing good judgment sanely adv., sanity n.

san-i-tar-y adj. free from bacteria or filth which endanger health

san-i-tize v. to make sanitary; to make clean or free of germs

sank v. past tense of sink

sa-pi-ent adj. wise

sap-phire n. a clear, deep-blue gem, used in jewelry

sar-casm n. insulting or mocking statement or remark sarcastic adj., sarcastically adj.

sar-dine n. small edible fish of the herring family, often canned in oil

sar-don-ic adj. scornful; mockingly cynical

sass n., Slang rudeness; a disrespectful manner of speech

sas-sa-fras n. dried root of a North American tree, used as flavoring

sat-el-lite n. natural or man-made object which orbits a celestial body

sat-in n. smooth, shiny fabric made of silk, nylon, or rayon, having a glossy face and dull back

sat-ire n. use of mockery, sarcasm, or humor in a literary work to ridicule or attack human vice

sat-is-fac-tion n. anything which brings about a happy feeling; the fulfillment of a need, appetite, or desire

sat-is-fy v. fulfill; to give assurance to

sat-u-rate v. to make completely wet; to soak or load to capacity saturation n.

sau-cer n. small shallow dish for holding a cup

sav-age adj. wild; uncivilized; brutal n. vicious or crude person -ly adv., -ry n.

sav-ior n. one who saves Christ Savior

sa-voir-faire n. social skill

sa-vor n. the taste or smell of something to truly enjoy savory adj.

say v. speak aloud; to express oneself in words; to indicate; to show n. chance to speak

scab n. stiff, crusty covering which forms over a healing wound *Slang* person who continues to work while others are on strike

sca-bies n. contagious skin disease characterized by severe itching, caused by a mite under the skin

scald v. burn with steam or a hot liquid

scal-lop n. marine shellfish

scalp n. skin which covers the top of the human head

scal-pel n. small, straight knife with a narrow, pointed blade, used in surgery

scamp n. scheming or tricky person

scan v. examine all parts closely; to look at quickly scan, scanner n.

scan-dal n. something which brings disgrace when exposed to the public; gossip

scan-di-um n. metallic element symbolized by Sc.

scant adj. not plentiful or abundant; inadequate

scant-ling n. dimensions of material used in building

scap-u-la n., pl. scapulae one pair of large, flat, triangular bones which form the back of the shoulder -ar adj.

scar n. permanent mark which remains on the skin after a sore or injury has healed

scarce adj. not common or plentiful; rare scarceness n.

scar-la-ti-na n. mild form of scarlet fever

scar-let n. bright or vivid red

scat-ter v. spread around

scav-en-ger n. an animal, as a vulture, which feeds on decaying or dead animals or plant matter

sce-nar-i-o n. synopsis of a dramatic plot

scene n. view; the time and place where an event occurs; a public display of temper

scent n. smell; an odor v. to smell

sched-ule n. list or written chart which shows the times at which events will happen

scheme n. plan of action; an orderly combination of related parts; a secret plot

schol-ar n. student with a strong interest in learning

school n. place for teaching and learning

schoon-er n. sailing vessel with two or more masts

sci-ence n. study and theoretical explanation of natural phenomena in an orderly way; knowledge acquired through experience scientific adj.

scis-sors pl., n. a cutting tool

scle-ro-sis n., pl. scleroses a hardening of a part of the body, as an artery

scold v. accuse or reprimand harshly

sconce n. wall bracket for holding candles

scoop n. mall, shovel-like tool v. lift up or out

scoot v. go suddenly and quickly

scope n. range or extent of one's actions

scope suff. device for seeing or discovering

scorch v. burn slightly, changing the color and taste of something; to parch with heat

scorn n. contempt; disdain v. treat with scorn scornful adj.

scor-pi-on n.

an arachnid having an upright tail tipped with a poisonous sting

scour v. clean by rubbing with an abrasive agent

scout v. observe activities in order to obtain information n. person whose job is to obtain information

scow n. a large barge with a flat bottom and square ends, used to transport freight, gravel, or other cargo

scowl v. make an angry look; to frown

scrab-ble v. scratch about frantically, as if searching for something scrabbler n.

scrag-gly adj. messy; irregular

scrap n. small section or piece

scrape v. rub a surface with a sharp object in order to clean *Slang* embarrassing situation

scrawl n. write or draw quickly and often illegibly

scraw-ny adj. very thin; skinny

scream v. utter a long, sharp cry, as of fear or pain n. long piercing cry

screech v. make a shrill, harsh noise

screw n.

a metal piece that resembles a nail, having a spiral thread which is used for fastening things together; a propeller on a ship v. to join by twising

scrim-shaw n. art of carving designs on whale ivory or whalebone

scrip-ture n. sacred writing Scriptures the Bible

scroll *n.* roll of parchment or similar material used in place of paper

scro-tum *n., pl.* **scrota** external sac of skin which encloses the testes **scrotal** *adj.*

scrub *v.* clean something by rubbing; *Slang* cancel

scrump-tious *adj., Slang* delightful

scru-ple *n.* principle which governs one's actions **scrupulous** *adj.*

scu-ba *n.* apparatus used by divers for underwater breathing

scuff *v.* drag or scrape the feet while walking

sculp-tor *n.* person who creates statues from clay, marble, or other material

scum *n.* thin layer of waste matter floating on top of a liquid

scurf *n.* flaky dry skin; dandruff

scur-ry *v.* move quickly

scut-tle *n.* small opening with a movable lid in the hull of a ship

scythe *n.* tool with a long handle and curved, single-edged blade, used for cutting hay, grain and grass

sea *n.* body of salt water which covers most of the earth

seal *n.*

a large aquatic mammal with a sleek body and large flippers; a device having a raised emblem, used to certify a signature or the authenticity of a document

seam *n.* line formed at the joint of two pieces of material

sear *v.* wither or dry up; to shrivel; to burn or scorch

search *v.* look over carefully **search, searcher** *n.*

sea-son *n.* one of the four parts of the year **seasonal** *adj.,*

seat *n.* place or spot, as a chair, stool, or bench, on which to sit

se-cede *v.* withdraw from an organization or group **secessionist** *n.*

se-clude *v.* isolate

sec-ond *n.* unit of time equal to 1/60 of a minute; a very short period of time; an object which does not meet first class standards

sec-on-dar-y *adj.* not being first in importance; inferior

~~ret *n.* knowledge kept from others; a ~~ystery

sec-re-tary *n., pl.* **secretaries** person hired to write and keep records for an executive or an organization

secretarial *adj.*

se-crete *v.* produce and give off; to release or discharge

sec-tion *n.* part or division of something; a separate part

sec-u-lar *adj.* relating to something worldly

se-cure *adj.* safe and free from doubt or fear; sturdy or strong; not likely to fail *v.* tie down, fasten, lock, or otherwise protect from risk or harm **-ly** *adv.*

se-cu-ri-ty *n., pl.* **securities** state of being safe and free from danger or risk; protection

se-date *adj.* serene and composed *v.* to keep or be kept calm through the use of drugs **sedative** *n.*

sed-i-ment *n.* material which floats in or settles to the bottom of a liquid **sedimentary** *adj.,* **sedimentation** *n.*

se-duce *v.* tempt and draw away from proper conduct **seducer, seduction** *n.,* **sedative** *adj.*

see *v.* have the power of sight; to understand

seed *n.* fertilized plant ovule with an embryo, capable of producing an offspring

seek *v.* search for; to try to reach; to attempt **seeker** *n.*

seem *v.* appear to be; to have the look of **seeming** *adj.*

seep *v.* leak or pass through slowly **seepage** *n.*

seer *n.* person who predicts the future

seg-ment *n.* any of the parts into which a thing is divided *v.* divide **-al** *adj.*

seg-re-gate *v.* separate or isolate from others

seg-re-ga-tion *n.* act of separating people based on the color of their skin

seine *n.* fishing net with weights on one edge and floats on the other

seize *v.* grasp or take possession forcibly

sel-dom *adv.* not often

se-lect *v.* to choose from a large group; to make a choice **selection** *adj.,* **-or**

se-le-ni-um *n.* element symbolized by Se.

self *n., pl.* **selves** complete and essential being of a person

self—de-fense *n.* act of defending oneself or one's belongings

sell *v.* exchange a product or service for money **seller** *n.*

se-man-tics *n.* study of word meanings and the relationships between symbols and signs

sem-a-phore *n.* system for signaling by using flags, lights or arms in various positions **semaphore** *v.*

se-men *n.* secretion of the male reproductive system, thick and whitish in color and containing sperm

se-mes-ter *n.* one of two periods of time in which a school year is divided

sem-i-an-nu-al *adj.* occurring twice a year

sem-i-co-lon *n.* punctuation mark (;) having a degree of separation stronger than a comma but less than a period

sem-i-nar *n.* course of study for students engaged in advanced study of a particular subject

sem-i-nar-y *n., pl.* seminaries school that prepares ministers, rabbis, or priests for their religious careers -ian *n.*

send *v.* cause something to be conveyed from one place to another; to dispatch

se-nile *adj.* having a mental deterioration often associated with old age senility *n.*

sen-ior *adj.* being the older of two; of higher office or rank; referring to the last year of high school or college seniority *n.*

sense *n.* sensation; feeling; the physical ability which allows a person to be aware of things around him; the five senses: taste, smell, touch, sight, and hearing

sen-si-bil-i-ty *n., pl.* sensibilities ability to receive sensations

sen-si-ble *adj.* capable of being perceived through the senses; sensitive; having good judgment sensibly *adv.*

sen-si-tive *adj.* capable of intense feelings sensitivity *n.*

sen-sor *n.* device which responds to a signal

sen-su-al *adj.* preoccupied with the gratification of the senses sensuality *n.*, sensualous *adj.*

sent *v.* past tense of send

sen-tence *n.* series of words arranged to express a single complete thought; a prison term for a convicted person

sen-ti-ment *n.* feelings of affection; an idea, opinion, thought, or attitude based on emotion rather than reason sentimental *adj.*

sen-ti-nel *n.* who guards

se-pal *n.* one of the leaves which forms a calyx in a flower

sep-a-rate *v.* divide or keep apart by placing a barrier between; to go in different directions; to set apart from others; *adj.* single; individual separation *n.*

se-quence *n.* set arrangement; a number of connected events; the regular order

ser-e-nade *n.* music performed as a romantic expression of love

se-rene *adj.* calm; peaceful serenity *n.*

serf *n.* slave owned by a lord during the Middle Ages

serge *n.* twilled, durable woolen cloth

se-ri-al *adj.* arranged in a series with one part presented at a time

se-ries *pl. n.* number of related items which follow one another

se-ri-ous *adj.* sober; grave; not trivial; important seriously *adv.*,

ser-mon *n.* message or speech delivered by a clergyman during a religious service

ser-pent *n.* snake

ser-rate *adj.* having sharp teeth; having a notched edge serration *n.*

se-rum *n., pl.* serums *or* sera yellowish fluid part of the blood which remains after clotting

ser-vant *n.* one employed to care for someone or his property

serve *v.* to take care of; to wait on; to prepare and supply; to complete a term of duty

serv-ice *n.* help given to others; a religious gathering; the military

ses-a-me *n.* tropical plant and its edible seeds

ses-sion *n.* meeting or series of meetings; a meeting set for a specific purpose

set *v.* to put or place; to cause to do; to regulate; to adjust; to arrange; to place in a frame or mounting

set-tee *n.* small couch or bench with arms and a back

set-tle *v.* arrange or put in order; to restore calm

sev-er *v.* cut off or separate severance *n.*

sev-er-al *adj.* being more than one or two, but not many; being separate severally *adv.*

se-vere *adj.* strict; stern; hard; not fancy; extremely painful severely *adv.*, severity *n.*

sew *v.* fasten or fix; to make stitches with thread and needle

sew-age *n.* solid waste material carried away by a sewer

sew-er *n.* conduit or drain pipe used to carry away waste

sex *n.* one of two divisions, male and female, into which most living things are grouped; sexual intercourse

sex-tet *n.* group of six people or things

shab-by *adj.* worn-out; ragged

shack *n.* small, poorly built building

shad *n., pl.* shad *or* shads edible fish which swims upstream to spawn shad-ow *n.* area from which light is blocked; a shaded area shadowy *adj.*

shaft *n.* long, narrow part of something; a beam or ray of light; a long, narrow underground passage

shal-low *adj.* not deep; lacking intellectual depth

sham *n.* person who is not genuine but pretends to be; a cover for pillows

sham-ble *v.* walk while dragging one's feet

shame *n.* painful feeling of embarrassment or disgrace brought on by doing something wrong; dishonor; disgrace

shank *n.* portion of the leg between the ankle and the knee; a cut of meat from the leg of an animal, such as a lamb

shape *n.* outline or configuration of something; the form of a human body

share *n.* part or portion given to or by one person; one of equal parts, as the capital stock in a corporation *v.* divide or distribute portions sharer *n.*

shark *n.*

large marine fish which eats other fish and is dangerous to man

sharp *adj.* having a thin edge or a fine point; capable of piercing or cutting; clever; quick-witted; painful

shat-ter *v.* burst suddenly into pieces

shave *v.* remove a thin layer; to cut body hair, as the beard, by using a razor; to come close to

she *pron.* female previously indicated by name

shear *v.* trim, cut, or remove the fleece or hair with a sharp instrument -er *n.*

sheath *n.* cover or case for a blade, as a sword

shed *v.* pour out or cause to pour; to throw off without penetrating; to cast off or leave behind, especially by a natural process

sheen *n.* luster

sheep *n., pl.* sheep

cud-chewing thick-fleeced mammal, widely domesticated for meat and wool

sheer *adj.* very thin; almost transparent; complete; absolute; very steep, almost

perpendicular

sheet *n.* large piece of cloth for covering a bed; a single piece of paper

shelf *n., pl.* shelves flat piece of wood, metal, plastic, or other rigid material attached to a wall or within another structure, used to hold or store things

shell *n.* hard outer covering of certain organisms

shel-ter *n.* something which gives protection or cover

shelve *v.* put aside; to place on a shelf

shep-herd *n.* person who takes care of a flock of sheep

sher-bet *n.* sweet frozen dessert made with fruit juices, milk or water, egg white, and gelatin

sher-iff *n.* high ranking lawenforcement officer

shield *n.* piece of protective metal or wood held in front of the body; anything which serves to conceal or protect; a badge or emblem shield *v.*, shielder *n.*

shift *n.* group of people who work together; a woman's loose-fitting dress; *v.* change direction or place

shim-mer *v.* shine with a faint sparkle shimmerer *n.*, shimmery *adj.*

shin *n.* front part of the leg from the knee to the ankle

shine *v.* give off light; to direct light; to polish shoes

shiner *n.* black eye

shin-gle *n.* thin piece of material, as asbestos, used to cover a roof or side of a house shingler *n.*

shin-gles *pl., n., Pathol.* acute, inflammatory viral infection, characterized by skin eruptions along a nerve path

ship *n.* large vessel for deep-water travel or transport; *v.* send or transport

ship-yard *n.* place where ships are built or repaired

shirt *n.* garment worn on the upper part of the body

shiv-er *v.* tremble or shake with excitement or chill shiver *n.*, shivery *adj.*

shoe *n.* outer cover for a foot

shone *v.* past tense of shine

shoot *v.* kill or wound with a missile, as a bullet, fired from a weapon; to discharge or throw rapidly

shore *n.* land bordering a body of water

short *adj.* having little height or length; less than normal in distance, time, or other qualities; less than the needed amount; shorts underpants or outerpants which end at the knee or above; shortage a lack in the amount needed;

short-change give less than the correct amount, as change for money; **short circuit** an electrical malfunction

shot *n.* discharging of a gun, rocket, or other device; an attempt; a try; an injection

should *v.* past tense of shall, used to express obligation, duty, or expectation

shoul-der *n.* part of the body located between the neck and upper arm

should-n't *contr.* should not

shout *v.* to yell; *n.* a loud cry

shov-el *n.* tool with a long handle and a scoop, used for picking up material or for digging

show *v.* put within sight; to point out; to explain; to put on display

shrank *v.* past tense of shrink

shrap-nel *n., pl.* **shrapnel** large shell containing metal fragments

shred *n.* a narrow strip or torn fragment; a small amount

shrew *n.* a small mouse-like mammal, having a narrow, pointed snout

shriek *n.* loud, sharp scream or noise

shrill *adj.* high-pitched, sharp sound

shrimp *n., pl.* **shrimp** or **shrimps** small, edible shellfish

shrink *v.* make or become less or smaller; to pull back from; to flinch; *Slang* psychiatrist

shroud *n.* a cloth in which a body is wrapped for burial; *v.* to cover

shrug *v.* to raise the shoulders briefly to indicate doubt or indifference shrug *n.*

shrunk *v.* past tense of shrink

shuck *n.* outer husk that covers an ear of corn

shud-der *v.* tremble uncontrollably, as from fear

shun *v.* avoid deliberately

shut *v.* move a door, drawer, or other object to close an opening; to lock up; to cease or halt operations

shy *adj.* bashful; timid; easily frightened

sib-ling *n.* one of two or more children from the same parents

sick *adj.* in poor health; ill; nauseated; morbid **sickness** *n.*

sick-le *n.*

tool with a curved blade attached to a handle, used for cutting grass or grain

side *n.* surface between the front and back or top and bottom of an object

SIDS *abbr., n.* Sudden Infant Death Syndrome; an unexpected death of a

seemingly healthy baby

siege *n.* the action of surrounding a town or port in order to capture it; a prolonged sickness

si-er-ra *n.* rugged chain of mountains or hills

si-es-ta *n.* rest or short nap

sieve *n.* meshed or perforated device which allows small particles to pass through but which holds back larger particles; a device for separating liquids from solids **sieve** *v.*

sigh *v.* to exhale a long, deep breath, usually when tired, sad, or relieved **sigh** *n.*

sight *n.* the ability to see with the eyes; the range or distance one can see

sign *n.* a piece of paper, wood, metal, etc., with information written on it; a gesture that tells or means something

sig-nal *n.* a sign which gives a warning; the image or sound sent by television or radio

sig-na-ture *n.* the name of a person, written by that person; a distinctive mark which indicates identity

sig-nif-i-cance *n.* quality of being important

sig-ni-fy *v.* express or make known by a sign; to indicate

signification *n.,* **significant** *adj.*

si-lence *n.* state or quality of being silent; quiet

silent *adj.* making no sound; not speaking; mute

silk *n.* soft, thread-like fiber spun by silkworms; thread or fabric made from silk

sil-ly *adj.* foolish; lacking good sense, seriousness, or substance **silliness** *n.*

sil-ver *n.* soft, white metallic element used in tableware, jewelry, and coins

sim-i-lar *adj.* almost the same, but not identical

sim-mer *v.* to cook just below boiling; to be near the point of breaking, as with emotion

sim-ple *adj.* easy to do or understand; not complicated; ordinary

sim-plic-i-ty *n.* state of being easy to understand

sim-pli-fy *v.* to make easy or simple **simplification** *n.*

sim-u-late *v.* to have the appearance, effect, or form of simulation, **simulator** *n.*

si-mul-ta-ne-ous *adj.* occurring at exactly the same time **simultaneously** *adj.*

sin *n.* breaking of a religious law or a law of God

since *adv.* at a time before the present;
prep. during the time later than

sin-cere *adj.* honest; not deceitful;
genuine; true **sincerely** *adv.*, **-ity** *n.*

sing *v.* to use the voice to make musical
tones; to make a humming or whis-
tling sound **singer** *n.*

singe *v.* to slightly burn the surface of
something

sin-gle *adj.* of or referring to only one,
separate; individual; unmarried

sin-gu-lar *adj.* separate; one; extraordinary; denoting a single unit, thing or
person

sink *v.* to submerge beneath a surface; to
go down slowly

si-nus *n., pl.* **sinuses** *Anat.* body cavity;
one of eight air spaces in the bones of
the face which drain into the nasal
cavity

sip *v.* drink in small amounts

si-phon *also* **syphon** *n.* tube through
which liquid from one container can
be drawn into another by forced air
pressure **siphon** *v.*

sir *n.* respectful term used when ad-
dressing a man

si-ren *n.* whistle which makes a loud
wailing noise, as a warning or signal

sit *v.* rest the body with the weight on
the buttocks; to cover eggs for hatching

siz-a-ble *adj.* large in size or dimensions

size *n.* measurement or dimensions of
something

siz-zle *v.* make a hissing sound, as of fat
frying

skate *n.*

one of numerous rays
having pectoral fins
and a rhomboidal
shaped body; device
with rollers or a
blade which attaches to the shoe and
allows one to glide over ice or roll
over a wooden or cement surface

skate-board *n.* narrow piece of wood
with wheels attached

skel-e-ton *n.* framework of bones that
protects and supports the soft tissues
and organs

skep-tic *n.* person who doubts or questions **skepticism** *n.*, **skeptical** *adj.*,
skeptically *adv.*

sketch *n.* rough drawing or outline; a
brief literary composition **sketchy** *adj.*

skew *v.* turn or slant; *n.* slant

skid *v.* slide to the side of the road; to

slide along without rotating

skill *n.* ability gained through practice;
expertise **skilled** *adj.*

skim *v.* remove the top layer; to remove
floating matter

skimp *v.* economize; to hold back **-y** *adj.*

skin *n.* tough, outside covering of man
and some animals; the outside layer of
a vegetable or fruit

skirt *n.* piece of clothing that extends
down from the waist

skull *n.* bony part of the skeleton which
protects the brain

skunk *n.*

a black mammal with
white streaks down
its back, which sprays
an unpleasant smell-
ing liquid when an-
noyed or frightened

sky *n., pl.* **skies** upper atmosphere above
the earth; the celestial regions

slab *n.* thick piece or slice

slack *adj.* not taut or tense; sluggish;
lacking in strength

slain *v.* past tense of slay

slam *v.* shut with force; to strike with a
loud impact

slam-mer *n., Slang* jail or prison

slan-der *n.* false statement that
deliberately does harm to another's
reputation **slanderous** *adj.*

slang *n.* informal language that contains
made-up words or common words
used in a different or uncommon way

slant *v.* lie in an oblique position; to
slope; to report on something giving
only one side or viewpoint

slap *n.* sharp blow with an open hand

slash *v.* cut with a fast sweeping stroke;
to reduce or limit greatly *n.* long cut

slate *n.* fine grained rock that splits into
thin layers, often used as a writing surface or roofing material **slate** *v.*

slaugh-ter *v.* kill livestock for food; to
kill in great numbers; *Slang* to soundly
defeat **slaughterer** *n.*

slave *n.* person held against his will and
made to work for another

sled *n.* vehicle with runners, used to
travel on snow or ice

sleek *adj.* smooth and shiny; neat and
trim **sleekly** *adv.*

sleep *n.* natural state of rest for the mind
and body; *v.* to rest in sleep

sleet *n.* rain that is partially frozen; a
combination of snow and rain

sleeve *n.* part of a garment which covers

the arm; a case for something

sleigh *n.* vehicle mounted on runners, usually pulled over ice and snow by horses

slen-der *adj.* slim; inadequate in amount slenderly *adv.*

slept *v.* past tense of sleep

slice *n.* thin cut; a portion or share

slick *adj.* smooth and slippery; quick; smart; clever

slick-er *n.* raincoat made of yellow oilcloth

slight *adj.* minor in degree; unimportant

slim *adj.* slender; meager; not much

slime *n.* wet, slippery substance -y *adj.*

sling *n.* piece of material, as leather, or a strap which secures something; a piece of fabric worn around the neck used to support an injured hand or arm

slip *v.* move in a smooth, quiet way; to fall or lose one's balance; *Slang* to become less active, alert, or strong

slith-er *v.* slide or slip in an indirect manner; to move like a snake slithery *adj.*

sliv-er *n.* thin, narrow piece of something that has been broken off sliver *v.*

slob-ber *v.* dribble from the mouth slobber *n.*

slo-gan *n.* phrase used to express the aims of a cause

slope *v.* slant upward or downward

slosh *v.* to splash in a liquid, as water sloshy *adj.*

slot *n.* narrow, thin groove or opening; *Slang* place or scheduled time for an event

sloth *n.* laziness; a slow mammal found in South America

slouch *n.* drooping or sagging posture; a lazy person

slow *adj.* moving at a low rate of speed; requiring more time than usual; not lively; sluggish; not interestin *adv.* at less speed; in a slow manner slowly *adv.*, slowness *n.*

slug *n.* slow animal related to the snail; a bullet or a lump of metal

sluice *n.* man-made ditch used to move water

slum *n.* crowded urban neighborhood marked by poverty

slum-ber *v.* to sleep; to doze; *n.* sleep slumberer *n.*

slump *v.* fall or sink suddenly

slur *v.* to slide over without careful consideration; to pronounce unclearly; *n.* an insult

slush *n.* melting snow slushy *adj.*

slut *n.* woman of bad character; a pros-

titute

sly *adj.* cunning; clever; sneaky slyly *adv.*, slyness *n.*

smack *v.* slap; press and open the lips with a sharp noise small *adj.* little in size, quantity, or extent; unimportant smallness *n.*

small-pox *n.* acute, contagious disease marked by high fever and sores on the skin

smart *adj.* intelligent; clever

smash *v.* break into small pieces; to ruin

smear *v.* spread or cover with a sticky, oily, or moist substance; *Slang* discredit one's reputation

smell *v.* notice an odor by means of the olfactory sense organs; *n.* odor

smelt *v.* heat metals or their ores to a high temperature in order to obtain pure metallic constituents

smile *n.* grin

smirk *v.* smile in a conceited way smirk, smirker *n.*

smite *v.* hit with great force using the hand

smock *n.* loose-fitting garment worn as a protection for one's clothes while working

smog *n.* mixture of smoke and fog smoggy *adj.*

smoke *n.* cloud of vapor released into the air when something is burning

smolder *v.* burn slowly without a flame and with little smoke smolder *n.*

smooth *adj.* not irregular; flat; without lumps; *adv.* evenly; *v.* to make less difficult

smor-gas-bord *n.* buffet meal with a variety of foods to choose from

smother *n.* failure to receive enough oxygen to survive; *v.* conceal smothery *adj.*

smudge *v.* soil by smearing with dirt; *n.* dirty mark or smear

smug *adj.* complacent with oneself; self-satisfied

smug-gle *v.* import or export goods illegally without paying duty fees smuggler *n.*

snack *n.* small amount of food taken between meals

snag *n.* stump or part of a tree; a pull in a piece of fabric

snake *n.* any of a large variety of scaly reptiles, having a long tapering body; *Slang* an untrustworthy person

snap *v.* break suddenly with a sharp, quick sound; to fly off under tension

snare *n.* anything that entangles or entraps; a trap with a noose, used to catch small animals

snarl *v.* speak in an angry way; to cause confusion; to tangle or be tangled

snatch *v.* seize or grasp something suddenly

sneak *v.* act or move in a quiet, sly way; *n.* person who acts in a secret, underhanded way

sneer *v.* express scorn by the look on one's face

sneeze *v.* expel air from the nose suddenly and without control

sniff *v.* inhale through the nose in short breaths with a noise

snip *v.* cut off in small pieces and with quick strokes

snipe *n., pl.* snipe or snipes bird with a long bill which lives in marshy places; *v.* to shoot at people from a hidden position **sniper** *n.*

snob *n.* a person who considers himself better than anyone else

snoop *v., Slang* prowl or spy; *n.* one who snoops

snore *v.* to breath with a harsh noise while sleeping **snorer** *n.*

snor-kel *n.* tube that extends above the water, used for breathing while swimming face down

snort *n.* force air through the nostrils with a loud, harsh nois; *Slang* inhale a narcotic through the nose

snow *n.* vapor that forms crystals in cold air and falls to the ground in white flakes **snow** *v.*

snub *v.* treat with contempt or in an unfriendly way

snuff *v.* draw air in through the nostrils **snuff** *n.*

snug *adj.* warm, pleasant, comfortable and safe

so *adv.* to a degree or extent as a result; likewise; also; indeed; *conj.* in order that; therefore

soap *n.* cleansing agent made of an alkali and a fat, and used for washing

soar *v.* glide or fly high without any noticeable movement; to rise higher than usual

sob *v.* weep with short, quick gasps

so-ber *adj.* not drunk or intoxicated; serious; solemn **soberly** *adv.*, **soberness** *n.*

soc-cer *n.* game in which two teams of eleven men each try to kick a ball into the opposing team's goal

so-cia-ble *adj.* capable of friendly social relations; enjoying the company of others **sociableness** *n.*, **sociably** *adv.*

socialism *n.* system in which people as a whole, and not individuals, control and own all property

so-ci-e-ty *n., pl.* societies people working together for a common purpose; companionship

so-ci-ol-o-gy *n.* study of society and the development of human society **sociologist** *n.*

sock *n.* short covering for the foot, ankle, and lower part of the leg; a hard blow

sock-et *n.* hollow opening into which something is fitted

so-da *n.* sodium carbonate; a flavored, carbonated drink

sod-den *adj.* completely saturate; very wet; lacking in expression

so-di-um *n.* metallic element symbolized by Na.

sod-om-y *n.* anal sexual intercourse

so-fa *n.* upholstered couch with arms and a back

soft *adj.* not stiff or hard; not glaring or harsh; mild or pleasant; gentle in sound

soft-ware *n.* in computer science, data, as routines, programs and languages, which is essential to the operation of computers

sog-gy *adj.* saturated with a liquid or moisture

sol-ace *n.* comfort in a time of trouble, grief, or misfortune **solacer** *n.*

so-lar *adj.* relating to or connected with the sun; utilizing the sun for power or light; measured by the earth's movement around the sun

so-lar-i-um *n., pl.* -ia *or* -ums a glassed-in room exposed to the sun's rays

solar system *n.* the sun and the planets, asteroids, and comets that orbit it

sol-der *n.* alloy, as lead or tin, which is melted and used to mend or join other pieces of metal

soldier *n.* enlisted person who serves in the military

sole *n.* bottom of a foot or shoe; single, the only one

sol-emn *adj.* very serious; characterized by dignity; sacred -ity, -ness *n.*

so-lic-it *v.* try to obtain; to ask earnestly; to beg or entice a person persistently **solicition** *n.*

sol-id *adj.* having a definite firm shape and volume; having no crevices; not hollow; having height, weight and length; with-out interruption -ify *v.*

sol-i-taire *n.* single gemstone set by itself; a card game played by one person

sol-i-tude *n.* act of being alone or secluded; isolation

so-lo *n.* musical composition written for and performed by one person or played by one instrument

sol-u-ble *adj.* capable of being dissolved solubility *n.*

solve *v.* find the answer to solvable *adj.*

som-ber *adj.* dark; gloomy; melancholy

some *adj.* being an indefinite number or quantity; unspecified; *pron.* undetermined or indefinite quantity

some-day *adv.* an unspecified future time

somehow *adv.* in a way

som-nam-bu-lism *n.* act of walking during sleep

son *n.* male offspring

song *n.* piece of poetry put to music; the act or sound of singing

son-ic *adj.* pertaining to sound or the speed of sound

son-net *n.* poem made up of fourteen lines

soon *adv.* in a short time; in the near future; quickly

soot *n.* black powder generated by incomplete combustion of a fuel, such as coal or wood

soothe *v.* make comfortable; to calm

sop *v.* soak up a liquid; to absorb

so-pran-o *n., pl.* sopranos *or* soprani highest female singing voice

sor-did *adj.* filthy, very dirty; morally corrupt

sore *adj.* tender or painful to the touch, as an injured part of the body; severe or extreme

so-ror-i-ty *n., pl.* sororities social organization for women

sor-rel *n.* any of several herbs with sour-tasting leaves, used in salads

sor-row *n.* anguish; mental suffering; an expression of grief -ful *adj.*, -fully *adv.*

sor-ry *adj.* feeling or showing sympathy or regret; worthless

sort *n.* collection of things having common attributes or similar qualities

sought *v.* past tense of seek

soul *n.* spirit in man that is believed to be separate from the body and is the source of a person's emotional, spiritual, and moral nature

sound *n.* sensation received by the ears from air, water, noise, and other sources; *v.* make a sound; *adj.* free from flaw, disease, or damage soundless *adj.*, soundly *adv.*

soup *n.* liquid food made by boiling meat and/or vegetables, in water

sour *adj.* sharp to the taste; acid; unpleasant sourly *adv.*

source *n.* any point of origin or beginning

south *n.* direction opposite of north; *adv.* to or towards the south; *adj.* from the south southerly *adj.*, southerner *n.*

south-paw *n.* left-handed person

sou-ve-nir *n.* item kept as a remembrance of something or someplace

sov-er-eign *n.* ruler with supreme power; a monarch

soviet *adj.* having to do with the Soviet Union

sow *v.* scatter or throw seeds on the ground for growth; *n.* a female pig

space *n.* unlimited area in all directions in which events occur and have relative direction; an interval of time; the area beyond the earth's atmosphere

spade *n.* tool with a flat blade used for digging, heavier than a shovel spade *v.*

spa-ghet-ti *n.* pasta made in long, thin pieces

span *n.* the section between two limits or supports; *v.* to extend across

spare *v.* to refrain from injuring, harming or destroying; to refrain from using

spark *n.* glowing or incandescent particle, as one released from a piece of burning wood or one produced by means of friction; *v.* to give off sparks

spar-kle *v.* emit or reflect light

spar-row *n.* small bird with grayish or brown plumage

sparse *adj.* scant; thinly distributed sparsely *adv.*

spasm *n.* involuntary muscle contraction

spat-ter *v.* scatter or splash a liquid

spat-u-la *n.* kitchen utensil with a flexible blade for mixing soft substances

spawn *n.* eggs of fish or other water animals, as oysters or frogs; *v.* to lay eggs

speak *v.* utter words; to express a thought in words

speak-er *n.* person who speaks, usually before an audience

spear *n.* weapon with a long shaft and a sharply pointed head; *v.* strike, pierce

spear-mint *n.* mint plant yielding an aromatic oil used as a flavoring

spe-cial-ist *n.* person, such as a doctor, who devotes his practice to one particular field

spe-cial-ize *v.* focus one's efforts or interests in one field of activity or study

spec-i-men *n.* sample; a representative of a particular thing

speck *n.* small particle, mark, or spot

spec-ta-cle *n.* public display of something unusual **spectacled** *adj.*

speech *n.* ability, manner, or act of speaking; a talk before the public

speed *n.* rate of action or movement; quickness; rapid motion; *Slang* a drug used strictly as a stimulant

spell *v.* say out loud or write in proper order the letters which make up a word; to relieve

spellbind *v.* fascinate or hold as if by magic

spend *v* give out; to use up; to pay; to exhaust

sperm *n.* male cell of reproduction; semen

sphere *n., Math* round object with all points the same distance from a given point; globe, ball, or other rounded object **spherical** *adj.*

sphinx *n., pl.* **sphinxes** *or* **sphinges** ancient Egyptian figure having the head of a man, male sheep, or hawk and the body of a lion; a very mysterious person

spice *n.* pungently aromatic plant used as flavoring in food, as nutmeg, cinnamon, pepper, or curry **spicy** *adj.*

spi-der *n.*

eight-legged insect with a body divided into two parts, spinning webs as a means of capturing and holding its prey

spike *n.* large, thick nail

spill *v.* allow or cause something to flow or run out of something

spin *v.* draw out fibers and twist into thread; to run something around and around **spinner** *n.*

spin-ach *n.* widely cultivated plant with green leaves which are used in salads

spine *n.* spinal column; the backbone; the back of a bound book

spin-ster *n.* unmarried woman; an old maid

spir-it *n.* vital essence of man, considered divine in origin the mind; the Holy Ghost

spir-i-tual *adj.* of, like, or pertaining to the nature of spirit; relating to religion; sacred **-ity** *n.,* **-ize** *v.*

spite *n.* hatred or malicious bitterness; a grudge; ill will **-ful** *adj.,* **-fully** *adv.*

spit-toon *n.* a cuspidor or receptacle for spit

spitz *n.* small dog with a tail which curls over its back

splash *v.* spatter a liquid; to wet or soil with liquid; to make a splash **splashy** *adj.*

splash-down *n.* landing of a missile or spacecraft in the ocean

spleen *n., Anat.* highly vascular, flattened organ which filters and stores blood, located below the diaphragm

splen-did *adj.* illustrious; magnificent

splice *v.* join together by wearing, overlapping, and binding the ends **splice** *n.*

splotch *n.* discolored and irregularly shaped spot

splutter *v.* make a slight, short spitting sound **splutter** *n.*

spoil *v.* destroy the value, quality, or usefulness

sponge *n.* any of a number of marine creatures with a soft, porous skeleton which soaks up liquid **spongy** *adj.*

spon-ta-ne-ous *adj.* done from one's own impulse without apparent external cause **spontaneousity** *n.,* **spontaneously** *adv.*

spoof *n.* deception; nonsense

spook *n., Slang* a ghost; *v.* scare or frighten **spooky** *adj.*

spool *n.* small cylinder for holding thread, tape or wire

spoon *n.* eating or cooking utensil; a shiny metallic fishing lure *Slang* make love, as by kissing or caressing **-ful** *n.*

spo-rad-ic *adj.* occurring occasionally or at irregular intervals **sporadically** *adv.*

spore *n., Bot.* reproductive singlecelled structure produced by nonflowering plants; any cell capable of developing into a new organism, seed, or germ

spouse *n.* one's husband or wife; a marriage partner

spout *v.* pour out forcibly, as under pressure; to cause to shoot forth **spouter** *n.*

sprain *n.* wrenching or twisting of a muscle or joint

sprawl *v.* sit or lie in an ungraceful manner; to develop haphazardly **sprawler** *n.*

spray *n.* liquid dispersed in a fine mist or droplets; *v.* disperse or send forth in a spray **sprayer** *n.*

spread *v.* unfold or open fully; to apply or distribute over an area; to force apart; to extend or expand **spread** *v.*

spree *n.* excessive indulgence in an activity; a binge

spright-ly *adj.* Vivacious, lively **sprightliness** *n.*

sprin-kle *v.* scatter in small particles or drops; to rain in small drops **sprinkle** *n.*

sprint *n.* short, fast race **sprinter** *n.*

sprock-et *n., Mech.* tooth-like projection from the rim of a wheel

sprung *v.* past tense of spring

spry *adj.* quick; brisk; energetic

spud *n., Slang* potato

spur *n.* sharp, projecting device worn on a rider's boot, used to nudge a horse

sput-nik *n.* unmanned Soviet earth satellite

sput-ter *v.* throw off small particles in short bursts; to speak in a confused or agitated manner

spu-tum *n., pl.* **sputa** saliva or mucus that is expectorated

spy *n., pl.* **spies** secret agent who obtains information; one who watches other people secretly

squab-ble *v.* engage in a petty argument

squad *n.* small group organized to perform a specific job

squan-der *v.* spend extravagantly or wastefully

square *n.* parallelogram with four equal sides; an implement having a T or L shape used to measure right angles; *Math.* to square root *n.* number which when multiplied by itself gives the given number

squash *n.*
edible fruit of the gourd family; a sport played in a walled court with a hard rubber ball and racket

squat *v.* sit on the heels; to crouch; to settle on a piece of land in order to obtain legal title

squaw *n.* American Indian woman

squeak *v.* utter a sharp, penetrating sound

squea-mish *adj.* easily shocked or nauseated **squeamishly** *adv.*

squeeze *v.* press together; to extract by using pressure

squint *v.* view something through partly closed eyes

squirm *n.* twist the body in a wiggling motion **squirm** *v.*

squir-rel *n.*
rodent with gray or brown fur, having a long bushy tail and dark eyes

squirt *v.* eject in a thin stream or jet; to wet with a squirt

sta-bi-lize *v.* make firm; to keep from changing **stabilizeation, stabilizer** *n.*

sta-ble *n.* building for lodging and feeding horses or other farm animals; *adj.* standing firm and resisting change

stac-ca-to *adj., Music* Marked by sharp emphasis **staccato** *n. & adv.*

stack *n.* large pile of straw or hay; any systematic heap or pile; a chimney

sta-di-um *n., pl.* **-dia** large structure for holding athletic events or other large gatherings

staff *n., pl.* **staffs** *or* **staves** pole or rod used for a specific purpose; the people employed to assist in the day-to-day affairs of running a business, organization, or government; *Mil.* a group of people on an executive or advisory board; *Music* the horizontal lines on which notes are written

stag *n.* adult male of various animals; a man who attends a social gathering without a woman companion

stag-ger *v.* to walk unsteadily; to totter *adj.* strongly affected by defeat, misfortune, or loss of strength

stag-nant *adj.* not flowing; standing still; foul from not moving; inactive **stagnate** *v.*

stair *n.* step or a series of steps

staircase *n.* series or a flight of steps that connect one level to another

stake *n.* bet placed on a game of chance; a sharpened piece of wood for driving into the ground

stale *adj.* having lost freshness; deteriorated; lacking in interest; dull

stalk *n.* main axis of a plant *v.* approach in a stealthy manner

stal-lion *n.* uncastrated, fully grown male horse

sta-men *n., pl.* **stamens** *Bot.* pollen-producing organs of a flower

stam-i-na *n.* physical or moral endurance

stam-mer *v.* make involuntary halts or repetitions of a sound or syllable while speaking

stamp *v.* put the foot down with force; to imprint or impress with a die, mark, or design *n.* a postage stamp

stam-pede *n.* sudden rush of panic, as of a herd of horses or cattle

stance *n.* posture or position of a standing person or animal

stand *v.* to be placed in or maintain an erect or upright position; to take an upright position; to remain unchanged; to maintain a conviction; to resist *n.* a device on which something rests; a small booth for selling or displaying items

stand-ard *n.* model which stands for or is accepted as a basis for comparison

stand-ing *n.* status, reputation, or achievement; a measure of esteem *adj.* unchanging

sta-ple *n.* principle commodity grown in an area; a major element; a metal fastener designed to hold materials such as cloth or paper **staple** *v.*, **stapler** *n.*

star *n., Astron.* self-luminous body that is a source of light; any of the celestial bodies that can be seen in the night sky; a symbol having five or six points and resembling a star

star-board *n.* right side of a ship or boat

starch *n.* nutrient carbohydrates that are found in foods such as rice and potatoes *v.* to stiffen clothing by using starch **starchiness** *n.*, **starchy** *adj.*

stare *v.* look with an intent, direct gaze **stare**, **starer** *n.*

stark *adj.* bare; total; complete; forbidding in appearance **starkness** *n.*, **starkl**y *adv.*

star-ling *n.* common black or brown bird

star-tle *v.* cause a sudden surprise; to shock **startle** *n.*

starve *v.* suffer or die from not having food; to suffer from the need of food, love, or other necessities **starvation** *n.*

stat-ic *adj.* not moving *n.* random noise heard on a radio **-ally** *adv.*

sta-tion *n.* place where someone or something is directed to stand; a scheduled stopping place; the place from which radio and television programs are broadcast

sta-tion-ar-y *adj.* not movable; unchanging

sta-tion-er-y *n.* writing paper and envelopes

sta-tis-tic *n.* estimate using an average or mean on the basis of a sample taken; numerical data

stat-ue *n.* form sculpted from wood, clay, metal, or stone

stave *n.* narrow piece of wood used in forming part of a container, as a barrel

stay *v.* remain; to pause; to maintain a position; to halt or stop; to postpone or delay an execution *n.* short visit

stead *n.* position, place, or job of another

stead-y *adj.* firmly placed, fixed or set; not changing

steal *v.* take another person's property; to move in a sly way; to move secretly *Slang* real bargain

steam *n.* water in the form of vapor; the visible mist into which vapor is condensed by cooling **steam** *v.*, **steamy** *adj.*

steel *n.* various mixture of iron, carbon, and other elements; a strong material that can be shaped when heated **steely** *adj.*

ste-nog-ra-phy *n.* skill of writing in shorthand **stenographer** *n.*

step *n.* single completed movement in walking, dancing, or running; the distance of such a step; the part of a ladder that one places the feet on in ascending or descending *Music* musical scale; a degree

ste-re-o *n.* record player with stereophonic sound

ster-e-o-type *n.* conventional opinion or belief; a metal printing plate

ster-ile *adj.* free from microorganisms; sanitary; unable to reproduce

ster-ling *n.* alloy of 92.5% silver and another metal, as copper

stern *adj.* inflexible; harsh *n.* rear of a boat or ship **sternly** *adv.*, **sternness** *n.*

ster-num *n., pl.* **-nums** *or* **-na** long, flat bone located in the chest wall, connecting the collarbones and the cartilage of the first seven pairs of ribs **sternumal** *adj.*

steth-o-scope *n.*

instrument used to listen to the internal sounds of the body

stew *v.* cook slowly; to simmer; to boil *n.* dish of stewed meat and potatoes *Slang* to worry

stick *n.* slender piece of wood; a club, rod, or walking stick *v.* put a hole in something; to pierce; to cling; to become jammed

stiff *adj.* not flexible; not easily bent; awkward *n., Slang* dead body **-ness** *n.*

sti-fle *v.* suffocate; to cut off; to suppress; to keep back

stig-ma *n., pl.* **-mata** *or* **-mas** mark of disgrace **stigmata** part of a flower where pollen is deposited at pollination **stigmatic** *adj.*

still *adj.* silent; calm; peaceful; until now or another time *adv.* nevertheless **stillness** *n.*

stillbirth *n.* birth of a dead fetus

stilt *n.* one of a pair of long poles with foot supports, used for walking

stim-u-lant *n.* agent which arouses or accelerates physiological activity

stim-u-late *v.* excite to a heightened activity; to quicken **stimulation** *n.*

stim-u-lus *n., pl.* -**li** something that excites to action

stin-gy *adj.* not giving freely; cheap

stink *v.* give off a foul odor that is highly offensive

stip-u-late *v.* settle something by agreement; to establish conditions of agreement **stipulation** *n.*

stir *v.* mix a substance by moving round and round; to agitate or provoke

stir-rup *n.* loop extending from a horse's saddle, used to support the rider's foot

stitch *n.* in sewing, a single loop formed by a needle and thread; the section of loop of thread

stock-ade *n.* barrier placed around a fort for protection

stock-ing *n.* knitted covering for the foot

stock-y *adj.* sturdy and compact; built sturdily

stole *n.* long, narrow scarf that is usually worn around a woman's shoulders, as a mink stole *v.* past tense of steal

stom-ach *n., Anat.* organ into which food passes from the esophagus; one of the primary organs of digestion *v.* tolerate or stand; to put up with

stood *v.* past tense of stand

stool *n.* seat without a backrest and arms; a small version of this on which to rest the feet; a bowel movement

stoop *v.* bend the body forward and downward from the waist *n.* porch attached to a house

stop *v.* cease; to halt; to refrain from moving, operating, or acting; to block or obstruct

stor-age *n.* act of storing or keeping; in Computer Science, the part of a computer in which all information is held; the memory

store *n.* business offering merchandise for sale; a supply to be used in the future *v.* supply; to accumulate

stork *n.* large, wading bird

storm *n.* atmospheric condition marked by strong winds with rain, sleet, hail, or snow *v.* charge or attack with a powerful force

sto-ry *n., pl.* -**ies.** narration of a fictional tale or account; a lie; a level in a building or house

stout *adj.* strong; sturdy; substantial; courageous

stove *n.* apparatus in which oil, electricity, gas, or other fuels are consumed to provide the heat for cooking

stow *v.* pack or put away

strad-dle *v.* sit or stand with the legs on

either side of something; to favor both sides of an issue -**er** *n.*

straight *adj.* being without bends, angles, or curves; upright; erect; honest; undiluted; unmodified; heterosexual **straightly** *adv.*

strain *v.* stretch beyond a proper limit; to injure by putting forth too much effort; to pass through a sieve to separate small particles from larger ones

strait *n.* narrow passageway which connects two bodies of water

strand *n.* land that borders a body of water; one of the threads that are twisted together to form a rope *v.* leave in a difficult situation

strange *adj.* not previously known or experienced;odd; peculiar; inexperienced; alien -**ly** *adv.*

stran-ger *n.* person unknown; a newcomer; an alien

stran-gle *v.* kill by choking **strangler** *n.*

strap *n.* long, narrow strip of leather or other material used to secure objects

strat-e-gy *n., pl.* -**ies** skillful planning and managing of an activity -**gic** *adj.*

stra-tum *n., pl.* -**ta** *or* -**tums** horizontal layer, as of the earth's crust

straw *n.* stalk of dried, threshed grain; a slender, plastic or paper straw used to suck up a liquid

straw-ber-ry *n.*

low plant with white flowers and red fruit; the fruit of this plant

stray *v.* roam or wander *n.* lost or wandering animal or person *adj.* lost **strayer** *n.*

streak *n.* narrow line or stripe that is different from the surrounding area; a run of good or bad luck *v.* rush or move rapidly; to make a streak **streaky** *adj.*

stream *n.* small body of flowing water; a steady or continuous succession or procession. *v.* flow in or like a stream

street *n.* public thoroughfare in a town or city with buildings on either or both sides

strength *n.* quality of being strong; power in general; degree of concentration or potency

strengthen *v.* grow strong or stronger

stren-u-ous *adj.* necessitating or characterized by vigorous effort or exertion **strenuously** *adv.*

stress *n.* special significance; an emphasis given to a specific syllable, word, action, or plan; strain or pressure stressful adj.

stretch v. extend fully; to extend forcibly beyond proper limits; to prolong n. state or act of stretching stretchable, stretchy adj.

strew v. scatter about

strick-en adj. suffering, as from an emotion, illness, or trouble

strict adj. holding to or observing rules exactly; imposing absolute standards strictly adv., -ness n.

stride v. walk with a long, sweeping step

strike v. hit with the hand; to ignite, as with a match; to afflict suddenly with a disease; to discover; to conclude or make; to stop working as a protest against something or in favor of rules or demands presented to an employer

string n. strip of thin twine, wire, or catgut used on stringed musical instruments; a series of related acts, items, or events; in Computer Science, data arranged in an ascending or descending sequence according to a command within the data

strin-gent adj. of or relating to strict requirements; marked by obstructions or scarcity stringently adv.

strip v. take off the outer covering; to divest or pull rank; to remove one's clothes; to rob

stripe n. streak, band, or strip of a different color or texture; a piece of material or cloth worn on the sleeve of a uniform to indicate rank, award, or service

stroke n. movement of striking; a sudden action with a powerful effect; a single movement made by the hand or as if by a brush or pen Path. sudden interruption of the blood supply to the brain v. pass the hand over gently

stroll v. walk in a slow, leisurely way

strong adj. exerting or possessing physical power; durable; difficult to break strongly adv.

struc-ture n. construction made up of a combination of related parts structure v., structural adj.

strug-gle v. put forth effort against opposition

strych-nine n. extremely poisonous alkaloid derived from certain plants, used to kill rodents and as a neural stimulant

stub n. short, projecting part; the short end of something after the main part has been removed or used

stub-born adj. inflexible; difficult to control, handle, or manage

stuc-co n., pl. -coes or -cos fine plaster used to coat exterior walls and to decorate interior walls

stud n. upright post, as in a building frame, to which sheets of wallboard or paneling are fastened; a small removable button used as an ornament; a male horse used for breeding stud v.

stu-dent n. person who studies at a school or college

stu-di-o n. place of work for an artist, photographer, or other creative person; a place for filming movies

stud-y n., pl. -ies process of applying the mind to acquire knowledge

stum-ble v. trip and nearly fall over something; to come upon unexpectedly

stump n. part of a tree which remains after the top is cut down v. puzzle or be puzzled; to walk heavily; to campaign

stun v. render senseless by or as if by a blow

stu-pen-dous adj. astonishing or highly impressive -ness n., stupendously adv.

stu-pid adj. slow in apprehension or understanding stupidity n.

stur-dy adj. possessing robust strength and health -ily adv., sturdiness n.

stur-geon n. large freshwater fish highly valued as a source of caviar

stut-ter v. speak with involuntary repetitions of sound stutter n.

sty n., pl. sties inflammation of the edge of an eyelid

style n. method, manner, or way of performing, speaking, or clothing; elegance, grace, or excellence in performance or appearance style v., stylish adj.

suave adj. ingratiating; smoothly pleasant in manner

sub- prefix. beneath, under, or below

sub-con-scious adj. below the level of consciousness

sub-due v. bring under control by influence, training, persuasion or force

sub-ject n. word in a sentence that defines a person or thing; a person who is under the control of another's governing power subjection n.

sub-jec-tive adj. taking place within, relating to or preceding from an individual's emotions or mind subjectively adv., subjectivity n.

sub-ma-rine adj. operating or existing

beneath the surface of the sea n. ship that travels underwater **submariner** n.

sub-merge v. plunge under the surface of the water

sub-mit v. give into or surrender to another's authority **submission,** **-tal** n., **submissive** adj.

sub-or-di-nate adj. being of lower class or rank; minor; inferior **-ation** n., **subordinative** adj.

sub-poe-na n. legal document requiring a person to appear in court for testimony

sub-se-quent adj. following in time, place, or order **subsequently** adv., **subsequentness** n.

sub-side v. move to a lower level or sink; to become less intense

sub-sid-i-ar-y adj., pl., n. **-ies.** providing assistance in a lesser capacity **subsidiaries** pl., n.

sub-si-dy n., pl. **-dies.** financial aid granted directly to a private commercial enterprise from the government

sub-sist v. have continued existence

sub-soil n. layer of earth that comes after the surface soil

sub-stance n. matter or material of which anything consists

sub-sti-tute n. something or someone that takes the place of another

sub-ten-ant n. a person who rents property from a tenant

sub-ter-ra-ne-an adj. located, situated, or operating underground

sub-ti-tle n. explanatory title, as in a document, book, etc.; a written translation that appears at the bottom of a foreign motion picture screen

sub-tract v. deduct or take away from

sub-trop-i-cal adj. pertaining to regions adjacent to the tropics

sub-urb n. residential community near a large city **suburban** adj.

sub-way n. underground electrical-lypowered train, usually used as a means of transportation

suc-ceed v. accomplish what is attempted; to come next or to follow

suc-cess n. achievement of something intended or desired; attaining wealth, fame, or prosperity

suc-ces-sion n. act or process of following in order; sequence; series; the order, sequence or act by which something changes hands

suc-ces-sive adj. following in order or sequence **-ly** adv., **-ness** n.

suc-cu-lent adj. juicy; full of juice or sap **-ence** n., **succulently** adv.

such adj. of this or that kind or thing; a great degree or extent in quality pron. of a particular degree or kind; a person or thing of such

suck v. pull liquid in the mouth by means of a vacuum created by the lips and tongue n. action of sucking

su-crose n. sugar obtained from the sugar beet or sugar cane

suc-tion n. process or act of sucking

sud-den adj. happening very quickly without warning or notice; sharp; abrupt; marked by haste **-ly** adv.

suds pl., n. bubbles or soapy water **sudsy** adv.

suede n. leather with a soft, napped finish

su-et n. hard fat around the kidney and loins of sheep

suf-fer v. feel pain or distress; to sustain injury, loss, or damage **sufferer** n.

suf-fi-cient adj. as much that is needed or desired

suf-fix n. form affixed to the end of a word

suf-fo-cate v. kill by depriving something or someone of oxygen **suffocation** n.

sugar n. sweet, watersoluble, crystal-like carbohydrate Slang nickname for someone

sug-gest v. give an idea for action or consideration; to imply; hint or intimate

sug-ges-tion n. act of suggesting; a slight insinuation; hint

su-i-cide n. act of taking one's own life **suicidal** adj.

suit n. set of articles, as clothing, to be used or worn together; in cards, one of the four sets: spades, hearts, clubs, and diamonds that make up a deck v. meet the requirements of; to satisfy

sul-fur also **sulphur** n. light, yellow, non-metallic element occurring naturally in both combined and free form, used in making matches, gunpowder and medicines

sulk v. to be sullenly silent

sul-len adj. ill-humored, melancholy; gloomy; depressing

sul-try adj. hot and humid; muggy

sum n. result obtained by adding; the whole amount, quantity, or number; summary

sum-ma-ry n., pl. **-ries.** giving the sum or substance adj. a statement covering the main points **summarily** adv.

sum-mer n. warmest of the four seasons, following spring and coming before autumn

sum-mit n. top and highest point,

degree, or level

sum-mons *n., pl.* **-monses** order or command to perform a duty; a notice to appear at a certain place

sun *n.* star around which other planets of the solar system orbit; the energy, visible light, and heat, that is emitted by the sun; sunshine **sunny** *adj.*

sun-down *n.* time of day the sun sets

sunk-en *adj.* submerged or deeply depressed in

su-per *adj.* exceeding a norm; in excessive intensity or degree; surpassing most others; superior in rank, status or position; excellent *n.* *Slang* superintendent of a building

su-perb *adj.* of firstrate quality **superbly** *adv.*

su-per-fi-cial *adj.* pertaining to a surface; concerned only with what is not necessarily real

su-pe-ri-or *adj.* of higher rank, grade, or dignity *n.* person who surpasses another in rank or excellence **-ity** *n.*, **superiorly** *adv.*

su-per-la-tive *adj.* of the highest degree of excellence; pertaining to the degree of comparison of an adverb or adjective that shows extreme extent or level **superlatively** *adv.*

su-per-nat-u-ral *adj.* order of existence beyond the natural world; pertaining to a divine power **supernaturaly** *adv.*

su-per-sede *v.* take the place of; to set aside

su-per-son-ic *adj., Aero.* characterized by a speed greater than that of sound

su-per-sti-tion *n.* belief founded, despite evidence that it is irrational; a belief, resulting from faith in magic or chance

su-per-vise *v.* have charge in directing the work of other people **supervision, supervisor** *n.*, **supervisory** *adj.*

sup-per *n.* last or evening meal of the day

sup-ple-ment *n.* part that compensates for what is lacking **-ary, -tal** *adj.*

sup-ply *v., pl., n.* **-plies.** provide with what is needed; to make available **supplier** *n.*

sup-port *v.* bear or hold the weight of; to tolerate; to give assistance or approval *n.* act of supporting **supportable, -ive** *adj.*, **-er** *n.*

sup-pose *v.* think or assume as true; to consider probable **supposed** *adj.*, **supposedly** *adv.*

su-preme *adj.* of the highest authority, rank, or power

sur-charge *n.* extra fee added to the cost of something; to overcharge

sure *adj.* firm and sturdy; being impossible to doubt; inevitable; not liable to fail

sur-face *n.* exterior or outside boundary of something

surge *v.* increase suddenly *n.* large swell of water

sur-geon *n.* physician who practices surgery

sur-ger-y *n., pl.* **-ies.** branch of medicine in which physical deformity or disease is treated by an operative procedure

sur-mise *v.* guess; conjecture

sur-mount *v.* overcome; be at the top

sur-name *n.* person's family last name

sur-pass *v.* go beyond the limits of; to be greater than

sur-plus *n.* amount beyond what is needed

sur-prise *v.* come upon unexpectedly or suddenly; to cause to feel amazed or astonished **surpriser** *n.*, **surprisingly** *adv.*

sur-ren-der *v.* give up or yield possession or power *n.* act of surrendering

sur-ro-gate *n.* person who puts himself in the place of another **surrogate** *v.*

sur-round *v.* extend around all edges of something; to enclose or shut in

sur-veil-lance *n.* close observation kept over one, especially as a suspect

sur-vive *v.* continue to exist; to outlast; to outlive

su-shi *n.* Japanese dish of thin slices of fresh, raw fish

sus-pect *v.* have doubt or distrust; to have a suspicion or inkling of someone or something **suspect** *n.*

sus-pend *v.* bar from a privilege for a certain time, as a means of punishment; to hang so as to allow free movement

sus-pense *n.* feeling of being insecure or undecided, resulting from uncertainty

sus-pi-cion *n.* instance of suspecting something wrong without proof

sus-tain *v.* hold up and keep from falling; to suffer or undergo an injury

su-ture *n.* stitching together or joining the edges of an incision or cut

swad-dle *v.* wrap closely, using a long strip of flannel or linen

swag-ger *v.* walk with a proud or conceited air

swan *n.*

a mostly pure white

bird having a long
neck and heavy body, related to geese
swap *v.* trade something for something in
return
swarm *n.* large number of insects, as
bees; a large group of persons or
things **swarm** *v.*, **swarmer** *n.*
swat *v.* hit something with a sharp blow
sway *v.* move or swing from right to left
or side by side; to exert influence or
control *n.* dominating power
swear *v.* make an affirmation under oath
swearer *n.*
sweat *v.* excrete a salty moisture from the
pores of the skin *Informal* work hard;
to cause to sweat *Slang* being impatient; having anxiety
sweat gland *n.*, *Anat.* one of the tubular
glands that secrete sweat externally
through pores
sweep *v.* touch very lightly; to remove or
clear away with a brush, broom, etc.;
to move with an even action
sweet *adj.* having a sugary, agreeable
flavor; arousing pleasant emotions; a
beloved or dear person
swell *v.* increase in size or bulk; to grow
in volume
swel-ter *v.* suffer from extreme heat
swerve *v.* turn aside from the regular
course
swift *adj.* moving with great speed; accomplished or occurring quickly
swiftly *adv.*, **swiftness** *n.*
swim *v.* move oneself through water by
moving parts of the body, as arms,
head, and legs
swin-dle *v.* cheat out of property or
money; to practice fraud **swindler** *n.*
swine *n.*, *pl.* swine hoofed mammal with
a snout, related to pigs and hogs; a
low, despicable person
swirl *v.* move with a whirling, rotating
motion **swirl** *n.*
swiv-el *n.* coupling device, ring, or pivot
that allows attached parts to rotate or
move freely **swivel** *v.*
sword *n.* weapon with a long, pointed
cutting blade
syl-la-ble *n.*, *Phonet.* word or part of one
that consists of a single vocal impulse,
usually consisting of one or more
vowels or consonants
sym-bol *n.* something that stands for or
represents something else
symbolical *adj.*
sym-me-try *n.*, *pl.* -tries. balance in form,
size, and position of parts that are on
two sides of an axis
sym-pa-thet-ic *adj.* having or showing

kindness or sympathy for others
symathize *v.*
sym-pa-thy *n.*, *pl.* -thies. mutual understanding or affection during a time of
sadness or loss
sym-pho-ny *n.*, *pl.* -nies. large orchestra
with wind, percussion and string sections
symp-tom *n.* sign of change in a body's
functions or appearance
symptomatic *adj.*
syn-a-gogue *n.* place for Jewish worship
and prayer
syn-chro-nize *v.* operate or take place at
the same time
syn-di-cate *n.* organization set up to
carry out business transactions
syn-drome *n.* set of concurrent symptoms
that indicate or characterize a disorder
or disease
syn-o-nym *n.* word that means the same
or nearly the same as another
synonymous *adj.*
syn-op-sis *n.*, *pl.* -ses. shortened statement or narrative
syn-tax *n.* way in which words are put
together or arranged to form sentences and phrases
syn-the-sis *n.* the combination of elements or parts to form a whole
synthesist *n.*
syn-the-size *v.* to produce or combine
by synthesis
syn-the-siz-er *n.* electronic equipment
used to produce and control sound
syn-ton-ic *adj.* adaptive and normally
responsive to the interpersonal or social environment **syntonically** *adv.*
syph-i-lis *n.* infectious venereal disease
transmissible by direct contact and
usually progressing in severity
syph-i-lol-o-gy *n.* a branch medicine
dealing with syphilis
sy-ringe *n.* medical instrument used to
inject or draw fluids
syr-up *n.* sticky, thick, sweet liquid, used
as a topping for food
sys-tal-ic *adj.* to be marked by regular
dilatation and contraction
sys-tem *n.* method or way of doing something **systemless** *adj.*
sys-to-le *n.*, *Physiol.* regular rhythmic
contraction of the heart that pumps
blood through the aorta and pulmo-
nary artery **systolic** *adj.*
sy-zy-gial *adj.* to be pertaining to syzygy
syz-y-gy *n.* a configuration of three celestial bodies in one gravitational system
such as the moon, the sun, and earth
when an eclipse is taking place

T, t The twentieth letter of the English alphabet.

tab *n.* strip, flap, or small loop that projects from something *slang* bill or total, as for a meal

tab-a-nid *n.* member of large bloodsucking insects such as the horse fly

tab-ard *n.* a type of domestic cat that has a coat which is mottled and striped

tab-er-na-cle *n.* portable shelter or structure used by the Jews during their journey out of Egypt

ta-bes *nl* the wasting that comes with or is accompanying a chronic disease

ta-bes for-sa-lis *n.* disease of the spinal cord

ta-bla *n.* a type of drum which is usually used in pairs of different sizes in the Hindu music

tab-la-ture *n.* a tabular surface or structure

ta-ble *n.* article of furniture
v. put off something until another time

tab-leau *n.* a striking picture representation

table-cloth *n.* a type of covering that is placed on the top of tables for protection or for decoration

ta-ble-ful *n.* the amount that a table is able to accomodate

ta-ble--hop *v.* to go from one table to another in order to talk with one's friends such as in a restaurant

ta-ble-land *n.* braod flat land; a plateau

table salt *n.* the salt that is suitable for use in cooking and at the table for the food

table-spoon *n.* a unit of measure; a large spoon for serving food

table sugar *n.* a type of white sugar which is granulated and used in foods

tab-let *n.* pad used for writing

ta-ble talk *n.* the conversation which is informal and takes place at the dinner table

ta-ble ten-nis *n.* a type of game that is like lawn tennis and is played on a table top with a plastic ball and wooden paddles

ta-ble-top *n.* a top of a table

ta-ble-ware *n.* the utensils such as forks, knives, and plates that are used on the table to eat with

ta-ble wine *n.* a type of wine that is wserved with the food and does not have more than 14 percent alcohol

tab-loid *n.* small newspaper

ta-boo *n.* custom or rule against doing, using, or mentioning something

tab-u-lar *adj.* pertaining to or arranged in a table or list

ta-chis-to-scope *n.* instrument for testing visual perception

ta-chom-e-ter *n.* instrument for measuring velocity and speed

tach-y-car-di-a *adj.* rapid heart movement or action

ta-chyg-ra-phy *n.* the art of shorthand; stenography

tac-it *adj.* understood; expressed or implied nonverbally; implicit

tac-i-turn *adj.* speaking infrequently taciturnity *n.*

tack-le *n.* equipment used for fishing or other sports or occupations **tackled** *v.*

tacky *adj.* slightly sticky; shabby; lacking style or good taste

ta-co *n.*, *pl.* -cos type of Mexican or Spanish food made of a tortilla

tact *n.* having the ability to avoid what would disturb or offend someone

tac-tic *n.* way or method of working toward a goal

tad *n.* small boy; an insignificant degree or amount

tad-pole *n.*

the early stage in the growth of a frog or toad during which it breathes by external gills, has a long tail, and lives in the water; a polliwog

tae-ni-a-sis *n.* a sickness due to the presence of tapeworms

taf-fe-ta *n.* stiff, smooth fabric of rayon, nylon, or silk **taffetized** *adj.*

taff-rail *n.* rail around the stern of a boat or ship

taf-fy *n.* candy made from sugar, butter and flavoring

taf-fy pull *n.* an informal party where guest make and pull taffy

tag *n.* piece of plastic, metal, paper, or other material that is attached to something in order to identify it; children's game **tagger** *n.*

tag-board *n.* very sturdy cardboard used to make posters, and signs

tail *n.* posterior extremity, extending from the end or back of an animal **Tails** opposite side of a coin from heads

tai-lor *n.* one whose profession is making, mending, and altering clothing *v.* adapt for a specific purpose

taint *v.* spoil, contaminate, or pollute *n.* blemish or stain

take *v.* seize or capture; to get possession of; to move to a different place; to choose

talc n. soft, fine-grained, smooth mineral used in making talcum powder

tale n. story or recital of relating events that may or may not be true

tal-ent n. aptitude, or ability of a person **talented** adj.

talk v. communicate by words or speech; to engage in chatter or gossip

tall adj. greater than average height; of a designated or specified height; imaginary, as a tall tale **tallness** n.

tal-low n. hard fat rendered from sheep or cattle, used to make candles, lubricants, and soap **tallow** adj.

tal-ly n., pl. **-ies** record or counting of money, amounts, or scores

tal-on n. long, curved claw found on birds or animals

tam-bou-rine n.

percussion instrument made of a small drum with jingling metal disks around the rim

tame adj. not wild or ferocious; domesticated or manageable v. make docile or calm **tamely** adv., **tamer, tameness** n.

tam-per v. change, meddle, or alter something; to use corrupt measures; to scheme **tamperproof** adj., **tamperer** n.

tan-dem n. any arrangement that involves two or more things, animals, or persons arranged one behind the other

tang n. sharp, distinct taste, smell, or quality

tan-gent n. line that touches a curved line but does not intersect or cross it; a sudden change from one course to another **tangency** n., **tangential** adj.

tan-ger-ine n. small citrus fruit

tan-gi-ble adj. capable of being appreciated or felt by the sense of touch **tangibly** adv.

tan-gle v. mix, twist, or unite in a confused manner making separation difficult **tangle, tanglement** n.

tank n. large container for holding or storing a gas or liquid **tankful** n.

tan-ta-lize v. tease or tempt by holding or keeping something just out of one's reach **tantalizer** n.

tan-ta-lum n. metallic element symbolized by Ta

tan-trum n. fit; an outburst or a rage of bad temper

tap v. strike repeatedly, usually while making a small noise; to strike or touch gently

tape n. narrow strip of woven fabric

ta-per n. very slender candle v. become gradually smaller or thinner at one end

tap-es-try n., pl. **-ies** thick fabric woven with designs and figures

tap-i-o-ca n. bead-like substance used for thickening and for puddings

taps n. pl. Mil. bugle call that signals lights out, also sounded at memorial and funeral services

tar-dy adj. late; not on time **tardily** adv., **tardiness** n.

tar-get n. object marked to shoot at; an aim or goal

tar-iff n. duty or tax on merchandise coming into or going out of a country

tar-nish v. become discolored or dull; to lose luster; to spoil **tarnishable** adj.

tar-ot n. set of 22 cards used for fortune-telling, each card showing a virtue, an elemental force, or a vice

tar-pau-lin n. sheet of waterproof canvas used as a protective covering

tar-ry v. linger, or delay

tart adj. sharp; sour; cutting, biting in tone or meaning **tartly** adv., **tartness** n.

task n. bit of work, usually assigned by another; a job

tas-sel n. ornamental decoration made from a bunch of string or thread

taste n. ability to sense or determine flavor in the mouth; a personal liking or dislike **tasteful, tasteless** adj., **taster** n.

tat-tle v. reveal the secrets of another by gossiping

tattle-tale n. one who betrays secrets concerning others; a person, usually a child, who informs on others

tat-too n. permanent design or mark made on the skin by pricking and inserting an indelible dye **tattooer** n.

taught v. past tense of teach

taut adj. tight; emotionally strained **tautly** adv., **tautness** n.

tau-tol-o-gy n., pl. **-ies** redundancy; a statement which is an unnecessary repetition of the same idea

tav-ern n. inn; an establishment or business licensed to sell alcoholic beverages **taverner** n.

tax n. payment imposed and collected

from individuals or businesses by the government *v.* strain

tax--ex-empt *adj.* exempted from tax

tax-i *v.* move along the ground or water surface on its own power before taking off

taxi-cab *n.* vehicle for carrying passengers for money

tax-i-der-my *n.* art or profession of preparing, stuffing, and mounting animal skins **taxidermist** *n.*

tea *n.* small tree or bush which grows where the climate is very hot and damp; a drink made by steeping the dried leaves of this shrub in boiling water

teach *v.* communicate skill or knowledge; to give instruction **teaching** *n.*, **teachable** *adj.*

teach-er *n.* person who teaches; one who instructs

tear *v.* become divided into pieces; to separate; to rip into parts or pieces

tear *n.* fluid secreted by the eye to moisten and cleanse *v.* to cry **teary** *adj.*

tease *v.* make fun of; to bother; to annoy

tech-ne-tium *n.* metallic element symbolized by Tc.

tech-ni-cal *adj.* expert; derived or relating to technique; related to industry or mechanics **technically** *adv.*

tech-nique *n.* technical procedure or method of doing something

tech-nol-o-gy *n., pl.* -ies application of scientific knowledge to serve man in industry, commerce, medicine and other fields

te-di-ous *adj.* boring; taking a long time **tediously** *adv.*

tee *n.*

a peg used to hold a golf ball on the first stoke toward a hole or goal post; a peg used to support a football during a field goal attempt

teem *v.* swarm or crowd; to abound; to be full of

teens *pl., n.* ages between 13 and 19; the years of one's life between 13 and 19

teeth *pl., n.* plural of tooth

tel-e-cast *n.* television broadcast **telecast** *v.*

tel-e-gram *n.* message sent or received by telegraph

tel-e-graph *n.* system for communicating; a transmission sent by wire or radio

tel-e-phone *n.* system or device for transmitting conversations by wire

tel-e-pho-to *adj.* relating to a camera lens which produces a large image of a distant object **telephotograph** *n.*

tel-e-scope *n.* instrument which contains a lens system which makes distant objects appear larger and nearer **telescopic** *adj.*

tel-ex *n.* teletype communications by means of automatic exchanges

tell *v.* relate or describe; to command or order

tem-per *n.* state of one's feelings **temperable** *adj.*

tem-per-a-ment *n.* personality; a characteristic way of thinking, reacting

tem-per-ance *n.* moderation; restraint from drinking alcoholic beverages

tem-per-ate *adj.* avoiding extremes; moderate **temperately** *adv.*

tem-per-a-ture *n.* measure of heat or cold in relation to the body or environment; an elevation in body temperature above the normal 98.6

tem-pest *n.* severe storm, with snow, hail, rain, or sleet

tem-ple *n.* place of worship

tem-po *n., pl.* -pos *or* -pi *Mus.* rate of speed at which a musical composition is to be played

tem-po-rar-y *adj.* lasting for a limited amount of time

tempt *n.* encourage or draw into a foolish or wrong course of action

te-na-cious *adj.* persistent; stubborn **tenaciously** *adv.*, **tenaciousness** *n.*

ten-ant *n.* person who pays rent to occupy another's property **-able** *adj.*

Ten Commandments *n.* ten rules of moral behavior which were given to Moses by God

tend *v.* to be inclined or disposed; to look after

ten-den-cy *n., pl.* -ies disposition to act or behave in a particular way

ten-der *adj.* fragile; soft; not hard or tough; painful or sore when touched

ten-don *n.* band of tough, fibrous tissues that connect a muscle and bone

ten-dril *n.*

a thread-like part of a climbing plant which attaches itself to a support

ten-nis *n.* sport played with a ball and racket by 2 or 4 people

tren-or *n.* adult male singing voice, above a baritone

tense *adj.* taut or stretched tightly; nervous **tense** *v.*

ten-sion *n.* condition of stretching or the state of being stretched **tensionless** *adj.*

tent *n.* portable shelter made by stretchin material over a supporting framework

ten-ta-cle *n.* long, unjointed, flexible body part that projects from certain invertebrates, as the octopus

ten-ta-tive *adj.* experimental; not definite **tentatively** *adv.*

ten-ure *n.* the right, state, or period of holding something, as an office or property **-ed, -ial** *adj.*

tep-id *adj.* lukewarm

ter-cen-ten-a-ry *n., pl.* **-ries.** time span of 300 years

term *n.* phrase or word; a limited time or duration

ter-mi-nal *adj.* of, forming, or located at the end; final

ter-mi-nate *v.* bring to a con-clusion or end **termination** *n.*

ter-mite *n.* winged or wingless insect which lives in large colonies feeding on wood

ter-race *n.* open balcony or porch

ter-ra cot-ta *n.* hard, baked clay used in ceramic pottery

ter-rain *n.* surface of an area, as land

ter-ra-pin *n.* edible turtle of North America

ter-res-tri-al *adj.* something earthly; not heavenly

ter-ri-ble *adj.* causing fear or terror; intense; extreme; horrid **terribly** *adv.*, **terriblness** *n.*

ter-rif-ic *adj.* terrifying *Informal* excellent; causing amazement **terrifically** *adv.*

ter-ri-fy *v.* fill with fear or terror; to frighten; to menace **terrified, terrifying** *adj.*

ter-ri-to-ry *n., pl.* **-ies** area, usually of great size, which is controlled by a particular government **territorial** *adj.*

ter-ror *n.* extreme fear

ter-ror-ism *n.* the use of intimidation to attain one's goals or to advance one's cause

terse *adj.* brief; using as few words as possible without loss of force or clearness **tersely** *adj.*, **terseness** *n.*

test *n.* examination to determine one's knowledge, skill, intelligence or other qualities **tester** *n.*

tes-ta-ment *n.* legal document which states how one's personal property is to be distributed upon his death

Testament *n.* one of the two sections of the Bible **Testamentary** *adj.*

tes-tate *adj.* having left a valid will

tes-ti-fy *v.* give evidence while under oath **testifier** *n.*

tes-ti-mo-ni-al *n.* formal statement; a gift, dinner, reception, or other sign of appreciation given to a person as a token of esteem

tes-ti-mo-ny *n., pl.* **-ies** a solemn affirmation made under oath

tes-tis *n., pl.* **testes** sperm producing gland of the male

test tube *n.*

a thin glass tube closed at one end, used in biology and chemistry

teth-er *n.* rope or chain which fastens an animal to something

text *n.* actual wording of an author's work; the main part of a book **textual** *adj.*

text-book *n.* book used by students to prepare their lessons

tex-tile *n.* cloth made by weaving; yarn or fiber for making cloth **textile** *adj.*

tex-ture *n.* look, surface, or feel of something

thal-li-um *n.* metallic element resembling lead, symbolized by Tl.

than *conj.* in comparison with or to something

thank *v.* express one's gratitude; to credit

thank-ful *adj.* feeling or showing gratitude

thanks *pl., n.* expression of one's gratitude

that *adj., pl.* **those** person or thing present or being mentioned

thaw *v.* change from a frozen state to a liquid or soft state; to melt **thaw** *n.*

the-a-tre or **the-a-ter** *n.* building adapted to present dramas, motion pictures, plays, or other performances

the-at-ri-cal *adj.* extravagant; designed for show, display, or effect **theatricals** *n.*

theft *n.* act or crime of stealing; larceny

their *adj. & pron.* possessive case of they

the-ism *n.* belief in the existence of God **theist** *n.*, **theistic** *adj.*

them *pron.* objective case of they

theme *n.* topic or subject of something

them-selves *pron.* them or they; a form of the third person plural pronoun

then *adv.* at that time; soon or immediately *adj.* being or acting in or belonging to or at that time

thence adv. from that place

thenceforth, thence-for-ward adv. from that time on

the-oc-ra-cy n., pl. -ies government by God or by clergymen who think of themselves as representatives of God -tic adj., -tically adv.

the-ol-o-gy n., pl. -ies religious study of the nature of God, beliefs -ian n.

the-o-rize v. analyze theories

the-o-ry n., pl. -ies general principle or explanation which covers the known facts

ther-a-peu-tics n. medical treatment of disease **therapeutist** n.

ther-a-py n., pl. -ies treatment of certain diseases **therapist** n.

there adv. in, at, or about that place; toward, into, or to

thereabouts, thereafter, thereby, therefore, therefrom, adv.

ther-mal adj. having to do with or producing heat

ther-mo-plas-tic ad. pliable and soft when heated or warm but hard when cooled **thermoplastic** n.

ther-mo-stat n.

device that automatically responds to temperature changes and activates equipment to adjust the temperature to correspond with the setting on the device

the-sau-rus n., pl. -ruses or -ri book which contains synonyms and antonyms

these pron. plural of this

the-sis n., pl. -ses formal argument or idea; a paper written by a student that develops an idea

they pron. two or more beings just mentioned

they'd contr. they had

they'll contr. they will

they're contr. they are

they've contr. they have

thick adj. having a heavy or dense consistency

thief n., pl. **thieves** person who steals

thieve v. take by theft **thievery** n.

thigh n. part of the leg between the hip and the knee of man

thim-ble n.

a small cap-like protection for the finger, worn while sewing

thin adj. having very little depth or ex-

tent from one side or surface to the other; not fat; slender **thinly** adv.

thing n. something not recognized or named; an idea, or conception

things one's belongings

think v. exercise thought; to use the mind **thinkable** adj.

third n. next to the second in time or place; the last in a series of three

thirst n. uncomfortably dry feeling in the throat and mouth; a desire for liquids

this pron., pl. **these** person or thing that is near, present, or just mentioned

this-tle n. prickly plant usually producing a purplish or yellowish flower

thith-er adv. to that place; there

thong n. narrow strip of leather used for binding

tho-rax n., pl. -raxes or -races section or part of the human body between the neck and abdomen

tho-ri-um n. radioactive metallic element symbolized by Th.

thorn n. sharp, pointed, woody projection on a plant stem **thorny** adj.

thor-ough adj. complete; intensive **thoroughly** adv.

thor-ough-bred adj. being of a pure breed of stock

thor-ough-fare n. public highway, road or street

those adj. & pron. plural of that

though adv. nevertheless; in spite of

thought n. process, act, or power of thinking; an idea

thoughtful, thoughtless adj.

thrash v. to beat or strike with a whip; to move violently about; to defeat **thrasher** n.

threat n. expression or warning of intent to do harm

thresh v. to separate seed from a harvested plant mechanically

thresh-old n. horizontal piece of wood or other material which forms a door-sill

threw v. past tense of throw

thrice adv. three times

thrift n. careful use of money and other resources

thrill n. feeling of sudden intense excitement, fear, or joy

thrilling adj., **thrillingly** adv.

thrive v. to prosper; to be healthy; to do well in a position

throat n. front section or part of the neck containing passages for food and air

throb v. to beat, move, or vibrate in a

pulsating way

throm-bo-sis *n., pl.* -ses development of a blood clot in a blood vessel or in the heart cavity

throng *n.* large group or crowd *v.* to crowd around or into

throt-tle *n.* valve which controls the flow of fuel to an engine

through *prep.* from the beginning to the end

through-out *prep., adv.* in every place; everywhere; at all times

throw *v.* to toss or fling through the air with a motion of the arm

thru *prep., adv. & adj.* through

thrush *n.* small songbird having a brownish upper body and spotted breast

thrust *v.* to push; to shove with sudden or vigorous force

thru-way *or* **throughway** *n.* major highway; an expressway

thud *n.* dull thumping sound

thug *n.* tough or violent gangster **thuggish** *adj.*

thumb *n.* short first digit of the hand

thump *n.* blow with something blunt or heavy

thun-der *n.* loud explosive sound made as air is suddenly expanded by heat and then quickly contracted again

thus *adv.* in this or that way

thwack *v.* strike hard, using something flat

thwart *v.* prevent from happening

thy *adj.* pertaining to oneself

thyme *n.* an aromatic mint herb whose leaves are used in cooking

thy-roid *adj. Anat.* pertaining to the thyroid gland

thy-rox-ine *n.* hormone secreted by the thyroid gland

ti-ar-a *n.* bejeweled crown

tick *n.* one of a series of rhythmical tapping sounds made by a clock; a small bloodsucking parasite

tick-et *n.* printed slip of paper or cardboard allowing its holder to enter a specified event or to enjoy a privilege

tick-le *v.* to stroke lightly so as to cause laughter; to amuse or delight -ler *n.*

tid-bit *n.* choice bit of food, news, or gossip

tide *n.* rise and fall of the surface level of the ocean

tid-ings *pl., n.* news; information about events

ti-dy *adj.* well arranged; neat; orderly **tidiness** *n.*

tie *v.* to secure or bind with a rope or other similar material; to make a bow or knot in; to match an opponent's score

tier *n.* layer or row placed one above the other **tiered** *adj.*

ti-ger *n.*

large carnivorous cat having tawny fur with black stripes

tiger-eye *n.* yellow-brown gemstone

tight *adj.* set closely together; bound or securely firm; not loose *adv.* firmly

tight-en *v.* to become or make tighter **tightener** *n.*

tights *pl., n.* skintight stretchable garment

till *prep. & conj.* until; unless or before *v.* to cultivate; to plow.

till-er *n.* machine or person that tills land

tilt *v.* to tip, as by raising one end

tim-ber *n.* wood prepared for building

timber line *n.* height on a mountain beyond which trees cannot grow

time *n.* continuous period measured by clocks, watches, and calendars *adj.* of or pertaining to time

tim-id *adj.* shy

tin *n.* white, soft, malleable me-tallic element, symbolized by Sn.

tinc-ture *n.* tinge of color; an alcohol solution of some medicinal substance

tin-der *n.* readily combustible substance or material

tine *n.* narrow pointed spike or prong, as of a fork or antler

tinge *v.* to impart a faint trace of color *n.* trace of color

tin-gle *v.* to feel a stinging or prickling sensation

tin-kle *v.* to produce a slight, sharp series of metallic ringing sounds

tin-ny *adj.* pertaining to or composed of tin

tin-sel *n.* thin strips of glittering material used for decorations

tint *n.* slight amount or trace of color *v.* to color

ti-ny *adj.* minute; very small

tip-ple *v.* drink an alcoholic beverage to excess

tip-sy *adj.* partially intoxicated

ti-rade *n.* long, violent speech

tire *v.* become or make weary *n.* outer covering for a wheel, usually made of rubber, serving to absorb shock and to provide traction

tis-sue n., *Biol.* similar cells and their products developed by plants and animals

ti-ta-ni-um n. metallic element symbolized by Ti.

tithe n. income given voluntarily for the support of a church

tithe v., **tither** n.

tit-il-late v. excite or stimulate in a pleasurable way

ti-tle n. identifying name of a book, poem, play, or other creative work; a name or mark of distinction indicating a rank or an office

to prep. toward, opposite or near; in contact with; as far as; used as a function word indicating an action, movement, or condition suggestive of movement; indicating correspondence, dissimilarity, similarity, or proportion

toad n. tailless amphibian

toaster n. device for toasting bread

to-bac-co n. plant widely cultivated for its leaves

to-bog-gan n. long sled-like vehicle without runners

to-day adv. on or during the present day

tod-dle v. walk unsteadily

toddler n. small child

tod-dy n., pl. -ies drink made with hot water, sugar, spices, and liquor

toe n. one of the extensions from the front part of a foot; the part of a stocking, boot or shoe

tof-fee n. chewy candy made of butter and brown sugar

to-geth-er adv. in or into one group, mass, or body; regarded jointly

toil v. to labor very hard and continuously **toilsome** adj.

toi-let n. porcelain apparatus with a flushing device, used as a means of disposing body wastes

toi-lette n. act of washing, dressing, or grooming oneself

tol-er-ate v. to put up with; to endure; to suffer

toll n. fixed charge for travel across a bridge or along a road v. to sound a bell in repeated single, slow tones

tom n. male turkey or cat

tom-a-hawk n. ax used as a weapon or tool by North American Indians

to-ma-to n., pl. -toes garden plant cultivated for its edible fruit; the fruit of such a plant

tomb n. vault for burying the dead; a grave

tomb-stone n. stone used to mark a grave

to-mor-row n. day after the present day

ton n. measurement of weight equal to 2,000 pounds

tone n. vocal or musical sound that has a distinct pitch v. to change or soften the color

tongs pl., n. implement with two long arms joined at one end

tongue n.

muscular organ attached to the floor of the mouth, used in tasting, chewing, and speaking

ton-ic n. medicine or other agent used to restore health

to-night n. this night; the night that is coming

ton-sil n. one of a pair of tissue similar to lymph nodes, found on either side of the throat

ton-sil-lec-to-my n. surgical re-moval of tonsils

too adv. also; as well; more than is needed

tool n. implement used to perform a task **tooling** n.

tooth n., pl. teeth one of the hard, white structures rooted in the jaw and used for chewing and biting; the small, notched, projecting part of any object, such as a gear, comb or saw **toothed, toothless** adj.

to-pog-ra-phy n., pl. -ies detailed description of a region or place

top-ple v. to fall; to overturn

torch n. stick of resinous wood which is burned to give light *Slang* to set fire to

tor-ment n. extreme mental anguish or physical pain v. to cause terrible pain; to pester, harass, or annoy

-ingly adv., **tormentor** n.

tor-na-do n., pl. -does *or* -dos whirling, violent windstorm accompanied by a funnel-shaped cloud that travels a narrow path over land

tor-pid adj. having lost the power of motion or feeling; dormant **torpidity** n., **torpidly** adv.

tor-rent n. swift, violent stream **torrential** adj.

tor-rid adj. parched and dried by the heat **torridly** adv.

tor-sion n. act or result of twisting **torsional** adj.

tor-so n., pl. -sos *or* -si trunk of the human body

tort n., *Law* wrongful act requiring compensation for damages

tor-toise *n.* turtle that lives on the land

tor-tu-ous *adj.* marked by repeated bends, turns, or twists; devious

tor-ture *n.* infliction of intense pain as punishment

tot *n.* young child; a toddler

to-tal *n.* whole amount or sum; the entire quantity *adj.* absolute; complete

to-tal-i-tar-i-an *adj.* characteristic of a government controlled completely by one party

tote *v.* carry something on one's arm or back

to-tem *n.* animal or plant regarded as having a close relationship to some family clan or group

tot-ter *v.* walk unsteadily

tou-can *n.* brightly colored tropical bird having a very large thin bill

touch *v.* allow a part of the body, as the hands, to feel or come into contact with; join; to come next to; to have an effect on; to move emotionally **touchable** *adj.*

tough *adj.* resilient and strong enough to withstand great strain without breaking or tearing; difficult to cut or chew *n.* unruly person; a thug **toughness** *n.*

tou-pee *n.* wig worn to cover a bald spot on one's head

tour *n.* trip with visits to points of interest; a journey **tourism, tourist** *n.*

tour-na-ment *n.* contest involving a number of competitors for a title or championship

tour-ni-quet *n.* device used to temporarily stop the flow of blood through an artery

tou-sle *v.* to mess up

tout *v.* to solicit customers

tow *v.* drag or pull, as by a chain or rope

to-ward or towards *prep.* in the direction of; just before; somewhat before; regarding

tow-el *n.* absorbent piece of cloth used for drying or wiping

tow-er *n.* very tall building or structure; a skyscraper **towering** *adj.*

town *n.* collection of houses and other buildings larger than a village and smaller than a city

tox-e-mi-a *n., Pathol.* blood poisoning; a condition in which the blood contains toxins

tox-ic *adj.* relating to a toxin; destructive, deadly, or harmful

tox-in *n.* poisonous substance produced by chemical changes in plant and animal tissue

toy *n.* object designed for the enjoyment of children; a small trinket; a bauble

trace *n.* visible mark or sign of a thing, person, or event; something left by some past agent or event

track *n.* mark, as a footprint, left by the passage of anything; a regular course; a set of rails on which a train runs; a circular or oval course for racing

tract *n.* extended area, as a stretch of land

trac-tor *n.* diesel or gasoline-powered vehicle used in farming

tractor trailer *n.* large truck having a cab and no body

trade *n.* business or occupation; skilled labor; a craft; an instance of selling or buying; a swap **trader** *n.*

trade-mark *n.* brand name which is legally the possession of one company and cannot be used by another

tra-di-tion *n.* customs passed down from one generation to another -*al adj.*

tra-duce *v.* to betray

traf-fic *n.* passage or movement of vehicles; trade, buying and selling

trag-e-dy *n., pl.* -ies extremely sad or fatal event or course of events

trail *v.* to draw, drag, or stream along behind; to follow in the tracks of

trail-er *n.* one who trails; a large vehicle that transports objects and is pulled by another vehicle

trait *n.* quality or distinguishing feature, such as one's character

trai-tor *n.* person who betrays his country

tra-jec-to-ry *n., pl.* -ies curved line or path of a moving object

tram-mel *n.* long, large net used to catch birds or fish

tramp *v.* to plod or walk with a heavy step

tram-ple *v.* to tread heavily; to stomp; to inflict injury, pain **trampler** *n.*

tram-po-line *n.* canvas device on which an athlete or acrobat may perform

trance *n.* stupor, daze, mental state, or condition, such as produced by drugs or hypnosis

tran-quil *adj.* very calm, quiet

trans-act *v.* to perform, carry out, conduct, or manage business in some way **transaction, transactor** *n.*

tran-scend *v.* to pass beyond; to exceed;

to surpass

tran-scribe *v.* to make copies of something; to adopt or arrange

tran-script *n.* written copy

trans-crip-tion *n.* process or act of transcribing

trans-fer *v.* remove, shift, or carry from one position to another **transferable** *adj.*

trans-fig-ure *v.* change the outward appearance or form **-ation** *n.*

trans-fix *v.* to pierce; to hold motionless, as with terror, awe or amazement **transfixion** *n.*

trans-form *v.* change or alter completely in nature, form or function **transformation**

trans-fuse *v.* transfer liquid by pouring from one place to another **transfusion**

trans-gress *v.* to go beyond the limit or boundaries

tran-sient *adj.* not staying or lasting very long; moving from one location to another **transiently** *adv.*

tran-sit *n.* passage or travel from one point to another

trans-late *v.* change from one language to another while retaining the original meaning **translation, translator** *n.*

trans-lu-cent *adj.* diffusing and admitting light but not allowing a clear view of the object

trans-mis-sion *n.* act or state of transmitting *Mech.* gears and associated parts of an engine which transmit power to the driving wheels of an automobile or other vehicle

trans-mit *v.* dispatch or convey from one thing, person, or place to another

trans-mute *v.* change in nature, kind, or substance

tran-som *n.* small, hinged window over a doorway

trans-par-ent *adj.* admitting light so that images and objects can be clearly viewed; obvious **transparency** *n.*

tran-spire *v.* to happen; to take place **transpiration** *n.*

trans-port *v.* carry or move from one place to another

trans-pose *v.* reverse the place or order of

trans-sex-u-al *n.* person whose sex has been changed surgically

tra-peze *n.* short horizontal bar suspended by two ropes, used for acrobatic exercise or stunts

trau-ma *n., pl.* **-mas** *or* **-mata** severe wound caused by a sudden physical injury; an emotional shock causing lasting and substantial damage to a person's psychological development

tra-vail *n.* strenuous mental or physical exertion

trav-el *v.* journey or move from one place to another

tra-verse *v.* pass over, across, or through

trawl *n.* strong fishing net which is dragged through water

tray *n.* flat container having a low rim, used for carrying, holding, or displaying something

treach-er-ous *adj.* disloyal; deceptive **treachery** *n.*

tread *v.* to walk along, on, or over; to trample

treas-ure *n.* hidden riches; something regarded as valuable

treas-ur-y *n., pl.* **-ies** place where public or private funds are kept

treat-ment *n.* manner or act of treating; medical care

trek *v.* make a slow and arduous journey **trekker** *n.*

trel-lis *n.* latticework frame used for supporting vines

trem-ble *v.* shake involuntarily, as with fear or from cold **trembler** *n.*, **trembly** *adj.*

tre-men-dous *adj.* extremely huge, large, or vast *Slang* wonderful

trem-or *n.* quick, shaking movement; any continued and involuntary trembling or quavering of the body

trench *n.* ditch; long, narrow excavation in the ground

trend *n.* general inclination, direction, or course; a fad

tres-pass *v.* infringe upon another's property

tres-tle *n.* bar or beam supported by four legs

tri-al *n.* in law, the examination and hearing of a case before a court of law

tri-an-gle *n., Geom.*

plane figure bounded by three sides and having three angles **-ar** *adj.*

tribe *n.* group of people composed of several villages, districts, or other groups which share a common language, culture, and name

trib-u-la-tion *n.* great distress or suffering

trib-un-al *n.* decision making body

trib-ute *n.* action of respect or gratitude to someone

tri-ceps *n.*, *Anat.* large muscle at the back of the upper arm

trick *n.* action meant to fool, as a scheme; a prank; a feat of magic **tricky** *adj.*

trick-er-y *n.* deception

trick-le *v.* flow in droplets or a small stream **trickle** *n.*

tri-col-or *n.* French color in the flag **tricolored** *adj.*

tri-cy-cle *n.* small vehicle having three wheels, propelled by pedals

tri-dent *n.* long spear with three prongs, used as a weapon

tried *adj.* tested and proven reliable or useful

tri-en-ni-al *adj.* happening every third year; lasting for a time period of three years

tri-fle *n.* something of little value or importance; a dessert made with cake, jelly, wine, and custard

tri-ni-tro-tol-u-ene *n.* very powerful explosive, abbreviated as TNT

trin-ket *n.* small piece of jewelry

tri-o *n.* set or group of three

trip *n.* travel from one place to another; a journey; a loss of balance

tripe *n.* stomach lining of oxen or similar animals, used as food

trip-le *adj.* having three parts

trip-let *n.* one of three born at the same time

tri-pod *n.* three-legged stand

trite *adj.* used too often; common

tri-umph *v.* be victorious *n.* victory **triumphantly** *adv.*

triv-i-al *adj.* insignificant; of little value or importance

trol-ley *n.* streetcar powered by electricity from overhead lines

tro-phy *n.*, *pl.* **-ies** prize or object, such as a plaque, awarded to someone for his success, victory, or achievement

tro-po-sphere *n.* lowest atmosphere between the earth's surface and the stratosphere

troth *n.* good faith; the act of pledging one's fidelity

trou-ble *n.* danger; affliction; need; distress; an effort *v.* bother; to worry; to be bothered **troubler** *n.*

trough *n.* long, narrow, shallow container, especially one that holds food or water for animals

trounce *v.* whip or beat

troupe *n.* group, especially of the performing arts

trou-sers *pl.*, *n.* outer garment that covers the body from the waist down

trous-seau *n.* wardrobe, linens, and other similar articles of a bride

tru-ant *n.* person who is absent from school without permission **truancy** *n.*

truce *n.* agreement to stop fighting; a cease fire

trudge *v.* walk heavily and wearily; plod

true *adj.* in accordance with reality or fact; not false; real; loyal; faithful

trunk *n.*

the long snout of an elephant; main part of a tree; sturdy box used for travel or storage

truss *v.* fasten or tie securely *Med.* support or device worn to keep a hernia in place

trust *n.* confidence or faith in a person or thing

trust-y *adj.* reliable

truth *n.*, *pl.* **truths** facts corresponding with actual events or happenings; sincerity or honesty

truthful *adj.*, **truthfully** *adv.*

try *v.* make an attempt; to make an effort; to strain; to hear or conduct a trial; to place on trial **trying** *adj.*

tryst *n.* meeting between lovers; a prearranged meeting

tsu-na-mi *n.* extensive and destructive ocean wave caused by an underwater earthquake

tub *n.* round, low, flat-bottomed, vessel with handles on the side

tu-ba *n.* large, brass wind instrument having a low range

tu-ber *n.*

the underground stem of certain plants, as the potato, with buds from which new plants arise

tu-ber-cu-lo-sis *n.* contagious lung disease of humans and animals caused by microorganisms

tuck *n.* flattened fold of material, usually stitched in place

tuft *n.* small cluster of feathers, threads, hair, or other material fastened or growing closely together

tug *v.* strain and pull vigorously *n.* hard pull

tu-i-tion *n.* payment for instruction, as at a private school or college

tu-lip *n.* bulb-bearing plant, having upright cup-like blossoms.

tum-ble *v.* fall or cause to fall; to perform acrobatic rolls, somersaults, and similar maneuvers

tum-ble-down *adj.* ramshackle; in need of repair

tum-brel *n.* cart which can discharge its load by tilting

tu-mor *n., Pathol.* swelling on or in any part of the body; an abnormal growth which may be malignant or benign

tu-mult *n.* confusion and noise of a crowd; a riot

tu-na *n., pl.* **-na** *or* **-nas** any of several large marine food fish

tun-dra *n.* treeless area in the arctic regions having a subsoil which is permanently frozen

tune *n.* melody which is simple and easy to remember; agreement

tung-sten *n.* element also known as wolfram, symbolized by W.

tu-nic *n.* loose garment extending to the knees, worn by ancient Romans and Greeks

tun-nel *n.* underground or underwater passageway

tur-ban *n.* Moslem headdress that consists of a long scarf wound around the head

tur-bu-lent *adj.* marked by a violent disturbance

tu-reen *n.* large dish used to serve soup or stew

turf *n.* layer of earth with its dense growth of grass and matted roots

tur-moil *n.* state of confusion or commotion

turn-key *n.* person in charge of the keys at a prison

turn-over *n.* process or act of turning over; an upset; a change or reversal

tur-pen-tine *n.* thick sap of certain pine trees; a clear liquid manufactured from this sap

tur-tle *n.*

a scaly-skinned animal having a soft body covered with a hard shell into which the head, legs, and tail can be retracted

tusk *n.* long, curved tooth, as of an elephant or walrus

tus-sle *n.* hard fight or struggle with a problem or person **tussle** *v.*

tu-tor *n.* person who teaches another

person privately

tu-tu *n.* very short ballet skirt

tux-e-do *n.* semiformal dress suit worn by men

tweak *v.* pinch and twist sharply

twice *adv.* double; two times

twid-dle *v.* to turn or twirl in an aimless way

twig *n.* small branch which grows from a larger branch on a tree

twi-light *n.* soft light of the sky between sunset and darkness

twill *n.* weave that produces the parallel rib on the surface of a fabric

twine *v.* weave or twist together

twinge *n.* sudden, sharp pain

twin-kle *v.* gleam or shine with quick flashes; to sparkle

twirl *v.* to rotate or cause to turn around and around

twist-er *n., Slang* tornado; a cyclone; one that twists

twit *v.* tease about a mistake

twitch *v.* move or cause to move with a jerky movement

twit-ter *v.* utter a series of chirping sounds; to chatter nervously

two-bits twenty-five cents

two-faced double-dealing

ty-coon *n., Slang* business person of wealth and power

tyke *n.* small child

type *n.* class or group of persons or things

ty-phoid *n., Path.* acute, infectious disease caused by germs in drink or food, resulting in high fever and intestional hemorrhaging

ty-phoon *n.* tropical hurricane

typ-ist *n.* operator of a type-writer

ty-po *n., Slang* error in typewriting or in setting type; any printed error which was not the fault of the author

ty-ran-no-sau-rus *n.*

large, flesh-eating dinosaur which walked on its hind legs

tyr-an-ny *n.* harsh, absolute, and unfair rule by a king or other ruler; complete control

tyr-an-nize *v.* rule or control completely

ty-rant *n.* absolute, unjust, or cruel ruler control unfairly

ty-ro *n.* a novice; a beginner

U, u The twenty-first letter of the English alphabet.

obi-qui-none *n.* the quinone which is able to function as an electron transfer agent in the Kreb's cycle

ubiq-ui-ty *n.* a presence in many places or locations at the same time

ud-der *n.* milk-producing organ pouch of some female animals, having two or more teats

ugh *interj.* used to express disgust or horror

ug-li-fy *v.* to make something ugly

ug-ly *adj.* offensive; unpleasant to look at

uh *interj.* to express hesitation.

u-ku-le-le *n.* small, four-stringed musical instrument

ul-cer *n.* festering, inflamed sore on a mucous membrane or on the skin that results in the destruction of the tissue

ul-na *n., Anat.* one of the two bones of the forearm

ul-ti-mate *adj.* final; ending; most extreme **ultimately** *adv.*

ul-ti-ma-tum *n., pl* **-tums, -ta** final demand, proposal, or choice

ultra- *prefix.* beyond the scope, range, or limit of something

ul-tra-mod-ern *adj.* extremely advanced or modern in style

ul-tra-son-ic *adj.* relating to sound frequencies inaudible to humans

ul-tra-vi-o-let *adj.* producing radiation having wave-lengths just shorter than those of visible light and longer than those of X rays

um-bil-i-cal cord *n.*

structure by which a fetus is attached to its mother, serving to supply food and dispose of waste

um-brel-la *n.* collapsible frame covered with plastic or cloth, held above the head as protection from sun or rain

um-pire *n.* in sports, the person who rules on plays in a game *v.* act as an umpire

ump-teen *adj., Slang* indefinitely large number

un- *prefix* reverse or opposite of an act; removal or release from

un-able *adj.* not having the mental capabilities

un-ac-com-pa-nied *adj.* alone; without a companion *Mus.* Solo

un-ac-count-a-ble *adj.* without an explanation; mysterious; not responsible

un-ac-cus-tomed *adj.* not used to or in the habit of; not ordinary

u-nan-i-mous *adj.* agreed to completely; based on the agreement of all

un-armed *adj.* lacking means for protection

un-as-sum-ing *adj.* modest and not showy

un-at-tach-ed *adj.* not engaged, going steady, or married

un-a-void-able *adj.* inevitable; unstoppable **-ly** *adv.*

un-a-ware *adj.* not realizing

un-bear-a-ble *adj.* not possible to endure; intolerable

un-be-coming *adj.* unattractive; not pleasing; not proper, polite or suitable for the situation

un-be-known *or* **unbeknownst** *adj.* not known; without one's knowledge

un-be-liev-able *adj.* incredible; hard to accept; not to be believed

un-called for *adj.* not necessary or needed; not requested

un-can-ny *adj.* strange, odd, or mysterious; exceptional

un-cer-tain *adj.* doubtful; not sure; not known; hard to predict

un-chang-ed *adj.* having nothing new or different

un-civ-i-lized *adj.* without culture or refinement; without an established cultural

un-cle *n.* brother of one's mother or father

un-clean *adj.* immoral; dirty; not decent

un-clothe *v.* uncover or undress

un-com-fort-a-ble *adj.* disturbed; not at ease physically or mentally

un-com-mon *adj.* rare; odd; unusual; extraordinary

un-com-pro-mis-ing *adj.* firm; unwilling to give in or to compromise

un-con-cern *n.* lack of interest; disinterest; indifference

un-con-di-tion-al *adj.* without conditions **unconditionally** *adv.*

un-con-scious *adj.* not mentally aware; done without thought; not on purpose

un-con-sti-tu-tion-al *adj.* contrary to the constitution or the basic laws of a state or country

un-couth *adj.* acting or speaking crudely, unrefined; clumsy or awkward

un-cov-er *v.* remove the cover from something; to disclose

un-de-cid-ed *adj.* unsettled; having made no firm decision; open to change

un-de-ni-able *adj.* not open to doubt or

denial; not possible to contradict

un-der *prep.* below, in place or position; in a place lower than another; less in degree, number, or other quality; inferior in rank, quality, or character; during the reign or period; in accordance with; less than the required amount; insufficient

under *prefix.* location beneath or below; lower in importance or rank

un-der-brush *n.* small bushes, vines, and plants that grow under tall trees

un-der-clothes *pl., n.* clothes worn next to the skin; underwear

un-der-de-vel-oped *adj.* not fully mature or grown; lacking modern communications and industry

un-der-foot *adj.* underneath or below the feet; being so close to one's feet as to be in the way

un-der-go *v.* to have the experience of; to be subjected to

un-der-grad-u-ate *n.* college or university student studying for a bachelor's degree

un-der-hand *adj.* done deceitfully and secretly **underhandedly** *adv.*

un-der-line *v.* to draw a line directly under something

un-der-mine *v.* to weaken; to make less strong

un-der-neath *adv.* beneath or below; on the under side; lower

un-der-pass *n.* road or walk that goes under another

un-der-priv-i-leged *adj.* deprived of economic and social advantages

un-der-rate *v.* rate or value below the true worth

un-der-score *v.* emphasize

un-der-sell *v.* sell for less than a competitor

un-der-side *n.* side or part on the bottom

un-der-stand *v.* comprehend; to realize

un-der-stand-a-ble *adj.* able to comprehend **-ly** *adv.*

un-der-state *v.* make too little of the actual situation **-ment** *n.*

un-der-stood *adj.* agreed upon by all

un-der-stud-y *v.* to learn another person's part or role in order to be able to replace him if necessary

un-der-take *v.* set about to do a task; to pledge oneself to a certain job; to attempt

un-der-tak-er *n.* person who prepares the dead for burial

un-der-tone *n.* low, quiet voice; a pale or subdued color visible through other colors

un-der-tow *n.* underwater current which runs in the opposite direction of the surface current

un-der-wa-ter *adj.* occurring, happening or used beneath the surface of the water

un-der-write *v.* sign or write at the end of something; to finance; to assume a risk by means of insurance assume responsibility for; to undertake to pay a written pledge of money **underwriter** *n.*

un-de-sir-a-ble *adj.* offensive; not wanted **undesirably** *adv.*

un-do *v.* cancel; to reverse; to loosen or unfasten

un-done *adj.* not finished; unfastened; ruined

un-du-late *v.* to move from side to side with a flowing motion; to have a wavy shape **undulation** *n.*

un-dy-ing *adj.* without end

un-earth *v.* dig up from the earth; to find or discover

unearthly *adj.* strange; not from this world

un-eas-y *adj.* feeling or causing distress or discomfort; embarrassed

un-em-ployed *adj.* without a job; without work **unemployment** *n.*

un-e-qual *adj.* not even; not fair; not of the same size or time

un-e-ven *adj.* not equal; varying in consistency or form; not balanced

un-e-vent-ful *adj.* lacking in significance; calm

un-expect-ed *adj.* surprising; happening without warning **-ly** *adv.*

un-fail-ing *adj.* constant, unchanging

un-fair *adj.* not honest; marked by a lack of justice

un-faith-ful *adj.* breaking a promise or agreement; without loyalty

un-fa-mil-iar *adj.* not knowing; strange; foreign

unfavorable *adj.*, not desired; harmful; unpleasant

un-feel-ing *adj.* without sympathy; hardhearted; without sensation

un-fit *adj.* not suitable; not qualified; in poor body or mental health

un-fold *v.* open up the folds of and lay flat; to reveal gradually

un-fore-seen *adj.* not anticipated or expected

un-for-get-ta-ble *adj.* impossible or hard to forget; memorable

un-for-tu-nate *adj.* causing or having bad luck, damage, or harm

un-found-ed *adj.* not founded or based on fact; groundless; lacking a factual basis

un-friend-ly *adj.* showing a lack of kindness; not friendly

un-furl *v.* unroll or unfold; to open up or out

un-fur-nished *adj.* without furniture

un-god-ly *adj.* wicked; evil; lacking reverence for God **ungodliness** *n.*

un-grate-ful *adj.* not thankful; no appreciation

un-guent *n.* healing or soothing salve; ointment

un-happy *adj.* sad; without laughter or joy; not satisfied or pleased

un-heard *adj.* not heard; not listened to

un-heard--of *adj.* not known or done before; without precedent

un-hook *v.* release or undo from a hook

u-ni-corn *n.*

mythical animal resembling a horse, with a horn in the center of its forehead

u-ni-cy-cle *n.* one wheeled vehicle with pedals

un-i-den-ti-fied flying object *n.* flying object that cannot be explained or identified

u-ni-form *n.* identical clothing worn by the members of a group to distinguish them from the general population **uniformly** *adv.*

u-ni-fy *v.* come together as one; to unite

un-in-hab-it-ed *adj.* not lived in; empty

un-in-ter-est-ed *adj.* having no interest or concern in; not interested

un-ion *n.* act of joining together of two or more groups or things; a group of countries or states joined under one government; a mar-riage; an organized body of employees who work together to upgrade their working conditions and wages **Union The United States**

u-nique *adj.* unlike any other; sole

u-ni-sex *adj.* adaptable and appropriate for both sexes

u-ni-son *n.* in music, the exact sameness of pitch, as of a tone

u-nit *n.* any one of several parts regarded as a whole; an exact quantity that is used as a standard of measurement; a special section

u-nite *v.* join or come together for a common purpose

United Nations *n.* international organization formed in 1945; comprised of nearly all the countries of the world whose purpose is to promote security, economic development, and peace

United States of America *n.* country bordering the Atlantic and Pacific Oceans, Mexico, and Canada

u-ni-ty *n., pl.* -ies fact or state of being one; accord; agreement; harmony

u-ni-valve *n.* mollusk having a one-piece shell, such as a snail

u-ni-ver-sal *adj.* having to do with the world or the universe in its entirety

u-ni-verse *n.* the world, stars, planets, space, and all that is contained

u-ni-ver-si-ty *n., pl.* -ies educational institution offering undergraduate and graduate degrees in a variety of academic areas

un-just *adj.* not fair; lacking justice or fairness

un-kempt *adj.* poorly groomed; messy

un-kind *adj.* harsh; lacking in sympathy, concern, or understanding

un-known *adj.* strange; unidentified; not known; not familiar

un-lead-ed *adj.* containing no lead

un-like *prep.* dissimilar; not alike; not equal in strength or quantity

un-lim-it-ed *adj.* having no boundaries or limitations

un-load *v.* take or remove the load; to unburden; to dispose or get rid of by selling in volume

un-lock *v.* open, release, or unfasten a lock; open with a key

un-loose *v.* loosen or undo; to release

un-luck-y *adj.* unfortunate; having bad luck; disappointing or unsuitable **unluckily** *adv.*

un-manned *adj.* designed to operate or be operated without a crew of people

un-men-tion-a-ble *adj.* improper or unsuitable

un-mis-tak-a-ble *adj.* very clear and evident; understood; obvious

un-mor-al *adj.* having no moral knowledge

un-nat-u-ral *adj.* abnormal or unusual; strange; artificial

un-nec-es-sar-y *adj.* not needed; not appropriate **unnecessarily** *adv.*

un-nerve *v.* frighten; to upset

un-num-bered *adj.* countless; not identified by number

un-oc-cu-pied *adj.* empty; not occupied

un-pack *v.* remove articles out of trunks,

suitcases, or boxes

un-pleas-ant *adj.* not agreeable; not pleasant

un-pop-u-lar *adj.* not approved or liked

un-pre-dict-a-ble *adj.* not capable or being foretold; not reliable

un-pre-pared *adj.* not equipped or ready

un-pro-fes-sion-al *adj.* contrary to the standards of a profession; having no professional status

un-prof-it-a-ble *adj.* showing or giving no profit; serving no purpose

un-qual-i-fied *adj.* lacking the proper qualifications; unreserved

un-rav-el *v.* to separate threads; to solve; to clarify; to come apart

un-re-al *adj.* having no substance or reality

un-rea-son-a-ble *adj.* not according to reason; exceeding all reason-able limits

un-re-li-a-ble *adj.* unable to be trusted; not dependable

un-re-served *adj.* done or given without reserve; unlimited

un-re-strained *adj.* not held back, forced, or affected

un-ru-ly *adj.* disorderly; difficult to subdue or control

un-sat-is-fac-to-ry *adj.* unacceptable; not pleasing

un-screw *v.* to loosen or unfasten by removing screws from

un-scru-pu-lous *adj.* without morals, guiding principles, or rules

un-seat *v.* cause to lose one's seat; to force out of office

un-sel-fish *adj.* willing to share; thinking of another's well-being before one's own

un-set-tle *v.* cause to be upset or excited; to disturb

un-sheathe *v.* draw a sword from a sheath or other case

un-sight-ly *adj.* not pleasant to look at; ugly

un-skilled *adj.* having no skills or training in a given kind of work

un-sound *adj.* having defects; not solidly made

un-speak-a-ble *adj.* of or relating to something which can not be expressed

un-sta-ble *adj.* not steady or firmly fixed; having the tendency to fluctuate or change

un-stead-y *adj.* not secure; unstable; variable

un-sub-stan-tial *adj.* lacking strength, weight, or solidity

un-suit-a-ble *adj.* unfitting; not suitable;

not appropriate for a specific circumstance

un-tan-gle *v.* free from snarls or entanglements

un-thank-ful *adj.* ungrateful

un-think-a-ble *adj.* unimaginable

un-ti-dy *adj.* messy; showing a lack of tidiness

un-tie *v.* unfasten or loosen; to free from a restraint or bond

un-til *prep.* up to the time of *conj.* to the time when; to the degree or place

un-time-ly *adj.* premature; before the expected time

un-told *adj.* not revealed; not told; inexpressible; cannot be described

un-touch-a-ble *adj.* cannot be touched; incapable of being obtained or reached

un-true *adj.* not true; contrary to the truth; not faithful; disloyal

un-truth *n.* something which is not true **untruthful** *adj.*

un-used *adj.* not put to use; never having been used

un-u-su-al *adj.* not usual; uncommon **unusually** *adv.*

un-ut-ter-a-ble *adj.* incapable of being described or expressed; unpronounceable

un-veil *v.* remove a veil from; to uncover; to reveal

un-war-y *adj.* not cautious or careful; careless

un-whole-some *adj.* unhealthy; morally corrupt or harmful

un-will-ing *adj.* reluctant; not willing

un-wind *v.* undo or reverse the winding of; to untangle

un-wise *adj.* lacking good judgment or common sense

un-wor-thy *adj.* not deserving; not becoming or befitting; lacking merit or worth; shameful **-iness** *n.*

up-beat *n.,* *Mus.* relatively unaccented beat preceding the down beat *adj.* optimistic; happy

up-bring-ing *n.* process of teaching and rearing a child

up-draft *n.* upward current of air

up-grade *v.* increase the grade, rank, or standard of

up-hol-ster *v.* cover furniture with fabric covering

up-keep *n.* cost and work needed to keep something in good condition

up-on *prep.* on

up-per *adj.* higher in status, position or location *n.* the part of a shoe to which the sole is attached

up-per--class *adj.* economically or socially superior

up-right *adj.* having a vertical direction or position; honest *n.* something standing vertically

up-ris-ing *n.* revolt; a rebellion; an insurrection

up-roar *n.* confused, loud noise; a commotion

up-root *v.* detach completely by pulling up the roots

up-set *v.* capsize; to turn over; to throw into confusion or disorder; to overcome; to beat unexpectedly *adj.* capsized; overturned; distressed; troubled

up-stage *adj. & adv.* toward or at the back part of a stage

up-start *n.* one who has risen quickly to power or wealth

up-tight *adv.* nervous, or tense

up-ward *or* **upwards** *adv.* from a lower position to or toward a higher one

u-ra-ni-um *n.* hard, heavy, shiny metallic element that is radioactive

urge *v.* encourage, push, or drive; to recommend persistently and strongly

ur-gent *adj.* requiring immediate attention

urine *n.* in man and other mammals, the yellowish fluid waste produced by the kidneys

Us *pl., pron.* objective case of we; used as an indirect object, direct object

us-a-ble *or* **useable** *adj.* fit or capable of being used **usability** *n.*, **usably** *adv.*

us-age *n.* way or act of using something; the way words are used

use *v.* put into action; to employ for a special purpose; to employ on a regular basis; to exploit for one's own advantage

u-su-al *adj.* ordinary or common; regular; customary **usually** *adv.*, **usualness** *n.*

u-surp *v.* take over by force without authority **usurpation, -er** *n.*

u-ten-sil *n.* tool, implement, or container

u-ter-us *n.* organ of female mammals33 within which young develop and grow before birth **uterine** *adj.*

u-til-i-ty *n., pl.* **-ies** state or quality of being useful; a company which offers a public service

u-til-ize *v.* make or put to use

ut-most *adj.* of the greatest amount or degree; most distant **utmost** *n.*

u-to-pi-a *n.* condition or place of perfection or complete harmony

u-vu-la *n.* fleshy projection which hangs above the back of the tongue

V, v The twenty-second letter of the English alphabet.

va-cant *adj.* empty; not occupied

va-cate *v.* leave; to cease

va-ca-tion *n.* period of time away from work for pleasure, relaxation, or rest

vac-ci-nate *v.* inject with a vaccine so as to produce immunity to an infectious disease

vac-ci-na-tion *n.* inoculation with a vaccine

vac-cine *n.* solution of weakened or killed microorganisms, as bacteria or viruses, injected into the body to produce immunity to a disease

vac-u-um *n., pl.* **vacuums, -ua** space which is absolutely empty; a void

vag-a-bond *n.* homeless person who wanders from place to place

va-gar-y *n., pl.* **vagaries** eccentric or capricious action or idea

va-gi-na *n., pl.* **vaginas, -nae** *Anat.* canal or passage extending from the uterus to the external opening of the female reproductive system

va-gi-ni-tis *n.* inflammation of the vagina

va-grant *n.* roaming from one area to another without a job

vague *adj.* not clearly expressed; not sharp or definite **vaguely** *adv.*

vain *adj.* conceited; lacking worth or substance **vainly** *adv.*

val-ance *n.* decorative drapery across the top of a window

vale *n.* a valley

val-e-dic-to-ri-an *n.* student ranking highest in a graduating class

val-en-tine *n.* card or gift sent to one's sweetheart on Valentine's Day, February 14th

val-et *n.* man who takes care of another man's clothes and other personal needs; a hotel employee

val-iant *adj.* brave; exhibiting valor **valiance, valor** *n.*

val-id *adj.* founded on facts or truth *Law* binding; having legal force **validity**

val-ley *n., pl.* **valleys** low land between ranges of hills

val-or *n.* bravery **valorous** *adj.*

val-u-a-ble *adj.* of great value or importance **valuableless** *adj.*

val-ue *n.* quality or worth of something that makes it valuable; material worth

valve *n.* movable mechanism which opens and closes to control the flow of a substance through a pipe or other passageway

va-moose *v. Slang* leave in a hurry

vam-pire *n.* in folklore, a dead person

believed to rise from the grave at night to suck the blood of sleeping persons; a person who preys on others

vampire bat *n.*

a tropical bat that feeds on the blood of living mammals.

van *n.* large closed wagon or truck

va-na-di-um *n.* metallic element symbolized by

van-dal-ism *n.* malicious defacement or destruction of private or public property

vane *n.* metal device that turns in the direction the wind is blowing

va-nil-la *n.* flavoring extract used in cooking and baking

van-ish *v.* disappear suddenly; to drop out of sight

van-i-ty *n., pl.,* vanities conceit; extreme pride in one's ability

van-tage *n.* superior position; an advantage

va-por *n.* moisture or smoke sus-pended in air, as mist or fog vaporish, vaporous *adj.*

var-i-able *adj.* changeable; tending to vary; inconstant variableness *n.,* variably *adv.*

var-i-ance *n.* state or act of varying; difference; conflict

var-i-a-tion *n.* result or process of varying; the degree or extent of varying

var-i-e-gat-ed *adj.* having marks of different colors variegate *v.*

va-ri-e-ty *n., pl.,* varieties state or character of being varied or various; a number of different kinds; an assortment

var-i-ous *adj.* of different kinds

var-mint *n., Slang* a troublesome animal; an obnoxious person

var-nish *n.* solution paint used to coat or cover a surface with a hard, transparent, shiny film

var-si-ty *n., pl.,* varsities best team representing a college, university, or school

var-y *v.* change; to make or become different; to be different

vas-cu-lar *adj., Biol.* having to do with vessels circulating fluids, as blood

va-sec-to-my *n., pl.* vasectomies method of male sterilization

vast *adj.* very large or great in size vastly *adv.,* vastness *n.*

vault *n.* room for storage and safekeeping, as in a bank, usually made of steel; a burial chamber

veg-e-ta-ble *n.* plant, as the tomato, green beans, lettuce, raised for the edible part

veg-e-tar-i-an *n.* person whose diet is limited to vegetables

veg-e-ta-tion *n.* plants or plant life which grow from the soil

ve-hi-cle *n.* a motorized device for transporting goods, equipment, or passengers

veil *n.* a piece of transparent cloth worn on the head or face for concealment or protection

vein *n., Anat.*

vessel which transports blood back to the heart after passing through the body vein *v.*

ve-lour *n.* soft velvet-like woven cloth

vel-vet *n.* fabric made of rayon, cotton, or silk

vend-er *or* vendor *n.* person who sells, as a peddler

ven-det-ta *n.* fight or feud between blood-related persons

ven-er-a-ble *adj.* meriting or worthy of respect by reason of dignity, position, or age

venereal disease *n.* contagious disease, as syphilis, or gonorrhea, which is typically acquired through sexual intercourse

ve-ne-tian blind *n.* window blind having thin, horizontal slats

ven-i-son *n.* edible flesh of a deer

ven-om *n.* poisonous substance secreted by some animals, as scorpions or snakes venomous *adj.*

ve-nous *adj.* of or relating to veins

vent *n.* means of escape or passage from a restricted area; an opening which allows the escape of vapor, heat, or gas

ven-ti-late *v.* expose to a flow of fresh air for refreshing, curing, or purifying purposes ventilation, ventilator *n.*

ven-ture *n.* course of action involving risk, chance, or danger, especially a business investment

ven-ue *n.* place where a crime or other cause of legal action occurs; the locale of a gathering

verb *n.* part of speech which expresses action, existence, or occurrence

ver-bal *adj.* expressed in speech; expressed orally; not written; relating to or derived from a verb *n.* an adjective, noun or other word which is based on a verb and retains some characteristics of a verb verbally *adv.*, **verbalize** *v.*

ver-ba-tim *adv.* word for word

ver-be-na *n.* American garden plant

verge *n.* extreme edge or rim; margin; the point beyond which something begins

ver-min *n.* a destructive, annoying animal which is harmful to one's health

ver-sa-tile *adj.* having the capabilities of doing many different things; having many functions or uses

verse *n.* writing that has a rhyme; poetry; a subdivision of a chapter of the Bible

ver-sion *n.* an account or description told from a particular point of view; a translation from another language, especially a translation of the Bible

ver-so *n.*, *pl.* **versos** left-hand page

ver-sus *prep.* against; in contrast to; as an alternative of

ver-te-bra *n.*, *pl.* **vertebrae, vertebras** one of the bony or cartilaginous segments making up the spinal column

ver-tex *n.*, *pl.* **vertexes, vertices** highest or topmost point; the pointed top of a triangle

ver-ti-cal *adj.* in a straight up-and-down direction

ver-y *adv.* to a high or great degree; truly; absolutely; exactly

ves-per *n.* evening prayer service; a bell to call people to such a service

ves-sel *n.* hollow or concave utensil, as a bottle, kettle, container, or jar; a hollow craft designed for navigation on water

vest *n.* a sleeveless garment open or fastening in front, worn over a shirt

ves-tige *n.* trace or visible sign of something that no longer exists **vestigial** *adj.*, **vestigially** *adj.*

ves-try *n.*, *pl.* **vestries** room in a church used for meetings

vet *n.*, *Slang* veterinarian; a veteran

vet-er-an *n.* person with a long record or experience in a certain field; one who has served in the military

vet-er-i-nar-i-an *n.* one who is trained and authorized to give medical treatment to animals

vet-er-i-nar-y *adj.* pertaining to the science and art of prevention and treatment of animals

ve-to- *n.*, *pl.* **vetoes** power of a government executive, as the President or a governor, to reject a bill passed by the legislature

vex *v.* to bother or annoy

vi-a *prep.* by way of; by means of

vi-a-duct *n.* bridge, resting on a series of arches

vi-al *n.* small, closed container used especially for liquids

vi-brate *v.* move or make move back and forth or up and down

vi-car-i-ous *adj.* undergoind or serving in the place of someone or something else; experienced through sympathetic or imaginative participation in the experience of another

vice *n.* immoral habit or practice; evil conduct

vi-ce ver-sa *adv.* with the order or meaning of something reversed

vi-chy-ssoise *n.* a soup made from potatoes, chicken stock, and cream, flavored with leeks or onions and usually served cold

vi-cin-i-ty *n.*, *pl.* **-ies** surrounding area or district; the state of being near in relationship or space

vi-cious *adj.* dangerously aggressive; having the quality of immorality

vic-tim *n.* person who is harmed or killed by another **victimize** *v.*

vic-tor *n.* person who conquers; the winner

vic-to-ri-ous *adj.* being the winner in a contest **victoriously** *adv.*

vic-to-ry *n.*, *pl.* **victories** defeat of those on the opposite side

vid-e-o *adj.* being, related to, or used in the reception or transmission of television

vid-e-o disc *n.* disc containing recorded images and sounds

vid-e-o game *n.* computerized game displaying on a display screen

vid-e-o term-in-al *n. Computer Science* computer device having a cathoderay tube for displaying data on a screen

vie *v.* strive for superiority

view *n.* act of examining or seeing; a judgment or opinion

vig-il *n.* a watch with prayers kept on the night before a religious feast; a period of surveillance

vig-or *n.* energy or physical strength; intensity of effect or action

vile *adj.* morally disgusting, miserable, and unpleasant

vil-la *n.* a luxurious home in the country; a country estate

vil-lage *n.* incorporated settlement, usually smaller than a town

vil-lain *n.* evil or wicked person

vin-ai-grette *n.* a small ornamental bottle with a periorated top, used for holding an aromatic preparation such as smelling salts

vin-di-cate *v.* to clear of suspicion; to set free vindication *n.*

vin-dic-tive *adj.* showing or possessing a desire for revenge; spiteful

vine *n.* plant whose stem needs support as it climbs or clings to a surface

vin-e-gar *n.* a tart, sour liquid derived from cider or wine

vin-tage *n.* the grapes or wine produced from a particular district in one season

vi-nyl *n.* variety of shiny plastics, similar to leather, often used for clothing and for covering furniture

vi-o-la *n.* stringed instrument, slightly larger and deeper in tone than a violin

vi-o-late *v.* break the law or a rule; to disrupt or disturb a person's privacy violation *n.*

vi-o-lence *n.* physical force or activity used to cause harm, damage, or abuse

vi-o-let *n.* small, low-growing plant with blue, purple, or white flowers; a purplish-blue color

vi-o-lin *n.* a small stringed instrument, played with a bow

vi-per *n.* a poisonous snake; an evil or treacherous person

vir-gin *n.* person who has never had sexual intercourse *adj.* in an unchanged or natural state

Vir-go *n.* the sixth sign of the zodiac; a person born betweeb August 23rd and September 22nd

vir-ile *adj.* having the qualities and nature of a man; capable of sexual performance in the male

vir-tu *n.* the love or knowledge of fine objects of art

vir-tue *n.* morality, goodness or uprightness; a special type of goodness

vi-rus *n.* any of a variety of microscopic organisms which cause diseases

vi-sa *n.* an offical authorization giving permission on a passport to enter a specific country

vis-cid *adj.* sticky; having an adhesive quality

vise or **vice** *n.* a tool in carpentry and metalwork having two jaws to hold things in position

vis-i-bil-i-ty *n., pl.* -ies degree or state of being visible; the distance that one is able to see clearly

vis-i-ble *adj.* apparent; exposed to view

vi-sion *n.* power of sight; the ability to see; an image created in the imagina-

tion; a supernatural appearance

vis-it *v.* journey to or come to see a person or place *n.* a professional or social call *Slang* to chat

vi-su-al *adj.* visible; relating to seeing or sight

vi-tal *adj.* essential to life; very important

vi-ta-min *n.* any of various substances which are found in foods and are essential to good health

vit-re-ous *adj.* related to or similar to glass

vi-va-cious *adj.* filled with vitality or animation; lively

viv-id *adj.* bright; brilliant; intense; having clear, lively, bright colors

viv-i-fy *v.* give life to

vo-cab-u-lar-y *n., pl.* vocabularies list or group of words and phrases, usually in alphabetical order; all the words that a person uses or understands

vo-cal *adj.* of or related to the voice; uttered by the voice; to speak freely and loudly *n.* vocal sound

vogue *n.* leading style or fashion; popularity

void *adj.* containing nothing; empty; not inhabited

voile *n.* a fine, soft, sheer fabric used for making light clothing and curtains

volt-age *n.* amount of electrical power, given in terms of the number of volts

vol-ume *n.* capacity or amount of space or room; a book; a quantity; the loudness of a sound

vo-lup-tu-ous *adj.* full of pleasure; delighting the senses; sensuous; luxury

vom-it *v.* eject contents of the stomach through the mouth

vo-ra-cious *adj.* having a large appetite; insatiable

vote *n.* expression of one's choice by voice, by raising one's hand, or by secret ballot voter *n.*

vouch *v.* verify or support as true; to guarantee

vow *n.* solemn pledge or promise, especially one made to God; a marriage vow

vow-el *n.* sound of speech made by voicing the flow of breath within the mouth; a letter representing a vowel

vul-gar *adj.* showing poor manners; crude; improper; immoral or indecent

vul-ner-a-ble *adj.* open to physical injury or attack

vulnerability *n.,* **vulnerably** *adv.*

vul-ture *n.* large bird of the hawk family, living on dead animals; a greedy person

W, w The twenty-third letter of the English alphabet.

wacky *adj.* amusingly or absurdly irrational

wad *n.* small crumpled mass or bundle

wad-dle *v.* walk with short steps and swing from side to side **waddle, waddler** *n.*

wade *v.* walk through a substance as mud or water which hampers one's steps

wad-able *adj.* having the capability of being wadded

wad-ding *n.* materials for wadding or wads; a sheet of loose fibers that is used for stuffing

wad-dle *v.* to walk with short steps and swing from side to side

wa-fer *n.* small, thin, crisp cracker, cookie, or candy

waf-fle *n.* pancake batter cooked in a waffle iron

waft *v.* drift or move gently, as by the motion of water or air **waft** *n.*

wag *v.* move quickly from side to side or up and down *n.* playful, witty person **waggish** *adj.*

wage *n.* payment of money for labor or services *v.* to conduct

wa-ger *v.* make a bet

wag-on *n.* four-wheeled vehicle used to transport goods; a station wagon; a child's four-wheeled cart with a long handle

waif *n.* abandoned, homeless, or lost child

wail *n.* loud, mournful cry or weep

waist *n.* narrow part of the body between the thorax and hips **waisted** *adj.*

wait *v.* stay in one place in expectation of; to await; to put off until a later time or date

wait-er *n.* man who serves food at a restaurant

wait-ress *n.* woman who serves food at a restaurant

waive *v.* forfeit of one's own free will; to postpone or dispense with

wake *v.* come to consciousness, as from sleep *n.* vigil for a dead body.

walk *v.* move on foot over a surface; to pass over, go on

walk-out *n.* labor strike against a company

wall *n.* vertical structure to separate or enclose an area *v.* to provide or close up, as with a wall

wal-la-by *n.* small or medium-sized kangaroo

wal-let *n.* flat folding case for carrying

paper money

wal-lop *n.* powerful blow; an impact *v.* to move with disorganized haste **walloper** *n.*

wall-pa-per *n.* decorative paper for walls, usually having a colorful pattern

wal-nut *n.* edible nut with a hard, light-brown shell; the tree on which this nut grows

wal-rus *n.*

large marine mammal of the seal family, having flippers, tusks, and a tough hide

waltz *n.* ballroom dance

wam-pum *n.* polished shells, once used as currency by North American Indians *Slang* Money

wand *n.* slender rod used by a magician

wan-der *v.* travel about aimlessly; to roam; to stray **wanderer** *n.*

wane *v.* decrease in size or extent; to decrease gradually *n.* gradual deterioration

wan-gle *v.* resort to devious methods in order to obtain something wanted **wangler** *n.*

want *v.* wish for or desire; to need; to lack; to fail to possess a required amount

war *n.* armed conflict among states or nations

ward *n.* section in a hospital.
v. to keep watch over someone or something

ware *n.* manufactured items of the same general kind; items or goods for sale

ware-house *n.* large building used to store merchandise

warm *adj.* moderate heat; neither hot or cold

warn *v.* give notice or inform beforehand; to call to one's attention; to alert

warp *v.* become bent out of shape; to deviate from a proper course

war-rant *n.* written authorization giving the holder legal power to search, seize, or arrest **warrantable** *adj.*

war-ri-or *n.* one who fights in a war or battle

war-y *adj.* marked by caution; alert to danger

wash *v.* cleanse by the use of water; to remove dirt

wash--and--wear *adj.* requiring little or

no ironing after washing

wash-board *n.* corrugated board on which clothes are rubbed in the process of washing

washed--out *adj., Slang* tired

wash-er *n.* small disk usually made of rubber or metal having a hole in the center, used with nuts and bolts; a washing machine

wash-ing *n.* clothes and other articles that are washed or to be washed; cleaning

was-n't *contr.* was not

wasp *n.* any of various insects, having a slim body with a constricted abdomen, the female capable of inflicting a painful sting

waste *v.* to be thrown away; to be available but not used completely -ful *adj.*

watch *v.* view carefully; to guard; to keep informed

watch-dog *n.* dog trained to guard someone or his property

watch-ful *adj.* carefully observant or attentive watchfully *adv.*

watch-man *n.* person hired to keep watch; a guard

wa-ter *n.* clear liquid making up oceans, lakes, and streams; the body fluids as tears or urine

water moccasin *n.* venomous snake

water polo *n.* water game between two teams

water power *n.* power or energy produced by swift-moving water

wa-ter-proof *adj.* capable of preventing water from penetrating.

wa-ter-shed *n.* The raised area between two regions that divides two sections drained by different river sources

wa-ter--ski *v.* travel over water on a pair of short, broad skis while being pulled by a motorboat

wa-ter-spout *n.* tube or pipe through which water is discharged

water table *n.* upper limit of the portion of the ground completely saturated with water

wa-ter-tight *adj.* closed or sealed so tightly that no water can enter

wa-ter-way *n.* navigable body of water; a channel for water

wa-ter-y *adj.* containing water; diluted; lacking effectiveness wateriness *n.*

watt *n.* unit of electrical power represented by current of one ampere, produced by the electromotive force of one volt

wave *v.* move back and forth or up and down; to motion with the hand

wa-ver *v.* sway unsteadily; to move back and forth; to weaken in force waver *n.*, waveringly *adv.*

wax *n.* natural yellowish substance made by bees, solid when cold and easily melted or softened when heated

way *n.* manner of doing something; a tendency or characteristic

way-far-er *n.* person who travels on foot

way-lay *v.* attack by ambush

way-ward *adj.* unruly; unpredictable

we *pl., pron.* used to refer to the person speaking and one or more other people

weak *adj.* having little energy or strength; easily broken; having inadequate skills weakness *n.*, weakly *adv.*

wealth *n.* abundance of valuable possessions or property

wean *v.* accustom an infant or small child to food other than a mother's milk or bottle

weap-on *n.* device which can be used to harm another person

wear *v.* to have on or put something on the body; to display wearable *adj.*

wea-ri-some *adj.* tedious, boring or tiresome

wea-ry *adj.* exhausted; tired; feeling fatigued wearily *adv.*, -iness *n.*

wea-sel *n.* mammal with a long tail and short legs; a sly, sneaky person

weath-er *n.* condition of the air or atmosphere in terms of humidity, temperature, and similar features

weath-er-man *n.* man who reports or forecasts the weather

weather vane *n.*

device that turns, indicating the direction of the wind

weave *v.* make a basket, cloth, or other item by interlacing threads or other strands of material

web *n.*

cobweb; piece of interlacing material which forms a woven structure

wed *v.* take as a spouse; to marry

we'd *contr.* we had; we should

wed-ding *n.* marriage ceremony; an act of joining together in close association

wedge *n.* tapered, triangular piece of wood or metal used to split logs, to add leverage, and to hold something

open or ajar

weed *n.* unwanted plant which interferes with the growth of grass, vegetables, or flowers

week *n.* period of seven days, beginning with Sunday and ending with Saturday

week-day *n.* any day of the week except Saturday or Sunday

week-end *n.* end of the week from the period of Friday evening through Sunday evening

weep *v.* to shed tears; to express sorrow, joy, or emotion

wee-vil *n.* small beetle having a downward-curving snout

weigh *v.* determine the heaviness of an object by using a scale; to consider carefully in one's mind

weight *n.* amount that something weighs; heaviness; a heavy object used to hold or pull something down

weight-less *adj.* lacking the pull of gravity; having little weight

weight-y *adj.* burdensome; important

weird *adj.* having an extraordinary or strange character **weirdly** *adv.*

weird-o *n., Slang* person who is very strange

wel-come *v.* extend warm hospitality; to accept gladly

weld *v.* unite metallic parts by applying heat and sometimes pressure, allowing the metals to bond together

wel-fare *n.* state of doing well; governmental aid to help the disabled or disadvantaged

well *n.* hole in the ground which contains a supply of water; a shaft in the ground through which gas and oil are obtained

we'll *contr.* we will; we shall

well--be-ing *n.* state of being healthy, happy, or prosperous

well--done *adj.* completely cooked; done properly

well--groomed *adj.* clean, neat, and properly cared for

well--known *adj.* widely known

well--man-nered *adj.* polite; having good manners

well--mean-ing *adj.* having good intentions

well--to--do *adj.* having more than enough wealth

welsh *v., Slang* cheat by avoiding a payment to someone; to neglect an obligation

welt *n.* strip between the sole and upper part of a shoe; a slight swelling on the body

wel-ter-weight *n.* boxer weighing between 136 and 147 pounds

went *v.* past tense of go

wept *v.* past tense of weep

were *v.* second person singular past plural of be

we're *contr.* we are

were-n't *contr.* were not

west *n.* direction of the setting sun **western** *adj.*

whack *v.* strike with a hard blow, to slap *n.* an attempt

whale *n.* very large mammal resembling a fish which lives in salt water

wharf *n.* pier or platform built at the edge of water so that ships can load and unload

what *pron.* which one; which things; which type or kind

what-ev-er *pron.* everything or anything *adj.* no matter what

what's *contr.* what is

wheat *n.* grain ground into flour, used to make breads and similar foods

wheel *n.* a circular disk which turns on an axle

wheel-bar-row *n.* vehicle having one wheel, used to transport small loads

wheel-chair *n.* a mobile chair for disabled persons

wheel-er *n.* anything that has wheels

wheeze *v.* breathe with a hoarse whistling sound *n.* high whistling sound

whelk *v.* any of various large water snails, sometimes edible

when *adv.* at what time; at which time *pron.* what or which time *conj.* while; at the time that

whence *adv.* from what source or place; from which

when-ev-er *adv.* at any time; when *conj.* at whatever time

where *adv.* at or in what direction or place; in what direction or place

where-a-bouts *adv.* near, at, or in a particular location *n.* approximate location

where-as *conj.* it being true or the fact; on the contrary

where-by *conj.* through or by which

wher-ev-er *adv.* in any situation or place

whet *v.* to make sharp; to stimulate

wheth-er *conj.* indicating a choice; alternative possibilities; either

whet-stone *n.* stone used to sharpen scissors, knives, and other implements

whew *n., interj.* used to express relief; or tiredness

whey *n.* clear, water-like part of milk that separates from the curd

which *pron.* what one or ones; the one previously; whatever one or ones; whichever

which-ev-er *pron.* any; no matter which or what

whiff *n.* slight puff; a light current of air; a slight breath or odor

while *n.* length or period of time *conj.* during the time that; even though; at the same time

whim *n.* sudden desire or impulse

whim-per *v.* make a weak, soft crying sound

whim-si-cal *adj.* impulsive; erratic; light and spontaneous **whimsically** *adv.*

whine *v.* make a squealing, plaintive sound; to complain in an irritating, childish fashion

whin-ny *v.* neigh in a soft gentle way

whip *v.* spank repeatedly with a rod or stick; to punish by whipping *n.* flexible stick or rod used to herd or beat animals **whipper** *n.*

whip-lash *n.* injury to the spine or neck caused by a sudden jerking motion of the head

whip-poor-will *n.* brownish nocturnal bird of North America

whir *v.* move with a low purring sound

whirl *v.* rotate or move in circles; to twirl; to move

whirl-pool *n.* circular current of water

whirl-wind *n.* violently whirling mass of air; a tornado

whirl-y-bird *n., Slang* helicopter

whisk *v.* move with a sweeping motion; move quickly or lightly

whisk-er *n.* hair that grows on a man's face; the long hair near the mouth of dogs, cats, and other animals

whiskers

man's beard
whis-key *n.* alcoholic beverage distilled from rye, barley, or corn

whis-per *v.* speak in a very low tone; to tell in secret

whis-tle *v.* make a clear shrill sound by blowing air through the teeth, through puckered lips, or through a special instrument

white *n.* color opposite of black; the part of something that is white or light in color, as an egg or the eyeball; a member of the Caucasian group of people

white-cap *n.* wave having a top of white foam

white--col-lar *adj.* relating to an employee whose job does not require manual labor

white-wash *n.* mixture made of lime and other ingredients and used for whitening fences and exterior walls

whith-er *adv.* what state, place, or circumstance; wherever

whit-tle *v.* cut or carve off small shavings from wood with a knife; to remove or reduce gradually **whittler** *n.*

who *pron.* which or what certain individual, person, or group

who'd *contr.* who would; who had

who-ev-er *pron.* whatever person; all or any persons

whole *adj.* complete; having nothing missing; not divided or in pieces

whole-heart-ed *adj.* sincere; totally committed

whole-sale *n.* sale of goods in large amounts to a retailer

whole-some *adj.* contributing to good mental or physical health **wholesomely** *adv.*, **-ness** *n.*

whole wheat *adj.* made from the wheat kernel with nothing removed

who'll *contr.* who shall; who will

whol-ly *adv.* totally; exclusively

whom *pron.* form of who used as the direct object of a verb or the object of the preposition

whom-ev-er *pron.* form of whoever used as the object of a preposition or the direct object of a verb

whooping cough *n.* infectious disease of the throat and breathing passages

whooping crane *n.* large bird of North America, nearly extinct

whoosh *v.* make a rushing or gushing sound, as a rush of air

whop-per *n.* something of extraordinary size *Slang* a lie

whore *n.* prostitute

who's *contr.* who is; who has

whose *pron.* belonging to or having to do with one's belongings

why *adj.* for what reason or purpose *conj.* cause, purpose, or reason for which *interj.* expressing surprise or disagreement

wick *n.* soft strand of fibers which extends from a candle or lamp

wick-er *n.* thin, pliable twig used to make furniture and baskets

wick-et *n.* wire hoop in the game of croquet

wide *adj.* broad; covering a large area; completely extended or open *adv.* over a large area; full extent

wide-spread *adj.* fully spread out; over a broad area

wid-ow *n.* woman whose husband is no longer living

wid-ow-er *n.* man whose wife is no longer living

width *n.* distance or extent of something from side to side'

wield *v.* use or handle something skillfully; to employ power effectively

wie-ner *n.* frankfurter; a hot dog

wife *n.* married female

wig *n.* artificial or human hair woven together to cover baldness or a bald spot on the head

wig-gle *v.* squirm; to move with rapid side-to-side motions -er *n.*

wig-wam *n.* Indian dwelling place

wild *adj.* living in a natural, untamed state; not occupied by man; not civilized; strange and unusual *adv.* out of control *n.* wilderness region not cultivated or settled by man

wild-cat *n.* medium-sized wild, feline animal; one with a quick temper

wil-der-ness *n.* unsettled area; a region left in its uncultivated or natural state

wild-life *n.* animals and plants living in their natural environments

will *n.* mental ability to decide or choose for oneself; strong desire or determination; a legal document stating how one's property is to be distributed after death

wil-low *n.* large tree, usually having narrow leaves and slender flexible twigs

wilt *v.* cause or to become limp; to lose force; to deprive of courage or energy

win *v.* defeat others; to gain victory in a contest; to receive *n.* victory; the act of winning winner *n.*

winch *n.* apparatus with one or more drums on which a cable or rope is wound, used to lift heavy loads

wind *n.* natural movement of air windy *adj.*

wind *v.* wrap around and around something; to turn, to crank *n.* turning or twisting

wind-bag *n., Slang* person who talks excessively without saying anything of importance

wind-fall *n.* sudden or unexpected stroke of good luck

wind instrument *n.* musical instrument which produces sound when a person forces his breath into it

wind-mill *n.* machine operated or powered by the wind

win-dow *n.* opening built into a wall for light and air; a pane of glass

win-dow--shop *v.* look at merchandise in store windows without going inside to buy

wind-pipe *n.* passage in the neck used for breathing; the trachea

wine *n.* drink containing 10-15% alcohol by volume, made by fermenting grapes

wing *n.* one of the movable appendages that allow a bird or insect to fly; one of the airfoils on either side of an aircraft

wing-spread *n.* extreme measurement from the tips or outer edges of the wings of an aircraft, bird, or other insect

wink *v.* shut one eye as a signal or message

win-ning *adj.* defeating others; captivating *n.* victory

win-some *adj.* very pleasant; charming

win-ter *n.* coldest season, coming between autumn and spring *adj.* relating to or typically of winter

win-ter-green *n.* small plant having aromatic evergreen leaves

wipe *v.* clean by rubbing; to take off by rubbing *n.* act or instance of wiping

wis-dom *n.* ability to understand what is right, true, or enduring; good judgment; knowledge

wise *adj.* having superior intelligence; having great learning; having a capacity for sound judgment marked by deep understanding wisely *adv.*

wish *v.* desire or long for something; to command or request *n.* longing or desire

wish-ful *adj.* having or expressing a wish; hopeful wishfully *adv.*

wish-y--wash-y *adj., Slang* not purposeful; indecisive

wisp *n.* tuft or small bundle of hay, straw, or hair; a thin piece wispy *adj.*

wit *n.* ability to use words in a clever way; a sense of humor

witch *n.* person believed to have magical powers; a mean, ugly, old woman

with *prep.* in the company of; near or alongside; having, wearing or bearing

with-draw *v.* take away; to take back; to retreat

with-draw-al *n.* process of with-drawing; a retreat; the act of removing money from an account

whither *v.* dry up or wilt from a lack of moisture; to lose freshness or vigor

with-hold *n.* hold back or keep

withholding tax *n.* tax on income held back by an employer in payment of one's income tax

with-in *adv.* inside the inner part; inside the limits; inside the limits of time, distance, or degree

with-out *adv.* on the outside; not in possession of

prep. something or someone lacking

with-stand *v.* endure

wit-ness *n.* person who has seen, experienced, or heard something; something serving as proof or evidence

wit-ty *adj.* amusing or cleverly humorous

wiz-ard *n.* very clever person; a person thought to have magical powers *Slang* one with amazing skill

wob-ble *v.* move unsteadily from side to side, as a rocking motion

woe *n.* great sorrow or grief; misfortune

wok *n.* convex metal cooker for stir-frying food

woke *v.* past tense of wake

wolf *n.* carnivorous animal found in northern areas; a fierce person *v.* eat quickly and with greed

wolfish *adj.*, **wolfishly** *adv.*

woman *n.* mature adult human female; a person who has feminine qualities

womanhood *n.* state of being a woman

womb *n.* uterus; place where development occurs

won *v.* past tense of win

won-der *n.* feeling of amazement or admiration *v.* feel admiration; feel uncertainty

won-der-ment *n.* feeling or state of amazement

won-drous *adj.* wonderful; marvelous

won't *contr.* will not

won-ton *n.* noodle dumpling filled with minced pork and served in soup

wood *n.* hard substance which makes up the main part of trees

wood-chuck *n.*

rodent having short legs and a heavyset body, which lives in a burrow

wood-en *adj.* made of wood; resembling wood; stiff; lifeless; lacking flexibility

wood-peck-er *n.* bird which uses its bill for drilling holes in trees looking for insects to eat

word *n.* meaningful sound which stands for an idea; a comment

word processing *n.* system which produces typewritten documents with automated type and editing equipment

world *n.* planet Earth; the universe; the human race

worm *n.*

a samll, thin animal having a long, flexible, rounded or flattened body

worn *adj.* made weak or thin from use; exhausted

wor-ry *v.* concerned or troubled; to tug at repeatedly; to annoy; to irritate

wor-ship *n.* reverence for a sacred object; high esteem or devotion for a person *v.* revere; attend a religious service **worshiper** *n.*

worst *adj.* bad; most inferior; most disagreeable

worth *n.* quality or value of something; personal merit

wor-thy *adj.* valuable or useful; deserving admiration or honor

would-n't *contr.* would not

wound *n.* laceration of the skin *v.* injure by tearing, cutting, or piercing the skin

wow *interj.* expression of amazement, surprise, or excitement

wran-gle *v.* quarrel noisily

wrap *v.* fold in order to protect something; encase or enclose

wrath *n.* violent anger or fury

wreak *v.* inflict punishment upon another person

wreck *v.* ruin or damage by accident or deliberately

wrench *n.*

a tool used to grip, turn, or twist an object, as a bolt or nut

wrest *v.* twist or pull away in a violent way

wretch *n.* extremely unhappy person; a miserable person

wrig-gle *v.* squirm; move by turning and twisting

wrin-kle *n.* small crease on the skin or on fabric

writ *n., Law* written court document directed to a public official or individual ordering a specific action

wrong *adj.* incorrect; against moral standards; not suitable **wrongly** *adv.*

wrote *v.* past tense of write

wrought *adj.* fashioned; formed; beatened or hammered into shape

X, x The twenty-fourth letter of the English alphabet.

xan-thate *n.* salt of xanthic acid

xan-thic *adj.* colors that tend to be yellow and yellows in flowers

xan-thip-pe *n.* wife; female which is like a shrew

xan-tho-chroid *adj.* light-haired, Caucasion peoples

x-axis *n.* in Cartesian coordinate system, the horizontal line of a two-dimensional plane

X chro-mo-some *n.* sex female chromosome, associated with female characteristics; occurs paired in the female and single in the male chromosome pair

xe-non *n.* colorless, odorless gaseous element found in small quantities in the air, symbolized by Xe.

xen-o-phobe *n.* person who dislikes, fears, and mistrusts foreigners or anything strange **xenophobia** *n.*

X--Ra-di-a-tion *n.* treatment with X-rays

X ray *n.* energy that is radiated with a short wavelength and high penetrating power; a black and white negative image or picture of the interior of the body

xy-lo-phone *n.*

musical instrument consisting of mounted wooden bars which produce a ringing musical sound when struck with two small wooden hammers **xylophonist** *n.*

Y, y The twenty-fifth letter of the English alphabet.

yacht *n.* small sailing vessel powdered by wind or motor, for pleasure cruises

yak *n.* longhaired ox of Tibet and mountains of central Asia

yam *n.*

edible root; a variety of the sweet potato

yap *v.* bark in a high pitched, sharp way *Slang* talk in a loud, or stupid manner

yard *n.* unit of measure that equals 36 inches or 3 feet; ground around a house

yarn *n.* twisted fibers, as of wool, used in knitting or weaving *Slang* involved tale or story

yawn *v.* inhale a deep breath with the mouth open wide

Y-Chro-mo-some *n.* sex chromosome associated with male characteristics

ye *pron.* you, used especially in religious contexts, as hymns

yea *adv.* yes; indeed; truly

yeah *adv., Slang* yes

year *n.* period of time starting on January 1st and continuing through December 31st

yearn *v.* feel a strong craving

yeast *n.* fungi or plant cells used to make baked goods rise or fruit juices ferment

yell *v.* cry out loudly *n.* loud cry; cheer to show support for an athletic team

yel-low *n.* bright color of a lemon; the yolk of an egg *v.* make or become yellow *adj.* of the color yellow *Slang* cowardly

yellow fever *n.* acute infectious disease of the tropics, spread by the bite of a mosquito

yeo-man *n.* owner of a small farm; a petty officer who acts as a clerk

yes *adv.* express agreement

yes-ter-day *n.* day before today; a former or recent time *adv.* on the day before the present day

yet *adv.* up to now; at this time *conj.* nevertheless; but

yew *n.* evergreen tree having poisonous flat, dark-green needles and poisonous red berries

yield *v.* bear or bring forward; give up possession

yo-del *v.* sing in a way so that the voice changes from normal to a high shrill sound and then back again

yo-ga *n.* system of exercises which helps the mind and the body in order to achieve tranquillity and spiritual insight

yo-gurt *n.* thick custard-like food made from curdled milk and often mixed with fruit

yoke *n.* wooden bar used to join together two animals working together, as oxen

yo-del *n.* very unsophisticated country person; a bumpkin

yolk *n.* yellow, nutritive part of an egg

Yom Kip-pur *n.* Jewish holiday observed with fasting and prayer for the forgiveness of sins

you *pron.* person or persons addressed

you all *pron., Slang* y'all southern variation used for two or more people in direct address

you'd *contr.* you had; you would

you'll *contr.* you will; you shall

young *adj.* of or relating to the early stage of life *n.* offspring of an animal **youngster** *n.*

your *adj.* belonging to you or yourself or the person spoken to

you're *contr.* you are

your-self *pron.* form of you for emphasis when the object of a verb and the subject is the same

you've *contr.* you have

yowl *v.* make a loud, long cry or howl **yowl** *n.*

yt-ter-bi-um *n.* metallic element symbolized by Yb.

yule *n.* Christmas

yule-tide *n.* Christmas season

Z, z The twenty-sixth letter of the English alphabet.

za-ny *n., pl* **-nies** clown; person who acts silly or foolish *adj.* typical of being clownish **zaniness** *n.*, **zannily** *adv.*

zap *v., Slang* destroy; do away with

zeal *n.* great interest or eagerness

zeal-ot *n.* fanatical person; a fanatic

zeal-ous *adj.* full of interest; eager; passionate **zealously** *adv.*

ze-bra *n.*

African mammal of the horse family having black or brown stripes on a white body

zeph-yr *n.* gentle breeze

ze-ro *n., pl.* **-ros, -roes** number or symbol "0"; nothing; point from which degrees or measurements on a scale begin; the lowest point *v.* aim, point at, or close in on *adj.* pertaining to zero; non-existing

zest *n.* enthusiasm; a keen quality **zestful** *adj.*, **zestfully, zesty** *adj.*

zig-zag *n.* pattern with sharp turns in alternating directions *adv.* move in a zigzag course or path

zilch *n., Slang* nothing; zero

zil-lion *n., Slang* extremely large number

zinc *n.* bluish-white crystalline metallic element, used as a protective coating for steel and iron, symbolized by Zn.

zip *n.* act or move with vigor or speed *v.* move with energy, speed, or facility; open or close with a zipper *Slang* energy; zero; nothing

zip code *n.* system to speed the delivery of mail by assigning a five digit number, plus four to each postal delivery location in the United States

zip-per *n.* fastener consisting of two rows of plastic or metal teeth that are interlocked by means of sliding a tab

zir-co-ni-um *n.* metallic element symbolized by Zr.

zit *n., Slang* pimple

zo-di-ac *n.* unseen path followed through the heavens by the moon, sun, and most planets; area divided into twelve astrological signs, bearing the name of a constellation

zom-bie *n.* person who resembles the walking dead

zone *n.* area or region set apart from its surroundings by some characteristic

zonk *v., Slang* stun; render senseless with alcohol or drugs

zoo *n., pl.* **zoos** public display or collection of living animals

zo-ol-o-gy *n.* science that deals with animals, animal life, and the animal kingdom **zoologist** *n.*

zoom *v.* move with a continuous, loud sound; move upward sharply

zuc-chi-ni *n., pl.* **-ni** summer squash that has a dark-green, smooth rind

zwie-back *n.* sweetened bread which is baked to make it crisp

zy-mur-gy *n.* chemistry of fermentation processes

NEW WEBSTER'S
THESAURUS

DICTIONARY FORMAT
OF
SYNONYMS AND ANTONYMS

a *(SYN.)* any, one.

abandon *(SYN.)* relinquish, resign, surrender, leave, give up, cease, forsake, waive, desert, quit, vacate, abjure, entirely, abdicate, leave undone, discard, evacuate, withdraw.
(ANT.) support, keep, fulfill, uphold, depend, stay, maintain, embrace, cherish, favor, adopt, join, engage, unite, retain.

abandoned *(SYN.)* depraved, wicked, deserted, desolate, forsaken, rejected, cast off, profligate, degraded, loose, unrestrained, marooned, immoral, evil.
(ANT.) befriended, cherished, chaste, moral, respectable, virtuous, righteous.

abase *(SYN.)* make humble, reduce, bring down, degrade, demote, mock, scorn, belittle, shame, make lower, despise, humiliate.
(ANT.) exalt, cherish, elevate, uplift, respect, dignify.

abash *(SYN.)* disconcert, bewilder, confuse, put off, discompose, nonplus.
(ANT.) comfort, relax, hearten, nerve.

abashed *(SYN.)* confused, ashamed, embarrassed, mortified, humiliated.

abate *(SYN.)* lessen, curtail, reduce, decrease, restrain, decline, stop, moderate, subside, slow, diminish, slacken.
(ANT.) grow, prolong, increase, extend, intensify, quicken, enhance, accelerate.

abbey *(SYN.)* nunnery, convent, cloisters, monastery.

abbot *(SYN.)* friar, monk.

abbreviate *(SYN.)* shorten, lessen, abridge, condense, curtail, reduce, cut, compress, trim, restrict, clip, contract.
(ANT.) lengthen, increase, expand, extend, prolong, enlarge, augment.

abbreviation *(SYN.)* abridgment, reduction, shortening, condensation.
(ANT.) expansion, extension, amplification, lengthening, dilation.

abdicate *(SYN.)* relinquish, renounce, vacate, waive, desert, forsake, abolish, quit, abandon, surrender, resign.
(ANT.) maintain, defend, stay, retain, uphold.

abdomen *(SYN.)* paunch, belly, stomach.

abduct *(SYN.)* carry off, take, kidnap.

aberrant *(SYN.)* capricious, devious, irregular, unnatural, abnormal, unusual.
(ANT.) methodical, regular, usual, fixed, ordinary.

aberration *(SYN.)* oddity, abnormality, irregularity, deviation, quirk, monster, abortion, nonconformity, eccentricity.
(ANT.) norm, conformity, standard, normality.

abet *(SYN.)* support, connive, encourage, conspire, help, incite, aid, assist.
(ANT.) deter, check, hinder, frustrate, oppose, discourage, resist.

abettor *SYN.)* accomplice, ally, confederate, associate, accessory.
(ANT.) opponent, rival, enemy.

abeyance *(SYN.)* inaction, cessation, pause, inactivity, rest, suspension, recess, dormancy, remission.
(ANT.) ceaselessness, continuation, continuity.

abhor *(SYN.)* dislike, hate, loathe, execrate, avoid, scorn, detest, despise.

abhorrent *(SYN.)* loathsome, horrible, detestable, nauseating, hateful, despicable, disgusting, foul, offensive, terrible, revolting.

abide *(SYN.)* obey, accept, tolerate, endure, dwell, stay, reside.

ability *(SYN.)* aptness, capability, skill, dexterity, faculty, power, talent, aptitude, efficiency, aptitude, capacity, expertness, effectiveness,
(ANT.) incapacity, incompetency, weakness, ineptitude, inability, disability.

abject *(SYN.)* sordid, infamous, miserable, wretched, mean, base, contempt.

abjure *(SYN.)* relinquish, renounce, vacate, waive, desert, quit, leave, forsake, forewear, abdicate, resign, surrender.
(ANT.) cling to, maintain, uphold, stay.

able *(SYN.)* qualified, competent, fit, capable, skilled, having power, efficient, clever, talented, adequate, skillful.
(ANT.) inadequate, trained, efficient, incapable, weak, incompetent, unable.

abnegation *(SYN.)* rejection, renunciation, self-denial, abandonment, refusal, relinquishment, abjuration.

abnormal *(SYN.)* uncommon, unnatural, odd, irregular, monstrous, eccentric, insane, unusual, weird, strange.
(ANT.) standard, natural, usual, normal, average.

aboard *(SYN.)* on board.

abode *(SYN.)* dwelling, habitat, hearth, home, residence, address, quarters, lodging place, domicile.

abolish *(SYN.)* end, eradicate, annul, cancel, revoke, destroy, invalidate, overthrow, obliterate, abrogate, erase, exterminate, wipe out, eliminate.

(ANT.) promote, restore, continue, establish, sustain.

abominable *(SYN.)* foul, dreadful, hateful, revolting, vile, odious, loathsome, detestable, bad, horrible, terrible, awful, nasty, obnoxious, disgusting, unpleasant.
(ANT.) delightful, pleasant, agreeable, commendable, admirable, noble, fine.

abominate *(SYN.)* despise, detest, hate, dislike, abhor, loathe.
(ANT.) love, like, cherish, approve, admire.

abomination *(SYN.)* detestation, hatred, disgust, loathing, revulsion, antipathy, horror.

abort *(SYN.)* flop, fizzle, miscarry, abandon, cancel.

abortion *(SYN.)* fiasco, disaster, failure, defeat.

abortive *(SYN.)* unproductive, vain, unsuccessful, useless, failed, futile.
(ANT.) rewarding, effective, profitable, successful.

abound *(SYN.)* swarm, plentiful, filled, overflow, teem.
(ANT.) scarce, lack.

about *(SYN.)* relating to, involving, concerning, near, around, upon, almost, approximately, of, close to, nearby, ready to, nearly.

about-face *(SYN.)* reversal, backing out, shift, switch.

above *(SYN.)* higher than, overhead, on, upon, over, superior to.
(ANT.) under, beneath, below.

aboveboard *(SYN.)* forthright, open, frank, honest, overt, plain, straightforward, guileless, trustworthy.
(ANT.) underhand, ambiguous, sneaky, wily.

abracadabra *(SYN.)* voodoo, magic, charm, spell.

abrasion *(SYN.)* rubbing, roughness, scratching, scraping, friction, chap, chafe, chapping, scrape.

abrasive *(SYN.)* hurtful, sharp, galling, annoying, grating, cutting, irritating, caustic.
(ANT.) pleasant, soothing, comforting, agreeable.

abreast *(SYN.)* beside, side by side, alongside.

abridge *(SYN.)* condense, cut, abbreviate, make shorter, contract, shorten, reduce, summarize, curtail.

(ANT.) increase, lengthen, expand, extend.

abridgment *(SYN.)* digest, condensation, summary, abbreviation, shortening.
(ANT.) lengthening, expansion, enlargement.

abroad *(SYN.)* away, overseas, broadly, widely.
(ANT.) at home, privately, secretly.

abrogate *(SYN.)* rescind, withdraw, revoke, annul, cancel, abolish, repeal.

abrupt *(SYN.)* sudden, unexpected, blunt, curt, craggy, precipitous, sharp, hasty, unannounced, harsh, precipitate, brusque, rude, rough, short, steep.
(ANT.) foreseen, smooth, warm, courteous, gradual, smooth, expected, anticipated.

abscess *(SYN.)* pustule, sore, wound, inflammation.

absence *(SYN.)* nonexistence, deficiency, lack, need, shortcoming.
(ANT.) attendance, completeness, existence, presence.

absent *(SYN.)* away, truant, abroad, departed, inattentive, lacking, not present, out, off.
(ANT.) attending, attentive watchful, present.

absent-minded *(SYN.)* inattentive, daydreaming, preoccupied, absorbed, distrait, bemused, dreaming, forgetful.
(ANT.) observant, attentive, alert.

absolute *(SYN.)* unconditional, entire, actual, complete, thorough, total, perfect, essential, supreme, ultimate, unrestricted, positive, unqualified, whole.
(ANT.) partial, conditional, dependent accountable, restricted, qualified, limited, fragmentary, imperfect, incomplete.

absolutely *(SYN.)* positively, really, doubtlessly.
(ANT.) doubtfully, uncertainly.

absolution *(SYN.)* pardon, forgiveness, acquittal, mercy, dispensation, amnesty, remission.

absolutism *(SYN.)* autarchy, dictatorship, authoritarianism.

absolve *(SYN.)* exonerate, discharge, acquit, pardon, forgive, clear, excuse.
(ANT.) blame, convict, charge, accuse.

absorb *(SYN.)* consume, swallow up, engulf, assimilate, imbibe, engage, engross, take in, integrate, incorporate, occupy, suck up.
(ANT.) discharge, dispense, emit, exude,

leak, eliminate, bore, tire, weary, drain.

absorbent (SYN.) permeable, spongy, pervious, porous.
(ANT.) moisture-proof, waterproof, impervious.

absorbing (SYN.) engaging, exciting, engaging, engrossing, entertaining, thrilling, intriguing, pleasing, fascinating.
(ANT.) dull, boring, tedious, tiresome.

abstain (SYN.) forbear, forego, decline, resist, hold back, withhold, refrain.
(ANT.) pursue.

abstemious (SYN.) abstinent, sparing, cautious, temperate, ascetic, self-disciplined, continent, sober.
(ANT.) uncontrolled, indulgent, abandoned, excessive.

abstinence (SYN.) fasting, self-denial, continence, forbearance, sobriety, refrain, do without, abstention.
(ANT.) gluttony, greed, excess, self-indulgence, pursue.

abstract (SYN.) part, appropriate, steal, remove, draw from, separate, purloin, unconcrete, abridge, summarize.
(ANT.) return, concrete, unite, add, replace, specific, clear, particular, restore.

abstracted (SYN.) parted, removed, stolen, abridged, taken away.
(ANT.) replaced, returned, alert, united, added.

abstraction (SYN.) idea, image, generalization, thought, opinion, impression, notion.
(ANT.) matter, object, thing, substance.

abstruse (SYN.) arcane, obscure, complicated, abstract, refined, mandarin, esoteric, metaphysical.
(ANT.) uncomplicated, direct, obvious, simple.

absurd (SYN.) ridiculous, silly, unreasonable, foolish, irrational, nonsensical, impossible, inconsistent, preposterous, self-contradictory, unbelievable.
(ANT.) rational, sensible, sound, meaningful, consistent, reasonable.

absurdity (SYN.) foolishness, nonsense, farce, drivel, joke, paradox, babble, drivel, senselessness, folly.

abundance (SYN.) ampleness, profusion, large amount, copiousness, plenty.
(ANT.) insufficiency, want, absence, dearth, scarcity.

abundant (SYN.) ample, overflowing, plentiful, rich, teeming, large amount, profuse, abounding.

(ANT.) insufficient, scant, not enough, scarce, deficient, rare, uncommon, absent.

abuse (SYN.) maltreatment, misuse, reproach, defamation, dishonor, mistreat, damage, ill-use, reviling, aspersion, desecration, invective, insult, outrage, profanation, perversion, upbraiding, disparagement, misemploy, misapply, hurt, harm, injure, scold, berate.
(ANT.) plaudit, respect, appreciate, commendation, protect, praise, cherish.

abusive (SYN.) harmful, insulting, libelous, hurtful, slanderous, nasty, defamatory, injurious, scathing, derogatory.
(ANT.) supportive, helpful, laudatory, complimentary.

abut (SYN.) touch, border, meet, join, verge on, connect with.

abutment (SYN.) pier, buttress, bulwark, brace, support.

abysmal (SYN.) immeasurable, boundless, endless, stupendous, profound, unbelievable, infinite, overwhelming, consummate.

abyss (SYN.) depth, chasm, void, infinitude, limbo, unknowable.

academic (SYN.) learned, scholarly, theoretical, erudite, bookish, formal, pedantic.
(ANT.) ignorant, practical, simple, uneducated.

academy (SYN.) college, school.

accede (SYN.) grant, agree, comply, consent, yield, endorse, accept, admit.
(ANT.) dissent, disagree, differ, oppose.

accelerate (SYN.) quicken, dispatch, facilitate, hurry, rush, speed up, forward, hasten, push, expedite.
(ANT.) hinder, retard, slow, delay, quicken.

accent (SYN.) tone, emphasis, inflection, stress, consent.

accept (SYN.) take, approve, receive, allow, consent to, believe, adopt, admit.
(ANT.) ignore, reject, refuse.

acceptable (SYN.) passable, satisfactory, fair, adequate, standard, par, tolerable, unobjectionable.
(ANT.) poor, substandard, inadmissible.

access (SYN.) entrance, approach, course, gateway, door, avenue.

accessible (SYN.) nearby, attainable, achievable, affable, democratic, accommodating.
(ANT.) remote, unobtainable, unachiev-

able, standoffish, forbidding, unfriendly.

accessory *(SYN.)* extra, addition, assistant, supplement, contributory, accomplice.

accident *(SYN.)* casualty, disaster, misfortune, mishap, chance, calamity, contingency, fortuity, misadventure, mischance, injury, event, catastrophe.
(ANT.) purpose, intention, calculation.

accidental *(SYN.)* unintended, chance, casual, fortuitous, contingent, unplanned, unexpected, unforeseen.
(ANT.) calculated, planned, willed, intended, intentional, on purpose, deliberate.

acclaim *(SYN.)* eminence, fame, glory, honor, reputation, credit, applaud, distinction, approve, notoriety.
(ANT.) infamy, obscurity, disapprove, reject, disrepute.

acclimated *(SYN.)* adapted, habituated, acclimatized, accommodated, seasoned, inured, used to, weathered, reconciled.

accolade *(SYN.)* praise, honor, acclaim, recognition, applause, kudos, bouquet, crown, testimonial, acclamation, salute.

accommodate *(SYN.)* help, assist, aid, provide for, serve, oblige, hold, house.
(ANT.) inconvenience.

accommodating *(SYN.)* obliging, helpful, willing, kind, cooperative, gracious, cordial, sympathetic, unselfish.
(ANT.) unfriendly, selfish, hostile, uncooperative.

accommodation *(SYN.)* change, alteration, adaptation, convenience, adjustment, acclimatization, aid, help, boon, kindness, service, courtesy.
(ANT.) inflexibility, rigidity, disservice, stubbornness, disadvantage.

accommodations *(SYN.)* housing, lodgings, room, place, quarters, board.

accompany *(SYN.)* chaperon, consort with, escort, go with, associate with, attend, join.
(ANT.) abandon, quit, leave, desert, avoid, forsake.

accomplice *(SYN.* accessory, ally, associate, partner in crime, assistant, sidekick, confederate.
(ANT.) opponent, rival, enemy, adversary.

accomplish *(SYN.)* attain, consummate, achieve, do, execute, carry out, fulfill, complete, effect, perform, finish.
(ANT.) fail, frustrate, spoil, neglect, defeat.

accomplished *(SYN.)* proficient, skilled, finished, well-trained, gifted, masterly, polished, able.
(ANT.) unskilled, amateurish, crude.

accomplishment *(SYN.)* deed, feat, statute, operation, performance, action, achievement, transaction.
(ANT.) cessation, inhibition, intention, deliberation.

accord *(SYN.)* concur, agree, award, harmony, conformity, agreement, give, tale, sum, statement, record, grant.
(ANT.) difference, quarrel, disagreement.

accordingly *(SYN.)* consequently, therefore, whereupon, hence, so, thus.

accost *(SYN.)* approach, greet, speak to, address.
(ANT.) avoid, shun.

account *(SYN.)* description, chronicle, history, narration, reckoning, rate, computation, detail, narrative, relation, recital, consider, believe, deem, record, explanation, report, tale, story, anecdote, reason, statement, tale, ledger.
(ANT.) confusion, misrepresentation, distortion.

accountable *(SYN.)* chargeable, answerable, beholden, responsible, obliged, liable.

account for *(SYN.)* justify, explain, substantiate, illuminate, clarify, elucidate.

accredited *(SYN.)* qualified, licensed, deputized, certified, commissioned, vouched for, empowered.
(ANT.) illicit, unofficial, unauthorized.

accrue *(SYN.)* amass, collect, heap, increase, accumulate, gather, hoard.
(ANT.) disperse, dissipate, waste, diminish.

accrued *(SYN.)* accumulated, totaled, increased, added, enlarged, amassed, expanded.

accumulate *(SYN.)* gather, collect, heap, increase, accrue, assemble, compile, hoard, amass.
(ANT.) spend, give away, diminish, dissipate.

accumulation *(SYN.)* heap, collection, pile, store, hoard, stack, aggregation.

accurate *(SYN.)* perfect, just, truthful, unerring, meticulous, correct, all right.
(ANT.) incorrect, mistaken, false, wrong.

accursed *(SYN.)* ill-fated, cursed, condemned, doomed, bedeviled, ruined.
(ANT.) fortunate, hopeful.

accusation *(SYN.)* charge, incrimination,

indictment, arraignment.
(ANT.) pardon, exoneration, absolve.
accuse *(SYN.)* incriminate, indict, censure, tattle, denounce, charge, arraign, impeach, blame.
(ANT.) release, vindicate, exonerate, acquit, absolve, clear.
accustom *(SYN.)* addict, familiarize, condition.
accustomed *(SYN.)* familiar with, used to, comfortable with.
(ANT.) strange, unusual, rare, unfamiliar.
ace *(SYN.)* champion, star, king, queen, winner, head.
acerbity *(SYN.)* bitterness, harshness, unkindness, sourness, acidity, unfriendliness, acrimony, coldness, sharpness.
(ANT.) sweetness, gentleness, kindness, tenderness.
ache *(SYN.)* hurt, pain, throb.
achieve *(SYN.)* do, execute, gain, obtain, acquire, accomplish, realize, perform, complete, accomplish, finish, fulfill, reach, attain, secure, procure.
(ANT.) fail, lose, fall short.
achievement *(SYN.)* feat, accomplishment, attainment, exploit, realization, performance, completion, deed.
(ANT.) botch, dud, mess, omission, defeat, failure.
acid *(SYN.)* tart, sour, bitter, mordant, biting, biting.
(ANT.) pleasant, friendly, bland, mild, sweet.
acknowledge *(SYN.)* allow, admit, agree to, concede, recognize, answer, grant, accept, receive.
(ANT.) reject, refuse, disavow, refute, deny.
acme *(SYN.)* summit, top, zenith, peak, crown.
(ANT.) bottom.
acquaint *(SYN.)* inform, teach, enlighten, notify, tell.
acquaintance *(SYN.)* fellowship, friendship, cognizance, knowledge, intimacy, familiarity, companionship, associate, colleague, companion.
(ANT.) inexperience, unfamiliarity, ignorance.
acquiesce *(SYN.)* submit, agree, concur, assent, comply, consent, succomb.
(ANT.) refuse, disagree, rebel, argue.
acquire *(SYN.)* attain, earn, get, procure, assimilate, obtain, secure, gain, appropriate.
(ANT.) miss, surrender, lose, forego, forfeit.
aquirement *(SYN.)* training, skill, learning, achievement, attainment, education, information.
aquisition *(SYN.)* procurement, gain, gift, purchase, proceeds, possession, grant.
aquisitive *(SYN.)* greedy, avid, hoarding, covetous.
acquit *(SYN.)* forgive, exonerate, absolve, cleanse, pardon, excuse, excuse, discharge, found not guilty.
(ANT.) doom, saddle, sentence, condemn.
acrid *(SYN.)* bitter, sharp, nasty, stinging, harsh.
(ANT.) pleasant, sweet.
acrimonious *(SYN.)* sharp, sarcastic, acerb, waspish, cutting, stinging, testy.
(ANT.) soft, kind, sweet, pleasant, soothing.
acrobat *(SYN.)* athlete, gymnast.
act *(SYN.)* deed, doing, feat, execution, accomplishment, performance, action, operation, transaction, law, decree, statute, edict, achievement, exploit, statute, judgment, routine, pretense.
(ANT.) inactivity, deliberation, intention, cessation.
acting *(SYN.)* officiating, substituting, surrogate, temporary, delegated.
action *(SYN.)* deed, achievement, feat, activity, exploit, movement, motion, play, behavior, battle, performance, exercise.
(ANT.) idleness, inertia, repose, inactivity, rest.
activate *(SYN.)* mobilize, energize, start, propel, nudge, push.
(ANT.) paralyze, immobilize, stop, deaden.
active *(SYN.)* working, operative, alert, agile, nimble, supple, sprightly, busy, brisk, lively, quick, industrious, energetic, vigorous, industrious, occupied, vivacious, dynamic, engaged.
(ANT.) passive, inactive, idle, dormant, lazy, lethargic.
activism *(SYN.)* engagement, confrontation, agitation, commitment, aggression, fervor, zeal.
(ANT.) detachment, lethargy, disengagement, fence-sitting.
activist *(SYN.)* militant, doer, enthusiast.
activity *(SYN.)* action, liveliness, motion, vigor, agility, exercise, energy, quick-

ness, enterprise, movement, briskness.
(ANT.) idleness, inactivity, dullness, sloth.
actor (SYN.) performer, trouper, entertainer.
actual (SYN.) true, genuine, certain, factual, authentic, concrete, real.
(ANT.) unreal, fake, bogus, nonexistent, false.
actuality (SYN.) reality, truth, deed, occurrence, fact, certainty.
(ANT.) theory, fiction, falsehood, supposition.
acute (SYN.) piercing, severe, sudden, keen,sharp, perceptive, discerning, shrewd, astute, smart, intelligent.
(ANT.) bland, mild, dull, obtuse, insensitive.
adamant (SYN.) unyielding, firm, obstinate.
(ANT.) yielding.
adapt (SYN.) adjust, conform, accommodate, change, fit, alter, vary, modify.
(ANT.) misapply, disturb.
add (SYN.) attach, increase, total, append, sum, affix, augment, adjoin, put together, unite, supplement.
(ANT.) remove, reduce, deduct, subtract, detach, withdraw.
address (SYN.) greet, hail, accost, speak to, location, residence, home, abode, dwelling, speech, lecture, greeting, oration, presentation.
(ANT.) avoid, pass by.
adept (SYN.) expert, skillful, proficient.
(ANT.) unskillful.
adequate (SYN.) capable, commensurate, fitting, satisfactory, sufficient, enough, ample, suitable, plenty, fit.
(ANT.) lacking, scant, insufficient, inadequate.
adhere (SYN.) stick fast, grasp, hold, keep, retain, cling, stick to, keep, cleave.
(ANT.) surrender, abandon, release, separate, loosen.
adherent (SYN.) follower, supporter.
(ANT.) renegade, dropout, defector.
adjacent (SYN.) next to, near, bordering, adjoining, touching, neighboring.
(ANT.) separate, distant, apart.
adjoin (SYN.) connect, be close to, affix, attach.
(ANT.) detach, remove,
adjoining (SYN.) near to, next, next to, close to, touching, bordering.
(ANT.) distant, remote, separate.
adjourn (SYN.) postpone, defer, delay,

suspend, discontinue, put off.
(ANT.) begin, convene, assemble.
adjust (SYN.) repair, fix, change, set, regulate, settle, arrange, adapt, suit, accommodate, modify, very, alter, fit.
administer (SYN.) supervise, oversee, direct, manage, rule, govern, control, conduct, provide, give, execute, preside, apply, contribute, help.
administration (SYN.) conduct, direction, management, supervision.
admirable (SYN.) worthy, fine, praisedeserving, commendable, excellent.
admiration (SYN.) pleasure, wonder, esteem, approval.
(ANT.) disdain, disrespect, contempt.
admire (SYN.) approve, venerate, appreciate, respect, revere. esteem, like.
(ANT.) abhor, dislike, despise, loathe, detest, hate.
admissible (SYN.) fair, justifiable, tolerable, allowable, permissible.
(ANT.) unsuitable, unfair, inadmissible.
admission (SYN.) access, admittance, entrance, pass, ticket.
admit (SYN.) allow, assent, permit, acknowledge, welcome, concede, agree, confess, accept, grant, own up to.
(ANT.) deny, reject, dismiss, shun, obstruct.
admittance (SYN.) access, entry, entrance.
admonish (SYN.) caution, advise against, warn, rebuke, reprove, censure.
(ANT.) glorify, praise.
admonition (SYN.) advice, warning, caution, reminder, tip.
ado (SYN.) trouble, other, fuss, bustle, activity, excitement, commotion, action, hubbub, upset, confusion, turmoil.
(ANT.) tranquillity, quietude.
adolescent (SYN.) young, youthful, immature, teen-age.
(ANT.) grown, mature, adult.
adoration (SYN.) veneration, reverence, glorification, worship homage.
adore (SYN.) revere, venerate, idolize, respect, love, cherish, esteem, honor.
(ANT.) loathe, hate, despise.
adorn (SYN.) trim, bedeck, decorate, ornament, beautify, embellish, glamorize, enhance, garnish, embellish.
(ANT.) mar, spoil, deform, deface, strip, bare.
adrift (SYN.) floating, afloat, drifting, aimless, purposeless, unsettled.

(ANT.) purposeful, stable, secure, well-organized.

adroit *(SYN.)* adept, apt, dexterous, skillful, clever, ingenious, expert.
(ANT.) awkward, clumsy, graceless, unskillful, oafish.

adult *(SYN.)* full-grown, mature.
(ANT.) infantile, immature.

advance *(SYN.)* further, promote, bring forward, propound, proceed, aggrandize, elevate, improve, adduce, allege, propose, progress, move, advancement, improvement, promotion, up-grade.
(ANT.) retard, retreat, oppose, hinder, revert, withdraw, flee, retardation.

advantage *(SYN.)* edge, profit, superiority, benefit, mastery, leverage, favor, vantage, gain.
(ANT.) handicap, impediment, obstruction, disadvantage, detriment, hindrance, loss.

adventure *(SYN.)* undertaking, occurrence, enterprise, happening, event, project, occurrence, incident, exploit.

adventurous *(SYN.)* daring, enterprising, rash, bold, chivalrous.
(ANT.) cautious, timid, hesitating.

adversary *(SYN.)* foe, enemy, contestant, opponent, antagonist.
(ANT.) ally, friend.

adverse *(SYN.)* hostile, counteractive, unfavorable, opposed, disastrous, contrary, antagonistic, opposite, unlucky, unfriendly, unfortunate.
(ANT.) favorable, propitious, fortunate, friendly, beneficial.

adversity *(SYN.)* misfortune, trouble, calamity, distress, hardship, disaster.
(ANT.) benefit, happiness.

advertise *(SYN.)* promote, publicize, make known, announce, promulgate.

advertisement *(SYN.)* commercial, billboard, want ad, handbill, flyer, poster, brochure, blurb.

advice *(SYN.)* counsel, instruction, suggestion, warning, information, caution, exhortation, admonition, recommendation, plan, tip, guidance, opinion.

advisable *(SYN.)* wise, sensible, prudent, suitable, fit, proper, fitting.
(ANT.) ill-considered, imprudent, inadvisable.

advise *(SYN.)* recommend, suggest, counsel, caution, warn, admonish.

adviser *(SYN.)* coach, guide, mentor, counselor.

advocate *(SYN.)* defend, recommend, support.
(ANT.) opponent, adversary, oppose, opponent.

aesthetic *(SYN.)* literary, artistic, sensitive, tasteful, well-composed.
(ANT.) tasteless.

affable *(SYN.)* pleasant, courteous, sociable, friendly, amiable, gracious, approachable, communicative.
(ANT.) unfriendly, unsociable.

affair *(SYN.)* event, occasion, happening, party, occurrence, matter, festivity, business, concern.

affect *(SYN.)* alter, modify, concern, regard, move, touch, feign, pretend, influence, sway, transform, change, impress.

affected *(SYN.)* pretended, fake, sham, false.

affection *(SYN.)* fondness, kindness, emotion, love, feeling, tenderness, attachment, disposition, endearment, liking, friendly, friendliness, warmth.
(ANT.) aversion, indifference, repulsion, hatred, repugnance, dislike, antipathy.

affectionate *(SYN.)* warm, loving, tender, fond, attached.
(ANT.) distant, unfeeling, cold.

affirm *(SYN.)* aver, declare, swear, maintain, endorse, certify, state, assert, ratify, pronounce, say, confirm, establish.
(ANT.) deny, dispute, oppose, contradict, demur, disclaim.

afflict *(SYN.)* trouble, disturb, bother, agitate, perturb.
(ANT.) soothe.

affliction *(SYN.)* distress, grief, misfortune, trouble.
(ANT.) relief, benefit, easement.

affluent *(SYN.)* wealthy, prosperous, rich, abundant, ample, plentiful, well-off, bountiful, well-to-do.
(ANT.) poor.

afford *(SYN.)* supply, yield, furnish.

affront *(SYN.)* offense, slur, slight, provocation, insult.

afraid *(SYN.)* faint-hearted, frightened, scared, timid, fearful, apprehensive, cowardly, terrified.
(ANT.) assured, composed, courageous, bold, confident.

after *(SYN.)* following, subsequently, behind, despite, next.
(ANT.) before.

again *(SYN.)* anew, repeatedly, afresh.
against *(SYN.)* versus, hostile to, opposed to, in disagreement.
(ANT.) pro, with, for, in favor of.
age *(SYN.)* antiquity, date, period, generation, time, senility, grow old, senescence, mature, dotage, ripen, mature, era, epoch.
(ANT.) youth, childhood.
aged *(SYN.)* ancient, elderly, old.
(ANT.) youthful, young.
agency *(SYN.)* office, operation.
agent *(SYN.)* performer, doer, worker, actor, operator.
aggravate *(SYN.)* intensify, magnify, annoy, irritate, increase, heighten, nettle, make worse, irk, vex, provoke, embitter, worsen.
(ANT.) soften, soothe, appease, pacify, mitigate, ease, relieve.
aggregate *(SYN.)* collection, entirety, sum, accumulate, total, amount to, compile, conglomeration.
(ANT.) part, unit, ingredient, element.
aggression *(SYN.)* assault, attack, invasion, offense.
(ANT.) defense.
aggressive *(SYN.)* offensive, belligerent, hostile, attacking, militant, pugnacious.
(ANT.) timid, withdrawn, passive, peaceful, shy.
aghast *(SYN.)* surprised, astonished, astounded, awed, thunderstruck, flabbergasted, bewildered.
agile *(SYN.)* nimble, graceful, lively, active, alert, fast, quick, athletic, spry.
(ANT.) inept, awkward, clumsy.
agility *(ANT.)* quickness, vigor, liveliness, energy, activity, motion.
(ANT.) dullness, inertia, idleness, inactivity.
agitate *(SYN.)* disturb, excite, perturb, rouse, shake, arouse, disconcert, instigate, inflame, provoke, jar, incite, stir up, toss.
(ANT.) calm, placate, quiet, ease, soothe.
agitated *(SYN.)* jumpy, jittery, nervous, restless, restive, upset, disturbed, ruffled.
agony *(SYN.)* anguish, misery, pain, suffering, torture, ache, distress, throe, woe, torment, grief.
(ANT.) relief, ease, comfort.
agree *(SYN.)* comply, coincide, conform, oncur, assent, accede, tally, settle, harmonize, unite, yield, consent.

(ANT.) differ, disagree, protest, contradict, argue, refuse.
agreeable *(SYN.)* amiable, charming, gratifying, pleasant, suitable, pleasurable, welcome, pleasing, acceptable, friendly, cooperative.
(ANT.) obnoxious, offensive, unpleasant, disagreeable, quarrelsome, contentious, touchy.
agreement *(SYN.)* harmony, understanding, unison, contract, pact, stipulation, alliance, deal, bargain, treaty, contract, arrangement, settlement, accord, concord.
(ANT.) variance, dissension, discord, disagreement, difference, misunderstanding.
agriculture *(SYN.)* farming, gardening, tillage, husbandry, cultivation, agronomy.
ahead *(SYN.)* before, leading, forward, winning, inadvance.
(ANT.) behind.
aid *(SYN.)* remedy, assist, helper, service, support, assistant, relief, help.
(ANT.) obstruct, hinder, obstacle, impede, hindrance.
ail *(SYN.)* bother, trouble, perturb, disturb, suffer, feel sick.
ailing *(SYN.)* sick, ill.
(ANT.) hearty, hale, well.
ailment *(SYN.)* illness, disease, affliction, sickness.
aim *(SYN.)* direction, point, goal, object, target, direct, try, intend, intention, end, objective.
aimless *(SYN.)* directionless, adrift, purposeless.
air *(SYN.)* atmosphere, display, reveal, expose, publicize.
(ANT.) conceal, hide.
airy *(SYN.)* breezy, light, gay, lighthearted, graceful, fanciful.
aisle *(SYN.)* corridor, passageway, lane, alley, opening, artery.
ajar *(SYN.)* gaping, open.
akin *(SYN.)* alike, related, connected, similar, affiliated, allied.
alarm *(SYN.)* dismay, fright, signal, warning, terror, apprehension, affright, consternation, fear, siren, arouse, startle, bell.
(ANT.) tranquillity, composure, security, quiet, calm, soothe, comfort.
alarming *(SYN.)* appalling, daunting, shocking.
(ANT.) comforting, calming, soothing.

alcoholic *(SYN.)* sot, drunkard, tippler, inebriate.

alert *(SYN.)* attentive, keen, clear-witted, ready, nimble, vigilant, watchful, observant.
(ANT.) logy, sluggish, dulled, list-less.

alias *(SYN.)* anonym, assumed name.

alibi *(SYN.)* story, excuse.

alien *(SYN.)* adverse, foreigner, strange, remote, stranger, different, extraneous.
(ANT.) germane, kindred, relevant, akin, familiar, accustomed.

alight *(SYN.)* debark, deplane, detrain, disembark.
(ANT.) embark, board.

alive *(SYN.)* existing, breathing, living, live, lively, vivacious, animated.
(ANT.) inactive, dead, moribund.

allay *(SYN.)* soothe, check, lessen, calm, lighten, relieve, soften, moderate, quite.
(ANT.) excite, intensify, worsen, arouse.

allege *(SYN.)* affirm, cite, claim, declare, maintain, state, assert.
(ANT.) deny, disprove, refute, contradict, gainsay.

allegiance *(SYN.)* faithfulness, duty, devotion, loyalty, fidelity, obligation.
(ANT.) treachery, disloyalty.

allegory *(SYN.)* fable, fiction, myth, saga, parable, legend.
(ANT.) history, fact.

alleviate *(SYN.)* diminish, soothe, solace, abate, assuage, allay, soften, mitigate, extenuate, relieve, let up, ease, slacken, relax, weaken.
(ANT.) increase, aggravate, augment, irritate.

alley *(SYN.)* footway, byway, path, passageway, aisle, corridor, opening, lane.

alliance *(SYN.)* combination, partnership, union, treaty, coalition, association, confederacy, marriage, pact, agreement, relation, interrelation, understanding, relationship.
(ANT.) separation, divorce, schism.

allot *(SYN.)* divide, mete, assign, give, measure, distribute, allocate, share, grant, dispense, deal, apportion.
(ANT.) withhold, retain, keep, confiscate, refuse.

allow *(SYN.)* authorize, grant, acknowledge, admit, let, permit, sanction, consent, concede, mete, allocate.
(ANT.) protest, resist, refuse, forbid, object, prohibit.

allowance *(SYN.)* grant, fee, portion, ration, allotment.

allude *(SYN.)* intimate, refer, insinuate, hint, advert, suggest, imply, mention.
(ANT.) demonstrate, specify, state, declare.

allure *(SYN.)* attract, fascinate, tempt, charm, infatuate, captivate.

ally *(SYN.)* accomplice, associate, confederate, abettor, assistant, friend, partner.
(ANT.) rival, enemy, opponent, foe, adversary.

almighty *(SYN.)* omnipotent, powerful.

almost *(SYN.)* somewhat, nearly.
(ANT.) completely, absolutely.

alms *(SYN.)* dole, charity, donation, contribution.

aloft *(SYN.)* overhead.

alone *(SYN.)* desolate, unaided, only, isolated, unaided, lone, secluded, lonely, deserted, solitary, single, apart, solo, separate.
(ANT.) surrounded, attended, accompanied, together.

aloof *(SYN.)* uninterested, uninvolved, apart, away, remote, unsociable, standoffish, separate, disdainful, distant.
(ANT.) warm, outgoing, friendly, cordial.

also *(SYN.)* in addition, likewise, too, besides, furthermore, moreover, further.

alter *(SYN.)* adjust, vary, deviate, modify, reserved, change.
(ANT.) maintain, preserve, keep.

alteration *(SYN.)* difference, adjustment, change, modification.
(ANT.) maintenance, preservation.

altercation *(SYN.)* controversy, dispute, argument, quarrel.

alternate *(SYN.)* rotate, switch, spell, interchange.
(ANT.) fix.

alternative *(SYN.)* substitute, selection, option, choice, replacement, possibility.

although *(SYN.)* though, even if, even though, despite, notwithstanding.

altitude *(SYN.)* elevation, height.
(ANT.) depth.

altogether *(SYN.)* totally, wholly, quite, entirely, thoroughly, completely.
(ANT.) partly.

altruism *(SYN.)* kindness, tenderness, generosity, charity, benevolence, liberality.
(ANT.) selfishness, unkindness, cruelty, inhumanity.

always *(SYN.)* evermore, forever, per-

petually, ever, unceasingly, continually, constantly, eternally, everlastingly.
(ANT.) never, rarely, sometimes, occasionally.

amalgamate *(SYN.)* fuse, unify, unite, commingle, merge, blend, combine, consolidate.
(ANT.) decompose, disintegrate, separate.

amass *(SYN.)* collect, accumulate, heap up, gather, increase, compile, assemble, store up.
(ANT.) disperse, dissipate, spend.

amateur *(SYN.)* beginner, dilettante, learner, dabbler, neophyte, apprentice, novice, nonprofessional, tyro.
(ANT.) expert, master, adept, professional, authority.

amaze *(SYN.)* surprise, flabbergast, stun, dumb-found, astound, bewilder, aghast, thunderstruck, astonish.
(ANT.) bore, disinterest, tire.

ambiguous *(SYN.)* uncertain, vague, obscure, dubious, equivocal, unclear, deceptive.
(ANT.) plain, clear, explicit, obvious, unequivocal, unmistakable, certain.

ambition *(SYN.)* eagerness, goal, incentive, aspiration, yearning, longing, desire.
(ANT.) indifference, satisfaction, indolence, resignation.

ambitious *(SYN.)* aspiring, intent upon.
(ANT.) indifferent.

amble *(SYN.)* saunter, stroll.

ambush *(SYN.)* trap, hiding place.

amend *(SYN.)* change, mend, better, correct, improve.
(ANT.) worsen.

amends *(SYN.)* compensation, restitution, payment, reparation, remedy, redress.

amiable *(SYN.)* friendly, good-natured, gracious, pleasing, agreeable, outgoing, kindhearted, kind, pleasant.
(ANT.) surly, hateful, churlish, disagreeable, ill-natured, ill-tempered, cross, captious, touchy.

amid *(SYN.)* among, amidst, surrounded by.

amiss *(SYN.)* wrongly, improperly, astray, awry.
(ANT.) properly, rightly, right, correctly, correct.

ammunition *(SYN.)* shot, powder, shells, bullets.

among *(SYN.)* between, mingled, mixed amidst, amid, betwixt, surrounded by.
(ANT.) separate, apart.

amorous *(SYN.)* amatory, affectionate, loving.

amount *(SYN.)* sum, total, quantity, number, price, value, measure.

ample *(SYN.)* broad, large, profuse, spacious, copious, liberal, plentiful, full, bountiful, abundant, great, extensive, generous, wide, enough, sufficient, roomy.
(ANT.) limited, insufficient, meager, small, lacking, cramped, confined, inadequate.

amplification *(SYN.)* magnification, growth, waxing, accrual, enhancement, enlargement, heightening, increase.
(ANT.) decrease, diminishing, reduction, contraction.

amplify *(SYN.)* broaden, develop, expand, enlarge, extend.
(ANT.) confine, restrict, abridge, narrow.

amuse *(SYN.)* divert, please, delight, entertain, charm.
(ANT.) tire, bore.

amusement *(SYN.)* diversion, pastime, entertainment, pleasure, enjoyment, recreation.
(ANT.) tedium, boredom.

amusing *(SYN.)* pleasant, funny, pleasing, entertaining, comical.
(ANT.) tiring, tedious, boring.

analogous *(SYN.)* comparable, corresponding, like, similar, correspondent, alike, correlative, parallel, allied, akin.
(ANT.) different, opposed, incongruous, divergent.

analysis *(SYN.)* separation, investigation, examination.

analyze *(SYN.)* explain, investigate, examine, separate.

ancestral *(SYN.)* hereditary, inherited.

ancestry *(SYN.)* family, line, descent, lineage.
(ANT.) posterity.

anchor *(SYN.)* fix, attach, secure, fasten.
(ANT.) detach, free, loosen.

ancient *(SYN.)* aged, old-fashioned, archaic, elderly, antique, old, primitive.
(ANT.) new, recent, current, fresh.

anecdote *(SYN.)* account, narrative, story, tale.

anesthetic *(SYN.)* opiate, narcotic, sedative, painkiller, analgesic.

angel *(SYN.)* cherub, archangel, seraph.

(ANT.) demon, devil.
angelic *(SYN.)* pure, lovely, heavenly, good, virtuous, innocent, godly, saintly. *(ANT.) devilish.*
anger *(SYN.)* exasperation, fury, ire, passion, rage, resentment, temper, indignation, animosity, irritation, wrath, displeasure, infuriate, arouse, nettle, annoyance, exasperate. *(ANT.) forbearance, patience, peace, self-control.*
angry *(SYN.)* provoked, wrathful, furious, enraged, incensed, exasperated, maddened, indignant, irate, mad, inflamed. *(ANT.) happy, pleased, calm, satisfied, content, tranquil.*
anguish *(SYN.)* suffering, torment, torture, distress, pain, heartache, grief, agony, misery. *(ANT.) solace, relief, joy, comfort, peace, ecstasy, pleasure.*
animal *(SYN.)* beast, creature.
animate *(SYN.)* vitalize, invigorate, stimulate, enliven, alive, vital, vigorous. *(ANT.) dead, inanimate.*
animated *(SYN.)* gay, lively, spry, vivacious, active, vigorous, chipper, snappy. *(ANT.) inactive.*
animosity *(SYN.)* grudge, hatred, rancor, spite, bitterness, enmity, opposition, dislike, hostility, antipathy. *(ANT.) good will, love, friendliness, kindliness.*
annex *(SYN.)* join, attach, add, addition, wing, append.
annihilate *(SYN.)* destroy, demolish, end, wreck, abolish.
announce *(SYN.)* proclaim, give out, make known, notify, publish, report, herald, promulgate, advertise, broadcast, state, tell, declare, publicize. *(ANT.) conceal, withhold, suppress, bury, stifle.*
announcement *(SYN.)* notification, report, declaration, bulletin, advertisement, broadcast, promulgation, notice, message. *(ANT.) silence, hush, muteness, speechlessness.*
annoy *(SYN.)* bother, irk, pester, tease, trouble, vex, disturb, inconvenience, molest, irritate, harry, harass. *(ANT.) console, gratify, soothe, accommodate, please, calm, comfort.*
annually *(SYN.)* once a year.
anoint *(SYN.)* grease, oil.

answer *(SYN.)* reply, rejoinder, response, retort, rebuttal, respond. *(ANT.) summoning, argument, questioning, inquiry, query, ask, inquire.*
antagonism *(SYN.)* opposition, conflict, enmity, hostility, animosity. *(ANT.) geniality, cordiality, friendliness.*
antagonist *(SYN.)* adversary, rival, enemy, foe, opponent. *(ANT.) ally, friend.*
antagonize *(SYN.)* against, provoke, counter, oppose, embitter. *(ANT.) soothe.*
anthology *(SYN.)* garland, treasury, collection.
anticipate *(SYN.)* await, foresee, forecast, hope for, expect.
anticipated *(SYN.)* expected, foresight, hoped, preconceived. *(ANT.) dreaded, reared, worried, doubted.*
antics *(SYN.)* horseplay, fun, merrymaking, pranks, capers, tricks, clowning.
antipathy *(SYN.)* hatred.
antiquated *(SYN.)* old, out-of-date, outdated, old-fashion.
antique *(SYN.)* rarity, curio, old, ancient, old-fashioned, archaic, out-of-date. *(ANT.) new, recent, fresh.*
anxiety *(SYN.)* care, disquiet, fear, concern, solicitude, trouble, worry, apprehension, uneasiness, distress, foreboding. *(ANT.) nonchalance, assurance, confidence, contentment, peacefulness, placidity, tranquillity.*
anxious *(SYN.)* troubled, uneasy, perturbed, apprehensive, worried, concerned, desirous, bothered, agitated, eager, fearful. *(ANT.) tranquil, calm, peaceful.*
anyway *(SYN.)* nevertheless, anyhow.
apartment *(SYN.)* suite, flat, dormitory.
apathy *(SYN.)* unconcern, indifference, lethargy. *(ANT.) interest, feeling.*
aperture *(SYN.)* gap, pore, opening, cavity, chasm, abyss, hole, void. *(ANT.) connection, bridge, link.*
apex *(SYN.)* acme, tip, summit, crown, top.
apologize *(SYN.)* ask forgiveness.
apology *(SYN.)* defense, excuse, confession, justification, alibi, explanation, plea. *(ANT.) denial, complaint, dissimulation,*

accusation.

apostate *(SYN.)* nonconformist, unbeliever, dissenter, heretic, schismatic.
(ANT.) saint, conformist, believer.

appall *(SYN.)* shock, stun, dismay, frighten, terrify, horrify.
(ANT.) edify, please.

appalling *(SYN.)* fearful, frightful, ghastly, horrid, repulsive, terrible, dire, awful.
(ANT.) fascinating, beautiful, enchanting, enjoyable.

apparatus *(SYN.)* rig, equipment, furnishings, gear, tackle.

apparel *(SYN.)* clothes, attire, garb, clothing, garments, dress, robes.

apparent *(SYN.)* obvious, plain, self-evident, clear, manifest, transparent, unmistakable, palpable, unambiguous, ostensible, illusory, visible, seeming, evident, understandable.
(ANT.) uncertain, indistinct, dubious, hidden, mysterious.

apparition *(SYN.)* illusion, ghost, phantom, vision, fantasy, dream.

appeal *(SYN.)* plea, petition, request, entreaty, request, plead, petition, beseech, beg, entreat, attract.
(ANT.) repulse, repel.

appear *(SYN.)* look, arrive, emanate, emerge, arise, seem, turn up.
(ANT.) vanish, withdraw, exist, disappear, evaporate.

appearance *(SYN.)* advent, arrival, aspect, demeanor, fashion, guise, apparition, manner, mien, look, presence.
(ANT.) disappearance, reality, departure, vanishing.

appease *(SYN.)* calm, compose, lull, quiet, relieve, assuage, pacify, satisfy, restraint, lesson, soothe, check, ease, alleviate, still, allay, tranquilize.
(ANT.) excite, arouse, incense, irritate, inflame.

append *(SYN.)* supplement, attach, add.

appendage *(SYN.)* addition, tail, supplement.

appetite *(SYN.)* zest, craving, desire, liking, longing, stomach, inclination, hunger, thirst, relish, passion.
(ANT.) satiety, disgust, distaste, repugnance.

appetizer *(SYN.)* hors d'oeuvre.

applaud *(SYN.)* cheer, clap, hail, approve, praise, acclaim.
(ANT.) disapprove, denounce, reject,

criticize, condemn.

appliance *(SYN.)* machine, tool, instrument, device, utensil, implement.

applicable *(SYN.)* fitting, suitable, proper, fit, usable, appropriate, suited.
(ANT.) inappropriate, inapplicable.

apply *(SYN.)* affix, allot, appropriate, use, employ, petition, request, devote, avail, pertain, attach, ask, administer, petition, assign, relate, utilize.
(ANT.) give away, demand, detach, neglect, ignore.

appoint *(SYN.)* name, choose, nominate, designate, elect, establish, assign, place.
(ANT.) discharge, fire, dismiss.

appointment *(SYN.)* rendezvous, meeting, designation, position, engagement, assignment.
(ANT.) discharge, dismissal.

appraise *(SYN.)* value, evaluate, place a value on.

appreciate *(SYN.)* enjoy, regard, value, prize, cherish, admire, go up, improve, rise, respect, think highly of, esteem, appraise.
(ANT.) belittle, misunderstand, apprehend, degrade, scorn, depreciate, undervalue.

apprehend *(SYN.)* seize, capture, arrest, understand, dread, fear, grasp, perceive.
(ANT.) release, lose.

apprehension *(SYN.)* fear, misgiving, dread, uneasiness, worry, fearfulness, anticipation, capture, seizure.
(ANT.) confidence, composure, self-assuredness.

apprehensive *(SYN.)* worried, afraid, uneasy, bothered, anxious, concerned, perturbed, troubled, fearful.
(ANT.) relaxed.

apprentice *(SYN.)* amateur, recruit, novice, learner, beginner.
(ANT.) experienced, professional, master.

approach *(SYN.)* greet, inlet, come near, advance, access, passageway.
(ANT.) avoid, pass by, retreat.

appropriate *(SYN.)* apt, particular, proper, fitting, suitable, applicable, loot, pillage, purloin, rob, steal, embezzle, assign, becoming, apportion, authorize.
(ANT.) improper, contrary, inappropriate, buy, repay, restore, return, unfit, inapt.

approval *(SYN.)* commendation, consent, praise, approbation, sanction, assent, endorsement, support.

(ANT.) reproach, censure, reprimand, disapprove.

approve *(SYN.)* like, praise, authorize, confirm, endorse, appreciate, think well of, ratify, commend, sanction.

(ANT.) criticize, nullify, disparage, frown on, disapprove, deny.

approximate *(SYN.)* near, approach, roughly, close.

(ANT.) correct.

apt *(SYN.)* suitable, proper, appropriate, fit, suited, disposed, liable, inclined, prone, clever, bright, alert, intelligent, receptive.

(ANT.) ill-becoming, unsuitable, unlikely, slow, retarded, dense.

aptness *(SYN.)* capability, dexterity, power, qualification, skill, ability, aptitude.

(ANT.) incompetency, unreadiness, incapacity.

aptitude *(SYN.)* knack, talent, gift, ability.

aqueduct *(SYN.)* gully, pipe, canal, waterway, channel.

arbitrary *(SYN.)* unrestricted, absolute, despotic, willful, unreasonable, unconditional, author-itative.

(ANT.) contingent, qualified, fair, reasonable, dependent, accountable.

arbitrate *(SYN.)* referee, settle, mediate, umpire, negotiate.

architecture *(SYN.)* structure, building, construction.

ardent *(SYN.)* fervent, fiery, glowing, intense, keen, impassioned, fervid, hot, passionate, earnest, eager, zealous, enthusiastic.

(ANT.) cool, indifferent, nonchalant, apathetic.

ardor *(SYN.)* enthusiasm, rapture, spirit, zeal, fervent, eager, glowing, eagerness.

(ANT.) unconcern, apathy, disinterest, indifference.

arduous *(SYN.)* laborious, hard, difficult, burdensome, strenuous, strained.

(ANT.) easy.

area *(SYN.)* space, extent, region, zone, section, expanse, district, neighborhood, size.

argue *(SYN.)* plead, reason, wrangle, indicate, prove, show, dispute, denote, imply, object, bicker, discuss, debate, disagree.

(ANT.) reject, spurn, ignore, overlook, agree, concur.

argument *(SYN.)* debate, dispute, discussion, controversy.

(ANT.) harmony, accord, agreement.

arid *(SYN.)* waterless, dry, flat, dull, unimaginative, stuffy.

(ANT.) fertile, wet, colorful.

arise *(SYN.)* enter, institute, originate, start, open, commence, emerge, appear.

(ANT.) terminate, end, finish, complete, close.

aristocrat *(SYN.)* noble, gentleman, peer, lord, nobleman.

(ANT.) peasant, commoner.

arm *(SYN.)* weapon, defend, equip, empower, fortify.

armistice *(SYN.)* truce, pact, deal, understanding, peace, treaty, contract, alliance, agreement.

army *(SYN.)* troops, legion, military, forces, militia.

aroma *(SYN.)* smell, odor, fragrance, perfume, scent.

arouse *(SYN.)* stir, animate, move, pique, provoke, kindle, disturb, excite, foment, stimulate, awaken.

(ANT.) settle, soothe, calm.

arraign *(SYN.)* charge, censure, incriminate, indict, accuse.

(ANT.) acquit, release, vindicate, exonerate, absolve.

arraignment *(SYN.)* imputation, charge, accusation, incrimination.

(ANT.) pardon, exoneration, exculpation.

arrange *(SYN.)* classify, assort, organize, place, plan, prepare, devise, adjust, dispose, regulate, order, group, settle, adapt, catalog, systematize, distribute, prepare.

(ANT.) jumble, scatter, disorder, confuse, disturb, disarrange.

arrangement *(SYN.)* display, grouping, order, array.

array *(SYN.)* dress, adorn, attire, clothe, arrange, order, distribute, arrangement, display, exhibit.

(ANT.) disorder, disorganization, disarray.

arrest *(SYN.)* detain, hinder, restrain, seize, withhold, stop, check, obstruct, apprehend, interrupt, catch, capture.

(ANT.) free, release, discharge, liberate.

arrival *(SYN.)* advent, coming.

(ANT.) leaving, departure.

arrive *(SYN.)* come, emerge, reach, visit, land, appear.

(ANT.) exit, leave, depart, go.

arrogance (SYN.) pride, insolence.
(ANT.) humbleness, modesty, humility.

arrogant (SYN.) insolent, prideful, scornful, haughty, cavalier, proud.
(ANT.) modest, humble.

art (SYN.) cunning, tact, artifice, skill, aptitude, adroitness, painting, drawing, design, craft, dexterity, composition, ingenuity.
(ANT.) clumsiness, innocence, unskillfulness, honesty.

artery (SYN.) aqueduct, pipe, channel.

artful (SYN.) clever, sly, skillful, knowing, deceitful, tricky, crafty, cunning.
(ANT.) artless.

article (SYN.) story, composition, treatise, essay, thing, report, object.

artifice (SYN.) trick, clever, scheme, device.

artificial (SYN.) bogus, fake, affected, feigned, phony, sham, unreal, synthetic, assumed, counterfeit, unnatural, man-made, unreal, manufactured, false, feigned, pretended.
(ANT.) genuine, natural true, real, authentic.

artisan (SYN.) worker, craftsman, mechanic.

artist (SYN.) actor, actress, painter, sculptor, singer, designer.

artless (SYN.) innocent, open, frank, simple, honest, candid, natural, unskilled, ignorant, truthful, sincere.
(ANT.) artful.

ascend (SYN.) rise, scale, tower, mount, go up, climb.
(ANT.) fall, sink, descend, go down.

ascertain (SYN.) solve, learn, clear up, answer.

ascribe (SYN.) attribute, assign.

ashamed (SYN.) shamefaced, humiliated, abashed, mortified, embarrassed.
(ANT.) proud.

ask (SYN.) invite, request, inquire, query, question, beg, solicit, demand, entreat, claim, interrogate, charge, expect.
(ANT.) order, reply, insist, answer.

askance (SYN.) side-ways.

askew (SYN.) disorderly, crooked, awry, twisted.
(ANT.) straight.

asleep (SYN.) inactive, sleeping, dormant.
(ANT.) alert, awake.

aspect (SYN.) appearance, look, view, outlook, attitude, viewpoint, phase, part, feature, side.

aspersion (SYN.) dishonor, insult, misuse, outrage, reproach, defamation, abuse, disparagement.
(ANT.) plaudit, respect, commendation, approval.

asphyxiate (SYN.) suffocate, stifle, smother, choke, strangle, throttle.

aspiration (SYN.) craving, desire, hope, longing, objective, passion, ambition.

aspire (SYN.) seek, aim, wish for, strive, desire, yearn for.

ass (SYN.) mule, donkey, burro, silly, dunce, stubborn, stupid, fool.

assail (SYN.) assault, attack.

assassinate (SYN.) purge, kill, murder.

assault (SYN.) invade, strike, attack, assail, charge, bombard, onslaught.
(ANT.) protect, defend.

assemble (SYN.) collect, gather, meet, congregate, connect, manufacture.
(ANT.) disperse, disassemble, scatter.

assembly (SYN.) legislature, congress, council, parliament.

assent (SYN.) consent to, concede, agree, approval, accept, comply, permission.
(ANT.) deny, dissent, refusal, denial, refuse.

assert (SYN.) declare, maintain, state, claim, express, defend, press, support, aver, uphold, consent, accept, comply, affirm, allege, emphasize.
(ANT.) deny, refute, contradict, decline.

assertion (SYN.) statement, affirmation, declaration.
(ANT.) contradiction, denial.

assess (SYN.) calculate, compute, estimate, levy, reckon, tax, appraise.

asset (SYN.) property, wealth, capitol, resourses, goods.

assign (SYN.) apportion, ascribe, attribute, cast, allot, choose, appropriate, name, elect, appoint, distribute, designate, specify.
(ANT.) release, relieve, unburden, discharge.

assignment (SYN.) task, job, responsibility, duty.

assimilate (SYN.) digest, absorb, blot up.

assist (SYN.) help, promote, serve, support, sustain, abet, aid, back.
(ANT.) prevent, impede, hinder, hamper.

assistance (SYN.) backing, help, patronage, relief, succor, support.
(ANT.) hostility, resistance, antagonism, counteraction.

assistant *(SYN.)* accomplice, ally, associate, confederate, abettor.
(ANT.) rival, enemy, adversary.

associate *(SYN.)* affiliate, ally, join, connect, unite, combine, link, mingle, partner, mix.
(ANT.) separate, disconnect, divide, disrupt, estrange.

association *(SYN.)* organization, club, union, society, fraternity, sorority, companionship, fellowship.

assorted *(SYN.)* varied, miscellaneous, classified, different, several, grouped, various.
(ANT.) alike, same.

assortment *(SYN.)* collection, variety, mixture, conglomeration.

assuage *(SYN.)* calm, quiet, lessen, relieve, ease, allay, moderate, alleviate, restrain.

assume *(SYN.)* arrogate, affect, suspect, believe, appropriate, take, pretend, usurp, simulate, understand, postulate, presume, suppose.
(ANT.) doff, demonstrate, prove, grant, concede.

assumption *(SYN.)* presumption, guess, theory, supposition, conjecture, postulate.

assurance *(SYN.)* confidence, conviction, self-reliance, surety, firmness, courage, promise, pledge, certainty, assertion, security, word, assuredness.
(ANT.) humility, shyness, suspicion, modesty.

assure *(SYN.)* promise, convince, warrant, guarantee, pledge.
(ANT.) equivocate, deny.

astonish *(SYN.)* astound, amaze, surprise, shock.
(ANT.) tire, bore.

astound *(SYN.)* shock, amaze, astonish, stun, surprise, floor.

asunder *(SYN.)* divided, separate, apart.
(ANT.) together.

asylum *(SYN.)* shelter, refuge, home, madhouse, institution.

athletic *(SYN.)* strong, active, able-bodied, gymnastic, muscular, well-built.

atone *(SYN.)* repay, make up.

atrocious *(SYN.)* horrible, savage, brutal, ruthless, dreadful, awful, horrifying, horrid, unspeakable, ghastly.
(ANT.) good, kind.

attach *(SYN.)* connect, adjoin, annex, join, append, stick, unite, adjoin, affix.

(ANT.) unfasten, untie, detach, separate, disengage.

attachment *(SYN.)* friendship, liking, regard, adherence, affection, devotion.
(ANT.) estrangement, opposition, alienation, aversion.

attack *(SYN.)* raid, assault, besiege, abuse, censure, offense, seige, onslaught, denunciation, aggression, bombardment, push, criticism, invade.
(ANT.) surrender, defense, opposition, aid, defend, protect, repel.

attain *(SYN.)* achieve, acquire, accomplish, gain, get, reach, win, complete, finish, secure, procure, arrive, fulfill, obtain, effect.
(ANT.) relinquish, discard, abandon, desert.

attainment *(SYN.)* exploit, feat, accomplishment, realization, performance.
(ANT.) omission, defeat, failure, neglect.

attempt *(SYN.)* essay, experiment, trial, try, undertaking, endeavor, effort.
(ANT.) laziness, neglect, inaction.

attend *(SYN.)* accompany, escort, watch, be serve, care for, follow, lackey, present, frequent, protect, guard.
(ANT.) desert, abandon, avoid.

attendant *(SYN.)* waiter, servant, valet.

attention *(SYN.)* consideration, heed, circumspection, notice, watchfulness, observance, application, reflection, study, care, alertness, mindfulness.
(ANT.) negligence, indifference, omission, oversight, disregard.

attentive *(SYN.)* careful, awake, alive, considerate, heedful, mindful, wary, assiduous, diligent, aware, alert.
(ANT.) indifferent, unaware, oblivious, apathetic.

attest *(SYN.)* testify, swear, vouch, certify.

attire *(SYN.)* apparel, dress, clothe.

attitude *(SYN.)* standpoint, viewpoint, stand, pose, aspect, position, posture, disposition, opinion.

attorney *(SYN.)* lawyer.

attract *(SYN.)* enchant, interest, pull, fascinate, draw, tempt, infatuate, entice, lure, charm, captivate, allure.
(ANT.) deter, repel, repulse, alienate.

attractive *(SYN.)* enchanting, winning, engaging, pleasant, pleasing, seductive, magnetic, charming, inviting, alluring.
(ANT.) unattractive, obnoxious, repellent, repulsive, forbidding.

attribute *(SYN.)* give, apply, place, trait, characteristic, feature, nature, credit, quality, assign, ascribe.

audacious *(SYN.)* daring, bold, arrogant, foolhardy, cavalier, haughty, insolent. *(ANT.) humble, shy.*

audacity *(SYN.)* effrontery, fearlessness, temerity, boldness. *(ANT.) humility, meekness, circumspection, fearfulness.*

audible *(SYN.)* distinct, bearable, plain, clear. *(ANT.) inaudible.*

augment *(SYN.)* enlarge, increase, raise, expand, broaden, extend.

auspicious *(SYN.)* lucky, timely, favorable, promising, fortunate. *(ANT.) untimely, unfortunate.*

austere *(SYN.)* stern, severe, harsh, strict. *(ANT.) lenient, soft.*

authentic *(SYN.)* real, true, genuine, pure, accurate, reliable, legitimate, factual, actual, correct, verifiable, authoritative, trustworthy. *(ANT.) false, spurious, artificial, counterfeit, erroneous.*

authenticate *(SYN.)* validate, warrant, guarantee, verify, certify.

author *(SYN.)* father, inventor, maker, originator, writer, composer.

authoritative *(SYN.)* certain, secure, commanding, sure, tried, trustworthy, safe, influential, dependable. *(ANT.) uncertain, unreliable, dubious, fallible, questionable.*

authority *(SYN.)* dominion, justification, power, permission, authorization, importance, domination, supremacy. *(ANT.) incapacity, denial, prohibition, weakness, impotence.*

authorize *(SYN.)* permit, sanction, legalize, assign, enable, approve, empower. *(ANT.) forbid, prohibit.*

autocrat *(SYN.)* monarch, ruler, tyrant, dictator.

autograph *(SYN.)* endorse, sign, approve.

automatic *(SYN.)* self-acting, mechanical, spontaneous, uncontrolled, involuntary, self-working, self-moving. *(ANT.) hand-operated, intentional, deliberate, manual.*

automobile *(SYN.)* auto, car.

auxiliary *(SYN.)* assisting, helping, aiding.

avail *(SYN.)* help, profit, use, value, benefit, serve, advantage.

available *(SYN.)* obtainable, convenient, ready, handy, accessible, prepared. *(ANT.) unavailable, out of reach, inaccessible, unobtainable.*

avarice *(SYN.)* lust, greed.

average *(SYN.* moderate, ordinary, usual, passable, fair, intermediate, medium, median, mediocre, mean, middling. *(ANT.) outstanding, exceptional, extraordinary, unusual.*

averse *(SYN.)* unwilling, opposed, forced, against, involuntary. *(ANT.) willing.*

aversion *(SYN.)* disgust, dislike, distaste, hatred, loathing, abhorrence, antipathy. *(ANT.) devotion, enthusiasm, affection, love.*

avert *(SYN.)* avoid, prevent, prohibit. *(ANT.) invite.*

avid *(SYN.)* greedy, eager.

avocation *(SYN.)* side-line, hobby.

avoid *(SYN.)* elude, forestall, evade, escape, dodge, avert, forbear, eschew, free, shun. *(ANT.) oppose, meet, confront, encounter, seek.*

award *(SYN.)* reward, prize, medal, gift, trophy.

aware *(SYN.)* mindful, perceptive, informed, apprised, realizing, conscious, observant, knowing, cognizant. *(ANT.) unaware, insensible, ignorant, oblivious.*

away *(SYN.)* absent, departed, distracted, gone, not at home. *(ANT.) present, attentive, at home, attending.*

awe *(SYN.)* surprise, respect, dread, astonishment, alarm.

awful *(SYN.)* frightful, horrible, awe-inspiring, dire, terrible, unpleasant, imposing, solemn, appalling, cruel, wicked, brutal, savage, dreadful. *(ANT.) humble, lowly, pleasant, nice, commonplace.*

awkward *(SYN.)* inept, unpolished, clumsy, gauche, rough, ungraceful, ungainly, cumbersome. *(ANT.) adroit, graceful, polished, skillful.*

awry *(SYN.)* askew, wrong, twisted, crooked, disorderly. *(ANT.) straight, right.*

axiom *(SYN.)* fundamental, maxim, principle, theorem, adage, apothegm, byword, aphorism.

babble *(SYN.)* twaddle, nonsense, gibberish, prattle, balderdash, rubbish, chatter, baby talk, poppycock, jabber, maunder, piffle.

baby *(SYN.)* newborn, infant, neonate, babe, teeny, small, wee, little, undersized, midget, papoose, protect, cosset, pamper.

babyish *(SYN.)* infantile, childish, baby, whiny, unreasonable, immature, puerile, foolish, dependent.
(ANT.) mature, adult, sensible, reasonable, grown-up.

back *(SYN.)* help, assist, endorse, support, second, ratify, approve, stand by, approve, posterior, rear.
(ANT.) anterior, front, face, undercut, veto, undermine, progress, flow, leading, close, accessible, near.

backbiting *(SYN.)* gossip, slander, abuse, malice, cattiness, aspersion, derogation, belittling, badmouthing.
(ANT.) compliments, praise, loyalty, friendliness, approval.

backbone *(SYN.)* vertebrae, spine, pillar, support, staff, mainstay, basis, courage, determination, toughness, character.
(ANT.) timidity, weakness, cowardice, spinelessness.

backbreaking *(SYN.)* exhausting, fatiguing, tough, tiring, demanding, wearying, wearing, difficult.
(ANT.) light, relaxing, undemanding, slight.

back down *(SYN.)* accede, concede, acquiesce, yield, withdraw, renege.
(ANT.) persevere, insist.

backer *(SYN.)* underwriter, benefactor, investor, patron, sponsor, supporter.

backfire *(SYN.)* flop, boomerang, fail, founder, disappoint.
(ANT.) succeed.

background *(SYN.)* training, training, practice, knowledge, experience.

backing *(SYN.)* help, support, funds, money, assistance, grant, advocacy, subsidy, sympathy, endorsement.
(ANT.) criticism, detraction, faultfinding.

backlog *(SYN.)* inventory, reserve, hoard, amassment, accumulation.

backslide *(SYN.)* relapse, revert, return, weaken, regress, renege.

backward *(SYN.)* dull, sluggish, stupid, loath, regressive, rearward, underdeveloped, slow, retarded.

(ANT.) progressive, precocious, civilized, advanced, forward.

bad *(SYN.)* unfavorable, wrong, evil, immoral, sinful, faulty, improper, unwholesome, wicked, corrupt, tainted, harmful, injurious, defective, poor, imperfect, inferior, substandard, contaminated, inappropriate, unsuited, rotten, unsuitable, sorry, upset, sick, suffering, unpleasant, disagreeable.
(ANT.) good, honorable, reputable, moral, excellent.

badger *(SYN.)* tease, question, annoy, pester, bother, taunt, bait, provoke, torment, harass, hector.

baffle *(SYN.)* confound bewilder, perplex, puzzle, mystify, confuse, frustrate, bewilder.
(ANT.) inform, enlighten.

bag *(SYN.)* catch, snare, poke, sack.

bait *(SYN.)* enticement, captivate, ensnare, tease, torment, pester, worry, entrap, question, entice, lure, trap, harass, tempt, badger.

balance *(SYN.)* poise, stability, composure, remains, residue, equilibrium, compare, weigh, equalize.
(ANT.) unsteadiness, instability.

bald *(SYN.)* bare, hairless, nude, open, uncovered, simple.
(ANT.) covered, hairy.

baleful *(SYN.)* evil immoral sinful, destructive, detrimental, noxious, wicked, bad, villainous, injurious.
(ANT.) good, moral, reputable, excellent, harmless.

balk *(SYN.)* unwilling, obstinate, stubborn, hesitate, check, stop.
(ANT.) willing.

ball *(SYN.)* cotillion, dance, globe, sphere, spheroid.

ballad *(SYN.)* poem, song, ditty.

balloon *(SYN.)* puff up, enlarge, swell.
(ANT.) shrivel, shrink.

ballot *(SYN.)* choice, vote, poll.

balmy *(SYN.)* soft, gentle, soothing, fragrant, mild.
(ANT.) tempestuous, stormy.

ban *(SYN.)* prohibit, outlaw, disallow, block, bar, exclude, obstruct, prohibition, taboo, forbid.
(ANT.) allow, permit.

banal *(SYN.)* hackneyed, corny, vapid, trite, overused, humdrum.
(ANT.) striking, original, fresh, stimulating, novel.

band *(SYN.)* company, association, crew, group, society, belt, strip, unite, gang.

bandit *(SYN.)* thief, robber, highwayman, outlaw, marauder.

bang *(SYN.)* hit, strike, slam.

banish *(SYN.)* drive away, eject, exile, oust, deport, dismiss, expel.
(ANT.) receive, accept, shelter, admit, harbor, embrace, welcome.

bank *(SYN.)* barrier, slope, storage, treasury, row, series, string, shore.

banner *(SYN.)* colors, standard, pennant, flag.

banquet *(SYN.)* feast, celebration, festival, dinner, regalement, affair.

banter *(SYN.)* joke, tease, jest.

bar *(SYN.)* counter, impediment, saloon, exclude, obstacle, barricade, obstruct, shut out, hindrance, forbid, block, barrier, obstruction.
(ANT.) allow, permit, aid, encouragement.

barbarian *(SYN.)* brute, savage, boor, ruffian, rude, uncivilized, primitive, uncultured, coarse, cruel, barbaric, crude.
(ANT.) permit, allow, encouragement.

barbarous *(SYN.)* savage, remorseless, cruel, uncivilized, rude, unrelenting, merciless, crude, ruthless, inhuman.
(ANT.) kind, civilized, polite, humane, refined, tasteful, cultivated.

barber *(SYN.)* coiffeur, hairdresser.

bare *(SYN.)* naked, nude, uncovered, undressed, unclothed, unfurnished, plain, barren, empty, disclose, reveal, publicize, bald, expose, scarce, mere.
(ANT.) dressed, garbed, conceal, covered, hide, disguise, clothed.

barefaced *(SYN.)* impudent, bold, insolent, brazen, shameless, audacious, impertinent, rude.

barely *(SYN.)* hardly, scarcely, just.

bargain *(SYN.)* agreement, arrangement, deal, contract, arrange, sale.

baroque *(SYN.)* ornamented, elaborate, embellished, ornate.

barren *(SYN.)* unproductive, bare, unfruitful, infertile, sterile, childless.
(ANT.) productive, fruitful, fertile.

barricade *(SYN.)* fence, obstruction, shut in, fortification, barrier.
(ANT.) free, open, release.

barrier *(SYN.)* fence, wall, bar, railing, obstacle, hindrance, fortification, restraint, impediment, limit, barricade.
(ANT.) assistance, aid, encouragement.

barter *(SYN.)* exchange, deal, trade.

base *(SYN.)* bottom, rest, foundation, establish, found, immoral, evil, bad, wicked, depraved, selfish, worthless, cheap, debased, poor, support, stand, low, abject, menial.
(ANT.) exalted, righteous, lofty, esteemed, noble, honored, refined, valuable.

bashful *(SYN.)* timorous, abashed, shy, coy, timid, diffident, modest, sheepish, embarrassed, shame-faced, humble, recoiling, uneasy, awkward, ashamed.
(ANT.) fearless, out-going, adventurous, gregarious, aggressive, daring.

basic *(SYN.)* underlying, chief, essential, main, fundamental.
(ANT.) subsidiary, subordinate.

basis *(SYN.)* presumption, support, base, principle, groundwork, presupposition, foundation, postulate, ground, assumption, premise, essential.
(ANT.) implication, trimming, derivative, superstructure.

basket *(SYN.)* hamper, creel, dossier, bassinet.

bastion *(SYN.)* mainstay, support, staff, tower, stronghold.

bat *(SYN.)* strike, hit, clout, stick, club, knock, crack.

batch *(SYN.)* group, set, collection, lot, cluster, bunch, mass, combination.

bath *(SYN.)* washing, shower, tub, wash, dip, soaping.

bathe *(SYN.)* launder, drench, swim, cover, medicate, immerse, wet, dip, soak, suffuse, rinse, saturate.

bathing suit *(SYN.)* maillot, swimsuit, trunks.

bathos *(SYN.)* mawkishness, soppiness, slush, sentimentality.

bathroom *(SYN.)* powder room, toilet, bath, lavatory.

baton *(SYN.)* mace, rod, staff, billy, crook, stick, fasces.

battalion *(SYN.)* mass, army, swarm, mob, drove, horde, gang, legion, regiment.

batten *(SYN.)* thrive, flourish, fatten, wax, expand, bloom, boom, grow.
(ANT.) decrease, weaken, fail.

batter *(SYN.)* pound, beat, hit, pommel, wallop, bash, smash, mixture, strike.

battery *(SYN.)* series, troop, force, rally, muster, set.

battle *(SYN.)* strife, fray, combat,

struggle, contest, skirmish, conflict, fight, war, flight, warfare, action, campaign, strive against. (ANT.) truce, concord, agreement, settlement, harmony, accept, concur, peace.

battlement (SYN.) parapet, crenellation, rampart, fort, bastion, stronghold, escarpment.

bauble (SYN.) plaything, toy, trinket.

bawd (SYN.) procuress, prostitute.

bawdy (SYN.) vulgar, smutty, filthy, dirty, obscene, pornographic.

bawl (SYN.) sob, shout, wail, cry loudly, bellow, weep, cry.

bawl out (SYN.) scold, upbraid, censure, berate, reprove, reprimand.

bay (SYN.) inlet, bayou, harbor, lagoon, cove, sound, gulf.

bazaar (SYN.) fair, market, marketplace.

beach (SYN.) sands, seashore, waterfront, seaside, strand, coast, shore.

beacon (SYN.) light, signal, watchtower, guide, flare, warning, alarm.

bead (SYN.) globule, drop, pill, blob.

beak (SYN.) nose, bill, proboscis.

beam (SYN.) gleam, ray, girder, cross-member, pencil, shine, glisten, smile, glitter, gleam.

beaming (SYN.) joyful, bright, happy, radiant, grinning. (ANT.) sullen, gloomy, threatening, scowling.

bear (SYN.) carry, support, take, uphold, suffer, convey, allow, stand, yield, endure, tolerate, produce, sustain, brook, transport, undergo, permit, suffer, abide, tolerate. (ANT.) evade, shun, avoid, refuse, dodge.

bearable (SYN.) sufferable, supportable, manageable, tolerable. (ANT.) terrible, painful, unbearable, awful, intolerable.

bearing (SYN.) course, direction, position, posture, behavior, manner, carriage, relation, reference, connection, application, deportment, air, way, conduct.

bearings (SYN.) orientation, whereabouts, location, direction, position, reading, course.

bear on (SYN.) affect, relate to.

bear out (SYN.) confirm, substantiate, justify, verify, prove.

bear up (SYN.) carry on, endure.

bear with (SYN.) tolerate, forbear.

beast (SYN.) monster, savage, brute, creature, animal.

beastly (SYN.) detestable, mean, low, hateful, loathsome, nasty, unpleasant, despicable, obnoxious, brutal, brutish, offensive. (ANT.) considerate, sympathetic, refined, humane, fine, pleasant.

beat (SYN.) pulse, buffet, pound, defeat, palpitate, hit, thump, belabor, knock, overthrow, thrash, pummel, rout, smite, throb, punch, subdue, pulsate, dash, strike, overpower, vanquish, conquer, batter, conquer, overcome, blow. (ANT.) stroke, fail, defend, surrender, shield.

beaten (SYN.) disheartened, dejected, licked, discouraged, hopeless, downcast, down, depressed. (ANT.) eager, hopeful, cheerful.

beatific (SYN.) uplifted, blissful, elated, happy, wonderful, joyful, divine. (ANT.) awful, hellish, ill-fated, accursed.

beating (SYN.) whipping, drubbing, flogging, lashing, scourging, walloping.

beau (SYN.) lover, suitor, swain, admirer.

beautiful (SYN.) pretty, fair, lovely, charming, comely, handsome, elegant, attractive. (ANT.) repulsive, hideous, unsightly, foul, homely, plainness, unattractive, ugly, ugliness.

beauty (SYN.) handsomeness, fairness, charm, pulchritude, attractiveness, loveliness, comeliness, grace, allegiance. (ANT.) ugliness, disfigurement, homeliness, plainness, deformity, eyesore.

becalm (SYN.) calm, quiet, smooth, still, hush, repose, settle.

because (SYN.) inasmuch as, as, since, for.

because of (SYN.) as a result of, as a consequence of.

beckon (SYN.) call, signal, summon, motion, gesture, wave.

becloud (SYN.) obfuscate, confuse, befog, confound, obscure, muddle. (ANT.) illuminate, clarify, solve.

become (SYN.) change, grow, suit, be appropriate, befit.

becoming (SYN.) suitable, meet, befitting, appropriate, fitting, seemly, enhancing, attractive, pleasing, flattering, tasteful, smart, adorning, ornamental. (ANT.) unsuitable, inappropriate, incongruent, ugly, unattractive, improper.

bed (SYN.) layer, cot, vein, berth, stratum, couch, accumulation, bunk, deposit, cradle.

bedazzle (SYN.) glare, blind, dumbfound, flabbergast, bewilder, furbish, festoon.

bedeck (SYN.) deck, adorn, beautify, smarten, festoon, garnish.

bedevil (SYN.) worry, fret, irk, torment, harass, pester, nettle, tease, vex, plague.
(ANT.) soothe, calm, delight, please.

bedlam (SYN.) tumult, uproar, madhouse, commotion, confusion, racket, rumpus, pandemonium.
(ANT.) calm, peace.

bedraggled (SYN.) shabby, muddy, sodden, messy, sloppy.
(ANT.) dry, neat, clean, well-groomed.

bedrock (SYN.) basis, foundation, roots, basics, essentials, fundamentals, bottom, bed, substratum, core.
(ANT.) top, dome, apex, nonessentials.

bedroom (SYN.) chamber, bedchamber.

beef (SYN.) brawn, strength, heft, gripe, sinew, fitness, huskiness, might.

beef up (SYN.) reinforce, vitalize, nerve, buttress, strengthen.
(ANT.) sap, weaken, enervate, drain.

beefy (SYN.) solid, strong, muscular, heavy, stocky.

befall (SYN.) occur, come about, happen.

before (SYN.) prior, earlier, in advance, formerly.
(ANT.) behind, following, afterward, latterly, after.

befriend (SYN.) welcome, encourage, aid, stand by.
(ANT.) dislike, shun, desert, avoid.

befuddle (SYN.) stupefy, addle, confuse, rattle, disorient.

beg (SYN.) solicit, ask, implore, supplicate, entreat, adjure, petition, beseech, request, importune, entreat, implore.
(ANT.) grant, cede, give, bestow, favor.

beget (SYN.) sire, engender, produce, create, propagate, originate, breed, generate, procreate, father.
(ANT.) murder, destroy, kill, abort, prevent, extinguish.

beggar (SYN.) scrub, tatterdemalion, pauper, wretch, ragamuffin, vagabond, raveling.

begin (SYN.) open, enter, arise, initiate, commence, start, inaugurate, originate, institute, create.
(ANT.) terminate, complete, finish, close,

end, stop.

beginner (SYN.) nonprofessional, amateur, apprentice.
(ANT.) veteran, professional.

beginning (SYN.) outset, inception, origin, source, commencement, start, opening, initiation, inauguration.
(ANT.) termination, completion, end, close, consummation, closing, ending, finish.

begrime (SYN.) soil, dirty, smear, muddy, splotch, tarnish.
(ANT.) wash, clean, freshen, launder.

begrudge (SYN.) resent, envy, stint, withhold, grudge.

begrudging (SYN.) hesitant, reluctant, resentful, unwilling, forced.
(ANT.) willing, eager, quick, spontaneous.

beguiling (SYN.) enchanting, interesting, delightful, intriguing, engaging, bewitching, attractive, enthralling, captivating.
(ANT.) boring, dull, unattractive, tedious.

behalf (SYN.) benefit, welfare, support, aid, part, interest.

behave (SYN.) deport, comport, manage, act, demean, bear, interact, carry, operate, conduct.
(ANT.) rebel, misbehave.

behavior (SYN.) manners, carriage, disposition, action, deed, bearing, deportment, conduct, demeanor.
(ANT.) rebelliousness, misbehavior.

behead (SYN.) decapitate, guillotine, decollate.

behest (SYN.) order, command, decree, mandate, bidding.

behind (SYN.) after, backward, at the back, in back of.
(ANT.) frontward, ahead, before.

behold (SYN.) look, see, view, notice, observe, perceive, sight.
(ANT.) overlook, ignore.

being (SYN.) life, existing, existence, living, actuality, organism, individual.
(ANT.) death, nonexistence, expiration.

belabor (SYN.) repeat, reiterate, pound, explain, expatiate, din.

belated (SYN.) late, delayed, overdue, tardy.
(ANT.) well-timed, early.

belch (SYN.) emit, erupt, gush, disgorge, bubble, eructation, burp.

beleaguered (SYN.) bothered, beset, annoyed, beset, harassed, badgered, vexed, plagued, victimized.

belie *(SYN.)* distort, misrepresent, twist, disappoint.

belief *(SYN.)* trust, feeling, certitude, opinion, conviction, persuasion, credence, confidence, reliance, faith, view, creed, assurance.
(ANT.) heresy, denial, incredulity, distrust, skepticism, doubt.

believe *(SYN.)* hold, apprehend, fancy, support, accept, conceive, suppose, imagine, trust, credit.
(ANT.) doubt, reject, distrust, disbelieve, question.

believer *(SYN.)* adherent, follower, devotee, convert, zealot.
(ANT.) doubter, critic, scoffer, skeptic.

belittle *(SYN.)* underrate, depreciate, minimize, decry, disparage, diminish, demean, slight, discredit, militant, depreciate, humiliate.
(ANT.) esteem, admire, flatter, overrate, commend.

bell *(SYN.)* pealing, ringing, signal, tolling, buzzer, chime.

belligerent *(SYN.)* aggressive, warlike, hostile, offensive, combative, militant.
(ANT.) easygoing, compromising, peaceful.

bellow *(SYN.)* thunder, roar, scream, shout, yell, howl.

bellwether *(SYN.)* leader, pilot, guide, ringleader, boss, shepherd.

belly *(SYN.)* stomach, abdomen, paunch.

belonging *(SYN.)* loyalty, relationship, kinship, acceptance, rapport.

belongings *(SYN.)* property, effects, possessions.

beloved *(SYN.)* adored, sweet, loved, cherished, prized, esteemed, valued, darling.

below *(SYN.)* under, less, beneath, underneath, lower.
(ANT.) aloft, overhead, above, over.

belt *(SYN.)* girdle, sash, strap, cummerbund, band, waistband, whack, hit, wallop, punch.

bemoan *(SYN.)* mourn, lament, grieve, sorrow, regret, deplore.

bend *(SYN.)* turn, curve, incline, submit, bow, lean, crook, twist, yield, stoop, crouch, agree, suppress, oppress, mold, kneel, deflect, subdue, influence.
(ANT.) resist, straighten, break, stiffen.

beneath *(SYN.)* under, below.
(ANT.) above, over.

benediction *(SYN.)* thanks, blessing, prayer.

beneficial *(SYN.)* salutary, good, wholesome, advantageous, useful, helpful, serviceable, profitable.
(ANT.) harmful, destructive, injurious, disadvantageous, un-wholesome, deleterious, detrimental.

benefit *(SYN.)* support, help, gain, avail, profit, account, favor, aid, good, advantage, serve, interest, behalf, service.
(ANT.) handicap, calamity, trouble, disadvantage, distress.

benevolence *(SYN.)* magnanimity, charity, tenderness, altruism, humanity, philanthropy, generosity, liberality, beneficence, good will.
(ANT.) malevolence, unkindness, cruelty, selfishness, inhumanity.

benevolent *(SYN.)* kindhearted, tender, merciful, generous, altruistic, obliging, kind, good, well-wishing, philanthropy, liberal, unselfish, kindly, disposed, openhearted, humane, benign, friendly.
(ANT.) malevolent, greedy, wicked, harsh.

bent *(SYN.)* curved, crooked, resolved, determined, set, inclined, firm, decided.
(ANT.) straight.

berate *(SYN.)* scold.

beseech *(SYN.)* appeal, entreat, plead, ask, beg, implore.

beset *(SYN.)* surround, attack.

besides *(SYN.)* moreover, further, except for, also, as well, furthermore.

besiege *(SYN.)* assault, attack, siege, bombard, raid, charge.

bespeak *(SYN.)* engage, reserve, indicate, show, signify, express.

best *(SYN.)* choice, prime, select.
(ANT.) worst.

bestial *(SYN.)* brutal, beastly, savage, cruel.

bestow *(SYN.)* confer, place, put, award, give, present.
(ANT.) withdraw, withhold.

bet *(SYN.)* gamble, give, stake, wager, pledge, ante.

betray *(SYN.)* reveal, deliver, expose, mislead, trick, deceive, exhibit, show.
(ANT.) shelter, protect, safeguard.

betrothal *(SYN.)* marriage, engagement, contract.

better *(SYN.)* superior, preferable, improve.
(ANT.) worsen.

between *(SYN.)* among, betwixt.

beware *(SYN.)* take care, watch out, look sharp, be careful.

bewilder *(SYN.)* perplex, confuse, mystify, baffle, puzzle, overwhelm. *(ANT.)* clarify, enlighten.

bewitch *(SYN.)* captivate, charm, delight, enchant.

beyond *(SYN.)* past, farther, exceeding.

bias *(SYN.)* slant, inclination, proneness, turn, bent, penchant, tendency, disposition, propensity, partiality, predisposition, leaning, proclivity, prejudice, influence, warp, slanting, predilection. *(ANT.)* fairness, justice, even-handedness, equity, detachment, impartiality.

bible *(SYN.)* guide, handbook, gospel, manual, sourcebook, guidebook.

bibulous *(SYN.)* guzzling, intemperate, winebibbing, sottish, alcoholic. *(ANT.)* sober, moderate.

bicker *(SYN.)* dispute, argue, wrangle, quarrel. *(ANT.)* go along with, agree.

bid *(SYN.)* order, command, direct, wish, greet, say, offer, instruct, invite, purpose, tender, proposal.

bidding *(SYN.)* behest, request, decree, call, charge, beck, summons, solicitation, invitation, instruction, mandate.

bide *(SYN.)* stay, tarry, delay, wait, remain.

big *(SYN.)* large, huge, bulky, immense, colossal, majestic, august, monstrous, hulking, gigantic, massive, great, enormous, tremendous, outgoing, important, kind, big-hearted, considerable, generous, grand. *(ANT.)* small, little, tiny, immature, petite.

big-hearted *(SYN.)* good-natured, liberal, generous, unselfish, open-handed, unstinting, charitable, magnanimous. *(ANT.)* cold, selfish, mean, uncharitable.

bigoted *(SYN.)* intolerant, partial, prejudiced, biased, unfair, chauvinist.

bigotry *(SYN.)* bias, blindness, intolerance, unfairness, prejudice, ignorance, passion, sectarianism. *(ANT.)* acceptance, open-mindedness.

big-shot *(SYN.)* somebody, brass hat, big gun. *(ANT.)* underling, nobody, nebbish, cipher.

bijou *(SYN.)* gem, bauble, jewel, ornament.

bile *(SYN.)* spleen, rancor, anger, bitterness, peevishness, ill-humor, nastiness, resentment, discontent, irascibility. *(ANT.)* cheerfulness, affability, pleasantness.

bilge *(SYN.)* hogwash, drivel, gibberish, rubbish, bosh, foolishness, twaddle.

bilious *(SYN.)* petulant, crabby, ill-natured, cross, peevish, crotchety, cranky. *(ANT.)* happy, agreeable, pleasant, good-natured.

bilk *(SYN.)* defraud, trick, cheat, hoodwink, deceive, fleece, rook, bamboozle.

bill *(SYN.)* charge, invoice, account, statement.

billet *(SYN.)* housing, quarters, berth, shelter, barrack, installation.

billingsgate *(SYN.)* swearing, scurrility, cursing, abuse, vulgarity, gutter, profanity.

billow *(SYN.)* surge, swell, rise, rush, peaking, magnification, amplification, augmentation, increase, intensification. *(ANT.)* lowering, decrease.

bin *(SYN.)* cubbyhole, box, container, chest, cubicle, crib, receptacle, can.

bind *(SYN.)* connect, restrain, band, fasten, oblige, obligate, engage, wrap, connect, weld, attach, tie, require, restrict. *(ANT.)* unlace, loose, unfasten, untie, free.

binding *(SYN.)* compulsory, obligatory, mandatory, compelling, unalterable, imperative, indissoluble, unconditional, unchangeable, hard-and-fast. *(ANT.)* adjustable, flexible, elastic, changeable.

binge *(SYN.)* fling, spree, carousal, toot.

birth *(SYN.)* origin, beginning, infancy, inception. *(ANT.)* finish, decline, death, disappearance, end.

biscuit *(SYN.)* bun, roll, cake, muffin, bread, rusk.

bit *(SYN.)* fraction, portion, scrap, fragment, particle, drop, speck, harness, small amount, restraint, morsel, sum.

bite *(SYN.)* gnaw, chew, nip, sting, pierce, mouthful, snack, morsel.

biting *(SYN.)* cutting, sharp, acid, sneering, sarcastic. *(ANT.)* soothing, kind, gentle, agreeable.

bitter *(SYN.)* distasteful, sour, acrid, pungent, piercing, vicious, severe,

biting, distressful, stinging, distressing, ruthless, hated, hostile, grievous, harsh, painful, tart.
(ANT.) sweet, mellow, pleasant, delicious.

bizarre (SYN.) peculiar, strange, odd, uncommon, queer, unusual.
(ANT.) usual, everyday, ordinary, inconspicuous.

black (SYN.) sooty, dark, ebony, inky, swarthy, soiled, filthy, dirty, stained, somber, depressing, sad, dismal, gloomy.
(ANT.) white, clean, pristine, glowing, pure, cheerful, light-skinned, sunny, bright.

blackball (SYN.) turn down, ban, blacklist, exclude, snub, reject, debar.
(ANT.) accept, include, invite, ask, bid.

blacken (SYN.) tar, ink, black, darken, besoot, smudge, begrime, discredit, defile, dull, dim, tarnish, ebonize, denounce, sully, libel, blemish, defame.
(ANT.) exalt, honor, whiten, brighten, shine, bleach.

blackmail (SYN.) bribe, payment, bribery, extortion, shakedown, coercion.

blackout (SYN.) faint, coma, unconsciousness, oblivion, amnesia, stupor, swoon.

bladder (SYN.) saccule, sac, vesicle, pouch, pod, cell, blister, container, cyst.

blade (SYN.) cutter, lancet, knife, sword.

blah (SYN.) lifeless, flat, jejune, lukewarm, stale, insipid, tasteless, pedestrian, tedious, dreary, uninteresting.
(ANT.) spirited, fascinating, vibrant, vigorous.

blame (SYN.) upbraid, criticize, fault, guilt, accuse, rebuke, charge, implicate, impeach, tattle, condemn, indict, responsibility, censure, denounce, reproach.
(ANT.) exonerate, credit, honor, absolve.

blameless (SYN.) moral, innocent, worthy, faultless.
(ANT.) blameworthy, culpable, guilty.

blanch (SYN.) whiten, bleach, decolorize, peroxide, fade, wash out, dim, dull.

bland (SYN.) soft, smooth, gentle, agreeable, vapid, insipid, mild, polite.
(ANT.) harsh, outspoken, disagreeable.

blandish (SYN.) praise, compliment, overpraise, cajole, puff, adulate, salve, fawn, court, toady, butter up, please,

jolly.
(ANT.) insult, deride, criticize, belittle.

blandisher (SYN.) adulator, booster, sycophant, eulogist, apple polisher, flunkey.
(ANT.) knocker, faultfinder, be-littler.

blandishment (SYN.) applause, cajolery, honey, adulation, plaudits, acclaim, fawning, compliments.
(ANT.) carping, belittling, criticism, deprecation.

blank (SYN.) unmarked, expressionless, uninterested, form, area, void, vacant, empty.
(ANT.) marked, filled, alert, animated.

blanket (SYN.) quilt, coverlet, cover, comforter, robe, padding, carpet, wrapper, mantle, envelope, housing, coat, comprehensive, universal, across-the-board, panoramic, omnibus.
(ANT.) limited, detailed, restricted, precise.

blare (SYN.) roar, blast, resound, jar, scream, swell, clang, peal, trumpet, toot, hoot.

blasphemous (SYN.) profane, irreverent, impious, godless, ungodly, sacrilegious, irreligious.
(ANT.) reverent, reverential, religious, pious.

blasphemy (SYN.) profanation, impiousness, cursing, irreverence, sacrilege, abuse, ecration, swearing, contempt.
(ANT.) respect, piety, reverence, devotion.

blast (SYN.) burst, explosion, discharge, blow-out.

blasted (SYN.) blighted, withered, ravaged, decomposed, spoiled, destroyed.

blastoff (SYN.) launching, expulsion, launch, shot, projection.

blatant (SYN.) shameless, notorious, brazen, flagrant, glaring, bold, obvious.
(ANT.) deft, subtle, insidious, devious.

blaze (SYN.) inferno, shine, flare, marking, fire, outburst, holocaust, notch, flame.
(ANT.) die, dwindle.

bleach (SYN.) pale, whiten, blanch, whitener.
(ANT.) darken, blacken.

bleak (SYN.) dreary, barren, cheerless, depressing, gloomy, windswept, bare, cold, dismal, desolate, raw, chilly.
(ANT.) lush, hopeful, promising, cheer-

ful.

bleary *(SYN.)* hazy, groggy, blurry, fuzzy, misty, clouded, overcast, dim, blear.
(ANT.) clear, vivid, precise, clear-cut.

bleed *(syn.)* pity, lose blood, grieve, sorrow.

blemish *(SYN.)* injury, speck, flaw, scar, disgrace, imperfection, stain, fault, blot.
(ANT.) purity, embellishment, adornment, perfection.

blend *(SYN.)* beat, intermingle, combine, fuse, unify, consolidate, unite, amalgamate, conjoin, mix, coalesce, intermix, join, merge, compound, combination, stir, mixture, commingle, mingle.
(ANT.) separate, decompose, analyze, disintegrate.

bless *(SYN.)* thank, celebrate, extol, glorify, adore, delight, praise, gladden, exalt.
(ANT.) denounce, blaspheme, slander, curse.

blessed *(SYN.)* sacred, holy, consecrated, dedicated, hallowed, sacrosanct, beatified, joyful, delighted, joyous, sainted, canonized, blissful.
(ANT.) miserable, sad, dispirited, cheerless.

blessing *(SYN.)* benison, sanction, favor, grace, benediction, invocation, approbation, approval, compliment, bounty, windfall, gift, benefit, advantage, kindness, felicitation, invocation.
(ANT.) disapproval, execration, curse, denunciation, malediction, rebuke, displeasure, condemnation, adversity, misfortune, mishap, calamity.

blight *(SYN.)* decay, disease, spoil, sickness, wither, ruin, damage, harm, decaying, epidemic, affliction, destroy.

blind *(SYN.)* sightless, unmindful, rash, visionless, ignorant, unsighted, unconscious, discerning, heedless, oblivious, purblind, un-knowing, screen, unaware, thoughtless, shade, unthinking, cover, curtain, without thought, headlong.
(ANT.) discerning, sensible, calculated, perceiving, perceptive, aware.

blink *(SYN.)* bat, glance, flicker, wink, twinkle.

bliss *(SYN.)* ecstasy, rapture, glee, elation, joy, blessedness, gladness, happiness, delight, felicity, blissfulness.
(ANT.) woe, sadness, sorrow, grief,

unhappiness, torment, wretchedness, misery.

blissful *(SYN.)* happy, elated, rapturous, ecstatic, paradisiacal, joyous, enraptured.

blister *(SYN.)* bleb, swelling, welt, sore, blob, bubble, inflammation, boil, canker.

blithe *(SYN.)* breezy, merry, airy, lighthearted, light, gay, fanciful, graceful.
(ANT.) morose, grouchy, low-spirited, gloomy.

blitz *(SYN.)* strike, onslaught, thrust, raid, lunge, drive, incursion, assault, sally.

blizzard *(SYN.)* storm, snowstorm, snowfall, gale, tempest, blast, blow, swirl.

bloat *(SYN.)* distend, puff up, inflate, swell.
(ANT.) deflate.

blob *(SYN.)* bubble, blister, pellet, globule.

block *(SYN.)* clog, hinder, bar, impede, close, obstruct, barricade, blockade, obstruction, hindrance, obstacle, impediment, retard, check, stop.
(ANT.) forward, promote, aid, clear, advance, advantage, assist, further, open.

blockade *(SYN.)* barrier, fortification, obstruction, barricade.

blockhead *(SYN.)* dunce, dolt, fool, sap, idiot, simpleton, chump, booby, bonehead, woodenhead.

blood *(SYN.)* murder, gore, slaughter, bloodshed, ancestry, lineage, heritage.

bloodcurdling *(SYN.)* hair-raising, terrifying, alarming, chilling, stunning, scary.

bloodless *(SYN.)* dead, torpid, dull, drab, cold, colorless, passionless, lackluster.
(ANT.) passionate, vital, ebullient, animated, vivacious.

bloodshed *(SYN.)* murder, killing, slaying, blood bath, massacre, carnage.

bloodthirsty *(SYN.)* murderous, cruel.

bloody *(SYN.)* cruel, pitiless, bloodthirsty, inhuman, ruthless, ferocious, murderous.
(ANT.) kind, gentle.

bloom *(SYN.)* thrive, glow, flourish, blossom, flower.
(ANT.) wane, decay, dwindle, shrivel, wither.

blooming *(SYN.)* flush, green, vigorous, thriving, vital, abloom, healthy, fresh, booming.

(ANT.) flagging, declining, whithering.

blooper *(SYN.)* muff, fluff, error, bungle, botch, blunder, fumble, howler, indiscretion.

blossom *(SYN.)* bloom, flower, flourish.

(ANT.) shrink, wither, dwindle, fade.

blot *(SYN.)* stain, inkblot, spot, inkstain, blemish, dishonor, disgrace, spatter, obliterate, soil, dry.

blot out *(SYN.)* wipe out, destroy, obliterate, abolish, annihilate, cancel, expunge, strike out, shade, darken, shadow, overshadow, obfuscate, cloud, eclipse.

blow *(SYN.)* hit, thump, slap, cuff, box, shock, move, drive, spread, breeze, puff, whistle, inflate, enlarge.

blowout *(SYN.)* blast, explosion, burst.

blue *(SYN.)* sapphire, azure, gloomy, sad, unhappy, depressed, dejected, melancholy.

(ANT.) cheerful, optimistic, happy.

blueprint *(SYN.)* design, plan, scheme, chart, draft, prospectus, outline, proposal, conception, project, layout.

blues *(SYN.)* dumps, melancholy, depression, doldrums, moodiness, dejection, despondency, gloominess, moroseness.

bluff *(SYN.)* steep, perpendicular, vertical, abrupt, precipitous, rough, open, frank, hearty, blunt, fool, mislead, pretend, deceive, fraud, lie, fake, deceit.

blunder *(SYN.)* error, flounder, mistake, stumble.

blunt *(SYN.)* solid, abrupt, rough, dull, pointless, plain, bluff, edgeless, unceremonious, obtuse, rude, outspoken, unsharpened, rounded, worn, crude, direct, impolite, short, curt, gruff.

(ANT.) tactful, polite, subtle, polished, suave, sharp, keen, pointed, diplomatic.

blur *(SYN.)* sully, dim, obscure, stain, dull, confuse, cloud, smear, stain, smudge.

(ANT.) clear, clarify.

blush *(SYN.)* redden.

board *(SYN.)* embark, committee, wood, mount, cabinet, food, get on, lumber.

boast *(SYN.)* vaunt, flaunt, brag, glory, crow, exaggerate, bragging.

(ANT.) humble, apologize, minimize, deprecate.

body *(SYN.)* remains, bulk, mass, carcass, form, company, corpus, society, firm-ness, group, torso, substance, collection, cadaver, trunk, group, throng, company, crowd, band.

(ANT.) spirit, intellect, soul.

bogus *(SYN.)* counterfeit, false, pretend, fake, phony.

(ANT.) genuine.

boil *(SYN.)* seethe, bubble, pimple, fume, pimple, cook, swelling, rage, foam, simmer, stew.

boisterous *(SYN.)* rough, violent, rowdy, noisy, tumultuous.

(ANT.) serene.

bold *(SYN.)* daring, forward, pushy, striking, brave, dauntless, rude, prominent, adventurous, fearless, insolent, conspicuous, defiant, arrogant, cavalier, brazen, unafraid, intrepid, courageous, valiant, heroic, gallant, disrespectful, impudent, shameless.

(ANT.) modest, bashful, cowardly, timid, retiring, flinching, fearful, timorous, polite, courteous, deferential.

bolt *(SYN.)* break away, fastener, flee, take flight, lock.

bombard *(SYN.)* shell, open fire, bomb, rake, assail, attack.

bond *(SYN.)* fastener, rope, tie, cord, connection, attachment, link, tie, promise.

(ANT.) sever, separate, untie, disconnect.

bondage *(SYN.)* slavery, thralldom, captivity, imprisonment, servitude, confinement, vassalage, enslavement.

(ANT.) liberation, emancipation, free, independence, freedom.

bonds *(SYN.)* chains, cuffs, fetters, shackles, irons, bracelets.

bone up *(SYN.)* learn, master, study, relearn.

bonus *(SYN.)* more, extra, premium, gift, reward, bounty.

bony *(SYN.)* lean, lank, thin, lanky, rawboned, fleshless, skinny, gangling, weight.

(ANT.) plump, fleshy, stout.

book *(SYN.)* manual, textbook, work, booklet, monograph, brochure, tract, volume, pamphlet, treatise, publication, hardcover, paperback, novel, workbook, text.

bookish *(SYN.)* formal, scholarly, theoretical, academic, learned, scholastic, erudite.

(ANT.) simple, ignorant.

boom *(SYN.)* advance, grow, flourish, progress, gain, increase, roar, beam, rumble, reverberate, thunder, prosper, swell, thrive, pole, rush.
(ANT.) decline, fail, recession.

booming *(SYN.)* flourishing, blooming, thriving, vigorous, prospering, exuberant.
(ANT.) waning, dying, failing, declining.

boon *(SYN.)* gift, jolly, blessing, pleasant, godsend, windfall.

boondocks *(SYN.)* sticks, backwoods.

boor *(SYN.)* lout, clown, oaf, yokel, rustic, vulgarian, ruffian.

boorish *(SYN.)* coarse, churlish, uncivil, ill-mannered, ill-bred, uncivilized, crude, uncouth.
(ANT.) polite, cultivated, cultivated, well-mannered.

boost *(SYN.)* push, lift, help, hoist, shove.
(ANT.) depress, lower, belittle, submerge, disparage, decrease, decline, reduction, downturn.

booster *(SYN.)* supporter, fan, rooter, plugger, follower.

boot *(SYN.)* shoe, kick.

booth *(SYN.)* enclosure, cubicle, stand, compartment, box.

bootless *(SYN.)* purposeless, ineffective, profitless, useless.
(ANT.) favorable, successful, useful.

bootlicker *(SYN.)* flunky, fawner, toady, sycophant.

booty *(SYN.)* prize, plunder, loot.

booze *(SYN.)* spirits, drink, liquor, alcohol.

border *(SYN.)* fringe, rim, verge, boundary, edge, termination, brink, limit, brim, outskirts, frontier, margin.
(ANT.) interior, center, mainland, core, middle.

borderline *(SYN.)* unclassifiable, indeterminate, halfway, obscure, inexact, indefinite, unclear.
(ANT.) precise, absolute, definite.

border on *(SYN.)* approximate, approach, resemble, echo, parallel, connect.

bore *(SYN.)* tire, weary, hole, perforate, pierce, drill.
(ANT.) arouse, captivate, excite, interest.

boredom *(SYN.)* ennui, doldrums, weariness, dullness, tedium.
(ANT.) stimulation, motive, activity, stimulus, excitement.

boring *(SYN.)* monotonous, dull, dead, flat, tedious, wearisome, trite, prosaic, humdrum, long-winded.

born *(SYN.)* hatched, produced.

borrow *(SYN.)* copy, adopt, simulate, mirror, assume, usurp, plagiarize, take.
(ANT.) allow, advance, invent, originate, credit, lend.

bosom *(SYN.)* chest, breast, feelings, thoughts, mind, interior, marrow, heart.

boss *(SYN.)* director, employer, oversee, direct, foreman, supervisor, manager.
(ANT.) worker, employee, underling.

bossy *(SYN.)* overbearing, arrogant, domineering, lordly, tyrannical, high-handed, arbitrary, oppress.
(ANT.) flexible, easy-going, cooperative.

botch *(SYN.)* blunder, bungle, fumble, goof, muff, mishandle, mismanage.
(ANT.) perform, realize.

bother *(SYN.)* haunt, molest, trouble, annoy, upset, fleeting, transient, harass, inconvenience, momentary, disturb, passing, pester, tease, irritate, worry, vex.
(ANT.) prolonged, extended, long, protracted, lengthy, comfort, solace.

bothersome *(SYN.)* irritating, vexatious, worrisome, annoying, distressing, troublesome, disturbing.

bottle *(SYN.)* container, flask, vessel, decanter, vial, ewer, jar.

bottleneck *(SYN.)* obstacle, obstruction, barrier, block, blockage, detour.

bottom *(SYN.)* basis, fundament, base, groundwork, foot, depths, lowest part, underside, foundation, seat, buttocks, rear, behind.
(ANT.) top, peak, apex, summit, topside.

bough *(SYN.)* branch, arm, limb.

bounce *(SYN.)* recoil, ricochet, rebound.

bound *(SYN.)* spring, vault, hop, leap, start, surrounded, jump, limit, jerk, boundary, bounce, skip, tied, shackled, trussed, fettered, certain, sure, destined, compelled, required.
(ANT.) unfettered, free.

boundary *(SYN.)* bound, limit, border, margin, outline, circumference, perimeter, division, frontier, edge.

boundless *(SYN.)* limitless, endless, inexhaustible, unlimited, eternal, infinite.
(ANT.) restricted, narrow, limited.

bounteous *(SYN.)* plentiful, generous, liberal, abundant.
(ANT.) scarce.

bountiful *(SYN.)* bounteous, fertile, plentiful, generous, abundant.
(ANT.) sparing, infertile, scarce.
bounty *(SYN.)* generosity, gift, award, bonus, reward, prize, premium.
bourgeois *(SYN.)* common, ordinary, commonplace, middle-class, conventional.
(ANT.) upper-class, unconventional, loose, aristocratic.
bout *(SYN.)* round, contest, conflict, test, struggle, match, spell, fight.
bow *(SYN.)* bend, yield, kneel, submit, stoop.
bowels *(SYN.)* entrails, intestines, innards, guts, stomach.
bowl *(SYN.)* container, dish, pot, pottery, crock, jug, vase.
bowl over *(SYN.)* fell, floor, overturn, astound, nonplus, stagger, jar.
bow out *(SYN.)* give up, withdraw, retire, resign, abandon.
box *(SYN.)* hit, fight, crate, case, container.
boxer *(SYN.)* prizefighter, fighter.
boy *(SYN.)* male, youngster, lad, kid, fellow, buddy, youth.
(ANT.) girl, man.
boycott *(SYN.)* picket, strike, ban, revolt, blackball.
boy friend *(SYN.)* date, young man, sweetheart, courtier, beau.
brace *(SYN.)* strengthen, tie, prop, support, tighten, stay, strut, bind, truss, crutch.
bracelet *(SYN.)* armband, bangle, circlet.
bracing *(SYN.)* stimulating, refreshing, restorative, fortifying, invigorating.
bracket *(SYN.)* join, couple, enclose, relate, brace, support.
brag *(SYN.)* boast, flaunt, vaunt, bluster, swagger.
(ANT.) demean, debase, denigrate, degrade, depreciate, deprecate.
braid *(SYN.)* weave, twine, wreath, plait.
brain *(SYN.)* sense, intelligence, intellect, common sense, understanding, reason.
(ANT.) stupid, stupidity.
brake *(SYN.)* decelerate, stop, curb.
(ANT.) accelerate.
branch *(SYN.)* shoot, limb, bough, tributary, offshoot, part, division, expand, department, divide, spread, subdivision.
brand *(SYN.)* make, trademark, label,

kind, burn, trade name, mark, stamp, blaze.
brave *(SYN.)* bold, daring, gallant, valorous, adventurous, heroic, magnanimous, chivalrous, audacious, valiant, courageous, fearless, intrepid, unafraid.
(ANT.) weak, cringing, timid, cowardly, fearful, craven.
brawl *(SYN.)* racket, quarrel, fracas, riot, fight, melee, fray, disturbance, dispute, disagreement.
brawn *(SYN.)* strength, muscle.
(ANT.) weakness.
brazen *(SYN.)* immodest, forward, shameless, bold, brassy, impudent, insolent, rude.
(ANT.) retiring, self-effacing, modest, shy.
breach *(SYN.)* rupture, fracture, rift, break, crack, gap, opening, breaking, quarrel, violation.
(ANT.) observation.
break *(SYN.)* demolish, pound, rack, smash, burst, rupture, disobey, violate, crack, infringe, crush, squeeze, transgress, fracture, shatter, wreck, crash, atomize, disintegrate, collapse, splinter, crack, gap, breach, opening, rupture.
(ANT.) restore, heal, join, renovate, mend, repair.
breed *(SYN.)* engender, bear, propagate, father, beget, rear, conceive, train, generate, raise, procreate, nurture, create, mother, produce, originate, generate, raise, train, nurture.
(ANT.) murder, abort, kill.
breeze *(SYN.)* air, wind, zephyr, breath.
(ANT.) calm.
breezy *(SYN.)* jolly, spry, active, brisk, energetic, lively, carefree, spirited.
brevity *(SYN.)* briefness, conciseness.
(ANT.) length.
brew *(SYN.)* plot, plan, cook, ferment, prepare, scheme.
bribe *(SYN.)* buy off.
bridle *(SYN.)* control, hold, restrain, check, harness, curb, restraint, halter.
(ANT.) release, free, loose.
brief *(SYN.)* curt, short, fleeting, passing, compendious, terse, laconic, succinct, momentary, transient, temporary, concise, compact, condensed.
(ANT.) long, extended, prolonged, lengthy, protracted, comprehensive, exten-

sive, exhaustive.

brigand (SYN.) bandit, robber, thief.

bright (SYN.) luminous, gleaming, clever, witty, brilliant, lucid, vivid, clear, smart, intelligent, lustrous, clever, shining, shiny, sparkling, shimmering, radiant, cheerful, lively, gay, happy, lighthearted, keen, promising, favorable, encouraging.
(ANT.) sullen, dull, murky, dark, gloomy, dim, lusterless, boring, colorless, stupid, backward, slow.

brilliant (SYN.) bright, clear, smart, intelligent, sparkling, shining, alert, vivid, splendid, radiant, glittering, talented, ingenious, gifted.
(ANT.) mediocre, dull, lusterless, second-rate.

brim (SYN.) border, margin, lip, rim, edge.
(ANT.) middle, center.

bring (SYN.) fetch, take, carry, raise, introduce, propose.
(ANT.) remove, withdraw.

brink (SYN.) limit, verge, rim, margin, edge.

brisk (SYN.) fresh, breezy, cool, lively, spry, refreshing, spirited, jolly, energetic, quick, active, animated, nimble, spry, agile, sharp, keen, stimulating, invigorating.
(ANT.) musty, faded, stagnant, decayed, hackneyed, slow, lethargic, sluggish, still, dull, oppressive.

briskness (SYN.) energy, exercise, motion, rapidity, agility, action, quickness, activity, vigor, liveliness, movement.
(ANT.) inertia, idleness, sloth, dullness, inactivity.

bristle (SYN.) flare up, anger, rage, seethe, get mad.

brittle (SYN.) crumbling, frail, breakable, delicate, splintery, crisp, fragile, weak.
(ANT.) tough, enduring, unbreakable, thick, strong, sturdy, flexible, elastic, supple.

broach (SYN.) set afoot, introduce, inaugurate, start, mention, launch, advance.

broad (SYN.) large, wide, tolerant, expanded, vast, liberal, sweeping, roomy, expansive, extended, general, extensive, full.
(ANT.) restricted, confined, narrow, con-

stricted, slim, tight, limited, negligible.

broadcast (SYN.) distribute, announce, publish, scatter, circulate, spread, send, transmit, relay.

broaden (SYN.) spread, widen, amplify, enlarge, extend, increase, add to, expand, stretch, deepen, magnify.
(ANT.) tighted, narrow, constrict, straiten.

broad-minded (SYN.) unprejudiced, tolerant, liberal, unbigoted.
(ANT.) prejudiced, petty, narrowminded.

brochure (SYN.) booklet, pamphlet, leaflet, mailing, circular, tract, flier.

broil (SYN.) cook, burn, heat, roast, bake, scorch, fire, grill, singe, sear, toast.

broken (SYN.) flattened, rent, shattered, wrecked, destroyed, reduced, smashed, crushed, fractured, ruptured, interrupted, burst, separated.
(ANT.) whole, integral, united, repaired.

brokenhearted (SYN.) disconsolate, forlorn, heartbroken, sad, grieving.

bromide (SYN.) banality, platitude, stereotype, commonplace, slogan, proverb.

brooch (SYN.) clasp, pin, breastpin, broach.

brood (SYN.) study, consider, ponder, reflect, contemplate, meditate, young, litter, offspring, think, muse, deliberate.

brook (SYN.) rivulet, run, branch, stream, creek.

brother (SYN.) comrade, man, kinsman, sibling.
(ANT.) sister.

brotherhood (SYN.) kinship, kindness, fraternity, fellowship, clan, society, brotherliness, bond, association, relationship, solidarity.
(ANT.) strife, discord, acrimony, opposition.

brotherly (SYN.) affectionate, fraternal, cordial, sympathetic, benevolent, philanthropic, humane, kindred, communal, altruistic.

brow (SYN.) forehead, eyebrow.

browbeat (SYN.) bully, domineer, bulldoze, intimidate, henpeck, oppress, grind.

brown study (SYN.) contemplation, reflection, reverie, musing, thoughtfulness, deliberation, rumination, self-communion.

browse *(SYN.)* scan, graze, read, feed.

bruise *(SYN.)* hurt, injure, wound, damage, abrasion, injury, contusion, mark, damage, harm, wound.

brunt *(SYN.)* force, impact, shock, strain, oppression, severity.

brush *(SYN.)* rub, wipe, clean, bushes, remove, shrubs, broom, whisk, paintbrush, hairbrush, underbrush, thicket.

brush-off *(SYN.)* dismissal, snub, slight, rebuff, turndown, go-by.

brusque *(SYN.)* sudden, curt, hasty, blunt, rough, steep, precipitate, rugged, craggy, gruff, surly, abrupt, short, bluff. *(ANT.)* smooth, anticipated, courteous, expected, gradual, personable.

brutal *(SYN.)* brute, cruel, inhuman, rude, barbarous, gross, sensual, ferocious, brutish, coarse, bestial, carnal, remorseless, ruthless, savage, mean, savage, pitiless, barbaric. *(ANT.)* kind, courteous, humane, civilized, gentle, kindhearted, mild.

brute *(SYN.)* monster, barbarian, beast, animal, wild, savage.

bubble *(SYN.)* boil, foam, seethe, froth.

buccaneer *(SYN.)* sea robber, privateer, pirate.

buck *(SYN.)* spring, jump, vault, leap.

bucket *(SYN.)* pot, pail, canister, can.

buckle *(SYN.)* hook, fastening, fastener, bend, wrinkle, clip, clasp, distort, catch, strap, fasten, collapse, yield, warp.

bud *(SYN.)* develop, sprout.

buddy *(SYN.)* companion, comrade, friend, partner, pal.

budge *(SYN.)* stir, move.

budget *(SYN.)* schedule, ration.

buff *(SYN.)* shine, polish, burnish, rub, wax.

buffet *(SYN.)* bat, strike, clout, blow, knock, beat, crack, hit, slap, cabinet, counter, server.

buffoon *(SYN.)* jester, fool, clown, jokester, zany, comedian, chump, boor, dolt.

bug *(SYN.)* fault, hitch, defect, catch, snag, failing, rub, flaw, snarl, weakness, annoy, pester, hector, vex, nag, nettle.

bugbear *(SYN.)* bogy, specter, demon, devil, fiend.

build *(SYN.)* found, rear, establish, constructed, raise, set up, erect, assemble. *(ANT.)* raze, destroy, overthrow, demolish, undermine.

building *(SYN.)* residence, structure, house, edifice.

buildup *(SYN.)* gain, enlargement, increase, praise, commendation, promotion, jump, expansion, uptrend, testimonial, plug, puff, blurb, endorsement, compliment. *(ANT.)* reduction, decrease, decline.

bulge *(SYN.)* lump, protuberance, bump, swelling, protrusion, extend, protrude. *(ANT.)* hollow, shrink, contract, depression.

bulk *(SYN.)* lump, magnitude, volume, size, mass, most, majority.

bulky *(SYN.)* great, big, huge, large, enormous, massive, immense, monstrous, clumsy, cumbersome, unwieldy. *(ANT.)* tiny, little, small, petite, handy, delicate.

bull *(SYN.)* push, force, press, drive, thrust, bump.

bulldoze *(SYN.)* cow, bully, coerce, thrust, push.

bulletin *(SYN.)* news, flash, message, statement, newsletter, circular.

bullheaded *(SYN.)* dogged, stiff-necked, stubborn, mulish, rigid, pigheaded, willful, tenacious, unyielding. *(ANT.)* flexible, submissive, compliant.

bully *(SYN.)* pester, tease, intimidate, harass, domineer.

bulwark *(SYN.)* wall, bastion, abutment, bank, dam, rampart, shoulder, parapet, backing, maintainer, embankment, safeguard, reinforcement, sustainer.

bum *(SYN.)* idler, loafer, drifter, hobo, wretch, dwadler, beggar, vagrant.

bumbling *(SYN.)* bungling, inept, blundering, clumsy, incompetent, awkward, maladroit, lumbering, ungainly. *(ANT.)* facile, handy, dexterous, proficient.

bump *(SYN.)* shake, push, hit, shove, prod, collide, knock, bang, strike.

bumpkin *(SYN.)* hick, yokel, rustic, yahoo.

bumptious *(SYN.)* arrogant, self-assertive, conceited, forward, overbearing, pushy, boastful, obtrusive. *(ANT.)* sheepish, self-effacing, retiring, shrinking, unobtrusive, diffident.

bumpy *(SYN.)* uneven, jolting, rough, jarring, rocky, coarse, craggy, irregular. *(ANT.)* flat, smooth, flush, polished, level.

bunch *(SYN.)* batch, bundle, cluster.

company, collection, flock, group.

bundle *(SYN.)* package, mass, collection, batch, parcel, packet, box, carton, bunch.

bungalow *(SYN.)* ranch house, cabana, cabin, cottage, lodge, summer house, villa.

bungle *(SYN.)* tumble, botch, foul up, boggle, mess up, louse up, blunder.

bunk *(SYN.)* berth, rubbish, nonsense, couch, bed, cot.

buoyant *(SYN.)* light, jolly, spirited, effervescent, blithe, sprightly, lively, resilient, vivacious, afloat, floating, cheery, cheerful, gay.
(ANT.) hopeless, dejected, sullen, depressed, heavy, despondent, sinking, low, pessimistic, downcast, glum.

burden *(SYN.)* oppress, afflict, trouble, encumber, tax, weight, load, worry, contents, trial, lade, overload.
(ANT.) lighten, alleviate, ease, mitigate, console, disburden.

burdensome *(SYN.)* arduous, cumbersome, bothersome, oppressive, irksome, trying, hard, difficult.

bureau *(SYN.)* office, division, department, unit, commission, board, chest, dresser.

bureaucrat *(SYN.)* clerk, official, functionary, servant, politician.

burglar *(SYN.)* thief, robber.

burial *(SYN.)* interment, funeral.

burly *(SYN.)* husky, beefy, heavyset, brawny, strapping.
(ANT.) skinny, scrawny.

burn *(SYN.)* scorch, blaze, scald, sear, char, incinerate, fire, flare, combust, flame, consume.
(ANT.) quench, extinguish.

burnish *(SYN.)* polish, shine, buff, wax, rub.

burrow *(SYN.)* tunnel, search, seek, dig, excavate, hunt, den, hole.

burst *(SYN.)* exploded, broken, erupt.

bury *(SYN.)* hide, inhume, conceal, immure, cover, inter, entomb, secrete.
(ANT.) reveal, display, open, raise, disinter.

business *(SYN.)* employment, profession, trade, work, art, engagement, vocation, occupation, company, concern, firm, partnership, corporation.
(ANT.) hobby, avocation, pastime.

bustle *(SYN.)* noise, flurry, action, trouble, fuss, ado, stir, excitement,

commotion.
(ANT.) calmness, composure, serenity, peacefulness.

bustling *(SYN.)* humming, busy, stirring, vibrant, bubbling, alive, active, moving, jumping, astir, zealous, enterprising.

busy *(SYN.)* careful, industrious, active, patient, assiduous, diligent, perseverant, hardworking, engaged, employed.
(ANT.) unconcerned, indifferent, apathetic, lethargic, careless, inactive, unemployed, lazy, indolent.

busybody *(SYN.)* gossip, tattletale, pry, meddler, snoop.

but *(SYN.)* nevertheless, yet, however, though, although, still.

butcher *(SYN.)* kill, murder, slaughter, assassinate, slay, massacre.
(ANT.) save, protect, vivify, animate, resuscitate.

butt *(SYN.)* bump, ram, bunt, shove, jam, drive, punch, blow, push, thrust, propulsion.

buttocks *(SYN.)* hind end, rump, posterior, backside, behind, bottom, rear, butt.

button *(SYN.)* clasp, close, fasten, hook.

buttress *(SYN.)* support, brace, stay, frame, prop, reinforcement, bulwark, backing, encourage, sustain, reassure, boost, bolster, steel.

buxom *(SYN.)* well-developed, chesty, ample, fleshy, full-figured, zaftig.

buy *(SYN.)* procure, get, purchase, acquire, obtain.
(ANT.) vend, sell.

buzz *(SYN.)* whir, hum, thrum, drone, burr.

by *(SYN.)* near, through, beside, with, from, at, close to.

bygone *(SYN.)* bypast, former, earlier, past, older, erstwhile, onetime, forgotten.
(ANT.) immediate, present, current, modern.

bypass *(SYN.)* deviate from, go around, detour around.

by-product *(SYN.)* offshoot, spin-off, effect, extra, outgrowth, bonus, appendage, side effect, supplement, extension, side issue, rider.

bystander *(SYN.)* onlooker, watcher, viewer, observer, witness, kibitzer.

byway *(SYN.)* passage, detour, path.

byword *(SYN.)* adage, proverb, axiom, shibboleth, apothegm, motto, slogan.

cab *(SYN.)* coach, taxi, car, hack, taxicab, carriage.

cabin *(SYN.)* cottage, shack, shanty, hut, dwelling, house.

cabinet *(SYN.)* ministry, council, committee, case, cupboard.

cable *(SYN.)* wire, cord, rope, telegraph.

cache *(SYN.)* bury, hide, cover, store.

cad *(SYN.)* knave, rascal, scoundrel, rogue.

cafe *(SYN.)* coffeehouse.

cafeteria *(SYN.)* cafe, diner, restaurant.

cagey *(SYN.)* cunning, wary, clever, tricky, cautious, shrewd, evasive. *(ANT.) innocent, straightfoward, guileless, naive.*

calamity *(SYN.)* ruin, disaster, casualty, distress, hardship, trouble, misfortune, bad luck, catastrophe. *(ANT.) blessing, fortune, welfare.*

calculate *(SYN.)* count, compute, figure, estimate, consider, tally, determine, measure, subtract, add, divide, multiply, judge, reckon. *(ANT.) guess, miscalculate, assume, conjecture.*

calculating *(SYN.)* crafty, shrewd, scheming, cunning. *(ANT.) simple, guileless, direct, ingenuous.*

calculation *(SYN.)* figuring, reckoning, computation, estimation. *(ANT.) guess, assumption.*

calendar *(SYN.)* timetable, schedule, diary.

call *(SYN.)* designate, name, yell, cry, ask, shout, speak, cry out, call out, exclaim, command, term, label, phone, ring up, collect, waken, awaken, ring, wake, arouse, rouse, outcry, need, demand, claim, assemble, telephone, occasion, invite.

calling *(SYN.)* occupation, profession, trade.

callous *(SYN.)* insensitive, impenitent, obdurate, unfeeling, indurate, hard, insensible, heartless. *(ANT.) soft, compassionate, tender.*

calm *(SYN.)* appease, lull, quiet, soothe, composed, tranquilize, dispassionate, still, imperturbable, peaceful, pacify, alloy, assuage, unruffled, mild, tranquil, smooth, serene, cool, level-headed, unexcited, aloof, detached, stillness, calmness, serenity, composure.

(ANT.) tempestuous, disturbed, emotional, turmoil, incite, inflame, roiled, incense, upheaval, excite, upset, disturb, arouse.

campaign *(SYN.)* movement, cause, crusade.

can *(SYN.)* tin, container.

canal *(SYN.)* gully, tube, duct, waterway.

cancel *(SYN.)* eliminate, obliterate, erase, delete, nullify, repeal, revoke, cross out, expunge, void, recall, set aside, abolish, rescind. *(ANT.) perpetuate, confirm, ratify, enforce, enact.*

candid *(SYN.)* free, blunt, frank, plain, open, sincere, honest, straightforward, direct, outspoken. *(ANT.) sly, contrived, wily, scheming.*

candidate *(SYN.)* applicant, aspirant, nominee.

canine *(SYN.)* pooch, dog, puppy.

canny *(SYN.)* artful, skillful, shrewd, clever, cautious, cunning, careful.

canopy *(SYN.)* awning, screen, shelter, cover.

cant *(SYN.)* dissimulation, patois, jargon, shoptalk, deceit, argot, pretense. *(ANT.) honesty, condor, frankness, truth.*

cantankerous *(SYN.)* crabby, grouchy, irritable, surly, ill-natured, grumpy, irascible.

canyon *(SYN.)* gulch, gully, arroyo, ravine, gorge.

cap *(SYN.)* top, cover, crown, beat, lid, excel.

capability *(SYN.)* aptness, ability, capacity, aptitude, dexterity, power, efficiency, qualification. *(ANT.) incapacity, disability, incompetency.*

capable *(SYN.)* clever, qualified, able, efficient, competent, skilled, fit, skillful, accomplished, fitted. *(ANT.) unfitted, incapable, incompetent, unskilled, inept, inadequate.*

capacity *(SYN.)* capability, power, ability, talent, content, skill, volume, size. *(ANT.) inability, stupidity, incapacity, impotence.*

cape *(SYN.)* pelisse, cloak, mantle, neck, point, headland, peninsula.

caper *(SYN.)* romp, frisk, cavort, frolic, gambol.

capital *(SYN.)* leading, chief, important, property, wealth, money, city, cash, assets, principal, resources, major, primary, first, funds.

(ANT.) unimportant, trivial, secondary.

capricious *(SYN.)* undependable, erratic, inconstant, fickle, changeable, irregular, inconsistent, unstable.

captain *(SYN.)* commander, authority, supervisor, leader, skipper, commander, master, officer.

caption *(SYN.)* heading, title, headline.

captivate *(SYN.)* fascinate, charm, delight.

captive *(SYN.)* convict, prisoner, hostage.

captivity *(SYN.)* detention, imprisonment, custody, confinement, bondage, slavery.

(ANT.) liberty, freedom.

capture *(SYN.)* catch, grip, apprehend, clutch, arrest, snare, seize, nab, seizure, catching, grasp, take prisoner, grab, recovery, trap.

(ANT.) set free, lose, liberate, throw, free, release.

car *(SYN.)* auto, automobile, motorcar, vehicle.

carcass *(SYN.)* remains, frame, corpse, form, bulk, mass, corpus, association, body, cadaver.

(ANT.) mind, spirit, intellect, soul.

cardinal *(SYN.)* chief, primary, important, prime, leading, major, essential.

(ANT.) subordinate, secondary, auxiliary.

care *(SYN.)* concern, anxiety, worry, caution, solicitude, charge, ward, attention, regard, supervision, consider, consideration, keeping, protection, attend, watch, supervise, keep, guardianship, custody.

(ANT.) neglect, disregard, indifference, unconcern, negligence.

career *(SYN.)* occupation, profession, job, calling, vocation, trade.

carefree *(SYN.)* lighthearted, happy, unconcerned, breezy, jolly, uneasy, nonchalant, happy-go-lucky, lively.

careful *(SYN.)* prudent, thoughtful, attentive, cautious, painstaking, scrupulous, heedful, circumspect, vigilant, guarded, discreet, watchful, wary, concerned, meticulous, thorough, lax, negligent.

(ANT.) nice, careful, heedless, messy, careless, accurate, incautious, sloppy, meticulous.

careless *(SYN.)* imprudent, heedless, un-

concerned, inattentive, lax, indiscreet, desultory, reckless, negligent.

(ANT.) careful, nice, cautious, painstaking, prudent, accurate.

caress *(SYN.)* hug, fondle, embrace, pet, pat, stroke, kiss, cuddle.

(ANT.) spurn, vex, buffet, annoy, tease.

cargo *(SYN.)* freight, load, freightload, shipment.

caricature *(SYN.)* exaggeration, parody, spoof, takeoff, lampoon, satire, burlesque.

carnage *(SYN.)* massacre, liquidation, slaughter, genocide, butchery, extermination, annihilation.

carnal *(SYN.)* base, corporeal, animal, lustful, worldly, sensual, bodily, gross, fleshy, voluptuous.

(ANT.) intellectual, spiritual, exalted, temperate.

carnival *(SYN.)* fete, fair, jamboree, festival.

carol *(SYN.)* hymn, song, ballad.

carp *(SYN.)* pick, praise, complain.

carpet *(SYN.)* mat, rug.

carping *(SYN.)* discerning, exact, captions, accurate, fastidious, important, hazardous.

(ANT.) superficial, cursory, approving, encouraging, unimportant, insignificant.

carriage *(SYN.)* bearing, conduct, action, deed, behavior, demeanor, disposition, deportment.

carry *(SYN.)* convey, transport, support, bring, sustain, bear, hold, move, transfer, take.

(ANT.) drop, abandon.

carry off *(SYN.)* seize, abduct, capture, kidnap.

(ANT.) set free, let go. liberate.

carry on *(SYN.)* go on, continue, proceed, misbehave.

(ANT.) stop.

carry out *(SYN.)* succeed, complete, fulfill, win, accomplish, effect.

carve *(SYN.)* hew, shape, cut, whittle, chisel, sculpt.

case *(SYN.)* state, covering, receptacle, condition, instance, example, occurrence, happening, illustration, sample, suit, action, claim, lawsuit, crate, container, carton, box.

cash *(SYN.)* currency, money.

casket *(SYN.)* coffin, box, crate.

cast *(SYN.)* fling, toss, throw, pitch,

form, company, shape, sort, mold, hurl, sling, shed, direct, impart, turn, actors, players, type, variety.

caste *(SYN.)* class, grade, order, category, status, elegance, set, rank, station, social standing, denomination, excellence, genre.

castle *(SYN.)* mansion, palace, chateau.

casual *(SYN.)* chance, unexpected, informal, accidental, incidental, offhand, unplanned, relaxed, fortuitous, unintentional, spontaneous.
(ANT.) planned, expected, calculated, formal, deliberate, dressy, premeditated, pretentious.

casualty *(SYN.)* calamity, fortuity, mishap, loss, injured, dead, wounded, accident, contingency, victim, sufferer, misfortune.
(ANT.) design, purpose, intention, calculation.

catalog *(SYN.)* classify, roll, group, list, inventory, directory, index, record, file.

catastrophe *(SYN.)* mishap, calamity, disaster, adversity, accident, ruin.
(ANT.) fortune, boon, triumph, blessing, advantage, welfare.

catch *(SYN.)* hook, snare, entrap, ensnare, capture, grip, apprehend, grasp, take, grab, nab, arrest, contract, snare, seize, apprehension, latch, bolt, pin, clasp, trap.
(ANT.) lose, free, liberate, throw, release.

catching *(SYN.)* contagious, pestilential, communicable, infectious, virulent.
(ANT.) noncommunicable, healthful.

catchy *(SYN.)* tricky, misleading, attractive.

category *(SYN.)* class, caste, kind, order, genre, rank, classification, sort, elegance, type, set, excellence.

cater *(SYN.)* coddle, oblige, serve, humor, baby, mollycoddle, pamper, spoil, indulge, provide.

cause *(SYN.)* effect, incite, create, induce, inducement, occasion, incentive, prompt, principle, determinant, reason, origin, motive.

caustic *(SYN.)* bitter, disagreeable, distasteful, acrid, sour, spiteful, pungent, tart, painful, cruel, insulting, peevish, mean, ruthless, malicious, hateful, harsh.
(ANT.) mellow, sweet, delicious, pleasant.

caution *(SYN.)* heed, vigilance, care, prudence, counsel, warning, wariness, advice, warn, injunction, admonish, watchfulness.
(ANT.) carelessness, heedlessness, incaution, abandon, recklessness.

cautious *(SYN.)* heedful, scrupulous, attentive, prudent, thoughtful, discreet, guarded, circumspect, vigilant, watchful, wary, careful.
(ANT.) improvident, headstrong, heedless, foolish, forgetful, indifferent.

cavalcade *(SYN.)* column, procession, parade.

cavalier *(SYN.)* contemptuous, insolent, haughty, arrogant.

cave *(SYN.)* grotto, hole, shelter, lair, den, cavern.

cave in *(SYN.)* fall in, collapse.

cavity *(SYN.)* pit, hole, crater.

cavort *(SYN.)* caper, leap, frolic, hop, prance.

cease *(SYN.)* desist, stop, abandon, discontinue, relinquish, end, terminate, leave, surrender, resign.
(ANT.) occupy, continue, persist, begin, endure, stay.

cede *(SYN.)* surrender, relinquish, yield.

celebrate *(SYN.)* honor, glorify, commemorate, keep, solemnize, extol, observe, commend, praise.
(ANT.) decry, overlook, profane, disregard, disgrace.

celebrated *(SYN.)* eminent, glorious, distinguished, noted, illustrious, famed, well-known, popular, renowned, famous.
(ANT.) obscure, hidden, anonymous, infamous, unknown.

celebrity *(SYN.)* somebody, personage, heroine, hero, dignitary, notable.

celestial *(SYN.)* godlike, holy, supernatural, divine, paradisiacal, utopian, transcendent, superhuman.
(ANT.) diabolical, profane, mundane, wicked.

cement *(SYN.)* solidify, weld, fasten, secure.

cemetery *(SYN.)* graveyard.

censure *(SYN.)* denounce, reproach, upbraid, blame, disapproval, reprehend, condemn, criticism, disapprove, criticize, reprove.
(ANT.) commend, approval, forgive, approve, praise, applaud, condone.

center *(SYN.)* heart, core, midpoint, middle, nucleus, inside, hub, focus.
(ANT.) rim, boundary, edge, border, periphery, outskirts.

central *(SYN.)* chief, necessary, main, halfway, dominant, mid, middle, inner, focal, leading, fundamental, principal.
(ANT.) side, secondary, incidental, auxiliary.

ceremonious *(SYN.)* correct, exact, precise, stiff, outward, external, solemn, formal.
(ANT.) material, unconventional, easy, heartfelt.

ceremony *(SYN.)* observance, rite, parade, formality, pomp, ritual, protocol, solemnity.
(ANT.) informality, casualness.

certain *(SYN.)* definite, assured, fixed, inevitable, sure, undeniable, positive, confident, particular, special, indubitable, secure, unquestionable.
(ANT.) probable, uncertain, doubtful, questionable.

certainly *(SYN.)* absolutely, surely, definitely.
(ANT.) dubiously, doubtfully, questionably.

certainty *(SYN.)* confidence, courage, security, assuredness, firmness, assertion, statement.
(ANT.) humility, bashfulness, modest, shyness.

certificate *(SYN.)* affidavit, document.

certify *(SYN.)* validate, affirm, verify, confirm, authenticate, substantiate.

certitude *(SYN.)* confidence, belief, conviction, feeling, faith, persuasion, trust.
(ANT.) doubt, incredulity, denial, heresy.

cessation *(SYN.)* ending, finish, stoppage, termination, conclusion, end.

chafe *(SYN.)* heat, rub, warm, annoy, disturb.

chagrin *(SYN.)* irritation, mortification, embarrassment, annoyance, vexation, worry, bother, shame, annoy, irk, humiliation, irritate, vex, frustrate, humiliate, embarrass, mortify, exasperate, disappoint, disappointment.

chain *(SYN.)* fasten, bind, shackle, restrain.

chairman *(SYN.)* speaker.

challenge *(SYN.)* question, dare, call, summon, threat, invite, threaten, demand.

chamber *(SYN.)* cell, salon, room.

champion *(SYN.)* victor, winner, choice, best, conqueror, hero, support, select.

chance *(SYN.)* befall, accident, betide, disaster, opportunity, calamity, occur, possibility, prospect, happen, luck, fate, take place.
(ANT.) design, purpose, inevitability, calculation, certainty, intention.

change *(SYN.)* modification, alternation, alteration, mutation, variety, exchange, shift, alter, transfigure, veer, vary, variation, substitution, substitute, vicissitude.
(ANT.) uniformity, monotony, settle, remain, endure, retain, preserve, steadfastness, endurance, immutability, stability.

changeable *(SYN.)* fitful, fickle, inconstant, unstable, shifting, wavering.
(ANT.) stable, uniform, constant, unchanging.

channel *(SYN.)* strait, corridor, waterway, artery, duct, canal, way, trough, groove, passageway.

chant *(SYN.)* singing, incantation, hymn, intone, sing, carol, psalm, song, ballad.

chaos *(SYN.)* confusion, jumble, turmoil, anarchy, disorder, muddle.
(ANT.) organization, order, tranquillity, tidiness, system.

chaotic *(SYN.)* confused, disorganized, disordered, messy.
(ANT.) neat, ordered, systematic, organized.

chap *(SYN.)* break, fellow, person, crack, split, man, rough, individual, boy.

chaperon *(SYN.)* associate with, escort, convoy, accompany, consort with.
(ANT.) avoid, desert, leave, abandon, quit.

chapter *(SYN.)* part, section, division.

char *(SYN.)* scorch, singe, burn, sear.

character *(SYN.)* description, class, kind, repute, mark, individuality, disposition, traits, personality, reputation, symbol, features, quality, eccentric, nature.

characteristic *(SYN.)* exclusive, distinctive, special, mark, feature, property, typical, unique, attribute. distinguishing, trait, quality.

charge *(SYN.)* arraignment, indictment, accusation, sell for, attack, assail, assault, indict, blame, allegation, care, custody, imputation.
(ANT.) pardon, flee, exculpation, excuse,

absolve, retreat, exoneration.

charitable *(SYN.)* benevolent, generous, liberal, altruistic, kind, obliging, considerate, unselfish.
(ANT.) petty, mean, harsh, wicked, greedy, narrow-minded, stingy, malevolent.

charity *(SYN.)* benevolence, kindness, magnanimity, altruism, generosity.
(ANT.) malevolence, cruelty, selfishness.

charm *(SYN.)* allure, spell, enchantment, attractiveness, magic, witchery, amulet, talisman, lure, enchant, bewitch, fascinate, captivate.

charmer *(SYN.)* siren, temptress, enchantress, vamp, seductress, seducer, enchanter.

charming *(SYN.)* attractive, enchanting, fascinating, alluring, appealing, winsome, agreeable, bewitching, winning.
(ANT.) revolting, repugnant, repulsive.

chart *(SYN.)* design, plan, cabal, plot, sketch, stratagem, map, diagram, conspiracy, graph, intrigue.

charter *(SYN.)* lease, hire, rent, alliance.

chase *(SYN.)* hunt, run after, pursue, trail, follow, persist, scheme.
(ANT.) escape, flee, abandon, elude, evade.

chasm *(SYN.)* ravine, abyss, canyon, gorge.

chaste *(SYN.)* clear, immaculate, innocent, sincere, bare, clean, modest, pure, decent, virtuous, virginal, sheer, absolute, spotless.
(ANT.) polluted, tainted, foul, impure, sinful, worldly, sullied, defiled.

chasten *(SYN.)* chastise, restrain, punish, discipline.

chastise *(SYN.)* punish, castigate, correct.
(ANT.) release, acquit, free, exonerate.

chat *(SYN.)* argue, jabber, blab, plead, consult, converse, lecture, discuss, talk, conversation, tattle.

chatter *(SYN.)* dialogue, lecture, speech, conference, talk, discourse.
(ANT.) silence, correspondence, writing.

cheap *(SYN.)* poor, common, inexpensive, shabby, low-priced, beggary, lowcost, shoddy, mean, inferior.
(ANT.) honorable, dear, noble, expensive, costly, well-made, elegant, dignified.

cheat *(SYN.)* deceive, fool, bilk, outwit, victimize, dupe, gull, hoodwink, circumvent, swindler, cheater, trickster, phony,

fraud, defraud, charlatan, crook, chiseler, con artist, hoax, swindle.

check *(SYN.)* dissect, interrogate, analyze, contemplate, inquire, question, scrutinize, arrest, stop, halt, block, curb, control, investigate, review, examine, test, counterfoil, stub, barrier, watch.
(ANT.) overlook, disregard, advance, foster, continue, promote, omit, neglect.

checkup *(SYN.)* medical examination, physical.

cheek *(SYN.)* nerve, effrontery, impudence, gall, impertinence.

cheer *(SYN.)* console, gladden, comfort, encourage, applause, encouragement, joy, glee, gaiety, mirth, soothe, sympathize, approval, solace.
(ANT.) depress, sadden, discourage, derision, dishearten, discouragement, antagonize.

cheerful *(SYN.)* glad, jolly, joyful, gay, happy, cherry, merry, joyous, lighthearted.
(ANT.) mournful, sad, glum, depressed, gloomy, sullen.

cherish *(SYN.)* prize, treasure, appreciate, nurse, value, comfort, hold dear, foster, nurture, sustain.
(ANT.) disregard, neglect, deprecate, scorn, reject, undervalue, abandon.

chest *(SYN.)* bosom, breast, coffer, box, case, trunk, casket, dresser, commode, cabinet, chifforobe.

chew *(SYN.)* gnaw, munch, bite, nibble.

chic *(SYN.)* fashionable, modish, smart, stylish, trendy.

chide *(SYN.)* admonish, rebuke, scold, reprimand, criticize, reprove.
(ANT.) extol, praise, commend.

chief *(SYN.)* chieftain, head, commander, captain, leader, principal, master, boss, leading, ruler.
(ANT.) servant, subordinate, secondary, follower, incidental, accidental, auxiliary, attendant.

chiefly *(SYN.)* mainly, especially, mostly.

childish *(SYN.)* immature, childlike, infantile, babyish.
(ANT.) mature, adult, seasoned, grownup.

chill *(SYN.)* coolness, cold, cool, coldness, brisk, frosty.
(ANT.) hot, warm, heat, heated, warmth.

chilly *(SYN.)* cold, frigid, freezing, arctic, cool, icy, passionless, wintry, unfeeling.

(ANT.) fiery, heated, passionate, ardent.

chirp *(SYN.)* peep, cheep, twitter, tweet, chirrup.

chivalrous *(SYN.)* noble, brave, polite, valorous, gallant, gentlemanly, courteous.
(ANT.) crude, rude, impolite, un-civil.

chivalry *(SYN.)* courtesy, nobility, gallantry, knighthood.

choice *(SYN.)* delicate, elegant, fine, dainty, exquisite, pure, refined, subtle, splendid, handsome, option, selection, beautiful, minute, pretty, pick, select, uncommon, rare, precious, valuable, thin, small.
(ANT.) coarse, rough, thick, blunt, large.

choke *(SYN.)* throttle, gag, strange.

choose *(SYN.)* elect, decide between, pick, select, cull, opt.
(ANT.) reject, refuse.

chop *(SYN.)* hew, cut, fell, mince.

chore *(SYN.)* routine, task, job, duty, work.

chronic *(SYN.)* persistent, constant, lingering, continuing, perennial, unending, sustained, permanent.
(ANT.) fleeting, acute, temporary.

chronicle *(SYN.)* detail, history, narrative, account, description, narration, recital.
(ANT.) misrepresentation, confusion, distortion.

chuckle *(SYN.)* titter, laugh, giggle.

chum *(SYN.)* friend, pal, buddy, companion.

cinema *(SYN.)* effigy, film, etching, appearance, drawing, engraving, illustration, likeness, image, panorama, painting, picture, photograph.

circle *(SYN.)* disk, ring, set, group, class, club, surround, encircle, enclose, round.

circuit *(SYN.)* circle, course, journey, orbit, revolution, tour.

circuitous *(SYN.)* distorted, devious, indirect, roundabout swerving, crooked, tortuous.
(ANT.) straightforward, straight, direct, honest.

circular *(SYN.)* chubby, complete, curved, bulbous, cylindrical, round, ringlike, globular, entire, rotund.
(ANT.) straight.

circumference *(SYN.)* border, perimeter, periphery, edge.

circumspection *(SYN.)* care, worry, solicitude, anxiety, concern, caution, attention, vigilance.
(ANT.) neglect, negligence, indifference.

circumstance *(SYN.)* fact, event, incident, condition, happening, position, occurrence, situation.

circumstances *(SYN.)* facts, conditions, factors, situation, background, grounds, means, capital, assets, rank, class.

cite *(SYN.)* affirm, assign, allege, advance, quote, mention, declare, claim, maintain.
(ANT.) refute, gainsay, deny, contradict.

citizen *(SYN.)* native, inhabitant, national, denizen, subject, dweller, resident.

city *(SYN.)* metropolis, municipality, town.

civil *(SYN.)* courteous, cultivated, accomplished, public, municipal, respectful, genteel, polite, considerate, gracious, urban.
(ANT.) uncouth, uncivil, impertinent, impolite, boorish.

civilization *(SYN.)* cultivation, culture, education, breeding, enlightenment, society, refinement.
(ANT.) ignorance, vulgarity.

civilize *(SYN.)* refine, tame, polish, cultivate, instruct, teach.

claim *(SYN.)* aver, declare, allege, assert, affirm, express, state, demand, maintain, defend, uphold.
(ANT.) refute, deny, contradict.

clamor *(SYN.)* cry, din, babel, noise, racket, outcry, row, sound tumult, shouting, shout, uproar.
(ANT.) hush, serenity, silence, tranquillity, stillness, quiet.

clan *(SYN.)* fellowship, kindness, solidarity, family, brotherliness, association, fraternity.
(ANT.) discord, strife, opposition, acrimony.

clandestine *(SYN.)* covert, hidden, latent, private, concealed, secret, unknown.
(ANT.) exposed, known, conspicuous, obvious.

clarify *(SYN.)* educate, explain, expound, decipher, illustrate, clear, resolve, define, interpret, unfold.
(ANT.) darken, obscure, baffle, confuse.

clash *(SYN.)* clank, crash, clang, conflict, disagreement, opposition, collision, struggle, mismatch, contrast, disagree,

collide, interfere.
(ANT.) accord, agreement, harmony, blend, harmonize, match, agree.
clasp *(SYN.)* grip, hold, grasp, adhere, clutch, keep, have, maintain, possess, occupy, retain, support, confine, embrace, fastening, check, detain, curb, receive.
(ANT.) relinquish, vacate, surrender, abandon.
class *(SYN.)* category, denomination, caste, kind, genre, grade, rank, order, elegance, classification, division, sort, family, species, set, excellence.
classic *(SYN.)* masterpiece.
classification *(SYN.)* order, category, class, arrangement, ordering, grouping, organization.
classify *(SYN.)* arrange, class, order, sort, grade, group, index.
clause *(SYN.)* condition, paragraph, limitation, article.
claw *(SYN.)* hook, talon, nail, scratch.
clean *(SYN.)* mop, tidy, neat, dustless, clear, unsoiled, immaculate, unstained, untainted, pure, dust, vacuum, scour, decontaminate, wipe, sterilize, cleanse, scrub, purify, wash, sweep.
(ANT.) stain, soil, pollute, soiled, impure, dirty, stain.
cleanse *(SYN.)* mop, purify, wash, sweep.
(ANT.) stain, soil, dirty, pollute.
clear *(SYN.)* fair, sunny, cloudless, transparent, apparent, limpid, distinct, intelligible, evident, unmistakable, understandable, unclouded, uncloudy, light, bright, certain, manifest, lucid, plain, obvious, unobstructed.
(ANT.) obscure, unclear, muddled, confused, dark, cloudy, blocked, obstructed, questionable, dubious, blockaded, foul, overcast.
clearly *(SYN.)* plainly, obviously, evidently, definitely, surely, certainly.
(ANT.) questionably, dubiously.
clemency *(SYN.)* forgiveness, charity, compassion, grace, mercy, leniency, pity, mildness.
(ANT.) punishment, vengeance, retribution.
clerical *(SYN.)* ministerial, pastoral, priestly, celestial, holy, sacred, secretarial.
clerk *(SYN.)* typist, office worker, office girl, saleslady, salesperson, salesclerk.

clever *(SYN.)* apt, dexterous, quick, adroit, quick-witted, talented, bright, skillful, witty, ingenious, smart, intelligent, shrewd, gifted, expert, sharp.
(ANT.) unskilled, slow, stupid, backward, maladroit, bungling, dull, clumsy.
cleverness *(SYN.)* intellect, intelligence, comprehension, mind, perspicacity, sagacity, fun.
(ANT.) sobriety, stupidity, solemnity, commonplace, platitude.
client *(SYN.)* patron, customer.
cliff *(SYN.)* scar, tor, bluff, crag, precipice, escarpment.
climate *(SYN.)* aura, atmosphere, air, ambience.
climax *(SYN.)* apex, culmination, peak, summit, consummation, height, acme, zenith.
(ANT.) depth, base, anticlimax, floor.
climb *(SYN.)* mount, scale, ascend.
(ANT.) descend.
clip *(SYN.)* snip, crop, cut, mow, clasp.
cloak *(SYN.)* conceal, cover, disguise, clothe, cape, guard, envelop, hide, mask, protect, shield.
(ANT.) divulge, expose, reveal, bare, unveil.
clod *(SYN.)* wad, hunk, gobbet, lump, chunk, clot, gob, dunce, dolt, oaf, fool.
clog *(SYN.)* crowd, congest, cram, overfill, stuff.
cloister *(SYN.)* monastery, priory, hermitage, abbey, convent.
close *(SYN.)* adjacent, adjoining, immediate, unventilated, stuffy, abutting, neighboring, dear, oppressive, mean, impending, nearby, near, devoted.
(ANT.) afar, faraway, removed, distant.
close *(SYN.)* seal, shut, clog, stop, obstruct, cease, conclude, complete, end, terminate, occlude, finish.
(ANT.) unlock, begin, open, unbar, inaugurate, commence, start.
closet *(SYN.)* cabinet, locker, wardrobe, cupboard.
cloth *(SYN.)* fabric, goods, material, textile.
clothe *(SYN.)* garb, dress, apparel.
(ANT.) strip, undress.
clothes *(SYN.)* array, attire, apparel, clothing, dress, garb, dress, garments, raiment, drapery, vestments.
(ANT.) nudity, nakedness.
clothing *(SYN.)* attire, clothes, apparel,

array, dress, drapery, garments, garb, vestments.

(ANT.) nudity, nakedness.

cloud *(SYN.)* fog, mist, haze, mass, collection, obscure, dim, shadow.

cloudy *(SYN.)* dim, dark, indistinct, murky, mysterious, indefinite, vague, sunless, clouded, obscure, overcast, shadowy.

(ANT.) sunny, clear, distinct, limpid, lucid, clarified, cloudless, clearheaded, brilliant, bright.

club *(SYN.)* society, association, set, circle, organization, bat, cudgel, stick, blackjack.

clue *(SYN.)* sign, trace, hint, suggestion.

clumsy *(SYN.)* bungling, inept, rough, unpolished, bumbling, awkward, ungraceful, gauche, ungainly, unskillful, untoward.

(ANT.) polished, skillful, neat, graceful, dexterous, adroit.

cluster *(SYN.)* batch, clutch, group, bunch, gather, pack, assemble, crowd.

clutch *(SYN.)* grip, grab, seize, hold.

coalition *(SYN.)* combination, association, alliance, confederacy, entente, league, treaty.

(ANT.) schism, separation, divorce.

coarse *(SYN.)* unpolished, vulgar, refined, rough, smooth, impure, rude, crude, gruff, gross, cultivated, delicate, cultured.

(ANT.) delicate, smooth, refined, polished, genteel, cultivated, suave, fine, cultured.

coast *(SYN.)* seaboard, seashore, beach, shore, drift, glide, ride.

coax *(SYN.)* urge, persuade, wheedle, cajole.

(ANT.) force, bully, coerce.

coddle *(SYN.)* pamper, baby, spoil, indulge.

code *(SYN.)* crypt, cryptogram, cipher.

coerce *(SYN.)* constrain, compel, enforce, force, drive, oblige, impel.

(ANT.) prevent, persuade, convince, induce.

coercion *(SYN.)* emphasis, intensity, energy, dint, might potency, power, vigor, strength, compulsion, force, constraint, violence.

(ANT.) impotence, frailty, feebleness, weakness, persuasion.

cognizance *(SYN.)* apprehension, erudi-

tion, acquaintance, information, learning, knowledge, lore, science, scholarship, understanding.

(ANT.) illiteracy, misunderstanding, ignorance.

cognizant *(SYN.)* conscious, aware, apprised informed, mindful, observant, perceptive.

(ANT.) unaware, ignorant, oblivious, insensible.

coherent *(SYN.)* logical, intelligible, sensible, rational, commonsensical, reasonable.

coiffeur *(SYN.)* hairdresser.

coiffure *(SYN.)* haircut, hairdo.

coincide *(SYN.)* acquiesce, agree, accede, assent, consent, comply, correspond, concur, match, tally, harmonize, conform.

(ANT.) differ, disagree, protest, contradict.

coincidence *(SYN.)* accident, chance.

(ANT.) plot, plan, pre-arrangement, scheme.

coincident *(SYN.)* identical, equal, equivalent, distinguishable, same, like.

(ANT.) distinct, contrary, disparate, opposed.

coincidental *(SYN.)* unpredicted, unexpected, chance, unforeseen, accidental, fortuitous.

cold *(SYN.)* cool, freezing, chilly, frigid, icy, frozen, wintry, arctic, unfriendly, indifferent, phlegmatic, stoical, passionless, chill, unemotional, heartless, unfeeling.

(ANT.) hot, torrid, fiery, burning, ardent, friendly, temperate, warm, passionate.

collapse *(SYN.)* descend, decrease, diminish, fail, downfall, failure, decline, fall, drop, sink, subside, topple.

(ANT.) soar, steady, limb, mount, arise.

colleague *(SYN.)* companion, attendant, comrade, associate, crony, co-worker, mate, friend, partner.

(ANT.) enemy, stranger, adversary.

collect *(SYN.)* assemble, amass, concentrate, pile, accumulate, congregate, obtain, heap, gather, solicit, secure, procure, raise, get, mass, hoard, consolidate.

(ANT.) divide, dole, assort, dispel, distribute, disperse.

collected *(SYN.)* cool, calm, composed,

peaceful, imperturbable, placid, sedate, quiet.

(ANT.) excited, violent, aroused, agitated.

collection (SYN.) amount, conglomeration, sum, entirety, aggregation, hoard, accumulation, pile, store, aggregate, total, whole.

(ANT.) part, unit, particular, element, ingredient.

collide (SYN.) hit, smash, crash, strike.

collision (SYN.) conflict, combat, duel, battle, encounter, crash, smash, fight, contention, struggle, discord.

(ANT.) concord, amity, harmony, consonance.

collusion (SYN.) combination, cabal, intrigue, conspiracy, plot, treason, treachery.

color (SYN.) hue, paint, pigment, complexion, dye, shade, tone, tincture, stain, tint, tinge.

(ANT.) paleness, transparency, achromatism.

colorful (SYN.) impressive, vivid, striking, full-color, multicolored, offbeat, weird, unusual.

(ANT.) flat, dull, uninteresting.

colossal (SYN.) enormous, elephantine, gargantuan, huge, immense, gigantic, prodigious.

(ANT.) little, minute, small, miniature, diminutive, microscopic, tiny.

combat (SYN.) conflict, duel, battle, collision, encounter, fight, contest, oppose, war, contention, struggle, discord.

(ANT.) consonance, harmony, concord, yield, surrender, succumb, amity.

combination (SYN.) association, confederacy, alliance, entente, league, compounding, mixture, blend, composite, federation, mixing, compound, blending, union.

(ANT.) separation, division, schism, divorce.

combine (SYN.) adjoin, associate, accompany, conjoin, connect, link, mix, blend, couple, unite, join.

(ANT.) detach, disjoin, divide, separate, disconnect.

come (SYN.) near, approach, reach, arrive, advance.

(ANT.) depart, leave, go.

comedian (SYN.) comic, wit, humorist, gagman, wag.

comely (SYN.) charming, elegant, beauteous, beautiful, fine, lovely, pretty, handsome lovely.

(ANT.) hideous, repulsive, foul, unsightly.

come-on (SYN.) lure, inducement, enticement, temptation, premium.

comfort (SYN.) contentment, ease, enjoyment, relieve, consolation, relief, cheer, console, calm, satisfaction, soothe, encourage, succor, luxury, solace.

(ANT.) depress, torture, discomfort, upset, misery, disturb, agitate, affliction, discompose, uncertainty, suffering.

comfortable (SYN.) pleasing, agreeable, convenient, cozy, welcome, acceptable, relaxed, restful, cozy, gratifying, easy, contented, rested, satisfying, pleasurable.

(ANT.) miserable, distressing, tense, strained, troubling, edgy, uncomfortable.

comical (SYN.) droll, funny, humorous, amusing, ludicrous, witty, ridiculous, odd, queer.

(ANT.) sober, solemn, sad, serious, melancholy.

command (SYN.) class, method, plan regularity, rank, arrangement, series, sequence, point, aim, conduct, manage, guide, bid, system, succession, bidding, direct, order, demand, direction, rule, dictate, decree.

(ANT.) consent, obey, misdirect, distract, deceive, misguide, license, confusion.

commandeer (SYN.) take, possession, seize, confiscate, appropriate.

commanding (SYN.) imposing, masterful, assertive, authoritative, positive.

commence (SYN.) open, start.

(ANT.) stop, end, terminate, finish.

commend (SYN.) laud, praise, applaud, recommend.

(ANT.) censure, blame, criticize.

commendable (SYN.) deserving, praiseworthy.

(ANT.) bad, deplorable, lamentable.

commendation (SYN.) approval, applause, praise, recommendation, honor, medal.

(ANT.) criticism, condemnation, censure.

commensurate (SYN.) keep, celebrate, observe, honor, commend, extol, glorify, laud, praise, honor.

(ANT.) decry, disgrace, disregard, over-look, profane, dishonor.

comment (SYN.) assertion, declaration, annotation, explanation, review, commentary, report, remark, observation, utterance, criticism, statement.

commerce (SYN.) business, engagement, employment, art, trade, marketing, enterprise, occupation.
(ANT.) hobby, pastime, avocation.

commission (SYN.) board, committee, command, permit, order, permission, delegate, authorize, deputize, entrust.

commit (SYN.) perpetrate, perform, obligate, do, commend, consign, relegate, bind, delegate, empower, pledge, entrust, authorize, trust.
(ANT.) neglect, mistrust, release, free, miscarry, fail, loose.

commitment (SYN.) duty, promise, responsibility, pledge.

committee (SYN.) commission, bureau, board, delegate, council.

commodious (SYN.) appropriate, accessible, adapted, favorable, handy, fitting, timely.
(ANT.) inconvenient, troublesome, awkward.

commodity (SYN.) article, merchandise, wares, goods.

common (SYN.) ordinary, popular, familiar, mean, low, general, vulgar, communal, mutual, shared, natural, frequent, prevalent, joint, conventional, plain, usual, universal.
(ANT.) odd, exceptional, scarce, noble, extraordinary, different, separate, outstanding, rare, unusual, distinctive, refined.

commonplace (SYN.) common, usual, frequent, ordinary, everyday.
(ANT.) distinctive, unusual, original.

commonsense (SYN.) perceptible, alive, apprehensible, aware, awake, cognizant, conscious, comprehending, perceptible.
(ANT.) unaware, impalpable, imperceptible.

commotion (SYN.) confusion, chaos, disarray, ferment, disorder, stir, tumult, agitation.
(ANT.) tranquillity, peace, certainty, order.

communicable (SYN.) infectious, virulent, catching, transferable, contagious.
(ANT.) hygienic, noncommunicable,

healthful.

communicate (SYN.) convey, impart, inform, confer, disclose, reveal, relate, tell, advertise, publish, transmit, publicize, divulge.
(ANT.) withhold, hide, conceal.

communication (SYN.) disclosure, transmission, declaration, announcement, notification, publication, message, report, news, information.

communicative (SYN.) unreserved, open, frank, free, straightforward, unrestrained.
(ANT.) close-mouthed, secretive.

communion (SYN.) intercourse, fellowship, participation, association, sacrament, union.
(ANT.) nonparticipation, alienation.

community (SYN.) public, society, city, town, village, township.

compact (SYN.) contracted, firm, narrow, snug, close, constricted, packed, vanity, treaty, agreement, tense, taught, tight, niggardly, close-fisted, parsimonious, com-pressed, stingy.
(ANT.) slack, open, loose, relaxed, unconfined, unfretted, sprawling, lax.

companion (SYN.) attendant, comrade, consort, friend, colleague, partner, crony, mate, associate.
(ANT.) stranger, enemy, adversary.

companionship (SYN.) familiarity, cognizance, acquaintance, fellowship, knowledge, intimacy.
(ANT.) unfamiliarity, inexperience, ignorance.

company (SYN.) crew, group, band, party, throng, house, assemblage, troop, fellowship, association, business, concern, partnership, corporation, companionship, firm.
(ANT.) seclusion, individual, solitude, dispersion.

comparable (SYN.) allied, analogous, alike, akin, like, correspondent, correlative, parallel.
(ANT.) opposed, incongruous, dissimilar, unalike, different, divergent.

compare (SYN.) discriminate, match, differentiate, contrast, oppose.

comparison (SYN.) likening, contrasting, judgment.

compartment (SYN.) division, section.

compassion (SYN.) mercy, sympathy, pity, commiseration, condolence.

(ANT.) *ruthlessness, hardness, brutality, inhumanity, cruelty.*

compassionate *(SYN.)* sympathizing, benign, forbearing, good, tender, affable, humane, indulgent, kind, sympathetic, kindly.

(ANT.) *inhuman, merciless, unkind, cold-hearted, unsympathetic, cruel.*

compatible *(SYN.)* consistent, agreeing, conforming, accordant, congruous, harmonious, cooperative, agreeable, constant, consonant, correspondent.

(ANT.) *discrepant, paradoxical, disagreeable, contradictory.*

compel *(SYN.)* drive, enforce, coerce, constrain, force, oblige, impel.

(ANT.) *induce, coax, prevent, wheedle, persuade, cajole, convince.*

compensate *(SYN.)* remunerate, repay, reimburse, recompense, balance.

compensation *(SYN.)* fee, earnings, pay, payment, recompense, allowance, remuneration, remittance, settlement, stipend, repayment, salary, wages.

(ANT.) *present, gratuity, gift.*

compete *(SYN.)* rival, contest, oppose, vie.

(ANT.) *reconcile, accord.*

competence *(SYN.)* skill, ability, capability.

competent *(SYN.)* efficient, clever, capable, able, apt, proficient, skillful, fitted, qualified.

(ANT.) *inept, incapable, unfitted, awkward, incompetent, in-adequate.*

competition *(SYN.)* contest, match, rivalry, tournament.

competitor *(SYN.)* rival, contestant, opponent.

(ANT.) *ally, friend, colleague.*

complain *(SYN.)* lament, murmur, protest, grouch, grumble, regret, moan, remonstrate, whine, repine.

(ANT.) *rejoice, praise, applaud, approve.*

complaint *(SYN.)* protest, objection, grievance.

complement *(SYN.)* supplement, complete.

(ANT.) *clash, conflict.*

complete *(SYN.)* consummate, entire, ended, full, thorough, finished, full, whole, concluded, over, done, terminate, unbroken, total, undivided.

(ANT.) *unfinished, imperfect, incomplete, start, partial, begin, commence,*

lacking.

completion *(SYN.)* achievement, attainment, end, conclusion, close, finish, wind-up, accomplishment, realization.

(ANT.) *omission, neglect, failure, defeat.*

complex *(SYN.)* sophisticated, compound, intricate, involved, perplexing, elaborate, complicated.

(ANT.) *basic, simple, rudimentary, uncompounded, uncomplicated, plain.*

complexion *(SYN.)* paint, pigment hue, color, dye, stain, tincture, tinge, tint, shade.

(ANT.) *paleness, transparency, achromatism.*

compliant *(SYN.)* meek, modest, lowly, plain, submissive, simple, unostentatious, unassuming, unpretentious.

(ANT.) *proud, vain, arrogant, haughty, boastful.*

complicated *(SYN.)* intricate, involved, complex, compound, perplexing.

(ANT.) *simple, plain, uncompounded.*

compliment *(SYN.)* eulogy, flattery, praise, admiration, honor, adulation, flatter, commendation, tribute.

(ANT.) *taunt, affront, aspersion, insult, disparage, criticism.*

complimentary *(SYN.)* gratis, free.

comply *(SYN.)* assent, consent, accede, acquiesce, coincide, conform, concur, tally.

(ANT.) *differ, dissent, protest, disagree.*

component *(SYN.)* division, fragment, allotment, moiety, apportionment, scrap, portion, section, share, segment, ingredient, organ.

(ANT.) *whole, entirety.*

comport *(SYN.)* carry, conduct, behave, act, deport, interact, operate, manage.

compose *(SYN.)* forge, fashion, mold, make, construct, create, produce, shape, form, constitute, arrange, organize, make up, write, invent, devise, frame.

(ANT.) *misshape, dismantle, disfigure, destroy.*

composed *(SYN.)* calm, cool, imperturbable, placid, quiet, unmoved, sedate, peaceful, collected, tranquil.

(ANT.) *aroused, violent, nervous, agitated, perturbed, excited.*

composer *(SYN.)* author, inventor, creator, maker, originator.

composition *(SYN.)* paper, theme, work,

essay, compound, mixture, mix.

composure *(SYN.)* calmness, poise, control, self-control, self-possession.
(ANT.) anger, rage, turbulence, agitation.

compound *(SYN.)* blend, confound, jumble, consort, aggregate, complicated, combination, combined, mixture, complex, join.
(ANT.) segregate, separate, divide, simple, sort.

comprehend *(SYN.)* apprehend, discern, learn, perceive, see, grasp, understand.
(ANT.) mistake, misunderstand, ignore.

comprehension *(SYN.)* insight, perception, understanding, awareness, discernment.
(ANT.) misconception, insensibility.

comprehensive *(SYN.)* wide, inclusive, complete, broad, full.
(ANT.) fragmentary, partial, limited, incomplete.

compress *(SYN.)* press, compact, squeeze, pack, crowd.
(ANT.) spread, stretch, expand.

comprise *(SYN.)* contain, hold, embrace.
(ANT.) emit, encourage, yield, discharge.

compulsion *(SYN.)* might, energy, potency, strength, vigor.
(ANT.) persuasion, impotence, frailty.

compulsory *(SYN.)* required, obligatory, necessary, unavoidable.
(ANT.) elective, optional, free, unrestricted.

computation *(SYN.)* reckoning, record.
(ANT.) misrepresentation.

compute *(SYN.)* count, calculate, determine, figure, reckon.
(ANT.) conjecture, guess, miscalculate.

comrade *(SYN.)* attendant, companion, colleague, associate, friend.
(ANT.) stranger, enemy, adversary.

con *(SYN.)* cheat, bamboozle, trick, swindle.

conceal *(SYN.)* disguise, cover, hide, mask, screen, secrete, veil, withhold.
(ANT.) reveal, show, disclose, expose.

concede *(SYN.)* permit, suffer, tolerate, grant, give, admit, acknowledge, allow, yield.
(ANT.) forbid, contradict, protest, refuse, deny, negate, resist.

conceit *(SYN.)* pride, vanity, complacency, conception, idea, egotism, self-esteem, caprice, fancy, whim.

(ANT.) humility, meekness, humbleness, modesty.

conceited *(SYN.)* proud, arrogant, vain, smug, egotistical.
(ANT.) humble, modest, self-effacing.

conceive *(SYN.)* design, create, imagine, understand, devise, concoct, perceive, frame, grasp, invent.
(ANT.) imitate, reproduce, copy.

concentrate *(SYN.)* localize, focus, condense, ponder, meditate, center, scrutinize.
(ANT.) scatter, diffuse, dissipate, disperse.

concentrated *(SYN.)* compressed, thick, dense.
(ANT.) sparse, quick, dispersed.

concept *(SYN.)* fancy, conception, image, notion, idea, sentiment, thought.
(ANT.) thing, matter, substance, entity.

conception *(SYN.)* consideration, deliberation, fancy, idea, notion, regard, thought, view.

concern *(SYN.)* matter, anxiety, affair, disturb, care, business, solicitude, interest, affect, involve, touch, trouble, interest, worry.
(ANT.) unconcern, negligence, disinterest, tire, bore, calm, soothe, indifference.

concerning *(SYN.)* regarding, about, respecting.

concerted *(SYN.)* united, joint, combined.
(ANT.) individual, unorganized, separate.

concession *(SYN.)* admission, yielding, granting.
(ANT.) insistence, demand.

concise *(SYN.)* pity, neat, brief, compact, succinct, terse.
(ANT.) wordy, lengthy, verbose, prolix.

conclude *(SYN.)* decide, achieve, close, complete, end, finish, terminate, arrange, determine, settle, perfect, perform.
(ANT.) start, begin, commence.

concluding *(SYN.)* extreme, final, last, terminal, utmost.
(ANT.) first, foremost, opening, initial.

conclusion *(SYN.)* end, finale, termination, deduction, close, settlement, decision, finish, resolution, determination, completion, issue, judgment.
(ANT.) commencement, inception, opening, start, beginning.

conclusive *(SYN.)* decisive, eventual, final, terminal, ultimate.
(ANT.) original, first, inaugural.

concord *(SYN.)* agreement, unison, understanding, accordance, stipulation.
(ANT.) disagreement, discord, dissension.

concrete *(SYN.)* solid, firm, precise, definite, specific.
(ANT.) undetermined, vague, general.

concur *(SYN.)* agree, assent, consent, accede.
(ANT.) dissent, protest, differ.

condemn *(SYN.)* denounce, reproach, blame, upbraid, convict, rebuke, doom, judge, censure, reprehend, punish, reprobate, sentence.
(ANT.) condone, forgive, absolve, praise, applaud, extol, approve, pardon, laud, excuse, commend.

condense *(SYN.)* shorten, reduce, abridge, abbreviate, concentrate, digest, compress, diminish.
(ANT.) enlarge, increase, swell, expand.

condition *(SYN.)* circumstance, state, situation, case, plight, requirement, position, necessity, stipulation, predicament, provision, term.

conditional *(SYN.)* dependent, relying.
(ANT.) casual, original, absolute.

condolence *(SYN.)* commiseration, concord, harmony, pity, sympathy, warmth.
(ANT.) harshness, indifference, unconcern.

conduct *(SYN.)* control, deportment, supervise, manage, behavior, deed, actions, act, behave, manners, deportment.

confederate *(SYN.)* ally, abettor, assistant.
(ANT.) enemy, rival, opponent, adversary.

confederation *(SYN.)* combination, league, union, marriage, treaty.
(ANT.) separation, divorce.

confer *(SYN.)* gossip, grant, speak, tattle, blab, chat, deliberate, consult, award, give, bestow, talk, mutter.
(ANT.) retrieve, withdraw.

confess *(SYN.)* avow, acknowledge, admit, concede, grant, divulge, reveal.
(ANT.) disown, renounce, deny, conceal.

confession *(SYN.)* defense, justification, excuse, apology.
(ANT.) dissimulation, denial, complaint.

confidence *(SYN.)* firmness, self-reliance, assurance, faith, trust, pledge, declaration, self-confidence, reliance, self-assurance, courage, statement.
(ANT.) distrust, shyness, mistrust, bashfulness, diffidence, doubt, modesty, suspicion.

confident *(SYN.)* certain, sure, dauntless, self-assured.
(ANT.) uncertain, timid, shy.

confine *(SYN.)* enclose, restrict, hinder, fence, limit, bound.
(ANT.) release, expose, free, expand, open.

confirm acknowledge, establish, settle, substantiate, approve, fix, verify, assure, validate, ratify, corroborate, strengthen.
(ANT.) disclaim, deny, disavow.

confirmation *(SYN.)* demonstration, experiment, test, trail, verification.
(ANT.) fallacy, invalidity.

confirmed *(SYN.)* regular, established, habitual, chronic.
(ANT.) occasional, infrequent.

conflict *(SYN.)* duel, combat, fight, collision, discord, encounter, interference, inconsistency, contention, struggle, opposition, clash, oppose, battle, controversy, contend, engagement, contest, variance.
(ANT.) consonance, harmony, amity.

confiscate *(SYN.)* capture, catch, gain, purloin, steal, take, clutch, grip, seize, get, obtain, bear.

conflagration *(SYN.)* flame, glow, heat, warmth, fervor, passion, vigor.
(ANT.) apathy, cold, quiescence.

conform *(SYN.)* adapt, comply, yield, submit, obey, adjust, agree, fit, suit.
(ANT.) misapply, misfit, rebel, vary, disagree, disturb.

conformity *(SYN.)* congruence, accord, agreement, correspondence.

confound *(SYN.)* confuse, baffle, perplex, puzzle, bewilder.

confront *(SYN.)* confront, defy, hinder, resist, thwart, withstand, bar.
(ANT.) submit, agree, support, succumb.

confuse *(SYN.)* confound, perplex, mystify, dumbfound, baffle, puzzle, jumble, mislead, mix up, mistake, bewilder.
(ANT.) explain, instruct, edify, illumine, enlighten, illuminate, solve.

confused *(SYN.)* deranged, indistinct,

disordered, muddled, bewildered, disconcerted, disorganized, per-plexed.

(ANT.) organized, plain, clear, obvious.

confusion *(SYN.)* commotion, disarray, agitation, disorder, chaos, ferment, stir, perplexity, tumult, bewilderment, disarrangement, uncertainty, muss, mess, turmoil.

(ANT.) order, tranquillity, enlightenment, comprehension, understanding, tidiness, organization, peace.

congregate *(SYN.)* gather, foregather, meet, convene.

(ANT.) scatter, dispel, disperse, dissipate.

congress *(SYN.)* parliament, legislature, assembly.

congruous *(SYN.)* agreeing, conforming, constant, correspondent.

(ANT.) incongruous, inconsistent, discrepant.

conjecture *(SYN.)* law, supposition, theory.

(ANT.) proof, fact, certainty.

conjunction *(SYN.)* combination, junction, connection, link.

(ANT.) separation, disconnection, separation, diversion.

connect *(SYN.)* adjoin, link, combine, relate, join, attach, unite, associate, attribute, affix.

(ANT.) detach, separate, disjoin, untie, dissociation, disconnect, disassociation, unfasten.

connection *(SYN.)* conjunction, alliance, link, affinity, bond, tie, association, relationship, union.

(ANT.) isolation, dissociation, separation, disassociation, disunion.

conquer *(SYN.)* master, beat, humble, defeat, overcome, rout, win, succeed, achieve, gain, overpower, quell, subdue, crush, vanquish.

(ANT.) cede, yield, retreat, surrender.

conquest *(SYN.)* triumph, victory, achievement.

(ANT.) surrender, failure, defeat.

conscientious *(SYN.)* upright, straight, honest, incorruptible, scrupulous.

(ANT.) careless, irresponsible, slovenly.

conscious *(SYN.)* cognizant, informed, perceptive, aware, intentional, sensible, awake, purposeful, deliberate, sensible.

(ANT.) unaware, insensible, asleep, comatose, ignorant.

consecrate *(SYN.)* exalt, extol, hallow,

honor.

(ANT.) mock, degrade, debase, abuse.

consecrated *(SYN.)* holy, divine, devout, spiritual.

(ANT.) evil, worldly, secular.

consent *(SYN.)* permission, leave, agree, let, assent, agreement, license, permit.

(ANT.) refusal, opposition, denial, dissent, prohibition.

consequence *(SYN.)* outcome, issue, result, effect, significance, importance.

(ANT.) impetus, cause.

consequential *(SYN.)* significant, important, weighty.

(ANT.) trivial, unimportant, minor, insignificant.

consequently *(SYN.)* hence, thence, therefore.

conservative *(SYN.)* conventional, reactionary, cautious, moderate, careful.

(ANT.) radical, liberal, rash, foolhardy, reckless.

conserve *(SYN.)* save, retain, reserve, guard, keep, support, sustain.

(ANT.) dismiss, neglect, waste, reject, discard.

consider *(SYN.)* heed, ponder, contemplate, examine, study, weigh, reflect, think about, regard, deliberate, respect.

(ANT.) ignore, overlook, disdain, disregard, neglect.

considerable *(SYN.)* much, noteworthy, worthwhile, significant, important.

considerate *(SYN.)* careful, considerate, heedful, prudent, kind, thoughtful, polite, introspective, reflective.

(ANT.) thoughtless, heedless, inconsiderate, selfish, rash.

consideration *(SYN.)* kindness, care, heed, politeness, empathy, notice, watchfulness, kindliness, thoughtfulness, courtesy, concern, sympathy, thought, attention, reflection, fee, pay, study.

(ANT.) omission, oversight, negligence.

consistent *(SYN.)* conforming, accordant, compatible, agreeing, faithful, constant, harmonious, expected, regular, congruous, correspondent.

(ANT.) paradoxical, discrepant, contrary, antagonistic, opposed, eccentric, inconsistent, incongruous.

consolation *(SYN.)* enjoyment, sympathy, relief, ease, contentment, comfort, solace.

(ANT.) discomfort, suffering, discouragement, torture, burden, misery.

console *(SYN.)* solace, comfort, sympathize with, assuage, soothe.
(ANT.) worry, annoy, upset, disturb, distress.

consolidate *(SYN.)* blend, combine, conjoin, fuse, mix, merge, unite.
(ANT.) decompose, separate, analyze, disintegrate.

consort *(SYN.)* companion, comrade, friend.
(ANT.) stranger, enemy, adversary.

conspicuous *(SYN.)* distinguished, clear, manifest, salient, noticeable, striking, obvious, prominent, visible.
(ANT.) hidden, obscure, neutral, common, inconspicuous.

conspiracy *(SYN.)* machination, combination, treason, intrigue, cabal, treachery, plot, collusion.

conspire *(SYN.)* plan, intrigue, plot, scheme.

constancy *(SYN.)* devotion, faithfulness, accuracy, precision, exactness.
(ANT.) faithlessness, treachery, perfidy.

constant *(SYN.)* continual, invariable, abiding, permanent, faithful, invariant, true, ceaseless, enduring, unchanging, steadfast, unchangeable, loyal, stable, immutable, staunch, steady, fixed.
(ANT.) fickle, irregular, wavering, off-and-on, infrequent, occasional, mutable.

constantly *(SYN.)* eternally, ever, evermore, forever, unceasingly.
(ANT.) rarely, sometimes, never, occasionally.

consternation *(SYN.)* apprehension, dismay, alarm, fear, fright, dread, horror, terror.
(ANT.) bravery, courage, boldness, assurance.

constitute *(SYN.)* compose, found, form, establish, organize, create, appoint, delegate, authorize, commission.

constitution *(SYN.)* law, code, physique, health, vitality.

constrain *(SYN.)* necessity, indigence, need, want, poverty.
(ANT.) luxury, freedom, uncertainty.

construct *(SYN.)* build, form, erect, make, fabricate, raise, frame.
(ANT.) raze, demolish, destroy.

construction *(SYN.)* raising, building, fabricating.

constructive *(SYN.)* useful, helpful, valuable.
(ANT.) ruinous, destructive.

construe *(SYN.)* explain, interpret, solve, render, translate.
(ANT.) distort, confuse, misconstrue.

consult *(SYN.)* discuss, chatter, discourse, gossip, confer, report, rumor, deliberate, speech, talk.
(ANT.) writing, correspondence, silence.

consume *(SYN.)* engulf, absorb, use up, use, expend, exhaust, devour, devastate, destroy, engross.
(ANT.) emit, expel, exude, discharge.

consumer *(SYN.)* user, buyer, purchaser.

consummate *(SYN.)* close, conclude, do finish, perfect, terminate.

consummation *(SYN.)* climax, apex, culmination, peak.
(ANT.) depth, base, floor.

contact *(SYN.)* meeting, touching.

contagious *(SYN.)* infectious, virulent, communicable, catching.
(ANT.) noncommunicable, healthful, hygienic.

contain *(SYN.)* embody, hold, embrace, include, accommodate, repress, restrain.
(ANT.) emit, encourage, yield, discharge.

contaminate *(SYN.)* corrupt, sully, taint, defile, soil, pollute, dirty, infect, poison.
(ANT.) purify.

contemplate *(SYN.)* imagine, recollect, consider, study, reflect upon, observe, deliberate, muse, ponder, plan, intend, view, regard, think about, reflect, think, mean.
(ANT.) forget, guess, conjecture.

contemplative *(SYN.)* simultaneous, meditative, thoughtful, contemporaneous, pensive, studious.
(ANT.) inattentive, indifferent, thoughtless.

contemporary *(SYN.)* modern, present, simultaneous, fashionable, coexisting, contemporaneous, up-to-date.
(ANT.) old, antecedent, past, ancient, succeeding, bygone.

contempt *(SYN.)* detestation, malice, contumely, disdain, derision, scorn.
(ANT.) respect, reverence, admiration, esteem, awe.

contemptible *(SYN.)* base, mean, vile, vulgar, nasty, low, detestable, selfish, miserable, offensive.
(ANT.) generous, honorable, noble, ex-

alted, admirable.
contemptuous *(SYN.)* disdainful, sneering, scornful, insolent.
(ANT.) modest, humble.
contend *(SYN.)* dispute, combat, contest, assert, claim, argue, maintain.
content *(SYN.)* pleased, happy, contented, satisfied.
(ANT.) restless, dissatisfied, discontented.
contented *(SYN.)* delighted, fortunate, gay, happy, joyous, lucky, merry.
(ANT.) gloomy, blue, depressed.
contention *(SYN.)* combat, duel, struggle, discord, battle, variance.
(ANT.) concord, harmony, amity, consonance.
contentment *(SYN.)* delight, happiness, gladness, pleasure, satisfaction.
(ANT.) misery, sorrow, grief, sadness, despair.
contest *(SYN.)* dispute, debate, competition, tournament, oppose, discuss, quarrel, squabble.
(ANT.) allow, concede, agree, assent.
continence *(SYN.)* forbearance, temperance.
(ANT.) self-indulgence, excess, intoxication.
contingency *(SYN.)* likelihood, possibility, occasion, circumstance.
contingent *(SYN.)* depending, subject.
(ANT.) independent, original, casual.
continual *(SYN.)* constant, unceasing, everlasting, unremitting, endless, continuous, uninterrupted, regular, connected, consecutive, ceaseless.
(ANT.) periodic, rare, irregular, occasional, interrupted.
continue *(SYN.)* proceed, extend, endure, persist, resume, renew, recommence, last, remain, last, prolong, pursue.
(ANT.) check, cease, discontinue, stop, suspend.
continuous *(SYN.)* continuing, uninterrupted, ceaseless, unceasing, incessant, constant.
(ANT.) intermittent, irregular, sporadic.
contract *(SYN.)* condense, diminish, reduce, bargain, restrict, agreement, compact, pact, shrink, get, treaty, shorten.
(ANT.) lengthen, extend, swell, expand, elongate.
contraction *(SYN.)* reduction, shorten-

ing.
(ANT.) enlargement, expansion, extension.
contradict *(SYN.)* gainsay, counter, oppose, confute, dispute.
(ANT.) verify, confirm, agree, support.
contradictory *(SYN.)* inconsistent, conflicting, incompatible, paradoxical, unsteady.
(ANT.) congruous, consistent, correspondent.
contrary *(SYN.)* disagreeable, perverse, hostile, stubborn, opposite, opposing, opposed, disagreeing, disastrous, conflicting, headstrong, unlucky.
(ANT.) lucky, agreeable, propitious, favorable, like, obliging, similar, complementary, tractable, fortunate.
contrast *(SYN.)* differentiate, compare, distinction, disagreement, distinguish, differ, discriminate, difference, oppose.
(ANT.) agreement, similarity, likeness.
contribute *(SYN.)* grant, give, donate, bestow, provide, offer.
(ANT.) deny, withhold.
contribution *(SYN.)* grant, gift, offering, donation.
contrition *(SYN.)* grief, regret, self-reproach.
(ANT.) self-satisfaction, complacency.
contrive *(SYN.)* devise, intend, plan, make, invent, plot, hatch, form, project, arrange, manage, man-euver, scheme, sketch.
control *(SYN.)* govern, regulate, rule, command, dominate, direct, manage, check, repress, curb, management, mastery, direction, restraint, superintend, restrain.
(ANT.) ignore, forsake, follow, submit, abandon.
controversy *(SYN.)* disagreement, dispute, debate.
(ANT.) agreement, harmony, accord, concord, decision.
convenience *(SYN.)* accessibility, aid, benefit, help, service, availability.
(ANT.) inconvenience.
convenient *(SYN.)* adapted, appropriate, fitting, favorable, handy, suitable, accessible, nearby, ready, available, advantageous, timely.
(ANT.) inconvenient, troublesome, awkward.
convention *(SYN.)* meeting, conference,

assembly, practice, custom, rule.

conventional *(SYN.)* common, regular, usual, everyday, habitual, routine, accustomed.
(ANT.) exotic, unusual, bizarre, extraordinary.

conversant *(SYN.)* aware, intimate, familiar, versed, close, friendly, sociable.
(ANT.) affected, distant, cold, reserved.

conversation *(SYN.)* colloquy, dialogue, chat, parley, discussion, talk.

converse *(SYN.)* jabber, talk, argue, comment, harangue, plead, rant, spout, discuss, chat, talk, speak, reason.

conversion *(SYN.)* alteration, change, mutation, modification, metamorphosis.

convert *(SYN.)* change, alter, alter, turn, transform, shift, modify, exchange, win over, vary, veer.
(ANT.) establish, stabilize, settle, retain.

convey *(SYN.)* carry, bear, communicate, transport, transmit, support, sustain.
(ANT.) drop, abandon.

conveyance *(SYN.)* van, car, train, truck, plane.

convict *(SYN.)* felon, offender, criminal.

conviction *(SYN.)* opinion, position, view, faith, belief, confidence, feeling, reliance, trust.
(ANT.) doubt, heresy, incredulity, denial.

convince *(SYN.)* persuade, assure, exhort, induce, influence.
(ANT.) deter, compel, restrain, dissuade.

convivial *(SYN.)* jolly, social, jovial, gregarious.
(ANT.) solemn, stern, unsociable.

convoy *(SYN.)* with, attend, chaperone.
(ANT.) avoid, desert, quit, leave.

cool *(SYN.)* frosty, chilly, icy, cold, wintry, quiet, composed, collected, distant, unfriendly, quiet, moderate.
(ANT.) hot, warm, heated, overwrought, excited, hysterical, friendly, outgoing.

cooperate *(SYN.)* unite, combine, help, contribute, support.

coordinate *(SYN.)* attune, harmonize, adapt, match, balance.

copious *(SYN.)* ample, abundant, bountiful, overflowing, plentiful, profuse, rich.
(ANT.) scant, scarce, insufficient, meager, deficient.

copy *(SYN.)* facsimile, exemplar, imitation, duplicate, reproduction, likeness, print, carbon, transcript.

(ANT.) prototype, original.

cordial *(SYN.)* polite, friendly, affable, genial, earnest, gracious, warm, ardent, warmhearted, hearty, sincere.
(ANT.) unfriendly, cool, aloof, hostile, ill-tempered, reserved.

core *(SYN.)* midpoint, heart, kernel, center, middle.
(ANT.) outskirts, border, surface, outside, boundary, rim.

corporation *(SYN.)* business, organization, crew, group, troop, society, company, conglomerate, firm.
(ANT.) individual, dispersion, seclusion.

corpse *(SYN.)* cadaver, carcass, remains, body, form.
(ANT.) spirit, soul, mind, intellect.

corpulent *(SYN.)* obese, portly, chubby, stout.
(ANT.) slim, thin, slender, lean, gaunt.

correct *(SYN.)* true, set right, faultless, impeccable, proper, accurate, precise, mend, right, rebuke, punish, amend, rectify, better, emend, caution, discipline, exact, strict.
(ANT.) condone, aggravate, false, inaccurate, wrong, untrue, faulty.

correction *(SYN.)* order, improvement, regulation, instruction, amendment, emendation, remedy, rectification, repair, training, punishment.
(ANT.) confusion, turbulence, chaos.

correlative *(SYN.)* allied, correspondent, like, similar, parallel.
(ANT.) different, opposed, divergent.

correspond *(SYN.)* compare, coincide, match, agree, suit, fit, write.
(ANT.) differ, diverge, vary.

correspondent *(SYN.)* allied, alike, comparable, like, parallel, similar.
(ANT.) different, opposed, divergent, dissimilar.

corridor *(SYN.)* hallway, hall, foyer, passage, lobby, passageway.

corrode *(SYN.)* erode.

corrupt *(SYN.)* crooked, untrustworthy, treacherous, debased, unscrupulous, wicked, evil, low, contaminated, perverted, bribe, depraved, corrupted, demoralize, degrade, venal, putrid, tainted, dishonest, impure.
(ANT.) upright, honest, pure, sanctify, edify, purify, sanctified, scrupulous.

corrupted *(SYN.)* crooked, dishonest, impure, spoiled, unsound.

cost *(SYN.)* price, value, damage, charge, loss, sacrifice, penalty, worth.

costly *(SYN.)* dear, expensive.

(ANT.) cheap, inexpensive.

costume *(SYN.)* dress, clothes, apparel, clothing, garb.

couch *(SYN.)* davenport, sofa, loveseat.

council *(SYN.)* caution, instruction, committee, cabinet, board, suggestion.

counsel *(SYN.)* guidance, attorney, lawyer, counselor, hint, imply, opinion, advice, offer, advise.

(ANT.) declare, dictate, insist.

count *(SYN.)* consider, number, enumerate, total, figure, compute, tally, estimate.

(ANT.) conjecture, guess, miscalculate.

countenance *(SYN.)* visage, face, aspect, support, appearance, approval, encouragement, favor.

(ANT.) forbid, prohibit.

counteract *(SYN.)* thwart, neutralize, offset, counterbalance, defeat.

counterfeit *(SYN.)* false, fraudulent, pretended, pretend, sham, imitate, forgery, artificial, bogus, fake, spurious, imitation, unreal.

(ANT.) authentic, natural, real, genuine, true.

country *(SYN.)* state, nation, forest, farmland.

(ANT.) city.

couple *(SYN.)* team, pair, accompany, associate, attach, combine, connect, brace, join, link, unite.

(ANT.) detach, separate, disjoin, disconnect.

courage *(SYN.)* fearlessness, boldness, chivalry, fortitude, mettle, spirit, daring, bravery, prowess, intrepidity, valor, resolution.

(ANT.) fear, timidity, cowardice.

courageous *(SYN.)* bold, dauntless, brave, daring, intrepid, valorous, plucky, fearless, heroic, valiant.

(ANT.) fearful, weak, timid, cowardly.

course *(SYN.)* passage, advance, path, road, progress, way, direction, bearing, route, street, track, trail, way.

courteous *(SYN.)* civil, respectful, polite, genteel, well-mannered, gracious, refined.

(ANT.) discourteous, rude, uncivil, impolite, boorish.

courtesy *(SYN.)* graciousness, politeness, respect.

(ANT.) discourtesy, rudeness.

covenant *(SYN.)* agreement, concord, harmony, unison, compact, stipulation.

(ANT.) variance, discord, dissension, difference.

cover *(SYN.)* clothe, conceal, disguise, curtain, guard, envelop, mask, cloak, shield, hide, screen, protect, embrace, top, lid, covering, stopper, protection, refuge, spread, overlay, include, veil.

(ANT.) bare, expose, reveal.

covert *(SYN.)* potential, undeveloped, concealed, dormant.

(ANT.) explicit, visible, manifest.

covetous *(SYN.)* grasping, greedy, acquisitive, avaricious.

(ANT.) generous.

coward *(SYN.)* dastard, milquetoast, cad.

(ANT.) hero.

cowardice *(SYN.)* dread, dismay, fright, dismay, panic, terror, timidity.

(ANT.) fearlessness, courage, bravery.

cowardly *(SYN.)* fearful, timorous, afraid, faint-hearted, yellow, pusillanimous, spineless.

cower *(SYN.)* wince, flinch, cringe, quail, tremble.

coy *(SYN.)* embarrassed, sheepish, shy, timid.

(ANT.) fearless, outgoing, bold, adventurous, daring.

crack *(SYN.)* snap, break, split.

cracker *(SYN.)* wafer, biscuit, saltine.

craft *(SYN.)* talent, skill, expertness, ability, cunning, guile, deceit, trade, profession, occupation.

crafty *(SYN.)* covert, clever, cunning, skillful, foxy, tricky, sly, underhand, shrewd.

(ANT.) frank, sincere, gullible, open, guileless, ingenuous.

craggy *(SYN.)* rough, rugged, irregular, uneven.

(ANT.) level, sleek, smooth, fine, polished.

crank *(SYN.)* cross, irritable, bad-tempered, testy.

(ANT.) cheerful, happy.

crash *(SYN.)* smash, shatter, dash.

crave *(SYN.)* want, desire, hunger for.

(ANT.) relinquish, renounce.

craving *(SYN.)* relish appetite, desire, liking, longing, passion.

(ANT.) renunciation, distaste, disgust.

crazy *(SYN.)* delirious, deranged, idiotic, mad, insane, imbecilic, demented, foolish, maniacal.
(ANT.) sane, sensible, sound, rational, reasonable.
creak *(SYN.)* squeak.
create *(SYN.)* fashion, form, generate, engender, formulate, make, originate, produce, cause, ordain, invent, beget, design, construct, constitute.
(ANT.) disband, abolish, terminate, destroy, demolish.
creative *(SYN.)* imaginative, ingenious, original, resourceful, clever, inventive, innovative, mystical.
(ANT.) unromantic, dull, literal.
credence *(SYN.)* confidence, faith, feeling, opinion, trust.
(ANT.) doubt, incredulity, denial.
credible *(SYN.)* conceivable, believable.
(ANT.) inconceivable, unbelievable.
credit *(SYN.)* believe, accept, belief, trust, faith, merit, honor, apprehend, fancy, hold, support.
(ANT.) doubt, reject, question, distrust.
creditable *(SYN.)* worthy, praiseworthy.
(ANT.) dishonorable, discreditable, shameful.
credulous *(SYN.)* trusting, naive, believing, gullible, unsuspicious.
(ANT.) suspicious.
creed *(SYN.)* belief, precept, credo, faith, teaching.
(ANT.) practice, deed, conduct, performance.
creek *(SYN.)* brook, spring, stream, rivulet.
crime *(SYN.)* offense, insult, aggression, wrongdoing, wrong, misdeed.
(ANT.) right, gentleness, innocence, morality.
criminal *(SYN.)* unlawful, crook, gangster, outlaw, illegal, convict, delinquent, offender, malefactor, culprit, felonious, felon, transgressor.
cripple *(SYN.)* hurt, maim, damage, injure.
crippled *(SYN.)* deformed, disabled, maimed, hobbling, limping, unconvincing, unsatisfactory.
(ANT.) robust, sound, vigorous, athletic.
crisis *(SYN.)* conjuncture, emergency, pass, pinch, acme, climax, contingency, juncture, exigency, strait.
(ANT.) calm, normality, stability, equi-

librium.
crisp *(SYN.)* crumbling, delicate, frail, brittle.
(ANT.) calm, normality, stability.
criterion *(SYN.)* measure, law, rule, principle, gauge, proof.
(ANT.) fancy guess, chance, supposition.
critic *(SYN.)* reviewer, judge, commentator, censor, defamer, slanderer, faultfinder.
critical *(SYN.)* exact, fastidious, caviling, faultfinding, accurate, condemning, reproachful, risky, dangerous, momentous, carping, acute, hazardous, hypercritical, perilous, decisive, important.
(ANT.) shallow, uncritical, approving, insignificant, trivial, unimportant.
criticize *(SYN.)* examine, analyze, inspect, blame, censure, appraise, evaluate, scrutinize, reprehend.
(ANT.) neglect, overlook, approve.
critique *(SYN.)* criticism, inspection, review.
crony *(SYN.)* colleague, companion, chum, buddy, comrade, friend, mate.
(ANT.) stranger, enemy, adversary.
crooked *(SYN.)* twisted, corrupt, hooked, curved, criminal, dishonest, degraded, bent, zigzag, impaired.
(ANT.) improved, raised, straight, honest, vitalized, upright, enhanced.
crop *(SYN.)* fruit, produce, harvest, cut, mow, reaping, result, yield.
cross *(SYN.)* mix, mingle, traverse, interbreed, annoyed, irritable, cranky, testy, angry, mean, ill-natured.
(ANT.) cheerful.
crouch *(SYN.)* duck, stoop.
crow *(SYN.)* boast, brag.
crowd *(SYN.)* masses, flock, host, squeeze, mob, multitude, populace, press, cramp, throng, swarm.
crown *(SYN.)* coronet, apex, crest, circlet, pinnacle, tiara, skull, head, top, zenith.
(ANT.) base, bottom, foundation, foot.
crude *(SYN.)* rude, graceless, unpolished, green, harsh, rough, coarse, illprepared, unfinished, raw, boorish, unrefined, uncouth.
(ANT.) finished, refined, polished, cultured, genteel, cultivated.
cruel *(SYN.)* ferocious, mean, heartless, unmerciful, malignant, savage, brutal, pitiless, inhuman, ruthless, merciless, barbarous.

(ANT.) humane, forbearing, kind, compassionate, merciful, benevolent, kindhearted, gentle.
cruelty *(SYN.)* harshness, meanness, savagery, brutality.
(ANT.) compassion, kindness.
crumb *(SYN.)* jot, grain, mite, particle, shred.
(ANT.) mass, bulk, quantity.
crunch *(SYN.)* champ, gnaw, nibble, pierce.
crush *(SYN.)* smash, break, crash.
cry *(SYN.)* yowl, yell, roar, shout, bellow, scream, wail, weep, bawl, sob.
cryptic *(SYN.)* puzzling, mysterious, enigmatic, hidden, secret, vague, obscure, occult, unclear.
cull *(SYN.)* elect, choose, pick, select.
(ANT.) reject, refuse.
culpable *(SYN.)* guilty, blameworthy.
(ANT.) innocent.
culprit *(SYN.)* delinquent, felon, offender.
cultivate *(SYN.)* plant, seed, farm, till, refine, educate, teach.
cultivation *(SYN.)* farming, horticulture, tillage, agriculture.
cultural *(SYN.)* civilizing, educational, elevating, instructive.
culture *(SYN.)* humanism, upbringing, cultivation, breeding, education, learning, civilization, enlightenment, cultivation, refinement.
(ANT.) illiteracy, vulgarity, ignorance.
cultured *(SYN.)* sophisticated, worldly.
(ANT.) crude, simple, uncouth, ingenuous.
cumbersome *(SYN.)* bulky, clumsy, awkward, unmanageable.
(ANT.) handy.
cunning *(SYN.)* clever, wily, crafty, foxy, skillful, tricky, ingenious, foxiness, ability, skill, wiliness, devious, shrewdness, slyness, cleverness, crooked.
(ANT.) gullible, honest, naive, openness, straightforward, simple, direct.
curb *(SYN.)* check, restraint, hinder, hold, limit, control, stop, suppress.
(ANT.) aid, loosen, incite, encourage.
cure *(SYN.)* help, treatment, heal, medicine, restorative, relief, remedy.
curiosity *(SYN.)* marvel, rarity, phenomenon, admiration, amazement, bewilderment, wonder.
(ANT.) apathy, indifference, expectation.

curious *(SYN.)* interrogative, interested, peculiar, queer, nosy, peeping, prying, inquisitive, snoopy, inquiring, unusual.
(ANT.) unconcerned, incurious, ordinary, indifferent, uninterested, common.
current *(SYN.)* up-to-date, contemporary, present, new, tide, stream, modern.
(ANT.) antiquated, old, bygone, ancient, past.
curse *(SYN.)* ban, oath, denounce, swear, condemn.
(ANT.) boon, blessing, advantage.
cursory *(SYN.)* frivolous, shallow, slight.
(ANT.) complete, deep, profound, thorough.
curt *(SYN.)* hasty, short, abrupt, brusque, brief, blunt, rude, harsh.
(ANT.) friendly, smooth, gradual, polite, courteous.
curtail *(SYN.)* condense, contract, diminish, reduce, limit, abbreviate.
(ANT.) lengthen, extend.
curtain *(SYN.)* blind, drapery, drape, shade.
curve *(SYN.)* crook, deflect, bend, bow, incline, turn, twist.
(ANT.) resist, stiffen, straighten.
cushion *(SYN.)* pillow, pad, check, absorb.
custodian *(SYN.)* guard, keeper, guardian, watchman.
custody *(SYN.)* guardianship, care.
(ANT.) neglect, disregard, indifference.
custom *(SYN.)* fashion, rule, routine, practice, usage.
customary *(SYN.)* common, usual, regular, everyday, general.
(ANT.) exceptional, irregular, rare, unusual, abnormal.
customer *(SYN.)* patron, client, buyer.
cut *(SYN.)* slash, gash, prick, slit, sever, cleave, mow, incision, chop, lop, slice.
cut back *(SYN.)* decrease, reduce.
cut in *(SYN.)* butt in, interfere.
cut off *(SYN.)* cease, end, stop, terminate.
cut short *(SYN.)* stop, finish, end, quit.
cutthroat *(SYN.)* killer, executioner, murderer, assassin, merciless, ruthless, insensitive, pitiless.
cutting *(SYN.)* bitter, stern, caustic, scathing, harsh, acerbic.
cylindrical *(SYN.)* circular, curved, plump, rotund, spherical, round.

dab *(SYN.)* coat, pat, smear.

dabble *(SYN.)* splatter, toy, splash, fiddle, putter.

dabbler *(SYN.)* amateur, dilettante, tinkerer, trifler.

(ANT.) master, expert, scholar, specialist, authority.

daft *(SYN.)* crazy, foolish, insane. dagger *(SYN.)* knife, dirk, blade.

daily *(SYN.)* every day, diurnal, regularly.

dainty *(SYN.)* slender, pleasing, delicate, frail, pleasant, pretty, petite, graceful, beautiful, fine, elegant.

(ANT.) uncouth, vulgar, coarse, tough.

dally *(SYN.)* dawdle, linger, lag, delay, loiter.

(ANT.) rush, hurry, dash, get going, bustle.

dam *(SYN.)* dike, levee, barrier, slow, stop, check, obstruct, block.

(ANT.) free, release, loose, unleash.

damage *(SYN.)* spoil, deface, impair, mar, hurt, injury, impairment, destruction, injure, harm.

(ANT.) repair, benefit, mend, rebuild, improve, ameliorate.

dame *(SYN.)* woman, lady.

damn *(SYN.)* denounce, descry, doom, curse, reprove, blame.

(ANT.) bless, honor, glorify, praise, accept, applaud, commend, consecrate.

damnable *(SYN.)* blameworthy, evil, detestable, execrable, outrageous, bad, sinful, horrible.

(ANT.) good, commendable, worthy, praiseworthy.

damp *(SYN.)* humid, dank, moisture, wetness, dampness, humidity.

(ANT.) arid, dry.

dampen *(SYN.)* wet, depressed, moisten, dull, suppress, sprinkle, discouraged, retard, slow, inhibit, deaden, muffle.

(ANT.) dehumidify, increase, encourage.

dance *(SYN.)* bounce, flit, skip, sway, prance, bob, glide, caper, cavort, frisk.

dandle *(SYN.)* jounce, joggle, bounce, jiggle, nestle, cuddle, caress.

dandy *(SYN.)* coxcomb, fop, swell, great, fine, wonderful, excellent.

(ANT.) rotten, terrible, awful, miserable, slob.

danger *(SYN.)* jeopardy, risk, threat, hazard, uncertainty, peril.

(ANT.) safety, immunity, security, defense.

dangerous *(SYN.)* risky, insecure, threatening, critical, perilous, unsafe, uncertain, hazardous.

(ANT.) trustworthy, secure, protected, safe.

dangle *(SYN.)* droop, swing, flap, hang, sag.

dank *(SYN.)* moist, muggy, wet.

(ANT.) dry.

dapper *(SYN.)* spruce, trim, natty, smart, well-tailored, dashing, neat.

(ANT.) untidy, sloppy, shabby, messy, unkempt.

dappled *(SYN.)* spotted, flecked, brindled, variegated, piebald, pied.

(ANT.) uniform, solid, unvaried.

dare *(SYN.)* brave, call, question, defy, risk, challenge, summon.

daredevil *(SYN.)* lunatic, thrill-seeker, madcap, adventurer.

daring *(SYN.)* foolhardy, chivalrous, rash, fearless, courageous, intrepid, valiant, courage, bravery, brave, precipitate, bold.

(ANT.) timid, cowardice, timidity, cautious.

dark *(SYN.)* somber, obscure, gloomy, black, unilluminated, dim, evil, hidden, secret, swarthy, murky, opaque, dismal, mournful, sable, sullen, shadowy, sinister, dusky, mystic, shadowy, unlit, sunless, shaded, wicked, occult.

(ANT.) lucid, light, happy, cheerful, illuminated, pleasant.

darling *(SYN.)* dear, adored, sweetheart, favorite, cherished.

(ANT.) uncherished, unlovable, disagreeable, rejected, forlorn.

darn *(SYN.)* repair, mend.

dart *(SYN.)* scurry, arrow, barb, hurry, dash, throw, missile, run, hasten, scamper, toss, rush, cast.

dash *(SYN.)* pound, thump, beat, smite, buffet, thrash, smash, break, scurry, run, dart, rush, scamper, hint, pinch, hit, strike.

(ANT.) stroke, hearten, encourage, defend.

dashing *(SYN.)* swashbuckling, dapper, flamboyant, handsome.

(ANT.) dull, colorless, shabby, lifeless.

dastardly *(SYN.)* mean-spirited, craven, cowardly, mean, rotten, villainous, dishonorable.

(ANT.) heroic, brave, high-minded, courageous.

data *(SYN.)* information, statistics, proof, facts, evidence.

date *(SYN.)* interview, appointment, commitment, engagement, meeting, rendezvous, regale, entertain.

dated *(SYN.)* out-of-date, old-fashioned, outmoded.

(ANT.) latest, now, current, fashionable, hot.

daub *(SYN.)* coat, grease, soil, scribble, cover, stain, smear, scrawl.

daunt *(SYN.)* discourage, dishearten, intimidate, frighten, deter.

(ANT.) enspirit, encourage.

dauntless *(SYN.)* fearless, brave, bold, courageous, intrepid, valiant.

(ANT.) fearful, timid, cowardly.

dawn *(SYN.)* sunrise, start, outset, daybreak, origin, commencement.

(ANT.) dusk, sunset, nightfall, end, conclusion, finish.

daydream *(SYN.)* woolgather, muse.

daze *(SYN.)* perplex, stun, puzzle, bewilder, upset, confuse, ruffle, confusion, stupor, bewilderment.

dazzle *(SYN.)* surprise, stun, astonish, impress, bewilder, stupefy.

dead *(SYN.)* departed, lifeless, deceased, insensible, inanimate, dull, defunct, gone, lifeless, unconscious, inoperative, inactive, inert, motionless, spiritless.

(ANT.) animate, functioning, active, living, alive, stirring.

deaden *(SYN.)* anesthetize, numb, paralyze.

deadlock *(SYN.)* standstill, impasse, stalemate.

deadly *(SYN.)* lethal, mortal, fatal, deathly, baleful.

deaf *(SYN.)* stone-deaf, unhearing, unheeding, unaware, unheedful, stubborn, oblivious, inattentive.

(ANT.) aware, conscious.

deafening *(SYN.)* vociferous, noisy, stentorian, resounding, loud.

(ANT.) soft, inaudible, subdued.

deal *(SYN.)* act, treat, attend, cope, barter, trade, bargain, apportion, give, distribute, deliver.

dear *(SYN.)* valued, esteemed, expensive, beloved, costly, darling, high-priced, loved, precious.

(ANT.) hateful, reasonable, inexpensive, cheap, unwanted.

dearth *(SYN.)* shortage, lack, scarcity.

death *(SYN.)* decease, extinction, demise, passing.

(ANT.) life.

debase *(SYN.)* lower, degrade, alloy, adulterate, defile, humiliate, depress, abase, pervert, corrupt.

(ANT.) restore, improve, vitalize, enhance.

debate *(SYN.)* wrangle, discuss, plead, argue, discussion, contend, argument, controversy, dispute.

(ANT.) agreement, reject, accord, ignore, spurn.

debonair *(SYN.)* urbane, sophisticated, refined, dapper, well-bred.

debris *(SYN.)* rubbish, litter, junk, wreckage, refuse, detritus, ruins, trash, residue.

debt *(SYN.)* amount due, liability, obligation.

decay *(SYN.)* decrease, spoil, ebb, decline, waste, disintegrate, wane, dwindle, molder, deteriorate, perish, wither, rot, collapse, rottenness, putrefy, die, decompose.

(ANT.) progress, rise, increase, grow, flourish.

deceased *(SYN.)* lifeless, departed, dead, insensible, defunct.

(ANT.) living, alive.

deceit *(SYN.)* duplicity, cheat, fraud, chicanery, trick, cunning, deception, guile, beguilement, deceitfulness, dishonesty, wiliness.

(ANT.) truthfulness, openness, forthrightness, honesty, candor.

deceitful *(SYN.)* false, fraudulent, insincere, dishonest, deceptive.

(ANT.) sincere, honest.

deceive *(SYN.)* cheat, defraud, hoodwink, mislead, swindle.

decency *(SYN.)* decorum, dignity, propriety, respectability.

decent *(SYN.)* befitting, fit, suitable, becoming, respectable, adequate, seemly, fitting, comely, appropriate, proper, tolerable, decorous.

(ANT.) vulgar, gross, improper, unsuitable, indecorous, reprehensible, indecent, coarse.

deception *(SYN.)* trick, cheat, sham, deceit, trickery, craftiness, treachery, beguilement, cunning.

(ANT.) openness, frankness, candor, probity, truthfulness, honesty.

deceptive *(SYN.)* specious, fallacious, deceitful, false, delusive, unreliable, il-

lusive, tricky, dishonest, deceiving, misleading, delusory.
(ANT.) honest, real, genuine, true, truthful, authentic.
decide (SYN.) resolve, determine, terminate, conclude, close, settle, adjudicate, choose, end.
(ANT.) waver, hesitate, vacillate, doubt, suspend.
decipher (SYN.) render, unravel, construe, solve, decode, translate, elucidate, determine.
(ANT.) misconstrue, distort, misinterpret, confuse.
decision (SYN.) resolution, determination, settlement.
decisive (SYN.) determined, firm, decided, unhesitating, resolute.
declaration (SYN.) pronouncement, notice, affirmation, statement, announcement, assertion.
declare (SYN.) assert, promulate, affirm, tell, broadcast, express, proclaim, aver, say, pronounce, profess, announce.
(ANT.) deny, withhold, conceal, suppress.
decline (SYN.) descend, decay, dwindle, refuse, incline, wane, sink, depreciate, deny, diminish, weaken.
(ANT.) accept, ascend, ameliorate, increase.
decompose (SYN.) rot, disintegrate, molder, decay, crumble.
decorate (SYN.) trim, paint, deck, enrich, color, beautify, enhance, furbish, furnish, adorn, ornament.
(ANT.) uncover, mar, deface, defame, debase.
decoration (SYN.) ornamentation, embellishment, adornment, furnishing, award, citation, medal.
decoy (SYN.) lure, bait.
decrease (SYN.) lessen, wane, deduct, diminish, curtail, deduct, remove, lessening, decline.
(ANT.) expansion, increase, enlarge, expand, grow.
decree (SYN.) order, edict, statute, declaration, announce, act.
decrepit (SYN.) feeble, puny, weakened, infirm, enfeebled, languid, rickety, weak, run-down, tumble-down, dilapidated, faint.
(ANT.) strong, forceful, vigorous, energetic, lusty.
decry (SYN.) lower, belittle, derogate,

minimize, undervalue.
(ANT.) praise, commend, magnify, aggrandize.
dedicate (SYN.) sanctify, consecrate, hallow, devote, assign.
dedicated (SYN.) disposed, true, affectionate, fond, wedded.
(ANT.) indisposed, detached, untrammeled, disinclined.
deduct (SYN.) lessen, shorten, abate, remove, eliminate, curtail, subtract.
(ANT.) grow, enlarge, add, increase, amplify, expand.
deed (SYN.) feat, transaction, action, performance, act, operation, achievement, document, certificate, title, accomplishment.
(ANT.) intention, cessation, inactivity, deliberation.
deem (SYN.) hold, determine, believe, regard, reckon, judge, consider, account, expound, view.
deep (SYN.) bottomless, low, unplumbed, acute, obscure, involved, absorbed.
(ANT.) shallow.
deface (SYN.) spoil, impair, damage, mar, hurt, scratch, mutilate, disfigure, injure, harm.
(ANT.) mend, benefit, repair, enhance.
defamation (SYN.) invective. reproach, upbraiding, abuse, insult, outrage, reviling, desecration.
(ANT.) respect, approval, laudation, commendation.
default (SYN.) loss, omission, lack, failure, want, dereliction.
(ANT.) victory, achievement, sufficiency, success.
defeat (SYN.) quell, vanquish, beat, overcome, overthrow, subdue, frustrate, spoil, conquest.
(ANT.) submit, retreat, cede, yield, surrender, capitulate, lose.
defect (SYN.) shortcoming, fault, omission, blemish, imperfection, forsake, leave, weakness, failure.
(ANT.) perfection, flawlessness, support, join, completeness.
defective (SYN.) faulty, imperfect, inoperative, flawed, inoperable.
(ANT.) flawless, perfect, faultless.
defend (SYN.) screen, espouse, justify, protect, vindicate, fortify, assert, guard, safeguard, shield. (ANT.) oppose, assault, submit, attack, deny.
defense (SYN.) resistance, protection,

bulwark, fort, barricade, trench, rampart, fortress.

defer *(SYN.)* postpone, delay.
(ANT.) speed, hurry, expedite.

deference *(SYN.)* fame, worship, adoration, reverence, admiration, respect, fame, dignity, homage.
(ANT.) dishonor, derision, reproach, contempt.

defiant *(SYN.)* rebellious, antagonistic, obstinate.
(ANT.) yielding, submissive.

deficient *(SYN.)* lacking, short, incomplete, defective, scanty, insufficient, inadequate.
(ANT.) enough, ample, sufficient, adequate.

defile *(SYN.)* pollute, march, corrupt, dirty, file, debase, contaminate.
(ANT.) purify.

define *(SYN.)* describe, fix, establish, label, designate, set, name, explain.

definite *(SYN.)* fixed, prescribed, certain, specific, exact, determined, distinct, explicit, correct.
(ANT.) indefinite, confused, undetermined, equivocal.

definitely *(SYN.)* certainly, assuredly, absolutely, positively, surely.

definition *(SYN.)* sense, interpretation, meaning, explanation.

deft *(SYN.)* handy, adroit, clever, adept, dexterous, skillful, skilled.
(ANT.) inept, clumsy, maladroit, awkward.

defunct *(SYN.)* lifeless, dead, departed, expired, extinct, spiritless, inanimate.
(ANT.) living, alive, stirring.

defy *(SYN.)* hinder, oppose, withstand, attack, resist, confront, challenge, flout, dare, thwart.
(ANT.) yield, allow, relent, surrender, submit, accede.

degenerate *(SYN.)* dwindle, decline, weaken, deteriorate, decrease.
(ANT.) ascend, ameliorate, increase, appreciate.

degrade *(SYN.)* crush, reduce, subdue, abash, humble, lower, shame, demote, downgrade, abase, mortify.
(ANT.) praise, elevate, honor.

degree *(SYN.)* grade, amount, step, measure, rank, honor, extent.

deign *(SYN.)* condescend, stoop.

dejected *(SYN.)* depressed, downcast, sad, disheartened, blue, discouraged.

(ANT.) cheerful, happy, optimistic.

delectable *(SYN.)* tasty, delicious, savory, delightful, sweet, luscious.
(ANT.) unsavory, distasteful, unpalatable, acrid.

delegate *(SYN.)* emissary, envoy, ambassador, representative, commission, deputize, authorize.

delete *(SYN.)* erase, cancel, remove.
(ANT.) add.

deleterious *(SYN.)* evil, unwholesome, base, sinful, bad, wicked, immoral, destructive, injurious, hurtful, damaging, detrimental, unsound.
(ANT.) moral, excellent, reputable, healthful, healthy, helpful, constructive, good.

deliberate *(SYN.)* studied, willful, intended, contemplated, premeditated, planned, methodical, designed.
(ANT.) fortuitous, hasty, accidental.

delicate *(SYN.)* frail, critical, slender, dainty, pleasing, fastidious, exquisite, precarious, demanding, sensitive, savory, fragile, weak.
(ANT.) tough, strong, coarse, clumsy, hearty, hale, vulgar, rude.

delicious *(SYN.)* tasty, luscious, delectable, sweet, savory.
(ANT.) unsavory, distasteful, unpalatable, unpleasant, acrid.

delight *(SYN.)* joy, bliss, gladness, pleasure, ecstasy, happiness, rapture.
(ANT.) revolt, sorrow, annoyance, displeasure, disgust, displease, revulsion, misery.

delightful *(SYN.)* pleasing, pleasant, charming, refreshing, pleasurable.
(ANT.) nasty, disagreeable, unpleasant.

delirious *(SYN.)* raving, mad, giddy, frantic, hysterical, violent.

deliver *(SYN.)* impart, publish, rescue, commit, communicate; free, address, offer, save, give, liberate,
(ANT.) restrict, confine, capture, enslave, withhold, imprison.

deluge *(SYN.)* overflow, flood.

delusion *(SYN.)* mirage, fantasy, phantasm, vision, dream, illusion, phantom, hallucination.
(ANT.) substance, actuality.

delve *(SYN.)* dig, look, search, scoop, explore, hunt.

demand *(SYN.)* claim, inquire, ask, need, require, obligation, requirement, ask for, necessitate.

(ANT.) tender, give, present, waive, relinquish, offer.

demean (SYN.) comport, bear, operate, carry, act, manage, deport.

demeanor (SYN.) manner, way, conduct, actions, behavior.

demented (SYN.) insane, crazy, mad, mental, psychotic, lunatic.

demolish (SYN.) ruin, devastate, ravage, annihilate, wreck, destroy, raze, exterminate, obliterate.

(ANT.) erect, make, save, construct, preserve, build, establish.

demolition (SYN.) wrecking, destruction.

(ANT.) erection, construction.

demon (SYN.) fiend, monster, devil, ogre, spirit.

demonstrate (SYN.) evince, show, prove, display, illustrate, describe, explain, manifest, exhibit.

(ANT.) hide, conceal.

demonstration (SYN.) exhibit, show, presentation, exhibition, display, rally.

demur (SYN.) waver, falter, delay, stutter, doubt, vacillate, hesitate, scruple.

(ANT.) proceed, decide, resolve, continue.

demure (SYN.) meek, shy, modest, diffident, retiring, bashful, coy.

den (SYN.) cave, lair, cavern.

denial (SYN.) disallowance, proscription, refusal, prohibition.

denounce (SYN.) condemn, blame, reprove, reprehend, censure, reproach, upbraid, reprobate.

(ANT.) condone, approve, forgive, commend, praise.

dense (SYN.) crowded, slow, close, obtuse, compact, dull, stupid, compressed, thick, concentrated, packed, solid.

(ANT.) sparse, quick, dispersed, clever, dissipated, empty, smart, bright.

dent (SYN.) notch, impress, pit, nick.

deny (SYN.) refuse, withhold, dispute, disavow, forbid, refute, contradict, abjure, confute, gainsay.

(ANT.) confirm, affirm, admit, confess, permit, allow, concede, assert.

depart (SYN.) quit, forsake, withdraw, renounce, desert, relinquish, die, perish, decease.

(ANT.) tarry, remain, come, abide, stay, arrive.

departure (SYN.) valediction, farewell.

depend (SYN.) trust, rely, confide.

dependable (SYN.) secure, trustworthy, certain, safe, trusty, reliable, tried.

(ANT.) unreliable, fallible, dubious, uncertain.

dependent (SYN.) relying, contingent, subordinate, conditional.

(ANT.) original, casual, absolute, independent.

depict (SYN.) explain, recount, describe, portray, characterize, relate, narrate.

deplore (SYN.) repine, lament, bemoan, wail, bewail, weep, grieve, regret.

deport (SYN.) exile, eject, oust, banish, expel, dismiss, ostracize, dispel, exclude.

(ANT.) receive, admit, shelter, accept, harbor.

deportment (SYN.) deed, behavior, manner, action, carriage, disposition, bearing, demeanor.

deposit (SYN.) place, put, bank, save, store, sediment, dregs, addition, entry.

(ANT.) withdraw, withdrawal.

depreciate (SYN.) dwindle, decrease, decay, belittle, disparage, weaken, minimize, descend, deteriorate.

(ANT.) ascend, ameliorate, praise, increase, applaud, appreciate.

depress (SYN.) deject, dishearten, sadden, dampen, devaluate, devalue, lessen, lower, cheapen, reduce, dispirit, discourage, sink.

(ANT.) exalt, cheer, exhilarate.

depression (SYN.) hopelessness, despondency, pessimism, dip, cavity, pothole, hole, despair, gloom, melancholy, sadness, sorrow, recession, decline, desperation, discouragement.

(ANT.) eminence, elation, optimism, happiness, confidence, elevation, hope.

deprive (SYN.) bereave, deny, strip.

(ANT.) provision, supply, provide.

derelict (SYN.) decrepit, shabby, dilapidated, neglected, forsaken, deserted, remiss, abandoned, lax.

dereliction (SYN.) want, lack, failure, miscarriage, loss, default, deficiency, omission, fiasco.

(ANT.) sufficiency, success, achievement, victory.

derision (SYN.) irony, satire, banter, raillery, sneering, gibe, ridicule.

derivation (SYN.) source, birth, inception, start, beginning, spring, commencement, foundation, origin.

(ANT.) issue, end, outcome, harvest, product.

derive (SYN.) obtain, acquire, get,

receive.

descend *(SYN.)* wane, lower, move, slope, incline, decline, slant, sink.
(ANT.) increase, appreciate, ameliorate, ascend.

descendant *(SYN.)* child, issue, progeny, offspring.

describe *(SYN.)* portray, picture, recount, depict, relate, characterize, represent, narrate.

description *(SYN.)* history, record, recital, account, computation, chronicle, reckoning, narration, detail, narrative.
(ANT.) misrepresentation, confusion, caricature.

desecration *(SYN.)* profanation, insult, defamation, reviling, abuse, maltreatment, aspersion, perversion, dishonor.
(ANT.) respect, commendation, approval, laudation.

desert *(SYN.)* forsake, wilderness, resign, abjure, abandon, wasteland, waste, leave, surrender, abdicate, quit, barren, uninhabited.
(ANT.) uphold, defend, stay, maintain, accompany, join, support.

deserter *(SYN.)* runaway, renegade, fugitive, defector.

deserts *(SYN.)* right, compensation, due, reward, requital, condign.

deserve *(SYN.)* earn, warrant, merit.

design *(SYN.)* drawing, purpose, outline, devise, intend, draw, contrive, draft, cunning, plan, artfulness, delineation, scheming, sketch, intent, invent, objective, mean, contrivance, plotting, intention, create.
(ANT.) candor, accident, result, chance.

designate *(SYN.)* manifest, indicate, show, specify, denote, reveal, name, appoint, select, assign, disclose, signify, imply, nominate, intimate.
(ANT.) divert, mislead, conceal, falsify, distract.

desirable *(SYN.)* coveted, wanted.

desire *(SYN.)* longing, craving, yearning, appetite, lust, long for, crave, covet, want, request, ask, need, wish, aspiration, urge.
(ANT.) hate, aversion, loathing, abomination, detest, loathe, abhor, distaste.

desist *(SYN.)* cork, stop, cease, hinder, terminate, abstain, halt, interrupt, seal, arrest, plug, bar.
(ANT.) promote, begin, speed, proceed,

start.

desolate *(SYN.)* forlorn, waste, bare, lonely, abandoned, wild, deserted, uninhabited, empty, sad, miserable, wretched, unhappy, bleak, forsaken.
(ANT.) crowded, teeming, populous, happy, cheerful, fertile, attended.

despair *(SYN.)* discouragement, pessimism, depression, hopelessness, despondency, gloom, desperation.
(ANT.) elation, optimism, hope, joy, confidence.

desperado *(SYN.)* criminal, crook, thug, gangster, hoodlum.

desperate *(SYN.)* reckless, determined, despairing, wild, daring, hopeless, despondent, audacious.
(ANT.) optimistic, composed, hopeful, collected, calm, assured.

despicable *(SYN.)* vulgar, offensive, base, vile, contemptible, selfish, low, mean, worthless, nasty.
(ANT.) noble, exalted, admirable, generous, worthy, dignified.

despise *(SYN.)* hate, scorn, detest, loathe, disdain, abhor, condemn, dislike, abominate.
(ANT.) honor, love, approve, like, admire.

despite *(SYN.)* notwithstanding.

despoil *(SYN.)* plunder, rob, loot.

despondent *(SYN.)* sad, dismal, depressed, somber, ejected, melancholy, doleful, sorrowful.
(ANT.) joyous, cheerful, merry, happy.

despot *(SYN.)* tyrant, ruler, oppressor, dictator.

despotic *(SYN.)* authoritative, unconditional, absolute, tyrannous, entire, unrestricted.
(ANT.) dependent, conditional, qualified, accountable.

destiny *(SYN.)* fate, portion, outcome, consequence, result, fortune, doom, lot.

destitute *(SYN.)* poor, penurious, needy, impecunious, poverty-stricken, impoverished, indigent.
(ANT.) opulent, wealthy, affluent, rich.

destroy *(SYN.)* raze, devastate, ruin, end, demolish, wreck, extinguish, annihilate, exterminate, obliterate, waste, slay, kill, eradicate.
(ANT.) make, construct, start, create, save, establish.

destroyed *(SYN.)* rent, smashed, interrupted, flattened, wrecked, broken, ruptured, crushed.

(ANT.) whole, repaired, integral, united.

destruction *(SYN.)* ruin, devastation, extinction, demolition.

(ANT.) beginning, creation.

destructive *(SYN.)* deadly, baneful, noxious, deleterious, injurious, pernicious, fatal, detrimental.

(ANT.) salutary, beneficial, creative.

detach *(SYN.)* deduct, remove, subtract, curtail, divide, shorten, decrease, disengage, reduce, separate, diminish.

(ANT.) hitch, grow, enlarge, increase, connect, amplify, attack, expand.

detail *(SYN.)* elaborate, commission, part, itemize, portion, division, fragment, assign, circumstance, segment.

detain *(SYN.)* impede, delay, hold back, retard, arrest, restrain, stay.

(ANT.) quicken, hasten, expedite, forward, precipitate.

detect *(SYN.)* discover, reveal, find, ascertain, determine, learn, originate, devise.

(ANT.) hide, screen, lose, cover, mask.

determinant *(SYN.)* reason, incentive, source, agent, principle, inducement.

(ANT.) result, effect, consequence, end.

determine *(SYN.)* decide, settle, end, conclude, ascertain, induce, fix, verify, resolve, establish, necessitate.

detest *(SYN.)* loathe, hate, despise.

(ANT.) savor, appreciate, like, love.

detriment *(SYN.)* injury, harm, disadvantage, damage.

(ANT.) benefit.

detrimental *(SYN.)* hurtful, mischievous, damaging, harmful.

(ANT.) salutary, advantageous, profitable, beneficial.

develop *(SYN.)* evolve, unfold, enlarge, amplify, expand, create, grow, advance, reveal, unfold, mature, elaborate.

(ANT.) wither, contract, degenerate, stunt, deteriorate, compress.

development *(SYN.)* growth, expansion, progress, unraveling, elaboration, evolution, maturing, unfolding.

(ANT.) compression, abbreviation, curtailment.

deviate *(SYN.)* deflect, stray, divert, diverge, wander, sidetrack, digress.

(ANT.) preserve, follow, remain, continue, persist.

device *(SYN.)* tool, utensil, means, channel, machine, agent, vehicle, gadget, ap-

paratus, tools, instrument, contrivance.

(ANT.) preventive, impediment, hindrance, obstruction.

devilish *(SYN.)* diabolical, fiendish, diabolic, satanic, demonic.

devious *(SYN.)* tortuous, winding, distorted, circuitous, tricky, crooked, roundabout, cunning, erratic, indirect.

(ANT.) straight, direct, straightforward, honest.

devise *(SYN.)* create, concoct, invent, originate.

devote *(SYN.)* assign, dedicate, give, apply.

(ANT.) withhold, relinquish, ignore, withdraw.

devoted *(SYN.)* attached, dedicated, prone, wedded, addicted, ardent, earnest, loyal, disposed, inclined, fond, affectionate, faithful.

(ANT.) untrammeled, disinclined, detached, indisposed.

devotion *(SYN.)* piety, zeal, ardor, loyalty, dedication, religiousness, consecration, affection, love, devoutness, fidelity, attachment.

(ANT.) unfaithfulness, aversion, alienation, indifference.

devour *(SYN.)* consume, gulp, gorge, waste, eat, ruin, swallow, destroy.

devout *(SYN.)* sacred, religious, spiritual, holy, theological, pietistic, pious, sanctimonious, reverent.

(ANT.) profane, skeptical, atheistic, secular, impious.

dexterity *(SYN.)* talent, capability, qualification, aptness, skill, ability.

(ANT.) unreadiness, incapacity, disability, incompetency.

dexterous *(SYN.)* clever, adroit, handy, deft, facile, skillful, skilled, proficient.

(ANT.) awkward, clumsy.

dialect *(SYN.)* slang, jargon, cant, speech, idiom, tongue, diction, vernacular.

(ANT.) nonsense, drivel, babble, gibberish.

dialogue *(SYN.)* interview, chat, discussion, conference, exchange, talk, conversation.

diary *(SYN.)* memo, account, journal, words.

dicker *(SYN.)* haggle, bargain, negotiate.

dictate *(SYN.)* deliver, speak, record, command, order, direct.

dictator *(SYN.)* oppressor, tyrant, despot, persecutor, overlord, autocrat.

die (SYN.) fade, wane, cease, depart, wither, decay, decline, sink, expire, perish, decease, go, diminish, fail, languish, decrease.
(ANT.) live, begin, grow, survive, flourish.

difference (SYN.) inequality, variety, disparity, discord, distinction, dissension, dissimilarity, disagreement, contrast, separation.
(ANT.) harmony, similarity, identity, agreement, likeness, compatibility, kinship, resemblance.

different (SYN.) unlike, various, distinct, miscellaneous, divergent, sundry, contrary, differing, diverse, variant, incongruous, divers, unalike, changed, dissimilar, opposite.
(ANT.) similar, congruous, same, alike, identical.

differentiate (SYN.) separate, discriminate, distinguish, perceive, detect, recognize, discern.
(ANT.) confuse, omit, mingle, confound, overlook.

difficult (SYN.) involved, demanding, arduous, trying, complicated, hard, laborious, perplexing, hard, intricate.
(ANT.) simple, easy, facile, effortless.

difficulty (SYN.) trouble, hardship, fix, predicament, trouble.
(ANT.) ease.

diffuse (SYN.) spread, sparse, scattered, scanty, dispersed, thin, rare.
(ANT.) concentrated.

dig (SYN.) burrow, excavate, appreciate, understand.

digest (SYN.) consume, eat, reflect on, study, shorten, consider, summarize, abridge, abstract, abridgment, synopsis.

dignified (SYN.) serious, solemn, noble, stately, elegant.

dignify (SYN.) honor, elevate.
(ANT.) shame, degrade, humiliate.

dignity (SYN.) stateliness, distinction, bearing.

digress (SYN.) divert, wander, bend, stray, deflect, sidetrack, crook.
(ANT.) preserve, continue, remain, follow, persist.

dilate (SYN.) increase, widen, amplify, enlarge, augment, expand.
(ANT.) shrink, contract, restrict, abridge.

dilemma (SYN.) fix, strait, condition, scrape, difficulty, plight.
(ANT.) ease, calmness, satisfaction, comfort.

diligent (SYN.) patient, busy, hardworking, active, perseverant, assiduous, industrious, careful.
(ANT.) unconcerned, indifferent, apathetic, lethargic, careless.

dim (SYN.) pale, shadowy, faint, faded, unclear, vague, darken, dull, indistinct.
(ANT.) brighten, brilliant, bright, illuminate, glaring.

dimension (SYN.) size, importance, measure, extent.

diminish (SYN.) suppress, lower, decrease, shrink, wane, abate, reduce, lessen, assuage.
(ANT.) enlarge, revive, amplify, increase.

diminutive (SYN.) small, wee, tiny, little, minute.
(ANT.) large, big, great, gigantic, huge.

din (SYN.) tumult, clamor, sound, babble, outcry, row, noise, racket.
(ANT.) quiet, stillness, hush.

dine (SYN.) lunch, eat, sup, feed.

dingy (SYN.) dull, dark, dismal, dirty, drab, murky, gray.
(ANT.) cheerful, bright.

dip (SYN.) immerse, plunge, submerge, wet, swim.

diplomacy (SYN.) knack, dexterity, skill, address, poise, tact, finesse.
(ANT.) vulgarity, blunder, awkwardness, incompetence.

diplomatic (SYN.) politic, adroit, tactful, discreet, judicious, gracious, polite, discriminating.
(ANT.) rude, churlish, gruff, boorish, impolite, coarse.

dire (SYN.) horrible, terrible, appalling, fearful, harrowing, grievous, ghastly, awful, horrid, terrifying, dreadful, frightful, horrifying, monstrous, horrendous, repulsive.
(ANT.) lovely, enchanting, fascinating, beautiful, enjoyable.

direct (SYN.) rule, manage, bid, order, level, command, conduct, regulate, point, indicate, show, aim, control, sight, guide, instruct, train, govern.
(ANT.) swerving, untruthful, misguide, distract, indirect, crooked, deceive.

direction (SYN.) way, order, course, instruction, tendency, management, route, trend, guidance, administration, supervision, inclination.

directly (SYN.) immediately, straight.

dirt (SYN.) pollution, soil, filthiness,

filth.
(ANT.) cleanliness, cleanness.
dirty *(SYN.)* muddy, base, pitiful, filthy, shabby, foul, soiled, nasty, mean, grimy, low, obscene, untidy, indecent, unclean, messy, squalid, contemptible, sloppy.
(ANT.) pure, neat, wholesome, clean, presentable.
disability *(SYN.)* inability, weakness, handicap, incapacity, injury, unfitness, incompetence, impotence.
(ANT.) power, ability, strength, capability.
disable *(SYN.)* weaken, incapacitate, cripple.
(ANT.) strengthen.
disabled *(SYN.)* deformed, limping, weak, crippled, maimed, defective, unsatisfactory, halt, unconvincing, feeble.
(ANT.) vigorous, athletic, sound, agile, robust.
disadvantage *(SYN.)* drawback, hindrance, handicap, inconvenience, obstacle.
(ANT.) advantage, benefit, convenience.
disagree *(SYN.)* quarrel, dispute, differ, conflict.
(ANT.) agree.
disagreement *(SYN.)* nonconformity, variance, difference, objection, challenge, remonstrance, dissent.
(ANT.) assent, acceptance, compliance, agreement.
disappear *(SYN.)* end, fade out, vanish.
(ANT.) emerge, appear.
disappoint *(SYN.)* fail, displease, mislead, dissatisfy.
(ANT.) please, satisfy, gratify.
disappointment *(SYN.)* dissatisfaction, defeat, discouragement, failure.
(ANT.) pleasure, satisfaction, gratification.
disapprove *(SYN.)* object to, disfavor, oppose.
(ANT.) approve.
disarm *(SYN.)* paralyze, demilitarize.
disaster *(SYN.)* casualty, mishap, misfortune, catastrophe, accident, adversity, ruin, calamity.
(ANT.) fortune, advantage, welfare.
disavow *(SYN.)* reject, revoke, disclaim, retract, disown.
(ANT.) recognize, acknowledge.
disband *(SYN.)* scatter, split, dismiss, separate.
disbelief *(SYN.)* doubt, incredulity, skep-

ticism.
(ANT.) certainty, credulity.
discard *(SYN.)* scrap, reject.
discern *(SYN.)* distinguish, see, descry, separate, differentiate, perceive, discriminate, detect, observe, recognize.
(ANT.) omit, confuse, overlook, mingle, confound.
discernment *(SYN.)* perception, sharpness, intelligence, perspicacity, acuity, keenness.
(ANT.) dullness, stupidity.
discharge *(SYN.)* remove, relieve, dismiss, banish, unburden, shoot, fire, explosion, eject, detonation, liberation, release, unload, discard, send.
(ANT.) retain, employ, enlist, hire, accept, recall, detain.
disciple *(SYN.)* learner, follower, student, adherent, supporter, scholar, pupil, votary, devotee.
(ANT.) guide, leader.
discipline *(SYN.)* training, order, instruction, drill, restraint, regulation, practice, correction, control, self-control, train, teach, exercise.
(ANT.) carelessness, sloppiness, confusion, negligence, messiness, chaos, turbulence.
disclaim *(SYN.)* retract, reject, deny, renounce, disavow, revoke.
(ANT.) recognize, acknowledge.
disclose *(SYN.)* show, divulge, betray, uncover, discover, reveal, expose.
(ANT.) hide, cloak, mask, cover, obscure, conceal.
discomfit *(SYN.)* malaise, concern, confuse, baffle, perplex, disconcert.
discomfort *(SYN.)* malaise, concern, anxiety, uneasiness.
disconcerted *(SYN.)* disturbed, agitated, upset.
disconnect *(SYN.)* divide, separate, unhook, disengage, detach.
(ANT.) connect, bind, attach, unify, engage.
disconsolate *(SYN.)* depressed, downcast, sorrowful, dejected, dismal, sad, unhappy, wretched, somber, cheerless, morose, lugubrious, miserable, mournful.
(ANT.) delightful, merry, glad, cheerful, happy.
discontent *(SYN.)* displeased, disgruntled, unhappy, dissatisfied, vexed.
discontinue *(SYN.)* postpone, delay, ad-

journ, stay, stop, defer, suspend, end, cease, interrupt.

(ANT.) prolong, persist, continue, start, begin, proceed, maintain.

discord (SYN.) disagreement, conflict.

(ANT.) concord, accord, agreement.

discourage (SYN.) hamper, obstruct, restrain, block, dishearten, retard, check, dispirit, thwart, depress, hinder, stop.

(ANT.) expedite, inspire, encourage, promote, inspirit, assist, further.

discourteous (SYN.) gruff, rude, vulgar, blunt, impolite, saucy, uncivil, boorish, rough.

(ANT.) stately, courtly, civil, dignified, genteel.

discover (SYN.) find out, invent, expose, ascertain, devise, reveal, learn, determine, detect.

(ANT.) hide, screen, cover, conceal, lose.

discredit (SYN.) disbelieve, dishonor, doubt, disgrace, shame.

discreet (SYN.) politic, discriminating, judicious, adroit, prudent, cautious, wise, tactful, careful, diplomatic.

(ANT.) incautious, rude, coarse, boorish, tactless, imprudent, indiscreet, careless, gruff.

discrepant (SYN.) incompatible, wavering, contrary, irreconcilable, unsteady, illogical, contradictory.

(ANT.) correspondent, compatible, consistent.

discriminating (SYN.) exact, particular, critical, accurate, discerning.

(ANT.) unimportant, shallow, insignificant, superficial.

discrimination (SYN.) perspicacity, discernment, racism, wisdom, bias, sagacity, intolerance, prejudice, intelligence, understanding.

(ANT.) thoughtlessness, senselessness, arbitrariness.

discuss (SYN.) gossip, plead, discourse, blab, lecture, talk, chat, spout, mutter, deliberate, consider, reason, comment.

discussion (SYN.) speech, chatter, lecture, conference, talk, dialogue, conversation, rumor.

(ANT.) silence, correspondence, writing.

disdain (SYN.) derision, hatred, contempt, scorn, contumely, reject, haughtiness, detestation.

(ANT.) respect, esteem, reverence, admire, prize, honor, admiration, awe,

regard.

disdainful (SYN.) haughty, scornful, arrogant, contemptuous.

(ANT.) awed, admiring, regardful.

disease (SYN.) malady, disorder, ailment, illness, affliction, infirmity, complaint, sickness.

(ANT.) soundness, health, vigor.

disentangle (SYN.) unwind, untie, clear, unravel, unknot, unsnarl, untangle.

disfigured (SYN.) deformed, marred, defaced, scarred.

disgrace (SYN.) odium, chagrin, shame, mortification, embarrassment, humiliate, scandal, dishonor, mortification.

(ANT.) renown, glory, respect, praise, dignity, honor.

disgraceful (SYN.) ignominious, shameful, discreditable, disreputable, scandalous, dishonorable.

(ANT.) renowned, esteemed, respectable, honorable.

disguise (SYN.) excuse, simulation, pretension, hide, camouflage, make-up, cover-up, mask, conceal, screen, affectation, pretext.

(ANT.) show, reality, actuality, display, reveal, sincerity, fact.

disgust (SYN.) offend, repulse, nauseate, revolt, sicken.

(ANT.) admiration, liking.

disgusting (SYN.) repulsive, nauseating, revolting, nauseous, repugnant

dish (SYN.) serve, container, give, receptacle.

dishearten (SYN.) depress, sadden, discourage.

disheveled (SYN.) mussed, sloppy, rumpled, untidy.

dishonest (SYN.) crooked, impure, unsound, false, contaminated, venal, corrupt, putrid, thievish, vitiated, tainted.

(ANT.) upright, honest, straightforward.

dishonor (SYN.) disrepute, scandal, indignity, chagrin, mortification, shame, obloquy, defamation, humiliation, disgrace, scandal.

(ANT.) renown, glory, praise, honor, dignity.

disinclined (SYN.) unwilling, reluctant, loath.

disingenuous (SYN.) tricky, deceitful, scheming, dishonest, underhanded, cunning, artful, crafty, insidious.

disintegrate (SYN.) decompose, dwindle, spoil, decay, wane, ebb, decline, rot.

(ANT.) increase, flourish, rise, grow.

disinterested *(SYN.)* unbiased, open-minded, neutral, impartial, unprejudiced.

dislike *(SYN.)* aversion, dread, reluctance, abhorrence, disinclination, hatred, repugnance.
(ANT.) devotion, affection, enthusiasm, attachment.

disloyal *(SYN.)* false, treasonable, apostate, unfaithful, recreant, treacherous, untrue, perfidious, traitorous, faithless.
(ANT.) true, devoted, constant, loyal.

dismal *(SYN.)* dark, lonesome, somber, bleak, dull, sad, doleful, sorrowful, cheerless, depressing, dreary, funeral, gloomy, melancholy.
(ANT.) lively, gay, happy, lighthearted, charming, cheerful.

dismantle *(SYN.)* take apart, wreck, disassemble.

dismay *(SYN.)* disturb, bother, dishearten, horror, alarm, bewilder, frighten, scare, discourage, confuse.
(ANT.) encourage, hearten.

dismiss *(SYN.)* remove, discharge, discard, release, liberate, exile, banish, eject, oust.
(ANT.) retain, detain, engage, hire, accept, recall.

disobedient *(SYN.)* refractory, forward, unruly, insubordinate, defiant, rebellious, undutiful.
(ANT.) submissive, compliant, obedient.

disobey *(SYN.)* invade, break, violate, infringe, defile.

disorder *(SYN.)* tumult, chaos, jumble, confusion, muddle, turmoil, anarchy.
(ANT.) organization, neatness, system, order.

disorganization *(SYN.)* jumble, confusion, muddle, anarchy.
(ANT.) system, order.

disorganized *(SYN.)* muddled, confused, indistinct, bewildered, mixed.
(ANT.) organized, lucid, clear, plain.

disown *(SYN.)* deny, renounce, reject, repudiate, forsake, disinherit.

disparaging *(SYN.)* belittling, deprecatory, discrediting, deprecating.

disparage *(SYN.)* undervalue, depreciate, lower, belittle, derogate, minimize, decry, discredit.
(ANT.) exalting, praise, aggrandize, magnify, commend.

disparagement *(SYN.)* lowering, decry-

ing, undervaluing, belittling, minimizing.
(ANT.) praise, exalting, aggrandizement, magnification.

dispassionate *(SYN.)* calm, cool, composed, controlled, unemotional, imperturbable.

dispatch *(SYN.)* throw, impel, transmit, emit, cast, finish, report, message, send, speed, achieve, conclude, communication, promptness, discharge.
(ANT.) reluctance, get, retain, bring, slowness, hold.

dispel *(SYN.)* disseminate, scatter, disperse, separate, diffuse.
(ANT.) collect, accumulate, gather.

dispense *(SYN.)* deal, give, allot, assign, apportion, mete, distribute, grant, allocate, measure.
(ANT.) refuse, withhold, confiscate, retain, keep.

disperse *(SYN.)* dissipate, scatter, disseminate, diffuse, separate, dispel.
(ANT.) collect, amass, gather, assemble, accumulate.

dispirited *(SYN.)* downhearted, unhappy, dejected, disheartened, sad, depressed, melancholy.
(ANT.) cheerful, happy, optimistic.

displace *(SYN.)* remove, transport, lodge, shift, move.
(ANT.) retain, leave, stay, remain.

display *(SYN.)* parade, exhibit, show, expose, reveal, demonstrate, showing, uncover, flaunt.
(ANT.) hide, cover, conceal.

displeasure *(SYN.)* dislike, disapproval, dissatisfaction, distaste, discontentment.

disposal *(SYN.)* elimination, adjustment, removal, release, arrangement, administration, settlement.

dispose *(SYN.)* settle, adjust, arrange.

disposition *(SYN.)* behavior, character, deed, deportment, action, manner, bearing, temperament, nature, demeanor, personality, carriage.

dispossess *(SYN.)* eject, expel, evict, oust, dislodge.

disprove *(SYN.)* refute, deny, invalidate, controvert.

dispute *(SYN.)* squabble, debate, argument, controversy, contention, disagreement, bicker, contest, argue, contend, quarrel, contradict, discuss, deny, oppose, altercate.
(ANT.) harmony, concord, agreement,

allow, concur, agree, concede, decision.

disregard *(SYN.)* slight, omit, ignore, inattention, oversight, skip, neglect, overlook.
(ANT.) regard, include.

disrepair *(SYN.)* ruin, decay, dilapidation, destruction.

disreputable *(SYN.)* dishonored, notorious, dishonorable, disgraced.

disrespectful *(SYN.)* fresh, impertinent, rude, impolite, impudent.
(ANT.) polite, respectful, courteous.

dissect *(SYN.)* examine, cut, analyze.

disseminate *(SYN.)* publish, circulate, spread, publish, broadcast.

dissent *(SYN.)* objection, challenge, disagreement, protest, remon-strance, difference, nonconformity, variance, noncompliance.
(ANT.) assent, acceptance, compliance, agreement.

dissertation *(SYN.)* thesis, treatise, disquisition.

dissimilar *(SYN.)* diverse, unlike, various, distinct, contrary, sundry, different, miscellaneous.
(ANT.) same, alike, similar, congruous.

dissimulation *(SYN.)* pretense, deceit, sanctimony, hypocrisy, cant.
(ANT.) honesty, candor, openness, frankness, truth.

dissipate *(SYN.)* misuse, squander, dwindle, consume, waste, lavish, diminish.
(ANT.) save, conserve, preserve, accumulate, economize.

dissolve *(SYN.)* liquefy, end, cease, melt, fade, disappear.

distant *(SYN.)* stiff, cold, removed, far, afar, unfriendly, remote, far-away, separated, aloof, reserved.
(ANT.) nigh, friendly, close, cordial, near.

distasteful *(SYN.)* disagreeable, unpleasant, objectionable.

distend *(SYN.)* swell, widen, magnify, expand, enlarge.

distinct *(SYN.)* plain, evident, lucid, visible, apparent, different, separate, individual, obvious, manifest, clear.
(ANT.) vague, indistinct, uncertain, obscure, ambiguous.

distinction *(SYN.)* importance, peculiarity, trait, honor, fame, characteristic, repute, quality, renown, prominence, attribute, property.

(ANT.) nature, substance, essence, being.

distinctive *(SYN.)* odd, exceptional, rare, individual, eccentric, special, strange.
(ANT.) ordinary, general, common, normal.

distinguish *(SYN.)* recognize, differentiate, divide, classify, descry, discern, separate, perceive, detect.
(ANT.) mingle, conjoin, blend, found, omit, confuse, overlook.

distinguished *(SYN.)* eminent, illustrious, renowned, celebrated, elevated, noted, important, famous, prominent.
(ANT.) ordinary, common, unknown, undistinguished, obscure, unimportant.

distort *(SYN.)* contort, falsify, twist, misrepresent.

distract *(SYN.)* occupy, bewilder, disturb, divert, confuse.
(ANT.) focus, concentrate.

distracted *(SYN.)* abstracted, preoccupied, absent.
(ANT.) attentive, attending, watchful, present.

distraction *(SYN.)* entertainment, confusion, amusement, diversion.

distress *(SYN.)* torment, misery, trouble, worry, pain, agony, torture, anguish, anxiety, disaster, wretchedness, peril, danger, suffering.
(ANT.) joy, solace, comfort, relief.

distribute *(SYN.)* deal, sort, allot, mete, classify, share, issue, dole, apportion, allocate, dispense, group.

district *(SYN.)* domain, place, territory, country, region, division, neighborhood, section, area, land.

distrust *(SYN.)* scruple, unbelief, suspect, mistrust, hesitation,- suspense, uncertainty, doubt, suspicion, ambiguity.
(ANT.) faith, conviction, trust, belief, determination.

disturb *(SYN.)* perturb, vex, confuse, worry, agitate, derange, unsettle, perplex, rouse, bother, trouble, annoy, interrupt, discompose.
(ANT.) quiet, order, calm, settle, pacify, soothe.

disturbance *(SYN.)* disorder, commotion, confusion, riot, fight, brawl.
(ANT.) calm, tranquillity, serenity.

disturbed *(SYN.)* neurotic, psychopathic, psychoneurotic, psychotic.
(ANT.) normal.

diverge *(SYN.)* fork, separate.
(ANT.) converge, join, merge.

diverse *(SYN.)* unlike, various, different, several.

diversify *(SYN.)* change, modify, alter.

diversion *(SYN.)* entertainment, sport, distraction, amusement, recreation.

divert *(SYN.)* detract, amuse, confuse, distract, deflect, entertain, tickle.

(ANT.) tire, bore, weary.

divide *(SYN.)* share, split, detach, cleave, apportion, sunder, part, distribute, allocate, disunite, estrange, separate, allot, sever.

(ANT.) merge, unite, convene, join, gather, combine.

divine *(SYN.)* holy, supernatural, godlike, transcendent, celestial, heavenly.

(ANT.) mundane, wicked, blasphemous, profane, diabolical.

division *(SYN.)* partition, separation, sharing, section, segment, part, portion.

(ANT.) union, agreement.

divorce *(SYN.)* disjoin, disconnect, separate, divide.

divulge *(SYN.)* discover, release, expose, show, betray, reveal, admit, disclose, uncover.

(ANT.) hide, conceal, cloak, cover.

dizzy *(SYN.)* staggering, unsteady, giddy, light-headed, confused.

(ANT.) rational, clearheaded, unconfused.

do *(SYN.)* effect, conduct, perform, work, suffice, accomplish, finish, transact, serve, discharge, execute, complete, carry on, make, settle, conclude, fulfill, consummate, produce, terminate, observe, practice.

docile *(SYN.)* pliant, tame, complaint, teachable, obedient, submissive, yielding.

(ANT.) unruly, obstinate, ungovernable, mulish.

dock *(SYN.)* moor, clip, anchor, tie.

doctor *(SYN.)* heal, treat, medic, remedy, cure.

doctrine *(SYN.)* tenet, precept, belief, dogma, teaching, principle, creed.

(ANT.) deed, practice, conduct, perform.

doctrinaire *(SYN.)* formal, dogmatic, overbearing, authoritarian, formal, arrogant, magisterial.

(ANT.) skeptical, indecisive, fluctuating.

document *(SYN.)* report, minute, memorial, vestige, account, note, trace.

dodge *(SYN.)* equivocate, recoil, elude, evade, avoid, duck.

dogma *(SYN.)* tenet, doctrine, belief, teaching, creed.

(ANT.) deed, practice, conduct, performance.

dogmatic *(SYN.)* formal, domineering, authoritarian, doctrinaire, opinionated, dictatorial, positive, arrogant, authoritative, overbearing, doctrinal, magisterial.

(ANT.) skeptical, indecisive, fluctuating.

doing *(SYN.)* feat, performance, act, deed, action, accomplishment, transaction.

(ANT.) intention, inactivity, cessation, inhibition.

dole *(SYN.)* deal, spread, allot, relief, divide, apportion, alms, welfare, distribute, dispense.

doleful *(SYN.)* dark, depressed, sad, dismal, dejected, bleak, dull, blue, sorrowful, unhappy, morose, lone-some, mournful, somber.

(ANT.) gay, lively, cheerful, joyous.

dolt *(SYN.)* blockhead, dunce.

domain *(SYN.)* place, division, region, territory, empire, country, charge, kingdom, realm, quarter, dominion, bailiwick, jurisdiction, land.

domestic *(SYN.)* family, tame, native, servant, homemade, household, internal.

(ANT.) alien, foreign, outside.

domesticate *(SYN.)* train, tame, housebreak, teach.

domicile *(SYN.)* dwelling, residence, home, abode.

dominate *(SYN.)* control, manage, rule, influence, subjugate, command, govern, tyrannize, direct, regulate.

(ANT.) follow, ignore, abandon, submit, forsake.

domination *(SYN.)* mastery, sway, ascendancy, transcendence.

don *(SYN.)* wear, slip on.

donation *(SYN.)* gift, bequest, present, benefaction, grant, contribution, offering, largess, boon.

(ANT.) earnings, purchase, deprivation, loss.

done *(SYN.)* complete, concluded, finished, over, terminated.

doom *(SYN.)* fortune, issue, result, destruction, destiny, consequence, fate, outcome, destine, ruin, death, lot.

doomed *(SYN.)* fated, predestined, destined, foreordained.

dormant *(SYN.)* unemployed, inert, lazy,

unoccupied, idle, indolent.
(ANT.) working, employed, occupied, active, industrious.
dose *(SYN.)* quantity, amount, portion.
dote *(SYN.)* indulge, treasure, coddle, pamper, spoil.
(ANT.) ignore.
double *(SYN.)* copy, fold, duplicate.
doubt *(SYN.)* distrust, incredulity, suspicion, hesitation, uncertainty, question, ' scruple, ambiguity, skepticism, suspect, mistrust, unbelief, suspense.
(ANT.) conviction, belief, determination, trust, certainty.
doubtful *(SYN.)* uncertain, unsettled, dubious, questionable, unsure, undetermined.
doubtless *(SYN.)* certainly, undoubtedly, assuredly, positively, unquestionably.
dour *(SYN.)* gloomy, sulky, crabbed, morose, fretful.
(ANT.) joyous, pleasant, amiable, merry.
douse *(SYN.)* immerse, quench, dip, dunk, extinguish.
dowdy *(SYN.)* messy, unkempt, untidy, sloppy, shabby, frowzy.
downcast *(SYN.)* sad, disheartened, unhappy, downhearted, dejected, dispirited, discourage, depressed, glum.
downfall *(SYN.)* destruction, comedown.
downgrade *(SYN.)* reduce, lower, diminish, decrease, depreciate.
(ANT.) improve, upgrade, appreciate.
downhearted *(SYN.)* glum, discouraged, depressed, gloomy, downcast, sad, dejected.
(ANT.) enthusiastic, cheerful, happy.
downpour *(SYN.)* cloudburst, deluge, flood.
downright *(SYN.)* totally, positively, completely, definitely.
dowry *(SYN.)* endowment, gift, settlement, talent, ability.
drab *(SYN.)* flat, dull, lifeless, unattractive.
draft *(SYN.)* air, induction, wind, enrollment, drawing, outline.
drag *(SYN.)* heave, pull, tug, crawl, draw, tarry, tow, haul, delay.
drain *(SYN.)* empty, deprive, dry, filter, spend, tap, exhaust, waste, sap, use.
(ANT.) fulfill, fill.
drama *(SYN.)* show, play, production, piece.
dramatist *(SYN.)* playwright.
drape *(SYN.)* flow, cover, hang.

drastic *(SYN.)* severe, rough, extreme, violent, tough, intense.
draw *(SYN.)* tug, obtain, trace, lure, drag, attract, persuade, induce, haul, write, remove, extend, stretch, take out, allure, pull, prolong, extract, tow, draft, delineate, unsheathe, lure, depict, entice, sketch, infer.
(ANT.) shorten, contract, propel, alienate, drive.
drawback *(SYN.)* snag, hitch, disadvantage, handicap, deficiency, difficulty, check, obstacle, hindrance, impediment.
(ANT.) gain, benefit, windfall, advantage.
drawing *(SYN.)* likeness, print, view, engraving, portrait, sketch, illustration, picture, resemblance, scene.
drawn *(SYN.)* tired, haggard, taut, strained, harrowed, weary, tense, sapped, spent.
(ANT.) rested, relaxed, energetic, fresh.
draw out *(SYN.)* protract, extend, persist, prolong, lengthen, sustain, continue.
(ANT.) reduce, curtail, shorten, abridge.
draw up *(SYN.)* draft, write out, prepare, compose, indite, formulate, wait, stay.
dread *(SYN.)* awe, horror, fear, terror, alarm, reverence, apprehension, foreboding.
(ANT.) courage, boldness, assurance, confidence.
dreadful *(SYN.)* dire, inspiring, ghastly, appalling, horrid, impressive, terrible, awful, frightful, horrible, bad, hideous, awesome, outrageous, repulsive.
(ANT.) fascinating, beautiful, enjoyable, enchanting, lovely.
dream *(SYN.)* fantasy, wish, hope, vision, daydream, reverie, imagine, fantasize, fancy, invent, muse.
dream up *(SYN.)* cook up, create, think up, concost, contrive, originate, imagine, devise.
dreary *(SYN.)* dull, sad, bleak, lonesome, gloomy, chilling, somber, depressing, dismal, cheerless, dark.
(ANT.) lively, hopeful, gay, cheerful, bright, joyous.
dregs *(SYN.)* riffraff, scum, outcasts, dross, leftovers, flotsam.
drench *(SYN.)* wet, bathe, flood, soak, saturate.
dress *(SYN.)* garb, frock, gown, clothing, costume, apparel, attire, wardrobe, garments, vesture, clothes, habit, wear,

don, robe, raiment.
(ANT.) undress, strip, divest, disrobe.
dresser (SYN.) dude, clotherhorse, fop, dandy.
dressing (SYN.) bandage, seasoning, medicine, sauce.
dressy (SYN.) flashy, swank, showy, dapper.
(ANT.) dowdy, drab, frumpy, shabby, tacky.
dribble (SYN.) fall, drip, leak, slaver, slobber.
drift (SYN.) roam, tendency, meander, sail, float, direction, wander, intention, stray.
drifter (SYN.) hobo, tramp, vagabond.
drill (SYN.) employment, lesson, task, use, activity, operation, training.
(ANT.) relaxation, indolence, rest, idleness, repose.
drink (SYN.) gulp, swallow, imbibe, beverage, refreshment, potion.
drip (SYN.) dribble, drop, trickle.
drive (SYN.) impel, coerce, oblige, force, push, direct, constrain, journey, urge, enforce, trip, handle, ride, propel, control, run, compel.
drivel (SYN.) slaver, drool, spit, spittle, dribble, slobber, saliva, nonsense, twaddle, rubbish, babble, gibberish.
driver (SYN.) motorist, operator, teamster, trucker, motorman, pilot, coachman.
droll (SYN.) laughable, funny, amusing, witty, comical.
(ANT.) sober, sad, solemn, melancholy.
drone (SYN.) buzz, hum, loafer, idler, nonworker.
drool (SYN.) drivel, slaver, dribble, spit, gibber, jabber, twaddle, trickle, salivate.
droop (SYN.) dangle, weaken, hang, sink, fail, settle, sag, weary, languish, despond.
(ANT.) stand, tower, extend, rise, straighten.
drop (SYN.) droop, dribble, topple, collapse, downward, drip, trickle, tumble, gob, droplet, reduction, slump, slip, decrease, fall, dismiss, decline.
(ANT.) ascend, mount, steady, arise, soar.
drop out (SYN.) back out, withdraw, stop, forsake, abandon, give up, leave, quit.
droppings (SYN.) faces, dung, waste, manure, excrement, ordure, guano.

dross (SYN.) dregs, impurity, leftovers, residue, debris, leavings, remains.
drove (SYN.) flock, herd.
drown (SYN.) sink, inundate, submerge, immerse.
drowse (SYN.) nap, doze, catnap, snooze, sleep, slumber, rest, drop off, repose.
drowsy (SYN.) dozing, torpid, soothing, dreamy, sleepy, comatose, sluggish, lulling, dull, calming, restful, lethargic.
(ANT.) alert, awake, sharp, keen, acute.
drub (SYN.) wallop, thrash, beat, thump, cane, flog, rout, outclass, overcome, belabor, pummel, defeat, outplay.
drubbing (SYN.) walloping, flogging, beating, pounding, pommeling, thwacking, thrashing, rout, licking, clobbering.
drudge (SYN.) work, labor, hack, slave, toil, grub, grind, toiler, flunky, menial, servant.
drudgery (SYN.) toil, travail, effort, task, work, endeavor, labor.
(ANT.) recreation, indolence, leisure.
drug (SYN.) remedy, medicine, stupefy, anesthetize, numb, benumb.
drugged (SYN.) numb, doped, numbed, stupefied, dazed, groggy, benumbed.
druggist (SYN.) apothecary, chemist, pharmacologist.
drunk (SYN.) tight, intoxicated, soused, drunken, inebriated, alcoholic, sozzled, besotted, sot, toper, boozer, wino, rummy, dipsomaniac, lush, tipsy.
drunkard (SYN.) sot, drunk, alcoholic, lush.
dry (SYN.) thirsty, dehydrated, vapid, plain, arid, uninteresting, drained, parched, barren, waterless, dull, tedious, boring, desiccated, tiresome.
(ANT.) fresh, wet, soaked, fascinating, attractive, lively, moist, interesting.
dub (SYN.) nickname, name, christen, call, style, term, confer, bestow, denominate, entitle, characterize, tag, label.
dubious (SYN.) unsure, uncertain, undecided, hesitant, spurious, unreliable, puzzling, untrustworthy, questionable, ambiguous.
(ANT.) decided, fixed, irrefutable, definite, genuine, unquestionable, sound, authentic, trustworthy.
duck (SYN.) douse, dip, submerse, submerge, immerse, plunge, wet, souse, drench, engulf, avoid, shun, lower, bob, hedge, shy, evade, swerve, quail.

(ANT.) raise, confront, face, elevate, cope with, undertake, assume, face up to.

duct *(SYN.)* pipe, tube, passage, vein, canal, funnel, gutter, main, trough, artery.

due *(SYN.)* payable, unpaid, owing, owed, imminent, expected.

duel *(SYN.)* competition, contest, engagement, rivalry, combat, strife, encounter, battle, conflict, dispute, strive.

dues *(SYN.)* assessment, fees, cost, levy, admission, fare, toll, demand, contribution.

duffer *(SYN.)* bungler, slouch, blunderer, novice, incompetent, fumbler, lummox. *(ANT.) master, expert, pro.*

dull *(SYN.)* commonplace, slow, sad, dreary, boring, stupid, uninteresting, blunt, tedious, dulled, dumb, tiring, monotonous, obtuse, tiresome, dense, unimaginative, unfeeling, dead, lifeless, dismal. *(ANT.) clear, animated, interesting, lively.*

dullard *(SYN.)* dolt, dunce, moron, clod, blockhead, numskull.

dumb *(SYN.)* dull, witless, ignorant, mute, speechless, brainless, dense, stupid, senseless. *(ANT.) discerning, bright, alert, clever, intelligent.*

dumbfound *(SYN.)* stagger, stun, nonplus, stupefy, overwhelm, amaze, confuse, startle, bewilder, surprise, astonish.

dumfounded *(SYN.)* shocked, astonished, flabbergasted, astounded, stunned.

dump *(SYN.)* heap, fling down, drop, empty, unload, clear out, dispose of, tipple, discharge, overturn, upset, dismiss, abandon. *(ANT.) store, fill, load, hoard, pack.*

dunce *(SYN.)* deadhead, nitwit, booby, idiot, ignoramus, numskull, noddy, fool.

dungeon *(SYN.)* jail, prison, keep, cell.

dunk *(SYN.)* plunge, douse, submerge, dip. *(ANT.) uplift, elevate, recover.*

dupe *(SYN.)* sucker, victim, gull, pushover, fool, cheat, deceive, defraud.

duplicate *(SYN.)* replica, replicate, facsimile, copy, reproduce, clone, double, twin, transcript. *(ANT.) prototype.*

duplicity *(SYN.)* dissimulation, deception, hypocrisy, deceitfulness, insin-

cerity, artifice, cant, guile. *(ANT.) openness, artlessness, candor, straightforwardness, genuineness.*

durability *(SYN.)* might, strength, force, sturdiness, intensity, potency, vigor. *(ANT.) weakness, frailty, feebleness.*

durable *(SYN.)* constant, firm, fixed, unchangeable, enduring, abiding, lasting. *(ANT.) unstable, temporary, perishable, transitory.*

duration *(SYN.)* time, term, period, while, stage, era, epoch, interim.

duress *(SYN.)* force, demand, compulsion, emergency, pressure.

dusky *(SYN.)* sable, black, dark, darkish, swarthy, tawny, gloomy, overcast, misty, obscure, opaque, shadowy. *(ANT.) light, fair, white, pale, shining, clear, bright.*

dusty *(SYN.)* sooty, unclean, dirty, musty, grubby, unswept, crumbly, friable, chalky, disintegrated, messy, grimy. *(ANT.) polished, immaculate, clean, shiny.*

dutiful *(SYN.)* docile, faithful, obedient. *(ANT.) disobedient, willful, unruly, headstrong.*

duty *(SYN.)* bond, responsibility, accountability, faithfulness, function, obligation, conscience, assignment, part, engagement. *(ANT.) freedom, choice.*

dwarf *(SYN.)* midget, runt, reduce, stunt, minimize, tiny. *(ANT.) mammoth, colossus, monster, giant.*

dwell *(SYN.)* inhabit, roost, settle, abide, live, reside.

dwelling *(SYN.)* seat, quarters, abode, home, hearth, residence, house, domicile.

dwell on *(SYN.)* insist, linger over, harp on, emphasize. *(ANT.) skip, neglect, skim over, disregard.*

dwindle *(SYN.)* wane, decrease, diminish, fade, subside, ebb, shrivel, lessen. *(ANT.) enlarge, wax, increase, grow, gain.*

dying *(SYN.)* failing, expiring, waning, passing, final, declining, receding, dwindling, vanishing. *(ANT.) thriving, booming, flourishing.*

dynamic *(SYN.)* active, forceful, kinetic, energetic, motive, mighty, vigorous. *(ANT.) sleepy, stable, inert, fixed, dead.*

eager *(SYN.)* avid, hot, anxious, fervent, enthusiastic, impatient, ardent, impassioned, yearning.
(ANT.) unconcerned, apathetic, impassioned, dull, uninterested, indifferent.

early *(SYN.)* betimes, opportune, first, beforehand, advanced, soon, shortly.
(ANT.) retarded, late, tardy, belated, overdue.

earmark *(SYN.)* peculiarity, characteristic, brand, sign, stamp, trademark.

earn *(SYN.)* attain, win, get, achieve, obtain, gain, deserve, realize, collect, net, acquire, merit.
(ANT.) lose, waste, consume, forfeit.

earnest *(SYN.)* sincere, decided, determined, intent, serious, eager, resolute.
(ANT.) indifferent, frivolous, insincere.

earnings *(SYN.)* wages, pay, salary, income.

earth *(SYN.)* globe, dirt, land, world, turf, soil, sod, ground.

earthly *(SYN.)* mundane, everyday, worldly.
(ANT.) heavenly.

earthy *(SYN.)* earthlike, coarse, earthen, crude, unrefined, vulgar.
(ANT.) tasteful, elegant, polished, refined.

ease *(SYN.)* lighten, alleviate, pacify, soothe, allay, comfort, contentedness, assuage, reduce, rest, facilitate, relaxation, calm, repose, mitigate, contentment, relax.
(ANT.) worry, disturb, confound, aggravate, difficulty, effort, trouble, intensify, distress.

easily *(SYN.)* readily, effortlessly, smoothly, naturally, facilely.
(ANT.) hardly, ardously, painfully, laboriously.

easiness *(SYN.)* repose, comfort, satisfaction, contentment, liberty, leisure, facility, simplicity.
(ANT.) unrest, torment, arduousness, difficulty, discomfort.

easy *(SYN.)* light, simple, facile, gentle, effortless, unhurried, comfortable, pleasant, cozy, relaxed, plain, uncomplicated, restful.
(ANT.) hard, demanding, awkward, strict, difficult, formal.

easygoing *(SYN.)* calm, mild, complacent, relaxed, unconcerned, serene, uncritical, cheerful, carefree, unhurried.
(ANT.) severe, demanding, stern, strict, harsh.

eat *(SYN.)* consume, swallow, dine, corrode, chew, lunch, devour, feast, breakfast, erode.

eavesdrop *(SYN.)* spy, listen, snoop, overhear.

eavesdropper *(SYN.)* monitor, listener, snoop, spy.

ebb *(SYN.)* diminish, recede, decline, decrease, retreat, lessen.
(ANT.) wax, grow, thrive, increase, swell.

ebullient *(SYN.)* vivacious, buoyant, exuberant.
(ANT.) lethargic, sad, gloomy, depressed.

eccentric *(SYN.)* odd, irregular, unusual, abnormal, peculiar.
(ANT.) ordinary, conventional, normal.

eccentricity *(SYN.)* kink, idiosyncracy, whim, freak, caprice, foible, quirk, oddness, strangeness, aberration.
(ANT.) normality, conventionality, ordinariness.

ecclesiastical *(SYN.)* religious, churchly, clerical.

echelon *(SYN.)* rank, level, grade, place, status.

echo *(SYN.)* response, imitation, suggestion, trace, reaction, imitate, repeat.

eclectic *(SYN.)* selective, diverse, broad, liberal, comprehensive.
(ANT.) limited, narrow, rigid, confined.

eclipse *(SYN.)* conceal, screen, hide, cover, obscure, overcast, veil.

economical *(SYN.)* saving, thrifty, careful, frugal, provident, sparing.
(ANT.) wasteful, extravagant, lavish, improvident, prodigal.

economize *(SYN.)* pinch, scrimp, save.

economy *(SYN.)* saving, thrift.

ecstasy *(SYN.)* frenzy, gladness, delight, madness, joy, glee, exaltation, pleasure, trance, rapture.
(ANT.) misery, melancholy, sadness.

ecstatic *(SYN.)* overjoyed, thrilled, delighted, happy, elated.

edge *(SYN.)* margin, brim, verge, brink, border, keenness, extremity, boundary, trim, periphery, hem, rim, sting.
(ANT.) dullness, center, bluntness.

edgy *(SYN.)* tense, touchy, nervous, irritable.

edict *(SYN.)* declaration, order, ruling, decree, pronouncement, command, law, proclamation.

edifice *(SYN.)* construction, building, establishment.

edit *(SYN.)* check, revise, correct, amend.

educate *(SYN.)* instruct, teach, school, train.

education *(SYN.)* training, development, knowledge, learning, cultivation, schooling, instruction, study.

eerie *(SYN.)* weird, fearful, ghastly, spooky, strange.

efface *(SYN.)* obliterate, erase.

effect *(SYN.)* produce, consequence, evoke, cause, make, complete, outcome, result, determine.

effective *(SYN.)* efficient, practical, productive.
(ANT.) *useless, wasteful, ineffective.*

efficiency *(SYN.)* efficacy, capability, effectiveness, competency, ability.
(ANT.) *wastefulness, inability.*

efficient *(SYN.)* efficacious, skillful, capable, adept, competent, useful, effectual, effective, apt, proficient.
(ANT.) *inefficient, unskilled, ineffectual, incompetent.*

effort *(SYN.)* labor, endeavor, pains, essay, trial, exertion, struggle, strain, try, attempt, strife, toil.

effortless *(SYN.)* simple, easy.

egg *(SYN.)* stir, ovum, incite, urge, arouse, embryo, provoke.

egghead *(SYN.)* scholar, intellectual, pedant.

egoism *(SYN.)* self-interest, conceit, pride, selfishness, egotism.
(ANT.) *modesty, generosity, selflessness.*

eject *(SYN.)* expel, remove, oust, eliminate.
(ANT.) *include.*

elaborate *(SYN.)* detail, develop, decorated, decorative, ornate, complex.
(ANT.) *simplify, simple, unadorned.*

elapse *(SYN.)* expire.

elastic *(SYN.)* yielding, flexible, adaptable, pliable.

elated *(SYN.)* delighted, rejoicing, overjoyed, jubilant.
(ANT.) *sad, unhappy.*

elder *(SYN.)* senior.
(ANT.) *younger.*

elderly *(SYN.)* aged, old.
(ANT.) *young, youthful.*

elect *(SYN.)* pick, appoint, choose.

electrify *(SYN.)* shock, charge, stir, upset, generate, agitate.

elegant *(SYN.)* tasteful, refined, cultivated, choice, polished, superior, fine.
(ANT.) *crude, coarse, unpolished, taste-*

less.

elementary *(SYN.)* simple, primary, basic, uncomplicated, initial, beginning, fundamental.
(ANT.) *involved, complex, sophisticated, complicated.*

elevate *(SYN.)* raise, lift.
(ANT.) *lower, drop.*

elf *(SYN.)* devil, fairy, imp.

elicit *(SYN.)* summon.

eligible *(SYN.)* fit, suitable, qualified.

eliminate *(SYN.)* expel, eject, remove, dislodge, extirpate, erase, oust.
(ANT.) *admit, involve.*

elite *(SYN.)* nobility, upper-class, aristocracy, gentry.
(ANT.) *mob, proletariat.*

elongate *(SYN.)* extend, prolong, lengthen.

elope *(SYN.)* escape, flee.

eloquent *(SYN.)* expressive, fluent, articulate, glib, meaningful.
(ANT.) *inarticulate.*

else *(SYN.)* different, another, other.

elude *(SYN.)* escape, miss, avoid, dodge.
(ANT.) *add, include.*

emaciated *(SYN.)* wasted, thin, starved, withered, shriveled, gaunt, shrunken, drawn, undernourished.

emancipate *(SYN.)* liberate, free, deliver, save.
(ANT.) *restrain.*

embankment *(SYN.)* shore, dam, bank, fortification, buttress.

embargo *(SYN.)* prohibition, restriction, restraint.

embark *(SYN.)* board, depart.

embarrass *(SYN.)* discomfit, rattle, distress, hamper, fluster, entangle, abash, mortify, hinder, perplex, confuse, shame, trouble.
(ANT.) *relieve, encourage, help.*

embassy *(SYN.)* ministry, legation, consulate.

embed *(SYN.)* root, inset, enclose, plant.

embellish *(SYN.)* adorn, decorate, ornament.

embezzle *(SYN.)* pilfer, misuse, rob, misappropriate, steal, take.

embitter *(SYN.)* provoke, arouse, alienate, anger, inflame.

emblem *(SYN.)* token, mark, symbol, badge.

embody *(SYN.)* comprise, cover, embrace, include.

embrace *(SYN.)* espouse, accept, receive,

comprehend, contain, welcome, comprise, cover, clasp, include, adopt, hug.
(ANT.) spurn, reject, bar, exclude, repudiate.

embroider (SYN.) decorate, adorn, stitch, trim, overstate, embellish, ornament, exaggerate, magnify.

emerge (SYN.) surface, show, appear.

emergency (SYN.) strait, pass, crisis, urgency, predicament, pinch.

eminent (SYN.) renowned, glorious, distinguished, noted, celebrated, elevated, glorious, important, conspicuous, prominent, famous.
(ANT.) ordinary, commonplace, unknown, undistinguished, common.

emissary (SYN.) envoy, minister, delegate, agent, spy.

emit (SYN.) expel, breathe, shoot, hurl, ooze, vent, belch, discharge.

emotion (SYN.) passion, turmoil, perturbation, affection, sentiment, feeling, trepidation, agitation.
(ANT.) dispassion, indifference, tranquillity, calm, restraint.

emotional (SYN.) ardent, passionate, stirring, zealous, impetuous, overwrought, enthusiastic.
(ANT.) tranquil, calm, placid.

emphasis (SYN.) accent, stress, insistence.

emphatic (SYN.) positive, definite, forceful, energetic, strong.
(ANT.) lax, quiet, unforceful.

employ (SYN.) avail, use, devote, apply, utilize, engage, sign, hire, retain, service, contract.
(ANT.) reject, discard.

employee (SYN.) laborer, worker, servant.
(ANT.) boss, employer.

employer (SYN.) owner, boss, management, proprietor, manager, superintendent, supervisor.
(ANT.) employee, worker.

employment (SYN.) occupation, work, business, position, job, service, engagement.
(ANT.) leisure, idleness, slothfulness.

empower (SYN.) enable, sanction, permit, warrant.

empty (SYN.) void, devoid, unfilled, barren, senseless, unoccupied, unfurnished, vacant, blank, evacuate, unload, hollow.
(ANT.) supplied, full, occupied.

emulate (SYN.) follow, imitate, copy.

enable (SYN.) authorize, empower, sanction, qualify.

enact (SYN.) legislate, portray, pass, stage, represent.

enchant (SYN.) charm, titillate, fascinate, bewitch, delight, thrill, captivate.
(ANT.) tire, bore.

encircle (SYN.) comprise, include, bound, encompass.

enclose (SYN.) envelop, confine, bound, surround, encompass, encircle, circumscribe.
(ANT.) open, exclude, distend, expose, develop.

encompass (SYN.) include, surround, encircle.

encore (SYN.) repetition, repeat, again.

encounter (SYN.) battle, meet, oppose, run into, face, collide.

encourage (SYN.) incite, favor, cheer, impel, countenance, inspirit, exhilarate, animate, hearten, embolden, support.
(ANT.) deter, dispirit, deject, dissuade.

encroach (SYN.) interfere, trespass, intrude, infringe.

encumber (SYN.) hamper, load, burden.

end (SYN.) completion, object, close, aim, result, conclusion, finish, extremity, intent, halt, stop, limit, purpose, cessation, expiration, termination.
(ANT.) opening, start, introduction, beginning, launch, inception.

endanger (SYN.) imperil, hazard, risk.
(ANT.) secure.

endear (SYN.) allure, charm.

endeavor (SYN.) strive, struggle, exertion, attempt, try, labor.

endless (SYN.) constant, nonstop, continuous, incessant, everlasting.

endorse (SYN.) approve, accept, sign, confirm, pass.

endow (SYN.) provide, furnish, bestow, give, contribute.
(ANT.) divest.

endure (SYN.) experience, undergo, sustain, last, bear, continue, remain, undergo, persist, brook, tolerate, suffer.
(ANT.) wane, die, perish, succumb, fail.

enemy (SYN.) foe, antagonist, rival, opponent, competitor, adversary, opposition.
(ANT.) colleague, ally, friend, accomplice.

energy (SYN.) strength, vim, force, power, stamina, vigor, might.
(ANT.) feebleness, lethargy.

enervate *(SYN.)* enfeeble, weaken, debilitate, exhaust, devitalize.
(ANT.) invigorate.

enfold *(SYN.)* clasp, surround, wrap, embrace, hug.

enforce *(SYN.)* make, drive, compel, execute, force.

engage *(SYN.)* absorb, occupy, employ, hold, involve, hire, agree, engross, retain, promise, commit, entangle.
(ANT.) fire, disengage, discharge, dismiss.

engaged *(SYN.)* affianced, betrothed, busy, occupied.

engaging *(SYN.)* fascinating, appealing, enticing, interesting, tempting, lovely, beguiling, charming, enchanting, engrossing, delightful, exquisite.
(ANT.) ordinary, boring.

engender *(SYN.)* develop, breed, cause, generate, produce.

engineer *(SYN.)* direct, conduct, guide, lead, manage.

engrave *(SYN.)* print, cut, impress, inscribe, carve, sketch.

engross *(SYN.)* engage, enthrall, occupy, fascinate, absorb.

engulf *(SYN.)* flood, swallow.

enhance *(SYN.)* better, uplift, improve.

enigma *(SYN.)* mystery, stumper, riddle.

enigmatic *(SYN.)* perplexing, confusing, puzzling, baffling, mystifying.

enjoy *(SYN.)* savor, like, relish.

enjoyment *(SYN.)* pleasure, delight, gratification.
(ANT.) abhorrence, displeasure.

enlarge *(SYN.)* widen, distend, amplify, broaden, extend, increase, augment, expand, dilate.
(ANT.) diminish, shrink, contract, decrease, wane, restrict.

enlighten *(SYN.)* inform, illuminate, clarify, teach, instruct.
(ANT.) confuse.

enlist *(SYN.)* enroll, prompt, join, induce, enter, register, persuade.
(ANT.) quit, leave, abandon.

enliven *(SYN.)* inspire, brighten, stimulate.

enmity *(SYN.)* antagonism, hatred, animosity, malignity, ill-will, antipathy, hostility, unfriendliness.
(ANT.) love, like, friendliness.

enormity *(SYN.)* heinousness, wickedness, barbarity, atrociousness.

enormous *(SYN.)* vast, huge, colossal, immense, gargantuan, elephantine, gigantic, stupendous, large.
(ANT.) small, slight, tiny, minute, infinitesimal, diminutive, little.

enough *(SYN.)* ample, adequate, sufficient, plenty.
(ANT.) inadequate, insufficient.

enrage *(SYN.)* anger, provoke, madden, inflame.
(ANT.) appease, soothe, calm.

enrich *(SYN.)* better, improve.

enroll *(SYN.)* record, list, recruit, register, enlist, write, induct.
(ANT.) quit, leave, abandon.

enshrine *(SYN.)* bury, entomb.

ensign *(SYN.)* banner, colors, flag, officer.

enslave *(SYN.)* keep, hold, capture.

ensue *(SYN.)* arise, succeed, follow, result.

ensure *(SYN.)* guarantee, assure, protect, defend, cover.

entangle *(SYN.)* confuse, snare, involve, ravel, snarl, tangle, trap.

enter *(SYN.)* join, go inside.

enterprise *(SYN.)* fete, deed, venture, project, adventure, undertaking, ambition, business, exploit.

enterprising *(SYN.)* energetic, resourceful.
(ANT.) lazy, indolent, sluggish, unresourceful.

entertain *(SYN.)* cheer, gladden, hold, consider, please, contemplate, divert, amuse, harbor, fascinate, interest.
(ANT.) repulse, tire, bore, disgust, annoy.

enthrall *(SYN.)* captivate, fascinate, enchant, charm, thrill.

enthusiasm *(SYN.)* fervor, fanaticism, zeal, ardor, intensity, devotion, excitement, eagerness, fervency, earnestness.
(ANT.) indifference, ennui, apathy, unconcern, detachment.

enthusiastic *(SYN.)* earnest, zealous, eager.
(ANT.) aloof, indifferent, unconcerned.

entice *(SYN.)* lure, attract, seduce.

entire *(SYN.)* complete, intact, whole, undivided.
(ANT.) divided, separated, incomplete, partial.

entirely *(SYN.)* altogether, thoroughly, wholly, solely.

entitle *(SYN.)* call, label, name, empower, allow, authorize, license, title.

entourage *(SYN.)* train, company, retinue, escort.

entrance *(SYN.)* inlet, portal, doorway, fascinate, entry, intrigue, door, thrill. *(ANT.)* exit.

entreat *(SYN.)* implore, beg, plead.

entreaty *(SYN.)* plea, appeal.

entrust *(SYN.)* commit, charge, assign, delegate, consign, commission.

enumerate *(SYN.)* count, tally, list, number.

enunciate *(SYN.)* announce, express, speak, state.

envelop *(SYN.)* embrace, cover, conceal, surround, wrap.

environment *(SYN.)* neighborhood, habitat, surroundings, setting.

envision *(SYN.)* picture, imagine, visualize.

envoy *(SYN.)* delegate, emissary, representative, agent, messenger.

envy *(SYN.)* covetousness, jealousy, spitefulness, covet. *(ANT.)* indifference, generosity.

epicure *(SYN.)* gourmand, gourmet, connoisseur, gastronome, epicurean, aesthete.

epidemic *(SYN.)* prevalent, scourge, plague, catching, widespread, pestilence, infectious.

episode *(SYN.)* happening, affair, occurrence, event, experience.

epoch *(SYN.)* age.

equal *(SYN.)* even, uniform, like, alike, equitable, same, identical, commensurate, equivalent, regular, parallel. *(ANT.)* different, unequal, irregular, uneven.

equilibrium *(SYN.)* stability, steadiness, balance, firmness.

equip *(SYN.)* fit, rig, provide, outfit, prepare, furnish.

equipment *(SYN.)* utensils, material, apparatus.

equitable *(SYN.)* square, rightful, fair, due, just, fit. *(ANT.)* partial, biased, unjust, uneven.

equity *(SYN.)* impartiality, fairness, justness, justice, fair-mindedness, evenhandedness.

equivalent *(SYN.)* match, rival, equal, like, replacement.

equivocal *(SYN.)* oblique, ambiguous, vague, indeterminate, uncertain, obscure. *(ANT.)* clear, precise, explicit, certain,

clear-cut, definite.

equivocate *(SYN.)* temporize, evade, hedge, quibble, fudge, waffle, straddle.

era *(SYN.)* epoch, cycle, age, time, period.

eradicate *(SYN.)* remove, demolish, eliminate.

erase *(SYN.)* obliterate, remove, cancel. *(ANT.)* add, include.

erect *(SYN.)* upright, build, straight, raise, construct, vertical. *(ANT.)* flat, horizontal, raze, flatten, demolish.

erection *(SYN.)* building, construction, raising, fabrication.

erode *(SYN.)* rust, consume, disintegrate.

erotic *(SYN.)* carnal, fleshy, amatory, prurient, lewd, wanton, passionate, lecherous.

err *(SYN.)* slip, misjudge.

errand *(SYN.)* chore, duty, task, exercise.

errant *(SYN.)* roving, rambling, wandering, vagrant.

erratic *(SYN.)* irregular, abnormal, uneven, occasional, sporadic, changeable, unsteady, odd, eccentric, strange, extraordinary, unconventional, bizarre, peculiar, uncertain, unusual, unstable. *(ANT.)* regular, steady, normal, ordinary.

erroneous *(SYN.)* wrong, mistaken, incorrect, inaccurate, false, untrue. *(ANT.)* true, right, correct, accurate.

error *(SYN.)* inaccuracy, fault, slip, oversight, fallacy, mistake, blunder.

erudite *(SYN.)* sage, wise, learned, deep, profound.

erupt *(SYN.)* vomit.

escapade *(SYN.)* caper, antic, stunt, trick, prank.

escape *(SYN.)* shun, avoid, flee, decamp, elude, flight, avert, departure, abscond, fly, evade. *(ANT.)* meet, confront, invite, catch.

escort *(SYN.)* conduct, lead, attend, accompany, protection, guard, guide, convoy, usher, squire.

especially *(SYN.)* unusually, principally, mainly, particularly, primarily.

essay *(SYN.)* test, thesis, undertake, paper, try.

essence *(SYN.)* substance, character, nature, principle, odor, meaning, basis, smell, perfume.

essential *(SYN.)* vital, intrinsic, basic, requisite, fundamental, indispensable, critical, requirement, necessity, necessary, important.

(ANT.) dispensable, unimportant, inessential.

establish (SYN.) prove, fix, found, settle, institute, raise, verify, conform, form, sanction, ordain, begin, organize.

(ANT.) upset, discontinue, scatter, disperse, refute, abolish, unsettle.

esteem (SYN.) revere, deem, appreciate, honor, value, think, admire, respect, hold, prize, reverence, regard.

(ANT.) scorn, disdain, depreciate, disregard, contempt, abhor.

estimate (SYN.) calculate, gauge, judge, rate, evaluate, compute, value, figure.

estimation (SYN.) judgment, viewpoint, opinion.

etch (SYN.) stamp, engrave, impress.

eternal (SYN.) undying, immortal, ceaseless, infinite, everlasting, deathless, perpetual, endless, timeless.

(ANT.) mortal, transient, finite, brief, temporary, passing.

etiquette (SYN.) decorum, formality.

evacuate (SYN.) withdraw, depart, leave, vacate.

evade (SYN.) miss, avoid, bypass.

(ANT.) confront, meet, face.

evaluate (SYN.) value, appraise, assay.

evaporate (SYN.) disappear, vanish.

(ANT.) condense, appear.

even (SYN.) smooth, level, still, square, same, flat, balanced, equal, parallel, identical.

(ANT.) irregular, bumpy, unbalanced, unequal, divergent.

evening (SYN.) twilight, dusk, sunset.

(ANT.) sunrise, dawn.

event (SYN.) issue, end, result, circumstance, occurrence, incident, consequence, happening, episode, outcome.

even-tempered (SYN.) composed, calm, cool.

(ANT.) hotheaded.

eventual (SYN.) consequent, ultimate.

(ANT.) present, current.

eventually (SYN.) ultimately.

ever (SYN.) continuously, always, constantly.

(ANT.) never.

everlasting (SYN.) permanent, ceaseless, endless, continual.

evermore (SYN.) always.

everyday (SYN.) commonplace, common, usual, ordinary, customary.

(ANT.) rare.

evict (SYN.) oust, put out, expel.

evidence (SYN.) grounds, clue, facts, testimony, data, sign, proof.

evident (SYN.) apparent, clear, obvious, indubitable, plain, conspicuous, patent, manifest, open, unmistakable.

(ANT.) hidden, unclear, uncertain, obscure, concealed.

evil (SYN.) immoral, harmful, badness, sinful, injurious, woe, bad, wicked.

(ANT.) goodness, moral, useful, upright, virtuous, beneficial, virtue, advantageous.

evoke (SYN.) summon, prompt.

evolve (SYN.) grow, advance, develop, result, emerge, unfold.

exact (SYN.) correct, faultless, errorless, detailed, accurate.

(ANT.) inaccurate, inexact, faulty.

exaggerate (SYN.) stretch, expand, amplify, embroider, heighten, overstate, caricature, magnify, enlarge.

(ANT.) understate, minimize, diminish, depreciate.

exalt (SYN.) erect, consecrate, raise, elevate, extol, dignify.

(ANT.) humble, degrade, humiliate.

examination (SYN.) investigation, inspection, test, scrutiny.

examine (SYN.) assess, contemplate, question, review, audit, notice, inquire, analyze, check, investigate, dissect, inspect, survey.

(ANT.) omit, disregard, overlook.

example (SYN.) pattern, archetype, specimen, illustration, model, instance, prototype, sample.

(ANT.) rule, concept, principle.

exasperate (SYN.) aggravate, anger, madden, irritate.

excavate (SYN.) unearth, dig, burrow.

exceed (SYN.) excel, beat, surpass, top.

exceedingly (SYN.) extremely, very, especially, unusually, surprisingly.

excel (SYN.) better, beat, surpass.

excellence (SYN.) distinction, superiority.

(ANT.) poorness, inferiority, badness.

excellent (SYN.) wonderful, fine, marvelous, superior.

(ANT.) poor, terrible, bad, inferior.

except (SYN.) omitting, barring, but, reject, excluding, save, exclude.

exception (SYN.) affront, offense, exclusion, deviation, omission, anomaly.

exceptional (SYN.) different, irregular, strange, unusual, abnormal.

excerpt (SYN.) abstract, extract.

excess (SYN.) surplus, intemperance, extravagance, immoderation, profusion, abundant, profuse, superfluity.
(ANT.) want, sparse, lack, dearth.

exchange (SYN.) barter, interchange, substitute, trade, change, swap.

excite (SYN.) arouse, incite, agitate, stimulate, awaken, disquiet.
(ANT.) lull, quiet, bore, pacify.

exclaim (SYN.) vociferate, cry, call out, cry out, ejaculate, shout.

exclamation (SYN.) shout, outcry, clamor.

exclude (SYN.) omit, restrain, hinder, bar, except, prevent.
(ANT.) welcome, involve, embrace, admit, accept, include.

exclusion (SYN.) exception, bar, rejection.
(ANT.) inclusion.

exclusive (SYN.) restricted, limited, restrictive, choice, selective, fashionable.
(ANT.) common, general, ordinary, unrestricted, unfashionable.

excursion (SYN.) voyage, tour, trip.

excuse (SYN.) exculpate, forgive, remit, acquit, free, pardon, condone, explanation, overlook, exempt, reason, justify, absolve.
(ANT.) revenge, punish, convict.

execute (SYN.) complete, accomplish, do, achieve, kill, perform.

exemplify (SYN.) show, illustrate.

exempt (SYN.) excuse, free, except, release.

exercise (SYN.) drill, task, use, activity, lesson, training, exertion, application, gymnastics, operation, practice.
(ANT.) rest, indolence, repose.

exertion (SYN.) attempt, effort, strain, endeavor.

exhale (SYN.) blow, breathe out.

exhaust (SYN.) drain, tire, empty, wear out, use, finish, fatigue.
(ANT.) renew, refresh, replace.

exhaustive (SYN.) comprehensive, thorough, extensive, complete.
(ANT.) incomplete.

exhibit (SYN.) demonstrate, display, reveal, betray, present, show, flaunt.
(ANT.) hide conceal, disguise.

exhilarate (SYN.) gladden, refresh, cheer, excite, stimulate.

exhort (SYN.) advise, coax, press, urge, prompt.

exile (SYN.) expulsion, proscription, deportation, ostracism, expatriation, deport, extradition, expel, banishment.
(ANT.) retrieval, welcome, recall, admittance, reinstatement.

exist (SYN.) stand, live, occur, be.

exit (SYN.) leave, depart.

exodus (SYN.) leaving, exit, parting, departure.

exonerate (SYN.) acquit, clear.

exorbitant (SYN.) unreasonable, outrageous, overpriced, preposterous, excessive.
(ANT.) normal, reasonable.

exotic (SYN.) strange, vivid, foreign, gay.
(ANT.) dull, native.

expand (SYN.) unfold, enlarge, broaden, spread, inflate, swell, grow.
(ANT.) contract, shrivel, shrink.

expect (SYN.) await, think, hope, anticipate.

expedient (SYN.) helpful, desirable, rush, hasten, useful, fitting, sensible.
(ANT.) delay.

expedition (SYN.) trek, speed, trip, haste, voyage, journey, hurry.

expel (SYN.) exile, dislodge, discharge, excommunicate, oust, eject, dismiss, banish, disown.
(ANT.) favor, recall, invite, admit.

expend (SYN.) consume, waste, spend, exhaust.
(ANT.) ration, reserve, conserve.

expense (SYN.) charge, cost, payment, price.

expensive (SYN.) costly, dear.
(ANT.) modest, inexpensive, cheap.

experience (SYN.) occurrence, episode, sensation, happening, existence, background, feeling, living, encountering, knowledge.

experienced (SYN.) expert, qualified, accomplished, skilled, practiced.
(ANT.) untutored, inexperienced, naive.

experiment (SYN.) trial, test, prove, research, examine, try, verify.

expert (SYN.) adept, handy, skillful, clever, specialist, authority, skilled, knowledgeable, ingenious.
(ANT.) untrained, unskilled, inexperienced.

expire (SYN.) terminate, die, cease, perish, pass, end, disappear.
(ANT.) commence, continue.

explain (SYN.) illustrate, decipher, expound, clarify, resolve, define, unravel,

elucidate, unfold, justify, interpret.
(ANT.) darken, baffle, obscure.
explanation (SYN.) definition, description, interpretation, account, reason, justification, excuse.
explicit (SYN.) lucid, definitive, specific, express, clear, manifest.
(ANT.) vague, implicit, ambiguous.
exploit (SYN.) feat, deed, accomplishment, adventure.
explore (SYN.) research, hunt, probe, search, investigate, look, examine.
explosion (SYN.) bang, boom, blowup, flare-up, blast, detonation, outbreak, convulsion, furor, tantrum, paroxysm.
explosive (SYN.) fiery, rabid, eruptive, volcanic, fulminatory, inflammatory.
(ANT.) stable, inert, peaceful, calm.
exponent (SYN.) explicator, spokesman, supporter, expounder, interpreter.
expose (SYN.) uncover, display, bare, open, unmask, reveal.
(ANT.) hide, conceal, mask, covered.
exposition (SYN.) fair, bazaar, show, expo, exhibition.
expound (SYN.) clarify, present, explain, lecture, demonstrate.
express (SYN.) voice, tell, send, say, ship, declare, state, precise, specific, swift, describe.
expression (SYN.) declaration, statement, look.
expressive (SYN.) suggestive, meaningful, telling, significant, thoughtful.
(ANT.) unthinking, meaningless, nondescript.
expressly (SYN.) precisely, exactly, definitely, clearly.
(ANT.) tentatively, vaguely, ambiguously.
expulsion (SYN.) ejection, discharge, removal, elimination.
expunge (SYN.) blot out, erase, cancel, obliterate, delete, efface, remove.
expurgate (SYN.) cleanse, purge, censor, edit, emasculate, abridge, blip.
exquisite (SYN.) delicate, delightful, attractive, dainty, beautiful, elegant, fine, superb, lovely, excellent, perfect.
(ANT.) vulgar, dull, ugly, unattractive.
extant (SYN.) subsisting, remaining, surviving, present, existing.
(ANT.) lost, defunct, extinct, vanished.
extemporaneous (SYN.) casual, impromptu, offhand.
extemporize (SYN.) improvise, devise.
extend (SYN.) lengthen, stretch, increase,

offer, give, grant, magnify, expand.
(ANT.) abbreviate, shorten, curtail.
extension (SYN.) expansion, increase, stretching, enlargement.
extensive (SYN.) vast, wide, spacious, broad.
(ANT.) narrow, cramped, confined, restricted.
extent (SYN.) length, degree, range, amount, measure, size, compass, reach, magnitude, scope, expanse, area.
extenuating (SYN.) exculpating, excusable, qualifying, justifying, softening.
exterior (SYN.) surface, face, outside, covering, outer, external.
(ANT.) inside, lining, interior, inner, internal.
exterminate (SYN.) slay, kill, destroy.
external (SYN.) outer, exterior, outside.
(ANT.) inner, internal, inside, interior.
externals (SYN.) images, effects, look, appearance, veneer, aspect.
extinct (SYN.) lost, dead, gone, vanished.
(ANT.) present, flourishing, alive, extant.
extinction (SYN.) eclipse, annihilation, obliteration, death, extirpation.
extinguish (SYN.) suppress, smother, quench.
extol (SYN.) laud, eulogize, exalt, praise.
(ANT.) denounce, belittle, discredit, disparage.
extra (SYN.) surplus, spare, additional.
extract (SYN.) remove, withdraw, essence.
(ANT.) penetrate, introduce.
extraordinary (SYN.) unusual, wonderful, marvelous, peculiar, noteworthy, remarkable, uncommon, exceptional.
(ANT.) commonplace, ordinary, usual.
extravagant (SYN.) excessive, exaggerated, lavish, wasteful, extreme.
(ANT.) prudent, frugal, thrifty, economical, provident.
extreme (SYN.) excessive, overdone, outermost, limit, greatest, utmost, furthest, endmost, extravagant.
(ANT.) reasonable, modest, moderate.
extricate (SYN.) rescue, free, clear, release, liberate.
exuberant (SYN.) buoyant, ebullient, vivacious.
(ANT.) sad, depressed.
exult (SYN.) rejoice, delight.
eye (SYN.) watch, view, stare, look, inspect, glance.

fable *(SYN.)* legend, parable, myth, fib, falsehood, fiction, tale, story.

fabled *(SYN.)* legendary, famous, famed, historic.

fabric *(SYN.)* goods, textile, material, cloth, yard goods.

fabricate *(SYN.)* assemble, make, construct, produce, create, manufacture, form.

(ANT.) raze, destroy, demolish.

fabrication *(SYN.)* deceit, lie, falsehood, untruth, forgery, prevarication, deception.

(ANT.) verity, reality, actuality, truth, fact.

fabulous *(SYN.)* amazing, marvelous, unbelievable, fantastic, astounding, astonishing, striking.

(ANT.) ordinary, commonplace, credible, proven, factual.

facade *(SYN.)* deception, mask, front, show, pose, veneer, guise, affectation.

face *(SYN.)* cover, mug, front, assurance, countenance, audacity, visage, expression, look, features, facade, encounter, meet, surface.

(ANT.) rear, shun, avoid, evade, back, timidity.

facet *(SYN.)* perspective, view, side, phase.

facetious *(SYN.)* jocular, pungent, humorous, funny, clever, droll, witty, playful, jesting.

(ANT.) sober, serious, grave, weighty.

face to face *(SYN.)* opposing, nose to nose, confronting.

facile *(SYN.)* simple, easy, quick, uncomplicated, clever, fluent, skillful.

(ANT.) complex, difficult, complicated, laborious, hard, ponderous, painstaking, arduous.

facilitate *(SYN.)* help, speed, ease, promote, accelerate, expedite.

facilities *(SYN.)* aid, means, resources, conveniences.

facility *(SYN.)* ability, skill, ease, skillfulness, material.

(ANT.) effort, difficulty, labor.

facsimile *(SYN.)* reproduction, likeness, replica.

fact *(SYN.)* reality, deed, certainty, act, incident, circumstance, occurrence, event, truth, actuality.

(ANT.) falsehood, fiction, delusion.

faction *(SYN.)* clique, party, sect.

factitious *(SYN.)* false, sham, artificial, spurious, unnatural, affected.

(ANT.) natural, real, genuine, artless.

factor *(SYN.)* part, certain, element, basis, cause.

factory *(SYN.)* installation, plant, mill, works.

factual *(SYN.)* true, correct, accurate, sure, genuine, authentic.

(ANT.) incorrect, erroneous, fabricated, invented.

faculty *(SYN.)* power, capacity, talent, staff, gift, ability, qualification, ability, skill.

fad *(SYN.)* fashion, vogue, mania, rage.

faddish *(SYN.)* ephemeral, modish, temporary, passing, fleeting.

(ANT.) lasting, permanent, enduring, classic.

fade *(SYN.)* pale, bleach, weaken, dim, decline, sink, discolor, fail, diminish, droop.

fagged *(SYN.)* exhausted, tired, weary, jaded, pooped, worn.

fail *(SYN.)* neglect, weaken, flunk, miss, decline, disappoint, fade.

(ANT.) succeed, achieve, accomplish.

failing *(SYN.)* fault, foible, imperfection, frailty, defect, peccadillo, shortcoming.

(ANT.) steadiness, strength, integrity, firmness.

failure *(SYN.)* miscarriage, omission, decline, deficiency, fiasco, lack, dereliction, failing, unsuccessfulness, loss, default, want, insufficiency, decay.

(ANT.) conquest, accomplishment, success, triumph, victory, hit, luck, achievement.

faint *(SYN.)* timid, faded, languid, halfhearted, dim, pale, wearied, feeble, indistinct, weak.

(ANT.) strong, sharp, forceful, glaring, clear, distinct, conspicuous, brave.

faint-hearted *(SYN.)* shy, cowardly, timid, bashful.

(ANT.) fearless, brave, stouthearted, courageous.

fair *(SYN.)* pale, average, light, sunny, mediocre, bright, just, clear, lovely, market, blond, honest, equitable, impartial, reasonable, comely, exposition.

(ANT.) ugly, fraudulent, foul, outstanding, dishonorable, unfair.

fairly *(SYN.)* equally, evenly, rather, impartially, passably, justly, squarely, somewhat.

fair-minded *(SYN.)* reasonable, fair, just,

open-minded, honest, unprejudiced, impartial, evenhanded.
(ANT.) bigoted, narrow-minded, unjust, close-minded, partisan.

fairness *(SYN.)* equity, justice, evenhandedness, honesty.
(ANT.) favoritism, partiality, bias, one-sidedness.

fairy *(SYN.)* leprechaun, gnome, elf, pixie, sprite.

faith *(SYN.)* dependence, trust, reliance, creed, loyalty, doctrine, confidence, dogma, tenet, persuasion, constancy, credence, fidelity, religion, belief.
(ANT.) mistrust, disbelief, doubt, infidelity.

faithful *(SYN.)* staunch, true, devoted, trusty, loyal, constant, credible, steadfast, strict, trust-worthy, accurate.
(ANT.) untrustworthy, faithless, inaccurate, wrong, false, disloyal, erroneous, treacherous.

faithless *(SYN.)* treacherous, unfaithful, disloyal, perfidious, untrue.
(ANT.) loyal, true, unwavering, constant, faithful.

fake *(SYN.)* falsify, distort, pretend, feign, fraud, counterfeit, cheat, false, artificial, phony, imitation, forgery, mock.
(ANT.) honest, pure, real, genuine, authentic.

falderal *(SYN.)* foolery, jargon, nonsense, gibberish, blather, balderdash.

fall *(SYN.)* drop, decline, diminish, droop, topple, decrease, sink, hang, descend, subside, plunge, collapse.
(ANT.) soar, climb, steady, rise, ascend.

fallacious *(SYN.)* untrue, false, wrong, erroneous, deceptive, illusory, delusive.
(ANT.) accurate, true, exact, real, factual.

fallacy *(SYN.)* mistake, error, illusion, sophism, misconception, deception.

fall back *(SYN.)* retreat, recede, retire, withdraw, concede.
(ANT.) progress, advance, gain, prosper, proceed.

fallow *(SYN.)* idle, unprepared, unproductive, inactive.
(ANT.) prepared, productive, cultivated.

false *(SYN.)* incorrect, wrong, deceitful, fake, imitation, counterfeit.
(ANT.) genuine, loyal, true, honest.

falsehood *(SYN.)* untruth, lie, fib, story.
(ANT.) truth.

falsify *(SYN.)* misquote, distort, misstate, mislead, adulterate.

falter *(SYN.)* stumble, tremble, waver, hesitate, flounder.

fame *(SYN.)* distinction, glory, mane, eminence, credit, reputation, renown, acclaim, notoriety.
(ANT.) infamy, obscurity, anonymity, disrepute.

famed *(SYN.)* known, renowned, famous.
(ANT.) obscure, unknown, anonymous.

familiar *(SYN.)* informal, intimate, close, acquainted, amicable, knowing, cognizant, well-acquainted, versed, unreserved, friendly, sociable, affable, aware, known, courteous, intimate.
(ANT.) unfamiliar, distant, affected, reserved.

familiarity *(SYN.)* sociability, acquaintance, awareness, frankness, intimacy, understanding, knowledge, fellowship.
(ANT.) distance, ignorance, reserve, presumption, constraint, haughtiness.

family *(SYN.)* kin, tribe, folks, group, relatives.

famine *(SYN.)* want, deficiency, starvation, need.
(ANT.) excess, plenty.

famous *(SYN.)* distinguished, noted, glorious, illustrious, famed, celebrated, well-known, eminent, renowned, prominent, esteemed.
(ANT.) obscure, hidden, unknown.

fan *(SYN.)* arouse, spread, admirer, enthusiast, devotee, stir, aficionado, whip, follower.

fanatic *(SYN.)* bigot, enthusiast, zealot.

fancy *(SYN.)* love, dream, ornate, imagine, suppose, imagination, taste, fantasy, ornamented, elaborate, think.
(ANT.) plain, undecorated, simple, unadorned.

fantastic *(SYN.)* strange, unusual, odd, wild, unimaginable, incredible, unbelievable, unreal, bizarre, capricious.
(ANT.) mundane, ordinary, staid, humdrum.

fantasy *(SYN.)* illusion, dream, whim, hallucination, delusion, caprice, mirage, daydream, fancy.
(ANT.) bore.

far *(SYN.)* removed, much, distant, remote, estranged, alienated.
(ANT.) close, near.

fare *(SYN.)* prosper, eat, passenger, thrive, toll, progress, succeed.

farewell *(SYN.)* good-by, valediction, departure, leaving.
(ANT.) welcome, greeting.
farm *(SYN.)* grow, harvest, cultivate, ranch, hire, charter, plantation.
fascinate *(SYN.)* charm, enchant, bewitch, attract, enthrall.
fashion *(SYN.)* create, shape, style, mode, make, custom, form, manner, method, way, vogue.
fashionable *(SYN.)* chic, smart, stylish, modish, elegant, voguish.
(ANT.) dowdy, unfashionable.
fast *(SYN.)* fleet, firm, quick, swift, inflexible, stable, secure, expeditious, rapid, steady, solid, constant, speedy.
(ANT.) insecure, sluggish, unstable, loose, slow, unsteady.
fasten *(SYN.)* secure, bind, tie, join, fix, connect, attach, unite.
(ANT.) open, loose, free, loosen, release, separate.
fastidious *(SYN.)* choosy, selective, discriminating, picky, meticulous.
fat *(SYN.)* stout, plump, chubby, pudgy, obese, oily, fleshy, greasy, fatty, portly, corpulent, paunchy, wide, thick, rotund.
(ANT.) slim, gaunt, emaciated, thin, slender.
fatal *(SYN.)* killing, lethal, doomed, disastrous, deadly, fateful, mortal.
(ANT.) nonfatal.
fate *(SYN.)* end, fortune, doom, issue, destiny, necessity, portion, result, lot, chance, luck, outcome, consequence, kismet.
father *(SYN.)* cause, sire, breed, originate, founder, inventor.
fatherly *(SYN.)* protective, paternal, kind, paternalistic.
fathom *(SYN.)* penetrate, understand, interpret, comprehend.
fatigue *(SYN.)* weariness, lassitude, exhaustion, enervation, languor, tiredness.
(ANT.) vivacity, rejuvenation, energy, vigor.
fault *(SYN.)* defect, flaw, mistake, imperfection, shortcoming, error, weakness, responsibility, omission, blemish, blame, failure.
(ANT.) perfection, completeness.
faultfinding *(SYN.)* carping, censorious, critical, caviling, nit-picking.
faulty *(SYN.)* imperfect, broken, defective, damaged, impaired.
(ANT.) flawless, perfect, whole.

favor *(SYN.)* rather, resemble, liking, service, prefer, approval, like, support, patronize, benefit.
(ANT.) deplore, disapprove.
favorite *(SYN.)* prized, pet, choice, darling, treasured, preferred.
favoritism *(SYN.)* prejudice, bias, partiality.
(ANT.) fairness, impartiality.
fear *(SYN.)* horror, terror, fright, trepidation, alarm, consternation, dismay, cowardice, panic, anxiety, dread, scare, apprehension.
(ANT.) fearlessness, boldness, courage, assurance.
fearless *(SYN.)* bold, brave, courageous, gallant, dauntless, confident.
(ANT.) timid, fearful, cowardly.
feast *(SYN.)* dinner, banquet, barbecue.
feat *(SYN.)* performance, act, operation, accomplishment, achievement, doing, transaction, deed.
(ANT.) intention, deliberation, cessation.
feature *(SYN.)* trait, quality, characteristic, highlight, attribute.
fee *(SYN.)* payment, pay, remuneration, charge, recompense.
feeble *(SYN.)* faint, puny, exhausted, impair, delicate, weak, enervated, frail, powerless, forceless, sickly, decrepit, ailing.
(ANT.) strong, forceful, powerful, vigorous, stout.
feed *(SYN.)* satisfy, nourish, food, fodder, forage.
feel *(SYN.)* sense, experience, perceive.
feeling *(SYN.)* opinion, sensibility, tenderness, affection, impression, belief, sensation, sympathy, thought, passion, sentiment, attitude, emotion.
(ANT.) fact, imperturbability, anesthesia, insensibility.
fellowship *(SYN.)* clan, society, brotherhood, fraternity, camaraderie, companionship, comradeship, association.
(ANT.) dislike, discord, distrust, enmity, strife, acrimony.
felonious *(SYN.)* murderous, criminal, larcenous.
feminine *(SYN.)* womanly, girlish, ladylike, female, maidenly, womanish.
(ANT.) masculine, male, virile.
ferocious *(SYN.)* savage, fierce, wild, blood-thirsty, brutal.
(ANT.) playful, gentle, harmless, calm.
fertile *(SYN.)* rich, fruitful, teeming,

plenteous, bountiful, prolific, luxuriant, productive, fecund.
(ANT.) *unproductive, barren, sterile.*
festival (SYN.) feast, banquet, regalement, celebration.
festive (SYN.) joyful, gay, joyous, merry, gala, jovial, jubilant.
(ANT.) *sad, gloomy, mournful, morose.*
fetching (SYN.) charming, attractive, pleasing, captivating, winsome.
feud (SYN.) dispute, quarrel, strife, argument, conflict, controversy.
(ANT.) *amity, understanding, harmony, peace.*
fiber (SYN.) line, strand, thread, string.
fickle (SYN.) unstable, capricious, restless, changeable, inconstant, variable.
(ANT.) *stable, constant, trustworthy, steady, reliable, dependable.*
fiction (SYN.) fabrication, romance, falsehood, tale, allegory, narrative, fable, novel, story, invention.
(ANT.) *verity, reality, fact, truth.*
fictitious (SYN.) invented, make-believe, imaginary, fabricated, unreal, counterfeit, feigned.
(ANT.) *real, true, genuine, actual, proven.*
fidelity (SYN.) fealty, devotion, precision, allegiance, exactness, constancy, accuracy, faithfulness, loyalty.
(ANT.) *treachery, disloyalty.*
fidget (SYN.) squirm, twitch, wriggle.
fiendish (SYN.) devilish, demonic, diabolical, savage, satanic.
fierce (SYN.) furious, wild, savage, violent, ferocious, vehement.
(ANT.) *calm, meek, mild, gentle, placid.*
fight (SYN.) contend, scuffle, struggle, battle, wrangle, combat, brawl, quarrel, dispute, war, skirmish, conflict.
figure (SYN.) design, pattern, mold, shape, form, frame, reckon, calculate, compute, determine.
fill (SYN.) glut, furnish, store, stuff, occupy, gorge, pervade, content, stock, fill up, supply, sate, replenish, satisfy.
(ANT.) *void, drain, exhaust, deplete, empty.*
filter (SYN.) screen, strainer, sieve.
filth (SYN.) pollution, dirt, sewage, foulness.
(ANT.) *cleanliness, innocence, purity.*
filthy (SYN.) foul, polluted, dirty, stained, unwashed, squalid.
(ANT.) *pure, clean, unspoiled.*

final (SYN.) ultimate, decisive, concluding, ending, terminal, last, conclusive, eventual, latest.
(ANT.) *inaugural, rudimentary, beginning, initial, incipient, first, original.*
finally (SYN.) at last, eventually, ultimately.
find (SYN.) observe, detect, discover, locate.
fine (SYN.) thin, pure, choice, small, elegant, dainty, splendid, handsome, delicate, nice, powdered, beautiful, minute, exquisite, subtle, pretty, refined.
(ANT.) *thick, coarse, rough, blunt, large.*
finicky (SYN.) fussy, meticulous, finical, fastidious, prim.
finish (SYN.) consummate, close, get done, terminate, accomplish, conclude, execute, perform, complete, end, achieve, fulfill, do, perfect.
(ANT.) *open, begin, start, beginning.*
fire (SYN.) vigor, glow, combustion, passion, burning, conflagration, ardor, flame, blaze, intensity, fervor.
(ANT.) *apathy, cold.*
firm (SYN.) solid, rigid, inflexible, stiff, unchanging, steadfast, dense, hard, unshakable, compact, business, company, corporation, partnership.
(ANT.) *weak, limp, soft, drooping.*
first (SYN.) chief, primary, initial, pristine, beginning, foremost, primeval, earliest, prime, primitive, original.
(ANT.) *subordinate, last, least, hindmost, latest.*
fishy (SYN.) suspicious, questionable, doubtful.
(ANT.) *believable, credible.*
fit (SYN.) adjust, suit, suitable, accommodate, conform, robust, harmonize, belong, seizure, spasm, attack, suited, appropriate, healthy, agree, adapt.
(ANT.) *misfit, disturb, improper.*
fitful (SYN.) variable, restless, fickle, capricious, unstable, changeable.
(ANT.) *trustworthy, stable, constant, steady.*
fitting (SYN.) apt, due, suitable, proper.
(ANT.) *improper, unsuitable, inappropriate.*
fix (SYN.) mend, regulate, affix, set, tie, repair, attach, settle, link, bind, determine, establish, define, place, rectify, stick, limit, adjust, fasten.
(ANT.) *damage, change, mistreat, displace, alter, disturb, mutilate.*

fixation *(SYN.)* fetish, obsession, infatuation, compulsion.

flair *(SYN.)* style, dash, flamboyance, drama, gift, knack, aptitude.

flamboyant *(SYN.)* showy, flashy, ostentatious, gaudy, ostentatious.

flame *(SYN.)* blaze, fire.

flash *(SYN.)* flare, flame, wink, twinkling, instant, gleam.

flashy *(SYN.)* tawdry, tasteless, pretentious, garish, flamboyant.

flat *(SYN.)* vapid, stale, even, smooth, tasteless, horizontal, dull, level, insipid, uninteresting, lifeless, boring.
(ANT.) tasty, racy, hilly, savory, stimulating, interesting, broken, sloping.

flattery *(SYN.)* compliment, praise, applause, blarney, acclaim.

flaunt *(SYN.)* exhibit, show off, display, parade.
(ANT.) conceal, hide, disguise.

flavor *(SYN.)* tang, taste, savor, essence, quality, character, season, spice.

flaw *(SYN.)* spot, imperfection, blemish, fault, deformity, blotch.

flee *(SYN.)* fly, abscond, hasten, escape, run away, decamp, evade.
(ANT.) remain, appear, stay, arrive.

fleece *(SYN.)* filch, rob, purloin, swindle, defraud, pilfer, cheat.

fleet *(SYN.)* rapid, swift, quick, fast.
(ANT.) unhurried, sluggish, slow.

fleeting *(SYN.)* brief, swift, passing, temporary.
(ANT.) stable, fixed, lasting, permanent.

fleshy *(SYN.)* overweight, chubby, stocky, plump, obese, stout.
(ANT.) spare, underweight, skinny.

flexible *(SYN.)* lithe, resilient, pliable, tractable, complaint, elastic, yielding, adaptable, agreeable, supple, pliant, easy, ductile.
(ANT.) hard, unbending, firm, brittle, inflexible, rigid, fixed.

flighty *(SYN.)* giddy, light-headed, frivolous, irresponsible.
(ANT.) solid, responsible, steady.

flimsy *(SYN.)* wobbly, weak, frail, fragile, unsteady, delicate, thin.
(ANT.) durable, stable, firm, strong.

fling *(SYN.)* pitch, throw, toss, fun, celebration, party.

flippant *(SYN.)* disrespectful, sassy, insolent, brazen, rude, impertinent.
(ANT.) courteous, polite, mannerly.

flit *(SYN.)* flutter, scurry, hasten, dart, skim.

flock *(SYN.)* gathering, group, flight, swarm, herd, school.

flog *(SYN.)* thrash, lash, switch, strike, paddle.

flood *(SYN.)* overflow, deluge, inundate, cascade.

florid *(SYN.)* gaudy, fancy, ornate, embellished.
(ANT.) spare, simple, plain, unadorned.

flourish *(SYN.)* succeed, grow, prosper, wave, thrive, bloom.
(ANT.) wither, wane, die, decline.

flout *(SYN.)* disdain, scorn, spurn, ignore, taunt, ridicule, mock.

flow *(SYN.)* proceed, abound, spout, come, stream, run, originate, emanate, result, pour, squirt, issue, gush, spurt.

fluctuate *(SYN.)* vary, oscillate, change, waver, hesitate, vacillate.
(ANT.) persist, stick, adhere, resolve.

fluent *(SYN.)* graceful, glib, flowing.

fluid *(SYN.)* liquid, running, liquefied.

flush *(SYN.)* abundant, flat, even, level.

fluster *(SYN.)* rattle, flurry, agitate, upset, perturb, quiver, vibrate.

fly *(SYN.)* flee, mount, shoot, decamp, hover, soar, flit, flutter, sail, escape, rush, spring, glide, abscond, dart, float.
(ANT.) sink, descend, plummet.

foam *(SYN.)* suds, froth, lather.

foe *(SYN.)* opponent, enemy, antagonist, adversary.
(ANT.) associate, ally, friend, comrade.

fog *(SYN.)* haze, mist, cloud, daze, confusion, stupor, vapor, smog.

foible *(SYN.)* frailty, weakness, failing, shortcoming, kink.

foist *(SYN.)* misrepresent, insinuate, falsify.

fold *(SYN.)* lap, double, overlap, clasp, pleat, tuck.

follow *(SYN.)* trail, observe, succeed, ensue, obey, chase, comply, accompany, copy, result, imitate, heed, adopt.
(ANT.) elude, cause, precede, avoid, flee.

follower *(SYN.)* supporter, devotee, henchman, adherent, partisan, votary, attendant, disciple, successor.
(ANT.) master, head, chief, dissenter.

following *(SYN.)* public, disciples, supporters, clientele, customers.

folly *(SYN.)* imprudence, silliness, foolishness, indiscretion, absurdity, imprudence, imbecility, stupidity, extravagance.

(ANT.) reasonableness, judgment, sense, prudence, wisdom.

fond *(SYN.)* affectionate, loving, attached, tender, devoted.

(ANT.) hostile, cool, distant, unfriendly.

fondness *(SYN.)* partiality, liking, affection.

(ANT.) hostility, unfriendliness.

food *(SYN.)* viands, edibles, feed, repast, nutriment, sustenance, diet, bread, provisions, meal, rations, victuals, fare.

(ANT.) want, hunger, drink, starvation.

fool *(SYN.)* oak, dunce, jester, idiot, simpleton, buffoon, harlequin, dolt, blockhead, numskull, clown, dope, trick, deceive, nincompoop.

(ANT.) scholar, genius, sage.

foolish *(SYN.)* senseless, irrational, crazy, silly, brainless, idiotic, simple, nonsensical, stupid, preposterous, asinine.

(ANT.) sane, sound, sensible, rational, judicious, wise, reasonable, prudent.

footing *(SYN.)* base, basis, foundation.

footloose *(SYN.)* uncommitted, free, detached, independent.

(ANT.) engaged, rooted, involved.

forbearance *(SYN.)* moderation, abstinence, abstention, continence.

(ANT.) greed, excess, intoxication.

forbid *(SYN.)* disallow, prevent, ban, prohibit, taboo, outlaw.

(ANT.) approve, let, allow, permit.

forbidding *(SYN.)* evil, hostile, unfriendly, sinister, scary, repulsive.

(ANT.) pleasant, beneficent, friendly.

force *(SYN.)* energy, might, violence, vigor, intensity, dint, power, constraint, coercion, vigor, compel, compulsion, oblige, make, coerce, strength.

(ANT.) weakness, frailty, persuasion, feebleness, impotence, ineffectiveness.

forceful *(SYN.)* dynamic, vigorous, energetic, potent, drastic, intense.

(ANT.) lackadaisical, insipid, weak.

foreboding *(SYN.)* misgiving, suspicion, apprehension, presage, intuition.

forecast *(SYN.)* prophesy, predict, predetermine.

foregoing *(SYN.)* above, former, preceding, previous, prior.

(ANT.) later, coming, below, follow.

foreign *(SYN.)* alien, strange, exotic, different, unfamiliar.

(ANT.) commonplace, ordinary, familiar.

foreigner *(SYN.)* outsider, alien, new-comer, stranger.

(ANT.) native.

foreman *(SYN.)* super, boss, overseer, supervisor.

forerunner *(SYN.)* harbinger, proclaimer, informant.

foresee *(SYN.)* forecast, expect, anticipate, surmise, envisage.

forest *(SYN.)* grove, woodland, wood, copse, woods.

forestall *(SYN.)* hinder, thwart, prevent, obstruct, repel.

foretell *(SYN.)* soothsay, divine, predict.

forever *(SYN.)* evermore, always, everlasting, hereafter, endlessly.

(ANT.) fleeting, temporarily.

forfeit *(SYN.)* yield, resign, lose, sacrifice.

forgive *(SYN.)* exonerate, clear, excuse, pardon.

(ANT.) impeach, accuse, blame, censure.

forgo *(SYN.)* relinquish, release, surrender, waive, abandon.

(ANT.) keep, retain, safeguard.

forlorn *(SYN.)* pitiable, desolate, dejected, woeful, wretched.

(ANT.) optimistic, cherished, cheerful.

form *(SYN.)* frame, compose, fashion, arrange, construct, make up, devise, create, invent, mold, shape, forge, organize, produce, constitute, make.

(ANT.) wreck, dismantle, destroy, misshape.

formal *(SYN.)* exact, stiff, correct, outward, conformist, conventional, affected, regular, proper, ceremonious, decorous, methodical, precise, solemn, external, perfunctory.

(ANT.) heartfelt, unconstrained, easy, unconventional.

former *(SYN.)* earlier, one-time, previous, erstwhile, prior.

formidable *(SYN.)* alarming, frightful, imposing, terrible, terrifying, dire, fearful, forbidding.

(ANT.) weak, unimpressive, ordinary.

forsake *(SYN.)* abandon, desert, forgo, quit, discard, neglect.

forte *(SYN.)* gift, capability, talent, specialty, aptitude, bulwark.

forth *(SYN.)* out, onward, forward.

forthright *(SYN.)* honest, direct, candid, outspoken, blunt sincere, plain, explicit.

forthwith *(SYN.)* instantly, promptly, immediately.

(ANT.) afterward, later, ultimately, slowly.

fortify (SYN.) bolster strengthen, buttress, barricade, defend.

fortuitous (SYN.) successful, benign, lucky, advantageous, propitious, happy, favored, chance.

(ANT.) unlucky, condemned, persecuted.

fortunate (SYN.) happy, auspicious, fortuitous, successful, favored, advantageous, benign, charmed, lucky, felicitous, blessed, propitious, blissful.

(ANT.) ill-fated, cheerless, unlucky, unfortunate, cursed, condemned.

fortune (SYN.) chance, fate, lot, luck, riches, wealth, kismet, destiny.

fortuneteller (SYN.) soothsayer, clairvoyant, forecaster, oracle, medium.

forward (SYN.) leading, front, promote, elevate, advance, first, ahead, onward, further, foremost, aggrandize.

(ANT.) withhold, retard, hinder, retreat, oppose.

foul (SYN.) base, soiled, dirty, mean, unclean, polluted, impure, vile, evil, muddy, wicked, rainy, stormy, despicable, filthy.

(ANT.) pure, neat, wholesome, clean.

found (SYN.) organize, establish.

foundation (SYN.) support, root, base, underpinning, ground-work, bottom, establishment, substructure, basis.

(ANT.) top, cover, building.

foxy (SYN.) cunning, sly, artful, crafty, wily, sharp, shrewd, slick.

fraction (SYN.) fragment, part, section, morsel, share, piece.

fracture (SYN.) crack, break, rupture.

fragile (SYN.) delicate, frail, weak, breakable, infirm, brittle, feeble.

(ANT.) tough, hardy, sturdy, strong, stout, durable.

fragment (SYN.) scrap, piece, bit, remnant, part, splinter, segment.

fragrance (SYN.) odor, smell, scent, perfume, aroma.

fragrant (SYN.) aromatic, scented, perfumed.

frail (SYN.) feeble, weak, delicate, breakable, fragile.

(ANT.) sturdy, strong, powerful.

frame (SYN.) support, framework, skeleton, molding, border, mount.

frank (SYN.) honest, candid, open, unreserved, direct, sincere, straight-forward.

(ANT.) tricky, dishonest.

frantic (SYN.) frenzied, crazed, raving, panicky.

(ANT.) composed, stoic.

fraud (SYN.) deception, guile, swindle, deceit, artifice, imposture, trick, cheat, imposition, duplicity, chicanery.

(ANT.) sincerity, fairness, integrity.

fraudulent (SYN.) tricky, fake, dishonest, deceitful

fray (SYN.) strife, fight, battle, struggle, tussle, combat, brawl, melee, skirmish.

(ANT.) truce, agreement, peace, concord.

freak (SYN.) curiosity, abnormality, monster, oddity.

free (SYN.) munificent, clear, autonomous, immune, open, freed, bountiful, liberated, unfastened, immune, emancipated, unconfined, unobstructed, easy, artless, loose, familiar, bounteous, unrestricted, liberal, independent, careless, frank, exempt.

(ANT.) stingy, clogged, illiberal, confined, parsimonious.

freedom (SYN.) independence, privilege, familiarity, unrestraint, liberty, exemption, liberation, immunity, license.

(ANT.) servitude, constraint, bondage, slavery, necessity.

freely (SYN.) liberally, generously, unstintingly.

freight (SYN.) chipping, cargo, load, shipment.

frenzy (SYN.) craze, agitation, excitement.

frequent (SYN.) usual, habitual, common, often, customary, general.

(ANT.) unique, rare, solitary, uncommon, exceptional, infrequent, scanty.

fresh (SYN.) recent, new, additional, modern, further, refreshing, natural, brisk, novel, inexperienced, late, current, sweet, pure, cool.

(ANT.) stagnant, decayed, musty, faded.

fret (SYN.) torment, worry, grieve, anguish.

fretful (SYN.) testy, irritable, touchy, peevish, short-tempered.

(ANT.) calm.

friend (SYN.) crony, supporter, ally, companion, intimate, associate, advocate, comrade, mate, patron, acquaintance, chum, defender.

(ANT.) stranger, adversary.

friendly (SYN.) sociable, kindly, affable, genial, companionable, social, neigh-

borly, amicable.
(ANT.) hostile, antagonistic, reserved.
friendship *(SYN.)* knowledge, familiarity, fraternity, acquaintance, intimacy, fellowship, comradeship, cognizance.
(ANT.) unfamiliarity, ignorance.
fright *(SYN.)* alarm, fear, panic, terror.
frighten *(SYN.)* scare, horrify, daunt, affright, appall, terrify, alarm, terrorize, astound, dismay, startle, panic.
(ANT.) soothe, embolden, compose, reassure.
frigid *(SYN.)* cold, wintry, icy, glacial, arctic, freezing.
fringe *(SYN.)* hem, edge, border, trimming, edging.
frisky *(SYN.)* animated, lively, peppy, vivacious.
frolic *(SYN.)* play, cavort, romp, frisk, gambol.
front *(SYN.)* facade, face, start, beginning, border, head.
(ANT.) rear, back.
frontier *(SYN.)* border, boundary.
frugal *(SYN.)* parsimonious, saving, stingy, provident, temperate, economical, sparing.
(ANT.) extravagant, wasteful, self-indulgent, intemperate.
fruitful *(SYN.)* fertile, rich, bountiful, teeming, fecund, productive, luxuriant, prolific.
(ANT.) lean, unproductive, barren, sterile.
fruitless *(SYN.)* barren, futile, vain, sterile, unproductive.
(ANT.) fertile, productive.
frustrate *(SYN.)* hinder, defeat, thwart, circumvent, outwit, foil, baffle, disappoint, balk, discourage, prevent.
(ANT.) promote, fulfill, accomplish, further.
fugitive *(SYN.)* refugee, deserter, runaway.
fulfill *(SYN.)* do, effect, complete, accomplish, realize.
full *(SYN.)* baggy, crammed, entire, satiated, flowing, perfect, gorged, soaked, complete, filled, packed, extensive, plentiful, replete, voluminous.
(ANT.) lacking, devoid, partial, empty, depleted.
full-fledged *(SYN.)* schooled, expert, professional, adept, qualified, top-flight, senior, full-blown, trained, able.
(ANT.) inexperienced, green, untried,

untrained.
full-grown *(SYN.)* ripe, adult, mature, developed, grown-up, complete.
(ANT.) green, young, unripe, adolescent.
fullness *(SYN.)* glut, repletion, enough, satiety, satiation, sufficiency, all, totality, satisfaction, overload, wholeness, aggregate, everything, sum.
(ANT.) need, want, hunger, lack, insufficiency, privation, emptiness, incompleteness.
full-scale *(SYN.)* major, all-out, lavish, comprehensive, unlimited, maximum.
(ANT.) indifferent, partial, minor, halfhearted.
fulsome *(SYN.)* disgusting, repulsive, nauseating, repellent, revolting.
fume *(SYN.)* gas, steam, smoke, rage, rave, vapor.
fun *(SYN.)* merriment, pleasure, enjoyment, gaiety, sport, amusement.
function *(SYN.)* operation, activity, affair, ceremony, gathering, party.
fundamental *(SYN.)* basic, essential, primary, elementary.
funny *(SYN.)* odd, droll, ridiculous, queer, farcical, laughable, comic, curious, amusing, humorous, witty.
(ANT.) solemn, sad, sober, melancholy.
furious *(SYN.)* angry, enraged.
(ANT.) serene, calm.
furnish *(SYN.)* yield, give, endow, fit, produce, equip, afford, decorate, supply, appoint.
(ANT.) divest, denude, strip.
furor *(SYN.)* commotion, tumult, turmoil.
furthermore *(SYN.)* moreover, also, further.
furtive *(SYN.)* surreptitious, secret, hidden, clandestine.
(ANT.) honest, open.
fury *(SYN.)* wrath, anger, frenzy, rage, violence, fierceness.
(ANT.) calmness, serenity.
fuss *(SYN.)* commotion, bother, pester, annoy, irritate.
futile *(SYN.)* pointless, idle, vain, useless, worthless, minor.
(ANT.) weighty, important, worth-while, serious, valuable.
future *(SYN.)* approaching, imminent, coming, impending.
(ANT.) former, past.
fuzzy *(SYN.)* indistinct, blurred.
(ANT.) lucid, clear.

gab *(SYN.)* jabber, babble, chatter, prattle, gossip.

gabble *(SYN.)* chatter, babble, jabber, blab, prate, gaggle, prattle, blather, gibberish.

gabby *(SYN.)* chatty, talkative, wordy, verbose.

gad *(SYN.)* wander, roam, rove, ramble, meander, cruise.

gadabout *(SYN.)* gypsy, wanderer, rambler.

gadget *(SYN.)* contrivance, device, doodad, jigger, thing, contraption.

gaffe *(SYN.)* blunder, boner, mistake, gaucherie, error, howler.

gag *(SYN.)* witticism, crack jest, joke.

gaiety *(SYN.)* joyousness, cheerfulness, high-spiritedness, joyfulness, light-heartedness.

(ANT.) melancholy, sadness, depression.

gain *(SYN.)* acquire, avail, account, good, interest, attain, favor, achieve, get, secure, advantage, earn, profit, procure, service, obtain, improvement, increase, behalf, net, reach, win, benefit.

(ANT.) trouble, lose, calamity, forfeit, handicap, lose, distress.

gainful *(SYN.)* lucrative, rewarding, profitable, beneficial, payable, productive.

(ANT.) unproductive, unprofitable, unrewarding.

gainsay *(SYN.)* refute, contradict, controvert, deny, refuse, inpugn, contravene, disavow, differ.

(ANT.) maintain, aver, affirm, asseverate.

gait *(SYN.)* stride, walk, tread, step.

gala *(SYN.)* ball, party, carnival, fete, festival.

gale *(SYN.)* burst, surge, outburst.

gall *(SYN.)* nerve, audacity, impudence, annoy, vex, anger, provoke, irritate.

gallant *(SYN.)* bold, brave, courageous, valorous, valiant, noble, polite, fearless, heroic, chivalrous.

gallantry *(SYN.)* valor, daring, courage, prowess, heroism, manliness, dauntlessness, graciousness, attentiveness, coquetry, gentleness, fearlessness, chivalrousness.

(ANT.) poltroonery, timidity, cowardice, cravenness, cloddishness.

gallery *(SYN.)* passageway, hall, aisle, hallway, passage, corridor.

galling *(SYN.)* vexing, irritating, annoying, distressful, irksome.

galore *(SYN.)* abounding, plentiful, profuse, rich, overflowing.

gamble *(SYN.)* game, wager, bet, hazard, risk, venture, chance.

gambol *(SYN.)* romp, dance, cavort, frolic.

game *(SYN.)* fun, contest, merriment, pastime, match, play, amusement, recreation, diversion, entertainment, competition, sport.

(ANT.) labor, hardship, work, business.

gamut *(SYN.)* extent, scope, sweep, horizon, range.

gang *(SYN.)* group, troop, band, company, horde, crew.

gangling *(SYN.)* rangy, lean, skinny, tall, lanky.

gangster *(SYN.)* crook, hoodlum, gunman, criminal.

gap *(SYN.)* cavity, chasm, pore, gulf, aperture, abyss, interval, space, hole, void, pore, break, opening.

gape *(SYN.)* ogle, stare, gawk.

garb *(SYN.)* clothing, dress, vesture, array, attire, clothes, drapery, apparel, garments, costume, raiment.

(ANT.) nudity, nakedness.

garbage *(SYN.)* refuse, waste, trash, rubbish.

garbled *(SYN.)* twisted, confused, distorted.

gargantuan *(SYN.)* colossal, monumental, giant, huge, large, enormous.

garments *(SYN.)* drapery, dress, garb, apparel, array, attire, clothes, vesture, raiment, clothing.

(ANT.) nakedness, nudity.

garnish *(SYN.)* decorate, embellish, trim, adorn, enrich, beautify, deck, ornament.

(ANT.) expose, strip, debase, uncover, defame.

garrulous *(SYN.)* chatty, glib, verbose, talkative, communicative, voluble.

(ANT.) silent, uncommunicative, laconic, reticent, taciturn.

gash *(SYN.)* lacerate, slash, pierce, cut, hew, slice.

gasp *(SYN.)* pant, puff, wheeze.

gather *(ANT.)* assemble, collect, garner, harvest, reap, deduce, judge, amass, congregate, muster, cull, glean, accumulate, convene.

(ANT.) scatter, disperse, distribute, disband, separate.

gathering *(SYN.)* meeting, crowd, throng, company, assembly.

gaudy *(SYN.)* showy, flashy, loud, bold, ostentatious.

gaunt *(ANT.)* lank, diaphanous, flimsy, gauzy, narrow, rare, scanty, meager, gossamer, emaciated, scrawny, tenuous, thin, fine, lean, skinny, spare, slim, slight, slender, diluted.

(ANT.) wide, fat, thick, broad, bulky.

gay *(SYN.)* merry, lighthearted, joy- ful, cheerful, sprightly, jolly, happy, joyous, gleeful, jovial, colorful, bright, glad.

(ANT.) glum, mournful, sad, depressed, sorrowful, somber, sullen.

gaze *(SYN.)* look, stare, view, watch, examine, observe, glance, behold, discern, seem, see, survey, witness, inspect, goggle, appear.

(ANT.) hide, overlook, avert, miss.

geld *(SYN.)* neuter, alter, spay, castrate.

gem *(SYN.)* jewel, semiprecious stone.

general *(SYN.)* ordinary, universal, usual, common, customary, regular, vague, miscellaneous, indefinite, inexact.

(ANT.) definite, particular, exceptional, singular, rare, particular, precise, exact, specific.

generally *(SYN.)* ordinarily, usually, customarily, normally, mainly.

(ANT.) seldom, infrequently, rare.

generate *(SYN.)* produce, bestow, impart, concede, permit, acquiesce, cede, relent, succumb, surrender, pay, supply, grant, relent, bear, afford, submit, waive, allow, breed, accord, accede, abdicate, resign, relinquish, surrender, quit.

(ANT.) assert, refuse, struggle, resist, dissent, oppose, deny, strive.

generation *(SYN.)* age, date, era, period, seniority, senescence, senility, time, epoch, dotage.

(ANT.) infancy, youth, childhood.

generosity *(SYN.)* magnanimity, benevolence, humanity, kindness, philanthropy, tenderness, altruism, liberality, charity, beneficence.

(ANT.) selfishness, malevolence, cruelty, inhumanity, unkindness.

generous *(SYN.)* giving, liberal, unselfish, magnanimous, bountiful, munificent, charitable, big, noble, beneficent.

(ANT.) greedy, stingy, selfish, covetous, mean, miserly.

genesis *(SYN.)* birth, root, creation, source, origin, beginning.

genius *(SYN.)* intellect, adept, intellectual, sagacity, proficient, creativity, ability, inspiration, faculty, originality, aptitude, brain, gift, prodigy, talent.

(ANT.) dullard, stupidity, dolt, shallowness, moron, ineptitude, obtuseness.

genre *(SYN.)* chaste, order, set, elegance, class, excellence, kind, caste, denomination, grade.

genteel *(SYN.)* cultured, polished, polite, refined, elegant.

(ANT.) discourteous, churlish, common.

gentle *(SYN.)* peaceful, placid, tame, serene, relaxed, docile, benign, soothing, calm, soft, mild, amiable, friendly, kindly, cultivated.

(ANT.) nasty, harsh, rough, fierce, mean, violent, savage.

genuine *(SYN.)* real, true, unaffected, authentic, sincere, bona fide, unadulterated, legitimate, actual, veritable, definite, proven.

(ANT.) false, sham, artificial, fake, counterfeit, bogus, pretended, insincere, sham.

genus *(SYN.)* kind, race, species, type, variety, character, family, breed, sort.

germ *(SYN.)* pest, virus, contamination, disease, pollution, taint, infection, contagion, poison, ailment.

germinate *(SYN.)* vegetate, pullulate, sprout, develop, grow.

gesture *(SYN.)* omen, signal, symbol, emblem, indication, note, token, symptom, movement, sign, motion, indication.

get *(SYN.)* obtain, receive, attain, gain, achieve, acquire, procure, earn, fetch, carry, remove, prepare, take, ready, urge, induce, secure.

(ANT.) lose, surrender, forfeit, leave, renounce.

ghastly *(SYN.)* frightful, horrible, horrifying, frightening, grisly, hideous, dreadful.

ghost *(SYN.)* phantom, spook, apparition, specter, trace, hint, vestige, spirit.

ghoulish *(SYN.)* weird, eerie, horrifying, gruesome, sinister, scary.

giant *(SYN.)* monster, colossus, mammoth, superman, gigantic.

(ANT.) small, tiny, dwarf, runt, midget, infinitesimal.

gibe *(SYN.)* sneer, jeer, mock, scoff, boo, hoot, hiss.

(ANT.) approve.

giddy *(SYN.)* reeling, dizzy, flighty, silly, scatterbrained.

(ANT.) serious.

gift *(SYN.)* endowment, favor, gratuity,

bequest, talent, charity, present, largess, donation, grant, aptitude, boon, offering, faculty, genius, benefaction.
(ANT.) purchase, loss, ineptitude, deprivation, earnings, incapacity.

gigantic *(SYN.)* huge, colossal, immense, large, vast, elephantine, gargantuan, prodigious, mammoth, monumental, enormous.
(ANT.) small, tiny, minute, diminutive, little.

giggle *(SYN.)* chuckle, jeer, laugh, roar, snicker, titter, cackle, guffaw, mock.

gild *(SYN.)* cover, coat, paint, embellish, sweeten, retouch, camouflage.

gingerly *(SYN.)* gentle, cautiously, carefully, gently.
(ANT.) roughly.

gird *(SYN.)* wrap, tie, bind, belt, encircle, surround, get set, prepare.
(ANT.) untie.

girl *(SYN.)* female, lass, miss, maiden, damsel.

girth *(SYN.)* measure, size, width, dimensions, expanse, proportions.

gist *(SYN.)* connotation, explanation, purpose, significance, acceptation, implication, interpretation, meaning.
(ANT.) redundancy.

give *(SYN.)* bestow, contribute, grant, impart, provide, donate, confer, deliver, present, furnish, yield, develop, offer, produce, hand over, award, allot, deal out, mete out, bend, sacrifice, supply.
(ANT.) withdraw, take, retain, keep, seize.

given *(SYN.)* handed over, presented, supposed, stated, disposed, assumed, inclined, bent.

glacier *(SYN.)* frigid, icy, iceberg.

glad *(SYN.)* happy, cheerful, gratified, delighted, joyous, merry, pleased, exulting, charmed, thrilled, satisfied, tickled, gay, bright.
(ANT.) sad, depressed, dejected, melancholy, unhappy, morose, somber, despondent.

gladness *(SYN.)* bliss, contentment, happiness, pleasure, well-being, beatitude, delight, satisfaction, blessedness.
(ANT.) sadness, sorrow, despair, misery, grief.

glade *(SYN.)* clearing.

gladiator *(SYN.)* battler, fighter, competitor, combatant, contender, contestant.

glamorous *(SYN.)* spellbinding, fascinating, alluring, charming, bewitching, entrancing, captivating, enchanting, attractive, appealing, enticing, enthralling.

glamour *(SYN.)* charm, allure, attraction, magnetism, fascination.

glance *(SYN.)* eye, gaze, survey, view, examine, inspect, discern, look, see, witness, peek, regard, skim, reflect, glimpse, behold, observe.
(ANT.) hide, miss, avert, overlook.

glare *(SYN.)* flash, dazzle, stare, glower, glow, shine, glaze, burn, brilliance, flare, blind, scowl.

glaring *(SYN.)* flagrant, obvious, blatant, prominent, dazzling.

glass *(SYN.)* cup, tumbler, goblet, pane, crystal.

glassy *(SYN.)* blank, empty, emotionless, vacant, fixed, expressionless.

glaze *(SYN.)* buff, luster, cover, wax, gloss, coat, polish, shellac.

gleam *(SYN.)* flash, glimmer, glisten, shimmer, sparkle, twinkle, glare, beam, glow, radiate, glimmering, shine, burn, reflection, blaze.

glean *(SYN.)* reap, gather, select, harvest, pick, separate, cull.

glee *(SYN.)* mirth, joy, gladness, enchantment, delight, cheer, bliss, elation, merriment.
(ANT.) depression, misery, dejection.

glen *(SYN.)* ravine, valley.

glib *(SYN.)* smooth, suave, flat, plain, polished, sleek, urbane.
(ANT.) rough, rugged, blunt, harsh, bluff.

glide *(SYN.)* sweep, sail, fly, flow, slip, coast, cruise, move easily, skim, slide.

glimmer *(SYN.)* blink, shimmer, flicker, indication, hint, clue, suggestion.

glimpse *(SYN.)* notice, glance, peek, see, impression, look, flash.

glint *(SYN.)* flash, gleam, peek, glance, glimpse, sparkle, glitter.

glisten *(SYN.)* shimmer, shine, glimmer, twinkle, glitter, glister, sparkle.

glitch *(SYN.)* mishap, snag, hitch, malfunction.

glitter *(SYN.)* glisten, glimmer, sparkle, shine, twinkle.

gloat *(SYN.)* triumph, exult, glory, rejoice, revel.

global *(SYN.)* universal, international, worldwise.

globe *(SYN.)* orb, ball, world, earth, map, universe, sphere.

gloom *(SYN.)* bleakness, despondency, misery, sadness, woe, darkness, dejection, obscurity, blackness, shadow, shade, dimness, shadows, melancholy. *(ANT.) joy, mirth, exultation, cheerfulness, light, happiness, brightness, frivolity.*

gloomy *(SYN.)* despondent, dismal, glum, somber, sorrowful, sad, dejected, disconsolate, dim, dark, morose, dispirited, moody, grave, pensive. *(ANT.) happy, merry, cheerful, highspirited, bright, sunny, joyous.*

glorify *(SYN.)* enthrone, exalt, honor, revere, adore, dignify, enshrine, consecrate, praise, worship, laud, venerate. *(ANT.) mock, dishonor, debase, abuse, degrade.*

glorious *(SYN.)* exalted, high, noble, splendid, supreme, elevated, lofty, raised, majestic, famous, noted, stately, distinguished, celebrated, renowned, famed, magnificent, grand, proud, impressive, elegant, sublime. *(ANT.) ridiculous, low, base, ignoble, terrible, ordinary.*

glory *(SYN.)* esteem, praise, respect, reverence, admiration, honor, dignity, worship, eminence, homage, deference. *(ANT.) dishonor, disgrace, contempt, reproach, derision.*

gloss *(SYN.)* luster, shine, glow, sheen.

glossary *(SYN.)* dictionary, thesaurus, wordbook, lexicon.

glossy *(SYN.)* smooth, glistening, shiny, sleek, polished. *(ANT.) matte, dull.*

glow *(SYN.)* beam, glisten, radiate, shimmer, sparkle, glare, blaze, scintillate, shine, light, gleam, burn, flare, flame, radiate, dazzle, blush, redden, heat, warmth, flicker.

glower *(SYN.)* scowl, stare, frown, glare. *(ANT.) beam, grin, smile.*

glowing *(SYN.)* fiery, intense, passionate, zealous, enthusiastic, ardent, eager, fervent, favorable, impassioned, keen, complimentary, vehement. *(ANT.) cool, indifferent, apathetic, nonchalant.*

glue *(SYN.)* bind, fasten, cement, paste.

glum *(SYN.)* morose, sulky, fretful, crabbed, sullen, dismal, dour, moody. *(ANT.) joyous, merry, amiable, gay, pleasant.*

glut *(SYN.)* gorge, sate, content, furnish, fill, pervade, satiate, stuff, replenish, fill up, satisfy, stock. *(ANT.) empty, exhaust, deplete, void,* drain.

glutton *(SYN.)* pig, hog, greedy eater.

gluttony *(SYN.)* ravenousness, piggishness, devouring, hoggishness, insatiability, swinishness, voraciousness. *(ANT.) satisfaction, fullness.*

gnarled *(SYN.)* twisted, knotted, rugged, knobby, nodular.

gnash *(SYN.)* gnaw, crunch, grind.

gnaw *(SYN.)* chew, eat, gnash, grind, erode.

go *(SYN.)* proceed, depart, flee, move, vanish, exit, walk, quit, fade, progress, travel, become, fit, agree, leave, suit, harmonize, pass, travel, function, operate, withdraw. *(ANT.) stay, arrive, enter, stand, come.*

goad *(SYN.)* incite, prod, drive, urge, push, shove, jab, provoke, stimulate.

goal *(SYN.)* craving, destination, desire, longing, objective, finish, end, passion, aim, object, aspiration.

gobble *(SYN.)* devour, eat fast, gorge, gulp, stuff.

goblet *(SYN.)* cup, glass.

goblin *(SYN.)* troll, elf, dwarf, spirit.

godlike *(SYN.)* holy, supernatural, heavenly, celestial, divine, transcendent. *(ANT.) profane, wicked, blasphemous, diabolical, mundane.*

godly *(SYN.)* pious, religious, holy, pure, divine, spiritual, righteous, saintly.

golden *(SYN.)* shining, metallic, bright, fine, superior, nice, excellent, valuable. *(ANT.) dull, inferior.*

gong *(SYN.)* chimes, bells.

good *(SYN.)* honest, sound, valid, cheerful, honorable, worthy, conscientious, moral, genuine, humane, kind, fair, useful, skillful, adequate, friendly, genial, proficient, pleasant, exemplary, admirable, virtuous, reliable, precious, benevolent, excellent, pure, agreeable, gracious, safe, commendable. *(ANT.) bad, imperfect, vicious, undesirable, unfriendly, unkind, evil.*

good-by *(SYN.)* so long, farewell.

good-bye *(SYN.)* farewell.

good-hearted *(SYN.)* good, kind, thoughtful, kindhearted, considerate. *(ANT.) evil-hearted.*

good-humored *(SYN.)* pleasant, goodnatured, cheerful, sunny, amiable. *(ANT.) petulant, cranky.*

goodness *(SYN.)* good, honesty, integrity, virtue, righteousness.

(ANT.) sin, evil, dishonesty, corruption, badness.

goods (SYN.) property, belongings, holdings, possessions, merchandise, wares.

good will (SYN.) agreeability, harmony, willingness, readiness.

gore (SYN.) impale, penetrate, puncture, gouge.

gorge (SYN.) ravine, devour, stuff, gobble, valley, defile, pass, cram, fill.

gorgeous (SYN.) grand, ravishing, glorious, stunning, brilliant, divine, splendid, dazzling, beautiful, magnificent.

(ANT.) homely, ugly, squalid.

gory (SYN.) bloody.

gossamer (SYN.) dainty, fine, filmy, delicate, sheer, transparent.

gossip (SYN.) prate, rumor, prattle, hearsay, meddler, tattler, chatter, talk, chat, blabbermouth.

gouge (SYN.) scoop, dig, carve, burrow, excavate, chisel, notch.

gourmet (SYN.) gourmand, gastronome, connoisseur.

govern (SYN.) manage, oversee, reign, preside over, supervise, direct, command, sway, administer, control, regulate, determine, influence, guide, lead, head, rule.

(ANT.) assent, submit, acquiesce, obey, yield.

government (SYN.) control, direction, rule, command, authority.

governor (SYN.) controller, administrator, director, leader, manager.

gown (SYN.) garment, robe, frock, dress, costume, attire.

grab (SYN.) snatch, grip, clutch, seize, grasp, capture, pluck.

grace (SYN.) charm, beauty, handsomeness, loveliness, dignify, fairness, honor, distinguish, sympathy, attractiveness, elegance, clemency, excuse, pardon, thanks, blessing, prayer, pulchritude.

(ANT.) eyesore, homeliness, deformity, ugliness, disfigurement.

graceful (SYN.) elegant, fluid, natural, supple, beautiful, comely, flowing, lithe.

(ANT.) clumsy, awkward, gawky, ungainly, deformed.

gracious (SYN.) warm-hearted, pleasing, friendly, engaging, agreeable, kind, amiable, kindly, nice, good, courteous, polite, generous, good-natured.

(ANT.) surly, hateful, churlish, rude, disagreeable, impolite, thoughtless, discourteous, ill-natured.

grade (SYN.) kind, rank, elegance, denomination, sort, arrange, category, classify, rate, group, place, mark, incline, slope, excellence, caste, order.

gradual (SYN.) deliberate, sluggish, dawdling, laggard, slow, leisurely, moderate, easy, delaying.

(ANT.) quick, swift, fast, speedy, rapid.

graduate (SYN.) pass, finish, advance.

graft (SYN.) fraud, theft, cheating, bribery, dishonesty, transplant, corruption.

grain (SYN.) speck, particle, plant, bit, seed, temper, fiber, character, texture, markings, nature, tendency.

grand (SYN.) great, elaborate, splendid, royal, stately, noble, considerable, outstanding, distinguished, impressive, prominent, majestic, fine, dignified, large, main, principal.

(ANT.) unassuming, modest, insignificant, unimportant, humble.

grandeur (SYN.) resplendence, majesty, distinction, glory.

grandiose (SYN.) grand, lofty, magnificent, stately, noble, pompous, dignified, imposing, sublime, majestic.

(ANT.) lowly, ordinary, common, undignified, humble.

grandstand (SYN.) bleachers, gallery.

granite (SYN.) stone, rock.

grant (SYN.) confer, allocate, deal, divide, mete, appropriation, assign, benefaction, distribute, allowance, donate, award, mete out, deal out, consent, bestow, give, measure.

(ANT.) refuse, withhold, confiscate, keep, retain.

granular (SYN.) grainy, sandy, crumbly, rough, gritty.

graph (SYN.) design, plan, stratagem, draw up, chart, sketch, cabal, machination, outline, plot, scheme, diagram.

graphic (SYN.) vivid, lifelike, significant, meaningful, pictorial, descriptive, representative.

grapple (SYN.) grip, seize, clutch, clasp, grasp, fight, struggle.

grasp (SYN.) clutch, grip, seize, apprehend, capture, snare, hold, clasp, comprehend, reach, grab, understand, grapple, possession, control, domination, command, perceive, trap.

(ANT.) release, lose, throw, liberate.

grasping (SYN.) possessive, greedy, selfish, acquisitive, mercenary.

(ANT.) *liberal, unselfish, generous.*

grate (SYN.) file, pulverize, grind, scrape, scratch, scrape, annoy, irritate.

grateful (SYN.) beholden, obliged, appreciative, thankful, indebted.
(ANT.) *ungrateful, unappreciative, grudging, thankless.*

gratify (SYN.) charm, gladden, please, satisfy.
(ANT.) *frustrate.*

gratifying (SYN.) contentment, solace, relief, comfort, ease, succor, consolation, enjoyment.
(ANT.) *suffering, torment, affliction, discomfort, torture, misery.*

grating (SYN.) harsh, rugged, severe, stringent, coarse, gruff, jarring, rigorous, strict.
(ANT.) *smooth, melodious, mild, gentle, soft.*

gratis (SYN.) complimentary, free.

gratitude (SYN.) gratefulness, thankfulness, appreciation.
(ANT.) *ungratefulness.*

gratuity (SYN.) tip, bonus, gift, donation.

grave (SYN.) sober, grim, earnest, serious, important, momentous, sedate, solemn, somber, imposing, vital, essential, staid, consequential, thoughtful.
(ANT.) *light, flighty, trivial, insignificant, unimportant, trifling, merry, gay, cheery, frivolous.*

gravel (SYN.) stones, pebbles, grain.

gravitate (SYN.) incline, tend, lean, approach, toward.

gravity (SYN.) concern, importance, seriousness, pull, movement.
(ANT.) *triviality.*

graze (SYN.) scrape, feed, rub, brush, contact, skim.

grease (SYN.) fat, oil, lubrication.

greasy (SYN.) messy, buttery, waxy, fatty.

great (SYN.) large, numerous, eminent, illustrious, big, gigantic enormous, immense, vast, weighty, fine, important, countless, prominent, vital, huge, momentous, serious, famed, dignified, excellent, critical, renowned, majestic, august, elevated, noble, grand.
(ANT.) *minute, common, menial, ordinary, diminutive, small, paltry, unknown.*

greed (SYN.) piggishness, lust, desire, greediness, avarice, covetousness.
(ANT.) *unselfishness, selflessness, generosity.*

greedy (SYN.) selfish, devouring, raven-

ous, avaricious, covetous, rapacious, gluttonous, insatiable, voracious.
(ANT.) *full, generous, munificent, giving, satisfied.*

green (SYN.) inexperienced, modern, novel, recent, further, naive, fresh, natural, raw, unsophisticated, undeveloped, immature, unripe, additional, brisk, artless.
(ANT.) *hackneyed, musty, decayed, faded, stagnant.*

greenhorn (SYN.) tenderfoot, beginner, apprentice, amateur, novice.

greenhouse (SYN.) hothouse.

greet (SYN.) hail, accost, meet, address, talk to, speak to, welcome, approach.
(ANT.) *pass by, avoid.*

gregarious (SYN.) outgoing, civil, affable, communicative, hospitable, sociable.
(ANT.) *inhospitable, antisocial, disagreeable, hermitic.*

grief (SYN.) misery, sadness, tribulation, affliction, heartache, woe, trial, anguish, mourning, distress, lamentation.
(ANT.) *happiness, solace, consolation, comfort, joy.*

grief-stricken (SYN.) heartsick, ravaged, devastated, wretched, forlorn, desolate, wretched.
(ANT.) *joyous, blissful, content.*

grievance (SYN.) injury, wrong, injustice, detriment, complaint, damage, prejudice, evil, objection, protest, accusation, harm.
(ANT.) *improvement, benefit, repair.*

grieve (SYN.) lament, brood over, mourn, weep, wail, sorrow, distress, bemoan, hurt, deplore.
(ANT.) *revel, carouse, celebrate, rejoice, gladden, soothe.*

grieved (SYN.) contrite, remorseful, beggarly, mean, pitiful, shabby, vile, sorrowful, pained, hurt, sorry, contemptible, worthless.
(ANT.) *splendid, delighted, cheerful, impenitent, unrepentant.*

grievous (SYN.) gross, awful, outrageous, shameful, lamentable, regrettable.
(ANT.) *agreeable, comforting, pleasurable.*

grill (SYN.) cook, broil, question, interrogate, barbecue, grating, gridiron, cross-examine.

grim (SYN.) severe, harsh, strict, merciless, fierce, horrible, inflexible, adamant, ghastly, frightful, unyielding, rigid, stern.

(ANT.) *pleasant, lenient, relaxed, amiable, congenial, smiling.*

grimace (SYN.) expression, sneer, scowl, mope.

grimy (SYN.) unclean, grubby, soiled.

grin (SYN.) beam, smile, smirk.

grind (SYN.) mill, mash, powder, crush, crumble, pulverize, smooth, grate, sharpen, even.

grip (SYN.) catch, clutch, apprehend, trap, arrest, grasp, hold, bag, suitcase, lay hold of, clench, command, control, possession, domination, comprehension, understanding, seize.

(ANT.) *release, liberate, lose, throw.*

gripe (SYN.) protest, lament, complaint, grumbling.

grit (SYN.) rub, grind, grate, sand, gravel, pluck, courage, stamina.

groan (SYN.) sob, wail, howl, moan, whimper, wail, complain.

groggy (SYN.) dazed, dopy, stupefied, stunned, drugged, unsteady.

(ANT.) *alert.*

groom (SYN.) tend, tidy, preen, curry, spouse, consort.

groove (SYN.) furrow, channel, track, routine, slot, scratch.

groovy (SYN.) marvelous, delightful, wonderful.

grope (SYN.) fumble, feel around.

gross (SYN.) glaring, coarse, indelicate, obscene, bulky, great, total, whole, brutal, grievous, aggregate, earthy, rude, vulgar, entire, enormous, plain, crass, rough, large.

(ANT.) *appealing, delicate, refined, proper, polite, cultivated, slight, comely, trivial, decent.*

grotesque (SYN.) strange, weird, odd, incredible, fantastic, monstrous, absurd, freakish, bizarre, peculiar, deformed, disfigured, unnatural, queer.

grotto (SYN.) tunnel, cave, hole, cavern.

grouch (SYN.) protest, remonstrate, whine, complain, grumble, murmur, mope, mutter, repine.

(ANT.) *praise, applaud, rejoice, approve.*

grouchy (SYN.) cantankerous, grumpy, surly.

(ANT.) *cheerful, contented, agreeable, pleasant.*

ground (SYN.) foundation, presumption, surface, principle, underpinning, premise, base, bottom, fix, basis, soil, land, earth, set, root, support, establish, dirt, presupposition.

(ANT.) *implication, superstructure, trimming, derivative.*

groundless (SYN.) baseless, unfounded, unwarranted, needless.

grounds (SYN.) garden, lawns, dregs, foundation, leftovers, reason, sediment, cause, basis, premise, motive.

groundwork (SYN.) support, bottom, base, underpinning, premise, presupposition, principle, basis.

(ANT.) *trimming, implication, derivative, superstructure.*

group (SYN.) crowd, clock, party, troupe, swarm, bunch, brook, assembly, herd, band, mob, brood, class, throng, cluster, flock, lot, collection, pack, horde, gathering, aggregation.

(ANT.) *disassemble.*

grouse (SYN.) mutter, grumble, gripe, scold, growl, complain.

grovel (SYN.) creep, crawl, cower, cringe, slouch, stoop, scramble.

groveling (SYN.) dishonorable, lowly, sordid, vile, mean, abject, despicable, ignoble, menial, servile, vulgar, ignominious.

(ANT.) *lofty, noble, esteemed, exalted, righteous.*

grow (SYN.) extend, swell, advance, develop, enlarge, enlarge, germinate, mature, expand, flower, raise, become, cultivate, increase, distend.

(ANT.) *wane, shrink, atrophy, decay, diminish, contract.*

growl (SYN.) complain, snarl, grumble, gnarl, roar, clamor, bellow.

grown-up (SYN.) full-grown, adult, of age, mature, big, senior.

(ANT.) *little, childish, budding, junior, juvenile.*

growth (SYN.) expansion, development, unfolding, maturing, progress, elaboration, evolution.

(ANT.) *degeneration, deterioration, curtailment, abbreviation, compression.*

grub (SYN.) gouge, dig, scoop out, burrow, tunnel, excavate, plod, toil, drudge.

grubby (SYN.) unkempt, grimy, slovenly, dirty.

(ANT.) *tidy, spruce, neat, clean, well-groomed.*

grudge (SYN.) malevolence, malice, resentment, bitterness, spite, animosity, enmity, rancor, ill will.

(ANT.) kindness, love, benevolence, affection, good will, friendliness, toleration.

grudgingly *(SYN.)* reluctantly, unwillingly, under protest, involuntarily.

grueling *(SYN.)* taxing, exhausting, excruciating, trying, arduous, grinding, crushing.

(ANT.) effortless, easy, light, simple.

gruesome *(SYN.)* hideous, frightful, horrible, loathsome, ghastly, horrifying, grisly.

(ANT.) agreeable, soothing, delightful, charming.

gruff *(SYN.)* scratchy, crude, incomplete, unpolished, stormy, brusque, rude, rough, uncivil, churlish, violent, harsh, imperfect, craggy, irregular, deep, husky, approximate, tempestuous, blunt.

(ANT.) civil, courteous, polished, calm, even, sleek, smooth, finished, gentle, placid, pleasant, tranquil. **grumble** *(SYN.)* protest, mutter, complain.

grumpy *(SYN.)* ill-tempered, cranky, grouchy, surly, cross-grained, crabbed, fractious, pettish, disgruntled, moody.

(ANT.) winsome, amiable, pleasant, cheery.

guarantee *(SYN.)* bond, pledge, token, warrant, earnest, surety, bail, commitment, promise, secure, swear, assure, sponsor, certify, warranty, insure, endorse, security.

guarantor *(SYN.)* voucher, sponsor, warrantor, signatory, underwriter, surety, seconder.

guaranty *(SYN.)* warranty, token, deposit, earnest, pledge, gage, collateral, stake.

guard *(SYN.)* protect, shield, veil, cloak, conceal, disguise, envelop, preserve, hide, defend, cover, sentry, protector, shroud, curtain.

(ANT.) unveil, expose, ignore, neglect, bare, reveal, disregard, divulge.

guarded *(SYN.)* discreet, cautious, careful.

(ANT.) audacious, reckless, indiscreet, careless.

guardian *(SYN.)* curator, keeper, protector, custodian, patron, watchdog, champion.

guess *(SYN.)* estimate, suppose, think, assume, reason, believe, reckon, speculate, notion, surmise, hypothesis, imagine, consider, opinion, conjecture.

(ANT.) know.

guest *(SYN.)* caller, client, customer, patient, visitor, company.

(ANT.) host.

guide *(SYN.)* manage, supervise, conduct, direct, lead, steer, escort, pilot, show, squire, usher, control, affect, influence, regulate.

(ANT.) follower, follow.

guild *(SYN.)* association, union, society.

guile *(SYN.)* deceitfulness, fraud, wiliness, trick, deceit, chicanery, cunning, deception, craftiness, sham, sneakiness, cheat.

(ANT.) sincerity, openness, honesty, truthfulness, candor, frankness.

guileless *(SYN.)* open, innocent, naive, sincere, simple, candid.

(ANT.) treacherous, plotting.

guilt *(SYN.)* sin, blame, misstep, fault, offense.

guilty *(SYN.)* culpable, to blame, responsible, at fault, criminal, blameworthy.

(ANT.) blameless, innocent, guiltless.

guise *(SYN.)* aspect, pretense, mien, look, air, advent, apparition, appearance, dress, garb, coat, cover, clothes, show, manner, form, demeanor, arrival.

gulch *(SYN.)* gorge, valley, gully, ravine, canyon.

gulf *(SYN.)* ravine, cut, break, crack, chasm, canyon, abyss, cleft, separation, bay, sound, inlet.

gullible *(SYN.)* trustful, naive, innocent, unsuspecting, deceivable, unsuspicious, believing.

(ANT.) skeptical, sophisticated.

gully *(SYN.)* ditch, gorge, ravine, valley, gulch, gulf.

gulp *(SYN.)* devour, swallow, gasp, repress, choke.

gun *(SYN.)* fire, shoot, weapon, discharge, pistol, firearm, revolver.

gush *(SYN.)* pour, spurt, stream, rush out, spout, flood, flush, chatter, babble, flow.

gust *(SYN.)* blast, wind, outbreak, outburst, eruption.

gutter *(SYN.)* ditch, groove, drain, channel, trench, sewer, trough.

gymnasium *(SYN.)* playground, arena, court, athletic field.

gymnastics *(SYN.)* drill, exercise, acrobatics, calisthenics.

gyp *(SYN.)* swindle, cheat, defraud.

gypsy *(SYN.)* nomad.

habit *(SYN.)* usage, routine, compulsion, use, wont, custom, disposition, practice, addiction, fashion.

habitation *(SYN.)* abode, domicile, lodgings, dwelling, home.

habitual *(SYN.)* general, usual, common, frequent, persistent, customary, routine, regular, often.

(ANT.) solitary, unique, exceptional, occasional, unusual, scanty, rare.

habituated *(SYN.)* used, accustomed, adapted, acclimated, comfortable, familiarized, addicted, settled.

hack *(SYN.)* cleave, chop, slash, hew, slice, pick, sever, mangle.

hackneyed *(SYN.)* stale, stereotyped, trite, commonplace, ordinary, banal, common, unique.

(ANT.) novel, stimulating, modern, fresh, creative, momentous.

hag *(SYN.)* beldam, crone, vixen, granny, ogress, harridan, virage.

haggard *(SYN.)* drawn, careworn, debilitated, spent, gaunt, worn.

(ANT.) bright, fresh, clear-eyed, animated.

haggle *(SYN.)* dicker, bargain.

hail *(SYN.)* welcome, approach, accost, speak to, address, greet.

(ANT.) pass by, avoid.

hair-do *(SYN.)* hairstyle, coiffure.

hairdresser *(SYN.)* beautician, barber.

hairless *(SYN.)* shorn, glabrous, bald, baldpated, depilitated.

(ANT.) hirsute, hairy, unshaven.

hair-raising *(SYN.)* horrifying, exciting, alarming, thrilling, startling, frightful, scary, breathtaking.

hairy *(SYN.)* bearded, shaggy, hirsute, bewhiskered.

hale *(SYN.)* robust, well, wholesome, hearty, healthy, sound, salubrious.

(ANT.) noxious, frail, diseased, delicate, infirm, injurious.

half-baked *(SYN.)* crude, premature, makeshift, illogical, shallow.

half-hearted *(SYN.)* uncaring, indifferent, unenthusiastic, cool.

(ANT.) eager, enthusiastic, earnest.

half-wit *(SYN.)* dope, simpleton, nitwit, dunce, idiot, fool.

hall *(SYN.)* corridor, lobby, passage, hallway, vestibule, foyer.

hallow *(SYN.)* glorify, exalt, dignify, aggrandize, consecrate, elevate, ennoble, raise, erect.

(ANT.) dishonor, humiliate, debase, degrade.

hallowed *(SYN.)* holy, sacred, beatified, sacrosanct, blessed, divine.

hallucination *(SYN.)* fantasy, mirage, dream, vision, phantasm, appearance, aberration, illusion.

halt *(SYN.)* impede, obstruct, terminate, stop, hinder, desist, check, arrest, abstain, discontinue, hold, end, cork, interrupt, bar, cease.

(ANT.) start, begin, proceed, speed, beginning, promote.

halting *(SYN.)* imperfect, awkward, stuttering, faltering, hobbling, doubtful, limping, wavering.

(ANT.) decisive, confident, smooth, graceful, facile.

hammer *(SYN.)* beat, bang, whack, pound, batter, drive, tap, cudgel.

hamper *(SYN.)* prevent, impede, thwart, restrain, hinder, obstruct.

(ANT.) help, assist, encourage, facilitate.

hamstrung *(SYN.)* disabled, helpless, paralyzed.

hand *(SYN.)* assistant, helper, support, aid, farmhand, laborer.

handicap *(SYN.)* retribution, penalty, disadvantage, forfeiture, hindrance, chastisement.

(ANT.) reward, pardon, compensation, remuneration.

handily *(SYN.)* readily, skillfully, easily, dexterously, smoothly, adroitly, deftly.

handkerchief *(SYN.)* bandanna, scarf.

handle *(SYN.)* hold, touch, finger, clutch, grip, manipulate, feel, grasp, control, oversee, direct, treat, steer, supervise, run, regulate.

hand out *(SYN.)* disburse, distribute, deal, mete, circulate.

hand over *(SYN.)* release, surrender, deliver, yield, present, fork over.

handsome *(SYN.)* lovely, pretty, fair, comely, beautiful, charming, elegant, good-looking, large, generous, liberal, beauteous, fine.

(ANT.) repulsive, ugly, unattractive, stingy, small, mean, petty, unsightly, meager, homely, foul, hideous.

handy *(SYN.)* suitable, adapted, appropriate, favorable, fitting, near, ready, close, nearby, clever, helpful, useful, timely, accessible.

(ANT.) inopportune, troublesome, awkward, inconvenient.

hang *(SYN.)* drape, hover, dangle, suspend, kill, sag, execute, lynch.

hang in *(SYN.)* continue, endure, remain, persevere, resist, persist.

hang-up *(SYN.)* inhibition, difficulty, snag, hindrance, block.

hanker *(SYN.)* wish, yearn, long, desire, pine, thirst, covet.

haphazard *(SYN.)* aimless, random, purposeless, indiscriminate, accidental.
(ANT.) determined, planned, designed, deliberate.

hapless *(SYN.)* ill-fated, unfortunate, jinxed, luckless, wretched.

happen *(SYN.)* occur, take place, bechance, betide, transpire, come to pass, chance, befall.

happening *(SYN.)* episode, event, scene, incident, affair, experience, phenomenon, transaction.

happiness *(SYN.)* pleasure, gladness, delight, beatitude, bliss, contentment, satisfaction, joy, joyousness, blessedness, joyfulness, felicity, elation, well-being.
(ANT.) sadness, sorrow, misery, grief.

happy *(SYN.)* gay, joyous, cheerful, fortunate, glad, merry, contented, satisfied, lucky, blessed, pleased, opportune, delighted.
(ANT.) gloomy, morose, sad, sorrowful, miserable, inconvenient, unlucky, depressed, blue.

happy-go-lucky *(SYN.)* easygoing, carefree, unconcerned.
(ANT.) prudent, responsible, concerned.

harangue *(SYN.)* oration, diatribe, lecture, tirade, exhortation.

harass *(SYN.)* badger, irritate, molest, pester, taunt, torment, provoke, tantalize, worry, aggravate, annoy, nag, plague, vex.
(ANT.) please, soothe, comfort, delight, gratify.

harbinger *(SYN.)* sign, messenger, proclaim, forerunner, herald.

harbor *(SYN.)* haven, port, anchorage, cherish, entertain, protect, shelter.

hard *(SYN.)* difficult, burdensome, arduous, rigid, puzzling, cruel, strict, unfeeling, severe, stern, impenetrable, compact, tough, solid, onerous, rigorous, firm, intricate, harsh, perplexing.
(ANT.) fluid, brittle, effortless, gentle, tender, easy, simple, plastic, soft, lenient, flabby, elastic.

hard-boiled *(SYN.)* unsympathetic, tough, harsh, unsentimental.

harden *(SYN.)* petrify, solidify.
(ANT.) loose, soften.

hardheaded *(SYN.)* stubborn, obstinate, unyielding, headstrong.

hardhearted *(SYN.)* merciless, hard, unmerciful, callous, pitiless, ruthless.

hardly *(SYN.)* barely, scarcely.

hard-nosed *(SYN.)* shrewd, practical.

hardship *(SYN.)* ordeal, test, effort, affliction, misfortune, trouble, experiment, proof, essay, misery, examination, difficulty, tribulation.
(ANT.) consolation, alleviation.

hardy *(SYN.)* sturdy, strong, tough, vigorous.
(ANT.) frail, decrepit, feeble, weak, fragile.

harm *(SYN.)* hurt, mischief, misfortune, mishap, damage, wickedness, cripple, injury, evil, detriment, ill, infliction, wrong.
(ANT.) favor, kindness, benefit, boon.

harmful *(SYN.)* damaging, injurious, mischievous, detrimental, hurtful, deleterious.
(ANT.) helpful, salutary, profitable,, advantageous, beneficial.

harmless *(SYN.)* protected, secure, snag, dependable, certain, painless, innocent, trustworthy.
(ANT.) perilous, hazardous, insecure, dangerous, unsafe.

harmonious *(SYN.)* tuneful, melodious, congenial, amicable.
(ANT.) dissonant, discordant, disagreeable.

harmony *(SYN.)* unison, bargain, contract, stipulation, pact, agreement, accordance, concord, accord, understanding, unity, coincidence.
(ANT.) discord, dissension, difference, variance, disagreement.

harness *(SYN.)* control, yoke.

harry *(SYN.)* vex, pester, harass, bother, plague.

harsh *(SYN.)* jarring, gruff, rugged, severe, stringent, blunt, grating, unpleasant, tough, stern, strict, unkind, rigorous, cruel, coarse.
(ANT.) smooth, soft, gentle, melodious, soothing, easy, mild.

harvest *(SYN.)* reap, gather, produce, yield, crop, gain, acquire, fruit, result, reaping, proceeds, glean, garner.
(ANT.) plant, squander, lose, sow.

haste *(SYN.)* speed, hurry, rush, rapidity, flurry, scramble.
(ANT.) sloth, sluggishness.

hasten *(SYN.)* hurry, sprint, quicken, rush, precipitate, accelerate, scurry, run, scamper, dispatch, press, urge, dash, expedite, speed.
(ANT.) retard, tarry, detain, linger, dawdle, delay, hinder.

hasty *(SYN.)* quick, swift, irascible, lively, nimble, brisk, active, speedy, impatient, testy, sharp, fast, rapid.
(ANT.) slow, dull, sluggish.

hat *(SYN.)* helmet, bonnet.

hatch *(SYN.)* breed, incubate, brood.

hate *(SYN.)* loathe, detest, despise, disfavor, hatred, abhorrence, abominate, abhor, dislike.
(ANT.) love, cherish, admire, like.

hateful *(SYN.)* loathsome, detestable, offensive.
(ANT.) likable, loving, admirable.

hatred *(SYN.)* detestation, dislike, malevolence, enmity, rancor, ill will, loathing, hate, hostility, abhorrence, aversion, animosity.
(ANT.) friendship, affection, attraction.

haughty *(SYN.)* proud, stately, vainglorious, arrogant, disdainful, overbearing, supercilious, vain.
(ANT.) meek, ashamed, lowly, humble.

haul *(SYN.)* draw, pull, drag, tow.

have *(SYN.)* own, possess, seize, hold, control, occupy, acquire, undergo, maintain, experience, receive, gain, affect, include, contain, get, take, obtain.
(ANT.) surrender, abandon, renounce, lose.

havoc *(SYN.)* devastation, ruin, destruction.

hazard *(SYN.)* peril, chance, dare, risk, offer, conjecture, jeopardy, danger.
(ANT.) safety, defense, protection, immunity.

hazardous *(SYN.)* perilous, precarious, threatening, unsafe, dangerous, critical, menacing, risky.
(ANT.) protected, secure, safe.

hazy *(SYN.)* uncertain, unclear, ambiguous, dim, obscure, undetermined, vague, unsettled, indefinite.
(ANT.) specific, clear, lucid, precise, explicit.

head *(SYN.)* leader, summit, top, culmination, director, chief, master, commander, supervisor, start, source, crest,

beginning, crisis.
(ANT.) foot, base, bottom, follower, subordinate, underling.

headstrong *(SYN.)* obstinate, stubborn, willful.
(ANT.) easygoing, amenable.

headway *(SYN.)* movement, progress.

heady *(SYN.)* thrilling, intoxicating, exciting, electrifying.

heal *(SYN.)* restore, cure.

healthy *(SYN.)* wholesome, hale, robust, sound, well, vigorous, strong, hearty, healthful, hygienic, salubrious, salutary.
(ANT.) noxious, diseased, unhealthy, delicate, frail, infirm, injurious.

heap *(SYN.)* collection, mound, increase, store, stack, pile, gather, accumulate, amass, accrue, accumulation, collect.
(ANT.) dissipate, scatter, waste, diminish, disperse.

hear *(SYN.)* heed, listen, detect, harken, perceive, regard.

heart *(SYN.)* middle, center, sympathy, nucleus, midpoint, sentiment, core, feeling, midst.
(ANT.) outskirts, periphery, border, rim, boundary.

heartache *(SYN.)* anguish, mourning, sadness, sorrow, affliction, distress, grief, lamentation, tribulation.
(ANT.) happiness, joy, solace, comfort, consolation.

heartbroken *(SYN.)* distressed, forlorn, mean, paltry, worthless, contemptible, wretched, crestfallen, disconsolate, downhearted, comfortless, brokenhearted, low.
(ANT.) noble, fortunate, contented, significant.

hearten *(SYN.)* encourage, favor, impel, urge, promote, sanction, animate, cheer, exhilarate, cheer.
(ANT.) deter, dissuade, deject, discourage, dispirit.

heartless *(SYN.)* mean, cruel, ruthless, hardhearted, pitiless.
(ANT.) sympathetic, kind.

heart-rending *(SYN.)* heartbreaking, depressing, agonizing.

hearty *(SYN.)* warm, earnest, ardent, cordial, sincere, gracious, sociable.
(ANT.) taciturn, aloof, cool, reserved.

heat *(SYN.)* hotness, warmth, temperature, passion, ardor, zeal, inflame, cook, excitement, warm.
(ANT.) cool, chill, coolness, freeze, cold-

ness, chilliness, iciness, cold.

heated *(SYN.)* vehement, fiery, intense, passionate.

heave *(SYN.)* boost, hoist, raise.

heaven *(SYN.)* empyrean, paradise.

heavenly *(SYN.)* superhuman, god-like, blissful, saintly, holy, divine, celestial, angelic, blessed.
(ANT.) *wicked, mundane, profane, blasphemous, diabolical.*

heavy *(SYN.)* weighty, massive, gloomy, serious, ponderous, cumbersome, trying, burdensome, harsh, grave, intense, dull, grievous, concentrated, severe, oppressive, sluggish.
(ANT.) *brisk, light, animated.*

heckle *(SYN.)* torment, harass, tease, hector, harry.

heed *(SYN.)* care, alertness, circumspection, mindfulness, consider, watchfulness, reflection, study, attention, notice, regard, obey, ponder, respect, meditate, mind, observe, deliberate, examine, contemplate, esteem, application.
(ANT.) *negligence, oversight, over look, neglect, ignore, disregard, indifference, omission.*

heedless *(SYN.)* sightless, headlong, rash, unmindful, deaf, unseeing, oblivious, ignorant, inattentive, disregardful, blind.
(ANT.) *perceiving, sensible, aware, calculated, discerning.*

height *(SYN.)* zenith, peak, summit, tallness, mountain, acme, apex, elevation, altitude, prominence, maximum, pinnacle, culmination.
(ANT.) *base, depth, anticlimax.*

heighten *(SYN.)* increase, magnify, annoy, chafe, intensify, amplify, aggravate, provoke, irritate, concentrate, nettle.
(ANT.) *soothe, mitigate, palliate, soften, appease.*

heinous *(SYN.)* abominable, grievous, atrocious.

hello *(SYN.)* greeting, good evening, good afternoon, good morning.
(ANT.) *farewell, good-bye, so long.*

help *(SYN.)* assist, support, promote, relieve, abet, succor, back, uphold, further, remedy, encourage, aid, facilitate, mitigate.
(ANT.) *afflict, thwart, resist, hinder, impede.*

helper *(SYN.)* aide, assistant, supporter.

helpful *(SYN.)* beneficial, serviceable,

wholesome, useful, profitable, advantageous, good, salutary.
(ANT.) *harmful, injurious, useless, worthless, destructive, deleterious, detrimental.*

helpfulness *(SYN.)* assistance, cooperation, usefulness, serviceability, kindness, neighborliness, willingness, collaboration, supportiveness, readiness.
(ANT.) *antagonism, hostility, opposition.*

helpless *(SYN.)* weak, feeble, dependent, disabled, inept, unresourceful, incapable, incompetent.
(ANT.) *resourceful, enterprising.*

helplessness *(SYN.)* impotence, feebleness, weakness, incapacity, ineptitude, invalidism, shiftless, awkwardness.
(ANT.) *power, strength, might, potency.*

helter-skelter *(SYN.)* haphazardly, chaotically, irregularly.

hem *(SYN.)* bottom, border, edge, rim, margin, pale, verge, flounce, boundary, fringe, brim, fence, hedge, frame.

hem in *(SYN.)* enclose, shut in, confine, restrict, limit.

hence *(SYN.)* consequently, thence, therefore, so, accordingly.

herald *(SYN.)* harbinger, crier, envoy, forerunner, precursor, augury, forecast.

herculean *(SYN.)* demanding, heroic, titanic, mighty, prodigious, laborious, arduous, overwhelming, backbreaking.

herd *(SYN.)* group, pack, drove, crowd, flock, gather.

heretic *(SYN.)* nonconformist, sectarian, unbeliever, sectary, schismatic, apostate, dissenter.

heritage *(SYN.)* birthright, legacy, patrimony, inheritance.

hermit *(SYN.)* recluse, anchorite, eremite.

hero *(SYN.)* paladin, champion, idol.

heroic *(SYN.)* bold, courageous, fearless, gallant, valiant, valorous, brave, chivalrous, adventurous, dauntless, intrepid, magnanimous.
(ANT.) *fearful, weak, cringing, timid, cowardly.*

heroism *(SYN.)* valor, bravery, gallant, dauntless, bold, courageous, fearless.

hesitant *(SYN.)* reluctant, unwilling, disinclined, loath, slow, averse.
(ANT.) *willing, inclined, eager, ready, disposed.*

hesitate *(SYN.)* falter, waver, pause, doubt, demur, delay, vacillate, wait, stammer, stutter, scruple.

(*ANT.*) *proceed, resolve, continue, decide, persevere.*

hesitation (*SYN.*) distrust, scruple, suspense, uncertainty, unbelief, ambiguity, doubt, incredulity, skepticism.

(*ANT.*) *determination, belief, certainty, faith, conviction.*

hidden (*SYN.*) undeveloped, unseen dormant, concealed, quiescent, latent, potential, inactive.

(*ANT.*) *visible, explicit, conspicuous, evident.*

hide (*SYN.*) disguise, mask, suppress, withhold, veil, cloak, conceal, screen, camouflage, pelt, skin, leather, cover.

(*ANT.*) *reveal, show, expose, disclose, uncover, divulge.*

hideous (*SYN.*) frightful, ugly, shocking, frightening, horrible, terrible, horrifying, terrifying, grisly, gross.

(*ANT.*) *lovely, beautiful, beauteous.*

high (*SYN.*) tall, eminent, exalted, elevated, high-pitched, sharp, lofty, proud, shrill, raised, strident, prominent, important, powerful, expensive, dear, high-priced, costly, grave, serious, extreme, towering.

(*ANT.*) *low, mean, tiny, stunted, short, base, lowly, deep, insignificant, unimportant, inexpensive, reasonable, trivial, petty, small.*

highly (*SYN.*) extremely, very, extraordinarily, exceedingly.

high-minded (*SYN.*) lofty, noble, honorable.

(*ANT.*) *dishonorable, base.*

high-priced (*SYN.*) dear, expensive, costly.

(*ANT.*) *economical, cheap.*

high-strung (*SYN.*) nervous, tense, wrought-up, intense.

(*ANT.*) *calm.*

highway (*SYN.*) parkway, speedway, turnpike, superhighway, freeway.

hilarious (*SYN.*) funny, side-splitting, hysterical.

(*ANT.*) *depressing, sad.*

hinder (*SYN.*) hamper, impede, block, retard, stop, resist, thwart, obstruct, check, prevent, interrupt, delay, slow, restrain.

(*ANT.*) *promote, further, assist, expedite, advance, facilitate.*

hindrance (*SYN.*) interruption, delay, interference, obstruction, obstacle, barrier.

hinge (*SYN.*) rely, depend, pivot.

hint (*SYN.*) reminder, allusion, suggestion, clue, tip, taste, whisper, implication, intimate, suspicion, mention, insinuation.

(*ANT.*) *declaration, affirmation, statement.*

hire (*SYN.*) employ, occupy, devote, apply, enlist, lease, rent, charter, rental, busy, engage, utilize, retain, let, avail.

(*ANT.*) *reject, banish, discard, fire, dismiss, discharge.*

history (*SYN.*) narration, relation, computation, record, account, chronicle, detail, description, narrative, annal, tale, recital.

(*ANT.*) *confusion, misrepresentation, distortion, caricature.*

hit (*SYN.*) knock, pound, strike, hurt, pummel, beat, come upon, find, discover, blow, smite.

hitch (*SYN.*) tether, fasten, harness, interruption, hindrance, interference.

hoard (*SYN.*) amass, increase, accumulate, gather, save, secret, store, cache, store, accrue, heap.

(*ANT.*) *dissipate, scatter, waste, diminish, squander, spend, disperse.*

hoarse (*SYN.*) deep, rough, husky, raucous, grating, harsh.

(*ANT.*) *clear.*

hoax (*SYN.*) ploy, ruse, wile, device, cheat, deception, antic, imposture, stratagem, stunt, guile, fraud.

(*ANT.*) *openness, sincerity, candor, exposure, honesty.*

hobbling (*SYN.*) deformed, crippled, halt lame, unconvincing, unsatisfactory, defective, feeble, disabled maimed, weak.

(*ANT.*) *robust, vigorous, agile, sound, athletic.*

hobby (*SYN.*) diversion, pastime, avocation.

(*ANT.*) *vocation, profession.*

hobo (*SYN.*) derelict, vagrant, vagabond, tramp.

hoist (*SYN.*) heave, lift, elevate, raise, crane, elevator, derrick.

hold (*SYN.*) grasp, occupy, possess, curb, contain, stow, carry, adhere, have, clutch, keep, maintain, clasp, grip, retain, detain, accommodate, restrain, observe, conduct, check, support.

(*ANT.*) *vacate, relinquish, surrender, abandon.*

holdup *(SYN.)* heist, robbery, stickup, delay, interruption, slowdown.

hole *(SYN.)* cavity, void, pore, opening, abyss, chasm, gulf, aperture, tear, pit, burrow, lair, den, gap.

hollow *(SYN.)* unfilled, vacant, vain, meaningless, flimsy, false, hole, cavity, depression, hypocritical, depressed, empty, pit, insincere.
(ANT.) *sound, solid, genuine, sincere, full.*

holocaust *(SYN.)* fire, burning, extermination, butchery, disaster, massacre.

holy *(SYN.)* devout, divine, blessed, consecrated, sacred, spiritual, pious, sainted, religious, saintly, hallowed.
(ANT.) *worldly, sacrilegious, unconsecrated, evil, profane, secular.*

homage *(SYN.)* reverence, honor, respect.

home *(SYN.)* dwelling, abode, residence, seat, quarters, hearth, domicile, family, house, habitat.

homely *(SYN.)* uncommonly, disagreeable, ill-natured, ugly, vicious, plain, hideous, unattractive, deformed, surly, repellent, spiteful.
(ANT.) *fair, handsome, pretty, attractive, comely, beautiful.*

homesick *(SYN.)* lonely, nostalgic.

honest *(SYN.)* sincere, trustworthy, truthful, fair, ingenuous, candid, conscientious, moral, upright, open, frank, forthright, honorable, just, straightfoward.
(ANT.) *fraudulent, tricky, deceitful, dishonest, lying.*

honesty *(SYN.)* frankness, openness, fairness, sincerity, trustworthiness, justice, candor, honor, integrity, responsibility, uprightness.
(ANT.) *deceit, dishonesty, trickery, fraud, cheating.*

honor *(SYN.)* esteem, praise, worship, admiration, homage, glory, respect, admire, heed, dignity, revere, value, deference, venerate, reverence, consider, distinction, character, principle, uprightness, honesty, adoration.
(ANT.) *scorn, dishonor, despise, neglect, abuse, shame, reproach, disdain, contempt, derision, disgrace.*

honorable *(SYN.)* fair, noble, creditable, proper, reputable, honest, admirable, true, trusty, eminent, respectable, esteemed, just, famed, illustrious, noble,

virtuous, upright.
(ANT.) *infamous, disgraceful, shameful, dishonorable, ignominious.*

honorary *(SYN.)* gratuitous, complimentary.

hoodlum *(SYN.)* crook, gangster, criminal, hooligan, mobster.

hop *(SYN.)* jump, leap.

hope *(SYN.)* expectation, faith, optimism, anticipation, expectancy, confidence, desire, trust.
(ANT.) *pessimism, despair, despondency.*

hopeful *(SYN.)* optimistic, confident.
(ANT.) *despairing, hopeless.*

hopeless *(SYN.)* desperate, despairing, forlorn, fatal, incurable, disastrous.
(ANT.) *promising, hopeful.*

hopelessness *(SYN.)* gloom, discouragement, depression, pessimism, despondency.
(ANT.) *optimism, confidence, elation.*

horde *(SYN.)* host, masses, press, rabble, swarm, throng, bevy, crush, mob, multitude, crowd, populace.

horizontal *(SYN.)* even, level, plane, flat, straight, sideways.
(ANT.) *upright, vertical.*

horrendous *(SYN.)* awful, horrifying, terrible, dreadful, horrid, ghastly.
(ANT.) *splendid, wonderful.*

horrible *(SYN.)* awful, dire, ghastly, horrid, repulsive, frightful, appalling, horrifying, dreadful, ghastly, fearful.
(ANT.) *enjoyable, enchanting, beautiful, lovely, fascinating.*

horrid *(SYN.)* repulsive, terrible, appalling, dire, awful, frightful, fearful, shocking, horrible, horrifying, horrid, ghastly, dreadful, revolting, hideous.
(ANT.) *fascinating, enchanting, enjoyable, lovely, beautiful.*

horror *(SYN.)* dread, awe, hatred, loathing, foreboding, alarm, apprehension, aversion, terror.
(ANT.) *courage, boldness, assurance, confidence.*

horseplay *(SYN.)* tomfoolery, clowning.

hospital *(SYN.)* infirmary, clinic, sanatorium, rest home, sanitarium.

hospitality *(SYN.)* warmth, liberality, generosity, graciousness, welcome.

hostile *(SYN.)* unfriendly, opposed, antagonistic, inimical, adverse, warlike.
(ANT.) *friendly, favorable, amicable, cordial.*

hostility *(SYN.)* grudge, hatred, rancor,

spite, bitterness, enmity, malevolence.
(ANT.) love, friendliness, good will.
hot *(SYN.)* scorching, fervent, hot-
blooded, passionate, peppery, ardent,
burning, fiery, impetuous, scalding,
heated, sizzling, blazing, frying, roasting, warm, intense, torrid, pungent.
*(ANT.) indifferent, apathetic, impassive,
passionless, bland, frigid, cold, freezing,
cool, phlegmatic.*
hot air *(SYN.)* bombast, blather, gabble.
hotbed *(SYN.)* sink, nest, well, den, nurs-
ery, cradle, source, incubator, seedbed.
hot-blooded *(SYN.)* passionate, ardent,
excitable, wild, fervent, fiery, impetuous, rash, brash, intense, impulsive.
(ANT.) stolid, impassive, cold, staid.
hotel *(SYN.)* hostel, motel, inn, hostelry.
hotheaded *(SYN.)* rash, touchy, short-
tempered, reckless, unruly.
(ANT.) levelheaded, cool-headed, calm.
hound *(SYN.)* harry, pester, harass.
hourly *(SYN.)* frequently, steadily, constantly, unfailingly, perpetually, cease-
lessly, continually, incessantly.
(ANT.) occasionally, seldom.
house *(SYN.)* building, residence, abode,
dwelling.
housebreaker *(SYN.)* robber, thief, prowler, cracksman, burglar.
household *(SYN.)* manage, family, home.
householder *(SYN.)* homeowner.
housing *(SYN.)* lodgings, shelter, dwelling, lodgment, case, casing, quarters,
domicile, enclosure, console, bracket.
hovel *(SYN.)* cabin, hut, sty, shack, shed.
hover *(SYN.)* hang, drift, poise, stand by,
linger, impend, waver, hand around.
however *(SYN.)* notwithstanding, still,
nevertheless, but, yet.
howl *(SYN.)* bellow, yowl, wail, yell, cry.
hub *(SYN.)* pivot, center, core, heart,
axis, basis, focus, nucleus.
hubbub *(SYN.)* uproar, tumult, commotion, clamor, bustle, racket, confusion.
*(ANT.) peacefulness, stillness, silence,
quiet, quiescence.*
huckster *(SYN.)* peddler, adman, hawker,
salesman, pitchman.
huddle *(SYN.)* mass, herd, bunch, crowd,
cram, gather, shove, flock, ball, conglomeration, knot, medley, scrum.
hue *(SYN.)* pigment, tint, shade, dye,
complexion, paint, color, tone, tincture.
*(ANT.) transparency, achromatism,
paleness.*

huffy *(SYN.)* sensitive, vulnerable, testy,
offended, thin-skinned, touchy, irascible, cross, offended.
(ANT.) tough, placid, stolid, impassive.
hug *(SYN.)* embrace, coddle, caress, kiss,
pet, press, clasp, fondle, cuddle.
(ANT.) tease, vex, spurn, buffet, annoy.
huge *(SYN.)* great, immense, vast, ample,
big, capacious, extensive, gigantic,
enormous, vast, tremendous, large,
wide, colossal.
(ANT.) short, small, mean, little, tiny.
hulking *(SYN.)* massive, awkward, bulky,
ponderous, unwieldy, overgrown, lum-
pish, oafish.
hullabaloo *(SYN.)* clamor, uproar, din,
racket, tumult, hubbub, commotion,
noise, blare.
(ANT.) calm, peace, silence.
hum *(SYN.)* whir, buzz, whizz, purr,
croon, murmur, intone, vibrate.
human *(SYN.)* manlike, hominid, mortal,
fleshly, individual, person, tellurian.
humane *(SYN.)* lenient, tender, tolerant,
compassionate, clement, forgiving, kind,
forbearing, thoughtful, kindhearted,
kindly, gentle, merciful.
*(ANT.) remorseless, cruel, heartless, piti-
less, unfeeling, brutal.*
humanist *(SYN.)* scholar, sage, savant.
humanitarian *(SYN.)* benefactor, philanthropist.
humanitarianism *(SYN.)* good will,
beneficence, philanthropy, humanism.
humanity *(SYN.)* generosity, magnanimity, tenderness, altruism, beneficence, kindness, charity, philanthropy.
*(ANT.) selfishness, unkindness, cruelty,
inhumanity.*
humble *(SYN.)* modest, crush, mortify,
simple, shame, subdue, meek, abase,
break, plain, submissive, compliant, unpretentious, unassuming, abash, unostentatious, lowly, polite, courteous,
unpretending, degrade.
*(ANT.) praise, arrogant, exalt, illustrious,
boastful, honor, elevate.*
humbly *(SYN.)* deferentially, meekly,
respectfully, unassumingly, diffidently,
modestly, subserviently, submissively.
*(ANT.) insolently, proudly, grandly, ar-
rogantly.*
humbug *(SYN.)* drivel, gammon, bosh,
nonsense, rubbish, inanity.
humdrum *(SYN.)* commonplace, prosy,
mundane, insipid, tedious, routine, dull,

boring.

(ANT.) interesting, stimulating, arresting, striking, exciting.

humid *(SYN.)* moist, damp, misty, muggy, wet, watery, vaporous.

(ANT.) parched, dry, desiccated.

humiliate *(SYN.)* corrupt, defile, depress, pervert, abase, degrade, disgrace, adulterate, humble, shame, lower, impair, deprave, depress.

(ANT.) restore, raise, improve, vitalize.

humiliation *(SYN.)* chagrin, dishonor, ignominy, abasement, mortification, disrepute, odium, disgrace, shame.

(ANT.) honor, praise, dignity, renown.

humor *(SYN.)* jocularity, wit, temperament, sarcasm, irony, joking, amusement, facetiousness, joke, disposition, waggery, fun, clowning, satire, mood.

(ANT.) sorrow, gravity, seriousness.

humorous *(SYN.)* funny, ludicrous, witty, curious, queer, amusing, comical, farcical, laughable, droll.

(ANT.) sober, unfunny, melancholy, serious, sad, solemn.

hunger *(SYN.)* desire, longing, inclination, relish, stomach, zest, craving, liking, passion.

(ANT.) satiety, repugnance, disgust, distaste, renunciation.

hungry *(SYN.)* famished, thirsting, craving, avid, longing, starved, ravenous.

(ANT.) gorged, satisfied, full, sated.

hunt *(SYN.)* pursuit, investigation, examination, inquiry, pursue, track, chase, search, quest, seek, probe, scour, exploration.

(ANT.) cession, abandonment.

hurl *(SYN.)* throw, cast, propel, fling, toss, pitch, thrust.

(ANT.) retain, pull, draw, haul, hold.

hurried *(SYN.)* rushed, hasty, swift, headlong, slipshod, careless, impulsive, superficial.

(ANT.) deliberate, slow, dilatory, thorough, prolonged.

hurry *(SYN.)* quicken, speed, ado, rush, accelerate, run, hasten, race, urge, bustle, expedite, precipitate.

(ANT.) retard, tarry, hinder, linger, dawdle, delay, hinder.

hurt *(SYN.)* damage, harm, grievance, detriment, pain, injustice, injure, abuse, distress, disfigured, mar, afflict, insult, wound, dishonor, wrong, mischief.

(ANT.) improvement, repair, compliment, help, praise, benefit.

hurtful *(SYN.)* harmful, damaging, maleficent, injurious, baleful, noxious.

(ANT.) remedial, good, salutary.

hurtle *(SYN.)* charge, collide, rush, crash, lunge, bump, fling.

husband *(SYN.)* spouse, mate.

hush *(SYN.)* quiet, silence, still.

husk *(SYN.)* shell, hull, pod, skin, covering, crust, bark.

husky *(SYN.)* strong, muscular.

(ANT.) feeble, weak.

hustle *(SYN.)* hasten, run, hurry, speed.

hut *(SYN.)* cottage, shanty, cabin, shed.

hutch *(SYN.)* box, chest, locker, trunk, coffer, bin.

hybrid *(SYN.)* mule, mixture, crossbreed, cross, mongrel, mutt, composite.

hygiene *(SYN.)* cleanliness, sanitation, health, hygienics, prophylaxis.

hygienic *(SYN.)* robust, strong, well, wholesome, hale, healthy, sound, salubrious.

(ANT.) frail, noxious, infirm, delicate, diseased, injurious.

hyperbole *(SYN.)* puffery, exaggeration, embellishment, overstatement, ballyhoo, amplification, magnification.

hypercritical *(SYN.)* faultfinding, captious, censorious, finicky, exacting, carping, querulous, nagging, finical, hairsplitting.

(ANT.) lax, easygoing, indulgent, lenient, tolerant.

hypnotic *(SYN.)* soothing, opiate, sedative, soporific, entrancing, spellbinding, arresting, charming, engaging, gripping.

hypnotize *(SYN.)* entrance, dazzle, mesmerize, fascinate, spellbind.

hypocrisy *(SYN.)* pretense, deceit, dissembling, fakery, feigning, pharisaism, sanctimony, cant, dissimulation.

(ANT.) openness, candor, truth, directness, forthrightness, honesty, frankness.

hypocrite *(SYN.)* cheat, deceiver, pretender, dissembler, fake, charlatan.

hypocritical *(SYN.)* dissembling, twofaced, insincere, dishonest, duplicitous, deceitful, phony.

(ANT.) heartfelt, true, genuine, honest.

hypothesis *(SYN.)* law, theory, supposition, conjecture.

(ANT.) proof, fact, certainty.

hypothetical *(SYN.)* conjectural, speculative, theoretical.

(ANT.) actual.

idea (SYN.) conception, image, opinion, sentiment, concept, fancy, notion, thought, impression.
(ANT.) thing, matter, entity, object, substance.

ideal (SYN.) imaginary, supreme, unreal, visionary, perfect, faultless, fancied, exemplary, utopian.
(ANT.) imperfect, actual, material, real, faulty.

idealistic (SYN.) extravagant, dreamy, fantastic, fanciful, ideal, maudlin, imaginative, mawkish, sentimental, poetic, picturesque.
(ANT.) practical, literal, factual, prosaic.

identify (ANT.) recollect, apprehend, perceive, remember, confess, acknowledge, name, describe, classify.
(ANT.) ignore, forget, overlook, renounce, disown, repudiate.

identity (SYN.) uniqueness, personality, character, individuality.

ideology (SYN.) credo, principles, belief.

idiom (SYN.) language, speech, vernacular, lingo, dialect, jargon, slang, tongue.
(ANT.) babble, gibberish, drivel, nonsense.

idiot (SYN.) buffoon, harlequin, dolt, jester, dunce, blockhead, imbecile, numbskull, simpleton, oaf, nincompoop, fool, moron.
(ANT.) philosopher, genius, scholar, sage.

idiotic (SYN.) asinine, absurd, brainless, irrational, crazy, nonsensical, senseless, preposterous, silly, ridiculous, simple, stupid, foolish, inane, moronic, halfwitted, simpleminded, dimwitted.
(ANT.) prudent, wise, sagacious, judicious, sane, intelligent, bright, brilliant, smart.

idle (SYN.) unemployed, dormant, lazy, inactive, unoccupied, indolent, slothful, inert, unused.
(ANT.) occupied, working, employed, active, industrious, busy, engaged.

idol (SYN.) unoccupied, unused, inactive, unemployed.

idolize (SYN.) revere, worship, adore.
(ANT.) despise.

ignoble (SYN.) dishonorable, ignominious, lowly, menial vile, sordid, vulgar, abject, base, despicable, groveling, mean, vile.

(ANT.) righteous, lofty, honored, esteemed, noble, exalted.

ignominious (SYN.) contemptible, abject, despicable, groveling, dishonorable, ignoble, lowly, low, menial, mean, sordid, servile, vulgar, vile.
(ANT.) lofty, noble, esteemed, righteous, exalted.

ignorant (SYN.) uneducated, untaught, uncultured, illiterate, uninformed, unlearned, unlettered, untrained, unaware, unmindful.
(ANT.) cultured, literate, educated, erudite, informed, cultivated, schooled, learned, lettered.

ignore (SYN.) omit, slight, disregard, overlook, neglect, skip.
(ANT.) notice, regard, include.

ill (SYN.) diseased, ailing, indisposed, morbid, infirm, unwell, unhealthy, sick, unhealthy.
(ANT.) robust, strong, healthy, well, sound, fit.

ill-use (SYN.) defame, revile, vilify, misemploy, disparage, abuse, traduce, asperse, misapply, misuse.
(ANT.) protect, cherish, respect, honor, praise.

ill-advised (SYN.) injudicious, ill-considered, imprudent.

ill-at-ease (SYN.) nervous, uncomfortable, uneasy.
(ANT.) comfortable.

illegal (SYN.) prohibited, unlawful, criminal, illicit, outlawed, illegitimate.
(ANT.) permitted, lawful, honest, legal, legitimate.

illiberal (SYN.) fanatical, bigoted, intolerant, narrow-minded, dogmatic, prejudiced.
(ANT.) progressive, liberal radical.

illicit (SYN.) illegitimate, criminal, outlawed, unlawful, prohibited, illegal, unauthorized.
(ANT.) legal, honest, permitted, lawful, licit.

ill-natured (SYN.) crabby, cranky, grouchy, cross, irascible.

illness (SYN.) complaint, infirmity, ailment, disorder, malady, sickness.
(ANT.) healthiness, health, soundness, vigor.

illogical (SYN.) absurd, irrational, preposterous.

ill-tempered (SYN.) crabby, cranky,

cross, grouchy.

ill-treated *(SYN.)* harmed, mistreated, abused, maltreated.

illuminate *(SYN.)* enlighten, clarify, irradiate, illustrate, light, lighten, explain, interpret, clarify, elucidate, brighten, illumine.
(ANT.) obscure, confuse, darken, obfuscate, shadow, complicate.

illusion *(SYN.)* hallucination, vision, phantom, delusion, fantasy, dream, mirage.
(ANT.) substance, actuality, reality.

illusive *(SYN.)* fallacious, delusive, false, specious, misleading, deceptive, deceitful, delusory.
(ANT.) real, truthful, authentic, genuine, honest.

illustrate *(SYN.)* decorate, illuminate, adorn, show, picture, embellish, demonstrate.

illustration *(SYN.)* likeness, painting, picture, print, scene, sketch, view, engraving, drawing, panorama, photograph, cinema, etching, effigy, film, appearance, portrayal, resemblance, image, portrait.

illustrator *(SYN.)* painter, artist.

illustrious *(SYN.)* prominent, eminent, renowned, famed, great, vital, elevated, majestic, noble, excellent, dignified, big, gigantic, enormous, immense, huge, vast, large, countless, numerous, celebrated, critical, momentous, august, weighty, grand, fine, magnificent, serious, important.
(ANT.) menial, common, minute, diminutive, small, obscure, ordinary, little.

image *(SYN.)* reflection, likeness, idea, representation, notion, picture, conception.

imaginary *(SYN.)* fanciful, fantastic, unreal, whimsical.
(ANT.) actual, real.

imagination *(SYN.)* creation, invention, fancy, notion, conception, fantasy, idea.

imaginative *(SYN.)* inventive, poetical, fanciful, clever, creative, mystical, visionary.
(ANT.) prosaic, dull, unromantic, literal.

imagine *(SYN.)* assume, surmise, suppose, conceive, dream, pretend, conjecture, fancy, opine, envisage, think, envision, guess, picture.

imbecile *(SYN.)* idiot, numbskull, simpleton, blockhead, dolt, dunce, jester, buffoon, harlequin, nincompoop, clown, fool, oaf.
(ANT.) scholar, genius, philosopher, sage.

imbibe *(SYN.)* absorb, consume, assimilate, engulf, engage, occupy, engross.
(ANT.) dispense, exude, discharge, emit.

imitate *(SYN.)* duplicate, mimic, follow, reproduce, mock, ape, counterfeit, copy, simulate, impersonate.
(ANT.) invent, distort, alter, diverge.

imitation *(SYN.)* replica, reproduction copy, duplicate, facsimile, transcript, exemplar.
(ANT.) prototype, original.

immaculate *(SYN.)* clean, spotless, unblemished.
(ANT.) dirty.

immature *(SYN.)* young, boyish, childish, youthful, childlike, puerile, girlish, juvenile, callow.
(ANT.) old, senile, aged, elderly, mature.

immeasurable *(SYN.)* unlimited, endless, eternal, immense, interminable, unbounded, immeasurable, boundless, illimitable, infinite.
(ANT.) limited, confined, bounded, finite, circumscribed.

immediate *(SYN.)* present, instant, instantaneous, near, close, next, prompt, direct.
(ANT.) distant, future.

immediately *(SYN.)* now, presently, instantly, promptly, straightway, directly, instantaneously, forthwith.
(ANT.) sometime, hereafter, later, shortly, distantly.

immense *(SYN.)* enormous, large, gigantic, huge, colossal, elephantine, great, gargantuan, vast.
(ANT.) small, diminutive, little, minuscule, minute, petit, tiny.

immensity *(SYN.)* hugeness, enormousness, vastness.

immerse *(SYN.)* plunge, dip, dunk, sink, submerge, engage, absorb, engross, douse.
(ANT.) uplift, elevate, recover.

immigration *(SYN.)* settlement, colonization.
(ANT.) exodus, emigration.

imminent *(SYN.)* nigh, impending, overhanging, approaching, menacing, threatening.

(ANT.) retreating, afar, distant, improbable, remote.

immoderation (SYN.) profusion, surplus, extravagance, excess, intemperance, superabundance.

(ANT.) lack, want, deficiency, dearth, paucity.

immoral (SYN.) sinful, wicked, corrupt, bad, indecent, profligate, unprincipled, antisocial, dissolute.

(ANT.) pure, high-minded, chaste, virtuous, noble.

immortal (SYN.) infinite, eternal, timeless, undying, perpetual, ceaseless, endless, deathless, everlasting.

(ANT.) mortal, transient, finite, ephemeral, temporal.

immune (SYN.) easy, open, autonomous, unobstructed, free, emancipated, clear, independent, unrestricted, exempt, liberated, familiar, loose, unconfined, frank, unfastened, careless, freed.

(ANT.) confined, impeded, restricted, subject.

immutable (SYN.) constant, faithful, invariant, persistent, unchanging, unalterable, continual, ceaseless, enduring, fixed, permanent, abiding, perpetual, unwavering.

(ANT.) mutable, vacillating, wavering, fickle.

impact (SYN.) striking, contact, collision.

impair (SYN.) harm, injure, spoil, deface, destroy, hurt, damage, mar.

(ANT.) repair, mend, ameliorate, enhance, benefit.

impart (SYN.) convey, disclose, inform, tell, reveal, transmit, notify, confer, divulge, communicate, relate.

(ANT.) hide, withhold, conceal.

impartial (SYN.) unbiased, just, honest, fair, reasonable, equitable.

(ANT.) fraudulent, dishonorable, partial.

impartiality (SYN.) indifference, unconcern, impartiality, neutrality, disinterestedness, apathy, insensibility.

(ANT.) passion, ardor, fervor, affection.

impasse (SYN.) standstill, deadlock, stalemate.

impede (SYN.) hamper, hinder, retard, thwart, check, encumber, interrupt, bar, clog, delay, obstruct, block, frustrate, restrain, stop.

(ANT.) assist, pro te, help, advance, further.

impediment (SYN.) barrier, bar, block, difficulty, check, hindrance, snag, obstruction.

(ANT.) assistance, help, aid, encouragement.

impel (SYN.) oblige, enforce, drive, coerce, force, constrain.

(ANT.) induce, prevent, convince, persuade.

impending (SYN.) imminent, nigh, threatening, overhanging, approaching, menacing.

(ANT.) remote, improbable, afar, distant, retreating.

impenetrable (SYN) rigid, tough, harsh, strict, unfeeling, rigorous, intricate, arduous, penetrable, cruel, difficult, severe, stern, firm, hard, compact.

(ANT.) soft, simple, gentle, tender, brittle, fluid, flabby, elastic, lenient, easy, effortless.

imperative (SYN.) critical, instant, important, necessary, serious, urgent, cogent, compelling, crucial, pressing, impelling, importunate, exigent, insistent.

(ANT.) trivial, insignificant, unimportant, petty.

imperceptible (SYN.) invisible, indiscernible, unseen, indistinguishable.

(ANT.) seen, evident, visible, perceptible.

imperfection (SYN.) flaw, shortcoming, vice, defect, blemish, failure, mistake, omission, fault, error.

(ANT.) correctness, perfection, completeness.

imperil (SYN.) jeopardize, risk, endanger, hazard, risk.

(ANT.) guard, insure.

impersonal (SYN.) objective, detached, disinterested.

(ANT.) personal.

impersonate (SYN.) mock, simulate, imitate, ape, counterfeit, mimic, copy, duplicate.

(ANT.) alter, invent, diverge, distort.

impertinence (SYN) impudence, presumption, sauciness, effrontery, audacity, rudeness, assurance, boldness, insolence.

(ANT.) truckling, politeness, diffidence, subserviency.

impertinent (SYN.) rude, offensive, insolent, disrespectful, arrogant, brazen, impudent, insulting, contemptuous, abusive.

(ANT.) polite, respectful, considerate, courteous.

impetuous (SYN.) rash, heedless, quick, hasty, careless, passionate, impulsive.

(ANT.) cautious, reasoning, careful, prudent, thoughtful, calculating.

implicate (SYN.) reproach, accuse, blame, involve, upbraid, condemn, incriminate, rebuke, censure.

(ANT.) exonerate, absolve, acquit.

implore (SYN.) beg, pray, request, solicit, crave, entreat, beseech, ask, importune, supplicate, adjure, appeal, petition.

(ANT.) give, cede, bestow, favor, grant.

imply (SYN.) mean, involve, suggest, connote, hint, mention, indicate, insinuate, signify.

(ANT.) state, assert, declare, express.

impolite (SYN.) rude, unpolished, impudent, boorish, blunt, discourteous, rough, saucy, surly, savage, insolent, gruff, uncivil, coarse, ignorant, crude, illiterate, raw, primitive, vulgar, untaught.

(ANT.) genteel, courteous, courtly, dignified, polite, stately, noble, civil.

import (SYN.) influence, significance, stress, emphasis, importance, value, weight.

(ANT.) triviality, insignificance.

important (SYN.) critical, grave, influential, momentous, well-known, pressing, relevant, prominent, primary, essential, weighty, material, considerable, famous, principle, famed, sequential, notable, significant, illustrious, decisive.

(ANT.) unimportant, trifling, petty, trivial, insignificant, secondary, anonymous, irrelevant.

impose (SYN.) levy, require, demand.

imposing (SYN.) lofty, noble, majestic, magnificent, august, dignified, grandiose, high, grand, impressive, pompous, stately.

(ANT.) ordinary, undignified, humble, common, lowly.

imposition (SYN.) load, onus, burden.

impossible (SYN.) preposterous.

impregnable (SYN.) safe, invulnerable, secure, unassailable.

(ANT.) vulnerable.

impress (SYN.) awe, emboss, affect,

mark, imprint, indent, influence.

impression (SYN.) influence, indentation, feeling, opinion, mark, effect, depression, guess, thought, belief, dent, sensibility.

(ANT.) fact, insensibility.

impressive (SYN.) arresting, moving, remarkable, splendid, thrilling, striking, majestic, grandiose, imposing, commanding, affecting, exciting, touching, stirring.

(ANT.) regular, unimpressive, commonplace.

impromptu (SYN.) casual, unprepared, offhand, extemporaneous.

improper (SYN.) unfit, unsuitable, inappropriate, naughty, indecent, unbecoming.

(ANT.) fitting, proper, appropriate.

improve (SYN.) better, reform, refine, ameliorate, amend, help, upgrade, rectify.

(ANT.) debase, vitiate, impair, corrupt, damage.

improvement (SYN) growth, advance, progress, betterment, development, advancement, progression.

(ANT.) relapse, regression, decline, retrogression, delay.

imprudent (SYN.) indiscreet, thoughtless, desultory, lax, neglectful, remiss, careless, inattentive, heedless, inconsiderate, reckless, ill-advised, irresponsible, unconcerned.

(ANT.) careful, meticulous, accurate.

impudence (SYN.) boldness, insolence, rudeness, sauciness, assurance, effrontery, impertinence, presumption, audacity.

(ANT.) politeness, truckling, subserviency, diffidence.

impudent (SYN.) forward, rude, abrupt, prominent, striking, bold, fresh, impertinent, insolent, pushy, insulting, brazen.

(ANT.) bashful, flinching, polite, courteous, cowardly, retiring, timid.

impulse (SYN.) hunch, whim, fancy, urge, caprice, surge, pulse.

impulsive (SYN.) passionate, rash, spontaneous, heedless, careless, hasty, quick, impetuous.

(ANT.) reasoning, calculating, careful, prudent, cautious.

impure (SYN.) dishonest, spoiled, tainted, contaminated, debased, corrupt, profligate, unsound, putrid, corrupted, crooked, depraved, vitiated, venal.

imputation *(SYN.)* diary, incrimination, arraignment, indictment.
(ANT.) *exoneration, pardon, exculpation.*

inability *(SYN.)* incompetence, incapacity, handicap, disability, impotence, weakness.
(ANT.) *power, strength, ability, capability.*

inaccurate *(SYN.)* false, incorrect, mistaken, untrue, askew, wrong, awry, erroneous, fallacious, imprecise, faulty, amiss.
(ANT.) *right, accurate, true, correct.*

inactive *(SYN.)* lazy, unemployed, indolent, motionless, still, inert, dormant, idle, unoccupied.
(ANT.) *employed, working, active, industrious, occupied.*

inadequate *(SYN.)* insufficient, lacking, short, incompléte, defective, scanty.
(ANT.) *satisfactory, enough, adequate, ample, sufficient.*

inadvertent *(SYN.)* careless, negligent, unthinking, thoughtless.

inane *(SYN.)* trite, insipid, banal, absurd, silly, commonplace, vapid, foolish, stupid, hackneyed.
(ANT.) *stimulating, novel, fresh, original, striking.*

inanimate *(SYN.)* deceased, spiritless, lifeless, gone, dull, mineral, departed, dead, insensible, vegetable, unconscious.
(ANT.) *living, stirring, alive, animate.*

inattentive *(SYN.)* absent-minded, distracted, abstracted, preoccupied.
(ANT.) *watchful, attending, attentive.*

inaugurate *(SYN.)* commence, begin, open, originate, start, arise, launch, enter, initiate.
(ANT.) *end, terminate, close, complete, finish.*

incense *(SYN.)* anger, enrage, infuriate.

incentive *(SYN.)* impulse, stimulus, inducement, encouragement.
(ANT.) *discouragement.*

inception *(SYN.)* origin, start, source, opening, beginning, outset, commencement.
(ANT.) *end, termination, close, completion, consummation.*

incessant *(SYN.)* perennial, uninterrupted, continual, ceaseless, continuous, unremitting, eternal, constant, unceasing, unending, perpetual, everlasting.
(ANT.) *rare, occasional, periodic, interrupted.*

incident *(SYN.)* happening, situation, occurrence, circumstance, condition, event, fact.

incidental *(SYN.)* casual, contingent, trivial, undesigned, chance, fortuitous, accidental, secondary, unimportant, unintended.
(ANT.) *intended, fundamental, planned, calculated, willed, decreed.*

incidentally *(SYN.)* by the way.

incinerate *(SYN.)* sear, char, blaze, scald, singe, consume, scorch, burn.
(ANT.) *quench, put out, extinguish.*

incisive *(SYN.)* neat, succinct, terse, brief, compact, condensed, neat, summary, concise.
(ANT.) *wordy, prolix, verbose, lengthy.*

incite *(SYN.)* goad, provoke, urge, arouse, encourage, cause, stimulate, induce, instigate, foment.
(ANT.) *quiet, bore, pacify, soothe.*

inclination *(SYN.)* bent, preference, desire, slope, affection, bent, bias, disposition, bending, penchant, incline, attachment, predisposition, predication, tendency, prejudice, slant, lean, leaning.
(ANT.) *nonchalance, apathy, distaste, aversion, reluctance, disinclination, uprightness, repugnance.*

incline *(SYN.)* slope, nod, lean.
(ANT.) *straighten.*

include *(SYN.)* contain, hold, accommodate, embody, encompass, involve, comprise, embrace.
(ANT.) *omit, exclude, discharge.*

income *(SYN.)* earnings, salary, wages, revenue, pay, return, receipts.

incomparable *(SYN.)* peerless, matchless, unequaled.

incompetency *(SYN.)* inability, weakness, handicap, impotence, disability, incapacity.
(ANT.) *strength, ability, power, capability.*

incomprehensible *(SYN.)* unintelligible, indecipherable.

inconceivable *(SYN.)* unbelievable, unimaginable, impossible.
(ANT.) *possible, believable.*

incongruous *(SYN.)* inconsistent, contrary, incompatible, irreconcilable, contradictory, unsteady, incongruous, wavering, paradoxical, vacillating, discrepant, illogical.
(ANT.) consistent, compatible, correspondent.

inconsiderate *(SYN.)* unthinking, careless, unthoughtful, unmindful.
(ANT.) logical, consistent.

inconsistency *(SYN)* discord, variance, contention, conflict, controversy, interference.
(ANT.) harmony, concord, amity, consonance.

inconsistent *(SYN.)* fickle, wavering, variable, changeable, contrary, unstable, illogical, contradictory, irreconcilable, discrepant, paradoxical, incompatible, self-contradictory, incongruous, unsteady, fitful, shifting.
(ANT.) unchanging, steady, logical, stable, uniform, constant.

inconspicuous *(SYN.)* retiring, unnoticed, unostentatious.
(ANT.) obvious, conspicuous.

inconstant *(SYN.)* fickle, shifting, changeable, fitful, vacillating, unstable, wavering.
(ANT.) stable, constant, steady, uniform, unchanging.

inconvenient *(SYN.)* awkward, inappropriate, untimely, troublesome.
(ANT.) handy, convenient.

incorrect *(SYN.)* mistaken, wrong, erroneous, inaccurate.
(ANT.) proper, accurate, suitable.

increase *(SYN.)* amplify, enlarge, grow, magnify, multiply, augment, enhance, expand, intensify, swell, raise, greaten, prolong, broaden, lengthen, expansion, accrue, extend, heighten.
(ANT.) diminish, reduce, atrophy, shrink, shrinkage, decrease, lessening, lessen, contract.

incredible *(SYN.)* improbable, unbelievable.
(ANT.) plausible, credible, believable.

incriminate *(SYN.)* charge, accuse, indict, arraign, censure.
(ANT.) release, exonerate, acquit, absolve, vindicate.

incrimination *(SYN.)* imputation, indictment, accusation, charge, arraignment.

(ANT.) exoneration, pardon, exculpation.

indebted *(SYN.)* obliged, grateful, beholden, thankful, appreciative.
(ANT.) unappreciative, thankless.

indecent *(SYN.)* impure, obscene, pornographic, coarse, dirty, filthy, smutty, gross, disgusting.
(ANT.) modest, refined, decent, pure.

indeed *(SYN.)* truthfully, really, honestly, surely.

indefinite *(SYN.)* unsure, uncertain, vague, confused, unsettled, confusing.
(ANT.) decided, definite, equivocal.

independence *(SYN.)* liberation, privilege, freedom, immunity, familiarity, liberty, exemption, license.
(ANT.) necessity, constraint, compulsion, reliance, dependence, bondage, servitude.

independent *(SYN.)* free, unrestrained, voluntary, autonomous, self-reliant, uncontrolled, unrestricted.
(ANT.) enslaved, contingent, dependent, restricted.

indestructible *(SYN.)* enduring, lasting, permanent, unchangeable, abiding, constant, fixed, stable, changeless.
(ANT.) unstable, temporary, transitory, ephemeral.

indicate *(SYN.)* imply, denote, signify, specify, intimate, designate, symbolize, show, manifest, disclose, mean, reveal.
(ANT.) mislead, falsify, distract, conceal, falsify.

indication *(SYN.)* proof, emblem, omen, sign, symbol, token, mark, portent, gesture, signal.

indict *(SYN.)* charge, accuse, incriminate, censure, arraign.
(ANT.) acquit, vindicate, absolve, exonerate.

indictment *(SYN.)* incrimination, arraignment, imputation, charge.
(ANT.) pardon, exoneration, exculpation.

indifference *(SYN.)* unconcern, apathy, impartiality, disinterestedness, insensibility, neutrality.
(ANT.) ardor, passion, affection, fervor.

indifferent *(SYN.)* uncaring, insensitive, cool, unconcerned.
(ANT.) caring, concerned, earnest.

indigence *(SYN.)* necessity, destitution, poverty, want, need, privation, penury.
(ANT.) wealth, abundance, plenty,

riches, affluence.

indigenous *(SYN.)* inborn, native, inherent, domestic, aboriginal, plenty, endemic, innate, natural.

indigent *(SYN.)* wishing, covetous, demanding, lacking, requiring, wanting, claiming, craving.

indignant *(SYN.)* irritated, irate, angry, aroused, exasperated.

(ANT.) calm, serene, content.

indignation *(SYN.)* ire, petulance, passion, choler, anger, wrath, temper, irritation, exasperation, animosity, resentment, rage.

(ANT.) self-control, peace, forbearance, patience.

indignity *(SYN.)* insolence, insult, abuse, affront, offense.

(ANT.) homage, apology, salutation.

indirect *(SYN.)* winding, crooked, devious, roundabout, cunning, tricky, tortuous, circuitous, distorted, erratic, swerving.

(ANT.) straightforward, direct, straight, honest.

indiscretion *(SYN.)* imprudence, folly, absurdity, extravagance.

(ANT.) prudence, sense, wisdom, reasonableness, judgment.

indispensable *(SYN.)* necessary, fundamental, basic, essential, important, intrinsic, vital.

(ANT.) optional, expendable, peripheral, extrinsic.

indistinct *(SYN.)* cloudy, dark, mysterious, vague, blurry, ambiguous, cryptic, dim, obscure, enigmatic, abstruse, hazy, blurred, unintelligible.

(ANT.) clear, lucid, bright, distinct.

indistinguishable *(SYN.)* identical, like, coincident, equal, same, equivalent.

(ANT.) dissimilar, opposed, contrary, disparate, distinct.

individual *(SYN.)* singular, specific, unique, distinctive, single, particular, undivided, human, apart, marked, person, different, special, separate.

(ANT.) universal, common, general, ordinary.

individuality *(SYN.)* symbol, description, mark, kind, character, repute, class, standing, sort, nature, disposition, reputation, sign.

indolent *(SYN.)* slothful, lazy, idle, inactive, slow, sluggish, torpid, supine, inert.

(ANT.) diligent, active, assiduous, vigorous, zestful, alert.

indomitable *(SYN.)* insurmountable, unconquerable, invulnerable, impregnable, unassailable.

(ANT.) weak, puny, powerless, vulnerable.

induce *(SYN.)* evoke, cause, influence, persuade, effect, make, originate, prompt, incite, create.

inducement *(SYN.)* incentive, motive, purpose, stimulus, reason, impulse, cause, principle, spur, incitement.

(ANT.) result, attempt, action, effort, deed.

induct *(SYN.)* instate, establish, install.

(ANT.) eject, oust.

indulge *(SYN.)* humor, satisfy, gratify.

indulgent *(SYN.)* obliging, pampering, tolerant, easy.

indurate *(SYN.)* impenitent, hard, insensible, tough, obdurate, callous, unfeeling.

(ANT.) soft, compassionate, tender, sensitive.

industrious *(SYN.)* hard-working, perseverant, busy, active, diligent, assiduous, careful, patient.

(ANT.) unconcerned, indifferent, lethargic, careless, apathetic, lazy, indolent, shiftless.

inebriated *(SYN.)* drunk, tight, drunken, intoxicated, tipsy.

(ANT.) sober, clearheaded, temperate.

ineffective *(SYN.)* pliant, tender, vague, wavering, defenseless, weak, inadequate, poor, irresolute, frail, decrepit, delicate, vacillating, assailable, exposed, vulnerable.

(ANT.) sturdy, robust, strong, potent, powerful.

inept *(SYN.)* clumsy, awkward, improper, inappropriate.

(ANT.) adroit, dexterous, adept, appropriate, proper, apt, fitting.

inequity *(SYN.)* wrong, injustice, unfairness, grievance, injury.

(ANT.) righteousness, lawfulness, equity, justice.

inert *(SYN.)* lazy, dormant, slothful, inactive, idle, indolent, motionless, unmoving, fixed, static.

(ANT.) working, active, industrious, occupied.

inertia *(SYN.)* indolence, torpidity, idle-

ness, slothfulness, indolence, sluggishness, supineness.
(ANT.) assiduousness, activity, alertness,
diligence.
inevitable (SYN.) definite, fixed, positive,
sure, undeniable, indubitable, certain,
assured, unquestionable, secure.
(ANT.) uncertain, probable, doubtful,
questionable.
inexpensive (SYN.) low-priced, cheap, inferior, mean, beggarly, common, poor,
shabby, modest, economical.
(ANT.) expensive, costly, dear.
inexperienced (SYN.) naive, untrained,
uninformed, green.
(ANT.) experienced, skilled, sophisticated, trained, seasoned.
inexplicable (SYN.) hidden, mysterious,
obscure, secret, dark, cryptic, enigmatical, incomprehensible, occult, recondite,
inscrutable, dim.
(ANT.) plain, simple, clear, obvious, explained.
infamous (SYN.) shocking, shameful,
scandalous.
infantile (SYN.) babyish, naive, immature, childish.
(ANT.) mature, grownup, adult.
infect (SYN.) pollute, poison, contaminate, defile, sully, taint.
(ANT.) purify, disinfect.
infection (SYN.) virus, poison, ailment,
disease, pollution, pest, germ, taint,
contamination, contagion.
infectious (SYN.) contagious, virulent,
catching, communicable, pestilential,
transferable.
(ANT.) noncommunicable, hygienic,
healthful.
infer (SYN.) understand, deduce, extract.
inference (SYN.) consequence, result,
conclusion, corollary, judgment, deduction.
(ANT.) preconception, foreknowledge,
assumption, presupposition.
inferior (SYN.) secondary, lower, poorer,
minor, subordinate, mediocre.
(ANT.) greater, superior, better, higher.
infinite (SYN.) immeasurable, interminable, unlimited, unbounded, eternal,
boundless, illimitable, immense, endless, vast, innumerable, numberless,
limitless.
(ANT.) confined, limited, bounded, circumscribed, finite.

infinitesimal (SYN.) minute, microscopic, tiny, submicroscopic.
(ANT.) gigantic, huge, enormous.
infirm (SYN.) feeble, impaired, decrepit,
forceless, languid, puny, powerless,
enervated, weak, exhausted.
(ANT.) stout, vigorous, forceful, lusty,
strong.
infirmity (SYN.) disease, illness, malady,
ailment, sickness, disorder, complaint.
(ANT.) soundness, health, vigor, healthiness.
inflame (SYN.) fire, incite, excite, arouse.
(ANT.) soothe, calm.
inflammation (SYN.) infection, sore-
ness, irritation.
inflammatory (SYN.) instigating, inciting,
provocative.
inflate (SYN.) expand, swell, distend.
(ANT.) collapse, deflate.
inflexible (SYN.) firm, stubborn,
headstrong, immovable, unyielding, uncompromising, dogged, contumacious,
determined, obstinate, rigid, unbending,
unyielding, steadfast.
(ANT.) submissive, compliant, docile,
amenable, yielding, flexible, giving, elastic.
inflict (SYN.) deliver, deal, give, impose,
apply.
influence (SYN.) weight, control, effect,
sway.
influenced (SYN.) sway, affect, bias, control, actuate, impel, stir, incite.
influential (SYN.) important, weighty,
prominent, significant, critical, decisive,
momentous, relevant, material, pressing, consequential, grave.
(ANT.) petty, irrelevant, mean, trivial,
insignificant.
inform (SYN.) apprise, instruct, tell,
notify, advise, acquaint, enlighten, impart, warn, teach, advise, relate.
(ANT.) delude, mislead, distract, conceal.
informal (SYN.) simple, easy, natural,
unofficial, familiar.
(ANT.) formal, distant, reserved, proper.
informality (SYN.) friendship, frankness,
liberty, acquaintance, sociability, intimacy, unreserved.
(ANT.) presumption, constraint, reserve,
distance, haughtiness.
information (SYN.) knowledge, data, intelligence, facts.

informative *(SYN.)* educational, enlightening, instructive.

informer *(SYN.)* tattler, traitor, betrayer.

infrequent *(SYN.)* unusual, rare, occasional, strange.

(ANT.) commonplace, abundant, usual, ordinary, customary, frequent, numerous.

ingenious *(SYN.)* clever, skillful, talented, adroit, dexterous, quick-witted, bright, smart, witty, sharp, apt, resourceful, imaginative, inventive, creative.

(ANT.) dull, slow, awkward, bungling, unskilled, stupid.

ingenuity *(SYN.)* cunning, inventiveness, resourcefulness, aptitude, faculty, cleverness, ingenuousness.

(ANT.) ineptitude, clumsiness, dullness, stupidity.

ingenuous *(SYN.)* open, sincere, honest, candid, straightforward, plain, frank, truthful, free, naive, simple, innocent, unsophisticated.

(ANT.) scheming, sly, contrived, wily.

ingredient *(SYN.)* component, element, constituent.

inhabit *(SYN.)* fill, possess, absorb, dwell, occupy, live.

(ANT.) relinquish, abandon, release.

inherent *(SYN.)* innate, native, congenital, inherent, intrinsic, inborn, inbred, natural, real.

(ANT.) extraneous, acquired, external, extrinsic.

inhibit *(SYN.)* curb, constrain, hold back, restrain, bridle, hinder, repress, suppress, stop, limit.

(ANT.) loosen, aid, incite, encourage.

inhuman *(SYN.)* merciless, cruel, brutal, ferocious, savage, ruthless, malignant, barbarous, barbaric, bestial.

(ANT.) kind, benevolent, forbearing, gentle, compassionate, merciful, humane, humane.

inimical *(SYN.)* hostile, warlike, adverse, antagonistic, opposed, unfriendly.

(ANT.) favorable, amicable, cordial.

iniquitous *(SYN.)* baleful, immoral, pernicious, sinful, wicked, base, bad, evil, noxious, unsound, villainous, unwholesome.

(ANT.) moral, good, excellent, honorable, reputable.

iniquity *(SYN.)* injustice, wrong, grievance, unfairness, injury.

(ANT.) lawful, equity, righteousness, justice.

initial *(SYN.)* original, first, prime, beginning, earliest, pristine, chief, primeval, primary, foremost, basic, elementary.

(ANT.) latest, subordinate, last, least, hindmost, final, terminal.

initiate *(SYN.)* institute, enter, arise, inaugurate, commence, originate, start, open, begin.

(ANT.) terminate, complete, end, finish, close, stop.

initiative *(SYN.)* enthusiasm, energy, vigor, enterprise.

injure *(SYN.)* harm, wound, abuse, dishonor, damage, hurt, impair, spoil, disfigure, affront, insult, mar.

(ANT.) praise, ameliorate, help, preserve, compliment, benefit.

injurious *(SYN.)* detrimental, harmful, mischievous, damaging, hurtful, deleterious, harmful, destructive.

(ANT.) profitable, helpful, advantageous, salutary, beneficial, useful.

injury *(SYN.)* harm, detriment, damage, injustice, wrong, prejudice, grievance, mischief.

(ANT.) repair, benefit, improvement.

injustice *(SYN.)* unfairness, grievance, iniquity, wrong, injury.

(ANT.) righteousness, justice, equity, lawfulness.

inmate *(SYN.)* patient, prisoner.

inn *(SYN.)* motel, lodge, hotel.

innate *(SYN.)* native, inherent, congenital, innate, real, inborn, natural, intrinsic, inbred.

(ANT.) extraneous, acquired, external, extrinsic.

innocent *(SYN.)* pure, sinless, blameless, innocuous, lawful, naive, faultless, virtuous, not guilty.

(ANT.) guilty, corrupt, sinful, culpable, sophisticated, wise, worldly.

innocuous *(SYN.)* naive, pure, innocent, blameless, virtuous, lawful, faultless, innocuous, sinless.

(ANT.) sinful, corrupt, unrighteous, culpable, guilty.

inquire *(SYN.)* ask, solicit, invite, demand, claim, entreat, interrogate, query, beg, request, question, investigate, examine.

(ANT.) dictate, insist, reply, command,

order.

inquiring *(SYN.)* prying, searching, curious, inquisitive, peering, snoopy, peeping, meddling, interrogative.
(ANT.) unconcerned, indifferent, uninterested, incurious.

inquiry *(SYN.)* investigation, quest, research, examination, interrogation, exploration, query, question, scrutiny, study.
(ANT.) inattention, inactivity, disregard, negligence.

inquisitive *(SYN.)* meddling, peeping, nosy, interrogative, peering, searching, prying, snoopy, inquiring, curious.
(ANT.) unconcerned, indifferent, incurious, uninterested.

insane *(SYN.)* deranged, mad, foolish, idiotic, demented, crazy, delirious, maniacal, lunatic.
(ANT.) sane, rational, reasonable, sound, sensible, coherent.

insanity *(SYN.)* delirium, aberration, dementia, psychosis, lunacy, madness, frenzy, mania, craziness, derangement.
(ANT.) stability, rationality, sanity.

insecure *(SYN.)* uneasy, nervous, uncertain, shaky.
(ANT.) secure.

insensitive *(SYN.)* unfeeling, impenitent, callous, hard, indurate, obdurate, tough.
(ANT.) soft, compassionate, tender, sensitive.

insight *(SYN.)* intuition, acumen, penetration, discernment, perspicuity.
(ANT.) obtuseness.

insignificant *(SYN.)* trivial, paltry, petty, small, frivolous, unimportant, insignificant, trifling.
(ANT.) momentous, serious, important, weighty.

insincere *(SYN.)* false, dishonest, deceitful.
(ANT.) honest, sincere.

insinuate *(SYN.)* imply, mean, suggest, connote, signify, involve.
(ANT.) express, state, assert.

insipid *(SYN.)* tasteless, dull, stale, flat, vapid.
(ANT.) racy, tasty, savory, exciting.

insist *(SYN.)* command, demand, require.

insolence *(SYN.)* boldness, presumption, sauciness, effrontery, audacity, assurance, impertinence, rudeness.

(ANT.) politeness, truckling, diffidence, subserviency.

insolent *(SYN.)* arrogant, impertinent, insulting, rude, brazen, contemptuous, abusive, offensive, disrespectful.
(ANT.) respectful, courteous, polite, considerate.

inspect *(SYN.)* observe, discern, eye, behold, glance, scan, stare, survey, view, regard, see, watch, witness, examine, investigate.
(ANT.) overlook, miss, avert, hide.

inspection *(SYN.)* examination, retrospect, survey, revision, reconsideration, critique, criticism, review.

inspiration *(SYN.)* creativity, aptitude, genius, originality, ability, faculty, sagacity, talent, proficient, master, gift, adept, intellectual, thought, impulse, idea, notion, hunch.
(ANT.) dullard, moron, shallowness, ineptitude, stupidity, obtuseness, dolt.

install *(SYN.)* establish.

instance *(SYN.)* occasion, illustration, occurrence, example, case.

instant *(SYN.)* flash, moment.

instantaneous *(SYN.)* hasty, sudden unexpected, rapid, abrupt, immediate.
(ANT.) slowly, anticipated, gradual.

instantly *(SYN.)* now, presently, directly, forthwith, immediately, rapidly straightaway, at once, instantaneously.
(ANT.) sometime, distantly, hereafter, later, shortly.

instinct *(SYN.)* intuition, feeling.

instinctive *(SYN.)* offhand, voluntary, willing, spontaneous, automatic, impulsive, extemporaneous.
(ANT.) rehearsed, planned, compulsory, prepared, forced.

institute *(SYN.)* ordain, establish, raise, form, organize, sanction, fix, found, launch, begin, initiate.
(ANT.) overthrow, upset, demolish, abolish, unsettle.

instruct *(SYN.)* teach, tutor, educate, inform, school, instill, train, inculcate, drill.
(ANT.) misinform, misguide.

instruction *(SYN.)* advise, warning, information, exhortation, notification, admonition, caution, recommendation, counsel, suggestion, teaching, training, education, command, order.

instrument *(SYN.)* channel, device, uten-

sil, tool, agent, apparatus, means, vehicle, medium, agent, implement.
(ANT.) obstruction, hindrance, preventive, impediment.

insubordinate *(SYN.)* rebellious, unruly, defiant, disorderly, disobedient, undutiful, refractory, intractable, mutinous.
(ANT.) obedient, compliant, submissive, dutiful.

insufficient *(SYN.)* limited, lacking, deficient, short, inadequate.
(ANT.) ample, protracted, abundant, big, extended.

insulation *(SYN.)* quarantine, segregation, seclusion, withdrawal, isolation, loneliness, alienation, solitude.
(ANT.) union, communion, association, fellowship, connection.

insult *(SYN.)* insolence, offense, abuse, dishonor, affront, insult, indignity, offend, humiliate, outrage.
(ANT.) compliment, homage, apology, salutation, flatter, praise.

integrated *(SYN.)* mingled, mixed, combined, interspersed, desegregated, nonsectarian, interracial.
(ANT.) separated, divided, segregated.

integrity *(SYN.)* honesty, openness, trustworthiness, fairness, candor, justice, rectitude, sincerity, uprightness, soundness, wholeness, honor, principle, virtue.
(ANT.) fraud, deceit, cheating, trickery, dishonesty.

intellect *(SYN.)* understanding, judgment.

intellectual *(SYN.)* intelligent.

intelligence *(SYN.)* reason, sense, intellect, understanding, mind, ability, skill, aptitude.
(ANT.) feeling, passion, emotion.

intelligent *(SYN.)* clever, smart, knowledgeable, well-informed, alert, discerning, astute, quick, enlightened, smart, bright, wise.
(ANT.) insipid, obtuse, dull, stupid, slow, foolish, unintelligent, dumb.

intend *(SYN.)* plan, prepare, scheme, contrive, outline, design, sketch, plot, project, delineate.

intense *(SYN.)* brilliant, animated, graphic, lucid, bright, expressive, vivid, deep, profound, concentrated, serious, earnest.
(ANT.) dull, vague, dusky, dim, dreary.

intensify *(SYN.)* accrue, augment, amplify, enlarge, enhance, extend, expand, heighten, grow, magnify, raise, multiply.
(ANT.) reduce, decrease, contract, diminish.

intent *(SYN.)* purpose, design, objective, intention, aim.
(ANT.) accidental, result, chance.

intensity *(SYN.)* force, potency, power, toughness, activity, durability, fortitude, vigor, stamina.
(ANT.) weakness, feebleness, infirmity, frailty.

intention *(SYN.)* intent, purpose, objective, plan, expectation, aim, object.
(ANT.) chance, accident.

intentional *(SYN.)* deliberate, intended, studied, willful, contemplated, premeditated, designed, voluntary, purposeful, planned.
(ANT.) fortuitous, accidental, chance.

intentionally *(SYN.)* purposefully, deliberately, maliciously.
(ANT.) accidentally.

interest *(SYN.)* attention, concern, care, advantage, benefit, profit, ownership, credit, attract, engage, amuse, entertain.
(ANT.) apathy, weary, disinterest.

interested *(SYN.)* affected, concerned.
(ANT.) unconcerned, indifferent, uninterested.

interesting *(SYN.)* engaging, inviting, fascinating, attractive.
(ANT.) boring, tedious, uninteresting, wearisome.

interfere *(SYN.)* meddle, monkey, interpose, interrupt, tamper, butt in, intervene.

interference *(SYN.)* prying, intrusion, meddling, obstacle, obstruction.

interior *(SYN.)* internal, inmost, inner, inward, inside, center.
(ANT.) outer, adjacent, exterior, external, outside.

interject *(SYN.)* intrude, introduce, insert, inject, interpose.
(ANT.) overlook, avoid, disregard.

interminable *(SYN)* immense, endless, immeasurable, unlimited, vast, unbounded, boundless, eternal, infinite.
(ANT.) limited, bounded, circumscribed, confined.

internal *(SYN.)* inner, interior, inside, intimate, private.
(ANT.) outer, external, surface.

interpose *(SYN.)* arbitrate, inject, intervene, meddle, insert, interject, introduce, intercede, intrude, interfere.
(ANT.) overlook, avoid, disregard.

interpret *(SYN.)* explain, solve, translate, construe, elucidate, decode, explicate, render, unravel, define, understand.
(ANT.) misinterpret, falsify, confuse, distort, misconstrue.

interrogate *(SYN.)* quiz, analyze, inquire, audit, question, contemplate, assess, dissect, notice, scan, review, view, check, survey, scrutinize, examine.
(ANT.) overlook, omit, neglect, disregard.

interrupt *(SYN.)* suspend, delay, postpone, defer, adjourn, stay, discontinue, intrude, interfere.
(ANT.) prolong, persist, continue, maintain, proceed.

interval *(SYN.)* pause, gap.

intervene *(SYN.)* insert, intercede, meddle, inject, introduce, interpose, mediate, interfere, interrupt, intrude.
(ANT.) overlook, avoid, disregard.

intimacy *(SYN.)* fellowship, friendship, acquaintance, frankness, familiarity, unreserved, liberty.
(ANT.) presumption, distance, haughtiness, constraint, reserve.

intimate *(SYN.)* chummy, confidential, friendly, loving, affectionate, close, familiar, near, personal, private, secret.
(ANT.) conventional, formal, ceremonious, distant.

intimation *(SYN.)* reminder, implication, allusion, hint, insinuation.
(ANT.) declaration, statement, affirmation.

intolerant *(SYN.)* fanatical, narrowminded, prejudiced, bigoted, illiberal, dogmatic, biased.
(ANT.) tolerant, radical, liberal, progressive, broad-minded, fair.

intoxicated *(SYN.)* inebriated, tipsy, drunk, tight, drunken, high.
(ANT.) sober, temperate, clearheaded.

intrepid *(SYN.)* brave, fearless, insolent, abrupt, rude, pushy, adventurous, daring, courageous, prominent, striking, forward, imprudent.
(ANT.) timid, bashful, flinching, cowardly, retiring.

intricate *(SYN.)* compound, perplexing, complex, involved, complicated.

intrigue *(SYN.)* design, plot, cabal, machination, stratagem, scheme, attract, charm, interest, captivate.

intrinsic *(SYN.)* natural, inherent, inbred, congenital, inborn, native.
(ANT.) extraneous, acquired, external, extrinsic.

introduce *(SYN.)* acquaint, present, submit, present, offer, propose.

introduction *(SYN.)* preamble, prelude, beginning, prologue, start, preface.
(ANT.) finale, conclusion, end, epilogue, completion.

intrude *(SYN.)* invade, attack, encroach, trespass, penetrate, infringe, interrupt.
(ANT.) vacate, evacuate, abandon, relinquish.

intruder *(SYN.)* trespasser, thief, prowler, robber.

intuition *(SYN.)* insight, acumen, perspicuity, penetration, discernment, instinct, clairvoyance.

invade *(SYN.)* intrude, violate, infringe, attack, penetrate, encroach, trespass.
(ANT.) vacate, abandon, evacuate, relinquish.

invalidate *(SYN.)* annul, cancel, abolish, revoke, abrogate.
(ANT.) promote, restore, sustain, establish, continue.

invaluable *(SYN.)* priceless, precious, valuable.
(ANT.) worthless.

invasion *(SYN.)* assault, onslaught, aggression, attack, intrusion.
(ANT.) surrender, opposition, resistance, defense.

invective *(SYN.)* insult, abuse, disparagement, upbraiding, reproach, defamation, aspersion.
(ANT.) laudation, plaudit, commendation.

invent *(SYN.)* devise, fabricate, design, concoct, frame, conceive, contrive, create, originate, devise.
(SYN.) reproduce, copy, imitate.

inventive *(SYN.)* fanciful, imaginative, visionary, poetical, clever, creative.
(ANT.) unromantic, literal, dull, prosaic.

inventiveness *(SYN)* cunning, cleverness, ingeniousness, aptitude.
(ANT.) ineptitude, clumsiness, dullness, stupidity.

invert *(SYN.)* upset, turn about, trans-

pose, countermand, revoke, reverse, overturn, repeal.
(ANT.) *maintain, stabilize, endorse.*
investigate (SYN.) look, probe, ransack, scrutinize, ferret, examine, seek, explore, search, scour, inspect, study.
investigation (SYN.) exploration, interrogation, quest, question, scrutiny, inquiry, query, examination, study, research.
(ANT.) *inattention, disregard, inactivity, negligence.*
invigorating (SYN.) bracing, fortifying, vitalizing, stimulating.
invincible (SYN.) insurmountable, unconquerable, impregnable, indomitable, invulnerable, unassailable.
(ANT.) *powerless, weak, vulnerable.*
invisible (SYN.) indistinguishable, unseen, imperceptible, indiscernible.
(ANT.) *evident, visible, seen, perceptible.*
invite (SYN.) bid, ask, encourage, request, urge.
inviting (SYN.) appealing, attractive, tempting, luring, alluring.
(ANT.) *unattractive, uninviting.*
involuntary (SYN.) reflex, uncontrolled, automatic, unintentional.
(SYN.) *voluntary, willful.*
involve (SYN.) include, embrace, entangle, envelop, incriminate, embroil, implicate, contain, complicate, confuse.
(ANT.) *separate, disconnect, extricate, disengage.*
involved (SYN.) compound, intricate, complicated, complex, perplexing.
(ANT.) *plain, uncompounded, simple.*
invulnerable (SYN.) indomitable, unassailable, invincible, unconquerable, insurmountable, impregnable.
(ANT.) *weak, puny, powerless, vulnerable.*
irate (SYN.) incensed, enraged, angry.
ire (SYN.) indignation, irritation, wrath, anger, animosity, fury, passion, temper, exasperation, petulance, rage.
(ANT.) *peace, patience, conciliation, self-control, forbearance.*
irk (SYN.) irritate, bother, disturb, pester, trouble, vex, tease, chafe, annoy, inconvenience, provoke.
(ANT.) *console, soothe, accommodate, gratify.*
irrational (SYN.) inconsistent, preposterous, self-contradictory, un-

reasonable, absurd, foolish, nonsensical, ridiculous.
(ANT.) *sensible, sound, rational, consistent, reasonable.*
irregular (SYN.) eccentric, unusual, aberrant, devious, abnormal, unnatural, capricious, variable, unequal, disorderly, unsettled, random, disorganized.
(ANT.) *regular, methodical, fixed, usual, ordinary, even.*
irrelevant (SYN.) foreign, unconnected, remote, alien, strange.
(ANT.) *germane, relevant, akin, kindred.*
irresolute (SYN.) frail, pliant, vacillating, ineffective, wavering, weak, yielding, fragile, pliable.
(ANT.) *robust, potent, sturdy, strong, powerful.*
irresponsible (SYN.) unreliable.
irritable (SYN.) hasty, hot, peevish, testy, irascible, fiery, snappish, petulant, choleric, excitable, touchy.
(ANT.) *composed, agreeable, tranquil, calm.*
irritate (SYN.) irk, molest, bother, annoy, tease, disturb, inconvenience, vex, trouble, pester, inflame, chafe.
(ANT.) *console, gratify, accommodate, soothe, pacify, calm.*
irritable (SYN.) peevish, testy, sensitive, touchy.
(ANT.) *happy, cheerful.*
irritation (SYN.) chagrin, mortification, vexation, annoyance, exasperation, pique.
(ANT.) *pleasure, comfort, gratification, appeasement.*
isolate (SYN.) detach, segregate, separate, disconnect.
(ANT.) *happy, cheerful.*
isolated (SYN.) lone, single, alone, desolate, secluded, solitary, deserted, sole.
(ANT.) *surrounded, accompanied.*
isolation (SYN.) quarantine, seclusion, separation, solitude, alienation, retirement, loneliness, withdrawal, segregation, detachment.
(ANT.) *fellowship, union, association, communion, connection.*
issue (SYN.) flow, proceed, result, come, emanate, originate, abound, copy, number, edition, problem, question, concern, publish, distribute, circulate, release.
itemize (SYN.) register, detail, record.

jab (SYN.) thrust, poke, nudge, prod, shove, jolt, boost, tap, slap, rap, thwack, push.

jabber (SYN.) mumble, gossip, prattle, chatter, gab, palaver.

jacent (SYN.) level, flatness, plane, proneness, recline.

jacinth (SYN.) decoration, ornament, embellishment.

jack (SYN.) fellow, guy, boy, toiler, guy, man, worker.

jackal (SYN.) puppet, drone, slave, legman, flunky, slavery, tool, servility, vassal.

jackass (SYN.) fool, idiot, dope, dunce, ignoramus, imbecile, ninny, simpleton, blockhead.

jacket (SYN.) wrapper, envelope, coat, sheath, cover, casing, folder, enclosure, skin.

jack-of-all-trades (SYN.) man friday, expert, proficient, amateur, adept, handyman, dab, master, specialist, mastermind, generalist.

jade (SYN.) hussy, wanton, trollop, harlot, common, whore, ignoble, wench, hag, shrew.

jaded (SYN.) exhausted, bored, tired, fatigued, satiated, weary, hardened.

jag (SYN.) notch, snag, protuberance, barb, dent, cut, nick, serration, indentation, point.

jagged (SYN.) crooked, bent, ragged, pointy, notched, aquiline, furcated, aduncous, serrated.
(ANT.) smooth.

jail (SYN.) stockade, prison, reformatory, penitentiary, keep, dungeon, brig, confine, lock up, detain, imprison, hold captive, coop, cage, house of detention, incarcerate.

jailbird (SYN.) convict, parolee, con, inmate, prisoner.

jailer (SYN.) guard, keeper, turnkey, warden.

jam (SYN.) force, pack, ram, crowd, push, wedge, squeeze, stuff, load, cram, press, crush, marmalade, jelly, conserve, preserve.

jamboree (SYN.) celebration, fete, spree, festival, festivity, carousal.

jangle (SYN.) rattle, vibrate, clank, clatter, dissonance, discord, quarrel, din, discord, dispute.

janitor (SYN.) custodian, door-keeper,

caretaker, superintendent, gatekeeper.

jape (SYN.) lampoon, banter, joke, jest, tease, ridicule.

jar (SYN.) rattle, shake, bounce, jolt.

jargon (SYN.) speech, idiom, dialect, vernacular, diction, argot, phraseology, language, patois, parlance, slang.
(ANT.) gibberish; babble, nonsense, drivel.

jaundiced (SYN.) biased; prejudiced.
(ANT.) fair.

jaunt (SYN.) journey, trip, tour, excursion, outing, voyage, expedition.

jaunty (SYN.) lively, vivacious, bouyant, winsome, frisky, showy, dapper, breezy, airy.

jazzy (SYN.) garish, vivacious, loud, splashy, exaggerated, flashy.

jealous (SYN.) covetous, desirous of, envious.

jealousy (SYN.) suspicion, envy, resentfulness, greed, covetousness.
(ANT.) tolerance, indifference, geniality, liberality.

jeer (SYN.) taunt, mock, scoff, deride, make fun of, gibe, sneer.
(ANT.) flatter, praise, compliment, laud.

jeering (SYN.) mockery, sneering, derision, sarcasm, irony, ridicule.

jell (SYN.) finalize, congeal, set, solidify, shape up, take form.

jeopardize (SYN.) risk, dare, expose, imperil, chance, venture, conjecture, hazard, endanger.
(ANT.) know, guard, determine.

jerk (SYN.) quiver, twitch, shake, spasm, jolt, yank, fool.

jerkwater (SYN.) remote, hick, backwoods, unimportant, one-horse.

jest (SYN.) mock, joke, tease, fun, witticism, quip.

jester (SYN.) fool, buffoon, harlequin, clown.
(ANT.) sage, genius, scholar, philosopher.

jet (SYN.) squirt, spurt, gush, inky, coalblack, nozzle.

jettison (SYN.) heave, discharge, throw, eject, cast off, dismiss.

jetty (SYN.) pier, breakwater, bulwark, buttress.

jewel (SYN.) ornament, gemstone, gem, bauble, stone.

jib (SYN.) shrink, shy, dodge, retreat, balk.

jig (SYN.) caper, prance, jiggle, leap, skip.

jiggle (SYN.) shimmy, agitate, jerk, twitch, wiggle.

jilt (SYN.) abandon, get rid of, reject, desert, forsake, leave.

jingle (SYN.) chime, ring, tinkle.

jinx (SYN.) hex, whammy, nemesis, curse, evil eye.

jittery (SYN.) jumpy, nervous, quivering, shaky, skittery.

job (SYN.) toil, business, occupation, post, chore, stint, career, duty, employment, profession, trade, work, situation, labor, assignment, position, undertaking, calling, task.

jobless (SYN.) idle, unoccupied, inactive, unemployed.

jocularity (SYN.) humor, wit, joke, facetiousness, waggery.
(ANT.) sorrow, gravity.

jocund (SYN.) mirthful, elated, pleasant, cheerful, merry, gay, jovial, frolicsome.

jog (SYN.) gait, trot, sprint, run, lope.

join (SYN.) conjoin, unite, attach, accompany, associate, assemble, fit, couple, combine, fasten, unite, clasp, put together, go with, adjoin, link, connect.
(ANT.) separate, disconnect, split, sunder, part, divide, detach.

joint (SYN.) link, union, connection, junction, coupling, common, combined, mutual, connected.
(ANT.) divided, separate.

joke (SYN.) game, jest, caper, prank, anecdote, quip, tease, antic, banter, laugh.

joker (SYN.) wisecracker, humorist, comedian, trickster, comic, jester, wit, punster.

jolly (SYN.) merry, joyful, gay, happy, sprightly, pleasant, jovial, gleeful, spirited, cheerful, glad.
(ANT.) mournful, depressed, sullen, glum.

jolt (SYN.) sway, waver, startle, rock, jar, totter, jerk, bounce, quake, bump, shake.

josh (SYN.) poke fun at, kid, tease, ridicule.

jostle (SYN.) shove, push, bump, thrust.

jot (SYN.) note, write, record.

jounce (SYN.) bounce, jolt, bump, jostle, jar, shake.

journal (SYN.) account, diary, log, chronicle, magazine, newspaper, record.

journey (SYN.) tour, passage, cruise, voyage, pilgrimage, jaunt, trip, outing, expedition, junket, excursion, travel.

joust (SYN.) tournament, contest, skirmish, competition, fight.

jovial (SYN.) good-natured, kindly, merry, good-humored, good-hearted, joyful, jolly, gleeful.
(ANT.) solemn, sad, serious, grim.

joy (SYN.) pleasure, glee, bliss, elation, mirth, felicity, rapture, delight, transport, exultation, gladness, happiness, festivity, satisfaction, merriment, ecstasy.
(ANT.) grief, depression, unhappiness, sorrow, misery, gloom, sadness, affliction.

joyful (SYN.) gay, lucky, opportune, cheerful, happy, blissful, jovial, merry, gleeful, delighted, glad, contented, fortunate.
(ANT.) gloomy, sad, blue, solemn, serious, grim, morose, glum, depressed.

joyous (SYN.) jolly, gay, blithe, merry, gleeful, cheerful, jovial.
(ANT.) sad, gloomy, sorrowful, melancholy.

jubilant (SYN.) exulting, rejoicing, overjoyed, triumphant, gay, elated, delighted.
(ANT.) dejected.

jubilee (SYN.) gala, holiday, celebration, festival, fete.

judge (SYN.) umpire, think, estimate, decide, arbitrator, condemn, decree, critic, appreciate, adjudicator, determine, arbiter, magistrate, arbitrate, justice, consider, mediate, referee, evaluate.

judgment (SYN.) wisdom, perspicacity, discernment, decision, common sense, estimation, verdict, understanding, intelligence, discretion, opinion, sense, discrimination.
(ANT.) thoughtlessness, senselessness, arbitrariness.

judicial (SYN.) legal, judicatory, forensic.

judicious (SYN.) sensible, wise, well-advised, thoughtful.
(ANT.) ignorant.

jug (SYN.) bottle, jar, flask, flagon, pitcher.

juice (SYN.) broth, liquid, sap, distillation, serum, fluid.

jumble *(SYN.)* disarrangement, tumult, agitation, ferment, turmoil, commotion, confuse, mix, muddle, scramble, disorder.
(ANT.) peace, arrange, compose, certainty, tranquillity.

jumbo *(SYN.)* huge, big, immense, enormous, giant, colossal, monstrous, mammoth, gigantic, tremendous.
(ANT.) mini, midget, dwarf, small, little, tiny.

jump *(SYN.)* leap, caper, skip, bound, jerk, vault, hop, spring.

jumpy *(SYN.)* touchy, excitable, nervous, sensitive.
(ANT.) tranquil, calm, unruffled.

junction *(SYN.)* coupling, joining, union, crossroads, intersection, weld, connection, linking, meeting, tie-up, seam, joint.
(ANT.) separation.

jungle *(SYN.)* woods, thicket, undergrowth, forest, bush.

junior *(SYN.)* secondary, inferior, minor, lower, younger.

junk *(SYN.)* rubbish, scraps, trash, waste, dump, discard, castoffs, debris.

junky *(SYN.)* tawdry, ramshackle, tattered, tacky, shoddy.

jurisdiction *(SYN.)* power, commission, warrant, authority, authorization, magistacy, sovereignty.

just *(SYN.)* fair, trustworthy, precise, exact, candid, upright, honest, impartial, lawful, rightful, proper, legal, truthful, merely, only, conscientious.
(ANT.) tricky, dishonest, unjust, corrupt, lying, deceitful.

justice *(SYN.)* justness, rectitude, equity, law, fairness, impartiality, right.
(ANT.) unfairness, inequity, wrong, partiality.

justifiable *(SYN.)* allowable, tolerable, admissible, warranted.
(ANT.) unsuitable, inadmissible.

justify *(SYN.)* uphold, excuse, defend, acquit, exonerate, absolve, clear, vindicate.
(ANT.) convict.

jut *(SYN.)* project, protrude, stick out.
(ANT.) indent, recess.

juvenile *(SYN.)* puerile, youthful, childish, babyish, youngster, youth, young, child.
(ANT.) old, aged, adult, mature.

kaiser *(SYN.)* czar, caesar, caliph, mogul, padishah, tycoon, khan, landamman, cazique.

kavass *(SYN.)* badel, macebearer, constable.

keck *(SYN.)* vomit, belch, retch.

keen *(SYN.)* clever, cunning, acute, penetrating, exact, severe, shrewd, wily, astute, sharp, bright, intelligent, smart, sharp-witted, witty, cutting, fine, quick.
(ANT.) stupid, shallow, dull, blunted, slow, bland, gentle, obtuse, blunt.

keep *(SYN.)* maintain, retain, observe, protect, confine, sustain, continue, preserve, save, guard, restrain, reserve, obey, support, honor, execute, celebrate, conserve, have, tend, detain, commemorate, hold.
(ANT.) abandon, disobey, dismiss, discard, ignore, neglect, lose, reject, relinquish.

keeper *(SYN.)* warden, jailer, ranger, gaoler, guard, turnkey, watchman, escort, custodian.

keeping *(SYN.)* congeniality, uniformity, consentaneousness, conformance, congruity, union.

keepsake *(SYN.)* reminder, memorial, relic, souvenir, memento, hint, remembrance.

keg *(SYN.)* container, drum, tub, barrel, receptacle, reservatory, capsule, cask, tank.

kelpie *(SYN.)* sprite, nixie, naiad, pixy.

kelson *(SYN.)* bottom, sole, toe, foot, root, keel.

kempt *(SYN.)* neat, trim, tidy, spruce, cleaned.

ken *(SYN.)* field, view, vision, range, scope.

kennel *(SYN.)* swarm, flock, covy, drove, herd, pound, doghouse.

kerchief *(SYN.)* neckcloth, hankerchief, scarf, headpiece, babushka.

kern *(SYN.)* peasant, carle, serf, tike, tyke, countryman.

kernel *(SYN.)* marrow, pith, backbone, soul, heart, core, nucleus.

ketch *(SYN.)* lugger, cutter, clipper, ship, barge, sloop.

kettle *(SYN.)* pan, caldron, vat, pot, teapot, vessel, receptacle, receiver, tureen.

key *(SYN.)* opener, explanation, tone, lead, cause, source, note, pitch, answer, clue.

keynote *(SYN.)* core, model, theme, pattern, standard, gist.

keystone *(SYN.)* backbone, support.

khan *(SYN.)* master, czar, kaiser, padishah, caesar.

kick *(SYN.)* punt, remonstrate, boot.

kickback *(SYN.)* repercussion, backfire, rebound.

kickoff *(SYN.)* beginning, opening, commencement, outset, start.

kid *(SYN.)* joke, tease, fool, jest, tot, child.

kidnap *(SYN.)* abduct, snatch, shanghai.

kill *(SYN.)* execute, put to death, slay, butcher, assassinate, murder, cancel, destroy, slaughter, finish, end, annihilate, massacre. *(ANT.)* save, protect, animate, resuscitate, vivify.

killing *(SYN.)* massacre, genocide, slaughter, carnage, butchery, bloodshed.

killjoy *(SYN.)* wet blanket, sourpuss, party-pooper.

kin *(SYN.)* relatives, family, folks, relations.

kind *(SYN.)* humane, affable, compassionate, benevolent, merciful, tender, sympathetic, breed, indulgent, forbearing, kindly, race, good, thoughtful, character, benign, family, sort, species, variety, class, type, gentle. *(ANT.)* unkind, cruel, merciless, severe, mean, inhuman.

kindle *(SYN.)* fire, ignite, light, arouse, excite, set afire, stir up, trigger, move, provoke, inflame. *(ANT.)* pacify, extinguish, calm.

kindly *(SYN.)* warm, kind-hearted, kind, warm-hearted. *(ANT.)* mean, cruel.

kindred *(SYN.)* family, relations, relatives, consanguinity, kinsfolk, affinity. *(ANT.)* strangers, disconnection.

kinetic *(SYN.)* vigorous, active, dynamic, energetic, mobile, forceful.

king *(SYN.)* sovereign, ruler, chief, monarch, potentate.

kingdom *(SYN.)* realm, empire, monarchy, domain.

kingly *(SYN.)* kinglike, imperial, regal, royal, majestic.

kink *(SYN.)* twist, curl, quirk, complication.

kinship *(SYN.)* lineage, blood, family, stock, relationship.

kismet *(SYN.)* fate, end, fortune, destiny.

kiss *(SYN.)* pet, caress, fondle, cuddle, osculate, embrace. *(ANT.)* vex, spurn, annoy, tease, buffet.

kit *(SYN.)* outfit, collection, furnishings, equipment, rig, gear, set.

knack *(SYN.)* cleverness, readiness, deftness, ability, ingenuity, skill, talent, aptitude, talent, know-how, art, adroitness, skillfulness. *(ANT.)* inability, clumsiness, awkwardness, ineptitude.

knave *(SYN.)* rogue, rascal, villain, scoundrel.

knead *(SYN.)* combine, massage, blend.

knickknack *(SYN.)* trinket, bric-a-brac, trifle.

knife *(SYN.)* sword, blade.

knightly *(SYN.)* valiant, courageous, gallant, chivalrous, noble.

knit *(SYN.)* unite, join, mend, fasten, connect, combine, heal.

knob *(SYN.)* doorknob, handle, protuberance, bump.

knock *(SYN.)* thump, tap, rap, strike, hit, jab, punch, beat, pound, bang, hammer, thwack.

knockout *(SYN.)* stunning, overpowering, stupefying, overwhelming.

knoll *(SYN.)* hill, elevation, hump, mound, butte.

knot *(SYN.)* cluster, gathering, collection, group, crowd, twist, snarl, tangle.

know *(SYN.)* perceive, comprehend, apprehend, recognize, understand, discern, discriminate, ascertain, identify, be aware, distinguish. *(ANT.)* doubt, suspect, dispute, ignore.

knowing *(SYN.)* sage, smart, wise, clever, sagacious, shrewd.

knowledge *(SYN.)* information, wisdom, erudition, learning, apprehension, scholarship, lore, cognizance. *(ANT.)* misunderstanding, ignorance, stupidity, illiteracy.

knurl *(SYN.)* gnarl, knot, projection, burl, node, lump.

kosher *(SYN.)* permitted, okay, fit, proper, acceptable.

kowtow *(SYN.)* stoop, bend, kneel, genuflect, bow.

kudos *(SYN.)* acclaim, praise, approbation, approval.

label (SYN.) mark, tag, title, name, marker, stamp, sticker, ticket, docket, identity.

labor (SYN.) toil, travail, effort, task, childbirth, work, parturition, striving, workers, effort, industry, workingmen, strive, exertion, employment, drudgery, endeavor.
(ANT.) recreation, indolence, idleness, leisure.

laboratory (SYN.) lab, workroom, workshop.

laborer (SYN.) wage earner, helper, worker, toiler, coolie, blue-collar worker.

laborious (SYN.) tiring, difficult, hard, burdensome, industrious, painstaking.
(ANT.) simple, easy, relaxing, restful.

labyrinth (SYN.) complex, maze, tangle.

lace (SYN.) openwork, fancywork, embroidery, edging.

lacerate (SYN.) mangle, tear roughly.

laceration (SYN.) cut, wound, puncture, gash, lesion, injury.

lack (SYN.) want, need, shortage, dearth, scarcity, require.
(ANT.) profusion, quantity, plentifulness.

lackey (SYN.) yesman, stooge, flatterer, flunky.

lacking (SYN.) insufficient, short, deficient, incomplete, defective, scanty.
(ANT.) satisfactory, enough, ample, sufficient, adequate.

lackluster (SYN.) dull, pallid, flat, lifeless, drab, dim.

laconic (SYN.) short, terse, compact, brief, curt, succinct, concise.

lacquer (SYN.) polish, varnish, gild.

lad (SYN.) youth, boy, fellow, stripling.

laden (SYN.) burdened, loaded, weighted.

ladle (SYN.) scoop, dipper.

lady (SYN.) matron, woman, dame, gentlewoman.

ladylike (SYN.) feminine, womanly, maidenly, womanish, female.
(ANT.) masculine, male, virile, mannish, manly.

lag (SYN.) dawdle, loiter, linger, poke, dilly-dally, straggle, delay, tarry, slowdown.

laggard (SYN.) dallier, idler, lingerer, slowpoke, dawdler.

lair (SYN.) retreat, burrow, den, nest, mew, hole.

lambaste (SYN.) berate, castigate, scold, censure.

lame (SYN.) feeble, maimed, disabled, crippled, deformed, hobbling, unconvincing, weak, poor, inadequate, halt, defective, limping.
(ANT.) vigorous, convincing, plausible, athletic, robust, agile, sound.

lament (SYN.) deplore, wail, bemoan, bewail, regret, grieve, mourning, lamentation, moaning, wailing, weep, mourn, sorrow.
(ANT.) celebrate, rejoice.

lamentable (SYN.) unfortunate, deplorable.

lamp (SYN.) light, beam, illumination, shine, insight, knowledge, understanding, radiance, luminosity, incandescence.
(ANT.) shadow, darkness, obscurity, gloom.

lampoon (SYN.) skit, tirade, burlesque, parody, satire.

lance (SYN.) cut, pierce, perforate, stab, puncture, impale, knife.

land (SYN.) earth, continent, ground, soil, domain, estate, field, realm, plain, surface, arrive, descend, country, island, region, alight, shore, sod, tract, farm.

landlord (SYN.) owner, landholder, landowner, proprietor.

landmark (SYN.) keystone, monument, milestone, point, cornerstone.

landscape (SYN.) panorama, environs, countryside, scenery, scene.

landslide (SYN.) rockfall, glissade, avalanche.

lane (SYN.) alley, way, road, path, aisle, pass, channel, avenue, artery, passage.

language (SYN.) dialect, tongue, speech, lingo, jargon, cant, diction, idiom, patter, phraseology, vernacular, words, lingo, talk, slang.
(ANT.) gibberish, nonsense, babble, drivel.

languid (SYN.) feeble, drooping, irresolute, debilitated, dull, lethargic, weak, faint, listless, wearied.
(ANT.) forceful, strong, vigorous.

languish (SYN.) decline, sink, droop, wither, waste, fail, wilt, weaken.
(ANT.) revive, rejuvenate, refresh, renew.

languor (SYN.) weariness, depression, torpor, inertia, apathy.

lanky (SYN.) skinny, gaunt, lean, scrawny, slender, thin.
(ANT.) chunky, stocky, obese, fat.

lantern *(SYN.)* torch, light, lamp, flashlight.

lap *(SYN.)* drink, lick, fold over.

lapse *(SYN.)* decline, sink, go down, slump.

larceny *(SYN.)* pillage, robbery, stealing, theft, burglary, plunder.

lard *(SYN.)* grease, fat.

large *(SYN.)* great, vast, colossal, ample, extensive, capacious, sizable, broad, massive, grand, immense, big, enormous, huge, giant, mammoth, wide. *(ANT.)* *tiny, little, short, small.*

largely *(SYN.)* chiefly, mainly, principally, mostly.

lariat *(SYN.)* lasso, rope.

lark *(SYN.)* fling, frolic, play, fun, spree, joke, revel, celebration.

lascivious *(SYN.)* lecherous, raunchy, lustful, wanton, lewd. .

lash *(SYN.)* thong, whip, rod, cane, blow, strike, hit, beat, knout.

lass *(SYN.)* maiden, girl, damsel. *(ANT.)* *woman.*

lasso *(SYN.)* lariat, rope, noose, snare.

last *(SYN.)* terminal, final, ultimate, remain, endure, concluding, latest, utmost, end, conclusive, hindmost, continue, extreme. *(ANT.)* *first, initial, beginning, opening, starting, foremost.*

latch *(SYN.)* clasp, hook, fastener, lock, closing, seal, catch.

late *(SYN.)* overdue, tardy, behind, advanced, delayed, new, slow, recent. *(ANT.)* *timely, early.*

lately *(SYN.)* recently, yesterday.

latent *(SYN.)* potential, undeveloped, unseen, dormant, secret, concealed, inactive, hidden, obscured, covered, quiescent. *(ANT.)* *visible, evident, conspicuous, explicit, manifest.*

lather *(SYN.)* suds, foam, froth.

lateral *(SYN.)* sideways, glancing, tangential, marginal, skirting, side.

latitude *(SYN.)* range, scope, freedom, extent.

latter *(SYN.)* more recent, later. *(ANT.)* *former.*

lattice *(SYN.)* grating, screen, frame, trellis, openwork, framework, grid.

laud *(SYN.)* commend, praise, extol, glorify, compliment. *(ANT.)* *criticize, belittle.*

laudable *(SYN.)* creditable, praiseworthy, commendable, admirable.

laudation *(SYN.)* applause, compliment, flattery, praise, commendation, acclaim, extolling, glorification. *(ANT.)* *criticizing, condemnation, reproach, disparagement, censure.*

laugh *(SYN.)* chuckle, giggle, snicker, cackle, titter, grin, smile, roar, guffaw, jeer, mock.

laughable *(SYN.)* funny, amusing, comical, humorous, ridiculous.

launch *(SYN.)* drive, fire, propel, start, begin, originate, set afloat, initiate. *(ANT.)* *finish, stop, terminate.*

launder *(SYN.)* bathe, wash, scrub, scour.

laurels *(SYN.)* glory, distinction, recognition, award, commendation, reward, honor.

lavatory *(SYN.)* toilet, washroom, bathroom, latrine.

lavish *(SYN.)* squander, waste, dissipate, scatter, abundant, free, plentiful, liberal, extravagant, ample, wear out, prodigal, generous, spend. *(ANT.)* *economize, save, conserve, accumulate, sparing, stingy, preserve.*

law *(SYN.)* decree, formula, statute, act, rule, ruling, standard, principle, ordinance, proclamation, regulation, order, edict.

lawful *(SYN.)* legal, permissible, allowable, legitimate, authorized, constitutional, rightful. *(ANT.)* *prohibited, criminal, illicit, illegal, illegitimate.*

lawless *(SYN.)* uncivilized, uncontrolled, wild, savage, untamed, violent. *(ANT.)* *obedient, law-abiding, tame.*

lawlessness *(SYN.)* chaos, anarchy.

lawn *(SYN.)* grass, meadow, turf.

lawyer *(SYN.)* counsel, attorney, counselor.

lax *(SYN.)* slack, loose, careless, vague, lenient, lazy. *(ANT.)* *firm, rigid.*

lay *(SYN.)* mundane, worldly, temporal, place, dispose, bet, wager, hazard, risk, stake, site, earthly, profane, laic, arrange, location, put, set, ballad, deposit, position, song, secular. *(ANT.)* *spiritual, unworldly, remove, misplace, disturb, mislay, disarrange, ecclesiastical, religious.*

lay off *(SYN.)* discharge, bounce, fire, dismiss.

layout *(SYN.)* plan, arrangement, design.

lazy *(SYN.)* slothful, supine, idle, inactive, sluggish, inert, indolent, torpid.
(ANT.) alert, ambitious, forceful, diligent, active, assiduous.

lea *(SYN.)* pasture, meadow.

leach *(SYN.)* remove, extract, seep, dilute, wash out.

lead *(SYN.)* regulate, conduct, guide, escort, direct, supervise, command, come first, steer, control.
(ANT.) follow.

leader *(SYN.)* master, ruler, captain, chief, commander, principal, director, head, chieftain.
(ANT.) follower, servant, disciple, subordinate, attendant.

leading *(SYN.)* dominant, foremost, principal, first, main, primary.

league *(SYN.)* entente, partnership, association, confederacy, coalition, society, alliance, federation, union.
(ANT.) separation, schism.

leak *(SYN.)* dribble, flow, drip, opening, perforation.

lean *(SYN.)* rely, tilt, slim, slender, slope, incline, tend, trust, bend, tendency, slant, depend, spare, scant, lanky, thin, meager, inclination, narrow, sag.
(ANT.) rise, heavy, fat, erect, straighten, portly, raise.

leaning *(SYN.)* trend, proclivity, bias, tendency, bent, predisposition, proneness.
(ANT.) disinclination, aversion.

leap *(SYN.)* vault, skip, caper, dive, hurdle, jump, bound, start, hop, plunge, spring.

learn *(SYN.)* gain, find out, memorize, acquire, determine.

learned *(SYN.)* erudite, knowing, enlightened, deep, wise, discerning, scholarly, intelligent, educated, sagacious.
(ANT.) simple, uneducated, ignorant, illiterate, unlettered, foolish.

learning *(SYN.)* science, education, lore, apprehension, wisdom, knowledge, scholarship, erudition.
(ANT.) misunderstanding, ignorance, stupidity.

lease *(SYN.)* charter, let, rent, engage.

leash *(SYN.)* chain, strap, shackle, collar.

least *(SYN.)* minutest, smallest, tiniest, trivial, minimum, fewest, slightest.
(ANT.) most.

leave *(SYN.)* give up, retire, desert, abandon, withdraw, relinquish, will,
depart, quit, liberty, renounce, go, bequeath, consent, allowance, permission, freedom, forsake.
(ANT.) come, stay, arrive, tarry, remain, abide.

lecherous *(SYN.)* lustful, sensual, carnal, lascivious.

lecture *(SYN.)* talk, discussion, lesson, instruct, speech, conference, sermon, report, recitation, address, oration, discourse.
(ANT.) writing, meditation, correspondence.

ledge *(SYN.)* eaves, ridge, shelf, rim, edge.

lee *(SYN.)* shelter, asylum, sanctuary, haven.

leech *(SYN.)* barnacle, bloodsucker, parasite.

leer *(SYN.)* eye, grimace, ogle, wink, squint.

leeway *(SYN.)* reserve, allowance, elbowroom, slack, clearance.

leftovers *(SYN.)* scraps, remains, residue, remainder.

legacy *(SYN.)* bequest, inheritance, heirloom.

legal *(SYN.)* legitimate, rightful, honest, allowable, allowed, permissible, lawful, permitted, authorized.
(ANT.) illicit, illegal, prohibited, illegitimate.

legalize *(SYN.)* authorize, ordain, approve, sanction.

legate *(SYN.)* envoy, agent, representative, emissary.

legend *(SYN.)* saga, fable, allegory, myth, parable, tale, story, folklore, fiction, chronicle.
(ANT.) history, facts.

legendary *(SYN.)* fictitious, traditional, mythical, imaginary, fanciful.

legible *(SYN.)* plain, readable, clear, distinct.
(ANT.) illegible.

legion *(SYN.)* outfit, unit, troop, regiment, company, battalion, force, army, team, division.

legislation *(SYN.)* resolution, ruling, lawmaking, regulation, enactment, statute, decree.

legislator *(SYN.)* statesman, congressman, senator, politician, lawmaker.

legitimate *(SYN.)* true, real, bona fide, lawful, proper, right, valid, correct, unadulterated, authentic, rightful, legal, sincere.

(ANT.) *sham, counterfeit, artificial, false.*

leisure *(SYN.)* respite, intermission, ease, relaxation, rest, calm, tranquillity, recreation, peace, pause.

(ANT.) *motion, commotion, tumult, agitation, disturbance.*

leisurely *(SYN.)* sluggish, laggard, unhurried, relaxed, casual, dawdling, slow, deliberate.

(ANT.) *hurried, swift, pressed, rushed, forced, fast, speedy, quick.*

lend *(SYN.)* entrust, advance, confer.

length *(SYN.)* reach, measure, extent, distance, span, longness, stretch.

lengthen *(SYN.)* stretch, prolong, draw, reach, increase, grow, protract, extend.

(ANT.) *shrink, contract, shorten.*

leniency *(SYN.)* grace, pity, compassion, mildness, charity, mercy, clemency.

(ANT.) *vengeance, punishment, cruelty.*

lenient *(SYN.)* tender, humane, clement, tolerant, compassionate, merciful, relaxed, forgiving, gentle, mild, lax, kind.

(ANT.) *unfeeling, pitiless, brutal, remorseless.*

leprechaun *(SYN.)* gnome, imp, goblin, fairy, elf, sprite, banshee.

lesion *(SYN.)* wound, blemish, sore, trauma, injury.

less *(SYN.)* fewer, smaller, reduced, negative, stinted.

(ANT.) *more.*

lessen *(SYN.)* shorten, reduce, deduct, subtract, curtail, diminish, shrink, dwindle, decline, instruction, teaching, remove, decrease.

(ANT.) *swell, grow, enlarge, increase, expand, multiply, amplify.*

lesson *(SYN.)* exercise, session, class, assignment, section, recitation.

let *(SYN.)* admit, hire out, contract, allow, permit, consent, leave, grant, rent.

(ANT.) *deny.*

letdown *(SYN.)* disillusionment, disappointment.

lethal *(SYN.)* mortal, dangerous, deadly, fatal, devastating.

lethargic *(SYN.)* sluggish, logy, slow, listless, phlegmatic, lazy.

(ANT.) *vivacious, energetic.*

lethargy *(SYN.)* numbness, stupor, daze, insensibility, torpor.

(ANT.) *wakefulness, liveliness, activity,*

readiness.

letter *(SYN.)* note, letter, mark, message, character, symbol, sign, memorandum.

letup *(SYN.)* slowdown, slackening, lessening, abatement, reduction.

levee *(SYN.)* dike, breakwater, dam, embankment.

level *(SYN.)* smooth, even, plane, equivalent, uniform, horizontal, equal, flatten, equalize, raze, demolish, flat.

(ANT.) *uneven, sloping, hilly, broken.*

level-headed *(SYN.)* reasonable, sensible, calm, collected, cool.

leverage *(SYN.)* clout, power, influence, weight, rank.

levity *(SYN.)* humor, triviality, giddiness, hilarity, fun, frivolity.

levy *(SYN.)* tax, duty, tribute, rate, assessment, exaction, charge, custom.

(ANT.) *wages, remuneration, gift.*

lewd *(SYN.)* indecent, smutty, coarse, gross, disgusting, impure.

(ANT.) *pure, decent, refined.*

liability *(SYN.)* indebtedness, answerability, obligation, vulnerability.

liable *(SYN.)* answerable, responsible, likely, exposed to, subject, amenable, probable, accountable.

(ANT.) *immune, exempt, independent.*

liaison *(SYN.)* union, coupling, link, connection, alliance.

liar *(SYN.)* fibber, falsifier, storyteller, fabricator, prevaricator.

libel *(SYN.)* slander, calumny, vilification, aspersion, defamation.

(ANT.) *defense, praise, applause, flattery.*

liberal *(SYN.)* large, generous, unselfish, openhanded, broad, tolerant, kind, unprejudiced, open-minded, lavish, plentiful, ample, abundant, extravagant, extensive.

(ANT.) *restricted, conservative, stingy, confined.*

liberality *(SYN.)* kindness, philanthropy, beneficence, humanity, altruism, benevolence, generosity, charity.

(ANT.) *selfishness, cruelty, malevolence.*

liberate *(SYN.)* emancipate, loose, release, let go, deliver, free, discharge.

(ANT.) *subjugate, oppress, jail, confine, restrict, imprison.*

liberated *(SYN.)* loose, frank, emancipated, careless, liberal, freed, autonomous, exempt, familiar.

(ANT.) subject clooped restricted

impeded.

liberty *(SYN.)* permission, independence, autonomy, license, privilege, emancipation, self-government, freedom.
(ANT.) constraint, imprisonment, bondage, captivity.

license *(SYN.)* liberty, freedom, liberation, permission, exemption, authorization, warrant, allow, consent, permit, sanction, approval, unrestraint.
(ANT.) servitude, constraint, bondage, necessity.

lick *(SYN.)* taste, lap, lave.

lid *(SYN.)* top, cover, cap, plug, cork, stopper.

lie *(SYN.)* untruth, fib, illusion, delusion, falsehood, fiction, equivocation, prevarication, repose, location, perjury, misinform, site, recline, similitude.
(ANT.) variance, truth, difference.

life *(SYN.)* sparkle, being, spirit, vivacity, animation, buoyancy, vitality, existence, biography, energy, liveliness, vigor.
(ANT.) demise, lethargy, death, languor.

lift *(SYN.)* hoist, pick up, elevate, raise, heft.

light *(SYN.)* brightness, illumination, beam, gleam, lamp, knowledge, brilliance, fixture, bulb, candle, fire, ignite, burn, dawn, incandescence, flame, airy, unsubstantial, dainty, luminosity, shine, radiance, giddy, enlightenment, weightless, understanding.
(ANT.) darken, gloom, shadow, extinguish, darkness.

lighten *(SYN.)* diminish, unburden, reduce, brighten.

light-headed *(SYN.)* giddy, silly, dizzy, frivolous.
(ANT.) sober, clear-headed, rational.

lighthearted *(SYN.)* carefree, merry, gay, cheerful, happy, glad.
(ANT.) somber, sad, serious, melancholy.

like *(SYN.)* fancy, esteem, adore, love, admire, care for, prefer, cherish.
(ANT.) disapprove, loathe, hate, dislike.

likely *(SYN.)* liable, reasonable, probable, possible.

likeness *(SYN.)* similarity, resemblance, representation, image, portrait.
(ANT.) difference.

likewise *(SYN.)* besides, as well, also, too, similarly.

liking *(SYN.)* fondness, affection, partiality.

(ANT.) antipathy, dislike.

limb *(SYN.)* arm, leg, member, appendage, part, bough.

limber *(SYN.)* bending, flexible, elastic, pliable.
(ANT.) inflexible, stiff.

limbo *(SYN.)* exile, banishment, purgatory.

limelight *(SYN.)* spotlight, notice, notoriety, fame, prominence.

limerick *(SYN.)* jingle, rhyme.

limit *(SYN.)* terminus, bound, extent, confine, border, restriction, .boundary, restraint, edge, frontier, check, end, limitation.
(ANT.) endlessness, vastness, boundlessness.

limn *(SYN.)* depict, portray, sketch, paint, illustrate.

limp *(SYN.)* soft, flabby, drooping, walk, limber, supple, flexible, hobble, stagger.
(ANT.) stiff.

limpid *(SYN.)* clear, open, transparent, unobstructed.
(ANT.) cloudy.

line *(SYN.)* row, file, series, array, sequence, wire, seam, wrinkle, crease, boundary, arrangement, kind, type, division.

lineage *(SYN.)* race, family, tribe, nation, strain, folk, people, ancestry, clan.

linger *(SYN.)* wait, rest, bide, delay, dwadle, stay, loiter, remain, dilly-dally, tarry.
(ANT.) leave, expedite.

lingo *(SYN.)* vernacular, dialect, language, jargon, speech.

link *(SYN.)* unite, connector, loop, couple, attach, connective, connection, coupling, juncture, bond.
(ANT.) separate, disconnect, split.

lip *(SYN.)* edge, brim, rim.

liquid *(SYN.)* watery, fluent, fluid, flowing.
(ANT.) solid, congealed.

liquidate *(SYN.)* pay off, settle, defray.

liquor *(SYN.)* spirits, alcohol, drink, booze.

lissom *(SYN.)* nimble, quick, lively, flexible, agile.

list *(SYN.)* roll, register, slate, enumeration, series.

listen *(SYN.)* overhear, attend to, heed, hear, list, hearken.
(ANT.) ignore, scorn, disregard, reject.

listless *(SYN.)* uninterested, tired,

lethargic, unconcerned, apathetic.
(ANT.) active.
literal (SYN.) exact, verbatim, precise, strict, faithful.
literally (SYN.) actually, exactly, really.
literate (SYN.) informed, educated, learned, intelligent, versed, knowledgeable.
(ANT.) unread, illiterate, ignorant, unlettered.
literature (SYN.) books, writings, publications.
lithe (SYN.) supple, flexible, bending, limber, pliable.
(ANT.) stiff.
litigious (SYN.) quarrelsome, disputatious, argumentative.
litter (SYN.) rubbish, trash, scatter, clutter, strew, debris, rubble, disorder.
little (SYN.) tiny, petty, miniature, diminutive, puny, wee, significant, small, short, brief, bit, trivial.
(ANT.) huge, large, big, long, immense.
liturgy (SYN.) ritual, sacrament, worship, service.
live (SYN.) dwell, reside, abide, survive, exist, alive, occupy, stay, active, surviving.
(ANT.) die.
livelihood (SYN.) keep, sustenance, support, subsistence, job, trade, profession, vocation.
lively (SYN.) blithe, vivaciousness, clear, vivid, active, frolicsome, brisk, fresh, animated, energetic, live, spry, vigorous, quick, nimble, bright, exciting, supple.
(ANT.) stale, dull, listless, slow, vapid.
livestock (SYN.) animals, cattle.
livid (SYN.) grayish, furious, pale, enraged.
living (SYN.) support, livelihood, existent, alive.
load (SYN.) oppress, trouble, burden, weight, freight, afflict, encumber, pack, shipment, cargo, lade, tax.
(ANT.) lighten, console, unload, mitigate, empty, ease.
loafer (SYN.) loiterer, bum, idler, sponger, deadbeat.
loan (SYN.) credit, advance, lend.
loath (SYN.) reluctant, unwilling, opposed.
loathe (SYN.) dislike, despise, hate, abhor, detest, abominate.
(ANT.) love, approve, like, admire.
loathsome (SYN.) foul, vile, detestable,

revolting, abominable, atrocious, offensive, odious.
(ANT.) pleasant, commendable, alluring, agreeable, delightful.
lob (SYN.) toss, hurl, pitch, throw, heave.
lobby (SYN.) foyer, entry, entrance, vestibule, passageway, entryway.
local (SYN.) limited, regional, restricted, particular.
locality (SYN.) nearness, neighborhood, district, vicinity.
(ANT.) remoteness.
locate (SYN.) discover, find, unearth, site, situate, place.
located (SYN.) found, residing, positioned, situated, placed.
location (SYN.) spot, locale, station, locality, situation, place, area, site, vicinity, position, zone, region.
lock (SYN.) curl, hook, bolt, braid, ringlet, plait, close, latch, tuft, fastening, bar, hasp, fasten, tress.
(ANT.) open.
locker (SYN.) wardrobe, closet, cabinet, chest.
locket (SYN.) case, lavaliere, pendant.
locomotion (SYN.) movement, travel, transit, motion.
locution (SYN.) discourse, cadence, manner, accent.
lodge (SYN.) cabin, cottage, hut, club, chalet, society, room, reside, dwell, live, occupy, inhabit, abide, board, fix, settle.
lodger (SYN.) guest, tenant, boarder, occupant.
lofty (SYN.) high, stately, grandiose, towering, elevated, exalted, sublime, majestic, scornful, proud, grand, tall, pompous.
(ANT.) undignified, lowly, common, ordinary.
log (SYN.) lumber, wood, board, register, record, album, account, journal, timber.
logical (SYN.) strong, effective, telling, convincing, reasonable, sensible, rational, sane, sound, cogent.
(ANT.) crazy, illogical, irrational, unreasonable, weak.
logy (SYN.) tired, inactive, lethargic, sleepy, weary.
loiter (SYN.) idle, linger, wait, stay, tarry, dilly-dally, dawdle.
loll (SYN.) hang, droop, recline, repose, relax.
lone (SYN.) lonely, sole, unaided, single, deserted, isolated, secluded, apart

alone, solitary.

(ANT.) *surrounded, accompanied.*

loner (SYN.) recluse, maverick, outsider, hermit.

loneliness (SYN.) solitude, isolation, seclusion, alienation.

lonely (SYN.) unaided, isolated, single, solitary, lonesome, unaccompanied, deserted, alone, desolate.

(ANT.) *surrounded, attended.*

lonesome (SYN.) secluded, remote, unpopulated, barren, empty, desolate.

long (SYN.) lengthy, prolonged, wordy, elongated, extended, lingering, drawn out, lasting, protracted, extensive, length, prolix, far-reaching, extended.

(ANT.) *terse, concise, abridged, short.*

long-standing (SYN.) persistent, established.

long-winded (SYN.) boring, dull, wordy.

(ANT.) *curt, terse.*

look (SYN.) gaze, witness, seem, eye, behold, see, watch, scan, view, appear, stare, discern, glance, examine, examination, peep, expression, appearance, regard, study, contemplation, survey.

(ANT.) *overlook, hide, avert, miss.*

loom (SYN.) emerge, appear, show up.

loop (SYN.) ringlet, noose, spiral, fastener.

loose (SYN.) untied, unbound, lax, vague, unrestrained, dissolute, limp, undone, baggy, disengaged, indefinite, slack, careless, heedless, unfastened, free, wanton.

(ANT.) *restrained, steady, fastened, secure, tied, firm, fast, definite, inhibited.*

loosen (SYN.) untie, undo, loose, unchain.

(ANT.) *tie, tighten, secure.*

loot (SYN.) booty, plunder, take, steal, rob, sack, rifle, pillage, ravage, devastate.

lope (SYN.) run, race, bound, gallop.

lopsided (SYN.) unequal, twisted, uneven, askew, distorted.

loquacious (SYN.) garrulous, wordy, profuse, chatty, verbose.

lord (SYN.) peer, ruler, proprietor, nobleman,. master, owner, boss, governor.

lore (SYN.) learning, knowledge, wisdom, stories, legends beliefs, teachings.

lose (SYN.) misplace, flop, fail, sacrifice, forfeit, mislay, vanish, surrender.

(ANT.) *succeed, locate, place, win, discover, find.*

loss (SYN.) injury, damage, want, hurt, need, bereavement, trouble, death, failure, deficiency.

lost (SYN.) dazed, wasted, astray, forfeited, preoccupied, used, adrift, bewildered, missing, distracted, consumed, misspent, absorbed, confused, mislaid, gone, destroyed.

(ANT.) *found, anchored.*

lot (SYN.) result, destiny, bunch, many, amount, fate, cluster, group, sum, portion, outcome, number, doom, issue.

lotion (SYN.) cosmetic, salve, balm, cream.

lottery (SYN.) wager, chance, drawing, raffle.

loud (SYN.) vociferous, noisy, resounding, stentorian, clamorous, sonorous, thunderous, shrill, blaring, roaring, deafening.

(ANT.) *soft, inaudible, murmuring, subdued, quiet, dulcet.*

lounge (SYN.) idle, loaf, laze, sofa, couch, davenport, relax, rest, lobby, salon, divan.

louse (SYN.) scoundrel, knave, cad, rat.

lousy (SYN.) revolting, grimy, rotten, dirty, disgusting.

lovable (SYN.) charming, attractive, delightful, amiable, sweet, cuddly, likeable.

love (SYN.) attachment, endearment, affection, adoration, liking, devotion, warmth, tenderness, friendliness, adore, worship, like, cherish, fondness.

(ANT.) *loathing, detest, indifference, dislike, hate, hatred.*

loveliness (SYN.) grace, pulchritude, elegance, charm, attractiveness, comeliness, fairness, beauty.

(ANT.) *ugliness, eyesore, disfigurement, deformity.*

lovely (SYN.) handsome, fair, charming, pretty, attractive, delightful, beautiful, beauteous, exquisite, comely.

(ANT.) *ugly, unsightly, homely, foul, hideous, repulsive.*

lover (SYN.) fiance, suitor, courter, sweetheart, beau.

loving (SYN.) close, intimate, confidential, affectionate, friendly.

(ANT.) *formal, conventional, ceremonious, distant*

low *(SYN.)* mean, vile, despicable, vulgar, abject, groveling, contemptible, lesser, menial.

(ANT.) righteous, lofty, esteemed, noble.

lower *(SYN.)* subordinate, minor, secondary, quiet, soften, disgrace, degrade, decrease, reduce, diminish, lessen, inferior.

(ANT.) greater, superior, increase, better.

low-key *(SYN.)* subdued, muted, calm, controlled, restrained, understated, gentle.

lowly *(SYN.)* lowborn, humble, base, low, mean, common, average, simple, modest.

(ANT.) royal, noble.

loyal *(SYN.)* earnest, ardent, addicted, inclined, faithful, devoted, affectionate, prone, fond, patriotic, dependable, true.

(ANT.) indisposed, detached, disloyal, traitorous, untrammeled.

loyalty *(SYN.)* devotion, steadfastness, constancy, faithfulness, fidelity, patriotism, allegiance.

(ANT.) treachery, falseness, disloyalty.

lubricate *(SYN.)* oil, grease, anoint.

lucent *(SYN.)* radiant, beaming, vivid, illuminated, lustrous.

lucid *(SYN.)* plain, visible, clear, intelligible, unmistakable, transparent, limpid, translucent, open, shining, light, explicit, understandable, clear-cut, distinct.

(ANT.) unclear, vague, obscure.

luck *(SYN.)* chance, fortunate, fortune, lot, fate, fluke, destiny, karma, providence.

(ANT.) misfortune.

lucky *(SYN.)* favored, favorable, auspicious, fortunate, successful, felicitous, benign.

(ANT.) unlucky, condemned, unfortunate, persecuted.

lucrative *(SYN.)* well-paying, profitable, high-paying, productive, beneficial.

ludicrous *(SYN.)* absurd, ridiculous, preposterous.

lug *(SYN.)* pull, haul, drag, tug.

luggage *(SYN.)* bags, valises, baggage, suitcases, trunks.

lugubrious *(SYN.)* mournful, sad, gloomy, somber, melancholy.

lukewarm *(SYN.)* unenthusiastic, tepid, spiritless, detached, apathetic, mild.

lull *(SYN.)* quiet, calm, soothe, rest, hush, stillness, pause, break, intermission, recess, respite, silence.

lumber *(SYN.)* logs, timber, wood.

luminous *(SYN.)* beaming, lustrous, shining, glowing, gleaming, bright, light, alight, clear, radiant.

(ANT.) murky, dull, dark.

lummox *(SYN.)* yokel, oaf, bumpkin, clown, klutz.

lump *(SYN.)* swelling, protuberance, mass, chunk, hunk, bump.

lunacy *(SYN.)* derangement, madness, aberration, psychosis, craziness.

(ANT.) stability, rationality.

lunge *(SYN.)* charge, stab, attack, thrust, push.

lurch *(SYN.)* topple, sway, toss, roll, rock, tip, pitch.

lure *(SYN.)* draw, tug, drag, entice, attraction, haul, attract, temptation, persuade, pull, draw on, allure.

(ANT.) drive, alienate, propel.

lurid *(SYN.)* sensational, terrible, melodramatic, startling.

lurk *(SYN.)* sneak, hide, prowl, slink, creep.

luscious *(SYN.)* savory, delightful, juicy, sweet, pleasing, delectable, palatable, delicious, tasty.

(ANT.) unsavory, nauseous, acrid.

lush *(SYN.)* tender, succulent, ripe, juicy.

lust *(SYN.)* longing, desire, passion, appetite, craving, aspiration, urge.

(ANT.) hate, aversion, loathing, distaste.

luster *(SYN.)* radiance, brightness, glister, honor, fame, effulgence, gloss, sheen, shine, gleam, glow, glitter, brilliance, splendor.

(ANT.) dullness, obscurity, darkness.

lustful *(SYN.)* amorous, sexy, desirous, passionate, wanton.

lusty *(SYN.)* healthy, strong, mighty, powerful, sturdy, strapping, hale, hardy, rugged, hefty, robust.

(ANT.) weak.

luxuriant *(SYN.)* abundant, flourishing, dense, lush, rich.

luxurious *(SYN.)* rich, lavish, deluxe, splendid.

(ANT.) simple, crude, sparse.

luxury *(SYN.)* frills, comfort, extravagance, elegance, splendor, prosperity, swankiness, well-being, grandeur.

(ANT.) poverty.

lyric *(SYN.)* musical, text, words, libretto.

lyrical *(SYN.)* poetic, musical.

macabre *(SYN.)* ghastly, grim, horrible, gruesome.

maceration *(SYN.)* dilution, washing.

machination *(SYN.)* hoax, swindle, card-sharping, cunning, plot, cabal, con-spriracy.

machinator *(SYN.)* stragetist, schemer, schemist.

machine *(SYN.)* motor, mechanism, device, contrivance.

machinist *(SYN.)* engineer.

macilent *(SYN.)* gaunt, lean, lank, meager, emaciated.

mactation *(SYN.)* immolation, self-immolation, infanticide.

macula *(SYN.)* mole, patch, freckle, spot.

maculate *(SYN.)* bespot, stipple.

maculation *(SYN.)* irisation, striae, iridescence, spottiness.

mad *(SYN.)* incensed, crazy, insane, angry, furious, delirious, provoked, enraged, demented, maniacal, exasperated, wrathful, crazy, mentally ill, deranged.
(ANT.) sane, calm, healthy, rational, lucid, cheerful, happy.

madam *(SYN.)* dame, woman, lady, matron, mistress.

madden *(SYN.)* anger, annoy, infuriate, enrage, provoke, convulse, asperate, outrage.
(ANT.) please, mollify, calm.

madder *(SYN.)* ruddle.

madness *(SYN.)* derangement, delirium, aberration, mania, insanity, craziness, frenzy, psychosis.
(ANT.) stability, rationality.

maelstrom *(SYN.)* surge, rapids, eddy, white water, riptide.

magazine *(SYN.)* journal, periodical, arsenal, armory.

magic *(SYN.)* sorcery, wizardry, charm, legerdemain, enchantment, black art, necromancy, voodoo, conjuring, witchcraft.

magical *(SYN.)* mystical, marvelous, magic, miraculous, bewitching, spellbinding.

magician *(SYN.)* conjuror, sorcerer, wizard, witch, artist, trickster.

magistrate *(SYN.)* judge, adjudicator.

magnanimous *(SYN.)* giving, bountiful, beneficent, unselfish.
(ANT.) stingy, greedy, selfish.

magnate *(SYN.)* leader, bigwig, tycoon, chief, giant.

magnet *(SYN.)* enticer, enticement, lure, temptation.

magnetic *(SYN.)* pulling, attractive, alluring, drawing, enthralling, seductive.

magnetism *(SYN.)* allure, irresistibility, attraction, appeal.

magnificence *(SYN.)* luxury, grandeur, splendor, majesty, dynamic, mesmerizing.

magnificent *(SYN.)* rich, lavish, luxurious, splendid, wonderful, extraordinary, impressive.
(ANT.) simple, plain.

magnify *(SYN.)* heighten, exaggerate, amplify, expand, stretch, caricature, increase, enhance.
(ANT.) compress understate, depreciate, belittle.

magnitude *(SYN.)* mass, bigness, size, area, volume, dimensions, greatness, extent, measure, importance, consequence, significance.

maid *(SYN.)* chambermaid, servant, maidservant.

maiden *(SYN.)* original, foremost, first, damsel, lass, miss.
(ANT.) accessory, secondary.

mail *(SYN.)* dispatch, send, letters, post, correspondence.

maim *(SYN.)* disable, cripple, hurt, wound, injure, mangle, mutilate, incapacitate.

main *(SYN.)* essential, chief, highest, principal, first, leading, cardinal, supreme, foremost.
(ANT.) supplemental, subordinate, auxiliary.

mainstay *(SYN.)* buttress, pillar, refuge, reinforcement, support, backbone.

maintain *(SYN.)* claim, support, uphold, defend, vindicate, sustain, continue, allege, contend, preserve, affirm, keep, justify, keep up.
(ANT.) neglect, oppose, discontinue, resist, deny.

maintenance *(SYN.)* subsistence, livelihood, living, support, preservation, upkeep.

majestic *(SYN.)* magnificent, stately, noble, august, grand, imposing, sublime, lofty, high, grandiose, dignified, royal, kingly, princely, regal.
(ANT.) humble, lowly, undignified, common, ordinary.

majesty *(SYN.)* grandeur, dignity, nobility, splendor, distinction, eminence.

major *(SYN.)* important, superior, larger, chief, greater, uppermost.
(ANT.) inconsequential, minor.

make *(SYN.)* execute, cause, produce, establish, assemble, create, shape, compel, fashion, construct, build, fabricate, manufacture, form, become.
(ANT.) unmake, break, undo, demolish.

make-believe *(SYN.)* pretend, imagined, simulated, false, fake, unreal.

maker *(SYN.)* inventor, creator, producer, builder, manufacturer, originator.

makeshift *(SYN.)* proxy, deputy, understudy, expedient, agent, lieutenant, alternate, substitute, equivalent.
(ANT.) sovereign, head, principal.

make-up *(SYN.)* composition, formation, structure, cosmetics.

malady *(SYN.)* disease, illness, sickness, ailment, infirmity, disorder, affliction.
(ANT.) vigor, healthiness, health.

malaise *(SYN.)* anxiety, apprehension, dissatisfaction, uneasiness, nervousness, disquiet, discontent.

male *(SYN.)* masculine, virile.
(ANT.) female, womanly, feminine.

malcontent *(SYN.)* displeased, ill-humored, querulous, discontented, quarrelsome.

malefactor *(SYN.)* perpetrator, gangster, hoodlum, wrongdoer, troublemaker, criminal, scoundrel, evildoer, lawbreaker.

malevolence *(SYN.)* spite, malice, enmity, rancor, animosity.
(ANT.) love, affection, toleration, kindness.

malfunction *(SYN.)* flaw, breakdown, snag, glitch, failure.

malice *(SYN.)* spite, grudge, enmity, ill will, malignity, animosity, rancor, resentment, viciousness, grudge, bitterness.
(ANT.) love, affection, toleration, benevolence, charity.

malicious *(SYN.)* hostile, malignant, virulent, bitter, rancorous, evil-minded, malevolent, spiteful, wicked.
(ANT.) kind, benevolent, affectionate.

malign *(SYN.)* misuse, defame, revile, abuse, traduce, asperse, misapply, disparage.

(ANT.) praise, cherish, protect, honor.

malignant *(SYN.)* harmful, deadly, killing, lethal, mortal, destructive, hurtful, malicious.
(ANT.) benign, harmless.

malingerer *(SYN.)* quitter, idler, goldbrick.

malleable *(SYN.)* meek, tender, soft, lenient, flexible, mild, compassionate, supple.
(ANT.) tough, rigid, unyielding, hard.

malodorous *(SYN.)* reeking, fetid, smelly, noxious, vile, rancid, offensive,

malpractice *(SYN.)* wrongdoing, misdeed, abuse, malfeasance, error, mismanagement, dereliction, fault, sin, misconduct.

maltreat *(SYN.)* mistreat, ill-treatment, abuse.

maltreatment *(SYN.)* disparagement, perversion, aspersion, invective, defamation, profanation.
(ANT.) respect, approval, laudation, commendation.

mammoth *(SYN.)* enormous, immense, huge, colossal, gigantic, gargantuan, ponderous.
(ANT.) minuscule, tiny, small.

man *(SYN.)* person, human being, society, folk, soul, individual, mortal, fellow, male, gentleman.
(ANT.) woman.

manacle *(SYN.)* chain, shackle, cuff, handcuff, bond.

manage *(SYN.)* curb, govern, direct, bridle, command, regulate, repress, check, restrain, dominate, guide, lead, supervise, superintend, control, rule.
(ANT.) forsake, submit, abandon, mismanage, bungle.

manageable *(SYN.)* willing, obedient, docile, controllable, tractable, submissive, governable, wieldy, untroublesome.
(ANT.) recalcitrant, unmanageable, wild.

management *(SYN.)* regulation, administration, supervision, direction, control.

manager *(SYN.)* overseer, superintendent, supervisor, director, boss, executive.

mandate *(SYN.)* order, injunction, command, referendum, dictate, writ, directive, commission.

mandatory *(SYN.)* compulsory, required, obligatory, imperative, necessary. *(ANT.) optional.*

maneuver *(SYN.)* execution, effort, proceeding, enterprise, working, action, operation, agency, instrumentality. *(ANT.) rest, inaction, cessation.*

mangle *(SYN.)* tear apart, cut, maim, wound, mutilate, injure, break, demolish.

mangy *(SYN.)* shoddy, frazzled, seedy, threadbare, shabby, ragged, sordid.

manhandle *(SYN.)* maltreat, maul, abuse, ill-treat.

manhood *(SYN.)* maturity, manliness. *(ANT.) youth.*

mania *(SYN.)* insanity, enthusiasm, craze, desire, madness.

manic *(SYN.)* excited, hyped up, agitated.

manifest *(SYN.)* open, evident, lucid, clear, distinct, unobstructed, cloudless, apparent, intelligible, apparent. *(ANT.) vague, overcast, unclear, cloudy, hidden, concealed.*

manifesto *(SYN.)* pronouncement, edict, proclamation, statement, declaration.

manifold *(SYN.)* various, many, multiple, numerous, abundant, copious, profuse. *(ANT.) few.*

manipulate *(SYN.)* manage, feel, work, operate, handle, touch, maneuver.

manly *(SYN.)* strong, brave, masculine, manful, courageous, stalwart.

man-made *(SYN.)* artificial. *(ANT.) natural.*

manner *(SYN.)* air, demeanor, custom, style, method, deportment, mode, habit, practice, way, behavior, fashion.

mannerism *(SYN.)* eccentricity, quirk, habit, peculiarity, idiosyncrasy, trait.

mannerly *(SYN.)* well-bred, gentlemanly, courteous, suave, polite, genteel.

manor *(SYN.)* land, mansion, estate, domain, villa, castle, property, palace.

manslaughter *(SYN.)* murder, killing, assassination, homicide, elimination.

mantle *(SYN.)* serape, garment, overgarment, cover, cloak, wrap.

manual *(SYN.)* directory, guidebook, handbook, physical, laborious, menial.

manufacture *(SYN.)* construct, make, assemble, fabricate, produce, fashion, build.

manure *(SYN.)* fertilizer, droppings, waste, compost.

manuscript *(SYN.)* copy, writing, work, paper, composition, document.

many *(SYN.)* numerous, various, divers, multitudinous, sundry, multifarious, several, manifold, abundant, plentiful. *(ANT.) infrequent, meager, few, scanty.*

map *(SYN.)* sketch, plan, chart, graph, itinerary.

mar *(SYN.)* spoil, hurt, damage, impair, harm, deface, injure. *(ANT.) repair, benefit, mend.*

marathon *(SYN.)* relay, race, contest.

maraud *(SYN.)* invade, plunder, loot, ransack, ravage, raid.

march *(SYN.)* promenade, parade, pace, hike, walk, tramp.

margin *(SYN.)* boundary, border, rim, edge.

marginal *(SYN.)* unnecessary, nonessential, borderline, noncritical. *(ANT.) essential.*

marine *(SYN.)* naval, oceanic, nautical, ocean, maritime.

mariner *(SYN.)* seafarer, gob, seaman, sailor.

marionette *(SYN.)* doll, puppet.

maritime *(SYN.)* shore, coastal, nautical.

mark *(SYN.)* stain, badge, stigma, vestige, sign, feature, label, characteristic, trace, brand, trait, scar, indication, impression, effect, imprint, stamp, brand.

marked *(SYN.)* plain, apparent, noticeable, evident, decided, noted, special, noteworthy.

market *(SYN.)* supermarket, store, bazaar, mart, stall, marketplace, plaza, emporium.

maroon *(SYN.)* desert, leave behind, forsake, abandon, jettison.

marriage *(SYN.)* wedding, matrimony, nuptials, espousal, union, alliance, association. *(ANT.) divorce, celibacy, separation.*

marrow *(SYN.)* center, core, gist, essential, soul.

marry *(SYN.)* wed, espouse, betroth.

marsh *(SYN.)* bog, swamp, mire, everglade, estuary.

marshal *(SYN.)* adjutant, officer, order, arrange, rank.

mart *(SYN.)* shop, market, store.

martial *(SYN.)* warlike, combative, militant, belligerent. *(ANT.) peaceful.*

martyr *(SYN.)* victim, sufferer, tortured,

torment, plague, harass, persecute.

marvel *(SYN.)* phenomenon, wonder, miracle, astonishment, sensation.

marvelous *(SYN.)* rare, wonderful, extraordinary, unusual, exceptional, miraculous, wondrous, amazing, astonishing, astounding. *(ANT.)* usual, common, ordinary. commonplace.

mascot *(SYN.)* pet, amulet, charm.

masculine *(SYN.)* robust, manly, virile, strong, bold, male, lusty, vigorous, hardy, mannish. *(ANT.)* weak, emasculated, feminine, effeminate, womanish, female, unmasculine.

mash *(SYN.)* mix, pulverize, crush, grind, crumble, granulate.

mask *(SYN.)* veil, disguise, cloak, secrete, withhold, hide, cover, protection, protector, camouflage, conceal, screen. *(ANT.)* uncover, reveal, disclose, show, expose.

masquerade *(SYN.)* pretend, disguise, pose, impersonate, costume party.

mass *(SYN.)* society, torso, body, remains, association, carcass, bulk, company, pile, heap, quantity, aggregation. *(ANT.)* spirit, mind, intellect.

massacre *(SYN.)* butcher, murder, carnage, slaughter, execute, slay, genocide, killing, butchery, extermination. *(ANT.)* save, protect, vivify, animate.

massage *(SYN.)* knead, rub, stroke.

masses *(SYN)* populace, crowd, multitude, people.

massive *(SYN.)* grave, cumbersome, heavy, sluggish, ponderous, serious, burdensome, huge, immense, tremendous, gigantic. *(ANT.)* light, animated, small, tiny, little.

mast *(SYN.)* pole, post.

master *(SYN.)* owner, employer, leader, ruler, chief, head, lord, teacher, manager, holder, commander, overseer, expert, maestro, genius, captain, director, boss. *(ANT.)* slave, servant.

masterful *(SYN.)* commanding, bossy, domineering, dictatorial, cunning, wise, accomplished, skillful, sharp.

masterly *(SYN.)* adroit, superb, skillful, expert. *(ANT.)* awkward, clumsy.

mastermind *(SYN.)* prodigy, sage, guru, mentor.

masterpiece *(SYN.)* prizewinner, classic, perfection, model.

mastery *(SYN.)* sway, sovereignty, domination, transcendence, ascendancy, influence, jurisdiction, prestige.

masticate *(SYN.)* chew.

mat *(SYN.)* cover, rug, pallet, bedding, pad.

match *(SYN.)* equivalent, equal, contest, balance, resemble, peer, mate.

matchless *(SYN.)* peerless, incomparable, unequaled, unrivaled, excellent. *(ANT.)* ordinary, unimpressive.

mate *(SYN.)* friend, colleague, associate, partner, companion, comrade. *(ANT.)* stranger, adversary.

material *(SYN.)* sensible, momentous, germane, bodily, palpable, important, physical, essential, corporeal, tangible, substance, matter, fabric. *(ANT.)* metaphysical, spiritual, insignificant, mental, immaterial, irrelevant, intangible.

materialize *(SYN.)* take shape, finalize, embody, incarnate, emerge, appear.

maternal *(SYN.)* motherly. *(ANT.)* fatherly.

mathematics *(SYN.)* measurements, computations, numbers, calculation, figures.

matrimony *(SYN.)* marriage, wedding, espousal, union. *(ANT.)* virginity, divorce.

matrix *(SYN.)* template, stamp, negative, stencil, mold, form, die, cutout.

matron *(SYN.)* lady.

matted *(SYN.)* tangled, clustered, rumpled, shaggy, knotted, gnarled, tousled.

matter *(SYN.)* cause, thing, substance, occasion, material, moment, topic, stuff, concern, theme, subject, consequence, affair, business, interest. *(ANT.)* spirit, immateriality.

mature *(SYN.)* ready, matured, complete, ripe, consummate, mellow, aged, seasoned, full-grown. *(ANT.)* raw, crude, undeveloped, young, immature, innocent.

maudlin *(SYN.)* emotional, mushy, sentimental, mawkish.

maul *(SYN.)* pummel, mistreat, manhandle, beat, batter, bruise, abuse.

mausoleum *(SYN.)* shrine, tomb, vault.

maverick *(SYN.)* nonconformist, oddball,

outsider, dissenter, loner.

mawkish *(SYN.)* sentimental, emotional, nostalgic.

maxim *(SYN.)* rule, code, law, proverb, principle, saying, adage, motto.

maximum *(SYN.)* highest, largest, head, greatest, supremacy, climax. *(ANT.) minimum.*

may *(SYN.)* can, be able.

maybe *(SYN.)* feasibly, perchance, perhaps, possibly. *(ANT.) definitely.*

mayhem *(SYN.)* brutality, viciousness, ruthlessness.

maze *(SYN.)* complex, labyrinth, network, muddle, confusion, snarl, tangle.

meadow *(SYN.)* field, pasture, lea, range, grassland.

meager *(SYN.)* sparse, scanty, mean, frugal, deficient, slight, paltry, inadequate. *(ANT.) ample, plentiful, abundant, bountiful.*

meal *(SYN.)* refreshment, dinner, lunch, repast, breakfast.

mean *(SYN.)* sordid, base, intend, plan, propose, expect, indicate, denote, say, signify, suggest, express, average, nasty, middle, contemptible, offensive, vulgar, unkind, cruel, despicable, vile, low, medium. *(ANT.) dignified, noble, exalted, thoughtful, gentle, openhanded, kind, generous, admirable.*

meander *(SYN.)* wind, stray, wander, twist

meaning *(SYN.)* gist, connotation, intent, purport, drift, acceptation, implication, sense, import, interpretation, denotation, signification, explanation, purpose, significance.

meaningful *(SYN.)* profound, deep, expressive, important, crucial.

meaningless *(SYN.)* nonsensical, senseless, unreasonable, preposterous.

means *(SYN.)* utensil, channel, agent, money, riches, vehicle, apparatus, device, wealth, support, medium, instrument. *(ANT.) preventive, impediment, hindrance.*

measly *(SYN.)* scanty, puny, skimpy, meager, petty.

measure *(SYN.)* law, bulk, rule, criterion, size, volume, weight, standard, dimension, breadth, depth, test, touchstone, trial, length, extent, gauge.

(ANT.) guess, chance, supposition.

measureless *(SYN.)* immeasurable, immense, boundless, limitless, infinite, vast. *(ANT.) figurable, ascertainable, measurable.*

meat *(SYN.)* lean, flesh, food.

mecca *(SYN.)* target, shrine, goal, sanctuary, destination.

mechanic *(SYN.)* repairman, machinist.

mechanism *(SYN.)* device, contrivance, tool, machine, machinery.

medal *(SYN.)* decoration, award, badge, medallion, reward, ribbon, prize, honor.

meddle *(SYN.)* tamper, interpose, pry, snoop, intrude, interrupt, interfere, monkey.

meddlesome *(SYN.)* forward, bothersome, intrusive, obtrusive.

media *(SYN.)* tools, instruments, implements.

mediate *(SYN.)* settle, intercede, umpire, intervene, negotiate, arbitrate, referee.

medicinal *(SYN.)* helping, healing, remedial, therapeutic, corrective.

medicine *(SYN.)* drug, medication, remedy, cure, prescription, potion.

mediocre *(SYN.)* medium, mean, average, moderate, fair, ordinary. *(ANT.) outstanding, exceptional.*

meditate *(SYN.)* remember, muse, think, judge, mean, conceive, contemplate, deem, suppose, purpose, consider, picture, reflect, believe, plan, reckon.

medium *(SYN.)* modicum, average, middling, median. *(ANT.) extreme.*

medley *(SYN.)* hodgepodge, mixture, assortment, conglomeration, mishmash, miscellany.

meek *(SYN.)* subdued, dull, tedious, flat, docile, domesticated, tame, insipid, domestic. *(ANT.) spirited, exciting, savage, wild.*

meet *(SYN.)* fulfill, suffer, find, collide, gratify, engage, connect, converge, encounter, unite, join, satisfy, settle, greet, answer, undergo, answer, meeting, contest, match, assemble, discharge, gather, convene, congregate, confront, intersect. *(ANT.) scatter, disperse, separate, cleave.*

melancholy *(SYN.)* disconsolate, dejected, despondent, glum, somber, pensive, moody, dispirited, depressed, gloomy, dismal, doleful, depression, downcast, gloom, sadness, sad, grave, downhearted, sorrowful. *(ANT.) happy, cheerful, merry.*

meld *(SYN.)* unite, mix, combine, fuse, merge, blend, commingle, amalgamate.

melee *(SYN.)* battle royal, fight, brawl, free-for-all, fracas.

mellow *(SYN.)* mature, ripe, aged, cured, full-flavored, sweet, smooth, melodious, develop, soften. *(ANT.) unripened, immature.*

melodious *(SYN.)* lilting, musical, lyric, dulcet, mellifluous, tuneful, melodic.

melodramatic *(SYN.)* dramatic, ceremonious, affected, stagy, histrionic, overwrought, sensational, stagy. *(ANT.) unemotional, subdued, modest.*

melody *(SYN.)* strain, concord, music, air, song, tune, harmony.

melt *(SYN.)* dissolve, liquefy, blend, fade out, vanish, dwindle, disappear, thaw. *(ANT.) freeze, harden, solidify.*

member *(SYN.)* share, part, allotment, moiety, element, concern, interest, lines, faction, role, apportionment. *(ANT.) whole.*

membrane *(SYN.)* layer, sheath, tissue, covering.

memento *(SYN.)* keepsake, token, reminder, trophy, sign, souvenir, remembrance.

memoirs *(SYN.)* diary, reflections, experiences, autobiography, journal, confessions.

memorable *(SYN.)* important, historic, significant, unforgettable, noteworthy, momentous, crucial, impressive. *(ANT.) passing, forgettable, transitory, commonplace.*

memorandum *(SYN.)* letter, mark, token, note, indication, remark, message.

memorial *(SYN.)* monument, souvenir, memento, remembrance, commemoration, reminiscent, ritual, testimonial.

memorize *(SYN.)* study, remember.

memory *(SYN.)* renown, remembrance, reminiscence, fame, retrospection, recollection, reputation. *(ANT.) oblivion.*

menace *(SYN.)* warning, threat, intimidation, warn, threaten, imperil, forebode.

menagerie *(SYN.)* collection, zoo, kennel.

mend *(SYN.)* restore, better, refit, sew, remedy, patch, correct, repair, rectify,

ameliorate, improve, reform, recover, fix. *(ANT.) hurt, deface, rend, destroy.*

mendacious *(SYN.)* dishonest, false, lying, deceitful, deceptive, tricky. *(ANT.) honest, truthful, sincere, creditable.*

mendicant *(SYN.)* ragamuffin, vagabond, beggar.

menial *(SYN.)* unskilled, lowly, degrading, tedious, humble, routine.

mental *(SYN.)* reasoning, intellectual, rational, thinking, conscious, reflective, thoughtful. *(ANT.) physical.*

mentality *(SYN.)* intellect, reason, understanding, liking, disposition, judgment, brain, inclination, faculties, outlook. *(ANT.) materiality, corporeality.*

mention *(SYN.)* introduce, refer to, reference, allude, enumerate, speak of.

mentor *(SYN.)* advisor, tutor, sponsor, guru, teacher, counselor, master, coach.

mercenary *(SYN.)* sordid, corrupt, venal, covetous, grasping, avaricious, greedy. *(ANT.) liberal, generous.*

merchandise *(SYN.)* stock, wares, goods, sell, commodities, promote, staples, products.

merchant *(SYN.)* retailer, dealer, trader, storekeeper, salesman, businessman.

merciful *(SYN.)* humane, kindhearted, tender, clement, sympathetic, forgiving, tolerant, forbearing, lenient, compassionate, tenderhearted, kind. *(ANT.) remorseless, cruel, unjust, mean, harsh, unforgiving, vengeful, brutal, unfeeling, pitiless.*

merciless *(SYN.)* carnal, ferocious, brute, barbarous, gross, ruthless, cruel, remorseless, bestial, savage, rough, pitiless, inhuman. *(ANT.) humane, courteous, merciful, openhearted, kind, civilized.*

mercurial *(SYN.)* fickle, unstable, volatile, changeable, inconstant, capricious, flighty.

mercy *(SYN.)* grace, consideration, kindness, clemency, mildness, forgiveness, pity, charity, sympathy, leniency, compassion. *(ANT.) punishment, retribution, ruthlessness, cruelty, vengeance.*

mere *(SYN.)* only, simple, scant, bare. *(ANT.) substantial, considerable.*

merely *(SYN.)* only, barely, simply, hardly.

meretricious *(SYN.)* gaudy, sham, bogus, tawdry, flashy, garish.

merge *(SYN.)* unify, fuse, combine, amalgamate, unite, blend, commingle. *(ANT.)* separate, decompose, analyze.

merger *(SYN.)* cartel, union, conglomerate, trust, incorporation, combine, pool.

meridian *(SYN.)* climax, summit, pinnacle, zenith, peak, acme, apex, culmination.

merit *(SYN.)* worthiness, earn, goodness, effectiveness, power, value, virtue, goodness, quality, deserve, excellence, worth. *(ANT.)* sin, fault, lose, consume.

merited *(SYN.)* proper, deserved, suitable, adequate, earned. *(ANT.)* unmerited, improper.

meritorious *(SYN.)* laudable, excellent, commendable, good, praise-worthy, deserving.

merry *(SYN.)* hilarious, lively, festive, joyous, sprightly, mirthful, blithe, gay, cheery, joyful, jolly, happy, gleeful, jovial, cheerful. *(ANT.)* sorrowful, doleful, morose, gloomy, sad, melancholy.

mesh *(SYN.)* grid, screen, net, complex.

mesmerize *(SYN.)* enthrall, transfix, spellbind, bewitch, charm, fascinate, hypnotize.

mess *(SYN.)* dirtiness, untidiness, disorder, confusion, muddle, trouble, jumble, difficulty, predicament, confuse, dirty.

message *(SYN.)* letter, annotation, memo, symbol, indication, sign, note, communication, memorandum, observation, token.

messenger *(SYN.)* bearer, agent, runner, courier, liaison, delegate, page.

messy *(SYN.)* disorderly, dirty, confusing, confused, disordered, sloppy, untidy, slovenly. *(ANT.)* orderly, neat, tidy.

metallic *(SYN.)* grating, harsh, clanging, brassy, brazen.

metamorphosis *(SYN.)* transfiguration, change, alteration, rebirth, mutation.

mete *(SYN.)* deal, assign, apportion, divide, give, allocate, allot, measure. *(ANT.)* withhold, keep, retain.

meteoric *(SYN.)* flashing, blazing, swift, brilliant, spectacular, remarkable.

meter *(SYN.)* record, measure, gauge.

method *(SYN.)* order, manner, plan, way, mode, technique, fashion, approach, design, procedure. *(ANT.)* disorder.

methodical *(SYN.)* exact, definite, ceremonious, stiff, accurate, distinct, unequivocal. *(ANT.)* easy, loose, informal, rough.

meticulous *(SYN.)* precise, careful, exacting, fastidious, fussy, perfectionist.

metropolitan *(SYN.)* civic, city, municipal.

mettle *(SYN.)* intrepidity, resolution, boldness, prowess, bravery, fearlessness. *(ANT.)* fear, timidity, cowardice.

microscopic *(SYN.)* tiny, precise, fine, detailed, minute, infinitesimal, minimal. *(ANT.)* general, huge, enormous.

middle *(SYN.)* midpoint, nucleus, center, midst, median, central, intermediate, core. *(ANT.)* end, rim, outskirts, beginning, border, periphery.

middleman *(SYN.)* dealer, agent, distributor, broker, representative, intermediary.

midget *(SYN.)* gnome, shrimp, pygmy, runt, dwarf. *(ANT.)* giant.

midst *(SYN.)* center, heart, middle, thick.

midway *(SYN.)* halfway, midmost, inside, central, middle.

mien *(SYN.)* way, semblance, manner, behavior, demeanor, expression, deportment.

miff *(SYN.)* provoke, rile, chagrin, irk, irritate, affront, offend, annoy, exasperate.

might *(SYN.)* force, power, vigor, potency, ability, strength. *(ANT.)* frailty, vulnerability, weakness.

mighty *(SYN.)* firm, fortified, powerful, athletic, potent, muscular, robust, strong, cogent. *(ANT.)* feeble, weak, brittle, insipid, frail, delicate.

migrant *(SYN.)* traveling, roaming, straying, roving, rambling, transient, meandering. *(ANT.)* stationary.

migrate *(SYN.)* resettle, move, emigrate, immigrate, relocate, journey.

(ANT.) *stay, remain, settle.*

migratory *(SYN.)* itinerant, roving, mobile, vagabond, unsettled, nomadic, wandering.

mild *(SYN.)* soothing, moderate, gentle, tender, bland, pleasant, kind, meek, calm, amiable, compassionate, temperate, peaceful, soft.
(ANT.) *severe, turbulent, stormy, excitable, violent, harsh, bitter.*

milieu *(SYN.)* environment, background, locale, setting, scene, circumstances.

militant *(SYN.)* warlike, belligerent, hostile, fighting, pugnacious, aggressive, combative.
(ANT.) *peaceful.*

military *(SYN.)* troops, army, service, soldiers.

milksop *(SYN.)* namby-pamby, weakling, sissy, coward.

mill *(SYN.)* foundry, shop, plant, factory, manufactory.

millstone *(SYN.)* load, impediment, burden, encumbrance, hindrance.

mimic *(SYN.)* simulate, duplicate, copy, imitate, mock, counterfeit, simulate.
(ANT.) *invent, distort, alter.*

mince *(SYN.)* shatter, fragment, chop, smash.

mind *(SYN.)* intelligence, psyche, disposition, intention, understanding, intellect, spirit, brain, inclination, mentality, soul, wit, liking, brain, sense, watch, faculties, judgment, reason.
(ANT.) *matter, corporeality.*

mindful *(SYN.)* alert, aware, watchful, cognizant, watchful, sensible, heedful.

mine *(SYN.)* shaft, lode, pit, excavation, drill, dig, quarry, source.

mingle *(SYN.)* unite, coalesce, fuse, merge, combine, amalgamate, unify, conjoin, mix, blend, commingle.
(ANT.) *separate, analyze, sort, disintegrate.*

miniature *(SYN.)* small, little, tiny, midget, minute, minuscule, wee, petite, diminutive.
(ANT.) *outsize.*

minimize *(SYN.)* shorten, deduct, belittle, decrease, reduce, curtail, lessen, diminish, subtract.
(ANT.) *enlarge, increase, amplify.*

minimum *(SYN.)* lowest, least, smallest, slightest.
(ANT.) *maximum.*

minister *(SYN.)* pastor, clergyman, vicar, parson, curate, preacher, prelate, chaplain, cleric, deacon, reverend.

minor *(SYN.)* poorer, lesser, petty, youth, inferior, secondary, smaller, unimportant, lower.
(ANT.) *higher, superior, major, greater.*

minority *(SYN.)* youth, childhood, immaturity.

minstrel *(SYN.)* bard, musician.

mint *(SYN.)* stamp, coin, strike, punch.

minus *(SYN.)* lacking, missing, less, absent, without.

minute *(SYN.)* tiny, particular, fine, precise, jiffy, instant, moment, wee, exact, detailed, microscopic.
(ANT.) *large, general, huge, enormous.*

miraculous *(SYN.)* spiritual, supernatural, wonderful, marvelous, incredible, preternatural.
(ANT.) *commonplace, natural, common, plain, everyday, human.*

mirage *(SYN.)* vision, illusion, fantasy, dream, phantom.
(ANT.) *reality, actuality.*

mire *(SYN.)* marsh, slush, slime, mud.

mirror *(SYN.)* glass, reflector, reflect.

mirth *(SYN.)* joy, glee, jollity, joyousness, gaiety, joyfulness, laughter, merriment.
(ANT.) *sadness, gloom, seriousness.*

misadventure *(SYN.)* accident, adversity, reverse, calamity, catastrophe, hardship, mischance, setback.

misappropriate *(SYN.)* embezzle, steal, purloin, plunder, cheat, filch, defraud.

misbehave *(SYN.)* trespass, act badly.
(ANT.) *behave.*

miscalculate *(SYN.)* miscount, blunder, confuse, err, mistake, misconstrue.

miscarriage *(SYN.)* omission, want, decay, fiasco, default, deficiency, loss, abortion, prematurity.
(ANT.) *success, sufficiency, achievement.*

miscarry *(SYN.)* flounder, fall short, falter, go wrong, fail.
(ANT.) *succeed.*

miscellaneous *(SYN.)* diverse, motley, indiscriminate, assorted, sundry, heterogeneous, mixed, varied.
(ANT.) *classified, selected, homogeneous, alike, ordered.*

miscellany *(SYN.)* medley, gallimaufry, jumble, potpourri, mixture, collection.

mischief *(SYN.)* injury, harm, damage, evil, ill, prankishness, rascality, roguishness, playfulness, wrong, detriment, hurt.

(ANT.) kindness, boon, benefit.

mischievous (SYN.) roguish, prankish, naughty, playful.

(ANT.) well-behaved, good.

misconduct (SYN.) transgression, delinquency, wrongdoing, negligence.

miscreant (SYN.) rascal, wretch, rogue, sinner, criminal, villain, scoundrel.

miscue (SYN.) blunder, fluff, mistake, error, lapse.

misdemeanor (SYN.) infringement, transgression, violation, offense, wrong.

miser (SYN.) cheapskate, tightwad, skinflint.

(ANT.) philanthropist.

miserable (SYN.) abject, forlorn, comfortless, low, worthless, pitiable, distressed, heartbroken, disconsolate, despicable, wretched, uncomfortable, unhappy, poor, unlucky, paltry, contemptible, mean.

(ANT.) fortunate, happy, contented, joyful, content, wealthy, honorable, lucky, noble, significant.

miserly (SYN.) stingy, greedy, acquisitive, tight, tightfisted, cheap, mean, parsimonious, avaricious.

(ANT.) bountiful, generous, spendthrift, munificent, extravagant, openhanded, altruistic.

misery (SYN.) suffering, woe, evil, agony, torment, trouble, distress, anguish, grief, unhappiness, anguish, tribulation, calamity, sorrow.

(ANT.) fun, pleasure, delight, joy.

misfit (SYN.) crank, loner, deviate, fifth wheel, individualist.

misfortune (SYN.) adversity, distress, mishap, calamity, accident, catastrophe, hardship, ruin, disaster, affliction.

(ANT.) success, blessing, prosperity.

misgiving (SYN.) suspicion, doubt, mistrust, hesitation, uncertainty.

misguided (SYN.) misdirected, misled, misinformed, wrong, unwise, foolish, erroneous, unwarranted, ill-advised.

mishap (SYN.) misfortune, casualty, accident, disaster, adversity, reverse.

(ANT.) intention, calculation, purpose.

mishmash (SYN.) medley, muddle, gallimaufry, hodge-podge, hash.

misjudge (SYN.) err, mistake, miscalculate.

mislay (SYN.) misplace, lose.

(ANT.) discover, find.

mislead (SYN.) misdirect, deceive, misinform, deceive, delude.

misleading (SYN.) fallacious, delusive, deceitful, false, deceptive, illusive.

(ANT.) real, genuine, truthful, honest.

mismatched (SYN.) unfit, unsuitable, incompatible, unsuited.

misplace (SYN.) lose, mislay, miss.

(ANT.) find.

misrepresent (SYN.) misstate, distort, falsify, twist, belie, garble, disguise.

miss (SYN.) lose, want, crave, yearn for, fumble, drop, error, slip, default, omit, lack, need, desire, fail.

(ANT.) suffice, have, achieve, succeed.

misshapen (SYN.) disfigured, deformed, grotesque, malformed, ungainly, gnarled, contorted.

missile (SYN.) grenade, shot, projectile.

missing (SYN.) wanting, lacking, absent, lost, gone, vanished.

mission (SYN.) business, task, job, stint, work, errand, assignment, delegation.

missionary (SYN.) publicist, evangelist, propagandist.

mist (SYN.) cloud, fog, haze, steam, haze.

mistake (SYN.) slip, misjudge, fault, blunder, misunderstand, confuse, inaccuracy, misinterpret, error.

(ANT.) truth, accuracy.

mistaken (SYN.) false, amiss, incorrect, awry, wrong, misinformed, confused, inaccurate, askew.

(ANT.) true, correct, suitable, right.

mister (SYN.) young man, gentleman, esquire, fellow, buddy.

mistreat (SYN.) wrong, pervert, oppress, harm, maltreat, abuse.

mistrust (SYN.) suspect, doubt, distrust, dispute, question, skepticism, apprehension.

(ANT.) trust.

misunderstand (SYN.) misjudge, misinterpret, jumble, confuse, mistake.

(ANT.) perceive, comprehend.

misunderstanding (SYN) clash, disagreement, dispute, conflict, misinterpretation.

misuse (SYN.) defame, malign, abuse, misapply, traduce, asperse, revile, vilify.

(ANT.) protect, honor, respect, cherish.

mite (SYN.) particle, mote, smidgen,

trifle, iota, corpuscle.

mitigate *(SYN.)* soften, soothe, abate, assuage, relieve, allay, diminish.
(ANT.) irritate, agitate, increase.

mix *(SYN.)* mingle, blend, consort, fuse, alloy, combine, jumble, fraternize, associate, concoct, commingle, amalgamate, confound, compound, join.
(ANT.) divide, sort, segregate, dissociate, separate.

mixture *(SYN.)* diversity, variety, strain, sort, change, kind, confusion, heterogeneity, jumble, mess, assortment, breed, mix, hodge-podge, subspecies.
(ANT.) likeness, sameness, homogeneity, monotony.

moan *(SYN.)* wail, groan, cry, lament.

moat *(SYN.)* fortification, ditch, trench, entrenchment.

mob *(SYN.)* crowd, host, populace, swarm, riot, bevy, horde, rabble, throng, multitude.

mobile *(SYN.)* free, movable, portable.
(ANT.) stationary, immobile, fixed.

mock *(SYN.)* taunt, jeer, deride, scoff, scorn, fleer, ridicule, tease, fake, imitation, sham, gibe, sneer, fraudulent, flout.
(ANT.) praise, applaud, real, genuine, honor, authentic, compliment.

mockery *(SYN.)* gibe, ridicule, satire, derision, sham, banter, irony, sneering, scorn, travesty, jeering.
(ANT.) admiration, praise.

mode *(SYN.)* method, fashion, procedure, design, manner, technique, way, style, practice, plan.
(ANT.) disorder, confusion.

model *(SYN.)* copy, prototype, type, example, ideal, imitation, version, facsimile, design, style, archetype, pattern, standard, mold.
(ANT.) reproduction, imitation.

moderate *(SYN.)* lower, decrease, average, fair, reasonable, abate, medium, conservative, referee, umpire, suppress, judge, lessen, assuage.
(ANT.) intensify, enlarge, amplify.

moderation *(SYN.)* sobriety, forbearance, self-control, restraint, continence, temperance.
(ANT.) greed, excess, intoxication.

moderator *(SYN.)* referee, leader, arbitrator, chairman, chairperson, master of cermonies, emcee.

modern *(SYN.)* modish, current, recent, novel, fresh, contemporary, new.
(ANT.) old, antiquated, past, bygone, ancient.

modernize *(SYN.)* refurnish, refurbish, improve, rebuild, renew, renovate.

modest *(SYN.)* unassuming, virtuous, bashful, meek, shy, humble, decent, demure, unpretentious, prudish, moderate, reserved.
(ANT.) forward, bold, ostentatious, conceited, immodest, arrogant.

modesty *(SYN.)* decency, humility, propriety, simplicity, shyness.
(ANT.) conceit, vanity, pride.

modicum *(SYN.)* particle, fragment, grain, trifle, smidgen, bit.

modification *(SYN.)* alternation, substitution, variety, change, alteration.
(ANT.) uniformity, monotony.

modify *(SYN.)* shift, vary, alter, change, convert, adjust, temper, moderate, curb, exchange, transform, veer.
(ANT.) settle, establish, retain, stabilize.

modish *(SYN.)* current, fashionable, chick, stylish, voguish.

modulate *(SYN.)* temper, align, balance, correct, regulate, adjust, modify.

module *(SYN.)* unit, measure, norm, dimension, component, gauge.

modus operandi *(SYN.)* method, technique, system, means, process, workings, procedure.

mogul *(SYN.)* bigwig, personage, figure, tycoon, magnate, potentate.

moiety *(SYN.)* part, scrap, share, allotment, piece, division, portion.

moist *(SYN.)* damp, humid, dank, muggy, clammy.

moisten *(SYN.)* wet, dampen, sponge.
(ANT.) dry.

moisture *(SYN.)* wetness, mist, dampness, condensation, evaporation, vapor, humidity.
(ANT.) aridity, dryness.

mold *(SYN.)* make, fashion, organize, produce, forge, constitute, create, combine, construct, form, pattern, format.
(ANT.) wreck, dismantle, destroy, misshape.

moldy *(SYN.)* dusty, crumbling, dank, old, deteriorating.

molest *(SYN.)* irk, disturb, trouble, annoy, pester, bother, vex, inconvenience.

(ANT.) console, accommodate.

mollify *(SYN.)* soothe, compose, quiet, humor, appease, tranquilize, pacify.

molt *(SYN.)* slough off, shed, cast off.

molten *(SYN.)* fusible, melted, smelted, redhot.

moment *(SYN.)* flash, jiffy, instant, twinkling, gravity, importance, consequence, seriousness.

momentary *(SYN.)* concise, pithy, brief, curt, terse, laconic, compendious.

(ANT.) long, extended, prolonged.

momentous *(SYN.)* critical, serious, essential, grave, material, weighty, consequential, decisive, important.

(ANT.) unimportant, trifling, mean, trivial, tribial, insignificant.

momentum *(SYN.)* impetus, push, thrust, force, impulse, drive, vigor, propulsion, energy.

monarch *(SYN.)* ruler, king, queen, empress, emperor, sovereign.

monastic *(SYN.)* withdrawn, dedicated, austere, unworldly, celibate, abstinent, ascetic.

monastery *(SYN.)* convent, priory, abbey, hermitage, cloister.

money *(SYN.)* cash, bills, coin, notes, currency, funds, specie, capital.

monger *(SYN.)* seller, hawker, huckster, trader, merchant, shopkeeper, retailer, vendor.

mongrel *(SYN.)* mixed-breed, hybrid, mutt.

monitor *(SYN.)* director, supervisor, advisor, observe, watch, control.

monkey *(SYN.)* tamper, interfere, interrupt, interpose.

monogram *(SYN.)* mark, stamp, signature

monograph *(SYN.)* publication, report, thesis, biography, treatise, paper, dissertation.

monologue *(SYN.)* discourse, lecture, sermon, talk, speech, address, soliloquy, oration.

monomania *(SYN.)* obsessiveness, passion, single-mindedness, extremism.

monopoly *(SYN.)* corner, control, possession.

monotonous *(SYN.)* dull, slow, tiresome, boring, humdrum, dilatory, tiring, irksome, tedious, burdensome, wearisome.

(ANT.) interesting, riveting, quick, fascinating, exciting, amusing.

monsoon *(SYN.)* storm, rains.

monster *(SYN.)* brute, beast, villain, demon, fiend, wretch.

monstrous *(SYN.)* tremendous, huge, gigantic, immense, enormous, revolting, repulsive, shocking, horrible, hideous, terrible.

(ANT.) diminutive, tiny, miniature, small.

monument *(SYN.)* remembrance, memento, commemoration, souvenir, statue, shrine.

monumental *(SYN.)* enormous, huge, colossal, immense, gigantic, important, significant.

(ANT.) trivial, insignificant, tiny, miniature.

mood *(SYN.)* joke, irony, waggery, temper, disposition, temperament, sarcasm.

(ANT.) sorrow, gravity.

moody *(SYN.)* morose, fretful, crabbed, changeable, sulky, dour, short-tempered, testy, temperamental, irritable, peevish, glum.

(ANT.) good-natured, even-tempered, merry, gay, pleasant, joyous.

moor *(SYN.)* tether, fasten, tie, dock, anchor, bind.

moorings *(SYN.)* marina, slip, harbor, basin, landing, dock, wharf, pier, anchorage.

moot *(SYN.)* unsettled, questionable, problematical, controversial, contestable.

mop *(SYN.)* wash, wipe, swab, scrub.

mope *(SYN.)* gloom, pout, whine, grumble, grieve, sulk, fret.

(ANT.) rejoice.

moral *(SYN.)* just, right, chaste, good, virtuous, pure, decent, honest, upright, ethical, righteous, honorable, scrupulous.

(ANT.) libertine, immoral, unethical, licentious, amoral, sinful.

morale *(SYN.)* confidence, spirit, assurance.

morality *(SYN.)* virtue, strength, worth, chastity, probity, force, merit.

(ANT.) fault, sin, corruption, vice.

morals *(SYN.)* conduct, scruples, guidelines, behavior, life style, standards.

morass *(SYN.)* fen, march, swamp, mire.

morbid *(SYN.)* sickly, unwholesome, unhealthy, ghastly, awful, horrible, shocking.

(ANT.) pleasant, healthy.
more *(SYN.)* further, greater, farther, extra, another.
(ANT.) less.
moreover *(SYN.)* further, in addition, also, furthermore, besides.
mores *(SYN.)* standards, rituals, rules, customs, conventions, traditions.
moron *(SYN.)* subnormal, dunce, blockhead, imbecile, retardate, simpleton.
morose *(SYN.)* gloomy, moody, fretful, crabbed, sulky, glum, dour, surly, downcast, sad, unhappy.
(ANT.) merry, gay, amiable, joyous, pleasant.
morsel *(SYN.)* portion, fragment, bite, bit, scrap. amount, piece, taste, tidbit.
(ANT.) whole, all, sum.
mortal *(SYN.)* fatal, destructive, human, perishable, deadly, temporary, momentary, final.
(ANT.) superficial, divine, immortal.
mortgage *(SYN.)* stake, post, promise, pledge.
mortician *(SYN.)* funeral director, embalmer.
mortified *(SYN.)* embarrassed, humiliated, abashed, ashamed.
mortify *(SYN.)* humiliate, crush, subdue, abase, degrade, shame.
(ANT.) praise, exalt, elevate.
mortuary *(SYN.)* morgue, crematory, funeral parlor.
most *(SYN.)* extreme, highest, supreme, greatest, majority.
(ANT.) least.
mostly *(SYN.)* chiefly, generally, largely, mainly, principally, especially, primarily.
mother *(SYN.)* bring about, produce, breed, mom, mama, watch, foster, mind, nurse, originate, nurture.
(ANT.) father.
motif *(SYN.)* keynote, topic, subject, theme.
motion *(SYN.)* change, activity, movement, proposition, action, signal, gesture, move, proposal.
(ANT.) stability, immobility, equilibrium, stillness.
motionless *(SYN.)* still, undisturbed, rigid, fixed, stationary, unresponsive, immobilized.
motivate *(SYN.)* move, prompt, stimulate, induce, activate, propel, arouse.
motive *(SYN.)* inducement, purpose,

cause, incentive, reason, incitement, idea, ground, principle, stimulus, impulse, spur.
(ANT.) deed, result, attempt, effort.
motley *(SYN.)* heterogeneous, mixed, assorted, sundry, diverse, miscellaneous.
(ANT.) ordered, classified.
motor *(SYN.)* engine, generator, machine.
mottled *(SYN.)* streaked, flecked, dappled, spotted, speckled.
motto *(SYN.)* proverb, saying, adage, byword, saw, slogan, catchword, aphorism.
mound *(SYN.)* hillock, hill, heap, pile, stack, knoll, accumulation, dune.
mount *(SYN.)* scale, climb, increase, rise, prepare, ready, steed, horse, tower.
(ANT.) sink, descend.
mountain *(SYN.)* alp, mount, pike, peak, ridge, height, range.
mountebank *(SYN.)* faker, rascal, swindler, cheat, fraud.
mounting *(SYN.)* backing, pedestal, easel, support, framework, background.
mourn *(SYN.)* suffer, grieve, bemoan, sorrow, lament, weep, bewail.
(ANT.) revel, celebrate, carouse.
mournful *(SYN.)* sorrowful, sad, melancholy, gloomy, woeful, rueful, disconsolate.
(ANT.) joyful, cheerful, happy.
mourning *(SYN.)* misery, trial, distress, affliction, tribulation, sorrow, woe.
(ANT.) happiness, solace, comfort, joy.
mousy *(SYN.)* quiet, reserved, dull, colorless, withdrawn, shy, bashful.
move *(SYN.)* impel, agitate, persuade, induce, push, instigate, advance, stir, progress, propel, shift, drive, retreat, proceed, stir, transfer, budge, actuate.
(ANT.) halt, stop, deter, rest.
movement *(SYN.)* activity, effort, gesture, move, proposition, crusade, action, change, motion.
(ANT.) stillness, immobility, equilibrium.
moving *(SYN.)* poignant, stirring, touching.
mow *(SYN.)* prune, cut, shave, crop, clip.
much *(SYN.)* abundance, quantity, mass, ample, plenty, sufficient, substantial.
mucilage *(SYN.)* adhesive, glue, paste.
muck *(SYN.)* filth, mire, dirt, rot, sludge, sewage.
muddle *(SYN.)* disorder, chaos, mess.
muddled *(SYN.)* disconcerted, confused, mixed, bewildered, perplexed.

(ANT.) plain, lucid, organized.

muff (SYN.) blunder, bungle, spoil, mess, fumble.

muffle (SYN.) soften, deaden, mute, quiet, drape, shroud, veil, cover. (ANT.) louden, amplify.

mug (SYN.) cup, stein, goblet, tankard.

muggy (SYN.) damp, warm, humid, stuffy, sticky, dank.

mulct (SYN.) amerce, punish, penalize.

mulish (SYN.) obstinate, stubborn, headstrong, rigid, tenacious, willful.

multifarious (SYN.) various, many, numerous, diversified, several, manifold. (ANT.) scanty, infrequent, scarce, few.

multiply (SYN.) double, treble, increase, triple, propagate, spread, expand. (ANT.) lessen, decrease.

multitude (SYN.) crowd, throng, mass, swarm, host, mob, army, legion. (ANT.) scarcity, handful.

mum (SYN.) mute, silent, quiet, still, close-mouthed, secretive.

mumble (SYN.) stammer, whisper, hesitate, mutter. (ANT.) shout, yell.

mundane (SYN.) temporal, earthly, profane, worldly, lay, secular, common. (ANT.) unworldly, religious.

municipal (SYN.) urban, metropolitan.

munificent (SYN.) bountiful, full, generous, forthcoming, satisfied. (ANT.) voracious, insatiable, grasping, ravenous, devouring.

murder (SYN.) homicide, kill, slay, slaughter, butcher, killing, massacre, assassinate, execute. (ANT.) save, protect, vivify, animate.

murderer (SYN.) slayer, killer, assassin.

murky (SYN.) gloomy, dark, obscure, unclear, impenetrable. (ANT.) cheerful, light.

murmur (SYN.) mumble, whine, grumble, whimper, lament, mutter, complaint, remonstrate, complain, repine. (ANT.) praise, applaud, rejoice.

muscle (SYN.) brawn, strength, power, fitness, vigor, vim, stamina, robustness.

muse (SYN.) ponder, brood, think, meditate, ruminate, reflect.

museum (SYN.) exhibit hall, treasure house, gallery, repository.

mushroom (SYN.) multiply, proliferate, flourish, spread, grow, pullulate.

music (SYN.) symphony, harmony, consonance.

musical (SYN.) tuneful, melodious, dulcet, lyrical, harmonious.

muss (SYN.) mess, disarray, rumple, litter, clutter, disarrange. (ANT.) fix, arrange.

must (SYN.) ought to, should, duty, obligation, ultimatum.

muster (SYN.) cull, pick, collect, harvest, accumulate, garner, reap, deduce. (ANT.) separate, disband, scatter.

musty (SYN.) mildewed, rancid, airless, dank, stale, decayed, rotten, funky.

mute (SYN.) quiet, noiseless, dumb, taciturn, hushed, peaceful, speechless, uncommunicative, silent. (ANT.) raucous, clamorous, noisy.

mutilate (SYN.) tear, cut, clip, amputate, lacerate, dismember, deform, castrate.

mutinous (SYN.) revolutionary, rebellious, unruly, insurgent, turbulent, riotous. (ANT.) dutiful, obedient, complaint.

mutiny (SYN.) revolt, overthrow, rebellion, rebel, coup, uprising, insurrection.

mutter (SYN.) complain, mumble, whisper, grumble, murmur.

mutual (SYN.) correlative, interchangeable, shared, alternate, joint, common, reciprocal. (ANT.) unshared, unrequited, separate, dissociated.

muzzle (SYN.) restrain, silence, bridle, bind, curb, suppress, gag, stifle, censor.

myopia (SYN.) incomprehension, folly, shortsightedness, obtuseness, insensibility.

myriad (SYN.) considerable, many.

mysterious (SYN.) hidden, mystical, secret, cryptic, incomprehensible, occult, dim, dark, inexplicable, enigmatical, inscrutable, obscure, recondite, puzzling, strange. (ANT.) simple, obvious, clear, plain.

mystery (SYN.) riddle, difficulty, enigma, puzzle, strangeness, conundrum. (ANT.) solution, key, answer, resolution.

mystical (SYN.) secret, cryptic, hidden, dim, obscure, dark, cabalistic. (ANT.) simple, explained, plain, clear.

mystify (SYN.) puzzle, confound, bewilder, stick, get, floor, bamboozle.

myth (SYN.) fable, parable, allegory, fiction, tradition, lie, saga, legend. (ANT.) history.

nag *(SYN.)* badger, harry, provoke, tease, bother, annoy, molest, taunt, vex, torment, worry, annoy, pester, irritate, pick on, horse, torment.
(ANT.) please, comfort, soothe.

nail *(SYN.)* hold, fasten, secure, fix, seize, catch, snare, hook, capture.
(ANT.) release.

naive *(SYN.)* frank, unsophisticated, natural, artless, ingenuous, simple, candid, open, innocent.
(ANT.) worldly, cunning, crafty.

naked *(SYN.)* uncovered, unfurnished, nude, bare, open, unclad, stripped, exposed, plain, mere, simple, barren, unprotected, bald, defenseless, unclothed, undressed.
(ANT.) covered, protected, dressed, clothed, concealed, suppressed.

name *(SYN.)* title, reputation, appellation, style, fame, repute, renown, denomination, appoint, character, designation, surname, distinction, christen, denominate, mention, specify, epithet, entitle, call, label.
(ANT.) anonymity, misnomer, hint, misname.

nap *(SYN.)* nod, doze, sleep, snooze, catnap, siesta, slumber, drowse, forty winks.

narcissistic *(SYN.)* egotistical, egocentric, self-centered, egotistic.

narcotics *(SYN.)* opiates, drugs, sedatives, tranquilizers, barbiturates.

narrate *(SYN.)* recite, relate, declaim, detail, rehearse, deliver, review, tell, describe, recount.

narrative *(SYN.)* history, relation, account, record, chronicle, detail, recital, description, story, tale.
(ANT.) distortion, caricature, misrepresentation.

narrow *(SYN.)* narrow-minded, illiberal, bigoted, fanatical, prejudiced, close, restricted, slender, cramped, confined, meager, thin, tapering, tight.
(ANT.) progressive, liberal, wide.

narrow-minded *(SYN.)* close-minded, intolerant, partisan, arbitrary, bigoted.
(ANT.) tolerant, liberal, broad-minded.

nascent *(SYN.)* prime, introductory, emerging, elementary.

nasty *(SYN.)* offensive, malicious, selfish, mean, disagreeable, unpleasant, foul, dirty, filthy, loathsome, disgusting, polluted, obscene, indecent, sickening,

nauseating, obnoxious, revolting, odious.
(ANT.) generous, dignified, noble, admirable, pleasant.

nation *(SYN.)* state, community, realm, nationality, commonwealth, kingdom, country, republic, land, society, tribe.

native *(SYN.)* domestic, inborn, inherent, natural, aboriginal, endemic, innate, inbred, indigenous, hereditary, original, local.
(ANT.) alien, stranger, foreigner, outsider, foreign.

natty *(SYN.)* chic, well-dressed, sharp, dapper.

natural *(SYN.)* innate, genuine, real, unaffected, characteristic, native, normal, regular, inherent, original, simple, inbred, inborn, hereditary, typical, authentic, honest, legitimate, pure, customary.
(ANT.) irregular, false, unnatural, formal, abnormal.

naturally *(SYN.)* typically, ordinarily, usually, indeed, normally, plainly, of course, surely, certainly.
(ANT.) artificially.

nature *(SYN.)* kind, disposition, reputation, character, repute, world, quality, universe, essence, variety, features, traits.

naught *(SYN.)* nought, zero, nothing.

naughty *(SYN.)* unmanageable, insubordinate, disobedient, mischievous, unruly, bad, misbehaving, disorderly, wrong, evil, rude, improper, indecent.
(ANT.) obedient, good, well-behaved.

nausea *(SYN.)* sickness, vomiting, upset, queasiness, seasickness.

nauseated *(SYN.)* unwell, sick, queasy, squeamish.

nautical *(SYN.)* naval, oceanic, marine, ocean.

naval *(SYN.)* oceanic, marine, nautical, maritime.

navigate *(SYN.)* sail, cruise, pilot, guide, steer.

near *(SYN.)* close, nigh, dear, adjacent, familiar, at hand, neighboring, approaching, impending, proximate, imminent, bordering.
(ANT.) removed, distant, far, remote.

nearly *(SYN.)* practically, close to, approximately, almost.

neat *(SYN.)* trim, orderly, precise, clear, spruce, nice, tidy, clean, well-kept, clever, skillful, adept, apt, tidy, dapper, smart, proficient, expert, handy, well-done, shipshape, elegant, well-organized.

(ANT.) unkempt, sloppy, dirty, slovenly, messy, sloppy, disorganized.

nebulous *(SYN.)* fuzzy, indistinct, indefinite, clouded, hazy.

(ANT.) definite, distinct, clear.

necessary *(SYN.)* needed, expedient, unavoidable, required, essential, indispensable, urgent, imperative, inevitable, compelling, compulsory, obligatory, needed, exigent.

(ANT.) optional, nonessential, contingent, casual, accidental, unnecessary, dispensable, unneeded.

necessity *(SYN.)* requirement, fate, destiny, constraint, requisite, poverty, exigency, compulsion, want, essential, prerequisite.

(ANT.) option, luxury, freedom, choice, uncertainty.

necromancy *(SYN.)* witchcraft, charm, sorcery, conjuring, wizardry.

need *(SYN.)* crave, want, demand, claim, desire, covet, wish, lack, necessity, requirement, poverty, require, pennilessness.

needed *(SYN.)* necessary, indispensable, essential, requisite.

(ANT.) optional, contingent.

needle *(SYN.)* goad, badger, tease, nag, prod, provoke.

needless *(SYN.)* nonessential, unnecessary, superfluous, useless, purposeless.

needy *(SYN.)* poor, indigent, impoverished penniless, destitute.

(ANT.) affluent, well-off, wealthy, well-to-do.

nefarious *(SYN.)* detestable, vicious, wicked, atrocious, horrible, vile.

negate *(SYN.)* revoke, void, cancel, nullify.

neglect *(SYN.)* omission, default, heedlessness, carelessness, thoughtlessness, disregard, negligence, oversight, omission, ignore, slight, failure, overlook, omit, skip, pass over, be inattentive, miss.

(ANT.) diligence, do, protect, watchfulness, care, attention, careful, attend, regard, concern.

negligent *(SYN.)* imprudent, thoughtless, lax, careless, inattentive, indifferent, remiss, neglectful.

(ANT.) careful, nice, accurate, meticulous.

negligible *(SYN.)* trifling, insignificant, trivial, inconsiderable.

(ANT.) major, vital, important.

negotiate *(SYN.)* intervene, talk over, mediate, transact, umpire, referee, arbitrate, arrange, settle, bargain.

neighborhood *(SYN.)* environs, nearness, locality, district, vicinity, area, section, locality.

(ANT.) remoteness.

neighboring *(SYN.)* bordering, near, adjacent, next to, surrounding, adjoining.

neighborly *(SYN.)* friendly, sociable, amiable, affable, companionable, congenial, kind, cordial, amicable.

(ANT.) distant, reserved, cool, unfriendly, hostile.

neophyte *(SYN.)* greenhorn, rookie, amateur, beginner, apprentice, tyro, student.

nepotism *(SYN.)* bias, prejudice, partronage, favoritism.

nerve *(SYN.)* bravery, spirit, courage, boldness, rudeness, strength, stamina, bravado, daring, impudence, mettle, impertinence.

(ANT.) frailty, cowardice, weakness.

nervous *(SYN.)* agitated, restless, excited, shy, timid, upset, disturbed, shaken, rattle, high-strung, flustered, tense, jittery, strained, edgy, perturbed, fearful.

(ANT.) placid, courageous, confident, calm, tranquil, composed, bold.

nest *(SYN.)* den, refuge, hideaway.

nestle *(SYN.)* cuddle, snuggle.

net *(SYN.)* snare, trap, mesh, earn, gain, web, get, acquire, secure, obtain.

nettle *(SYN.)* irritate, vex, provoke, annoy, disturb, irk, needle, pester.

neurotic *(SYN.)* disturbed, psychoneurotic.

neutral *(SYN.)* nonpartisan, uninvolved, detached, impartial, cool, unprejudiced, indifferent, inactive.

(ANT.) involved, biased, partisan.

neutralize *(SYN.)* offset, counteract, nullify, negate.

nevertheless *(SYN.)* notwithstanding, however, although, anyway, but, regardless.

new *(SYN.)* modern, original, newfangled, late, recent, novel, young, firsthand, fresh, unique, unusual.

(ANT.) antiquated, old, ancient, ob-

solete, outmoded.

newborn *(SYN.)* baby, infant, cub, suckling.

news *(SYN.)* report, intelligence, information, copy, message, advice, tidings, knowledge, word, story, data.

next *(SYN.)* nearest, following, closest, successive, succeeding, subsequent.

nibble *(SYN.)* munch, chew, bit.

nice *(SYN.)* pleasing, pleasant, agreeable, thoughtful, satisfactory, friendly, enjoyable, gratifying, desirable, fine, good, cordial.
(ANT.) nasty, unpleasant, disagreeable, unkind, inexact, careless, thoughtless.

niche *(SYN.)* corner, nook, alcove, cranny, recess.

nick *(SYN.)* cut, notch, indentation, dash, score, mark.

nickname *(SYN.)* byname, sobriquet.

nigh *(SYN.)* close, imminent, near, adjacent, approaching, bordering, neighboring, impending.
(ANT.) removed, distant.

nightmare *(SYN.)* calamity, horror, torment, bad dream.

nil *(SYN.)* zero, none, nought, nothing.

nimble *(SYN.)* brisk, quick, active, supple, alert, lively, spry, light, fast, speedy, swift, agile.
(ANT.) slow, heavy, sluggish, clumsy.

nincompoop *(SYN.)* nitwit, idiot, fool, moron, blockhead, ninny, idiot, simpleton.

nip *(SYN.)* bite, pinch, chill, cold, squeeze, crispness, sip, small.

nippy *(SYN.)* chilly, sharp, bitter, cold, penetrating.

nit-picker *(SYN.)* fussbudget, precise, purist, perfectionist.

nitty-gritty *(SYN.)* essentials, substance, essence.

noble *(SYN.)* illustrious, exalted, dignified, stately, eminent, lofty, grand, elevated, honorable, honest, virtuous, great, distinguished, majestic, important, prominent, magnificent, grandiose, aristocratic, upright, well-born.
(ANT.) vile, low, base, mean, dishonest, common, ignoble.

nocturnal *(SYN.)* nightly.

nod *(SYN.)* bob, bow, bend, tip, signal.

node *(SYN.)* protuberance, growth, nodule, cyst, lump, wen.

noise *(SYN.)* cry, sound, din, babel, racket, uproar, clamor, outcry, tumult,

outcry, sounds, hubbub, bedlam, commotion, rumpus, clatter.
(ANT.) quiet, stillness, hush, silence, peace.

noisome *(SYN.)* repulsive, disgusting, revolting, obnoxious, malodorous, rotten, rancid.

noisy *(SYN.)* resounding, loud, clamorous, vociferous, stentorian, tumultuous.
(ANT.) soft, dulcet, subdued, quiet, silent, peaceful.

nomad *(SYN.)* gypsy, rover, traveler, roamer, migrant, vagrant, wanderer.

nominate *(SYN.)* propose, choose, select.

nomination *(SYN.)* appointment, naming, choice, selection, designation.

nominee *(SYN.)* aspirant, contestant, candidate, competitor.

nonbeliever *(SYN.)* skeptic, infidel, atheist, heathen.

nonchalant *(SYN.)* unconcerned, indifferent, cool, casual, easygoing.

noncommittal *(SYN.)* neutral, tepid, undecided, cautious, guarded, uncommunicative.

nonconformist *(SYN.)* protester, rebel, radical, dissenter, renegade, dissident, eccentric.

nondescript *(SYN.)* unclassifiable, indescribable, indefinite.

nonentity *(SYN.)* nothing, menial, nullity.

nonessential *(SYN.)* needless, unnecessary.

nonpareil *(SYN.)* unsurpassed, exceptional, paramount, unrivaled.

nonplus *(SYN.)* confuse, perplex, dumfound, mystify, confound, puzzle, baffle, bewilder.
(ANT.) illumine, clarify, solve, explain.

nonsense *(SYN.)* balderdash, rubbish, foolishness, folly, ridiculousness, stupidity, absurdity, poppycock, trash.

nonsensical *(SYN.)* silly, preposterous, absurd, unreasonable, foolish, irrational, ridiculous, stupid, senseless.
(ANT.) sound, consistent, reasonable.

nonstop *(SYN.)* constant, continuous, unceasing, endless.

nook *(SYN.)* niche, corner, recess, cranny, alcove.

noose *(SYN.)* snare, rope, lasso, loop.

normal *(SYN.)* ordinary, uniform, natural, unvaried, customary, regular, healthy, sound, whole, usual, typical, characteristic, routine, standard.
(ANT.) rare, erratic, unusual, abnormal.

normally *(SYN.)* regularly, frequently, usually, customarily.

nosy *(SYN.)* inquisitive, meddling, peering, searching, prying, snooping.
(ANT.) unconcerned, incurious, uninterested.

notable *(SYN.)* noted, unusual, uncommon, noteworthy, remarkable, conspicuous, distinguished, distinctive, celebrity, starts, important, striking, special, memorable, extraordinary, rare, exceptional, personality.
(ANT.) commonplace, ordinary, usual.

notch *(SYN.)* cut, nick, indentation, gash.

note *(SYN.)* sign, annotation, letter, indication, observation, mark, symbol, comment, remark, token, message, memorandum, record, memo, write, list, inscribe, notice.

noted *(SYN.)* renowned, glorious, celebrated, famous, illustrious, well-known, distinguished, famed, notable.
(ANT.) unknown, hidden, infamous, ignominious.

noteworthy *(SYN.)* consequential, celebrated, exceptional, prominent.

notice *(SYN.)* heed, perceive, hold, mark, behold, descry, recognize, observe, attend to, remark, note, regard, see, sign, announcement, poster, note, advertisement, observation, warning.
(ANT.) overlook, disregard, skip.

notify *(SYN.)* apprise, acquaint, instruct, tell, advise, warn, teach, inform, report, remind, announce, mention, reveal.
(ANT.) mislead, delude, conceal.

notion *(SYN.)* image, conception, sentiment, abstraction, thought, idea, impression, fancy, understanding, view, opinion, concept.
(ANT.) thing, matter, substance, entity.

notorious *(SYN.)* celebrated, renowned, famous, well-known, popular, infamous.

nourish *(SYN.)* strengthen, nurse, feed, supply, nurture, sustain, support.

nourishment *(SYN.)* nutriment, food, sustenance, support.
(ANT.) starvation, deprivation.

novel *(SYN.)* fiction, narrative, allegory, tale, fable, story, romance, invention, different, unusual, strange, original, new, unique, fresh, firsthand, odd.
(ANT.) verity, history, truth, fact.

novice *(SYN.)* beginner, amateur, newcomer, greenhorn, learner, apprentice, freshman, dilettante.

(ANT.) expert, professional, adept, master.

now *(SYN.)* today, at once, right away, immediately, at this time, present.
(ANT.) later.

noxious *(SYN.)* poisonous, harmful, damaging, toxic, detrimental.
(ANT.) harmless.

nucleus *(SYN.)* core, middle, heart, focus, hub, kernel.

nude *(SYN.)* naked, unclad, plain, open, defenseless, mere, bare, exposed, unprotected, simple, stripped, uncovered.
(ANT.) dressed, concealed, protected, clothed, covered.

nudge *(SYN.)* prod, push, jab, shove, poke, prompt.

nugget *(SYN.)* clump, mass, lump, wad, chunk, hunk.

nuisance *(SYN.)* annoyance, bother, irritation, pest.

nullify *(SYN.)* abolish, cross out, delete, invalidate, obliterate, cancel, expunge, repeal, annul, revoke, quash, rescind.
(ANT.) perpetuate, confirm, enforce.

numb *(SYN.)* unfeeling, dull, insensitive, deadened, anesthetized, stupefied.

number *(SYN.)* quantity, sum, amount, volume, aggregate, total, collection, sum, numeral, count, measure, portion, bulk, figure, multitude, digit.
(ANT.) zero, nothing, nothingness.

numeral *(SYN.)* figure, symbol, digit.

numerous *(SYN.)* many, several, manifold, multifarious, various, multitudinous, diverse, abundant, sundry, numberless, infinite.
(ANT.) scanty, infrequent, meager, few, scarce.

numskull *(SYN.)* fool, nitwit, blockhead, ninny.

nuptials *(SYN.)* marriage, wedding, espousal, wedlock, matrimony.
(ANT.) virginity, divorce, celibacy.

nurse *(SYN.)* tend, care for, nourish, nurture, feed, foster, train, mind, attend.

nurture *(SYN.)* hold dear, foster, sustain, appreciate, prize, bring up, rear, value, treasure, cherish.
(ANT.) dislike, disregard, abandon.

nutriment *(SYN.)* food, diet, sustenance, repast, meal, fare, edibles.
(ANT.) hunger, want, starvation.

nutrition *(SYN.)* nourishment, sustenance, food, nutriment.

oaf *(SYN.)* boor, clod, clown, lummox, fool, lout, dunce, bogtrotter.

oasis *(SYN.)* shelter, haven, retreat, refuge.

oath *(SYN.)* promise, pledge, vow, profanity, curse, agreement, commitment, swearword.

obdurate *(SYN.)* insensible, callous, hard, tough, unfeeling, insensitive, impenitent, indurate.
(ANT.) soft, compassionate, tender.

obedience *(SYN.)* docility, submission, subservience, compliance, conformability.
(ANT.) rebelliousness, disobedience.

obedient *(SYN.)* dutiful, yielding, tractable, compliant, submissive.
(ANT.) rebellious, intractable, insubordinate, obstinate.

obese *(SYN.)* portly, fat, pudgy, chubby, plump, rotund, stout, thickset, corpulent, stocky.
(ANT.) slim, gaunt, lean, thin, slender.

obey *(SYN.)* submit, yield, mind, comply, listen to, serve, conform.
(ANT.) resist, disobey.

obfuscate *(SYN.)* bewilder, complicate, fluster, confuse.

object *(SYN.)* thing, aim, intention, design, end, objective, particular, mark, purpose, goal, target, article.
(ANT.) assent, agree, concur, approve, acquiesce.

objection *(SYN.)* disagreement, protest, rejection, dissent, challenge, noncompliance, difference, nonconformity, recusancy, disapproval, criticism, variance.
(ANT.) acceptance, compliance, agreement, assent.

objectionable *(SYN.)* improper, offensive, unbecoming, deplorable.

objective *(SYN.)* aspiration, goal, passion, desire, aim, hope, purpose, drift, design, ambition, end, object, intention, intent, longing, craving.
(ANT.) biased, subjective.

objectivity *(SYN.)* disinterest, neutrality, impartiality.

obligate *(SYN.)* oblige, require, pledge, bind, force, compel.

obligation *(SYN.)* duty, bond, engagement, compulsion, account, contract, ability, debt.
(ANT.) freedom, choice, exemption.

oblige *(SYN.)* constrain, force, impel, enforce, coerce, drive, gratify.

(ANT.) persuade, convince, allure, free, induce, disoblige, prevent.

obliging *(SYN.)* considerate, helpful, thoughtful, well-meaning, accommodating.
(ANT.) discourteous.

obliterate *(SYN.)* terminate, destroy, eradicate, raze, extinguish, exterminate, annihilate, devastate, wipe out, ravage, blot out, erase.
(ANT.) make, save, construct, establish, preserve.

oblivious *(SYN.)* sightless, unmindful, headlong, rash, blind, senseless, ignorant, forgetful, undiscerning, preoccupied, unconscious, heedless.
(ANT.) sensible, aware, calculated, perceiving, discerning.

oblong *SYN.)* rectangular, elliptical, elongated.

obloquy *(SYN.)* defamation, rebuke, censure.

obnoxious *(SYN.)* hateful, offensive, nasty, disagreeable, repulsive, loathsome, vile, disgusting, detestable, wretched, terrible, despicable, dreadful.

obscene *(SYN.)* indecent, filthy, impure, dirty, gross, lewd, pornographic, coarse, disgusting, bawdy, offensive, smutty.
(ANT.) modest, pure, decent, refined.

obscure *(SYN.)* cloudy, enigmatic, mysterious, abstruse, cryptic, dim, indistinct, dusky, ambiguous, dark, indistinct, unintelligible, unclear, shadowy, fuzzy, blurred, vague.
(ANT.) clear, famous, distinguished, noted, illumined, lucid, bright, distinct.

obsequious *(SYN.)* fawning, flattering, ingratiating.

observance *(SYN.)* protocol, ritual, ceremony, rite, parade, pomp, solemnity, formality.
(ANT.) omission.

observant *(SYN.)* aware, alert, careful, mindful, watchful, heedful, considerate, attentive, anxious, circumspect, cautious, wary.
(ANT.) unaware, indifferent, oblivious.

observation *(SYN.)* attention, watching, comment, opinion, remark, notice, examination.

observe *(SYN.)* note, behold, discover, notice, perceive, eye, detect, inspect, keep, commemorate, mention, utter, watch, examine, mark, view, express, see, celebrate.

(ANT.) neglect, overlook, disregard, ignore.

observer (SYN.) examiner, overseer, lookout, spectator, bystander, witness, watcher.

obsession (SYN.) preoccupation, mania, compulsion, passion, fetish, infatuation.

obsolete (SYN.) old, out-of-date, ancient, archaic, extinct, old-fashioned, discontinued, obsolescent, venerable, dated, antiquated.
(ANT.) modern, stylish, current, recent, fashionable, extant.

obstacle (SYN.) block, hindrance, barrier, impediment, snag, check, deterrent, stoppage, hitch, bar, difficulty, obstruction.
(ANT.) help, aid, assistance, encouragement.

obstinate (SYN.) firm, headstrong, immovable, stubborn, determined, dogged, intractable, uncompromising, inflexible, willful, bullheaded, contumacious, obdurate, unbending, unyielding, pertinacious.
(ANT.) yielding, docile, amenable, submissive, pliable, flexible, compliant.

obstruct (SYN.) clog, barricade, impede, block, delay, hinder, stop, close, bar.
(ANT.) promote, clear, aid, help, open, further.

obstruction (SYN.) block, obstacle, barrier, blockage, interference.

obtain (SYN.) get, acquire, secure, win, procure, attain, earn, gain, receive, assimilate.
(ANT.) surrender, forfeit, lose, forego, miss.

obtrusive (SYN.) blatant, garish, conspicuous.

obtuse (SYN.) blunt, dull, slow-witted, unsharpened, stupid, dense, slow.
(ANT.) clear, interesting, lively, bright, animated, sharp.

obviate (SYN.) prevent, obstruct, forestall, preclude, intercept, avert, evade.

obvious (SYN.) plain, clear, evident, palpable, patent, self-evident, apparent, distinct, understandable, manifest, unmistakable.
(ANT.) concealed, hidden, abstruse, obscure.

obviously (SYN.) plainly, clearly, surely, evidently, certainly.

occasion (SYN.) occurrence, time, happening, excuse, opportunity, chance.

occasional (SYN.) random, irregular, sporadic, infrequent, periodically, spasmodic.
(ANT.) chronic, regular, constant.

occasionally (SYN.) seldom, now and then, infrequently, sometimes, irregularly.
(ANT.) regularly, often.

occlude (SYN.) clog, obstruct, choke, throttle.

occupant (SYN.) tenant, lodger, boarder, dweller, resident, inhabitant.

occupation (SYN.) employment, business, enterprise, job, trade, vocation, work, profession, matter, interest, concern, affair, activity, commerce, trading, engagement.
(ANT.) hobby, pastime, avocation.

occupy (SYN.) dwell, have, inhabit, absorb, hold, possess, fill, busy, keep.
(ANT.) relinquish, abandon, release.

occur (SYN.) take place, bechance, come about, befall, chance, transpire, betide, happen.

occurrence (SYN.) episode, event, issue, end, result, consequence, happening, circumstance, outcome.

ocean (SYN.) deep, sea, main, briny.

odd (SYN.) strange, bizarre, eccentric, unusual, single, uneven, unique, queer, quaint, peculiar, curious, unmatched, remaining, singular.
(ANT.) matched, common, typical, normal, familiar, even, usual, regular.

odious (SYN.) obscene, depraved, vulgar, despicable, mean, wicked, sordid, foul, base, loathsome, depraved, vicious, displeasing, hateful, revolting, offensive, repulsive, horrible, obnoxious, vile.
(ANT.) decent, upright, laudable, attractive, honorable.

odor (SYN.) fume, aroma, fragrance, redolence, smell, stink, scent, essence, stench.

odorous (SYN.) scented, aromatic, fragrant.

odyssey (SYN.) crusade, quest, journey, voyage.

offbeat (SYN.) uncommon, eccentric, strange, unconventional, peculiar.

off-color (SYN.) rude, improper, earthy, suggestive, salty.

offend (SYN.) annoy, anger, vex, irritate, displease, provoke, hurt, grieve, pain, disgust, wound, horrify, stricken, insult, outrage.

(ANT.) flatter, please, delight.

offender *(SYN.)* criminal, culprit, lawbreaker, miscreant.

offense *(SYN.)* indignity, injustice, transgression, affront, outrage, misdeed, sin, insult, atrocity, aggression, crime. *(ANT.) morality, gentleness, innocence, right.*

offensive *(SYN.)* attacking, aggressive, unpleasant, revolting, disagreeable, nauseous, disgusting. *(ANT.) pleasing, defending, defensive, pleasant, attractive, agreeable.*

offer *(SYN.)* suggestion, overture, proposal, present, suggest, propose, try, submit, attempt, tender. *(ANT.) withdrawal, denial, rejection.*

offhand *(SYN.)* informal, unprepared, casual, impromptu, spontaneous. *(ANT.) considered, planned, calculated.*

office *(SYN.)* position, job, situation, studio, berth, incumbency, capacity, headquarters, duty, task, function, work, post.

officiate *(SYN.)* regulate, administer, superintend, oversee, emcee.

offset *(SYN.)* compensate, counterbalance, cushion, counteract, neutralize, soften, balance.

offshoot *(SYN.)* outgrowth, addition, byproduct, supplement, appendage, accessory, branch.

offspring *(SYN.)* issue, children, progeny, descendants.

often *(SYN.)* frequently, repeatedly, commonly, generally, many times, recurrently. *(ANT.) seldom, infrequently, rarely, occasionally, sporadically.*

ogle *(SYN.)* gaze, stare, eye, leer.

ogre *(SYN.)* fiend, monster, devil, demon.

ointment *(SYN.)* lotion, pomade, balm, emollient.

old *(SYN.)* antique, senile, ancient, archaic, old-fashioned, superannuated, obsolete, venerable, antiquated, elderly, discontinued, abandoned, aged. *(ANT.) new, youthful, recent, modern, young.*

old-fashioned *(SYN.)* outmoded, old, dated, ancient. *(ANT.) modern, fashionable, current, new.*

olio *(SYN.)* potpourri, variety, mixture, jumble.

omen *(SYN.)* sign, gesture, indication, proof, portent, symbol, token, emblem, signal.

ominous *(SYN.)* unfavorable, threatening, sinister, menacing.

omission *(SYN.)* failure, neglect, oversight, default. *(ANT.) inclusion, notice, attention, insertion.*

omit *(SYN.)* exclude, delete, cancel, eliminate, ignore, neglect, skip, leave out, drop, miss, bar, overlook, disregard. *(ANT.) insert, notice, enter, include, introduce.*

omnipotent *(SYN.)* all-powerful, almighty, divine.

oncoming *(SYN.)* imminent, approaching, arriving, nearing.

onerous *(SYN.)* intricate, arduous, hard, perplexing, difficult, burdensome, puzzling. *(ANT.) simple, easy, facile, effortless.*

one-sided *(SYN.)* unfair, partial, biased, prejudiced. *(ANT.) impartial, neutral.*

ongoing *(SYN.)* advancing, developing, continuing, progressive.

onlooker *(SYN.)* witness, spectator, observer, bystander.

only *(SYN.)* lone, sole, solitary, single, merely, but, just.

onset *(SYN.)* commencement, beginning, opening, start, assault, attack, charge, offense, onslaught. *(ANT.) end.*

onslaught *(SYN.)* invasion, aggression, attack, assault, offense, drive, criticism, onset, charge, denunciation. *(ANT.) vindication, defense, surrender, opposition, resistance.*

onus *(SYN.)* load, weight, burden, duty.

onward *(SYN.)* ahead, forward, frontward. *(ANT.) backward.*

ooze *(SYN.)* seep, leak, drip, flow, filter.

opacity *(SYN.)* obscurity, thickness, imperviousness.

opaque *(SYN.)* murky, dull, cloudy, filmy, unilluminated, dim, obtuse, indistinct, shadowy, dark, obscure. *(ANT.) light, clear, bright.*

open *(SYN.)* uncovered, overt, agape, unlocked, passable, accessible, unrestricted, candid, plain, clear, exposed, unclosed, unobstructed, free, disengaged, frank, unoccupied, public, honest, ajar, available.

open *(SYN.)* unbar, unfold, exhibit, spread, unseal, expand, unfasten.
(ANT.) close, shut, conceal, hide.

open-handed *(SYN.)* kind, generous, charitable, lavish, extravagant, bountiful.
(ANT.) mean, stingy.

openhearted *(SYN.)* frank, honest, candid, sincere, ingenuous, straightforward.
(ANT.) insincere, devious.

opening *(SYN.)* cavity, hole, void, abyss, aperture, chasm, pore, gap, loophole.

openly *(SYN.)* sincerely, frankly, freely.
(ANT.) secretly.

open-minded *(SYN.)* tolerant, fair, just, liberal, impartial, reasonable, unprejudiced.
(ANT.) prejudiced, bigoted.

operate *(SYN.)* comport, avail, behave, interact, apply, manage, utilize, demean, run, manipulate, employ, act, exploit, exert, exercise, practice, conduct.
(ANT.) neglect, waste.

operation *(SYN.)* effort, enterprise, mentality, maneuver, action, instrumentality, performance, working, proceeding, agency.
(ANT.) inaction, cessation, rest, inactivity.

operative *(SYN.)* busy, active, industrious, working, effective, functional.
(ANT.) inactive, dormant.

opiate *(SYN.)* hypnotic, tranquilizer, narcotic.

opinion *(SYN.)* decision, feeling, notion, view, idea, conviction, belief, judgment, sentiment, persuasion, impression.
(ANT.) knowledge, fact, misgiving, skepticism.

opinionated *(SYN.)* domineering, overbearing, arrogant, dogmatic, positive, magisterial, obstinate, pertinacious.
(ANT.) questioning, fluctuating, indecisive, skeptical, open-minded, indecisive.

opponent *(SYN.)* competitor, foe, adversary, contestant, enemy, rival, contender, combatant, antagonist.
(ANT.) comrade, team, ally, confederate.

opportune *(SYN.)* fitting, suitable, appropriate, proper, favorable, felicitous.

opportunity *(SYN.)* possibility, chance, occasion, time, contingency, opening.
(ANT.) obstacle, disadvantage, hin-

drance.

oppose *(SYN.)* defy, resist, withstand, combat, bar, counteract, confront, thwart, struggle, fight, contradict, hinder, obstruct.
(ANT.) submit, support, agree, cooperate, succumb.

opposed *(SYN.)* opposite, contrary, hostile, adverse, counteractive, unlucky, antagonistic, unfavorable, disastrous.
(ANT.) lucky, benign, propitious, fortunate, favorable.

opposite *(SYN.)* reverse, contrary, different, unlike, opposed.
(ANT.) like, same, similar.

opposition *(SYN.)* combat, struggle, discord, collision, conflict, battle, fight, encounter, discord, controversy, inconsistency, variance.
(ANT.) harmony, amity, concord, consonance.

oppress *(SYN.)* harass, torment, vex, afflict, annoy, harry, pester, hound, worry, persecute.
(ANT.) encourage, support, comfort, assist, aid.

oppression *(SYN.)* cruelty, tyranny, persecution, injustice, despotism, brutality, abuse.
(ANT.) liberty, freedom.

oppressive *(SYN.)* difficult, stifling, burdensome, severe, domineering, harsh, unjust, overbearing, overwhelming.

oppressor *(SYN.)* bully, scourge, slavedriver.

opprobrium *(SYN.)* disgrace, contempt, reproach, shame, discredit.

opt *(SYN.)* choose, prefer, pick, select.

optical *(SYN.)* seeing, visual.

optimism *(SYN.)* faith, expectation, optimism, anticipation, trust, expectancy, -confidence, hope.
(ANT.) despair, pessimism, despondency.

optimistic *(SYN.)* happy, cheerful, bright, glad, pleasant, radiant, lighthearted.
(ANT.) pessimistic.

option *(SYN.)* preference, choice, selection, alternative, election, self-determination.

optional *(SYN.)* selective, elective, voluntary.
(ANT.) required.

opulence *(SYN.)* luxury, abundance, fortune, riches, wealth, plenty, affluence.
(ANT.) need, indigence, want, poverty.

opulent *(SYN.)* wealthy, rich, prosperous,

well-off, affluent, well-heeled.

oracle *(SYN.)* authority, forecaster, wizard, seer, mastermind, clairvoyant.

oral *(SYN.)* voiced, sounded, vocalized, said, uttered, verbal, vocal, spoken. *(ANT.)* recorded, written, documentary.

orate *(SYN.)* preach, lecture, sermonize.

oration *(SYN.)* address, lecture, speech, sermon, discourse, recital, declamation.

orb *(SYN.)* globe, sphere, ball, moon.

orbit *(SYN.)* path, lap, course, circuit, revolution, revolve, circle.

orchestra *(SYN.)* ensemble, band.

orchestrate *(SYN.)* coordinate, direct, synchronize, organize.

ordain *(SYN.)* constitute, create, order, decree, decide, dictate, command, rule, bid, sanction, appoint. *(ANT.)* terminate, disband.

ordeal *(SYN.)* hardship, suffering, test, affliction, trouble, fortune, proof, examination, trial, experiment, tribulation, misery. *(ANT.)* consolation, alleviation.

order *(SYN.)* plan, series, decree, instruction, command, system, method, aim, arrangement, class, injuction, mandate, instruct, requirement, dictate, bidding. *(ANT.)* consent, license, confusion, disarray, irregularity, permission.

order *(SYN.)* guide, command, rule, direct, govern, manage, regulate, bid, conduct. *(ANT.)* misguide, deceive, misdirect, distract.

orderly *(SYN.)* regulated, neat, well-organized, disciplined, methodical, shipshape. *(ANT.)* sloppy, messy, haphazard, disorganized.

ordinarily *(SYN.)* commonly, usually, generally, mostly, customarily, normally.

ordinary *(SYN.)* common, habitual, normal, typical, usual, conventional, familiar, accustomed, customary, average, standard, everyday, inferior, mediocre, regular, vulgar, plain. *(ANT.)* uncommon, marvelous, extraordinary, remarkable, strange.

ordance *(SYN.)* munitions, artillery.

organ *(SYN.)* instrument, journal, voice.

organic *(SYN.)* living, biological, animate.

organism *(SYN.)* creature, plant, microorganism.

organization *(SYN.)* order, rule, system, arrangement, method, plan, regularity, scheme, mode, process. *(ANT.)* irregularity, chaos, disarrangement, chance, disorder, confusion.

organize *(SYN.)* assort, arrange, plan, regulate, systematize, devise, categorize, classify, prepare. *(ANT.)* jumble, disorder, disturb, confuse, scatter.

organized *(SYN.)* planned, neat, orderly, arranged.

orient *(SYN.)* align, fit, accustom, adjust.

orifice *SYN.)* vent, slot, opening, hole.

origin *(SYN.)* birth, foundation, source, start, commencement, inception, beginning, derivation, infancy, parentage, spring, cradle. *(ANT.)* product, issue, outcome, end.

original *(SYN.)* primary, fresh, new, initial, pristine, creative, first, primordial, inventive, primeval, novel, introductory. *(ANT.)* banal, trite, subsequent, derivative, later, modern, terminal.

originality *(SYN.)* unconventionality, genius, novelty, creativity, imagination.

originate *(SYN.)* fashion, invent, cause, create, make, initiate, inaugurate, organize, institute, produce, engender, commence, found, establish, form, begin, arise, generate, formulate. *(ANT.)* demolish, terminate, annihilate, disband, destroy.

originator *(SYN.)* creator, inventor, discoverer. *(ANT.)* follower, imitator.

ornament *(SYN.)* decoration, ornamentation, adornment, embellishment, trimming, garnish.

ornamental *(SYN.)* ornate, decorative.

ornate *SYN.)* florid, overdone, elaborate, showy, flowery, pretentious.

ornery *(SYN.)* disobedient, firm, unruly, stiff, rebellious, stubborn, headstrong, willful, contrary, rigid, mean, difficult, malicious, cross, disagreeable. *(ANT.)* pleasant.

orthodox *(SYN.)* customary, usual, conventional, correct, proper, accepted. *(ANT.)* different, unorthodox.

oscillate *(SYN.)* vary, change, hesitate, waver, undulate, fluctuate, vacillate. *(ANT.)* persist, resolve, adhere, stick, decide.

ostentation *(SYN.)* parade, show, boasting, pageantry, vaunting, pomp. display, flourish.

(ANT.) reserve, humility, unobtrusiveness, modesty.

ostentatious (SYN.) flashy, showy, overdone, fancy, pretentious, garish.

ostracize (SYN.) hinder, omit, bar, exclude, blackball, expel, prohibit, shout out, prevent, except.

(ANT.) welcome, accept, include, admit.

other (SYN.) distinct, different, extra, further, new, additional, supplementary.

ought (SYN.) must, should, be obliged.

oust (SYN.) eject, banish, exclude, expatriate, ostracize, dismiss, exile, expel.

(ANT.) shelter, accept, receive, admit, harbor.

ouster (SYN.) expulsion, banishment, ejection, overthrow.

outbreak (SYN.) riot, revolt, uprising, disturbance, torrent, eruption, outburst.

outburst (SYN.) outbreak, eruption, torrent, ejection, discharge.

outcast (SYN.) friendless, homeless, deserted, abandoned, forsaken, disowned, derelict, forlorn, rejected.

outclass (SYN.) outshine, surpass.

outcome (SYN.) fate, destiny, necessity, doom, portion, consequence, result, end, fortune, effect, issue, aftermath.

outcry (SYN.) scream, protest, clamor, noise, uproar.

outdated (SYN.) old-fashioned, unfashionable, old, outmoded.

(ANT.) stylish.

outdo (SYN.) outshine, defeat, excel, beat, surpass.

outer (SYN.) remote, exterior, external.

outfit (SYN.) garb, kit, gear, furnish, equip, rig, clothing, provisions.

outgoing (SYN.) leaving, departing, friendly, congenial, amicable.

(ANT.) unfriendly, incoming.

outgrowth (SYN.) effect, outcome, upshot, fruit, result, consequence, product, by-product, development.

outing (SYN.) journey, trip, excursion, jaunt, expedition, junket.

outlandish (SYN.) peculiar, odd, weird, curious, strange, queer, exotic, bazaar.

(ANT.) ordinary, common.

outlast (SYN.) survive, endure, outlive.

outlaw (SYN.) exile, bandit, outcast, badman, convict, criminal, fugitive, desperado.

outlay (SYN.) expense, costs, spending, disbursement, expenditure, charge.

outlet (SYN.) spout, opening, passage.

outline (SYN.) form, sketch, brief, draft, figure, profile, contour, chart, diagram, skeleton, delineation, plan, silhouette.

outlook (SYN.) viewpoint, view, prospect, opportunity, position, attitude, future.

outlying (SYN.) external, remote, outer, out-of-the-way, surburban, rural.

outmoded (SYN.) unfashionable, oldfashioned.

(ANT.) up-to-date, modern.

outnumber (SYN.) exceed.

output (SYN.) yield, crop, harvest, proceeds, productivity, production.

outrage (SYN.) aggression, transgression, vice, affront, offense, insult, indignity, atrocity, misdeed, trespass, wrong.

(ANT.) morality, right, gentleness, innocence.

outrageous (SYN.) shameful, shocking, disgraceful, insulting, nonsensical, absurd, foolish, crazy, excessive, ridiculous, bizarre, preposterous, offensive.

(ANT.) prudent, reasonable, sensible.

outright (SYN.) entirely, altogether, completely, quite, fully, thoroughly.

outset (SYN.) inception, origin, start, commencement, opening, source.

(ANT.) end, completion, termination, consummation, close.

outside (SYN.) covering, exterior, surface, facade, externals, appearance.

(ANT.) intimate, insider.

outsider (SYN.) immigrant, stranger, foreigner, alien, newcomer, bystander.

(ANT.) countryman, friend, acquaintance, neighbor, associate.

outsmart (SYN.) outmaneuver, outwit.

outspoken (SYN.) rude, impolite, unceremonious, brusque, unrestrained, vocal, open, straight-foward, blunt, unreserved, frank, forthright, rough.

(ANT.) suave, tactful, shy, polished, polite, subtle.

outstanding (SYN.) well-known, important, prominent, leading, eminent, distinguished, significant, conspicuous.

(ANT.) insignificant, unimportant.

outward (SYN.) apparent, outside, exterior, visible.

outweigh (SYN.) predominate, supersede, counteract, dwarf.

outwit (SYN.) baffle, trick, outsmart, bewilder, outdo, outmaneuver, confuse.

oval (SYN.) egg-shaped, elliptical, ovular.

ovation (SYN.) fanfare, homage, applause, tribute, cheers, acclamation.

overall *(SYN.)* comprehensive, complete, general, extensive, wide-spread, entire.

overbearing *(SYN.)* domineering, masterful, autocratic, dictatorial, arrogant, bossy, imperious, haughty. *(ANT.)* humble.

overcast *(SYN.)* dim, shadowy, cloudy, murky, dark, mysterious, gloomy, somber, dismal, hazy, indistinct. *(ANT.)* sunny, bright, distinct, limpid, clear.

overcome *(SYN.)* quell, beat, crush, surmount, rout, humble, conquer, subjugate, defeat, subdue, upset, vanquish. *(ANT.)* retreat, surrender, capitulate, cede, lose.

overconfident *(SYN.)* egotistical, presumptuous, arrogant, conceited.

overdo *(SYN.)* stretch, exaggerate, enlarge, magnify, exhaust, overexert, strain.

overdue *(SYN.)* tardy, advanced, slow, delayed, new. *(ANT.)* timely, early, beforehand.

overflow *(SYN.)* run over, flood, spill, cascade, inundate.

overflowing *(SYN.)* ample, plentiful, teeming, abundant, copious, profuse. *(ANT.)* insufficient, scant, deficient, scarce.

overhang *(SYN.)* protrude, extend, projection.

overhaul *(SYN.)* recondition, rebuild, service, repair, condition, revamp.

overhead *(SYN.)* high, above, aloft, expenses, costs.

overjoyed *(SYN.)* enchanted, delighted, ecstatic, enraptured, elated, blissful. *(ANT.)* depressed.

overlap *(SYN.)* overhang, extend, superimpose.

overload *(SYN.)* burden, weight, oppress, afflict, weigh, trouble, encumber, tax. *(ANT.)* ease, lighten, console, alleviate, mitigate.

overlook *(SYN.)* miss, disregard, exclude, cancel, omit, skip, ignore, drop, delete, neglect, exclude, watch, eliminate. *(ANT.)* notice, enter, include, introduce, insert.

overly *(SYN.)* exceedingly, needlessly, unreasonably.

overpass *(SYN.)* span, bridge, viaduct.

overpower *(SYN.)* overcome, conquer, defeat, surmount, vanquish, overwhelm.

(ANT.) surrender.

overrated *(SYN.)* exaggerated, misrepresented.

overrule *(SYN.)* disallow, nullify, cancel, override, repeal, revoke.

overrun *(SYN.)* spread, exceed, beset, infest, flood, abound.

oversee *(SYN.)* direct, run, operate, administer, superintend, boss, manage, supervise.

overseer *(SYN.)* leader, ruler, master, teacher, chief, commander, lord, employer, manager, head. *(ANT.)* slave, servant.

overshadow *(SYN.)* dominate, control, outclass, surpass, domineer.

oversight *(SYN.)* omission, charge, superintendence, surveillance, inattention, error, inadvertence, neglect, mistake, inspection, control, slip, negligence, management. *(ANT.)* scrutiny, care, attention, observation.

overstep *(SYN.)* surpass, exceed, trespass, transcend, impinge, violate, intrude.

overt *(SYN.)* honest, candid, frank, plain, open, apparent, straightforward.

overtake *(SYN.)* outdistance, reach, catch, pass.

overthrow *(SYN.)* defeat, demolish, overcome, destroy, ruin, rout, vanquish, subvert, reverse, supplant, overturn, overpower, upset. *(ANT.)* revive, restore, construct, regenerate, reinstate.

overture *(SYN.)* offer, bid, proposal, prelude, introduction, presentation, recommendation. *(ANT.)* finale.

overturn *(SYN.)* demolish, overcome, vanquish, upset, supplant, destroy. *(ANT.)* uphold, construct, build, preserve, conserve.

overweight *(SYN.)* pudgy, stout, heavy, obese, fat.

overwhelm *(SYN.)* crush, surmount, vanquish, conquer, astonish, surprise, bewilder, astound, startle, overcome, overpower, defeat.

overwrought *(SYN.)* distraught, hysterical.

owe *(SYN.)* be liable, be indebted.

own *(SYN.)* monopolize, hold, possess, maintain, have.

owner *(SYN.)* landholder, partner, proprietor, possessor.

pace *(SYN.)* rate, gait, step.

pacific *(SYN.)* peaceful, calm, serene, undisturbed, composed, imperturbable, placid, still, tranquil, unruffled, peaceable, quiet.
(ANT.) turbulent, wild, excited, frantic.

pacify *(SYN.)* appease, lull, relieve, quell, soothe, allay, assuage, calm, satisfy, compose, placate, alleviate.
(ANT.) incense, inflame, arouse, excite.

pack *(SYN.)* prepare, stow, crowd, stuff, bundle, parcel, load, crowd, gang, mob.

package *(SYN.)* parcel, packet, load, bundle, box, bottle, crate.

packed *(SYN.)* filled, complete, plentiful, crammed, fall, replete, gorged, satiated, copious, entire, extensive.
(ANT.) lacking, depleted, devoid, vacant, insufficient, partial, empty.

pageant *(SYN.)* show, display, spectacle.

pain *(SYN.)* twinge, ache, pang, agony, distress, grief, anguish, throe, paroxysm, suffering, misery.
(ANT.) happiness, pleasure, comfort, relief, solace, ease, delight, joy.

painful *(SYN.)* hurting, galling, poignant, bitter, grievous, agonizing, aching.
(ANT.) sweet, pleasant, soothing.

painting *(SYN.)* image, picture, portrayal, scene, view, sketch, illustration, panorama, likeness, representation.

pair *(SYN.)* team, couple, mate, match.

palatial *(SYN.)* majestic, magnificent, sumptuous, luxurious.

pale *(SYN.)* colorless, white, pallid, dim, faint, whiten, blanch.
(ANT.) flushed, ruddy, bright, dark.

pamphlet *(SYN.)* leaflet, brochure.

pang *(SYN.)* throb, pain, hurt.

panic *(SYN.)* fear, terror, fright, alarm, apprehension, trembling, horror, dread.
(ANT.) tranquillity, composure, calmness, serenity, calm, soothe.

pant *(SYN.)* wheeze, puff, gasp.

pantry *(SYN.)* cupboard, storeroom.

paper *(SYN.)* journal, newspaper, document, article, essay.

parable *(SYN.)* fable, saga, legend, myth, allegory, chronicle, fiction.
(ANT.) history, fact.

ade *(SYN.)* procession, cavalcade, succession, train, file, cortege, retinue, sequence, march, review, pageant, strut.

paradise *(SYN.)* utopia, heaven.

paradoxical *(SYN.)* unsteady, contradic-

tory, discrepant, incompatible, inconsistent, vacillating, wavering, illogical.
(ANT.) correspondent, compatible, congruous, consistent.

parallel *(SYN.)* allied, analogous, comparable, corresponding, akin, similar, correlative, alike, like, resembling, equal, counterpart, likeness, correspondence, resemble, equal, match.
(ANT.) opposed, different, incongruous.

paralyze *(SYN.)* numb, deaden.

paraphernalia *(SYN.)* effect, gear, belonging, equipment.

parcel *(SYN.)* packet, package, bundle.

parched *(SYN.)* dry, arid, thirsty, drained, dehydrated, desiccated.
(ANT.) moist, damp.

pardon *(SYN.)* absolution, forgiveness, remission, acquittal, amnesty, excuse, exoneration, forgive, acquit.
(ANT.) sentence, penalty, conviction, punishment, condemn.

pardon *(SYN.)* condone, overlook, remit, absolve, acquit, forgive, excuse, remit.
(ANT.) punish, chastise, accuse, condemn, convict.

pare *(SYN.)* skin, peel, reduce, trim, shave, crop.

parley *(SYN.)* interview, talk, conference, chat, dialogue, colloquy.

paroxysm *(SYN.)* twinge, pang, ache, pain.
(ANT.) ease, relief, comfort.

parsimonious *(SYN.)* avaricious, miserly, penurious, stingy, acquisitive, greedy.
(ANT.) munificent, extravagant, bountiful, altruistic, generous.

part *(SYN.)* piece, section, allotment, portion, segment, element, member, concern, side, interest, lines, role, apportionment, division, share, fragment, ingredient, organ, party, moiety, section, fraction, participation, divide.
(ANT.) whole, entirety.

part *(SYN.)* separate, sever, divide, sunder.
(ANT.) join, combine, unite, convene.

partake *(SYN.)* dispense, parcel, allot, assign, distribute, partition, appropriate, divide, portion, share.
(ANT.) condense, aggregate, combine.

partial *(SYN.)* unfinished, undone, incomplete, prejudiced, unfair.
(SYN.) comprehensive, complete.

partiality *(SYN.)* preconception, bias, predisposition, bigotry.

(ANT.) reason, fairness, impartiality.
participant *(SYN.)* associate, colleague, partner, shareholder.
participate *(SYN.)* join, share, partake.
participation *(SYN.)* communion, sacrament, union, intercourse, association, fellowship.
(ANT.) nonparticipation, alienation.
particle *(SYN.)* mite, crumb, scrap, atom, corpuscle, grain, iota, shred, smidgen, grain, speck, bit, spot.
(ANT.) quantity, bulk, mass.
particular *(SYN.)* peculiar, unusual, detailed, specific, fastidious, individual, distinctive, singular, circumstantial, exact, careful, squeamish, special.
(ANT.) general, rough, universal, comprehensive, undiscriminating.
partisan *(SYN.)* follower, successor, adherent, attendant, henchman, devotee, disciple, votary.
(ANT.) leader, chief, master, head.
partition *(SYN.)* distribution, division, separation, screen, barrier, separator, divider, wall.
(ANT.) unification, joining.
partly *(SYN.)* comparatively, partially, somewhat.
partner *(SYN.)* colleague, comrade, friend, crony, consort, associate, companion, mate, participant.
(ANT.) stranger, enemy, adversary.
party *(SYN.)* company, gathering, crowd, group.
pass *(SYN.)* proceed, continue, move, go, disregard, ignore, exceed, gap, permit, permission, admission, throw, toss.
(ANT.) note, consider, notice.
pass by *(SYN.)* dodge, avert, elude, free, ward, shun, eschew avoid, forbear.
(ANT.) meet, confront, oppose, encounter.
passable *(SYN.)* fair, average, mediocre, acceptable, adequate, satisfactory.
(ANT.) worst, excellent, first-rate, exceptional, extraordinary, superior.
passage *(SYN.)* section, passageway, corridor, section, voyage, tour, crossing.
passenger *(SYN.)* traveler, tourist, rider, voyager, commuter.
passion *(SYN.)* feeling, affection, turmoil, sentiment, perturbation, agitation, emotion, trepidation, zeal, rapture, excitement, desire, love, liking, fondness, enthusiasm.
(ANT.) tranquillity, indifference, calm,

restraint, dispassion, apathy, coolness.
passionate *(SYN.)* fiery, ardent, burning, glowing, irascible, fervid, excitable hot, impetuous, emotional, impulsive, excited, zealous, enthusiastic, earnest, sincere.
(ANT.) quiet, calm, cool, apathetic, deliberate.
passive *(SYN.)* relaxed, idle, stoical, enduring, inert, inactive, patient, submissive.
(ANT.) dynamic, active, aggressive.
password *(SYN.)* watchword.
past *(SYN.)* done, finished, gone, over, former.
(ANT.) future, present, ahead.
pastime *(SYN.)* match, amusement, diversion, fun, play, sport, contest, merriment, recreation, entertainment, hobby.
(ANT.) quiescence, labor, apathy, business.
patch *(SYN.)* restore, fix, repair, ameliorate, correct, rectify, remedy, sew, mend, better.
(ANT.) rend, deface, destroy, hurt, injure.
patent *(SYN.)* conspicuous, apparent, obvious, clear, evident, unmistakable, open, overt, manifest, indubitable, protection, control, copyright, permit.
(ANT.) hidden, concealed, obscure, covert.
path *(SYN.)* avenue, street, trail, walk, course, road, route, thoroughfare, channel, way, track, lane, footpath, pathway, walkway.
pathetic *(SYN.)* piteous, sad, affecting, moving, poignant, pitiable, touching, pitiful, touching.
(ANT.) funny, comical, ludicrous.
patience *(SYN.)* perseverance, composure, endurance, fortitude, longsuffering, forbearance, calmness, passiveness, serenity, courage, persistence.
(ANT.) restlessness, nervousness, impatience, unquite, impetuosity.
patient *(SYN.)* indulgent, stoical, forbearing, composed, assiduous, passive, uncomplaining, resigned, persistent, untiring, persevering, submissive, resigned, serene, calm, quiet, unexcited, unruffled.
(ANT.) turbulent, high-strung, chafing, clamorous, hysterical.
patrol *(SYN.)* inspect, watch, guard.

patron (SYN.) purchaser, buyer, client, customer.

patronize (SYN.) support.

pattern (SYN.) guide, example, original, model, design, figure, decoration.

paunchy (SYN.) fat, pudgy, stout, plump, portly, rotund, corpulent, obese, stocky. (ANT.) slim, slender, gaunt, lean, thin.

pause (SYN.) falter, hesitate, waver, demur, doubt, scruple, delay, vacillate, hesitation, rest, interruption, break, delay, intermission, recess. (ANT.) proceed, continue, decide, resolve, persevere, continuity, perpetuate.

pawn (SYN.) tool, puppet, stooge.

pay (SYN.) earnings, salary, allowance, stipend, wages, payment, compensation, recompense. (ANT.) gratuity, present, gift.

payable (SYN.) unpaid, due, owed, owing.

peace (SYN.) hush, repose, serenity, tranquillity, silence, stillness, calmness, quiescence, calm, quietude, rest, quiet, peacefulness, pact. (ANT.) noise, tumult, agitation, disturbance, excitement.

peaceable (SYN.) mild, calm, friendly, peaceful, amiable, gentle, pacific. (ANT.) aggressive, hostile, warlike.

peaceful (SYN.) pacific, calm, undisturbed, quiet, serene, mild, placid, gentle, tranquil, peaceable. (ANT.) noisy, violent, agitated, turbulent, disturbed, disrupted, riotous.

peak (SYN.) climax, culmination, summit, zenith, height, acme, consummation, apex, top, point, crest. (ANT.) depth, floor, base, anticlimax, base, bottom.

peculiar (SYN.) odd, eccentric, extraordinary, unusual, individual, particular, striking, rare, exceptional, distinctive, strange, unfamiliar, uncommon, queer, curious, outlandish. (ANT.) ordinary, common, normal, general, regular, unspecial.

peculiarity (SYN.) characteristic, feature, mark, trait, quality, attribute, property, distinctiveness.

pedantic (SYN.) formal, scholastic, erudite, academic, learned, bookish, theoretical, scholarly. (ANT.) simple, common-sense, ignorant, practical, unlearned.

peddle (SYN.) sell, vend, hawk.

pedestrian (SYN.) stroller, walker.

pedigree (SYN.) descent, line, parentage, lineage, ancestry, family.

peek (SYN.) glimpse, look, peer, peep.

peel (SYN.) rind, skin, peeling.

peep (SYN.) squeak, cheep, chirp.

peer (SYN.) match, rival, equal, parallel, peep, glimpse, examine, peek, scrutinize.

peeve (SYN.) nettle, irk, irritate, annoy, vex.

peevish (SYN.) ill-natured, irritable, waspish, touchy, petulant, snappish, fractious, ill-tempered, fretful. (ANT.) pleasant, affable, good-tempered, genial, good-natured.

pen (SYN.) coop, enclosure, cage.

penalize (SYN.) dock, punish.

penalty (SYN.) fine, retribution, handicap, punishment, chastisement, disadvantage, forfeiture, forfeit. (ANT.) remuneration, compensation, reward, pardon.

penchant (SYN.) disposition, propensity, tendency, partiality, inclination, bent, tendency, slant, bias. (ANT.) justice, fairness, equity, impartiality.

penetrate (SYN.) bore, hole, pierce, enter.

penetrating (SYN.) profound, recondite, abstruse, deep, solemn, piercing, puncturing, boring, sharp, acute. (ANT.) superficial, trivial, shallow, slight.

peninsula (SYN.) spit, headland, neck, point.

penitent (SYN.) remorseful, sorrowful, regretful, contrite, sorry, repentant. (ANT.) remorseless, objurgate.

penniless (SYN.) poor, destitute, impecunious, needy, poverty-stricken, needy. (ANT.) rich, wealthy, affluent, opulent, prosperous, well-off.

pensive (SYN.) dreamy, meditative, thoughtful, introspective, reflective, contemplative. (ANT.) thoughtless, heedless, inconsiderate, precipitous, rash.

penurious (SYN.) avaricious, greedy, parsimonious, miserly, stingy, acquisitive, tight. (ANT.) munificent, extravagant, bountiful, generous, altruistic.

penury (SYN.) poverty, want, destitution,

necessity, indigence, need, privation.
(ANT.) riches, affluence, abundance, plenty, wealth.
people *(SYN.)* humans, person.
perceive *(SYN.)* note, conceive, see, comprehend, understand, discern, recognize, apprehend, notice, observe, distinguish, understand, grasp.
(ANT.) overlook, ignore, miss.
perceptible *(SYN.)* sensible, appreciable, apprehensible.
(ANT.) imperceptible, absurd, impalpable.
perception *(SYN.)* understanding, apprehension, conception, insight, comprehension, discernment.
(ANT.) misconception, ignorance, misapprehension, insensibility.
perceptive *(SYN.)* informed, observant, apprised, cognizant, aware, conscious, sensible, mindful, discerning, sharp, acute, observant.
(ANT.) unaware, ignorant, oblivious, insensible.
perfect *(SYN.)* ideal, whole, faultless, immaculate, complete, superlative, absolute, unqualified, utter, sinless, holy, finished, blameless, entire, excellent, pure, flawless, ideal.
(ANT.) incomplete, defective, imperfect, deficient, blemished, lacking, faulty, flawed.
perfectionist *(SYN.)* purist, pedant.
perform *(SYN.)* impersonate, pretend, act, play, do, accomplish, achieve, complete.
performance *(SYN.)* parade, entertainment, demonstration, movie, show, production, ostentation, spectacle, presentation, offering.
performer *(SYN.)* entertainer, actress, actor.
perfume *(SYN.)* cologne, scent, essence.
perfunctory *(SYN.)* decorous, exact, formal, external, correct, affected, methodical, precise, stiff, outward, proper, solemn.
(ANT.) unconventional, easy, unconstrained, natural, heartfelt.
perhaps *(SYN.)* conceivable, possible, maybe.
(ANT.) absolutely, definitely.
peril *(SYN.)* jeopardy, risk, danger, hazard.
(ANT.) safety, immunity, protection, defense, security.

perilous *(SYN.)* menacing, risky, hazardous, critical, dangerous, precarious, unsafe, insecure, threatening.
(ANT.) safe, firm, protected, secure.
period *(SYN.)* era, age, interval, span, tempo, time, epoch, duration, spell, date.
periodical *(SYN.)* uniform, customary, orderly, systematic, regular, steady.
(ANT.) exceptional, unusual, abnormal, rare, erratic.
perish *(SYN.)* die, sink cease, decline, decay, depart, wane, wither, languish, expire, cease, pass away.
(ANT.) grow, survive, flourish, begin, live.
perishable *(SYN.)* decomposable, decayable.
permanent *(SYN.)* constant, durable, enduring, abiding, fixed, changeless, unchangeable, lasting, indestructible, stable, continuing, long-lived, persistent, persisting, everlasting, unchanging, unaltered.
(ANT.) unstable, transient, ephemeral, temporary, transitory, passing, inconstant, fluctuating.
permeate *(SYN.)* penetrate, pervade, run through, diffuse, fill, saturate, infiltrate.
permissible *(SYN.)* allowable, fair, tolerable, admissible, justifiable, probable, warranted.
(ANT.) unsuitable, inadmissible, irrelevant.
permission *(SYN.)* authorization, liberty, permit, authority, consent, leave, license, freedom.
(ANT.) refusal, prohibition, denial, opposition.
permissive *(SYN.)* easy, tolerant, openminded, unrestrictive.
(ANT.) restrictive.
permit *(SYN.)* let, tolerate, authorize, sanction, allow, grant, give.
(ANT.) refuse, resist, forbid, protest, object, prohibit, disallow.
perpendicular *(SYN.)* standing, upright, vertical.
(ANT.) horizontal.
perpetrate *(SYN.)* commit, perform, do.
(ANT.) neglect, fail, miscarry.
perpetual *(SYN.)* everlasting, immortal, ceaseless, endless, timeless, undying, infinite, eternal, unceasing, continuing, continual, continuous, permanent, constant, eternal.

(ANT.) transient, mortal, finite, temporal ephemeral, inconstant, intermittent, fluctuating.

perpetually (SYN.) continually, ever, incessantly, eternally, forever, always, constantly.

(ANT.) rarely, sometimes, never, occasionally, fitfully.

perplex (SYN.) confuse, dumbfound, mystify, puzzle, bewilder, confound, nonplus.

(ANT.) solve, explain, illumine, instruct, clarify.

perplexed (SYN.) confused, disorganized, mixed, bewildered, deranged, disordered, muddled, disconcerted.

(ANT.) plain, obvious, clear, lucid, organized.

perplexing (SYN.) intricate, complex, involved, compound, complicated.

(ANT.) uncompounded, plain, simple.

persecute (SYN.) harass, hound, torment, worry, vex, torture, harry, afflict, annoy, oppress, pester, ill-treat, victimize, maltreat.

(ANT.) support, comfort, assist, encourage, aid.

persevere (SYN.) remain, abide, endure, last, persist, continue.

(ANT.) vacillate, desist, discontinue, cease, waver, lapse.

perseverance (SYN.) persistency, constancy, pertinacity, steadfastness, tenacity, industry.

(ANT.) sloth, cessation, laziness, idleness, rest.

persist (SYN.) endure, remain, abide, persevere, continue, last.

(ANT.) vacillate, waver, desist, cease, discontinue, stop.

persistence (SYN.) persistency, constancy, perseverance, steadfastness, tenacity.

(ANT.) cessation, rest, sloth, idleness.

persistent (SYN.) lasting, steady, obstinate, stubborn, fixed, enduring, immovable, constant, indefatigable, dogged.

(ANT.) wavering, unsure, hesitant, vacillating.

person (SYN.) human, individual, somebody, someone.

personal (SYN.) secret, private.

(ANT.) general, public.

personality (SYN.) make-up, nature, disposition, character.

perspicacity (SYN.) intelligence, understanding, discernment, judgment, wisdom, sagacity.

(ANT.) thoughtlessness, stupidity, arbitrariness, senselessness.

persuade (SYN.) entice, coax, exhort, prevail upon, urge, allure, induce, influence, win over, convince.

(ANT.) restrain, deter, compel, dissuade, coerce, discourage.

persuasion (SYN.) decision, feeling, notion, view, sentiment, conviction, belief, opinion.

(ANT.) knowledge, skepticism, fact, misgiving.

persuasive (SYN.) winning, alluring, compelling, convincing, stimulating, influential.

(ANT.) dubious, unconvincing.

pertain (SYN.) refer, relate, apply.

pertinacious (SYN.) firm, obstinate, contumacious, head-strong, dogged, inflexible, obdurate, uncompromising, determined, immovable, unyielding.

(ANT.) yielding, docile, amenable, submissive, compliant.

pertinent (SYN.) apt, material, relevant, relating, applicable, to the point, germane, apropos, apposite, appropriate.

(ANT.) unrelated, foreign, alien, extraneous.

perturbed (SYN.) agitated, disturbed, upset, flustered.

pervade (SYN.) penetrate, saturate, fill, diffuse, infiltrate, run through, permeate.

perverse (SYN.) obstinate, ungovernable, sinful, contrary, fractious, peevish, forward, disobedient, wicked, intractable, petulant.

(ANT.) docile, agreeable, tractable, obliging.

perversion (SYN.) maltreatment, outrage, desecration, abuse, profanation, misuse, reviling.

(ANT.) respect.

pervert (SYN.) deprave, humiliate, impair, debase, corrupt, degrade, abase, defile.

(ANT.) improve, raise, enhance.

perverted (SYN.) wicked, perverse, sinful.

pest (SYN.) annoyance, bother, nuisance, bother, irritant, irritation.

pester (SYN.) disturb, annoy, irritate, tease, bother, chafe, inconvenience, molest, trouble, vex, harass, torment, worry.

(ANT.) console, soothe, accommodate, gratify.

pet (SYN.) darling, favorite, caress.

petition (SYN.) invocation, prayer, request, appeal, entreaty, supplication, suit, plea, application, solicitation, entreaty.

petty (SYN.) paltry, trivial, frivolous, small, unimportant, trifling, insignificant.

(ANT.) important, serious, weighty, momentous, grand, vital, significant, generous.

petulant (SYN.) irritable, ill-natured, fretful, snappish, peevish, ill-tempered, waspish, touchy.

(ANT.) pleasant, affable, good-tempered, genial, good-natured.

phantom (SYN.) apparition, ghost, specter.

phase (SYN.) period, stage, view, condition.

phenomenon (SYN.) occurrence, fact, happening, incident.

philanthropy (SYN.) kindness, benevolence, charity, generosity, tenderness, liberality, humanity, magnanimity, altruism.

(ANT.) unkindness, inhumanity, cruelty, malevolence, selfishness.

phlegmatic (SYN.) unfeeling, passionless, listless, cold, lethargic, sluggish, slow, lazy.

(ANT.) passionate, ardent, energetic.

phony (SYN.) counterfeit, artificial, ersatz, fake, synthetic, unreal, spurious, feigned, assumed, bogus, sham, false, forged.

(ANT.) real, genuine, natural, true.

phrase (SYN.) expression, term, word, name.

physical (SYN.) material, bodily, carnal, corporeal, natural, somatic, corporal.

(ANT.) spiritual, mental.

pick (SYN.) cull, opt, select, elect, choose.

(ANT.) reject, refuse.

picture (SYN.) etching, image, painting, portrait, print, representation, sketch, appearance, cinema, effigy, engraving, scene, view, illustration, panorama, resemblance, likeness, drawing, photograph.

piece (SYN.) portion, bit, fraction, morsel, scrap, fragment, amount, part,

quantity, unit, section, portion.

(ANT.) sum, whole, entirety, all, total.

piecemeal (SYN.) gradually, partially.

(ANT.) whole, complete, entire.

pierce (SYN.) puncture, perforate.

pigheaded (SYN.) inflexible, stubborn, obstinate.

pigment (SYN.) shade, tint, color, dye, hue, complexion, tincture, stain, tinge.

(ANT.) transparency, paleness.

pile (SYN.) accumulation, heap, collection, amass.

pilgrim (SYN.) wanderer, traveler.

pilgrimage (SYN.) trip, journey, tour, expedition.

pillar (SYN.) support, prop, column, shaft.

pillow (SYN.) bolster, cushion, pad.

pilot (SYN.) helmsman, aviator, steersman.

pin (SYN.) clip, fastening, peg, fastener.

pinch (SYN.) squeeze, nip.

pinnacle (SYN.) crown, zenith, head, summit, chief, apex, crest, top.

(ANT.) bottom, foundation, base, foot.

pioneer (SYN.) guide, pilgrim, pathfinder, explorer.

pious (SYN.) devout, religious, spiritual, consecrated, divine, hallowed, holy, saintly, sacred, reverent.

(ANT.) worldly, sacrilegious, evil, secular, profane, irreligious, impious.

pirate (SYN.) plunderer, buccaneer, privateer.

pistol (SYN.) gun, revolver, weapon, handgun.

pit (SYN.) well, cavity, hole, excavation.

pitch (SYN.) throw, cast, toss, propel, hurl, fling, thrust, establish.

(ANT.) retain, draw, hold, pull, haul.

pitcher (SYN.) jug.

piteous (SYN.) poignant, touching, affecting, moving, pitiable, sad, pathetic.

(ANT.) funny, ludicrous, comical.

pitfall (SYN.) lure, snare, wile, ambush, bait, intrigue, trick, trap, artifice, net, snare.

pitiable (SYN.) poignant, touching, moving, affecting, sad.

(ANT.) ludicrous, funny, comical.

pitiful (SYN.) distressing, pathetic, pitiable.

pitiless (SYN.) unmerciful, mean, unpitying, merciless, cruel.

(ANT.) gentle, kind.

pity (SYN.) sympathy, commiseration,

condolence, mercy, compassion, charity, mercy.

(ANT.) *ruthlessness, hardness, cruelty, inhumanity, brutality, vindictiveness.*

pivotal (SYN.) crucial, critical, essential, central.

(ANT.) *peripheral, unimportant.*

place (SYN.) lay, arrange, dispose, put, deposit, space, region, location, plot, area, spot.

(ANT.) *mislay, remove, disarrange, disturb, misplace.*

placid (SYN.) pacific, serene, tranquil, calm, imperturbable, composed, peaceful, quiet, still, undisturbed, unruffled.

(ANT.) *wild, frantic, turbulent, stormy, excited.*

plagiarize (SYN.) recite, adduce, cite, quote, paraphrase, repeat, extract.

(ANT.) *retort, contradict, misquote, refute.*

plague (SYN.) hound, pester, worry, harass, annoy, persecute, torment, vex, afflict, badger, torture, epidemic, trouble.

(ANT.) *encourage, aid, comfort, assist, support.*

plain (SYN.) candid, simple, flat, smooth, clear, evident, sincere, unpretentious, level, distinct, absolute, visible, open, frank, palpable, undecorated, ordinary, unembellished, unadorned.

(ANT.) *embellished, abstruse, abrupt, rough, broken, insincere, adorned, fancy, elaborate, beautiful, ornamented.*

plan (SYN.) design, purpose, sketch, devise, invent, contrive, intend, draw, create, scheme, plot, method, procedure.

plane (SYN.) level, airplane.

plastic (SYN.) pliable, moldable, supple, flexible, synthetic.

platform (SYN.) stage, pulpit.

plausible (SYN.) likely, practical, credible, feasible, possible, probable.

(ANT.) *impracticable, impossible, visionary.*

play (SYN.) entertainment, amusement, pastime, sport, game, fun, diversion, recreation, show, performance, drama, theatrical.

(ANT.) *work, labor, boredom, toil.*

playful (SYN.) sportive, frolicsome, frisky.

plaything (SYN.) game, trinket, toy, gadget.

playwright (SYN.) scriptwriter, dramatist.

plea (SYN.) invocation, request, appeal, entreaty, supplication, petition, suit.

plead (SYN.) beseech, defend, rejoin, supplicate, discuss, beg, appeal, ask, implore, argue, entreat.

(ANT.) *deprecate, deny, refuse.*

pleasant (SYN.) agreeable, welcome, suitable, charming, pleasing, amiable, gratifying, acceptable, pleasurable, enjoyable, nice, satisfying, satisfactory, acceptable, affable, mild, friendly.

(ANT.) *offensive, disagreeable, obnoxious, unpleasant, horrid, sour, difficult, nasty.*

please (SYN.) satisfy, suffice, fulfill, content, appease, gratify, satiate, compensate, remunerate.

(ANT.) *dissatisfy, annoy, tantalize, frustrate, displease, vex.*

pleasing (SYN.) luscious, melodious, sugary, delightful, agreeable, honeyed, mellifluous, engaging, pleasant, charming, engaging.

(ANT.) *repulsive, sour, acrid, bitter, offensive, irritating, annoying.*

pleasure (SYN.) felicity, delight, amusement, enjoyment gratification, happiness, joy, satisfaction, gladness, wellbeing.

(ANT.) *suffering, pain, vexation, trouble, affliction, discomfort, torment.*

pledge (SYN.) promise, statement, assertion, declaration, assurance, agreement, oath, commitment, agree, vow, swear.

pledge (SYN.) bind, obligate, commit.

(ANT.) *renounce, release, neglect, mistrust.*

plentiful (SYN.) ample, profuse, replete, bountiful, abundant, plenteous, luxurious, fullness, fruitful, copious.

(ANT.) *rare, scanty, deficient, scarce, insufficient.*

plenty (SYN.) fruitfulness, bounty, fullness, abundance.

(ANT.) *want, scarcity, need.*

pliable (SYN.) elastic, supple, flexible, compliant, pliant, resilient, ductile.

(ANT.) *rigid, unbending, hard, brittle, stiff.*

plight (SYN.) dilemma, situation, difficulty, condition, predicament, fix, scrape, state.

(ANT.) *satisfaction, ease, comfort, calmness.*

plot *(SYN.)* design, plan, scheme, cabal, conspiracy, diagram, sketch, graph, chart, machination, intrigue.

plotting *(SYN.)* cunning, scheming, objective, artfulness, contrivance, purpose, intent, design.

(ANT.) accident, chance, result, candor, sincerity.

ploy *(SYN.)* ruse, guile, antic, deception, hoax, subterfuge, wile, cheat, artifice, fraud, trick.

(ANT.) honesty, sincerity, openness, exposure, candor.

pluck *(SYN.)* yank, snatch, jerk, pull.

plug *(SYN.)* cork, stopper.

plump *(SYN.)* obese, portly, stout, thickset, rotund, chubby, fat, paunchy, stocky, corpulent, pudgy, stout, fleshy.

(ANT.) slim, thin, gaunt, lean, slender, skinny.

plunder *(SYN.)* ravage, strip, sack, rob, pillage, raid, loot.

plunge *(SYN.)* immerse, dip, submerge.

pocketbook *(SYN.)* purse, handbag.

poem *(SYN.)* lyric, verse, poetry.

poetry *(SYN.)* rhyme, verse.

pogrom *(SYN.)* massacre, carnage, slaughter, butchery.

poignant *(SYN.)* pitiable, touching, affecting, impressive, sad, tender, moving, heart-rending.

point *(SYN.)* direct, level, train, aim, locality, position, spot, location.

(ANT.) distract, misguide, deceive, misdirect.

pointed *(SYN.)* keen, sharp, penetrating, shrewd, witty, quick, acute, penetrating, cutting, piercing, astute, severe.

(ANT.) shallow, stupid, bland, blunt, gentle.

pointless *(SYN.)* vain, purposeless.

poise *(SYN.)* composure, self-possession, equanimity, equilibrium, carriage, calmness, balance, self-control, assurance, control, dignity.

(ANT.) rage, turbulence, agitation, anger, excitement.

poison *(SYN.)* corrupt, sully, taint, infect, befoul, defile, contaminate, venom, toxin, virus.

(ANT.) purify, disinfect.

poke *(SYN.)* punch, stab, thrust, jab.

policy *(SYN.)* procedure, system, rule, approach, tactic.

polish *(SYN.)* brighten, shine, finish, brightness, gloss.

(ANT.) tarnish, dull.

polished *(SYN.)* glib, diplomatic, urbane, refined, sleek, suave, slick.

(ANT.) rough, blunt, bluff, harsh, rugged.

polite *(SYN.)* civil, refined, well-mannered, accomplished, courteous, genteel, urbane, well-bred, cultivated, considerate, thoughtful, mannerly, respectful.

(ANT.) uncouth, impertinent, rude, boorish, uncivil, discourteous.

pollute *(SYN.)* contaminate, poison, taint, sully, infect, befoul, defile, dirty.

(ANT.) purify, disinfect, clean, clarify.

pomp *(SYN.)* flourish, pageantry, vaunting, show, boasting, ostentation, parade, display.

(ANT.) reserve, humility, modesty.

pompous *(SYN.)* high, magnificent, stately, august, dignified, grandiose, noble, majestic, lofty, imposing, arrogant, vain, pretentious.

(ANT.) lowly, undignified, humble, common, ordinary.

ponder *(SYN.)* examined, study, contemplate, investigate, meditate, muse, scrutinize, cogitate, reflect, weigh, deliberate, consider.

ponderous *(SYN.)* burdensome, trying, gloomy, serious, sluggish, massive, heavy, cumbersome, grievous, grave, dull, weighty.

(ANT.) light, animated, brisk.

poor *(SYN.)* penniless, bad, deficient, destitute, inferior, shabby, wrong, scanty, pecunious, indigent, needy, poverty-stricken, unfavorable, impoverished, penniless.

(ANT.) wealthy, prosperous, rich, fortunate, good, excellent.

poppycock *(SYN.)* rubbish, babble, twaddle, nonsense.

popular *(SYN.)* favorite, general, common, familiar, prevalent, liked, prevailing, well-liked, approved, accepted, celebrated, admired, ordinary.

(ANT.) unpopular, esoteric, restricted, exclusive.

populous *(SYN.)* dense, thronged, crowded.

porch *(SYN.)* patio, veranda.

pornographic *(SYN.)* impure, indecent, obscene, coarse, dirty, filthy, lewd, smutty, offensive, disgusting.

(ANT.) refined, modest, pure, decent.

port (SYN.) harbor, refuge, anchorage.

portable (SYN.) transportable, movable.

portal (SYN.) entry, doorway, opening, inlet, entrance.
(ANT.) exit, departure.

portend (SYN.) foreshadow, presage, foretoken.

portentous (SYN.) significant, critical, momentous.
(ANT.) trivial.

portion (SYN.) share, bit, parcel, part, piece, section, fragment, division, quota, segment, allotment.
(ANT.) whole, bulk.

portly (SYN.) majestic, grand, impressive, dignified, stout, fat, heavy, obese.
(ANT.) slender, thin, slim.

portrait (SYN.) painting, representation, picture, likeness.

portray (SYN.) depict, picture, represent, sketch, describe, delineate, paint.
(ANT.) misrepresent, caricature, suggest.

pose (SYN.) model.

position (SYN.) caste, site, locality, situation, condition, standing, incumbency, office, bearing, posture, berth, place, job, pose, rank, attitude, location, place, spot, station, job, situation, occupation.

positive (SYN.) sure, definite, fixed, inevitable, undeniable, indubitable, assured, certain, unquestionable, unmistakable.
(ANT.) uncertain, doubtful, questionable, probably, unsure, dubious, confused, negative, adverse.

positively (SYN.) unquestionably, surely, certainly, absolutely.

possess (SYN.) own, obtain, control, have, seize, hold, occupy, affect, hold, control.
(ANT.) surrender, abandon, lose, renounce.

possessed (SYN.) entranced, obsessed, consumer, haunted, enchanted.

possession (SYN.) custody, ownership, occupancy.

possessions (SYN.) commodities, effects, goods, property, merchandise, wares, wealth, belongings, stock.

possible (SYN.) likely, practical, probable, feasible, plausible, credible, practicable.
(ANT.) visionary, impossible, improbable.

possibility (SYN.) opportunity, chance,

contingency, occasion.
(ANT.) obstacle, disadvantage, hindrance.

possible (SYN.) feasible, practical, practicable, doable.

possibly (SYN.) perchance, perhaps, maybe.

post (SYN.) position, job, berth, incumbency, situation, shaft, pole, fort, base, station.

postpone (SYN.) delay, stay, suspend, discontinue, defer, adjourn, interrupt, put off.
(ANT.) persist, prolong, maintain, continue, proceed.

postulate (SYN.) principle, adage, saying, proverb, truism, byword, aphorism, axiom, fundamental, maxim.

potency (SYN.) effectiveness, capability, skillfulness, efficiency, competency, ability.
(ANT.) wastefulness, inability, ineptitude.

potent (SYN.) mighty, influential, convincing, effective.
(ANT.) feeble, weak, powerless, impotent.

potential (SYN.) likely, possible, dormant, hidden, latent.

pouch (SYN.) container, bag, sack.

pound (SYN.) buffet, beat, punch, strike, thrash, defeat, subdue, pulse, smite, belabor, knock, thump, overpower, palpitate, rout, vanquish.
(ANT.) fail, surrender, stroke, defend, shield.

pour (SYN.) flow.

pout (SYN.) brood, sulk, mope.

poverty (SYN.) necessity, need, want, destitution, privation, indigence, distress.
(ANT.) plenty, abundance, wealth, riches, affluence, richness, comfort.

power (SYN.) potency, might, authority, control, predominance, capability, faculty, validity, force, vigor, command, influence, talent, ability, dominion, competency.
(ANT.) incapacity, fatigue, weakness, disablement, impotence, ineptitude.

powerful (SYN.) firm, strong, concentrated, enduring, forcible, robust, sturdy, tough, athletic, forceful, hale, impregnable, hardy, mighty, potent.
(ANT.) feeble, insipid, brittle, delicate, fragile, weak, ineffectual, powerless.

practical *(SYN.)* sensible, wise, prudent, reasonable, sagacious, sober, sound, workable, attainable.
(ANT.) stupid, unaware, impalpable, imperceptible, absurd, impractical.
practically *(SYN.)* almost, nearly.
practice *(SYN.)* exercise, habit, custom, manner, wont, usage, drill, tradition, performance, action, repetition.
(ANT.) inexperience, theory, disuse, idleness, speculation.
practiced *(SYN.)* able, expert, skilled, adept.
(ANT.) inept.
prairie *(SYN.)* plain, grassland.
praise *(SYN.)* applaud, compliment, extol, laud, glorify, commend, acclaim, eulogize, flatter, admire, celebrate, commendation, approval.
(ANT.) criticize, censure, reprove, condemn, disparage, disapprove, criticism, negation.
pray *(SYN.)* supplicate, importune, beseech, beg.
prayer *(SYN.)* plea, suit, appeal, invocation, supplication, petition, entreaty, request.
preach *(SYN.)* teach, urge, moralize, lecture.
preamble *(SYN.)* overture, prologue, beginning, introduction, prelude, start, foreword, preface.
(ANT.) end, finale, completion, conclusion, epilogue.
precarious *(SYN.)* dangerous, perilous, threatening, menacing, critical, risky, unsafe, hazardous.
(ANT.) secure, firm, protected, safe.
precaution *(SYN.)* foresight, forethought, care.
precedence *(SYN.)* preference, priority.
precedent *(SYN.)* model, example.
precept *(SYN.)* doctrine, tenet, belief, creed, teaching, dogma.
(ANT.) practice, conduct, performance, deed.
precious *(SYN.)* dear, useful, valuable, costly, esteemed, profitable, expensive, priceless, dear.
(ANT.) poor, worthless, cheap, mean, trashy.
precipice *(SYN.)* bluff, cliff.
precipitate *(SYN.)* speedy, swift, hasty, sudden.
precipitous *(SYN.)* unannounced, sudden, harsh, rough, unexpected, sharp,

abrupt, hasty, craggy, steep, precipitate.
(ANT.) expected, smooth, anticipated, gradual.
precise *(SYN.)* strict, exact, formal, rigid, definite, unequivocal, prim, ceremonious, distinct, accurate, correct.
ANT.) loose, easy, vague, informal, careless, erroneous.
precisely *(SYN.)* specifically, exactly.
precision *(SYN.)* correction, accuracy, exactness.
preclude *(SYN.)* hinder, prevent, obstruct, forestall, obviate, thwart, impede.
(ANT.) permit, aid, expedite, encourage, promote.
preclusion *(SYN.)* omission, exception, exclusion.
(ANT.) standard, rule, inclusion.
predicament *(SYN.)* dilemma, plight, situation, condition, fix, difficulty, strait, scrape.
(ANT.) satisfaction, comfort, east, calmness.
predict *(SYN.)* forecast, foretell.
prediction *(SYN.)* forecast, prophecy.
predilection *(SYN.)* attachment, inclination, affection, bent, desire, penchant, disposition, preference.
ANT.) repugnance, aversion, apathy, distaste, nonchalance.
predominant *(SYN.)* highest, paramount, cardinal, foremost, main, first, leading, supreme, principal, essential, prevalent, dominant, prevailing.
(ANT.) subsidiary, auxiliary, supplemental, minor, subordinate.
predominate *(SYN.)* prevail, outweigh, rule.
preface *(SYN.)* foreword, introduction, preliminary, prelude, prologue, preamble.
prefer *(SYN.)* select, favor, elect, fancy.
preference *(SYN.)* election, choice, selection, alternative, option.
prejudice *(SYN.)* bias, favoritism, unfairness, partiality.
prejudiced *(SYN.)* fanatical, narrowminded, dogmatic, bigoted, illiberal, intolerant.
(ANT.) radical, liberal, tolerant, progressive.
preliminary *(SYN.)* introductory, preparatory, prelude, preface.
premature *(SYN.)* early, untimely, unex-

pected.

(ANT.) timely.

premeditated *(SYN.)* intended, voluntary, contemplated, designed, intentional, willful, deliberate, studied.

(ANT.) fortuitous, accidental.

premeditation *(SYN.)* intention, deliberation, forethought, forecast.

(ANT.) hazard, accident, impromptu, extemporization.

premise *(SYN.)* basis, presupposition, assumption, postulate, principle, presumption.

(ANT.) superstructure, derivative, trimming, implication.

preoccupied *(SYN.)* abstracted, distracted, absorbed, meditative, inattentive, absent, absent-minded.

(ANT.) attentive, alert, conscious, present, attending, watchful.

prepare *(SYN.)* contrive, furnish, ready, predispose, condition, fit, arrange, plan, qualify, make ready, get ready.

preposterous *(SYN.)* foolish, nonsensical, silly, contradictory, unreasonable, absurd, inconsistent, irrational, self-contradictory.

(ANT.) sensible, rational, consistent, sound, reasonable.

prerequisite *(SYN.)* essential, requirement, necessity, condition, demand.

prerogative *(SYN.)* grant, right, license, authority, privilege.

(ANT.) violation, encroachment, wrong, injustice.

prescribe *(SYN.)* order, direct, designate.

presence *(SYN.)* nearness, attendance, closeness; vicinity, appearance, bearing, personality.

present *(SYN.)* donation, gift, today, now, existing, current, largess, donate, acquaint, introduce, being, give, gratuity, boon, grant.

(ANT.) reject, spurn, accept, retain, receive.

presentable *(SYN.)* polite, well-bred, respectable, well-mannered.

presently *(SYN.)* shortly, soon, directly, immediately.

preserve *(SYN.)* protect, save, conserve, maintain, secure, rescue, uphold, spare, keep, can, safeguard, defend, rescue.

(ANT.) impair, abolish, destroy, abandon, squander, injure.

preside *(SYN.)* officiate, direct, administrate.

press *SYN.)* impel, shove, urge, hasten, push, compress, squeeze, hug, crowd, propel, force, drive, embrace, smooth, iron, insist on, pressure, promote, urgency, jostle.

(ANT.) oppose, pull, falter, drag, retreat, ignore.

pressing *(SYN.)* impelling, insistent, necessary, urgent, compelling imperative, instant, serious, important, cogent, exigent, importunate.

(ANT.) unimportant, trifling, insignificant, petty, trivial.

pressure *(SYN.)* force, influence, stress, press, compulsion, urgency, constraint, compression.

(ANT.) relaxation, leniency, ease, recreation.

prestige *(SYN.)* importance, reputation, weight, influence, renown, fame, distinction.

presume *(SYN.)* guess, speculate, surmise, imagine, conjecture, apprehend, believe, think, assume, suppose, deduce.

(ANT.) prove, ascertain, demonstrate, know, conclude.

presumption *(SYN.)* boldness, impertinence, insolence, rudeness, assurance, effrontery, impudence, assumption, audacity, supposition, sauciness.

(ANT.) politeness, truckling, diffidence.

presumptuous *(SYN.)* bold, impertinent, fresh, imprudent, rude, forward, arrogant.

presupposition *(SYN.)* basis, principle, premise, assumption, postulate.

(ANT.) superstructure, derivative, implication.

pretend *(SYN.)* feign, stimulate, act, profess, make believe, imagine, fake, sham, affect.

(ANT.) expose, reveal, display, exhibit.

pretense *(SYN.)* mask, pretext, show, affection, disguise, garb, semblance, simulation, fabrication, lie, excuse, falsification, deceit, subterfuge.

(ANT.) sincerity, actuality, truth, fact, reality.

pretentious *(SYN.)* gaudy, ostentatious.

(ANT.) simple, humble.

pretty *(SYN.)* charming, handsome, lovely, beauteous, fair, comely, attractive, beautiful, elegant.

(ANT.) repulsive, foul, unsightly, homely, plain, hideous.

prevail *(SYN.)* win, succeed, predominate, triumph.
(ANT.) yield, lose.

prevailing *(SYN.)* common, current, general, habitual, steady, regular, universal.

prevalent *(SYN.)* ordinary, usual, common, general, familiar, popular, prevailing, widespread, universal, frequent.
(ANT.) odd, scarce, exceptional, extraordinary.

prevent *(SYN.)* impede, preclude, forestall, stop, block, check, halt, interrupt, deter, slow, obviate, hinder, obstruct, thwart.
(ANT.) expedite, help, allow, abet, aid, permit, encourage, promote.

previous *(SYN.)* former, anterior, preceding, prior, antecedent, earlier, aforesaid, foregoing.
(ANT.) subsequent, following, consequent, succeeding, later.

prey *(SYN.)* raid, seize, victimize.

price *(SYN.)* worth, cost, expense, charge, value.

pride *(SYN.)* self-respect, vanity, glory, superciliousness, haughtiness, conceit, arrogance, self-importance, pretension, egotism, satisfaction, fulfillment, enjoyment, self-esteem.
(ANT.) modesty, shame, humbleness, lowliness, meekness, humility.

prim *(SYN.)* formal, puritanical, priggish, prudish.

primarily *(SYN.)* mainly, chiefly, firstly, essentially, originally.
(ANT.) secondarily.

primary *(SYN.)* first, principal, primeval, pristine, beginning, original, initial, fundamental, elementary, chief, foremost, earliest, main, prime.
(ANT.) subordinate, last, secondary, least, hindmost, latest.

prime *(SYN.)* first, primary, chief, excellent, best, superior, ready.

primeval *(SYN.)* fresh, primary, novel, inventive, creative, primordial, original, first, new, initial.
(ANT.) trite, modern, subsequent, banal, later, terminal, derivative.

primitive *(SYN.)* antiquated, early, primeval, prehistoric, uncivilized, uncultured, simple, pristine, old, aboriginal, unsophisticated, rude, rough, primary.
(ANT.) sophisticated, modish, civilized, cultured, cultivated, late.

primordial *(SYN.)* pristine, inventive, novel, creative, original, first, initial, new, primary.
(ANT.) trite, terminal, banal, modern, derivative, subsequent, later.

principal *(SYN.)* first, leading, main, supreme, predominant, chief, foremost, highest, prime, primary, leader, headmaster, paramount, essential, cardinal.
(ANT.) supplemental, secondary, auxiliary, subsidiary, accessory, minor, subordinate.

principle *(SYN.)* law, method, axiom, rule, propriety, regulation, maxim, formula, order, statute.
(ANT.) exception, hazard, chance, deviation.

print *(SYN.)* issue, reprint, publish, letter, sign, fingerprint, mark, picture, lithograph, engraving, etching.

prior *(SYN.)* previous, aforesaid, antecedent, sooner, earlier, preceding, former, foregoing.
(ANT.) succeeding, following, later, consequent, subsequent.

prison *(SYN.)* brig, jail, stockade, penitentiary.

pristine *(SYN.)* primordial, creative, first, original, fresh, inventive, novel, primary, initial.
(ANT.) trite, terminal, derivative, modern, banal, subsequent, plagiarized, later.

private *(SYN.)* concealed, hidden, secret, clandestine, unknown, personal, surreptitious, covert, individual, particular, special, latent.
(ANT.) exposed, known, closed, general, public, conspicuous, disclosed, obvious.

privation *(SYN.)* necessity, penury, destitution, need, poverty, want.
(ANT.) wealth, affluence, abundance, plenty, riches.

privilege *(SYN.)* liberty, right, advantage, immunity, freedom, license, favor, sanction.
(ANT.) restriction, inhibition, prohibition, disallowance.

prize *(SYN.)* compensation, bonus, award, premium, remuneration, reward, bounty, esteem, value, rate, recompense, requital.
(ANT.) charge, punishment, wages, earnings, assessment.

probable *(SYN.)* presumable, likely.

probe *(SYN.)* stretch, reach, investigate,

examine, examination, scrutiny, scrutinize, inquire, explore, inquiry, investigation, extend.
(ANT.) miss, short.
problem (SYN.) dilemma, question, predicament, riddle, difficulty, puzzle.
procedure (SYN.) process, way, fashion, form, mode, conduct, practice, manner, habit, system, operation, management, plan.
proceed (SYN.) progress, continue, issue, result, spring, thrive, improve, advance, emanate, rise.
(ANT.) retard, withhold, withdraw, hinder, retreat, oppose.
proceeding (SYN.) occurrence, business, affair, deal, negotiation, transaction, deed.
proceedings (SYN.) account, record, document.
proceeds (SYN.) result, produce, income, reward, intake, fruit, profit, store, yield, product, return, harvest, crop.
process (SYN.) method, course, system, procedure, operation, prepare, treat.
procession (SYN.) cortege, •parade, sequence, train, cavalcade, file, retinue, succession.
proclaim (SYN.) declare, assert, make known, promulgate, state, assert, broadcast, express, announce, aver, advertise, tell, publish, profess.
proclamation (SYN.) declaration, announcement, promulgation.
procrastinate (SYN.) waver, vacillate, defer, hesitate, delay, postpone.
procreate (SYN.) generate, produce, beget, engender, originate, propagate, sire, create, father.
(ANT.) murder, destroy, abort, kill, extinguish.
procure (SYN.) secure, gain, win, attain, obtain, get, acquire, earn.
(ANT.) lose.
prod (SYN.) goad, nudge, jab, push.
prodigious (SYN.) astonishing, enormous, immense, monstrous, remarkable, marvelous, huge, amazing, astounding, stupendous, monumental.
(ANT.) insignificant, commonplace, small.
produce (SYN.) harvest, reaping, bear, result, originate, bring about, store, supply, make, create, crop, proceeds, bring forth, occasion, breed, generate, cause, exhibit, show, demonstrate,

fabricate, hatch, display, manufacture, exhibit, give, yield.
(ANT.) conceal, reduce, destroy, consume, waste, hide.
product (SYN.) outcome, result, output, produce, goods, commodity, stock, merchandise.
productive (SYN.) fertile, luxuriant, rich, bountiful, fruitful, creative, fecund, teeming, plenteous, prolific.
(ANT.) wasteful, unproductive, barren, impotent, useless, sterile.
profanation (SYN.) dishonor, insult, outrage, aspersion, defamation, ·invective, misuse, abuse, reviling, maltreatment, desecration, perversion.
(ANT.) plaudit, commendation, laudation, respect, approval.
profane (SYN.) deflower, violate, desecrate, pollute, dishonor, ravish, debauch.
profess (SYN.) declare, assert, make known, state, protest, announce, aver, express, broadcast, avow, tell.
(ANT.) suppress, conceal, repress, withhold.
profession (SYN.) calling, occupation, vocation, employment.
(ANT.) hobby, avocation, pastime.
proffer (SYN.) extend, tender, volunteer, propose, advance.
(ANT.) reject, spurn, accept, receive, retain.
proficient (SYN.) competent, adept, clever, able, cunning, practiced, skilled, versed, ingenious, accomplished, skillful, expert.
(ANT.) untrained, inexpert, bungling, awkward, clumsy.
profit (SYN.) gain, service, advantage, return, earnings, emolument, improvement, benefit, better, improve, use, avail.
(ANT.) waste, loss, detriment, debit, lose, damage, ruin.
profitable (SYN.) beneficial, advantageous, helpful, wholesome, useful, gainful, favorable, beneficial, serviceable, salutary, productive, good.
(ANT.) harmful, destructive, injurious, deleterious, detrimental.
profligate (SYN.) corrupt, debased, tainted, unsound, vitiated, contaminated, crooked, depraved, impure, venal.
profound (SYN.) deep, serious, knowing,

wise, intelligent, knowledgeable, recondite, solemn, abstruse, penetrating.
(ANT.) trivial, slight, shallow, superficial.

profuse (SYN.) lavish, excessive, extravagant, improvident, luxuriant, prodigal, wasteful, exuberant, immoderate, plentiful.
(ANT.) meager, poor, economical, sparse, skimpy.

profusion (SYN.) immoderation, superabundance, surplus, extravagance, intemperance, superfluity.
(ANT.) lack, paucity, death, want, deficiency.

program (SYN.) record, schedule, plan, agenda, calendar.

progress (SYN.) advancement, improvement, development, betterment, advance, movement, improve, progression.
(ANT.) delay, regression, relapse, retrogression, decline.

progression (SYN.) gradation, string, train, chain, arrangement, following, arrangement, order.

prohibit (SYN.) hinder, forbid, disallow, obstruct, prevent, stop, ban, interdict, debar.
(ANT.) help, tolerate, allow, sanction, encourage, permit.

prohibition (SYN.) prevention, ban, embargo, restriction.
(ANT.) allowance, permission.

prohibitive (SYN.) forbidding, restrictive.

project (SYN.) design, proposal, scheme, contrivance, outline, homework, activity, purpose, bulge, protrude, throw, cast, device, plan.
(ANT.) production, accomplishment, performance.

prolific (SYN.) fertile, rich, fruitful, teeming, fecund, bountiful, luxuriant, productive, plenteous.
(ANT.) unproductive, barren, sterile, impotent.

prolong (SYN.) extend, increase, protract, draw, stretch, lengthen.
(ANT.) shorten.

prominent (SYN.) distinguished, illustrious, outstanding, renowned, influential, famous, well-known, noted, notable, important, conspicuous, eminent, leading, celebrated.
(ANT.) low, vulgar, ordinary, common.

promise (SYN.) assurance, guarantee,

pledge, undertaking, agreement, bestowal, word, contract, oath, vow.

promote (SYN.) advance, foster, encourage, assist, support, further, aid, help, elevate, raise, facilitate, forward.
(ANT.) obstruct, demote, hinder, impede.

prompt (SYN.) punctual, timely, exact, arouse, evoke, occasion, induce, urge, ineffect, cite, suggest, hint, cause, mention, propose, make, precise, originate.
(ANT.) laggardly, slow, tardy, dilatory.

promptly (SYN.) immediately, instantly, straightway, forthwith, directly, instantaneously, presently.
(ANT.) later, sometime, hereafter, distantly, shortly.

promulgate (SYN.) declare, known, protest, affirm, broadcast, profess, assert, proclaim, state, aver, tell.
(ANT.) repress, conceal, withhold.

prone (SYN.) apt, inclined, disposed, likely, predisposed.

pronounce (SYN.) proclaim, utter, announce, articulate, enunciate.

pronounced (SYN.) clear, definite.
(ANT.) minor, unnoticeable.

proof (SYN.) evidence, verification, confirmation, experiment, demonstration, testimony, trial, protected, impenetrable, corroboration, test.
(ANT.) fallacy, invalidity, failure.

propagate (SYN.) create, procreate, sire, beget, breed, father, originate, produce.
(ANT.) extinguish, kill, abort, destroy.

propel (SYN.) drive, push, transfer, actuate, induce, shift, persuade, move.
(ANT.) stay, deter, halt, rest, stop.

propensity (SYN.) leaning, proneness, trend, drift, aim, inclination, bias, proclivity, tendency, predisposition.
(ANT.) disinclination, aversion.

proper (SYN.) correct, suitable, decent, peculiar, legitimate, right, conventional, decent, just, well-mannered, seemly, fit, appropriate, fitting, respectable, special.

property (SYN.) real estate, effects, possessions, quality, characteristic, merchandise, stock, possession, land, wealth, belongings, attribute, trait.
(ANT.) poverty, destitution, want, deprivation.

prophecy (SYN.) augury, prediction.

prophesy (SYN.) foretell, predict, augur.

prophet (SYN.) fortuneteller, oracle, seer, soothsayer, clairvoyant.

propitious (SYN.) lucky, opportune, advantageous, favorable, fortunate, promising, happy.

proportion *(SYN.)* steadiness, poise, composure, relation, balance, equilibrium, comparison, section, part, arrange, adjust, symmetry.
(ANT.) unsteadiness, imbalance, fall.

proposal *(SYN.)* plan, proposition, tender, scheme, program, offer, suggestion, overture.
(ANT.) rejection, acceptance, denial.

propose *(SYN.)* offer, proffer, recommend, plan, mean, expect, move, design, propound, present, tender.
(ANT.) fulfill, perform, effect.

proposition *(SYN.)* proposal, motion.

propound *(SYN.)* bring forward, offer, advance, allege, propose, assign.
(ANT.) retreat, hinder, withhold, retard.

proprietor *(SYN.)* master, owner.
(ANT.) slave, servant.

prosaic *(SYN.)* commonplace, common, everyday, ordinary, routine.
(ANT.) exciting, different, extraordinary.

proscribe *(SYN.)* forbid, ban, prohibit.
(ANT.) permit, allow.

prospect *(SYN.)* anticipation, expectation, candidate, buyer, explore, search.

prospective *(SYN.)* planned, proposed.

prosper *(SYN.)* succeed, win, achieve, gain, rise, prevail, flourish, thrive.
(ANT.) miscarry, wane, miss, fail.

prosperous *(SYN.)* rich, wealthy, affluent, well-to-do, sumptuous, well-off, flourishing, thriving, opulent, luxurious.
(ANT.) impoverished, indigent, beggarly, needy, destitute, poor.

prostrate *(SYN.)* prone, supine, overcome, recumbent, crushed.

protect *(SYN.)* defend, preserve, save, keep, conserve, safeguard, maintain, guard, shield, secure.
(ANT.) impair, abandon, destroy, abolish, injure.

protection *(SYN.)* safeguard, shelter, security, bulwark, fence, guard, safety, assurance, defense, refuge, shield.

protest *(SYN.)* dissent, noncompliance, disagree, objection, disagreement, challenge, difference, complaint, nonconformity, variance, opposition, remonstrate, reject, disapprove, complain, object, rejection.
(ANT.) acquiesce, assent, compliance, concur, comply, acceptance, approval.

prototype *(SYN.)* model, archetype,

specimen, instance, illustration, example, pattern, sample.
(ANT.) rule, concept, precept, principle.

protract *(SYN.)* extend, strain, distend, expand, spread, stretch, elongate, distort, lengthen.
(ANT.) tighten, contract, loosen, shrink.

protuberance *(SYN.)* prominence, projection, bulge, protrusion, swelling.

proud *(SYN.)* overbearing, vain, arrogant, haughty, stately, vain, glorious, disdainful, prideful, conceited, egotistical, self-important, supercilious.
(ANT.) humble, meek, ashamed, lowly.

prove *(SYN.)* manifest, verify, confirm, demonstrate, establish, show, affirm, examine, corroborate, try, test.
(ANT.) contradict, refute, disprove.

proverb *(SYN.)* maxim, byword, saying, adage, byword, saw, motto, apothegm.

proverbial *(SYN.)* common, well-known.

provide *(SYN.)* supply, endow, afford, produce, yield, give, fit, equip, furnish, bestow, fit out.
(ANT.) strip, denude, divest, despoil.

provident *(SYN.)* saving, thrifty, economical, frugal, sparing.
(ANT.) wasteful, lavish, extravagant.

provision *(SYN.)* supply, fund, condition, arrangement, accumulation, reserve, store, hoard.

provisions *(SYN.)* stock, supplies, store.

provoke *(SYN.)* excite, stimulate, agitate, arouse, incite, stir up, vex, bother, disquiet, excite, irritate, annoy, anger.
(ANT.) quell, allay, pacify, calm, quiet.

prowess *(SYN.)* fortitude, mettle, boldness, fearlessness, courage, chivalry, bravery, resolution.
(ANT.) pusillanimity, fear, cowardice, timidity.

prowl *(SYN.)* sneak, slink, lurk.

proximate *(SYN.)* nigh, imminent, adjacent, neighboring, bordering, close, impending, approaching.
(ANT.) removed, distant, far.

proximity *(SYN.)* vicinity, nearness.

proxy *(SYN.)* representative, equivalent, makeshift, alternate, deputy, substitute, expedient, lieutenant.
(ANT.) sovereign, head, principal, master.

prudence *(SYN.)* watchfulness, care, heed, vigilance, wariness, carefulness, tact, judgment, wisdom, common, foresight, caution.

(ANT.) rashness, recklessness, abandon, foolishness, carelessness.

prudent *(SYN.)* reasonable, sensible, sound, discreet, practical, judicious, sagacious, sensible, provident, sage, intelligent, sober, careful, wise.
(ANT.) stupid, unaware, absurd.

pry *(SYN.)* peer, peep, meddle, peek.

prying *(SYN.)* inquisitive, meddling, curious, inquiring, nosy, peering, searching, interrogative, snoopy.
(ANT.) unconcerned, incurious, indifferent, uninterested.

psyche *(SYN.)* judgment, reason, understanding, brain, intellect, mentality, soul, mind, faculties, spirit.
(ANT.) materiality, body, matter, corporality.

psychosis *(SYN.)* derangement, insanity, madness, delirium, dementia, frenzy, lunacy, mania, aberration.
(ANT.) stability, rationality, sanity.

public *(SYN.)* common, civil, governmental, federal, unrestricted, people, society, open.

publish *(SYN.)* distribute, issue, declare, announce, reveal, proclaim, publicize, bring out.

pulchritude *(SYN.)* elegance, grace, loveliness, attractiveness, comeliness, fairness, handsomeness, charm, beauty.
(ANT.) ugliness, eyesore, deformity, homeliness, disfigurement.

pull *(SYN.)* attract, induce, prolong, draw, tow, drag, remove, take out, persuade, allure, entice, extract.
(ANT.) shorten, alienate, drive, propel.

pulsate *(SYN.)* beat, throb, palpitate.

pummel *(SYN.)* punish, correct, castigate, discipline, chastise, strike.
(ANT.) release, acquit, free, exonerate.

pump *(SYN.)* interrogate, question, ask, inquire, quiz, examine, query.
(ANT.) state, answer, respond, reply.

punctual *(SYN.)* timely, prompt, exact, ready, nice, precise.
(ANT.) laggardly, tardy, dilatory, late.

punish *(SYN.)* correct, pummel, chasten, reprove, strike, castigate, chastise.
(ANT.) release, exonerate, reward, pardon, acquit, free.

punishment *(SYN.)* correction, discipline.
(ANT.)· turbulence, chaos, confusion.

puny *(SYN.)* feeble, impaired, exhausted, infirm, unimportant, weak, decrepit, trivial, enervated, frail, powerless, force-

less, delicate.
(ANT.) strong, forceful, lusty, vigorous.

pupil *(SYN.)* learner, student, undergraduate.

purchase *(SYN.)* get, procure, buy, shopping, acquire, obtain.
(ANT.) sell, dispose of, vend.

pure *(SYN.)* chaste, absolute, clean, immaculate, untainted, spotless, guiltless, modest, virgin, bare, unmixed, simple, undiluted, uncontaminated, innocent, chaste, undefiled, genuine, clear.
(ANT.) corrupt, mixed, defiled, foul, tainted, adulterated, polluted, tarnished.

purely *(SYN.)* entirely, completely.

purify *(SYN.)* cleanse, wash, clean, mop, sweep.
(ANT.) soil, dirty, sully, stain, pollute.

puritanical *(SYN.)* prim, stiff.
(ANT.) permissive.

purloin *(SYN.)* loot, plagiarize, steal, pilfer, burglarize, plunder, pillage, snitch, embezzle, swipe.
(ANT.) repay, return, refund, buy.

purport *(SYN.)* import, meaning, explanation, acceptation, drift, sense, significance, purpose, intent, gist.

purpose *(SYN.)* intention, end, goal, aim, objective, application, use, drift, object, intent, design.
(ANT.) hazard, accident, fate.

pursue *(SYN.)* persist, track follow, hunt, hound, chase, trail.
(ANT.) evade, abandon, flee, elude.

pursuit *(SYN.)* hunt, chase.

push *(SYN.)* jostle, shove, urge, press, thrust, force, drive, crowd, hasten, shove, propel, promote.
(ANT.) ignore, falter, halt, drag, oppose.

pushy *(SYN.)* impudent, abrupt, prominent, insolent, forward, brazen, conspicuous, bold, striking.
(ANT.) retiring, timid, cowardly, bashful.

put *(SYN.)* set, place, state, express, say, assign, attach, establish.

putrefy *(SYN.)* disintegrate, decay, rot, waste, spoil, decompose.
(ANT.) grow, increase, luxuriate.

putrid *(SYN.)* decayed, rotten, moldy, decomposed.

puzzle *(SYN.)* mystery, mystify, confound, perplex, riddle, conundrum, confusion, question, bewilder, confuse, dumfound, enigma, problem.
(ANT.) key, solution, solve, explain, answer, resolution, illumine, clue.

quack *(SYN.)* faker, fake, fraud, gaggle, clack, gabble, bluffer, cackle, dissembler, charlatan, impostor.

quackery *(SYN.)* charlatanism, deceit, make-believe, fakery, duplicity, dissimulation, pretense, fraudulence, sham, counterfeiting, show.

(ANT.) integrity, probity, veracity, sincerity, honesty.

quaff *(SYN.)* swig, swill, swallow, lap up, sip, drink, ingurgitate, guzzle, imbibe.

quagmire *(SYN.)* swamp, bog, fen, ooze, morass, slough, marsh, plight, predicament, dilemma, impasse, fix, entanglement, quicksand, hole, quandary.

quail *(SYN.)* recoil, cower, flinch, blench, wince, falter, shrink, shake, hesitate, faint, droop.

(ANT.) brave, resist, defy, withstand.

quaint *(SYN.)* odd, uncommon, old-fashioned, antique, antiquated, queer, unusual, curious, eccentric, peculiar, picturesque, singular, whimsical, droll, charming, fanciful, droll, strange.

(ANT.) usual, normal, common, novel, ordinary, modern, current, commonplace, familiar.

quake *(SYN.)* shake, tremble, shudder, quiver, pulsate, stagger, shiver, temblor, vibrate, quaver, throb, earthquake.

qualification *(SYN.)* efficiency, adaptation, restriction, aptness, skill, ability, faculty, talent, power, aptitude, competence, suitability, capability, fitness, condition, dexterity.

(ANT.) unreadiness, incapacity, disability.

qualified *(SYN.)* clever, skillful, efficient, suitable, able, capable, fit, fitted, suited, bounded, limited, contingent, eligible, delimited, adept, circumscribed, equipped, modified, competent.

(ANT.) deficient, inept, impotent, categorical, unlimited, unfitted, unfit, incapable, unsuitable, inadequate.

qualify *(SYN.)* fit, suit, befit, ready, prepare, empower, lessen, moderate, soften, capacitate, condition, adapt, label, designate, name, call, equip, train, restrict, restrict, limit, change.

(ANT.) unfit, incapacitate, disable, disqualify, enlarge, reinforce, aggravate.

quality *(SYN.)* trait, feature, attribute, value, peculiarity, grade, caliber, character, distinction, rank, condition, status, characteristic, kind, nature, constitu-

tion, mark, type, property.

(ANT.) nature, inferiority, mediocrity, triviality, indifference, inferior, shoddy, second-rate, being, substance, essence.

qualm *(SYN.)* doubt, uneasiness, anxiety, suspicion, skepticism, question, pang, compunction, twinge, regret, uncertainty, demur, fear, remorse, misgiving.

(ANT.) security, comfort, confidence, easiness, invulnerability, firmness.

quandary *(SYN.)* predicament, perplexity, confusion, uncertainty, puzzle, plight, bewilderment, fix, difficulty, entanglement, impasse, doubt, dilemma.

(ANT.) ease, relief, certainty, assurance.

quantity *(SYN.)* sum, measure, volume, content, aggregate, bulk, mass, portion, amount, number, multitude, extent.

(ANT.) zero, nothing.

quarantine *(SYN.)* segregate, separate, confine, isolate, seclude.

quarrel *(SYN.)* contention, argument, affray, dispute, altercation, squabble, feud, difference, disagree, bicker, differ, spar, fight, bickering, tiff, argue, disagreement, spat.

(ANT.) peace, friendliness, reconciliation, amity, agreement, sympathy, accord, concur, support, agree, unity, harmony.

quarrelsome *(SYN.)* testy, contentious, edgy, peevish, irritable, snappish, argumentative, disputatious, cranky, belligerent, combative, disagreeable.

(ANT.) genial, friendly, peaceful, easygoing, peaceable, tempered.

quarry *(SYN.)* prey, quest, game, victim, goal, aim, prize, objective.

quarter *(SYN.)* place, source, fount, well, origin, mainspring, ruth, mercy, pity, compassion, clemency, spring, benevolence, forbearance.

(ANT.) ruthlessness, brutality, cruelty, barbarity, harshness, ferocity.

quarters *(SYN.)* residence, rooms, lodgings, dwelling, flat, billets, chambers, accommodations.

quash *(SYN.)* void, annul, overthrow, nullify, suppress, cancel, quench, quell, repress, invalidate.

(ANT.) reinforce, sustain, authorize, sanction, validate, incite.

quasi *(SYN.)* would-be, partial, synthetic, nominal, imitation, bogus, sham, counterfeit, mock.

(ANT.) certified, real, legitimate.

quaver *(SYN.)* tremble, shake, hesitate,

trill, oscillate, waver, vibrate, shiver, quiver, falter, quake.

quay *(SYN.)* dock, wharf, pier, jetty, bank.

queasy *(SYN.)* sick, squeamish, nauseated, uneasy, queer, restless, nauseous, uncomfortable.
(ANT.) untroubled, comfortable, easy, relaxed.

queen *(SYN.)* empress, diva, doyenne, goddess, star.

queer *(SYN.)* odd, quaint, curious, unusual, droll, strange, peculiar, extraordinary, singular, uncommon, eccentric, weird, funny, nutty, screwy, wacky, deviant, whimsical.
(ANT.) familiar, usual, normal, common, commonplace, plain, patent, conventional, ordinary.

queerness *(SYN.)* oddity, oddness, freakishness, strangeness, singularity, outlandishness, anomaly, weirdness.
(ANT.) normality, familiarity, commonness, standardization.

quell *(SYN.)* subdue, calm, pacify, quiet, cool, hush, appease, lull, mollify, reduce, crush, smother, suppress, stifle, extinguish.
(ANT.) encourage, foment, arouse, foster, incite.

quench *(SYN.)* extinguish, stop, suppress, sate, allay, abate, stifle, slacken, put out, slake, satisfy.
(ANT.) set, light, begin, start, kindle.

querulous *(SYN.)* faultfinding, fretful, carping, critical, complaining, censorious, captious, petulant.
(ANT.) pleased, easygoing, contented, carefree.

query *(SYN.)* inquire, interrogate, demand, investigate, probe, examine, question, inquiry, ask.
(ANT.) answer.

quest *(SYN.)* investigation, interrogation, research, examination, search, question, exploration, seek, pursue, journey, hunt, pursuit, explore, query.
(ANT.) negligence, inactivity, disregard.

question *(SYN.)* interrogate, quiz, doubt, ask, pump, challenge, inquiry, uncertainty, interview, suspect, inquire, dispute, demand, examine, query.
(ANT.) accept, solution, reply, assurance, rejoinder, state, answer, result, response, attest, avow, confidence, respond.

questionable *(SYN.)* uncertain, doubtful, dubious, implausible, debatable, hypothetical, unlikely.
(ANT.) obvious, assured, indubitable, proper, unimpeachable, seemly, conventional, sure, certain.

queue *(SYN.)* file, row, line, series, chain, tier, sequence, string.

quibble *(SYN.)* cavil, shift, evasion, equivocation, dodge, sophism, prevaricate, quiddity, palter.

quick *(SYN.)* rapid, touchy, shrewd, active, hasty, testy, nimble, irascible, discerning, fast, swift, precipitate, excitable, speedy, sharp, impatient, acute, abrupt, curt, brisk, clever, keen, sensitive, lively.
(ANT.) inattentive, dull, gradual, patient, slow, unaware, unhurried, backward, deliberate, sluggish.

quicken *(SYN.)* expedite, forward, rush, hurry, accelerate, push, hasten, dispatch, facilitate, speed.
(ANT.) slow, impede, hinder, hamper, delay, kill, deaden, retard, block.

quickly *(SYN.)* soon, rapidly, fast, at once, promptly, presently, swiftly, hastily, fleety, headlong.
(ANT.) deliberately, slowly, later, gradually.

quickness *(SYN.)* energy, vigor, intensity, action, movement, briskness, exercise, motion, rapidity, agility, enterprise.
(ANT.) sloth, idleness, inertia, dullness.

quick-witted *(SYN.)* astute, shrewd, alert, keen, penetrating, quick, knowing, intelligent, clever.
(ANT.) slow, dull, unintelligent, plodding.

quiescent *(SYN.)* latent, resting, silent, tranquil, undeveloped, still, quiet, dormant, secret, unseen, inactive.
(ANT.) visible, aroused, evident, active, patent, astir, manifest.

quiet *(SYN.)* meek, passive, hushed, peaceful, calm, patient, quiescent, motionless, tranquil, gentle, undisturbed, mild, peace, silent, quiescence, hush, modest, quietude, rest, tranquillity, calmness, repose, silence, placid, serenity, soundless, immobile, still.
(ANT.) disturbed, agitation, excitement, loud, disturbance, restless, noisy, boisterous, anxious, perturbed, noise, agitated.

quietness *(SYN.)* tranquillity, repose, calm, silence, quietude, calmness, stillness, quietism, muteness, noiselessness, placidity, seclusion, soundlessness.

(ANT.) flurry, disturbance, fuss, turbulence, agitation, uproar, tumult.

quintessence *(SYN.)* heart, soul, extract, essence, distillation, core.

(ANT.) contingency, adjunct, excrescence, nonessential.

quip *(SYN.)* jest, sally, wisecrack, witticism, joke, jibe, pleasantry.

quirk *(SYN.)* mannerism, idiosyncrasy, foible, peculiarity, oddity, quiddity, vagary, habit, trait, eccentricity.

quirky *(SYN.)* odd, weird, whimsical, peculiar, pixilated, erratic, kinky.

(ANT.) normal, conventional, steady.

quisling *(SYN.)* collaborationist, traitor, subversive, betrayer.

(ANT.) partisan, loyalist.

quit *(SYN.)* leave, stop, desist, depart, abandon, resign, withdraw, refrain, retreat, cease, vacate, end, relinquish, discontinue, halt, lay off, surrender.

(ANT.) persevere, remain, stay, endure, persist, abide, continue.

quite *(SYN.)* somewhat, rather, completely, truly, absolutely, really, entirely.

(ANT.) hardly, merely, barely, somewhat.

quitter *(SYN.)* shirker, dropout, defeatist, piker, loser, malingerer.

quiver *(SYN.)* quake, shake, shudder, tremble, vibrate, shiver.

quixotic *(SYN.)* unrealistic, romantic, visionary, impractical, idealistic, chimerical, lofty, fantastic, fey.

(ANT.) pragmatic, realistic, prosaic, practical.

quiz *(SYN.)* challenge, interrogate, inquire, pump, doubt, question, ask, dispute, test, query, examine.

(ANT.) reply, say, inform, respond, accept, answer, state.

quizzical *(SYN.)* teasing, coy, mocking, derisive, insolent, arch, bantering, puzzled, questioning, baffled.

(ANT.) respectful, obsequious, uninterested, normal, everyday, usual, serious, attentive.

quota *(SYN.)* share, portion, apportionment, ratio, proportion, allotment.

quotation *(SYN.)* quote, selection, excerpt, repetition, cutting, reference.

quote *(SYN.)* refer to, recite, paraphrase, adduce, repeat, illustrate, cite, echo, plagiarize.

(ANT.) retort, contradict, refute.

rabble *(SYN.)* throng, mob, horde, crowd.

rabid *(SYN.)* frantic, frenzied, violent, raging, raving, zealous, fanatical.

(ANT.) normal, sound, sober, moderate.

race *(SYN.)* meet, run, clan, stock, lineage, strain, match, course, stream, hasten, compete, folk, competition, dash, contest, contend, hurry, speed, tribe.

(ANT.) linger, dawdle, dwell.

rack *(SYN.)* frame, framework, bracket, scaffold, skeleton.

racket *(SYN.)* sound, cry, babel, noise, uproar, hubbub, clamor, fuss, disturbance, din, tumult, fracas, clatter.

(ANT.) stillness, hush, silence, quiet, tranquillity, peace.

racy *(SYN.)* interesting, vigorous, lively, spirited, animated, entertaining.

radiance *(SYN.)* luster, brilliancy, brightness, splendor, effulgence, glowing.

(ANT.) gloom, darkness, obscurity.

radiant *(SYN.)* showy, superb, brilliant, illustrious, dazzling, grand, shining, bright, effulgent, beaming, sumptuous.

(ANT.) dark, unimpressive, dull, dim, lusterless, ordinary.

radiate *(SYN.)* spread, emit, diffuse, shed, irradiate, shine, gleam, illuminate.

radical *(SYN.)* ultra, innate, essential, organic, complete, revolutionary, insurgent, natural, total, fundamental, extreme, basic, original, thorough.

(ANT.) extraneous, moderate, conservative, superficial, shallow, established.

radius *(SYN.)* orbit, reach, extent, scope, sphere, range, sweep.

raft *(SYN.)* pontoon, platform, float.

rag *(SYN.)* dishcloth, dishrag, cloth.

ragamuffin *(SYN.)* tatterdemalion, wretch, beggar, vagabond, mendicant.

rage *(SYN.)* passion, ire, exasperation, fashion, fad, vogue, craze, anger, temper, fury, irritation, mania, rave, rant, storm, fume, overflow, wrath.

(ANT.) peace, forbearance, conciliation, patience.

raging *(SYN.)* raving, severe, passionate, boisterous, violent, fierce, wild, passionate, acute, intense, powerful.

(ANT.) feeble, soft, calm, quiet.

ragged *(SYN.)* tattered, torn, worn, shredded, seedy, threadbare, shabby.

raid *(SYN.)* assault, attack, invasion, arrest, invade, seizure, maraud, foray.

rail *(SYN.)* railing, fence, bar.

railing *(SYN.)* balustrade, banister, barrier, fence.

rain *(SYN.)* shower, drizzle, rainstorm, sprinkle, deluge, down-pour.

raise *(SYN.)* grow, muster, elevate, heave, cultivate, awake, rouse, excite, enlarge, increase, rise, breed, hoist, bring up, rear, gather, exalt, lift.
(ANT.) destroy, decrease, lessen, cut, depreciate, lower, abase, debase, drop, demolish, level.

rakish *(SYN.)* dapper, dashing, smart, debonair, natty, swanky, showy.

rally *(SYN.)* muster, convoke, summon, convene, convention, assemblage.

ramble *(SYN.)* err, amble, saunter, wander, roam, saunter, walk, deviate, stroll, digress, stray.
(ANT.) stop, linger, stay, halt, settle.

rambling *(SYN.)* incoherent, erratic.
(ANT.) straightfoward, coherent.

rambunctious *(SYN.)* stubborn, defiant, unruly, aggressive, contrary.

ramification *(SYN.)* aftermath, extension, branch, offshoot, result, consequence.

rampage *(SYN.)* tumult, outbreak, uproar, rage, frenzy, ebullition, storm.

rampant *(SYN.)* excessive, flagrant, boisterous, menacing.
(ANT.) bland, calm, mild.

ramshackle *(SYN.)* rickety, decrepit, flimsy, dilapidated, shaky.

rancid *(SYN.)* spoiled, rank, tainted, sour, musty, putrid, rotten, purtrescent.
(ANT.) pure, fresh, wholesome, fragrant.

rancor *(SYN.)* spite, grudge, malice, animosity, malevolence, hostility.
(ANT.) kindness, toleration, affection.

random *(SYN.)* haphazard, chance, unscheduled, unplanned, casual.
(ANT.) intentional, specific, particular.

range *(SYN.)* expanse, extent, limit, area, grassland, pasture, plain, change, wander, roam, travel, rove.

rank *(SYN.)* estate, blood, range, grade, standing, hue, eminence, level, class, order, classify, dense, wild, rotten, degree, standing, arrange, sort, row.
(ANT.) shame, disrepute, stigma, humiliation.

ransack *(SYN.)* pillage, loot, rummage, plunder, despoil, ravish, search.

ransom *(SYN.)* release, deliverance, compensation, redeem.

rant *(SYN.)* declaim, rave, harangue.

rap *(SYN.)* thump, knock, blow, whack.

rapacious *(SYN.)* greedy, wolfish, avaricious, ravenous, grasping, predatory.

rapid *(SYN.)* speedy, quick, swift, fast.
(ANT.) deliberate, halting, sluggish, slow.

rapidity *(SYN.)* motion, enterprise, action, vigor, liveliness, activity, quickness, exercise, energy.
(ANT.) sloth, dullness, inertia, idleness.

rapine *(SYN.)* destruction, pillage, robbery, marauding, spoiling.

rapport *(SYN.)* harmony, fellowship, agreement, mutuality, accord, empathy.

rapture *(SYN.)* joy, gladness, ecstasy, bliss, transport, exultation, delight, happiness, enchantment, ravishment.
(ANT.) woe, misery, wretch, depression.

rare *(SYN.)* unique, strange, precious, uncommon, infrequent, choice, singular, occasional, unusual, fine, matchless, undone, incomparable, scarce.
(ANT.) worthless, common, commonplace, usual, everyday, customary.

rarely *(SYN.)* scarcely, hardly infrequently, occasionally, sparingly, barely.
(ANT.) usually, continually, often.

rascal *(SYN.)* scoundrel, villain, trickster, rogue, scamp, swindler, imp, prankster.

rash *(SYN.)* quick, careless, passionate, thoughtless, hotheaded, reckless, foolhardy, eruption, dermatitis, heedless.
(ANT.) thoughtful, considered, prudent, reasoning, calculating, careful.

raspy *(SYN.)* gruff, harsh, dissonant, grinding, hoarse, grating, strident.

rate *(SYN.)* try, adjudicate, consider, decide, condemn, decree, estimate, speed, pace, measure, judge, arbitrate, velocity, ratio, evaluate, evaluate.

ratify *(SYN.)* validate, certify, confirm, establish, support, endorse, uphold.

rating *SYN.)* assessment, position, assignment, status, classification.

ration *(SYN.)* portion, allowance, distribute, measure, allotment, share, percentage.

rational *(SYN.)* sound, wise, sane, intelligent, sober, sensible, judicious, sober.
(ANT.) irrational, absurd, insane.

rationality *(SYN.)* cause, aim, intelligence, reason, basis, understanding, ground, argument, mind, sense.

raucous *(SYN.)* raspy, harsh, grating, hoarse, discordant, rowdy.
(ANT.) dulcet, pleasant, sweet.

ravage *(SYN.)* ruin, despoil, strip, waste, destroy, pillage, plunder, sack, havoc.
(ANT.) conserve, save, accumulate.

rave *(SYN.)* rage, storm, laud, praise.

ravenous *(SYN.)* hungry, voracious, craving, starved, gluttonous, famished.
(ANT.) replete, gorged, satiated, full.

ravine *(SYN.)* chasm, gorge, crevasse, canyon, abyss.

ravish *(SYN.)* violate, debauch.

ravishing *(SYN.)* enchanting, captivating, bewitching, fascinating, alluring.
(ANT.) loathsome, disgusting, repulsive.

raw *(SYN.)* harsh, rough, coarse, unrefined, undone, uncooked, unprocessed, crude, unpolished, natural.
(ANT.) finished, refined, processed.

ray *(SYN.)* beam.

raze *(SYN.)* ravage, wreck, destroy, flatten, annihilate, obliterate, demolish.
(ANT.) make, erect, construct, preserve, establish, save.

reach *(SYN.)* overtake, arrive at, extent, distance, scope, range, extend, attain, stretch.
(ANT.) fail, miss.

react *(SYN.)* result, reply, respond.
(ANT.) overlook, disregard.

reaction *(SYN.)* result, response, reception, repercussion.

readable *(SYN.)* understandable, distinct, legible, plain, clear, comprehensible.
(ANT.) obliterated, illegible, defaced.

readily *(SYN.)* quickly, promptly, easily.

ready *(SYN.)* mature, ripe, complete, seasonable, done, arrange, prompt, prepared, completed, quick, mellow.
(ANT.) undeveloped, immature, green.

real *(SYN.)* true, actual, positive, authentic, genuine, veritable.
(ANT.) counterfeit, unreal, fictitious, false, sham, supposed.

realization *(SYN.)* completion, achievement, performance, accomplishment, comprehension, insight.
(ANT.) failure.

realize *(SYN.)* discern, learn, comprehend, appreciate, perfect, actualize, understand, apprehend, know, see.
(ANT.) misunderstand, misapprehend.

really *(SYN.)* truly, actually, honestly,

undoubtedly, positively, genuinely.
(ANT.) questionably, possibly, doubtfully.

realm *(SYN.)* land, domain, farm, kingdom, sphere, department, estate, world.

reap *(SYN.)* gather, harvest, gain, glean, produce, cut, pick, acquire, garner.
(ANT.) plant, seed, sow, lose, squander.

reaping *(SYN.)* proceeds, result, crop, yield, fruit, produce.

rear *(SYN.)* posterior, raise, lift, train, nurture, rump, back, elevate, construct, build, foster.

reason *(SYN.)* intelligence, objective, understanding, mind, aim, argument, cause, aim, judgment, common sense, sanity, gather, assume, sake, motive.

reasonable *(SYN.)* prudent, rational, logical, sage, sound, moderate, intelligent, sensible, discreet.
(ANT.) unaware, imperceptible, insane, absurd, stupid, illogical, irrational.

rebel *(SYN.)* revolutionary, traitor, mutineer, mutiny, revolt, disobey.

rebellion *(SYN.)* revolt, uprising, coup, overthrow, insurrection, revolution.
(ANT.) submission, obedience, repression, peace.

rebellious *(SYN.)* unruly, forward, defiant, undutiful, disobedient.
(ANT.) obedient, compliant, submissive.

rebirth *(SYN.)* renascence, renaissance, revival.

rebuff *(SYN.)* snub, oppose, resist, reject, refuse, slight, opposition.
(ANT.) welcome, encourage, support.

rebuild *(SYN.)* restore, renew, refresh, reconstruct, renovate.

rebuke *(SYN.)* chide, scold, reproach, censure, upbraid, scolding, condemn.
(ANT.) praise, exonerate, absolve.

rebuttal *(SYN.)* contradiction, defense, answer.
(ANT.) argument, validation, corroboration.

recall *(SYN.)* recollect, remembrance, withdraw, retract, remember, recollection, reminisce, mind, memory, remind.
(ANT.) forget, overlook, ignore.

recede *(SYN.)* withdraw, ebb, retire, retreat.

receive *(SYN.)* entertain, acquire, admit, accept, shelter, greet, obtain, welcome.
(ANT.) reject, offer, give, bestow, discharge, impart.

recent (SYN.) novel, original, late, new, newfangled, fresh, modern, current. (ANT.) old, antiquated, ancient.

reception (SYN.) gathering, party.

recess (SYN.) hollow, opening, nook, cranny, dent, respite, rest, break, pause. (ANT.) gather, convene.

recession (SYN.) slump, depression.

recipe (SYN.) instructions, formula, prescriptions, procedure, method.

recital (SYN.) history, account, relation, chronicle, narrative, detail, narration. (ANT.) distortion, confusion, misrepresentation.

recite (SYN.) describe, narrate, declaim, rehearse, tell, mention, repeat, detail, recapitulate, report, list, relate, deliver.

reckless (SYN.) thoughtless, inconsiderate, careless, imprudent, rash, indiscreet, unconcerned. (ANT.) careful, nice, accurate.

reclaim (SYN.) reform, rescue, reinstate, regenerate, recycle.

recline (SYN.) stretch, sprawl, repose, rest, lounge, loll, incline.

recluse (SYN.) hermit, eremite, loner, anchorite.

recognize (SYN.) remember, avow, own, know, admit, apprehend, recollect, recall, concede, acknowledge, confess. (ANT.) disown, ignore, renounce.

recollect (SYN.) recall, remember, memory, reflect, call to mind, reminisce. (ANT.) forget.

recollection (SYN.) remembrance, retrospection, impression, recall. (ANT.) forgetfulness, oblivion.

recommend (SYN.) hind, refer, advise, commend, suggest, counsel, allude, praise, approve, intimatem advocate. (ANT.) disapprove, declare, insist.

recommendation (SYN.) instruction, justice, trustworthiness, counsel, admonition, caution, integrity, uprightness. (ANT.) fraud, deceit, trickery, cheating.

reconcile (SYN.) meditate, unite, adapt, adjust, settle, reunite, appease.

recondition (SYN.) rebuild, overhaul, restore, service.

reconsider (SYN.) ponder, reevaluate, mull over, reflect, reassess.

record (SYN.) enter, write, register, chronicle, history, account, document.

recount (SYN.) report, convey, narrate,

tell, detail, recite, describe, repeat.

recoup (SYN.) regain, recover, repay, retrieve.

recover (SYN.) regain, redeem, recapture, retrieve, salvage, better, improve, mend, heal. (ANT.) debilitate, succumb, worsen.

recreation (SYN.) entertainment, amusement, enjoyment, diversion, fun.

recrimination (SYN.) vindication, reproach, dissension, accusation, countercharge.

recruit (SYN.) trainee, beginner, volunteer, draftee, select, enlist, novice.

recuperate (SYN.) regain, retrieve, cure, recapture, redeem, rally, convalesce, revive, recover, repossess, restore. (ANT.) sicken, weaken, lose, regress, forfeit.

redeem (SYN.) claim, recover, repossess, regain, reclaim, cash in, retrieve.

reduce (SYN.) lessen, decrease, lower, downgrade, degrade, suppress, lower, abate, diminish. (ANT.) enlarge, swell, raise, elevate, revive, increase, amplify.

reduction (SYN.) shortening, abridgment, abbreviation. (ANT.) amplification, extension, enlargement.

reek (SYN.) odor, stench, stink, smell.

refer (SYN.) recommend, direct, commend, regard, concern, relate, suggest, mention.

referee (SYN.) judge, arbitrator, umpire, arbiter, moderator, mediator, intermediary.

reference (SYN.) allusion, direction, mention, concern, respect, referral.

refine (SYN.) purify, clarify, improve, clean. (ANT.) pollute, debase, muddy, downgrade.

refined (SYN.) purified, cultured, cultivated, courteous, courtly. (ANT.) rude, coarse, crude, vulgar.

refinement (SYN.) culture, enlightenment, education, civilization. (ANT.) vulgarity, ignorance, boorishness.

reflect (SYN.) muse, mirror, deliberate, cogitate, think, reproduce, ponder, consider, reason, meditate, contemplate.

reflection (SYN.) warning, conception, intelligence, appearance, likeness, image, cogitation, notification.

reform *(SYN.)* right, improve, correction, change, amend, improvement, better, betterment, correct, rectify.
(ANT.) spoil, damage, aggravate, vitiate.
refresh *(SYN.)* exhilarate, renew, invigorate.
(ANT.) exhaust, tire.
refreshing *(SYN.)* bracing, cool, brisk, fresh.
refreshment *(SYN.)* food, snack, drink, nourishment, exhilaraton, stimulation.
refuge *(SYN.)* safety, retreat, shelter, asylum, sanctuary, harbor.
(ANT.) peril, exposure, jeopardy, danger.
refuse *(SYN.)* spurn, rebuff, decline, reject, trash, rubbish, withhold, disallow, waste, garbage, deny, demur.
(ANT.) allow, accept, welcome, grant.
refute *(SYN.)* rebut, disprove, confute, falsify, controvert, contradict.
(ANT.) prove, confirm, accept, establish.
regain *(SYN.)* redeem, retrieve, recover, repossess, recapture.
(ANT.) lose.
regalement *(SYN.)* feast, dinner, celebration, entertainment.
regard *(SYN.)* estimate, value, honor, affection, notice, care, consideration, consider, relation, respect, attend, thought, reference, care, attention, esteem, concern, liking.
(ANT.) neglect, disgust, antipathy.
regards *(SYN.)* salutations, greetings, good wishes, respects, remembrances.
regenerate *(SYN.)* improve, reconstruct, remedy, reestablish, rebuild.
regime *(SYN.)* direction, government, administration, management, dynasty, command, leadership.
regimented *(SYN.)* ordered, directed controlled, orderly, rigid, disciplined.
(ANT.) loose, free, unstructured.
region *(SYN.)* belt, place, spot, territory, climate, area, zone, locality, station, locale.
register *(SYN.)* catalog, record, book, list, roll, enter, roster, chronicle.
regressive *(SYN.)* revisionary, retrograde.
(ANT.) progressive, civilized, advanced.
regret *(SYN.)* sorrow, qualm, lament, grief, compunction, bemoan, concern, scruple, misgiving, remorse, contrition.
(ANT.) obduracy, complacency.
regular *(SYN.)* steady, orderly, natural,

normal, customary, usual, habitual, even, uniform, systematic, unvaried, methodical, symmetrical.
(ANT.) odd, exceptional, unusual, irregular, abnormal, rare.
regulate *(SYN.)* control, manage, govern, direct, legislate, set, adjust, systematize.
regulation *(SYN.)* method, rule, axiom, guide, control, standard, canon, precept, restraint, requirement.
(ANT.) chaos, deviation, hazard, turbulence, confusion.
rehabilitate *(SYN.)* renew, restore, rebuild, reestablish, repair, reconstruct.
rehearse *(SYN.)* repeat, practice, train, learn, coach, prepare, perfect, direct.
reign *(SYN.)* dominion, power, rule, sovereignty, govern, domination.
reimburse *(SYN.)* recompense, remunerate, compensate, remit.
rein *(SYN.)* restriction, bridle, check, deterrent, curb, restraint, barrier, control.
reinforce *(SYN.)* brace, strengthen, fortify, intensify, support.
reiterate *(SYN.)* reproduce, recapitulate, duplicate, repeat, rephrase.
reject *(SYN.)* spurn, rebuff, decline, renounce, expel, discard, withhold, deny, refuse.
(ANT.) endorse, grant, welcome, accept.
rejection *(SYN.)* dissent, nonconformity, variance, challenge, remonstrance, difference, noncompliance.
(ANT.) assent, acceptance, compliance.
rejoice *(SYN.)* celebrate, delight, enjoy, revel, exhilarate, elate.
rejuvenate *(SYN.)* refresh, rekindle, overhaul, revitalize, animate, invigorate.
(ANT.) deplete, weaken, exhaust, enervate.
relapse *(SYN.)* worsen, deteriorate, regress, weaken, fade, worsen, sink fail.
(ANT.) strengthen, progress, advance, get well, rehabilitate.
relate *(SYN.)* refer, beat, report, describe, tell, correlate, narrate, recount, compare, connect.
relation *(SYN.)* entente, compact, coalition, alliance, connection, relationship, association, partnership, similarity, kinsman, treaty, marriage.
(ANT.) separation, divorce.
relationship *(SYN.)* link, tie, alliance, connection, union, bond, affinity, con-

junction.

(ANT.) separation, disunion.

relative (SYN.) dependent, proportional, about, pertinent, regarding.

relax (SYN.) slacken, loosen, repose, rest, recline, unwind.

(ANT.) increase, tighten, intensify.

relaxation (SYN.) comfort, ease, rest, enjoyment, lull, recess, breather, loafing.

relaxed (SYN.) welcome, pleasing, casual, acceptable, informal, restful, agreeable.

(ANT.) formal, planned, wretched, distressing, troubling.

release (SYN.) liberate, emancipate, relinquish, proclaim, publish, liberation, announce, deliver, free, discharge.

(ANT.) restrict, imprison, subjugate.

relegate (SYN.) entrust, authorize, remand, refer, assign.

relent (SYN.) cede, yield, surrender, give, relax, abdicate, relinquish, waive.

(ANT.) strive, assert, struggle.

relentless (SYN.) eternal, stubborn, tenacious, dogged, ceaseless, incessant, ceaseless, persistent, determined.

relevant (SYN.) related, material, apt, applicable, fit, relating, germane.

(ANT.) foreign, alien, unrelated.

reliable (SYN.) trusty, tried, certain, secure, trustworthy, dependable.

(ANT.) unreliable, eccentric, questionable, erratic, dubious.

reliance (SYN.) faith, confidence, trust.

(ANT.) mistrust, doubt, skepticism.

relic (SYN.) remains, fossil, throwback, heirloom, souvenir, keepsake, heirloom.

relief (SYN.) help, aid, comfort, ease, backing, patronage, alms, support.

(ANT.) hostility, defiance, antagonism, resistance.

relieve (SYN.) diminish, soothe, calm, abate, pacify, ease, lessen, replace, spell, lighten, comfort, alleviate.

(ANT.) disturb, irritate, agitate, trouble, aggravate, worry.

religion (SYN.) tenet, belief, dogma, faith, creed, persuasion.

religious (SYN.) godly, reverent, faithful, devout, zeal, pious, divine, holy, devoted, sacred, theological.

(ANT.) profane, irreligious, skeptical, impious, lax, atheistic.

religiousness (SYN.) love, zeal, affection, devoutness, fidelity, ardor.

(ANT.) indifference, apathy, un-

faithfulness.

relinquish (SYN.) capitulate, submit, yield, abandon, cede, sacrifice, disclaim.

(ANT.) overcome, conquer, rout, resist.

relish (SYN.) enjoyment, satisfaction, delight, gusto, appreciation, condiment, like, enjoy, enthusiasm.

(ANT.) distaste, antipathy, disfavor, dislike.

reluctance (SYN.) disgust, hatred, repulsion, abhorrence, distaste, repugnance, aversion.

(ANT.) enthusiasm, affection, devotion.

reluctant (SYN.) slow, averse, hesitant, unwilling, loath, disinclined, balky.

(ANT.) ready, eager, willing, disposed.

rely (SYN.) confide, trust, lean, depend.

(ANT.) mistrust, disbelieve, question, distrust.

remain (SYN.) survive, rest, stay, abide, halt, endure, dwell, tarry, continue, linger.

(ANT.) finish, leave, terminate, dissipate.

remainder (SYN.) leftover, residue, rest, surplus, balance, excess.

remains (SYN.) residue, balance, rest, remnants, relics, discards, waste, junk.

remark (SYN.) comment, state, utterance, mention, note, observe, observation, annotation, declaration, statement.

remarkable (SYN.) exciting, impressive, overpowering, unusual, affecting, thrilling, splendid, special, noteworthy, extraordinary, touching, august.

(ANT.) ordinary, unimpressive, commonplace, average, regular.

remedy (SYN.) redress, help, cure, relief, medicine, restorative, rectify, alleviate, medication, correct, reparation.

remember (SYN.) recollect, reminisce, recall, memorize, mind, retain, remind.

(ANT.) forget, overlook, disregard.

remembrance (SYN.) monument, memory, recollection, memento, recall, keepsake, souvenir, retrospection.

remiss (SYN.) delinquent, lax, careless, negligent, oblivious, forgetful, absentminded, sloppy, irresponsible.

remit (SYN.) send, pay, forward, forgive, pardon, overlook, excuse, reimburse.

remittance (SYN.) payment.

remnant (SYN.) remains, remainder, rest, residue, trace, relic.

remodel (SYN.) remake, reshape,

rebuild, redecorate, renovate, modify, change, alter, convert, refurbish, update.

remonstrate *(SYN.)* grouch, protest, complain, grumble, murmur, repine, dispute.
(ANT.) rejoice, applaud, praise.

remorse *(SYN.)* sorrow, qualm, contrition, regret, compunction, repentance.
(ANT.) obduracy, complacency.

remorseless *(SYN.)* savage, unrelenting, crude, barbaric, merciless, cruel, fiendish, brutal, callous.
(ANT.) kind, refined, polite, civilized.

remote *(SYN.)* inconsiderable, removed, slight, far, unlikely, distant, inaccessible, unreachable, isolated, sequestered.
(ANT.) visible, nearby, current, near, close.

remove *(SYN.)* transport, eject, move, vacate, withdraw, dislodge, transfer, doff, displace, eliminate, murder, kill, oust, extract.
(ANT.) insert, retain, leave, stay, keep.

removed *(SYN.)* aloof, distant, cool, remote.

remuneration *(SYN.)* wages, payment, pay, salary, compensation, reimbursement, reward.

render *(SYN.)* become, make, perform, do, offer, present, give, submit.

rendition *(SYN.)* interpretation, version, depiction, expression, characterization.

renegade *(SYN.)* defector, insurgent, dissenter, rebel, maverick, mutineer, betrayer.

renege *(SYN.)* let down, doublecross, deceive.

renew *(SYN.)* restore, renovate, overhaul, revise, modernize, reshape, redo.

renounce *(SYN.)* resign, disown, revoke, abandon, quit, retract, forgo, leave, forsake, abdicate, reject, relinquish, deny.
(ANT.) assert, uphold, recognize, maintain.

renovate *(SYN.)* restore, rehabilitate, rebuild, refresh, renew, overhaul, redesign.

renown *(SYN.)* honor, reputation, eminence, acclaim, glory, repute, luster, fame, notability.
(ANT.) obscurity, anonymity, disgrace.

renowned *(SYN.)* noted, famous, distinguished, well-known, glorious, celebrated.

(ANT.) unknown, infamous, hidden, obscure.

rent *(SYN.)* payment, rental, let, lease, hire.

repair *(SYN.)* rebuilding, mend, renew, tinker, correct, patch, restore, adjust, reconstruction, remedy, amend, rehabilitation, retrieve.
(ANT.) harm, break.

repartee *(SYN.)* badinage, banter.

repast *(SYN.)* feast, banquet, meal, refreshment, snack.

repeal *(SYN.)* end, cancel, nullify, annul, quash, abolish, cancellation, rescind, abolition, abrogate.

repeat *(SYN.)* reiterate, restate, redo, rehearse, quote, remake, relate, iterate, reproduce.

repeated *(SYN.)* continuous, frequent, recurrent, continual.

repel *(SYN.)* check, repulse, rebuff, reject, decline, discourage.
(ANT.) lure, attract.

repellent *(SYN.)* sickening, offensive, disgusting, nauseating, repugnant, obnoxious.

repent *(SYN.)* deplore, regret, rue, lament.

repentance *(SYN.)* penitence, remorse, sorrow, compunction, qualm, grief.
(ANT.) obduracy, complacency.

repentant *(SYN.)* regretful, sorrowful, contrite, sorry, penitent.
(ANT.) remorseless, obdurate.

repetitious *(SYN.)* repeated, monotonous, boring, tiresome, humdrum.

repine *(SYN.)* protest, lament, complain, whine, regret, grouch, murmur, grumble.
(ANT.) rejoice, applaud, praise.

replace *(SYN.)* alternate, return, reinstate.

replacement *(SYN.)* understudy, proxy, second, alternate, substitute, replica, surrogate.

replenish *(SYN.)* store, pervade, fill, stock, occupy, supply.
(ANT.) empty, void, deplete, exhaust, drain.

replica *(SYN.)* reproduction, copy, exemplar, imitation, duplicate, facsimile.
(ANT.) prototype.

reply *(SYN.)* retort, rejoinder, answer, retaliate, respond, confirmation.

(ANT.) summoning, inquiry.
report *(SYN.)* declare, herald, publish, announce, summary, publish, advertise.
(ANT.) suppress, conceal, withhold, bury.
reporter *(SYN.)* journalist.
repose *(SYN.)* hush, quiet, tranquillity, rest, peace, slumber, calm, stillness, sleep, calmness, dormancy.
(ANT.) tumult, excitement, agitation.
reprehensible *(SYN.)* criminal, immoral, damnable, culpable, wrong, wicked.
represent *(SYN.)* picture, draw, delineate, portray, depict, denote, symbolize.
(ANT.) misrepresent, caricature.
representation *(SYN.)* effigy, film, likeness, portrait, print, scene, appearance, drawing, scene, view, cinema.
representative *(SYN.)* delegate, agent, substitute, surrogate.
repress *(SYN.)* limit, stop, check, bridle, curb, restrain, constrain, suppress.
(ANT.) loosen, aid, incite, liberate, encourage.
reprimand *(SYN.)* rate, scold, vituperate, berate, lecture, blame, admonish, upbraid.
(ANT.) praise, approve.
reproach *(SYN.)* defamation, dishonor, insult, profanation, abuse, disparagement, misuse, reviling.
(ANT.) respect, laudation, approval, plaudit.
reproduction *(SYN.)* replica, copy, exemplar, transcript, duplicate, photocopy.
reproof *(SYN.)* rebuke, punishment, blame, censure, disapproval, scorn, disdain, admonition.
repugnance *(SYN.)* disgust, hatred, reluctance, abhorrence, aversion, loathing, antipathy, distaste, repulsion.
(ANT.) devotion, affection, enthusiasm, attachment.
repulsive *(SYN.)* repellent, ugly, homely, deformed, horrid, offensive, plain, uncomely.
(ANT.) fair, pretty, attractive, handsome.
reputable *(SYN.)* honest, upstanding, trustworthy, straightforward, upright, reliable.
(ANT.) notorious, corrupt, disreputable.
reputation *(SYN.)* class, nature, standing, name, fame, kind, renown, prominence, character, distinction, disposition, repute.
repute *(SYN.)* class, nature, standing, kind, character, reputation, disposition, sort.
request *(SYN.)* sue, implore, petition, desire, appeal, question, entreaty, beseech, ask, pray, supplicate.
(ANT.) require.
require *(SYN.)* exact, need, order, command, order, lack, claim, demand, want.
requirement *(SYN.)* demand, need, necessity, condition, provision, prerequisite.
requisite *(SYN.)* vital, necessary, basic, fundamental, indispensable, essential, needed.
(ANT.) casual, nonessential, peripheral, accidental.
rescind *(SYN.)* annul, quash, revoke, abolish, invalidate, abrogate, withdraw.
rescue *(SYN.)* liberate, ransom, release, deliver, deliverance, liberation.
research *(SYN.)* exploration, quest, scrutiny, exploration, interrogation, query, examination, study, investigation.
(ANT.) inattention, disregard, negligence.
resemblance *(SYN.)* parity, similitude, analogy, likeness, correspondence.
(ANT.) distinction, difference.
resemble *(SYN.)* duplicate, mirror, look like.
resentfulness *(SYN.)* envy, jealousy, covetousness, suspicion.
(ANT.) liberality, geniality, tolerance, difference.
resentment *(SYN.)* displeasure, bitterness, indignation, rancor, outrage, hostility.
(ANT.) complacency, understanding, good will.
reservation *(SYN.)* skepticism, restriction, objection, limitation, doubt.
reserve *(SYN.)* fund, hold, keep, store, accumulation, save, stock, maintain, supply.
(ANT.) waste, squander.
reserved *(SYN.)* cautious, fearful, timorous, wary, aloof, chary, sheepish, restrained, proper, unfriendly, bashful, diffident.
(ANT.) forward, bold, wild, immodest, brazen, abandoned, friendly.

reside *(SYN.)* inhabit, dwell, abide, live, lie.

residence *(SYN.)* home, dwelling, stay, seat, abode, quarters, domicile, living quarters.

residue *(SYN.)* balance, remainder, rest, ashes, remnants, dregs, leftovers, ends.

resign *(SYN.)* vacate, withdraw, leave, surrender, quit.

resignation *(SYN.)* perseverance, endurance, fortitude, composure, forbearance.
(ANT.) unquiet, nervousness, impatience.

resigned *(SYN.)* forbearing, stoical, assiduous, passive, accepting, composed, uncomplaining.
(ANT.) turbulent, chafing.

resilience *(SYN.)* rubbery, springy, buoyant, elasticity.
(ANT.) unresponsive, fixed, rigid, stolid.

resist *(SYN.)* defy, attack, withstand, hinder, confront, oppose.
(ANT.) relent, allow, yield, accede.

resolute *(SYN.)* firm, resolved, set, determined, decided.
(ANT.) irresolute, wavering, vacillating.

resolution *(SYN.)* resolve, courage, determination, persistence, statement, verdict, recommendation, decision, steadfastness, dedication, perseverance.
(ANT.) indecision, inconstancy.

resolve *(SYN.)* determination, resolution, courage, settle, decide, persistence, determine, confirm, decision, steadfastness.
(ANT.) integrate, indecision, inconstancy.

resort *(SYN.)* motel, lodge, hotel, solve.

resound *(SYN.)* echoe, ring, reverberate.

resource *(SYN.)* store, source, supply, reserve.

resourceful *(SYN.)* inventive, ingenious, creative, clever, imaginative, skillful.

respect *(SYN.)* honor, approval, revere, heed, value, admire, esteem, point, detail, admiration, reverence, regard, feature, particular, venerate, consider.
(ANT.) disrespect, neglect, abuse, scorn, disregard, despise.

respectable *(SYN.)* becoming, respected, proper, seemly, tolerable, decent, acceptable, fair, adequate, passable, suitable, honorable, valuable.
(ANT.) unsavory, vulgar, gross, disreputable, reprehensible.

respectful *(SYN.)* courteous, polite, well-behaved, well-bred, compliant, submissive.
(ANT.) disobedient, impertinent, rude, flippant.

respite *(SYN.)* deferment, adjournment, suspension.

respond *(SYN.)* rejoin, answer, reply, acknowledge, retort.
(ANT.) overlook, disregard.

response *(SYN.)* reply, acknowledgment, answer, retort, rejoinder.
(ANT.) summoning, inquiry.

responsibility *(SYN.)* duty, obligation, accountability, trust-worthiness, trust, liability, commitment.

responsible *(SYN.)* answerable, chargeable, trustworthy, liable, accountable, able, capable, upstanding, reliable, solid, indebted, creditable.
(ANT.) careless, free, negligent.

rest *(SYN.)* ease, intermission, calm, quiet, balance, surplus, repose, lounge, inactivity, motionlessness, immobility, standstill, relax, remainder, excess, surplus, relaxation, slumber, peace, tranquillity, leisure.
(ANT.) tumult, commotion, motion, agitation.

restful *(SYN.)* peaceful, quiet, tranquil, calm.
(ANT.) tumultuous, upsetting, agitated, disturbed.

restitution *(SYN.)* recompense, satisfaction, refund, amends, retrieval.

restive *(SYN.)* balky, disobedient, fractious, impatient, unruly, fidgety, uneasy.

restless *(SYN.)* sleepless, unquiet, transient, active, agitated, disturbed, jumpy, nervous, uneasy, disquieted, irresolute.
(ANT.) quiet, tranquil, calm, peaceable.

restore *(SYN.)* repair, recover, rebuild, reestablish, renovate, return, renew, mend, reinstall, revive, rehabilitate, replace.

restrain *(SYN.)* limit, curb, constraint, stop, bridle, control, reserve, constrain, repress, check, suppress, hinder.
(ANT.) incite, aid, loosen.

restraint *(SYN.)* order, self-control, reserve, control, regulation, limitation, confinement.
(ANT.) freedom, liberty, confusion.

restrict *(SYN.)* fetter, restrain, confine, limit, engage, attach, connect, link, tie, bind.

(ANT.) broaden, enlarge, untie, loose, free.

restriction *(SYN.)* curb, handicap, check, boundary, ban, limitation, control, deterrent.

result *(SYN.)* effect, issue, outcome, resolve, end, consequence, happen, determination, conclusion, reward, aftermath.

(ANT.) cause, beginning, origin.

resume *(SYN.)* restart, continue, recommence, reassume.

resurgence *(SYN.)* rebirth, comeback, recovery, revival, resuscitation, rejuvenation, renewal.

resuscitate *(SYN.)* restore, revive, resurrect.

retain *(SYN.)* keep, hold, recall, remember, employ, hire, engage.

retainer *(SYN.)* aide, assistant, lackey, attendant, servant.

retaliate *(SYN.)* repay, revenge, return, avenge.

(ANT.) condone, forgive, overlook, excuse, forget.

retard *(SYN.)* detain, slacken, defer, impede, hold back, delay, postpone.

(ANT.) accelerate, speed, hasten, rush.

retention *(SYN.)* reservation, acquisition, holding, tenacity, possession.

reticent *(SYN.)* reserved, subdued, quiet, shy, withdrawn, restrained, bashful, silent.

(ANT.) outspoken, forward, opinionated.

retire *(SYN.)* resign, quit, abdicate, depart, vacate.

retiring *(SYN.)* timid, bashful, withdrawn, modest, reticent, quiet, reserved.

(ANT.) gregarious, assertive, bold.

retort *(SYN.)* reply, answer, response, respond, rejoin, rejoinder, retaliate.

(ANT.) summoning, inquiry.

retreat *(SYN.)* leave, depart, retire, withdraw, retirement, withdrawal, departure, shelter, refuge.

(ANT.) advanced.

retrench *(SYN.)* reduce, scrape, curtail.

retribution *(SYN.)* justice, vengeance, reprisal, punishment, comeuppance, vindictiveness, revenge, retaliation.

retrieve *(SYN.)* regain, recover, recapture, repossess, reclaim, salvage, recoup.

retrograde *(SYN.)* regressive, backward, declining, deteriorating, worsening.

(ANT.) onward, progression, advanced.

return *(SYN.)* restoration, replace, revert, recur, restore, retreat.

(ANT.) keep, take, retain.

reveal *(SYN.)* discover, publish, communicate, impart, uncover, tell, betray, divulge, disclose.

(ANT.) conceal, cover, obscure, cloak, hide.

revel *(SYN.)* rejoice, wallow, bask, enjoy, delight, savor, gloat, luxuriate, relish.

revelation *(SYN.)* hallucination, dream, phantoms, apparition, ghost, mirage, specter, daydream, suprise, shocker.

(ANT.) verity, reality.

revelry *(SYN.)* merriment, merry-making, carousal, feasting, gala, festival.

revenge *(SYN.)* vindictiveness, reprisal, requital, vengeance, repayment, repay, retribution, reparation.

(ANT.) reconcile, forgive, pity.

revenue *(SYN.)* take, proceeds, income, profit, return.

revere *(SYN.)* admire, honor, worship, respect, venerate, adore.

(ANT.) ignore, despise.

reverence *(SYN.)* glory, worship, homage, admiration, dignity, renown, respect, esteem, veneration, adoration, honor.

(ANT.) dishonor, derision, reproach.

reverent *(SYN.)* honoring, respectful, adoring, pious, devout, humble.

(ANT.) impious, disrespectful.

reverse *(SYN.)* overthrow, unmake rescind, opposite, invert, contrary, rear, back, misfortune, defeat, catastrophe, upset, countermand, revoke.

(ANT.) vouch, stabilize, endorse, affirm.

revert *(SYN.)* revive, relapse, backslide, rebound, retreat, recur, go back.

(ANT.) keep, take, appropriate.

review *(SYN.)* reconsideration, examination, commentary, retrospection, restudy, journal, synopsis, study, reexamine, critique, inspection.

revile *(SYN.)* defame, malign, vilify, abuse, traduce, asperse, scandalize, smear.

(ANT.) honor, respect, cherish, protect.

revise *(SYN.)* change, alter, improve, correct, amend, update, rewrite, polish.

revision *(SYN.)* inspection, survey, retrospection, commentary, critique.

revival *(SYN.)* renaissance, exhumation, resurgence, renewal, revitalization.

revive *(SYN.)* refresh, lessen, decrease, renew, reduce, lower, abate, reanimate, diminish, reawaken, rejuvenate, suppress.
(ANT.) increase, amplify, intensify.

revoke *(SYN.)* nullify, cancel, abolish, quash, rescind, abrogate.

revolt *(SYN.)* mutiny, rebel, disgust, revolution, uprising, rebellion, upheaval, takeover, insurgence, abolish.

revolting *(SYN.)* hateful, odious, abominable, foul, vile, detestable, loathsome, repugnant, obnoxious, sickening.
(ANT.) delightful, agreeable, pleasant.

revolution *(SYN.)* rebellion, mutiny, turn, coup, revolt, overthrow, cycle, spin, uprising.

revolutionary *(SYN.)* insurgent, extremist, radical, subversive, mutinous.

revolve *(SYN.)* spin, wheel, rotate, circle, circle, turn, whirl, gyrate.
(ANT.) travel, proceed, wander.

revolver *(SYN.)* gun, pistol.

revulsion *(SYN.)* reversal, rebound, backlash, withdrawal, recoil.

reward *(SYN.)* bounty, premium, meed, award, compensation, prize, recompense, bonus, remuneration, accolade, wages.
(ANT.) charge, wages, punishment.

rewarding *(SYN.)* pleasing, productive, fruitful, profitable, favorable, satisfying, gratifying, fulfilling.

rhetoric *(SYN.)* style, verbosity, expressiveness, eloquence, fluency, flamboyance.

rhyme *(SYN.)* poem, verse, poetry, ballad, ditty, rhapsody, sonnet.

ribald *(SYN.)* suggestive, off-color, indecent, spicy, rude, vulgar.

rich *(SYN.)* ample, costly, wealthy, fruitful, prolific, abundant, well-off, affluent, plentiful, fertile, bountiful, luxuriant.
(ANT.) poor, unfruitful, beggarly, barren, impoverished, scarce, scanty, unproductive, destitute.

rickety *(SYN.)* unsound, unsteady, flimsy, unstable, shaky, decrepit, wobbly.
(ANT.) steady, solid, sturdy.

ricochet *(SYN.)* recoil, backfire, rebound, bounce, deviate, boomerang.

rid *(SYN.)* free, clear, shed, delivered,

eliminate, disperse, unload, purge.

riddle *(SYN.)* puzzle, mystery, conundrum, problem, question, enigma.
(ANT.) key, solution, answer, resolution.

ride *(SYN.)* tour, journey, motor, manage, drive, control, guide.

ridge *(SYN.)* hillock, backbone, spine, crest, mound, hump.

ridicule *(SYN.)* gibe, banter, mock, jeering, deride, tease, taunt, satire, mockery, derision.
(ANT.) praise, respect.

ridiculous *(SYN.)* silly, nonsensical, absurd, accurate, inconsistent, farcical, proper, laughable, apt, preposterous, foolish.
(ANT.) sound, reasonable, consistent.

rife *(SYN.)* widespread, abundant, innumerable, rampant, teeming.

rifle *(SYN.)* plunder, pillage, rummage, ransack, rob, steal.

rift *(SYN.)* crevice, fault, opening, crack, flaw, fissure, split, breach, opening.

right *(SYN.)* correct, appropriate, suitable, ethical, fit, real, legitimate, justice, factual, just, directly, virtue, true, definite, straight, honorably, seemly.
(ANT.) immoral, unfair, wrong, bad, improper.

righteous *(SYN.)* ethical, chaste, honorable, good, virtuous, good, noble.
(ANT.) sinful, libertine, amoral, licentious.

rigid *(SYN.)* strict, unyielding, stiff, stern, austere, rigorous, inflexible, stringent, unbendable, severe, harsh, unbending.
(ANT.) supple, flexible, mild, compassionate, pliable, limp, relaxed.

rigorous *(SYN.)* unfeeling, rough, strict, blunt, cruel, hard, severe, grating, coarse, jarring, stern, stringent.
(ANT.) soft, mild, tender, gentle, smooth.

rile *(SYN.)* irritate, nettle, hector, exasperate, provoke, gripe.

rim *(SYN.)* verge, frontier, border, outskirts, edge, brink, lip, limit, termination, boundary, fringe, brim, margin.
(ANT.) core, mainland, center.

rind *(SYN.)* layer, cover, skin, hide, peel, crust, bark.

ring *(SYN.)* fillet, band, loop, circlet, circle, surround, encircle, peal, sound, resound, jingle, tinkle.

ringleader *(SYN.)* provoker, troublemaker, leader, instigator, chief, inciter, agitator.

rinse *(SYN.)* launder, cleanse, wash, soak, immerse, laundering, rinsing, immerse, bathe, clean.

riot *(SYN.)* disturbance, disorder, outburst, commotion, insurgence, uproar, panic, boisterousness, lark, hoot, wow, sensation, caper, roister, frolic, eruption, confusion, tumult, revolt.

riotous *(SYN.)* boisterous, wild, rambunctious, roisterous, tumultuous, turbulent, noisy, loud, rowdy, rollicking.

rip *(SYN.)* tear, rend, wound, rive, cleave, cut, slit, slash, lacerate, shred, scramble, dart, dash, split, disunite.
(ANT.) unite, join, repair.

ripe *(SYN.)* ready, finished, mature, complete, full-grown, develop, mellow, seasonable, full-fledged, primed, disposed, keen, avid, consummate.
(ANT.) raw, crude, undeveloped, premature, unprepared, unripe, immature.

ripen *(SYN.)* grow, season, age, mature, mellow, develop, progress, maturate.

rip into *(SYN.)* assail, lash out at, attack, charge.

rip-off *(SYN.)* fraud, dishonesty, gyp, racket, swindle, exploitation, heist, theft, extortion, thievery, larceny, shakedown.

riposte *(SYN.)* rejoinder, comeback, quip, retort, response, reply, wisecrack.

ripple *(SYN.)* wave, ruffle, wavelet, gurgle, undulate, gurgle, corrugation, rumple, crumple, spurtle, dribble, bubble.

rise *(SYN.)* thrive, awaken, ascend, climb, mount, tower, arise, wake, scale, flourish, prosper, advance, proceed, soar.
(ANT.) fall, drop, plunge, fade, slump, decline, sinking, depression, waning, comedown, setback, retrogression, descend.

risk *(SYN.)* hazard, peril, danger, endanger, chance, jeopardy, threat, vulnerability, contingency, precariousness, shakiness.
(ANT.) protection, safety, immunity, defense.

risky *(SYN.)* menacing, chancy, threatening, critical, perilous, insecure, unsafe, dicey, unsound, dangerous.
(ANT.) guarded, safe, certain, firm, secure.

rite *(SYN.)* pomp, solemnity, ceremony, observance, ceremonial, formality.

ritual *(SYN.)* pomp, solemnity, ceremony, parade, rite, ritualism, prescription, routine, custom, tradition.

rival *(SYN.)* enemy, opponent, contestant, compete, foe, adversary, oppose, competitor, contest, antagonist.
(ANT.) colleague, confederate, allay, collaborator, helpmate, teammate.

rivalry *(SYN.)* contest, struggle, duel, race, vying, opposition, contention, competition.
(ANT.) alliance, collaboration, partnership, cooperation, teamwork, coalition.

river *(SYN.)* brook, stream, headstream, watercourse, tributary, creek.

rivet *(SYN.)* weld, bolt, fasten, attach, secure, bind, join, staple, nail, couple.

road *(SYN.)* street, way, highway, pike, drive, highway, expressway, boulevard.

roam *(SYN.)* err, saunter, deviate, rove, range, wander, digress, ramble, stroll.
(ANT.) stop, linger, stay, halt, settle.

roar *(SYN.)* cry, bellow, yell, shout, yowl, howl, bawl, hoot, bang, boom, blast, blare, scream, whoop, holler, yelp.

roast *(SYN.)* deride, ridicule, kid, ride, mock, tease, twit, parody, burlesque.

rob *(SYN.)* fleece, steal, despoil, pilfer, pillage, sack, loot, plunder, burglarize, ransack, hold up, rip off, thieve.

robbery *(SYN.)* larceny, plundering, thievery, stealing, theft, pillage, swiping, caper, snatching, burglary, plunder.

robe *(SYN.)* housecoat, bathrobe, dressing gown, caftan, muumuu, smock, cape.

robot *(SYN.)* computer, android, automaton, pawn, workhorse, drudge, laborer.

robust *(SYN.)* well, hearty, hale, sound, healthy, strong, able-bodied, stalwart.
(ANT.) fragile, feeble, debilitated, reserved, refined, puny, frail, delicate, infirm.

rock *(SYN.)* pebble, boulder, stone, gravel, granite, roll, sway, swagger, limestone.

rocky *(SYN.)* unstable, faint, rocklike, stony, pebbly, gravelly, trembly, rough, bumpy, formidable, quavering, challenging, unsteady, dizzy.
(ANT.) effortless, easy, slight, simple, sound, rugged, stout, hardy, strong,

robust.

rod *(SYN.)* bar, pole, wand, stick, pike, staff, billy, baton.

rogue *(SYN.)* criminal, rascal, outlaw, scoundrel, scamp, good-for-nothing, villain.

roguish *(SYN.)* prankish, playful, mischievous, elfish, waggish, devilish, tricky.
(ANT.) grave, humorless, solemn, staid, lawabiding.

roil *(SYN.)* churn, muddy, rile, mire, disturb.

roister *(SYN.)* bluster, swagger, swashbuckle, vaunt, bluff, flourish, rollick.

role *(SYN.)* task, part, function, characterization, portrayal, face, character.

roll *(SYN.)* revolve, rotate, whirl, swing, rock, waver, reel, lumber, swagger, stagger, progress, proceed, turn, spin.

rollicking *(SYN.)* spirited, animated, frolicsome, exuberant, lighthearted, carefree.

roll up *(SYN.)* amass, collect, accumulate, gather.

romance *(SYN.)* affair, enchantment, novel, tale, adventure, enterprise, daring, story.

romantic *(SYN.)* poetic, mental, dreamy, fanciful, imaginative, extravagant, impractical, exaggerated, wild, idealistic, mawkish, ideal, maudlin.
(ANT.) homely, faint-hearted, familiar, unromantic, pessimistic, unemotional, cynical, literal, prosaic, factual.

romp *(SYN.)* caper, gambol, frolic, play, conquer, triumph, horseplay, frisk.
(ANT.) defeat, rout.

room *(SYN.)* enclosure, cell, chamber, space, stay, lodge, cubicle, reside.

roomy *(SYN.)* broad, large, wide, sizable, generous, capacious, ample, spacious, extensive, commodious, vast.
(ANT.) tight, limited, crowded, confined, narrow.

roost *(SYN.)* coop, henhouse, perch, hutch, residence, abode, hearth, lodgings.

root *(SYN.)* reason, bottom, groundwork, cause, support, base, underpinning, beginning, mainspring, source, basis.
(ANT.) cover, top, building.

rooted *(SYN.)* fixed, fast, firm, steadfast, immovable, stationary.

root for *(SYN.)* back, support, boost,

sponsor, promote, bolster, encourage, hail, cheer.

root out *(SYN.)* dispose of, uproot, cut out, pluck out.

rope *(SYN.)* string, wire, cord, cable, line, strand, rigging, ropework, cordage.

ropy *(SYN.)* wiry, stringy, viscous, threadlike, viscoid.

roster *(SYN.)* list, census, muster, enrollment, listing, register.

rosy *(SYN.)* reddish, pink, healthy, fresh, cheerful, bright, happy, glowing, flushed, promising, favorable.
(ANT.) pale, pallid, gray, wan, disheartening, ashen, unfavorable, gloomy.

rot *(SYN.)* putrefy, waste, decay, mold, decompose, dwindle, spoil, decline, decomposition, wane, rotting, ebb.
(ANT.) increase, rise, grow, luxuriate.

rotary *(SYN.)* axial, rotating, turning, gyral, revolving, rolling, whirling, rotational.

rotate *(SYN.)* spin, twirl, wheel, circle, twist, orbit, invert, swivel, gyrate, wind, alternate, recur, intermit, pivot.
(ANT.) stop, arrest, stand.

rotation *(SYN.)* turning, rolling, succession, gyration, revolution, return, rhythm, swirling, spinning, whirling.

rote *(SYN.)* repetition, system, convention, routine, mechanization, habitude, habit, custom, perfunctoriness.

rotten *(SYN.)* decayed, decomposed, spoiled, putrid, contaminated, tainted.
(ANT.) unspoiled, pure, sweet, fresh.

rough *(SYN.)* jagged, scratchy, crude, incomplete, severe, craggy, stormy, rugged, unpolished, approximate, uneven, irregular, bumpy, coarse, unpolished, rude.
(ANT.) calm, polished, civil, mild, refined, placid, gentle, smooth, sleek, sophisticated, suave.

roughly *(SYN.)* nearly, about, approximately.

round *(SYN.)* rotund, chubby, curved, bulbous, entire, complete, spherical, circular, bowed.
(ANT.) slender, trim, slim, thin, lean.

roundness *(SYN.)* sphericalness, globularity, rotundity, globularness, sphericity.

rouse *(SYN.)* waken, awaken, stimulate, excite, summon, arise, stir.
(ANT.) rest, calm, sleep, restrain, sedate.

rousing *(SYN.)* exciting, galvanic,

stimulating, electric, moving, exhilarating, stirring, breathtaking, inciting. *(ANT.) flat, uninteresting, drab, monotonous, boring, tiresome, slow, dull.*

rout *(SYN.)* defeat, beat, quell, vanquish, conquer, humble, subdue, scatter. *(ANT.) cede, retreat, surrender.*

route *(SYN.)* street, course, trail, way, avenue, passage, thoroughfare, track, road, path.

routine *(SYN.)* way, habit, use, custom, practice, fashion, method, system, channel, circuit. *(ANT.) unusual, rate, uncommon.*

rover *(SYN.)* traveler, adventurer, wanderer, voyager.

row *(SYN.)* file, order, series, rank, progression, sequence, arrangement.

rowdy *(SYN.)* disorderly, unruly, brawling, roughneck, scrapper.

royal *(SYN.)* lordly, regal, noble, courtly, ruling, stately, dignified, supreme, majestic, sovereign, imperial, kingly. *(ANT.) servile, common, low, humble, vulgar.*

rub *(SYN.)* shine, polish, scour, scrape.

rubbish *(SYN.)* debris, garbage, trash, waste, junk, clutter.

ruddy *(SYN.)* rosy, reddish, healthy, robust, blushing, sanguine.

rude *(SYN.)* gruff, impudent, blunt, impolite, boorish, insolent, saucy, rough, crude, unmannerly, coarse, impertinent. *(ANT.) courtly, civil, stately, genteel, calm, dignified, polished, courteous, cultivated, polite.*

rudimentary *(SYN.* essential, primary, fundamental, original, imperfect.

rue *(SYN.)* lament, repine, sorrow, deplore, regret, bemoan.

ruffian *(SYN.)* crook, hoodlum, thug.

ruffle *(SYN.)* rumple, disarrange, disorder, disturb, trimming, frill.

rug *(SYN.)* floor-covering, carpet.

rugged *(SYN.)* jagged, craggy, scratchy, irregular, uneven, harsh, severe, tough. *(ANT.) smooth, level, even.*

ruin *(SYN.)* wreck, exterminate, devastate, annihilate, raze, demolish, spoil, wreck, destroy, destruction, devastation, disintegration, decay. *(ANT.) save, establish, preserve.*

ruination *(SYN.)* obliteration, annihilation, havoc, catastrophe.

rule *(SYN.)* law, guide, order, regulation,

sabotage *(SYN.)* subversion, treason, treachery, damage, disable, subvert.

sack *(SYN.)* pouch, bag.

sacrament *(SYN.)* communion, fellowship, association, intercourse, participation, union. *(ANT.) nonparticipation, alienation.*

sacred *(SYN.)* consecrated, blessed, devout, divine, holy, hallowed, pious, religious, spiritual, saintly. *(ANT.) profane, evil, sacrilegious, worldly, secular, blasphemous.*

sad *(SYN.)* dejected, cheerless, despondent, depressed, disconsolate, doleful, downhearted, glum, saddening. *(ANT.) happy, cheerful, glad, merry.*

safe *(SYN.)* dependable, certain, harmless, secure, snug, trustworthy. *(ANT.) hazardous, dangerous, unsafe, insecure, perilous.*

safeguard *(SYN.)* fence, bulwark, protection, shelter, refuge, shield, guard, defense, security.

sag *(SYN.)* incline, bend, lean, slant, tend, depend, rely, trust, fail. *(ANT.) rise, raise, erect, straighten.*

sagacity *(SYN.)* erudition, discretion, foresight, insight, information, judgment, intelligence, knowledge, learning, reason, prudence, sageness, sense. *(ANT.) foolishness, imprudence, stupidity, nonsense.*

sage *(SYN.)* intellectual, disciple, learner, savant, scholar, pupil, student, wise, judicious, sagacious, rational, logical, scholar, expert. *(ANT.) dunce, fool, dolt, idiot.*

saintly *(SYN.)* virtuous, moral, holy, devout, righteous, good.

sake *(SYN.)* motive, reason, purpose, benefit, advantage, welfare.

salary *(SYN.)* compensation, allowance, earnings, pay, fee, payment, recompense, wages. *(ANT.) gratuity, present, gift.*

salient *(SYN.)* distinguished, clear, manifest, noticeable, prominent, obvious, striking, visible. *(ANT.) hidden, inconspicuous, obscure.*

salubrious *(SYN.)* healthy, hale, sound, robust, strong, well, hygienic, wholesome, salutary. *(ANT.) diseased, delicate, frail, injurious, infirm, noxious.*

saloon *(SYN.)* pub, bar.

salutary *(SYN.)* beneficial, advantageous,

profitable, useful, wholesome.
(ANT.) *destructive, deleterious, detrimental, injurious, harmful.*
salute (SYN.) receive, greet.
salvage (SYN.) retrieve, rescue, recover.
salvation (SYN.) release, rescue, deliverance.
same (SYN.) equal, coincident, equivalent, like, indistinguishable.
(ANT.) *disparate, contrary, dissimilar, opposed, distinct.*
sample (SYN.) example, case, illustration, model, instance, pattern, prototype, specimen, token.
sanction (SYN.) approval, approbation, authorization, authority, let, permit.
(ANT.) *reproach, reprimand, stricture, censure, object, forbid, refuse, resist.*
sanctuary (SYN.) harbor, haven, asylum, refuge, retreat, shelter.
(ANT.) *danger, hazard, exposure, jeopardy, peril.*
sane (SYN.) balanced, rational, normal, sound, reasonable.
(ANT.) *crazy, insane, irrational.*
sanguinary (SYN.) bloody, sanguineous, gory, blood-stained.
sanguine (SYN.) confident, optimistic.
sanitary (SYN.) purified, clean, hygienic, disinfected.
(ANT.) *soiled, fouled, unclean, dirty.*
sap (SYN.) undermine, exhausted, drain, weaken.
sarcastic (SYN.) biting, acrimonious, cutting, caustic, derisive, sardonic, satirical, ironic, sneering.
(ANT.) *agreeable, affable, pleasant.*
sardonic (SYN.) bitter, caustic, acrimonious, severe, harsh.
(ANT.) *mellow, pleasant, sweet.*
satanic (SYN.) demonic, fiendish, diabolic, diabolical.
sate (SYN.) fill up, fill, occupy, furnish, pervade, stock, replenish, store, supply, content, gorge, satiate, stuff, satisfy.
(ANT.) *empty, drain, deplete, void.*
satiate (SYN.) compensate, appease, content, fulfill, please, gratify, remunerate, suffice.
(ANT.) *displease, dissatisfy, annoy, frustrate, tantalize.*
satire (SYN.) cleverness, fun, banter, humor, irony, raillery, pleasantry.
(ANT.) *platitude, sobriety, commonplace, solemnity, stupidity.*
satirical (SYN.) biting, caustic,

acrimonious, cutting, ironic, derisive, sarcastic, sneering, sardonic, taunting.
(ANT.) *agreeable, affable, pleasant.*
satisfaction (SYN.) blessedness, beatitude, bliss, delight, contentment, felicity, pleasure, enjoyment.
(ANT.) *grief, misery, sadness, despair.*
satisfactory (SYN.) ample, capable, adequate, commensurate, enough, sufficient, fitting, suitable, okay.
(ANT.) *scant, lacking, deficient, unsatisfactory, poor.*
satisfy (SYN.) compensate, appease, content, gratify, fulfill, suitable.
(ANT.) *displease, dissatisfy, annoy, frustrate, tantalize.*
saturate (SYN.) fill, diffuse, infiltrate, penetrate, permeate, run through.
saucy (SYN.) insolent, bold, impudent, impertinent.
(ANT.) *shy, demure.*
savage (SYN.) brutal, cruel, barbarous, ferocious, inhuman, merciless, malignant, ruthless, wild, uncivilized, uncultivated, rough, rugged, natural.
(ANT.) *compassionate, forbearing, benevolent, gentle, humane, kind, merciful, tame, cultivated.*
save (SYN.) defend, conserve, keep, maintain, guard, preserve, protect, safeguard, rescue, secure, uphold, spare, free, liberate, salvage.
(ANT.) *abolish, destroy, abandon, impair, injure.*
savory (SYN.) delectable, delightful, delicious, palatable, luscious, tasty.
(ANT.) *distasteful, nauseous, acrid, unpalatable, unsavory.*
say (SYN.) converse, articulate, declare, express, discourse, harangue, talk, speak, tell, utter, remark, state.
(ANT.) *hush, refrain, be silent.*
saying (SYN.) aphorism, adage, byword, maxim, proverb, motto.
scalding (SYN.) hot, scorching, burning, torrid, warm, fervent, ardent, fiery, impetuous, intense, pungent, peppery.
(ANT.) *cool, cold, freezing, passionless, frigid, bland.*
scale (SYN.) balance, proportion, ration, range, climb, mount.
scamp (SYN.) troublemaker, rascal.
scan (SYN.) examine, study.
scandal (SYN.) chagrin, humiliation, abashment, mortification, dishonor, disgrace, disrepute, odium.

(ANT.) *glory, honor, dignity, praise.*
scandalize *(SYN.)* asperse, defame, abuse, disparage, revile, vilify, traduce.
(ANT.) *honor, respect, cherish.*
scandalous *(SYN.)* disgraceful, discreditable, dishonorable, ignominious, disreputable, shameful.
(ANT.) *honorable, renowned, esteemed.*
scant *(SYN.)* succinct, summary, concise, terse, inadequate, deficient, insufficient, limited, lacking.
(ANT.) *ample, big, extended, abundant, protracted.*
scanty *(SYN.)* inadequate, scarce, sparse, insufficient, meager.
(ANT.) *abundant, plentiful.*
scarce *(SYN.)* occasional, choice, infrequent, exceptional, incomparable, precious, singular, rare, uncommon, unique, sparse, scanty.
(ANT.) *frequent, ordinary, usual, customary, abundant, numerous, worthless.*
scarcely *(SYN.)* barely, hardly.
scarcity *(SYN.)* want, insufficiency, lack, need, dearth.
(ANT.) *abundance.*
scare *(SYN.)* alarm, papal, affright, astound, dismay, daunt, frighten, intimidate, horrify, terrorize, shock.
(ANT.) *compose, reassure, soothe.*
scared *(SYN.)* apprehensive, afraid, fainthearted, frightened, fearful, timid.
(ANT.) *bold, assured, courageous, composed, sanguine.*
scarf *(SYN.)* kerchief.
scatter *(SYN.)* dispel, disperse, diffuse, disseminate, separate, dissipate, spread.
(ANT.) *assemble, accumulate, amass, gather, collect.*
scene *(SYN.)* exhibition, view, display.
scent *(SYN.)* fragrance, fume, aroma, incense, perfume, odor, redolence, stench, stink, smell.
schedule *(SYN.)* program, timetable.
scheme *(SYN.)* conspiracy, cabal, design, machination, intrigue, plot, plan, chart, stratage, diagram, graph, sketch, program, delineate, design, devise.
scheming *(SYN.)* create, design, intend, mean, draw, sketch, purpose.
scholar *(SYN.)* intellectual, pupil, learner, disciple, sage, student, savant, teacher, professor.
(ANT.) *dunce, idiot, fool, ignoramus.*
scholarly *(SYN.)* bookish, erudite, formal, academic, learned, pedantic,

theoretical, scholastic.
(ANT.) *practical, simple, ignorant.*
scholarship *(SYN.)* cognizance, erudition, apprehension, information, learning, knowledge, science, wisdom.
(ANT.) *illiteracy, stupidity, ignorance, misunderstanding.*
science *(SYN.)* enlightenment, discipline, knowledge, scholarship.
(ANT.) *superstition, ignorance.*
scoff *(SYN.)* ridicule, belittle, mock.
scold *(SYN.)* berate, blame, lecture, rate, rebuke, censure, admonish, reprehend, upbraid, reprimand, criticize.
(ANT.) *commend, praise, approve.*
scope *(SYN.)* area, compass, expanse, amount, extent, magnitude, degree, measure, reach, size, range.
scorch *(SYN.)* burn, char, consume, blaze, incinerate, sear, singe, scald.
(ANT.) *put out, quench, extinguish.*
score *(SYN.)* reckoning, tally, record, mark, rating.
scorn *(SYN.)* contumely, derision, contempt, detestation, hatred, disdain, despise, hate, spurn, refuse, reject.
(ANT.) *esteem, respect, awe.*
scornful *(SYN.)* disdainful, contemptuous.
scoundrel *(SYN.)* rogue, villain, cad.
scour *(SYN.)* wash, clean, scrub.
scourge *(SYN.)* affliction, lash, whip.
scowl *(SYN.)* glower, frown, glare.
scramble *(SYN.)* combine, mix, blend, hasten, clamber, climb.
scrap *(SYN.)* fragment, rag, apportionment, part, portion, piece, section, share, segment, crumb, junk.
(ANT.) *whole, entirety.*
scrape *(SYN.)* difficulty, dilemma, condition, fix, predicament, plight, situation, strait, scour, rub, scratch.
(ANT.) *comfort, ease, calmness.*
scratch *(SYN.)* scrape, scar.
scrawny *(SYN.)* gaunt, skinny, spindly.
(ANT.) *husky, burly.*
scream *(SYN.)* screech, shriek, yell.
screech *(SYN.)* yell, cry, scream, shriek.
screen *(SYN.)* partition, cover, separation, protection.
scrimp *(SYN.)* skimp, save, economize, conserve.
script *(SYN.)* penmanship, hand, handwriting, text, lines.
scrounge *(SYN.)* sponge, borrow.
scrub *(SYN.)* cleanse, mop, purify, clean,

sweep, wash, scour.

(ANT.) pollute, dirty, stain, sully.

scrupulous *(SYN.)* conscientious, candid, honest, honorable, fair, just sincere, truthful, upright, painstaking, critical.

(ANT.) dishonest, fraudulent, lying deceitful, tricky, careless.

scrutinize *(SYN.)* criticize, appraise, evaluate, examine, inspect, analyze.

(ANT.) neglect, overlook, approve.

scurrilous *(SYN.)* insulting, outrageous.

scurry *(SYN.)* scamper, scramble, hasten, hustle, hurry.

scuttle *(SYN.)* swamp, ditch, sink.

seal *(SYN.)* emblem, stamp, symbol, crest, signet.

search *(SYN.)* exploration, examination, investigation, inquiry, pursuit, quest, explore, scrutinize, investigate, hunt, probe, rummage, ransack, seek, scour.

(ANT.) resignation, abandonment.

searching *(SYN.)* inquiring, inquisitive, interrogative, nosy, curious, peeping, peering, snoopy, prying.

(ANT.) indifferent, unconcerned, incurious, uninterested.

season *(SYN.)* mature, perfect, ripen, develop, age.

seasoned *(SYN.)* veteran, skilled.

secede *(SYN.)* quit, withdraw, resign.

secluded *(SYN.)* deserted, desolate, isolated, alone, lonely, lone, unaided, only, sole, solitary, single, separate, isolated, sheltered, hidden, secret.

(ANT.) attended, surrounded, accompanied.

seclusion *(SYN.)* insulation, isolation, loneliness, alienation, quarantine, segregation, separation, retirement.

(ANT.) fellowship, union, connection, association, communion.

secondary *(SYN.)* minor, poorer, inferior, lower, subordinate.

(ANT.) greater, higher, superior.

secret *(SYN.)* concealed, hidden, latent, covert, private, surreptitious, unknown.

(ANT.) disclosed, exposed, known, obvious, conspicuous, open, public.

secrete *(SYN.)* clothe, conceal, cover, cloak, curtain, envelop, disguise, hide, mask, guard, protect, shroud, veil.

(ANT.) divulge, reveal, expose, unveil.

sect *(SYN.)* segment, denomination, faction, group.

section *(SYN.)* district, country, domain, dominion, division, land, place,

province, territory, subdivision.

secular *(SYN.)* lay earthly, laic, mundane, temporal, profane, worldly, temporal.

(ANT.) religious, spiritual, unworldly, ecclesiastical.

secure *(SYN.)* certain, definite, fixed, assured, indubitable, positive, inevitable, undeniable, sure, unquestionable, firm,

(ANT.) probable, questionable, uncertain, doubtful, loose, endangered, free.

security *(SYN.)* bond, earnest, pawn, bail, guaranty, pledge, token, surety.

sedate *(SYN.)* controlled, serene, calm, composed, unruffled.

sediment *(SYN.)* residue, lees, dregs, grounds.

see *(SYN.)* contemplate, descry, behold, discern, espy, distinguish, glimpse, inspect, look at, observe, perceive, scan, watch, view, witness, regard, examine, study, notice, eye.

seek *(SYN.)* explore, hunt, examine, look, investigate, probe, ransack, search, scour, rummage, scrutinize.

seem *(SYN.)* look, appeal.

(ANT.) exist, be, disappear, withdraw, vanish.

segment *(SYN.)* apportionment, division, fragment, moiety, allotment, part, portion, piece, scrap, share, section, element, faction, ingredient, interest, side.

(ANT.) whole, entirety.

segregate *(SYN.)* exclude, separate.

(ANT.) include, combine.

seize *(SYN.)* check, detain, hinder, apprehend, arrest, obstruct, stop, restrain, withhold, grab, grasp, clutch.

(ANT.) free, liberate, release, activate, discharge, loosen.

seldom *(SYN.)* infrequently, scarcely, rarely.

select *(SYN.)* cull, opt, pick, choose, elect, prefer.

(ANT.) reject, refuse.

selection *(SYN.)* election, choice, alternative, option, preference.

self-denial *(SYN.)* abstinence, continence, abstention, forbearance, fasting, sobriety, moderation, temperance.

(ANT.) gluttony, excess, greed, intoxication, self-indulgence.

self-important *(SYN.)* egotistical, proud, conceited, egocentric.

self-indulgence *(SYN.)* egotism, narrowness, self-centeredness, self-seeking, stinginess, ungenerousness.

(ANT.) *charity, magnanimity, altruism, liberality.*

selfish *(SYN.)* illiberal, narrow, self-centered, self-seeking, mercenary, stingy, ungenerous, greedy, mean, miserly.

(ANT.) *charitable.*

self-satisfied *(SYN.)* smug, complacent.

sell *(SYN.)* market, retail, merchandise, vend, trade, barter.

send *(SYN.)* discharge, emit, dispatch, cast, propel, impel, throw, transmit, forward, ship, convey, mail.

(ANT.) *get, hold, retain, receive, bring.*

senescence *(SYN.)* dotage, senility, age, seniority.

(ANT.) *infancy, youth, childhood.*

senile *(SYN.)* antiquated, antique, aged, ancient, archaic, obsolete, old, elderly, old-fashioned, venerable.

(ANT.) *new, youthful, young, modern.*

senior *(SYN.)* superior, older, elder.

(ANT.) *minor, junior.*

sensation *(SYN.)* feeling, image, impression, apprehension, sense, sensibility, perception, sensitiveness.

(ANT.) *insensibility, torpor, stupor, apathy.*

sensational *(SYN.)* exciting, marvelous, superb, thrilling, startling, spectacular.

sense *(SYN.)* drift, connotation, acceptation, explanation, gist, implication, intent, import, interpretation, purport, meaning, purpose, signification, significance, sensation, perception.

sense *(SYN.)* perception, sensation, feeling, awareness, insight, consciousness, appreciate, discern, perceive.

senseless *(SYN.)* dense, dull, crass, brainless, dumb, obtuse, foolish, stupid.

(ANT.) *discerning, intelligent, alert, clever, bright.*

sensibility *(SYN.)* sensation, emotion, feeling, passion, tenderness, sentiment.

(ANT.) *coldness, imperturbability, anesthesia, insensibility, fact.*

sensible *(SYN.)* apprehensible, perceptible, appreciable, alive, aware, awake, cognizant, comprehending, perceiving, conscious, sentient, intelligent, discreet, practical, judicious, prudent, sagacious, reasonable, sage, sober, wise, sound.

(ANT.) *impalpable, imperceptible, absurd, stupid, unaware, foolish.*

sensitive *(SYN.)* perceptive, prone, impressionable, responsive, susceptible,

sentient, tender, sore, delicate, tender, tense, touchy, nervous, keen.

(ANT.) *dull, hard, callous, insensitive.*

sensual *(SYN.)* lascivious, earthy, lecherous, carnal, sensory, voluptuous, wanton, erotic, lustful, sexual, indecent.

(ANT.) *chaste, ascetic, abstemious, virtuous, continent.*

sentence *(SYN.)* convict, condemn.

(ANT.) *acquit, pardon, absolve acquit.*

sentiment *(SYN.)* affection, emotion, sensation, feeling, sensibility, passion, tenderness, impression, opinion, attitude.

(ANT.) *coldness, imperturbability, anesthesia, insensibility, fact.*

sentimental *(SYN.)* extravagant, fanciful, fantastic, dreamy, fictitious, idealistic, ideal, maudlin, imaginative, mawkish, poetic, romantic, picturesque.

(ANT.) *literal, practical, prosaic.*

separate *(SYN.)* part sever, sunder, divide, allot, dispense, share, distribute, disconnect, split, isolate, segregate, different, distinct, independent.

(ANT.) *convene, join, gather, combine.*

separation *(SYN.)* insulation, isolation, loneliness, alienation, quarantine, seclusion, retirement, solitude, segregation, withdrawal.

(ANT.) *communion, fellowship, union, association, connection.*

sequence *(SYN.)* chain, graduation, order, progression, arrangement, following, series, succession, train, string.

serene *(SYN.)* composed, imperturbable, calm, dispassionate, pacific, placid, peaceful, quiet. tranquil, still, undisturbed, unruffled.

(ANT.) *frantic, turbulent, wild, excited, stormy, agitated, turbulent.*

serenity *(SYN.)* calmness, hush, calm, quiet, peace, quiescence, quietude, rest, repose, stillness, silence, tranquillity.

(ANT.) *tumult, excitement, noise, agitation, disturbance.*

series *(ANT.)* following, chain, arrangement, graduation, progression, order, sequence, train, string.

serious *(SYN.)* important, momentous, great, earnest, grave, sedate, sober, staid, alarming, solemn, critical, dangerous, risky, solemn.

(ANT.) *trivial, informal, relaxed, small.*

servant *(SYN.)* attendant, butler, domestic, valet, manservant, maid.

serve (SYN.) assist, attend, help, succor, advance, benefit, forward, answer, promote, content, satisfy, suffice, supply, distribute, wait on, aid.
(ANT.) command, direct, dictate, rule.

service (SYN.) advantage, account, avail, benefit, behalf, favor, good, gain, profit, interest.
(ANT.) distress, calamity, trouble, handicap.

serviceable (SYN.) beneficial, good, helpful, advantageous, profitable, salutary, wholesome, useful.
(ANT.) destructive, deleterious, detrimental, injurious, harmful.

servile (SYN.) base, contemptible, despicable, abject, groveling, dishonorable, ignominious, ignoble, lowly, low, menial, mean, sordid, vulgar, vile.
(ANT.) honored, exalted, lofty, esteemed, righteous, noble.

servitude (SYN.) confinement, captivity, bondage, imprisonment, slavery.
(ANT.) liberation, freedom.

set (SYN.) deposit, dispose, lay, arrange, place, put, position, pose, station, appoint, fix, assign, settle, establish.
(ANT.) mislay, misplace, disturb, remove, disarrange.

settle (SYN.) close, conclude, adjudicate, decide, end, resolve, agree upon, establish, satisfy, pay, lodge, locate, reside, determine, abide, terminate.
(ANT.) suspend, hesitate, doubt, vacillate, waver.

settlement (SYN.) completion, close, end, finale, issue, conclusion, termination, deduction, decision, inference.
(ANT.) commencement, prelude, start, inception, beginning.

sever (SYN.) part, divide, sunder, split, cut, separate.
(ANT.) convene, connect, gather, join, unite, combine.

several (SYN.) some, few, a handful.

severe (SYN.) arduous, distressing, acute, exacting, hard, harsh, intense, relentless, rigorous, sharp, stern, rigid, stringent, strict, cruel, firm, unyielding, unmitigated, difficult, unpleasant, dangerous, violent.
(ANT.) genial, indulgent, lenient, yielding, merciful, considerate.

sew (SYN.) mend, patch, fix, stitch, refit, restore, repair.
(ANT.) destroy, hurt, deface, injure.

shabby (SYN.) indigent, impecunious, needy, penniless, worn, ragged, destitute, poor, threadbare, deficient, inferior, scanty.
(ANT.) rich, wealthy, ample, affluent, opulent, right, sufficient, good.

shack (SYN.) hovel, hut, shanty, shed.

shackle (SYN.) chain, fetter, handcuff.

shade (SYN.) complexion, dye, hue, paint, color, stain, pigment, darkness, shadow, tincture, dusk, gloom, blacken, darken, conceal, screen, tint, tinge.
(ANT.) transparency, paleness.

shadowy (SYN.) dark, dim, gloomy, murky, black, obscure, dusky, unilluminated, dismal, evil, gloomy, sinister, indistinct, hidden, vague, undefined, wicked, indefinite, mystic, secret, occult.
(ANT.) bright, clear, light, pleasant, lucid.

shady (SYN.) shifty, shaded, questionable, doubtful, devious.

shaggy (SYN.) hairy, unkempt, uncombed, woolly.

shake (SYN.) flutter, jar, jolt, quake, agitate, quiver, shiver, shudder, rock, totter, sway, tremble, vibrate, waver.

shaky (SYN.) questionable, uncertain, iffy, faltering, unsteady.
(ANT.) sure, definite, positive, certain.

shallow (SYN.) exterior, cursory, flimsy, frivolous, slight, imperfect, superficial.
(ANT.) complete, deep, abstruse, profound, thorough.

sham (SYN.) affect, act, feign, assume, pretend, simulate, profess.
(ANT.) exhibit, display, reveal, expose.

shame (SYN.) chagrin, humiliation, abashment, disgrace, mortification, dishonor, ignominy, embarrassment, disrepute, odium mortify, humiliate, abash, humble, opprobrium, scandal.
(ANT.) pride, glory, praise, honor.

shameful (SYN.) disgraceful, dishonorable, disreputable, discreditable, humiliating, ignominious, scandalous.
(ANT.) honorable, renowned, respectable, esteemed.

shameless (SYN.) unembarrassed, unashamed, brazen, bold, impudent.
(ANT.) demure, modest.

shape (SYN.) create, construct, forge, fashion, form, make, produce, mold, constitute, compose, arrange, combine, organize, frame, outline, figure, invent, appearance, pattern, cast, model.

devise.

(ANT.) disfigure, misshape, dismantle, wreck.

shapeless (SYN.) rough, amorphous, vague.

shapely (SYN.) attractive, well-formed, curvy, alluring.

(ANT.) shapeless.

share (SYN.) parcel, bit, part, division, portion, ration, piece, fragment, allotment, partake, apportion, participate, divide, section.

(ANT.) whole.

shared (SYN.) joint, common, reciprocal, correlative, mutual.

(ANT.) unrequited, dissociated.

sharp (SYN.) biting, pointed, cunning, acute, keen, rough, fine, cutting, shrill, cutting, pungent, witty, acrid, blunt, steep, shrewd.

(ANT.) gentle, bland, shallow, smooth, blunt.

sharpen (SYN.) whet, hone, strop.

shatter (SYN.) crack, rend, break, pound, smash, burst, demolish, shiver, infringe.

(ANT.) renovate, join, repair, mend.

shattered (SYN.) fractured, destroyed, reduced, separated, broken, smashed, flattened, rent, wrecked.

(ANT.) united, integral, whole.

shawl (SYN.) stole, scarf.

sheepish (SYN.) coy, embarrassed, shy, humble, abashed, diffident, timid, modest, timorous.

(ANT.) daring, outgoing, adventurous, gregarious.

sheer (SYN.) thin, transparent, clear, simple, utter, absolute, abrupt, steep, see-through.

sheet (SYN.) leaf, layer, coating, film.

shelter (SYN.) retreat, safety, cover, asylum, protection, sanctuary, harbor, guard, haven, security.

(ANT.) unveil, expose, bare, reveal.

shield (SYN.) envelop, cover, clothe, curtain, protest, protection, cloak, guard, conceal, defense, shelter, hide, screen, veil, shroud.

(ANT.) unveil, divulge, reveal, bare.

shift (SYN.) move, modify, transfer, substitute, vary, change, alter, spell, turn, transfigure.

(ANT.) settle, establish, stabilize.

shifting (SYN.) wavering, inconstant, changeable, fitful, variable, fickle.

(ANT.) uniform, stable, unchanging.

shiftless (SYN.) idle, lazy, slothful.

(ANT.) energetic.

shifty (SYN.) shrewd, crafty, tricky.

shilly-shally (SYN.) fluctuate, waver, hesitate, vacillate.

shimmer (SYN.) glimmer, shine, gleam.

(ANT.) dull.

shine (SYN.) flicker, glisten, glow, blaze, glare, flash, beam, shimmer, glimmer, radiate, brush, polish, twinkle, buff, luster, gloss, scintillate, radiance, gleam.

shining (SYN.) dazzling, illustrious, showy, superb, brilliant, effulgent, magnificent, splendid, bright.

(ANT.) ordinary, dull, unimpressive.

shiny (SYN.) bright, glossy, polished, glistening.

(ANT.) lusterless, dull.

shipshape (SYN.) clean, neat.

(ANT.) sloppy, messy.

shiver (SYN.) quiver, quake, quaver, tremble, shudder, shake, break, shatter.

shock (SYN.) disconcert, astonish, surprise, astound, amaze, clash, disturbance, bewilder, outrage, horrify, revolt, agitation, stagger, blow, impact, collision, surprise, startle, upset, stun.

(ANT.) prepare, caution, admonish.

shocking (SYN.) hideous, frightful, severe, appalling, horrible, awful, terrible, dire, fearful.

(ANT.) safe, happy, secure, joyous.

shore (SYN.) seaside, beach, coast.

(ANT.) inland.

short (SYN.) abrupt, squat, concise, brief, low, curtailed, dumpy, terse, inadequate, succinct, dwarfed, small, abbreviated, lacking, abridge, condensed, undersized, slight, little.

(ANT.) extended, ample, protracted.

shortage (SYN.) deficiency, deficit, shortfall.

(ANT.) surplus, enough.

shortcoming (SYN.) error, vice, blemish, failure, flaw, omission, failing.

(ANT.) perfection, completeness.

shorten (SYN.) curtail, limit, cut, abbreviate, reduce, abridge, lessen, restrict.

(ANT.) lengthen, elongate.

shortening (SYN.) reduction, abridgment, abbreviation.

(ANT.) enlargement, amplification.

short-handed (SYN.) understaffed.

shortly (SYN.) soon, directly, presently.

shortsighted (SYN.) myopic, nearsighted,

unimaginative, unthinking, thoughtless.

shout (*SYN.*) ejaculate, cry, yell, roar, vociferate, bellow, exclaim.

(*ANT.*) *whisper, intimate.*

shove (*SYN.*) propel, drive, urge, crowd, jostle, force, push, promote.

(*ANT.*) *retreat, falter, oppose, drag, halt.*

shovel (*SYN.*) spade.

show (*SYN.*) flourish, parade, point, reveal, explain, array, movie, production, display, exhibit, note, spectacle, demonstrate, entertainment, tell, usher, guide, prove, indicate, present, lead, demonstration.

showy (*SYN.*) ceremonious, stagy, affected, theatrical, artificial.

(*ANT.*) *unaffected, modest, unemotional, subdued.*

shred (*SYN.*) particle, speck, iota, mite, bit, smidgen, tear, slit, cleave, rip, disunite, wound, rend, mince, tatter, lacerate.

(*ANT.*) *bulk, unite, quantity, mend, aggregate, repair.*

shrewd (*SYN.*) cunning, covert, artful, stealthy, foxy, astute, ingenious, guileful, crafty, sly, surreptitious, wily, tricky, clever, intelligent, clandestine.

(*ANT.*) *frank, sincere, candid, open.*

shriek (*SYN.*) screech, scream, howl, yell.

shrill (*SYN.*) keen, penetrating, sharp, acute, piercing, severe.

(*ANT.*) *gentle, bland, shallow.*

shrink (*SYN.*) diminish, shrivel, dwindle.

shrivel (*SYN.*) wizen, waste, droop, decline, sink, dry, languish, wither.

(*ANT.*) *renew, refresh, revive, rejuvenate.*

shun (*SYN.*) escape, avert, forestall, avoid, forbear, evade, ward, elude, dodge, free.

(*ANT.*) *encounter, confront, meet.*

shut (*SYN.*) seal, finish, stop, close, terminate, conclude, clog, end, obstruct.

(*ANT.*) *begin, open, start, unbar, inaugurate, unlock, commence.*

shy (*SYN.*) reserved, fearful, bashful, retiring, cautious, demure, timid, shrinking, wary, chary.

(*ANT.*) *brazen, bold, immodest, self-confident, audacious.*

sick (*SYN.*) ill, morbid, ailing, unhealthy, diseased, unwell, infirm.

(*ANT.*) *sound, well, robust, strong.*

sickness (*SYN.*) illness, ailment, disease, complaint, disorder.

(*ANT.*) *soundness, healthiness, vigor.*

side (*SYN.*) surface, face, foe, opponent, rival, indirect, secondary, unimportant.

siege (*SYN.*) blockade.

sieve (*SYN.*) screen, strainer, riddle, colander.

sight (*SYN.*) eyesight, vision, scene, view, display, spectacle, eyesore.

sightless (*SYN.*) unmindful, oblivious, blind, unseeing, heedless, ignorant.

(*ANT.*) *sensible, discerning, aware, perceiving.*

sign (*SYN.*) omen, mark, emblem, token, suggestion, indication, clue, hint, approve, authorize, signal, gesture, symbol, portent.

signal (*SYN.*) beacon, sign, alarm.

significance (*SYN.*) connotation, drift, acceptation, explanation, implication, gist, importance, interpretation, intent, weight, meaning, purpose, purport, sense, signification.

significant (*SYN.*) grave, important, critical, material, indicative, meaningful, crucial, momentous, telling, vital, weighty.

(*ANT.*) *irrelevant, insignificant, meaningless, unimportant, negligible.*

signify (*SYN.*) designate, imply, denote, intimate, reveal, indicate, manifest, mean, communicate, show, specify.

(*ANT.*) *distract, divert, mislead, conceal, conceal.*

silence (*SYN.*) motionless, peaceful, placid, hushed, stillness, quiescent, still, soundlessness, quiet, tranquil, noiselessness, hush, muteness, undisturbed.

(*ANT.*) *strident, loud, racket, disturbed, clamor, agitated, perturbed.*

silent (*SYN.*) dumb, hushed, mute, calm, noiseless, quiet, peaceful, still, soundless, speechless, tranquil, uncommunicative, taciturn.

(*ANT.*) *communicative, loud, noisy, raucous, talkative, clamorous.*

silhouette (*SYN.*) contour, delineation, brief, draft, form, figure, outline, profile, plan, sketch.

silly (*SYN.*) asinine, brainless, crazy, absurd, foolish, irrational, witless, nonsensical, simple, ridiculous, stupid.

(*ANT.*) *sane, wise, judicious, prudent.*

similar (*SYN.*) alike, akin, allied, comparable, analogous, correlative, corresponding, correspondent, parallel, resembling, like.

(*ANT.*) *dissimilar, divergent, opposed,*

different, incongruous.

similarity *(SYN.)* likeness, parity, analogy, correspondence, resemblance, similitude.

(ANT.) distinction, variance, difference.

simple *(SYN.)* effortless, elementary, pure, easy, facile, mere, single, uncompounded, homely, humble, unmixed, plain, artless, naive, frank, natural, unsophisticated, open, asinine, foolish, credulous, silly.

(ANT.) artful, complex, intricate, adorned, wise.

simpleton *(SYN.)* idiot, fool, ignoramus.

simulate *(SYN.)* copy, counterfeit, duplicate, ape, imitate, impersonate, mock, mimic.

(ANT.) distort, diverge, alter, invent.

sin *(SYN.)* evil, crime, iniquity, transgress, guilt, offense, ungodliness, trespass, vice, transgression, wickedness, wrong.

(ANT.) purity, goodness, purity, virtue, righteousness.

sincere *(SYN.)* earnest, frank, heartfelt, genuine, candid, honest, open, true, straightforward, faithful, truthful, upright, trustworthy, unfeigned.

(ANT.) hypocritical, insincere, affected, dishonest, untruthful.

sincerity *(SYN.)* fairness, frankness, honesty, justice, candor, integrity, openness, responsibility, rectitude, uprightness.

(ANT.) deceit, dishonesty, cheating.

sinful *(SYN.)* bad, corrupt, dissolute, antisocial, immoral, licentious, profligate, evil, indecent, unprincipled, vicious.

(ANT.) pure, noble, virtuous.

sing *(SYN.)* chant, croon, hum, carol, intone, lilt, warble.

singe *(SYN.)* burn, char, consume, blaze, incinerate, scorch, sear, scald.

(ANT.) put out, quench, extinguish.

single *(SYN.)* individual, marked, particular, distinctive, separate, special, specific, lone, one, solitary, sole, unwed, unmarried, singular, unique.

(ANT.) ordinary, universal, general.

singular *(SYN.)* exceptional, eccentric, odd, peculiar, rate, extraordinary, strange, unusual, striking, characteristic, remarkable, rare, individual, distinctive, uncommon, special.

(ANT.) general, normal, ordinary.

sink *(SYN.)* diminish, droop, subside, hang, decline, fall, extend, downward, drop, descend.

(ANT.) mount, climb, soar, steady, arise.

sinless *(SYN.)* faultless, holy, immaculate, perfect, blameless, holy, consummate, ideal, excellent, superlative, supreme.

(ANT.) defective, faulty, blemished, imperfect.

sip *(SYN.)* drink, taste, swallow.

sire *(SYN.)* breed, create, father, engender, beget, generate, procreate, originate, produce, propagate.

(ANT.) destroy, ill, extinguish, murder, abort.

site *(SYN.)* place, position, location, situation, station, locality.

situation *(SYN.)* circumstance, plight, state, site, location, placement, locale, predicament, position, state, condition.

size *(SYN.)* bigness, bulk, dimensions, expanse, amplitude, measurement, area, extent, largeness, magnitude, mass, greatness, volume.

skeptic *(SYN.)* doubter, infidel, agnostic, deist, questioner, unbeliever.

(ANT.) believer, worshiper, adorer.

skepticism *(SYN.)* hesitation, questioning, wavering, doubting, distrust, mistrust, suspicion.

(ANT.) confidence, reliance, trust.

sketch *(SYN.)* draft, figure, form, outline, contour, delineation, drawing, picture, represent, silhouette, draw, profile.

sketchy *(SYN.)* indefinite, vague, incomplete, indistinct.

(ANT.) definite, detailed, complete.

skill *(SYN.)* cunning, deftness, dexterity, ability, adroitness, cleverness, talent, readiness, skillfulness.

(ANT.) ineptitude, inability.

skillful *(SYN.)* adept, clever, able, accomplished, competent, expert, ingenious, cunning, proficient, practiced, versed, skilled.

(ANT.) untrained, inept, clumsy, inexpert, bungling, awkward.

skimpy *(SYN.)* cheap, scanty, meager.

(ANT.) abundant, generous.

skin *(SYN.)* outside, covering, peel, rind, shell, pare.

skinny *(SYN.)* gaunt, thin, raw-boned.

(ANT.) fat, hefty, heavy.

skip *(SYN.)* drop, eliminate, ignore, exclude, cancel, delete, disregard, omit, overlook neglect, miss.

(ANT.) notice, introduce, include, insert.

skirmish *(SYN.)* brawl, battle, conflict, combat, dispute, encounter, contend, quarrel, squabble, scuffle, wrangle, struggle.

slack *(SYN.)* lax, limp, indefinite, free, disengaged, unbound, untied, unfastened, vague, dissolute, heedless, careless, unrestrained, limp, lazy, loose, inactive, sluggish, wanton.

(ANT.) restrained, tied, right, stiff, taunt, rigid, fast, inhibited.

slander *(SYN.)* libel, calumny, backbiting, aspersion, scandal, vilification.

(ANT.) praise, flattery, commendation, defense.

slang *(SYN.)* jargon, dialect.

slant *(SYN.)* disposition, inclination, bias, bent, partiality, slope, tilt, pitch, penchant, prejudice, proneness, proclivity, turn, incline, lean, tendency.

(ANT.) justice, fairness, impartiality, equity.

slash *(SYN.)* gash, cut, slit, lower, reduce.

slaughter *(SYN.)* butcher, kill, massacre, slay, butchering, killing.

slave *(SYN.)* bondservant, serf.

slavery *(SYN.)* captivity, imprisonment, serfdom, confinement, bondage, thralldom, servitude, enslavement.

(ANT.) freedom, liberation.

slay *(SYN.)* assassinate, kill, murder.

sleek *(SYN.)* smooth, polished, slick.

(ANT.) blunt, harsh, rough, rugged.

sleep *(SYN.)* drowse, nap, nod, catnap, repose, doze, rest, slumber, snooze.

sleepy *(SYN.)* tired, drowsy, nodding.

slender *(SYN.)* lank, lean, meager, emaciated, gaunt, scanty, rare, skinny, scrawny, slight, spare, trim, slim, tenuous, thin.

(ANT.) fat, broad, overweight, thick, wide, bulky.

slide *(SYN.)* glide, slip, skim, skid.

slight *(SYN.)* lank, lean, meager, emaciated, gaunt, fine, narrow, scanty, scrawny, skinny, sparse, small, rare, slender, spare, insignificant, tenuous, unimportant, slim, thin.

(ANT.) regard, notice, enormous, large, major, huge, include.

slim *(SYN.)* thin, slender, lank, slight, weak, insignificant, unimportant.

slip *(SYN.)* error, fault, inaccuracy, shift, err, slide, mistake, glide, blunder.

(ANT.) precision, truth, accuracy.

slipshod *(SYN.)* sloppy, careless.

(ANT.) careful.

slit *(SYN.)* slash, cut, tear, slot.

slogan *(SYN.)* catchword, motto.

slope *(SYN.)* incline, leaning, inclination, bending, slant.

sloth *(SYN.)* indolence, idleness, inactivity, inertia, supineness, sluggishness, torpidity.

(ANT.) alertness, assiduousness, diligence, activity.

slothful *(SYN.)* indolent, idle, inactive, lazy, inert, supine, sluggish, torpid.

(ANT.) alert, diligent, active, assiduous.

slovenly *(SYN.)* sloppy, bedraggled, unkempt, messy.

(ANT.) meticulous, neat.

slow *(SYN.)* deliberate, dull, delaying, dawdling, gradual, leisurely, tired, sluggish, unhurried, late, behindhand, delayed.

(ANT.) rapid, quick, swift, speedy, fast.

sluggish *(SYN.)* dull, deliberate, dawdling, delaying, laggard, gradual, leisurely, tired, slow, lethargic.

(ANT.) quick, rapid, fast, speedy, swift, energetic, vivacious.

slumber *(SYN.)* drowse, catnap, nod, doze, repose, sleep, rest, snooze.

slump *(SYN.)* drop, decline, descent.

sly *(SYN.)* covert, artful, astute, crafty, clandestine, foxy, furtive, cunning, insidious, guileful, stealthy, subtle, shrewd, tricky, surreptitious, underhand, wily, secretive.

(ANT.) sincere, ingenuous, open, candid.

small *(SYN.)* little, minute, petty, diminutive, puny, wee, tiny, trivial, slight, miniature.

(ANT.) immense, enormous, large, huge.

smart *(SYN.)* dexterous, quick, skillful, adroit, apt, clever, bright, witty, ingenious, sharp, intelligent.

(ANT.) foolish, stupid, unskilled, awkward, clumsy, bungling, slow, dumb.

smash *(SYN.)* burst, crush, demolish, destroy, break, crack, fracture, pound, fringe, rack, rupture, shatter, rend.

(ANT.) mend, renovate, restore, repair.

smear *(SYN.)* wipe, rub, spread.

smell *(SYN.)* fragrance, fume, odor, perfume, incense, aroma, fetidness, stench, stink, scent, sniff, detect, bouquet.

smidgen *(SYN.)* crumb, mite, small, bit, particle, shred, speck, scrap.

(ANT.) bulk, mass, quantity, aggregate.
smile grin.
(ANT.) frown.
smite *(SYN.)* knock, hit, dash, beat, belabor, buffet, pound, punch, pummel, thrash, thump, defeat, overthrow, overpower, subdue, vanquish, rout.
(ANT.) surrender, fail, defend, shield, stroke.
smooth *(SYN.)* polished, sleek, slick, glib, diplomatic, flat, level, plain, suave, urbane, even, unwrinkled.
(ANT.) rugged, harsh, rough, blunt, bluff, uneven.
smother *(SYN.)* suffocate, asphyxiate, stifle.
smutty *(SYN.)* disgusting, filthy, impure, coarse, dirty, lewd, offensive, obscene, pornographic.
(ANT.) modest, refined, decent, pure.
snag *(SYN.)* difficulty, bar, barrier, check, hindrance, obstruction.
(ANT.) assistance, help, encouragement.
snappish *(SYN.)* ill-natured, ill-tempered, fractious, irritable, fretful, peevish, testy, touchy, petulant.
(ANT.) good-tempered, pleasant, good-natured, affable, genial.
snappy *(SYN.)* quick, stylish, chic.
snare *(SYN.)* capture, catch, arrest, clutch, grasp, grip, lay, apprehend, seize, trap, net.
(ANT.) throw, release, lose, liberate.
snarl *(SYN.)* growl.
snatch *(SYN.)* grasp, seize, grab.
sneak *(SYN.)* steal, skulk, slink.
sneer *(SYN.)* fleer, flout, jeer, mock, gibe, deride, taunt, scoff, scorn.
(ANT.) laud, flatter, praise, compliment.
sneering *(SYN.)* derision, gibe, banter, jeering, mockery, raillery, sarcasm, ridicule, satire.
sniveling *(SYN.)* whimpering, sniffling, weepy, whining, blubbering.
snobbish *(SYN.)* uppity, conceited, snooty, snobby, snotty.
snoopy *(SYN.)* inquisitive, interrogative, curious, inquiring, meddling, peeping, prying, peering.
(ANT.) uninterested, incurious, unconcerned, indifferent.
snub *(SYN.)* rebuke, insult, slight.
snug *(SYN.)* constricted, close, contracted, compact, firm, narrow, taut, tense, stretched, tight, cozy, comfortable, sheltered.

(ANT.) loose, lax, slack, relaxed, open.
soak *(SYN.)* saturate, drench, steep, wet.
soar *(SYN.)* flutter, fly, flit, float, glide, sail, hover, mount.
(ANT.) plummet, sink, fall, descend.
sob *(SYN.)* weep, cry, lament.
sober *(SYN.)* sedate, serious, staid, earnest, grave, solemn, moderate.
(ANT.) ordinary, joyful, informal, boisterous, drunk, fuddled, inebriated.
sobriety *(SYN.)* forbearance, abstinence, abstention, self-denial, moderation, temperance.
(ANT.) self-indulgence, excess, intoxication.
social *(SYN.)* friendly, civil, gregarious, affable, communicative, hospitable, sociable, group, common, genial, polite.
(ANT.) inhospitable, hermitic, antisocial, disagreeable.
society *(SYN.)* nation, community, civilization, organization, club, association, fraternity, circle, association, company, companionship.
soft *(SYN.)* gentle, lenient, flexible, compassionate, malleable, meek, mellow, subdued, mild, tender, supple, yielding, pliable, elastic, pliant.
(ANT.) unyielding, rough, hard, tough, rigid.
soften *(SYN.)* assuage, diminish, abate, allay, alleviate, mitigate, relieve, soothe, solace.
(ANT.) irritate, increase, aggravate, agitate.
soil *(SYN.)* defile, discolor, spot, befoul, blemish, blight, stain, sully, earth, dirt, loam, dirty.
(ANT.) purify, honor, cleanse, bleach, decorate.
solace *(SYN.)* contentment, ease, enjoyment, comfort, consolation, relief, succor.
(ANT.) torture, torment, misery, affliction, discomfort.
sole *(SYN.)* isolated, desolate, deserted, secluded, unaided, lone, alone, only, single, solitary.
(ANT.) surrounded, accompanied, attended.
solemn *(SYN.)* ceremonious, imposing, formal, impressive, reverential, ritualistic, grave, sedate, earnest, sober, staid, serious, dignified.
(ANT.) ordinary, joyful, informal, boisterous, cheerful, gay, happy.

solicit *(SYN.)* beg, beseech, request, seek, pray.

solicitous *(SYN.)* anxious, concerned.

solicitude *(SYN.)* concern, worry, anxiety, care, attention, regard, vigilance, caution, wariness.
(ANT.) indifference, disregard, neglect, negligence.

solid *(SYN.)* hard, dense, compact, firm.
(ANT.) loose.

solitary *(SYN.)* isolated, alone, lonely, deserted, unaided, secluded, only, single, lone, sole.
(ANT.) surrounded, attended, accompanied.

solitude *(SYN.)* loneliness, privacy, refuge, retirement, seclusion, retreat, alienation, asylum, concealment.
(ANT.) publicity, exposure, notoriety.

solution *(SYN.)* explanation, answer.

solve *(SYN.)* explain, answer, unravel.

somatic *(SYN.)* corporeal, corporal, natural, material, bodily, physical.
(ANT.) spiritual, mental.

somber *(SYN.)* dismal, dark, bleak, doleful, cheerless, natural, physical, serious, sober, gloomy, grave.
(ANT.) lively, joyous, cheerful, happy.

sometimes *(SYN.)* occasionally.
(ANT.) invariably, always.

soon *(SYN.)* shortly, early, betimes, beforehand.
(ANT.) tardy, late, overdue, belated.

soothe *(SYN.)* encourage, console, solace, comfort, cheer, gladden, sympathize, calm, pacify.
(ANT.) dishearten, depress, antagonize, aggravate, disquiet, upset, unnerve.

soothing *(SYN.)* gentle, benign, docile, calm, mild, placid, peaceful, serene, soft, relaxed, tractable, tame.
(ANT.) violent, savage, fierce, harsh.

sophisticated *(SYN.)* cultured, worldly, blase, cultivated, urbane, cosmopolitan, suave, intricate, complex, advanced.
(ANT.) uncouth, ingenuous, simple, naive, crude.

sorcery *(SYN.)* enchantment, conjuring, art, charm, black, magic, voodoo, witchcraft, wizardry.

sordid *(SYN.)* vicious, odious, revolting, obscene, foul, loathsome, base, depraved, debased, vile, vulgar, abject, wicked, ignoble, despicable, mean, low, worthless, wretched, dirty, unclean.
(ANT.) upright, decent, honorable.

sore *(SYN.)* tender, sensitive, aching, hurting, painful.

sorrow *(SYN.)* grief, distress, heartache, anguish, misery, sadness, mourning, trial, tribulation, gloom, depression.
(ANT.) consolation, solace, joy, happiness, comfort.

sorrowful *(SYN.)* dismal, doleful, dejected, despondent, depressed, disconsolate, gloomy, melancholy, glum, moody, somber, sad, grave, aggrieved.
(ANT.) merry, happy, cheerful, joyous.

sorry *(SYN.)* hurt, pained, sorrowful, afflicted, grieved, contrite, repentant, paltry, poor, wretched, remorseful, mean, shabby, contemptible, worthless, vile, regretful, apologetic.
(ANT.) delighted, impenitent, cheerful, unrepentant, splendid.

sort *(SYN.)* class, stamp, category, description, nature, character, kind, type, variety.
(ANT.) peculiarity, deviation.

sound *(SYN.)* effective, logical, telling, binding, powerful, weighty, legal, strong, conclusive, valid.
(ANT.) weak, null, counterfeit.

sour *(SYN.)* glum, sullen, bitter, peevish, acid, rancid, tart, acrimonious, sharp, bad-tempered, unpleasant, cranky.
(ANT.) wholesome, kindly, genial, benevolent, sweet.

source *(SYN.)* birth, foundation, agent, determinant, reason, origin, cause, start, incentive, motive, spring, inducement, principle, beginning.
(ANT.) product, harvest, outcome, issue, consequence, end.

souvenir *(SYN.)* memento, monument, commemoration, remembrance.

sovereign *(SYN.)* monarch, king, emperor, queen, empress.

sovereignty *(SYN.)* command, influence, authority, predominance, control, sway.
(ANT.) debility, incapacity, disablement, ineptitude, impotence.

space *(SYN.)* room, area, location.

spacious *(SYN.)* capacious, large, vast, ample, extensive, wide, roomy, large.
(ANT.) limited, confined, narrow, small, cramped.

span *(SYN.)* spread, extent.

spare *(SYN.)* preserve, safeguard, uphold, conserve, protect, defend, rescue, reserve, additional, unoccupied.
(ANT.) impair, abolish, injure, abandon.

sparing *(SYN.)* economical, thrifty, frugal.
(ANT.) lavish.

sparkle *(SYN.)* gleam, glitter, twinkle, beam, glisten, radiate, shine, blaze.

spat *(SYN.)* quarrel, dispute, affray, wrangle, altercation.
(ANT.) peace, friendliness, agreement, reconciliation.

spawn *(SYN.)* yield, bear.

speak *(SYN.)* declare, express, say, articulate, harangue, converse, talk, utter.
(ANT.) refrain, hush, quiet.

special *(SYN.)* individual, uncommon, distinctive, peculiar, exceptional, unusual, extraordinary, different, particular.
(ANT.) general, widespread, broad, prevailing, average, ordinary.

specialist *(SYN.)* authority, expert.

species *(SYN.)* variety, type, kind, class, sort.

specific *(SYN.)* limited, characteristic, definite, peculiar, explicit, categorical, particular, distinct, precise.
(ANT.) generic, general, nonspecific.

specify *(SYN.)* name, call, mention, appoint, denominate, designate, define.
(ANT.) miscall, hint.

specimen *(SYN.)* prototype, example, sample, model, pattern, type.

speck *(SYN.)* scrap, jot, bit, mite, smidgen, crumb, iota, particle, spot.
(ANT.) quantity, bulk, aggregate.

spectacle *(SYN.)* demonstration, ostentation, movie, array, exhibition, show, display, performance, parade, splurge.

spectator *(SYN.)* viewer, observer.

speculate *(SYN.)* assume, deduce, surmise, apprehend, imagine, consider, view, think, guess, suppose, conjecture.
(ANT.) prove, demonstrate, conclude.

speech *(SYN.)* gossip, discourse, talk, chatter, lecture, conference, discussion, address, dialogue, articulation, accent.
(ANT.) silence, correspondence, writing, meditation.

speed *(SYN.)* forward, push, accelerate, hasten, rapidity, dispatch, swiftness.
(ANT.) impede, slow, block, retard.

spellbound *(SYN.)* fascinated, entranced, hypnotized, mesmerized, rapt.

spend *(SYN.)* pay, disburse, consume.
(ANT.) hoard, save.

spendthrift *(SYN.)* squanderer, profligate.

sphere *(SYN.)* globe, orb, ball, environment, area, domain.

spherical *(SYN.)* round, curved, globular.

spicy *(SYN.)* indecent, off-color, suggestive, indelicate.

spin *(SYN.)* revolve, turn, rotate, whirl, twirl, tell, narrate, relate.

spine *(SYN.)* vertebrae, backbone.

spineless *(SYN.)* weak, limp, cowardly.
(ANT.) brave, strong, courageous.

spirit *(SYN.)* courage, phantom, verve, fortitude, apparition, mood, soul, ghost.
(ANT.) listlessness, substance, languor.

spirited *(SYN.)* excited, animated, lively, active, vigorous, energetic.
(ANT.) indolent, lazy, sleepy.

spiritless *(SYN.)* gone, lifeless, departed, dead, insensible, deceased, unconscious.
(ANT.) stirring, alive, living.

spiritual *(SYN.)* sacred, unearthly, holy, divine, immaterial, supernatural.
(ANT.) material, physical, corporeal.

spite *(SYN.)* grudge, rancor, malice, animosity, malevolence, malignity.
(ANT.) kindness, toleration, affection.

spiteful *(SYN.)* vicious, disagreeable, surly, ill-natured.
(ANT.) pretty, beautiful, attractive, fair.

splendid *(SYN.)* glorious, illustrious, radiant, brilliant, showy, superb, bright.
(ANT.) ordinary, mediocre, dull.

splendor *(SYN.)* effulgence, radiance, brightness, luster, magnificence, display.
(ANT.) darkness, obscurity, dullness.

splinter *(SYN.)* fragment, piece, sliver, chip, shiver.

split *(SYN.)* rend, shred, cleave, disunite, sever, break, divide, opening, lacerate.
(ANT.) repair, unite, join, sew.

spoil *(SYN.)* rot, disintegrate, waste, decay, ruin, damage, mold, destroy.
(ANT.) luxuriate, grow, flourish.

spoken *(SYN.)* verbal, pronounced, articulated, vocal, uttered, oral.
(ANT.) written, documentary.

spokesman *(SYN.)* agent, representative.

spontaneous *(SYN.)* impulsive, voluntary, automatic, instinctive, willing, extemporaneous, natural, unconscious.
(ANT.) planned, rehearsed, forced, studied, prepared.

sport *(SYN.)* match, play, amusement, fun, pastime, entertainment, athletics.

sporting *(SYN.)* considerate, fair, sportsmanlike.

spot *(SYN.)* blemish, mark, stain, flaw, blot, location, place, site, splatter.

spotty (SYN.) erratic, uneven, irregular, inconsistent.
(ANT.) regular, even.
spout (SYN.) spurt, squirt, tube, nozzle.
spray (SYN.) splash, spatter, sprinkle.
spread (SYN.) unfold, distribute, open, disperse, unroll, unfurl, scatter, jelly.
(ANT.) shut, close, hide, conceal.
sprightly (SYN.) blithe, hopeful, vivacious, buoyant, lively, light, nimble.
(ANT.) hopeless, depressed, sullen, dejected, despondent.
spring (SYN.) commencement, foundation, start, beginning, inception, jump, cradle, begin, birth, bound, originate.
(ANT.) issue, product, end.
sprinkle (SYN.) strew, spread, scatter, rain.
spruce (SYN.) orderly, neat, trim, clear, nice.
(ANT.) unkempt, sloppy, dirty.
spry (SYN.) brisk, quick, agile, nimble, energetic, supple, alert, active, lively.
(ANT.) heavy, sluggish, inert, clumsy.
spur (SYN.) inducement, purpose, cause, motive, impulse, reason, incitement.
(ANT.) effort, action, result, attempt.
squabble (SYN.) bicker, debate, altercate, contend, discuss, argue, quarrel.
(ANT.) concede, agree, assent.
squalid (SYN.) base, indecent, grimy, dirty, pitiful, filthy, muddy, nasty.
(ANT.) wholesome, clean, pure.
squander (SYN.) scatter, lavish, consume, dissipate, misuse.
(ANT.) preserve, conserve, save, accumulate.
squeamish (SYN.) particular, careful.
stab (SYN.) stick, gore, pierce, knife, spear, bayonet.
stability (SYN.) steadiness, balance, proportion, composure, symmetry.
(ANT.) imbalance, fall, unsteadiness.
stable (SYN.) firm, enduring, constant, fixed, unwavering, steadfast, steady.
(ANT.) irresolute, variable, changeable.
stack (SYN.) mass, pile, mound, heap, accumulate.
staff (SYN.) pole, stick, club, personnel, crew, employees.
stage (SYN.) frame, platform, boards, theater, scaffold, period, phase, step, direct, produce, present.
stagger (SYN.) totter, sway, reel, vary, falter, alternate.
staid (SYN.) solemn, sedate, earnest, sober, grave.
(ANT.) joyful, informal, ordinary.
stain (SYN.) blight, dye, tint, befoul, spot, defile, mark, dishonor, disgrace, smirch, blot, tint, blemish, discolor, color, tinge.
(ANT.) honor, bleach, decorate, purify.
stair (SYN.) staircase, stairway, steps.
stake (SYN.) rod, pole, picket, post, pale, bet, wager, concern, interest.
stale (SYN.) tasteless, spoiled, old, inedible, dry, uninteresting, trite, flat, dull, vapid, insipid.
(ANT.) new, fresh, tasty.
stalk (SYN.) dog, follow, track, shadow, hunt.
stall (SYN.) hesitate, stop, delay, postpone.
stammer (SYN.) falter, stutter.
stamp (SYN.) crush, trample, imprint, mark, brand, block, seal, die.
stand (SYN.) tolerate, suffer, stay, stand up, endure, bear, abide, halt, arise, rise, remain, sustain, rest.
(ANT.) run, yield, advance.
standard (SYN.) law, proof, pennant, emblem, touchstone, measure, example, gauge, model, banner, symbol, test.
(ANT.) guess, chance, irregular, unusual, supposition.
standing (SYN.) rank, position, station, status.
standpoint (SYN.) position, viewpoint, attitude.
staple (SYN.) main, principal, chief, essential, necessary.
stare (SYN.) gaze.
stark (SYN.) utter, absolute, sheer, complete, rough, severe, harsh, grim.
start (SYN.) opening, source, commence, onset, surprise, shock, beginning, origin, begin, initiate, jerk, jump, advantage, lead, commencement, outset.
(ANT.) end, completion, termination, close.
startle (SYN.) astonish, disconcert, aback, alarm, shock, agitate, surprise, astound, amaze, stun.
(ANT.) caution, prepare, admonish, forewarn.
starved (SYN.) longing, voracious, hungry, craving, avid, famished.
(ANT.) satisfied, sated, gorged, full.
state (SYN.) circumstance, predicament, case, situation, condition, affirm, declare, express, nation, country, status,

assert, recite, tell, recount.

(ANT.) imply, conceal, retract.

stately *(SYN.)* lordly, elegant, regal, sovereign, impressive, magnificent, courtly, grand, imposing, majestic, noble, supreme, dignified.

(ANT.) low, common, mean, servile, humble, vulgar.

statement *(SYN.)* announcement, mention, allegation, declaration, thesis, assertion, report.

station *(SYN.)* post, depot, terminal, position, place.

statuesque *(SYN.)* imposing, stately, regal, majestic, dignified.

status *(SYN.)* place, caste, standing, condition, state, rank, position.

statute *(SYN.)* law, ruling, decree, rule.

(ANT.) intention, deliberation.

staunch *(SYN.)* faithful, true, constant, reliable, loyal, devoted.

(ANT.) treacherous, untrustworthy.

stay *(SYN.)* delay, continue, hinder, check, hold, hindrance, support, brace, line, rope, linger, sojourn, abide, halt, stand, rest, remain, tarry, arrest, wait.

(ANT.) hasten, progress, go, depart, advance, leave.

stead *(SYN.)* place.

steadfast *(SYN.)* solid, inflexible, constant, stable, unyielding, secure.

(ANT.) unstable, insecure, unsteady.

steadfastness *(SYN.)* persistence, industry, tenacity, constancy, persistency.

(ANT.) laziness, sloth, cessation.

steady *(SYN.)* regular, even, unremitting, stable, steadfast, firm, reliable, solid.

steal *(SYN.)* loot, rob, swipe, burglarize, pilfer, shoplift, embezzle, snitch.

(ANT.) restore, buy, return, refund.

stealthy *(SYN.)* sly, secret, furtive.

(ANT.) direct, open, obvious.

steep *(SYN.)* sharp, hilly, sheer, abrupt, perpendicular, precipitous.

(ANT.) gradual, level, flat.

steer *(SYN.)* manage, guide, conduct, lead, supervise, escort, navigate, drive, control, direct.

stem *(SYN.)* stalk, trunk, arise, check, stop, orginate, hinder.

stench *(SYN.)* odor, fetor, fetidness, stink, aroma, smell, fume, scent.

step *(SYN.)* stride, pace, stage, move, action, measure, come, go, walk.

stern *(SYN.)* harsh, rigid, exacting, rigorous, sharp, severe, strict, hard,

unyielding, unmitigated, stringent.

(ANT.) indulgent, forgiving, yielding, lenient, considerate.

stew *(SYN.)* ragout, goulash, boil, simmer.

stick *(SYN.)* stalk, twig, rod, staff, pole, pierce, spear, stab, puncture, gore, cling, adhere, hold, catch, abide, remain, persist.

stickler *(SYN.)* nitpicker, perfectionist, disciplinarian.

sticky *(SYN.)* tricky, delicate, awkward.

stiff *(SYN.)* severe, unbendable, unyielding, harsh, inflexible, unbending, rigid, firm, hard, solid, rigorous.

(ANT.) supple, yielding, compassionate, mild, lenient, resilient.

stifle *(SYN.)* choke, strangle, suffocate.

stigma *(SYN.)* trace, scar, blot, stain, mark, vestige.

still *(SYN.)* peaceful, undisturbed, but, mild, hushed, calm, patient, modest, nevertheless, motionless, meek, quiescent, stationary, besides, however, quiet, hush, tranquil, serene, placid.

(ANT.) agitated, perturbed, loud.

stimulate *(SYN.)* irritate, excite, arouse, disquiet, rouse, activate, urge, invigorate, animate, provoke.

(ANT.) quell, calm, quiet, allay.

stimulus *(SYN.)* motive, goad, arousal, provocation, encouragement.

(ANT.) discouragement, depressant.

stingy *(SYN.)* greedy, penurious, avaricious, mean, penny-pinching, cheap, selfish, miserly, tight, tightfisted.

(ANT.) munificent, generous, giving, extravagant, openhanded, bountiful.

stipend *(SYN.)* payment, earnings, salary, allowance, pay, compensation, wages.

(ANT.) gratuity, gift.

stipulate *(SYN.)* require, demand.

stir *(SYN.)* instigate, impel, push, agitate, induce, mix, rouse, move, propel.

(ANT.) halt, stop, deter.

stock *(SYN.)* hoard, store, strain, accumulation, supply, carry, keep, provision, fund, breed, sort.

(ANT.) sameness, likeness, homogeneity, uniformity.

stoical *(SYN.)* passive, forbearing, uncomplaining, composed, patient.

(ANT.) turbulent, chafing, hysterical.

stolid *(SYN.)* obtuse, unsharpened, dull, blunt, edgeless.

(ANT.) suave, tactful, polished, subtle.

stone *(SYN.)* pebble, gravel, rock.

stony *(SYN.)* insensitive, unsentimental, cold.

stoop *(SYN.)* bow, bend, lean, crouch.

stop *(SYN.)* terminate, check, abstain, hinder, arrest, close, bar, cork, halt, end, conclude, obstruct, finish, quit, pause, discontinue, stay, impede, cease. *(ANT.)* start, proceed, speed, begin.

store *(SYN.)* amass, hoard, collect, market, shop, reserve, supply, deposit, bank, save, accrue, increase, stock. *(ANT.)* dissipate, waste, disperse.

storm *(SYN.)* gale, tempest, tornado, thunderstorm, hurricane, rage, rant, assault, besiege.

stormy *(SYN.)* rough, inclement, windy, blustery, roaring, tempestuous. *(ANT.)* quiet, calm, tranquil, peaceful.

story *(SYN.)* yarn, novel, history, tale, falsehood, account, fable, anecdote, narrative, fabrication, lie, level, floor, fiction, report.

stout *(SYN.)* plump, obese, chubby, fat, paunchy, overweight, portly, heavy, sturdy, strong, pudgy, thickset. *(ANT.)* thin, slender, flimsy, gaunt, slim.

straight *(SYN.)* erect, honorable, square, just, direct, undeviating, unbent, right, upright, honest, uncurving, directly, n ral, correct, orderly, vertical. *(ANT.)* dishonest, bent, circuitous, twisted, crooked.

straightforward *(SYN.)* forthright, direct, open, candid, aboveboard. *(ANT.)* devious.

strain *(SYN.)* stock, kind, variety, stretch, breed, tighten, harm, injure, screen, filter, sprain, sort.

strainer *(SYN.)* colander, sieve, filter.

strait *(SYN.)* fix, situation, passage, condition, dilemma, channel, trouble, predicament, difficulty, distress, crisis. *(ANT.)* ease, calmness, satisfaction, comfort.

strange *(SYN.)* bizarre, peculiar, odd, abnormal, irregular, unusual, curious, uncommon, singular, extraordinary, foreign, eccentric, unfamiliar, queer. *(ANT.)* regular, common, familiar, conventional.

stranger *(SYN.)* foreigner, outsider, newcomer, alien, outlander, immigrant. *(ANT.)* friend, associate, acquaintance.

strap *(SYN.)* strip, belt, thong, band.

stratagem *(SYN.)* design, ruse, cabal, plot, machination, subterfuge, trick, wile, conspiracy.

strategy *(SYN.)* technique, management, tactics, approach.

stray *(SYN.)* ramble, rove, deviate, lost, strayed, wander, digress, roam, stroll. *(ANT.)* linger, stop, halt, settle.

stream *(SYN.)* issue, proceed, flow, come, abound, spout, run, brook.

street *(SYN.)* way, road, boulevard, avenue.

strength *(SYN.)* power, might, toughness, durability, lustiness, soundness, vigor, potency. *(ANT.)* weakness, frailty, feebleness.

strengthen *(SYN.)* verify, assure, confirm, fix, sanction, ratify, substantiate.

strenuous *(SYN.)* forceful, energetic, active, vigorous, determined.

stress *(SYN.)* urgency, press, emphasize, accentuate, accent, weight, strain, importance, compulsion, pressure. *(ANT.)* relaxation, lenience, ease.

stretch *(SYN.)* strain, expand, elongate, extend, lengthen, spread, distend, protract, distort. *(ANT.)* tighten, loosen, slacken, contract.

strict *(SYN.)* rough, stiff, stringent, harsh, unbending, severe, rigorous. *(ANT.)* easygoing, lenient, mild.

strife *(SYN.)* disagreement, conflict, discord, quarrel, difference, unrest. *(ANT.)* tranquillity, peace, concord.

strike *(SYN.)* pound, hit, smite, beat, assault, attack, affect, impress, overwhelm, sitdown, walkout, slowdown.

striking *(SYN.)* arresting, imposing, splendid, august, impressive, thrilling, stirring, awesome, aweinspiring. *(ANT.)* ordinary, unimpressive, commonplace, regular.

stringent *(SYN.)* harsh, rugged, grating, severe, gruff.

strip *(SYN.)* disrobe, undress, remove, uncover, peel, ribbon, band, piece.

stripped *(SYN.)* open, simple, bare, nude, uncovered, exposed, bald, plain, naked, barren, defenseless. *(ANT.)* protected, dressed, concealed.

strive *(SYN.)* aim, struggle, attempt, undertake, design, endeavor, try. *(ANT.)* omit, abandon, neglect, decline.

stroke *(SYN.)* rap, blow, tap, knock, feat, achievement, accomplishment, caress.

stroll *(SYN.)* amble, walk, ramble.

strong *(SYN.)* potent, hale, athletic,

mighty, sturdy, impregnable, resistant. *(ANT.) feeble, insipid, brittle, weak, bland, fragile.*

structure *(SYN.)* construction, framework, arrangement.

struggle *(SYN.)* fray, strive, fight, contest, battle, skirmish, oppose, clash. *(ANT.) peace, agreement, truce.*

stubborn *(SYN.)* obstinate, firm, determined, inflexible, obdurate, uncompromising, pigheaded, contumacious, rigid, unbending, intractable. *(ANT.) docile, yielding, amenable, submissive.*

student *(SYN.)* pupil, observer, disciple, scholar, learner.

studio *(SYN.)* workroom, workshop.

study *(SYN.)* weigh, muse, master, contemplate, reflect, examination, examine.

stuff *(SYN.)* thing, subject, material, theme, matter, substance, fill, ram, cram, pack, textile, cloth, topic. *(ANT.) spirit, immateriality.*

stumble *(SYN.)* sink, collapse, tumble, drop, topple, lurch, trip, fall. *(ANT.) steady, climb, soar, arise.*

stun *(SYN.)* shock, knock out, dumbfound, take, amaze, alarm. *(ANT.) forewarn, caution, prepare.*

stunning *(SYN.)* brilliant, dazzling, exquisite, ravishing. *(ANT.) drab, ugly.*

stunt *(SYN.)* check, restrict, hinder.

stupid *(SYN.)* dull, obtuse, half-witted, brainless, foolish, dumb, witless, idiotic. *(ANT.) smart, intelligent, clever, quick, bright, alert, discerning.*

stupor *(SYN.)* lethargy, torpor, daze, languor, drowsiness, numbness. *(ANT.) wakefulness, liveliness, activity.*

sturdy *(SYN.)* hale, strong, rugged, stout, mighty, enduring, hardy, well-built. *(ANT.) fragile, brittle, insipid, delicate.*

style *(SYN.)* sort, type, kind, chic, smartness, elegance.

subdue *(SYN.)* crush, overcome, rout, beat, reduce, lower, defeat, vanquish. *(ANT.) retreat, cede, surrender.*

subject *(SYN.)* subordinate, theme, case, topic, dependent, citizen, matter.

sublime *(SYN.)* lofty, raised, elevated, supreme, exalted, splendid, grand. *(ANT.) ordinary, vase, low, ridiculous.*

submerge *(SYN.)* submerse, dunk, sink, dip, immerse, engage, douse, engross. *(ANT.) surface, rise, uplift, elevate.*

submissive *(SYN.)* deferential, yielding, dutiful, compliant. *(ANT.) rebellious, intractable, insubordinate.*

submit *(SYN.)* quit, resign, waive, yield, tender, offer, abdicate, cede, surrender. *(ANT.) fight, oppose, resist, struggle, deny, refuse.*

subordinate *(SYN.)* demean, reduce, inferior, assistant, citizen, liegeman. *(ANT.) superior.*

subsequent *(SYN.)* later, following. *(ANT.) preceding, previous.*

subside *(SYN.)* decrease, lower, sink, droop, hang, collapse, downward. *(ANT.) mount, steady, arise, climb.*

subsidy *(SYN.)* support, aid, grant.

substance *(SYN.)* stuff, essence, importance, material, moment, matter. *(ANT.) spirit, immaterial.*

substantial *(SYN.)* large, considerable, sizable, actual, real, tangible, influential. *(ANT.) unimportant, trivial.*

substantiate *(SYN.)* strengthen, corroborate, confirm.

substitute *(SYN.)* proxy, expedient, deputy, makeshift, replacement, alternate, lieutenant, representative, surrogate, displace, exchange, equivalent. *(ANT.) sovereign, master, head.*

substitution *(SYN.)* change, mutation, vicissitude, alteration, modification. *(ANT.) uniformity, monotony.*

subterfuge *(SYN.)* pretext, excuse, cloak, simulation, disguise, garb, pretension. *(ANT.) reality, truth, actuality, sincerity.*

subtle *(SYN.)* suggestive, indirect. *(ANT.) overt, obvious.*

subtract *(SYN.)* decrease, reduce, curtail, deduct, diminish, remove, lessen. *(ANT.) expand, increase, add, enlarge, grow.*

succeed *(SYN.)* thrive, follow, replace, achieve, win, flourish, prevail, inherit. *(ANT.) flop, miscarry, anticipate, fail, precede.*

success *(SYN.)* advance, prosperity, luck. *(ANT.) failure.*

successful *(SYN.)* fortunate, favorable, lucky, triumphant.

succession *(SYN.)* chain, course, series, order, string, arrangement, progression, train, following.

successive *(SYN.)* serial, sequential.

succinct *(SYN.)* pithy, curt, brief, short, compendious, terse.

(ANT.) prolonged, extended, long, protracted.

succor (SYN.) ease, solace, comfort, enjoyment, consolation.

(ANT.) suffering, discomfort, torture, affliction, torment.

sudden (SYN.) rapid, swift, immediate, abrupt, unexpected, unforeseen, hasty.

(ANT.) slowly, anticipated.

suffer (SYN.) stand, experience, endure, bear, feel, allow, let, permit, sustain.

(ANT.) exclude, banish, overcome.

suffering (SYN.) distress, ache, anguish, pain, woe, misery, torment.

(ANT.) ease, relief, comfort.

sufficient (SYN.) fitting, enough, adequate, commensurate, satisfactory.

(ANT.) scant, deficient.

suffix (SYN.) ending.

(ANT.) prefix.

suggest (SYN.) propose, offer, refer, advise, hint, insinuate, recommend, allude.

(ANT.) dictate, declare, insist.

suggestion (SYN.) exhortation, recommendation, intelligence, caution, admonition, warning, advice.

suit (SYN.) conform, accommodate, fit.

(ANT.) misapply, disturb.

suitable (SYN.) welcome, agreeable, acceptable, gratifying.

(ANT.) offensive, disagreeable.

sullen (SYN.) moody, fretful, surly, crabbed, morose, dour.

(ANT.) merry, gay, pleasant, amiable.

sullen (SYN.) fretful, morose, crabbed, dismal, silent, sulky, bitter, sad, somber, glum, gloomy, dour, moody.

(ANT.) pleasant, joyous, amiable, merry.

sultry (SYN.) close, hot, stifling.

sum (SYN.) amount, total, aggregate, whole, increase, append, add.

(ANT.) sample, fraction, reduce, deduct.

summarize (SYN.) abstract, abridge.

(ANT.) restore, add, unite, return.

summary (SYN.) digest, outline, abstract, synopsis, concise, brief, short, compact.

summit (SYN.) peak, top, head, crest, zenith, apex, crown, pinnacle.

(ANT.) bottom, foundation, base, foot.

summon (SYN.) invoke, call, invite.

(ANT.) dismiss.

sundry (SYN.) miscellaneous, several, different, various, divers.

(ANT.) similar, identical, alike, same, congruous.

sunny (SYN.) cheery, cheerful, fair, joyful, happy, cloudless.

(ANT.) overcast, cloudy.

superannuated (SYN.) old, archaic, aged, senile, ancient, venerable, elderly.

(ANT.) youthful, modern, young.

superb (SYN.) splendid, wonderful, extraordinary, marvelous.

supercilious (SYN.) contemptuous, snobbish, overbearing, vainglorious, arrogant, haughty, stately.

(ANT.) meek, ashamed, lowly.

superficial (SYN.) flimsy, shallow, cursory, slight, exterior.

(ANT.) thorough, deep, - abstruse, profound.

superintend (SYN.) control, govern, rule, command, manage, direct, regulate.

(ANT.) ignore, follow, submit, abandon.

superintendence (SYN.) control, oversight, surveillance, management.

superintendent (SYN.) manager, supervisor, overseer, director, administrator.

superior (SYN.) greater, finer, better, employer, boss.

(ANT.) inferior.

superiority (SYN.) profit, mastery, advantage, good, service, edge, utility.

(ANT.) obstruction, harm, detriment, impediment.

superlative (SYN.) pure, consummate, sinless, blameless, holy, perfect, faultless, ideal, unqualified, immaculate.

(ANT.) lacking, defective, imperfect, deficient, blemished.

supernatural (SYN.) unearthly, preternatural, marvelous, miraculous.

(ANT.) plain, human, physical, common.

supervise (SYN.) rule, oversee, govern, command, direct, superintend, manage, control.

(ANT.) submit, forsake, abandon.

supervision (SYN.) oversight, inspection, surveillance, charge, management.

supervisor (SYN.) manager, boss, foreman, director.

supplant (SYN.) overturn, overcome.

(ANT.) uphold, conserve.

supple (SYN.) lithe, pliant, flexible, limber, elastic, pliable.

(ANT.) stiff, brittle, rigid, unbending.

supplement (SYN.) extension, complement, addition, extend, add.

supplicate (SYN.) beg, petition, solicit, adjure, beseech, entreat, ask, pray, crave.

(ANT.) cede, give, bestow, grant.

supplication (SYN.) invocation, plea, appeal, request, entreaty.

supply (SYN.) provide, inventory, hoard, reserve, store, accumulation, stock, furnish, endow, give.

support (SYN.) groundwork, aid, favor, base, prop, assistance, comfort, basis, succor, living, subsistence, encouragement, backing, livelihood, help, maintain.
(ANT.) discourage, abandon, oppose, opposition, attack.

supporter (SYN.) follower, devotee, adherent, henchman, attendant, disciple, votary.
(ANT.) master, head, chief.

suppose (SYN.) believe, presume, deduce, apprehend, think, assume, imagine, speculate, guess, conjecture.
(ANT.) prove, demonstrate, ascertain.

supposition (SYN.) theory, conjecture.
(ANT.) proof, fact.

suppress (SYN.) diminish, reduce, overpower, abate, lessen, decrease, subdue, lower.
(ANT.) revive, amplify, intensify, enlarge.

supremacy (SYN.) domination, predominance, ascendancy, sovereignty.

supreme (SYN.) greatest, best, highest, main, principal, cardinal, first, chief, foremost, paramount.
(ANT.) supplemental, minor, subsidiary, auxiliary.

sure (SYN.) confident, fixed, inevitable, certain, positive, trustworthy, reliable, unquestionable, convinced, steady, assured, unfailing, stable, firm, safe, solid, destined, fated, inevitable, indubitable.
(ANT.) probable, uncertain, doubtful.

surface (SYN.) outside, exterior, cover, covering.

surge (SYN.) heave, swell, grow.
(ANT.) wane, ebb, diminish.

surly (SYN.) disagreeable, hostile, unfriendly, ugly, antagonistic.

surmise (SYN.) judge, think, believe, assume, suppose, presume, guess, thought, suspect.

surname (SYN.) denomination, epithet, title, name, appellation, designation.

surpass (SYN.) pass, exceed, excel, outstrip, outdo.

surplus (SYN.) extravagance, intemperance, superabundance, excess, im-

moderation, remainder, extra, profusion, superfluity.
(ANT.) want, lack, dearth, paucity.

surprise (SYN.) miracle, prodigy, wonder, awe, phenomenon, marvel, bewilderment, wonderment, rarity.
(ANT.) expectation, triviality, indifference, familiarity.

surrender (SYN.) relinquish, resign, yield, abandon, sacrifice, submit, cede.
(ANT.) overcome, rout, conquer.

surreptitious (SYN.) sneaky, sneaking, underhead, sly, furtive. -
(ANT.) openhanded, open, straightforward.

surround (SYN.) confine, encompass, circle, encircle, girdle, fence, circumscribe, limit, envelop.
(ANT.) open, distend, expose, enlarge.

surveillance (SYN.) inspection, oversight, supervision, management, control.

survey (SYN.) scan, inspect, view, examine, inspection, examination.

survive (SYN.) live, remain, continue, persist.
(ANT.) die, fail, succumb.

suspect (SYN.) waver, disbelieve, presume, suppose, mistrust, distrust, question, suspected, assume, defendant, questionable, suspicious, doubt.
(ANT.) decide, believe, trust.

suspend (SYN.) delay, hang, withhold, interrupt, postpone, dangle, adjourn, poise, defer, swing.
(ANT.) persist, proceed, maintain.

suspicious (SYN.) suspecting, distrustful, doubtful, doubting, questioning, suspect, skeptical, unusual.

suspicion (SYN.) unbelief, distrust, suspense, uncertainty, doubt.
(ANT.) determination, conviction, faith, belief.

sustain (SYN.) bear, carry, undergo, foster, keep, prop, help, advocate, back, encourage, maintain, assist, suffer, approve, uphold, support.
(ANT.) discourage, betray, oppose, destroy.

sustenance (SYN.) fare, food, diet, rations, nutriment, edibles, victuals, repast, feed.
(ANT.) hunger, want, drink.

swallow (SYN.) gorge, gulp, eat, mouthful.

swallow up (SYN.) consume, absorb, engulf, assimilate.

(ANT.) *exude, dispense, expel, discharge.*

swamp *(SYN.)* fen, bog, marsh, quagmire, morass, flood, overcome, deluge.

swarm *(SYN.)* throng, horde, crowd.

swarthy *(SYN.)* sable, dark.

(ANT.) *bright, light.*

sway *(SYN.)* control, affect, stir, actuate, impel, impress, bend, wave, swing, persuade, influence.

swear *(SYN.)* declare, state, affirm, vouchsafe, curse, maintain.

(ANT.) *demur, oppose, deny, contradict.*

sweat *(SYN.)* perspiration, perspire.

sweeping *(SYN.)* extensive, wide, general, broad, tolerant, comprehensive, vast.

(ANT.) *restricted, confined.*

sweet *(SYN.)* engaging, luscious, pure, clean, fresh, melodious, winning, unsalted, pleasant, agreeable.

(ANT.) *bitter, harsh, nasty, irascible, discordant, irritable, acrid.*

swell *(SYN.)* increase, grow, expand, enlarge.

(ANT.) *diminish, shrink.*

swift *(SYN.)* quick, fast, fleet, speedy, rapid, expeditious.

swindle *(SYN.)* bilk, defraud, con, deceive, cheat, guile, imposture, deception, artifice, deceit, trick, chicanery.

(ANT.) *sincerity, honesty, fairness.*

swing *(SYN.)* rock, sway, wave.

switch *(SYN.)* shift, change, turn.

swoon *(SYN.)* faint.

symbol *(SYN.)* sign, character.

sympathetic *(SYN.)* considerate, compassionate, gentle, benevolent, good, tender, affable, merciful, thoughtful.

(ANT.) *unkind, merciless, unsympathetic, indifferent, intolerant, cruel.*

sympathize *(SYN.)* gladden, sheer, solace, comfort, encourage, soothe.

(ANT.) *depress, antagonize.*

sympathy *(SYN.)* compassion, agreement, tenderness, commiseration, pity.

(ANT.) *indifference, unconcern, antipathy, malevolence.*

symptom *(SYN.)* indication, sign.

synopsis *(SYN.)* outline, digest.

synthetic *(SYN.)* counterfeit, artificial, phony, unreal, bogus, sham.

(ANT.) *natural, true, genuine.*

system *(SYN.)* organization, procedure, regularity, arrangement, mode, order.

(ANT.) *confusion, chance, disorder.*

systematic *(SYN.)* orderly, organized.

(ANT.) *irregular, random.*

table *(SYN.)* catalog, list, schedule, postpone, chart, index, shelve, delay, put off.

tablet *(SYN.)* pad, notebook, capsule, sketchpad, pill, lozenge.

taboo *(SYN.)* banned, prohibited, forbidden, restriction.

(ANT.) *accepted, allowed, sanctioned.*

tacit *(SYN.)* understood, assumed, implied.

taciturn *(SYN.)* quiet, withdrawn, reserved.

tack *(SYN.)* add, join, attach, clasp, fasten.

tackle *(SYN.)* rigging, gear, apparatus, equipment, grab, seize, catch, down, throw, try, undertake.

tacky *(SYN.)* gummy, sticky, gooey.

tact *(SYN.)* dexterity, poise, diplomacy, judgment, savoir-faire, skill, finesse, sense, prudence, adroitness, address.

(ANT.) *incompetence, vulgarity, blunder, rudeness, awkwardness, insensitivity, grossness.*

tactful *(SYN.)* discreet, considerate, judicious, adroit, sensitive, diplomatic, skillful, discriminating, politic.

(ANT.) *coarse, gruff, tactless, boorish, unfeeling, churlish, rude.*

tactical *(SYN.)* foxy, cunning, proficient, deft, adroit, clever, expert.

(ANT.) *blundering, gauche, clumsy, inept.*

tactics *(SYN.)* plan, strategy, approach, maneuver, course, scheme.

tag *(SYN.)* sticker, label, mark, identification, marker, name.

tail *(SYN.)* rear, back, follow, end, shadow, pursue, trail, heel.

tailor *(SYN.)* modiste, couturier, modify, redo, shape, fashion.

taint *(SYN.)* spot, stain, tarnish, soil, mark, discolor.

(ANT.) *cleanse, disinfect, clean.*

tainted *(SYN.)* crooked, impure, vitiated, profligate, debased, spoiled, corrupted, depraved, dishonest, contaminated, putrid, unsound.

take *(SYN.)* accept, grasp, catch, confiscate, clutch, adopt, assume, receive, bring, attract, claim, necessitate, steal, ensnare, capture, demand, select, appropriate, obtain, captivate, hold, seize, win, escort, note, record, rob, shoplift, get, remove, gain, choose.

taking *(SYN.)* charming, captivating,

winning, attractive.

takeover *(SYN.)* revolution, merger, usurpation, confiscation.

tale *(SYN.)* falsehood, history, yarn, chronicle, account, fable, fiction, narration, story, narrative, anecdote.

talent *(SYN.)* capability, knack, skill, endowment, gift, cleverness, aptitude, ability, cleverness, genius.

(ANT.) ineptitude, incompetence, stupidity.

talented *(SYN.)* skillful, smart, adroit, dexterous, clever, apt, quick-witted, witty, ingenious.

(ANT.) dull, clumsy, awkward, unskilled, stupid, slow.

talk *(SYN.)* conversation, gossip, report, speech, communicate, discuss, confer, chatter, conference, preach, dialogue, reason, jabber, discourse, lecture, communication, consul, plead, argue, converse, rant, chat, mutter, speak, rangue, rumor, deliberate, discussion.

(ANT.) silence, correspondence, meditation, writing.

talkative *(SYN.)* glib, communicative, chattering, loquacious, voluble, garrulous, chatty.

(ANT.) uncommunicative, laconic, reticent, silent.

tall *(SYN.)* elevated, high, towering, big, lofty, imposing, gigantic.

(ANT.) tiny, low, short, small, stunted.

tally *(SYN.)* score, count, compute, reckon, calculate, estimate, list, figure, correspond, agree, match, check.

tame *(SYN.)* domesticated, dull, insipid, docile, broken, uninteresting, gentle, subdued, insipid, flat, unexciting, boring, empty, break, domesticate, mild, tedious, domestic, submissive.

(ANT.) spirited, savage, wild, exciting, animated, undomesticated.

tamper *(SYN.)* mix in, interrupt, interfere, meddle, interpose.

tang *(SYN.)* zest, sharpness, tartness, taste.

tangible *(SYN.)* material, sensible, palpable, corporeal, bodily.

(ANT.) metaphysical, mental, spiritual.

tangle *(SYN.)* confuse, knot, snarl, twist, ensnare, embroil, implicate.

tangy *(SYN.)* pungent, peppery, seasoned, sharp, tart.

tantalize *(SYN.)* tease, tempt, entice, titillate, stimulate, frustrate.

tantrum *(SYN.)* outburst, fit, fury, flare-up, conniption, rampage.

tap *(SYN.)* pat, rap, hit, strike, blow, faucet, spout, spigot, bunghole.

tape *(SYN.)* ribbon, strip, fasten, bandage, bind, record, tie.

taper *(SYN.)* narrow, candle, decrease, lessen.

tardy *(SYN.)* slow, delayed, overdue, late, belated.

(ANT.) prompt, timely, punctual, early.

target *(SYN.)* aim, goal, object, objective.

tariff *(SYN.)* duty, tax, levy, rate.

tarnish *(SYN.)* discolor, blight, defile, sully, spot, befoul, disgrace, stain.

(ANT.) honor, purify, cleanse, bleach, decorate, shine, gleam, sparkle.

tarry *(SYN.)* dawdle, loiter, linger, dally, remain, delay, procrastinate.

tart *(SYN.)* sour, acrid, pungent, acid, sharp, distasteful, bitter.

(ANT.) mellow, sweet, delicious, pleasant.

task *(SYN.)* work, job, undertaking, labor, chore, duty, stint.

taste *(SYN.)* tang, inclination, liking, sensibility, flavor, savor, try, sip, sample, zest, experience, undergo, appreciation, relish, discrimination, discernment, judgment.

(ANT.) indelicacy, disinclination, antipathy, insipidity.

tasteful *(SYN.)* elegant, choice, refined, suitable, artistic.

(ANT.) offensive, unbecoming.

tasteless *(SYN.)* flavorless, insipid, unpalatable, rude, unrefined, uncultivated, boorish, uninteresting.

tasty *(SYN.)* delectable, delicious, luscious, palatable, tempting.

tattered *(SYN.)* ragged, torn, shoddy, shabby, frazzled, frayed, tacky, seedy.

tattle *(SYN.)* inform, divulge, disclose, blab, reveal.

taunt *(SYN.)* tease, deride, flout, scoff, sneer, mock, annoy, pester, bother, ridicule, jeer.

(ANT.) praise, compliment, laud, flatter.

taunting *(SYN.)* ironic, caustic, cutting, sardonic, derisive, biting, acrimonious, sarcastic, satirical, sneering.

(ANT.) pleasant, agreeable, affable, amiable.

taut *(SYN.)* tight, constricted, firm, stretched, snug, tense, extended.

(ANT.) slack, loose, relaxed, open, lax.

tavern *(SYN.)* pub, bar, cocktail lounge.

tawdry *(SYN.)* pretentious, showy, vulgar, tasteless, sordid, garish.

tax *(SYN.)* duty, assessment, excise, levy, toll, burden, strain, tribute, tariff, assess, encumber, overload, impost, custom, exaction, rate. *(ANT.)* reward, gift, remuneration, wages.

taxi *(SYN.)* cab, taxicab.

teach *(SYN.)* inform, school, educate, train, inculcate, instruct, instill, tutor. *(ANT.)* misinform, misguide.

teacher *(SYN.)* tutor, instructor, professor, lecturer.

team *(SYN.)* company, band, party, crew, gang, group.

teamwork *(SYN.)* collaboration, cooperation.

tear *(SYN.)* rend, shred, sunder, cleave, rip, lacerate, teardrop, disunite, rend, divide, drop, wound, split, slit, sever. *(ANT.)* mend, repair, join, unite, sew.

tearful *(SYN.)* sad, weeping, crying, sobbing, weepy, lachrymose.

tease *(SYN.)* badger, harry, bother, irritate, nag, pester, taunt, vex, annoy, disturb, harass, worry, tantalize, plague, aggravate, provoke, torment. *(ANT.)* please, delight, soothe, comfort, gratify.

technical *(SYN.)* industrial, technological, specialized, mechanical.

technique *(SYN.)* system, method, routine, approach, procedure.

tedious *(SYN.)* boring, dilatory, humdrum, sluggish, monotonous, irksome, dreary, dull, tiring, burdensome, tiresome, wearisome, tardy. *(ANT.)* interesting, entertaining, engaging, exciting, amusing, quick.

teem *(SYN.)* abound, swarm.

teeming *(SYN.)* overflowing, bountiful, abundant, ample, profuse, plenteous, rich, copious. *(ANT.)* scant, scarce, deficient, insufficient.

teeter *(SYN.)* sway, hesitate, hem and haw, waver.

telecast *(SYN.)* broadcast.

televise *(SYN.)* telecast.

tell *(SYN.)* report, mention, state, betray, announce, recount, relate, narrate, rehearse, mention, utter, confess, disclose, direct, request, acquaint, instruct, notify, inform, discover, determine, reveal, divulge.

telling *(SYN.)* persuasive, convincing, forceful, effective.

telltale *(SYN.* revealing, informative, suggestive, meaningful.

temerity *(SYN.)* rashness, foolhardiness, audacity, boldness, recklessness, precipitancy. *(ANT.)* prudence, wariness, caution, hesitation, timidity.

temper *(SYN.)* fury, choler, exasperation, anger, passion, petulance, disposition, nature, rage, soothe, soften, wrath, indignation, irritation, pacify, animosity, mood, resentment. *(ANT.)* peace, self-control, forbearance, conciliation.

temperament *(SYN.)* humor, mood, temper, nature, disposition.

temperamental *(SYN.)* testy, moody, touchy, sensitive, irritable. *(ANT.)* calm, unruffled, serene.

temperance *(SYN.)* abstinence, sobriety, self-denial, forbearance, abstention. *(ANT.)* intoxication, excess, self-indulgence, gluttony, wantonness.

temperate *(SYN.)* controlled, moderate, cool, calm, restrained. *(ANT.)* excessive, extreme, prodigal.

tempest *(SYN.)* draft, squall, wind, blast, gust, storm, hurricane, commotion, tumult, zephyr. *(ANT.)* calm, tranquillity, peace.

tempo *(SYN.)* measure, beat, cadence, rhythm.

temporal *(SYN.)* mundane, earthly, lay, profane, worldly, terrestrial, laic. *(ANT.)* spiritual, ecclesiastical, unworldly, religious, heavenly.

temporary *(SYN.)* brief, momentary, shortlived, fleeting, ephemeral, passing, short, transient. *(ANT.)* lasting, permanent, immortal, everlasting, timeless, abiding.

tempt *(SYN.)* entice, allure, lure, attract, seduce, invite, magnetize.

tenacious *(SYN.)* persistent, determined, unchanging, unyielding.

tenable *(SYN.)* correct, practical, rational, reasonable, sensible, defensible.

tenacity *(SYN.)* perseverance, steadfastness, industry, constancy, persistence, pertinacity. *(ANT.)* laziness, rest, cessation, idleness, sloth.

tenant *(SYN.)* renter, lessee, lodger,

lease-holder, dweller, resident.

tend *(SYN.)* escort, follow, care for, lackey, watch, protect, take care of, attend, guard, serve.

tendency *(SYN.)* drift, inclination, proneness, leaning, bias, aim, leaning, disposition, predisposition, propensity, trend, impulse.
(ANT.) disinclination, aversion, deviation.

tender *(SYN.)* sympathetic, sore, sensitive, painful, gentle, meek, delicate, fragile, proffer, bland, mild, loving, offer, affectionate, soothing, propose, moderate, soft.
(ANT.) rough, severe, fierce, chewy, tough, cruel, unfeeling, harsh.

tenderfoot *(SYN.)* novice, apprentice, beginner, amateur.

tenderhearted *(SYN.)* kind, sympathetic, merciful, softhearted, understanding, sentimental, affectionate, gentle, sensitive.

tenderness *(SYN.)* attachment, kindness, love, affection, endearment.
(ANT.) repugnance, indifference, aversion, hatred, repulsive.

tenet *(SYN.)* dogma, belief, precept, doctrine, creed, opinion.
(ANT.) deed, conduct, practice, performance.

tense *(SYN.)* strained, stretched, excited, tight, nervous.
(ANT.) loose, placid, lax, relaxed.

tension *(SYN.)* stress, strain, pressure, anxiety, apprehension, distress.

tentative *(SYN.)* hypothetical, indefinite, probationary, conditional.

tenure *(SYN.)* administration, time, regime, term.

tepid *(SYN.)* temperate, mild, lukewarm.
(ANT.) boiling, scalding, passionate, hot.

term *(SYN.)* period, limit, time, boundary, duration, name, phrase, interval, session, semester, expression, word.

terminal *(SYN.)* eventual, final, concluding, decisive, ending, fatal, latest, last, ultimate, conclusive.
(ANT.) original, first, rudimentary, incipient, inaugural.

terminate *(SYN.)* close, end, finish, abolish, complete, cease, stop, conclude, expire, culminate.
(ANT.) establish, begin, initiate, start, commence.

terminology *(SYN.)* vocabulary, nomen-

clature, terms, phraseology.

terms *(SYN.)* stipulations, agreement, conditions, provisions.

terrible *(SYN.)* frightful, dire, awful, gruesome, horrible shocking, horrifying, terrifying, horrid, hideous, appalling, shocking.
(ANT.) secure, happy, joyous, pleasing, safe.

terrific *(SYN.)* superb, wonderful, glorious, great, magnificent, divine, colossal, sensational, marvelous.

terrify *(SYN.)* dismay, intimidate, startle, terrorize, appall, frighten, petrify, astound, alarm, affright, horrify, scare.
(ANT.) soothe, allay, reassure, compose, embolden.

territory *(SYN.)* dominion, province, quarter, section, country, division, region, domain, area, place, district.

terror *(SYN.)* fear, alarm, dismay, horror, dread, consternation, fright, panic.
(ANT.) calm, security, assurance, peace.

terse *(SYN.)* concise, incisive, succinct, summary, condensed, compact, neat, pithy, summary.
(ANT.) verbose, wordy, lengthy, prolix.

test *(SYN.)* exam, examination, trial, quiz, analyze, verify, validate.

testify *(SYN.)* depose, warrant, witness, state, attest, swear.

testimony *(SYN.)* evidence, attestation, declaration, proof, witness, confirmation.
(ANT.) refutation, argument, disproof, contradiction.

testy *(SYN.)* ill-natured, irritable, snappish, waspish, fractious, fretful, touchy, ill-tempered, peevish, petulant.
(ANT.) pleasant, affable, good-tempered, genial, good-natured.

tether *(SYN.)* tie, hamper, restraint, bridle.

text *(SYN.)* textbook, book, manual.

textile *(SYN.)* material, cloth, goods, fabric.

texture *(SYN.)* construction, structure, make-up, composition, grain, finish.

thankful *(SYN.)* obliged, grateful, appreciative.
(ANT.) thankless, ungrateful, resenting.

thaw *(SYN.)* liquefy, melt, dissolve.
(ANT.) solidify, freeze.

theater *(SYN.)* arena, playhouse, battlefield, stadium, hall.

theatrical *(SYN.)* ceremonious, melo-

dramatic, stagy, artificial, affected, dramatic, showy, dramatic, compelling.
(ANT.) unemotional, subdued, modest, unaffected.

theft (SYN.) larceny, robbery, stealing, plunder, burglary, pillage, thievery, depredation.

theme (SYN.) motive, topic, argument, subject, thesis, text, point, paper, essay, composition.

theoretical (SYN.) bookish, learned, scholarly, pedantic, academic, formal, erudite, scholastic.
(ANT.) practical, ignorant, common-sense, simple.

theory (SYN.) doctrine, guess, presupposition, postulate, assumption, hypothesis, speculation.
(ANT.) practice, verity, fact, proof.

therefore (SYN.) consequently, thence so, accordingly, hence, then.

thick (SYN.) compressed, heavy, compact, viscous, close, concentrated, crowded, syrupy, dense.
(ANT.) watery, slim, thin, sparse, dispersed, dissipated.

thief (SYN.) burglar, robber, criminal.

thin (SYN.) diluted, flimsy, lean, narrow, slender, spare, emaciated, diaphanous, gauzy, meager, slender, tenuous, slim, rare, sparse, scanty, lank, gossamer, scanty, slight.
(ANT.) fat, wide, broad, thick, bulky.

think (SYN.) picture, contemplate, ponder, esteem, intend, mean, imagine, deliberate, contemplate, recall, speculate, recollect, deem, apprehend, consider, devise, plan, judge, purpose, reflect, suppose, assume, meditate, muse.
(ANT.) forget, conjecture, guess.

thirst (SYN.) appetite, desire, craving, longing.

thirsty (SYN.) arid, dry, dehydrated, parched, craving, desirous.
(ANT.) satisfied.

thorn (SYN.) spine, barb, prickle, nettle, bramble.

thorough (SYN.) entire, complete, perfect, total, finished, unbroken, perfect, careful, thoroughgoing, consummate, undivided.
(ANT.) unfinished, careless, slapdash, imperfect, haphazard, lacking.

thoroughfare (SYN.) avenue, street, parkway, highway, boulevard.

(ANT.) byway.

though (SYN.) in any case, notwithstanding, however, nevertheless.

thought (SYN.) consideration, pensive, attentive, heedful, prudent, dreamy, reflective, introspective, meditation, notion, view, deliberation, sentiment, fancy, idea, impression, reasoning, contemplation, judgment, regard.
(ANT.) thoughtlessness.

thoughtful (SYN.) considerate, attentive, dreamy, pensive, provident, introspective, meditative, cautious, heedful, kind, courteous, friendly, pensive.
(ANT.) thoughtless, heedless, inconsiderate, rash, precipitous, selfish.

thoughtless (SYN.) inattentive, unconcerned, negligent, lax, desultory, inconsiderate, careless, imprudent, inaccurate, neglectful, indiscreet, remiss.
(ANT.) meticulous, accurate, nice, careful.

thrash (SYN.) whip, beat, defeat, flog, punish, flog, strap, thresh.

thread (SYN.) yarn, strand, filament, fiber, string, cord.

threadbare (SYN.) shabby, tacky, worn, ragged, frayed.

threat (SYN.) menace, warning, danger, hazard, jeopardy, omen.

threaten (SYN.) caution, warning, forewarn, menace, intimidate, loom.

threatening (SYN.) imminent, nigh, approaching, impending, overhanging, sinister, foreboding.
(ANT.) improbable, retreating, afar, distant, remote.

threshold (SYN.) edge, verge, start, beginning, doorsill, commencement.

thrift (SYN.) prudence, conservation, saving, economy.

thrifty (SYN.) saving, economical, sparing, frugal, provident, stingy, saving, parsimonious.
(ANT.) wasteful, spendthrift, intemperate, self-indulgent, extravagant.

thrill (SYN.) arouse, rouse, excite, stimulation, excitement, tingle.
(ANT.) bore.

thrive (SYN.) succeed, flourish, grow, prosper.
(ANT.) expire, fade, shrivel, die, fail, languish.

throb (SYN.) pound, pulsate, palpitate, beat, pulse.

throe (SYN.) pang, twinge, distress, suffering, pain, ache, grief, agony.

(ANT.) pleasure, relief, ease, solace, comfort.

throng (SYN.) masses, press, crowd, bevy, populace, swarm, rabble, horde, host, mass, teem, mob, multitude.

throttle (SYN.) smother, choke, strangle.

through (SYN.) completed, done, finished, over.

throughout (SYN.) all over, everywhere, during.

throw (SYN.) propel, cast, pitch, toss, hurl, send, thrust, fling.

(ANT.) retain, pull, draw, haul, hold

thrust (SYN.) jostle, push, promote, crowd, force, drive, hasten, push, press, shove, urge.

(ANT.) ignore, falter, retreat, drag, oppose, halt.

thug (SYN.) mobster, hoodlum, mugger, gangster, assassin, gunman.

thump (SYN.) blow, strike, knock, jab, poke, pound, beat, clout, bat, rap, bang.

thunderstruck (SYN.) amazed, astounded, astonished, awed, flabbergasted, surprised, dumbfounded, bewildered, spellbound.

thus (SYN.) hence, therefore, accordingly, so, consequently.

thwart (SYN.) defeat, frustrate, prevent, foil, stop, baffle, circumvent hinder, obstruct, disappoint, balk, outwit.

(ANT.) promote, accomplish, fulfill, help, further.

ticket (SYN.) stamp, label, tag, seal, token, pass, summons, certificate, ballot, sticker, slate, citation.

tickle (SYN.) delight, entertain, thrill, amuse, titillate, excite.

ticklish (SYN.) fragile, delicate, tough, difficult.

tidings (SYN.) message, report, information, word, intelligence, news.

tidy (SYN.) trim, clear, neat, precise, spruce, orderly, shipshape.

(ANT.) disheveled, unkempt, sloppy, dirty, slovenly.

tie (SYN.) bond, join, relationship, bind, restrict, fetter, connect, conjunction, association, alliance, union, fasten, engage, attach, restrain, oblige, link, affinity.

(ANT.) separation, disunion, unfasten, open, loose, untie, free, isolation.

tier (SYN.) line, row, level, deck, layer.

tiff (SYN.) bicker, squabble, argue, row, clash, dispute, altercation.

tight (SYN.) firm, taut, penny-pinching, constricted, snug, taut, parsimonious, secure, fast, strong, sealed, fastened, watertight, locked, close, compact, stingy.

(ANT.) slack, lax, open, relaxed, loose.

till (SYN.) plow, work, moneybox, depository, cultivate, vault.

tilt (SYN.) slant, slope, incline, tip, lean.

timber (SYN.) lumber, wood, logs.

time (SYN.) epoch, span, term, age, duration, interim, period, tempo, interval, space, spell, season.

timeless (SYN.) unending, lasting, perpetual, endless, immemorial.

(ANT.) temporary, mortal, temporal.

timely (SYN.) prompt, exact, punctual, ready, precise.

(ANT.) slow, dilatory, tardy, late.

timepiece (SYN.) clock, watch.

timetable (SYN.) list, schedule.

timid (SYN.) coy, humble, sheepish, abashed, embarrassed, modest, bashful, diffident, shamefaced, retiring, fearful, faint-hearted, shy, timorous.

(ANT.) gregarious, bold, daring, adventurous, fearless, outgoing.

tinge (SYN.) color, tint, dye, stain, flavor, imbue, season, impregnate.

tingle (SYN.) shiver, chime, prickle.

tinker (SYN.) potter, putter, fiddle with, dawdle, dally, dabble.

tinkle (SYN.) sound, peal, ring, jingle, chime, toll.

tint (SYN.) color, tinge, dye, stain, hue, tone, shade.

tiny (SYN.) minute, little, petty, wee, slight, diminutive, miniature, small, insignificant, trivial, puny.

(ANT.) huge, large, immense, big, enormous.

tip (SYN.) point, end, top, peak, upset, tilt, reward, gift, gratuity, clue, hint, suggestion, inkling.

tirade (SYN.) outburst, harangue, scolding.

tire (SYN.) jade, tucker, bore, weary, exhaust, weaken, wear out, fatigue.

(ANT.) restore, revive, exhilarate, amuse, invigorate, refresh.

tired (SYN.) weary, exhausted, fatigued, run-down, sleepy, faint, spent, wearied, worn, jaded.

(ANT.) rested, fresh, hearty, invigorated, energetic, tireless, eager.

tireless (SYN.) active, enthusiastic, energetic, strenuous.
(ANT.) exhausted, wearied, fatigued.
tiresome (SYN.) dull, boring, monotonous, tedious.
(ANT.) interesting.
titan SYN.) colossus, powerhouse, mammoth.
title (SYN.) epithet, privilege, name, appellation, claim, denomination, due, heading, ownership, right, deed, designation.
toast (SYN.) salutation, pledge, celebration.
toddle (SYN.) stumble, wobble, shuffle.
toil (SYN.) labor, drudgery, work, travail, performance, business, achievement, employment, occupation, slave, sweat, effort.
(ANT.) recreation, ease, vacation, relax, loll, play, leisure, repose.
token (SYN.) mark, sign, sample, indication, evidence, symbol.
tolerant (SYN.) extensive, vast, considerate, broad, patient, large, sweeping, liberal, wide.
(ANT.) intolerant, bigoted, biased, restricted, narrow, confined.
tolerate (SYN.) endure, allow, bear, authorize, permit, brook, stand, abide.
(ANT.) forbid, protest, prohibit, discriminating, unreasonable.
toll (SYN.) impost, burden, rate, assessment, duty, custom, excise, tribute, levy, burden, strain.
(ANT.) reward, wages, gift, remuneration.
tomb (SYN.) vault, monument, catacomb, grave, mausoleum.
tone (SYN.) noise, sound, mood, manner, expression, cadence.
tongs (SYN.) tweezers, hook, grapnel, forceps.
tongue (SYN.) diction, lingo, cant, jargon, vernacular, dialect, idiom, speech, phraseology.
(ANT.) nonsense, drivel, babble, gibberish.
too (SYN.) furthermore, moreover, similarly, also, in addition, besides, likewise.
tool (SYN.) devise, medium, apparatus, agent, implement, utensil, agent, vehicle, instrument.
(ANT.) preventive, hindrance, impediment, obstruction.

top (SYN.) crown, pinnacle, peak, tip, cover, cap, zenith, apex, crest, chief, head, summit.
(ANT.) bottom, foundation, base, foot.
topic (SYN.) subject, thesis, issue, argument, matter, theme, point.
topple (SYN.) collapse, sink, fall, tumble.
torment (SYN.) pain, woe, pester, ache, distress, misery, harass, throe, annoy, vex, torture, anguish, suffering, misery.
(ANT.) relief, comfort, ease, gratify, delight.
torpid (SYN.) sluggish, idle, lazy, inert, inactive, supine, slothful, indolent, motionless, lethargic.
(ANT.) alert, assiduous, diligent, active.
torpor (SYN.) lethargy, daze, numbness, stupor, drowsiness, insensibility, languor.
(ANT.) wakefulness, liveliness, activity, alertness, readiness.
torrent (SYN.) flood, downpour, deluge.
torrid (SYN.) scorching, ardent, impetuous, passionate, scalding, warm, fiery, hot-blooded, sultry, tropical, intense, sweltering, burning, hot.
(ANT.) passionless, impassive, cold, frigid, apathetic, freezing, phlegmatic, indifferent, temperate.
torso (SYN.) form, frame, body.
(ANT.) soul, mind, spirit, intellect.
torture (SYN.) anguish, badger, plague, distress, ache, torment, pester, pain, hound, agony, woe, worry, vex, persecute, suffering, throe, afflict, misery.
(ANT.) aid, relief, comfort, ease, support, encourage, mitigation.
toss (SYN.) throw, cast, hurl, pitch, tumble, thrust, pitch, fling, propel.
(ANT.) retain, pull, draw, haul, hold.
total (SYN.) entire, complete, concluded, finished, thorough, whole, entirely, collection, aggregate, conglomeration, unbroken, perfect, undivided, consummate, full.
(ANT.) part, element, imperfect, unfinished, ingredient, particular, lacking.
tote (SYN.) move, transfer, convey, drag, carry.
totter (SYN.) falter, stagger, reel, sway, waver, stumble, wobble.
touch (SYN.) finger, feel, handle, move, affect, concern, mention, hint, trace, suggestion, knack, skill, ability, talent.
touch-and-go (SYN.) dangerous, risky, perilous, hazardous.

touching *(SYN.)* pitiable, affecting, moving, sad, adjunct, bordering, tangent, poignant, tender, effective, impressive, adjacent.
(ANT.) removed, enlivening, animated, exhilarating.

touchy *(SYN.)* snappish, irritable, fiery, choleric, testy, hot, irascible, nervous, excitable, petulant, sensitive, shorttempered, jumpy, peevish.
(ANT.) composed, agreeable, tranquil, calm, serene, stolid, cool.

tough *(SYN.)* sturdy, difficult, trying, vicious, incorrigible, troublesome, hard, stout, leathery, strong, laborious, inedible, sinewy, cohesive, firm, callous, obdurate, vicious.
(ANT.) vulnerable, submissive, easy, brittle, facile, weak, fragile, compliant, tender, frail.

toughness *(SYN.)* stamina, sturdiness, fortitude, durability, intensity, force, might, stoutness, power, sturdiness, vigor.
(ANT.) weakness, feebleness, infirmity, frailty.

tour *(SYN.)* rove, travel, go, visit, excursion, ramble, journey, roam.
(ANT.) stop, stay.

tourist *(SYN.)* traveler, sightseer, vagabond, voyager.

tournament *(SYN.)* tourney, match, contest, competition.

tout *(SYN.)* vend, importune, peddle, solicit, sell, hawk.

tow *(SYN.)* tug, take out, unsheathe, haul, draw, remove, extract, pull, drag.
(ANT.) propel, drive.

towering *(SYN.)* elevated, exalted, high, lofty, tall, proud, eminent.
(ANT.) base, mean, stunted, small, tiny, low.

town *(SYN.)* hamlet, village, community, municipality.

toxic *(SYN.)* deadly, poisonous, fatal, lethal, harmful.
(ANT.) beneficial.

toy *(SYN.)* play, romp, frolic, gamble, stake, caper, plaything, wager, revel.

trace *(SYN.)* stigma, feature, indication, trait, mark, stain, scar, sign, trial, trace, suggestion, characteristic, vestige, symptoms.

track *(SYN.)* persist, pursue, follow, sign, mark, spoor, trace, path, route, road, carry, hunt, chase.

(ANT.) escape, evade, abandon, flee, elude.

tract *(SYN.)* area, region, territory, district, expanse, domain.

tractable *(SYN.)* yielding, deferential, submissive, dutiful, compliant, obedient.
(ANT.) rebellious, intractable, insubordinate, obstinate.

trade *(SYN.)* business, traffic, commerce, dealing, craft, occupation, profession, livelihood, swap, barter, exchange.

trademark *(SYN.)* logo, brand name, identification, emblem, insignia, monogram.

tradition *(SYN.)* custom, legend, folklore, belief, rite, practice.

traduce *(SYN.)* defame, malign, vilify, revile, abuse, asperse, scandalize, disparage.
(ANT.) protect, honor, cherish, praise, respect, support, extol.

tragedy *(SYN.)* unhappiness, misfortune, misery, adversity, catastrophe.

tragic *(SYN.)* miserable, unfortunate, depressing, melancholy, mournful.
(ANT.) happy, cheerful, comic.

trail *(SYN.)* persist, pursue, chase, follow, drag, draw, hunt, track.
(ANT.) evade, flee, abandon, elude, escape.

train *(SYN.)* direct, prepare, aim, point, level, teach, drill, tutor, bid, instruct, order, command.
(ANT.) distract, deceive, misguide, misdirect.

traipse *(SYN.)* roam, wander, saunter, meander.

trait *(SYN.)* characteristic, feature, attribute, peculiarity, mark, quality, property.

traitor *(SYN.)* turncoat, betrayer, spy, double-dealer, conspirator.

traitorous *(SYN.)* disloyal, faithless, apostate, false, recreant, perfidious, treasonable, treacherous.
(ANT.) devoted, true, loyal, constant.

tramp *(SYN.)* bum, beggar, rover, hobo, march, stamp, stomp, vagabond, wanderer, vagrant.
(ANT.) laborer, worker, gentleman.

trample *(SYN.)* crush, stomp, squash.

tranquil *(SYN.)* composed, calm, dispassionate, imperturbable, peaceful, pacific, placid, quiet, still, serene, undisturbed, unruffled.

(ANT.) *frantic, stormy, excited, disturbed, upset, turbulent, wild.*

tranquillity *(SYN.)* calmness, calm, hush, peace, quiet, quiescence, quietude, repose, serenity, rest, stillness, silence, placid.
(ANT.) disturbance, agitation, excitement, tumult, noise.

transact *(SYN.)* conduct, manage, execute, treat, perform.

transaction *(SYN.)* business, deal, affair, deed, settlement, occurrence, negotiation, proceeding.

transcend *(SYN.)* overstep, overshadow, exceed.

transcribe *(SYN.)* write, copy, rewrite, record.

transfer *(SYN.)* dispatch, send, transmit, remove, transport, transplant, consign, move, shift, reasign, assign, relegate.

transform *(SYN.)* change, convert, alter, modify, transfigure, shift, vary, veer.
(ANT.) establish, continue, settle, preserve, stabilize.

transgression *(SYN.)* atrocity, indignity, offense, insult, outrage, aggression, injustice, crime, misdeed, trespass, sin, wrong, vice.
(ANT.) innocence, morality, gentleness, right.

transient *(SYN.)* ephemeral, evanescent, brief, fleeting, momentary, temporary, short-lived.
(ANT.) immortal, abiding, permanent, lasting, timeless, established.

transition *(SYN.)* change, variation, modification.

translate *(SYN.)* decipher, construe, decode, elucidate, explicate, explain, interpret, solve, render, unravel.
(ANT.) distort, falsify, misinterpret, confuse, misconstrue.

transmit *(SYN.)* confer, convey, communicate, divulge, disclose, impart, send, inform, relate, notify, reveal, dispatch, tell.
(ANT.) withhold, hide, conceal.

transparent *(SYN.)* crystalline, clear, limpid, lucid, translucent, thin, evident, manifest, plain, evident, explicit, obvious, open.
(ANT.) opaque, muddy, turbid, thick, questionable, ambiguous.

transpire *(SYN.)* befall, bechance, betide, happen, chance, occur.

transport *(SYN.)* carry, bear, convey,

remove, move, shift, enrapture, transfer, lift, entrance, ravish, stimulate.

transpose *(SYN.)* change, switch, reverse.

trap *(SYN.)* artifice, bait, ambush, intrigue, net, lure, pitfall, ensnare, deadfall, snare, ruse, entrap, bag, trick, stratagem, wile.

trash *(SYN.)* refuse, garbage, rubbish, waste.

trashy *(SYN.)* insignificant, worthless, slight.

trauma *(SYN.)* ordeal, upheaval, jolt, shock, disturbance.

travail *(SYN.)* suffering, torment, anxiety, distress, anguish, misery, ordeal.

travel *(SYN.)* journey, go, touring, ramble, rove, voyage, cruise, tour, roam.
(ANT.) stop, stay, remain, hibernate.

travesty *(SYN.)* farce, joke, misrepresentation, counterfeit, mimicry.

treachery *(SYN.)* collusion, cabal, combination, intrigue, conspiracy, machination, disloyalty, betrayal, treason, plot.
(ANT.) allegiance, steadfastness, loyalty.

treason *(SYN.)* cabal, combination, betrayal, sedition, collusion, intrigue, conspiracy, machination, disloyalty, treachery, plot.

treasure *(SYN.)* cherish, hold dear, abundance, guard, prize, appreciate, value, riches, wealth, foster, sustain, nurture.
(ANT.) disregard, neglect, dislike, abandon, reject.

treat *(SYN.)* employ, avail, manipulate, exploit, operate, utilize, exert, act, exercise, practice, handle, manage, deal, entertain, indulge, host, negotiate, tend, attend, heal, use.
(ANT.) neglect, overlook, ignore, waste.

treaty *(SYN.)* compact, agreement, pact, bargain, covenant, alliance, marriage.
(ANT.) schism, separation, divorce.

trek *(SYN.)* tramp, hike, plod, trudge.

tremble *(SYN.)* flutter, jolt, jar, agitate, quake, quiver, quaver, rock, shake, shudder, shiver, totter, sway, vibrate, waver.

trembling *(SYN.)* apprehension, alarm, dread, fright, fear, horror, terror, panic.
(ANT.) composure, calmness, tranquillity, serenity.

tremendous *(SYN.)* enormous, huge, colossal, gigantic, great, large.

tremor *(SYN.)* flutter, vibration, palpitation.

trench *(SYN.)* gully, gorge, ditch, gulch, moat, dugout, trough.

trenchant *(SYN.)* clear, emphatic, forceful, impressive, meaningful.

trend *(SYN.)* inclination, tendency, drift, course, tendency, direction.

trendy *(SYN.)* modish, faddish, stylish, voguish, popular, current.

trepidation *(SYN.)* apprehension, alarm, dread, fright, fear, horror, panic, terror.
(ANT.) boldness, bravery, fearlessness, courage, assurance.

trespass *(SYN.)* atrocity, indignity, affront, insult, outrage, offense, aggression, crime, misdeed, injustice, vice, wrong, sin.
(ANT.) evacuate, vacate, relinquish, abandon.

trespasser *(SYN.)* invader, intruder, encroacher.

trial *(SYN.)* experiment, ordeal, proof, test, examination, attempt, effort, endeavor, essay, affliction, misery, hardship, suffering, difficulty, misfortune, tribulation, trouble.
(ANT.) consolation, alleviation.

tribe *(SYN.)* group, race, clan, bunch.

tribulation *(SYN.)* anguish, distress, agony, grief, misery, sorrow, torment, suffering, woe, disaster, calamity, evil, trouble, misfortune.
(ANT.) elation, delight, joy, fun, pleasure.

tribunal *(SYN.)* arbitrators, judges, decision-makers, judiciary.

trick *(SYN.)* artifice, antic, deception, device, cheat, fraud, hoax, guile, imposture, ruse, ploy, stratagem, trickery, deceit, jest, joke, prank, defraud, subterfuge, wile, stunt.
(ANT.) exposure, candor, openness, honesty, sincerity.

trickle *(SYN.)* drip, drop, dribble, leak, seep.

tricky *(SYN.)* artifice, antic, covert, cunning, foxy, crafty, furtive, guileful, insidious, sly, shrews, stealthy, surreptitious, subtle, underhand, wily.
(ANT.) frank, candid, ingenuous, sincere, open.

trifling *(SYN.)* insignificant, frivolous, paltry, petty, trivial, small, unimportant.
(ANT.) momentous, serious, important, weighty.

trigger *(SYN.)* generate, provoke,

prompt, motivate, activate.

trim *(SYN.)* nice, clear, orderly, precise, tidy, spruce, adorn, bedeck, clip, shave, prune, cut, shear, compact, neat, decorate, embellish, garnish.
(ANT.) deface, deform, spoil, mar, important, serious, momentous, weighty.

trimmings *(SYN.)* accessories, adornments, decorations, garnish, ornaments.

trinket *(SYN.)* bead, token, memento, bauble, charm, knickknack.

trio *(SYN.)* threesome, triad, triple.

trip *(SYN.)* expedition, cruise, stumble, err, journey, jaunt, passage, blunder, bungle, slip, excursion, tour, pilgrimage, voyage, travel.

trite *(SYN.)* common, banal, hackneyed, ordinary, stereotyped, stale.
(ANT.) modern, fresh, momentous, stimulating, novel, new.

triumph *(SYN.)* conquest, achievement, success, prevail, win, jubilation, victory, ovation.
(ANT.) succumb, failure, defeat.

triumphant *(SYN.)* celebrating, exultant, joyful, exhilarated, smug.

trivial *(SYN.)* insignificant, frivolous, paltry, petty, trifling, small, unimportant.
(ANT.) momentous, important weighty, serious.

troops *(SYN.)* militia, troopers, recruits, soldiers, enlisted men.

trophy *(SYN.)* award, memento, honor, testimonial, prize.

tropical *(SYN.)* sultry, sweltering, humid, torrid.

trouble *(SYN.)* anxiety, affliction, calamity, distress, hardship, grief, pain, misery, sorrow, woe, bother, annoyance, care, embarrassment, irritation, torment, pains, worry, disorder, problem, disturbance, care, effort, exertion, toil, inconvenience, misfortune, labor.
(ANT.) console, accommodate, gratify, soothe, joy, peace.

troublemaker *(SYN.)* rebel, scamp, agitator, demon, devil, ruffian.

troublesome *(SYN.)* bothersome, annoying, distressing, irksome, disturbing, trying, arduous, vexatious, arduous, difficult, burdensome, laborious, tedious.
(ANT.) amusing, accommodating, gratifying, easy, pleasant.

trounce *(SYN.)* lash, flog, switch, whack, punish, whip, stomp.

truant *(SYN.)* delinquent, absentee, vagrant, malingerer.

truce *(SYN.)* armistice, cease-fire, interval, break, intermission, respite.

trudge *(SYN.)* march, trek, lumber, hike.

true *(SYN.)* actual, authentic, accurate, correct, exact, genuine, real, veracious, veritable, constant, honest, faithful, loyal, reliable, valid, legitimate, steadfast, sincere, trustworthy.
(ANT.) *erroneous, counterfeit, false, spurious, fictitious, faithless, inconstant, fickle.*

truly *(SYN.)* indeed, actually, precisely, literally, really, factually.

truncate *(SYN.)* prune, clip, pare, shorten.

truss *(SYN.)* girder, brace, framework, shoring.

trust *(SYN.)* credence, confidence, dependence, reliance, faith, trust, depend on, rely on, reckon on, believe, hope, credit, commit, entrust, confide.
(ANT.) *incredulity, doubt, skepticism, mistrust.*

trusted *(SYN.)* trustworthy, reliable, true, loyal, staunch, devoted.

trustworthy *(SYN.)* dependable, certain, reliable, secure, safe, sure, tried, trust.
(ANT.) *fallible, dubious, questionable, unreliable, uncertain.*

truth *(SYN.)* actuality, authenticity, accuracy, correctness, exactness, honesty, fact, rightness, truthfulness, veracity, verisimilitude, verity.
(ANT.) *falsity, falsehood, fiction, lie, untruth.*

truthful *(SYN.)* frank, candid, honest, sincere, open, veracious, accurate, correct, exact, reliable.
(ANT.) *misleading, sly, deceitful.*

try *(SYN.)* endeavor, attempt, strive, struggle, undertake, afflict, test, prove, torment, trouble, essay, examine, analyze, investigate, effort, aim, design, aspire, intend, mean.
(ANT.) *decline, ignore, abandon, omit, neglect, comfort, console.*

trying *(SYN.)* bothersome, annoying, distressing, irksome, disturbing, troublesome, arduous, vexatious, burdensome, difficult, tedious.
(ANT.) *amusing, easy, accommodating, pleasant, gratifying.*

tryout *(SYN.)* audition, trial, chance, test.

tryst *(SYN.)* rendezvous, meeting, appointment.

tub *(SYN.)* basin, vessel, sink, bowl.

tube *(SYN.)* hose, pipe, reed.

tubular *(SYN.)* hollow, cylindrical.

tuck *(SYN.)* crease, fold, gather, bend.

tuft *(SYN.)* bunch, group, cluster.

tug *(SYN.)* pull, wrench, tow, haul, draw, yank, jerk.

tuition *(SYN.)* instruction, schooling, teaching, education.

tumble *(SYN.)* toss, trip, fall, sprawl, wallow, lurch, flounder, plunge, topple, stumble.

tumble-down *(SYN.)* ramshackle, decrepit, broken-down, dilapidated, rickety.

tumult *(SYN.)* chaos, agitation, commotion, confusion, disarray, disarrangement, disorder, noise, hubbub, ferment, stir, to-do, ado, jumble, disturbance, uproar, turmoil.
(ANT.) *peacefulness, order, peace, certainty, tranquillity.*

tune *(SYN.)* song, concord, harmony, air, melody, strain.
(ANT.) *aversion, discord, antipathy.*

tunnel *(SYN.)* passage, grotto, cave.

turbid *(SYN.)* dark, cloudy, thick, muddy, murky.

turbulent *(SYN.)* gusty, blustery, inclement, rough, roaring, stormy, tempestuous, disorderly, violent, tumultuous, unruly, windy.
(ANT.) *clear, calm, quiet, peaceful, tranquil.*

turf *(SYN.)* lawn, grassland, sod, grass.

turmoil *(SYN.)* chaos, agitation, commotion, confusion, disarray, disarrangement, disorder, jumble, uproar, ferment, stir, pandemonium, tumult.
(ANT.) *order, peace, certainty, quiet, tranquillity.*

turn *(SYN.)* circulate, circle, invert, rotate, revolve, spin, twist, twirl, whirl, wheel, avert, reverse, become, sour, spoil, ferment, deviate, deflect, divert, swerve, change, alter, transmute.
(ANT.) *fix, stand, arrest, stop, continue, endure, proceed, perpetuate.*

turncoat *(SYN.)* renegade, defector, deserter, rat, betrayer, traitor.
(ANT.) *loyalist.*

turret *(SYN.)* watchtower, belfry, steeple, tower, cupola, lookout.

tussle *(SYN.)* wrestle, struggle, contend,

battle, fight, scuffle.

tutor *(SYN.)* instruct, prime, school, teach, train, prepare, drill.

tweak *(SYN.)* squeeze, pinch, nip.

twig *(SYN.)* sprig, branch, shoot, stem.

twilight *(SYN.)* sunset, sundown, nightfall, eventide, dusk.

twin *(SYN.)* lookalike, imitation, copy, double, replica.

twine *(SYN.)* string, cordage, rope, cord.

twinge *(SYN.)* smart, pang, pain.

twinkle *(SYN.)* shine, gleam, glisten, sparkle, glitter, shimmer, scintillate.

twirl *(SYN.)* rotate, spin, wind, turn, pivot, wheel, swivel, whirl.

twist *(SYN.)* bow, bend, crook, intertwine, curve, incline, deflect, lean, braid, distort, contort, warp, interweave, stoop, turn.

(ANT.) resist, break, straighten, stiffen.

twitch *(SYN.)* fidget, shudder, jerk.

two-faced *(SYN.)* deceitful, insincere, hypocritical, false, untrustworthy.

(ANT.) straightforward, honest.

tycoon *(SYN.)* millionaire, industrialist, businessman.

tyke *(SYN.)* rascal, urchin, brat, ragamuffin, imp.

type *(SYN.)* mark, emblem, sign, category, symbol, character, class, description, nature, kind, variety, example, sample, sort, stamp, model, exemplar, pattern.

(ANT.) deviation, monstrosity, eccentricity, peculiarity.

typhoon *(SYN.)* hurricane, cyclone, storm, tornado, whirlwind, twister.

typical *(SYN.)* common, accustomed, conventional, familiar, customary, habitual ordinary, characteristic, normal, plain, representative, regular, symbolic, usual, vulgar.

(ANT.) marvelous, extraordinary, remarkable, odd, atypical, uncommon, strange.

typify *(SYN.)* symbolize, illustrate, signify, represent, incarnate, indicate.

tyrannize *(SYN.)* oppress, victimize, threaten, brutalize, coerce.

tyrannous *(SYN.)* arbitrary, absolute, authoritative, despotic.

(ANT.) conditional, accountable, contingent, qualified, dependent.

tyrant *(SYN.)* dictator, autocrat, despot, oppressor, slave driver, martinet, disciplinarian, persecutor.

ugly *(SYN.)* hideous, homely, plain, deformed, repellent, uncomely, repulsive, ill-natured, unsightly, nasty, unpleasant, wicked, disagreeable, spiteful, surly, vicious.

(ANT.) beautiful, fair, pretty, attractive, handsome, comely, good.

ultimate *(SYN.)* extreme, latest, final, concluding, decisive, hindmost, last, terminal, utmost, greatest, maximum.

(ANT.) foremost, opening, first, beginning, initial.

umbrage *(SYN.)* anger, displeasure.

umpire *(SYN.)* judge, referee, arbitrator.

unadulterated *(SYN.)* genuine, clear, clean, immaculate, spotless, pure, absolute, untainted, sheer, bare.

(ANT.) foul, sullied, corrupt, tainted, polluted, tarnished, defiled.

unalterable *(SYN.)* fixed, unchangeable, steadfast, inflexible.

unanimity *(SYN.)* accord, unity, agreement.

unannounced *(SYN.)* hasty, precipitate, abrupt, unexpected.

(ANT.) courteous, expected, anticipated.

unassuming *(SYN.)* humble, lowly, compliant, modest, plain, meek, simple, unostentatious, retiring, submissive, unpretentious.

(ANT.) haughty, showy, pompous, proud, vain, arrogant, boastful.

unattached *(SYN.)* apart, separate, unmarried, single, free, independent.

(ANT.) committed, involved, entangled.

unavoidable *(SYN.)* inescapable, certain, inevitable, unpreventable.

unawares *(SYN.)* abruptly, suddenly, unexpectedly, off guard.

unbalanced *(SYN.)* crazy, mad, insane, deranged.

unbearable *(SYN.)* insufferable, intolerable.

(ANT.) tolerable, acceptable.

unbeliever *(SYN.)* dissenter, apostate, heretic, schismatic, nonconformist, sectary, sectarian.

unbending *(SYN.)* firm, inflexible, decided, determined, obstinate.

(ANT.) flexible.

unbiased *(SYN.)* honest, equitable, fair, impartial, reasonable, unprejudiced, just.

(ANT.) partial, fraudulent, dishonorable.

unbroken *(SYN.)* complete, uninterrupted, continuous, whole.

unburden *(SYN.)* clear, disentangle, divest, free.

uncanny *(SYN.)* amazing, remarkable, extraordinary, strange.

uncertain *(SYN.)* dim, hazy, indefinite, obscure, indistinct, unclear, undetermined, unsettled, ambiguous, unsure, doubtful, questionable, dubious, vague. *(ANT.)* explicit, lucid, specific, certain, unmistakable, precise, clear.

uncertainty *(SYN.)* distrust, doubt, hesitation, incredulity, scruple, ambiguity, skepticism, uncertainty, suspense, suspicion, unbelief. *(ANT.)* faith, belief, certainty, conviction, determination.

uncivil *(SYN.)* impolite, rude, discourteous. *(ANT.)* polite.

uncivilized *(SYN.)* barbaric, barbarous, barbarian, brutal, crude, inhuman, cruel, merciless, rude, remorseless, uncultured, savage, unrelenting. *(ANT.)* humane, kind, polite, civilized, refined.

unclad *(SYN.)* exposed, nude, naked, bare, stripped, defenseless, uncovered, open, unprotected. *(ANT.)* concealed, protected, clothed, covered, dressed.

uncommon *(SYN.)* unusual, rare, odd, scarce, strange, peculiar, queer, exceptional, remarkable. *(ANT.)* ordinary, usual.

uncompromising *(SYN.)* determined, dogged, firm, immovable, contumacious, headstrong, inflexible, obdurate, intractable, obstinate, pertinacious, stubborn, unyielding. *(ANT.)* docile, compliant, amenable, yielding, submissive, pliable.

unconcern *(SYN.)* disinterestedness, impartiality, indifference, apathy, insensibility, neutrality. *(ANT.)* affection, fervor, passion, ardor.

unconditional *(SYN.)* unqualified, unrestricted, arbitrary, absolute, pure, complete, actual, authoritative, perfect, entire, ultimate, tyrannous. *(ANT.)* conditional, contingent, accountable, dependent, qualified.

unconscious *(SYN.)* lethargic, numb, comatose.

uncouth *(SYN.)* green, harsh, crude,

coarse, ill-prepared, rough, raw, unfinished, unrefined, vulgar, rude, impolite, discourteous, unpolished, ill-mannered, crass. *(ANT.)* well-prepared, cultivated, refined, civilized, finished.

uncover *(SYN.)* disclose, discover, betray, divulge, expose, reveal, impart, show. *(ANT.)* conceal, hide, cover, obscure, cloak.

undependable *(SYN.)* changeable, unstable, uncertain, shifty, irresponsible. *(ANT.)* stable, dependable, trustworthy.

under *(SYN.)* beneath, underneath, following, below, lower, downward. *(ANT.)* over, above, up, higher.

undercover *(SYN.)* hidden, secret.

undergo *(SYN.)* endure, feel, stand, bear, indulge, suffer, sustain, experience, let, allow, permit, feel, tolerate. *(ANT.)* overcome, discard, exclude, banish.

underhand *(SYN.)* sly, secret, sneaky, secretive, stealthy, crafty. *(ANT.)* honest, open, direct, frank.

undermine *(SYN.)* demoralize, thwart, erode, weaken, subvert, sabotage.

underscore *(SYN.)* emphasize, stress.

understand *(SYN.)* apprehend, comprehend, appreciate, conceive, discern, know, grasp, hear, learn, realize, see, perceive. *(ANT.)* misunderstand, mistake, misapprehend, ignore.

understanding *(SYN.)* agreement, coincidence, concord, accordance, concurrence, harmony, unison, compact, contract, arrangement, bargain, covenant, stipulation. *(ANT.)* variance, difference, discord, dissension, disagreement.

understudy *(SYN.)* deputy, agent, proxy, representative, agent, alternate, lieutenant, substitute. *(ANT.)* head, principal, sovereign, master.

undertake *(SYN.)* venture, attempt.

undertaking *(SYN.)* effort, endeavor, attempt, experiment, trial, essay. *(ANT.)* laziness, neglect, inaction.

undersigned *(SYN.)* casual, chance, contingent, accidental, fortuitous, incidental, unintended. *(ANT.)* decreed, planned, willed, calculated.

undesirable *(SYN.)* obnoxious, distasteful, objectionable, repugnant.
(ANT.) appealing, inviting, attractive.

undivided *(SYN.)* complete, intact, entire, integral, total, perfect, unimpaired, whole.
(ANT.) partial, incomplete.

undoing *(SYN.)* ruin, downfall, destruction, failure, disgrace.

undying *(SYN.)* endless, deathless, eternal, everlasting, ceaseless, immortal, infinite, perpetual, timeless.
(ANT.) transient, mortal, temporal, ephemeral, finite, impermanent.

unearthly *(SYN.)* metaphysical, ghostly, miraculous, marvelous, preternatural, superhuman, spiritual, foreign, strange, weird, supernatural.
(ANT.) physical, plain, human, natural, common, mundane.

uneducated *(SYN.)* uncultured, ignorant, illiterate, uninformed, unlearned, untaught, unlettered.
(ANT.) erudite, cultured, educated, literate, formed.

unemployed *(SYN.)* inert, inactive, idle, jobless, unoccupied.
(ANT.) working, occupied, active, industrious, employed.

uneven *(SYN.)* remaining, single, odd, unmatched, rugged, gnarled, irregular.
(ANT.) matched, even, flat, smooth.

unexceptional *(SYN.)* commonplace, trivial, customary.

unexpected *(SYN.)* immediate, hasty, surprising, instantaneous, unforeseen, abrupt, rapid, startling, sudden.
(ANT.) slowly, expected, gradual, predicted, anticipated, planned.

unfaithful *(SYN.)* treacherous, disloyal, deceitful,capricious.
(ANT.) true, loyal, steadfast, faithful.

unfasten *(SYN.)* open, expand, spread, exhibit, unbar, unlock, unfold, unseal.
(ANT.) shut, hide, conceal, close.

unfavorable *(SYN.)* antagonistic, contrary, adverse, opposed, opposite, disastrous, counteractive, unlucky.
(ANT.) benign, fortunate, lucky, propitious.

unfeeling *(SYN.)* hard, rigorous, cruel, stern, callous, numb, hard, strict, unsympathetic, severe.
(ANT.) tender, gentle, lenient, humane.

unfold *(SYN.)* develop, create, elaborate,
amplify, evolve, mature, expand.
(ANT.) wither, restrict, contract, stunt, compress.

unfurnished *(SYN.)* naked, mere, bare, exposed, stripped, plain, open, simple.
(ANT.) concealed, protected, covered.

ungainly *(SYN.)* clumsy, awkward, bungling, clownish, gawky.
(ANT.) dexterous, graceful, elegant.

unhappy *(SYN.)* sad, miserable, wretched, melancholy, distressed, depressed, wretched.
(ANT.) joyful, happy, joyous, cheerful.

unhealthy *(SYN.)* infirm, sick, diseased, sickly.
(ANT.) vigorous, well, healthy, hale.

uniform *(SYN.)* methodical, natural, customary, orderly, normal, consistent, ordinary, regular, unvarying, unchanging, systematic, steady, unvaried.
(ANT.) rare, unusual, erratic, abnormal, exceptional, changeable.

unimportant *(SYN.)* petty, trivial, paltry, trifling, insignificant, indifferent, minor, petty.

uninformed *(SYN.)* illiterate, uncultured, uneducated, ignorant, unlearned, untaught, unlettered.
(ANT.) informed, literate, erudite, cultured, educated.

uninhibited *(SYN.)* loose, open, liberated, free.
(ANT.) constrained, tense, suppressed.

unintelligible *(SYN.)* ambiguous, cryptic, dark, cloudy, abstruse, dusky, mysterious, indistinct, obscure, vague.
(ANT.) lucid, distinct, bright, clear.

uninteresting *(SYN.)* burdensome, dilatory, dreary, dull, boring, slow humdrum, monotonous, sluggish, tedious, tardy, wearisome, tiresome.
(ANT.) entertaining, exciting, quick, amusing.

union *(SYN.)* fusion, incorporation, combination, joining, concurrence, solidarity, agreement, unification, concord, harmony, alliance, unanimity, coalition, confederacy, amalgamation, league, concert, marriage.
(ANT.) schism, disagreement, separation, discord.

unique *(SYN.)* exceptional, matchless, distinctive, choice, peculiar, singular, rare, sole, single, incomparable, uncommon, solitary, unequaled.

(ANT.) typical, ordinary, commonplace, frequent, common.

unison *(SYN.)* harmony, concurrence, understanding, accordance, concord, agreeable, coincidence.
(ANT.) disagreement, difference, discord, variance.

unite *(SYN.)* attach, blend, amalgamate, combine, conjoin, associate, connect, embody, consolidate, join, link, fuse, unify, merge.
(ANT.) sever, divide, separate, sever, disrupt, disconnect.

universal *(SYN.)* frequent, general, popular, common, familiar, prevailing, prevalent, usual.
(ANT.) scarce, odd, regional, local, extraordinary, exceptional.

unkempt *(SYN.)* sloppy, rumpled, untidy, messy, bedraggled.
(ANT.) presentable, well-groomed, tidy, neat.

unkind *(SYN.)* unfeeling, unsympathetic, unpleasant, cruel, harsh.
(ANT.) considerate, sympathetic, amiable, kind.

unlawful *(SYN.)* illegitimate, illicit, illegal, outlawed, criminal, prohibited.
(ANT.) permitted, law, honest, legal, legitimate, authorized.

unlike *(SYN.)* dissimilar, different, distinct, contrary, diverse, divergent, opposite, incongruous, variant, miscellaneous, divers.
(ANT.) conditional, accountable, contingent, qualified, dependent.

unlucky *(SYN.)* cursed, inauspicious, unfortunate.
(ANT.) prosperous, fortunate, blessed.

unmerciful *(SYN.)* cruel, merciless, heartless, brutal.

unmistakable *(SYN.)* clear, patent, plain, visible, obvious.

unnecessary *(SYN.)* pointless, needless, superfluous, purposeless.

unoccupied *(SYN.)* empty, vacant, uninhabited.

unparalleled *(SYN.)* peerless, unequaled, rare, unique, unmatched.

unpleasant *(SYN.)* offensive, disagreeable, repulsive, obnoxious, unpleasing.

qualified *(SYN.)* inept, unfit, incapable, incompetent, unquestioned, absolute, utter.

unreasonable *(SYN.)* foolish, absurd, irrational, inconsistent, nonsensical, ridiculous, silly.
(ANT.) reasonable, sensible, sound, consistent, rational.

unruffled *(SYN.)* calm, smooth, serene, unperturbed.

unruly *(SYN.)* unmanageable, disorganized, disorderly, disobedient.
(ANT.) orderly.

unsafe *(SYN.)* hazardous, insecure, critical, dangerous, perilous, menacing, risky, precarious, threatening.
(ANT.) protected, secure, firm, safe.

unselfish *(SYN.)* bountiful, generous, liberal, giving, beneficent, magnanimous, openhanded, munificent.
(ANT.) miserly, stingy, greedy, selfish, covetous.

unsightly *(SYN.)* ugly, unattractive, hideous.

unsophisticated *(SYN.)* frank, candid, artless, ingenuous, naive, open, simple, natural.
(ANT.) sophisticated, worldly, cunning, crafty.

unsound *(SYN.)* feeble, flimsy, weak, fragile, sick, unhealthy, diseased, invalid, faulty, false.

unstable *(SYN.)* fickle, fitful, inconstant, capricious, changeable, restless, variable.
(ANT.) steady, stable, trustworthy, constant.

unswerving *(SYN.)* fast, firm, inflexible, constant, secure, stable, solid, steady, steadfast, unyielding.
(ANT.) sluggish, insecure, unsteady, unstable, loose, slow.

untainted *(SYN.)* genuine, pure, spotless, clean, clear, unadulterated, guiltless, innocent, chaste, modest, undefiled, sincere, virgin.
(ANT.) polluted, tainted, sullied, tarnished, defiled, corrupt, foul.

untamed *(SYN.)* fierce, savage, uncivilized, barbarous, outlandish, rude, undomesticated, desert, wild, frenzied, mad, turbulent, impetuous, wanton, boisterous, wayward, stormy, extravagant, tempestuous, foolish, rash, giddy, reckless.
(ANT.) quiet, gentle, calm, civilized, placid.

untidy *(SYN.)* messy, sloppy, disorderly, slovenly.

untoward *(SYN.)* disobedient, contrary, peevish, fractious, forward, petulant, obstinate, intractable, stubborn, perverse, ungovernable.
(ANT.) docile, tractable, obliging, agreeable.

unusual *(SYN.)* capricious, abnormal, devious, eccentric, aberrant, irregular, variable, remarkable, - extraordinary, odd, peculiar, uncommon, strange, exceptional, unnatural.
(ANT.) methodical, regular, usual, fixed, ordinary.

unyielding *(SYN.)* fast, firm, inflexible, constant, solid, secure, stable, steadfast, unswerving, steady.
(ANT.) sluggish, slow, insecure, loose, unsteady, unstable.

upbraid *(SYN.)* blame, censure, berate, admonish, rate, lecture, rebuke, reprimand, reprehend, scold, vituperate.
(ANT.) praise, commend, approve.

uphold *(SYN.)* justify, espouse, assert, defend, maintain, vindicate.
(ANT.) oppose, submit, assault, deny, attack.

upright *(SYN.)* undeviating, right, unswerving, direct, erect, unbent, straight, fair, vertical.
(ANT.) bent, dishonest, crooked, circuitous, winding.

uprising *(SYN.)* revolution, mutiny, revolt, rebellion.

uproar *(SYN.)* noise, disorder, commotion, tumult, disturbance.

upset *(SYN.)* disturb, harass, bother, annoy, haunt, molest, inconvenience, perplex, pester, tease, plague, trouble, worry, overturned, toppled, upend, capsize, fluster, agitate.
(ANT.) soothe, relieve, please, gratify.

upshot *(SYN.)* conclusion, result, outcome.

urbane *(SYN.)* civil, considerate, cultivated, courteous, genteel, polite, accomplished, refined, well-mannered.
(ANT.) rude, uncouth, boorish, uncivil.

urge *(SYN.)* craving, desire, longing, lust, appetite, aspiration, yearning, incite, coax, entice, force, drive, prod, press, plead, persuade, implore, beg, recommend, advise.
(ANT.) loathing, hate, distaste, aversion, coerce, deter, restrain, compel, dissuade, discourage.

urgency *(SYN.)* emergency, exigency, pass, pinch, strait, crisis.

urgent *(SYN.)* critical, crucial, exigent, imperative, impelling, insistent, necessary, instant, serious, pressing, cogent, important, importunate, immediate.
(ANT.) trivial, unimportant, petty, insignificant.

usage *(SYN.)* use, treatment, custom, practice, tradition.

use *(SYN.)* custom, practice, habit, training, usage, manner, apply, avail employ, operate, utilize, exert, exhaust, handle, manage, accustom, inure, train, exploit, manipulate, spend, expend, consume, exercise, work.
(ANT.) disuse, neglect, waste, ignore, overlook, idleness.

useful *(SYN.)* beneficial, helpful, good, serviceable, wholesome, advantageous.
(ANT.) harmful, injurious, deleterious, destructive, detrimental.

usefulness *(SYN.)* price, merit, utility, value, excellence, virtue, worth, worthiness.
(ANT.) useless, cheapness, valuelessness, uselessness.

useless *(SYN.)* bootless, empty, idle, pointless, vain, valueless, worthless, abortive, fruitless, unavailing, ineffectual, vapid.
(ANT.) profitable, potent, effective.

usher *(SYN.)* guide, lead.

usual *(SYN.)* customary, common, familiar, general, normal, habitual, accustomed, everyday, ordinary, regular.
(ANT.) irregular, exceptional, rare, extraordinary, abnormal.

utensil *(SYN.)* instrument, tool, vehicle, apparatus, device, implement.
(ANT.) preventive, hindrance, obstruction.

utilize *(SYN.)* use, apply, devote, busy, employ, occupy, avail.
(ANT.) reject, banish, discharge, discard.

utopian *(SYN.)* perfect, ideal, faultless, exemplary, supreme, visionary, unreal.
(ANT.) real, material, imperfect, actual, faulty.

utter *(SYN.)* full, perfect, whole, finished, entire, speak, say, complete, superlative, supreme, total, absolute, pronounce, unqualified, downright, express.
(ANT.) imperfect, deficient, lacking, faulty, incomplete.

vacancy *(SYN.)* void, emptiness, vacuum, hollowness, blankness, vacuity, depletion, nothingness.
(ANT.) plenitude, fullness, profusion, completeness.

vacant *(SYN.)* barren, empty, blank, bare, unoccupied, void, vacuous.
(ANT.) filled, packed, employed, full, replete, busy, engaged.

vacate *(SYN.)* abjure, relinquish, abdicate, renounce, abandon, resign, surrender, desert, waive, quit, leave.
(ANT.) stay, support, uphold, maintain.

vacation rest, holiday, recess, break.
(ANT.) labor, work, routine.

vacillate *(SYN.)* hesitate, oscillate, undulate, change, fluctuate, vary, waver.
(ANT.) adhere, persist, stick, decide.

vacillating *(SYN.)* contrary, illogical, contradictory, contrary, inconsistent, incongruous, incompatible, paradoxical, irreconcilable, unsteady, wavering.
(ANT.) correspondent, congruous, consistent, compatible.

vacuity *(SYN.)* space, emptiness, vacuum, void, blank, nothingness, ignorance, unawareness, senselessness, mindlessness, chatter, nonsense, froth, absurdity.
(ANT.) matter, fullness, content, substance, knowledge, intelligence.

vacuous *(SYN.)* dull, blank, uncomprehending, imbecillic, foolish, thoughtless, distracted, absent-minded.
(ANT.) responsive, alert, attentive, bright, intelligent, aware.

vacuum *(SYN.)* void, gap, emptiness, hole, chasm, nothingness, abyss.

vagabond *(SYN.)* pauper, ragamuffin, scrub, beggar, mendicant, starveling, wretch, tatterdemalion, hobo, tramp.
(ANT.) responsible, established, rooted, installed, reliable.

vagary *(SYN.)* notion, whim, fantasy, fancy, daydream, caprice, conceit, quirk, whimsy, impulse.

vagrant *(SYN.)* hobo, rover, tramp, beggar, bum, wanderer, vagabond.
(ANT.) settled, worker, laborer, rooted, ambitious, gentleman.

vague *(SYN.)* indefinite, hazy, dim, indistinct, ambiguous, obscure, undetermined, unclear, unsure, unsettled.
(ANT.) certain, spelled out, specific, lucid, clear, definite, distinct, explicit, precise, unequivocal.

vain *(SYN.)* fruitless, empty, bootless, futile, idle, abortive, ineffectual, unavailing, vapid, pointless, valueless, useless, trivial, unfruitful, worthless, unsuccessful, proud, conceited.
(ANT.) meek, modest, potent, rewarding, self-effacing, diffident, profitable, effective, humble.

vainglory *(SYN.)* conceit, pride, self-esteem, arrogance, self-respect, superciliousness, haughtiness, vanity.
(ANT.) shame, modesty, meekness, humility, lowliness.

valet *(SYN.)* groom, dresser, attendant, manservant.

valiant *(SYN.)* bold, brave, courageous, adventurous, audacious, chivalrous, daring, fearless, dauntless, heroic, brave, gallant, magnanimous, intrepid, unafraid, valorous, dauntless.
(ANT.) weak, fearful, cowardly, timid.

valid *(SYN.)* cogent, conclusive, effective, convincing, binding, efficacious, logical, powerful, legal, sound, weighty, well-founded, real, genuine, actual, true, trustworthy, authentic, strong, telling, logical, authentic.
(ANT.) weak, unconvincing, void, unproved, null, spurious, counterfeit.

validate *(SYN.)* corroborate, substantiate, support, confirm, prove, uphold, sustain, authenticate.
(ANT.) disprove, contradict, cancel.

valise *(SYN.)* satchel, bag, baggage.

valley *(SYN.)* dale, dell, lowland, basin, gully, vale, ravine.
(ANT.) highland, hill, upland, headland.

valor *(SYN.)* courage, heroism, bravery, boldness, intrepidity, fearlessness.

valuable *(SYN.)* profitable, useful, costly, precious, dear, expensive, worthy, important, high-priced, esteemed.
(ANT.) trashy, poor, cheap, worthless.

value *(SYN.)* price, merit, usefulness, value, virtue, utility, appreciate, prize, hold dear, treasure, excellence, benefit, cost, rate, evaluate, appraise, esteem, importance, worth, worthiness.
(ANT.) valuelessness, uselessness, cheapness.

vanish *(SYN.)* evaporate, disappear.
(ANT.) appear.

vanity *(SYN.)* complacency, egotism, pride, self-esteem, conceit, caprice, fancy, idea, conception, notion, haugh-

tiness, self-respect, whim, smugness, vainglory, arrogance, imagination.
(ANT.) meekness, humility, diffidence.
vanquish *(SYN.)* defeat, crush, humble, surmount, master, beat, conquer, overcome, rout, quell, subjugate, subdue.
(ANT.) surrender, cede, lose, retreat, capitulate.
vapid *(SYN.)* hackneyed, inane, insipid, trite, banal, commonplace.
(ANT.) striking, novel, fresh, original, stimulating.
vapor *(SYN.)* steam, fog, mist, smog, haze, steam.
variable *(SYN.)* fickle, fitful, inconstant, unstable, shifting, changeable, unsteady, wavering, vacillating.
(ANT.) unchanging, uniform, stable, unwavering, steady, constant.
variant *(SYN.)* dissimilar, different, distinct, contrary, diverse, divergent, opposite, unlike, incongruous, divers, sundry, various, miscellaneous.
(ANT.) similar, same, congruous, identical, alike.
variation *(SYN.)* change, alternation, alteration, substitution, variety, substitute, mutation, exchange, vicissitude.
(ANT.) uniformity, stability, monotony.
variety *(SYN.)* dissimilarity, diversity, heterogeneity, assortment, change, difference, medley, mixture, miscellany, variousness, form, type, class, breed, sort, kind, strain, stock.
(ANT.) likeness, monotony, uniformity, sameness, homogeneity.
various *(SYN.)* miscellaneous, sundry, divers, several, contrary, distinct, dissimilar, divergent, unlike, incongruous, opposite, different.
(ANT.) identical, similar, same, alike, congruous.
vary *(SYN.)* exchange, substitute, alter, change, modify, shift, convert, transform, transfigure, diversify, veer.
(ANT.) settle, stabilize, continue, establish, preserve.
vassalage *(SYN.)* confinement, captivity, imprisonment, slavery, thralldom.
(ANT.) liberation, freedom.
vast *(SYN.)* big, capacious, extensive, huge, great, ample, immense, wide, unlimited, enormous, measureless, large.
(ANT.) tiny, small, short, little.
vault *(SYN.)* caper, jerk, jump, leap,

bound, crypt, sepulcher, hop, spring, safe, start, tomb, grave, catacomb, skip.
vaunt *(SYN.)* crow, flaunt, glory, boast.
(ANT.) minimize, humble, deprecate, apologize.
vaunting *(SYN.)* flourish, display, ostentation, parade, show, pomp.
(ANT.) modesty, reserve, humility.
vehement *(SYN.)* excitable, fervent, ardent, burning, fiery, glowing, impetuous, hot, irascible, passionate.
(ANT.) calm, quiet, cool, apathetic, deliberate.
veil *(SYN.)* clothe, conceal, cover, cloak, web, hide, curtain, disguise, gauze, film, envelop, screen, mask, shield, film.
(ANT.) reveal, unveil, bare, divulge.
velocity *(SYN.)* quickness, rapidity, speed, swiftness.
venal *(SYN.)* greedy, mercenary, sordid, corrupt.
(ANT.) liberal, honorable, generous.
venerable *(SYN.)* antiquated, aged, antique, ancient, elderly, old, superannuated, old-fashion.
(ANT.) young, new, youthful, modern.
venerate *(SYN.)* approve, esteem, admire, appreciate, wonder, respect.
(ANT.) dislike, despise.
vengeance *(SYN.)* requital, reprisal, reparation, retribution, revenge.
(ANT.) forgiveness, remission, pardon, mercy.
venom *(SYN.)* toxin, poison, bitterness, spite, hate.
vent *(SYN.)* eject, emit, expel, shoot, spurt, emanate, hurl, shed, belch, discharge, breathe.
venture *(ANT.)* speculate, attempt, test, dare, hazard, gamble, chance, risk.
(ANT.) insure, secure, protect.
verbal *(SYN.)* oral, spoken, literal, unwritten, vocal.
(ANT.) printed, written, recorded.
verbose *(SYN.)* communicative, glib, chattering, chatty, garrulous, loquacious, talkative.
(ANT.) uncommunicative, silent.
verbosity *(SYN.)* long-windedness, verboseness, redundancy, wordiness.
(ANT.) terseness, laconic, conciseness.
verdict *(SYN.)* judgment, finding, opinion, decision.
verge *(SYN.)* lip, rim, edge, margin, brink, brim.

verification *(SYN.)* confirmation, demonstration, evidence, proof, test, experiment, testimony, trial.
(ANT.) terseness, laconic, conciseness.

verify *(SYN.)* confirm, substantiate, acknowledge, determine, assure, establish, approve, fix, settle, ratify, strengthen, corroborate, affirm, sanction.

veritable *(SYN.)* authentic, correct, genuine, real, true, accurate, actual.
(ANT.) false, fictitious, spurious, erroneous, counterfeit.

versed *(SYN.)* conversant, familiar, intimate, knowing, acquainted, aware.
(ANT.) inclined, level, prone, oblique.

version *(SYN.)* interpretation, rendition.

vertical *(SYN.)* erect, perpendicular, upright.
(ANT.) horizontal.

very *(SYN.)* exceedingly, extremely, greatly, considerably.

vessel *(SYN.)* craft, boat, ship.

vestige *(SYN.)* stain, scar, mark, brand, stigma, characteristic, trace, feature, trait, symptoms, hint, token, suggestion, indication.

veto *(SYN.)* refusal, denial, refuse, deny, negate, forbid, prohibit.
(ANT.) approve, approval.

vex *(SYN.)* embitter, exasperate, aggravate, annoy, chafe, bother, provoke, pester, plague, anger, nettle, anger.
(ANT.) soften soothe, palliate, mitigate.

vexation *(SYN.)* chagrin, irritation, annoyance, mortification, irritation, pique.
(ANT.) comfort, pleasure, appeasement, gratification.

vibrate *(SYN.)* flutter, jar, quake, jolt, quaver, agitate, transgression, wickedness, ungodliness, tremble, wrong.

vice *(SYN.)* iniquity, crime, offense, evil, guilt, sin, ungodliness, wickedness, depravity, corruption, wrong.
(ANT.) righteousness, virtue, goodness, innocence, purity.

vicinity *(SYN.)* district, area, locality, neighborhood, environs, proximity, nearness, adjacency.
(ANT.) remoteness, distance.

vicious *(SYN.)* bad, evil, wicked, sinful, corrupt, cruel, savage, dangerous.

victimize *(SYN.)* cheat, dupe, swindle, deceive, take advantage of.

victor *(SYN.)* champion, winner.
(ANT.) loser.

victory *(SYN.)* conquest, jubilation, triumph, success, achievement, ovation.
(ANT.) defeat, failure.

view *(SYN.)* discern, gaze, glance, behold, eye, discern, stare, watch, examine, witness, prospect, vision, vista, sight, look, panorama, opinion, judgment, belief, impression, perspective, range, regard, thought, observation, survey, scene, conception, outlook, inspect, observe.
(ANT.) miss, overlook, avert, hide.

viewpoint *(SYN.)* attitude, standpoint, aspect, pose, disposition, position, stand, posture.

vigilant *(SYN.)* anxious, attentive, careful, alert, circumspect, cautious, observant, wary, watchful, wakeful.
(ANT.) inattentive, neglectful, careless.

vigor *(SYN.)* spirit, verve, energy, zeal, fortitude, vitality, strength, liveliness.
(ANT.) listlessness.

vigorous *(SYN.)* brisk, energetic, active, blithe, animated, frolicsome, strong, spirited, lively, forceful, sprightly, vivacious, powerful, supple.
(ANT.) vapid, dull, listless, insipid.

vile *(SYN.)* foul, loathsome, base, depraved, debased, sordid, vulgar, wicked, abject, ignoble, mean, worthless, sinful, bad, low, wretched, evil, offensive, objectionable, disgusting.
(ANT.) honorable, upright, decent, laudable, attractive.

vilify *(SYN.)* asperse, defame, disparage, abuse, malign, revile, scandalize.
(ANT.) protect, honor, praise, cherish.

village *(SYN.)* hamlet, town.
(ANT.) metropolis, city.

villain *(SYN.)* rascal, rogue, cad, brute, scoundrel, devil, scamp.

villainous *(SYN.)* deleterious, evil, bad, base, iniquitous, unsound, sinful, unwholesome, wicked.
(ANT.) honorable, reputable, moral, good, excellent.

violate *(SYN.)* infringe, break.

violent *(SYN.)* strong, forcible, forceful.
(ANT.) gentle.

vindicate clear, assert, defend, absolve, excuse, acquit, uphold, support.
(ANT.) accuse, convict, abandon.

violate *(SYN.)* disobey, invade, defile, break, desecrate, pollute, dishonor, debauch, profane, deflower, ravish.

violence *(SYN.)* constraint, force, com-

pulsion, coercion.
(ANT.) weakness, persuasion, feebleness, impotence, frailty.
violent *(SYN.)* strong, forceful, powerful, forcible, angry, fierce, savage, passionate, furious.
(ANT.) gentle.
virgin *(SYN.)* immaculate, genuine, spotless, clean, clear, unadulterated, chaste, untainted, innocent, guiltless, pure, untouched, modest, maid, maiden, sincere, unused, undefiled, pure.
(ANT.) foul, tainted, defiled, sullied, polluted, corrupt.
virile *(SYN.)* hardy, male, mannish, lusty, bold, masculine, strong, vigorous.
(ANT.) feminine, unmanly, weak, effeminate, womanish, emasculated.
virtue *(SYN.)* integrity, probity, purity, chastity, goodness, rectitude, effectiveness, force, honor, power, efficacy, quality, strength, merit, righteousness, advantage, excellence, advantage.
(ANT.) fault, vice, lewdness, corruption.
virtuous *(SYN.)* good, ethical, chaste, honorable, moral, just, pure, righteous, upstanding, upright, scrupulous.
(ANT.) licentious, unethical, amoral, sinful, libertine, immoral.
virulent *(SYN.)* hostile, malevolent, malignant, bitter, spiteful, wicked.
(ANT.) kind, affectionate, benevolent.
vision *(SYN.)* dream, hallucination, mirage, eyesight, sight, fantasy, illusion, specter, revelation, phantom, spook, ghost, imagination, far-sightedness, keenness, foresight, apparition.
(ANT.) verity, reality.
visionary *(SYN.)* faultless, ideal, perfect, unreal, supreme.
(ANT.) real, actual, imperfect, faulty.
visit *(SYN.)* attend, see, call on, appointment.
visitor *(SYN.)* caller, guest.
vista *(SYN.)* view, scene, aspect.
vital *(SYN.)* cardinal, living, paramount, alive, essential, critical, basic, indispensable, urgent, life-and-death.
(ANT.) lifeless, unimportant, inanimate, nonessential.
vitality *(SYN.)* buoyancy, being, life, liveliness, existence, spirit, vigor.
(ANT.) death, lethargy, dullness, demise.
vitiate *(SYN.)* allay, abase, corrupt, adulterate, debase, defile, depress, deprave,

degrade, impair, humiliate, pervert, improve, restore, vitalize, restore.
vivacious *(SYN.)* lively, spirited.
vivid *(SYN.)* brilliant, striking, clear, bright, intense, lively, strong, graphic.
(ANT.) dim, dusky, vague, dull, dreary.
vocal *(SYN.)* said, uttered, oral, spoken, definite, outspoken, specific.
vocation *(SYN.)* commerce, employment, business, art, job, profession, trade, occupation, career, calling, work, trading.
(ANT.) pastime, hobby, avocation.
void *(SYN.)* barren, emptiness, space, annul, cancel, empty, bare, unoccupied, meaningless, invalid, useless, invalidate, worthless, vacant, barren.
(ANT.) employed, full, replete, engaged.
volatile *(SYN.)* effervescent, resilient, buoyant, animated, cheerful, hopeful, lively, sprightly, spirited, vivacious.
(ANT.) depressed, sullen, hopeless, dejected, despondent.
volition *(SYN.)* desire, intention, pleasure, preference, choice, decision, resolution, testament, wish, will.
(ANT.) disinterest, compulsion, indifference.
voluble *(SYN.)* glib, communicative, verbose, loquacious, chatty, chattering.
(ANT.) uncommunicative, laconic, taciturn, silent.
volume *(SYN.)* capacity, skill, power, talent, faculty, magnitude, mass, book, dimensions, quantity, amount, size.
(ANT.) stupidity, inability, impotence, incapacity.
voluntary *(SYN.)* extemporaneous, free, automatic, spontaneous, offhand.
(ANT.) forced, planned, required, rehearsed, compulsory, prepared.
volunteer *(SYN.)* extend, offer, present, advance, propose, tender, sacrifice.
(ANT.) receive, spurn, reject, accept, retain.
voodoo *(SYN.)* art, conjuring, legerdemain, magic, witchcraft, wizardry.
voracious *(SYN.)* insatiable, ravenous.
vow *(SYN.)* oath, pledge, swear, promise.
voyage *(SYN.)* tour, journey, excursion.
vulgar *(SYN.)* ordinary, popular, common, general, crude, coarse, low, rude, bad-mannered, obscene, unrefined.
(ANT.) polite, refined, select, aristocratic.
vulnerable *(SYN.)* unguarded, defenseless, unprotected.

wacky *(SYN.)* strange, crazy, peculiar.

wad *(SYN.)* hunk, clump, chunk.

wafer *(SYN.)* cracker, lozenge.

waft *(SYN.)* convey, glide, sail, float.

wage *(SYN.)* conduct, pursue, make.

wager *(SYN.)* stake, bet, play, gamble, speculate, risk, chance.

wages *(SYN.)* payment, compensation, fee, allowance, pay, salary, earnings, rate, recompense.

wagon *(SYN.)* carriage, buggy, cart, surrey, stagecoach.

waif *(SYN.)* guttersnipe, ragamuffin, tramp, vagrant, urchin.

wail *(SYN.)* mourn, moan, cry, bewail, lament, bemoan, sorrow.

wait *(SYN.)* linger, tarry, attend, bide, watch, delay, await, abide, stay, serve, pause, remain, postponement, rest, minister, expect.

(ANT.) hasten, act leave, expedite.

waive *(SYN.)* renounce, abandon, surrender, relinquish, forgo.

(ANT.) uphold, maintain.

wake *(SYN.)* awaken, rouse, waken, arouse, stimulate, activate.

(ANT.) doze, sleep.

waken *(SYN.)* wake, arouse, rouse, awaken, stimulate, activate.

(ANT.) doze, sleep.

walk *(SYN.)* step, stroll, march, amble, saunter, hike, lane, path, passage, preambulate.

wall *(SYN.)* barricade, divider, partition, panel, stockade.

wallow *(SYN.)* plunge, roll, flounder, grovel.

wan *(SYN.)* colorless, haggard, gaunt, pale, pallid, pasty, pale.

wander *(SYN.)* rove, stroll, deviate, ramble, digress, roam, traipse, range, err, meander, saunter.

(ANT.) linger, stop, settle.

wane *(SYN.)* abate, weaken, fade, ebb, decrease, wither, subside.

want *(SYN.)* penury, destitution, crave, desire, requirement, poverty, wish, require, need, privation.

(ANT.) wealth, plenty, abundance.

wanton *(SYN.)* lecherous, immoral, loose, lewd, salacious, lustful.

war *(SYN.)* battle, hostilities, combat, fight, strife, contention.

warble *(SYN.)* sing, trill, chirp.

ward *(SYN.)* annex, wing, section.

warden *(SYN.)* custodian, guard, guardian, keeper, turnkey, jailer, curator, gamekeeper.

ward off *(SYN.)* repel, thwart, deflect, foil, deter, forestall, repulse.

wardrobe *(SYN.)* chiffonier, bureau, closet, armoire.

warehouse *(SYN.)* arsenal, storehouse, depository.

wares *(SYN.)* merchandise, staples, inventory, commodities, goods.

wariness *(SYN.)* heed, care, watchfulness, caution, vigilance.

(ANT.) carelessness, abandon.

warlike *(SYN.)* hostile, unfriendly, combative, belligerent, antagonistic, pugnacious, bellicose, opposed, aggressive.

(ANT.) cordial, peaceful, amicable.

warm *(SYN.)* sincere, cordial, hearty, earnest, sympathetic, ardent, heated, gracious, temperate, enthusiastic, lukewarm, tepid, eager, sociable.

(ANT.) cool, aloof, taciturn, brisk, indifferent.

warmhearted *(SYN.)* loving, kind, kindhearted, friendly, generous.

warmth *(SYN.)* friendliness, cordiality, geniality, understanding, compassion.

warn *(SYN.)* apprise, notify, admonish, caution, advise, inform.

warning *(SYN.)* advice, information, caution, portent, admonition, indication, notice, sign.

warp *(SYN.)* turn, bend, twist, deprave.

warrant *(SYN.)* pledge, assurance, warranty, guarantee, authorize, approve, mandate, sanction.

warrior *(SYN.)* combatant, fighter, soldier, mercenary, guerrilla.

wary *(SYN.)* careful, awake, watchful, heedful, attentive, alive, mindful, cautious, thoughtful.

(ANT.) unaware, indifferent, careless, apathetic.

wash *(SYN.)* launder, cleanse, rub, touch, reach, border, wet, clean, scrub, bathe.

(ANT.) soil, dirty, stain.

washed-out *(SYN.)* bleached, dull, faded, pale, discolored, pallid.

waspish *(SYN.)* irritable, petulant, fractious, ill-tempered, snappish, touchy.

(ANT.) pleasant, genial.

waste *(SYN.)* forlorn, bleak, wild, solitary, dissipate, abandoned, spend, deserted, bare, consume, dwindle, decay, misspend, decrease, wither, wear, effluent, useless, unused, garbage, rub-

bish, refuse, trash, uninhabited.
(ANT.) cultivated, attended.

wasteful *(SYN.)* wanton, costly, lavish, extravagant.

watch *(SYN.)* inspect, descry, behold, distinguish, guard, attend, observe, contemplate, espy, perceive, look at, protect, chronometer, timepiece, patrol, vigil, duty, shift, regard, note, view, sentinel, watchman, sentry, discern.

watchdog *(SYN.)* lookout, guard, sentinel, sentry.

watchful *(SYN.)* alert, careful, attentive, vigilant, wary, cautious.

waterfall *(SYN.)* cascade, cataract.

watertight *(SYN.)* impregnable, solid.

wave *(SYN.)* ripple, whitecap, undulation, breaker, surf, swell, sea, surge, tide, flow, stream.

waver *(SYN.)* question, suspect, flicker, deliberate, doubt, distrust, hesitate, falter, stagger.
(ANT.) confide, trust, believe, decide.

wavering *(SYN.)* fickle, shifting, variable, changeable, vacillating, fitful.
(ANT.) unchanging, constant, uniform.

wavy *(SYN.)* rippling, serpentine, curly.

wax *(SYN.)* raise, heighten, expand, accrue, enhance, extend, multiply, enlarge, augment, amplify.
(ANT.) reduce, atrophy, diminish.

way *(SYN.)* habit, road, course, avenue, route, mode, system, channel, track, fashion, method, walk, approach, manner, technique, means, procedure, trail, proceed, progress, path, style.

waylay *(SYN.)* surprise, accost, ambush, attack, pounce, intercept.

wayward *(SYN.)* stubborn, headstrong, contrary, obstinate, naughty, disobedient, rebellious, refractory.

weak *(SYN.)* frail, debilitated, delicate, poor, wavering, infirm, bending, lame, defenseless, vulnerable, fragile, pliant, feeble, watery, diluted, undecided, irresolute, unsteady, yielding, tender.
(ANT.) strong, potent, sturdy, powerful.

weaken *(SYN.)* exhaust, sap, disable, devitalize.

weakling *(SYN.)* sissy, namby-pamby, milksop, milquetoast.

weakness *(SYN.)* incompetence, inability, impotence, handicap, fondness, affection, disability, incapacity, feebleness.
(ANT.) strength, ability, dislike, power.

wealth *(SYN.)* fortune, money, riches,

possessions, means, abundance, opulence, affluence, property, quantity, profession, luxury.
(ANT.) want, need.

wealthy *(SYN.)* rich, exorbitant, prosperous, affluent, successful.
(ANT.) poverty-stricken, poor, indigent, impoverished, beggarly, destitute, needy.

wear *(SYN.)* erode, fray, grind, apparel, clothes, garb, attire.

wearied *(SYN.)* weak, languid, faint, irresolute, feeble, timid.
(ANT.) brave, vigorous.

weary *(SYN.)* faint, spent, worn, tired, fatigued, exhausted, tiresome, bored, wearied, tedious, jaded.
(ANT.) rested, hearty, fresh.

weasel *(SYN.)* cheat, traitor, betrayer.

weave *(SYN.)* lace, interlace, plait, intertwine, braid, knit.

web *(SYN.)* netting, network, net, cobweb, trap, entanglement.

wed *(SYN.)* espouse, marry.

wedlock *(SYN.)* marriage, union, espousal, wedding, matrimony.

wedge *(SYN.)* chock, jam, lodge.

wee *(SYN.)* small, tiny, miniature, petite, microscopic, minute.

weep *(SYN.)* mourn, sob, bemoan, cry, lament, whimper, wail.

weigh *(SYN.)* heed, deliberate, consider, ponder, contemplate, reflect, evaluate.
(ANT.) neglect, ignore.

weight *(SYN.)* importance, emphasis, load, burden, import, stress, influence, heaviness, gravity, significance.
(ANT.) triviality, levity, insignificance, lightness, buoyancy.

weird *(SYN.)* odd, eerie, strange, unnatural, peculiar, spooky.

welcome *(SYN.)* take, entertain, greet, accept, receive, gain, greeting, shelter.
(ANT.) reject, bestow, impart, discharge.

weld *(SYN.)* solder, connect, fuse, bond.

welfare *(SYN.)* good, well-being, prosperity.

well *(SYN.)* hearty, happy, sound, hale, beneficial, good, convenient, expedient, healthy, favorably, fully, thoroughly, surely, adequately, satisfactorily, competently, certainly, completely, trim, undoubtedly, fit, profitable.
(ANT.) infirm, depressed, weak.

well-being *(SYN.)* delight, happiness, satisfaction, contentment, gladness.
(ANT.) sorrow, grief, sadness, despair.

well-bred (SYN.) cultured, polite, genteel, courtly, refined, cultivated.
(ANT.) crude, vulgar, boorish, rude.
well-known (SYN.) famous, illustrious, celebrated, noted, eminent, renowned.
(ANT.) unknown, ignominious, obscure.
wet (SYN.) moist, dank, soaked, damp, drenched, dampen, moisten.
(ANT.) arid, dry, parched.
wharf (SYN.) pier, dock.
wheedle (SYN.) coax, cajole, persuade.
whim (SYN.) fancy, notion, humor, quirk, caprice, inclination, vagary.
whimsical (SYN.) quaint, strange, curious, odd, unusual, droll, queer, eccentric, peculiar.
(ANT.) normal, common, usual, familiar.
whine (SYN.) whimper, moan, complain.
whip (SYN.) scourge, thrash, beat, lash.
whirl (SYN.) rotate, twirl, revolve, reel.
whole (SYN.) total, sound, all, intact, complete, well, hale, integral, unimpaired, healed, entire, uncut, undivided, unbroken, undamaged, intact, perfect.
(ANT.) partial, defective, deficient.
wholesome (SYN.) robust, well, hale, healthy, sound, salubrious, good, hygienic, salutary, nourishing, healthful, strong, nutritious, hearty.
(ANT.) frail, noxious, infirm, delicate, injurious, diseased.
wicked (SYN.) deleterious, iniquitous, immoral, bad, evil, base, ungodly, unsound, sinful, bitter, blasphemous, malicious, evil-minded, profane, baleful, hostile, rancorous, unwholesome.
(ANT.) moral, reputable, honorable.
wide (SYN.) large, broad, sweeping, extensive, vast, expanded.
(ANT.) restricted, narrow.
width (SYN.) extensiveness, breadth.
wield (SYN.) handle, brandish.
wild (SYN.) outlandish, uncivilized, untamed, irregular, wanton, foolish, mad, barbarous, rough, waste, desert, uncultivated, boisterous, unruly, savage, primitive, giddy, unrestrained, silly, wayward, uncontrolled, impetuous, crazy, ferocious, undomesticated, desolate.
(ANT.) quiet, gentle, placid, tame, restrained, civilized.
willful (SYN.) intentional, designed, contemplated, studied, premeditated.
(ANT.) fortuitous.
will (SYN.) intention, desire, volition,

decision, resolution, wish, resoluteness, choice, determination, pleasure.
(ANT.) disinterest, coercion, indifference.
willing (SYN.) agreeing, energetic, enthusiastic, consenting, agreeable, eager.
wilt (SYN.) sag, droop, weaken.
wily (SYN.) cunning, foxy, sly, crafty.
win (SYN.) gain, succeed, prevail, achieve, thrive, obtain, get, acquire, earn, flourish.
(ANT.) lose, miss, forfeit, fail.
wind (SYN.) gale, breeze, storm, gust, blast, air, breath, flurry, puff, blow, hurricane, typhoon, cyclone, tornado, suggestion, hint, clue, zephyr, squall, coil, crank, screw, meander, wander, twist, weave, draft.
winsome (SYN.) winning, agreeable.
wisdom (SYN.) insight, judgment, learning, sense, discretion, reason, prudence, erudition, foresight, intelligence, sageness, knowledge, information, sagacity.
(ANT.) nonsense, foolishness, stupidity, ignorance.
wise (SYN.) informed, sagacious, learned, penetrating, enlightened, advisable, prudent, profound, deep, erudite, scholarly, knowing, sound, intelligent, expedient, discerning.
(ANT.) simple, shallow, foolish.
wish (SYN.) crave, hanker, long, hunger, yearning, lust, craving, yearn, want, appetite, covet, longing, desire, urge.
(ANT.) hate, aversion, loathing, distaste.
wit (SYN.) sense, humor, pleasantry, satire, intelligence, comprehension, understanding, banter, mind, wisdom, intellect, wittiness, fun, drollery, humorist, wag, comedian, witticism.
(ANT.) solemnity, commonplace.
witch (SYN.) magician, sorcerer, enchanter, sorceress, enchantress, warlock.
witchcraft (SYN.) enchantment, magic, wizardry, conjuring, voodoo.
withdraw (SYN.) renounce, leave, abandon, recall, retreat, go, secede, desert, quit, retire, depart, retract, forsake.
(ANT.) enter, tarry, abide, place, stay.
wither (SYN.) wilt, languish, dry, shrivel, decline, fade, decay, sear, waste, wizen, weaken, droop, sink, fail, shrink.
(ANT.) renew, refresh, revive.
withhold (SYN.) forbear, abstain, repress, check, refrain.
(ANT.) persist, continue.
withstand (SYN.) defy, contradict, bar,

thwart, oppose, hinder, counteract.
(ANT.) succumb, cooperate, support.

witness *(SYN.)* perceive, proof, spectator, confirmation, see, attestation, watch, observe, eyewitness, declaration, notice, testimony.
(ANT.) refutation, contradiction, argument.

witty *(SYN.)* funny, talented, apt, bright, adroit, sharp, clever.
(ANT.) slow, dull, clumsy, awkward.

wizard *(SYN.)* magician, sorcerer.

wizardry *(SYN.)* voodoo, legerdemain, conjuring, witchcraft, charm.

woe *(SYN.)* sorrow, disaster, trouble, evil, agony, suffering, anguish, sadness, grief, distress, misery, torment, misfortune.
(ANT.) pleasure, delight, fun.

womanly *(SYN.)* girlish, womanish, female, ladylike.
(ANT.) mannish, virile, male, masculine.

wonder *(SYN.)* awe, curiosity, miracle, admiration, surprise, wonderment, marvel, conjecture, amazement, question, astonishment.
(ANT.) expectation, familiarity, indifference, apathy, triviality.

wonderful *(SYN.)* extraordinary, marvelous, astonishing, amazing, remarkable, astounding.

wont *(SYN.)* practice, use, custom, training, habit, usage, manner.
(ANT.) inexperience, disuse.

word *(SYN.)* phrase, term, utterance, expression, articulate.

wordy *(SYN.)* talkative, verbose, garrulous.

work *(SYN.)* opus, employment, achievement, performance, toil, business, exertion, occupation, labor, job, product, accomplishment, travail, effort.
(ANT.) recreation, leisure, vacation, ease.

working *(SYN.)* busy, active, industrious.
(ANT.) lazy, dormant, passive, inactive.

world *(SYN.)* globe, earth, universe.

worldly *(SYN.)* bodily, fleshy, animal, carnal, corporeal, gross, voluptuous.
(ANT.) refined, temperate, exalted, spiritual.

worn *(SYN.)* tired, jaded, exhausted, wearied, faint, weary.
(ANT.) invigorated, fresh, rested.

worry *(SYN.)* concern, trouble, disquiet, anxiety, fear, pain, harry, gall, grieve, persecute, annoy, disturb, fidget, chafe,

agonize, bother, haze, pester, uneasiness, fret.
(ANT.) console, comfort, contentment, satisfaction, peace.

worship *(SYN.)* honor, revere, adore, idolize, reverence, glorify, respect, deify, venerate.
(ANT.) curse, scorn, blaspheme, despise.

worth *(SYN.)* value, price, deserving, excellence, usefulness, worthiness, merit.
(ANT.) uselessness, valuelessness, cheapness.

worthless *(SYN.)* empty, idle, abortive, ineffectual, bootless, pointless, vain, unavailing.
(ANT.) meek, effective, modest, potent.

wound *(SYN.)* mar, harm, damage, hurt, dishonor, injure, spoil, wrong, disfigure.
(ANT.) compliment, benefit, preserve, help.

wrangle *(SYN.)* spat, bickering, affray, argument, dispute, quarrel, altercation, contention, squabble, disagreement.
(ANT.) peace, friendliness, reconciliation, harmony.

wrap *(SYN.)* cover, protect, shield, cloak, mask, clothe, curtain, guard, conceal.
(ANT.) reveal, bare, unveil, expose.

wrath *(SYN.)* fury, anger, irritation, rage, animosity, passion, temper, petulance, choler, resentment.
(ANT.) patience, conciliation, peace.

wreck *(SYN.)* ravage, devastation, extinguish, destroy, annihilate, damage, raze, demolish, destruction, ruin, devastate.
(ANT.) make, construct, preserve, establish.

wrench *(SYN.)* tug, jerk, twist.

wrestle *(SYN.)* fight, tussle, grapple.

wretch *(SYN.)* cad, scoundrel, rogue.

wretched *(SYN.)* forlorn, miserable, comfortless, despicable, low, worthless, disconsolate, sorry, mean, heartbroken.
(ANT.) noble, contented, happy, significant.

wring *(SYN.)* twist, extract.

writer *(SYN.)* creator, maker, author, father, composer.

wrong *(SYN.)* awry, incorrect, improper, amiss, naughty, inappropriate, criminal, faulty, erroneous, bad, evil, imprecise, inaccurate, askew, sin, incorrectness, false, unsuitable, impropriety, wickedness, immoral.
(ANT.) proper, true, correct, suitable.

wry *(SYN.)* amusing, witty, dry, droll.

yacht *(SYN.)* sailboat, boat, cruiser.

yank *(SYN.)* pull, wrest, draw, haul, tug, jerk, wrench, heave, extract.

yap *(SYN.)* howl, bark.

yard *(SYN.)* pen, confine, court, enclosure, compound, garden.

yardstick *(SYN.)* measure, criterion, gauge.

yarn *(SYN.)* wool, tale, narrative, thread, story, fiber, anecdote, spiel.

yaw *(SYN.)* tack, change course, pitch, toss. roll.

yawn *(SYN.)* open, gape.

yearly *(SYN.)* annually.

yearn *(SYN.)* pine, long for, want, desire, crave, wish.

yearning *(SYN.)* hungering, craving, desire, longing, appetite, lust, urge, aspiration, wish.

(ANT.) distaste, loathing, abomination, hate.

yell *(SYN.)* call, scream, shout, whoop, howl, roar, holler, wail, bawl.

yellow *(SYN.)* fearful, cowardly, chicken.

(ANT.) bold, brave.

yelp *(SYN.)* screech, squeal, howl, bark.

yen *(SYN.)* longing, craving, fancy, appetite, desire, lust, hunger.

yet *(SYN.)* moreover, also, additionally, besides.

yield *(SYN.)* produce, afford, breed, grant, accord, cede, relent, succumb, bestow, allow, permit, give way, submit, bear, surrender, supply, fruits, give up, abdicate, return, impart, harvest, permit, accede, acquiesce, crop, capitulate, pay, concede, generate, relinquish.

(ANT.) assert, deny, refuse, resist, struggle, oppose, strive.

yielding *(SYN.)* dutiful, submissive, compliant, obedient, tractable.

(ANT.) rebellious, intractable, insubordinate.

yoke *(SYN.)* tether, leash, bridle, harness.

yokel *(SYN.)* hick, peasant, hayseed, innocent.

young *(SYN.)* immature, undeveloped, youthful, underdeveloped, juvenile, junior, underage.

(ANT.) old, mature, elderly.

youngster *(SYN.)* kid, lad, stripling, minor, youth, child, fledgling.

(ANT.) adult, elder.

youthful *(SYN.)* childish, immature, young, boyish, childlike, callow, girlish, puerile.

(ANT.) old, elderly, senile, aged, mature.

yowl *(SYN.)* yell, shriek, cry, wail, whoop, howl, scream.

zany *(SYN.)* clownish, comical, foolish, silly, scatterbrained.

zap *(SYN.)* drive, vim, pep, determination.

zeal *(SYN.)* fervor, eagerness, passion, feverency, vehemence, devotion, intensity, excitement, earnestness, inspiration, warmth, ardor, fanaticism, enthusiasm.

(ANT.) unconcern, ennui, apathy, indifference.

zealot *(SYN.)* champion, crank, fanatic, bigot.

zealous *(SYN.)* enthusiastic, fiery, keen, eager, fervid, ardent, intense, vehement, fervent, glowing, hot, impassioned, passionate.

(ANT.) cool, nonchalant, apathetic.

zenith *(SYN.)* culmination, apex, height, acme, consummation, top, summit, pinnacle, climax, peak.

(ANT.) floor, nadir, depth, base, anticlimax.

zero *(SYN.)* nonexistent, nil, nothing, none.

zest *(SYN.)* enjoyment, savor, eagerness, relish, satisfaction, gusto, spice, tang, pleasure, exhilaration.

zestful *(SYN.)* delightful, thrilling, exciting, stimulating, enjoyable.

zip *(SYN.)* vigor, vim, energy, vitality, spirited, animation, provocative.

zone *(SYN.)* region, climate, tract, belt, sector, section, district, locality, precinct, territory.

zoo *(SYN.)* menagerie.

zoom *(SYN.)* zip, fly, speed, whiz, roar, race.

WEBSTER'S SPELLER

Edited by
Liz Kauffman

Proofread by
Marsha Tischner

This book was not published by the original publishers of the Webster's Speller, or by any of their successors.

Staff
Kim Nichols
Kathleen Flickinger
Cindy Carter
Marsha Tischner

WEBSTER'S
SPELLER

This **WEBSTER'S SPELLER** is designed for use in the school, in the office, and in the home, as a Quick Referance Guide to spelling and proper word hyphenation.

Words that contain double dashes (--) between letters indicates a hyphenated word. Single dashes (-) show syllabic division.

A

aard-vark
a-back
ab-a-cus
  ab-a-cus-es
  ab-a-ci
a-baft
  abaft-ment
  abaft-ed
ab-a-lo-ne
a-ban-don
  aban-doned
  aban-don-er
  aban-don-ment
a-base
  a-based
  a-bas-ing
  a-base-ment
a-bash
  a-bash-ment
a-bate
  a-bat-ed
  a-bat-ing
  a-bat-a-ble
  a-bate-ment
aba-tis
ab-at-oir
ab-ba-cy
  ab-ba-tial
ab-bess
ab-bey
  ab-beys
ab-bot
ab-bre-vi-a-tion
  ab-bre-vi-ate
  ab-bre-vi-at-ed
  ab-bre-vi-at-ing
  ab-bre-vi-a-tor
ab-di-cate
  ab-di-cat-ed
  ab-di-cat-ing
  ab-di-ca-tion
ab-do-men
  ab-dom-i-nal
  ab-dom-i-nal-ly
ab-duce
ab-duct
  ab-duc-tion
  ab-duc-tor
  ab-duct-ing
a-beam
a-bed
ab-er-rance
  ab-er-ran-cy
ab-er-rant
  ab-er-rant-ly
ab-er-ra-tion

ab-er-ra-tion-al
a-bet
  a-bet-ted
  a-bet-ting
  a-bet-ment
  a-bet-tor
  a-bet-ter
a-bey-ance
ab-hor
  ab-horred
  ab-hor-ring
  ab-hor-rence
  ab-hor-er
ab-hor-rence
ab-hor-rent
  ab-hor-rent-ly
a-bide
  a-bid-er
  a-bi-ded
  a-bid-ing
  a-bid-ance
a-bid-ing
  a-bid-ing-ly
a-bil-i-ty
  a-bil-i-ties
ab-ject
  ab-ject-ly
  ab-ject-ness
  ab-jec-tion
ab-jure
  ab-jured
  ab-jur-ing
  ab-ju-ra-tion
  ab-jur-er
ab-late
  ab-lat-ed
  ab-lat-ing
  ab-la-tion
  ab-la-tive
  ab-la-tive-ly
ab-laut
a-blaze
a-ble
  a-bler
  a-blest
  a-bly
a-ble-bod-ied
a-bloom
ab-lu-tion
  ab-lu-tion-ar-y
ab-ne-gate
  ab-ne-gat-ed
  ab-ne-gat-ing
  ab-ne-ga-tor
  ab-ne-ga-tion
ab-nor-mal

ab-nor-mal-ly
ab-nor-mal-i-ty
ab-nor-mal-i-ties
a-board
a-bode
a-boil
a-bol-ish
  a-bol-ish-a-ble
  a-bol-ish-er
  a-bol-ish-ment
ab-o-li-tion
  ab-o-li-tion-ary
  ab-o-li-tion-ism
  ab-o-li-tion-ist
a-b-oma-sum
  a-b-oma-sal
a-bom-i-na-ble
  a-bom-i-na-bly
a-bom-i-nate
  a-bom-i-nat-ed
  a-bom-i-nat-ing
  a-bom-i-na-tion
  a-bom-i-na-tor
ab-o-rig-i-ne
  ab-o-rig-i-nal
  ab-o-rig-i-nal-ly
a-born-ing
a-bort
  a-bort-er
a-bor-ti-fa-cient
a-bor-tion
a-bor-tion-ist
a-bor-tive
  a-bor-tive-ness
  a-bor-tive-ly
a-bout-face
a-bove-board
ab-ra-ca-dab-ra
abrad-ant
a-brade
  a-brad-ed
  a-brad-ing
  a-brad-a-ble
  a-brad-er
a-bra-sion
a-bra-sive
  a-bra-sive-ness
  a-bra-sive-ly
ab-re-act
a-breast
a-bridge
  a-bridged
  a-bridg-ing
  a-bridg-er
  a-bridg-a-ble
  a-bridg-ment

3

a-bridge-ment
a-broach
a-broad
ab-ro-gate
  ab-ro-gat-ed
  ab-ro-gat-ing
  ab-ro-ga-tion
ab-rupt
  abrupt-ness
  abrupt-ly
ab-scess
  ab-scessed
ab-scis-sa
  ab-scis-sas
  ab-scis-sae
ab-scis-sion
ab-scond
  ab-scond-er
ab-sence
ab-sent
  ab-sent-ly
ab-sen-tee
  ab-sen-tee-ism
ab-sent-mind-ed
  ab-sent-mind-ed-ly
  ab-sent-mind-ed-ness
ab-sinthe
ab-so-lute
  ab-so-lute-ness
  ab-so-lute-ly
  ab-so-lu-tion
  ab-so-lut-ism
  ab-so-lut-ist
ab-solve
  ab-solved
  ab-solv-ing
  ab-solv-a-ble
  ab-solv-er
ab-sorb
  ab-sorb-er
  ab-sorb-a-bil-i-ty
  ab-sorb-a-ble
  ab-sorb-en-cy
  ab-sorb-ent
  ab-sorb-tion
  ab-sorb-tive
  ab-sorp-tiv-i-ty
ab-sorb-ing
  ab-sorb-ing-ly
ab-stain
  ab-stain-er
  ab-sten-tion
  ab-sti-nence
  ab-sti-nent
ab-ste-mi-ous
  ab-ste-mi-ous-ly

ab-stract
  ab-stract-ly
  ab-strac-tion
  ab-strac-tive
ab-stract-ed
  ab-stract-ed-ly
  ab-stract-ed-ness
  ab-strac-tion-ism
  ab-strac-tion-ist
ab-struse
  ab-struse-ness
  ab-struse-ly
  ab-stru-si-ty
ab-surd
  ab-surd-ness
  ab-surd-i-ty
  ab-surd-i-ties
  ab-surd-ly
a-bub-ble
a-build-ing
a-bud-dance
a-bun-dant
  a-bun-dant-ly
a-buse
  a-bused
  a-bus-ing
  a-bus-er
  a-bus-a-ble
a-bu-sive
  a-bu-sive-ly
  a-bu-sive-ness
a-but
  a-but-ter
  a-but-ted
  a-but-ting
a-but-ment
a-but-tals
a-but-ting
a-buzz
a-bye
a-bysm
a-bys-mal
  a-bys-mal-ly
a-byss
  a-bys-sal
a-ca-cia
ac-a-deme
ac-a-dem-ic
  ac-a-dem-i-cal-ly
  ac-a-dem-i-cal
acad-e-mi-cian
a-cad-e-my
  a-cad-e-mies
a-can-thus
  a-can-thus-es
  a-can-thi

a cap-pel-la
ac-cede
  ac-ced-ed
  ac-ced-ing
ac-ce-le-ran-do
ac-cel-er-ate
  ac-cel-er-at-ed
  ac-cel-er-at-ing
  ac-cel-er-a-tive
  ac-cel-er-at-ing-ly
ac-cel-er-a-tion
ac-cel-er-a-tor
ac-cel-er-om-e-ter
ac-cent
  ac-cent-less
ac-cen-tu-al
  ac-cen-tu-al-ly
ac-cen-tu-ate
  ac-cen-tu-at-ed
  ac-cen-tu-at-ing
  ac-cen-tu-a-tion
ac-cept
  ac-cept-ing-ly
  ac-cept-ing-ness
  ac-cept-ance
  ac-cept-er
  ac-cept-or
ac-cept-a-ble
  ac-cept-a-bil-i-ty
  ac-cept-a-bly
  ac-cept-a-ble-ness
ac-cept-ed
  ac-cept-ed-ly
ac-cess
ac-ces-si-ble
  ac-ces-si-bil-i-ty
  ac-ces-si-ble-ness
  ac-ces-si-bly
ac-ces-sion
  ac-ces-sion-al
ac-ces-so-ry
  ac-ces-so-ri-ly
  ac-ces-so-ri-ness
ac-ci-dent
  ac-ci-dent-ly
  ac-ci-den-tal
  ac-ci-den-tal-ness
  ac-ci-den-tal-ly
ac-ci-dent--prone
ac-cip-i-ter
  ac-cip-i-trine
ac-claim
  ac-claim-er
ac-cla-ma-tion
ac-clam-a-to-ry
ac-cli-mate

4

ac-cli-mat-ed
ac-cli-mat-ing
ac-cli-ma-tion
ac-cli-ma-ti-za-tion
ac-cli-ma-tize
ac-cli-ma-tized
ac-cli-ma-tiz-er
ac-cli-ma-tiz-ing
ac-cli-ma-ti-za-tion
ac-cliv-i-ty
ac-cliv-i-ties
ac-co-lade
ac-com-mo-date
ac-com-mo-dat-ed
ac-com-mo-dat-ing
ac-com-mo-da-tive
ac-com-mo-dat-er
ac-com-mo-da-tion
ac-com-pa-ni-ment
ac-com-pa-nist
ac-com-pa-ny
ac-com-pa-nied
ac-com-pa-ny-ing
ac-com-pa-nies
ac-com-plice
ac-com-plish
ac-com-plish-a-ble
ac-com-plish-ment
ac-com-plish-er
ac-com-plished
ac-cord
ac-cord-ance
ac-cord-ing
ac-cord-ing-ly
ac-cor-dant
ac-cor-dant-ly
ac-cor-di-on
ac-cor-di-on-ist
ac-cost
ac-couche-ment
ac-cou-cheur
ac-count
ac-count-a-ble
ac-count-a-bil-i-ty
ac-count-a-bly
ac-count-a-ble-ness
ac-count-an-cy
ac-count-ant
ac-coun-tant-ship
ac-count-ing
ac-cou-tre-ment
ac-cred-it
ac-cred-i-table
ac-cred-i-ta-tion
ac-crete
ac-creting

ac-creted
ac-cre-tion
ac-cre-tive
ac-cre-tion-ary
ac-cru-al
ac-crue
ac-crued
ac-cru-ing
ac-cru-a-ble
ac-crue-ment
ac-cul-tur-ate
ac-cul-tur-ating
ac-cul-tur-ated
ac-cul-tur-a-tion
ac-cul-tur-a-tion-al
ac-cul-tur-a-tive
ac-cum-u-late
ac-cum-u-lat-ed
ac-cum-u-lat-ing
ac-cum-u-la-tion
ac-cu-mu-la-tive
ac-cu-mu-la-tive-ness
ac-cu-mu-la-tive-ly
ac-cum-u-la-tor
ac-cu-ra-cy
ac-cu-ra-cies
ac-cu-rate
ac-cu-rate-ly
ac-cu-rate-ness
ac-curs-ed
ac-curst
ac-curs-ed-ness
ac-curs-ed-ly
ac-cus-al
ac-cu-sa-tion
ac-cu-sa-tive
ac-cuse
ac-cus-er
ac-cus-ed
ac-cus-ing
ac-cu-sa-tion
ac-cu-sa-to-ry
ac-cus-ing-ly
ac-cus-tom
ac-cus-tom-a-tion
ac-cus-tomed
ac-cus-tomed-ness
ace-dia
a-cel-da-ma
a-cel-lu-lar
a-cen-tric
a-ceph-a-lous
a-ce-quia
a-cerb
a-cer-bi-ty
ac-er-o-la

ac-er-vate
ac-er-vate-ly
ac-er-va-tion
ac-e-tab-u-lar-ia
ac-e-tab-u-lum
ac-e-tab-u-lar
ac-et-al-de-hyde
ac-et-amide
ac-et-amin-o-phen
ac-et-an-i-lide
ac-e-tate
a-ce-tic
a-cet-i-fy
a-cet-i-fied
a-cet-i-fy-ing
a-ce-ti-fi-ca-tion
a-ce-ti-fi-er
ac-e-tone
ac-e-ton-ic
ac-e-to-phe-net-i-din
a-ce-tous
a-cet-y-late
a-cet-y-lat-ing
a-cet-y-lat-ed
a-cet-y-la-tion
a-cet-y-la-tive
a-ce-tyl-cho-line
a-ce-tyl-cho-lin-ic
a-cet-y-lene
a-cet-y-le-nic
ache
ached
ach-ing
ach-ing-ly
a-chene
a-chieve
a-chiev-ed
a-chiev-ing
a-chiev-a-ble
a-chiev-er
a-chieve-ment
a-chla-myd-e-ous
a-chlor-ly-dric
a-chon-drite
a-chon-drit-ic
a-chon-dro-pla-sia
a-chon-dro-plas-tic
ach-ro-mat-ic
ach-ro-ma-tic-i-ty
ach-ro-mat-i-cal-ly
ach-ro-ma-tize
a-cic-u-la
a-cic-u-late
a-cic-u-lar
ac-id
ac-id-ness

ac-id-ly
ac-id-ic
a-cid-i-fy
  a-cid-i-fied
  a-cid-i-fy-ing
  a-cid-i-fi-ca-tion
  a-cid-i-fi-er
a-cid-i-ty
ac-i-do-phile
ac-i-do-phil-ic
ac-i-do-sis
  ac-i-dot-ic
a-cid-u-late
  a-cid-u-lat-ed
  a-cid-u-lat-ing
  a-cid-u-la-tion
a-cid-u-lent
a-cid-u-lous
ac-i-nar
ac-i-nus
  ac-i-nous
ac-knowl-edge
  ac-knowl-edged
  ac-knowl-edg-ing
  ac-knowl-edge-a-ble
  ac-knowl-edg-er
  ac-knowl-edg-ment
  ac-knowl-edge-ment
ac-me
ac-ne
  ac-ned
ac-o-lyte
ac-o-nite
a-corn
a-cous-tic
  a-cous-ti-cal
  a-cous-ti-cal-ly
a-cous-tics
ac-quaint
ac-quaint-ance
  ac-quaint-ance-ship
ac-qui-esce
  ac-qui-esc-ed
  ac-qui-esc-ing
  ac-qui-es-cence
  ac-qui-es-cent
  ac-qui-es-cent-ly
ac-quire
  ac-quired
  ac-quir-ing
  ac-quir-er
  ac-quir-a-ble
  ac-quire-ment
  ac-qui-si-tion
ac-quit
  ac-quit-ted

ac-quit-ting
  ac-quit-tal
a-cre
a-cre-age
ac-rid
  acrid-i-ty
ac-ri-mo-ni-ous
  ac-ri-mo-ni-ous-ness
  ac-ri-mo-ni-ous-ly
ac-ri-mo-ny
ac-ro-bat
  ac-ro-bat-ic
ac-ro-nym
ac-ro-pho-bi-a
a-crop-o-lis
a-cros-tic
  a-cros-ti-cal-ly
a-cryl-ic
ac-ry-lo-ni-trile
act-ing
ac-tin-ia
  ac-tin-i-an
ac-tin-ic
  ac-tin-i-cal-ly
ac-tin-ism
ac-tin-i-um
ac-ti-nom-e-ter
  ac-ti-nom-e-try
ac-ti-no-mor-phic
  ac-ti-no-mor-phy
ac-ti-no-my-ces
  ac-ti-no-my-ce-tal
  ac-ti-no-my-co-sis
  ac-ti-no-my-cot-ic
ac-ti-non
ac-ti-no-zo-an
ac-tion
  ac-tion-a-ble
  ac-tion-a-bly
ac-ti-vate
  ac-ti-vat-ed
  ac-ti-vat-ing
  ac-ti-va-tion
  ac-ti-va-tor
ac-tive
  ac-tive-ly
  ac-tive-ness
ac-tiv-ism
  ac-tiv-ist
ac-tiv-i-ty
  ac-tiv-i-ties
ac-tor
ac-tress
ac-tu-al
  ac-tu-al-ly
  ac-tu-al-i-ty

ac-tu-al-i-ties
ac-tu-al-ize
  ac-tu-al-ized
  ac-tu-al-iz-ing
  ac-tu-al-i-za-tion
ac-tu-ar-y
  ac-tu-ar-ies
  ac-tu-ar-i-al
ac-tu-ate
  ac-tu-at-ed
  ac-tu-at-ing
  ac-tu-a-tion
  ac-tu-a-tor
a-cu-i-ty
  a-cu-i-ties
a-cu-men
a-cu-mi-nate
ac-u-punc-ture
a-cute
  a-cute-ly
  a-cute-ness
  a-cut-est
  a-cut-er
a-cy-clic
ac-yl
ad-age
a-da-gio
ad-a-mant
  ad-a-mant-ly
ad-a-man-tine
a-dapt
  a-dapt-er
  a-dapt-ed-ness
a-dapt-a-ble
  a-dapt-a-bil-i-ty
ad-ap-ta-tion
  ad-ap-ta-tion-al
  ad-ap-ta-tion-al-ly
a-dap-tive
  a-dap-tive-ly
  a-d-ap-tiv-i-ty
add
  add-a-ble
  add-i-ble
ad-dax
  ad-dax-es
ad-dend
ad-den-dum
  ad-den-da
ad-der
ad-dict
  ad-dic-tion
  ad-dict-ed
  ad-dic-tive
Ad-dis Ab-a-ba
Ad-di-son's dis-ease

6

ad-di-tion
ad-di-tion-al
ad-di-tion-al-ly
ad-di-tive
ad-di-tive-ly
ad-di-tiv-i-ty
ad-dle
ad-dress
ad-dress-er
ad-dress-ee
ad-dress-a-ble
ad-duce
ad-duc-ing
ad-duced
ad-duc-er
ad-duct
ad-duc-tion
ad-duc-tive
a-de-lan-ta-do
a-demp-tion
ad-e-nine
ad-e-ni-tis
ad-e-no-car-ci-no-ma
ad-e-no-hy-poph-y-sis
ad-e-noid
ad-e-noi-dal
ad-e-no-ma
aden-o-sine
a-dept
a-dept-ly
a-dept-ness
ad-e-qua-cy
ad-e-quate
ad-e-quate-ly
ad-e-quate-ness
ad-here
ad-hered
ad-her-ing
ad-her-ence
ad-her-ent
ad-her-ent-ly
ad-he-sion
ad-he-sion-al
ad-he-sive
ad-he-sive-ly
ad-he-sive-ness
ad hoc
ad ho-mi-nem
ad-i-a-bat-ic
a-dieu
ad in-fi-ni-tum
a-di-os
ad-i-pose
ad-i-pos-i-ty
ad-ja-cen-cy
ad-ja-cen-cies

ad-ja-cent
ad-ja-cent-ly
ad-jec-tive
ad-jec-ti-val
ad-join
ad-join-ing
ad-journ
ad-journ-ment
ad-judge
ad-judged
ad-judg-ing
ad-ju-di-cate
ad-ju-di-cat-ed
ad-ju-di-cat-ing
ad-ju-di-ca-tion
ad-ju-di-ca-tor
ad-junct
ad-junc-tive
ad-jure
ad-jured
ad-jur-ing
ad-ju-ra-tion
ad-ju-ra-to-ry
ad-jur-er
ad-just
ad-just-a-ble
ad-just-er
ad-jus-tor
ad-just-ment
ad-ju-tan-cy
ad-ju-tant
ad lib
ad libbed
ad lib-bing
ad-man
ad-men
ad-min-is-ter
ad-min-is-ter-ing
ad-min-is-tered
ad-min-is-trate
ad-min-is-trat-ing
ad-min-is-trated
ad-min-is-tra-tion
ad-min-is-tra-tive
ad-min-is-tra-tor
ad-min-is-tra-tive-ly
ad-min-is-tra-tion-al
ad-mi-ral
ad-mi-ral-ty
ad-mire
ad-mired
ad-mir-ing
ad-mi-ra-ble
ad-mi-ra-bly
ad-mi-ra-tion
ad-mi-rer

ad-mir-ing-ly
ad-mis-si-ble
ad-mis-si-bil-i-ty
ad-mis-sion
ad-mis-sive
ad-mit
ad-mit-ted
ad-mit-ting
ad-mit-ted-ly
ad-mit-tance
ad-mix
ad-mix-ture
ad-mon-ish
ad-mon-ish-er
ad-mo-ni-tion
ad-mon-i-to-ry
ad-mon-ish-ing-ly
ad-mon-ish-ment
a-do
a-do-be
ad-o-les-cence
ad-o-les-cent
ad-o-les-cent-ly
a-dopt
a-dopt-a-ble
a-dopt-er
a-dop-tion
a-dop-tive
a-dopt-a-bil-i-ty
a-dore
a-dored
a-dor-ing
a-dor-a-ble
ador-ing-ly
ad-o-ra-tion
a-dorn
a-dorn-ment
a-doze
ad-re-nal
ad-re-nal-ly
a-dren-a-line
a-drift
a-droit
a-droit-ly
a-droit-ness
ad-sorb
ad-sor-bent
ad-sorp-tion
ad-u-late
ad-u-lat-ed
ad-u-lat-ing
ad-u-la-tor
ad-u-la-to-ry
a-dult
a-dult-hood
a-dul-ter-ate

7

a-dul-ter-at-ed
a-dul-ter-at-ing
a-dul-ter-ant
a-dul-ter-a-tion
a-dul-ter-y
a-dul-ter-ies
a-dul-ter-er
a-dul-ter-ess
a-dul-ter-ous
ad-um-brate
ad-um-brat-ed
ad-um-brat-ing
ad va-lo-rem
ad-vance
ad-vanced
ad-vanc-ing
ad-vance-ment
ad-van-tage
ad-van-taged
ad-van-tag-ing
ad-van-ta-geous
ad-van-ta-geous-ly
ad-vent
ad-ven-ti-tious
ad-ven-tive
ad-ven-ture
ad-ven-tured
ad-ven-tur-ing
ad-ven-tur-er
ad-ven-tur-ess
ad-ven-tur-ous
ad-ven-ture-some
ad-verb
ad-ver-bi-al
ad-ver-sar-y
ad-ver-sar-ies
ad-verse
ad-verse-ly
ad-verse-ness
ad-ver-si-ty
ad-ver-si-ties
ad-vert
ad-vert-ence
ad-vert-ent
ad-ver-tise
ad-ver-tised
ad-ver-tis-ing
ad-ver-tis-er
ad-ver-tise-ment
ad-vice
ad-vise
ad-vised
ad-vis-ing
ad-vis-a-bil-i-ty
ad-vis-a-ble
ad-vis-a-bly

ad-vis-er
ad-vi-sor
ad-vis-ed-ly
ad-vise-ment
ad-vi-so-ry
ad-vo-ca-cy
ad-vo-ca-cies
ad-vo-cate
ad-vo-cat-ed
ad-vo-cat-ing
ad-vo-ca-tion
ae-gis
ae-on
aer-ate
aer-at-ed
aer-at-ing
aer-a-tion
aer-a-tor
aer-en-chy-ma
aer-i-al
aer-i-al-ly
aer-i-al-ist
aer-ie
aer-i-fy
aer-i-fi-ca-tion
aer-obe
aero-me-chan-ics
aero-naut-ics
aero-nau-ti-cal
aero-nau-tic
aero-pause
aer-o-plane
aer-o-sol
aero-sol-ize
aero-sol-iza-tion
aero-sol-iz-ing
aero-sol-ized
aer-o-space
aero-sphere
aero-stat
aero-stat-ics
aes-thete
aes-thet-ic
aes-thet-i-cal-ly
aes-thet-i-cal
afar
afeard
af-fa-ble
af-fa-bil-i-ty
af-fa-bly
af-fair
af-fect
af-fect-ing
af-fect-ing-ly
af-fec-tive
af-fec-ta-tion

af-fect-ed
af-fect-ed-ly
af-fect-ed-ness
af-fec-tion
af-fec-tion-ate
af-fec-tion-ate-ly
af-fec-tion-ate-ness
af-fer-ent
af-fer-ent-ly
af-fi-ance
af-fi-anced
af-fi-anc-ing
af-fi-da-vit
af-fil-i-ate
af-fil-i-at-ed
af-fil-i-at-ing
af-fin-i-ty
af-fin-i-ties
af-firm
af-firm-a-ble
af-firm-a-bly
af-fir-ma-tion
af-firm-a-tive
af-fix
af-fix-a-ble
af-fix-ment
af-fix-a-tion
af-fla-tus
af-flict
af-flic-tion
af-flu-ence
af-flu-ent
af-flu-ent-ly
af-fray
af-fri-cate
af-fric-a-tive
af-fri-ca-tion
af-front
af-ghan
afield
afire
aflame
af-la-tox-in
afloat
aflut-ter
afoot
afore
afore-men-tioned
afore-said
afore-thought
a for-ti-o-ri
afoul
afraid
afreet
afresh
af-ter

af-ter-ef-fect
af-ter-glow
af-ter--hours
af-ter-life
af-ter-most
af-ter-noon
af-ter-taste
af-ter-thought
af-ter-time
af-ter-ward
af-ter-wards
again
against
agape
aga-pe-ic
agar
ag-ate
ag-ate-ware
aga-ve
agaze
age
aged
ag-ing
age-ing
aged
age-less
age-long
agen-cy
agen-cies
agen-da
agen-da-less
agent
agen-tial
ag-glom-er-ate
ag-glom-er-at-ed
ag-glom-er-at-ing
ag-glom-er-a-tion
ag-glom-er-a-tive
ag-glu-ti-nate
ag-glu-ti-nat-ed
ag-glu-tin-at-ing
ag-glu-ti-na-tion
ag-glu-ti-na-tive
ag-gran-dize
ag-gran-dized
ag-gran-diz-ing
ag-gran-dize-ment
ag-gran-diz-er
ag-gra-vate
ag-gra-vat-ed
ag-gra-vat-ing
ag-gra-va-tion
ag-gre-gate
ag-gre-gat-ed
ag-gre-gat-ing
ag-gre-ga-tion

ag-gre-ga-tive
ag-gress
ag-gress-ive
ag-gress-ive-ly
ag-gress-ive-ness
ag-gres-sor
ag-gres-sion
ag-grieve
ag-grieved
ag-griev-ing
aghast
ag-ile
ag-ile-ly
agil-i-ty
agin-ner
agio
ag-i-tate
ag-i-tat-ed
ag-i-tat-ing
ag-i-tat-ed-ly
ag-i-ta-tion
ag-i-ta-tor
ag-i-ta-tion-al
agleam
aglow
agly-con
ag-nail
ag-nate
ag-na-tion
ag-nat-i-cal-ly
ag-nat-ic
ag-nize
ag-niz-ing
ag-nized
ag-no-men
ag-nom-i-na
ag-nos-tic
ag-nos-ti-cism
agog
ag-o-nal
agon-ic
ag-o-nist
ag-o-nis-tic
ag-o-nis-ti-cal-ly
ag-o-nis-ti-cal
ag-o-nize
ag-o-nized
ag-o-niz-ing
ag-o-niz-ing-ly
ag-o-ny
ag-o-nies
ag-o-ra-pho-bia
ag-o-ra-pho-bic
ag-o-ra-pho-bi-ac
agrar-i-an
agrar-i-an-ism

agree
agreed
agree-ing
agree-a-bil-i-ty
agree-a-ble
agree-a-ble-ness
agree-a-bly
agree-ment
ag-ri-busi-ness
ag-ri-cul-ture
ag-ri-cul-tur-al
ag-ri-cul-tur-ist
agron-o-my
ag-ro-nom-ic
ag-ro-nom-i-cal
agron-o-mist
ag-ro-nom-i-cal-ly
aground
ague
agu-ish-ly
agu-ish
aha
ahead
ahem
ahoy
aide-de-camp
ai-grette
ai-guille
ai-guil-lette
ai-ki-do
ail
ail-ing
ail-ment
ai-lan-thus
ai-ler-on
aim-less
air-less
air-less-ness
air-borne
air-brush
air-con-di-tion
air-con-di-tioned
air con-di-tion-er
air con-di-tion-ing
air-craft
air-field
air-mail
air-man
air-men
air-plane
air-port
air pres-sure
air-sick-ness
air-space
air-wave
airy

air-i-er
air-i-est
air-i-ness
air-i-ly
aisle
ajar
akim-bo
akin
al-a-bas-ter
al-a-bas-trine
a la carte
alack
alac-ri-ty
alac-ri-tous
alarm
alarm-ing
alarm-ing-ly
alarm-ist
alarm-ism
alas
alate
alat-ed
al-ba-core
al-ba-cores
al-ba-tross
al-ba-tross-es
al-be-do
al-be-it
al-bi-no
al-bi-nos
al-bi-nism
al-bum
al-bu-men
al-bu-min
al-bu-mi-nous
al-che-my
al-che-mist
al-che-mize
al-che-miz-ing
al-che-mized
al-co-hol
al-co-hol-ic
al-co-hol-ism
al-co-hol-i-cal-ly
al-cove
al-de-hyde
al-de-hy-dic
al-der
al-der-man
al-der-man-ic
ale-a-to-ry
alee
alert
alert-ness
alert-ly
ale-wife

ale-wives
al-ex-an-drine
al-ex-an-drite
alex-ia
al-fal-fa
al-fil-a-ria
al-for-ja
al-fres-co
al-ga
al-gae
al-gal
al-goid
al-ge-bra
al-ge-bra-ic
al-ge-bra-ic-al
al-ge-bra-ic-al-ly
al-ge-bra-ist
al-go-rithm
al-go-rith-mic
ali-as
ali-as-es
al-i-bi
al-i-bi-ing
al-i-bied
alien
alien-a-ble
alien-a-bil-i-ty
alien-ate
alien-at-ed
alien-at-ing
alien-ator
alien-ist
alien-ism
ali-form
alight
alight-ed
alit
alight-ing
alight-ment
align
align-ment
alike
al-i-ment
al-i-men-tal
al-i-men-tal-ly
al-i-men-ta-tion
al-i-men-ta-ry
al-i-men-ta-ry ca-nal
al-i-mo-ny
al-i-mo-nies
aline-ment
al-i-quant
al-i-quot
alive
alive-ness
al-ka-li

al-ka-lies
al-ka-lis
al-ka-line
al-ka-lin-i-ty
al-ka-lize
al-ka-lized
al-ka-liz-ing
al-ka-li-za-tion
al-ka-loid
al-ka-loi-dal
all-Amer-i-can
all-a-round
al-lay
al-layed
al-lay-ing
al-lay-er
al-le-ga-tion
al-lege
al-leged
al-leg-ing
al-lege-a-ble
al-leg-ed-ly
al-le-giance
al-le-go-ry
al-le-go-ries
al-le-gor-ic
al-le-gor-i-cal
al-le-gor-i-cal-ly
al-le-gor-ist
al-le-gret-to
al-le-gro
al-le-gros
al-ler-gen
al-ler-gen-ic
al-ler-gy
al-ler-gies
al-ler-gic
al-ler-gist
al-le-vi-ate
al-le-vi-at-ed
al-le-vi-at-ing
al-le-vi-a-tion
al-le-vi-a-tor
al-le-vi-a-tive
al-le-vi-a-to-ry
al-ley
al-leys
al-li-ance
al-lied
al-li-ga-tor
all--in-clu-sive
all--in-clu-sive-ness
al-lit-er-ate
al-lit-er-at-ed
al-lit-er-at-ing
al-lit-er-a-tive

al-lit-er-a-tive-ly
al-lit-er-a-tive-ness
al-lit-er-a-tion
al-lo-ca-ble
al-lo-cate
  al-lo-cat-ed
  al-lo-cat-ing
  al-lo-ca-tion
al-lo-cu-tion
al-log-a-mous
  al-log-a-my
al-lo-ge-ne-ic
al-lo-graph
  al-lo-graph-ic
al-lom-er-ism
  al-lom-er-ous
al-lo-path
al-lop-a-thy
  al-lo-path-ic
  al-lo-path-i-cal-ly
al-lop-a-thist
al-lo-phone
  al-lo-phon-ic
al-lo-pu-ri-nol
al-lo-ste-ric
  al-lo-ste-ri-cal-ly
al-lot
  al-lot-ted
  al-lot-ting
  al-lot-ment
  al-lot-ta-ble
  al-lot-ter
al-lo-trope
  al-lo-trop-ic
  al-lo-trop-cal-ly
al-lot-ro-py
  al-lot-ro-pism
al-lo-trope
  al-lo-trop-ic
  al-lo-trop-i-cal-ly
al-low
  al-low-a-ble
  al-low-a-bly
  al-low-ed-ly
al-low-ance
  al-low-anced
  al-low-anc-ing
al-loy
all--pow-er-ful
all--pur-pose
all right
all-spice
al-lude
  al-lud-ed
  al-lud-ing
al-lure

al-lured
al-lur-ing
al-lure-ment
al-lur-er
al-lur-ing-ly
al-lu-sion
  al-lu-sive
  al-lu-sive-ly
  al-lu-sive-ness
al-lu-via
al-lu-vi-al
al-lu-vi-um
  al-lu-viums
al-ly
al-lies
al-lied
  al-ly-ing
al-ma mat-er
al-ma-nac
al-man-dine
al-man-dite
al-mighty
  al-mighti-ness
al-mond
al-mo-ner
al-most
alms-giv-er
  alms-giv-ing
alms-house
al-ni-co
al-oe
aloft
alo-ha
alone
  alone-ness
along
along-shore
along-side
aloof
  aloof-ly
  aloof-ness
al-o-pe-cia
al-paca
al-pen-glow
al-pen-stock
al-pes-trine
al-pha
al-pha-bet
  al-pha-bet-ic
  al-pha-bet-i-cal
  al-pha-bet-i-cal-ly
  al-pha-bet-i-za-tion
  al-pha-bet-ize
  al-pha-bet-ized
  al-pha-bet-iz-ing
al-ready

al-so
al-tar
al-ter
  al-ter-a-bil-ity
  al-ter-a-ble
  al-ter-ant
  al-ter-a-tion
  al-ter-a-tive
al-ter-cate
  al-ter-cat-ing
  al-ter-cat-ed
  al-ter-ca-tion
al-ter e-go
al-ter-nate
  al-ter-nat-ed
  al-ter-nat-ing
  al-ter-nate-ly
  al-ter-na-tion
al-ter-na-tive
  al-ter-na-tive-ly
  al-ter-na-tive-ness
al-ter-na-tor
al-though
al-tim-e-ter
al-tim-e-try
al-ti-pla-no
al-ti-tude
al-to
al-to-cu-mu-lus
al-to-gether
al-to-re-lie-vo
al-to-stra-tus
al-tru-ism
  al-tru-is-tic
  al-tru-is-ti-cal-ly
  al-tru-ist
al-lu-mi-na
alu-mi-nate
alu-mi-nif-er-ous
al-u-min-i-um
alu-mi-nous
alu-mi-num
alum-na
  alum-nae
alum-nus
  alum-ni
al-ve-o-lar
  al-ve-o-lus
  al-ve-o-li
al-ways
alys-sum
amain
amal-gam
  amal-gam-a-ble
  amal-gam-ate
  amal-gam-at-ed

amal-gam-at-ing
amal-gam-a-tion
aman-u-en-ses
aman-u-en-ses
am-a-ryl-lis
amass
amass-ment
amass-er
am-a-teur
am-a-teur-ism
am-a-teur-ish
am-a-teur-ish-ly
am-a-teur-ish-ness
am-a-tive
am-a-tive-ness
am-a-tive-ly
am-a-to-ry
am-au-ro-sis
amaze
amazed
amaz-ing
amaz-ed-ly
amaz-ed-ness
amaze-ment
amaz-ing-ly
am-bas-sa-do-ri-al
am-ber
amber-gris
am-ber-jack
am-bi-dex-trous
am-bi-dex-trous-ly
am-bi-dex-ter-i-ty
am-bi-ance
am-bi-ence
am-bi-ent
am-big-u-ous
am-big-u-ous-ly
am-big-u-ous-ness
am-bi-gu-i-ty
am-bit
am-bi-tion
am-bi-tion-less
am-bi-tious
am-bi-tious-ly
am-bi-tious-ness
am-biv-a-lence
am-biv-a-lent
am-biv-a-lent-ly
am-bi-ver-sion
am-bi-ver-sive
am-bi-vert
am-ble
am-bled
am-bling
am-bler
am-blyg-o-nite

am-bly-opia
am-bo-cep-tor
am-bro-sia
am-bro-sial-ly
am-bro-sial
am-bro-type
ambs-ace
am-bu-la-crum
am-bu-lance
am-bu-la-to-ry
am-bu-lant
am-bu-late
am-bu-lat-ed
am-bu-lat-ing
am-bu-la-tion
am-bus-cade
am-bus-cad-ed
am-bus-cad-ing
am-bus-cad-er
am-bush
am-bush-ment
am-bush-er
ameba
amel-io-rate
amel-io-rat-ed
amel-io-rat-ing
amel-io-ra-ble
amel-io-ra-tion
amel-ior-a-tive
amel-io-ra-tor
amen
ame-na-ble
ame-na-bil-i-ty
ame-na-ble-ness
ame-na-bly
amend
amend-a-ble
amend-er
amend-ment
amends
amend-i-ty
amend-i-ties
amerce
amerced
amerc-ing
amerce-a-ble
amerce-ment
amerce-er
Amer-i-ca
Amer-i-can
Amer-i-cana
Amer-i-can-ism
am-e-thyst
am-e-thys-tine
am-e-tro-pia
ami-a-ble

ami-a-bil-i-ty
ami-a-bly
ami-a-ble-ness
ami-ca-ble
am-i-ca-bil-i-ty
am-i-ca-bly
am-i-ca-ble-ness
am-ice
amid
amidst
am-ide
amid-ic
amid-ships
ami-go
amine
amino acid
ami-no-ac-id-uria
ami-no-py-rine
amir
amiss
am-i-to-sis
am-i-tot-ic
am-i-tot-i-cal-ly
am-i-ty
am-me-ter
am-mi-no
am-mon-nia
am-mon-ic
am-mo-ni-ac
am-mo-ni-um
am-mo-ni-un chlo-ride
am-mu-ni-tion
am-ne-sia
am-ne-sic
am-nes-tic
am-nes-ty
am-ni-on
am-ni-ons
am-ni-on-ic
am-nia
am-ni-ot-ic
a-moe-ba
a-moe-bae
a-moe-bas
a-moe-bic
a-moe-ban
a-moe-boid
a-mok
a-mong
a-mongst
a-mon-til-la-do
a-mor-al
a-mo-ral-i-ty
a-mor-al-ism
a-mor-al-ly
amo-ret-to

12

am-or-ist
am-o-rous
  am-o-rous-ly
  am-o-rous-ness
a-mor-phism
a-mor-phous
  a-mor-phous-ness
  a-mor-phous-ly
am-or-tize
  am-or-tized
  am-or-tiz-ing
  am-or-ti-za-tion
  am-or-tiz-able
a-mount
a-mour
am-per-age
am-pere
am-per-sand
am-phet-a-mine
am-phib-ia
am-phib-i-an
am-phib-i-ous
  am-phib-i-ous-ly
  am-phib-i-ous-ness
am-phi-the-a-ter
  am-phi-the-at-ric
am-pho-ra
  am-phe-rae
  am-phe-ras
am-ple
  am-pler
  am-plest
  am-ple-ness
  am-ply
am-pli-fy
  am-pli-fied
  am-pli-fy-ing
  am-pli-fi-ca-tion
  am-pli-fi-er
am-pli-tude
am-pul
am-pu-tate
  am-pu-tat-ed
  am-pu-tat-ing
  am-pu-ta-tion
  am-pu-tee
a-muck
am-u-let
a-muse
  a-mused
  a-mus-ing
  a-muse-ment
  a-mus-ed
am-yl-ase
a-nach-ro-nism
  a-nach-ro-nis-tik

a-nach-ro-nis-ti-cal-ly
a-nach-ro-nous
an-a-con-da
an-aer-obe
an-aes-the-sia
an-aes-thet-ic
an-a-gram
  an-a-gram-mat-ic
  an-a-gram-mat-i-cal
  ana-gram-ma-tize
  ana-gram-ma-tized
  ana-gram-ma-tiz-ing
a-nal
an-a-lects
an-al-ge-sic
al-a-log
  an-a-log-i-cal
  an-a-log-i-cal-ly
a-nal-o-gize
  a-nal-o-gized
  a-nal-o-giz-ing
a-nal-o-gy
  a-nal-o-gies
  a-nal-o-gous
a-nal-y-sis
  a-nal-y-ses
an-a-lyst
  an-a-lyt-ic
  an-a-lyt-ics
an-a-lyze
  an-a-lyzed
  an-a-lyz-ing
  an-a-lyz-a-ble
  an-a-ly-za-tion
  an-a-lyz-er
an-a-pest
an-a-pes-tic
an-ar-chism
an-ar-chis-tic
an-ar-chy
  an-ar-chic
  an-ar-chi-cal
a-nath-e-ma
  a-nath-e-mas
  a-nath-e-ma-tize
  a-nath-e-ma-tized
  a-nath-e-ma-tiz-ing
  a-nath-e-mat-iz-a-tion
a-nat-o-mize
  a-nat-o-mized
  a-nat-o-mizing
  a-nat-o-mi-za-tion
a-nat-o-my
  a-nat-o-mies
  an-a-tom-i-cal
  an-a-tom-i-cal-ly

a-nat-o-mist
an-ces-tor
  an-ces-tral
  an-ces-tress
  an-ces-try
an-chor
  an-chor-age
an-cho-ress
an-cho-rite
an-cho-vy
an-cient
  an-cient-ly
  an-cient-ness
an-cil-lary
an-dan-te
and-i-ron
an-dro-gen
  an-drog-y-nous
  an-drog-y-ny
an-dros-ter-one
an-ec-dote
  an-ec-dot-age
  an-ec-do-tal
  an-ec-dot-ist
a-ne-mia
  a-ne-mic
an-e-mom-e-ter
an-e-mom-e-try
a-nem-o-ne
an-er-oid
an-es-the-sia
  an-es-thet-ic
  an-es-the-tize
  an-es-the-tized
  an-es-the-tiz-ing
an-eu-rysm
  an-eu-rism
  an-eu-rys-mal
a-new
an-ga-ry
an-gel
  an-gel-ic
  an-gel-i-cal
  an-gel-i-cal-ly
an-gel-i-ca
an-ger
an-gi-na
an-gi-na pec-to-ris
an-gi-o-sperm
  an-gi-o-sper-mous
an-gle
an-gler
an-gle-worm
an-gling
an-go-ra
an-gos-tu-ra bark

an-gry
  an-gri-ly
  an-gri-ness
ang-strom u-nit
an-guish
an-gu-lar
  an-gu-lar-i-ty
  an-gu-lar-ly
  an-gu-lar-ness
an-hy-dride
an-hy-drous
an-i-line
an-i-mad-vert
  an-i-mad-ver-sion
an-i-mal
  an-i-mal-cule
  an-i-mal-cu-lar
  an-i-mal-ism
  an-i-mal-i-ty
  an-i-mal-ize
  an-i-mal-ized
  an-i-mal-iz-ing
an-i-mate
  an-i-mat-ed
  an-i-mat-ing
  an-i-ma-tion
a-ni-ma-to
an-i-mism
  an-i-mis-tic
an-i-mos-i-ty
an-i-mus
an-i-on
an-ise
an-i-seed
an-i-sette
an-kle
an-kle-bone
an-klet
an-ky-lose
  an-ky-losed
  an-ky-los-ing
  an-ky-lo-sis
  an-ky-lot-ic
an-nal-ist
  an-nal-is-tic
an-nals
an-neal
an-ne-lid
  an-nel-i-dan
an-nex
  an-nex-a-tion
  an-nex-a-tion-ist
an-ni-hi-late
  an-ni-hi-lat-ed
  an-ni-hi-lat-ing
  an-ni-hi-la-tion

an-ni-hi-la-tor
an-ni-ver-sa-ry
  an-ni-ver-sa-ries
an-no Dom-i-ni
an-no-tate
  an-no-tat-ed
  an-no-tat-ing
  an-no-ta-tion
  an-no-ta-tor
an-nounce
  an-nounced
  an-nounc-ing
  an-nounce-ment
  an-nounc-er
an-noy
  an-noy-ance
  an-noy-er
an-nu-al
an-nu-i-ty
an-nu-i-tant
an-nul
  an-nulled
  an-nul-ling
  an-nul-ment
an-nu-lar
  an-nu-lar-i-ty
  an-nu-lar-ly
an-nu-late
an-nu-let
an-nu-lus
  an-nu-lus-es
an-nun-ci-a-tion
an-nun-ci-ate
  an-nun-ci-at-ed
  an-nun-ci-at-ing
  an-nun-ci-a-tor
an-ode
  an-od-ic
an-o-dyne
a-noint
  a-noint-er
  a-noint-ment
a-nom-a-ly
  a-nom-a-lism
  a-nom-a-lous
  a-nom-a-lous-ly
  a-nom-a-lous-ness
an-o-mie
  an-o-my
an-o-nym
  a-non-y-mous
  a-non-y-mous-i-ty
  a-non-y-mous-ly
  a-non-y-mous-ness
a-noph-e-les
an-oth-er

an-ox-ia
an-ser-ine
an-swer
  an-swer-a-ble
ant-ac-id
an-tag-o-nist
  an-tag-o-nism
  an-tag-o-nis-tic
  an-tag-o-nis-ti-cal-ly
  an-tag-o-nize
  an-tag-o-nized
  an-tag-o-niz-ing
ant-arc-tic
an-te
  an-ted
  an-te-ing
ant-eat-er
an-te--bel-lum
an-te-ced-ence
  an-te-ced-ent
  an-te-cede
  an-te-ced-ed
  an-te-ced-ing
  an-te-ce-dent-ly
an-te-cham-ber
an-te-choir
an-te-date
  an-te-dat-ed
  an-te-dat-ing
an-te-di-lu-vi-an
an-te-lope
  an-te-lopes
an-te me-rid-i-em
an-ten-na
  an-ten-nae
  an-ten-nas
an-te-pe-nult
  an-te-pe-nul-ti-mate
an-te-ri-or
an-te-room
an-them
an-ther
  an-ther-id-i-um
an-thol-o-gy
  an-thol-o-gies
  an-thol-o-gist
  an-thol-o-gize
  an-thol-o-giz-ing
an-tho-zo-an
an-thra-cene
  an-thra-cite
  an-thra-cit-ic
an-thrax
  an-thra-ces
an-thro-po-cen-tric
an-thro-po-gen-e-sis

14

an-thro-poid
an-thro-pol-o-gy
an-thro-po-log-ic
an-thro-po-log-i-cal
an-thro-pol-o-gist
an-thr-pom-e-try
an-thro-po-met-ric
an-ti-air-craft
an-ti-bi-o-sis
an-ti-bi-ot-ic
an-ti-bod-y
an-ti-bod-ies
an-tic
an-ti-christ
an-tic-i-pate
an-tic-i-pat-ed
an-tic-i-pat-ing
an-tic-i-pa-tion
an-tic-i-pa-tive
an-tic-i-pa-to-ry
an-ti-cler-i-cal
an-ti-cler-i-cal-ism
an-ti-cli-max
an-ti-cli-mac-tic
an-ti-cli-nal
an-ti-cline
an-ti-cy-clone
an-ti-dote
an-ti-dot-al
an-ti-fed-er-al
an-ti-fed-er-al-ist
an-ti-fed-er-al-ism
an-ti-freeze
an-ti-gen
an-ti-he-ro
an-ti-his-ta-mine
an-ti-log-a-rithm
an-ti-ma-cas-sar
an-ti-mis-sile
an-ti-mo-ny
an-ti-pas-to
an-tip-a-thy
an-ti-phon
an-tiph-o-nal
an-ti-pode
an-ti-quar-i-an
an-ti-quar-y
an-ti-quar-ies
an-ti-quate
an-ti-quat-ed
an-ti-quat-ing
an-ti-quat-ed
an-tique
an-tiqed
an-tiq-uing
an-tique-ly

an-tique-ness
an-tiq-ui-ty
an-tiq-ui-ties
an-ti-Sem-i-tism
an-ti-sep-sis
an-ti-sep-tic
an-ti-se-rum
an-ti-slav-er-y
an-ti-so-cial
an-tith-e-sis
an-tith-e-ses
an-ti-thet-i-cal
an-ti-tox-in
an-ti-tox-in
an-ti-trust
ant-ler
ant-ler-ed
an-to-nym
an-trum
an-tra
a-nus
an-vil
anx-i-e-ty
anx-i-e-ties
anx-ious
anx-ious-ness
an-y
an-y-bod-y
an-y-bod-ies
an-y-how
an-y-more
an-y-one
an-y-place
an-y-thing
an-y-way
an-y-where
an-y-wise
a-or-ta
a-or-tas
a-or-tae
a-or-tal
a-or-tic
a-pace
a-pache
a-part
a-part-heid
a-part-ment
ap-a-thy
ap-a-thet-ic
ap-a-thet-i-cal-ly
ape
a-per-ri-tif
ap-er-ture
a-pex
a-pex-es
a-pi-ces

ap-i-cal
a-pha-sia
a-phe-li-on
a-phe-lia
a-phid
a-phis
a-phi-des
aph-o-rism
aph-o-rist
aph-ro-dis-i-ac
a-pi-an
a-pi-ar-i-an
a-pi-a-rist
a-pi-ary
a-pi-ar-ies
a-pi-cul-ture
a-pi-cul-tur-al
a-pi-cul-tur-ist
a-piece
ap-ish
ap-ish-ly
ap-ish-ness
a-plomb
a-poc-a-lypse
a-poc-a-lyp-tic
a-poc-o-pe
a-poc-ry-phal
ap-o-gee
a-po-lit-i-cal
a-pol-o-get-ics
a-pol-o-gist
a-pol-o-gize
a-pol-o-gized
a-pol-o-giz-ing
a-pol-o-gy
a-pol-o-gies
a-pol-o-get-ic
a-pol-o-get-i-cal
ap-o-plec-tic
ap-o-plex-y
a-port
a-pos-ta-sy
a-pos-ta-sies
a-pos-tate
a-pos-ta-tize
a-pos-ta-tized
a-pos-to-tiz-ing
a pos-te-ri-o-ri
a-pos-tle
a-pos-tle-ship
a-pos-to-late
ap-os-tol-ic
ap-os-tol-i-cal
a-pos-tro-phe
a-poth-e-cary
a-poth-e-car-ies

ap-o-thegm
ap-o-phthegm
ap-o-theg-mat-ic
a-poth-e-o-sis
a-poth-e-o-ses
a-poth-e-o-size
a-poth-e-o-sized
a-poth-e-o-siz-ing
ap-pall
ap-palled
ap-pal-ling
ap-pal-ling-ly
ap-pa-rat-us
ap-pa-rat-us-es
ap-par-el
ap-par-ent
ap-pa-ri-tion
ap-pa-ri-tion-al
ap-peal
ap-peal-a-ble
ap-peal-er
ap-peal-ing-ly
ap-pear
ap-pear-ance
ap-pease
ap-peased
ap-peasing
ap-pease-ment
ap-peas-a-ble
ap-peas-er
ap-pel-lant
ap-pel-late
ap-pel-la-tion
ap-pel-la-tive
ap-pend
ap-pen-dage
ap-pend-ant
ap-pen-dec-to-my
ap-pen-di-ci-tis
ap-pen-dix
ap-pen-dix-es
ap-pen-di-ces
ap-per-cep-tion
ap-per-cep-tive
ap-per-tain
ap-pe-tite
ap-pe-tiz-er
ap-pe-tiz-ing
ap-plaud
ap-plause
ap-ple
ap-ple-jack
ap-pli-ance
ap-pli-ca-ble
ap-pli-ca-bil-i-ty
ap-pli-ca-ble-ness

ap-pli-cant
ap-pli-ca-tion
ap-pli-ca-tive
ap-pli-ca-to-ry
ap-pli-ca-tor
ap-plied
ap-ply
ap-ply-ing
ap-point
ap-point-a-ble
ap-point-ee
ap-point-er
ap-point-ment
ap-por-tion
ap-por-tion-ment
ap-pose
ap-posed
ap-pos-ing
ap-po-site
ap-po-si-tion
ap-po-si-tion-al
ap-pos-i-tive
ap-praise
ap-prais-al
ap-praised
ap-praiser
ap-prais-ing
ap-pre-ci-a-ble
ap-pre-ci-a-bly
ap-pre-ci-ate
ap-pre-ci-at-ed
ap-pre-ci-at-ing
ap-pre-ci-a-tion
ap-pre-ci-a-tive
ap-pre-hend
ap-pre-hen-si-ble
ap-pre-hen-sion
ap-pre-hen-sive
ap-pren-tice
ap-pren-tic-ed
ap-pren-tic-ing
ap-pre-tice-ship
ap-prise
ap-prised
ap-pris-ing
ap-prize
ap-proach
ap-proach-a-bil-i-ty
ap-proach-a-ble
ap-pro-ba-tion
ap-pro-ba-tive
ap-pro-ba-to-ry
ap-pro-pri-ate
ap-pro-pri-at-ed
ap-pro-pri-at-ing
ap-pro-pri-ate-ly

ap-pro-pri-a-tor
ap-pro-pri-a-tion
ap-pro-pri-a-tive
ap-prox-i-mate
ap-prox-i-mate-ly
ap-prox-i-ma-tion
ap-pur-te-nance
ap-pur-te-nant
ap-ri-cot
a-pri-o-ri
a-pron
ap-ro-pos
apt
apt-ly
apt-ness
ap-ter-ous
ap-ti-tude
aq-ua
aq-uas
aq-uae
a-qua-cul-ture
aq-ua-ma-rine
aq-ua-naut
aq-ua-plane
aquar-ia
aquar-i-um
aquar-i-ums
a-quat-ic
aq-ua-tint
aq-ue-duct
a-que-ous
aq-ui-line
ar-a-besque
ar-a-ble
a-rach-nid
a-rach-ni-dan
ar-ba-lest
ar-ba-lest-er
ar-ba-list
ar-bi-ter
ar-bi-tral
ar-bit-ra-ment
ar-bi-trar-y
ar-bi-trar-i-ly
ar-bi-trar-i-ness
ar-bi-trate
ar-bi-trat-ed
ar-bi-trat-ing
ar-bi-tra-ble
ar-bi-tra-tor
ar-bi-tra-tion
ar-bor
ar-bo-re-al
ar-bo-res-cent
ar-bo-re-ta
ar-bo-re-tum

ar-bo-re-tums
ar-bor-vi-tae
ar-bu-tus
arc
  arced
  arc-ing
ar-cade
ar-cane
arch
  arch-ly
  arch-ness
ar-cha-ic
ar-cha-ism
ar-cha-ist
ar-cha-is-tic
arch-an-gel
arch-bish-op
  arch-bish-op-ric
arch-dea-con
arch-di-o-cese
  arch-di-oc-e-san
arch-du-cal
arch-duch-ess
arch-duch-y
  arch-duch-ies
arch-duke
arch-en-e-my
  arch-en-e-mies
arch-er
  ar-cher-y
ar-che-type
  ar-che-typ-al
  ar-che-typ-i-cal
arch-fiend
ar-chi-e-pis-co-pal
  ar-chi-e-pis-co-pate
ar-chi-pel-a-goes
  ar-chi-pel-a-gos
ar-chi-tect
ar-chi-tec-ton-ic
ar-chi-tec-ture
ar-chi-trave
ar-chive
  ar-chi-val
  ar-chi-vist
ar-chon
arch-priest
arch-way
arc-tic
arc-tic cir-cle
ar-dent
  ar-dent-ly
ar-dor
ar-du-ous
  ar-du-ous-ly
  ar-du-ous-ness

ar-e-a
  ar-e-al
  ar-e-a-way
a-re-na
a-re-o-la
  a-re-o-lae
  a-re-o-las
ar-gent
ar-gen-tine
ar-gil
ar-gon
ar-go-sy
  ar-go-sies
ar-got
  ar-got-ic
ar-gue
  ar-gued
  ar-gu-ing
  ar-gu-a-ble
  ar-gu-er
  ar-gu-ment
  ar-gu-men-ta-tion
  ar-gu-men-ta-tive
ar-gyle
  ar-gyll
a-ri-a
ar-id
  a-rid-i-ty
a-right
a-rise
  a-rose
  a-ris-en
  a-ris-ing
ar-is-toc-ra-cy
  ar-is-toc-ra-cies
  aris-to-crat
  aris-to-crat-ic
a-rith-me-tic
  a-rith-met-i-cal
  a-rith-met-i-cal-ly
  a-rith-me-ti-cian
ar-ma-da
ar-ma-dil-lo
ar-ma-ment
ar-ma-ture
ar-mi-stice
ar-moire
ar-mor
ar-mor-er
ar-mor-y
  ar-mor-ies
arm-pit
ar-my
  ar-mies
ar-ni-ca
a-ro-ma

ar-o-mat-ic
  ar-o-mat-i-cal
a-round
a-rouse
  a-roused
  a-rous-ing
ar-peg-gi-o
  ar-peg-gi-os
ar-raign
  ar-raign-ment
ar-range
  ar-ranged
  ar-rang-er
  ar-rang-ing
  ar-range-ment
ar-rant
  ar-rant-ly
ar-ras
ar-ray
ar-rear
ar-rest
  ar-rest-er
  ar-rest-or
ar-ri-val
ar-rive
  ar-rived
  ar-riv-ing
ar-ro-gant
  ar-ro-gat-ed
  ar-ro-gat-ing
  ar-ro-ga-tion
ar-row
ar-row-head
ar-row-root
ar-roy-o
  ar-roy-os
ar-se-nal
ar-se-nate
ar-se-nic
ar-son
  ar-son-ist
ar-te-ri-al
ar-te-ri-o-scle-ro-sis
ar-ter-y
  ar-ter-ies
ar-te-sian well
art-ful
  art-ful-ly
  art-ful-ness
ar-thri-tis
  ar-thrit-ic
ar-thro-pod
  ar-throp-o-dal
  ar-throp-o-dous
ar-ti-choke
ar-ti-cle

ar-tic-u-lar
ar-tic-u-late
  ar-tic-u-lat-ed
  ar-tic-u-lat-ing
  ar-tic-u-late-ly
  ar-tic-u-late-ness
  ar-tic-u-lar-tor
  ar-tic-u-la-tion
  ar-tic-u-la-to-ry
ar-te-fact
  ar-ti-fact
ar-ti-fice
  ar-tif-i-cer
ar-ti-fi-cial
  ar-ti-fi-ci-al-i-ty
  ar-ti-fi-cial-ly
  ar-ti-fi-cial-ness
ar-til-ler-y
  ar-til-ler-ist
ar-ti-san
art-ist
ar-tiste
  ar-tis-tic
  ar-tis-ti-cal-ly
art-ist-ry
art-less
  art-less-ly
  art-less-ness
art-y
  ar-ti-ness
as-bes-tos
  as-bes-tus
as-cend
  as-cend-ance
  as-cend-ence
  as-cend-an-cy
  as-cend-en-cy
  as-cend-ant
  as-cend-ent
as-cen-sion
as-cent
as-cer-tain
  as-cer-tain-a-ble
  as-cer-tain-ment
as-cet-ic
  as-cet-is-al
  as-cet-i-cism
as-cot
as-cribe
  as-cribed
  as-crib-ing
  as-crib-a-ble
a-sep-sis
a-sep-tic
a-sex-u-al
  a-sex-u-al-i-ty

a-sex-u-al-ly
a-shamed
  a-sham-ed-ly
ash-en
ash-lar
  ash-ler
a-shore
ash-y
a-side
as-i-nine
a-skance
a-skew
a-slant
a-sleep
a-slope
a-so-cial
as-par-a-gus
as-pect
as-pen
as-per-i-ty
as-perse
  as-persed
  as-pers-ing
as-per-sion
as-phalt
  as-phal-tic
as-pho-del
as-phyx-ia
  as-phyx-i-ate
  as-phyx-i-at-ed
  as-phyx-i-at-ing
  as-phyx-i-a-tion
as-pic
as-pi-dis-tra
as-pir-ant
as-pi-rate
  as-pi-rat-ed
  as-pi-rat-ing
  as-pi-ra-tion
  as-pi-ra-tor
as-pire
  as-pired
  as-pir-ing
  as-pir-er
as-pi-rin
as-sail
  as-sail-a-ble
  as-sail-ant
as-sas-sin
as-sas-si-nate
  as-sas-si-nat-ed
  as-sas-si-na-tion
  as-sas-si-na-tor
as-sault
as-say
  as-say-er

as-sem-blage
as-sem-ble
  as-sem-bled
  as-sem-bling
  as-sem-bler
as-sem-bly
  as-sem-blies
as-sem-bly-man
  as-sem-bly-men
as-sent
  as-sent-er
as-sert
  as-sert-er
  as-ser-tion
as-ser-tive
  as-ser-tive-ly
  as-ser-tive-ness
as-sess
  as-sess-a-ble
  as-sess-ment
  as-sess-or
as-set
as-si-du-i-ty
as-sid-u-ous
  as-sid-u-ous-ly
  as-sid-u-ous-ness
as-sign
  as-sign-a-bil-i-ty
  as-sign-a-ble
  as-sign-a-bly
as-sig-na-tion
as-sign-ee
  as-sign-ment
as-sist
  as-sist-ance
as-sis-tant
as-size
as-so-ci-ate
  as-so-ci-at-ed
  as-so-ci-at-ing
  as-so-ci-a-tion
  as-so-ci-a-tive
as-so-nance
as-sort
  as-sor-ted
  as-sort-ment
as-suage
  as-suaged
  as-suag-ing
  as-suage-ment
as-sume
  as-sumed
  as-sum-ing
  as-sump-tion
as-sur-ance
as-sure

as-sured
as-sur-ing
as-sur-er
as-sur-ed-ly
as-ter
as-ter-isk
a-stern
as-ter-oid
as-ter-oi-dal
asth-ma
asth-mat-ic
a-stig-ma-tism
as-tig-mat-ic
a-stir
as-ton-ish
as-ton-ish-ing
as-ton-ish-ing-ly
as-ton-ish-ment
as-tound
as-tound-ing
a-strad-dle
as-tra-khan
as-tral
a-stray
a-stride
as-trin-gent
as-trin-gen-cy
as-tro-dome
as-tro-labe
as-trol-o-gy
as-trol-o-ger
as-tro-log-ic
as-tro-log-i-cal
as-tro-naut
as-tro-nau-tics
as-tro-nau-ti-cal
as-tro-nom-ic
as-tro-nom-i-cal-ly
as-tron-o-my
as-tron-o-mer
as-tro-phys-ics
as-tro-phys-i-cist
as-tute
as-tute-ly
as-tute-ness
a-sun-der
a-sy-lum
a-sym-me-try
asym-met-ric
asym-met-ri-cal
asym-met-ri-cal-ly
at-a-vism
at-a-vist
at-a-vis-tic
a-tax-ia
a-tax-ic

at-el-ier
ath-er-o-scle-ro-sis
a-thirst
ath-lete
ath-let-ic
ath-let-ics
a-thwart
a-tilt
at-las
at-las-es
at-mos-phere
at-oll
at-om
atom-ic
atom-i-cal
atom-i-cal-ly
ato-nal-i-ty
ato-nal
ato-nal-ly
a-tone
a-toned
a-ton-ing
a-tone-ment
a-ton-er
a-top
a-tri-um
a-tro-cious
a-tro-cious-ly
a-tro-cious-ness
a-troc-i-y
a-troc-i-ties
at-ro-phy
at-ro-phies
at-ro-phied
at-ro-pine
at-tach
at-tach-a-ble
at-tach-ment
at-tack
at-tain
at-tain-a-ble
at-tain-a-bil-i-ty
at-tain-a-ble-ness
at-tain-ment
at-tain-der
at-taint
at-tar
at-tempt
at-tempt-a-ble
at-tend
at-tend-ance
at-tend-ant
at-ten-tion
at-ten-tive
at-ten-u-ate
at-ten-u-at-ed

at-ten-u-at-ing
at-ten-u-a-tion
at-test
at-tes-ta-tion
at-tic
at-tire
at-tired
at-tir-ing
at-ti-tude
at-ti-tu-di-nize
at-ti-tu-di-nized
at-ti-tu-di-niz-ing
at-tor-ney
at-tract
at-tract-a-ble
at-trac-tive
at-tract-or
at-trac-tion
at-tri-bute
at-tri-but-ed
at-tri-but-ing
at-tri-but-a-ble
at-tri-bu-tion
at-trib-u-tive
at-tri-tion
at-tune
at-tuned
at-tun-ing
a-typ-i-cal
a-typ-ic
a-typ-i-cal-ly
au-burn
au cou-rant
auc-tion
auc-tion-eer
au-da-cious
au-da-cious-ness
au-dac-i-ty
au-di-ble
au-di-ble-ness
au-di-bly
au-di-ence
au-di-o
au-di-o-vis-u-al
au-dit
au-di-tion
au-dit-or
au-di-to-rium
au-di-to-ry
au-ger
aug-ment
aug-ment-a-ble
aug-ment-er
aug-men-ta-tion
aug-ment-a-tive
au-grat-in

au-gur
 au-gu-ry
 au-gu-ries
au-gust
 au-gust-ly
 au-gust-ness
auk
auld lang syne
au na-tu-rel
aunt
au-ra
 au-ras
 au-rae
au-ral
 au-ral-ly
au-re-ate
au-re-ole
au-re-voir
au-ri-cle
au-ric-u-lar
au-rif-er-ous
au-ro-ra
au-ro-ra bor-e-al-is
aus-cul-tate
 aus-cul-tat-ed
 aus-cul-tat-ing
 aus-cul-ta-tion
aus-tere
 aus-ter-i-ty
 aus-ter-i-ties
aus-tral
au-then-tic
 au-then-ti-cat-ed
 au-then-ti-cat-ing
 au-then-ti-ca-tion
 au-then-ti-ca-tor
au-thor
au-thor-i-tar-i-an
 au-thor-i-tar-i-an-ism
 au-thor-i-ta-tive
au-thor-i-ty
 au-thor-i-ties
au-thor-ize
 au-thor-ized
 au-thor-iz-ing
 au-thor-i-za-tion
au-thor-ship
au-to
au-to-bi-og-ra-phy
 au-to-bi-og-ra-phies
 au-to-bi-og-ra-pher
au-toc-ra-cy
 au-toc-ra-cies
au-to-crat
 au-to-crat-ic
 au-to-crat-i-cal

au-to-crat-i-cal-ly
au-toc-ra-cy
 au-toc-ra-cies
au-to-graph
au-to-mat
au-to-mat-ic
au-to-ma-tion
au-to-mate
 au-to-mat-ed
 au-to-mat-ing
au-tom-a-tism
au-tom-a-ton
 au-tom-a-tons
 au-tom-a-ta
au-to-mo-bile
au-to-mo-tive
au-to-nom-ic
 au-to-nom-i-cal-ly
au-ton-o-mous
 au-ton-o-mous-ly
au-ton-o-my
 au-ton-o-mies
 au-ton-o-mist
au-top-sy
au-to-sug-ges-tion
au-tumn
 au-tum-nal
aux-il-ia-ry
 aux-il-ia-ries
a-vail
 a-vail-a-bil-i-ty
 a-vail-a-ble-ness
 a-vail-ably
av-a-lanche
 av-a-lanched
 av-a-lanch-ing
a-vant-garde
av-a-rice
 av-a-ri-cious
 av-a-ri-cious-ly
 av-a-ri-cious-ness
a-vast
av-a-tar
a-ve
a-venge
 a-venged
 a-veng-ing
 a-veng-er
av-e-nue
a-ver
 a-verred
 a-ver-ring
 a-ver-ment
av-er-age
 av-er-aged
 av-er-ag-ing

a-verse
 a-verse-ly
a-ver-sion
a-vert
a-vi-ar-y
 avi-ar-ies
a-vi-a-tion
a-vi-a-tor
av-id
 a-vid-i-ty
 av-id-ly
av-o-ca-do
av-o-ca-tion
a-void
 avoid-a-ble
 a-void-ance
a-vow
 a-vow-er
a-vow-al
a-vowed
a-wait
a-wake
 a-woke
 a-wak-ed
 a-wak-ing
a-wak-en
 awak-en-ing
a-ward
a-ware
 a-ware-ness
awe
 awed
 aw-ing
a-weigh
awe-some
awe-struck
aw-ful
 aw-ful-ly
 aw-ful-ness
awk-ward
 awk-ward-ly
awl
awn
 awned
 awn-less
 awn-ing
a-wry
ax-i-al
 ax-i-al-ly
ax-i-om
ax-is
ax-le
a-zal-ea
az-i-muth
a-zo-ic
az-ure

B

bab-bitt
bab-ble
  bab-bled
  bab-bling
  bab-bler
ba-bel
ba-boon
ba-bush-ka
ba-by
  ba-bies
  ba-bied
  ba-by-ing
  ba-by-hood
  ba-by-ish
ba-by--sit
  ba-by--sat
  ba-by--sit-ting
  ba-by--sit-ter
bac-ca-lau-re-ate
bac-ca-rat
bac-cha-nal
  bac-cha-na-li-an
bac-chant
bac-chant-te
bach-e-lor
  bach-e-lor-hood
bac-il-lar-y
bac-cil-lus
  bac-cil-li
back-bite
  back-bit
  back-bit-ten
  back-bit-er
back-board
back-bone
back-drop
back-field
back-fire
  back-fired
  back-fir-ing
back-gam-mon
back-ground
back-hand
  back-hand-ed
back-ing
back-lash
back-log
back-side
back-slide
  back-slid
  back-slid-den
  back-slid-ing
  back-slid-er
back-spin
back-stage
back-stairs

back-stop
back-stretch
back-stroke
back-talk
back-up
back-ward
  back-wards
  back-ward-ness
back-wash
back-water
back-woods
  back-woods-man
ba-con
bac-ter-ia
  bac-ter-i-um
  bac-te-ri-al
  bac-te-ri-al-ly
bac-te-ri-cide
  bac-te-ri-ci-dal
bac-te-ri-ol-o-gy
  bac-te-ri-ol-o-gist
  bac-te-ri-o-log-i-cal
bac-te-ri-o-phage
bad
bade
badge
  badged
  badg-ing
  badg-er
bad-i-nage
bad-land
  bad-lands
bad-ly
bad-min-ton
bad-tem-pered
baf-fle
  baf-fled
  baf-fling
  baf-fler
bag
  bagged
  bag-ging
ba-gasse
bag-a-telle
ba-gel
bag-gage
bag-gy
  bag-gi-er
  bag-gi-est
bag-man
bagn-io
bag-pipe
  bag-pi-per
bah
bail
bail-iff

bail-i-wick
bails-man
  bails-men
bairn
bait
bake
  baked
  bak-ing
bak-er
  bak-er-y
  bak-er-ies
bak-ing pow-der
bak-ing so-da
bak-sheesh
bak-shish
bal-a-lai-ka
bal-ance
  bal-anced
  bal-anc-ing
  bal-anc-er
bal-brig-gan
bal-co-ny
  bal-co-nies
bald
  bald-ly
  bald-ness
bal-der-dash
bald-head
bal-dric
bale
  baled
  bal-ing
ba-leen
bale-ful
  bale-ful-ly
balk
  balk-er
bal-kan-ize
  bal-kan-ized
  bal-kan-iz-ing
  bal-kan-i-za-tion
balk-y
  balk-i-er
  balk-i-est
bal-lad
  bal-lade
  bal-lad-eer
  bal-lad-ry
bal-last
ball-bear-ing
bal-le-ri-na
bal-let
bal-lis-tic
  bal-lis-tics
  bal-lis-ti-cian
bal-loon

bal-lot
  bal-lot-ed
  bal-lot-ing
ball-room
bal-ly-hoo
balm
balm-y
  balm-ier
  balm-i-est
  balm-i-ly
  balm-i-ness
ba-lo-ney
bal-sa
bal-sam
bal-us-ter
bal-us-trade
bam-bi-no
  bam-bi-nos
bam-boo
bam-boo-zle
  bam-boo-zled
  bam-boo-zling
  bam-boo-zler
ban
  banned
  ban-ning
ba-nal
  ba-nal-i-ty
ban-nan-a
band-age
  band-aged
  band-ag-ing
ban-dana
  ban-dan-na
ban-deau
  ban-deaux
ban-de-role
ban-dit
  ban-dits
  ban-dit-ti
  ban-dit-ry
band-mas-ter
band-o-leer
  ban-do-lier
bands-man
  bands-men
band-stand
band-wa-gon
ban-dy
  ban-died
  ban-dy-ing
ban-dy--leg-ged
bane-ful
  ban-ful-ness
ban-gla-desh
ban-gle

ban-ish
  ban-ish-ment
ban-i-ster
ban-jo
bank
bank-er
bank-ing
bank-note
bank-roll
bank-rupt
  bank-rupt-cy
  bank-rupt-cies
ban-ner
banns
ban-quet
  ban-quet-ter
ban-quette
ban-shee
ban-tam
ban-tam-weight
ban-ter
  ban-ter-er
  ban-ter-ing-ly
ban-yan
ban-zal
ba-o-bab
bap-tism
  bap-tis-mal
bap-tist
  bap-tist-ery
  bap-tis-ter-ies
bap-tize
  bap-tized
  bap-tiz-er
  bap-tiz-ing
bar
  barred
  bar-ring
bar-bar-ic
bar-ba-rism
bar-bar-i-ty
  bar-bar-i-ties
bar-ba-rize
  bar-ba-rized
  bar-ba-riz-ing
bar-ba-rous
bar-be-cue
  bar-be-cued
  bar-be-cu-ing
bar-ber
bar-ber-ry
  bar-ber-ries
bar-ber-shop
bar-bi-tal
bar-bi-tu-rate
  bar-bi-tur-ic

bar-busse
bar-ca-role
bard
bare
  bar-er
  bar-est
  bare-ness
bare-back
bare-faced
bare-foot
bare-hand-ed
bare-ly
bar-gain
  bar-gain-er
barge
  barg-ed
  barg-ing
bar-i-tone
bar-i-um
bar-keep-er
bar-ken-tine
bark-er
bar-ley
bar-maid
bar-man
  bar-men
bar-mitz-vah
barm-y
bar-na-cle
barn-storm
  barn-storm-er
  barn-storm-ing
barn-yard
bar-o-graph
ba-rom-et-er
  bar-o-met-ric
  bar-o-met-ric-al
bar-on
  ba-ro-ni-al
bar-on-age
bar-on-ess
bar-on-et
  bar-on-et-age
  bar-on-et-cy
bar-o-ny
  bar-o-nies
ba-roque
barque
bar-quen-tine
bar-rack
bar-ra-cu-da
  bar-ra-cu-das
bar-rage
  bar-raged
  bar-rag-ing
bar-ra-try

22

bar-ra-tries
bar-ra-tor
bar-ra-trous
bar-rel
bar-reled
bar-relled
bar-rel-ling
bar-ren
bar-ren-ly
bar-ren-ness
bar-rette
bar-ri-cade
bar-ri-cad-ed
bar-ri-cad-ing
bar-ri-er
bar-ring
bar-ri-o
bar-ri-os
bar-ris-ter
bar-room
bar-row
bar-ten-der
bar-ter
bar-ter-er
ba-sal
ba-salt
base-ball
base-board
base-less
base-ment
bash-ful
bash-ful-ly
bash-ful-ness
ba-sic
ba-si-cal-ly
ba-sil
ba-sil-i-cia
bas-i-lisk
ba-sin
ba-sis
bas-ket
bas-ket-ball
bas-ket-ry
bas-re-lief
bas-si-net
bas-so
bas-soon
bass-wood
bas-tard
baste
bast-ed
bast-ing
bas-tille
bas-ti-on
bas-ti-oned
bat

bat-ted
bat-ting
bat-ter
batch
bate
bat-ed
bat-ing
bathe
bathed
bath-ing
bath-er
bath-i-nette
ba-thos
bath-robe
bath-room
bath-y-scaphe
bath-y-sphere
ba-tik
ba-tiste
bat-on
bat-ten
bat-ter
bat-tery
bat-tle
bat-tled
bat-tling
bat-tle dore
bat-tle-field
bat-tle-ment
bat-ty
bat-ti-er
bat-ti-est
bau-ble
bawd-y
bawd-i-er
bawd-i-est
bay-o-net
bay-o-net-ted
bay-o-net-ing
bay-ou
ba-zaar
ba-zoo-ka
beach
beach-comb-er
beach-head
bea-con
bead
bead-ed
bead-like
bead-y
bead-i-er
bead-i-est
beak
beaked
beak-er
beam

beam-ed
bear
bear-ing
bear-a-ble
bear-a-bly
bear-er
beard
beard-ed
beard-less
bear-skin
beast
beast-li-ness
beast-ly
beast-li-er
beast-li-est
beat
beat-en
beat-ing
beat-er
be-a-tif-ic
be-at-i-fy
be-at-i-fied
be-at-i-fi-ca-tion
be-at-i-tude
beat-nik
beau
beaus
beaux
beau geste
beau-te-ous
beau-te-ous-ly
beau-ti-cian
beau-ti-fy
beau-ti-fied
beau-ti-fy-ing
beau-ti-fi-ca-tion
beau-ti-fi-er
beau-ti-ful
beau-ti-ful-ly
beau-ty
beaux-arts
bea-ver
be-calm
be-cause
beck-on
be-cloud
be-come
be-com-ing
be-com-ing-ly
bed
bed-ded
bed-ding
be-daub
be-daz-zle
be-daz-zled
be-daz-zling

23

be-daz-zle-ment
bed-bug
bed-clothes
be-deck
be-dev-il
  be-dev-iled
  be-dev-il-ing
  be-dev-il-ment
be-dew
bed-fast
bed-fel-low
be-dim
  be-dimmed
  be-dim-ming
bed-lam
bed-pan
be-drag-gle
  be-drag-gled
  be-drag-gling
bed-rid-den
bed-rock
bed-room
bed-sore
bed-spread
bed-spring
bed-time
bee-bread
beech
beef
beef-eat-er
beef-steak
beef-y
  beef-i-er
  beef-i-est
bee-hive
bee-line
beer-y
  beer-i-er
  beer-i-est
beest-ings
bees-wax
bee-tle
  bee-tled
  bee-tling
bee-tle-browed
be-fall
  be-fall-en
  be-fall-ing
be-fit
  be-fit-ted
  be-fit-ting
be-fog
  be-fogged
  be-fog-ging
be-fore
be-fore-hand

be-foul
be-friend
be-fud-dle
  be-fud-dled
  be-fud-dling
beg
  beg-ged
  beg-ging
be-get
  be-get-ten
  be-got
  be-got-ten
beg-gar
  beg-gar-dom
  beg-gar-hood
  beg-gar-ly
be-gin
  be-gan
  be-gun
  be-gin-ning
  be-gin-ner
be-go-ni-a
be-grime
  be-grimed
  be-grim-ing
be-grudge
  be-grudged
  be-grudg-ing
  be-grudg-ing-ly
be-guile
  be-guiled
  be-guil-ing
  be-guil-er
be-half
be-have
  be-haved
  be-hav-ing
be-hav-ior
  be-hav-ior-ism
  be-hav-ior-ist
  be-hav-ior-is-tic
be-head
be-he-moth
be-hest
be-hind
be-hind-hand
be-hold
  be-hold-ing
  be-hold-er
  be-hold-en
be-hoove
  be-hooved
  be-hoov-ing
beige
he-ing
be-la-bor

be-lat-ed
  be-lat-ed-ly
  be-lat-ed-ness
be-lay
  be-lay-ed
  be-lay-ing
belch
bel-dam
be-lea-quer
bel-fry
  bel-fries
be-lie
  be-lied
  be-ly-ing
be-lief
be-lieve
  be-lieved
  be-liev-ing
  be-liev-a-ble
  be-liev-er
be-lit-tle
  be-lit-tled
  be-lit-tling
bel-la-don-na
bell-boy
bell bouy
belle
belles let-tres
bell-hop
bel-li-cose
  bel-li-cos-i-ty
bel-lig-er-ence
  bel-lig-er-en-cy
  bel-li-ger-ent
  bel-lig-er-ent-ly
bel-low
  bel-lows
bell-weth-er
bel-ly
  bel-lies
  bel-lied
  bel-ly-ing
bel-ly-ache
  bel-ly-ach-ing
bel-ly-but-ton
be-long
  be-long-ings
be-loved
be-low
belt
  belt-ed
belt-way
be-lu-ga
be-mire
  be-mired
  be-mir-ing

24

be-moan
be-muse
  be-mused
  be-mus-ing
bench
bend
  bend-ing
  bend-er
be-neath
ben-e-dict
ben-e-dic-tion
ben-e-fac-tion
ben-e-fac-tor
  ben-e-fac-tress
ben-e-fice
  ben-e-ficed
  ben-e-fic-ing
be-nef-i-cence
be-nef-i-cent
be-ne-fi-cial
  ben-e-fi-cial-ly
  ben-e-fi-ci-ar-ies
ben-e-fit
  ben-e-fit-ed
  ben-e-fit-ing
be-nev-o-lence
  be-nev-o-lent
  be-nev-o-lent-ly
be-night-ed
be-nign
  be-nig-ni-ty
  be-nig-ni-ties
  be-nign-ly
be-nig-nant
  be-nig-nan-cies
  be-nig-nan-cy
ben-i-son
ben-ny
  ben-nies
be-numb
bent
ben-zene
ben-zine
ben-zo-ate
ben-zo-in
ben-zol
be-queath
be-quest
be-rate
  be-rat-ed
  be-rat-ing
be-reave
  be-reaved
  be-reav-ing
be-reft
be-ret

ber-ga-mot
ber-i-ber-i
berke-li-um
ber-ry
  ber-ries
  ber-ried
  ber-ry-ing
ber-serk
berth
ber-tha
ber-yl
be-ryl-li-um
be-seech
  be-seeched
  be-seech-ing
  be-seech-ing-ly
be-set
  be-set-ting
be-shrew
be-side
  be-sides
be-siege
  be-sieged
  be-sieg-ing
  be-sieg-er
be-smear
be-smirch
bes-om
be-sot
  be-sot-ted
  be-sot-ting
be-spat-ter
be-speak
  be-speak-ing
best
bes-tial
  bes-tial-ly
  bes-ti-al-i-ty
  bes-ti-al-i-ties
be-stir
  be-stirred
  be-stir-ring
be-stow
  be-stow-al
be-strew
be-stride
  be-strid-den
  be-strid-ing
bet
  bet-ted
  bet-ting
be-ta
be-take
  be-tak-en
  be-tak-ing
  be-ta rays

be-ta-tron
be-tel
beth-el
be-tide
  be-tid-ed
  be-tid-ing
be-to-ken
be-tray
  be-tray-al
  be-tray-er
be-troth
  be-troth-al
  be-troth-ed
bet-ter
bet-ter-ment
bet-tor
be-tween
be-twixt
bev-el
  bev-eled
  bev-el-ing
bev-er-age
bev-y
  bev-ies
be-wail
be-ware
be-wil-der
  be-wil-der-ing-ly
  be-wil-der-ment
be-witch
  be-witch-er
  be-witch-ery
  be-witch-ing
  be-witch-ing-ly
  be-witch-ment
be-yond
be-zique
bi-an-nu-al
bi-as
  bi-ased
  bi-as-ing
bi-ax-i-al
  bi-ax-i-al-ly
bi-be-lot
Bi-ble
  Bib-li-cal
  Bib-li-cal-ly
bib-li-og-ra-phy
  bib-li-og-ra-phies
  bib-li-o-graphic
bib-li-o-ma-ni-a
  bib-li-o-ma-ni-ac
bib-li-o-phile
bib-u-lous
bi-cam-er-al
bi-car-bo-nate

25

bi-ce-te-nary
bi-cen-te-nar-ies
bi-cen-ten-ni-al
bi-ceps
bi-chlo-ride
bick-er
bi-con-cave
bi-con-vex
bi-cus-pid
bi-cus-pi-dal
bi-cus-pi-date
bi-cy-cle
bi-cy-cled
bi-cy-cling
bi-cy-cler
bi-cy-clist
bid
bid-den
bid-da-ble
bid-der
bid-dy
bid-dies
bide
bid-ed
bid-ing
bi-en-ni-al
bi-en-ni-al-ly
bier
bi-fid
bi-fo-cal
bi-fo-cals
bi-fur-cate
bi-fur-cat-ed
bi-fur-cat-ing
bi-fur-ca-tion
big
big-ger
big-gest
big-a-my
big-a-mies
big-a-mist
big-a-mous
big-heart-ed
big-horn
bight
big-no-ni-a
big-ot
big-ot-ed
big-ot-ed-ly
big-ot-ry
big-ot-ries
bi-jou
bi-joux
bi-ju-gous
bi-ki-ni
bi-lat-er-al

bi-lat-er-al-ly
bil-ber-ry
bil-ber-ries
bilge
bil-i-ary
bi-lin-gual
bil-ious
bilk
bill
bil-led
bil-ling
bil-la-bong
bill-board
bil-let
bil-let-doux
bill-fold
bill-hook
bil-liards
bil-lings-gate
bil-lion
bil-lion-are
bil-lionth
bil-low
bil-low-y
bil-low-ier
bil-low-i-est
bil-ly goat
bi-met-al-lism
bi-met-al-list
bi-me-tal-lic
bi-month-ly
bi-month-lies
bi-na-ry
bi-nate
bin-au-ral
bind
bind-ing
bind-er
bind-ery
bind-er-ies
binge
bin-go
bin-na-cle
bi-noc-u-lar
bi-no-mi-al
bio-chem-is-try
bio-chem-i-cal
bio-chem-ist
bi-o-cide
bi-o-e-col-o-gy
bi-o-en-gi-neer-ing
bi-o-gen-e-sis
bi-o-ge-net-ic
bi-og-ra-phy
bi-og-ra-pher
bi-o-graph-ic

bi-o-graph-i-cal
bi-o-graph-i-cal-ly
bi-ol-o-gy
bi-o-log-i-cal
bi-ol-o-gist
bi-o-met-rics
bi-o-nom-ics
bi-o-phys-ics
bi-o-phys-i-cal
bi-o-phys-i-cist
bi-op-sy
bi-op-sies
bi-o-sphere
bi-o-tin
bi-par-ti-san
bi-par-tite
bi-par-ti-tion
bi-ped
bi-ped-al
bi-plane
bi-po-lar
bi-po-lar-i-ty
birch
birch-en
bird-bath
bird-brain
bird-brained
bird-call
bird-ie
bird-lime
bird-man
bird's-eye
bi-ret-ta
birth-day
birth-mark
birth-place
birth-right
birth-stone
bis-cuit
bi-sect
bi-sec-tion
bi-sec-tor
bi-sex-u-al
bish-op
bish-op-ric
bis-muth
bi-son
bisque
bis-ter
bis-tered
bis-tro
bis-tros
bi-sul-fide
bitch
bite
bit-ten

bit-ing
bit-ing-ly
bit-stock
bit-ter
bit-ter-ish
bit-ter-ly
bit-ter-ness
bit-tern
bit-ter-root
bit-ters
bit-ter-sweet
bi-tu-men
bi-tu-mi-nous coal
bi-va-lent
bi-va-lence
bi-valve
bi-val-vu-lar
biv-ou-ac
biv-ou-acked
biv-ou-ack-ing
bi-week-ly
bi-week-lies
bi-year-ly
bi-zarre
bi-zarre-ly
bi-zarre-ness
blab
blab-bed
blab-bing
blab-ber
blab-ber-mouth
black-ball
black-ber-ry
black-ber-ries
black-bird
black-board
black-en
black-guard
black-head
black-ing
black-jack
black-list
black-mail
black-out
black-smith
black-snake
black-top
blad-der
blade
blad-ed
blame
blamed
blam-ing
blam-a-ble
blame-a-ble
blame-ful

blame-less
blame-less-ly
blame-less-ness
blame-wor-thy
blame-wor-thi-ness
blanch
blanc-er
blanch-ing
blanc-mange
bland
bland-ly
bland-ness
blan-dish
blan-dish-er
blan-dish-ment
blank
blank-ly
blank-ness
blan-ket
blare
blared
blar-ing
blar-ney
blas-pheme
blas-phemed
blas-phem-ing
blas-phem-er
blas-phem-ies
blas-phe-my
blast-ed
bas-tu-la
blat
blat-ted
blat-ting
bla-tant
bla-tan-cy
bla-tant-ly
blath-er
blaze
blazed
blaz-ing
bla-zer
bleach
bleach-er
bleak
bleak-ly
bleak-ness
blear
bleary
blear-i-ness
bleed
bleed-ing
bleed-er
blem-ish
blench
blend

blend-ed
blend-ing
blend-er
bless
bless-ed
bles-sing
bless-ed-ness
blind
blind-ing
blind-ing-ly
blind-ly
blind-ness
blind-fold
blind-man's bluff
blink-er
bliss
bliss-ful
bliss-ful-ly
bliss-ful-ness
blis-ter
blis-ter-y
blithe
blithe-ly
blithe-some
blithe-some-ly
blitz-krieg
bliz-zard
block
block-er
block-ade
block-ad-ed
block-ad-ing
block-ad-er
block-bus-ter
block-head
block-house
block-ish
block-ish-ly
blocky
blond
blood-curd-ling
blood bank
blood-ed
blood-hound
blood-less
blood-less-ly
blood-less-ness
blood-let-ting
blood pres-sure
blood re-la-tion
blood-shed
blood-shot
blood-stone
blood-suck-er
blood-thirst-y
blood-thirst-i-ly

bloody
  blood-i-er
  blood-i-est
  blood-ied
  blood-y-ing
  blood-i-ly
  blood-i-ness
bloom-ers
bloom-ing
  bloom-ing-ly
bloop-er
blos-som
blot , -
  blot-ted
  blot-ting
blotch
  blotchy
blot-ter
blow
  blown
  blow-ing
  blow-er
blow-fly
  blow-flies
blow-gun
blow-hole
blow-out
blow-pipe
blow-torch
blow-up
blow-y
blowz-y
blub-ber
  blub-bery
blu-cher
bludg-eon
blue
  blu-er
  blu-est
  blue-ness
blue-bell
blue-ber-ry
  blue-ber-ries
blue-bird
blue-blood-ed
blue-bon-net
blue-coat
blue-col-lar
blue-fish
blue-grass
blue-jac-ket
blue-nose
blue-pen-cil
blue-print
blu-et
blu-ing

blun-der
  blun-der-er
  blun-der-ing-ly
blun-der-buss
blunt
  blunt-ly
  blunt-ness
blur
  blur-red
  blur-ring
  blur-ry
blush
  blushed
  blush-ing
  blush-ing-ly
blus-ter
  blus-ter-er
  blus-ter-ing-ly
  blus-ter-ous
  blus-ter-y
bo-a
board-er
board-walk
boast
  boas-ter
  boast-ful
  boast-ful-ness
  boast-ing-ly
boat-house
boat-man
boat-swain
bob
  bob-bed
  bob-bing
  bob-bin
  bob-ble
  bob-bled
  bob-bling
bob-by-pin
bob-cat
bob-o-link
bob-sled
bob-tail
bob-white
bock
bode
  bod-ed
  bod-ing
bod-ice
bod-i-ly
bod-kin
bod-y
  bod-ied
  bod-y-ing
bod-y-guard
bog

  bog-gy
  bog-ging
bo-gey
bog-gle
  bog-gled
  bog-gling
  bog-gler
bo-gus
bo-gy
boil-er
bois-ter-ous
  bois-ter-ous-ly
  bois-ter-ous-ness
bo-la
  bo-las
bold
  bold-ly
  bold-ness
bold-face
bo-le-ro
bol-lix
boli-worm
boll weevil
bo-lo
bo-lo-gna
bo-lo-ney
bol-ster
  bol-ster-er
bolt
  bolt-ed
  bolt-er
bom-bard
  bom-bard-ment
bom-bar-dier
bom-bast
  bom-bas-tic
  bom-bas-ti-cal-ly
bomb-er
bomb-proof
bomb-shell
bomb-sight
bo-na fide
bo-nan-za
bon-bon
bond-age
bond-ed
bond-man
  bond-men
bonds-men
bone
  boned
  bon-ing
bone-head
bon-er
bon-fire
bon-go

bon-gos
bon-gies
bon-ho-mie
bo-ni-to
bon-net
bon-ny
bon-sai
bo-nus
  bo-nus-es
bon voy-age
bon-y
  bon-i-er
  bon-i-est
boo
  booed
  boo-ing
boo-by
  boo-bies
boo-by trap
boo-dle
boo-hoo
  boo-hooed
  boo-hoo-ing
book
  book-bind-er
book-case
book-end
book-ie
book-ish
  book-ish-ness
book-keep-ing
  book-keep-er
book-let
book-mak-er
book-mark
book-mo-bile
book-plate
book-sell-er
  book-sell-ing
book-stall
book-worm
boo-me-rang
boon docks
boon-dog-gle
boor
  boor-ish
  boor-ish-ness
boost
  boost-er
boot-black
boot-ee
boot-jack
boot-leg
  boot-legged
  boot-leg-ging
  boot-leg-ger

boot-less
  boot-less-ly
  boot-less-ness
boot-lick
  boot-lick-er
boo-ty
  boo-ties
booze
  booz-er
  booz-y
  booz-i-er
  booz-i-est
bo-rax
bor-der
  bor-der-ed
  bor-der-ing
  bor-der-land
  bor-der-line
bore
  bored
  bor-ing
  bor-er
bo-re-al
bore-dom
bo-ric
bo-ron
bor-ough
bor-row
  bor-row-er
borsch
bosh
bosk-y
bos-om
boss-ism
boss-y
  boss-i-er
  boss-i-est
  boss-i-ness
bo-sun
bot-a-ny
  bo-tan-i-cal
  bot-a-nist
  bot-a-nize
botch
  botchy
  botch-i-er
  botch-i-est
both-er
  both-er-some
bot-tle
  bot-tled
  bot-tling
  bot-tle-ful
  bot-tler
bot-tle-neck
bot-tom

bot-tom-less
bot-u-lism
bou-doir
bouf-fant
bough
bought
bouil-lon
boul-der
boul-e-vard
bounce
  bounced
  bounc-ing
bound
bound-a-ry
  bound-a-ries
bound-er
bound-less
  bound-less-ness
boun-te-ous
  boun-te-ous-ness
boun-ti-ful
boun-ty
  boun-ties
bou-quet
bour-bon
bour-geois
bour-geoi-sie
bou-tique
bou-ton-niere
bo-vine
bow-el
bow-er
bow-ery
bow-ie
bow-ing
bow-knot
bowl
bow-leg
  bow-leg-ged
bowl-er
bow-line
bow-ling
bow-man
  bow-men
bow-string
box
  box-ful
  box-fuls
box-car
box-er
box-ing
box of-fice
boy
  boy-hood
  boy-ish
  boy-ish-ly

boy-ish-ness
boy-cott
boy-friend
boy-sen-ber-ry
boy-sen-ber-ries
brace
bra-ced
brac-ing
brace-let
brac-er
bra-ces
brack-en
brack-et
brack-ish
brack-ish-ness
bract
brad
brad-ded
brad-ding
brae
brag
brag-ged
brag-ging
brag-gart
braid
braid-er
braid-ing
braille
brain-child
brain-less
brain-pow-er
brain-storm
brain-storm-ing
brain-wash-ing
brain-y
brain-i-er
brain-i-est
braise
braised
brais-ing
brake
braked
brak-ing
brake-man
brake-men
bram-ble
bram-bly
branch
branch-ed
brand
brand-er
brand-ish
brand-new
bran-dy
bran-dies
bran-died

bran-dy-ing
bra-sier
bras-se-rie
bras-se-ries
bras-siere
brassy
brass-i-er
brass-i-est
brat
brat-tish
brat-ty
bra-va-do
brave
braved
brav-ing
brave-ness
brav-ery
brav-er-ies
bra-vo
bra-vos
bra-vu-ra
brawl
braw-ler
brawn
brawn-i-ness
brawny
brawn-i-er
brawn-i-est
bra-zen
bra-zier
breach
bread
bread = ed
breadth-ways
bread-win-ner
break
break-ing
break-a-ble
break-age
break-a-way
break-down
brak-er
break-fast
break-neck
break-through
break-up
breast-bone
breast-plate
breath
breathe
breathed
breath-ing
breath-er
breath-ing
breath-tak-ing
breath-tak-ing-ly

breathy
breath-i-er
breath-i-est
breech-es
breech-load-er
bred
breed
breed-ing
breeze
breezy
breez-i-er
breez-i-est
breez-i-ness
breth-ren
bre-vet
bre-vet-ted
bre-vet-ting
bre-vi-a-ry
bre-vi-a-ries
brev-i-ty
brew
brew-er
brew-ery
brew-er-ies
bri-ar
bri-ary
bribe
bribed
brib-ing
brib-a-ble
birb-ery
brib-er-ies
bric-a-brac
brick-lay-er
brick-lay-ing
brick-work
bride
brid-al
bride-groom
brides-maid
bridge
bri-dle
bri-dled
bri-dling
brief
brief-ly
brief-ing
bri-er
bri-gade
bri-a-dier
brig-an-tine
bright
bright-ly
bright-ness
bright-en
bril-liance

30

bril-lian-cy
bril-liant
brim
brimmed
brim-ming
brim-stone
brine
briny
bring
bring-ing
brink
bri-oche
bri-quet
bri-quette
brisk
brisk-ly
brisk-ness
bris-ket
bris-tle
bris-tled
britch-es
brit-tle
broach
broached
broach-ing
broad-cast
broad-cast-ed
broad-cast-ing
broad-cloth
broad-mind-ed
broad-side
bro-cade
bro-cad-ed
bro-cad-ing
broc-co-li
bro-chure
broil-er
bro-ken
bro-ker
bro-ker-age
bro-mide
bro-mine
bron-chi
bron-chi-al
bron-chi-tis
bron-chue
bron-co
bron-cos
bron-to-saur
bronze
bronz-ed
bronz-ing
brooch
brood
brood-ing
brook

broom-stick
broth-el
broth-er
broth-er-in-law
broth-ers-in-law
broth-er-ly
brow-beat
brow-beat-en
brow-beat-ing
brown
brown-ie
browse
browsed
brows-ing
bru-in
bruise
bruis-ed
bruis-er
bruis-ing
brunch
bru-net
brusque
bru-tal
bru-tal-i-ty
bru-tal-ize
bru-tal-ized
bru-tal-iz-ing
bru-tal-i-za-tion
brut-ish
bub-ble
bub-bled
bub-bling
bub-bler
bu-bon-ic plague
buc-ca-neer
buck-a-roo
buck-board
buck-et
buck-et-ed
buck-et-ing
buck-eye
buck-le
buck-saw
buck-shot
buck-skin
buck-tooth
buck-teeth
buck-toothed
buck-wheat
bu-col-ic
bud
bud-ded
bud-ding
bud-dy
budge
budg-et

buff-er
buf-fet
buf-fet-ed
buf-fet = ing
buf-foon
buf-foon-ery
buf-foon-er-ies
buf-foon-ish
bug
bugged
bug-ging
bug-a-boo
bug-gy
bug-gi-er
bug-gi-est
bu-gle
bu-gled
bu-gling
bu-gler
build
build-er
build-ing
built--in
built-up
bulb
bul-ba-ceous
bul-bar
bul-bous
bulge
bulged
bulg-ing
bulgy
bulk-head
bulk-y
bulk-i-er
bulk-i-est
bulk-i-ly
bulk-i-ness
bull-dog
bull-doze
bull-dozed
bull-doz-ing
bull-doz-er
bul-let
bul-le-tin
bul-let-proof
bull-fight
bull-fight-er
bull-fight-ing
bull-finch
bull-head-ed
bul-lion
bull-pen
bull's-eye
bul-ly
bul-lies

bul-lied
bul-ly-ing
bul-rush
bul-wark
bum
bum-mer
bum-mest
bum-ble-bee
bump-er
bump-kin
bump-tious
bump-tious-ness
bump-y
bump-i-er
bump-i-est
bunch
bunchy
bunch-i-er
bunch-i-est
bun-co
bun-combe
bun-dle
bun-dled
bun-dling
bun-ga-low
bun-gle
bun-gled
bun-gling
bun-gler
bun-ion
bunk-er
bunk-house
bun-ko
bun-kum
bun-ny
bun-nies
bun-ting
bu-oy
buoy-an-cy
buoy-ant
buoy-ant-ly
bur-ble
bur-den
bur-den-some
bur-dock
bu-reau
bu-reaus
bu-reaux
bu-reauc-ra-cy
bu-reauc-ra-cies
bu-reau-crat
bu-reau-crat-ic
bu-rette
bur-geon
burg-er
bur-gess

bur-glar
bur-glar-ize
bur-glar-ized
bur-glar-iz-ing
bur-gla-ries
bur-gla-ry
bur-gle
bur-gled
bur-gling
bur-i-al
bur-lap
bur-lesque
bur-lesqued
bur-les-quing
bur-les-quer
bur-ly
bur-li-er
bur-li-est
bur-li-ness
burn
burn-ed
burnt
burn-ing
burn-a-ble
burn-er
bur-nish
bur-nish-er
bur-noose
burn-sides
burp
burr
burred
bur-ring
bur-ro
bur-ros
bur-row
bur-row-er
bur-sa
bur-sae
bur-sal
bur-sar
bur-sa-ri-al
bur-sa-ry
bur-sa-ries
bur-si-tis
burst
burst-ing
burst-er
bur-y
bur-ied
bur-y-ing
bus
bus-ed
bus-ing
bus-boy
bus-by

bus-bies
bushed
bush-el
bu-shi-do
bush-ing
bush-man
bush-men
bush-mas-ter
bush-rang-er
bush-whack
bush-whack-er
bush-whack-ing
bush-y
bush-i-er
bush-i-est
bush-i-ness
bus-i-ly
busi-ness
busi-ness-like
busi-ness-man
busi-ness-men
busi-ness-wom-an
bus-kin
bus-kined
bus-tard
bus-tle
bus-tled
bus-tling
bus-tler
bus-y
bus-i-er
bus-i-est
bus-ied
bus-y-ing
bu-ta-di-ene
bu-tane
butch-er
butch-ery
butch-er-ies
but-ler
butte
but-ter
but-tery
but-tock
but-ton
but-tress
bu-ty-ric
bux-om
buy
bought
buy-ing
buz-zard
buzz-er
by-gong
by-law
byte

32

C

ca-bal
  ca-balled
  ca-ball-ing
cab-a-la
  cab-a-lis-tic
  cab-a-lis-ti-cal
ca-bal-le-ro
ca-ba-na
cab-a-ret
cab-bage
cab-by
  cab-bies
ca-ber
cab-in
cab-i-net
cab-i-net-mak-er
cab-i-net-work
ca-ble
  ca-bled
  ca-bling
ca-ble-gram
cab-o-chon
ca-boo-dle
ca-boose
cab-ri-o-let
ca-ca-o
cach-a-lot
cache
  cached
  cach-ing
ca-chet
ca-cique
cack-le
ca-coph-o-ny
  ca-coph-o-nies
cac-tus
  cac-tus-es
cac-ti
cad
  cad-dish
ca-dav-er
  ca-dav-er-ous
cad-die
  cad-died
cad-dis fly
cad-dy
  cad-dies
ca-dence
ca-den-za
ca-det
cadge
  cadged
  cadg-ing
cad-mi-um
ca-dre
ca-du-ce-us

ca-du-cei
cea-su-ra
cae-su-rae
ca-fe
caf-e-te-ria
caf-feine
caf-tan
cage
  caged
cai-man
cairn
cais-son
cai-tiff
ca-jole
cake
  caked
cal-a-bash
cal-a-boose
cal-a-mine
ca-lam-i-ty
  ca-lam-i-ties
  ca-lam-i-tous
cal-cic
cal-ci-fy
  cal-ci-fied
  cal-ci-fy-ing
  cal-ci-fi-ca-tion
cal-ci-mine
cal-cite
cal-ci-um
cal-cu-la-ble
  cal-cu-la-bil-i-ty
cal-cu-late
  cal-cu-lat-ed
  cal-cu-lat-ing
  cal-cu-la-tion
cal-cu-la-tor
cal-cu-lus
  cal-cu-lus-es
cal-dron
cal-en-dar
cal-ends
calf
cal-i-ber
cal-i-brate
  cal-i-brat-ed
  cal-i-brat-ing
  cal-i-bra-tion
cal-i-co
  cal-i-coes
cal-i-per
ca-liph
  cal-iph-ate
cal-is-then-ics
cal-lig-ra-pher
cal-lig-ra-phy

call-ing
cal-li-o-pe
cal-lous
  cal-loused
cal-low
cal-lus
  cal-lus-es
calm
ca-lor-ic
cal-o-rie
  cal-o-ries
cal-o-rif-ic
cal-u-met
cal-um-ny
calve
  calved
ca-lyp-so
  ca-lyp-sos
ca-lyx
  ca-lyx-es
cal-y-ces
ca-ma-ra-de-rie
cam-ber
cam-bi-um
cam-bric
cam-el
ca-mel-lia
cam-eo
cam-era
cam-i-sole
cam-o-mile
cam-ou-flage
  cam-ou-flaged
  cam-ou-flag-ing
cam-paign
cam-pa-ni-le
  cam-pa-ni-les
camp-er
cam-phor
cam-pus
  cam-pus-es
camp-y
cam-shaft
can
  canned
  can-ning
ca-nal
  ca-naled
  ca-nal-ing
ca-nard
ca-nar-y
ca-nas-ta
can-can
can-cel
  can-celed
  can-cel-ing

can-cel-la-tion
can-cer
can-de-la-brum
can-did
can-di-da-cy
  can-di-da-cies
  can-di-date
can-died
can-dle
can-dor
can-dy
  can-dies
  can-died
  can-dy-ing
cane
ca-nine
can-is-ter
can-ker
  can-ker-ous
can-na-bis
canned
can-ner
can-nery
  can-ner-ies
can-ni-bal
can-non
can-not
can-ny
  can-nier
ca-noe
can-on
ca-non-i-cal
can-on-ize
  can-on-ized
  can-on-i-za-tion
can-o-py
can-ta-loup
  can-ta-loupe
  can-ta-lope
can-tan-ker-ous
can-ta-ta
can-teen
can-ter
can-ti-cle
can-ti-lev-er
can-to
  can-tos
can-ton
can-tor
can-vas
can-yon
ca-pa-bil-i-ty
  cap-pa-bil-i-ties
ca-pa-ble
  ca-pa-bly
ca-pa-cious

ca-pac-i-tate
  ca-pac-i-tat-ed
  ca-pac-i-tat-ing
ca-pac-i-ty
  ca-pac-i-ties
ca-per
ca-pi-as
cap-il-lar-i-ty
cap-il-lar-y
  cap-il-lar-ies
cap-i-tal
cap-i-ta-tion
ca-pit-u-late
  ca-pit-u-lat-ed
  ca-pit-u-lat-ing
  ca-pit-u-la-tor
ca-pon
ca-pote
ca-pric-cio
ca-price
  ca-pri-cious
  ca-pri-cious-ly
cap-ri-ole
  cap-ri-oled
  cap-ri-ol-ing
cap-size
cap-stan
cap-stone
cap-sule
  cap-su-lar
cap-tain
  cap-tain-cy
cap-tion
cap-tious
  cap-tious-ness
cap-ti-vate
cap-tive
  cap-tiv-i-ty
  cap-tiv-i-ties
cap-tor
cap-ture
  cap-tured
  cap-tur-ing
  cap-tur-er
car-a-cole
  car-a-coled
  car-a-col-ing
car-a-cul
ca-rafe
car-a-mel
car-a-pace
car-at
car-a-van
car-a-van-sa-ry
  car-a-van-sa-ries
car-a-vel

car-a-way
car-bide
car-bine
car-bo-hy-drate
car-bo-lat-ed
car-bol-ic
car-bon
car-bo-na-ceous
car-bo-nate
  car-bo-na-tion
car-bon di-ox-ide
car-bon-if-er-ous
car-bon-ize
  car-bon-ized
  car-bon-iz-ing
  car-bon-i-za-tion
car-bon mon-ox-ide
car-boy
car-bun-cle
car-bu-re-tor
car-ca-jou
car-cass
car-cin-o-gen
  car-cin-o-gen-ic
car-ci-no-ma
  car-ci-no-mas
  car-ci-no-ma-ta
car-da-mom
car-di-ac
car-di-gan
car-di-nal
car-di-o-graph
  car-di-og-ra-phy
ca-reen
ca-reer
care-ful
  care-ful-ly
  care-ful-ness
care-less
  care-less-ly
  care-less-ness
ca-ress
  ca-ress-ing-ly
car-et
care-worn
car-go
  car-goes
  car-gos
car-hop
car-i-bou
car-i-ca-ture
  car-i-ca-tured
  car-i-ca-tur-ing
  car-i-ca-tur-ist
car-ies
car-il-lon

car-il-lonned
car-i-lon-ning
car-i-lon-neur
car-mine
car-nage
car-nal
car-nal-i-ty
car-nal-ly
car-na-tion
car-nel-ian
car-ni-val
car-ni-vore
car-niv-o-rous
car-niv-o-rous-ly
car-niv-o-rous-ness
car-om
ca-rot-id
ca-rous-al
ca-rouse
ca-roused
ca-rous-ing
ca-rous-er
car-ou-sel
carp
car-pen-ter
car-pen-try
car-pet
car-pet-ing
car-pus
car-riage
car-ri-er
car-ri-ole
car-rot
car-roty
car-ry
car-ried
car-ry-ing
cart
cart-age
carte-blanche
car-tel
car-ti-lage
car-ti-lag-i-nous
car-tog-ra-phy
car-tog-ra-pher
car-to-graph-ic
car-ton
car-toon
car-toon-ist
car-tridge
cart-wheel
carve
car-vel
car-y-at-id
car-y-at-ids
car-y-at-i-des

ca-sa-ba
cas-cade
cas-cad-ed
cas-cad-ing
ca-sein
case-mate
case-mat-ed
case-ment
case-ment-ed
case-work
case-work-er
cash-ew
cash-ier
cash-mere
cas-ing
ca-si-no
cas-ket
cas-sa-ba
cas-sa-va
cas-se-role
cas-sette
cas-si-no
cas-sock
cas-socked
cas-so-wary
cas-so-war-ies
cast
cast-ing
cas-ta-net
cast-a-way
caste
cas-tel-lat-ed
cast-er
cas-ti-gate
cas-ti-gat-ed
cas-ti-gat-ing
cas-ti-ga-tion
cas-ti-ga-tor
cast i-ron
cas-tle
cas-tor
cas-trate
cas-trat-ed
cas-trat-ing
cas-trat-er
cas-tra-tion
cas-u-al
cas-u-al-ty
cas-u-al-ties
cas-u-ist
cas-u-is-tic
cas-u-ist-ry
cas-ist-ries
cas-u-ist
cas-u-ist-ic
cas-u-ist-ry

cas-u-ist-ries
cat-a-clysm
cat-a-cly-mal
cat-a-comb
cat-a-falque
cat-a-lep-sy
cat-a-lep-tic
cat-a-log
cat-a-loged
cat-a-log-ing
cat-a-log-er
cat-a-log-ist
ca-tal-pa
ca-tal-y-sis
ca-tal-y-ses
cat-a-lyt-ic
cat-a-lyst
cat-a-lyze
cat-a-lyzed
cat-a-lyz-ing
cat-a-ma-ran
cat-a-pult
cat-a-ract
ca-tarrh
ca-tas-tro-phe
cat-as-troph-ic
catch
caught
catch-ing
catch-er
catch-up
catch-y
catch-i-er
catch-i-est
cat-e-chism
cat-e-chis-mal
cat-e-chiz
cat-e-chu-men
cat-e-gor-i-cal
cat-e-gor-i-cal-ly
cat-e-go-ry
cat-a-go-ries
cat-e-gor-ize
cat-e-gor-ized
cat-e-gor-iz-ing
ca-ter
ca-ter-er
cat-er-pil-lar
ca-ter-waul
cat-fish
cat-fish-es
cat-gut
ca-thar-sis
ca-thar-ses
ca-thar-tic
ca-the-dral

cath-e-ter
cath-ode
cat-i-on
cat-nap
  cat-napped
  cat-nap-ping
cat-nip
cat's-paw
cat-sup
cat-tail
cat-tle
cat-ty
  cat-tier
  cat-ti-est
  cat-ti-ly
  cat-ti-ness
cat-ty-cor-ner
cau-cus
  cau-cus-es
  cau-cused
  cau-cus-ing
cau-dal
cau-date
  cau-dat-ed
cau-dle
caul-dron
cau-li-flow-er
caulk
  caulk-er
caus-al
  caus-al-ly
cau-sal-i-ty
  cau-sal-i-ties
cause-way
caus-tic
  caus-ti-cal-ly
cau-ter-ize
  cau-ter-ized
  cau-ter-iz-ing
  cau-ter-i-za-tion
cau-ter-y
  cau-ter-ies
cau-tion
  cau-tion-ary
cau-tious
cav-al-cade'
cav-a-lier
  cav-a-lier-ly
cav-al-ry
cave
ca-ve-at
cav-ern
  cav-ern-ous
cav-ier
cav-il
  cav-iled

cav-il-ing
cav-i-ty
  cav-i-ties
ca-vort
cay-enne
cay-man
  cay-mans
cay-use
ce-cum
ce-dar
cede
  ced-ed
  ced-ing
ce-dil-la
ceil-ing
cel-an-dine
cel-a-brant
cel-e-brate
  cel-e-brat-ed
  cel-e-brat-ing
  cel-e-bra-tion
  cel-e-bra-tor
ce-leb-ri-ty
  ce-leb-ri-ties
ce-ler-i-ty
cel-er-y
ce-les-tial
ce-li-ac
cel-i-ba-cy
  cel-i-bate
cel-lar
cel-lo
  cel-los
  cel-list
cel-lo-phane
cel-lu-lar
cel-lule
cel-lu-lose
ce-ment
cem-e-ter-y
ce-no-bite
cen-o-taph
cen-ser
cen-sor
  cen-so-ri-al
  cen-sor-ship
  cen-so-ri-ous
  cen-so-ri-ous-ly
  cen-so-ri-ous-ness
cen-sure
  cen-sured
  cen-sur-ing
  cen-sur-er
cen-sus
  cen-sus-es
  cen-sused

cen-sus-ing
cen-tare
cen-taur
cen-te-nar-i-an
cen-te-na-ry
  cen-te-nar-ies
cen-ten-ni-al
cen-ter
cen-ti-are
cen-ti-grade
cen-ti-gram
cen-ti-li-ter
cen-ti-me-ter
cen-tral
  cen-tral-ize
  cen-tral-ized
  cen-tral-iz-ing
cen-trif-u-gal
cen-tri-fuge
cen-trip-e-tal
cen-tu-ri-an
cen-tu-ry
  cen-tu-ries
ce-ram-ic
  ce-ram-ics
ce-re-al
cer-e-bel-lum
cer-e-bral
cer-e-brum
cer-e-mo-ni-al
  cer-e-mo-no-al-ism
cer-e-mo-ny
  cer-e-mo-nies
ce-rise
ce-ric
ce-ri-um
cer-tain
cer-tain-ty
  cer-tain-ties
cer-tif-i-cate
  cer-tif-i-ca-tion
cer-ti-fy
  cer-ti-fied
  cer-ti-fy-ing
cer-ti-tude
ce-ru-le-an
cer-vi-cal
cer-vix
  cer-vix-es
  cer-vi-ces
ces-sa-tion
ces-sion
cess-pool
ce-ta-cean
  ce-ta-ceous
chafe

chafed
chaf-ing
chaf-er
chaff
chaf-fer
chaff-er-er
cha-grin
cha-grined
cha-grin-ing
chain re-ac-tion
chair-man
chair-men
chaise-longue
chal-et
chal-ice
chalk
chalky
chal-lenge
chal-lenged
chal-leng-ing
cham-ber
cham-ber-maid
cha-me-le-on
cham-ois
cham-pagne
cham-pi-on
cham-pi-on-ship
chance-ful
chan-cel-lor
chanc-y
chanc-i-er
chanc-i-est
chan-de-lier
change
changed
chang-ing
chang-a-ble
chan-nel
chan-ti-cleer
cha-os
cha-ot-ic
cha-pa-re-jos
chap-ar-ral
cha-peau
cha-peaux
chap-el
chap-e-ron
chap-fall-en
chap-lain
chap-let
chap-ter
char
charred
char-ring
char-ac-ter
char-ac-ter-is-tic

char-ac-ter-is-ti-cal-ly
char-ac-ter-ize
char-ac-ter-ized
char-ac-ter-iz-ing
char-ac-ter-i-za-tion
char-ac-ter-iz-er
cha-rade
char-coal
charge
charged
charg-ing
charg-er
char-i-ot
char-i-ot-eer
cha-ris-ma
char-i-ta-ble
char-i-ta-ble-ness
char-i-ta-bly
char-i-ty
char-i-ties
cha-riv-a-ri
char-la-tan
char-la-tan-ism
char-ley horse
charm
char-nel
char-ter
char-treuse
char-wom-an
chary
char-i-er
char-i-est
chase
chased
chas-ing
chas-er
chasm
chas-sis
chaste
chaste-ly
chas-ten
chas-tise
chas-tised
chas-tis-ing
chas-tise-ment
chas-tis-er
chas-ti-ty
chat
chat-ted
chat-ting
cha-teau
cha-teaux
chat-e-laine
chat-tel
chat-ter
chat-ter-box

chat-ty
chat-ti-er
chat-ti-est
chat-ti-ly
chat-ti-ness
chauf-feur
chau-vin-ist
chau-vin-ism
chau-vin-is-tic
cheap
cheap-ly
cheap-ness
cheap-en
cheap-skate
cheat
check-er-board
check-list
check-mate
check-mat-ed
check-mat-ing
check-out
check-point
check-room
check-up
ched-dar
cheek-bone
cheek-y
cheek-i-er
cheek-i-est
cheek-i-ness
cheer-ful
cheer-ful-ly
cheer-ful-ness
cheer-lead-er
cheer-less
cheer-less-ly
cheer-less-ness
chee-y
cheer-i-er
cheer-i-est
cheer-i-ly
cheer-i-ness
cheese-burg-er
cheese-cake
cheese-cloth
chees-y
chees-i-er
chees-i-est
chees-i-ness
chee-tah
chem-i-cal
chem-i-cal-ly
che-mise
chem-ist
chem-is-try
chem-o-ther-a-py

che-nille
cher-ish
che-root
cher-ry
cher-ries
cher-ub
cher-ubs
cher-u-bim
che-ru-bic
cher-vil
chess-man
chess-men
chest-nut
chest-y
chest-i-er
chest-i-est
chev-ron
chew
chew-er
chi-a-ro-scu-ro
chi-can-ery
cha-can-er-ies
chi-chi
chick-a-dee
chic-ken
chic-ken-heart-ed
chic-le
chic-o-ry
chic-o-ries
chide
chid-ed
chief
chief-ly
chief-tain
chif-fon
chif-fo-nier
chi-gnon
chil-blain
chil-dren
child-bear-ing
child-birth
child-hood
child-ish
child-ish-ly
child-like
chili
chil-ies
chill
chill-ing-ly
chill-y
chill-i-er
chill-i-est
chill-i-ness
chi-me-ra
chi-mer-ic
chi-mer-i-cal

chi-mer-i-cal-ly
chi-mer-i-cal-ness
chim-ney
chim-pan-zee
chin
chinned
chin-ning
chi-na
chi-no
chi-nos
chi-noi-se-rie
chintz-y
chintz-i-er
chintz-i-est
chip
chipped
chip-ping
chip-munk
chip-per
chi-rog-ra-pher
chi-rog-ra-phy
chi-rop-o-dist
chi-ro-prac-tic
chi-ro-prac-tor
chis-el
chis-eled
chis-el-ing
chis-el-er
chit-chat
chi-tin
chit-ter-ling
chiv-al-ry
chiv-al-ries
chiv-al-ric
chiv-al-rous
chiv-al-rous-ly
chiv-al-rous-ness
chlo-rine
chlo-ro-form
clo-ro-phyll
chock-full
choc-o-late
choice
choice-ly
choice-ness
choir-boy
choke
choked
chok-ing
chok-er
chol-er
chol-era
chol-er-ic
cho-les-te-rol
choose
chose

cho-sen
choos-ing
choos-y
choos-i-er
choos-i-est
chop
chopped
chop-ping
chop-per
chop-pi-ness
chop-py
chop-pi-er
chop-i-est
chop-sticks
chop su-ey
cho-ral
cho-ral-ly
cho-rale
chord
chord-al
cho-rea
cho-re-og-ra-phy
cho-re-og-ra-pher
cho-re-o-graph-ic
cho-ric
chor-is-ter
chor-tle
chor-tled
chor-tling
cho-rus
cho-rus-es
cho-rused
cho-rus-ing
chos-en
chow-der
chow mein
chrism
Christ
chris-ten
chris-ten-ing
Chris-tian
Chis-ti-an-i-ty
Chris-ti-an-i-ties
Christ-mas
chro-mate
chro-mat-ic
chro-mat-i-cal-ly
chro-mat-ics
chro-ma-tin
chro-mic
chro-mi-um
chro-mo
chro-mus
chro-mo-lith-o-graph
chro-mo-some
chro-mo-sphere

chron-ic
chron-i-cal-ly
chron-i-cle
chron-i-cled
chron-i-cling
chron-i-cler
chron-o-log-i-cal
chron-o-log-i-cal-ly
chro-no-lo-gy
chro-nol-o-gies
chro-nol-o-gist
chro-nom-e-ter
chron-o-met-ric
chrys-a-lis
chry-sa-lis-es
chry-sal-i-des
chrys-an-the-mum
chrys-o-lite
chub-by
chub-bi-er
chub-bi-est
chub-bi-ness
chuck-full
chuck-le
chuck-led
chuck-ling
chuk-ker
chum-my
chum-mi-er
chum-mi-est
chunk
chunky
chunk-i-er
chunk-i-est
church
church-li-ness
church-ly
church-go-er
church-man
church-men
church-war-den
church-yard
churl-ish
churl-ish-ly
churl-ish-ness
churn-er
chut-ney
chutz-pah
ci-bo-ri-um
ci-bo-ria
ci-ca-da
ci-ca-das
ci-ca-dea
cic-a-trix
cic-a-tri-ces
cic-a-trize

cic-a-trized
cic-a-triz-ing
cic-e-ro-ne
ci-der
ci-gar
cig-a-rette
cil-ia
cil-i-ar-y
cil-i-ate
cin-cho-na
cinc-ture
cin-der
cin-e-ma
cin-e-mas
cin-e-mat-ic
cin-e-ma-to-graph
cin-e-ma-tog-ra-phy
cin-e-rar-i-um
cin-na-bar
cin-na-mon
cinque-foil
ci-on
ci-pher
cir-ca
cir-ca-di-an
cir-cle
cir-cled
cir-cling
cir-clet
cir-cuit
cir-cu-i-tous
cir-cu-i-tous-ly
cir-cu-i-tous-ness
cir-cu-lar
cir-cu-lar-ize
cir-cu-lar-ized
cir-cu-lar-iz-ing
cir-cu-lar-i-za-tion
cir-cu-la-tion
cir-cu-late
cir-cu-lat-ed
cir-cu-lat-ing
cir-cu-la-tive
cir-cu-la-tor
cir-cu-la-to-ry
cir-cum-am-bi-ent
cir-cum-cise
cir-cum-cised
cir-cum-cis-ing
cir-cum-cis-er
cir-cum-ci-sion
cir-cum-fer-ence
cir-cum-fer-en-tial
cir-cum-flex
cir-cum-flu-ent
cir-cum-fuse

cir-cum-fus-ing
cir-cum-fu-sion
cir-cum-lo-cu-tion
cir-cum-lo-cu-to-ry
cir-cum-nav-i-gate
cir-cum-nav-i-gat-ed
cir-cum-nav-i-gat-ing
cir-cum-nav-i-ga-tion
cir-cum-nav-i-ga-tor
cir-cum-scribe
cir-cum-scribed
cir-cum-scrib-ing
cir-cum-scrib-er
cir-cum-scrip-tion
cir-cum-scrip-tive
cir-cum-spect
cir-cum-stance
cir-cum-stan-tial
cir-cum-stan-ti-al-i-ty
cir-cum-stan-ti-at-ed
cir-cum-stan-ti-at-ing
cir-cum-stan-ti-a-tion
cir-cum-vent
cir-cum-ven-tion
cir-cum-ven-tive
cir-cus
cir-cus-es
cir-rho-sis
cir-rhot-ic
cir-rus
cis-tern
cit-a-del
cite
cit-ed
cit-ing
ci-ta-tion
cith-a-ra
cit-i-zen
cit-i-zen-ship
cit-i-zen-ry
cit-i-zen-ries
cit-rate
cit-ric
cit-ron
cit-ron-el-la
cit-rus
cit-tern
city
cit-ies
ci-ty-state
civ-et
civ-ic
civ-ics
civ-il
ci-vil-ian
ci-vil-i-ty

ci-vil-i-ties
civ-i-li-za-tion
civ-i-lize
  civ-i-lized
  civ-i-liz-ing
clab-ber
claim
  claim-a-ble
  claim-ant
  claim-er
clair-voy-ance
  clair-voy-ant
clam
  clammed
  clam-ming
clam-bake
clam-bar
clam-my
  clam-mi-er
  clam-mi-est
  clam-mi-ly
  clam-mi-ness
clam-or
  clam-or-ous
clan
  clan-nish
clan-des-tine
clang-or
  clang-or-ous
clans-man
  clans-men
clap
  clapped
  clap-ping
clap-board
clap-per
clap-trap
claque
clar-et
clar-i-fy
  clar-i-fied
  clar-i-fy-ing
  clar-i-fi-ca-tion
clar-i-net
  clar-i-net-ist
clar-i-on
clar-i-ty
class-a-ble
clas-sic
  clas-si-cal
  clas-si-cal-ly
clas-si-cism
  clas-si-cist
clas-si-fy
  clas-si-fied
  clas-si-fy-ing

clas-si-fi-er
  clas-si-fi-ca-tion
class-mate
class-room
class-y
  class-i-er
  class-i-est
clat-ter
clause
  claus-i-cle
  claus-tro-pho-bia
clav-i-chord
clav-i-cle
cla-vier
clay
  clay-ey
  clay-more
clean-cut
clean-er
clean-ly
  clean-li-er
  clean-li-est
  clean-li-ness
cleanse
  cleansed
  cleans-ing
  cleans-er
clean-up
clear
  clear-ly
  clear-ness
clear-ance
clear-cut
clear-ing
clear-sight-ed
cleav-age
cleave
  cleaved
  cleav-ing
cleav-er
clef
cleft
clem-en-cy
  clem-ent
clere-sto-ry
  clere-sto-ries
cler-gy
  cler-gies
cler-gy-man
  cler-gy-men
cler-ic
  cler-i-cal
  cler-i-cal-ism
  cler-i-cal-ist
clev-er
  clev-er-ly

clev-er-ness
clev-is
  clev-is-es
clew
cli-ent
cli-en-tele
cliff-hang-er
cli-mac-ter-ic
cli-mate
  cli-mat-ic
  cli-mat-i-cal
climb
  climb-a-ble
  climb-er
clinch-er
cling
  cling-ing
  cling-ing-ly
  cling-er
clin-ic
  clin-i-cal
  clin-i-cal-ly
clink-er
clip
  clipped
  clip-ping
clip-per
clique
  cliqu-ey
  cliqu-ish
clit-o-ris
clo-a-ca
  clo-a-cae
  clo-a-cal
clob-ber
clock-wise
clock-work
clod
  clod-dish
  clod-dy
clog
  clog-ged
  clog-ging
clois-ter
  clois-tral
close
  closed
  clos-ing
  clos-est
  close-ly
  close-ness
close-fist-ed
close-mouthed
clos-et
  clos-et-ed
  clos-et-ing

close-up
clo-sure
clot
  clot-ted
  clot-ting
clothe
  clothed
  cloth-ing
clothes-horse
clothes-line
clothes-pin
cloth-ier
clöth-ing
clo-ture
cloud-burst
cloud-y
  cloud-i-er
  cloud-i-est
  cloud-i-ly
  cloud-i-ness
clo-ven
clo-ver
clo-ver-leaf
clown
  clown-ish
cloy
  cloy-ing-ly
club
  clubbed
  club-bing
club-foot
club-house
clump
  clumpy
clum-sy
  clum-si-er
  clum-si-est
  clum-si-ly
  clum-si-ness
clus-ter
coach-man
  coach-men
co-ag-u-late
  co-ag-u-lat-ed
  co-ag-u-lat-ing
  co-ag-u-la-tion
co-a-lesce
  co-a-lesced
  co-a-les-cing
  co-a-les-cence
  co-a-les-cent
co-a-li-tion
coarse
  coars-er
  coars-est
  coars-en

coarse-ly
coast-er
coast-line
coat-ing
co-au-thor
coax
  coax-ing-ly
co-balt
cob-ble
  cob-bled
  cob-bling
cob-bler
cob-ble-stone
co-bra
cob-web
  cob-webbed
  cob-web-by
co-ca
co-caine
coc-cyx
  coc-cy-ges
  coc-cyg-e-al
coch-le-a
cock-ade
cock-a-too
cock-crow
cock-er span-iel
cock-eyed
cock-fight
cock-le
cock-le-bur
cock-le-shell
cock-ney
  cock-neys
cock-pit
cock-roach
cocks-comb
cock-sure
cock-tail
cocky
  cock-i-er
  cock-i-est
  cock-i-ness
co-coa
co-co-nut
co-coon
cod
  cod-fish
cod-dle
  cod-dled
  cod-dling
code
  cod-ed
  cod-ing
co-deine
codg-er

cod-i-cil
cod-i-fy
  cod-i-fied
  cod-i-fy-ing
  cod-i-fi-ca-tion
cod-liv-er oil
co-ed
co-ed-u-ca-tion
coe-len-ter-ate
co-e-qual
co-erce
  co-erced
  co-er-cing
  co-er-ci-ble
  co-er-cion
  co-er-cive
co-ex-ist
  co-ex-ist-ence
  co-ex-ist-ent
cof-fee
cof-fee-house
cof-fee-pot
cof-fer
cof-fin
co-gent
  co-gen-cy
  co-gent-ly
cog-i-tate
  cog-i-tat-ed
  cog-i-tat-ing
  cog-i-ta-ble
  cog-i-ta-tive
cog-nac
cog-nate
cog-ni-tion
  cog-ni-tive
cog-ni-zance
  cog-ni-zant
cog-wheel
co-hab-it
  co-hab-i-ta-tion
co-here
  co-hered
  co-her-ing
co-her-ent
  co-her-ence
  co-her-en-cy
  co-her-ent-ly
co-he-sion
co-he-sive
  co-hes-sive-ly
  co-hes-sive-ness
co-hort
coif-feur
coif-fure
  coif-fured

coif-fur-ing
coin-age
co-in-cide
  co-in-cid-ed
  co-in-cid-ing
  co-in-ci-dence
co-in-ci-den-tal
  co-in-ci-den-tal-ly
co-i-tion
co-i-tus
  co-i-tal
coke
  coked
  cok-ing
co-la
col-an-der
cold-blood-ed
cole-slaw
col-ic
  col-icky
col-i-se-um
co-li-tis
col-lab-o-rate
  col-lab-o-rat-ed
  col-lab-o-rat-ing
  col-lab-o-ra-tion
  col-lab-o-ra-tor
col-lage
col-lapse
  col-lapsed
  col-laps-ing
  col-lap-si-ble
col-lar
col-lar-bone
col-late
  col-lat-ed
  col-lat-ing
  col-la-tion
  col-la-tor
col-lat-er-al
col-league
col-lect
  col-lect-i-ble
  col-lec-tor
  col-lect-ed
  col-lec-tion
col-lec-tive
  col-lec-tive-ly
  col-lect-tiv-i-ty
  col-lec-tiv-ism
  col-lec-tiv-iz-e
  col-lec-tiv-iz-ing
  col-lec-tiv-i-za-tion
col-lege
  col-le-gi-al
col-le-gian

col-le-giate
col-lide
  col-lid-ed
  col-lid-ing
  col-li-sion
col-li-mate
  col-li-mat-ed
  col-li-mat-ing
  col-li-ma-tion
col-lo-cate
  col-lo-cat-ed
  col-lo-cat-ing
  col-lo-ca-tion
col-loid
col-lo-qui-al
  col-lo-qui-al-ly
  col-lo-qui-al-ism
col-lo-quy
  col-lo-quies
col-lu-sion
  col-lu-sive
co-logne
co-lon
colo-nel
co-lo-ni-al
  co-lo-ni-al-ism
  co-lo-ni-al-ist
col-o-nist
col-o-nade
col-o-ny
  col-o-nies
  col-o-nize
  col-o-nized
  col-o-niz-ing
  col-o-niz-er
  col-o-ni-za-tion
col-or
  col-or-er
  col-or-less
col-or-a-tion
col-or-blind
  col-or-blind-ness
col-or-cast
col-ored
col-or-fast
col-or-ful
col-or-ing
co-los-sal
co-los-sus
  co-los-si
colt-ish
col-um-bine
col-umn
  co-lum-nar
  co-lumned
  col-um-nist

co-ma
  co-mas
  co-ma-tose
com-bat
  com-bat-ed
  com-bat-ing
  com-bat-ant
  com-ba-tive
comb-er
com-bi-na-tion
  com-bi-na-tion-al
  com-bi-na-tive
com-bine
  com-bined
  com-bin-ing
  com-bin-a-ble
  com-bin-er
com-bo
  com-bos
com-bust-ti-ble
  com-bus-ti-bil-i-ty
con-bus-tion
  com-bus-tive
come
  com-ing
come-back
co-me-di-an
  co-me-di-enne
come-down
com-e-dy
  com-e-dies
come-ly
  come-li-ness
come-on
com-er
com-et
come-up-pance
com-fort
  com-fort-a-ble
  com-fort-a-bly
  com-fort-er
com-fy
  com-fi-er
  com-fi-est
com-ic
  com-i-cal
com-ing
com-i-ty
  com-i-ties
com-ma
  com-mas
com-mand
com-man-dant
com-man-deer
com-mand-er
  com-mand-er-ship

com-mand-ment
com-man-do
  com-man-dos
com-mem-o-rate
  com-mem-o-rat-ed
  com-mem-o-rat-ing
  com-mem-o-ra-ble
  com-mem-o-ra-tion
  com-mem-o-ra-tive
  com-mem-o-ra-to-ry
com-mence
  com-menced
  com-ménc-ing
com-mence-ment
com-mend
  com-mend-a-ble
  com-mend-a-bly
com-men-da-tion
  com-mend-a-to-ry
com-men-su-rate
  com-men-su-rate-ly
  com-men-su-ra-tion
com-ment
com-men-tary
  com-men-tar-ies
  com-men-ta-tor
com-merce
com-mer-cial
  com-mer-cial-ism
  com-mer-cial-ize
  com-mer-cial-ized
  com-mer-cial-iz-ing
com-mie
com-mis-er-ate
  com-mis-er-at-ed
  com-mis-er-at-ing
  com-mis-er-a-tion
  com-mis-er-a-tive
com-mis-sar
com-mis-sar-y
  com-mis-sar-ies
com-mis-sion
  com-mis-sioned
com-mis-sion-er
com-mit
  com-mit-ted
  com-mit-ting
  com-mit-ment
com-mit-tee
  com-mit-tee-man
  com-mit-tee-wo-man
com-mode
com-mo-di-ous
com-mod-i-ty
  com-mod-i-ties
com-mo-dore

com-mon
com-mon-al-ty
  com-mon-al-ties
com-mon-place
com-mons
com-mon-wealth
com-mo-tion
com-mu-nal
  com-mu-nal-i-ty
com-mune
  com-muned
  com-mun-ing
com-mu-ni-cant
com-mu-ni-cate
  com-mu-ni-cat-ed
  com-mu-ni-cat-ing
  com-mu-ni-ca-ble
  com-mu-ni-ca-tive
  com-mu-ni-ca-tion
com-mun-ion
  com-mun-ism
  com-mun-ist
com-mu-ni-ty
  com-mu-ni-ties
com-mu-nize
  com-mu-nized
  com-mu-niz-ing
com-mu-ta-tion
com-mu-ta-tor
com-mute
  com-mut-ed
  com-mut-ing
  com-mut-a-ble
com-mut-er
com-pact
com-pan-ion
  com-pan-ion-a-ble
  com-pan-ion-ship
com-pa-ny
  com-pa-nies
com-par-a-ble
  com-par-a-bil-ity
com-par-a-tive
com-pare
  com-pared
  com-par-ing
com-par-i-son
com-part-ment
  com-part-men-tal
  com-part-ment-ed
  com-part-men-tal-ize
com-pass
com-pas-sion
  com-pas-sion-ate
com-pat-ible
  com-pat-i-bly

com-pat-i-bil-i-ty
com-pa-tri-ot
com-peer
com-pel
  com-pelled
  com-pel-ling
com-pen-di-ous
  com-pen-di-um
com-pen-sate
  com-pen-sat-ed
  com-pen-sat-ing
  com-pen-sa-tive
  com-pen-sa-tor
  com-pen-sa-to-ry
com-pen-sa-tion
com-pete
  com-pet-ed
  com-pet-ing
com-pet-i-tor
com-pe-tence
  com-pe-ten-cy
com-pe-tent
com-pe-ti-tion
com-pet-i-tive
com-pile
  com-piled
  com-pil-ing
  com-pi-la-tion
com-pla-cence
  com-pla-cen-cy
  com-pla-cent
com-plain
com-plain-ant
com-plaint
com-plai-sance
  com-plai-sant
com-plect-ed
com-ple-ment
  com-ple-men-tal
  com-ple-men-ta-ry
com-plete
  com-plet-ed
  com-plet-ing
  com-plet-a-ble
com-ple-tion
com-plex
com-plex-ion
  com-plex-ioned
com-plex-i-ty
  com-plex-i-ties
com-pli-ance
  com-pli-an-cy
  com-pli-ant
com-pli-cate
  com-pli-cat-ed
  com-pli-cat-ing

com-pli-ca-tion
com-plic-i-ty
  com-plic-i-ties
com-pli-ment
  com-pli-men-ta-ri-ly
com-ply
  com-plied
  com-ply-ing
com-po-nent
com-port
com-port-ment
com-pose
  com-posed
  com-pos-ing
com-pos-er
com-pos-ite
com-po-si-tion
com-post
com-po-sure
com-pote
com-pound
com-pre-hend
  com-pre-hend-i-ble
com-pre-hen-si-ble
  com-pre-hen-si-bly
com-pre-hen-sion
com-pre-hen-sive
com-press
  com-presed
  com-press-i-ble
  com-press-i-bil-ity
com-pres-sion
com-pres-sor
com-prise
  com-prised
  com-pris-ing
com-pro-mise
  com-pro-mised
  com-pro-mis-ing
comp-trol-ler
com-pul-sion
com-pul-sive
com-pul-so-ry
com-punc-tion
com-pute
  com-put-ed
  com-put-ing
  com-pu-ta-tion
com-pu-ter
com-put-er-ize
  com-put-er-ized
  com-put-er-iz-ing
  com-put-er-i-za-tion
com-rade
  com-rade-ship
com-sat

con
  conned
  con-ning
con-cave
con-ceal
  con-ceal-a-ble
  con-ceal-ment
con-cede
  con-ced-ed
  con-ced-ing
con-ceit
  con-ceit-ed
con-ceive
  con-ceived
  con-ceiv-ing
  con-ceiv-a-ble
  con-ceiv-a-bly
con-cen-trate
  con-cen-tra-ted
  con-cen-trat-ing
  con-cen-tra-tive
  con-cen-tra-tion
con-cen-tric
  con-cen-tri-cal
  con-cen-tric-i-ty
con-cept
  con-cep-tu-al
con-cep-tion
  con-cep-tive
con-cep-tu-al-ize
  con-cep-tu-al-ized
  con-cep-tu-al-iz-ing
con-cern
  con-cerned
  con-cern-ing
con-cert
  con-cert-ed
  con-cer-ti-na
con-cert-mas-ter
  con-cer-to
con-ces-sion
  con-ces-sion-aire
conch
  conchs
con-cil-i-ate
  con-cil-i-at-ed
  con-cil-i-at-ing
  con-cil-i-a-tion
  con-cil-i-a-to-ry
con-cise
  con-cise-ness
  con-cise-ly
con-clave
con-clude
  con-clud-ed
  con-clud-ing

con-clu-sion
con-clu-sive
con-coct
  con-coc-tion
con-com-i-tant
  con-com-i-tance
con-cord
  con-cord-ance
  con-cord-ant
con-course
con-crete
  con-cret-ed
  con-cret-ing
con-cre-tion
  con-cre-tive
con-cu-bine
con-cur
  con-curred
  con-cur-ring
  con-cur-rence
  con-cur-rent
con-cus-sion
  con-cus-sive
con-demn
  con-dem-na-ble
  con-dem-na-tion
  con-dem-na-to-ry
con-dense
  con-densed
  con-dens-ing
  con-den-sa-ble
  con-den-sa-tion
  con-dens-er
con-de-scend
  con-de-scend-ing
  con-de-scen-sion
con-di-ment
con-di-tion
  con-di-tion-al
  con-di-tion-er
  con-di-tion-ed
con-dole
  con-doled
  con-dol-ing
  con-do-la-to-ry
  con-do-ler
con-do-lence
con-dom
con-do-min-i-um
con-done
  con-doned
  con-don-ing
  con-do-na-tion
con-dor
con-duce
  con-duced

44

con-duc-ing
con-duct
con-duct-i-bil-i-ty
con-duct-i-ble
con-duct-ance
con-duc-tion
con-fer-ence
con-fer-en-tial
con-fess
con-fess-ed-ly
con-fes-sion
con-fes-sion-al
con-fes-sor
con-fet-ti
con-fi-dant
con-fi-dante
con-fide
con-fid-ed
con-fid-ing
con-fi-dence
con-fi-dent
con-fi-den-tial
con-fig-u-ra-tion
con-fig-u-ra-tion-al
con-fine
con-fined
con-fin-ing
con-fine-ment
con-firm
con-firm-a-ble
con-fir-ma-tion
con-fir-ma-tive
con-fir-ma-to-ry
con-fir-med
con-firm-ed-ly
con-firm-ed-ness
con-fis-cate
con-fis-cat-ed
con-fis-cat-ing
con-fis-ca-tion
con-fis-ca-tor
con-fis-ca-to-ry
con-fla-gra-tion
con-flict
con-flict-ing
con-flic-tive
con-flic-tion
con-flu-ence
con-flu-ent
con-flux
con-form
con-form-ist
con-form-ism
con-form-a-ble
con-form-a-bly
con-form-ance

con-for-ma-tion
con-form-i-ty
con-form-i-ties
con-found
con-found-ed
con-found-ed-ly
con-front
con-fron-ta-tion
con-fuse
confused
con-fus-ing
con-fus-ed-ly
con-fus-ed-ness
con-fu-sion
con-fute
con-futed
con-fut-ing
con-fu-ta-tion
con-ga
con-gas
con-geal
con-geal-ment
con-gen-ial
con-ge-ni-al-i-ty
con-gen-ial-ly
con-gen-i-tal
con-ger
con-ge-ries
con-gest
con-ges-tion
con-ges-tive
con-glom-er-ate
con-glom-er-at-ing
con-glom-er-a-tion
con-grat-u-late
con-grat-u-lat-ed
con-grat-u-lat-ing
con-grat-u-la-tor
con-grat-u-la-to-ry
con-grat-u-la-tion
con-gre-gate
con-gre-gat-ed
con-gre-gat-ing
con-gre-ga-tion
con-gre-ga-tion-al
con-gress
con-gres-sion-al
con-gress-man
con-gress-men
con-gress-wom-an
con-gress-wom-en
con-gru-ent
con-gru-ent-ly
con-gru-ence
con-gru-en-cy
con-gru-en-cies

con-gru-i-ty
con-gru-i-ties
con-gru-ous
con-gru-ous-ly
con-ic
con-i-cal
co-ni-fer
con-jec-ture
con-jec-tured
con-jec-tur-ing
con-jec-tur-al
con-join
con-joint
con-joint-ly
con-ju-gal
con-ju-gal-ly
con-ju-gate
con-ju-gat-ed
con-ju-gat-ing
con-ju-ga-tion
con-ju-ga-tive
con-junc-tion
con-junc-tive
con-jur-a-tion
con-jure
con-jured
con-jur-ing
con-jur-er
con-nect
con-nec-tor
con-nec-tion
con-nec-tive
con-nip-tion
con-nive
con-nived
con-niv-ing
con-niv-ance
con-nois-seur
con-note
con-not-ed
con-not-ing
con-no-ta-tion
con-no-ta-tive
con-nu-bi-al
con-ni-bi-al-ly
con-quer
con-quer-a-ble
con-quer-or
con-quest
con-quis-ta-dor
con-quis-ta-dors
con-quis-ta-dor-es
con-san-quin-e-ous
con-san-quin-i-ty
con-science
con-sci-en-tious

con-sci-en-tious-ly
con-scious
con-scious-ly
con-scious-ness
con-script
con-scrip-tion
con-se-crate
con-se-crat-ed
con-se-crat-ing
con-se-cra-tive
con-se-cra-tion
con-sec-u-tive
con-sec-u-tive-ly
con-sen-sus
con-sent
con-sent-er
con-se-quence
con-se-quent
con-se-quent-ly
con-se-quen-tial
con-se-quen-ti-al-i-ty
con-se-quen-tial-ly
con-ser-va-tion
con-ser-va-tion-al
con-ser-va-tion-ist
con-serv-a-tive
con-serv-a-tism
con-ser-va-tive-ly
con-serv-a-to-ry
con-serv-a-to-ries
con-serve
con-served
con-serv-ing
con-serv-a-ble
con-serv-er
con-sid-er
con-sid-er-a-ble
con-sid-er-a-bly
con-sid-er-ate
con-sid-er-a-tion
con-sid-er-ing
con-sign
con-sign-er
con-sign-or
con-sign-ment
con-sign-ee
con-sist
con-sist-en-cy
con-sist-en-cies
con-sist-ence
con-sist-ent
con-sist-ent-ly
con-sis-to-ry
con-sis-to-ries
con-so-la-tion
con-sol-a-to-ry

con-sole
con-soled
con-sol-ing
con-sol-a-ble
con-sol-i-date
con-sol-i-dat-ed
con-sol-i-dat-ing
con-sol-i-da-tion
con-so-nant
con-so-nance
con-so-nant-ly
con-so-nan-tal
con-sort
con-sor-ti-um
con-sor-tia
con-spic-u-ous
con-spic-u-ous-ly
con-spic-u-ous-ness
con-spire
con-spired
con-spir-ing
con-spir-a-cy
con-spir-a-cies
con-spir-a-tor
con-spir-a-to-ri-al
con-spir-er
con-spir-ing-ly
con-sta-ble
con-sta-ble-ship
con-stab-u-lar-y
con-stab-u-lar-ies
con-stant
con-stan-cy
con-stant-ly
con-stel-la-tion
con-ster-na-tion
con-sti-pate
con-sti-pa-tion
con-stit-u-en-cy
con-stit-u-en-cies
con-stit-u-ent
con-sti-tute
con-sti-tu-tion
con-sti-tu-tion-al
con-sti-tu-tion-al-i-ty
con-sti-tu-tion-al-ly
con-strain
con-strain-a-ble
con-strained
con-straint
con-strict
con-stric-tive
con-stric-tion
con-stric-tor
con-struct
con-struc-tor

con-struc-tion
con-struc-tion-al
con-struc-tive
con-struc-tive-ly
con-struc-tive-ness
con-strue
con-strued
con-stru-ing
con-stru-a-ble
con-stru-er
con-sul
con-su-lar
con-sul-ship
con-su-late
con-sult
con-sul-ta-tion
con-sult-ant
con-sume
con-sumed
con-sum-ing
con-sum-a-ble
con-sum-er
con-sum-mate
con-sum-mat-ed
con-sum-mat-ing
con-sum-mate-ly
con-sum-ma-tion
con-sump-tion
com-sump-tive
con-tact
con-ta-gion
con-ta-gious
con-ta-gious-ness
con-tain
con-tain-a-ble
con-tain-er
con-tain-ment
con-tam-i-nate
con-tam-i-nat-ed
con-tam-i-nat-ing
con-tam-i-nant
con-tam-i-na-tion
con-tam-i-na-tive
con-tam-i-na-tor
con-tem-plate
con-tem-plat-ed
con-tem-plat-ing
con-tem-pla-tion
con-tem-pla-tive
con-tem-po-ra-ne-ous
con-tem-po-rar-y
con-tem-po-rar-ies
con-tempt
con-tempt-i-ble
con-tempt-i-bly
con-temp-tu-ous

con-temp-tu-ous-ly
con-tend
con-tend-er
con-tent
con-tent-ment
con-tent-ed
con-tent-ed-ly
con-tent-ed-ness
con-ten-tion
con-ten-tious
con-ten-tious-ly
con-ten-tious-ness
con-ter-mi-ous
con-test
con-test-a-ble
con-test-er
con-test-ant
con-text
con-tig-u-ous
con-ti-gu-i-ty
con-ti-gu-i-ties
con-tig-u-ous-ly
con-tig-u-ous-ness
con-ti-nence
con-ti-nen-cy
con-ti-nent
con-ti-nent-ly
con-ti-nen-tal
con-tin-gent
con-tin-gen-cies
con-tin-gent-ly
con-tin-u-al
con-tin-u-al-ly
con-tin-u-ance
con-tin-ue
con-tin-ued
con-tin-u-ing
con-tin-u-a-tion
con-tin-u-er
con-ti-nu-i-ty
con-ti-nu-i-ties
con-tin-u-ous
con-tin-u-ous-ly
con-tin-u-um
con-tin-ua
con-tort
con-tor-tion
con-tor-tive
con-tor-tion-ist
con-tour
con-tra-band
can-tra-cep-tive
con-tra-cep-tion
con-tract
con-tract-ed
con-tract-i-ble

con-trac-tu-al
con-trac-tion
con-trac-tive
con-trac-tile
con-trac-tor
con-tra-dict
con-tra-dict-a-ble
con-tra-dic-tion
con-tra-dic-to-ry
con-tra-dis-tinc-tion
con-trail
con-tral-to
con-tral-tos
con-tral-ti
con-trap-tion
con-tra-pun-tal
con-tra-ri-wise
con-tra-ry
con-tra-ries
con-tra-ri-ly
con-tra-ri-ness
con-trast
con-trast-a-ble
con-trast-ing-ly
con-tra-vene
con-tra-vened
con-tra-ven-ing
con-tra-ven-er
con-tra-ven-tion
con-trib-ute
con-trib-ut-ed
con-trib-ut-ing
con-trib-ut-a-ble
con-trib-u-tor
con-trib-u-tory
con-tri-bu-tion
con-trite
con-trite-ly
con-trite-ness
con-tri-tion
con-trive
con-triv-ed
con-triv-ing
con-triv-ance
con-trol
con-trolled
con-trol-ling
con-trol-la-ble
con-trol-ler
con-trol-ler-ship
con-tro-ver-sy
con-tro-ver-sies
con-tro-ver-sal
con-tro-ver-sial-ly
con-tro-vert
con-tu-me-ly

con-tu-me-lies
con-tuse
con-tused
con-tus-ing
con-tu-sion
co-nun-drum
cov-va-lesce
con-va-lesced
con-va-les-cing
con-va-les-cence
con-va-les-cent
con-vec-tion
con-vene
con-vened
con-ven-ing
con-ven-er
con-ven-ience
con-ven-ient
con-ven-ient-ly
con-vent
con-ven-tion
con-ven-tion-al
con-ven-tion-al-ism
con-ven-tion-al-ist
con-ven-tion-al-i-ty
con-ven-tion-al-i-ties
con-ven-tion-al-ize
con-ven-tion-al-ized
con-ven-tion-al-iz-ing
con-verge
con-verged
con-verg-ing
con-ver-gence
con-ver-gen-cy
con-ver-gent
con-ver-sant
con-ver-sa-tion
con-ver-sa-tion-al
con-ver-sa-tion-al-ist
con-verse
con-versed
con-vers-ing
con-verse-ly
con-ver-sion
con-vert
con-vert-er
con-vert-i-ble
con-vert-i-bil-i-ty
con-vert-i-bly
con-vex
con-vex-ly
con-vex-i-ty
con-vey
con-vey-a-ble
con-vey-ance
con-vey-er

con-vey-or
con-vict
con-vic-tion
  con-vic-tion-al
con-vince
  con-vinced
  con-vinc-ing
  con-vinc-er
  con-vinc-i-ble
con-viv-i-al
  con-viv-i-al-i-ty
  con-viv-i-al-ly
con-vo-ca-tion
  con-vo-ca-tion-al
con-voke
  con-voked
  con-vok-ing
  con-vok-er
con-vo-lute
  con-vo-lut-ed
  con-vo-lut-ing
  con-vo-lute-ly
  con-vo-lu-tion
con-voy
con-vulse
  con-vulsed
  con-vuls-ing
con-vul-sion
  con-vul-sive
  con-vul-sive-ly
co-ny
coo
  cooed
  coo-ing
  coo-ing-ly
cook-book
cook-er-y
  cook-e-ries
cook-out
cool
  cool-ish
  cool-ly
  cool-ness
cool-ant
cool-er
coo-lie
  coo-lies
coon-skin
coop-er
coop-er-age
co-op-er-ate
  co-op-er-at-ed
  co-op-er-at-ing
co-op-er-a-tion
co-op-er-a-tive
  co-op-er-a-tive-ly

co-opt
co-op-ta-tion
co-or-di-nate
  co-or-di-nat-ed
  co-or-di-nat-ing
  co-or-di-nate-ly
  co-or-di-na-tor
  co-or-di-na-tion
coo-tie
cop
  copped
  cop-ping
cope-stone
co-pi-lot
co-pi-ous
  co-pi-ous-ly
  co-pi-ous-ness
cop-out
cop-per
  cop-per-y
cop-per-head
cop-per-plate
cop-pice
cop-ra
copse
cop-u-la
  cop-u-las
  cop-u-lae
  cop-u-lar
cop-u-late
  cop-u-lat-ed
  cop-u-lat-ing
  cop-u-la-tion
cop-u-la-tive
  cop-u-la-tive-ly
copy
  cop-ies
  cop-ied
  cop-y-ing
cop-y-book
cop-y-cat
cop-y-ist
cop-y-right
co-quet
  co-quet-ted
  co-quet-ting
co-quet-ry
  co-quet-ries
co-quette
  co-quet-tish
  co-quet-tish-ly
cor-a-cle
cor-al
cor-bel
cord-age
cor-date

cor-date-ly
cor-dial
  cor-dial-i-ty
  cor-dial-ness
  cor-dial-ly
cor-dil-le-ra
cord-ite
cor-don
cor-do-van
cor-du-roy
cord-wood
core
  cored
  cor-ing
co-re-la-tion
co-re-spond-ent
co-ri-an-der
cor-ker
cork-screw
corn-cob
cor-nea
  cor-ne-al
cor-ner
cor-ner-stone
cor-net
  cor-net-ist
corn-flow-er
cor-nice
corn-starch
cor-nu-co-pi-a
corn-y
  corn-i-er
  conr-i-est
co-rol-la
cor-ol-lar-y
  cor-ol-lar-ies
co-ro-na
  co-ro-nas
  co-ro-nae
cor-o-nar-y
cor-o-na-tion
cor-o-ner
  cor-o-ner-ship
cor-o-net
  cor-o-net-ed
cor-po-ral
cor-po-rate
  cor-po-rate-ly
  cor-po-ra-tive
cor-po-ra-tion
cor-po-rat-ism
cor-po-re-al
  cor-po-re-al-i-ty
  cor-po-re-al-ness
corps
corpse

corps-man
 corps-men
cor-pu-lent
 cor-pu-lence
 cor-pu-len-cy
cor-pus
cor-pus-cle
 cor-pus-cu-lar
cor-ral
 cor-ralled
 cor-ral-ling
cor-rect
 cor-rect-a-ble
 cor-rect-i-ble
 cor-rect-ness
 cor-rec-tor
cor-rec-tion
 cor-rec-tion-al
cor-rec-tive
cor-re-late
 cor-re-lat-ed
 cor-re-lat-ing
cor-re-la-tion
cor-rel-a-tive
cor-re-spond
 cor-re-spond-ing
 cor-re-spond-ing-ly
cor-re-spond-ence
cor-re-spond-ent
cor-ri-dor
cor-ri-gi-ble
 cor-ri-gi-bil-i-ty
 cor-ri-gi-bly
cor-rob-o-rate
 cor-rob-o-rat-ed
 cor-rob-o-rat-ing
 cor-rob-o-ra-tion
 cor-rob-o-ra-tive
 cor-rob-o-ra-to-ry
cor-rode
 cor-rod-ed
 cor-rod-ing
 cor-rod-i-ble
cor-ro-sion
cor-ro-sive
cor-ru-gate
 cor-ru-gat-ed
 cor-ru-gat-ing
 cor-ru-ga-tion
cor-rupt
 cor-rupt-er
 cor-rup-ti-ble
 cor-rup-ti-bil-i-ty
 cor-rupt-ly
 cor-rupt-ness
 cor-rup-tion

cor-sage
cor-sair
cor-set
 cor-set-ed
cor-tex
 cor-ti-ces
 cor-ti-cal
 cor-ti-sone
co-run-dum
co-sig-na-to-ry
cos-met-ic
cos-mic
 cos-mi-cal-ly
cos-mog-o-ny
 cos-mog-o-nies
 cos-mo-gon-ic
 cos-mog-o-nist
cos-mog-o-ny
 cos-mog-o-nist
cos-mog-ra-phy
 cos-mog-ra-phies
 cos-mog-ra-pher
 cos-mo-graph-ic
cos-mol-o-gy
 cos-mol-o-gies
 cos-mo-log-ic
 cos-mol-o-gist
cos-mo-naut
cos-mo-pol-i-tan
 cos-mo-pol-i-tan-ism
cos-mop-o-lite
cos-mos
cost-ly
 cost-li-er
 cost-li-est
 cost-li-ness
cost--plus
cos-tume
 cos-tumed
 cos-tum-ing
cos-tum-er
co-sy
 co-si-er
 cos-i-est
co-te-rie
co-ter-mi-nous
co-til-lion
cot-tage
cot-ter
cot-ton
 cot-ton-y
cot-ton-mouth
cot-ton-seed
cot-ton-tail
cot-ton-wood
couch

coun-cil
 coun-cil-or
 coun-cil-man
 coun-cil-lor-ship
count
 count-a-ble
count-down
coun-te-nance
 coun-te-nanced
 coun-te-nanc-ing
 coun-te-nanc-er
count-er
coun-ter-act
 coun-ter-ac-tion
 coun-ter-ac-tive
coun-ter-at-tack
coun-ter-charge
 coun-ter-charged
 coun-ter-char-ging
coun-ter-claim
 coun-ter-claim-ant
coun-ter-clock-wise
coun-ter-cul-ture
coun-ter-es-pi-o-nage
coun-ter-feit
 coun-ter-feit-er
coun-ter-in-tel-li-gence
coun-ter-mand
coun-ter-meas-ure
coun-ter-of-fen-sive
coun-ter-pane
coun-ter-part
coun-ter-point
coun-ter-poise
 coun-ter-poised
 coun-ter-pois-ing
coun-ter-rev-o-lu-tion
coun-ter-sign
 coun-ter-sig-na-ture
coun-ter-sink
 coun-ter-sank
 coun-ter-sunk
coun-ter-spy
 coun-ter-spies
coun-ter-weight
coun-tees
 count-less
coun-tri-fied
coun-try
 coun-tries
coun-try-man
 coun-try-men
 coun-try-wom-an
 coun-try-wom-en
coun-try-side
coun-ty

coun-ties
coup
  coups
coup-le
  coup-led
  coup-ling
coup-ler
cou-pon
cour-age
  cou-ra-geous
cour-i-er
course
  coursed
  cours-ing
cours-er
cour-te-ous
  cour-te-ous-ly
cour-te-sy
  cour-te-sies
court-house
cour-ti-er
court-ly
  court-li-er
  court-li-est
  court-li-ness
court-mar-tial
  courts-mar-tial
  court-mar-tialed
  court-mar-tial-ling
court-room
court-ship
court-yard
cous-in
  cous-in-hood
  cous-in-ly
cou-tu-rier
cov-e-nant
  cov-e-nan-ter
  cov-e-nan-tor
cov-er
  cov-ered
  cov-er-ing
  cov-er-less
cov-er-age
cov-er-all
cov-er-let
cov-ert
  cov-ert-ly
  cov-ert-ness
cov-er-up
cov-et
  cov-et-a-ble
  cov-et-er
cov-et-ous
  cov-et-ous-ly
cov-ey

cow-ard
  cow-ard-ly
  cow-ard-li-ness
cow-ard-ice
cow-boy
cow-er
  cow-er-ing-ly
cow-hide
cowl
  cowled
cow-lick
cowl-ing
cow-man
  cow-men
co-work-er
cow-poke
cow-pox
cow-ry
  cow-rie
  cow-ries
cox-swain
coy
  coy-ly
  coy-ness
coy-o-te
coz-en
  coz-en-age
  coz-en-er
co-zy
  co-zi-er
  co-zi-est
  co-zi-ly
  co-zi-ness
crab
  crabbed
  crab-bing
  crab-by
  crab-bed-ly
  crab-bed-ness
crack-down
crack-er
crack-ing
crack-le
  crack-led
  crack-ling
crack-up
cra-dle
  cra-dled
  cra-dling
crafts-man
  crafts-man-ship
crafty
  craft-i-er
  craft-i-est
  craft-i-ly
  craft-i-ness

crag
  crag-ged
  crag-gy
  crag-gi-ness
cram
  crammed
  cram-ming
  cram-mer
cran-ber-ry
  cran-ber-ries
crane
  craned
  cran-ing
cra-ni-um
  cra-ni-ums
  cra-nia
  cra-ni-al
  cra-ni-ate
  cra-ni-al-ly
crank-case
crank-shaft
crank-y
  crank-i-er
  crank-i-est
  crank-i-ly
  crank-i-ness
cran-ny
  cran-nies
  cran-nied
crash-land
crass
  crass-ly
  crass-ness
crate
  crat-ed
  crat-ing
cra-ter
  cra-ter-al
  cra-tered
cra-vat
crave
  craved
  crav-ing
  crav-er
  crav-ing-ly
craw-fish
crawl
  crawl-y
  crawl-ing-ly
crawl-er
cray-fish
cray-on
craze
  craz-ing
cra-zy
  cra-zi-er

50

cra-zi-est
cra-zi-ly
cra-zi-ness
creak
creak-i-ly
creak-i-ness
creaky
creak-i-er
creak-i-est
cream
cream-i-ly
cream-i-ness
cream-y
cream-i-er
cream-i-est
cream-er
cream-er-y
cream-er-ies
crease
creased
creas-ing
creas-y
creas-i-er
creas-i-est
cre-ate
cre-at-ed
cre-at-ing
cre-a-tion
cre-a-tion-al
cre-a-tive
cre-a-tive-i-ty
cre-a-tor
crea-ture
cre-dence
cre-den-tial
cre-den-za
cred-i-ble
cred-i-bil-i-ty
cred-i-bly
cred-it
cred-it-a-ble
cred-it-a-bil-i-ty
cred-it-a-bly
cred-i-tor
cre-do
cre-dos
cred-u-lous
creek
creel
creep
crept
creep-ing
creepy
creep-i-er
creep-i-est
creep-i-ness

creep-er
cre-mate
cre-mat-ed
cre-mat-ing
cre-ma-tion
cre-ma-tor
cre-ma-to-ry
cre-ma-to-ri-um
cre-o-sote
crepe
creped
crep-ing
cre-pus-cu-lar
cres-cen-do
cres-cent
crest
crest-ed
crest-less
crest-fall-en
cre-ta-ceous
cre-tin-ism
cre-tonne
cre-vasse
crev-ice
crew-el
crib
cribbed
crib-bing
crib-ber
crib-bage
crick-et
cri-er
crim-i-nal
crim-i-nal-i-ty
crim-i-nal-ly
crim-i-nol-o-gy
crim-i-nol-o-gist
crimpy
crimp-i-er
crimp-i-est
crim-son
cringe
cringed
cring-ing
crin-kle
crin-kled
crin-kling
crin-kly
crin-kli-er
crin-kli-est
crip-ple
crip-pled
crip-pling
cri-sis
cri-ses
crisp

crisp-er
crisp-ness
crispy
crisp-i-er
crisp-i-est
criss-cross
cri-te-ri-on
cri-te-ria
crit-ic
crit-i-cal
crit-i-cal-ly
crit-i-cal-ness
crit-i-cism
crit-i-cize
crit-i-cized
crit-i-ciz-ing
crit-i-ciz-a-ble
cri-tique
crit-er
croak-y
croak-i-er
croak-i-est
croak-er
cro-chet
cro-cheted
cro-chet-ing
cro-chet-er
crock-ery
croc-o-dile
cro-cus
cro-cus-es
crois-sant
cro-ny
cro-nies
crook-ed
croon-er
crop
cropped
crop-ping
crop-per
cro-quette
cross-bar
cross-bones
cross-bow
cross-bred
cross-breed
cross-breed-ing
cross-coun-try
cross-cut
cross-ex-am-ine
cross-ex-am-ined
cross-ex-am-in-ing
cross-fer-ti-li-za-tion
cross-ing
cross-pol-li-na-tion
cross-pol-li-nate

cross-pur-pose
cross-ref-er-ence
cross-stitch
cross-ways
crotch-ety
  crotch-et-i-ness
crouch
croup
  croupy
crou-pi-er
crou-ton
crow-bar
crow's--foot
  crow's--feet
crow's--nest
cru-cial
  cru-ci-al-i-ty
  cru-cial-ly
cru-ci-ble
cru-ci-fix
cru-ci-fix-ion
cru-ci-form
cru-ci-fy
  cru-ci-fied
  cru-ci-fy-ing
crude
  crud-er
  crud-est
  crude-ly
  crude-ness
cru-di-ty
cru-di-ties
cru-el
  cru-el-ly
  cru-el-ness
  cru-el-ty
cru-et
cruise
  cruised
  cruis-ing
cruis-er
crul-ler
crum-ble
  crum-bled
  crum-bling
  crum-bly
crum-my
  crum-mi-er
  crum-mi-est
crum-pet
crum-ple
  crum-pled
  crum-pling
  crum-pler
  crum-ply
  crum-pli-er

crum-pli-est
crunchy
crunch-i-er
crunch-i-est
cru-sade
cru-sad-er
crush-er
crush-ing
crush-ing-ly
crus-ta-cean
crust-y
crust-i-er
crust-i-est
crust-i-ly
crust-i-ness
crux
  crux-es
cru-ces
cry
  cried
  cry-ing
cry-ba-by
cry-o-gen-ics
cry-o-sur-gery
crypt
  crypt-al
crypt-a-nal-y-sis
crypt-ic
  cryp-ti-cal
  cryp-ti-cal-ly
cryp-to-gram
cryp-to-graph
  cryp-tog-ra-phy
  cryp-to-graph-ic
  cryp-tog-ra-pher
crys-tal
crys-tal-line
crys-tal-lize
  crys-tal-lized
  crys-tal-liz-ing
  crys-tal-liz-er
  crys-tal-liz-a-ble
  crys-tal-li-za-tion
cub-by
  cub-bies
cu-by-hole
cube
  cubed
  cub-ing
cu-bic
cu-bi-cle
cub-ism
cu-bit
cuck-old
  cuck-old-ry
cuck-oo

cuck-oos
cuck-ooed
cuck-oo-ing
cu-cum-ber
cud-dle
  cud-dled
  cud-dling
  cud-dle-some
  cud-dly
  cud-dli-er
  cud-dli-est
cudg-el
  cudg-eled
  cudg-el-ing
cue
  cued
  cu-ing
cui-sine
cul-de-sac
  culs-de-sac
cu-li-nary
cul-mi-nant
cul-mi-nate
  cul-mi-nat-ed
  cul-mi-nat-ing
  cul-mi-na-tion
cu-lottes
cul-pa-ble
  cul-pa-bil-i-ty
  cul-pa-bly
cul-prit
cult
  cul-tic
cul-ti-vate
  cul-ti-vat-ed
  cul-ti-vat-ing
  cul-ti-va-tion
  cul-ti-va-ble
  cul-ti-vat-a-ble
  cul-ti-va-tor
cul-tur-al
cul-ture
  cul-tured
  cul-tur-ing
cul-vert
cum-ber
  cum-ber-some
cum-brance
cum lau-de
cum-mer-bound
cum-mu-late
  cum-mu-lat-ed
  cum-mu-lat-ing
  cum-mu-la-tion
  cum-mu-la-tive
cu-mu-lo-nim-bus

cu-mu-lo-nim-bus-es
cu-mu-lus
cu-mu-lous
cu-ne-i-form
cum-ni-lin-gus
cun-ning
 cun-ning-ly
 cun-ning-ness
cup
 cupped
 cup-ping
cup-board
cup-cake
cup-ful
 cup-fuls
cu-pid-i-ty
cu-po-la
cur-a-ble
 cur-a-bil-i-ty
 cur-a-bly
cu-rate
cur-a-tive
cu-ra-tor
 cu-ra-to-ri-al
 cu-ra-tor-ship
curb-ing
curb-stone
cur-dle
 cur-dled
 cur-dling
cure
 cured
 cur-ing
 cur-er
cure-all
cur-few
cu-ria
 cu-ri-ae
cu-ri-al
cu-rie
cu-ri-o
 cu-ri-os
cu-ri-os-i-ty
 cu-ri-os-i-ties
cu-ri-ous
cu-ri-um
curl
 curl-er
curl-i-cue
curl-ing
curly
 curl-i-er
 curl-i-est
 curl-i-ness
cur-rant
cur-ren-cy

cur-ren-cies
cur-rent
cur-ric-u-lum
 cur-ric-u-lums
 cur-ric-u-la
 cur-ri-c-u-lar
cur-rish
cur-ry
 cur-ries
 cur-ried
 cur-ry-ing
 cur-ri-er
cur-ry-comb
curse
cur-sive
 cur-sive-ly
cur-so-ry
 cur-so-ri-ly
 cur-so-ri-ness
curt
cur-tail
 cur-tail-ment
cur-tain
curt-sy
 curt-sies
 curt-sied
 curt-sy-ing
cur-va-ceous
cur-va-ture
curve
 cruved
 curv-ing
 curv-ed-nesss
cur-vi-lin-e-ar
cush-ion
cush-y
 cush-i-er
 cush-i-est
cus-pid
 cus-pi-dal
 cus-pi-date
 cus-pi-dor
cuss-ed
 cuss-ed-ly
 cuss-ed-ness
cus-tard
cus-to-dian
 cus-to-di-an-ship
cus-to-dy
 cus-to-dies
 cus-to-di-al
cus-tom
cus-tom-ary
 cus-tom-ar-ies
 cus-tom-ar-i-ly
 cus-tom-ar-i-ness

cus-tom-built
cus-tom-er
cus-tom-ize
 cus-tom-ized
 cus-tom-iz-ing
cus-tom-made
cu-ta-ne-ous
cut-back
cute
 cut-er
 cut-est
 cute-ly
 cute-ness
cu-ti-cle
cut-lery
cut-let
cut-ting
 cut-ting-ly
cut-tle
cut-up
cy-an-ic
cy-a-nide
cy-a-no-sis
cy-ber-na-tion
cy-ber-net-ics
cyc-la-men
cy-cle
cy-clic
cy-cli-cal
 cy-cli-cal-ly
cy-clom-e-ter
cy-clone
cy-clo-rama
 cy-clo-ram-ic
cy-clo-tron
cyg-net
cyl-in-der
 cy-lin-dric
 cy-lin-dri-cal
cym-bal
 cym-bal-ist
cyn-ic
 cyn-i-cism
cyn-i-cal
 cyn-i-cal-ly
cy-no-sure
cy-pher
cy-press
cyst
 cys-tic
cys-tic fi-bro-sis
cy-tol-o-gy
 cy-tol-o-gist
czar
czar-e-vitch
cza-ri-na

D

dab
  dabbed
  dab-bing
dab-ble
  dab-bled
  dab-bing
  dab-bler
dac-tyl
  dac-tyl-ic
dad-dy--long-legs
daf-fo-dil
daf-fy
  daf-fi-er
  daf-fi-est
dag-ger
da-guerre-o-type
dahl-ia
dai-ly
  dai-lies
dain-ty
  dain-ti-er
  dain-ti-est
  dain-ties
  dain-ti-ly
  dain-ti-ness
dai-qui-ri
dair-y
  dair-ies
dair-y-man
  dair-y-men
da-is
dai-sy
  dai-sies
dal-ly
  dal-lied
  dal-ly-ing
  dal-li-ance
dam-age
  dam-aged
  dam-ag-ing
  dam-age-a-ble
dam-a-scene
  dam-a-scened
  dam-a-scen-ing
dam-ask
damn
dam-na-ble
  dam-na-ble-ness
  dam-na-bly
dam-na-tion
damned
damp-en
damp-er
dam-sel
dam-son
dan-de-li-on

dan-der
dan-dle
  dan-dled
  dan-dling
dan-druff
dan-dy
  dan-dies
  dan-di-er
  dan-di-est
  dan-dy-ism
dan-ger
dan-ger-ous
  dan-ger-ous-ly
  dan-ger-ous-ness
dan-gle
  dan-gled
  dan-gling
  dan-gler
dank
  dank-ly
  dank-ness
dan-seuse
  dan-seus-es
dap-per
dap-ple
  dap-pled
  dap-pling
dare
  dared
  dar-ing
dare-dev-il
  dar-ing-ly
dark
  dark-ish
  dark-ly
  dark-ness
dark-en
dark-ling
dark-room
dar-ling
  dar-ling-ly
  dar-ling-ness
darn-er
dart-er
dash-board
dash-ing
das-tard
  das-tard-li-ness
  das-tard-ly
da-ta
date
  dat-ed
  dat-ing
  dat-a-ble
  dat-er
date-less

date-line
da-tive
da-tum
daub
  daub-er
daugh-ter
  daugh-ter-ly
  daugh-ter--in--law
  daugh-ters--in--law
daunt-less
  daunt-less-ly
  daunt-less-ness
dau-phin
dav-en-port
dav-it
daw-dle
  daw-dled
  daw-dling
  daw-dler
dawn
day-break
day-dream
  day-dream-er
day-light
day-time
daze
  dazed
  daz-ing
  daz-ed-ly
daz-zle
  daz-zled
  daz-zling
  daz-zler
  daz-zling-ly
dea-con
  dea-con-ry
  dea-con-ship
dea-con-ess
dead-beat
dead-en
  dead-en-er
dead-end
dead-line
dead-lock
dead-ly
  dead-li-er
  dead-li-est
  dead-li-ness
dead-pan
dead-wood
deaf
  deaf-ly
  deaf-ness
deaf-en
  deaf-en-ing-ly
deaf-mute

deal
  dealt
  deal-ing
  deal-er
dean-ship
dear
  dear-ly
  dear-ness
dearth
death
  death-less
  death-ly
death-blow
death-trap
death-watch
de-ba-cle
de-bar
  de-barred
  de-bar-ring
  de-bar-ment
de-bark
  de-bar-ka-tion
de-base
  de-based
  de-bas-ing
  de-base-ment
  de-bas-er
de-bate
  de-bat-ed
  de-bat-ing
  de-bat-a-ble
  de-bat-er
de-bauch
  de-bauch-er
  de-bauch-ment
  de-bauch-ery
  de-bauch-er-ies
deb-au-chee
de-ben-ture
de-bil-i-tate
  de-bil-i-tat-ed
  de-bil-i-tat-ing
  de-bil-i-ta-tion
de-bil-i-ty
  de-bil-i-ties
deb-it
deb-o-nair
de-bris
debt-or
de-bunk
  de-bunk-er
de-but
deb-u-tante
de-cade
dec-a-dent
  dec-a-dence

dec-a-dent-ly
dec-a-gon
dec-a-gram
dec-a-he-dron
  dec-a-he-drons
de-cal
de-camp
  de-camp-ment
de-cant
  de-cant-er
de-cap-i-tate
  de-cap-i-tat-ed
  de-cap-i-tat-ing
  de-cap-i-ta-tion
dec-a-pod
de-cath-lon
de-cay
de-crease
  de-creased
de-ceit
  de-ceit-ful
  de-ceit-ful-ly
  de-ceit-ful-ness
de-ceive
  de-ceived
  de-ceiv-ing
  de-ceiv-er
  de-ceiv-ing-ly
  de-ceiv-a-ble
de-cel-er-ate
  de-cel-er-at-ed
  de-cel-er-at-ing
  de-cel-er-a-tion
de-cen-cy
  de-cen-cies
de-cen-ni-al
  de-cen-ni-al-ly
de-cent
  de-cent-ly
de-cen-tral-ize
  de-cen-tral-ized
  de-cen-tral-iz-ing
  de-cen-tral-i-za-tion
de-cep-tion
  de-cep-tive
  de-cep-tive-ly
  de-cep-tive-ness
dec-i-bel
de-cide
  de-cid-ed
  de-cid-ing
  de-cid-a-ble
  de-cid-ed-ly
  de-cid-ed-ness
de-cid-u-ous
  de-cid-u-ous-ly

dec-i-mal
dec-i-mate
  dec-i-mat-ed
  dec-i-mat-ing
  dec-i-ma-tion
de-ci-pher
  de-ci-pher-a-ble
de-ci-sion
de-ci-sive
  de-ci-sive-ly
  de-ci-sive-ness
deck-le edge
de-claim
  dec-la-ma-tion
  de-clam-a-tory
de-clare
  de-clared
  de-clar-ing
  de-clar-a-tive
  de-clar-a-to-ry
  de-clar-er
  dec-la-ra-tion
de-clas-si-fy
  de-clas-si-fied
  de-clas-si-fy-ing
de-clen-sion
dec-li-na-tion
de-cline
  de-clined
  de-clin-ing
  de-clin-a-ble
de-cliv-i-ty
  de-cliv-i-ties
de-code
  de-cod-ed
  de-cod-ing
  de-cod-er
de-com-pose
  de-com-posed
  de-com-pos-ing
  de-com-po-si-tion
de-com-press
  de-com-pres-sion
de-con-tam-i-nate
  de-con-tam-i-nat-ed
  de-con-tam-i-nat-ing
  de-con-tam-i-na-tion
de-con-trol
  de-con-trolled
  de-con-trol-ling
de-cor
dec-o-rate
  dec-o-rat-ed
  dec-o-rat-ing
  dec-o-ra-tion
  dec-o-ra-tive

dec-o-ra-tive-ly
dec-o-ra-tor
dec-o-rous
dec-o-rous-ly
de-co-rum
de-coy
de-crease
de-creased
de-creas-ing
de-creas-ing-ly
de-cree
de-creed
de-cree-ing
de-crep-it
de-crep-i-tude
de-crep-it-ly
de-cre-scen-do
de-cre-scen-dos
de-cry
de-cried
de-cry-ing
de-cri-al
ded-i-cate
ded-i-cat-ed
ded-i-cat-ing
ded-i-ca-to-ry
ded-i-ca-tive
ded-i-ca-tion
de-duce
de-duc-i-ble
de-duct
de-duct-i-ble
de-duc-tion
de-duc-tive
de-duc-tive-ly
deep
deep-ly
deep-ness
deep-en
deep-root-ed
deep-seat-ed
deer-skin
de-es-ca-late
de-es-ca-lat-ed
de-es-ca-lat-ing
de-es-ca-la-tion
de-face
de-faced
de-fac-ing
de-face-ment
de-fac-er
de fac-to
de-fame
de-famed
de-fam-ing
def-a-ma-tion

de-fam-a-to-ry
de-fam-er
de-fault
de-fault-er
de-feat
de-feat-ism
de-feat-ist
def-e-cate
def-e-cat-ed
def-e-cat-ing
def-e-ca-tion
de-fect
de-fec-tion
de-fec-tor
de-fec-tive
de-fec-tive-ly
de-fec-tive-ness
de-fend
de-fend-er
de-fend-ant
de-fense
de-fense-less
de-fense-less-ly
de-fense-less-ness
de-fen-si-ble
de-fen-si-bil-i-ty
de-fen-si-bly
de-fen-sive
de-fen-sive-ly
de-fer
de-ferred
de-fer-ring
de-fer-ment
def-er-ence
def-er-en-tial
def-er-en-tial-ly
de-fi-ance
de-fi-ant
de-fi-ant-ly
de-fi-cient
de-fi-cien-cy
de-fi-cien-cies
de-fi-cient-ly
def-i-cit
de-file
de-filed
de-fil-ing
de-fine
de-fined
de-fin-ing
de-fin-er
de-fin-a-ble
de-fin-a-bly
def-i-nite
def-i-nite-ly
def-i-nite-ness

def-i-ni-tion
de-fin-i-tive
de-fin-i-tive-ly
de-flate
de-flat-ed
de-flat-ing
de-fla-tion
de-fla-tion-ary
de-flect
de-flec-tion
de-flec-tive
de-flec-tor
de-flow-er
de-fo-li-ate
de-fo-li-at-ed
de-fo-li-at-ing
de-for-est
de-for-est-a-tion
de-form
de-for-ma-tion
de-formed
de-form-i-ty
de-form-i-ties
de-fraud
de-fray
de-fray-al
de-fray-ment
de-fray-a-ble
de-frost
de-frost-er
deft
deft-ly
deft-ness
de-funct
de-fy
de-fied
de-fy-ing
de-fi-er
de-gen-er-ate
de-gen-er-at-ed
de-gen-er-at-ing
de-gen-er-ate-ly
de-gen-er-a-cy
de-gen-er-a-tion
de-gen-er-a-tive
de-grade
de-graded
de-grad-ing
deg-ra-da-tion
de-gree
de-his-cence
de-his-cent
de-hy-drate
de-hy-drat-ed
de-hy-drat-ing
de-hy-dra-tion

de-i-fy
de-i-fied
de-i-fy-ing
de-i-fi-ca-tion
de-i-fi-er
deign
de-ist
de-ism
de-is-tic
de-is-ti-cal
de-i-ty
de-i-ties
de-ject-ed
de-jec-ted-ly
de-jec-tion
de ju-re
de-lay
de-lay-er
de-lec-ta-ble
de-lec-ta-ble-ness
de-lec-ta-bly
de-lec-ta-tion
del-e-gate
del-e-gat-ed
del-e-gat-ing
del-e-ga-tion
de-lete
de-let-ed
de-let-ing
de-le-tion
del-e-te-ri-ous
de-lib-er-ate
de-lib-er-at-ed
de-lib-er-at-ing
de-lib-er-ate-ly
de-lib-er-ate-ness
de-lib-er-a-tion
de-lib-er-a-tive
de-lib-er-a-tor
del-i-ca-cy
del-i-ca-cies
del-i-cate
del-i-cate-ly
del-i-cate-ness
del-i-ca-tes-sen
de-li-cious
de-li-cious-ly
de-li-cious-ness
de-lim-it
de-lim-i-ta-tion
de-lin-e-ate
de-lin-e-at-ed
de-lin-e-at-ing
de-lin-e-a-tion
de-lin-e-a-tor
de-lin-quent

de-lin-quen-cy
de-lin-quen-cies
de-lir-i-um
de-lir-i-ums
de-lir-ia
de-lir-i-ous
de-lir-i-ous-ly
de-liv-er
de-liv-er-a-ble
de-liv-er-er
de-liv-er-ance
de-liv-ery
de-liv-er-ies
de-louse
de-loused
de-lous-ing
del-phin-i-um
del-ta
del-toid
de-lude
de-lud-ed
de-lud-ing
de-lud-er
de-lu-sive
de-lu-so-ry
de-lu-sive-ly
del-uge
del-uged
del-ug-ing
de-lu-sion
de-luxe
delve
delved
delv-ing
dem-a-gogue
dem-a-gogu-ery
dem-a-gog-ic
dem-a-gog-i-cal
de-mand
de-mand-er
de-mar-ca-tion
de-mean
de-mean-or
de-ment-ed
de-men-tia
de-mer-it
dem-i-god
de-mise
de-mised
de-mis-ing
dem-i-tasse
de-mo-bi-lize
de-mo-bi-lized
de-mo-bi-liz-ing
de-mo-bi-li-za-tion
de-moc-ra-cy

de-moc-ra-cies
dem-o-crat
dem-o-crat-ic
dem-o-crat-i-cal-ly
de-moc-ra-tize
de-moc-ra-tized
de-moc-ra-tiz-ing
de-moc-ra-ti-za-tion
de-mog-ra-phy
de-mog-ra-pher
dem-o-graph-ic
de-mol-ish
de-mol-ish-er
dem-o-li-tion
de-mon
de-mon-ic
de-mon-e-tize
de-mon-e-tized
de-mon-e-tiz-ing
de-mon-e-ti-za-tion
de-mo-ni-ac
de-mo-ni-a-cal
de-mon-ol-o-gy
de-mon-ol-o-gist
dem-on-strate
dem-on-strat-ed
dem-on-strat-ing
de-mon-stra-ble
de-mon-stra-bly
dem-on-stra-tion
de-mon-stra-tive
de-mon-stra-tive-ly
de-mon-stra-tive-ness
dem-on-stra-tor
de-mor-al-ize
de-mor-al-ized
de-mor-al-iz-ing
de-mor-al-i-za-tion
de-mor-al-iz-er
de-mote
de-mot-ed
de-mot-ing
de-mo-tion
de-mur
de-murred
de-mur-ring
de-mur-ral
de-mur-er
de-mur-est
de-mure-ly
de-mure-ness
de-mur-rage
de-nat-u-ral-ize
de-nat-u-ral-ized
de-nat-u-ral-iz-ing
de-nat-u-ral-i-za-tion

de-na-ture
de-na-tured
de-na-tur-ing
den-drite
den-dro-lite
den-drol-o-gy
den-e-ga-tion
de-ni-al
de-ni-er
den-im
den-i-zen
de-nom-i-nate
de-nom-i-nat-ed
de-nom-i-nat-ing
de-nom-i-na-tion
de-nom-i-na-tion-al
de-nom-i-na-tion-al-ism
de-nom-i-na-tive
de-nom-i-na-tor
de-note
de-not-ed
de-not-ing
de-no-ta-tion
de-noue-ment
de-nounce
de-nounced
de-noun-cing
de-nounce-ment
de-nun-ci-a-tion
de-nun-ci-a-to-ry
dense
den-ser
den-sest
dense-ly
dense-ness
den-si-ty
den-si-ties
den-tal
den-tate
den-ti-frice
den-tin
den-tist
den-tist-ry
den-ti-tion
den-ture
de-nude
de-nud-ed
de-nud-ing
den-u-da-tion
de-nun-ci-ate
de-nun-ci-at-ed
de-nun-ci-at-ing
de-nun-ci-a-tion
de-nun-ci-a-to-ry
de-ny
de-nied

de-ny-ing
de-o-dor-ant
de-o-dor-ize
de-o-dor-ized
de-o-dor-iz-ing
de-part
de-part-ed
de-part-ment
de-part-men-tal
de-par-ture
de-pend
de-pend-ence
de-pend-a-ble
de-pend-a-bly
de-pend-a-bil-i-ty
de-pend-en-cy
de-pend-en-cies
de-pend-ent
de-pict
de-pic-tion
de-pil-a-to-ry
de-pil-a-to-ries
de-plete
de-plet-ed
de-plet-ing
de-ple-tion
de-plor-a-ble
de-plor-a-bly
de-plore
de-plored
de-plor-ing
de-ploy
de-ploy-ment
de-po-nent
de-pop-u-late
de-pop-u-lat-ed
de-pop-u-lat-ing
de-pop-u-la-tion
de-port
de-por-ta-tion
de-port-ment
de-pose
de-posed
de-pos-ing
de-pos-a-ble
de-pos-it
de-pos-i-tor
dep-o-si-tion
de-pos-i-to-ry
de-pot
de-prave
de-praved
de-prav-ing
de-prav-i-ty
dep-re-cate
dep-re-cat-ed

dep-re-cat-ing
dep-re-cat-ing-ly
dep-re-ca-tion
dep-re-ca-to-ry
de-pre-ci-ate
de-pre-ci-at-ed
de-pre-ci-at-ing
de-pre-ci-a-tion
de-pre-ci-a-to-ry
de-pre-ci-a-tor
dep-re-date
dep-re-dat-ed
dep-re-dat-ing
dep-re-da-tion
de-press
de-pres-sant
de-pressed
de-pres-sion
de-prive
de-prived
de-priv-ing
dep-ri-va-tion
depth
dep-u-ta-tion
de-pute
de-put-ed
de-put-ing
dep-u-tize
dep-u-tized
dep-u-tiz-ing
dep-u-ty
dep-u-ties
dep-u-ty-ship
de-rail
de-rail-ment
de-range
de-ranged
de-rang-ing
de-range-ment
der-e-lict
der-e-lic-tion
de-ride
de-rid-ed
de-rid-ing
de-ri-sion
de-ri-sive
de-ri-sive-ly
de-ri-so-ry
der-i-va-tion
de-riv-a-tive
de-rive
de-rived
de-riv-ing
de-riv-a-ble
der-ma
der-mal

der-ma-tol-o-gy
  der-ma-to-log-i-cal
  der-ma-tol-o-gist
der-mis
der-o-gate
  der-o-gat-ed
  der-o-gat-ing
  der-o-ga-tion
de-rog-a-to-ry
  de-rog-a-to-ri-ly
der-rick
der-rin-ger
der-vish
des-cant
de-scend
  de-scend-a-ble
de-scend-ant
de-scent
de-scribe
  de-scribed
  de-scrib-ing
  de-scriba-ble
  de-scrib-er
de-scrip-tion
  de-scrip-tive
  de-scrip-tive-ly
  de-scrip-tive-ness
de-scry
  de-scried
  de-scry-ing
des-e-crate
  des-e-crat-ed
  des-e-crat-ing
  des-e-cra-tion
de-seg-re-gate
  de-seg-re-gat-ed
  de-seg-re-gat-ing
  de-seg-re-ga-tion
des-ert
de-sert
  de-sert-er
  de-ser-tion
de-serve
  de-served
  de-serv-ing
  de-serv-ed-ly
des-ha-bille
des-ic-cate
  des-ic-cat-ed
  des-ic-cat-ing
  des-ic-ca-tion
  des-ic-ca-tive
de-sid-er-a-tum
de-sign
des-ig-nate
  des-ig-nat-ed

des-ig-nat-ing
des-ig-na-tion
des-ig-na-tive
des-ig-na-tor
de-sign-ed-ly
de-sign-er
de-sign-ing
de-sire
  de-sired
  de-sir-ing
  de-sir-a-ble
  de-sir-a-bil-i-ty
  de-sir-a-bly
  de-sir-ous
de-sist
des-o-late
  des-o-lat-ed
  des-o-lat-ing
  des-o-late-ly
  des-o-la-tion
de-spair
  de-spair-ing
  de-spair-ing-ly
des-per-a-do
  des-per-a-does
des-per-ate
  des-per-ate-ly
  des-per-ate-ness
  des-per-a-tion
des-pi-ca-ble
  des-pi-ca-bly
de-spise
  de-spised
  de-spis-ing
de-spite
de-spoil
  de-spoil-er
  de-spo-li-a-tion
de-spond
  de-spond-en-cy
  de-spond-ence
  de-spond-ent
  de-spond-ent-ly
des-pot
  des-pot-ic
  des-pot-i-cal-ly
des-pot-ism
des-sert
des-ti-na-tion
des-tine
  des-tined
  des-tin-ing
des-ti-ny
  des-ti-nies
des-ti-tute
  des-ti-tu-tion

de-stroy
de-stroy-er
de-struc-tion
  de-struct-i-ble
  de-struct-i-bil-i-ty
de-struc-tive
  de-struc-tive-ly
  de-struc-tive-ness
des-ue-tude
des-ul-to-ry
  des-ul-to-ri-ly
de-tach
  de-tach-a-ble
de-tached
de-tach-ment
de-tail
  de-tailed
de-tain
  de-tain-ment
  de-tain-er
de-tect
  de-tect-a-ble
  de-tec-tion
de-tec-tive
  de-tec-tor
de-ten-tion
de-ter
  de-terred
  de-ter-ring
de-ter-gent
de-te-ri-o-rate
  de-te-ri-o-rat-ed
  de-te-ri-o-rat-ing
  de-te-ri-o-ra-tion
de-ter-mi-na-ble
de-ter-mi-nant
de-ter-mi-nate
de-ter-mi-na-tion
  de-ter-mi-na-tive
de-ter-mine
  de-ter-mined
  de-ter-min-ing
  de-ter-min-er
de-ter-mined
  de-ter-mined-ly
de-ter-min-ism
  de-ter-min-ist
de-ter-rent
  de-ter-rence
de-test
  de-test-a-ble
  de-test-a-bly
de-tes-ta-tion
de-throne
  de-throned
  de-thron-ing

de-throne-ment
det-o-nate
  det-o-nat-ed
  det-o-nat-ing
  det-o-na-tion
  det-o-na-tor
de-tour
de-tract
  de-trac-tion
  de-trac-tor
det-ri-ment
  det-ri-men-tal
  det-ri-men-tal-ly
de-tri-tus
deuce
deu-te-ri-um
de-val-u-ate
  de-val-u-at-ed
  de-val-u-at-ing
  de-val-u-a-tion
dev-as-tate
  dev-as-tat-ed
  dev-as-tat-ing
  dev-as-ta-tion
de-vel-op
  de-vel-op-ment
de-vel-op-er
de-vi-ate
  de-vi-at-ed
  de-vi-at-ing
  de-vi-ant
  de-vi-a-tion
de-vice
dev-il
  dev-il-ment
  dev-il-try
  dev-il-tries
  dev-il-ry
dev-il-ish
  dev-il-ish-ly
  dev-il-ish-ness
de-vi-ous
  de-vi-ous-ly
  de-vi-ous-ness
de-vise
  de-vised
  de-vis-ing
  de-vis-a-ble
  de-vis-al
  de-vi-see
  de-vi-sor
de-void
de-volve
  de-volved
  de-volv-ing
  dev-o-lu-tion

de-vote
  de-vot-ing
de-vot-ed
  de-vot-ed-ly
dev-o-tee
de-vo-tion
  de-vo-tion-al
de-vour
  de-vour-er
  de-vour-ing-ly
de-vout
  de-vout-ly
  de-vout-ness
dew-drop
dew-lap
dewy
  dew-i-er
  dew-i-est
  dew-i-ness
dew-y-eyed
dex-ter-ous
  dex-ter-i-ty
  dex-ter-ous-ly
dex-trose
di-a-be-tes
  di-a-bet-ic
di-a-bol-ic
  di-a-bol-i-cal
  di-a-bol-i-cal-ly
di-a-crit-ic
di-a-crit-i-cal
  di-a-crit-i-cal-ly
di-a-dem
di-ag-nose
  di-ag-nosed
  di-ag-nos-ing
  di-ag-no-sis
  di-ag-no-ses
  di-ag-nos-tic
  di-ag-nos-ti-cian
di-ag-o-nal
  di-ag-o-nal-ly
di-a-gram
  di-a-gramed
  di-a-gram-ing
  di-a-gram-mat-ic
  di-a-gram-mat-i-cal
di-al
  di-aled
  di-al-ing
di-a-lect
  di-a-lec-tal
di-a-lec-tic
  di-a-lec-ti-cal
  di-a-lec-ti-cian
di-a-logue

di-am-e-ter
di-a-met-ric
  di-a-met-ric-al
  di-a-met-ric-al-ly
dia-mond
dia-per
di-aph-a-nous
di-a-phragm
di-ar-rhea
di-a-ry
di-as-to-le
  di-as-tol-ic
di-a-ther-mic
di-a-tom
di-a-ton-ic
dib-ble
  dib-bled
  dib-bling
di-chot-o-my
  di-chot-o-mous
  di-cho-tom-ic
dic-tate
  dic-ta-tion
dic-ta-tor
  dic-ta-to-ri-al
  dic-ta-to-ri-al-ly
dic-tion-ary
dic-tum
di-dac-tic
  di-dac-ti-cally
di-er-e-ses
di-e-tary
di-e-tet-ic
  di-e-tet-i-cal
  di-e-tet-i-cal-ly
di-e-tet-ics
di-e-ti-cian
dif-fer-ence
  dif-fer-enced
  dif-fer-en-cing
dif-fer-ent
  dif-fer-ent-ly
dif-fer-en-tial
  dif-fer-en-tial-ly
dif-fer-en-ti-ate
  dif-fer-en-ti-at-ed
dif-fi-cult
  dif-fi-cult-ly
dif-fi-dence
  dif-fi-dent
  dif-fi-dent-ly
dif-fuse
  dif-fused
  dif-fus-ing
  dif-fuse-ness
  dif-fu-sion

60

di-gest
 di-gest-er
 di-gest-i-ble
 di-gest-i-bil-i-ty
 di-ges-tion
dig-ger
dig-gings
dig-it-al
dig-i-tal-is
dig-ni-fied
dig-ni-fy
 dig-ni-fy-ing
dig-ni-tary
 dig-ni-tar-ies
dig-ni-ty
di-gress
 di-gres-sion
 di-gres-sive
di-he-dral
di-lap-i-dat-ed
 di-lap-i-da-tion
dil-a-ta-tion
di-late
 di-lat-ed
 di-lat-ing
 di-lat-a-ble
 di-la-tion
dil-a-to-ry
 dil-a-to-ri-ly
di-lem-ma
dil-et-tan-te
 dil-et-tan-tes
dil-i-gence
 dil-i-gent
 dil-i-gent-ly
dil-ly-dal-ly
di-lute
 di-lut-ed
 di-lut-ing
 di-lute-ness
di-men-sion
 di-men-sion-al
di-min-ish
 di-min-ish-a-ble
di-min-u-en-do
 di-min-u-en-dos
dim-i-nu-tion
di-min-u-tive
 di-min-u-tive-ness
dim-ple
 dim-pled
 dim-pling
din-er
di-nette
din-ghy
 din-ghies

din-gy
 din-gi-er
 din-gi-est
 din-gi-ness
din-ner
di-no-saur
di-o-cese
di-oc-e-san
di-o-ram-a
diph-the-ri-a
di-plo-ma
di-plo-ma-cy
 di-plo-ma-cies
dip-lo-mat
 dip-lo-mat-ic
 dip-lo-mat-i-cal-ly
dip-per
dip-so-ma-nia
 dip-so-ma-ni-ac
dire
 dir-er
 dir-est
 dire-ness
di-rect
 di-rect-ness
di-rec-tion
 di-rec-tion-al
di-rec-tive
di-rect-ly
di-rec-tor
 di-rec-to-ri-al
 di-rec-tor-ship
di-rec-to-rate
di-rec-to-ry
 di-rec-to-ries
dis-a-ble
 dis-a-bling
 dis-a-bil-i-ty
 dis-a-ble-ment
dis-a-buse
 dis-a-bused
 dis-a-bus-ing
dis-ad-van-tage
 dis-ad-van-taged
dis-af-fect
 dis-af-fec-tion
 dis-af-fect-ed
dis-a-gree
 dis-a-gree-ing
 dis-a-gree-a-ble
 dis-a-gree-ment
dis-al-low
 dis-al-low-ance
dis-ap-pear
 dis-ap-pear-ance
dis-ap-point

dis-ap-point-ment
dis-ap-pro-ba-tion
dis-ap-prove
 dis-ap-prov-al
dis-arm
dis-ar-ma-ment
dis-ar-range
 dis-ar-ranged
 dis-ar-rang-ing
dis-ar-ray
dis-as-sem-ble
dis-as-ter
 dis-as-trous
 dis-as-trous-ly
dis-a-vow
 dis-a-vow-al
dis-band
 dis-band-ment
dis-bar
 dis-barred
 dis-bar-ring
dis-be-lieve
 dis-be-lief
 dis-be-liev-er
dis-burse
 dis-bursed
 dis-burs-ing
 dis-burs-er
dis-cern-ing
dis-cern-ment
dis-charge
 dis-charged
 dis-charg-ing
 dis-char-ger
dis-ci-ple
 dis-ci-ple-ship
dis-ci-pline
 dis-ci-plines
 dis-ci-pli-nary
dis-claim-er
dis-close
 dis-closed
 dis-clos-er
 dis-clo-sure
dis-coid
dis-col-or
 dis-col-or-a-tion
dis-com-fit
 dis-com-fi-ture
dis-com-fort
dis-com-mode
 dis-com-mod-ing
dis-com-pose
 dis-com-posed
 dis-com-pos-ing
dis-con-cert

dis-con-cert-ed
dis-con-nect
dis-con-nec-tion
dis-con-so-late
dis-con-tent
dis-con-tent-ed
dis-con-tin-ue
dis-con-tin-ued
dis-con-tin-u-ing
dis-con-tin-u-ous
dis-cord
dis-cord-ance
dis-cord-ant-ly
dis-count
dis-cour-age
dis-cour-ag-ing
dis-course
dis-coursed
dis-cours-ing
dis-cour-te-ous
dis-cour-te-sy
dis-cov-er
dis-cov-er-a-ble
dis-cov-er-er
dis-cov-er-y
dis-cov-er-ies
dis-cred-it
dis-cred-it-a-bly
dis-creet
dis-crep-an-cy
dis-crep-an-cies
dis-crete
dis-cre-tion
dis-cre-tion-ary
dis-crim-i-nate
dis-crim-i-nate-ly
dis-crim-i-na-to-ry
dis-crim-i-na-tor
dis-cur-sive
dis-cur-sive-ly
dis-cur-sive-ness
dis-cus
dis-cus-es
dis-cuss
dis-cuss-i-ble
dis-cus-sion
dis-dain
dis-dain-ful
dis-dain-ful-ly
dis-ease
dis-eased
dis-eas-ing
dis-em-bark
dis-em-body
dis-em-bod-ied
dis-em-bod-y-ing

dis-em-bow-el
dis-em-bow-eled
dis-em-bow-el-ing
dis-en-chant
dis-en-chant-ment
dis-en-cum-ber
dis-en-fran-chise
dis-en-fran-chised
dis-en-fran-chis-ing
dis-en-gage
dis-en-gaged
dis-en-gag-ing
dis-en-tan-gle
dis-en-tan-gled
dis-en-tan-gling
dis-es-tab-lish
dis-fa-vor
dis-fig-ure
dis-fig-ured
dis-fig-ur-ing
dis-fig-ure-ment
dis-fran-chise
dis-fran-chised
dis-fran-chis-ing
dis-gorge
dis-gorged
dis-gorg-ing
dis-grace
dis-graced
dis-grac-ing
dis-grace-ful
dis-grace-ful-ly
dis-grun-tle
dis-grun-tled
dis-grun-tling
dis-guise
dis-guised
dis-guis-ing
dis-guis-er
dis-gust
dis-gust-ed
dis-gust-ing
dis-ha-bille
dis-har-mo-ny
dis-har-mo-nies
dis-heart-en
dis-hev-eled
dis-hon-est
dis-hon-est-ly
dis-hon-es-ty
dis-hon-es-ties
dis-hon-or
dis-hon-or-a-ble
dis-hon-or-a-bly
dis-il-lu-sion
dis-in-cline

dis-in-clined
dis-in-fect
dis-in-her-it
dis-in-te-grate
dis-in-ter-es-ted
dis-in-ter-est-ed-ly
dis-junc-tion
dis-loy-al
dis-loy-al-ty
dis-o-be-di-ence
dis-or-der-ly
dis-o-ri-ent
dis-pas-sion
dis-pen-sa-tion
dis-pos-a-ble
dis-qual-i-fy
dis-qui-et
dis-re-spect
dis-re-spect-ful
dis-rup-tive
dis-rupt-er
dis-sat-is-fy
dis-sat-is-fy-ing
dis-sem-blance
dis-sem-i-nate
dis-sem-i-nat-ing
dis-sem-i-na-tor
dis-sent
dis-ser-tate
dis-ser-ta-ting
dis-ser-ta-tion
dis-serv-ice
dis-si-dent
dis-sim-i-lar
dis-sim-i-lar-i-ty
dis-sim-i-late
dis-sim-i-lat-ing
dis-sim-i-la-tive
dis-si-pate
dis-si-pa-tion
dis-so-nance
dis-so-nant
dis-suade
dis-sua-sion
dis-sua-sive
dis-tance
dis-taste
dis-taste-ful-ly
dis-tem-per
dis-til-late
dis-till-ery
dis-tinc-tion
dis-tin-guish
dis-tract
dis-tract-ing
dis-trib-ute

dis-trib-ut-ed
dis-tri-bu-tion
dis-tri-u-tor
dis-u-nite
di-van
di-verge
 di-ver-gence
 di-ver-gent
di-verse
di-ver-sion
div-i-dend
di-vi-sor
di-vulge
 di-vulg-ing
 di-vul-gence
do-a-ble
doc-tor-ate
doc-u-ment
dod-der
dog-ma
dog-mat-ic
 dog-mat-i-cal
dol-drums
dol-or-ous
dol-phin
do-mes-tic
do-mes-ti-cate
do-mes-tic-i-ty
dom-i-cile
 dom-i-cil-ing
dom-i-nance
dom-i-nant
dom-i-neer
do-min-ion
dop-ey
 dop-i-est
 dop-i-ness
dor-mant
dor-mer
dor-mi-to-ry
dos-age
dos-si-er
dou-ble-faced
dou-ble-take
dou-ble-time
doubt-a-ble
douche
dow-a-ger
dow-el
down-ward-ly
doz-ing
doz-en
drab-ness
drag-gle
drag-on
drain-age

dra-mat-ics
dra-per-y
dread-ful
drib-ble
 drib-bled
 drib-bling
 drib-bler
drill-ing
dri-ly
driv-el
 driv-eled
 driv-el-ing
driz-zle
 driz-zling
 driz-zly
drom-e-dar-y
droop
 droop-y
 droop-i-er
 droop-i-est
drop-per
dross
drought
 drought-y
 drought-i-er
 drought-i-est
drowned
drowse
 drowsed
 drows-ing
 drow-si-ness
drudge
drug-gist
dru-id
drum-mer
drunk-ard
drunk-en
 drunk-en-ly
 drunk-en-ness
dry-ad
du-al
 du-al-i-ty
du-al-ism
 du-al-ist
 du-al-is-tic
du-bi-ous
 du-bi-e-ty
 du-bi-ous-ly
 du-bi-ous-ness
du-cal
duch-ess
duck-ling
duct-less
duc-tile
du-el
 du-eled

du-el-ing
du-el-ist
duke-dom
dul-cet
dum-found
dump-ling
dunce
dung
dun-ga-ree
dun-geon
dun-nage
du-o-dec-i-mal
du-o-de-num
 du-o-de-na
 du-o-de-nal
du-pli-cate
 du-pli-cat-ing
 du-pli-ca-tor
du-plic-i-ty
du-ra-ble
 du-ra-bil-ity
 du-ra-bly
dur-ance
du-ra-tion
dur-ing
dust-er
du-ti-a-ble
du-ti-ful
 du-ti-ful-ly
 du-ti-ful-ness
dwarf
 dwarf-ish
dwell
 dewlt
 dwelled
 dwell-ing
dwin-dle
 dwin-dled
 dwin-dling
dye-stuff
dy-ing
dy-nam-ic
 dy-nam-i-cal
 dy-nam-i-cal-ly
 dy-na-mism
dy-na-mite
dy-na-mo
dy-nas-ty
 dy-nas-ties
dyne
dys-en-tery
dys-func-tion
dys-pep-sia
dys-pep-tic
 dys-pep-ti-cal
dys-tro-phy

ea-ger
  ea-ger-ly
  ea-ger-ness
ea-gle
ea-gle eyed
ea-glet
ear-ache
ear-drum
earl-dom
ear-ly
  ear-li-er
  ear-li-est
ear-mark
ear-muff
earn
  earn-er
ear-nest
  ear-nest-ly
  ear-nest-ness
earn-ings
ear-phone
ear-ring
earth-en
earth-ly
  earth-li-er
  earth-li-est
earth-quake
earth-y
ear-wax
ease
  eased
  eas-ing
ea-sel
ease-ment
eas-i-ly
  eas-i-ness
east-er-ly
east-ern
east-ern-most
east-ward
eas-y
  eas-i-er
  eas-i-est
eas-y-go-ing
eat
ebb
eb-on-y
  eb-on-ies
e-bul-lience
  e-bul-lient
  e-bul-li-tion
ec-cen-tric
  ec-cen-tri-cal-ly
  ec-cen-tric-i-ty
  ec-cen-tric-i-ties
ec-cle-si-as-tic

ec-cle-si-as-ti-cal
  ec-cle-si-as-ti-cal-ly
ech-e-lon
e-chi-no-derm
ech-o
e-cho-ic
e-clair
ec-lec-tic
  ec-lec-ti-cal-ly
  ec-lec-ti-cism
e-clipse
  e-clipsed
  e-clips-ing
e-clip-tic
e-col-o-gy
  e-c-o-log-ic
  e-c-o-log-i-cal
  e-col-o-gist
e-co-nom-ic
  e-co-nom-i-cal
e-co-nom-ics
e-con-o-mist
e-con-o-mize
  e-con-o-mized
  e-con-o-miz-ing
  e-con-o-miz-er
e-con-o-my
  e-con-o-mies
ec-o-sys-tem
ec-ru
ec-sta-sy
  ec-sta-sies
ec-stat-ic
  ec-stat-i-cal
ec-to-morph
  ec-to-mor-phic
ec-to-plasm
ec-u-men-i-cal
ec-u-men-ic
  ec-u-men-i-cal-ly
  ec-u-men-ism
ec-ze-ma
e-de-ma
  e-de-ma-ta
e-den-tate
edg-y
ed-i-ble
e-dict
ed-i-fice
ed-i-fy
  ed-i-fied
  ed-i-fy-ing
  ed-i-fi-ca-tion
ed-it
e-di-tion
ed-i-tor

ed-i-tor-ship
ed-i-to-ri-al
  ed-i-to-ri-al-ly
  ed-i-to-ri-al-ize
  ed-i-to-ri-al-lized
ed-u-cate
  ed-u-cat-ed
  ed-u-cat-ing
  ed-u-ca-ble
ed-u-ca-tor
ed-u-ca-tion
  ed-u-ca-tion-al
e-duce
  e-duced
  e-duc-ing
  e-duc-i-ble
  e-duc-tion
eel
ee-rie
  ee-ri-er
  ee-ri-est
  ee-ri-ly
ef-fect
  ef-fec-tive
  ef-fec-tive-ness
  ef-fec-tive-ly
ef-fec-tu-al
  ef-fec-tu-al-i-ty
ef-fec-tu-ate
  ef-fec-tu-at-ed
  ef-fec-tu-at-ing
ef-fem-i-nate
  ef-fem-i-na-cy
  ef-fem-i-na-cies
  ef-fem-i-nate-ly
ef-fete
ef-fi-ca-cious
ef-fi-ca-cy
  ef-fi-ca-cies
ef-fi-cien-cy
  ef-fi-cien-cies
ef-fi-cient
  ef-fi-cient-ly
ef-fi-gy
  ef-fi-gies
ef-flo-resce
ef-flu-ent
  ef-flu-ence
ef-flu-vi-um
  ef-flu-via
  ef-flu-vi-ums
  ef-flu-vi-al
ef-fort
  ef-fort-less
  ef-fort-less-ly
ef-fron-ter-y

ef-fron-ter-ies
ef-ful-gent
ef-ful-gence
ef-fuse
ef-fused
ef-fus-ing
ef-fu-sion
ef-fu-sive
ef-fu-sive-ly
egal-i-tar-i-an
egal-i-tar-i-an-ism
egg-nog
egg-plant
e-go
e-gos
e-go-cen-tric
e-go-ism
e-go-ist
e-go-is-tic
e-go-tism
e-go-tis-tic
e-go-tis-ti-cal
e-gre-gious
e-gre-gious-ly
e-gress
e-gret
ei-der-down
eight
eighth
eight-ball
eight-fold
eight-y
eight-ies
eight-i-eth
ei-ther
e-jac-u-late
e-jac-u-lat-ed
e-jac-u-lat-ing
e-jac-u-la-tion
e-ject
e-jec-tion
e-ject-ment
e-jec-tor
eke
eked
ek-ing
e-lab-o-rate
e-lab-o-rat-ed
e-lab-o-rat-ing
e-lab-o-rate-ly
e-lab-o-ra-tion
e-lapse
e-lapsed
e-laps-ing
e-las-tic
e-las-ti-cal-ly

e-las-tic-i-ty
e-late
e-lat-ed
e-lat-ing
e-la-tion
el-bow
el-bow-room
el-der
eld-er-ship
el-der-ly
eld-er-li-ness
eld-est
e-lect
e-lec-tion
e-lec-tion-eer
e-lec-tive
e-lec-tor
e-lec-tor-ate
e-lec-tric
e-lec-tri-cal
e-lec-tri-cal-ly
e-lec-tri-cian
e-lec-tric-i-ty
e-lec-tri-fy
e-lec-tri-fied
e-lec-tri-fy-ing
e-lec-tri-fi-ca-tion
elec-tro-car-di-o-graph
e-lec-tro-cute
e-lec-tro-cut-ed
e-lec-tro-cut-ing
e-lec-tro-cu-tion
e-lec-trode
e-lec-tro-dy-nam-ics
e-lec-trol-y-sis
e-lec-tro-lyze
e-lec-tro-lyzed
e-lec-tro-lyz-ing
e-lec-tro-lyte
e-lec-tro-lyt-ic
e-lec-tro-mag-net
e-lec-tro-mag-net-ism
e-lec-tro-mag-net-ic
e-lec-tron
e-lec-tron-ic
e-lec-tron-ics
e-lec-tron-i-cal-ly
e-lec-tro-plate
e-lec-tro-plat-ed
e-lec-tro-plat-ing
e-lec-tro-ther-a-py
e-lec-trum
el-ee-mos-y-nar-y
el-e-gant
el-e-gance
el-e-gan-cy

el-e-gant-ly
el-e-gy
el-e-gies
el-e-gi-ac
el-e-gist
el-e-gize
el-e-gized
el-e-giz-ing
el-e-ment
el-e-men-tal
el-e-men-tal-ly
el-e-men-ta-ry
el-e-men-ta-ri-ly
el-e-phant
el-e-phan-tine
el-e-vate
el-e-vat-ed
el-e-vat-ing
el-e-va-tion
el-e-va-tor
e-lev-en
e-lev-enth
elf
e-lic-it
el-i-gi-ble
el-i-gi-bil-i-ty
el-i-gi-bly
e-lim-i-nate
e-lim-i-nat-ed
e-lim-i-nat-ing
e-lim-i-na-tion
e-lim-i-na-tor
e-lite
e-lit-ism
e-lit-ist
e-lix-ir
el-lipse
el-lip-sis
el-lip-ses
el-lip-ti-cal
el-lip-tic
el-lip-ti-cal-ly
el-o-cu-tion
el-o-cu-tion-ary
el-o-cu-tion-ist
e-lon-gate
e-lon-gat-ed
e-lon-gat-ing
e-lon-ga-tion
e-lope
el-o-quence
el-o-quent
el-o-quent-ly
else-where
e-lu-ci-date
e-lu-ci-dat-ed

e-lu-ci-dat-ing
e-lu-ci-da-tion
e-lu-ci-da-tor
e-lude
e-lud-ed
e-lud-ing
e-lu-sion
e-lu-sive
e-lu-sive-ly
e-lu-sive-ness
elv-ish
e-ma-ci-ate
e-ma-ci-at-ed
e-ma-ci-at-ing
e-ma-ci-a-tion
em-a-nate
em-a-nat-ed
em-a-nat-ing
em-a-na-tion
e-man-ci-pate
e-man-ci-pat-ed
e-man-ci-pat-ing
e-man-ci-pa-tor
e-mas-cu-late
e-mas-cu-lat-ed
e-mas-cu-lat-ing
e-mas-cu-la-tion
em-balm
em-balm-er
em-balm-ment
em-bank-ment
em-bar-go
em-bar-goes
em-bar-goed
em-bar-go-ing
em-bark
em-bar-ka-tion
em-bark-ment
em-bar-rass
em-bar-rass-ing-ly
em-bar-rass-ment
em-bas-sy
em-bas-sies
em-bat-tle
em-bat-tled
em-bat-tling
em-bat-tle-ment
em-bed
em-bed-ded
em-bed-ding
em-bel-lish
em-bel-lish-ment
em-ber
em-bez-zle
em-bez-zled
em-bez-zling

em-bez-zle-ment
em-bez-zler
em-bit-ter
em-bit-ter-ment
em-bla-zon
em-bla-zon-er
em-blaz-on-ment
em-bla-zon-ry
em-blem
em-blem-at-ic
em-blem-at-i-cal
em-bod-y
em-bod-ied
em-bod-y-ing
em-bod-i-ment
em-bold-en
em-bo-lism
em-bo-lus
em-bos-om
em-boss
em-boss-ment
em-bou-chure
em-brace
em-braced
em-brac-ing
em-broi-der
em-broi-dery
em-broi-der-ies
em-broil
em-broil-ment
em-bry-o
em-bry-os
em-bry-on-ic
em-bry-ol-o-gy
em-cee
em-ceed
em-cee-ing
e-mend
em-er-ald
e-merge
e-merged
e-merg-ing
e-mer-gence
e-mer-gent
e-mer-gen-cy
e-mer-gen-ies
e-mer-i-tus
em-er-y
e-met-ic
em-i-grant
em-i-grate
em-i-grat-ed
em-i-grat-ing
em-i-gra-tion
em-i-nence
em-i-nent

em-i-ent-ly
em-i-nent do-main
em-is-sary
em-is-sar-ies
e-mis-sion
e-mis-sive
e-mit
e-mit-ted
e-mit-ting
e-mit-ter
e-mol-lient
e-mol-u-ment
e-mote
e-mot-ed
e-mot-ing
e-mo-tive
emo-tion
emo-tion-al
emo-ton-al-ly
emo-tion-al-ism
em-pan-el
em-pa-thize
em-pa-thized
em-pa-thiz-ing
em-pa-thy
em-pa-thet-ic
em-path-ic
em-per-or
em-pha-sis
em-pha-ses
em-pha-size
em-pha-sized
em-pha-siz-ing
em-phat-ic
em-phat-i-cal-ly
em-phy-se-ma
em-pire
em-pir-i-cal
em-pir-i-cal-ly
em-pir-i-cism
em-pir-i-cist
em-place-ment
em-ploy
em-ploy-a-ble
em-ploy-ee
em-ploy-er
em-ploy-ment
em-pori-um
em-po-ri-ums
em-po-ria
em-pow-er
em-press
emp-ty
emp-ti-er
emp-ti-est
emp-tied

emp-ty-ing
emp-ti-ly
emp-ti-ness
emp-ty--hand-ed
emp-ty--head-ed
e-mu
em-u-late
em-u-lat-ed
em-u-lat-ing
em-u-la-tion
e-mul-si-fy
e-mul-si-fied
e-mul-si-fy-ing
e-mul-si-fi-ca-tion
e-mul-si-fi-er
emul-sion
emul-sive
en-a-ble
en-a-bled
en-a-bling
en-act
e-nam-el
e-nam-eled
e-nam-el-ing
e-nam-el-er
e-nam-el-ware
en-am-or
en-am-ored-ness
en-camp
en-camp-ment
en-cap-su-late
en-cap-su-lat-ed
en-cap-su-lat-ing
en-cap-sule
en-case
en-cased
en-cas-ing
en-ceinte
en-ceph-a-li-tis
en-ceph-a-lit-ic
en-ceph-a-lon
en-ceph-a-la
en-chant
en-chant-er
en-chant-ress
en-chant-ing
en-chant-ing-ly
en-chant-ment
en-chi-la-da
en-cir-cle
en-cir-cled
en-cir-cling
en-cir-cle-ment
en-clave
en-close
en-closed

en-clos-ing
en-clo-sure
en-code
en-cod-ed
en-cod-ing
en-co-mi-ast
en-com-pass
en-com-pass-ment
en-core
en-coun-ter
en-cour-age
en-cour-aged
en-cour-ag-ing
en-cour-ag-ing-ly
en-croach
en-croach-er
en-croach-ment
en-crust
en-crus-ta-tion
en-cum-ber
en-cum-brance
en-cy-clo-pe-di-a
en-cy-clo-pe-dic
en-cy-clo-pe-di-cal
en-cy-clo-pe-di-cal-ly
en-cyst
en-dan-ger
en-dan-ger-ment
en-dear
en-dear-ment
en-dea-vor
en-dem-ic
en-dem-i-cal
en-dem-i-cal-ly
end-ing
end-less
end-less-ly
end-less-ness
end-most
en-do-crine
en-do-cri-nol-o-gy
en-do-crin-o-log-ic
en-do-crin-o-log-i-cal
en-do-cri-nol-o-gist
en-dog-e-nous
en-dorse
en-dorsed
en-dors-ing
en-dor-see
en-dor-ser
en-dorse-ment
en-do-sperm
en-dow
en-dow-ment
en-due
en-dued

en-du-ing
en-dur-ance
en-dure
en-dured
en-dur-ing
en-dur-a-ble
en-dur-a-bly
en-dur-ing-ness
end-ways
en-e-ma
en-e-my
en-e-mies
en-er-get-ic
en-er-get-i-cal
en-er-get-i-cal-ly
en-er-gize
en-er-gized
en-er-giz-ing
en-er-gi-zer
en-er-gy
en-er-gies
en-er-vate
en-er-vat-ed
en-er-vat-ing
en-er-va-tion
en-fee-ble
en-fee-bled
en-fee-bling
en-fee-ble-ment
en-fi-lade
en-fi-lad-ed
en-fi-lad-ing
en-fold
en-force
en-forced
en-forc-ing
en-force-a-ble
en-force-ment
en-forc-er
en-fran-chise
en-fran-chised
en-fran-chis-ing
en-fran-chise-ment
en-gage
en-gaged
en-gag-ing
en-gage-ment
en-gen-der
en-gine
en-gi-neer
en-gorge
en-gorged
en-gorg-ing
en-gorge-ment
en-grave
en-graved

en-grav-ing
en-grav-er
en-gross
  en-grossed
  en-gross-er
  en-gross-ing
  en-gross-ing-ly
  en-gross-ment
en-gulf
  en-gulf-ment
en-hance
  en-hanced
  en-hanc-ing
  en-hance-ment
e-nig-ma
  en-ig-mat-ic
  en-ig-mat-i-cal
  en-ig-mat-i-cal-ly
en-join
  en-join-er
  en-join-ment
en-joy
  en-joy-a-ble
  en-joy-a-ble-ness
  en-joy-a-bly
  en-joy-ment
en-large
  en-larged
  en-larg-ing
  en-large-a-ble
  en-larg-er
en-large-ment
en-light-en
  en-light-en-ment
en-list
  en-list-ed
  en-list-ment
en-liv-en
  en-liv-en-er
en-mesh
en-mi-ty
  en-mi-ties
en-no-ble
  en-no-bled
  en-no-bling
  en-no-ble-ment
  en-no-bler
en-nui
e-nor-mi-ty
  e-nor-mi-ties
e-nor-mous
  e-nor-mous-ly
  e-nor-mous-ness
e-nough
en-plane
  en-planed

en-plan-ing
en-rage
  en-raged
  en-rag-ing
en-rap-ture
  en-rap-tured
  en-rap-tur-ing
en-rich
  en-rich-er
  en-rich-ment
en-roll
  en-roll-ment
en route
en-sconce
  en-sconced
  en-sconc-ing
en-sem-ble
en-shrine
  en-shrin-ing
en-shroud
en-sign
en-si-lage
  en-si-laged
  en-si-lag-ing
en-slave
  en-slaved
  en-slav-ing
  en-slave-ment
  en-slav-er
en-snare
  en-snared
  en-snar-ing
  en-snare-ment
  en-snar-er
  en-snar-ing-ly
en-sue
  en-sued
  en-su-ing
  en-su-ing-ly
en-sure
  en-sured
  en-sur-ing
  en-sur-er
en-tail
  en-tail-er
  en-tail-ment
en-tan-gle
  en-tan-gled
  en-tan-gling
  en-tan-gle-ment
  en-tan-gler
en-tente
en-ter
  en-ter-a-ble
  en-ter-i-tis
en-tr-prise

en-ter-pris-ing
en-ter-pris-ing-ly
en-ter-tain
  en-ter-tain-er
  en-ter-tain-ing
  en-ter-tain-ing-ly
  en-ter-tain-ment
en-thrall
  en-thralled
  en-thrall-ing
  en-thrall-ment
en-throne
  en-throned
  en-thron-ing
  en-throne-ment
en-thuse
  en-thused
  en-thus-ing
en-thu-si-asm
en-thu-si-ast
  en-thu-si-as-tic
  en-thu-si-as-ti-cal-ly
en-tice
  en-ticed
  en-tic-ing
  en-tice-ment
  en-tic-er
  en-tic-ig-ly
en-tire
  en-tire-ly
  en-tire-ness
  en-tire-ty
  en-tire-ties
en-ti-tle
  en-ti-tled
  en-ti-tling
  en-ti-tle-ment
en-ti-ty
  en-ti-ties
en-to-mol-o-gy
  en-to-mol-o-gies
  en-to-mo-log-ic
  en-to-mo-log-i-cal
  en-to-mo-log-i-cal-ly
  en-to-mol-o-gist
en-tou-rage
en-trails
en-train
  en-train-er
en-trance
  en-trance-way
  en-tranced
  en-tranc-ing
  en-trance-ment
  en-tranc-ing-ly
en-trant

en-trap
  en-trapped
  en-trap-ping
  en-trap-ment
en-treat
  en-treat-ing-ly
  en-treat-ment
  en-treat-y
en-tree
en-trench
  en-trench-ment
  en-tre-pre-neur
  en-tre-pre-neur-i-al
  en-tre-pre-neur-ship
en-tro-py
en-trust
  en-trust-ment
en-try
  en-tries
en-twine
  en-twined
  en-twin-ing
e-nu-mer-ate
  e-nu-mer-at-ed
  e-nu-mer-at-ing
  e-nu-mer-a-tion
  e-nu-mer-a-tive
  e-nu-mer-a-tor
e-nun-ci-ate
  e-nun-ci-at-ed
  e-nun-ci-at-ing
  e-nun-ci-a-tion
  e-nun-ci-a-tive
  e-nun-ci-a-tor
en-u-re-sis
  en-u-ret-ic
en-vel-op
  en-vel-oped
  en-vel-op-ing
en-vi-a-ble
  en-vi-a-ble-ness
  en-vi-a-bly
en-vi-ous
  en-vi-ous-ly
  en-vi-ous-ness
en-vi-ron
  en-vi-ron-ment
  en-vi-ron-men-tal
  en-vi-ron-men-tal-ly
en-vi-rons
en-vis-age
  en-vis-aged
  en-vis-ag-ing
en-vi-sion
en-voy
en-vy

en-vies
en-vied
en-vy-ing
en-vi-er
en-vy-ing-ly
en-zyme
  en-zy-mat-ic
  en-zy-mat-i-cal-ly
e-on
ep-au-let
e-phed-rine
e-phem-er-al
  e-phem-er-al-ness
  e-phem-er-al-ly
ep-ic
  ep-i-cal
ep-i-cen-ter
ep-i-cure
  epi-cu-re-an
ep-i-dem-ic
  ep-i-dem-i-cal-ly
ep-i-der-mis
  ep-i-der-mal
  ep-i-der-mic
ep-i-glot-tis
ep-i-gram
ep-i-logue
  ep-i-log
epis-co-pa-cy
  epsi-co-pa-cies
epis-co-pal
epis-co-pa-lian
  epis-co-pa-lian-ism
epis-co-pate
ep-i-sode
  ep-i-sod-ic
  ep-i-sod-i-cal
  ep-i-sod-i-cal-ly
e-pis-te-mol-o-gy
  e-psi-te-mo-log-i-cal
  e-pis-te-mol-o-gist
e-pis-tle
e-pis-to-lar-y
ep-i-taph
  ep-i-taph-ic
  ep-i-taph-ist
ep-i-thet
  ep-i-thet-ic
  ep-i-thet-i-cal
e-pit-o-me
epit-o-mize
  epit-o-mized
  epit-o-miz-ing
ep-och
  ep-och-al
ep-ox-y

ep-ox-y res-in
ep-si-lon
eq-ua-ble
  eq-ua-bil-i-ty
  eq-ua-ble-ness
  eq-ua-bly
e-qual
  e-qualed
  e-qual-ling
  e-qual-ly
  e-qual-ness
e-qual-i-tar-i-an
  e-qual-i-tar-i-an-ism
e-qual-i-ty
  e-qual-i-ties
e-qual-ize
  e-qual-ized
  e-qual-iz-ing
  e-qual-i-za-tion
  e-qual-iz-er
e-qua-nim-i-ty
e-quate
  e-quat-ed
  e-quat-ing
e-qua-tion
  e-qua-tion-al
  e-qua-tion-al-ly
e-qua-tor
  e-qua-to-ri-al
  e-qua-to-ri-al-ly
e-ques-tri-an
  e-ques-tri-enne
e-qui-dis-tance
  e-qui-dis-tant
  e-qui-dis-tant-ly
e-qui-lat-er-al
e-qui-li-brate
  e-qui-li-brat-ed
  e-qui-li-brat-ing
  e-qui-li-bra-tion
  e-qui-i-bra-tor
e-qui-lib-ri-um
  e-qui-lib-ri-ums
  e-qui-lib-ria
e-quine
e-qui-noc-tial
e-qui-nox
e-quip
  e-quipped
  e-quip-ping
  e-quip-per
eq-ui-page
e-quip-ment
e-qui-poise
eq-ui-ta-ble
  eq-ui-ta-ble-ness

69

eq-ui-ta-bly
eq-ui-ty
  eq-ui-ties
e-quiv-a-lance
  e-quiv-a-len-cy
e-quiv-a-lent
  e-quiv-a-lent-ly
e-quiv-o-cal
  e-quiv-o-cal-ly
  e-quiv-o-cal-ness
e-quiv-o-cate
  e-quiv-o-cat-ed
  e-quiv-o-cat-ing
  e-quiv-o-ca-tor
  e-quiv-o-ca-tion
e-ra
e-rad-i-cate
  e-rad-i-cat-ed
  e-rad-i-cat-ing
  e-rad-i-ca-ble
  e-rad-i-ca-tion
  e-rad-i-ca-tive
  e-rad-i-ca-tor
e-rase
  e-rased
  e-ras-ing
  e-ras-a-bil-i-ty
  e-ras-a-ble
  e-ras-er
  e-ras-ure
e-rect
  e-rect-a-ble
  e-rect-er
  e-rec-tive
  e-rect-ly
  e-rect-ness
e-rec-tile
  e-rec-til-i-ty
e-rec-tion
e-rec-tor
er-go
er-mine
e-rode
  e-rod-ed
  e-rod-ing
e-rog-e-nous
e-ro-sion
e-rot-ic
  e-rot-i-cal-ly
e-rot-i-cism
err
  err-ing-ly
er-rand
er-rant
  er-rant-ly
er-rat-ic

er-rat-i-cal-ly
er-ra-tum
er-ra-ta
er-ro-ne-ous
  er-ro-ne-ous-ly
  er-ro-ne-ous-ness
er-ror
  er-ror-less
er-satz
erst-while
er-u-dite
  er-u-dite-ly
  er-u-dite-ness
er-u-di-tion
e-rupt
  e-rup-tion
  e-rup-tive
  e-rup-tive-ly
  e-rup-tive-ness
es-ca-lade
  es-ca-lad-ed
  es-ca-lad-ing
  es-ca-lad-er
es-ca-late
  es-ca-lat-ed
  es-ca-lat-ing
  es-ca-la-tion
  es-ca-la-tor
es-cal-lop
es-ca-pade
es-cape
  es-caped
  es-cap-ing
  es-cap-er
es-ca-pee
es-cap-ist
  es-cap-ism
es-carp-ment
es-chew
  es-chew-al
  es-chew-er
es-cort
es-cri-toire
es-crow
es-cutch-eon
  es-cutch-eoned
e-soph-a-gus
es-o-ter-ic
  es-o-ter-i-cal
  es-o-ter-i-cal-ly
es-pal-ier
es-pe-cial
  es-pe-cial-ly
  es-pe-cial-ness
es-pi-o-nage
es-pla-nade

es-pouse
  es-poused
  es-pous-ing
  es-pous-er
es-pous-al
es-pres-so
es-prit
es-prit de corps
es-py
  es-pied
  es-py-ing
es-quire
  es-quired
  es-quir-ing
es-say
  es-say-er
  es-say-ist
es-sence
es-sen-tial
  es-sen-ti-al-i-ty
  es-sen-tial-ly
  es-sen-tial-ness
es-tab-lish
  es-tab-lish-er
  es-tab-lish-ment
es-tate
es-teem
es-thete
  es-thet-ic
es-ti-ma-ble
  es-ti-ma-ble-ness
  es-ti-ma-bly
es-ti-mate
  es-ti-mat-ed
  es-ti-mat-ing
  es-ti-ma-tive
  es-ti-ma-tor
es-ti-ma-tion
es-trange
  es-tranged
  es-trang-ing
  es-trange-ment
  es-tran-ger
es-trus
es-tu-ar-y
  es-tu-ar-ies
  es-tu-ar-i-al
etch
  etch-er
  etch-ing
e-ter-nal
  e-ter-nal-ly
e-ter-ni-ty
e-ter-nize
  e-ter-nized
  e-ter-niz-ing

e-ter-ni-za-tion
eth-a-nol
e-ther
e-the-re-al
e-the-re-al-i-ty
e-the-re-al-ly
e-the-re-al-ness
e-the-re-al-ize
e-the-re-al-ized
e-the-re-al-iz-ing
e-the-re-al-i-za-tion
eth-ic
eth-i-cal
eth-i-cal-ly
eth-ics
eth-nic
eth-ni-cal
eth-ni-cal-ly
eth-nol-o-gy
eth-yl
eti-ol-o-gy
eti-o-log-ist
eti-o-log-i-cal
eti-o-log-i-cal-ly
et-i-quette
e-tude
et-y-mol-o-gy
et-y-mol-o-gies
et-y-mo-log-ic
et-y-mo-log-i-cal
et-y-mol-o-gist
eu-ca-lyp-tus
eu-ca-lyp-tus-es
eu-ca-lyp-ti
eu-gen-ic
eu-lo-gise
eu-lo-gized
eu-lo-giz-ing
eu-lo-gis-tic
eu-lo-gis-ti-cal-ly
eu-nuch
eu-phe-mism
eu-phe-mist
eu-phe-mis-tic
eu-phe-mis-ti-cal
eu-phe-mis-ti-cal-ly
eu-phe-mize
eu-phe-mized
eu-phe-miz-ing
eu-pho-ni-ous
eu-pho-ni-ous-ly
eu-pho-ni-ous-ness
eu-pho-ny
eu-phon-ic
eu-phon-i-cal
eu-phon-i-cal-ly

eu-pho-ria
eu-phor-ic
eu-re-ka
eu-tha-na-sia
e-vac-u-ate
e-vac-u-at-ed
e-vac-u-at-ing
e-vac-u-a-tion
e-vac-u-a-tive
e-vac-u-a-tor
e-vac-u-ee
e-vade
e-vad-ed
e-vad-ing
e-vad-a-ble
e-vad-er
e-vad-ing-ly
e-val-u-ate
e-val-u-at-ed
e-val-u-at-ing
e-val-u-a-tion
e-val-u-a-tor
ev-a-nesce
ev-a-nesced
ev-a-nesc-ing
ev-a-nes-cent
ev-a-nes-cence
ev-a-nes-cent-ly
e-van-gel
evan-gel-i-cal
evan-gel-ic
evan-gel-i-cal-ism
evan-gel-i-cal-ly
evan-gel-i-cal-ness
evan-ge-lism
evan-ge-lis-tic
evan-ge-lis-ti-cal-ly
evan-ge-list
evan-ge-lize
evan-ge-lized
evan-ge-liz-ing
evan-ge-li-za-tion
evan-ge-liz-er
e-vap-o-rate
e-vap-o-rat-ed
e-vap-o-rat-ing
e-vap-o-ra-ble
e-vap-o-ra-tion
e-vap-o-ra-tive
e-vap-o-ra-tor
e-va-sion
e-va-sive
e-va-sive-ly
e-va-sive-ness
e-ven
e-ven-ly

e-ven-ness
e-ven-hand-ed
eve-ning
e-vent
e-vent-ful
event-ful-ly
event-ful-ness
e-ven-tu-al
e-ven-tu-al-ly
e-ven-tu-al-i-ty
e-ven-tu-al-i-ties
e-ven-tu-ate
e-ven-tu-at-ed
e-ven-tu-at-ing
ev-er
ev-er-green
ev-er-last-ing
ev-er-last-ing-ly
ev-er-last-ing-ness
ev-er-more
e-vert
e-ver-si-ble
e-ver-sion
eve-ry
eve-ry-body
eve-ry-day
eve-ry-one
eve-ry-thing
eve-ry-where
e-vict
e-vic-tion
e-vic-tor
ev-i-dence
ev-i-denced
ev-i-denc-ing
ev-i-dent
ev-i-dent-ly
ev-i-den-tial
ev-i-den-tial-ly
e-vil
e-vince
e-vinced
e-vinc-ing
e-vin-ci-ble
e-vis-cer-ate
e-vis-cer-at-ed
e-vis-cer-at-ing
e-vis-cer-a-tion
e-voke
e-voked
e-vok-ing
ev-o-ca-tion
ev-o-lu-tion
ev-o-lu-tion-al
ev-o-lu-tion-ary
ev-o-lu-tion-ism

ev-ol-lu-tion-ist
e-volve
 e-volved
 e-volv-ing
 e-volv-a-ble
 e-volve-ment
 e-volv-er
ew-er
ex-ac-er-bate
 ex-ac-er-bat-ed
 ex-ac-er-bat-ing
 ex-ac-er-ba-tion
ex-act
 ex-act-a-ble
 ex-ac-tor
ex-act-ing
 ex-act-ing-ly
 ex-act-ing-ness
ex-act-i-tude
ex-act-ly
ex-ag-ger-ate
 ex-ag-ger-at-ed
 ex-ag-ger-at-ing
 ex-ag-ger-a-tion
 ex-ag-ger-a-tor
ex-alt
 ex-alt-er
 ex-al-ta-tion
ex-alt-ed
 ex-alt-ed-ly
 ex-alt-ed-ness
ex-am
ex-am-i-na-tion
ex-am-ine
 ex-am-ined
 ex-am-in-ing
 ex-am-in-a-ble
 ex-am-in-er
 ex-am-i-nee
ex-am-ple
 ex-am-pled
 ex-am-pling
ex-as-per-ate
 ex-as-per-at-ed
 ex-as-per-at-ing
 ex-as-per-a-tion
ex-ca-vate
 ex-ca-vat-ed
 ex-ca-cat-ing
 ex-ca-va-tion
 ex-ca-va-tor
ex-ceed
 ex-ceed-ing
 ex-ceed-ing-ly
ex-cel
 ex-celled

ex-cel-ling
ex-cel-lence
ex-cel-len-cy
 ex-cel-len-cies
ex-cel-lent
 ex-cel-lent-ly
ex-cel-si-or
ex-cept
 ex-cept-ing
 ex-cep-tion
 ex-cep-tion-a-ble
 ex-cep-tion-al
ex-cerpt
ex-cess
 ex-ces-sive
 ex-ces-sive-ly
 ex-ces-sive-ness
ex-change
 ex-changed
 ex-chang-ing
 ex-change-a-bil-i-ty
 ex-change-a-ble
 ex-chan-ger
ex-cheq-uer
ex-cise
 ex-cised
 ex-cis-ing
 ex-cis-a-ble
 ex-ci-sion
ex-cit-a-ble
 ex-cit-a-bil-i-ty
 ex-cit-a-bly
 ex-ci-ta-tion
ex-cite
 ex-cit-ed
 ex-cit-ing
ex-cit-ed
 ex-cit-ed-ly
 ex-cit-ed-ness
ex-cite-ment
ex-cit-ing
 ex-cit-ing-ly
ex-claim
ex-cla-ma-tion
 ex-clam-a-to-ry
 ex-clam-a-to-ri-ly
ex-clude
ex-clu-sion
ex-clu-sive
 ex-clu-sive-ly
 ex-clu-sive-ness
 ex-clu-siv-i-ty
ex-com-mu-ni-cate
ex-co-ri-ate
 ex-co-ri-at-ed
 ex-co-ri-at-ing

ex-co-ri-a-tion
ex-cre-ment
 ex-cre-men-tal
ex-cres-cense
 ex-cres-cent
ex-cre-ta
 ex-cre-tal
ex-crete
 ex-cret-ed
 ex-cret-ing
ex-cre-tion
ex-cru-ci-ate
 ex-cru-ci-at-ed
 ex-cru-ci-at-ing
 ex-cru-ci-at-ing-ly
 ex-cru-ci-a-tion
ex-cul-pate
 ex-cul-pat-ed
 ex-cul-pat-ing
 ex-cul-pa-tion
 ex-cul-pa-to-ry
ex-cur-sion
 ex-cur-sion-al
 ex-cur-sion-ary
 ex-cur-sion-ist
ex-cur-sive
 ex-cur-sive-ly
 ex-cur-sive-ness
ex-cus-a-to-ry
ex-cuse
ex-e-cra-ble
 ex-e-cra-ble-ness
 ex-e-cra-bly
ex-e-crate
 ex-e-crat-ed
 ex-e-crat-ing
 ex-e-cra-tive
 ex-e-cra-tor
ex-e-cra-tion
ex-e-cute
 ex-e-cut-ed
 ex-e-cut-ing
 ex-e-cut-a-ble
 ex-e-cut-er
ex-e-cu-tion
ex-e-cu-tion-er
ex-ec-u-tive
 ex-ec-u-tive-ly
ex-ec-u-tor
 ex-ec-u-tor-ship
ex-e-ge-sis
ex-em-pli-fy
 ex-em-pli-fied
 ex-em-pli-fy-ing
 ex-em-pli-fi-a-ble
 ex-em-pli-fi-ca-tion

ex-empt
ex-emp-tion
ex-er-cise
  ex-er-cised
  ex-er-cis-ing
  ex-er-cis-er
ex-ert
ex-er-tion
ex-fo-li-ate
  ex-fo-li-at-ed
  ex-fo-li-at-ing
  ex-fo-li-a-tion
ex-hal-la-tion
ex-hale
  ex-haled
  ex-hal-ing
  ex-hal-ant
ex-haust
ex-hib-it
  ex-hib-it-a-ble
  ex-hib-i-tor
  ex-hib-i-to-ry
ex-hi-bi-tion
  ex-hi-bi-tion-ism
  ex-hi-bi-tion-ist
  ex-hi-bi-tion-is-tic
ex-hil-a-rate
ex-hort
  ex-hor-ta-tive
  ex-hor-ta-to-ry
  ex-hort-er
  ex-hort-ing-ly
ex-hor-ta-tion
ex-hume
  ex-humed
  ex-hum-ing
ex-i-gen-cy
  ex-i-gen-cies
ex-i-gent
  ex-i-gent-ly
ex-ile
  ex-iled
ex-ist
  ex-ist-ence
  ex-ist-ent
ex-is-ten-tial
  ex-is-ten-tial-ly
ex-it
ex li-bris
ex-o-dus
ex of-fi-ci-o
ex-og-a-my
  ex-og-a-mous
ex-og-e-nous
  ex-og-e-nous-ly
ex-on-er-ate

ex-or-bi-tant
  ex-or-bi-tance
  ex-or-bi-tant-ly
ex-or-cise
  ex-or-cised
  ex-or-cis-ing
  ex-or-cism
  ex-or-cist
ex-o-tic
  ex-ot-i-cal-ly
  ex-ot-i-cism
ex-pand
  ex-pand-er
ex-panse
  ex-pan-si-ble
ex-pan-sion
  ex-pan-sion-ism
  ex-pan-sion-ist
ex-pan-sive
  ex-pan-sive-ly
  ex-pan-sive-ness
ex-pa-ti-ate
  ex-pa-ti-at-ed
  ex-pa-ti-at-ing
  ex-pa-ti-a-tion
ex-pa-tri-ate
  ex-pa-tri-at-ed
  ex-pa-tri-at-ing
  ex-pa-tri-a-tion
ex-pect
  ex-pect-a-ble
  ex-pect-a-bly
  ex-pect-ing-ly
ex-pect-an-cy
  ex-pect-an-cies
ex-pect-ant
  ex-pect-ant-ly
ex-pec-ta-tion
ex-pec-to-rate
  ex-pec-to-rat-ed
  ex-pec-to-rat-ing
  ex-pec-to-ra-tion
ex-pe-di-en-cy
ex-pe-di-ent
  ex-pe-di-ent-ly
ex-pe-dite
  ex-pe-dit-ed
  ex-pe-dit-ing
  ex-pe-dit-er
ex-pe-di-tion
  ex-pe-di-tion-ary
ex-pe-di-tious
  ex-pe-di-tious-ly
ex-pel
  ex-pelled
  ex-pel-ling

ex-pend
  ex-pend-a-ble
  ex-pend-a-bil-i-ty
ex-pend-i-ture
ex-pense
  ex-pen-sive
  ex-pen-sive-ly
  ex-pen-sive-ness
ex-pe-ri-ence
  ex-pe-ri-enced
  ex-pe-ri-enc-ing
ex-pe-ri-en-tial
  ex-pe-ri-en-tial-ly
ex-per-i-ment
  ex-per-i-men-ta-tion
  ex-per-i-men-tal
  ex-per-i-men-tal-ism
  ex-per-i-men-tal-ist
  ex-per-i-men-tal-ly
ex-pert
  ex-pert-ly
  ex-pert-ness
ex-per-tise
ex-pi-ra-tion
  ex-pir-a-to-ry
ex-pire
  ex-pired
  ex-pir-ing
ex-plain
  ex-plain-a-ble
  ex-plain-er
ex-pla-na-tion
  ex-plan-a-to-ry
  ex-plan-a-to-ri-ly
ex-ple-tive
ex-pli-ca-ble
ex-pli-cate
  ex-pli-cat-ed
  ex-pli-cat-ing
  ex-pli-ca-tion
  ex-pli-ca-tive
  ex-pli-ca-tor
ex-plic-it
  ex-plic-it-ly
  ex-plic-it-ness
ex-plode
  ex-plod-ed
  ex-plod-ing
  ex-plod-er
ex-ploit
  ex-ploit-a-ble
  ex-ploi-ta-tion
  ex-ploit-er
  ex-ploit-ive
ex-plore
  ex-plo-ra-tion

ex-plor-a-to-ry
ex-plor-er
ex-plo-sion
ex-plo-sive
ex-plo-sive-ly
ex-plo-sive-ness
ex-po-nent
ex-po-nen-tial
ex-po-nen-tial-ly
ex-port
ex-port-a-ble
ex-por-ta-tion
ex-port-er
ex-pose
ex-posed
ex-pos-ing
ex-pos-er
ex-po-si-tion
ex-pos-i-tor
ex-pos-i-to-ry
ex post fac-to
ex-pos-tu-late
ex-po-sure
ex-pound
ex-pound-er
ex-press
ex-press-er
ex-press-i-ble
ex-pres-sion
ex-pres-sive
ex-pres-sive-ly
ex-pres-sive-ness
ex-press-ly
ex-press-way
ex-pro-pri-ate
ex-pro-pri-at-ing
ex-pro-pri-a-tor
ex-pro-pri-a-tion
ex-pul-sion
ex-pul-sive
ex-punge
ex-pur-gate
ex-pur-ga-to-ry
ex-pur-ga-to-ri-al
ex-qui-site
ex-qui-site-ly
ex-qui-site-ness
ex-tant
ex-tem-po-ra-ne-ous
ex-tem-po-rize
ex-tem-po-rized
ex-tem-po-riz-ing
ex-tem-po-ri-za-tion
ex-tem-po-riz-er
ex-tend
ex-tend-i-bil-i-ty

ex-tend-i-ble
ex-tend-ed
ex-tend-ed-ly
ex-tend-ed-ness
ex-tend-er
ex-ten-si-ble
ex-ten-si-bil-i-ty
ex-ten-sion
ex-ten-sion-al
ex-ten-sive
ex-ten-sive-ly
ex-ten-sive-ness
ex-tent
ex-ten-u-ate
ex-te-ri-or
ex-te-ri-or-ly
ex-ter-mi-nate
ex-ter-mi-nat-ed
ex-ter-mi-nat-ing
ex-ter-mi-na-tion
ex-ter-mi-na-tor
ex-ter-nal
ex-ter-nal-ly
ex-tinct
ex-tinc-tion
ex-tin-guish
ex-tin-guish-a-ble
ex-tin-guish-er
ex-tin-guish-ment
ex-tir-pate
ex-tir-pat-ed
ex-tir-pat-ing
ex-tir-pa-tion
ex-tir-pa-tive
ex-tol
ex-tol-ler
ex-tol-lingly
ex-tol-ment
ex-tort
ex-tor-ter
ex-tor-tive
ex-tor-tion
ex-tra
ex-tract
ex-tract-a-ble
ex-trac-tive
ex-trac-tor
ex-trac-tion
ex-tra-cur-ric-u-lar
ex-tra-dite
ex-tra-ne-ous
ex-tra-ne-ous-ly
ex-tra-ne-ous-ness
ex-traor-di-nary
ex-traor-di-nar-i-ly
ex-trap-o-late

ex-trap-o-lat-ed
ex-trap-o-lat-ing
ex-trap-o-la-tion
ex-tra-sen-so-ry
ex-tra-ter-res-tri-al
ex-tra-ter-ri-to-ri-al
ex-trav-a-gance
ex-trav-a-gan-cy
ex-trav-a-gant
ex-trav-a-gant-ly
ex-trav-a-gan-za
ex-treme
ex-treme-ly
ex-treme-ness
ex-trem-ist
ex-trem-ism
ex-trem-i-ty
ex-trem-i-ties
ex-tri-cate
ex-tri-cat-ed
ex-tri-cat-ing
ex-tri-ca-ble
ex-tri-ca-tion
ex-trin-sic
ex-tro-vert
ex-tro-ver-sion
ex-trude
ex-u-ber-ance
ex-u-ber-ant
ex-u-ber-ant-ly
ex-ude
ex-ud-ed
ex-ud-ing
ex-u-da-tion
ex-ult
ex-ult-ant
ex-ult-ant-ly
ex-ul-at-tion
ex-ult-ing-ly
ex-ur-ban-ite
eye
eyed
eye-ing
eye-ball
eye-glass
eye-glass-es
eye-hole
eye-lash
eye-let
eye-lid
eye-o-pen-er
eye-o-pen-ing
eye-wit-ness
ey-rie
ey-ry
ey-ries

fa-ble
  fa-bled
fab-ric
fab-ri-cate
  fab-ri-cated
  fab-ri-cat-ing
  fab-ri-ca-tion
fab-u-lous
  fab-u-lous-ness
fa-cade
  fa-cades
face
  faced
  fac-ing
face card
face--lift
fac-et
fa-ce-tious
  fa-ce-tious-ly
fa-cial
  fa-cial-ly
fac-ile
  fac-ile-ly
  fac-ile-ness
fa-cil-i-tate
fa-cil-i-ty
fac-ing
fac-sim-i-le
fact
fac-tion
  fac-tion-al
  fac-tion-al-ly
fac-ti-tious
  fac-ti-tious-ly
fac-ti-tious-ness
fac-tor
fac-to-ry
  fac-to-ries
fac-to-tum
fac-tu-al
fac-ul-ty
fad
  fad-dish
  fad-dist
fade
  fad-ed
  fad-ing
fa-er-ie
  fa-ery
  fa-er-ies
fag
  faggged
  fag-ging
fag-got
fag-ot
Fahr-en-heit

fail-ing
  fail-ing-ly
fail-safe
fail-ure
faint
  faint-ly
  faint-ness
faint-heart-ed
fair
  fir-ness
fair-ground
fair-ly
fair-mind-ed
fair--trade
fair-y
  fair-ies
fair-y-like
fair-y tale
faith
  faith-ful
  faith-ful-less
fake
  faked
  fak-ing
  fak-er
fal-con
fal-con-ry
fall
  fall-en
  fall-ing
fal-la-cious
  fal-la-cious-ly
fal-la-cy
fall-guy
fal-li-ble
  fal-li-bly
fail-ing star
fall-out
fal-low
  fal-low-ness
false
  fals-er
  fals-est
false-hood
fal-si-fy
  fal-si-fied
  fal-si-fy-ing
  fal-si-fi-er
fal-si-ty
fal-ter
  fal-ter-er
  fal-ter-ing-ly
fame
famed
fa-mil-ial
fa-mil-iar

fa-mil-iar-ly
fa-mil-i-ar-i-ty
fa-mil-iar-ize
  fa-mil-iar-ized
  fa-mil-iar-iz-ing
fam-ily
  fam-i-lies
fam-ine
fam-ish
fam-ished
fa-mous
  fa-mous-ly
fan
  fan-like
  fan-ner
fa-nat-ic
  fa-nat-i-cal
fa-nat-i-cism
fa-nat-i-cize
  fa-nat-i-cized
fan-ci-er
fan-ci-ul
  fan-ci-ful-ly
fan-cy
  fan-cies
  fan-ci-ly
  fan-ci-ness
fan-cy-work
fan-fare
fang
fanged
fan-light
fan-tas-tic
  fan-tas-ti-cal
fan-ta-sy
  fan-ta-sies
far
  far-ther
  far-thest
far-a-way
farce
  farced
  farc-ing
far-ci-cal
  far-ci-cal-ly
fare
  fared
  far-ing
fare-well
far-fetched
far-flung
farm
farm-er
farm-hand
farm-house
farm-ing

farm-yard
far-off
far-reach-ing
  far-reach-ing-ly
far-see-ing
far-sight-ed
  far-sight-ed-ly
far-ther
far-ther-most
far-thest
fas-ci-a
  fas-ci-ae
fas-ci-cle
  fas-ci-cled
fas-ci-nate
  fas-ci-nat-ed
  fas-ci-nat-ing
fas-ci-na-tion
fas-cism
  fas-cist
  fa-scis-tic
fash-ion
fash-ion-ble
fast
fas-ten
  fas-ten-er
  fas-ten-ing
fas-tid-i-ous
  fas-ti-di-ous-ly
fat
  fat-ter
  fat-test
fa-tal
  fa-tal-ly
fa-tal-ism
  fa-tal-ist
fa-tal-i-ty
  fa-tal-i-ties
fate
  fat-ed
  fat-ing
fate-ful
  fate-ful-ly
  fate-ful-ness
fa-ther
fa-ther-hood
  fa-ther-ly
fa-ther-in-law
  fa-thers-in-law
fa-ther-land
fath-om
  fath-om-a-ble
  fath-om-less
fa-tique
  fa-tiqued
  fa-tiq-uing

fat-i-ga-ble
fat-ten
  fat-ten-er
fat-ty
  fat-ti-er
  fat-ti-est
  fat-ti-ness
  fat-tish
fa-tu-i-ty
  fa-tui-ties
fat-u-ous
  fat-u-ous-ly
  fat-u-ous-ness
fau-cet
fault
fault-find-er
  fault-find-ing
fault-less
  fault-less-ly
fault-less-ness
fault-y
  fault-i-er
  fault-i-est
  fault-i-ly
fau-na
  fau-nas
  fau-nae
faux pas
fa-vor
  fa-vor-ing-ly
fa-vor-a-ble
  fa-vor-ably
fa-vored
  fa-vored-ly
  fa-vored-ness
fa-vor-ite
fa-vor-it-ism
fawn
faze
  fazed
  faz-ing
fe-al-ty
fear
fear-ful
  fear-ful-ly
  fear-ful-ness
fear-less
  fear-less-ly
  fear-less-ness
fear-some
  fear-some-ly
  fear-some-ness
fea-si-ble
  fea-si-bil-i-ty
  fea-si-ble-ness
  fea-si-bly

feast
feat
feath-er
  fea-thered
feath-er-bed-ding
fea-ture
  fea-tured
  fea-tur-ing
fea-ture-ness
fe-brile
fe-ces
fe-cal
feck-less
fe-cund
  fe-cun-di-ty
fe-cun-date
  fe-cun-dat-ed
  fe-cun-da-tion
fed-er-al
fed-er-al-ism
fed-er-al-li-ist
fed-er-al-ize
  fed-er-al-ized
  fed-er-al-iz-ing
  fed-er-al-i-za-tion
  fed-er-al-ly
fed-er-ate
  fed-er-at-ed
  fed-er-at-ing
fed-er-a-tion
fee
fee-ble
  fee-bler
  fee-blest
  fee-bly
fee-ble-mind-ed
  fee-ble-mind-ed-ness
feed
  fed
  feed-ing
  feed-er
feed-back
feel
  feel-ing
feel-er
feel-ing
  feel-ing-ly
  feel-ing-ness
feign
  feigned
  feign-ed-ly
  feign-er
  feign-ing-ly
feint
feist-y
  feist-i-er

feist-i-est
fe-lic-i-tate
fe-lic-i-tat-ed
fe-lic-i-tat-ing
fe-lic-i-ta-tion
fe-lic-i-tous
fe-lic-i-tous-ly
fe-lic-i-ty
fe-lic-i-ties
fe-line
fe-line-ly
fe-line-i-ty
fell
fel-la-ti-o
fel-low
fel-low-ship
fe-lon
fel-o-ny
fel-o-nies
fe-lo-ni-ous
fe-lo-ni-ous-ly
fe-male
fem-i-nine
fem-i-nine-ly
fem-i-nine-ness
fem-i-nin-i-ty
fem-i-nism
fem-i-nist
fem-i-nis-tic
fem-i-nize
fem-i-nized
fem-i-niz-ing
fe-mur
fe-murs
fem-o-ra
fem-o-ral
fen
fen-ny
fen-ni-er
fen-ni-est
fence
fecned
fenc-ing
fenc-er
fen-der
fe-ral
fer-ment
fer-ment-a-ble
fer-men-ta-tion
fern
fern-er-y
fern-er-ies
fe-ro-cious
fe-ro-cious-ly
fe-ro-ci-ty
fer-ret

fer-ret-er
fer-ro-con-crete
fer-ro-mag-net-ic
fer-ru-gi-nous
fer-rule
fer-ry
fer-ries
fer-ry-boat
fer-ry-man
fer-tile
fer-tile-ly
fer-tile-ness
fer-til-i-ty
fer-ti-li-za-tion
fer-ti-li-za-tion-al
fer-ti-lize
fer-ti-lized
fer-ti-liz-ing
fer-ti-liz-a-ble
fer-ti-liz-er
fer-vent
fer-ven-cy
fer-vid
fer-vid-ly
fer-vid-ness
fer-vor
fes-ter
fes-ti-val
fes-tive
fes-tive-ly
fes-tive-ness
fes-tiv-i-ty
fes-toon
fes-toon-ery
fes-toon-er-ies
fe-tal
fetch
fetch-er
fetch-ing
fetch-ing-ly
fete
fet-id
fet-id-ly
fet-id-ness
fet-ish
fet-ish-ism
fet-ish-ist
fet-ish-is-tic
fet-lock
fet-ter
fet-tle
fe-tus
fe-tus-es
feud
feud-ist
feu-dal

feu-dal-ism
feu-dal-ist
feu-dal-is-tic
feu-dal-i-za-tion
feu-dal-ize
feu-dal-ized
feu-dal-iz-ing
fe-ver
fe-ver blis-ter
fe-ver-ish
fe-ver-ish-ly
fe-ver-ish-ness
fe-ver-ous
fe-ver-ous-ly
few
few-ness
fez-zes
fi-as-co
fi-as-cos
fi-as-coes
fi-at
fib
fi-ber
fi-bered
fi-ber-board
fi-ber-glass
fi-bril
fi-bril-la-tion
fi-broid
fi-brous
fib-u-la
fib-u-las
fib-u-lae
fick-le
fick-le-ness
fic-tion
fic-tion-al
fic-tion-al-ly
fic-ti-tious
fid-dle
fid-dler
fid-dled
fi-del-i-ty
fidg-et
fidg-ety
field-er
field-glass
fiend
fiend-ish
fiend-ish-ly
fiend-ish-ness
fierce
fierce-ly
fierce-ness
fier-y
fier-i-er

fier-i-est
fier-i-ly
fier-i-ness
fif-teen
fif-teenth
fifth
fif-ti-eth
fif-ty
fif-ties
fight
fight-er
fig-ment
fig-u-ra-tion
fig-u-ra-tive
fig-u-ra-tive-ly
fid-u-ra-tive-ness
fig-ure
fig-ured
fig-ur-ing
fig-ur-er
fig-ure-head
fig-ur-ine
fil-a-ment
fil-a-men-ta-ry
fil-a-ment-ed
fil-a-men-tous
filch
file
filed
fil-ing
fi-let
fi-let mi-gnon
fil-i-al
fil-i-al-ly
fil-i-bus-ter
fil-i-gree
fil-i-greed
fil-i-gree-ing
fil-lings
fill-er
fil-let
fill-ing
fil-lip
fil-ly
fil-lies
film-strip
film-y
film-i-er
film-i-est
film-i-ness
fil-ter
filth
filth-i-ness
filthy
filth-i-er
filth-i-est

fin
finned
fin-ning
fin-less
fin-like
fi-na-gled
fi-na-gling
fi-na-gler
fi-nal
fi-na-le
fi-nal-ist
fi-nal-i-ty
fi-nal-i-ties
fi-nal-ize
fi-nal-ized
fi-nal-iz-ing
fi-nal-ly
fi-nance
fi-nanced
fi-nanc-ing
fi-nan-cial
fi-nan-cial-ly
fin-an-cier
finch
find
found
find-ing
find-er
fine
fin-er
fin-est
fine-ly
fine-ness
fin-er-y
fin-er-ies
fi-nesse
fi-nessed
fi-ness-ing
fin-ger
fin-ger-bowl
fin-ger-ing
fin-ger-nail
fin-ger-print
fin-i-al
fin-i-cal
fin-i-cal-ly
fin-ick-y
fin-ick-ing
fin-is
fin-is-es
fin-ish
fin-ished
fin-ish-er
fi-nite
fi-nite-ly
fi-nite-ness

fire
fired
fir-ing
fir-er
fire-arm
fire-ball
fire-brand
fire-bug
fire-crack-er
fire-fight-er
fire-fly
fire-flies
fire-man
fire-place
fire-plug
fire-pow-er
fire-proof
fire-side
fire-trap
fire-wa-ter
fire-wood
fire-works
fir-ing-squad
firm
firm-ly
firm-ness
fir-ma-ment
first-born
first-hand
first-ling
first-ly
first-rate
first-string
fis-cal
fis-cal-ly
fish-er
fish-er-man
fish-er-men
fish-er-y
fish-er-ies
fish-hook
fish-ing
fish-wife
fish-wived
fish-y
fish-i-er
fish-i-est
fis-sle
fis-sion
fis-sure
fis-sured
fis-sur-ing
fist-ic
fist-i-cuff
fit
fit-ter

fit-test
fit-ted
fit-ting
fit-ly
fit-ness
fit-ful
  fit-ful-ly
  fit-ful-ness
fit-ting
  fit-ting-ly
  fit-ting-ness
five-fold
five-and-ten
fix
  fix-a-ble
  fixed
  fix-ed-ly
  fix-er
fix-a-tion
fix-a-tive
fix-ings
fix-i-ty
  fix-i-ties
fix-ture
fiz-zle
  fiz-zled
  fiz-zling
fiz-zy
  fiz-zi-er
  fiz-zi-est
flab-ber-gast
flab-by
  flab-bi-er
  flab-bi-est
  flab-bi-ly
  flab-bi-ness
flac-cid
flag
  flagged
  flag-ging
flag-el-lant
  flag-el-lat-ed
  flag-el-lat-ing
  flag-el-la-tion
fla-gi-tious
flag-on
flag-pole
flag-rank
fla-grant
  fla-grant-ly
flag-ship
flag-stone
flail
flair
flake
  flaked

flak-ing
flak-y
  flak-i-er
  flak-i-est
  flak-i-ness
flam-boy-ant
  flam-boy-ance
  flam-boy-an-cy
  flam-boy-ant-ly
flame
  flamed
  falm-ing
  flam-ing-ly
flam-ma-ble
flange
flank
  flank-er
flan-nel-ette
flap
  flapped
  flap-ping
  flap-per
flap-jack
flare
  flared
  flar-ing
flare-up
flash-back
flash-light
  flash-i-er
  flash-i-est
  flash-i-ly
  flash-i-ness
flask
flat
  flat-ly
  flat-ted
  flat-ting
  flat-ness
flat-car
flat-foot
  flat-foot-ed
  flat-foot-ed-ly
falt-ten
  flat-ten-er
flat-ter
  flat-ter-er
  flat-ter-ing-ly
flat-ter-y
  flat-ter-ies
flat-u-lent
  flat-u-lence
  flat-u-len-cy
  flat-u-lent-ly
flat-ware
flaunt

flaunt-er
flaunt-ing-ly
flanty
flaunt-i-er
flaunt-i-est
flau-tist
fla-vor
  fla-vored
  fla-vor-less
  fla-vor-ing
  flaw-less
fla-zen
flax-seed
flay-er
flea-bite
  flea-bit-ten
fleck
flec-tion
fledge
  fledged
  fledg-ing
fledg-ling
flee
  fled
  flee-ing
fleece
  fleeced
  fleec-ing
fleec-y
  fleec-i-er
  fleec-i-est
  fleec-i-ness
fleet
  fleet-ly
  fleet-ness
fleet-ing
  fleet-ing-ly
  fleet-ing-ness
flesh-ly
  flesh-li-er
  flesh-li-est
flesh-pots
flesh-y
  flesh-i-ert
  flesh-i-est
flesh-i-ness
flex-i-ble
  flex-i-bil-i-ty
  flex-i-bly
flex-ion
flex-or
flex-ure
fib-ber-ti-gib-bet
flick-er
  flick-er-ing
fli-er

flight
  flight-less
flight-y
  flight-i-er
  flight-i-est
  flight-i-ly
  flight-i-ness
flim-flam
  flim-flammed
  flim-flam-ming
firm-sy
  firm-si-er
  firm-si-est
  firm-si-ly
  firm-si-ness
flinch
  flinch-er
  flinch-ing-ly
fin-ders
fling
  flung
  fling-ing
flint-y
  flint-i-er
  flint-i-est
  flint-i-ness
flip
  flipped
  flip-ping
  flip-flop
flip-pant
  flip-pan-cy
  flip-pant-ly
flip-per
flirt-er
flir-ta-tion
  flir-ta-tious
flit
  flit-ted
  flit-ting
  flit-ter
float-a-ble
float-a-tion
float-er
float-ing
floc-cu-lent
  floc-cu-lence
flocked
flood-gate
flood-light
  flood-lit
floor-ing
floor-walk-er
floo-zy
  floo-zies
flop

flopped
  flop-ping
  flop-per
flop-house
flop-py
  flop-pi-er
  flop-pi-est
  flop-pi-ly
flo-ra
  flo-ras
  flo-rae
flo-ral
flo-res-cence
  flo-res-cent
flo-ret
flo-ri-cul-ture
  flo-ri-cul-tur-al
  flo-ri-cul-tur-ist
flor-id
  flo-rid-i-ty
  flor-id-ly
  flor-id-ness
flo-rist
floss
  flossy
  floss-i-er
  floss-i-est
flo-ta-tion
flo-til-la
flot-sam
flounce
  flounced
  flounc-ing
floun-der
flour-y
  flour-i-er
  flour-i-est
flour-ish
  flou-rish-ing
flow-er
  flow-ered
  flow-er-ing
flow-ery
  flow-er-i-ness
flub
  flubbed
  flub-bing
fluc-tu-ate
  fluc-tu-at-ed
  fluc-tu-at-ing
  fluc-tu-a-tion
flue
  flu-ent
  flu-ency
  flu-ent-ly
fluff

fluff-i-ness
fluff-y
  fluff-i-er
  fluff-i-est
flu-id
  flu-id-ly
  flu-id-ness
fluke
  fluky
  fluk-i-er
  fluk-i-est
flum-mer-y
  flum-mer-ies
flun-ky
  flunk-ies
flu-o-resce
  flu-o-resced
  flu-o-resc-ing
flu-o-res-cence
  flu-o-res-cent
flur-ry
  flur-ries
  flur-ried
  flur-ry-ing
flus-ter
flute
  flut-ed
  flut-ing
  flut-ist
flut-ter
  flut-ter-er
  flut-ter-ing-ly
  flut-tery
  flut-ter-i-er
  flut-ter-i-est
flux-ion
fly-brown
fly-by-night
fly-er
fly-ing
fly-leaf
  fly-leaves
fly-pa-per
fly-speck
fly-wheel
foal
foam
  foam-i-ness
  foam-y
  foam-i-er
  foam-i-est
fob
  fobbed
  fob-bing
fo-cal
  fo-cal-ize

fo-cal-lized
fo-cal-iz-ing
fo-cus
  fo-cus-es
  fo-cus-ing
  fo-cus-er
fod-der
foe-tus
  foe-tal
fog
  fogged
  fog-ging
fog-gy
  fog-gi-er
  fog-gi-est
  fog-gi-ly
  fog-gi-ness
fog-horn
fo-gy
  fo-gies
  fo-gy-ish
foi-ble
fold-er
fol-de-rol
fo-li-a-ceous
fo-li-age
fo-li-ate
  fo-li-at-ed
  fo-li-at-ing
  fol-li-a-tion
fo-li-o
  fo-li-os
  fol-li-oed
  fo-li-o-ing
folk-lore
  folk-lor-ist
flok-sy
  flok-si-er
  flok-si-est
  flok-si-ness
folk-ways
fol-li-cle
  fol-lic-u-lar
fol-low
  fol-low-er
  fol-low-ing
fol-ly
  fol-lies
fo-ment
  fo-men-ta-tion
  fo-ment-er
fon-dant
fon-dle
  fond-led
  fon-dling
  fon-dler

fond-ly
fond-ness
fon-due
food-stuff
fool-er-y
  fool-er-ies
fool-har-dy
  fool-har-di-ness
fool-proof
fools-cap
foot-age
foot-ball
foot-board
foot-can-dle
foot-ed
foot-fall
foot-hill
foot-hold
foot-ing
foot-lights
foot-loose
foot-note
  foot-not-ed
  foot-not-ing
foot-path
foot-print
foot-sore
foot-step
foot-stool
foot-wear
foot-work
foo-zle
  foo-zled
  foo-zling
fop
  fop-pery
  fop-per-ies
  fop-pish
  fop-pish-ly
  fop-pish-ness
for-age
  for-aged
  for-ag-ing
for-ay
for-bear
  for-bore
  for-borned
  for-bear-ing
  for-bear-ance
  for-bear-ing-ly
for-bid
  for-bade
  for-bid-den
  for-bid-ding
  for-bid-ding-ness
force

forced
forc-ing
forc-a-ble
force-less
forc-er
force-ful
  force-ful-ly
  force-ful-ness
for-ceps
for-ci-ble
  for-ci-bly
ford-a-ble
fore-arm
fore-bear
fore-bode
  fore-bod-ed
  fore-bod-ing
  fore-bod-er
fore-brain
fore-cast
  fore-cast-ed
  fore-cast-ing
  fore-cast-er
fore-close
  fore-closed
  fore-clos-ing
  fore-clo-sure
fore-fa-ther
fore-fin-ger
fore-foot
  fore-feet
fore-front
fore-gath-er
fore-go
  fore-went
  fore-gone
  fore-go-ing
fore-ground
fore-hand
  fore-hand-ed
  fore-hand-ed-ness
fore-head
for-eign
  for-eign-er
  for-eign-ness
fore-know
  fore-knew
  fore-known
  fore-know-ing
  fore-knowl-edge
fore-leg
fore-lock
fore-man
  fore-men
fore-most
fore-noon

fo-ren-sic
fore-or-dain
fore-quar-ter
fore-run
  fore-ran
  fore-run-ning
fore-run-ner
fore-see
  fore-saw
  fore-seen
  fore-see-ing
  fore-see-a-ble
  fore-se-er
fore-shad-ow
  fore-shad-ow-er
fore-sight
  fore-sight-ed
  fore-sight-ed-ness
fore-skin
for-est
fore-stall
for-est-a-tion
for-es-ter
for-es-try
fore-taste
  fore-tast-ed
  fore-tast-ing
fore-tell
  fore-told
  fore-tell-ing
  fore-tell-er
fore-thought
for-ev-er
for-ev-er-more
fore-warn
fore-word
for-feit
  for-feit-er
for-fei-ture
for-gath-er
forge
  forged
  forg-ing
  forg-er
for-ger-y
  fog-er-ies
for-get
  for-got
  for-got-ten
  for-get-ting
  for-get-ta-ble
  for-get-ter
for-get-ful
  for-get-ful-ly
  for-get-ful-ness
for-give

for-gave
for-giv-en
for-giv-ing
for-giv-a-ble
for-give-ness
for-giv-er
for-go
  for-went
  for-gone
  for-go-ing
  for-go-er
fork-loft
for-lorn
  for-lorn-ly
  for-lorn-ness
for-mal
  for-mal-ly
for-mal-ism
for-mal-i-ty
  for-mal-i-ties
for-mal-ize
  for-mal-ized
  for-mal-iz-ing
  for-mal-i-za-tion
for-mat
for-ma-tion
form-a-tive
for-mer
  for-mer-ly
for-mi-da-ble
  for-mi-da-ble-ness
  for-mi-da-bly
form-less
  form-less-ly
  form-less-ness
for-mu-la
  for-mu-las
  for-mu-lae
for-mu-lar-y
  for-mu-lar-ies
for-mu-late
  for-mu-lat-ed
  for-mu-lat-ing
  for-mu-la-tion
  for-mu-la-tor
for-ni-cate
  for-ni-cat-ed
  for-ni-cat-ing
  for-ni-cat-or
  for-ni-ca-tion
for-sake
  for-soke
  for-sak-en
  for-sak-ing
  for-sak-en-ly
for-swear

for-swore
for-sworn
for-swear-ing
for-swear-er
fort
forte
forth-com-ing
forth-right
  forth-right-ness
forth-with
for-ti-fi-ca-tion
for-ti-fy
  for-ti-fied
  for-ti-fy-ing
  for-ti-fi-er
for-tis-si-mo
for-ti-tude
fort-night
for-night-ly
  for-night-lies
for-tress
for-tu-i-tous
  for-tu-i-tous-ly
  for-tu-i-tous-ness
for-tu-nate
  for-tu-nate-ly
for-tune
for-tune-tell-er
  for-tune-tell-ing
for-ty
  for-ties
for-ty-nin-er
fo-rum
  fo-rums
  fo-ra
for-ward
  for-ward-er
  for-ward-ly
  for-ward-ness
fos-sil
fos-sil-ize
  fos-sil-ized
  fos-sil-iz-ing
  fos-sil-i-za-tion
fos-ter
  fos-tered
  fos-ter-ing
fought
fou-lard
found
foun-da-tion
  foun-da-tion-al
found-er
found-ling
found-ry
  found-ries

foun-tain	fran-tic	fres-coes
foun-tain-head	fran-ti-cal-ly	fres-cos
four-flush-er	fra-ter-nal	fres-coed
four-square	fra-ter-nal-ly	fres-co-ing
four-teen	fra-ter-ni-ty	fresh
four-teenth	fra-ter-ni-ties	fresh-ly
fourth	frat-er-nize	fresh-ness
fourth-ly	frat-ri-cide	fresh-en
fowl	frat-ri-cid-al	fresh-en-er
fowl-er	fraud-u-lent	fresh-et
fox-hole	fraud-u-lence	fresh-man
fox-i-er	fraught	fresh-men
fox-i-est	fraz-zle	fret
fox-i-ly	fraz-zled	fret-ted
fox-i-ness	fraz-zling	fret-work
foy-er	freak	fri-ary
fra-cas	freak-ish	fri-ar-ies
fra-cas-es	freck-le	fric-as-see
frac-tion	freck-led	fric-as-seed
frac-tion-al	freck-li-er	fric-tion
frac-tious	free	fric-tion-al
frac-tious-ly	fre-er	friend
frac-ture	free-ly	friend-less
frac-tured	free-bie	friend-ly
frac-tur-ing	free-boot-er	friend-li-er
frag-ile	free-dom	friend-li-est
fra-gil-i-ty	free-lance	frieze
frag-ment	free-lanced	fright-ful
frag-ment-al	free-lanc-ing	fright-ful-ly
frag-men-ter-i-ness	free-spoken	frig-id
frag-men-tary	free-spo-ken-ness	fri-gid-i-ty
frag-men-ta-tion	free-stone	frig-id-ly
frag-ment-ize	free-think-ing	frig-id-ness
frag-ment-ized	free-way	frilly
frag-ment-iz-ing	free-wheel	frill-i-er
fra-grance	freeze	frill-i-est
fra-grant	froze	fringe
fra-grant-ly	fro-zen	fringed
frail	freez-ing	fring-ing
frail-ty	freeze-dry	frip-pery
frail-ness	freeze-dried	frip-per-ies
frame	freeze-dry-ing	frisky
framed	freez-er	frisk-i-er
fram-ing	fre-net-ic	fit-ter
fram-er	fre-net-i-cal-ly	friv-o-lous
frame-up	fren-zy	fri-vol-i-ty
frame-work	fren-zies	frizz
franc	fren-zied	friz-zi-ness
fran-chise	fren-zy-ing	friz-zi-er
fran-chised	fre-quen-cy	friz-zle
frank	fre-quen-cies	friz-zled
frank-er	fre-quent	friz-zling
frank-ly	fre-quent-er	frol-ic
frank-ness	fre-quent-ly	frol-ick-ed
frank-furt-er	fre-quen-ta-tive	frol-ick-ing
frank-in-cense	fres-co	frol-ic-some

front-age
fron-tal-ly
fron-tier
frost
frost-ed
frost-bite
frost-bit
frost-bit-ten
frost-bit-ting
frost-ing
frost-y
frost-i-er
froth
froth-i-ness
frothy
froth-i-er
froth-i-est
frou-frou
fro-ward
frown
frown-ing-ly
frow-zy
frow-zi-er
fro-zen
fro-zen-ly
fro-zen-ness
fruc-ti-fy
fruc-ti-fied
fruc-ti-fy-ing
fruc-ti-fi-ca-tion
fru-gal
fru-gal-i-ty
fru-gal-i-ties
fru-gal-ly
fruit-ful
fruit-ful-ly
fru-i-tion
fruit-less-ly
fruity
frump
frump-ish
frump-i-est
frus-trate
frus-trat-ed
frus-trat-ing
frus-tra-tion
fry
fried
fry-ing
fry-er
fud-dle
fud-dled
fud-dling
fudge
fudged
fudg-ing

fu-el
fu-eled
fu-el-ing
fu-gi-tive
fu-gi-tive-ly
ful-crum
ful-crums
ful-cra
ful-fill
ful-filled
ful-fil-ling
ful-fil-ment
full
full-ness
ful-ly
full-back
ful-mi-nate
ful-mi-nat-ed
ful-mi-nat-ing
ful-mi-na-tion
ful-some
ful-some-ly
fum-ble
fum-bled
fum-bling
fum-bler
fume
fumed
fum-ing
fum-ing-ly
fu-mi-gate
fu-mi-gat-ed
fu-mi-gat-ing
func-tion
func-tion-less
func-tion-al
func-tion-al-ly
func-tion-ary
func-tion-ar-ies
fun-da-men-tal
fun-da-men-tal-ly
fun-da-men-tal-ism
fun-da-men-tal-ist
fu-ner-al
fu-ner-re-al
fun-gi-cide
fun-gi-cid-al
fun-gi-cid-al-ly
fun-gous
fun-gus
fun-gi
fun-gus-es
funic-u-lar
funk-y
funk-i-er
funk-i-est

fun-nel
fun-neled
fun-nel-ing
fun-ny
fun-ni-er
fun-ni-est
fur
furred
fur-ring
fur-bish
fu-ri-ous
fu-ri-ous-ly
fur-long
fur-lough
fur-nace
fur-nish
fur-nish-ings
fur-ni-ture
for-row
fur-ry
fur-ri-er
fur-ri-est
fur-ther
fur-ther-more
fur-ther-most
fur-thest
fur-tive
fur-tive-ly
fu-ry
fu-ries
fuse
fused
fus-ing
fu-see
fu-se-lage
fu-si-bil-i-ty
fu-si-ble
fu-si-form
fu-si-lade
fu-si-lad-ed
fu-si-lad-ing
fu-sion
fussy
fuss-i-er
fuss-i-est
fuss-i-ly
fus-tian
fus-ty
fu-tile
fu-til-i-ty
fu-til-i-ties
fu-ture
fu-tur-ism
fu-tur-is-tic
fu-tu-ri-ty
fuzz-y

G

gab
  gabbed
  gab-ber
gab-ar-dine
gab-ble
  gab-bled
  gab-bler
gab-by
  gab-bi-er
  gab-bi-est
ga-ble
  ga-bled
  ga-bling
gad
  gad-ded
  gad-ding
gad-a-bout
gad-fly
  gad-flies
gad-get
  gad-get-ry
gaffe
gaf-fer
gag
ga-ga
gai-e-ty
  gai-e-ties
gai-ly
gain-ful
gain-say
  gain-said
  gain-say-ing
gait
ga-la
ga-lac-tic
gal-ax-y
  gal-a-xies
gal-lant
gal-lant-ry
  gal-lant-ries
gal-ler-y
  gal-ler-ies
gal-ley
gal-li-cism
gal-li-mau-fry
  gal-li-mau-fries
gall-ing
gal-li-vant
gal-lon
gal-lop
gal-lows
  gal-lows-es
gall-stone
ga-loot
ga-lore
gal-van-ic

gal-va-nism
gal-va-nize
  gal-va-nized
gal-va-nom-e-ter
gam-bit
gam-ble
  gam-bled
  gam-bling
gam-bol
gam-brel
game
  gam-er
  gam-est
  gamed
  gam-ing
game-keep-er
game-some
game-ster
gam-ete
ga-met-ic
gam-in
gam-ma
gam-mon
gam-ut
gam-y
  gam-i-er
  gam-i-est
  gam-i-ly
  gam-i-ness
gan-der
gang-land
gan-gling
gan-gli-on
  gan-glia
  gan-gli-ons
gan-gly
  gan-gli-er
  gan-gli-est
gang-plank
gan-grene
  gan-grened
  gan-gren-ing
  gan-gre-nous
gang-ster
gang-way
gant-let
gan-try
  gan-tries
gap
  gapped
  gap-ping
ga-rage
  ga-raged
  ga-rag-ing
gar-bage
gar-ble

gar-bled
gar-bling
gar-den
gar-gan-tu-an
gar-gle
  gar-gled
  gar-gling
gar-goyle
gar-ish
gar-land
gar-ment
gar-ner
gar-net
gar-nish
gar-nish-ee
  gar-nish-ee-ing
gar-nish-ment
gar-ni-ture
gar-ret
gar-ri-son
gar-rote
  gar-rot-ed
  gar-rot-ing
  gar-rot-er
gar-ru-lous
gar-ter
gas
  gassed
  gas-sing
gas-e-ous
gas-i-fy
  gas-i-fied
  gas-i-fy-ing
  gas-i-fi-ca-tion
  gas-i-fi-er
gas-ket
gas-light
gas-lit
gas-o-line
gas-ser
gas-sy
  gas-si-er
  gas-si-est
  gas-si-ness
gas-tric
gas-ti-tis
gas-tro-in-tes-ti-nal
gas-tron-o-my
  gas-tro-nom-ic
  gas-tro-nom-i-cal
  gas-tro-nom-i-cal-ly
gas-works
gate-crash-er
  gate-crash-ing
gate-house
gate-keep-er

gate-post
gate-way
gath-er
  gath-er-ing
gauche
gau-cho
gaud-y
  gaud-i-er
  gaud-i-est
  gaud-i-ly
  gaud-i-ness
gauge
  gauged
  gaug-ing
gaunt-let
gauze
  gauz-i-er
  gauz-i-est
  gauz-i-ness
  gauzy
gay-e-ty
gaze
  gazed
  gaz-er
  gaz-ing
ga-ze-bo
  ga-ze-bos
  ga-ze-boes
ga-zelle
ga-zette
gaz-et-teer
gear-box
gear-ing
gear-shift
gear-wheel
gee
  geed
  gee-ing
gee-zer
gei-sha
gel
  gelled
  gel-ling
gel-a-tin
gel-at-i-nous
ge-la-tion
geld
  geld-ed
  geld-ing
  gelt
gel-id
gem
  gemmed
  gem-ming
gem-i-nate
  gem-i-nat-ed

gem-i-nat-ing
gem-i-nate-ly
gem-i-na-tion
gem-ol-o-gy
  gem-o-log-i-cal
  gem-ol-o-gist
gem-stone
gen-darme
gen-der
gene
ge-ne-al-o-gy
  ge-ne-a-log-i-cal
  ge-ne-al-o-gist
gen-er-al
gen-er-al-is-si-mo
  gen-er-al-is-si-mos
gen-er-al-ist
gen-er-al-i-ty
  gen-er-al-i-ties
gen-er-al-ize
  gen-er-al-ized
  gen-er-al-iz-ing
  gen-er-al-i-za-tion
  gen-er-al-iz-er
gen-er-ate
  gen-er-at-ed
  gen-er-at-ing
  gen-er-a-tive
  gen-er-a-tive-ly
gen-er-a-tion
gen-er-a-tor
ge-ner-ic
  ge-ner-i-cal
  ge-ner-i-cal-ly
gen-er-ous
  gen-er-os-i-ty
  gen-er-os-i-ties
gen-e-sis
ge-net-ic
  ge-net-i-cal-ly
  ge-net-ics
  ge-net-i-cist
gen-ial
  ge-ni-al-i-ty
ge-nie
  ge-nies
  ge-nii
gen-i-tal
gen-i-ta-lia
gen-i-tals
gen-ius
  gen-ius-es
gen-o-cide
  gen-o-ci-dal
gen-re
gen-teel

gen-tian
gen-tile
gen-til-i-ty
  gen-til-i-ties
gen-tle
  gen-tler
  gen-tlest
  gen-tly
gen-tle-folk
gen-tle-man
  gen-tle-men
gen-tle-wom-an
  gen-tle-wom-en
gen-try
gen-u-flect
  gen-u-flec-tion
  gen-u-flec-tor
gen-u-ine
ge-nus
  gen-e-ra
  ge-nus-es
ge-o-cen-tric
  ge-o-cen-tri-cal-ly
ge-o-chem-is-try
  ge-o-chem-i-cal
  ge-o-chem-ist
ge-ode
ge-o-des-ic
ge-o-gra-phy
  ge-o-gra-phies
  ge-o-gra-pher
  ge-o-gra-phic
  ge-o-graph-i-cal
ge-ol-o-gy
  ge-ol-o-gies
  ge-o-log-ic
  ge-o-log-i-cal
  ge-o-log-i-cal-ly
  ge-ol-o-gist
ge-o-met-ric
ge-om-e-try
  ge-om-e-tries
ge-o-phys-ics
  ge-o-phys-i-cal
  ge-o-phys-i-cist
ge-o-pol-i-tic
  ge-o-pol-i-tics
  ge-o-pol-o-tic
  ge-o-po-lit-i-cal
  ge-o-po-lit-i-cal-ly
ge-o-ther-mal
ger-bil
ger-i-at-ric
  ger-i-at-rics
  ger-i-a-tri-cian
  ger-i-at-rist

ger-mane
ger-mi-cide
  ger-mi-cid-al
ger-mi-nate
  ger-mi-nat-ed
  ger-mi-nat-ing
  ger-mi-na-tion
ger-on-tol-o-gy
  ger-on-tol-o-gist
ger-ry-man-der
ger-und
ges-so
ges-tate
  ges-tat-ed
  ges-tat-ing
  ges-ta-tion
ges-tic-u-late
  ges-tic-u-lat-ed
  ges-tic-u-lat-ing
  ges-tic-u-la-tion
  ges-tic-u-la-tive
  ges-tic-u-la-to-ry
  ges-tic-u-la-tor
ges-ture
  ges-tured
  ges-tur-ing
  ges-tur-er
ge-sund-heit
get-a-way
gew-gaw
gey-ser
ghast-ly
  ghast-li-er
  ghast-li-est
  ghast-li-ness
gher-kin
ghet-to
  ghe-tos
  ghet-toes
ghost-ly
  ghost-li-er
  ghost-li-est
  ghost-li-ness
ghost-write
  ghost-wrote
  ghost-writ-ten
  ghost-writ-ting
ghoul
gi-ant
gib-ber-ish
gib-bon
gibe
  gib-er
  gib-ing-ly
gib-let
gid-dy

gid-di-er
gid-di-est
gid-di-ly
gid-di-ness
gi-gan-tic
gi-gan-tism
gig-gle
  gig-gled
  gig-gling
  gig-gler
  gig-gly
  gig-gli-er
  gig-gli-est
gig-o-lo
gild-ed
gilt-edged
gim-crack
gim-let
gim-mick
gin-ger
gin-ger-bread
gin-ger-ly
  gin-ger-li-ness
gin-ger-snap
gin-ger-y
ging-ham
gird-er
gir-dle
  gir-dled
  gir-dling
girl-hood
girl-ish
girth
gist
give
  gave
  giv-en
  giv-ing
give-and-take
give-a-way
giz-zard
gla-cial
gla-cier
glad
  glad-der
  glad-dest
  glad-ly
  glad-ness
glad-den
glad-i-a-tor
  glad-i-a-to-ri-al
glad-i-o-lus
  glad-i-o-lus-es
  glad-i-o-la
glad-some
glam-or-ize

glam-or-ized
glam-or-iz-ing
glam-or-i-za-tion
glam-or-i-zer
glam-or-ous
  glam-or-ous-ly
  glam-or-ous-ness
glam-our
glance
  glanced
  glanc-ing
glan-du-lar
glare
  glared
  glar-ing
  glar-i-ness
  glar-y
  glar-i-er
  glar-i-est
glass-blow-ing
  glass-blow-er
glass-ful
glass-ware
glass-y
  glass-i-er
  glass-i-est
  glass-i-ly
  glass-i-ness
glau-co-ma
glaze
  glazed
  glaz-ing
gla-zier
gleam
  gleam-ing
  gleam-y
glean
  glean-er
  glean-ing
glee
  glee-ful
  glee-ful-ly
  glee-ful-ness
glen-gar-ry
glib
  glib-ber
  glib-best
  glib-ly
  glib-ness
glide
  glid-ed
  glid-ing
glim-mer
glimpse
  glimpsed
glis-san-do

glis-san-di
glis-san-dos
glis-ten
glit-ter
gloam-ing
gloat
  gloat-er
  gloat-ing
glob
glo-bal
  glob-al-ly
globe-trot-ter
  globe-trot-ting
glob-u-lar
glob-ule
glock-en-spiel
gloom-y
  gloom-i-er
  gloom-i-est
  gloom-i-ly
  gloom-i-ness
glo-ri-fy
  glo-ri-fied
  glo-ri-fy-ing
  glo-ri-fi-ca-tion
  glo-ri-fi-er
glo-ri-ous
  glo-ri-ous-ly
  glo-ri-ou-ness
glo-ry
  glo-ries
  glo-ried
  glo-ry-ing
glos-sa-ry
glos-sa-ries
glossy
  gloss-i-er
  gloss-i-est
  gloss-i-ly
  gloss-i-ness
glot-tis
  glot-tis-es
  glot-ti-des
glove
  gloved
  glov-ing
glow
  glow-er
  glow-ing
glow-worm
glu-cose
glue
  glued
  glu-ing
glum
  glum-mer

glum-mest
glut
  glut-ted
  glut-ting
glu-ten
glu-ti-nous
glut-ton
glut-ton-ous
  glut-tony
glyc-er-in
  glyc-er-ine
glyc-er-ol
gnarl
  gnarled
  gnarly
  gnarl-i-er
  gnarl-i-est
gnash
gnat
gnaw
  gnawed
  gnaw-ing
gneiss
gnome
gnu
  gnus
goad-ed
go-a-head
goal-keep-er
goat-ee
goat-herd
goat-skin
gob-ble
  gob-bled
  gob-bling
gob-ble-dy-ween
gob-let
gob-lin
go-cart
god-child
  god-chil-dren
  god-daugh-ter
  god-son
god-dess
good-fa-ther
god-head
god-less
  god-less-ness
god-like
god-ly
  god-li-er
  god-li-est
  god-li-ness
god-mo-ther
god-par-ent
god-send

go-get-ter
gog-gle
  gog-gled
  gog-gling
  gog-gle-eyed
  gog-gles
go-ing
goi-ter
gold-brick
gold-en
gold-smith
go-nad
gon-do-la
gon-do-lier
gon-er
gon-or-rhea
goo-ber
good-by
  good-bye
good-for-noth-ing
good-heart-ed
good-ish
good-look-ing
good-ly
  good-li-er
  good-li-est
good-na-tured
good-ness
good-tem-pered
good-y
  good-ies
goof-off
goof-y
  goof-i-er
  goof-i-est
  goof-i-ness
goose-ber-ry
  goose-ber-ries
gore
  gored
  gor-ing
gorge
  gorged
  gorg-ing
gor-geous
  gor-geous-ly
  gor-geous-ness
gor-y
  gor-i-er
  gor-i-est
gos-ling
gos-pel
gos-sa-mer
  gos-sa-mery
  gos-sa-mer-i-er
  gos-sa-mer-i-est

gos-sip
  gos-sip-ing
  gos-sipy
gouge
  gouged
  goug-ing
  goug-er
gou-lash
gourd
gour-met
  gour-mets
gout
  gouty
  gout-i-er
  gout-i-est
gov-ern
  gov-ern-a-ble
gov-ern-ess
gov-ern-ment
  gov-ern-men-tal
gov-er-nor
  gov-er-nor-ship
gow-and
gowned
grab
  grabbed
  grab-bing
  grab-ber
grace
  graced
  grac-ing
grace-ful
  grace-ful-ly
  grace-ful-ness
grace-less
gra-cious
gra-da-tion
grade
  grad-ed
  grad-ing
grad-er
gra-di-ent
grad-u-al
  grad-u-al-ly
  grad-u-al-ness
grad-u-ate
  grad-u-at-ed
  grad-u-at-ing
grad-u-ation
graf-fi-to
  graf-fi-ti
graft
  graft-age
  graft-er
  graft-ing
gra-ham

grain
grain-y
  grain-i-er
  grain-i-est
  grain-i-ness
gram
gram-mar
  gram-mar-i-an
gram-mat-i-cal
  gram-mat-i-cal-ly
gra-na-ry
  gra-na-ries
grand
  grand-ly
grand-child
  grand-daugh-ter
gran-dee
gran-deur
grand-fa-ther
gran-dil-o-quence
  gran-dil-o-quent
gran-di-ose
  gran-di-ose-ly
grand-moth-er
grand-par-ent
grand-son
grand-stand
grange
  grang-er
gran-ite
  gra-nat-ic
gran-ny
  gran-nies
gran-u-lar
  gran-u-lar-i-ty
gran-u-late
  gran-u-lat-ed
  gran-u-lat-ing
gran-u-la-tion
gran-ule
grape-fruit
grape-vine
graph-ic
  graph-i-cal
  graph-i-cal-ly
graph-ite
graph-ol-o-gy
  graph-ol-o-gist
grap-nel
grap-ple
  grap-pled
  grap-pling
  grap-pler
grass
  grass-y
  grass-i-er

grass-i-est
grass-hop-per
grass-land
grate
  grat-ed
  grat-ing
grate-ful
  grate-ful-ly
  grate-ful-ness
grat-i-fy
  grat-i-fied
  grat-i-fy-ing
gra-tis
grat-i-tude
gra-tu-i-tous
gra-tu-i-ty
  gra-tu-i-ties
grave
  graved
  grav-en
  grav-ing
  grav-er
  grave-ly
  grave-ness
grav-el
  grav-eled
  grav-el-ing
  grav-el-ly
grave-stone
grave-yard
grav-i-tate
  grav-i-tat-ed
  grav-i-tat-ing
grav-i-ta-tion
  grav-i-ta-tion-al
grav-i-ty
  grav-i-ties
gra-vy
  grav-ies
gray
  gray-ly
  gray-ness
gray-ling
graze
  grazed
  graz-ing
grease
  greas-ed
  greas-ing
greas-y
  greas-i-er
  greas-i-ness
great
  great-ly
great-coat
great-heart-ed

greed-y
greed-i-er
greed-i-est
greed-i-ly
greed-i-ness
green-back
green-er-y
green-er-ies
green-gro-cer
green-horn
green-house
green-hous-es
green-ing
green-ish
green-ish-ness
green-sward
greet
greet-er
greet-ing
gre-gar-i-ous
gre-gar-i-ous-ly
gre-gar-i-ous-ness
grem-lin
gren-a-dier
gren-a-dine
grey
grey-ly
grey-ness
grid-dle
grid-dle-cake
grid-i-ron
grief
griev-ance
grieve
grieved
griev-ing
griev-ous
griev-ous-ly
grif-fin
grif-fon
grill
gril-lage
grille
grill-room
grim
grim-mer
grim-mest
grim-ly
grim-ness
grim-ace
grim-aced
grim-ac-ing
grime
grimed
grim-ing
grim-y

grim-i-er
grim-i-est
grim-i-ly
grim-i-ness
grin
grin-ned
grin-ning
grin-ner
grind
ground
grind-ing
grind-er
grind-stone
grin-go
grin-gos
grip
gripped
grip-ping
gripe
griped
grip-er
grippe
gris-ly
gris-li-er
gris-li-est
gris-li-ness
gris-tle
gris-tly
gris-tli-er
gris-tli-est
grit
grit-ted
grit-ting
grit-ty
grit-ti-er
grit-ti-est
grit-ti-ly
grit-ti-ness
griz-zled
griz-zly
griz-zli-er
griz-zli-est
griz-zlies
groan
groan-er
gro-cer
gro-cer-y
gro-cer-ies
grog-gy
grog-gi-er
groin
grom-met
groom
groove
grooved
groov-er

groov-y
groov-i-er
groov-i-est
grope
groped
grop-ing
gros-grain
gross
gross-es
gross-ness
gro-tesque
gro-tesque-ly
gro-tesque-ness
grot-to
grot-toes
grot-tos
grouch
grouchy
grouch-i-er
grouch-i-est
ground-er
ground-less
ground-less-ly
ground-less-ness
ground-ling
ground-nut
ground-work
group-ie
grouse
groused
grous-ing
grous-er
grov-el
grov-eled
grov-el-er
grow
grow-ing
grow-er
growl
growl-er
grown-up
growth
grub
grubbed
grub-bing
grub-ber
grub-by
grub-bi-er
grub-bi-est
grub-stake
grub-staked
grub-stak-ing
grudge
grudged
grudg-ing
grudg-ing-ly

gru-el
gru-el-ing
grue-some
  grue-some-ly
gruff
  gruff-ly
  gruff-ness
grum-ble
  grum-bled
  grum-bling
  grum-bler
grump-y
  grump-i-er
  grump-i-ness
grunt
  grunt-er
  grunt-ing
gua-no
  gua-nos
guar-an-tee
  guar-an-teed
  guar-an-tee-ing
guar-an-tor
guar-an-ty
  guar-an-ties
  guar-an-ty-ing
guard-ed
  guard-ed-ly
guard-house
guard-i-an
guards-man
  guards-men
gua-va
gu-ber-na-to-ri-al
gudg-eon
guer-ril-la
  gue-ril-la
guess
  gues-ser
guess-work
guest
guf-faw
guid-ance
guide
  guid-ed
  guid-ing
guide-book
guide-post
gui-don
guid-hall
guile
  guile-ful
  guile-ful-ly
  guile-less
  guile-less-ly
guil-lo-tine

guil-lo-tined
  guil-lo-tin-ing
guilt
  guilt-less
  guilt-less-ly
guilt-y
  guilt-i-er
  guilt-i-ness
guin-ea
guise
gui-tar
  gui-tar-ist
gul-let
gul-li-ble
  gul-li-bil-i-ty
  gul-li-bly
gul-ly
  gul-lies
  gul-lied
  gul-ly-ing
gum
  gummed
  gum-ming
gum-bo
  gum-bos
gum-drop
gum-my
  gum-mi-er
  gum-mi-est
  gum-mi-ness
gump-tion
gum-shoe
  gum-shoed
gun
  gunned
  gun-ning
gun-boat
gun-fight
  gun-fight-er
gun-fire
gun-man
  gun-men
gun-ner
  gun-ner-y
gun-ny
  gun-nies
gun-ny-bag
gun-pow-der
gun-stock
gun-wale
gup-py
  gup-pies
gur-gle
  gur-gled
  gur-gling
gu-ru

gush-er
gush-ing
gush-y
  gush-i-er
  gush-i-est
  gush-i-ness
gus-set
gus-ta-to-ry
  gus-to
gust-y
  gust-i-er
  gust-i-est
gut
  gut-ted
  gut-ting
gut-ter
gut-tur-al
  gut-tur-al-ly
guz-zle
  guz-zled
  guz-zling
  guz-zler
gym-na-si-um
  gym-na-si-ums
  gym-na-sia
gym-nast
gym-nas-tic
  gym-nas-tics
gy-ne-col-o-gy
  gy-ne-co-log-ic
  gy-ne-co-log-i-cal
  gy-ne-col-o-gist
gyp
  gypped
  gyp-ping
gyp-sum
gyp-sy
  gyp-sies
gy-ral
gy-rate
  gy-rat-ed
  gy-rat-ing
  gy-ra-tion
  gy-ra-tor
  gy-ra-to-ry
gyr-fal-con
gy-roi-dal
gy-rom-e-ter
gy-ro-plane
gy-ro-scope
  gy-ro-scop-ic
gy-rose
gy-rus
gyve
  gyved
  gyv-ing

hab-da-lah
ha-be-as cor-pus
hab-er-dash-er
  hab-er-dash-ery
  hab-er-dash-er-ies
ha-bil-i-ment
hab-it
hab-it-a-ble
ha-bi-tant
hab-i-ta-tion
ha-bit-u-al
  ha-bit-u-al-ly
  ha-bit-u-al-ness
ha-bit-u-ate
  ha-bit-u-at-ed
  ha-bit-u-at-ing
  ha-bit-u-a-tion
ha-ci-en-da
  ha-ci-en-das
hack-le
  hack-led
  hack-ling
hack-ney
  hack-neyed
hack-saw
hadn't
had-ron
hae-mo-glo-bin
hae-mo-phil-i-a
haft
ha-gar
hag-gard
  hag-gard-ly
hag-gle
  hag-gled
  hag-gling
  hag-gler
ha-gi-ol-o-gy
  hag-i-ol-o-gies
  hag-i-ol-o-gist
hag-rid-den
haik
hai-ku
hail-fel-low
hail-stone
hail-storm
hair-breadth
hair-brush
hair-cut
hair-do
hair-dress-er
hair-dress-ing
hair-line
hair-pin
hair-split-ter
  hair-split-ting

hair-spring
hair-y
  hair-i-er
  hair-i-est
ha-la-tion
hal-cy-on
hale
  haled
  hal-ing
half-back
half-baked
half-breed
half-caste
half-heart-ed
  half-heart-ed-ly
half hour
half--life
  half-lives
half--mast
half--moon
half note
half step
half-tone
half-track
half-truth
half-way
half--wit
  half--wit-ted
hal-i-but
hal-i-to-sis
hall-mark
hal-lo
hal-low
  hal-lowed
hal-lu-ci-nate
  hal-lu-ci-nat-ed
  hal-lu-ci-nat-ing
hal-lu-ci-na-tion
  hal-lu-ci-na-to-ry
hal-lu-cin-o-gen
  hal-lu-cin-o-gen-ic
hal-lux
hall-way
ha-lo
  ha-los
  ha-loes
halo-phile
halt
  halt-ing
  halt-ing-ly
hal-ter
hal-ter-break
halve
  halved
  halv-ing
halv-ers

halves
hal-yard
ham-burg-er
ham-let
ham-mer
ham-mer-head
ham-mer-less
ham-mock
ham-my
  ham-mi-er
  ham-mi-est
hamp-er
ham-ster
ham-string
  ham-strung
  ham-string-ing
hand-bag
hand-ball
hand-bill
hand-book
hand-cuff
hand-ed
hand-ful
  hand-fuls
hand-i-cap
  hand-i-capped
  hand-i-cap-ping
  hand-i-cap-per
hand-i-craft
hand-i-ly
handi-ness
hand-i-work
han-ker-chief
han-dle
  han-dled
  han-dling
  han-dler
han-dle-bar
hand-made
hand-maid-en
hand--me--down
hand-out
hand-pick
  hand-picked
hand-rail
hand-shake
hand-some
  hand-som-er
  hand-som-est
  hand-some-ly
  hand-some-ness
hand-spike
hand-spring
hand-to-hand
hand--to--mouth
hand-work

hand-writ-ing
handy
  hand-i-er
  hand-i-est
handy-man
  handy-men
hang
  hung
  hanged
  hang-ing
hang-ar
hang-dog
hang-er
hang-er--on
hang-man
  hanf-men
hang-nail
hang-out
hang-o-ver
hang--up
hank-er
han-som
hap-haz-ard
  hap-haz-ard-ly
  hap-haz-ard-ness
hap-less
  hap-less-ly
hap-ly
hap-pen
hap-pen-ing
hap-pen-stance
hap-pi-ness
hap-py
  hap-pi-er
  hap-pi-est
  hap-pi-ly
hap-py--go--lucky
hara-kiri
ha-rangue
  ha-rangued
  ha-rangu-ing
ha-rass
  ha-rass-ment
har-bin-ger
har-bor
hard--bit-ten
hard--boiled
hard--core
hard-cov-er
hard-en
  hard-en-er
hard hat
hard-head-ed
hard-heart-ed
har-di-hood
har-di-ness

hard-ly
har-di-er
har-di-est
har-di-ly
hare-brained
hare-lip
har-em
har-le-quin
har-lot
  har-lot-ry
harm-ful
  harm-ful-ly
  harm-ful-ness
harm-less
  harm-less-ly
  harm-less-ness
har-mon-ic
  har-mon-i-cal-ly
har-mon-i-ca
har-mon-ics
har-mo-ni-ous
  har-mo-ni-ous-ly
har-mo-nize
  har-mo-nized
  har-mo-niz-ing
har-mo-ny
  har-mo-nies
har-ness
harp-ist
har-poon
harp-si-chord
har-py
  har-pies
har-que-bus
har-ri-dan
har-row
  har-row-ing
har-ry
  har-ried
  har-ry-ing
harsh
  harsh-ly
  harsh-ness
har-um-scar-um
har-vest
har-ves-ter
has--been
hash-ish
  hash-eesh
hasn't
has-sle
  has-sled
  has-sling
has-sock
has-ten
hasty

hast-i-er
hast-i-est
hast-i-ness
hatch-ery
  hatch-er-ies
hatch-et
hatch-way
hate
  hat-ed
  hat-ing
  hat-er
hate-ful
  hate-ful-ly
  hate-ful-ness
ha-tred
hat-ter
haugh-ty
  haugh-ti-er
  haugh-ti-est
  haugh-ti-ly
  haught-ti-ness
haul
  haul-age
haunch
  haunch-es
haunt-ed
  haunt-ing
hau-teur
ha-ven
have--not
haven't
hav-er-sack
havers
hav-oc
hawk
  hawk-ish
haw-ser
hay-loft
hay-mak-er
hay-mow
hay-seed
hay-stack
hay-wire
haz-ard
  haz-ard-ous
  haz-ard-ous-ly
  haz-ard-ou-ness
haze
  hazed
  haz-ing
ha-zel
ha-zel-nut
hazy
  ha-zi-er
  ha-zi-est
  ha-zi-ly

ha-zi-ness
head-ache
head-band
head-dress
head-er
head-first
  head-fore-most
head-gear
head-hunt-er
head-ing
head-land
head-less
head-light
head-line
  head-lined
  head-lin-ing
head-long
head-mas-ter
head-mis-tress
head-most
head--on
head-piece
head-quar-ters
head-set
head-stone
head-strong
head-wait-er
head-wa-ter
head-way
head-wind
heady
  head-i-er
  head-i-est
  head-i-ly
  head-i-ness
heal-er
health-ful
  health-ful-ly
healthy
  health-i-er
  health-i-est
  health-i-ness
heaped
hear
  heared
  hear-ing
  hear-er
hear-ken
hear-say
hearse
heart-ache
heart-break
  heart-break-ing
heart-brok-en
heart-burn
heart-en

heart-felt
hearth-stone
heart-less
  heart-less-ly
  heart-less-ness
heart-rend-ing
heart-sick
heart-strings
heart--to--heart
hearty
  heart-i-er
  heart-i-est
  heart-i-ly
  heart-i-ness
heat-ed
heat-er
heath
hea-then
heave
  heaved
  heav-ing
heav-en
heav-en-ly
heav-en-ward
  heav-en-wards
heavy
  heav-i-er
  heav-i-est
  heav-i-ly
  heav-i-ness
heavy--du-ty
heavy--hand-ed
heavy-weight
heck-le
  heck-led
  heck-ling
  heck-ler
hect-are
hec-tic
  hec-ti-cal-ly
hec-to-gram
hec-to-li-ter
hec-to-me-ter
hedge
  hedged
  hedg-ing
  hedg-er
he-do-nism
  he-do-nist
  he-do-nis-tic
hee-haw
hefty
  heft-i-er
  heft-i-est
he-ge-mo-ny
  he-ge-mo-nies

heg-e-mon-ic
he-gi-ra
heif-er
height-en
  height-en-er
hei-nous
  hei-nous-ly
  hei-nous-ness
heir-ess
heir-loom
heist
he-li-cop-ter
he-li-um
he-lix
  he-li-ces
  he-lix-es
hell--bent
hell-cat
hel-lion
hell-ish
  hell-ish-ly
  hell-ish-ness
hel-lo
  hel-los
helm
  helm-less
hel-met
  hel-met-ed
helms-man
  helms-men
help-er
help-ful
  help-ful-ly
  help-ful-ness
help-ing
help-less
  help-less-ly
  help-less-ness
help-mate
hel-er--skel-ter
hem
  hemmed
  hem-ming
he--man
  he--men
hemi-sphere
  hemi-spher-ic
  hemi-sper-i-cal
hem-lock
he-mo-glo-bin
he-mo-phil-ia
hem-or-rhage
  hem-or-rhag-ing
  hem-or-rhag-ic
hem-or-rhoid
  hem-or-rhoid-al

94

hemp-en
hem-stitch
hence-forth
hench-man
hench-men
  hench-man-ship
hen-na
hen-peck
hep-a-ti-tis
her-ald
  he-ral-dic
her-ald-ry
  her-ald-ries
herb-age
her-biv-o-rous
Her-cu-le-an
herd-er
herds-man
  herds-men
here-af-ter
he-red-i-tary
  he-red-i-tar-i-ly
  he-red-i-tar-i-ness
he-red-i-ty
  he-red-i-ties
here-in
here-of
her-e-sy
  her-e-sies
her-e-tic
  he-ret-i-cal
  he-ret-i-cal-ly
here-to
here-to-fore
here-upon
here-with
her-i-ta-ble
  her-i-ta-bil-i-ty
  her-i-ta-bly
her-i-tage
her-maph-ro-dite
  her-maph-ro-dit-ic
  her-maph-ro-dit-ism
her-met-ic
  her-met-i-cal
  her-met-i-cal-ly
her-mit
  her-mit-age
her-nia
  her-ni-al
  her-ni-a-tion
he-ro
  he-roes
  he-ro-ic
  he-ro-ical
  he-ro-ical-ly

her-o-in
her-o-ine
her-o-ism
her-on
her-ring-bone
  her-ring-boned
  her-ring-bon-ing
her-self
hes-i-tant
  hes-i-tan-cy
  hes-i-tan-cies
  hes-i-tant-ly
hes-i-tate
  hes-i-tat-ed
  hes-i-tat-ing
  hes-i-tat-er
  hes-i-ta-tor
  hes-i-tat-ing-ly
hes-i-ta-tion
het-ero-dox
  het-ero-doxy
het-er-o-ge-neous
  het-er-o-ge-ne-ity
  het-er-o-ge-neous-ly
het-ero-sex-u-al
  het-ero-sex-u-al-i-ty
hew
  hewed
  hewn
  hew-ing
  hew-er
hexa-gon
  hex-ag-o-nal
  hex-ag-o-nal-ly
hey-day
  hey-dey
hi-a-tus
  hi-a-tus-es
hi-ba-chi
hi-ber-nate
  hi-ber-nat-ed
  hi-ber-nat-ing
  hi-ber-na-tion
hi-bis-cus
hic-cup
  hic-cuped
  hic-cup-ing
hid-den
  hid-den-ness
hide
  hid
  hid-den
  hid-er
hide-bound
hid-eous
  hid-eous-ly

hid-eous-ness
hide-out
hi-er-ar-chy
  hi-er-ar-chies
  hi-er-ar-chal
  hi-er-ar-chic
  hi-er-ar-chi-cal
  hi-er-ar-chi-cal-ly
hi-ero-glyph
  hi-ero-glyph-ic
  hi-ero-glyph-i-cal
  hi-ero-glyph-i-cal-ly
hi--fi
high-ball
high-born
high-boy
high-brow
  high-browed
  high-brow-ism
high-er--up
high-fa-lu-tin
  high-fa-lu-ting
high--flown
high--grade
high--hand-ed
  high--hand-ed-ly
  high--hand-ed-ness
high--hat
high-land
high-light
high--mind-ed
  high--mind-ed-ly
  high--mind-ed-ness
high-ness
high--pressure
  high--pressured
  high--pressur-ing
high school
high seas
high--spir-it-ed
  high--spir-it-ed-ly
  high--spir-it-ed-ness
high--strung
high-tail
high--tension
high--toned
high-way
high-way-man
  high-way-men
hi-jack
  hi-jack-er
  hi-jack-ing
hike
  hiked
  hik-ing
  hik-er

95

hi-lar-i-ous
  hi-lar-i-ous-ly
  hi-lar-i-ous-ness
  hi-lar-i-ty
hill-bil-ly
  hill-bil-lies
hill-ock
hill-side
hill-top
hilly
  hill-i-er
  hill-i-est
him-self
hin-der
  hin-der-er
hind-most
hind-quar-ter
hin-drance
hind-sight
hinge
  hinged
  hing-ing
hint-er
  hint-ing-ly
hin-ter-land
hipped
hip-pie
hip-po
  hip-pos
hip-po-drome
hip-po-pot-a-mus
  hip-po-pot-a-mus-es
  hip-po-pot-a-mi
hire-ling
hir-sute
  hir-sute-ness
hiss
  hiss-er
his-ta-mine
  his-ta-min-ic
his-to-ri-an
his-tor-ic
his-tor-i-cal
  his-tor-i-cal-ly
  his-tor-i-cal-ness
his-to-ry
  his-to-ries
his-tri-on-ic
  his-tri-on-i-cal
  his-tri-on-i-cal-ly
his-tri-on-ics
hit
  hit-ting
hit--and--run
hitch
hitch-er

hitch-hike
  hitch-hiked
  hitch-hik-ing
  hitch-hik-er
hith-er-to
hive
  hived
  hiv-ing
hoary
  hoar-i-er
  hoar-i-est
  hoar-i-ness
hoard
  hoard-er
  hoard-ing
hoar-frost
hoarse
  hoarse-ly
  hoars-en
  hoarse-ness
hoax
  hoax-er
hob-ble
  hob-bled
  hob-bling
hob-by
  hob-bies
hob-by-horse
hob-gob-lin
hob-nail
  hob-nail-ed
hob-nob
  hob-nobbed
  hob-nob-bing
ho-bo
  ho-boes
  ho-bos
  ho-bo-ism
hock-er
hock-ey
ho-cus-po-cus
hodge-podge
hoe
  hoed
  hoe-ing
hoe-down
hog
  hogged
  hog-ging
hog-gish
  hog-gish-ly
  hog-gish-ness
hogs-head
hog--tie
  hog--tied
  hog--ty-ing

hog-wash
hoi pol-loi
hoist-er
ho-kum
hold-er
hold-ing
hold-out
hold-over
hold-up
hole
  holed
  hol-ing
  holey
hol-i-day
ho-li-ness
Hol-land
hol-ler
hol-low
  hol-low-ly
  hol-low-ness
hol-ly
  hol-lies
hol-ly-hock
hol-mi-um
ho-lo-caust
ho-lo-gram
hol-o-graph
hol-ster
ho-ly
  ho-li-er
  ho-li-est
  ho-lies
hom-age
hom-bre
  hom-bres
home-com-ing
home-less
  home-less-ness
home-ly
  home-li-er
  home-li-est
  home-li-ness
home-made
hom-er
home-sick
  home-sick-ness
home-spun
home-stead
  home-stead-er
home-ward
  home-wards
home-work
homey
  hom-i-er
  hom-i-est
  hom-i-ness

hom-i-cide
hom-i-let-ics
hom-i-ly
  hom-i-lies
homing pigeon
hom-i-ny
ho-mo-ge-neous
  ho-mo-ge-ne-ity
  ho-mo-ge-neous-ness
ho-mog-e-nize
  ho-mog-e-nized
  ho-mog-e-niz-ing
ho-mo-graph
ho-mol-o-gous
  ho-mol-o-gy
  ho-mol-o-gies
hom-onym
  hom-onym-ic
ho-mo-phone
  ho-mo-pho-nic
ho-mo-sex-u-al
  ho-mo-sex-u-al-i-ty
hone
  honed
  hon-ing
hon-est
  hon-est-ly
hon-es-ty
  hon-es-ties
hon-ey
  hon-eys
  hon-eyed
  hon-ied
  hon-ey-ing
hon-ey-bee
hon-ey-comb
hon-ey-moon
  hon-ey-moon-er
hon-ey-suck-le
  hon-ey-suck-led
hon-ky--tonk
hon-or
hon-or-able
  hon-or-ably
hon-o-rar-i-um
  hon-o-rar-i-ums
  hon-o-rar-ia
hon-or-ary
hon-or-if-ic
hood-ed
hood-lum
hoo-doo
  hoo-doo-ism
hood-wink
  hood-wink-er
hoo-ey

hoof
hoofs
hooves
hoofed
hooked
hook-er
hook-up
hoo-li-gan
  hoo-li-gan-ism
hoop
  hooped
  hoop-like
hoop-la
hoo-ray
hoose-gow
hoot
  hoot-er
  hoot-ing-ly
hop
  hopped
  hop-ping
  hop-er
hope-ful
  hope-ful-ly
  hope-ful-ness
hope-less
  hope-less-ly
  hope-less-ness
hop-head
hop-per
hop-scotch
horde
  hord-ed
  hord-ing
ho-ri-zon
hor-i-zon-tal
  hor-i-zon-tal-ly
hor-mone
  hor-mon-al
horn
  horned
  horn-like
  horny
  horn-i-er
  horn-i-est
hor-net
horn-swog-gle
  horn-swog-gled
  horn-swog-gling
hor-rol-o-gy
  ho-rol-o-ger
  ho-rol-o-gist
horo-scope
hor-ren-dous
  hor-ren-dous-ly
hor-ri-ble

hor-ri-bly
hor-rid
  hor-rid-ly
  hor-rid-ness
hor-ri-fy
  hor-ri-fied
  hor-ri-fy-ing
  hor-ri-fi-ca-tion
hor-ror
horse
  hors-es
  horsed
  hors-ing
horse-back
horse-fly
  horse-flies
horse-hair
horse-laugh
horse-men
  horse-man-ship
  horse-wom-an
  horse-wom-en
horse opera
horse-play
horse-pow-er
horse-rad-ish
horse-shoe
  horse-sho-er
horse-whip
  horse-whipped
  horse-whip-ping
hors-ey
  horsy
  hors-i-er
  hors-i-est
  hors-i-ly
  hors-i-ness
hor-ta-to-ry
hor-ti-cul-ture
  hor-ti-cul-tur-al
  hor-ti-cul-tur-ist
ho-san-na
hose
  hos-es
  hosed
  hos-ing
ho-siery
hos-pice
hos-pi-ta-ble
  hos-pi-ta-bly
hos-pi-tal
hos-pi-tal-i-ty
  hos-pi-tal-i-ties
hos-pi-tal-iza-tion
hos-pi-tal-ize
  hos-pi-tal-ized

hos-pi-tal-iz-ing
hos-tage
hos-tel
  hos-tel-ry
  hos-tel-ries
host-ess
hos-tile
  hos-tile-ly
hos-til-i-ty
  hos-til-i-ties
hos-tler
hot
  hot-ter
  hot-test
  hot-ly
hot-bed
hot--blood-ed
ho-tel
hot-head
  hot-head-ed
  hot-head-ed-ness
hot-house
hot-shot
hound
  hound-er
hour-glass
hour-ly
house
  hous-es
  housed
  hous-ing
house-boat
house-bro-ken
  house-break
  house-broke
  house-break-ing
house-fly
house-hold
house-keep-er
  house-keep-ing
house-maid
house-warm-ing
house-wife
  house-wives
  house-wife-ly
  house-wif-ery
house-work
hous-ing
hov-el
  hov-eled
  hov-el-ing
hov-er
  hov-er-er
  hov-er-ing
how-ev-er
how-it-zer

howl-er
how-so-ev-er
hoy-den
  hoy-den-ish
hob-bub
huck-le-ber-ry
  huck-le-ber-ries
huck-ster
hud-dle
  hud-dled
  hud-dling
  hud-dler
huffy
  huff-i-er
  huff-i-est
  huff-i-ly
  huff-i-ness
hug
  hugged
  hug-ging
  hug-ger
huge
  hug-er
  hug-est
  huge-ly
  huge-ness
hu-la
hulk-ing
hul-la-ba-loo
hum
  hummed
  hum-ming
  hum-mer
hu-man
  hu-man-ness
hu-mane
  hu-mane-ly
  hu-man-ness
hu-man-ism
  hu-man-ist
  hu-man-ist-ic
hu-man-i-tar-i-an-ism
hu-man-i-ty
  hu-man-i-ties
hu-man-ize
  hu-man-ized
  hu-man-iz-ing
  hu-man-i-za-tion
  hu-man-iz-er
hu-man-kind
hu-man-ly
hum-ble
  hum-bler
  hum-blest
  hum-bled
  hum-bling

  hum-ble-ness
  hum-bly
hum-bug
  hum-bugged
  hum-bug-ging
  hum-bug-ger
  hum-bug-gery
hum-ding-er
hum-drum
hu-mer-us
hu-mid
  hu-mid-ly
hu-mid-i-fy
  hu-mid-i-fied
  hu-mid-i-fy-ing
  hu-mid-i-fi-er
hu-mid-i-ty
hum-ming-bird
hum-mock
  hum-mocky
  hum-mock-i-er
  hum-mock-i-est
hu-mor
hu-mor-ist
  hu-mor-is-tic
hu-mor-ous
  hu-mor-ous-ly
  hu-mor-ous-ness
hump
  humped
  humpy
  hump-i-er
  hump-i-est
hump-back
hu-mus
hunch-back
  hunch-backed
hun-dred
hun-ger
hun-gry
  hun-gri-er
  hun-gri-est
  hun-gri-ly
  hun-gri-ness
hunt
  hunt-er
  hunt-ing
  hunt-ress
  hunts-man
  hunts-men
hur-dle
  hur-dled
  hur-dling
  hur-dler
hur-dy--gur-dy
  hur-dy--gur-dies

hurl-er
hurl-y--burl-y
  hurl-y—burl-ies
hur-rah
hur-ri-cane
hur-ry
  hur-ried
  hur-ry-ing
  hur-ried-ly
  hur-ry-ing-ly
hurt-ful
  hurt-ful-ly
  hurt-ful-ness
hurt-ing
hur-tle
  hur-tled
  hur-tling
hurt-less
hus-band
  hus-band-er
  hus-band-less
  hus-band-ly
  hus-band-man
  hus-band-ry
hush
husk-er
husk-ing
husky
  husk-i-er
  husk-i-est
  husk-i-ly
  husk-i-ness
  husk-ies
hus-sar
hus-sy
  hussies
hus-tings
hus-tle-
  hus-tled
  hus-tling
  hus-tler
hutch
hut-ment
huz-zah
  huz-za
hy-a-cinth
  hy-a-cin-thine
hy-a-line
hy-a-lite
hy-a-loid
hy-a-lo-plasm
hy-brid
  hy-brid-ism
  hy-brid-i-ty
hy-brid-ize
  hy-brid-ized

hy-brid-iz-er
hy-brid-iz-ing
hy-brid-i-za-tion
hy-da-thode
hy-da-tid
hy-dra
  hy-dras
  hy-dae
hy-dral-azine
hy-dran-gea
hy-drant
hy-dra-ted
hy-dra-ting
hy-dra-tion
hy-dra-tor
hy-drau-lic
  hy-drau-li-cal-ly
hy-drau-lics
hy-dro-car-bon
hy-dro-chlo-ric acid
hy-dro-dy-nam-ics
  hy-dro-dy-na-mic
hy-dro-elec-tric
hy-dro-gen
  hy-drog-e-nous
hy-dro-ly-sis
hy-drom-e-ter
  hy-dro-met-ric
  hy-dro-met-ri-cal
hy-drom-e-try
hy-dro-pho-bia
hy-dro-plane
  hy-dro-plan-er
  hy-dro-plan-ing
hy-dro-pon-ics
hy-dro-ther-a-py
  hy-dro-ther-a-pist
hy-drous
hy-drox-ide
hy-drox-yl
hy-dro-zo-an
hy-e-na
hy-giene
  hy-gien-ic
  hy-gien-i-cal-ly
  hy-gien-ist
hy-men
hy-me-ne-al
  hy-me-ne-al-ly
hym-nal
hy-per-bo-la
hy-per-bo-le
  hy-per-bo-lize
  hy-per-bo-lized
  hy-per-bo-liz-ing
hy-per-bol-ic

hy-per-crit-i-cal
  hy-per-crit-i-cal-ly
hy-per-sen-si-tive
  hy-per-sen-si-tiv-i-ty
hy-per-sex-u-al
  hy-per-sex-u-al-ity
hy-per-ten-sion
hy-per-thy-roid-ism
hy-phen
hy-phen-ate
  hy-phen-at-ed
  hy-phen-at-ing
hyp-no-sis
hyp-not-ic
hyp-no-tism
  hyp-no-tist
hyp-no-tize
  hyp-no-tized
  hyp-no-tiz-ing
hy-po
hy-po-chon-dria
  hy-po-chon-dri-ac
hy-poc-ri-sy
  hy-poc-ri-sies
  hyp-o-crite
hy-po-der-mic
hy-po-sen-si-tize
  hy-po-sen-si-tized
  hy-po-sen-si-tiz-ing
hy-po-ten-sion
hy-pot-e-nuse
hy-poth-e-cate
  hy-poth-e-cat-ed
  hy-poth-e-cat-ing
  hy-poth-e-ca-tion
  hy-poth-e-ca-tor
hy-poth-e-sis
  hy-poth-e-ses
  hy-poth-e-size
  hy-poth-e-siz-ing
hy-po-thet-i-cal
  hy-po-thet-i-cal-ly
hyp-ox-emia
hyp-ox-ia
hyp-sog-ra-phy
hy-son
hys-sop
hys-ter-ec-to-my
  hys-ter-ec-to-mies
hys-ter-e-sis
hys-te-ria
  hys-ter-ic
  hys-ter-i-cal
  hys-ter-i-cal-ly
hys-ter-ics

I

iamb
iat-ric
ibid
ibi-dem
ibis
  ibis-es
ice
  iced
  ic-ing
ice-boat
ice--cream
ice-man
  ice-men
ice--skate
icon
icon-o-clasm
  icon-o-clas-tic
icon-o-clast
ide-al-ize
  ide-al-ized
  ide-al-iz-ing
  ide-al-i-za-tion
ide-al-ly
idem
iden-ti-cal
  iden-ti-cal-ly
iden-ti-fi-a-ble
  iden-ti-fy-ing
  iden-ti-fi-a-bly
iden-ti-fi-ca-tion
iden-ti-fy
  iden-ti-fied
  iden-ti-fy-ing
  iden-ti-fi-er
iden-ti-ty
  iden-ti-ties
ides
id-i-o-cy
  id-i-o-cies
id-i-om
  id-i-o-mat-ic
  id-i-o-mat-i-cal-ly
id-i-o-syn-cra-sy
  id-i-o-syn-cra-sies
  id-i-o-syn-crat-ic
id-i-ot
  id-i-ot-ic
  id-i-ot-i-cal-ly
idle
idol
idol-ize
idyll
  idyl-lic
  idyl-lic-al-ly
ig-ne-ous
ig-nite

ig-ni-tion
ig-no-ble
  ig-no-bil-i-ty
  ig-no-bly
ig-no-mi-ny
  ig-no-min-ies
  ig-no-min-i-ous
  ig-no-min-i-ous-ly
ig-no-ra-mus
ig-no-rant
  ig-no-rance
  ig-no-rant-iy
ig-nore
  ig-nored
  ig-nor-ing
igua-na
ill--ad-vised
  ill--ad-vis-ed-ly
ill--bred
il-le-gal
  il-le-gal-i-ty
  il-le-gal-ly
il-leg-i-ble
  il-leg-i-bil-i-ty
  il-leg-i-bly
il-le-git-i-mate
  il-le-git-i-ma-cy
  il-le-git-i-ma-cies
  il-le-git-i-mate-ly
ill--fat-ed
ill--fa-vored
ill--got-ten
il-lib-er-al
il-lic-it
il-lim-it-able
il-lit-er-a-cy
  il-lit-er-a-cies
il-lit-er-ate
ill-ness
il-log-i-cal
ill-starred
ill-tem-pered
  ill-tem-pered-ly
ill-timed
il-lu-mi-nate
  il-lu-mi-nat-ed
  il-lu-mi-nat-ing
  il-lu-mi-na-tor
il-lu-mi-na-tion
il-lu-mine
  il-lu-mined
  il-lu-min-ing
ill-use
il-lu-sion
  il-lu-sive
  il-lu-sive-ly

  il-lu-sive-ness
il-lus-trate
  il-lus-trat-ed
  il-lus-trat-ing
il-lus-tra-tion
  il-lus-tra-tive
  il-lus-tra-tive-ly
  il-lus-tra-tor
il-lus-tri-ous
  il-lus-tri-ous-ly
im-age
  im-aged
im-ag-ing
  im-age-a-ble
  im-ag-er
im-ag-ery
  im-ag-eries
  im-ag-eri-al
imag-in-able
  imag-in-able-ness
  imag-in-ably
imag-i-nary
  imag-i-nar-ies
  imag-i-nar-i-ly
  imag-i-nar-i-ness
imag-i-na-tion
  imag-i-na-tion-al
imag-i-na-tive
  imag-i-na-tive-ly
imag-ine
  imag-ined
  imag-in-ing
im-bal-ance
im-be-cile
  im-be-cil-ic
  im-be-cile-ly
  im-be-cil-i-ty
imbed
  imbed-ded
  im-bed-ding
im-bibe
im-bro-glio
im-brue
  im-brued
  im-bru-ing
im-i-ta-ble
im-i-tate
  im-i-tat-ed
  im-i-tat-ing
  im-i-ta-tor
im-i-ta-tion
  im-i-ta-tive
im-mac-u-late
  im-mac-u-la-cy
  im-mac-u-late-ly
im-ma-nent

im-ma-nence
im-ma-ne-cy
im-ma-nent-ly
im-ma-te-ri-al
im-ma-te-ri-al-ness
im-ma-te-ri-al-i-ty
im-ma-te-ri-al-ize
im-ma-ture
im-ma-ture-ly
im-ma-ture-ness
im-ma-tu-ri-ty
im-meas-ur-a-ble
im-meas-ur-a-bly
im-me-di-a-cy
im-me-di-a-cies
im-me-di-ate
im-me-di-ate-ly
im-me-di-ate-ness
im-me-mo-ri-al
im-me-mo-ri-al-ly
im-mense
im-mese-ly
im-mese-ness
im-men-si-ty
im-merge
im-merged
im-merse
im-mersed
im-mers-ing
im-mer-sion
im-mi-grant
im-mi-grat-ed
im-mi-gra-tion
im-mi-gra-tor
im-mi-nent
im-mi-nence
im-mo-bile
im-mo-bil-i-ty
im-mo-bi-lize
im-mod-er-ate
im-mod-er-ate-ly
im-mod-er-ate-ness
im-mod-est
im-mod-est-ly
im-mod-es-ty
im-mo-late
im-mo-lat-ed
im-mo-lat-ing
im-mo-la-tion
im-mo-la-tor
im-mor-al
im-mor-al-ist
im-mo-ral-i-ty
im-mor-al-ly
im-mor-tal
im-mov-a-ble

im-mov-a-bli-i-ty
im-mov-a-bly
im-mune
im-mu-ni-ty
im-mu-ni-ties
im-mu-nize
im-mu-nized
im-mu-niz-ing
im-mu-ni-za-tion
im-mu-nol-o-gy
im-mure
im-mured
im-mur-ing
im-mu-ta-ble
im-mu-ta-bil-i-ty
im-mu-ta-bly
im-pact
im-pac-tion
im-pact-ed
im-pair
im-pair-er
im-pair-ment
im-pa-la
im-pal-as
im-pal-ae
im-pale
im-paled
im-pal-ing
im-pale-ment
im-pal-er
im-pal-pa-ble
im-pal-pa-bil-i-ty
im-pal-pa-bly
im-pan-el
im-pan-eled
im-pan-el-ing
im-part
im-par-tial
im-par-ti-al-i-ty
im-par-tial-ly
im-pass-able
im-pass-abil-i-ty
im-pass-able-ness
im-pass-ably
im-passe
im-pas-si-ble
im-pas-si-bil-i-ty
im-pas-si-bly
im-pas-sion
im-pas-sioned
im-pas-sioned-ly
im-pas-sive
im-pas-sive-ly
im-pas-sive-ness
im-pas-siv-i-ty
im-pa-tience

im-pa-tient
im-pa-tient-ly
im-peach
im-peach-a-ble
im-peach-ment
im-pec-ca-ble
im-pec-ca-bil-i-ty
im-pec-ca-bly
im-pe-cu-nious
im-pe-cu-nious-ly
im-pe-cu-nious-ness
im-pede
im-ped-ed
im-ped-ing
im-ped-i-ment
im-pel
im-pelled
im-pel-ling
im-pend
im-pend-ing
im-pen-e-tra-bil-i-ty
im-pen-e-tra-ble
im-pen-e-tra-ble-ness
im-pen-e-tra-bly
im-pen-i-tent
im-pen-i-tence
im-pen-i-tent-ly
im-per-a-tive
im-per-a-tive-ly
im-per-a-tive-ness
im-per-cep-ti-ble
im-per-cep-ti-bil-i-ty
im-per-cep-tive
im-per-cep-tive-ness
im-per-fect
im-per-fect-ly
im-per-fect-ness
im-per-fec-tion
im-pe-ri-al
im-pe-ri-al-ly
im-pe-ri-al-ism
im-pe-ri-al-ist
im-pe-ri-al-is-tic
im-pe-ri-al-is-ti-cal-ly
im-per-il
im-per-iled
im-per-il-ing
im-per-il-ment
im-pe-ri-ous
im-pe-ri-ous-ly
im-pe-ri-ous-ness
im-per-ish-able
im-per-ish-abil-i-ty
im-per-ish-able-ness
im-per-ish-ably
im-per-ma-nence

im-per-ma-nen-cy
im-per-ma-nent
  im-per-ma-nent-ly
im-per-me-able
  im-per-me-abil-i-ty
  im-per-me-able-ness
  im-per-me-ably
im-per-son-al
  im-per-son-al-i-ty
  im-per-son-al-i-ties
  im-per-son-al-ly
im-per-son-ate
  im-per-son-at-ed
  im-per-son-at-ing
  im-per-son-a-tion
  im-per-son-ator
im-per-ti-nent
  im-per-ti-nence
  im-per-ti-nent-ly
im-per-turb-able
  im-per-turb-ably
im-per-vi-ous
  im-per-vi-ous-ly
  im-per-vi-ous-ness
im-pe-ti-go
im-pet-u-os-i-ty
im-pet-u-ous
  im-pet-u-ous-ly
  im-pet-u-ous-ness
im-pe-tus
  im-pe-tus-es
im-pi-ety
  im-pi-eties
im-pinge
  im-pinged
  im-ping-ing
  im-pinge-ment
  im-ping-er
im-pi-ous
  im-pi-ous-ly
  im-pi-ous-ness
im-pla-ca-ble
  im-pla-ca-bil-i-ty
  im-pla-ca-ble-ness
  im-pla-ca-bly
im-plant
  im-plan-ta-tion
  im-plant-er
im-plau-si-ble
  im-plau-si-bly
  im-plau-si-bil-i-ty
im-ple-ment
  im-ple-men-tal
  im-ple-men-ta-tion
im-pli-cate
  im-pli-cat-ed

im-pli-cat-ing
im-pli-ca-tion
im-plic-it
  im-plic-it-ly
  im-plic-it-ness
im-plode
  im-ploded
  im-plod-ing
im-plore
  im-plored
  im-plor-ing
  im-plo-ra-tion
im-plo-sion
  im-plo-sive
im-ply
  im-plied
  im-ply-ing
im-po-lite
  im-po-lite-ly
  im-po-lite-ness
im-pol-i-tic
  im-pol-i-tic-ly
im-pon-der-a-ble
  im-pon-der-a-bil-i-ty
  im-pon-der-a-bly
im-pone
  im-poned
im-port
  im-port-a-ble
  im-port-er
im-por-tance
  im-por-tant
  im-por-tant-ly
im-por-ta-tion
im-por-tu-nate
  im-por-tu-nate-ly
im-por-tune
  im-por-tuned
  im-por-tun-ing
im-pose
  im-posed
  im-pos-ing
  im-pos-ter
  im-po-si-tion
im-pos-si-bil-i-ty
  im-pos-si-bil-i-ties
im-pos-si-ble
  im-pos-si-bly
im-post
im-pos-tor
im-pos-ture
im-po-tence
im-po-ten-cy
im-po-tent
  im-po-tent-ly
im-pound

im-pound-age
im-pov-er-ish
  im-pov-er-ish-ment
im-prac-ti-ca-ble
  im-prac-ti-ca-bil-i-ty
  im-prac-ti-ca-ble-ness
  im-prac-ti-ca-bly
im-prac-ti-cal
im-pre-cate
  im-pre-cat-ed
  im-pre-cat-ing
  im-pre-ca-tion
im-preg-na-ble
  im-preg-na-bil-i-ty
  im-preg-na-ble-ness
  im-preg-na-bly
im-preg-nate
  im-preg-nat-ed
  im-preg-nat-ing
  im-preg-na-tion
  im-preg-n-tor
im-pre-sa-rio
  im-pre-sa-ri-os
im-press
  im-press-er
  im-press-i-ble
  im-press-ment
im-pres-sion
  im-pres-sion-ist
im-pres-sion-a-ble
  im-pres-sion-a-bly
im-pres-sion-ism
  im-pres-sion-ist
  im-pres-sion-is-tic
im-pres-sive
  im-pres-sive-ly
  im-pres-sive-ness
im-pri-ma-tur
im-print
  im-print-er
im-pris-on
  im-pris-on-ment
im-prob-a-bil-i-ty
im-prob-a-ble
  im-prob-a-ble-ness
  im-prob-a-bly
im-promp-tu
im-prop-er
  im-prop-er-ly
  im-prop-er-ness
im-pro-pri-ety
  im-pro-pri-eties
im-prove
  im-proved
  im-prov-ing
  im-prov-a-bil-i-ty

im-prov-a-ble
im-prove-ment
im-prov-i-dence
im-prov-i-dent
im-prov-i-dent-ly
im-pro-vi-sa-tion
im-pro-vi-sa-tion-al
im-pro-vise
im-pro-vised
im-pro-vis-ing
im-pro-vis-er
im-pru-dence
im-pru-dent
im-pru-dent-ly
im-pugn
im-pugn-er
im-pulse
im-pul-sion
im-pul-sive
im-pu-ni-ty
im-pure
im-pure-ly
im-pure-ness
im-pu-ri-ty
im-pu-ri-ties
im-pute
im-put-ed
im-put-ing
im-put-able
im-put-a-tion
im-put-a-tive
im-put-er
in-a-bil-i-ty
in-ac-ces-si-ble
in-ac-ces-si-bil-i-ties
in-ac-ces-si-ble-ness
in-ac-ces-si-bly
in-ac-cu-rate
in-ac-cu-rate-ly
in-ac-cu-ra-cy
in-ac-cu-ra-cies
in-ac-tion
in-ac-tive
in-ac-tive-ly
in-ac-tiv-i-ty
in-ad-e-quate
in-ad-e-qua-cies
in-ad-e-qua-cy
in-ad-e-quate-ly
in-ad-mis-si-ble
in-ad-mis-si-bly
in-ad-ver-tence
in-ad-ver-ten-cy
in-ad-ver-tent
in-ad-ver-tent-ly
in-alien-a-ble

in-alien-a-bly
in-am-o-ra-ta
in-am-o-ra-tas
inane
inane-ly
inane-ness
inan-i-ty
inan-i-ties
in-an-i-mate
in-ap-pro-pri-ate
in-ap-pro-pri-ate-ly
in-ap-pro-pri-ate-ness
in-apt
in-apt-ti-tude
in-apt-ly
in-apt-ness
in-ar-tic-u-late
in-ar-tic-u-late-ly
in-ar-tic-u-late-ness
in-as-much as
in-at-ten-tion
in-at-ten-tive
in-at-ten-tive-ly
in-au-gu-ral
in-au-gu-rate
in-au-gu-rat-ed
in-au-gu-rat-ing
in-au-gu-ra-tion
in-aus-pi-cious
in-aus-pi-cious-ly
in-board
in-born
in-bred
in-breed
in-breed-ing
in-cal-cu-la-ble
in-cal-cu-la-bly
in-can-des-cent
in-can-des-cence
in-can-des-cent-ly
in-can-ta-tion
in-ca-pa-ble
in-ca-pa-bly
in-ca-pac-i-tate
in-ca-pac-i-tat-ed
in-ca-pac-i-tat-ing
in-ca-pac-i-ty
in-ca-pac-i-ties
in-car-cer-ate
in-car-cer-at-ed
in-car-cer-at-ing
in-car-cer-a-tion
in-car-nate
in-car-nat-ed
in-car-nat-ing
in-car-na-tion

in-cen-di-ary
in-cen-di-aries
in-cense
in-censed
-ceas-ing
in-cen-tive
in-cep-tion
in-ces-sant
in-ces-sant-ly
in-cest
in-ces-tu-ous
in-ces-tu-ous-ly
in-ces-tu-ous-ness
in-cho-ate
in-cho-ate-ly
in-cho-ate-ness
in-ci-dence
in-ci-dent
in-ci-den-tal
in-ci-den-tal-ly
in-cin-er-ate
in-cin-er-at-ed
in-cin-er-at-ing
in-cin-er-a-tion
in-cin-er-a-tor
in-cip-i-ent
in-cip-i-ent-ly
in-cise
in-cised
in-cis-ing
in-ci-sion
in-ci-sive
in-ci-sive-ly
in-ci-sive-ness
in-ci-sor
in-cite
in-cit-ed
in-cit-ing
in-cite-ment
in-cit-er
in-clem-en-cy
in-clem-ent
in-clem-ent-ly
in-cli-na-tion
in-cline
in-clined
in-clin-ing
in-clin-er
in-clude
in-clud-ed
in-clud-ing
in-clud-a-ble
in-clu-sion
in-clu-sive
in-clu-sive-ly
in-clu-sive-ness

103

in-cog-ni-to
in-cog-ni-tos
in-co-her-ence
in-co-her-ent
in-co-her-ent-ly
in-come
in-com-ing
in-com-men-su-ra-ble
in-com-men-su-ra-bly
in-com-men-su-rate
in-com-mo-di-ous
in-com-pa-ra-ble
in-com-pa-ra-bly
in-com-pat-i-bil-i-ty
in-com-pat-i-ble
in-com-pat-i-bly
in-com-pe-tence
in-com-pen-ten-cy
in-com-pe-tent
in-com-pe-tent-ly
in-com-plete
in-com-plete-ly
in-com-plete-ness
in-com-ple-tion
in-com-pre-hen-si-ble
in-com-pre-hen-si-bly
in-com-pre-hen-sion
in-con-ceiv-able
in-con-ceiv-ably
in-con-clu-sive
in-con-clu-sive-ly
in-con-clu-sive-ness
in-con-gru-ity
in-con-gru-ous
in-con-gru-ous-ly
in-con-gru-ous-ness
in-con-gru-i-ties
in-con-se-quen-tial
in-con-se-quen-tial-ly
in-con-sid-er-able
in-con-sid-er-ably
in-con-sid-er-ate
in-con-sid-er-ate-ly
in-con-sid-er-ate-ness
in-con-sis-tent
in-con-sist-ent-ly
in-con-sol-able
in-con-sol-able-ness
in-con-sol-ably
in-con-spic-u-ous
in-con-spic-u-ous-ly
in-con-stant
in-con-stan-cy
in-con-stan-cies
in-con-stant-ly
in-con-test-able

in-con-test-abil-i-ty
in-con-ti-nence
in-con-ti-nen-cy
in-con-ti-nent
in-con-ti-nent-ly
in-con-trol-la-ble
in-con-tro-vert-ible
in-con-ve-nience
in-con-ve-nien-cy
in-con-ve-nient
in-con-ve-nient-ly
in-con-ven-ienc-ing
in-con-vert-ible
in-con-vert-ibly
in-cor-po-rate
in-cor-po-rat-ed
in-cor-po-rat-ing
in-cor-po-ra-tion
in-cor-po-ra-tor
in-cor-po-re-al
in-cor-rect
in-cor-rect-ly
in-cor-ri-gi-ble
in-cor-ri-gi-bil-i-ty
in-cor-ri-gi-ble-ness
in-cor-ri-gi-bly
in-cor-rupt-ible
in-cor-rupt-ibil-i-ty
in-cor-rupt-ible-ness
in-cor-rupt-ibly
in-crease
in-creased
in-creas-ing
in-creas-able
in-creas-ing-ly
in-cred-i-ble
in-cred-i-bil-i-ty
in-cred-i-ble-ness
in-cred-i-bly
in-cre-du-li-ty
in-cred-u-lous
in-cred-u-lous-ness
in-cred-u-lous-ly
in-cre-ment
in-cre-men-tal
in-crim-i-nate
in-crim-i-nat-ed
in-crim-i-nat-ing
in-crim-i-na-tion
in-crim-i-na-tor
in-crim-i-na-to-ry
in-crust
in-crus-ta-tion
in-cu-bate
in-cu-bat-ed
in-cu-bat-ing

in-cu-ba-tion
in-cu-ba-tor
in-cu-bus
in-cu-bus-es
in-cul-cate
in-cul-cat-ed
in-cul-cat-ing
in-cul-ca-tion
in-cul-ca-tor
in-cul-pate
in-cul-pat-ed
in-cul-pat-ing
in-cul-pa-tion
in-cum-ben-cy
in-cum-ben-cies
in-cum-bent
in-cum-bent-ly
in-cur
in-curred
in-cur-ring
in-cur-able
in-cur-a-bil-i-ty
in-cur-a-ble-ness
in-cur-a-bly
in-cur-sion
in-cur-sive
in-debt-ed
in-debt-ed-ness
in-de-cen-cy
in-den-cies
in-de-cent
in-de-cent-ly
in-de-ci-sion
in-de-ci-sive
in-de-ci-sive-ly
in-de-ci-sive-ness
in-deed
in-de-fat-i-ga-ble
in-de-fat-i-ga-bil-i-ty
in-de-fat-i-ga-ble-ness
in-de-fat-i-ga-bly
in-def-i-nite
in-def-i-nite-ly
in-def-i-nite-ness
in-del-i-ble
in-del-i-bil-ity
in-del-i-ble-ness
in-del-i-bly
in-del-i-ca-cy
in-del-i-cate
in-del-i-cate-ness
in-del-i-cate-ly
in-dem-ni-fi-ca-tion
in-dem-ni-fy
in-dem-ni-fied
in-dem-ni-fy-ing

in-dem-ni-fi-er
in-dem-ni-ty
  in-dem-ni-ties
in-dent
in-den-ta-tion
  in-dent-ed
in-den-ture
  in-den-tured
  in-den-tur-ing
in-de-pen-dence
in-de-pen-den-cy
in-de-pen-dent
  in-de-pen-dent-ly
in-de-scib-able
  in-de-scrib-abil-ity
  in-de-scrib-able-ness
  in-de-scrib-ably
in-de-struc-ti-ble
  in-de-struc-ti-bil-i-ty
  in-de-struc-ti-ble-ness
  in-de-struc-ti-bly
in-det-mi-na-cy
in-de-ter-mi-nate
  in-de-ter-mi-nat-ly
  in-de-ter-mi-na-tion
in-dex
  in-dex-er
  in-dex-es
  in-di-ces
in-di-cate
  in-di-cat-ed
  in-di-cat-ing
  in-di-ca-tion
in-dic-a-tive
  in-dic-a-tive-ly
in-di-ca-tor
  in-dic-a-tory
in-dict
  in-dict-a-ble
  in-dict-er
  in-dict-or
  in-dict-ment
in-dif-fer-ence
in-dif-fer-ent
  in-dif-fer-ent-ist
  in-dif-fer-ent-ly
in-dig-e-nous
  in-dig-e-nous-ly
  in-dig-e-nous-ness
in-di-gent
  in-di-gent-ly
in-di-gest-ed
in-di-gest-ible
  in-di-gest-ibil-i-ty
  in-di-gest-ible-ness
in-di-ges-tion

in-di-ges-tive
in-dig-nant
  in-dig-ant-ly
in-dig-na-tion
in-dig-ni-ty
  in-dig-ni-ties
in-di-go
  in-di-goes
  in-di-gos
in-di-rect
  in-di-rect-ly
  in-di-rect-ness
in-dis-creet
  in-dis-creet-ly
  in-dis-creet-ness
in-dis-crete
in-dis-cre-tion
in-dis-crim-i-nate
  in-dis-crim-i-nate-iy
  in-dis-crim-i-nat-ing
  in-dis-crim-i-na-tion
in-dis-pens-able
  in-dis-pens-able-ness
  in-dis-pens-abil-i-ty
  in-dis-pens-ably
in-dis-pose
  in-dis-posed
  in-dis-pos-ing
  in-dis-po-si-tion
in-dis-sol-u-ble
  in-dis-sol-u-bil-i-ty
  in-dis-sol-u-ble-ness
  in-dis-sol-u-bly
in-di-um
in-di-vid-u-al
  in-di-vid-u-al-ly
in-di-vid-u-al-ism
  in-di-vid-u-al-ist
  in-di-vid-u-al-is-tic
in-di-vid-u-al-i-ty
  in-di-vid-u-al-i-ties
in-di-vid-u-al-ize
  in-di-vid-u-al-ized
  in-di-vid-u-al-iz-ing
in-doc-tri-nate
  in-doc-tri-nat-ed
  in-doc-tri-nat-ing
  in-doc-tri-na-tion
  in-doc-tri-na-tor
in-do-lence
  in-do-lent
  in-do-lent-ly
in-dom-i-ta-ble
  in-dom-i-ta-bil-i-ty
  in-dom-ita-ble-ness
  in-dom-i-ta-bly

in-door
in-doors
in-du-bi-ta-ble
  in-du-bi-ta-bil-i-ty
  in-dubi-ta-ble-ness
  in-du-bi-tab-ly
in-duce
  in-duced
  in-duce-ment
  in-duc-er
  in-duc-i-ble
  in-duc-ing
in-duct
  in-duct-ee
in-duc-tion
  in-duc-tive
in-dulge
  in-dulged
  in-dulg-ing
in-dul-gence
  in-dul-gent
  in-dul-gent-ly
in-dus-tri-al
  in-dus-tri-al-ly
  in-dus-tri-al-ness
in-dus-tri-al-ism
in-dus-tri-al-ize
  in-dus-tri-al-ist
  in-dus-tri-al-i-za-tion
  in-dus-tri-al-ized
  in-dus-tri-al-iz-ing
in-dus-tri-ous
  in-dus-tri-ous-ly
in-dus-try
  in-dus-tries
ine-bri-ate
  ine-bri-at-ed
  ine-bri-at-ing
  ine-bri-a-tion
  ine-bri-ety
in-ed-u-ca-ble
in-ef-fa-ble
  in-ef-fa-bil-i-ty
  in-ef-fa-ble-ness
  in-ef-fa-bly
in-ef-fec-tive
  in-ef-fec-tive-ly
  in-ef-fec-tive-ness
in-ef-fec-tu-al
  in-ef-fec-tu-al-i-ty
  in-ef-fec-tu-al-ly
  in-ef-fec-tu-al-ness
in-ef-fi-cient
  in-ef-fi-cien-cy
  in-ef-fi-cien-cies
  in-ef-ffi-cient-ly

in-el-i-gi-ble
  in-el-i-gi-bil-i-ty
  in-el-i-gi-bly
in-e-luc-ta-ble
in-ept
  in-ept-i-tude
  in-ept-ly
in-ept-ness
in-e-qual-i-ty
in-eq-ui-ta-ble
in-eq-ui-ty
  in-eq-ui-ties
in-ert
  in-ert-ly
  in-ert-ness
in-er-tia
  in-er-tial
in-es-cap-a-ble
in-es-cap-a-ble
in-es-ti-ma-ble
  in-es-ti-ma-bly
in-ev-i-ta-ble
  in-ev-i-ta-bil-i-ty
  in-ev-i-ta-ble-ness
  in-ev-i-ta-ble-ness
  in-ev-i-ta-bly
in-ex-haust-i-ble
  in-ex-haust-i-bil-i-ty
  in-ex-haust-i-ble-ness
  in-ex-haust-i-bly
in-ex-o-ra-ble
  in-ex-o-ra-bil-i-ty
  in-ex-o-ra-ble-ness
  in-ex-o-ra-bly
in-ex-pe-ri-ence
  in-ex-pe-ri-enced
in-ex-pert
  in-ex-per-ly
  in-ex-pert-ness
in-ex-pe-ri-ence
  in-ex-pe-ri-enced
in-ex-pert
  in-ex-pert-ly
  in-ex-pert-ness
in-ex-pi-a-ble
  in-ex-pi-a-ble-ness
  in-ex-pi-a-bly
in-ex-pli-ca-ble
  in-ex-pli-ca-bil-i-ty
  in-ex-pli-ca-ble-ness
  in-ex-pli-ca-bly
in-fal-li-ble
  in-fal-i-bil-i-ty
  in-fal-li-ble-ness
  in-fal-li-bly
in-fa-mous

in-fa-mous-ly
in-fa-mous-ness
in-fa-my
  in-fa-mies
in-fan-cy
  in-fan-cies
in-fant
  in-fant-hood
  in-fant-like
in-fan-tile
  in-fan-tine
  in-fan-til-i-ty
in-fan-try
  in-fan-tries
  in-fan-try-man
  in-fan-try-men
in-fat-u-ate
  in-fat-u-at-ed
  in-fat-u-at-ing
  in-fat-u-at-ed-ly
  in-fat-u-a-tion
in-fect
  in-fect-ed-ness
  in-fect-er
  in-fect-or
in-fec-tion
in-fec-tious
  in-fec-tious-ly
  in-fec-tious-ness
  in-fec-tive
in-fer
  inferred
  in-fer-ring
  in-fer-a-ble
  in-fer-a-bly
  in-fer-ence
  in-fer-er
in-fe-ri-or
  in-fe-ri-or-i-ty
  in-fe-ri-or-ly
in-fer-nal
in-fer-no
  in-fer-nos
in-fest
  in-fes-ta-tion
  in-fest-er
in-fi-del
in-fi-del-i-ty
  in-fi-del-i-ties
in-field
  in-field-er
in-fight-ing
  in-fight-er
in-fil-trate
  in-fil-trat-ed
  in-fil-trat-ing

in-fil-tra-tion
in-fil-tra-tive
in-fil-tra-tor
in-fi-nite
  in-fi-nite-ly
  in-fi-nite-ness
  in-fin-i-tude
in-fin-i-tes-i-mal
  in-fin-i-tes-i-mal-ty
in-fin-i-tive
  in-fin-i-tive-ly
in-fin-i-ty
  in-fin-i-ties
in-firm
  in-firm-lly
  in-firm-ness
in-fir-ma-ry
  in-fir-ma-ries
in-fir-mi-ty
  in-fir-mi-ties
in-flame
  in-flamed
  in-flam-ing
  in-flam-er
in-flam-ma-ble
  in-flam-ma-bil-i-ty
  in-flam-ma-ble-ness
  in-flam-ma-bly
in-flam-ma-tion
in-flam-ma-to-ry
in-flate
  in-flat-ed
  in-flat-ing
  in-flat-a-ble
  in-flat-ed-ness
  in-fla-tor
  in-flat-er
in-fla-tion
  in-fla-tion-ary
  in-fla-tion-ism
  in-fla-tion-ist
in-flect
  in-flec-tion
  in-flec-tion-al
  in-flec-tion-al-ly
  in-flec-tion-less
  in-flec-tive
  in-flec-tor
in-flex-i-ble
  in-flex-i-bil-i-ty
  in-flex-i-ble-ness
  in-flex-i-bly
in-flict
  in-flict-a-ble
  in-flict-er
  in-flict-or

in-flic-tion
in-flic-tive
in-flu-ence
in-flu-enced
in-flu-enc-ing
in-flu-ence-a-ble
in-flu-enc-er
in-flu-en-tial
in-flu-en-tial-ly
in-flu-en-za
in-flu-en-zal
in-flu-en-za-like
in-flux
in-form
in-formed
in-for-mer
in-for-mal
in-for-mal-i-ty
in-for-mal-ly
in-form-ant
in-for-ma-tion
in-for-ma-tion-al
in-for-ma-tive
in-for-ma-tive-ly
in-for-ma-tive-ness
in-for-ma-to-ry
in-frac-tion
in-fran-gi-ble
in-fran-gi-bil-i-ty
in-fran-gi-ble-ness
in-fran-gi-bly
in-fra-red
in-fra-struc-ture
in-fre-quent
in-fre-quen-cy
in-fre-quent-ly
in-fringe
in-fringed
in-fring-ing
in-fringe-ment
in-fring-er
in-fu-ri-ate
in-fu-ri-at-ed
in-fu-ri-at-ing
in-fu-ri-at-ing-ly
in-fu-ri-a-tion
in-fuse
in-fused
in-fus-ing
in-fus-er
in-fus-i-bil-i-ty
in-fus-i-ble
in-fu-sion
in-fu-sive
in-gen-ious
in-gen-ious-ly

in-gen-ious-ness
in-gest
in-ges-tion
in-ges-tive
in-glo-ri-ous
in-glo-ri-ous-ly
in-glo-ri-ous-ness
in-got
in-grain
in-grained
in-grate
in-gra-ti-ate
in-gra-ti-at-ed
in-gra-ti-at-ing
in-gra-ti-a-tion
in-grat-i-tude
in-gre-di-ent
in-group
in-grow-ing
in-grown
in-growth
in-gulf
in-hab-it
in-hab-it-a-ble
in-hab-i-ta-tion
in-hab-it-er
in-hab-it-ed
in-hab-it-ant
in-hal-ant
in-ha-la-tion
in-ha-la-tor
in-hale
in-haled
in-hal-ing
in-hal-er
in-here
in-hered
in-her-ing
in-her-ence
in-her-ent
in-her-ent-ly
in-he-sion
in-her-it
in-her-i-tor
in-her-i-tance
in-hib-it
in-hib-i-tive
in-hib-o-to-ry
in-hib-i-ter
in-hib-it-or
in-hi-bi-tion
in-hos-pi-ta-ble
in-hos-pi-tal-i-ty
in-hu-man
in-hu-man-i-ty
in-hu-mane

in-im-i-cal
in-im-i-ta-ble
in-iq-ui-ty
in-iq-ui-ties
in-iq-ui-tous
in-i-tial
in-i-tialed
in-i-tial-ing
in-i-tial-ly
in-i-ti-ate
in-i-ti-at-ed
in-i-ti-at-ing
in-i-ti-a-tion
in-i-ti-a-tor
in-i-ti-a-tive
in-ject
in-jec-tion
in-jec-tor
in-ju-di-cious
in-junc-tion
in-junc-tive
in-jur
in-jured
in-jur-ing
in-ju-ri-ous
in-ju-ry
in-ju-ries
in-jus-tice
ink-blot
ink-ling
inky
in-law
in-lay
in-laid
in-lay-ing
in-let
in-me-mo-ri-an
in-most
in-nards
in-nate
in-ner
in-ner-most
in-ner-sole
in-ner-vate
in-ner-vat-ed
in-ner-vat-ing
in-ner-va-tion
in-nerve
in-ning
inn-keep-er
in-no-cence
in-no-cent
in-no-cent-ly
in-noc-u-ous
in-no-vate
in-no-vat-ed

in-no-vat-ing
in-no-va-tion
in-no-va-tive
in-no-va-tor
in-nu-en-do
in-nu-en-dos
in-nu-en-does
in-nu-mer-a-ble
in-nu-mer-ous
in-nu-mer-a-bly
in-ob-serv-ance
in-ob-serv-ant
in-ob-serv-ant-ly
in-oc-u-lant
in-oc-u-late
in-oc-u-lat-ed
in-oc-u-lat-ing
in-oc-u-la-tion
in-oc-u-la-tor
in-oc-u-lum
in-of-fen-sive
in-op-er-a-ble
in-op-er-a-tive
in-op-por-tune
in-op-por-tun-i-ty
in-or-di-nate
in-pa-tient
in-pour
in-put
in-quest
in-qui-e-tude
in-quire
in-quiry
in-quir-ies
in-qui-si-tion
in-qui-si-tive
in-quis-i-tor
in-road
in-rush
in-sane
in-san-i-ty
in-san-i-ties
in-sa-tia-ble
in-sa-tia-bil-i-ty
in-sa-tia-bly
in-sa-ti-ate
in-scribe
in-scru-ta-ble
in-scru-ta-bil-i-ty
in-scru-ta-bly
in-seam
in-sect
in-sec-ti-cide
in-sec-ti-cid-al
in-se-cure
in-se-cu-ri-ty

in-sem-i-nate
in-sem-i-nat-ed
in-sem-i-nat-ing
in-sem-i-na-tion
in-sen-sate
in-sen-si-ble
in-sen-si-tive
in-sen-si-tiv-i-ty
in-sen-ti-ent
in-sep-a-ra-ble
in-sep-a-ra-bil-i-ty
in-sep-a-ra-bly
in-sert
in-sert-er
in-ser-tion
in-set
in-set-ting
in-shore
in-side
in-sid-er
in-sid-i-ous
in-sight
in-sight-ful
in-sig-nia
in-sig-nif-i-cant
in-sig-nif-i-cance
in-sin-cere
in-sin-cer-i-ty
in-sin-cer-i-ties
in-sin-u-ate
in-sin-u-at-ed
in-sin-u-at-ing
in-sin-u-a-tor
in-sin-u-a-tion
in-sip-id
in-sip-id-i-ty
in-sip-id-ness
in-sist
in-sist-ence
in-sist-ent
in-so-bri-e-ty
in-so-cia-ble
in-so-cia-bil-i-ty
in-so-cia-bly
in-so-far
in-sole
in-so-lent
in-so-lence
in-sol-u-ble
in-sol-u-bil-i-ty
in-sol-u-bly
in-solv-a-ble
in-sol-vent
in-sol-ven-cy
in-som-nia
in-som-ni-ac

in-so-much
in-spect
in-spec-tion
in-spec-tor
in-spi-ra-tion
in-spi-ra-tion-al
in-spire
in-spir-ing
in-spir-it
in-sta-ble
in-sta-bil-i-ty
in-stall
in-stan-ta-ne-ous
in-stant-ly
in-state
in-stat-ed
in-stat-ing
in-state-ment
in-stead
in-step
in-sti-gate
in-sti-gat-ed
in-sti-gat-ing
in-sti-ga-tion
in-sti-ga-tor
in-still
in-stinct
in-stinc-tive
in-stinc-tu-al
in-stinc-tive-ly
in-sti-tute
in-sti-tut-ed
in-sti-tut-ing
in-sti-tut-er
in-sti-tu-tor
in-sti-tu-tion
in-sti-tu-tion-al
in-sti-tu-tion-al-ism
in-sti-tu-tion-al-ize
in-sti-tu-tion-al-ized
in-struct
in-struc-tion
in-struc-tive
in-struc-tor
in-stru-ment
in-stru-men-tal
in-stru-men-ta-list
in-stru-men-ta-tion
in-sub-or-di-nate
in-sub-or-di-na-tion
in-sub-stan-tial
in-sub-stan-ti-al-i-ty
in-suf-fer-a-ble
in-suf-fer-a-bly
in-suf-fi-cient
in-suf-fi-cien-cy

in-su-lar
in-su-lar-i-ty
in-su-late
in-su-lat-ed
in-su-lat-ing
in-su-la-tion
in-su-la-tor
in-su-lin
in-sult
in-sop-port-a-ble
in-sup-press-i-ble
in-sur-ance
in-sure
in-sured
in-sur-ing
in-sur-er
in-sur-gent
in-sur-gence
in-sur-gen-cy
in-sur-mount-a-ble
in-sur-rec-tion
in-sur-rec-tion-ary
in-sus-cep-ti-ble
in-tact
in-take
in-tan-gi-ble
in-tan-gi-bil-i-ty
in-tan-gi-bly
in-te-ger
in-te-gral
in-te-gral-ly
in-te-grate
in-te-grat-ed
in-te-grat-ing
in-te-gra-tion
in-te-gra-tion-ist
in-teg-ri-ty
in-tel-lect
in-tel-lec-tu-al
in-tel-lec-tu-al-ism
in-tel-li-gence
in-tel-li-gent
in-tel-li-gent-ly
in-tel-li-gent-sia
in-tel-li-gi-ble
in-tel-li-gi-bil-i-ty
in-tel-li-gi-bly
in-tem-per-ance
in-tem-per-ate
in-tend
in-tend-er
in-tend-ed
in-tense
in-tense-ly
in-tense-ness
in-ten-si-fy

in-ten-si-fied
in-ten-si-fy-ing
in-ten-si-fi-ca-tion
in-ten-si-fi-er
in-ten-sion
in-ten-si-ty
in-ten-si-ties
in-ten-sive
in-ten-sive-ly
in-ten-sive-ness
in-tent
in-ten-tion
in-ten-tion-al
in-en-tion-al-ly
in-ten-tioned
in-ter
in-ter-act
in-ter-ac-tion
in-ter-breed
in-ter-bred
in-ter-bredd-ing
in-ter-cede
in-ter-ced-ed
in-ter-ced-ing
in-ter-ced-er
in-ter-cept
in-ter-cep-ter
in-ter-cept-or
in-ter-cep-tion
in-ter-cep-tive
in-ter-ces-sion
in-ter-change
in-ter-changed
in-ter-chang-ing
in-ter-chang-a-ble
in-ter-chng-a-bil-i-ty
in-ter-chang-a-bly
in-ter-col-le-gi-ate
in-ter-com
in-ter-com-mun-i-cate
in-ter-con-nect
in-ter-con-nec-tion
in-ter-con-ti-nen-tal
in-ter-course
in-ter-cul-tur-al
in-ter-cur-rent
in-ter-de-part-men-tal
in-ter-de-pend-ent
in-ter-de-pend
in-ter-de-pend-ence
in-ter-de-pend-en-cy
in-ter-dict
in-ter-dic-tion
in-ter-dis-ci-pli-nary
in-ter-est
in-ter-est-ed

in-ter-est-ed-ly
in-ter-est-ing
in-ter-face
in-ter-fa-cial
in-ter-faith
in-ter-fere
in-ter-ga-lac-tic
in-ter-im
in-te-ri-or
in-ter-ject
in-ter-jec-tion
in-ter-jec-to-ry
in-ter-ly-er
in-ter-leaf
in-ter-leaves
in-ter-leave
in-ter-leaved
in-ter-leav-ing
in-ter-line
in-ter-lined
in-ter-lin-ing
in-ter-link
in-ter-lock
in-ter-lo-cu-tion
in-ter-loc-u-tor
in-ter-loc-u-to-ry
in-ter-lope
in-ter-loped
in-ter-loped
in-ter-lop-ing
in-ter-lop-er
in-ter-lude
in-ter-nar
in-ter-na-ry
in-ter-mar-ry
in-ter-mar-ried
in-ter-mar-ry-ing
in-ter-mar-riage
in-ter-me-di-ary
in-ter-me-di-ar-ies
in-ter-me-di-ate
in-ter-me-di-at-ed
in-ter-me-di-at-ing
in-ter-me-di-a-tion
in-ter-me-di-a-tor
in-ter-mi-na-ble
in-ter-min-gle
in-ter-min-gledd
in-ter-min-gling
in-ter-mis-sion
in-ter-mis-sive
in-ter-mit
in-ter-mix
in-ter-mix-ture
in-tern
in-ter-ship

in-ter-nal
  in-ter-nal-ly
in-ter-nal-ize
  in-ter-nal-ized
  in-ter-nal-iz-ing
  in-ter-nal-i-za-tion
in-ter-na-tion-al
  in-ter-na-tion-al-i-ty
  in-ter-na-tion-al-ize
  in-ter-na-tion-al-ized
in-ter-na-tion-al-ism
in-tern-ee
in-tern-ist
in-tern-ment
in-ter-of-fice
in-ter-pen-e-trate
  in-ter-pen-e-tra-tion
in-ter-plan-e-tary
in-ter-play
in-ter-po-late
in-ter-pose
  in-ter-posed
  in-ter-pos-ing
  in-ter-pos-er
  in-ter-po-si-tion
in-ter-pret
  in-ter-pret-a-ble
  in-ter-pret-er
  in-ter-pre-tive
in-ter-pre-ta-tion
  in-ter-pre-ta-tion-al
  in-ter-pre-ta-tive
in-ter-re-late
  in-ter-re-lat-ed
  in-ter-re-alt-ing
in-ter-ro-gate
  in-ter-ro-gat-ed
  in-ter-ro-gat-ing
in-ter-ro-ga-tion
  in-ter-ro-ga-tion
  in-ter-ro-ga-tion-al
in-ter-rog-a-tive
in-ter-ro-ga-tor
in-ter-rupt
  in-ter-rup-tion
  in-ter-rup-tive
in-ter-rupt-er
  in-ter-rupt-or
in-terr-scho-las-tic
in-ter-sect
in-ter-sec-tion
in-ter-space
  in-ter-spaced
  in-ter-spac-ing
in-ter-sperse
  in-ter-spersed

  in-ter-spers-ing
  in-ter-sper-sion
in-ter-state
  in-ter-stel-lar
in-ter-tid-al
in-ter-twine
  in-ter-twined
  in-ter-twin-ing
in-ter-ur-ban
in-ter-val
in-ter-vence
in-ter-view
  in-ter-view-er
in-ter-weave
  in-ter-wove
  in-ter-weav-ing
  in-ter-wo-ven
in-tes-tate
in-tes-tine
  in-tes-ti-nal
in-ti-mate
  in-ti-mat-ed
  in-ti-mat-ing
  in-ti-mate-ly
  in-ti-ma-tion
in-tim-i-date
  in-tim-i-dat-ed
  in-tim-i-dat-ing
  in-tim-i-da-tion
  in-tim-i-da-tor
in-ti-tled
  in-ti-ling
in-to
in-tol-er-a-ble
  in-tol-er-a-bly
in-tol-er-ant
  in-tol-er-ance
in-tomb
in-to-mate
  in-to-nat-ed
  in-to-nat-ing
in-to-na-tion
in-tone
  in-toned
  in-ton-ing
  in-ton-er
in-tox-i-cant
in-tox-i-cate
  in-tox-i-cat-ed
  in-tox-i-cat-ing
  in-tox-i-ca-tion
in-trac-ta-ble
  in-trac-ta-bil-i-ty
in-tra-mu-ral
  in-tra-mu-ral-ly
in-tran-si-gent

in-tran-si-gence
in-tran-si-tive
in-tra-state
in-tra-ve-nous
in-trench
in-trep-id
  in-tre-pid-i-ty
in-tri-cate
  in-tri-ca-cy
  in-tri-ca-cies
  in-tri-cate-ness
in-trique
  in-tri-quing
in-trin-sic
  in-trin-si-cal
  in-trin-si-cal-ly
in-tro-duce
  in-tro-duced
  in-tro-duc-ing
  in-tro-duc-er
  in-tro-duc-tion
  in-tro-duc-to-ry
in-tro-spect
  in-tro-spec-tion
  in-tro-spec-tive
in-tro-ver-sion
  in-tro-ver-sive
in-tro-vert
  in-tro-vert-ed
in-trude
in-trust
in-tu-it
in-tu-i-tion
  in-tu-i-tion-al
in-tu-i-tive
in-un-date
  in-un-dat-ed
  in-un-dat-ing
  in-un-da-tion
  in-un-da-tor
in-ure
  in-ured
  in-ur-ing
in-vade
in-val-id
  in-va-lid-i-ty
in-val-i-date
  in-val-i-dat-ed
  in-val-i-dat-ing
  in-val-i-da-tion
  in-val-i-da-tor
in-va-lid-ism
in-val-u-a-ble
in-var-i-a-ble
  in-var-i-a-bil-i-ty
in-var-i-ant

in-var-i-ance
in-va-sion
in-va-sive
in-vec-tive
in-vent
in-vent-a-ble
in-ven-tor
in-ven-tion
in-ven-tive
in-ven-tive-ness
in-ven-to-ry
in-ven-to-ries
in-ven-to-ried
in-ven-to-ry-ing
in-verse
in-ver-sion
in-vert
in-ver-te-brate
in-vert-ed
in-vest
in-ves-tor
in-ves-ti-gate
in-ves-ti-gat-ed
in-ves-ti-gat-ing
in-ves-ti-ga-tion
in-ves-ti-ga-tor
in-ves-ti-ture
in-vest-ment
in-vet-er-ate
in-vid-i-ous
in-vig-or-ate
in-vig-or-at-ed
in-vig-or-at-ing
in-vig-or-ant
in-vig-or-a-tion
in-vig-or-a-tor
in-vin-ci-ble
in-vin-ci-bil-i-ty
in-vin-ci-bly
in-vi-o-la-ble
in-vi-o-la-bil-i-ty
in-vi-o-la-bly
in-vi-o-late
in-vis-i-ble
in-vis-i-bil-i-ty
in-vis-i-bly
in-vi-ta-tion
in-vi-ta-tion-al
in-vite
in-vit-ed
in-vit-ing
in-vit-er
in-vo-ca-tion
in-voice
in-voke
in-voked

in-vok-ing
in-vol-un-tary
in-vol-un-tar-i-ly
in-vo-lute
in-vo-lu-tion
in-volve
in-volved
in-volv-ing
in-volve-ment
in-volv-er
in-vul-ner-a-ble
in-ward
in-wards
in-ward-ly
in-ward-ness
in-waeve
in-wrought
io-dine
ion
ion-ic
ion-ize
ion-ized
ion-iz-ing
ion-i-za-tion
ion-iz-er
ion-o-sphere
iota
ip-so fac-to
iras-ci-ble
iras-ci-bil-i-ty
iras-ci-bly
irate
ir-i-des-cent
ir-i-des-cence
irid-i-um
iris
irk-some
iron
iron-er
iron-clad
iron-ic
iron-i-cal
iron-smith
iron-ware
iron-work
iron-work-er
iro-ny
iro-nies
ir-ra-di-ate
ir-ra-di-at-ed
ir-ra-di-at-ing
ir-ra-di-a-tion
ir-ra-di-a-ter
ir-rad-i-ca-ble
ir-ra-tion-al
ir-ra-tion-al-i-ty

ir-re-claim-a-ble
ir-rec-on-cil-a-ble
ir-rec-on-cil-a-bil-i-ty
ir-re-cov-er-a-ble
ir-re-duc-i-ble
ir-ref-u-ta-ble
ir-re-gard-less
ir-reg-u-lar
ir-reg-u-lar-i-ty
ir-rel-e-vant
ir-rel-e-vance
ir-rel-e-van-cy
ir-re-li-gion
ir-re-li-gious
ir-re-mis-si-ble
ir-re-mov-a-ble
ir-rep-a-ra-ble
ir-re-plac-a-ble
ir-re-press-i-ble
ir-re-press-i-bil-i-ty
ir-re-press-i-bly
ir-re-proach-a-ble
ir-re-sist-i-ble
ir-re-sist-i-bil-i-ty
ir-res-o-lute
ir-res-o-lu-tion
ir-re-spec-tive
ir-re-spon-si-ble
ir-re-spon-si-bil-i-ty
ir-re-spon-sive
ir-re-spon-sive-ness
ir-re-triev-a-ble
ir-re-triev-a-bil-i-ty
ir-re-triev-a-bly
ir-rev-o-ca-ble
ir-rev-o-ca-bil-i-ty
ir-ri-gate
ir-ri-gat-ed
ir-ri-ta-ble
ir-ri-tant
ir-ri-tate
ir-rupt
is-land
isle
iso-bar
iso-gloss
iso-late
iso-lat-ed
iso-met-ric
ison-o-my
iso-ton-ic
is-su-ance
is-sue
item
it-er-ate
ivo-ry

J

jab
jabbed
jab-bing
jab-ber
jab-ber-er
jac-a-mar
jac-a-ram-da
jack-al
jack-ass
jack-boot
jack-et
  jack-et-ed
jack-ham-mer
jack--in--the--box
  jack--in--the--box-es
jack-knife
  jack-kives
  jack-knifed
  jack-knif-ing
jack--of--all--trades
jack--o'--lan-tern
jack-pot
jack rab-bit
jac-o-net
jac-quard
jade
  jad-ed
  jad-ing
Jaf-fa
jag
  jag-ged
  jag-ging
jag-uar
jail-bird
jail-break
jail-er
ja-lopy
  ja-lop-ies
jal-ou-sie
jam
  jammed
  jam-ming
  jam-mer
jamb
jam-bo-ree
jan-gle
  jan-gled
  jan-gling
  jan-gler
  jan-gly
jan-i-tor
  jan-i-to-ri-al
jar
  jar-ful
  jarred
  jar-ring

jar-di-niere
jar-red
jar-gon
  jar-gon-ize
jas-mine
jas-sid
jaun-dice
  jaun-diced
  jaun-dic-ing
jaunt
  jaun-ty
  jaun-ti-er
  jaun-ti-est
  jaun-ti-ly
  jaun-ti-ness
jav-e-lin
jaw-bone
jaw-break-er
jay-gee
jay-walk
  jay-walk-er
jazz
  jazz-ist
  jazz-man
jazzy
  jazz-i-er
  jazz-i-est
  jazz-i-ly
  jazz-i-ness
jeal-ous
  jeal-ous-ies
jeep
jeer-er
je-hu
jel-li-fy
  jel-li-fies
  jel-li-fy-ing
jel-ly
  jel-lied
  jel-lies
  jel-ly-ing
  jel-ly-like
jel-ly bean
jel-ly-fish
jen-ny
  jen-nies
jeop-ar-dy
  jeop-ar-dize
  jeop-ar-dized
  jeop-ar-diz-ing
jerk
  jerk-er
  jerk-i-ly
  jerk-i-ness
  jerk-y
  jerk-i-er

jerk-i-est
jer-kin
jer-ry--build
  jer-ry--built
  jer-ry--build-ing
  jer-ry--build-er
jer-sey
jes-sa-mine
jest-er
  jest-ing
Je-sus
jet
  jet-ted
  jet-ting
  jet-lin-er
  jet-port
  jet-pro-polled
  jet-sam
  jet-ti-son
  jet-ty
  jet-ties
jew-el
  jew-eled
  jew-el-ing
  jew-el-er
  jew-el-ry
jibe
  jibed
  jib-ing
jif-fy
  jif-fies
jig
  jigged
  jig-ging
  jig-ger
jig-gle
  jig-gled
  jig-gling
  jig-gly
jig-saw
jilt-er
jim-dan-dy
jim-my
  jim-mies
  jim-mied
  jim-my-ing
jin-gle
  jin-gled
  jin-gling
jinx
jit-ney
  jit-neys
jit-ter
  jit-ters
  jit-tery
  jit-ter-bug

jit-ter-bugged
job
jobbed
job-bing
job-ber
job-hold-er
jock-ey
jock-eys
jock-eyed
jock-ey-ing
jock-strap
jo-cose
jo-cos-i-ty
jo-cund
jo-cun-di-ty
jodh-pur
jog
jogged
jog-ging
jog-ger
jog-gle
jog-gled
jog-gling
join-able
join-er
joint
joint-ed
joint-ly
joist
joke
joked
jok-ing
joke-ster
jok-ing-ly
jok-er
jol-ly
jol-li-er
jol-li-est
jol-lied
jol-ly-ing
jolt
jolt-er
jolt-ing-ly
jolty
jon-quil
jos-tle
jos-tled
jos-tling
jos-tler
jot
jott-ed
joule
jour-nal
jour-nal-ism
jour-nal-ist
jour-na-lis-tic

jour-nal-ize
jour-ney
jour-ney-man
jour-ney-men
joust
jo-vi-al
jo-vi-al-i-ty
jowl
jowled
jowy
joy-ful
joy-less
joy-ous
joy-ride
ju-bi-lant
ju-bi-lance
ju-bi-lan-cy
ju-bi-lar-i-an
ju-bi-la-tion
ju-bi-late
ju-bi-lat-ed
ju-bi-lat-ing
ju-bi-lee
judge
judged
judg-ing
judge-ment
judge-men-tal
ju-di-ca-ture
ju-di-cial
ju-di-cia-ry
ju-di-cious
Ju-dith
ju-do
jug
jugged
jug-gin
jug-ful
jug-gler
ju-gate
jug-u-lar
jug-u-lum
ju-gum
juice
juic-i-er
juic-i-est
juic-i-ly
juic-i-ness
ju-jit-su
juke-box
ju-lep
ju-li-enne
Ju-lius
Ju-ly
jum-ble
jum-bled

jum-bling
jum-bo
jum-bos
jump
jump-ing
jump-i-ness
jumpy
jump-er
jump--off
junc-tion
junc-ture
jun-gle
jun-ior
ju-ni-per
junk
junk-man
junky
jun-ket
junk-ie
jun-ta
Ju-pi-ter
ju-ris-dic-tion
ju-ris-dic-tion-al
ju-ris-pru-dence
ju-ris-pru-den-tial
ju-ris-pru-dent
ju-rist
ju-ris-tic
ju-ror
ju-ry
ju-ries
ju-ry-man
just
just-ly
just-ness
jus-tice
jus-tice-less
jus-tice-like
jus-ti-fi-ca-tion
jus-ti-fy
jus-ti-fied
jus-ti-fy-ing
jus-ti-fi-a-ble
jus-tif-i-ca-tory
jut
jut-ted
jut-ting
jute
ju-ve-nes-cence
ju-ve-nes-cent
ju-ve-nile
ju-ve-nil-i-ty
jux-ta-pose
jux-ta-posed
jux-ta-pos-ing
jux-ta-po-si-tion

113

K

ka-bob
kai-ser
ka-lei-do-scope
  ka-lei-do-scop-ic
ka-mi-ka-ze
kan-ga-roo
ka-olin
  ka-oline
ka-pok
ka-put
ka-ra-te
kar-ma
  kar-mic
ka-ty-did
kay-ak
kay-o
kedge
  kedged
  kedg-ing
keel-haul
keel-son
keen-ly
  keen-ness
keep-ing
keep-sake
keg-ler
kelp
ken-nel
  ken-neled
  ken-nel-ing
ke-no
ker-a-tin
ker-chief
ker-mis
ker-nel
ker-o-sene
kes-trel
ketch-up
ke-tone
ket-tle
ket-tle-drum
key
  keyed
key-board
key-hole
key-note
key-stone
kha-ki
  khak-is
kha-lif
khan
kib-butz
  kib-but-zim
ki-bitz-er
ki-bosh
kick-back

kick-off
kid
kid-nap
kid-ney
  kid-neys
kill-deer
kill-ing
kill-joy
kiln
kilo
  kil-os
kilo-cy-cle
ki-lo-gram
ki-lo-me-ter
ki-lo-ton
kil-o-watt
kilt
ki-mo-no
kin-der-gar-ten
kin-dle
  kin-dled
  kin-dling
kind-ly
  kind-li-er
  kind-li-est
kin-dred
kin-e-mat-ic
kin-e-scope
ki-net-ic
  ki-net-ics
kin-folk
king-bird
king-dom
king-fish
  king-fish-er
king-ly
king-pin
king-size
  king-sized
kink-y
  kink-i-er
  kink-i-est
kins-folk
kins-man
  kins-men
  kins-wom-an
ki-osk
kip-per
kir-mess
kis-met
kiss-a-ble
kiss-er
kitch-en
kitch-en-ette
kitch-en-ware
kite

kit-ed
kit-ing
kitsch
kit-ten
kit-ten-ish
  kit-ten-ish-ly
kit-ty
  kit-ties
kit-ty--cor-ner
ki-wi
klatch
  klatsch
klep-to-ma-nia
  klep-to-ma-ni-ac
knack
knap-sack
knave
knav-ery
knav-ish
  knav-ish-ly
knead
knee
  kneed
  knee-ing
knee-cap
knee--deep
kneel
  knelt
  kneel-ing
  kneel-er
knee-pan
knell
knick-knack
knife
  knives
  knifed
  knif-ing
  knife-like
knight
  knight-hood
  knight-ly
knight-er-rant
  knights-er-rant
  knight-er-rant-ry
knit
  knit-ted
  knit-ting
  knit-ter
knob
  knobbed
  knob-by
  knob-bi-er
  knob-bi-est
knock
knock-a-bout
knock-down

L

knock-er
knock--knee
  knock--kneed
knock-out
knoll
knot
  knot-ted
  knot-ting
  knot-less
  knot-like
  knot-ty
knot-hole
knout
know
  knew
  known
  know-ing
  know-a-ble
  know-er
know--how
know-ing-ly
knowl-edge
knowl-edge-able
know--noth-ing
knuck-le
  knuck-led
  knuck-ling
knurl
  knurled
  knurly
ko-ala
ko-bold
ko-el
ko-gas-in
kohl-ra-bi
  kohl-ra-bies
ko-la
ko-lin-sky
  ko-lin-skies
kook
  kooky
  kook-i-er
  kook-i-est
kook-a-bur-ra
ko-peck
ko-ru-na
ko-sher
kou-mis
kow-tow
krim-mer
kro-na
kro-ne
kryp-ton
ku-dos
ku-miss
kum-quat

la-bel
  la-beled
  la-bel-ing
  la-bel-er
la-bi-al
  la-bi-al-ly
la-bi-ate
la-bi-o-den-tal
la-bi-um
  la-bia
la-bor
  la-bor-er
lab-o-ra-to-ry
la-bored
la-bo-ri-ous
  la-bo-ri-ous-ly
  la-bo-ri-ous-ness
la-bor-sav-ing
la-bur-num
lab-y-rinth
  lab-y-rin-thine
  lab-y-rin-thi-an
lace
lac-er-ate
  lac-er-at-ed
  lac-er-at-ing
  lac-er-a-tion
lace-wing
la-ches
lach-ry-mal
lach-ry-mose
  lach-ry-mose-ly
lac-ing
lack-a-dai-si-cal
  lack-a-dai-si-cal-ly
lack-ey
lack-lus-ter
la-ci-nia
la-con-ic
  la-con-i-cal-ly
lac-quer
  lac-quer-er
la-crosse
lac-tate
  lac-tat-ed
  lac-tat-ing
  lac-ta-tion
lac-te-al
lac-tic
lac-tose
la-cu-na
  la-cu-nas
  la-cu-nae
lad-der
lad-die
lade

lad-ed
lad-en
lad-ing
la-dle
  la-dled
  la-dling
la-dy
  la-dy-bug
la-dy-fin-ger
la-dy--in--wait-ing
la-dy-like
la-dy-love
lag
  lagged
  lag-ging
la-ger
lag-gard
la-gniappe
la-goon
la-ic
  la-i-cal
  la-i-cal-ly
lair
laird
la-i-ty
  la-i-ties
lake-side
lal-la-tion
la-lop-a-thy
lam
  lammed
  lam-ming
la-ma
la-ma-sery
  la-ma-ser-ies
lam-baste
  lam-bast-ed
  lam-bast-ing
lam-ben-cy
lam-bent
  lam-bent-ly
lam-bre-quin
lamb-skin
lame
la-ment
  lam-en-ta-ble
  lam-en-ta-bly
  lam-en-ta-tion
lam-i-na
  lam-i-nae
  lam-i-nas
lam-i-nate
  lam-i-nat-ed
  lam-i-nat-ing
  lam-i-na-tion
lam-poon

lam-prey	lar-der	lat-i-tu-di-nar-i-an
lam-preys	large	la-trine
lance	larg-er	lat-ter
lanced	larg-est	lat-tice
lanc-ing	large-ly	lat-tied
lance-wood	lar-gess	lat-tic-ing
lan-dau	lar-ghet-to	lat-tice-work
land-ed	lar-ghet-tos	laud-able
land-ing	larg-ish	laud-ably
land-la-dy	lar-go	lau-da-num
land-la-dies	lar-gos	lau-da-to-ry
land-locked	lar-i-at	lau-da-tive
land-lord	lar-rup	laugh
land-lub-ber	lar-va	laugh-ter
land-own-er	lar-vae	launch
land-own-ing	lar-val	launch-er
land-own-er-ship	lar-yn-gi-tis	laun-der
land-slide	lar-ynx	laun-der-er
land-ward	lar-ynx-es	laun-dress
land-wards	lar-ynx-ges	laun-der-ette
lang syne	la-ryn-ge-al	laun-dry
lan-gauge	las-civ-i-ous	laun-dries
lan-quid	las-ci-v-i-ous-ly	lau-re-ate
lan-quid-ly	la-ser	lau-rel
lan-quish	lash	la-va
lan-quish-ing	lash-ing	la-a-liere
lan-quish-ing-ly	lash-er	lav-a-to-ry
lan-quor	las-sie	lav-a-to-ries
lan-guor-ous	las-si-tude	lave
lan-guor-ous-ly	las-so	laved
lank-ness	las-sos	lav-ing
lanky	las-soes	lav-en-der
lank-i-er	las-so-er	lav-ish
lank-i-est	last-ing	lav-ish-ly
lank-i-ness	last-ing-ly	la-vish-ness
lan-o-lin	last-ly	law-abid-ing
lan-tern	latch-key	law-break-er
lan-tha-num	late	law-break-ing
lan-yard	lat-er	law-ful
lap	lat-est	law-ful-ly
la-pel	late-ness	law-ful-ness
lap-ful	late-ly	law-less
lap-fuls	la-tent	law-less-ly
laps-ful	la-ten-cy	law-less-ness
lap-i-dary	la-tent-ly	law-mak-er
lap-i-dar-ies	lat-er-al	law-mak-ing
lap-in	lat-er-al-ly	lawn
lap-pet	la-tex	law-ren-ci-um
lapse	la-tex-es	law-suit
lapsed	lathe	law-yer
laps-ing	lath-er	lax
lar-board	lath-er-er	lax-i-ty
lar-ce-ny	lath-ery	lax-ly
lar-ce-nies	lath-ing	lax-ness
lar-ce-nous	lat-i-tude	lax-a-tive
larch	lat-i-tu-di-nal	lay-er

lay-ette
lay-man
lay-men
lay-off
lay-out
lay-over
laze
lazed
laz-ing
la-zy
la-zi-er
la-zi-est
la-zi-ly
la-zy-bones
lea
leach
lead
lead-ing
lead-en
lead-en-ly
lead-er
lead-er-less
lead-er-ship
leaf-age
leafy
leaf-i-er
leaf-i-est
leaque
leaqued
leaqu-ing
leak
leak-age
leak-i-ness
leaky
leak-i-er
leak-i-est
lean
lean-ly
lean-ness
lean-ing
lean--to
lean--tos
leap
leaped
leapt
leap-ing
leap-er
leap-frog
learn
learn-ed
learnt
learn-ing
learn-er
learn-ed-ly
learn-ed-ness
lease

· leased
leas-ing
leash
least-wise
least-ways
leath-er
leath-er-neck
leath-ery
leave
left
leav-ing
lev-er
leav-en
leaves
leave-talk-ing
lech-er
lech-er-ous
lech-er-ous-ly
lech-ery
lech-er-ies
lec-tern
lec-ture
lec-tured
lec-tur-ing
lec-tur-er
ledge
ledg-er
leech
leek
leer-ing-ly
leery
lee-ward
lee-way
left--hand-ed
left—hand-ed-ly
left—hand-ed-ness
left-ist
left-over
left--wing
left—wing-er
leg
legged
leg-ging
leg-a-cy
leg-a-cies
le-gal
le-gal-ly
le-gal-ist
le-gal-is-tic
le-gal-i-ty
le-gal-i-ties
le-gal-ize
le-gal-ized
le-gal-iz-ing
le-gal-i-za-tion
leg-ate

leg-a-tee
le-ga-tion
le-ga-to
leg-end
leg-end-ary
leg-er-de-main
leg-gy
leg-gi-er
leg-gi-est
leg-horn
leg-i-ble
leg-i-bil-i-ty
leg-i-bly
le-gion
le-gion-ary
le-gion-ar-ies
le-gion-naire
leg-is-late
leg-is-lat-ed
leg-is-la-tive
leg-is-la-tor
leg-is-la-tion
leg-is-la-ture
le-git
le-git-i-mate
le-git-i-mat-ed
le-git-i-mat-ing
le-git-i-ma-cy
le-git-i-mate-ly
le-git-i-mist
le-git-i-mize
le-git-i-mized
le-git-i-miz-ing
le-gume
le-gu-mi-nous
lei
leis
lei-sure
lei-sure-ly
lei-sure-li-ness
leit-mo-tif
lem-ming
lem-on
lem-on-ade
le-mur
lend
lent
lend-ing
lend-er
length
length-en
length-wise
lengthy
length-i-er
length-i-est
length-i-ly

length-i-ness
le-nient
  le-ni-ence
  le-ni-en-cy
  le-ni-ent-ly
len-i-tive
len-i-ty
lens
len-til
len-to
le-o-nine
leop-ard
  leop-ard-ess
le-o-tard
lep-er
lep-i-dop-ter-ous
lep-re-chaun
lep-ro-sy
lep-rous
les-bi-an
  les-bi-an-ism
le-sion
les-see
less-en
les-sor
least
let-down
le-thal
  le-thal-ly
leth-ar-gy
  leth-ar-gies
  le-thar-gic
  le-thar-gi-cal
let-ter
  let-ter-ed
let-ter-head
let-ter-ing
let-ter--per-fect
let-ter-press
let-tuce
let-up
leu-ke-mia
leu-ko-cyte
lev-ee
lev-el
  lev-eled
  lev-el-ing
  lev-el-er
  lev-el-ly
  lev-el-ness
lev-el-head-ed
  lev-el-head-ed-ness
lev-er
lev-er-age
le-vi-a-than
lev-i-tate

lev-i-tat-ed
lev-i-tat-ing
lev-i-ta-tion
lev-i-ty
levy
  lev-ies
  lev-ied
  lev-y-ing
lewd
  lewd-ly
  lewd-ness
lex-i-cog-ra-phy
  lex-i-cog-ra-pher
  lex-i-co-graph-ic
  lex-i-co-graph-i-cal
lex-i-con
li-a-bil-i-ty
  li-a-bil-i-ties
li-a-ble
li-ai-son
li-ar
li-ba-tion
li-bel
  li-beled
  li-bel-ing
  li-bel-er
li-bel-ous
  li-bel-ous-ly
lib-er-al
  lib-er-al-ly
  lib-er-al-ness
lib-er-al-ism
lib-er-al-i-ty
  lib-er-al-i-ties
lib-er-al-ize
  lib-er-al-ized
  lib-er-al-iz-ing
  lib-er-al-i-za-tion
lib-er-ate
  lib-er-at-ed
  lib-er-at-ing
  lib-er-a-tion
  lib-er-a-tor
lib-er-tar-i-an
lib-er-tine
  lib-er-tin-ism
lib-er-ty
  lib-er-ties
li-bid-i-nous
  li-bid-i-nous-ly
  li-bid-i-nous-ness
li-bi-do
  li-bid-in-al
li-brar-i-an
li-brary
  li-brar-ies

li-bret-to
  li-bret-tos
  li-bret-ist
li-cense
  li-censed
  li-cens-ing
  li-cen-see
  li-cens-er
li-cen-ti-ate
li-cen-tious
  li-cen-tious-ly
  li-cen-tious-ness
li-chee
li-chen
lic-it
lick-e-ty--split
lick-spit-tle
lic-o-rice
lid-ded
lief
liege
lien
lieu
lieu-ten-an-cy
lieu-ten-ant
life-blood
life-boat
life-guard
life-less
  life-less-ly
  life-less-ness
life-like
life-line
lif-er
life-sav-er
life--size
life--style
life-time
life-work
lift-off
lig-a-ment
lig-a-ture
  lig-tured
  lig-a-tur-ing
light-en
light-er
light-fin-gered
light-foot-ed
  light-foot-ed-ly
light-head-ed
  light-head-ed-ly
  light-head-ed-ness
light-heart-ed
  light-heart-ed-ly
  light-heart-ed-ness
light-house

light-ing
light-ly
light--mind-ed
  light--mind-ed-ly
  light--mind-ed-ness
light-ning
light-weight
light--year
lig-nite
like
  liked
  lik-ing
  lik-a-ble
  lik-a-ble-ness
  lik-a-ble-ness
like-li-hood
like-ly
  like-li-er
  like-li-est
like--mind-ed
lik-en
like-ness
like-wise
lik-ing
li-lac
lilt-ing
lily
  lil-lies
lil-y--liv-ered
li-ma
limb
limb-er
  lim-ber-ness
lim-bo
lime
  limed
  lim-ing
  limy
  lim-i-er
  lim-i-est
  lime-like
lime-light
  lime-light-er
lim-er-ick
lime-stone
lim-it
lim-it-a-ble
lim-i-ta-tive
lim-i-ter
lim-it-less
lim-i-ta-tion
lim-it-ed
  lim-it-ed-ly
  lim-it-ed-ness
lim-ou-sine
limp

limp-er
limp-ing-ly
limp-ly
limp-ness
lim-pet
lim-pid
  lim-pid-i-ty
  lim-pid-ly
  lim-pid-ness
lin-age
lin-den
line
  lined
  lin-ing
lin-e-age
lin-eal
lin-ea-ment
lin-ear
  lin-ear-ly
line-back-er
  line-back-ing
line-man
  line-men
lin-en
lin-er
line-up
lin-ger
  lin-ger-er
  lin-ger-ing-ly
lin-ge-rie
lin-go
  lin-goes
lin-gua fran-ca
lin-qual
  lin-qual-ly
lin-quist
lin-quis-tic
  lin-quis-tics
  lin-quis-ti-cal
  lin-quis-ti-cal-ly
lin-i-ment
lin-ing
link
  linked
  link-er
link-age
lin-net
li-no-leum
lin-seed
lint
  linty
  lint-i-er
  lint-i-est
lin-tel
li-on
  li-on-ess

  li-on-like
li-on-heart-ed
li-on-ize
  li-on-ized
  li-on-iz-ing
  li-on-i-za-tion
  li-on-iz-er
lip-py
  lip-pi-er
  lip-pi-est
lip-stick
liq-ue-fy
  liq-ue-fied
  liq-ue-fy-ing
  liq-ue-fac-tion
  liq-ue-fi-able
  liq-ue-fi-er
li-queur
liq-uid
  li-quid-i-ty
  li-quid-ness
  li-quid-ly
liq-ui-date
  liq-ui-dat-ed
  liq-ui-dat-ing
  liq-ui-da-tion
  liq-ui-da-tor
liq-uor
lisle
lisp
  lisp-ing-ly
lis-some
  lis-some-ly
  lis-some-ness
list
  list-ed
  list-er
  list-ing
lis-ten
  lis-ten-er
list-less
  list-less-ly
  list-less-ness
lit-a-ny
  lit-a-nies
li-tchi
  li-tchis
li-ter
lit-er-a-cy
lit-er-al
  lit-er-al-i-ty
  lit-er-al-ness
  lit-er-al-ly
lit-er-ary
  lit-er-ar-i-ly
  lit-er-ar-i-ness

lit-er-ate
  lit-er-ate-ly
lit-e-ra-ti
lit-er-a-ture
lithe
  lithe-some
  lithe-ly
  lithe-ness
lith-i-um
lith-o-graph
  lith-o-gra-pher
  lith-o-graph-ic
  lith-o-graph-i-cal-ly
li-thog-ra-phy
lit-i-gate
  lit-i-gat-ed
  lit-i-gat-ing
  lit-i-ga-tion
  lit-i-ga-tor
lit-ter
lit-ter-bug
lit-tle
  lit-tler
  lit-tlest
lit-to-ral
lit-ur-gy
  lit-ur-gies
  lit-ur-gist
  lit-ur-gic
  li-tur-gi-cal
liv-able
  live-able
  liv-able-ness
  live-able-ness
live-li-hood
live-long
live-ly
  live-li-er
  live-li-est
  live-li-ness
liv-en
  liv-en-er
liv-er
liv-er-wurst
liv-ery
  liv-er-ies
  liv-er-ied
  liv-er-y-man
  liv-er-y-men
live-stock
liv-id
  li-vid-i-ty
  liv-id-ness
  liv-id-ly
liv-ing
  liv-ing-ly

liv-ing-ness
liz-ard
lla-ma
lla-no
  lla-mos
load
  load-ed
  load-er
loaf
  loaves
  loaf-er
loamy
loath
  loath-ness
loathe
  loathed
  loath-ing
  loath-ing-ly
loath-some
  loath-some-ly
  loath-some-ness
lob
  lobbed
  lob-bing
lob-by
  lob-bies
  lob-by-ist
lobe
  lo-bar
  lo-bate
  lobed
lob-ster
lo-cal
  lo-cal-ly
lo-cale
lo-cal-i-ty
  lo-cal-i-ties
lo-cal-i-ties
lo-cal-ize
  lo-cal-ized
  lo-cal-iz-ing
  lo-cal-i-za-tion
lo-cate
  lo-cat-ed
  lo-cat-ing
  lo-ca-tor
lo-ca-tion
loch
lock-able
lock-er
lock-et
lock-jaw
lock-out
lock-smith
lock-up
lo-co

lo-co-mo-tion
lo-co-mo-tive
lo-co-weed
lo-cus
  lo-ci
lo-cust
lo-cu-tion
lode-stone
lodge
  lodged
  lodg-ing
  lodg-er
lofty
  loft-i-er
  loft-i-est
  loft-i-ly
lo-gan-ber-ry
  lo-gan-ber-ries
log-a-rithm
  log-a-rith-mic
  log-a-rith-mi-cal
  log-a-rith-mi-cal-ly
log-book
loge
log-ger
log-ger-hed
log-ic
  lo-gi-cian
log-i-cal
  log-i-cal-i-ty
  log-i-cal-ly
lo-gis-tic
  lo-gis-tics
  lo-gis-ti-cal
log-jam
lo-gy
  lo-gi-er
  lo-gi-est
loin-cloth
loi-ter
  loi-ter-er
lol-li-pop
lone-ly
  lone-li-er
  lone-li-est
  lone-li-ly
lon-er
lone-some
  lone-some-ly
  lone-some-ness
lon-gev-i-ty
long-ing
  long-ing-ly
lon-gi-tude
lon-gi-tu-di-nal
  lon-gi-tu-di-nal-ly

long-lived
long--play-ing
long-shore-man
  long-shore-men
long--suf-fer-ing
long--term
long--wind-ed
  long--wind-ed-ly
long-wise
look-out
loony
  loon-i-er
  loon-i-est
  loon-ies
loose
  loos-er
  loos-est
  loosed
  loos-ing
  loose-ly
  loose-ness
loos-en
loot-er
lop
  looped
  lop-ping
lope
  loped
  lop-ing
  lop-er
lop-sid-ed
lo-qua-cious
  lo-qua-cious-ly
  lo-quac-i-ty
  lo-quac-i-ties
lord-ly
  lord-li-er
  lord-li-est
lord-ship
lor-gnette
lor-ry
  lor-ries
lose
  lost
  los-ing
  los-a-ble
  los-er
lot
lo-tion
lot-tery
  lot-ter-ies
lot-to
lo-tus
  lo-tus-es
loud
  loud-ly

loud-ness
loud-mouthed
loud-speak-er
lounge
  lounged
  loung-ing
  loung-er
louse
  lice
lousy
  lous-i-er
  lous-i-est
  lous-i-ly
lou-ver
  lou-vered
love
  loved
  lov-ing
  lov-able
love-lorn
love-ly
  love-li-er
  love-li-est
lov-er
lov-ing
  loving-ly
low-er
low-er-case
low-er-ing
  low-er-ing-ly
low-ery
low--key
  low--keyed
low-land
  low-land-er
low-ly
  low-li-er
  low-li-est
loy-al
  loy-al-ist
  loy-al-ly
  loy-al-ties
loz-enge
lu-au
lub-ber
  lub-ber-li-ness
  lub-ber-ly
lu-beak
lu-bri-cate
  lu-bri-cat-ed
  lu-bri-cat-ing
  lu-bri-ca-tion
lu-cid
  lu-cid-i-ty
  lu-cid-ness
  lu-cid-ly

luck
  luck-i-er
  luck-i-est
lu-cra-tive
  lu-cra-tive-ly
  lu-cra-tive-ness
lu-cre
lu-cu-brate
  lu-cu-brat-ed
  lu-cu-brat-ing
  lu-cu-bra-tion
  lu-cu-bra-tor
lu-di-crous
  lu-di-crous-ly
  lu-di-crous-ness
lug
  lugged
  lug-ging
lug-gage
lug-ger
lug-sail
lu-gu-bri-ous
  lu-gu-bri-ous-ly
luke-warm
  luke-warm-ly
lull-a-by
  lull-a-bies
lum-ba-go
lum-bar
lum-ber
  lum-ber-ing-ly
  lum-ber-er
lum-ber-ing
lum-ber-jack
lum-ber-man
  lum-ber-men
lu-men
lu-mi-nary
  lu-mi-nar-ies
lu-mi-nes-cence
  lu-mi-nes-cent
lu-mi-nous
  lu-mi-nos-i-ty
  lu-mi-nous-ly
lum-mox
lumpy
lu-na-cy
  lu-na-cies
lu-nar
lu-nate
lu-na-tic
lunch
  lunch-er
lun-cheon
lunge
  lunged

lung-ing
lu-pine
lurch
lure
lured
lur-ing
lu-rid
lu-rid-ly
lu-rid-ness
lurk
lurk-er
lurk-ing-ly
lus-cious
lus-cious-ly
lush
lush-ly
lust
lust-ful
lust-ful-ly
lust-er
lus-ter-less
lus-trous
lus-trous-ly
lus-trous-ness
lusty
lut-ist
lux-u-ri-ant
lux-u-ri-ance
lux-u-ri-an-cy
lux-u-ri-ant-ly
lux-u-ri-ate
lux-u-ri-at-ed
lux-u-ri-at-ing
lux-u-ri-a-tion
lux-u-ri-ous
lux-u-ri-ous-ly
lux-u-ry
lux-u-ries
ly-ce-um
ly-ing
ly-ing--in
lymph
lym-phoid
lym-phat-ic
lynch
lynch-er
lynch-ing
lynx
lynx-es
lynx-eyed
lyre
ly-ric
lyr-i-cal
lyr-i-cal-ly
ly-ser-gic acid
ly-sine

ma-ca-bre
ma-ca-bre-ly
mac-ad-am
mac-ad-am-ize
mac-ad-am ised
mac-ad-am-iz-ing
mac-ad-am-i-za-tion
ma-caque
mac-a-ro-ni
ma-caw
mace
maced
mac-ing
mac-er-ate
mac-er-at-ed
mac-er-at-ing
mac-er-a-tion
mac-er-a-tor
ma-chete
mach-i-nate
ma-chine
ma-chin-ery
ma-chin-er-ies
ma-chin-ist
mack-er-el
mack-i-naw
mack-in-tosh
mac-in-tosh
mac-ro-cosm
mac-ro-cos-mic
mac-ro-cos-mi-cal-ly
ma-cron
mad
mad-der
mad-ly
mad-ness
mad-am
mes-dames
mad-cap
mad-den
mad-den-ing
mad-den-ing-ly
mad-e-moi-selle
mes-de-moi-selles
made-up
mad-house
mad-man
mad-men
ma-dras
mad-ri-gal
mad-ri-gal-ist
mael-strom
mae-stro-so
mag-a-zine
ma-gen-ta
mag-got

mag-goty
mag-ic
mag-i-cal
mag-i-cal-ly
ma-gi-cian
mag-is-te-ri-al
mag-is-te-ri-al-ly
mag-is-te-ri-al-ness
mag-is-tra-cy
mag-is-tra-cies
mag-is-trate
mag-ma
mag-mas
mag-ma-ta
mag-mat-ic
mag-nan-i-mous
mag-nan-i-mous-ly
mag-na-nim-i-ty
mag-na-nim-i-ties
mag-nate
mag-ne-sia
mag-ne-sian
mag-ne-sium
mag-net
mag-net-ic
mag-net-i-cal-ly
mag-net-ism
mag-net-ize
mag-net-ized
mag-net-iz-ing
mag-net-iz-a-ble
mag-net-i-za-tion
mag-net-iz-er
mag-ne-to
mag-ne-tos
mag-ne-tom-e-ter
mag-ne-to-met-ric
mag-ne-tom-e-try
mag-nif-i-cent
mag-nif-i-cence
mag-nif-i-cent-ly
mag-ni-fy
mag-ni-fied
mag-ni-fy-ing
maf-ni-fi-a-ble
mag-ni-fi-ca-tion
mag-ni-fi-er
mag-ni-tude
mag-no-lia
mag-num
mag-uey
ma-ha-ra-jah
ma-ha-ra-ni
ma-hat-ma
ma-hat-ma-ism
ma-hoe

ma-hog-a-ny
  ma-hog-a-nies
ma-hout
maid-en
mail-a-ble
mail-box
mail-man
  mail-men
maim
  maim-er
main-land
  main-land-er
main-ly
main-mast
main-sail
main-tain
  main-tain-a-ble
main-te-nance
maize
maj-es-ty
  maj-es-ties
  ma-jes-tic
  ma-jes-ti-cal
ma-jol-i-ca
ma-jor
ma-jor-do-mo
  ma-jor-do-mos
ma-jor-i-ty
  ma-jor-i-ties
make
  mak-a-ble
  mak-er
  mak-ing
make-shift
make-up
mal-a-dapt-ed
mal-ad-just-ment
  mal-ad-just-ed
mal-ad-min-is-ter
mal-adroit
  mal-adroit-ly
  mal-adroit-ness
mal-a-dy
  mal-a-dies
mal-aise
mal-a-prop
mal-a-prop-ism
ma-lar-ia
  ma-lar-i-al
  ma-lar-i-an
  ma-lar-i-ous
ma-lar-key
mal-con-tent
male-dict
male-dic-tion
  male-dic-to-ry

male-frac-tion
male-frac-tor
ma-lev-o-lent
  ma-lev-o-lence
  ma-lev-o-lent-ly
mal-fea-sance
  mal-fea-sant
mal-for-ma-tion
  mal-formed
mal-func-tion
mal-ice
  ma-li-cious
  ma-li-cious-ly
ma-lign
  ma-lign-er
  ma-lign-ly
ma-lig-nant
  ma-lig-nan-cy
  ma-lig-nan-cies
  ma-lig-nant-ly
ma-lin-ger
  ma-lin-ger-er
mal-lard
mal-lea-ble
  mal-lea-bil-i-ty
mal-let
ma-low
mal-nour-ished
mal-nu-tri-tion
mal-oc-clu-sion
mal-odor
  mal-odor-ous
  mal-odor-ous-ly
mal-prac-tice
  mal-prac-ti-tion-er
malt
  malty
  malt-i-er
mal-treat
  mal-treat-ment
mam-ma
  ma-ma
mam-mal
  mam-ma-li-an
mam-mam-ries
mam-mon
mam-moth
mam-my
  mam-mies
man
  manned
  man-ning
man-a-cle
  man-a-cled
  man-a-cling
man-age

man-aged
man-a-ging
man-age-a-ble
man-age-a-bil-i-ty
man-age-a-bly
man-age-ment
man-ag-er
  man-ag-er-ship
man-a-ge-ri-al
  man-a-ge-ri-al-ly
man-a-tee
man-da-la
man-da-rin
man-date
  man-dat-ed
  man-dat-ing
man-da-to-ry
  man-da-to-ries
  man-da-to-ri-ty
man-di-ble
  man-dib-u-lar
  man-dib-u-lary
  man-dib-u-late
man-do-lin
  man-do-lin-ist
man-drakes
man-drill
man-eat-er
  man-eat-ing
ma-neu-ver
  ma-neu-ver-a-nil-i-ty
  ma-neu-ver-a-ble
  ma-neu-ver-er
man-ga-nese
mange
man-ger
man-gle
  man-gled
  man-gling
man-go
  man-goes
  man-gos
man-grove
man-gy
  man-gi-er
  man-gi-est
  man-gi-ly
man-han-dle
  man-han-dled
  man-han-dling
man-hole
man-hood
man--hour
man-hunt
  man-hunt-er
ma-nia

man-ic
ma-ni-ac
ma-ni-a-cal
ma-ni-a-cal-ly
man-ic-de-pres-sive
man-i-cure
man-i-cur-eed
man-i-cur-ing
man-i-cur-ist
man-i-fest
man-i-fest-er
man-i-fest-ly
man-i-fes-ta-tion
man-i-fes-to
man-i-fes-tos
man-i-fes-toes
man-i-fold
man-i-kin
man-a-kin
man-ni-kin
ma-nila
ma-nil-la
ma-nip-u-late
man-kind
man-ly
man-li-er
man-li-est
man--made
man-na
man-ne-quin
man-ner
man-nered
man-ner-ism
man-ner-ly
man-ner-li-ness
man-nish
man--of--war
men--of--war
ma-nom-e-ter
man-or
ma-no-ri-al
man pow-er
man-sard
man-ser-vant
man-sion
man-sized
man-slaugh-ter
man-slay-er
man-til-la
man-tle
man-tled
man-tling
man-trap
man-u-al
man-u-al-ly
man-u-fac-ture

man-u-fac-tured
man-u-fac-tur-ing
man-u-fac-tur-a-ble
man-u-fac-tur-al
man-u-fac-tur-er
ma-nure
manu-script
many
man-y-sid-ed
map
mapped
map-ping
map-per
ma-ple
mar
marred
mar-ring
ma-ra-ca
mar-a-schi-no
mar-a-thon
ma-raud
ma-raud-er
mar-ble
mar-bled
mar-bling
mar-ble-ize
mar-ble-ized
mar-ble-iz-ing
mar-bly
mar-cel
mar-celled
mar-cel-ling
march-er
mar-chio-ness
mare's tail
mar-ga-rine
mar-gin
mar-gi-nal
mar-gi-na-lia
mar-gin-al-i-ty
mar-gin-al-ly
mar-gin-ate
mar-gin-ated
mar-gin-at-ing
mar-gin-a-tion
mar-gue-rite
mar-i-cul-ture
mari-gold
mar-i-jua-na
ma-rim-ba
ma-ri-na
mar-i-nade
mar-i-nad-ed
mar-i-nad-ing
mar-i-na-tion
mar-i-nate

mar-i-nat-ed
mar-i-nat-ing
mar-i-na-tion
ma-rine
mar-i-ner
mar-i-o-nette
mar-i-tal
mar-i-time
mar-jo-ram
marked
mark-ed-ly
mark-er
mar-ket
mar-ket-er
mar-ket-able
mar-ket-abil-i-ty
mar-ket-ing
mar-ket-place
mark-ing
marks-man
marks-men
marks-man-ship
mar-lin
mar-ma-lade
mar-mo-set
mar-mot
ma-roon
mar-quee
mar-quis
mar-quis-es
mar-quess
mar-quise
mar-quis-es
mar-riage
mar-riage-able
mar-riage-abil-i-ty
mar-ried
mar-row
mar-rowy
mar-row-bone
mar-ry
mar-ried
mar-ry-ing
mar-shall
mar-shaled
mar-shal-ing
marsh-mal-low
marshy
marsh-i-er
marsh-i-est
marsh-i-ness
mar-su-pi-al
mar-tial
mar-tin
mar-ti-ni
mar-ti-nis

124

mar-tyr
mar-tyr-ize
mar-tyr-ized
mar-tyr-iz-ing
mar-tyr-dom
mar-vel
mar-veled
mar-vel-ing
mar-vel-ous
mar-vel-ous-ly
mar-zi-pan
mas-cara
mas-cu-line
mas-cu-line-ness
mas-cu-lin-i-ty
mas-cu-lin-ize
mas-cu-lin-ized
mas-cu-lin-iz-ing
mash-er
mask
mask-like
masked
mas-och-ism
mas-och-ist
mas-och-is-tic
ma-son
ma-son-ic
ma-son-ary
ma-son-ries
masque
mas-quer-ade
mas-quer-ad-ed
mas-quer-ad-ing
mas-quer-ad-er
mas-sa-cre
mas-sa-cred
mas-sa-cring
mas-sa-cre
mas-sage
mas-saged
mas-sag-ing
mas-sag-er
mas-sag-ist
mas-seur
mas-sause
mas-seus-es
mas-sive
mass-pro-duce
mass-pro-duced
mass-pro-duc-ing
mass-pro-duc-er
mass-pro-duc-tion
massy
masss-i-er
mass-i-est
mass-i-ness

mas-tec-to-my
mas-tec-to-mies
mas-ter
mas-ter-ful
mas-ter-mind
mas-ter-piece
mas-tery
mas-ter-ies
mast-head
mas-tic
mas-ti-cate
mas-ti-ca-ted
mas-ti-ca-ting
mas-ti-ca-ble
mas-ti-ca-tion
mas-ti-ca-tor
mas-tiff
mast-odon
mas-toid
mas-tur-bate
mas-tur-bat-ed
mas-tur-bat-ing
mas-tur-ba-tion
mat
mat-ted
mat-ting
mat-a-dor
match-book
match-mak-er
match-mak-ing
mate
mat-ed
mat-ing
mate-less
ma-te-ri-al
ma-te-ri-al-ly
ma-te-ri-al-ism
ma-te-ri-al-ist
ma-te-ri-al-is-tic
ma-te-ri-al-is-ti-cal-ly
ma-te-ri-al-ize
ma-te-ri-al-ized
ma-te-ri-al-iz-ing
ma-te-ri-el
ma-ter-nal
ma-ter-nal-ism
ma-ter-nal-is-tic
ma-ter-nal-ly
ma-ter-ni-ty
ma-ter-ni-ties
math-e-mat-i-cal
math-e-mat-ic
math-e-mat-i-cal-ly
math-e-ma-ti-cian
math-e-mat-ics
ma-tin

mat-in-al
mat-i-nee
ma-tri-arch
ma-tri-ar-chal-ism
ma-tri-ar-chy
ma-tri-ar-chies
ma-tri-cide
ma-tric-u-lant
ma-tric-u-late
ma-tric-u-lat-ed
ma-tric-u-lat-ing
ma-tric-u-la-tion
ma-tri-lin-eal
mat-ri-mo-ny
mat-ri-mo-nies
mat-ri-mo-ni-al
ma-trix
ma-tri-ces
ma-trix-es
ma-tron
ma-tron-ly
mat-ter
mat-ter-of-course
mat-ter--of--fact
mat-ter-of--fact-ly
mat-ter--of--fact-ness
mat-ting
mat-tress
mat-u-rate
mat-u-rat-ed
mat-u-rat-ing
mat-u-ra-tion
ma-ture
ma-tur-i-ty
mat-zo
mat-zoth
mat-zos
maud-lin
mau-so-le-um
mau-so-le-ums
mau-so-lea
mauve
mav-er-ick
mawk-ish
max-im
max-i-mal
max-i-mal-ly
max-i-mize
max-i-mized
max-i-miz-ing
max-i-mum
max-i-mums
max-i-ma
may-be
may-flow-er
may-fly

may-flies
may-hem
may-on-naise
may-or
may-or-al
may-or-al-ty
may-or-al-ties
maze
mazed
maz-ing
ma-zy
ma-zi-er
ma-zi-est
ma-zi-ly
ma-zi-ness
mead-ow
mead-ow-lark
mea-ger
mea-ger-ly
mea-ger-ness
meal-time
meal-worm
mealy
meal-i-er
meal-i-est
meal-i-ness
meal-y-mouthed
mean
mean-ing
mean-ly
mean-ness
me-an-der
mean-ing-ful
mean-ing-ful-ly
mean-ing-less
mean-ing-less-ly
mean-ing-less-ness
meant
mean-time
mean-while
mea-sles
mea-sly
mea-sli-er
mea-sli-est
meas-ur-a-ble
meas-ur-a-bil-i-ty
meas-ur-a-bly
meas-ure
meas-ur-er
mea-sured
mea-sure-ment
meaty
meat-i-er
meat-i-est
meat-i-ness
mec-ca

me-chan-ic
mech-a-nism
mech-a-nis-tic
mech-a-nis-ti-cal-ly
mech-a-nize
mech-a-nized
mech-a-niz-ing
mech-a-ni-za-tion
mech-a-niz-er
med-al
med-aled
med-al-ing
me-dal-ic
me-dal-lion
med-dle
med-dled
med-dling
med-dler
med-dle-some
me-dia
me-di-al
me-di-an
me-di-an-ly
me-di-ate
me-di-at-ed
me-di-at-ing
me-di-a-tion
me-di-a-tive
me-di-a-to-ry
me-di-a-tor
med-ic
med-i-ca-ble
med-i-ca-bly
med-i-cal
med-i-cal-ly
me-di-ca-ment
med-i-cate
med-i-cat-ed
med-i-cat-ing
med-i-ca-tion
me-dic-i-nal
me-dic-i-nal-ly
med-i-cine
med-i-cined
med-i-cin-ing
med-i-co
me-di-e-val
me-di-e-val-ism
me-di-o-cre
me-di-oc-ri-ty
me-di-oc-ri-ties
med-i-tate
med-i-tat-ed
med-i-tat-ing
med-i-tat-ing-ly
med-i-ta-tor

med-i-ta-tion
med-i-ta-tive
Med-i-ter-ra-ne-an
me-di-um
me-dia
me-di-ums
med-ley
med-leys
meet-ing
meet-ing-house
meg-a-city
meg-a-cit-ies
mega-cy-cle
meg-a-lo-ma-nia
meg-a-lo-ma-ni-ac
meg-a-lo-ma-ni-a-cal
meg-a-lop-o-lis
meg-a-lo-pol-i-tan
mega-phone
mega-phoned
mega-phon-ing
mega-ton
mega-watt
mei-o-sis
mei-ot-ic
mel-a-mine
mel-an-cho-lia
mel-an-cho-li-ac
mel-an-choly
mel-an-chol-ies
mel-an-chol-ic
mel-an-chol-i-cal-ly
mel-an-chol-i-ty
mel-an-chol-i-ness
mel-a-nin
mel-a-no-ma
mel-a-no-mas
mel-a-no-ma-ta
me-lee
me-lio-rate
me-lio-rat-ed
me-lio-rat-ing
me-lio-ra-ble
me-lio-ra-tion
me-lio-ra-tor
mel-lif-lu-ous
mel-lif-lu-nt
mel-lif-lu-ous-ly
mel-low
me-lo-de-on
melo-dra-ma
melo-dra-mat-ic
melo-dra-mat-i-cal-ly
melo-dra-mat-ics
mel-o-dy
mel-o-dies

me-lod-ic
me-lod-i-cal-ly
me-lo-di-ous
me-lo-di-ous-ness
mel-on
melt
　melt-ed
　melt-ing
　melt-a-bil-i-ty
　melt-a-ble
　melt-er
mem-ber
　mem-bered
　mem-ber-less
mem-ber-ship
mem-brane
　mem-bra-nous
me-men-to
　me-men-tos
　me-men-toes
memo
mem-oir
mem-o-ra-bil-ia
mem-o-ra-ble
　mem-o-ra-bly
mem-o-ran-dum
　mem-o-ran-dums
　mem-o-ran-da
me-mo-ri-al
　me-mo-ri-al-ly
me-mo-ri-al-ize
　me-mo-ri-al-ized
　me-mo-ri-al-iz-ing
　me-mo-ri-al-i-za-tion
　me-mo-ri-al-iz-er
　me-mo-ri-al-ly
mem-o-rize
　mem-o-rized
　mem-o-riz-ing
　mem-o-riz-a-ble
　mem-o-ri-za-tion
mem-o-ry
　mem-o-ries
men-ace
　men-aced
　men-ac-ing
me-nag-er-ie
mend
　mend-able
men-da-cious
　men-da-cious-ly
　men-da-cious-ness
men-dac-i-ty
men-de-le-vi-um
men-di-cant
me-ni-al

me-ni-al-ly
me-nin-ges
men-in-gi-tis
me-nis-cus
　me-nis-cus-es
　me-nis-ci
men-o-pause
　men-o-pau-sal
me-nor-ah
men-sal
men-ses
men-stru-al
men-stru-a-tion
　men-stru-ate
　men-stru-at-ed
　men-stru-at-ing
men-sur-a-ble
men-tal
　men-tal-ly
men-tal-i-ty
　men-tal-i-ties
men-thol
　men-tho-lat-ed
men-tion
　men-tion-a-ble
　men-tion-er
men-tor
menu
me-ow
mep-ro-bam-ate
mer-can-tile
mer-can-til-ism
　mer-can-til-ist
mer-ce-nary
　mer-ce-nar-ies
　mer-ce-nar-ily
mer-cer-ize
　mer-cer-ized
　mer-cer-iz-ing
mer-chan-dise
　mer-chan-dised
　mer-chan-dis-ing
　mer-chan-dis-er
mer-chant
mer-chant-man
　mer-chant-men
mer-cu-ri-al
mer-cu-ry
　mer-cu-ries
mer-cy
　mer-cies
　mer-ci-ful
　mer-ci-ful-ly
　mer-ci-less
mere-ly
mer-e-tri-cious

mer-e-tri-cious-ly
mer-e-tri-cious-ness
merge
merged
merg-ing
mer-gence
merg-er
me-rid-i-an
me-rid-i-o-nal
me-ringue
mer-it
　mer-i-ted
　mer-it-ed-ly
　mer-it-less
mer-i-to-ri-ous
mer-maid
　mer-man
　mer-men
mer-ri-ment
mer-ry
　mer-ri-er
　mer-ri-est
　mer-ri-ness
mer-ry--go--round
mer-ry-mak-er
mer-ry-mak-ing
me-sa
mes-cal
mes-dames
mes-de-moi-selles
mesh-work
me-si-al
mes-mer-ism
　mes-mer-ic
　mes-mer-i-cal-ly
　mes-mer-ist
mes-mer-ize
　mes-mer-ized
　mes-mer-iz-ing
　mes-mer-i-za-tion
　mes-mer-iz-er
mes-o-morph
　mes-o-mor-phic
　mes-o-mor-phism
　mes-o-mor-phy
me-son
mes-o-sphere
mes-quite
mess
　mess-i-ly
　mess-i-ness
　messy
　mess-i-er
　mess-i-est
mes-sage
mes-sen-ger

mes-ti-zo
me-tab-o-lism
  met-a-bol-ic
  met-a-bol-i-cal
me-tab-o-lize
  me-tab-o-lized
  me-tab-o-liz-ing
met-al
  met-aled
  met-al-ing
met-al-ize
  met-al-ized
  met-al-iz-ing
me-tal-lic
  me-tal-li-cal-ly
met-al-loid
met-al-lur-gy
  met-al-lur-gic
  met-al-lur-gi-cal
  met-al-lur-gi-cal-ly
  met-al-lur-gist
met-al-work
  met-al-work-er
  met-al-work-ing
meta-mor-phism
  meta-mor-phic
meta-mor-phose
  meta-mor-phosed
  meta-mor-phos-ing
meta-mor-pho-sis
  meta-mor-pho-ses
met-a-phor
  met-a-phor-ic
  met-a-phor-i-cal
meta-phys-ic
meta-phys-ics
  meta-phys-i-cal
meta-tar-sus
  meta-tar-si
  meta-tar-sal
meta-zo-an
  meta-zo-al
  meta-zo-ic
mete
  met-ed
  met-ing
me-te-or
me-te-or-ic
me-te-or-ite
  me-te-or-it-ic
me-te-or-oid
me-te-o-rol-o-gy
  me-te-o-ro-log-i-cal
  me-te-o-rol-o-gist
me-ter
met-es-trus

meth-a-done
meth-ane
meth-a-nol
meth-od
me-thodi-cal
  me-thodi-cal-ly
meth-od-ize
  meth-od-ized
  meth-od-iz-ing
  meth-od-iz-er
meth-od-ol-o-gy
  meth-od-ol-o-gies
  meth-od-o-log-i-cal
  meth-od-ol-o-gist
me-tic-u-lous
  me-tic-u-los-i-ty
  me-tic-u-lous-ly
met-ric
met-ri-cal
  met-ri-cal-ly
met-ri-fi-ca-tion
met-ro
met-ro-nome
  met-ro-nom-ic
me-trop-o-lis
met-ro-pol-i-tan
  met-ro-pol-i-tan-ism
met-tle
met-tle-some
mez-za-nine
mez-zo
mi-as-ma
  mi-as-mas
  mi-as-ma-ta
  mi-as-mat-ic
  mi-as-mic
mi-ca
mi-crobe
  mi-cro-bi-al
  mi-cro-bi-an
  mi-cro-bic
mi-cro-bi-ol-o-gy
  mi-cro-bi-o-log-i-cal
  mi-cro-bi-ol-o-gist
mi-cro-copy
  mi-cro-cop-ies
mi-cro-cosm
  mi-cro-cos-mos
  mi-cro-cos-mic
  mi-cro-cos-mi-cal
mi-cro-film
mi-cro-gram
mi-cro-groove
mi-crom-e-ter
mi-crom-e-try
mi-cro-mi-cron

mi-cro-min-ia-ture
mi-cro-mil-li-me-ter
mi-cron
  mi-crons
  mi-cra
mi-cro-or-gan-ism
mi-cro-phone
  mi-cro-phon-ic
mi-cro-pho-to-graph
mi-cro-read-er
mi-cro-scope
  mi-cro-scop-i-cal
  mi-cro-scop-i-cal-ly
mi-cros-co-py
  mi-cros-co-pist
mi-cro-sec-ond
mi-cro-wave
mid-day
mid-dle
  mid-dles
  mid-dling
mid-dle--aged
mid-dle-man
  mid-dle-men
mid-dle-most
mid-dle-weight
mid-dy
  mid-dies
midg-et
mid-land
mid-night
mid-sec-tion
mid-ship
mid-ship-man
  mid-ship-men
midst
mid-sum-mer
mid-term
mid-way
mid-wife
  mid-wives
mid-wife-ry
mid-year
mien
mighty
  might-i-er
  might-i-est
  might-i-ly
  might-i-ness
mi-graine
mi-grant
mi-grate
  mi-grat-ed
  mi-grat-ing
  mi-gra-tion
  mi-gra-tor

mi-gra-to-ry
mi-la-dy
  mi-la-dies
mild
  mild-ly
  mild-ness
mil-dew
  mil-dewy
mile-age
mil-er
mile-stone
mi-lieu
  mi-lieus
mil-i-tant
  mil-i-tan-cy
  mil-i-tant-ness
mil-i-ta-rism
  mil-i-ta-ris-tic
  mil-i-ta-ris-ti-cal-ly
  mil-i-ta-rize
  mil-i-ta-rized
  mil-i-ta-riz-ing
  mil-i-ta-ri-za-tion
mil-i-tary
  mil-i-tar-i-ly
mi-li-tia
milk
  milk-er
  milky
  milk-i-er
  milk-i-est
milk-maid
milk-man
  milk-men
milk-weed
mill-board
mil-len-ni-um
  mil-len-nia
  mil-len-ni-al
mil-ler
mil-let
mill-li-am-pere
mil-li-bar
mil-li-gram
mil-li-li-ter
mil-li-me-ter
mil-li-mi-cron
mil-li-ner
mil-li-nery
mill-ing
mil-lion
  mil-lionth
mill-lion-aire
mil-li-sec-ond
mill-pond
mill-run

mill-stone
mill-stream
mi-lord
milt
mime
  mimed
  mim-ing
  mim-er
mim-e-o-graph
mim-ic
  mim-icked
  mim-ick-ing
  mim-i-cal
  mim-i-cal
  mim-ick-r
mim-ic-ry
  mim-ic-ries
min-able
  mine-able
min-e-ret
mince
  minced
  minc-ing
  minc-er
  minc-ing-ly
mince-meat
mind-ed
mind-less
  mind-less-ly
  mind-less-ness
min-er
mine-field
min-er-al
min-er-al-ize
  min-er-al-ized
  min-er-al-iz-ing
  min-er-al-i-za-tion
min-er-al-o-gy
  min-er-al-og-ical
  min-er-al-o-gist
min-e-stro-ne
mine-sweep-er
  mine-sweep-ing
min-gle
  min-gled
  min-gling
min-i-a-ture
  min-i-a-tur-ize
  min-i-a-tur-ized
  min-i-a-tur-iz-ing
  min-i-a-tur-i-za-tion
min-im
min-i-mal
  min-i-mal-ly
min-i-mize
  min-i-mized

  min-i-miz-ing
  min-i-mi-za-tion
  min-i-miz-er
min-i-mum
  min-i-mums
  min-i-ma
min-ing
min-ion
min-is-ter
  min-is-te-ri-al
min-is-trant
min-is-tra-tion
min-is-tries
min-now
mi-nor
mi-nor-i-ty
  mi-nor-i-ties
min-strel
mint-age
  mint-er
min-u-end
mi-nus
mi-nus-cule
min-ute
  min-ut-ed
  min-ut-ing
mi-nut-er
  mi-nut-est
min-ute-man
  min-ute-men
mi-nu-tia
  mi-nu-ti-ae
minx
mir-a-cle
mi-rac-u-lous
mi-rage
mire
  mired
  mir-ing
mir-ror
mirth
  mirth-ful
  mirth-ful-ly
  mirth-ful-ness
  mirth-less
mis-ad-ven-tage
mis-ad-vise
  mis-ad-vised
  mis-ad-vis-ing
mis-al-li-ance
mis-an-thrope
mis-an-tho-pist
  mis-an-throp-ic
  mis-an-throp-i-cal
  mis-an-thro-py
mis-ap-ply

mis-ap-plied
mis-ap-ply-ing
mis-ap-pli-ca-tion
mis-ap-pre-hend
mis-ap-pre-hen-sion
mis-ap-pro-pri-ate
mis-ap-pro-pri-at-ed
mis-ap-pro-pri-at-ing
mis-ap-pro-pri-a-tion
mis-be-have
mis-be-haved
mis-be-hav-ing
mis-be-hav-er
mis-be-ha-vior
mis-cal-cu-late
mis-cal-cu-lat-ed
mis-cal-cu-lat-ing
mis-cal-cu-la-tion
mis-cal-cu-la-tor
mis-call
mis-car-riage
mis-car-ry
mis-car-ried
mis-car-ry-ing
mis-ce-ge-na-tion
mis-ce-ge-net-ic
mis-cel-la-neous
mis-cel-la-ny
mis-cel-la-nies
mis-chance
mis-chief
mis-chie-vous
mis-che-vous-ly
mis-che-vous-ness
mis-ci-ble
mis-ci-bil-i-ty
mis-con-ceive
mis-con-ceived
mis-con-ceiv-ing
mis-con-ceiv-er
mis-con-cep-tion
mis-con-duct
mis-con-strue
mis-con-strued
mis-con-stru-ing
mis-con-struc-tion
mis-count
mis-cre-ant
mis-cue
mis-cued
mis-cu-ing
mis-deal
mis-dealt
mis-deal-ing
mis-deed
mis-de-mean-or

mis-di-rect
mis-di-rec-tion
mis-do
mis-did
mis-done
mis-do-ing
mis-em-ploy
mis-em-ploy-ment
mi-ser
mi-ser-li-ness
mi-ser-ly
mis-er-a-ble
mis-er-a-ble-ness
mis-er-a-bly
mis-ery
mis-er-ies
mis-fea-sance
mis-fire
mis-fired
mis-fir-ing
mis-fit
mis-fit-ted
mis-fit-ting
mis-for-tune
mis-giv-ing
mis-gov-ern
mis-gov-ern-ment
mis-guide
mis-guid-ed
mis-guid-ing
mis-guid-ance
mis-han-dle
mis-han-dled
mis-han-dling
mis-hap
mish-mash
mis-in-form
mis-in-form-ant
mis-in-form-er
mis-in-for-ma-tion
mis-in-ter-pret
mis-in-ter-pre-ta-tion
mis-in-ter-pret-er
mis-judge
mis-judged
mis-judg-ing
mis-judg-ment
mis-lay
mis-laid
mis-lay-ing
mis-lead
mis-led
mis-lead-ing
mis-lead-er
mis-man-age
mis-man-aged

mis-man-ag-ing
mis-man-age-ment
mis-match
mis-mate
mis-mat-ed
mis-mat-ing
mis-name
mis-named
mis-nam-ing
mis-no-mer
mi-sog-a-my
mi-sog-y-ny
mi-sog-y-nist
mi-sog-y-nous
mis-place
mis-placed
mis-plac-ing
mis-place-ment
mis-play
mis-print
mis-pri-sion
mis-prize
mis-prized
mis-priz-ing
mis-pro-nounce
mis-pro-nounced
mis-pro-nouc-ing
mis-pro-nun-ci-a-tion
mis-quote
mis-quoted
mis-quot-ing
mis-quo-ta-tion
mis-read
mis-read-ing
mis-rep-re-sent
mis-rep-re-sen-ta-tion
mis-rep-re-sen-ta-tive
mis-rule
mis-ruled
mis-rul-ing
mis-sal
mis-shape
mis-shaped
mis-shap-ing
mis-shap-en
mis-sile
miss-ing
mis-sion
mis-sion-ary
mis-sion-ar-ies
mis-sive
mis-spell
mis-spelled
mis-spel-ling
mis-spend
mis-spent

mis-spend-ing
mis-state
  mis-stat-ed
  mis-stat-ing
  mis-state-ment
mis-step
mist
  mist-i-ly
  mist-i-ness
mis-ta-a-ble
mis-take
  mis-took
  mis-tak-en
  mis-tak-ing
  mis-tak-en-ly
  mis-tak-er
mis-tle-toe
mis-tral
mis-treat
  mis-treat-ment
mis-tress
mis-tri-al
mis-trust
  mis-trust-ful
  mis-trust-ful-ly
  mis-trust-ing-ly
misty
  mist-i-er
  mist-i-est
mis-un-der-stand
  mis-un-der-stood
  mis-un-der-stand-ing
mis-us-age
mis-use
  mis-used
  mis-us-ing
  mis-us-er
mis-val-ue
  mis-val-ued
  mis-val-u-ing
mi-ter
  mi-tre
mi-ti-cide
  mi-ti-cid-al
mit-i-gate
  mit-i-gat-ed
  mit-i-gat-ist
  mit-i-ga-tion
  mit-i-ga-tive
  mit-i-ga-tor
  mit-i-ga-to-ry
mi-to-sis
mi-tral
mit-ten
mix
  mixed

mix-ing
mix-er
mix-ture
mix-up
miz-pah
miz-zen
mne-mon-ic
mne-mon-ics
moa
mob
  mobbed
  mob-bing
  mob-bish
mo-bile
  mo-bil-i-ty
mo-bi-lize
  mo-bi-lized
  mo-bi-liz-ing
  mo-bi-li-za-tion
mob-ster
moc-ca-sin
mo-cha
mock
  mock-er
  mock-ing-ly
mock-ery
  mock-er-ies
mock-ing-bird
mock-up
mod-al
  mo-dal-i-ty
  mod-al-ly
mod-el
  mod-eled
  mod-el-ing
  mod-el-er
mod-er-ate
  mod-er-at-ed
  mod-er-at-ing
  mod-er-ate-ly
  mod-er-ate-ness
mod-er-a-tion
mod-er-a-tor
  mod-er-a-tor-ship
mod-ern
mod-ern-ism
  mod-er-ist
  mod-er-ist-ic
mod-ern-ize
  mod-ern-ized
  mod-ern-iz-ing
  mod-ern-iz-er
  mod-ern-i-za-tion
mod-est
  mod-est-ly
  mod-est-ty

mod-es-ties
mod-i-cum
mod-i-fi-ca-tion
mod-i-fy
  mod-i-fied
  mod-i-fy-ing
  mod-i-fi-a-ble
  mod-i-fi-er
mod-ish
  mod-ish-ly
  mod-ish-ness
mo-diste
mod-u-late
  mod-u-lat-ed
  mod-u-lat-ing
mod-u-la-tion
  mod-u-la-tor
  mod-u-la-to-ry
mod-ule
mod-u-lar
mo-gulmo-hair
moi-ety
  moi-eties
moil
  moil-er
  moil-ing-ly
mois-ten
  moist-en-er
mois-ture
  mois-tur-ize
  mois-tur-ized
  mois-tur-iz-ing
  mois-tur-iz-er
mo-lar
mo-las-ses
mold
  mold-able
  mold-er
mold-board
mold-ing
moldy
  mold-i-er
  mold-i-est
  mold-i-ness
mol-e-cule
mole-hill
mole-skin
mo-lest
  mo-les-ta-tion
  mo-lest-er
mol-li-fy
  mol-li-fied
  mol-li-fy-ing
  mol-i-fi-ca-tion
  mol-li-fi-er
  mol-li-fy-ing-ly

mol-lusk
mol-ly-cod-dle
  mol-ly-cod-dled
  mol-ly-cod-dling
molt
  moult
  molt-er
mol-ten
  mol-ten-ly
mo-lyb-de-num
mo-ment
me-men-tary
  mo-men-tar-i-ly
  mo-men-tar-i-ness
mo-men-tous
  mo-men-tous-ly
  mo-men-tous-ness
mo-men-tum
mo-nad
  mo-nad-ic
  mo-nad-i-cal
  mo-nad-al
  mo-nad-i-cal-ly
mon-arch
  mo-nar-chal
  mo-nar-chal-ly
mo-nar-chi-cal
  mo-nar-chic
  mo-nar-chi-cal-ly
mon-ar-chism
  mon-ar-chist
  mon-ar-chis-tic
mon-ar-chy
  mon-ar-chies
  mon-as-tery
  mon-as-ter-ies
  mon-as-te-ri-al
mo-nas-tic
mo-nas-ti-cal
  mo-nas-ti-cal-ly
mo-nas-ti-cism
mon-au-ral
  mon-au-ral-ly
mon-e-tary
  mon-e-tar-i-ly
mon-e-tize
  mon-e-tized
  mon-e-tiz-ing
  mon-e-ti-za-tion
mon-ey
mon-ey-chang-er
mon-eyed
  mon-ied
mon-ey--mak-er
  mon-ey--mak-ing
mon-ger

mon-goose
  mon-gooses
mon-grel
mon-i-ker
mon-ism
  mon-ist
  mo-nis-tic
  mo-nis-ti-cal
  mo-nis-ti-cal-ly
mo-ni-tion
mon-i-tor
  mon-i-to-ri-al
monk
  monk-ish
  monk-ish-ly
mon-key
  mon-keys
  mon-keyed
  mon-key-ing
mon-key-shine
mon-chro-mat-ic
mon-o-chrome
  mon-o-chro-mic
  mon-o-chro-mi-cal
  mon-o-chro-mi-cal-ly
  mon-o-chrom-ist
mon-o-cle
  mon-o-cled
mon-o-cli-nal
mon-o-cline
  mon-o-cli-nal-ly
mon-o-cli-nous
mon-o-dist
mon-o-dy
  mon-o-dies
  mo-nod-ic
mo-noe-cious
  mo-noe-cious-ly
mo-nog-a-my
  mo-nog-a-mist
  mo-nog-a-mous
mon-o-gram
  mon-o-grammed
  mon-o-gram-ming
  mon-o-gram-mat-ic
mon-o-graph
  mo-nog-ra-pher
  mon-o-graph-ic
mon-o-lith
mon-o-logue
  mon-o-log
  mon-o-logu-ist
  mon-o-log-ist
mon-o-ma-nia
  mon-o-ma-ni-ac
  mon-o-ma-ni-a-cal

mon-o-met-al-lism
  mon-o-me-tal-lic
mo-no-mi-al
mon-nu-cle-o-sis
mon-o-pho-nic
mono-plane
mo-nop-o-lize
  mo-nop-o-lized
  mo-nop-o-liz-ing
  mo-nop-o-li-za-tion
  mo-nop-o-liz-er
mo-nop-o-ly
  mo-nop-o-lies
mono-rail
mon-o-syl-lab-ic
  mon-o-syl-lab-i-cal-ly
mon-o-syl-la-ble
mon-o-the-ism
  mon-o-the-ist
  mon-o-the-is-tic
  mon-o-the-is-ti-cal-ly
mon-o-tone
mo-not-o-nous
  mo-not-o-nous-ly
  mo-not-o-nous-ness
mo-not-o-ny
mone-treme
mono-type
  mon-o-typ-er
  mon-o-typ-ic
mon-o-va-lent
  mon-o-va-lence
  mon-o-va-len-cy
mon-ox-ide
mon-sei-gneur
  mes-sei-gneurs
mon-sieur
mon-soon
mon-ster
mon-stros-i-ty
  mon-stro-i-ties
mon-strous
  mon-strous-i-ties
mon-tage
month-ly
  month-lies
mon-u-ment
mon-u-men-tal
  mon-u-men-tal-ly
mooch
  mooch-er
moody
  mood-i-er
  mood-i-est
  mood-i-ly
  mood-i-ness

moon-beam
moon-light
moon-light-er
  moon-light-ing
moon-scape
moon-shine
  moon-shiner
moon-stone
moon-struck
moony
  moon-i-er
  moon-i-est
moor-ing
moot-ness
mop
  mopped
  mop-ping
mope
  moped
  mop-ing
  mop-er
  mop-ish
mop-pet
mo-raine
  mo-rain-al
  mo-rain-ic
mor-al
  mor-al-ly
mo-rale
mor-al-ist
  mor-al-is-tic
mo-ral-i-ty
  mo-ral-i-ties
mor-al-ize
  mor-al-ized
  mor-al-iz-ing
  mor-al-i-za-tion
  mor-al-iz-er
mo-rass
mor-a-to-ri-um
  mor-a-to-ri-ums
  mor-a-to-ria
mo-ray
mor-bid
  mor-bid-ly
  mor-bid-i-ty
  mor-bid-ness
mor-dant
  mor-dan-cy
  mor-dant-ly
more-over
mo-res
mor-ga-nat-ic
  mor-ga-nat-i-cal-ly
morque
mor-i-bund

mo-ri-on
morn-ing
morn-ing glo-ry
  morn-ing glo-ries
mo-roc-co
mo-ron
  mo-ron-ic
  mo-ron-i-cal-ly
mo-rose
  mo-rose-ly
  mo-rose-ness
mor-pheme
mor-phine
mor-phol-o-gy
  mor-pho-log-ic
  mor-pho-log-i-cal
  mor-phol-o-gist
mor-row
mor-sel
mor-tal
  mor-tal-ly
mor-tal-i-ty
  mor-tal-i-ties
mor-tar
mort-gage
  mort-gaged
  mort-gag-ing
  mort-gag-ee
  mort-gag-er
mor-ti-cian
mor-ti-fy
  mor-ti-fied
  mor-ti-fy-ing
  mor-ti-fi-ca-tion
mor-tise
  mor-tised
  mor-tising
mort-main
mor-tu-ary
  mor-tu-ar-ies
mo-sa-ic
Mo-ses
mo-sey
  mo-seyd
  mo-sey-ing
mosque
mos-qui-to
  mos-qui-toes
  mos-qui-tos
moss
most-ly
mo-tel
mo-tet
moth-ball
moth-eat-en
moth-er

moth-er-hood
moth-er-in-law
moth-er-ly
mo-tif
mo-tile
  mo-til-i-ty
mo-tion
  mo-tion-less
mo-ti-vate
  mo-ti-vat-ed
  mo-ti-vat-ing
  mo-ti-va-tion
mo-tive
mot-ley
mo-tor
mo-tor-bike
mo-tor-boat
mo-tor-bus
mo-tor-cade
mo-tor-cy-cle
  mo-tor-cy-cling
  mo-tor-cy-clist
mo-tor-ist
mo-tor-ize
  mo-tor-ized
  mo-tor-iz-ing
  mo-tor-i-za-tion
mo-tor-man
  mo-tor-men
mot-tle
  mot-tled
  mot-tling
  mot-tler
mound
mount
  mount-able
  mount-er
moun-tain
moun-tain-eer
moun-tain-ous
moun-te-bank
mount-ing
mourn
  mourn-er
mourn-ful
  mourn-ful-ly
  mourn-ful-ness
mourn-ing
  mourn-ing-ly
mouse
  moused
  mous-ing
mous-er
mous-tache
mousy
  mous-i-er

mous-i-est
mouth
  mouthed
  mouth-er
mouth-ful
  mouth-fuls
mouth-piece
mouthy
  mouth-i-er
  mouth-i-est
mou-ton
mov-able
  mov-a-bil-i-ty
  mov-a-bly
move
  moved
  mov-ing
move-ment
mov-ie
mow
mox-ie
mu-ci-lage
  mu-ci-lag-i-nous
muck
  mucky
mu-cous
  mu-cos-i-ty
mu-cus
mud
  mud-ded
  mud-ding
mud-dle
  mud-dled
  mud-dling
  mud-dler
mud-dy
  mud-di-er
  mud-di-est
mu-ez-zin
muf-fin
muf-ti
mug
  mugged
  mug-ging
  mug-ger
mug-gy
  mug-gi-er
  mug-gi-est
mu-lat-to
  mu-lat-toes
mul-ber-ry
  mul-ber-ries
mulch
mu-le-teer
mul-ish
  mul-ish-ly

mul-let
mul-li-gan
mul-li-ga-taw-ny
mul-lion
  mul-lioned
mul-ti-far-i-ous
  mul-ti-far-i-ous-ly
mul-ti-lat-er-al
mul-ti-mil-lion-aire
mul-ti-ple
mul-ti-ple scle-ro-sis
mul-ti-i-cand
mul-ti-pli-ca-tion
mul-ti-plic-i-ty
mul-ti-pli-er
mul-ti-ply
  mul-ti-plied
  mul-ti-ply-ing
  mul-ti-pli-a-ble
mul-ti-tude
mul-ti-tu-di-nous
  mul-ti-tu-di-nous-ly
mum-ble
mum-mer
mum-mery
mum-mi-fy
  mum-mi-fied
  mum-mi-fy-ing
  mum-mi-fi-ca-tion
mum-my
  mum-mies
  mum-mied
  mum-my-ing
munch
  munch-er
mun-dane
  mun-dane-ly
mu-nic-i-pal
  mu-nic-i-pal-ly
mu-nic-i-pal-i-ty
mu-nif-i-cent
  mu-nif-i-cence
  mu-nif-i-cent-ly
mu-ni-tion
mu-ral
  mu-ral-ist
mur-der
  mur-der-er
  mur-der-ess
mur-der-ous
  mur-der-ous-ly
mu-ri-at-ic ac-id
murky
  murk-i-er
  murk-i-est
  murk-i-ly

mur-mur
mur-rain
mus-cat
  mus-ca-tel
mus-cle
  mus-cled
  mus-cling
mus-cle--bound
mus-cu-lar
  mus-cu-lar-i-ty
  mus-cu-lar-ly
mus-cu-lar dys-tro-phy
mus-cu-la-ture
muse
  mused
  mus-ing
  mus-ing-ly
mu-se-um
mush
  mushy
  mush-i-er
  mush-i-est
mush-room
mu-sic
mu-si-cal
  mu-si-cal-ly
mu-si-cale
mu-si-cian
musk
  musky
  musk-i-er
  misk-i-est
mus-ket
mus-ke-teer
mus-ket-ry
musk-mel-on
musk-rat
mus-lin
muss
  mussy
  muss-i-er
mus-sel
mus-tache
mus-tang
mus-tard
mus-ter
mus-ty
  mus-ti-er
  mus-ti-est
  mus-ti-ly
mu-ta-ble
  mu-ta-bil-i-ty
  mu-ta-bly
mu-tant
mu-ta-tion
mu-tate

mu-tat-ed
mu-tat-ing
mu-ta-tion-al
mute
mut-ed
mut-ing
mute-ly
mute-ness
mu-ti-late
mu-ti-neer
mu-ti-ny
mu-ti-nies
mu-ti-nied
mu-ti-ny-ing
mu-ti-nous
mut-ter
mut-ter-er
mut-ton
mu-tu-al
mu-tu-al-i-ty
mu-tu-al-ly
muz-zle
my-col-o-gy
my-col-o-gist
my-na
my-nah
my-o-pia
my-op-ic
myr-i-ad
myr-mi-don
myrrh
myr-tle
mys-te-ri-ous
mys-te-ri-ous-ly
mys-tery
mys-ter-ies
mys-tic
mys-ti-cal
mys-ti-cal-ly
mys-ti-cism
mys-ti-fy
mys-ti-fied
mys-ti-fy-ing
mys-ti-fi-ca-tion
mys-tique
myth
myth-ic
myth-i-cal
myth-i-cal-ly
myth-i-cist
myth-i-cize
my-thol-o-gy
my-thol-o-gies
myth-o-log-ic
myth-o-log-i-cal
my-thol-o-gist

nab
nabbed
nab-bing
na-bob
na-cre
na-cre-ous
na-dir
nag
nagged
nag-ging
nag-ger
nail-er
na-ive
na-ive-ly
na-ive-te
na-ked
na-ked-ly
na-ked-ness
nam-by-pam-by
name
named
nam-ing
name-less
name-ly
name-sake
nan-keen
nan-kin
nan-ny
nan-nies
nap
napped
nap-ping
nap-per
na-palm
nape
naph-tha
naph-tha-lene
nap-kin
nar-cis-sism
nar-cism
nar-cis-sist
nar-co-sis
nar-cot-ic
nar-co-tize
nar-co-tized
nar-is
nar-es
nar-rate
nar-ra-ted
nar-ra-ting
nar-ra-tor
nar-ra-tion
nar-ra-tive
nar-ra-tive-ly
nar-row
nar-row-ly

nar-row-mind-ed
nary
na-sal
na-scent
scence
na-scen-cy
na-stur-tium
nas-ty
nas-ti-er
nas-ti-est
na-tal
na-tion
na-tion-hood
na-tion-al
na-tion-al-ly
na-tion-al-ism
na-tion-al-ist
na-tion-al-is-tic
na-tion-al-i-ty
na-tion-al-i-ties
na-tion-al-ize
na-tion-al-ized
na-tion-al-iz-ing
na-tion-al-i-za-tion
na-tion-wide
na-tive
na-tive-ly
na-tiv-i-ty
na-tiv-i-ties
nat-ty
nat-ti-er
nat-u-ral
nat-u-ral-ly
nat-u-ral-ness
nat-u-ral-ism
nat-u-ral-ist
nat-u-ral-is-tic
nat-u-ral-ized
nat-u-ral-iz-ing
nat-u-ral-i-za-tion
na-ture
naught
naugh-ty
naugh-ti-er
naugh-ti-est
nau-sea
nau-se-ate
nau-se-at-ed
nau-se-at-ing
nau-seous
nau-seous-ly
nau-ti-cal
nau-ti-cal-ly
nau-ti-lus
nau-ti-lus-es
nau-ti-li

na-val
na-vel
nav-i-ga-ble
nav-i-gate
  nav-i-gat-ed
  nav-i-gat-ing
nav-i-ga-tion
  nav-i-ga-tion-al
nav-i-ga-tor
na-vy
  na-vies
near
  near-ly
  near-ness
near-by
neat
  neat-ly
  neat-ness
neb-bish
neb-u-la
nec-es-sary
  nec-es-sar-ies
  nec-es-sar-i-ly
  ne-ces-si-tate
  ne-ces-si-ta-ting
ne-ces-si-ty
  ne-ces-si-ties
neck-er-chief
neck-ing
neck-lace
neck-tie
ne-crol-o-gy
  ne-crol-o-gies
nec-ro-man-cy
  nec-ro-man-cer
ne-cro-sis
  ne-crot-ic
nec-tar
  nec-tar-ine
need-ful
  need-ful-ly
  need-ful-ness
nee-dle
  nee-dled
  nee-dling
  nee-dle-like
  nee-dler
nee-dle-point
need-less
  need-less-ly
nee-dle-work
  nee-dle-work-er
needy
  need-i-er
  need-i-est
  need-i-ness

ne'er--do--well
ne-far-i-ous
  ne-far-i-ous-ly
  ne-far-i-ous-ness
ne-gate
  ne-ga-ted
  ne-ta-ting
ne-ga-tion
neg-a-tive
  neg-a-tive-ly
  neg-a-tive-ness
  neg-a-tive-i-ty
  neg-a-tiv-ism
ne-glect
  ne-glec-ter
  ne-glec-tor
  ne-glect-ful-ness
  ne-glect-ful
  ne-glect-ful-ly
neg-li-gee
neg-li-gent
  neg-li-gence
  neg-li-gent-ly
neg-li-gi-ble
  neg-li-gi-bly
  neg-li-gi-bil-i-ty
ne-go-tia-ble
  ne-go-tia-bil-i-ty
ne-go-ti-ate
  ne-go-ti-at-ed
  ne-go-ti-at-ing
  ne-go-ti-a-tion
  ne-go-ti-a-tor
neigh-bor
  neigh-bor-ing
  neigh-bor-ly
  neigh-bor-li-ness
  neigh-bor-hood
nei-ther
nem-e-sis
  nem-e-ses
neo-clas-sic
  neo-clas-si-cism
neo-lith-ic
ne-ol-o-gism
ne-ol-o-gy
ne-on
ne-o-phyte
ne-pen-the
  ne-pen-the-an
neph-ew
ne-phri-tis
  ne-phrit-ic
nep-o-tism
  nep-o-tist
nep-tu-ni-um

nerve
  nerved
  nerv-ing
  nerve-less
nerve--rack-ing
  nerve--wrack-ing
ner-vous
  ner-vous-ly
  ner-vous-ness
nervy
  nerv-i-er
  nerv-i-est
  nerv-i-ness
nes-tle
  nes-tled
  nes-tling
  nes-tler
net
  net-ted
  net-ting
neth-er
  neth-er-most
net-tle
  net-tled
  net-tling
net-work
neu-ral
  neu-ral-ly
  neu-ral-gia
  neu-ral-gic
neu-ras-the-nia
  neu-ra-then-ic
neu-ri-tis
  neu-rit-ic
neu-rol-o-gy
  neu-ro-log-i-cal
  neu-rol-o-gist
neu-ron
  neu-ron-ic
neu-ro-sis
  neu-ro-ses
neu-rot-ic
  neu-rot-i-cal-ly
neu-ter
neu-tral
  neu-tral-i-ty
  neu-tral-ly
neu-tral-ism
  neu-tral-ist
neu-tral-ize
  neu-tral-ized
  neu-tral-iz-ing
  neu-tral-i-za-tion
  neu-tral-iz-er
neu-tri-no
neu-tron

nev-er
nev-er-more
nev-er-the-less
new
  new-ish
  new-ness
new-born
new-com-er
new-el
new-fan-gled
new-ly
new-ly-wed
news-boy
news-cast
  news-cast-er
news-pa-per
  news-pa-per-man
news-print
news-reel
news-stand
newsy
  news-i-er
  news-i-est
newt
nex-us
ni-a-cin
nib-ble
  nib-bled
  nib-bling
  nib-bler
nib-lick
nice
  nic-er
  nic-est
  nice-ly
  nice-ness
nice-ty
  nice-ties
niche
nick-el
nick-el-ode-on
nick-name
nick-named
  nick-nam-ing
nic-o-tine
  nic-o-tin-ic
niece
nif-ty
  nif-ti-er
  nif-ti-est
nig-gard
  nig-gard-li-ness
  nig-gard-ly
nigh
  nigh-er
  nigh-est

night-cap
night-dress
night-fall
night-gown
night-hawk
night-in-gale
night-ly
night-mare
  night-mar-ish
night-shade
night-shirt
night-time
ni-hil-ism
  ni-hil-ist
  ni-hil-is-tic
nim-ble
  nim-bler
  nim-blest
  nim-ble-ness
  nim-bly
nim-bus
nin-com-poop
nine-pin
nine-teen
  nine-teenth
nine-ty
  nine-ties
  nine-ti-eth
nin-ny
  nin-nines
ninth
nip
  nipped
  nip-ping
  nip-per
nip-ple
nip-py
  nip-pi-er
  nip-pi-est
nir-va-na
nit
  nit-ty
  nit-ti-er
  nit-ti-est
ni-ter
nit-pick
ni-trate
  ni-trat-ed
  ni-trat-ing
  ni-tra-tion
  ni-tra-tor
ni-tric
ni-tro-gen
  ni-trog-e-nous
  ni-tro-glyc-er-in
  ni-trous ox-ide

nit-ty-grit-ty
nit-wit
no-be-li-um
no-bil-i-ty
  no-bil-i-ties
no-ble
no-body
noc-tur-nal
noc-turne
nod
  nod-ded
  nod-ding
  nod-der
node
  nod-al
nod-ule
  nod-u-lar
no-el
nog-gin
noise
  noised
  nois-ing
  noise-less
noi-some
  noi-some-ly
noisy
  nois-i-er
  nois-i-est
  nois-i-ly
no-mad
  no-mad-ic
  no-mad-i-cal-ly
  no-mad-ism
nom de plume
  noms de plume
no-men-cla-ture
nom-i-nal
  nom-i-nal-ly
nom-i-nate
  nom-i-nat-ed
  nom-i-nat-ing
  nom-i-na-tion
  nom-i-na-tor
  nom-i-na-tive
nom-i-nee
non-age
nonce
non-cha-lant
  non-cha-lance
  non-cha-lant-ly
non-com
  non-com-bat-ant
non-com-mit-tal
  non-com-mit-tal-ly
non-con-duc-tor
  non-con-duc-ing

non-con-form-ist
non-con-form-i-ty
non-de-script
non-en-ti-ty
non-en-ti-ties
none-the-less
non-in-ter-ven-tion
non-met-al
non-me-tal-lic
non-pa-reil
non-par-ti-san
non-par-ti-san-ship
non-plus
non-plused
non-plus-ing
non-prof-it
non-res-i-dent
non-res-i-dence
non-res-i-den-cy
non-res-i-den-cies
non-re-stric-tive
non-sec-tar-i-an
non-sense
non-sen-si-cal
non-sen-si-cal-ly
non se-qui-tur
non-stop
non-union
non-union-ism
non-union-ist
non-vi-o-lence
non-vi-o-lent
non-vi-o-lent-ly
noo-dle
noon
noon-day
noon-time
noose
noosed
noos-ing
nor-mal
nor-mal-cy
nor-mal-i-ty
nor-mal-ly
nor-mal-ize
nor-mal-ized
nor-mal-iz-ing
nor-mal-i-za-tion
north-east
north-east-ern
north-east-er
north-er
north-ern
north-ern-most
north-ern-er
north-ward

north-wards
north-ward-ly
north-west
nose
nosed
nos-ing
nose-gay
nos-tal-gia
nos-tal-gic
nos-tril
nos-trum
nosy
nos-i-er
nos-i-est
nos-i-ly
nos-i-ness
no-ta-ble
no-ta-rize
no-ta-rized
no-ta-riz-ing
no-ta-ri-za-tion
no-ta-ry
no-ta-ries
no-ta-tion
no-ta-tion-al
notch
notched
note
not-ed
not-ed
not-ed-ly
note-wor-thy
note-wor-thi-ness
noth-ing
noth-ing-ness
no-tice
no-ticed
no-tic-ing
no-tice-a-ble
no-tice-a-bly
no-ti-fy
no-ti-fied
no-ti-fy-ing
no-ti-fi-ca-tion
no-ti-fi-er
no-tion
no-to-ri-ous
no-to-ri-ous-ly
no-to-ri-e-ty
no-trump
nought
nour-ish
nour-ish-er
nour-ish-ing
nour-ish-ment
no-va

no-vas
nov-el
nov-el-ist
nov-el-is-tic
nov-el-ette
nov-el-ty
nov-el-ties
no-ve-na
no-ve-nae
nov-ice
no-vi-ti-ate
no-where
no-wise
nox-ious
nox-ious-ly
noz-zle
nu-ance
nub-bin
nu-bile
nu-cle-ar
nu-cle-us
nu-cle-us-es
nu-clei
nude
nude-ly
nude-ness
nu-di-ty
nudge
nudged
nudg-ing
nudg-er
nud-ism
nud-ist
nug-get
nui-sance
null
nul-li-ty
nul-li-ties
nul-li-fy
nul-li-fied
nul-li-fy-ing
nul-li-fi-ca-tion
nul-li-fi-er
numb
numb-ly
numb-ness
numb-ing
num-ber
num-ber-er
num-ber-less
numb-skull
nu-mer-al
num-er-al-ly
nu-mer-ate
nu-mer-at-ed
nu-mer-at-ing

nu-mer-a-tion
nu-mer-a-tor
nu-mer-i-cal
 nu-mer-i-cal-ly
nu-mer-ous
 nu-mer-ous-ly
nu-mis-mat-ics
 nu-mis-mat-ic
 nu-mis-mat-i-cal
 nu-mis-ma-tist
num-skull
nun-cio
 nun-ci-os
nun-nery
 nun-ner-ies
nup-tial
 nup-tial-ly
nurse
 nursed
 nurs-ing
 nurs-er
nurse-maid
nurs-ery
 nurs-er-ies
nur-ture
 nur-tured
 nur-tur-ing
 nur-tur-er
nut
 nut-ted
 nut-ting
nut-crack-er
nut-hatch
nut-meg
nu-tri-ent
 nu-tri-ment
nu-tri-tion
 nu-tri-tion-al
 nu-tri-tion-al-ly
 nu-tri-tion-ist
nu-tri-tious
 nu-tri-tious-ly
nu-tri-tive
 nu-tri-tive-ly
nut-shell
nut-ty
 nut-ti-er
 nut-ti-est
nuz-zle
 nuz-zled
 nuz-zling
ny-lon
nymph
 nym-phal
nym-pho-ma-nia
 nym-pho-ma-ni-ac

oaf
 oaf-ish
 oaf-ish-ly
oak-en
oa-kum
oar
 oared
 oars-man
 oars-men
oar-lock
oa-sis
 oa-ses
oat-en
oath
oat-meal
ob-bli-ga-to
 ob-bli-ga-tos
ob-du-rate
 ob-du-ra-cy
 ob-du-rate-ly
obe-di-ence
 obe-di-ent
 obe-di-ent-ly
obei-sance
 obei-sant
obe-lisk
obese
 obese-ness
 obes-i-ty
obey
 obey-er
ob-fus-cate
 ob-fus-ca-ted
 ob-fus-ca-ting
 ob-fus-ca-tion
obit
obit-u-ary
 obit-u-ar-ies
ob-ject
 ob-ject-less
 ob-ject-or
ob-jec-tion
 ob-jec-tion-a-ble
 ob-jec-tion-a-bly
ob-jec-tive
 ob-jec-tive-ly
 ob-jec-tive-ness
 ob-jec-tiv-i-ty
ob-jur-gate
 ob-jur-gat-ed
 ob-jur-gat-ing
 ob-jur-ga-tion
 ob-jur-ga-to-ry
ob-late
 ob-late-ly
 ob-late-ness

ob-li-gate
 ob-li-gat-ed
 ob-li-gat-ing
 ob-li-ga-tion
 ob-lig-a-to-ry
oblige
 obliged
 oblig-ing
 oblig-er
ob-lique
 ob-liqued
 ob-liqu-ing
 ob-lique-ly
oblit-er-ate
 oblit-er-at-ed
 oblit-er-at-ing
 oblit-er-a-tion
 oblit-er-a-tive
obliv-i-on
 obliv-i-ous
 obliv-i-ous-ly
ob-long
ob-lo-quy
 ob-lo-quies
ob-nox-ious
 ob-nox-ious-ly
oboe
obo-ist
ob-scene
 ob-scene-ly
 ob-scen-ity
 ob-scen-i-ties
ob-scure
 ob-scur-er
 ob-scur-est
 ob-scured
 ob-scur-ing
 ob-scure-ly
ob-se-qui-ous
 ob-se-qui-ous-ly
ob-se-quy
 ob-se-quies
ob-serv-able
 ob-serv-ably
ob-ser-vance
ob-ser-vant
 ob-ser-vant-ly
ob-ser-va-tion
 ob-ser-va-tion-al
ob-ser-va-to-ry
 ob-ser-va-to-ries
ob-serve
 ob-served
 ob-serv-ing
 ob-serv-ed-ly
 ob-serv-er

ob-serv-ing-ly
ob-sess
  ob-ses-sive
  ob-ses-sive-ly
ob-ses-sion
  ob-sid-i-an
ob-so-les-cent
  ob-so-les-cence
  ob-so-les-cent-ly
ob-so-lete
  ob-sta-cle
ob-ste-tri-cian
  ob-stet-rics
  ob-stet-ric
  ob-stet-ri-cal
ob-sti-nate
  ob-sti-na-cy
  ob-sti-na-cies
  ob-sti-nat-ly
ob-strep-er-ous
  ob-strep-er-ous-ly
ob-struct
  ob-struc-tive
  ob-struc-tor
ob-struc-tion
  ob-struc-tion-ism
  ob-struc-tion-ist
ob-tain
  ob-tain-a-ble
  ob-tain-er
  ob-tain-ment
ob-trude
  ob-trud-ed
  ob-trud-ing
  ob-trud-er
  ob-tru-sion
  ob-tru-sive
ob-tuse
  ob-tuse-ly
ob-verse
  ob-verse-ly
ob-vi-ate
  ob-vi-ated
  ob-vi-at-ing
  ob-vi-a-tion
  ob-vi-a-tor
ob-vi-ous
  ob-vi-ous-ly
oc-ca-sion
  oc-ca-sion-al
  oc-ca-sion-al-ly
oc-ci-dent
  oc-ci-den-tal
oc-clude
  oc-clud-ed
  oc-clud-ing

oc-clu-sive
oc-clu-sion
oc-cult
oc-cult-ism
  oc-cult-ist
oc-cu-pan-cy
  oc-cu-pan-cies
  oc-cu-pant
oc-cu-pa-tion
  oc-cu-pa-tion-al
  oc-cu-pa-tion-al-ly
oc-cu-py
  oc-cu-pied
  oc-cu-py-ing
  oc-cu-pi-er
oc-cur
  oc-curred
  oc-cur-ring
  oc-cur-rence
  oc-cur-rent
ocean
  oce-an-ic
ocean-og-ra-phy
  ocean-og-ra-pher
  ocean-o-graph-ic
oce-lot
ocher
  ocher-ous
  ochery
o'clock
oc-ta-gon
  oc-tag-o-nal
  oc-tag-o-nal-ly
oc-ta-he-dron
  oc-ta-he-drons
  oc-ta-he-dra
  oc-ta-he-dral
oc-tane
oc-tave
oc-ta-vo
oc-tet
oc-to-ge-nar-i-an
  oc-tog-e-nary
oc-to-pus
oc-u-lar
  oc-u-lar-ly
oc-u-list
odd
  odd-ly
  odd-ness
odd-ball
odd-i-ty
  odd-i-ties
od-ic
odi-ous
  odi-ous-ly

odi-um
odom-e-ter
odor
  odored
  odor-less
  odor-ous
  odor-ous-ly
odor-if-er-ous
  odor-if-er-ous-ly
od-ys-sey
oe-di-pal
of-fal
off-beat
off--col-or
of-fend
  of-fend-er
of-fense
  of-fense-less
of-fen-sive
  of-fen-sive-ly
  of-fen-sive-ness
of-fer
  of-fer-er
  of-fer-ing
of-fer-to-ry
  of-fer-to-ri-al
  of-fer-to-ries
off-hand
  off-hand-ed-ly
  off-hand-ed-ness
of-fice
of-fice-hold-er
of-fi-cer
of-fi-cial
  of-fi-cial-dom
  of-fi-cial-ism
  of-fi-cial-ly
of-fi-ci-ate
  of-fi-ci-at-ed
  of-fi-ci-at-ing
  of-fi-ci-a-tion
  of-fi-ci-a-tor
of-fi-cious
  of-fi-cious-ly
  of-fi-cious-ness
off-ing
off-set
  off-set-ting
off-shoot
off-shore
off-side
off-spring
off-stage
off--the--cuff
of-ten
of-ten-times

ogle
 ogled
 ogler
 ogling
ogre
 ogre-ish
ohm
 ohm-ic
ohm-age
ohm-me-ter
oil-cloth
oil-er
oil-skin
oily
 oil-i-er
 oil-i-est
 oil-i-ness
oint-ment
okra
old
 old-en
 old-er
 old-est
 old-ish
 old-ness
old--fash-ioned
old-ster
old--time
 old--tim-er
old--world
ole-ag-i-nous
 ole-ag-i-nous-ly
 ole-ag-i-nous-ness
oleo
oleo-mar-ga-rine
ol-fac-tion
ol-fac-to-ry
 ol-fac-to-ries
oli-garch
oli-gar-chic
 oli-gar-chi-cal
oli-gar-chy
 oli-gar-chies
oli-gop-oly
ol-ive
om-buds-man
 om-buds-men
om-elet
omen
om-i-nous
 om-i-nous-ly
 om-i-nous-ness
omis-sion
omit
 omit-ted
 omit-ting

om-ni-bus
 om-ni-bus-es
om-nip-o-tence
 om-nip-o-tent-ly
om-ni-pres-ence
om-ni-pres-ent
 om-ni-pres-ent-ly
om-ni-science
 om-ni-scient
 om-ni-scient-ly
om-ni-vore
om-niv-o-rous
 om-niv-o-rous-ly
 om-niv-o-rous-ness
onan-ism
 onan-ist
 onan-is-tic
once--over
on-com-ing
oner-ous
 oner-ous-ly
 oner-ous-ness
one-self
one--sid-ed
 one--sid-ed-ly
 one--sid-ed-ness
one-time
one--track
one--way
on-go-ing
on-ion
 on-ion-like
 on-iony
on-ion-skin
on--line
on-look-er
 on-look-ing
on-ly
on-o-mato-poe-ia
 on-o-mato-poe-ic
 on-o-mato-po-et-ic
on-rush
 on-rush-ing
on-set
on-shore
on-slaught
onto-
onus
on-ward
on-yx
oo-dles
ooze
 oozed
 oo-zi-er
 oo-zi-est
 oo-zi-ness

ooz-ing
oo-zy
opac-i-ty
 opac-i-ties
opal
opal-es-cence
 opal-es-cent
opaque
 opaque-ly
 opaque-ness
open
 open-er
 open-ly
 open-ness
open--air
open door
open--end
open--eyed
open-hand-ed
 open-hand-ed-ly
open house
open-ing
open--mind-ed
 open--mind-ed-ly
open-mouthed
open ses-a-me
open-work
opera
 op-er-at-ic
 op-er-at-i-cal-ly
op-er-a-ble
 op-er-a-bil-i-ty
 op-er-a-bly
opera glass
opera house
op-er-ate
 op-er-at-ed
 op-er-at-ing
op-er-a-tion
 op-er-a-tive
 op-er-a-tive-ly
op-er-a-tor
op-er-et-ta
oph-thal-mic
 oph-thal-mo-log-ic
 oph-thal-mol-o-gist
 oph-thal-mol-o-gy
opi-ate
opine
 opined
 opin-ing
opin-ion
 opin-ion-at-ed
 opin-ion-at-ed-ly
opi-um
opos-sum

op-po-nent
op-por-tune
  op-por-tune-ly
  op-por-tune-ness
op-por-fun-ism
  op-por-tun-ist
  op-por-tun-is-ty
op-por-tu-ni-ty
  op-por-tu-ni-ties
op-pos-able
  op-pos-a-bil-i-ty
op-pose
  op-posed
  op-pos-er
  op-pos-ing
  op-pos-ing-ly
op-po-site
  op-po-site-ly
op-po-si-tion
  op-po-si-tion-al
op-press
  op-pres-si-ble
  op-pres-sor
op-pres-sion
op-pres-sive
  op-pres-sive-ly
  op-pres-sive-ness
op-pro-bri-ous
  op-pro-bri-ous-ly
op-pro-bri-um
op-tic
  op-ti-cal
  op-ti-cal-ly
op-ti-cian
op-tics
op-ti-mal
op-ti-mism
  op-ti-mist
  op-ti-mis-tic
  op-ti-mis-ti-cal-ly
op-ti-mize
  op-ti-mi-za-tion
  op-ti-mized
  op-ti-miz-ing
op-ti-mum
  op-ti-ma
op-tion
  op-tion-al
  op-tion-al-ly
op-tom-e-trist
op-tom-e-try
  op-to-met-ric
  op-to-met-ri-cal
op-u-lence
op-u-lent
  op-u-lent-ly

opus
  opus-es
or-a-cle
  orac-u-lar
  orac-u-lar-i-ty
  orac-u-lar-ly
oral
  oral-ly
or-ange
  or-ange-ade
orang-utan
orate
  orat-ed
  orat-ing
ora-tion
or-a-tor
  or-a-tor-i-cal
  or-a-tor-i-cal-ly
or-a-to-rio
  or-a-to-ri-os
or-a-to-ry
or-bic-u-lar
  or-bic-u-lar-i-ty
  or-bic-u-lar-ly
or-bic-u-late
or-bit
  or-bit-al
  or-bit-er
or-chard
or-ches-tra
  or-ches-tral
  or-ches-tral-ly
or-ches-trate
  or-ches-trat-ed
  or-ches-trat-ing
  or-ches-tra-tion
or-chid
or-dain
  or-dain-er
  or-dain-ment
or-deal
or-der
  or-dered
  or-der-li-ness
  or-der-ly
or-di-nal
or-di-nance
  or-di-nari-ly
or-di-nary
  or-di-nari-ness
or-di-na-tion
ord-nance
or-dure
oreg-a-no
or-gan
  or-gan-dy

or-gan-ic
  or-gan-i-cal-ly
or-gan-ism
  or-gan-is-mal
  or-gan-is-mic
or-gan-ist
or-ga-ni-za-tion
  or-gan-i-za-tion-al
or-ga-nize
  or-ga-niz-able
  or-ga-nized
  or-ga-niz-er
  or-ga-niz-ing
  or-ga-niz-a-ble
or-gasm
  or-gas-mic
or-gi-as-tic
  or-gi-as-ti-cal-ly
or-gy
  or-gies
ori-ent
Ori-en-tal
ori-en-tal-ism
  ori-en-tal-ist
  ori-en-tal-ly
ori-en-tate
  ori-en-tat-ed
  ori-en-tat-ing
ori-en-ta-tion
or-i-fice
ori-ga-mi
orig-i-nal
  orig-i-nal-i-ty
  orig-i-nal-ly
orig-i-nate
  orig-i-nat-ed
  orig-i-nat-ing
  orig-i-na-tion
  orig-i-na-tive
  orig-i-na-tive-ly
  orig-i-na-tor
or-i-son
or-na-ment
  or-na-men-tal
  or-na-men-ta-tion
or-nate
  or-nate-ly
  or-nate-ness
or-nery
  or-ner-i-ness
or-ni-thol-o-gy
  or-ni-tho-log-ic
  or-ni-tho-log-i-cal
  or-ni-tho-log-i-cal-ly
  or-ni-thol-o-gist
oro-tund

oro-tun-di-ty
or-phan
  or-phan-hood
  or-phan-age
orth-odon-tics
  orth-odon-tic
  orth-odon-tist
or-tho-dox
  or-tho-dox-ly
  or-tho-dox-ness
or-tho-doxy
  or-tho-dox-ies
or-tho-gen-ic
or-thog-o-nal
  or-thog-o-nal-ly
or-thog-ra-phy
  or-tho-graph-ic
  or-tho-graph-i-cal
  or-tho-graph-i-cal-ly
  or-thog-ra-phies
  or-thog-ra-pher
or-tho-pe-dic
  or-tho-pe-dics
  or-tho-pe-dist
os-cil-late
  os-cil-lat-ed
  os-cil-lat-ing
  os-cil-la-tion
  os-cil-la-tor
  os-cil-la-to-ry
os-cil-lo-scope
os-cu-late
  os-cu-lat-ed
  os-cu-lat-ing
  os-cu-la-tion
  os-cu-la-to-ry
os-mi-um
os-mose
  os-mosed
  os-mos-ing
os-mo-sis
  os-mot-ic
  os-mot-i-cal-ly
os-prey
os-si-fy
  os-si-fied
  os-si-fi-er
  os-si-fy-ing
os-ten-si-ble
  os-ten-si-bly
os-ten-sive
  os-ten-sive-ly
os-ten-ta-tion
os-ten-ta-tious
  os-ten-ta-tious-ly
os-te-op-a-thy

os-teo-path
os-teo-path-ic
os-teo-path-i-cal-ly
os-tra-cism
os-tra-cize
  os-tra-cized
  os-tra-ciz-ing
os-trich
oth-er
  oth-er-ness
oth-er-wise
oth-er-world
  oth-er-world-ly
oti-ose
  oti-ose-ly
  oti-os-i-ty
ot-ter
ot-to-man
ought
ounce
our-self
our-selves
oust-er
out-bid
  out-bid-den
  out-bid-ding
  out-bid-der
out-board
out-bound
out-brave
  out-braved
  out-brav-ing
out-break
out-build-ing
out-burst
out-cast
out-come
out-cry
  out-cries
out-dat-ed
out-dis-tance
  out-dis-tanced
  out-dis-tanc-ing
out-do
  out-did
  out-do-ing
  out-done
out-door
out-er
out-er-most
outer space
out-face
  out-faced
  out-fac-ing
out-field
  out-field-er

out-fit
  out-fit-ted
  out-fit-ter
  out-fit-ting
out-flank
out-fox
out-grow
  out-grew
  out-grow-ing
  out-grown
out-growth
out-guess
out-ing
out-land-ish
  out-land-ish-ly
out-last
out-law
  out-law-ry
out-lay
  out-laid
  out-lay-ing
out-let
out-line
  out-lined
  out-lin-ing
out-live
  out-lived
  out-liv-ing
out-look
out-ly-ing
out-mod-ed
out-num-ber
out--of--date
out-post
out-put
out-rage
  out-raged
  out-rag-ing
out-ra-geous
  out-ra-geous-ly
out-range
  out-ranged
  out-rang-ing
out-rank
out-rig-ger
out-right
out-run
  out-ran
  out-run-ning
out-sell
  out-sell-ing
  out-sold
out-set
out-shine
  out-shin-ing
  out-shone

out-side
out-sid-er
out-smart
out-spo-ken
  out-spo-ken-ly
out-stand-ing
  out-stand-ing-ly
out-strip
  out-stripped
  out-strip-ping
out-ward
  out-ward-ly
  out-wards
out-wear
  out-wear-ing
  out-wore
  out-worn
out-weigh
out-wit
  out-wit-ted
  out-wit-ting
ova
oval
  oval-ly
ova-ry
  ovar-i-an
  ova-ries
ovate
ova-tion
ov-en
over
over-act
over-age
over-all
over-awe
  over-awed
  over-aw-ing
over-bear-ing
  over-bear-ing-ly
over-blown
over-board
over-build
  over-build-ing
  over-built
over-cast
over-charge
  over-charged
  over-charg-ing
over-coat
over-come
  over-came
over-com-pen-sa-tion
  over-com-pen-sate
  over-com-pen-sat-ed
  over-com-pen-sat-ing
over-con-fi-dence

over-con-fi-dent
over-do
  over-did
  over-do-ing
  over-done
over-dose
  over-dos-age
over-draft
over-draw
  over-draw-ing
  over-drawn
  over-drew
over-drive
over-due
over-em-pha-sis
  over-em-pha-size
  over-em-pha-sized
  over-em-pha-sizing
over-es-ti-mate
  over-es-ti-mat-ed
  over-es-ti-mat-ing
  over-es-ti-ma-tion
over-flow
  over-flowed
  over-flowing
  over-flown
over-gen-er-ous
over-grow
  over-grew
  over-grow-ing
  over-grown
over-growth
over-hand
  over-hand-ed
over-hang
  over-hang-ing
  over-hung
over-haul
  over-haul-ing
over-head
over-hear
  over-heard
  over-hear-ing
over-joy
  over-joyed
over-kill
over-land
over-lap
  over-lapped
  over-lap-ping
over-lay
  over-laid
  over-lay-ing
over-look
over-lord
over-ly

over-much
over-night
over-pass
over-play
over-pow-er
  over-pow-er-ing
over-rate
  over-rat-ed
  over-rat-ing
over-reach
over-ride
  over-rid-den
  over-rid-ing
  over-rode
over-rule
  over-ruled
  over-rul-ing
over-run
over-seas
over-see
  over-saw
  over-see-ing
  over-seen
over-seer
over-shad-ow
over-shoe
over-shoot
  over-shoot-ing
  over-shot
over-sight
over-sim-pli-fy
  over-sim-pli-fi-ca-tion
  over-sim-pli-fied
  over-sim-pli-fy-ing
over-size
over-sleep
  over-sleep-ing
  over-slept
over-spread
  over-spread-ing
over-state
  over-stat-ed
  over-state-ment
  over-stat-ing
over-stay
over-step
  over-stepped
  over-step-ping
over-strung
over-stuff
overt
  overt-ly
over-take
  over-tak-en
  over-tak-ing
  over-took

144

over-tax
over--the--coun-ter
over-throw
  over-threw
  over-thrown
  over-throw-ing
over-time
over-tone
over-ture
over-turn
over-view
over-ween-ing
  over-ween-ing-ly
over-weight
over-whelm
  over-whelm-ing
over-work
  over-worked
  over-work-ing
over-wrought
ovi-duct
ovip-a-rous
  ovip-ar-ous-ly
ovoid
  ovoi-dal
ovu-late
  ovu-lat-ed
  ovu-lat-ing
  ovu-la-tion
ovule
  ovu-lar
ovum
ova
owe
  owed
  ow-ing
owl-ish
own-er
ox-al-ic ac-id
ox-bow
ox-en
ox-ford
ox-i-da-tion
  ox-i-da-tive
  ox-i-dant
ox-ide
ox-i-dize
  ox-i-dized
  ox-i-diz-ing
ox-y-a-cet-y-lene
ox-y-gen
ox-y-gen-ate
  ox-y-gen-at-ed
  ox-y-gen-at-ing
  ox-y-gen-a-tion
oys-ter

pab-u-lum
pace
  paced
  pac-ing
  pac-er
pace-mak-er
pa-cif-ic
pa-cif-i-ca-tion
  pa-cif-i-ca-tor
  pa-cif-i-ca-to-ry
pac-i-fi-er
pac-i-fism
  pac-i-fist
pac-i-fy
  pac-i-fied
  pac-i-fy-ing
pack-age
  pack-ag-er
pack-er
pack-et
pack-ing
pad
  pad-ded
  pad-ding
pad-dle
pad-dock
pad-dy
  pad-dies
pad-lock
pae-an
  pe-an
pe-gan
  pe-gan-ism
page
  paged
  pag-ing
pag-eant
  pag-ent-ry
pag-i-nate
  pag-i-nat-ed
  pag-i-nat-ing
pa-go-da
pain
  pain-ful
  pain-less
pain-kil-ler
pains-tak-ing
  pains-tak-ing-ly
paint-er
pais-ley
pa-ja-mas
pal-ace
pal-at-a-ble
  pal-at-a-bil-i-ty
  pal-at-a-bly
pal-ate

pa-la-tial
  pa-la-tial-ly
pal-a-tiner
  pa-lat-i-nate
pa-lav-er
pale
pa-le-on-tol-o-gy
  pa-le-on-to-log-ic
  pa-le-on-to-log-i-cal
pal-ette
pal-imp-sest
pal-in-drome
pal-ing
pal-i-sade
  pal-i-sad-ed
  pal-i-sad-ing
pal-la-di-um
pall-bear-er
pal-let
pal-li-ate
  pal-li-at-ed
  pal-li-at-ing
  pal-li-a-tion
pal-lid
pal-lor
palm
  pal-ma-ceous
pal-mate
  pal-mate-ly
palm-er
palm-is-try
  palm-ist
palmy
  palm-i-er
  palm-i-est
pal-o-mi-no
  pal-o-mi-nos
pal-pa-ble
  pal-pa-bil-i-ty
  pal-pa-bly
pal-pate
  pal-pat-ed
  pal-pat-ing
pal-sy
  pal-sied
  pal-sy-ing
pal-ter
  pal-ter-er
pal-try
  pal-tri-er
  pal-tri-est
pam-pas*
  pam-pe-an
pam-per
  pam-per-er
pam-phlet

pan
  panned
  pan-ning
pan-a-ce-a
  pan-a-ce-an
pa-nache
pan-cake
pan-cre-as
  pan-cre-at-ic
pan-dem-ic
pan-de-mo-ni-um
pan-der
pan-el
  pan-eled
  pan-el-ing
pan-el-ist
pang
pan-ic
  pan-icked
  pan-ick-ing
pan-nier
  pan-ier
pan-o-ply
  pan-o-plies
  pan-o-plied
pan-ora-ma
  pan-oram-ic
  pan-oram-i-cal-ly
pan-sy
  pan-sies
pan-ta-loon
pan-the-ism
  pan-the-is-tic
pan-the-on
pan-ther
pan-ties
pan-to-mime
  pan-to-mimed
pan-try
  pan-tries
pant-suit
pant-y-hose
pa-pa
pa-pa-cy
  pa-pa-cies
pa-pal
pa-per
  pa-per-er
  pa-pery
pa-per-back
pa-pil-la
  pa-pil-pae
pa-poose
pap-ri-ka
pa-py-rus
par-a-ble

para-chute
  para-chut-ed
  para-chut-ing
  para-chut-ist
pa-rade
  pa-rad-ed
  pa-rad-ing
par-a-digm
  par-a-dig-mat-ic
par-a-dise
  par-a-di-si-a-cal
par-a-dox
  par-a-dox-i-cal
par-af-fin
par-a-gon
par-a-graph
  par-a-graph-er
par-a-keet
par-al-lax
  par-al-al-lac-tic
par-al-lel
  par-al-leled
  par-al-lel-ing
par-al-lel-o-gram
pa-ral-y-sis
  pa-ral-y-ses
  par-a-lyt-ic
par-a-lyze
  par-a-lyzed
  par-a-lyz-ing
par-a-me-cium
par-a-med-ic
pa-ram-e-ter
par-a-mount
  par-a-mount-cy
  par-a-mount-ly
par-amour
para-noia
  para-noid
par-a-pet
par-a-pher-nal-ia
para-phrase
  para-phrased
  para-phras-ing
para-ple-gia
  para-ple-gic
para-psy-chol-o-gy
par-a-site
  par-a-sit-ic
para-sol
par-a-sym-pa-thet-ic
para-thi-on
para-troop-er
para-ty-phoid
par-boil
par-cel

par-celed
  par-cel-ing
parch-ment
par-don
  par-don-a-ble
  par-don-a-bly
pare
  pared
  par-ing
par-e-gor-ic
par-ent
  pa-ren-tal
par-ent-age
pa-ren-the-sis
pa-re-sis
  pa-ret-ic
par-fait
pa-ri-ah
par-i-mu-tu-el
par-ish
  pa-rish-ion-er
par-i-ty
par-ka
par-lance
par-lay
  par-lay-ed
  par-lay-ing
par-ley
  par-leyed
  par-ley-ing
par-lia-ment
  par-lia-men-tar-ian
  par-lia-men-ta-ry
par-lor
pa-ro-chi-al
par-o-dy
  par-o-dies
  par-o-died
pa-role
  pa-roled
par-ot-id
par-ox-ysm
  par-ox-ys-mal
par-quet
  par-queted
  par-quet-ing
par-quet-ry
par-rot
  par-rot-like
  par-roty
par-ry
  par-ried
  par-ry-ing
parse
par-si-mo-ny
  par-si-mo-ni-ous

146

par-si-mo-ni-ous-ly
pars-ley
pars-nip
par-son-age
par-take
  par-took
  par-tak-en
part-ed
par-the-no-gen-e-sis
par-tial
  par-tial-ly
par-tial-i-ty
  par-tial-i-ties
par-tic-i-pant
par-tic-i-pate
  par-tic-i-pat-ed
  par-tic-i-pat-ing
par-ti-cip-i-al
par-ti-ci-ple
par-ti-cle
par-ti--col-ored
par-tic-u-lar
  par-tic-u-lar-ly
par-tic-u-lar-i-ties
par-tic-u-lar-ize
  par-tic-u-lar-ized
  par-tic-u-lar-iz-ing
par-tic-u-late
part-ing
par-ti-san
  par-ti-san-ship
par-tite
par-ti-tion
par-ti-tive
part-ly
part-ner
  part-ner-ship
par-tridge
  par-tridg-es
part--time
par-tu-ri-ent
par-tu-ri-tion
par-ty
  par-ties
par-ve-nu
pas-chal
pa-sha
pass-able
pass-ably
pass-sen-ger
pass-er-by
  pass-ers-by
pass-ing
pas-sion
  pas-sion-ies
pas-sion-ate

pas-sion-ate-ly
pas-sive
pas-ta
paste
  pas-ted
  pas-ting
paste-board
pas-tel
pas-teur-ize
  pas-teur-ized
  pas-teur-iz-ing
  pas-teur-i-za-tion
pas-tille
pas-time
pas-tor
pas-to-ral
pas-to-ral-ly
pas-tor-ate
pas-tra-mi
past-ry
  pas-tries
pas-ture
pas-ty
  past-i-er
  past-i-est
patch-work
patchy
  patch-i-er
  patch-i-est
pat-ent
  pa-ten-cy
  pat-ent-ly
pat-en-tee
pat-er-nal
  pat-ter-nal-ly
pa-ter-nal-ism
pa-ter-ni-ty
pa-thet-ic
path-find-er
pa-thol-o-gy
pa-thos
pa-tience
pa-tient
  pa-tient-ly
pat-i-na
pa-tio
  pa-tios
pa-tri-arch
pa-tri-ar-chy
  pa-tri-ar-chies
pa-tri-cian
pat-ri-mo-ny
  pat-ri-mo-nies
pa-tri-ot
  pa-tri-ot-ic
  pa-tri-ot-ism

pa-trol
  pa-trolled
  pa-trol-ling
pa-trol-man
  pa-trol-men
pa-tron
  pa-tron-ess
pa-tron-age
pa-tron-ize
  pa-tron-ized
  pa-tron-iz-ing
  pa-tron-iz-ing-ly
pat-ro-nym-ic
pat-sy
  pat-sies
pat-ter
pat-tern
  pat-terned
pat-ty
  pat-ties
pau-ci-ty
paunch
pau-per
  pau-per-ism
pause
  paused
  paus-ing
pa-vil-ion
pawn
  pawn-er
pawn-bro-ker
pay-a-ble
pay-ment
pay-off
peace
peace-able
  peace-ably
peace-ful
  peace-ful-ly
peach
pea-cock
peak-ed
pea-nut
pearl
  pear-ly
peas-ant
  peas-ant-ly
peaty
peb-ble
pe-can
pec-ca-dil-lo
  pec-ca-dil-loes
pec-ca-dil-los
peck-er
pec-tin
pec-to-ral

pec-u-late
  pec-u-lat-ed
  pec-u-lat-ing
pe-cu-liar
  pe-cu-liar-ly
  pe-cu-li-ar-i-ty
  pe-cu-li-ar-i-ties
pe-cu-ni-ary
ped-a-go-gue
ped-a-go-gy
ped-al
  ped-aled
  ped-al-ing
ped-ant
  pe-dan-tic
  pe-dan-ti-cal-ly
  ped-ant-ry
ped-dle
ped-es-tal
pe-des-tri-an
  pe-des-tri-an-ism
pe-di-at-ric
  pe-di-at-rics
pe-di-a-tri-cian
  pe-di-at-rist
ped-i-cure
  ped-i-cur-ist
ped-i-gree
  ped-i-greed
ped-i-ment
  ped-i-men-tal
  ped-i-ment-ed
pe-dom-e-ter
peep-hole
peer
peer-less
  peer-less-ly
peeve
  peeved
peev-ing
pee-vish
  pee-vish-ly
pee-wee
pe-jo-ra-tive
  pe-jo-ra-tive-ly
pe-koe
pel-let
pell--mell
pel-lu-cid
  pel-lu-cid-i-ty
  pel-lu-cid-ly
pelt-er
  pelt-ry
pel-vis
  pel-vis-es
  pel-ves

pel-vic
pem-mi-can
  pem-i-can
pe-nal
pe-nal-ize
  pe-nal-ized
  pe-nal-iz-ing
pen-al-ty
  pen-al-ties
pen-ance
pen-chant
pen-cil
pend-ant
pend-ent
  pend-en-cy
  pend-ent-ly
pend-ing
pen-du-lous
  pen-du-lous-ly
pen-du-lum
pen-a-tra-ble
  pen-a-tra-bil-i-ty
  pen-a-tra-bly
pen-e-trate
  pen-e-trat-ed
  pen-e-trat-ing
pen-e-tra-tion
pen-i-cil-lin
pen-in-su-la
  pen-in-su-lar
pe-nis
pen-i-tent
  pen-i-tence
  pen-i-ten-tial
pen-i-ten-tia-ry
  pen-i-ten-tia-ries
pen-knife
  pen-knives
pen-man-ship
pen-nant
pen-ni-less
pen-non
pen-ny
  pen-nies
pen-ny an-te
pe-nol-o-gy
  pe-no-log-i-cal
  pe-nol-o-gist
pen-sion
pen-sive
  pen-sive-ly
pen-ta-gon
  pen-tag-o-nal
  pen-tag-o-nal-ly
pen-tam-e-ter
pen-tath-lon

pent-up
pe-nult
  pe-nul-ti-ma
  pe-nul-ti-mate
pe-num-bra
  pe-num-bras
  pe-num-brae
  pe-num-bral
pe-nu-ri-ous
  pe-nu-ri-ous-ly
pen-u-ry
pe-on
  pe-on-age
pe-o-ny
  pe-on-ies
peo-ple
pep
  pepped
  pep-ping
pep-per
pep-pery
pep-py
  pep-pi-er
  pep-pi-est
pep-sin
pep-tic
per-am-bu-late
per-am-bu-la-tor
per an-num
per-cale
per cap-i-ta
per-ceive
  per-ceived
  per-ceiv-ing
  per-ceiv-a-ble
per-cent
  per-cent-age
per-cen-tile
per-cep-ti-ble
  per-cep-ti-bil-i-ty
  per-cep-ti-bly
per-cep-tion
  per-cep-tion-al
  per-cep-tu-al
  per-cep-tu-al-ly
perch
per-co-late
  per-co-lat-ed
  per-co-lat-ing
  per-co-la-tion
per-co-la-tor
per-cus-sion
  per-cus-sion-ist
per di-em
per-di-tion
per-e-gri-nate

pe-remp-to-ry
  pe-remp-to-to-ri-ly
pe-ren-ni-al
  pe-ren-ni-al-ly
per-fec-tion
  per-fec-tion-ist
per-fect-ly
per-fi-dy
  per-fid-i-ous
  per-fid-i-ous-ly
per-fo-rate
  per-fo-rat-ed
per-force
per-form
  per-form-a-ble
  per-form-er
per-for-mance
per-fume
  per-fumed
per-func-to-ry
  per-func-to-ri-ly
per-haps
per-i-gee
  per-i-ge-al
  per-i-ge-an
peri-he-li-on
  peri-he-lia
per-il
  per-il-ous
  per-il-ous-ly
pe-rim-e-ter
  per-i-met-ic
  per-i-met-ri-cal
pe-ri-od
pe-ri-od-ic
  pe-ri-o-dic-i-ty
pe-ri-od-i-cal
  pe-ri-od-i-cal-ly
pe-riph-ery
  pe-riph-er-ies
  pe-riph-er-al
  pe-riph-er-al-ly
per-i-phrase
peri-scope
  peri-scopic
  peri-scop-i-cal
per-ish
per-ish-able
  per-ish-abil-i-ty
  per-ish-ably
peri-stal-sis
  peri-stal-ses
  peri-style
peri-to-ne-um
  peri-to-ne-ums
  peri-to-nea

peri-to-ne-al
peri-to-ni-tis
peri-wig
peri-win-kle
per-jure
  per-jured
  per-jur-ing
  per-jur-er
per-ju-ry
  per-ju-ries
perky
  perk-i-er
  perk-i-est
per-ma-nent
per-me-able
  per-me-abil-i-ty
  per-me-ably
per-me-ate
  per-me-at-ed
  per-me-at-ing
  per-me-a-tion
  per-me-a-tive
per-mis-si-ble
  per-mis-si-bil-i-ty
  per-mis-si-bly
per-mis-sion
per-mis-sive
  per-mis-sive-ly
per-mit
  per-mit-ted
  per-mit-ting
  per-mit-ter
per-mu-ta-tion
per-ni-cious
  per-ni-cious-ly
per-ora-tion
per-ox-ide
  per-ox-id-ed
  per-ox-id-ing
per-pen-dic-u-lar
  per-pen-dic-u-lar-i-ty
  per-pen-dic-u-lar-ly
per-pe-trate
  per-pe-trat-ed
  per-pe-trat-ing
  per-pe-tra-tion
  per-pe-tra-tor
per-pet-u-al
  per-pet-u-al-ly
per-pet-u-ate
  per-pet-u-at-ed
  per-pet-u-at-ing
  per-pet-u-a-tion
  per-pet-ua-tor
per-pe-tu-ity
  per-pe-tu-ities

per-plex
  per-plexed
  per-plex-ing
  per-plex-ing-ly
  per-plex-ed-ly
  per-plex-i-ty
  per-plex-i-ties
per-qui-site
per-se-cute
  per-se-cut-ed
  per-se-cut-ing
  per-se-cu-tive
  per-se-cu-tor
  per-se-cu-tion
per-se-vere
  per-se-vered
  per-se-ver-ing
  per-sse-ver-ance
  per-se-ver-ing-ly
per-si-flage
per-sim-mon
per-sist
  per-sist-ence
  per-sis-ten-cy
per-sist-ent
  per-sist-ent-ly
per-snick-e-ty
per-son
per-son-able
per-son-age
per-son-al-i-ty
  per-son-al-i-ties
per-son-al-ize
  per-son-al-ized
  per-son-al-iz-ing
per-son-al-ly
per-so-na non gra-ta
per-son-ate
  per-son-at-ed
  per-son-at-ing
  per-son-a-tion
  per-son-a-tor
per-son-i-fy
  per-son-i-fied
  per-son-i-fy-ing
  per-son-i-fi-ca-tion
  per-son-i-fi-er
per-son-nel
per-spec-tive
  per-spec-tive-ly
per-spi-ca-cious
  per-spi-ca-cious-ly
  per-spi-cac-i-ty
per-spi-cu-i-ty
  per-spic-u-ous
  per-spic-u-ous-ly

per-spi-ra-tion
per-spire
  per-spired
  per-spiring
per-suade
  per-suad-ed
  per-suad-ing
  per-suad-a-ble
  per-suad-er
per-sua-sion
per-sua-sive
  per-sua-sive-ly
  per-sua-sive-ness
pert
  pert-ly
  pert-ness
per-tain
per-ti-na-cious
  per-ti-na-cious-ly
  per-ti-nac-i-ty
per-ti-nent
  per-ti-nence
  per-ti-nen-cy
  per-ti-nent-ly
per-turb
  per-turb-a-ble
  per-tur-ba-tion
pe-ruke
pe-ruse
  pe-rused
  pe-rus-ing
  pe-rus-al
  pe-rus-er
per-vade
  per-vad-ed
  per-vad-ing
  per-vad-er
  per-va-sion
  per-va-sive
  per-va-sive-ly
per-verse
  per-verse-ly
  per-verse-ness
  per-ver-si-ty
per-ver-sion
per-vert
  per-vert-ed
  per-vert-ed-ly
  per-vert-er
  per-vert-i-ble
per-vi-ous
  per-vi-ous-ness
pes-ky
  pes-ki-er
  pes-ki-est
  pesk-i-ly

pes-si-mism
  pes-si-mist
  pes-si-mist
  pes-si-mis-tic
  pes-si-mis-ti-cal-ly
pes-ter
pest-hole
pest-i-cide
pes-tif-er-ous
  pes-tif-er-ous-ly
per-ti-lence
  pes-ti-len-tial
pes-ti-lent.
  pes-ti-lent-ly
pes-tle
  pes-tled
  pes-tling
pet
  pet-ted
  pet-ting
  pet-ter
pet-al
  pet-aled
  pet-cock
pe-ter
pet-i-ole
pe-tite
  pe-tite-ness
pet-it four
pe-ti-tion
  pe-ti-tion-ary
  pe-ti-tion-er
pe-trel
pet-ri-fy
  pet-ri-fied
  pet-ri-fy-ing
  pe-tri-fac-tion
pe-tro-chem-is-try
  pe-tro-chem-i-cal
pet-rol
pet-ro-la-tum
pe-trol-leum
pet-ti-coat
pet-ti-fog
  pet-ti-fogged
  pet-ti-fog-ging
  pet-ti-fog-ger
  pet-ti-fog-gery
pet-tish
  pet-tish-ly
  pet-tish-ness
pet-ty
pet-ti-er
  pet-ti-est
  pet-ti-ly
  pet-ti-ness

pet-u-lant
  pet-u-lance
  pet-u-lan-cy
  pet-u-lant-ly
pe-tu-nia
pew-ter
pey-o-te
  pey-o-tes
pha-lanx
  pha-lanx-es
  pha-lang-es
pal-lus
  pal-li
  pahl-lus-es
  phal-lic
phan-tasm
  phan-tas-ma
  phan-tas-mal
  phan-tas-mic
phan-tas-ma-go-ria
  phan-tas-ma-go-ri-al
  phan-tas-ma-gor-ic
phan-ta-sy
  phan-ta-sies
phan-tom
phar-aoh
phar-ma-ceu-ti-cal
  phar-ma-cue-tic
  phar-ma-ceu-ti-cal-ly
phar-ma-cue-tics
phar-ma-cist
phar-ma-col-o-gy
  phar-ma-co-log-ic
  phar-ma-co-log-i-ca
  phar-ma-col-o-gist
phar-ma-co-poe-ia
  phar-ma-co-poe-ial
phar-ma-cy
  phar-ma-cies
phar-ynx
  pha-ryn-ges
  pha-ryn-ge-al
  pha-ryn-gal
phase
  phased
  phas-ing
  pha-sic
pheas-ant
phe-no-bar-bi-tal
phe-nol
  phe-nol-ic
phe-nom-e-non
  phe-nom-e-na
  phe-nom-e-nons
  phe-nom-e-nal
  phe-nom-e-nal-ly

phi-al
phi-lan-der
phi-lan-der-er
phi-lan-thro-py
phi-lan-thro-pies
phil-an-throp-ic
phil-an-throp-i-cal
phi-lan-thro-pist
phi-late-ly
phil-a-tel-ic
phil-a-tel-i-cal
phi-lat-e-list
phil-har-mon-ic
phil-o-den-dron
phil-o-den-drons
phil-o-den-dra
phi-log-o-gy
phi-lol-o-gist
phi-lol-o-ger
phil-o-lo-gi-an
phil-o-log-i-cal
phil-o-log-ic
phil-o-log-i-cal-ly
phi-los-o-pher
phil-o-soph-i-cal
phil-o-soph-ic
phil-o-soph-i-cal-ly
phi-los-o-phize
phi-los-o-phized
phi-los-o-phiz-ing
phi-los-o-phiz-er
phi-los-o-phy
phi-los-o-phies
phil-ter
phil-tered
phil-ter-ing
phle-bi-tis
phle-bit-ic
phle-bot-o-my
phle-bot-o-mist
phlegm
phleg-mat-ic
phleg-mat-i-cal
phleg-mat-i-cal-ly
phlox
pho-bia
pho-bic
phoe-be
phoe-nix
phone
phoned
phon-ing
pho-neme
pho-ne-mic
pho-net-ic
pho-net-ics

pho-net-i-cal
pho-net-i-cal-ly
phon-ic
phon-ics
pho-no-graph
pho-no-graph-ic
pho-no-graph-i-cal-ly
pho-nol-o-gy
pho-nol-o-gies
pho-no-log-ic
pho-no-log-i-cal
pho-no-log-i-cal-ly
pho-nol-o-gist
pho-ny
pho-ni-er
pho-ni-est
pho-nies
pho-ni-ness
phos-phate
phos-pho-res-cence
phos-pho-resce
phos-pho-resced
phos-pho-resc-ing
phos-pho-res-cent
phos-pho-res-cent-ly
phos-pho-rus
pho-to
pho-tos
pho-to-copy
pho-to-cop-ies
pho-to-cop-ied
pho-to-cop-y-ing
pho-to-e-lec-tric
pho-to-en-grav-ing
pho-to-en-grave
pho-to-en-graved
pho-to-en-grav-er
pho-to-flash
pho-to-gen-ic
pho-to-graph
pho-to-graph-er
pho-tog-ra-phy
pho-to-graph-ic
pho-to-graph-i-cal
pho-to-graph-i-cal-ly
pho-to-gra-vure
pho-to--off-set
pho-to-stat
pho-to-stat-ed
pho-to-stat-ing
pho-to-stat-ic
pho-to-syn-the-sis
phrase
phrased
phras-ing
phras-al

phrase-ol-o-gy
phre-net-ic
phre-nol-o-gy
phre-nol-o-gist
phy-lac-tery
phy-lac-ter-ies
phy-log-e-ny
phy-lo-gen-e-sis
phy-lo-ge-net-ic
phy-lo-gen-ic
phy-log-e-nist
phy-lu
phys-ic
phys-icked
phys-ick-ing
phys-i-cal
phys-i-cal-ly
phy-si-cian
phys-ics
phys-i-cist
phys-i-og-no-my
phys-i-og-no-mies
phys-i-og-nom-ic
phys-i-og-nom-i-cal
phys-i-og-no-mist
phys-i-og-ra-phy
phys-i-o-graph-ic
phys-i-o-graph-i-cal
phys-i-ol-o-gy
phys-i-o-log-ic
phys-i-o-log-i-cal
phys-i-o-log-i-cal-ly
phys-i-ol-o-gist
phys-i-o-ther-a-py
phy-sique
pi-a-nis-si-mo
pi-an-ist
pi-ano
pia-nos
pi-ano-forte
pi-az-za
pi-ca
pic-a-dor
pic-a-resque
pic-a-yune
pic-a-yun-ish
pic-ca-lil-li
pic-co-lo
pic-co-los
pic-co-lo-list
pick-ax
picked
pick-er-el
pick-et
pick-et-er
pick-ing

pick-le
 pick-led
 pick-ling
pick-pock-et
pick-up
picky
 pick-i-er
 pick-i-est
pic-nic
 pic-nicked
 pic-nick-ing
 pic-nick-er
pic-to-ri-al
 pic-to-ri-al-ly
pic-ture
 pic-tured
 pic-tur-ing
pic-tur-esque
 pic-tur-esque-ly
pid-dle
 pid-dled
 pid-dling
pid-gin
pie-bald
piece
 piec-er
piece-meal
piece-work
 piece-worker
pied
pier
pierce
 pierc-ed
 pierc-ing
pierc-ing-ly
pi-etism
 pi-etis-tic
 pi-etis-ti-cal
pi-ety
 pi-eties
pif-fle
pig
 pigged
 pig-ging
pi-geon
pe-geon-hole
 pi-geon-holed
 pi-geon-hol-ing
pi-geon--toed
pig-gish
 pig-ish-ly
 pig-gis-ness
pig-head-ed
 pig-head-ed-ly
 pig-head-ed-ness
pig-ment

pig-men-tary
pig-men-ta-tion
pig-pen
pig-skin
pig-sty
 pig-sties
pig-tail
pike
 piked
 pik-ing
pik-er
pi-las-ter
pil-chard
pile
 piled
 pil-ing
pil-fer
 pil-fer-age
 pil-fer-er
pil-grim
pil-grim-age
 pil-grim-aged
 pil-grim-ag-ing
pil-lage
 pil-laged
 pil-lag-ing
 pil-lag-er
pil-lar
pill-box
pil-lion
pil-lo-ry
 pil-lo-ries
 pil-lo-ry-ing
pil-low
pil-low-case
pi-lot
 pi-lot-age
 pi-lot-less
pi-lot-house
pi-men-to
 pi-men-tos
pim-ple
 pim-pled
 pim-ply
pin
 pinned
 pin-ning
pin-afore
pince-nez
pin-cers
pinch
 pinch-er
pinch-beck
pin-cush-ion
pin-dling
pine

pine-like
piney
pin-ing
pi-ne-al
pine-ap-ple
pin-feath-er
 pin-feath-ered
 pin-feath-ery
pin-fold
pin-head
 pin-head-ed
pin-hole
pin-ion
pink-eye
pink-ie
pinko
 pink-os
 pink-oes
pin-na
 pin-nas
 pin-nae
 pin-nal
pin-na-cle
 pin-na-cled
 pin-na-cling
pi-nate
 pin-nate-ly
 pin-na-tion
pi-noch-le
 pi-noc-le
pin-point
pin-prick
pin-set-ter
pin-tail
 pin-tailed
pin-tle
pin-to
 pin-tos
pin-up
pin-wheel
pin-worm
pi-o-neer
pi-ous
 pi-ous-ly
 pi-ous-ness
pip
 pipped
 pip-ping
pipe-line
 pipe-lined
 pipe-lin-ing
pip-er
pip-ing
pip-it
pip-pin
pip-squeak

pi-quant
  pi-quan-cy
  pi-quant-ly
pique
  piqued
  pi-quing
pi-ra-cy
  pi-ra-cies
pi-ra-nha
pi-rate
  pi-rat-ed
  pi-rat-ing
  pi-rat-i-cal
  pi-rat-i-cal-ly
pi-roque
pir-ou-ette
  pir-ou-et-ted
  pir-ou-et-ting
pi-sci-cul-ture
pis-ta-chio
  pis-ta-chi-os
pis-til
pis-til-late
pis-tol
  pis-toled
  pis-tol-ing
pis-ton
pit
  pit-ted
  pit-ting
pitch--blake
pitch-blend
pitch-er
pitch-fork
pitchy
  pitch-i-er
  pitch-i-est
pit-e-ous
  pit-e-ous-ly
pit-fall
pith
  pith-i-er
  pith-i-est
  pith-i-ly
piti-a-ble
  piti-anle-ness
  piti-a-bly
piti-ful
  piti-ful-ly
  piti-ful-ness
piti-less
  piti-less-ly
pit-man
  pit-men
pit-tance
pi-tu--tar-ies

pity
  pit-ies
  pit-ied
  pit-y-ing
  pit-y-ing-ly
piv-ot
  piv-ot-al
  piv-ot-al-ly
pix-i-lat-ed
pixy
  pix-ie
  pix-ies
piz-za
piz-ze-ria
piz-zi-ca-to
place-a-ble
  plac-a-bil-i-ty
  plac-a-bly
plac-ard
pla-cate
  pla-cat-ed
  pla-cat-ing
  pla-ca-tion
  pla-ca-tive
  pla-ca-to-ry
place
  placed
  plac-ing
pla-ce-bo
  pla-ce-bos
  pla-ce-boes
place-ment
pla-cen-ta
  pla-cen-tas
  pla-cen-tae
  pla-cen-tal
plac-er
plac-id
  pla-cid-i-ty
  plac-id-ness
pla-gal
pla-gia-rism
  pla-gia-rized
  pla-gia-riz-ing
  pla-gia-riz-er
pla-gia-ry
  pla-gia-ries
plaque
  plaqued
  pla-quing
  pla-quer
pla-guy
  pla-guey
  pla-gui-ly
plaid
plain

plain-ly
plain-ness
plain-song
plain-spo-ken
plain-tiff
plain-tive
  plain-tive-ly
plait
  plait-ing
plan
  planned
  plan-ning
  plan-less
  plan-ner
plane
  planed
  plan-ing
plan-er
plan-et
plan-e-tar-i-um
  plan-e-tar-i-ums
  plan-e-tar-ia
plan-e-tary
plan-e-told
plan-ish
  plan-ish-er
plank-ing
plank-ton
  plank-ton-ic
plant
  plant-able
  plant-like
plan-tain
plan-ta-tion
plant-er
plaque
plasm
plas-ma
  plas-mic
  plas-mat-ic
plas-ter
  plas-ter-er
  plas-ter-ing
  plas-ter-work
plas-ter-board
plas-tered
plas-tic
  plas-ti-cal-ly
  plas-tic-i-ty
  plas-ti-ciz-er
plat
  plat-ted
  plat-ting
plate
  plat-ed
  plat-ing

153

plat-er
pla-teau
  pla-teaus
  pla-teaux
plate-ful
  plate-fuls
plate-let
plat-form
plat-i-num
plat-i-tude
  plat-i-tu-di-nal
  plat-i-tu-di-nous
plat-i-tu-di-nize
  plat-i-tu-di-nized
  plat-i-tu-di-niz-ing
pla-ton-ic
  pla-ton-i-cal-ly
pla-toon
plat-ter
platy-pus
  platy-pus-es
  platy-pi
plau-dit
plau-si-ble
  plau-si-bil-i-ty
  plau-si-bly
play-act
  play-act-ing
play-back
play-bill
play-boy
play-er
play-ful
  play-ful-ly
  play-ful-ness
play-go-er
play-ground
play-house
  play-hous-es
play-let
play-mate
play-off
play-pen
play-thing
play-time
play-wright
pla-za
plea
plead
  plead-ed
  plead-ing
  plead-a-ble
  plead-er
pleas-ant
  pleas-ant-ly
  pleas-ant-ness

pleas-ant-ry
  pleas-an-trioes
please
  pleased
  pleas-ing
  pleas-ing-ly
  pleas-ing-ness
plea-sur-a-ble
  plea-sur-able-ness
  plea-sur-ably
pleas-ure
pleat
  pleat-ed
  pleat-er
plebe
ple-be-ian
pleb-i-scite
pledge
  pledged
  pledg-ing
  pledg-ee
  pledg-er
ple-na-ry
pleni-po-ten-tia-ry
  pleni-po-ten-tia-ries
plen-i-tude
plen-te-ous
  plen-te-ous-ly
plen-ti-ful
  plen-ti-ful-ly
plen-ty
pleth-o-ra
  ple-thor-ic
pleu-ra
  pleu-rae
  pleu-ral
pleu-ri-sy
  pleu-rit-ic
plex-us
  plex-us-es
pli-able
  pli-a-bil-i-ty
  pli-a-ble-ness
  pli-a-bly
pli-ant
  pli-an-cy
  pli-ant-ness
  pli-ant-ly
pli-ca-tion
pli-ers
plight
plink
plod
  plod-ded
  plod-ding
  plod-der

plop
  plopped
  plop-ping
plot
  plot-ted
  plot-ting
  plot-ter
plow
  plow-a-ble
  plow-er
  plow-man
plow-share
pluck
  pluck-er
plucky
  pluck-i-er
  pluck-i-est
  pluck-i-ly
  pluck-i-ness
plug
  plugged
  plug-ging
  plug-ger
plum-age
plumb-er
plumb-ing
plume
  plumed
  plum-ing
  plume-like
  plumy
  plum-i-er
  plum-i-est
plum-met
plump
  plump-er
  plump-ly
  plump-ness
plun-der
  plun-der-er
  plun-der-ous
plunge
  plunged
  plung-ing
  plung-er
plunk-er
plu-ral
  plu-ral-ly
  plu-ral-ize
  plu-ral-ized
  plu-ral-iz-ing
plu-ral-ism
  plu-ral-ist
  plu-ral-is-tic
plu-ral-i-ty
  plu-ral-i-ties

plush
plush-i-ness
plushy
plush-i-er
plush-i-est
plu-toc-ra-cy
plu-tac-ra-cies
plu-ta-crat
plu-to-cart-ic
plu-to-ni-um
plu-vi-al
ply
plied
ply-ing
ply-wood
pneu-mat-ic
pneu-mat-i-cal-ly
pneu-mat-ics
pneu-mo-nia
pneu-mon-ic
poach
poach-er
pock-et
pock-et-book
pock-et-ful
pock-et-knife
pock-et-knives
pock-mark
pock-marked
pod
pod-ded
pod-ding
pod-like
podgy
podg-i-er
podg-i-est
po-di-trist
po-di-a-try
po-di-um
po-dia
po-di-ums
po-esy
po-esies
po-et
po-et-ess
po-et-ize
po-et-ized
po-et-iz-ing
po-et-iz-er
po-et lau-re-ate
po-ets lau-re-ate
po-et-ry
po-go
po-grom
poi-gnant
poi-gnan-cy

poi-gnant-ly
poin-set-tia
point--blank
point-ed
point-ed-ly
point-ed-ness
point-er
poin-til-lism
poin-til-list
point-less
poise
poised
pois-ing
poi-son
poi-son-er
poi-son-ing
poi-son-ous
poi-son--pen
poke
poked
pok-ing
pok-er
poky
pok-i-er
pok-i-est
pok-i-ly
pok-i-ness
po-lar
po-lar-i-ty
po-lar-i-ties
po-lar-i-za-tion
po-lar-ize
po-lar-ized
po-lar-iz-ing
po-lar-iz-a-ble
po-lar-iz-er
pole
poled
pol-ing
pole-less
pole-cat
po-lem-ic
po-lem-i-cal
po-lem-i-cal-ly
po-lem-i-cist
po-lem-ics
pole-star
po-lice
po-liced
po-lic-ing
pol-i-cy
pol-i-cies
pol-i-o-my-e-li-tis
pol-ish
pol-ish-er
po-lite

po-lite-ly
po-lite-ness
pol-i-tic
po-lit-i-cal
po-lit-i-cal-ly
pol-i-ti-cian
po-lit-i-cize
po-lit-i-cized
po-lit-i-ciz-ing
pol-i-tick
pol-i-tick-er
pol-i-tics
pol-i-ty
pol-i-ties
pol-ka
pol-kaed
pol-ka-ing
poll
poll-ee
poll-er
pol-len
pol-li-nate
pol-li-nat-ed
pol-li-nat-ing
pol-li-na-tion
pol-li-na-tor
pol-li-wog
poll-ster
pol-lu-tant
pol-lute
pol-lut-ed
pol-lut-ing
pol-lu-ter
pol-lu-tion
po-lo
po-lo-ist
pol-o-naise
po-lo-ni-um
pol-ter-geist
poly-an-dry
poly-an-drous
poly-chro-mat-ic
poly-chrome
poly-es-ter
poly-eth-yl-ene
polyg-a-mist
polyg-a-my
polyg-a-mous
poly-glot
poly-gon
polyg-o-nal
polyg-o-nal-ly
poly-graph
poly-graph-ic
po-lyg-y-ny
po-lyg-y-nous

155

poly-he-dron
poly-he-drons
poly-he-dra
poly-he-dral
poly-mer
po-ly-mer-ize
po-ly-mer-ized
po-ly-mer-iz-ing
po-lym-er-ism
po-lym-er-i-za-tion
pol-y-mor-phism
pol-y-mor-phic
pol-y-mor-phous
poly-no-mi-al
pol-yp
poly-phon-ic
po-lyph-ony
poly-sty-rene
poly-syl-lab-ic
poly-syl-lab-i-cal-ly
poly-syl-la-ble
poly-tech-nic
poly-the-ism
poly-the-ist
poly-the-is-tic
poly-the-is-ti-cal
poly-un-sat-u-rat-ed
pom-ace
po-made
po-mad-ed
po-mad-ing
pome-gran-ate
pom-mel
pom-meled
pom-mel-ing
pom-pa-dour
pom-pon
pomp-ous
pom-pos-i-ty
pom-pous-ly
pon-cho
pon-der
pon-der-a-ble
pon-der-er
pon-der-ous
pon-der-ous-ly
pon-der-ou-ness
pon-iard
pon-tiff
pon-tif-i-cal
pon-tif-i-cal-ly
pon-tif-i-cate
pon-tif-i-cat-ed
pon-tif-i-cat-ing
pon-toon
po-ny

po-nies
po-nied
po-ny-ing
po-ny-tail
poo-dle
pool-room
poor
poor-ish
poor-ly
pop-corn
pop-ery
pop-ish
pop-eyed
pop-gun
pop-in-jay
pop-lar
pop-lin
pop-per
pop-py
pop-pies
pop-pied
pop-py-cock
pop-u-lace
pop-u-lar
pop-u-lar-ly
pop-u-lar-i-ty
pop-u-lar-ize
pop-u-lar-ized
pop-u-lar-iz-ing
pop-u-lar-i-za-tion
pop-u-lar-iz-er
pop-u-late
pop-u-lat-ed
pop-u-lat-ing
pop-u-la-tion
pop-u-lism
pop-u-list
pop-u-lous
pop-u-lous-ly
por-ce-lain
por-cine
por-cu-pine
pore
pored
por-ing
pork-er
por-nog-ra-phy
por-nog-ra-pher
por-no-graph-ic
por-no-graph-i-cal-ly
po-rous
po-rous-i-ty
po-rous-ly
po-rous-ness
por-poise
por-pios-es

por-ridge
port-a-ble
port-a-bil-i-ty
port-a-bly
por-tage
por-taged
por-tag-ing
por-tal
por-tend
por-tent
por-ten-tous
por-ter
por-ter-house
port-fo-lio
port-fo-lios
port-hole
por-ti-co
por-ti-coes
por-ti-cos
por-tion
por-tion-less
port-ly
port-li-er
port-li-est
por-trait
por-trat-ist
por-trai-ture
por-tray
por-tray-er
por-tray-al
pose
posed
pos-ing
pos-er
po-suer
pos-it
po-si-tion
po-si-tion-al
po-si-tion-er
pos-i-tive
pos-i-tive-ly
pos-i-tive-ness
pos-i-tiv-ism
pos-i-tron
pos-se
pos-sess
pos-ses-sor
pos-sessed
pos-ses-sion
pos-ses-sive
pos-ses-sive-ly
pos-ses-sive-ness
pos-si-bil-i-ty
pos-si-ble
pos-si-bly
pos-sum

post-age
post-box
post-date
post-dat-ed
post-dat-ing
post-er
pos-te-ri-or
pos-te-ri-or-i-ty
pos-ter-i-ty
post-grad-u-ate
post-haste
post-hu-mous
post-hu-mous-ly
post-lude
post-man
post-men
post-mark
post-mas-ter
post-mis-tress
post me-ri-di-em
post-mor-tem
post-na-sal
post-na-tal
post-na-tal-ly
post-paid
post-par-tum
post-pone
post-poned
post-pon-ing
post-pon-a-ble
post-pone-ment
post-pon-er
post-scipt
pos-tu-lant
pos-tu-late
pos-tu-lat-ed
pos-tu-lat-ing
pos-tu-la-tion
pos-tu-la-tor
pos-ture
pos-tured
pos-tur-ing
pos-tur-al
pos-tur-er
post-war
po-sy
po-sies
pot
pot-ted
pot-ting
po-ta-ble
pot-ash
po-tas-si-um
po-ta-to
po-ta-toes
pot-bel-ly

pot-bel-lied
pot-boil-er
po-tent
po-ten-cy
po-tent-ly
po-ten-tate
po-ten-tial
po-ten-ti-al-i-ty
po-ten-tial-ly
pot-hole
po-tion
pot-luck
pot-pour-ri
pot-sherd
pot-tage
pot-ter
pot-tery
pot-ter-ies
pot-ty
pot-ties
pot-ty--chair
pouch
pouched
pouchy
pouch-i-er
pouch-i-est
poul-tice
poul-ticed
poul-tic-ing
poul-try
pounce
pounced
pounc-ing
pound-age
pound--fool-ish
pour
pour-a-ble
pour-er
pout
pov-er-ty
pov-er-ty--strick-en
pow-der
pow-dery
pow-er
pow-er-boat
pow-er-ful
pow-er-ful-ly
pow-er-ful-ness
pow-er-house
pow-er-less
Pow-ha-tan
pow-wow
prac-ti-ca-ble
prac-ti-ca-bil-i-ty
prac-ti-ca-bly
prac-ti-cal

prac-ti-cal-i-ty
prac-ti-cal-ly
prac-tice
prac-ti-tio-ner
prae-di-al
pre-di-al
prag-mat-ic
prag-mat-i-cal
prag-mat-i-cal-ly
prag-ma-tism
prag-ma-tist
prag-ma-tis-tic
prai-rie
praise
praised
prais-ing
prais-er
praise-wor-thy
praise-wor-thi-ly
praise-wor-thi-ness
pra-line
prance
pranced
pranc-ing
pranc-er
prank
prank-ish
prank-ster
prate
prat-ed
prat-ing
prat-er
prat-ing-ly
prat-fall
prat-tle
prat-tled
prat-tling
prat-tler
prat-tling-ly
prawn
prawn-er
pray-er
pray-er-ful
preach
prach-er
preach-ify
preach-ified
preach-ify-ing
preach-ment
preachy
preach-i-er
preach-i-est
pre-ad-o-les-cence
pre-ad-o-les-cent
pre-am-ble
pre-ar-range

pre-ar-ranged
pre-ar-rang-ing
pre-ar-range-ment
pre-as-signed
pre-can-cel
pre-can-celed
pre-can-cel-ing
pre-can-cel-la-tion
pre-car-i-ous
pre-car-i-ous-ly
pre-car-i-ous-ness
pre-cau-tion
pre-cau-tion-ary
pre-cede
pre-ced-ed
pre-ced-ing
prec-e-dence
prec-e-dent
pre-cept
pre-cep-tive
pre-cep-tor
pre-cep-to-ri-al
pre-ces-sion
pre-ces-sion-al
pre-cinct
pre-cious
pre-ci-os-i-ty
pre-cious-ness
prec-i-pice
pre-cip-i-tous
pre-cip-i-tant
pre-cip-i-tant-ly
pre-cip-i-tate
pre-cip-i-tat-ed
pre-cip-i-tat-ing
pre-cip-i-ta-tive
pre-cip-i-ta-tor
pre-cip-i-ta-tion
pre-cip-i-tous
pre-cip-i-tous-ly
pre-cise
pre-cise-ness
pre-ci-sion
pre-ci-sion-ist
pre-clude
pre-clud-ed
pre-clud-ing
pre-clu-sion
pre-clu-sive
pre-co-cious
pre-coc-cious-ly
pre-coc-cious-ness
pre-coc-i-ty
pre-cog-ni-tion
pre-cog-ni-tive
pre-con-ceive

pre-con-ciev-ed
pre-con-ceiv-ing
pre-con-cep-tion
pre-cook
pre-cur-sor
pre-cur-so-ry
pre-date
pred-a-tor
pred-a-to-ry
pred-a-to-ri-ly
pre-dawn
pre-de-ces-sor
pre-des-ti-nate
pre-des-ti-nat-ed
pre-des-ti-nat-ing
pre-des-ti-na-tion
pre-des-tine
pre-des-tined
pre-des-tin-ing
pre-de-ter-mine
pre-de-ter-mined
pre-de-ter-min-ing
pre-de-ter-mi-na-tion
pred-i-ca-ble
pred-i-ca-bil-i-ty
pre-dic-a-ment
pred-i-cate
pred-i-cat-ed
pred-i-cat-ing
pred-i-ca-tion
pred-i-ca-tive
pre-dict
pre-dict-a-ble
pre-dict-a-bly
pre-dict-a-bil-i-ty
pre-dic-tion
pre-dic-tive
pre-di-lec-tion
pre-dis-po-si-tion
pre-dis-pose
pre-dis-posed
pre-dis-pos-ing
pre-dom-i-nant
pre-dom-i-nance
pre-dom-i-nan-cy
pre-dom-i-nate
pre-dom-i-nat-ed
pre-dom-i-nat-ing
pre-dom-i-na-tion
pre-em-i-nent
pre-em-i-nence
pre-empt
pre-emp-tor
pre-emp-tion
pre-emp-tive
preen-er

pre-ex-ist
pre-ex-ist-ence
pre-ex-ist-ent
pre-fab-ri-cate
pre-fab-ri-cat-ed
pre-fab-ri-cat-ing
pre-fab-ri-a-tion
pref-ace
pref-aced
pref-ac-ing
pref-a-to-ry
pre-fer
pre-ferred
pre-fer-ring
pre-fer-rer
pref-er-a-ble
pref-er-a-bil-i-ty
pref-er-a-bly
pref-er-ence
pref-er-en-tial
pref-er-en-tial-ly
pre-fer-ment
pre-fix
pre-flight
pre-form
preg-n-able
preg-na-bil-i-ty
preg-nan-cy
preg-nan-cies
preg-nant
pre-heat
pre-hen-sile
pre-hen-sil-i-ty
pre-his-tor-ic
pre-his-to-ry
pre-judge
pre-judged
pre-judg-ing
pre-judg-er
pre-judge-ment
prej-u-dice
prej-u-diced
prej-u-dic-ing
prej-u-di-cial
prej-u-di-cial-ly
prel-ate
prel-ate-ship
prel-a-ture
pre-lim-i-nar-y
pre-lim-i-nar-ies
pre-lim-i-nar-i-ly
prel-ude
prel-uded
prel-ud-ing
pre-ma-ture
pre-na-tu-ri-ty

158

pre-med-i-cal
pre-med-i-tate
pre-med-i-tat-ed
pre-med-i-tat-ing
pre-med-i-ta-tor
pre-med-i-tat-ed-ly
pre-med-i-ta-tive
pre-med-i-ta-tion
pre-men-stru-al
pre-mier
pre-mier-ship
pre-miere
prem-ise
prem-ised
prem-is-ing
pre-mi-um
pre-mo-ni-tion
pre-mon-i-to-ry
pre-mon-i-to-ri-ly
pre-na-tal
pre-na-tal-ly
pre-oc-cu-pa-tion
pre-oc-cu-py
pre-oc-cu-pied
pre-oc-cu-py-ing
prep-a-ra-tion
pre-par-a-to-ry
pre-par-a-to-ri-ly
pre-pare
pre-pared
pre-par-ing
pre-par-er
pre-par-ed-ness
pre-pay
pre-paid
pre-pay-ing
pre-pay-ment
pre-plan
pre-planned
pre-plan-ning
pre-pon-der-ant
pre-pon-der-ance
pre-pon-der-an-cy
pre-pon-der-ant-ly
pre-pon-der-ate
pre-pon-der-at-ed
pre-pon-der-at-ing
pre-pon-der-at-ing-ly
pre-pon-der-a-tion
prep-o-si-tion
prep-o-si-tion-al
pre-pos-sess
pre-pos-sess-ing
pre-pos-sess-ing-ly
pre-pos-ter-ous
pre-puce

pre-pu-tial
pre-re-cord
pre-re-ui-site
pre-rog-a-tive
pres-age
pres-aged
pres-ag-ing
pres-ag-er
pres-by-ter-y
pres-by-ter-ies
pre-school
pre-scribe
pre-scribed
pre-scrib-ing
pre-scrib-er
pre-script
pre-scrip-tion
pre-scrip-tive
pre-sea-son
pres-ence
pre-sent
pre-sent-er
pres-ent
pre-sent-a-ble
pre-sent-a-bil-i-ty
pre-sent-a-ble-ness
pre-sent-a-bly
pres-en-ta-tion
pres-ent-day
pres-ent-ly
pre-serv-a-tive
per-serve
pre-served
pre-serv-ing
pre-serv-a-ble
pres-er-va-tion
pre-serv-er
pre-side
pre-sid-ed
pre-sid-ing
pre-sid-er
pres-i-den-cy
pres-i-den-cies
pres-i-dent
pres-i-den-tial
press-board
press-ing
pres-sure
pres-sured
pres-sur-ing
pre-su-rize
pres-su-rized
pres-su-riz-ing
pres-su-riz-er
pres-sur-i-za-tion
press-work

pres-ti-dig-i-ta-tion
pres-ti-dig-i-ta-tor
pres-tige
pres-tig-ious
pres-to
pe-sum-a-ble
pre-sum-a-bly
pre-sume
pre-sumed
pre-sum-ing
pre-sum-er
pre-sump-tion
pre-sump-tive
pre-sum-tu-ous
pre-sup-pose
pre-sup-posed
pre-sup-pos-ing
pre-sup-po-si-tion
pre-tend
pre-tend-ed
pre-tend-er
pre-tense
pre-ten-sion
pre-ten-tious
pre-ten-tious-ness
pre-test
pre-text
pret-ti-fy
pret-ti-fied
pret-ti-fy-ing
pret-ti-fi-ca-tion
pret-ty
pret-ties
pret-tied
pret-ty-ing
pret-ti-ly
pret-ti-ness
pret-ty-ish
pret-zel
pre-vail
pre-vail-ing
prev-a-lent
prev-a-lence
pre-vent
pre-vent-a-ble
pre-vent-a-bil-i-ty
pre-vent-er
pre-ven-tion
pre-view
pre-vi-ous
pre-war
prey
prey-er
price-less
prick-er
prick-le

prick-ly
  prick-li-er
  prick-li-est
  prick-li-ness
pride
  prid-ed
  prid-ing
pride-ful
pri-er
priest
  priest-ess
  priest-hood
priest-ly
  priest-li-er
  priest-li-est
priest-li-ness
prig
  prig-gish
prim
  prim-mer
  prim-mest
  primmed
  prim-ming
  prim-ness
pri-ma-cy
  pri-ma-cies
pri-ma don-na
  pri-ma don-nas
pri-mal
pri-ma-ri-ly
pri-ma-ry
  pri-mar-ies
pri-mate
prime
  primed
  prim-ing
prime me-rid-i-an
prim-er
pr-me-val
prim-i-tive
pri-mo-gen-i-tor
pri-mo-gen-i-ture
pri-mor-di-al
  pri-mor-di-al-ly
primp
prim-rose
prince-ly
  prince-li-er
  prince-li-est
prin-cess
prin-ci-pal
  prin-ci-pal-ly
prin-ci-pal-i-ty
  prin-ci-pal-i-ties
prin-ci-ple
prin-ci-pled

print-a-ble
print-ing
print-out
pri-or
  pri-or-ate
  pri-or-ess
pri-or-i-ty
  pri-or-i-ties
pri-or-y
  pri-or-ies
prism
  pris-mat-ic
  pris-mat-i-cal-ly
pris-on
pris-on-er
pris-sy
  pris-si-er
  pris-si-est
  pris-si-ly
pris-tine
pri-va-cy
pri-vate
pri-va-tion
priv-et
priv-i-ledge
  priv-i-ledged
  priv-i-leg-ing
priv-y
  priv-ies
  priv-i-ly
prize
  prized
prize-fight
prob-a-bil-i-ty
  prob-a-bil-i-ties
prob-a-ble
  prob-a-bly
pro-bate
  pro-bat-ed
  pro-bat-ing
pro-ba-tion
  pro-ba-tion-al
  pro-ba-tion-ary
pro-na-tion-er
pro-ba-tive
probe
  probed
  prob-ing
  prob-er
prob-lem
prob-lem-at-ic
  pro-lem-at-i-cal
pro-bos-cis
  pro-bos-cis-es
  pro-bos-ci-des
pro-ce-dure

pro-ce-dur-al
pro-ce-dur-al-ly
pro-ceed
pro-ceed-ing
pro-ceeds
pro-ces-sion
pro-ces-sion-al
pro-claim
  pro-claim-er
proc-la-ma-tion
pro-cliv-i-ty
  pro-cliv-i-ties
pro-cras-ti-nate
  pro-cras-ti-nat-ed
  pro-cras-ti-nat-ing
  pro-cras-ti-na-tion
  pro-cras-ti-na-tor
pro-cre-ate
  pro-cre-at-ed
  pro-cre-at-ing
  pro-cre-a-tion
proc-tor
  proc-to-ri-al
proc-u-ra-tor
  proc-u-ra-to-ri-al
  proc-u-ra-tor-ship
pro-cure
  pro-cured
  pro-cur-ing
  pro-cure-ment
prod
  prod-ded
  prod-ding
  prod-dler
prod-i-gal
  prod-i-gal-i-ty
  prod-i-gal-ly
pro-di-gious
  pro-di-gious-ness
prod-i-gy
  prod-i-gies
pro-duce
  pro-duced
  pro-duc-ing
pro-duc-er
prod-uct
pro-duc-tion
pro-duc-tive
  pro-duc-tive-ness
  pro-duc-tiv-i-ty
pro-fane
  pro-faned
pro-fan-i-ty
pro-fess
  pro-fessed
  pro-fess-ed-ly

pro-fes-sion
pro-fes-sion-al
 pro-fes-sion-al-ism
pro-fes-sion-al-ize
 pro-fes-sion-al-ized
 pro-fes-sion-al-iz-ing
pro-fes-sor
 pro-fes-so-ri-al
 pro-fes-sor-ship
prof-fer
 prof-fer-er
pro-fi-cien-cy
pro-fi-cient
pro-file
 pro-filed
 pro-fil-ing
prof-it
 prof-it-less
prof-it-able
 prof-it-a-bil-i-ty
 prof-it-ably
prof-i-teer
prof-li-gate
 prof-li-ga-cy
pro-found
pro-fun-di-ty
 pro-fun-di-ties
pro-fuse
pro-fu-sion
pro-gen-i-tor
prog-e-ny
 prog-e-nies
pro-ges-ter-one
prog-no-sis
 prog-no-ses
 prog-nos-tic
prog-nos-ti-cate
 prog-nos-ti-cat-ed
 prog-nos-ti-cat-ing
 prog-nos-ti-ca-tion
 prog-nos-ti-ca-tive
 prog-nos-ti-ca-tor
pro-gram
prog-ress
pro-gres-sion
pro-gres-sive
 pro-gres-siv-ism
pro-hib-it
pro-hi-bi-tion
pro-hi-bi-tion-ist
pro-hib-i-tive
pro-ject
pro-jec-tile
pro-jec-tion
pro-jec-tion-ist
pro-jec-tive

pro-jec-tive-ly
pro-jec-tiv-i-ty
pro-jec-tor
pro-le-tar-i-at
 pro-le-tar-i-an
pro-lif-er-ate
 pro-lif-er-at-ed
pro-lif-ic
 pro-lif-i-ca-cy
pro-lix
 pro-lix-i-ty
pro-logue
 pro-logued
 pro-logu-ing
pro-long
 pro-lon-ga-tion
 pro-long-er
prom-e-nade
 prom-e-nad-ed
 prom-e-nad-ing
 prom-e-nad-er
prom-i-nence
prom-i-nent
 prom-i-nent-ly
pro-mis-cu-ity
 pro-mis-cu-i-ties
pro-mis-cu-ous
 pro-mis-cu-ous-ly
prom-ise
 prom-ised
 prom-is-ing
prom-is-so-ry
prom-on-to-ry
 prom-on-to-ries
pro-mote
 pro-mot-ed
 pro-mot-ing
 pro-mot-a-ble
pro-mot-er
pro-mo-tion
 pro-mo-tive
prompt
 prompt-er
 prompt-ly
pro-mul-gate
 pro-mul-gat-ed
 pro-mul-ga-tion
prone
prong
pro-noun
pro-nounce
 pro-nounced
 pro-nounce-ment
pron-to
pro-nun-ci-a-tion
proof

proof-read
prop
pro-pa-gan-da
pro-pa-gate
pro-pa-ga-tion
 pro-pa-ga-tion-al
pro-pane
pro-pel
 pro-pelled
 pro-pel-ling
pro-pel-lant
pro-pel-ler
pro-pen-si-ty
 pro-pen-si-ties
prop-er
proph-e-cy
 proph-e-cies
proph-e-sy
 proph-e-sied
 proph-e-sy-ing
proph-et
pro-phet-ic
 pro-phet-i-cal-ly
pro-phy-lax-is
pro-pin-qui-ty
pro-pi-ti-ate
 pro-pi-ti-at-ed
 pro-pi-ti-a-tion
pro-pi-tious
 pro-pi-tious-ly
pro-po-nent
pro-por-tion
 pro-por-tion-a-ble
 pro-por-tion-a-bly
pro-por-tion-al
 pro-por-tion-al-i-ty
pro-por-tion-ate
 pro-por-tion-at-ed
 pro-por-tion-at-ing
pro-pos-al
pro-pose
 pro-posed
prop-o-si-tion
 prop-o-si-tion-al
pro-pound
 pro-pound-er
pro-pri-e-tary
 pro-pri-e-tar-ies
pro-pri-etor
 pro-pri-e-tor-ship
pro-pri-ety
pro-pul-sion
pro-pul-sive
pro-rate
 pro-rat-ed
pro-sa-ic

pro-sa-i-cal-ly
pro-scribe
pro-scribed
pro-scrib-ing
pro-scrib-er
pro-scrip-tion
pro-srip-tive
prose
pros-e-cute
pros-e-cute-a-ble
pros-e-cu-tion
pros-e-cu-tor
pros-pect
pros-pec-tor
pro-spec-tive
pro-spec-tus
pros-per-i-ty
pros-per-ous
pros-tate
pros-the-sis
pros-the-ses
pros-thet-ic
pros-thet-ics
pros-the-tis
prosth-odon-tics
prosth-odon-tist
pros-ti-tute
pros-trate
pros-trat-ing
pros-tra-tor
pros-tra-tive
prosy
pros-i-er
pros-i-est
pro-tag-o-nist
pro-te-an
pro-tect
pro-tect-ing
pro-tec-tive
pro-tec-tor
pro-tec-tion
pro-tec-tion-ism
pro-tec-tion-ist
pro-tec-tor-ate
pro-tein
pro-test
prot-es-ta-tion
pro-tist
pro-tis-tan
pro-to-col
pro-ton
pro-to-plasm
pro-to-plas-mic
pro-to-type
pro-to-typ-i-cal
pro-to-typ-ic

pro-to-typ-i-cal-ly
pro-to-zo-an
pro-to-zo-ic
pro-tract
pro-trac-tion
pro-trac-tive
pro-trac-tile
pro-trac-tor
pro-trude
pro-trud-ed
pro-trud-ing
pro-tru-sion
pro-tru-sive
pro-tu-ber-ance
pro-tu-ber-ant
proud
proud-ly
prov-erb
pro-ver-bi-al
pro-ver-bi-al-ly
pro-vide
pro-vid-ed
pro-vid-ing
prov-i-dence
prov-i-den-tial
prov-i-dent
prov-ince
pro-vin-cial
pro-vin-cial-ism
pro-vi-sion
pro-vi-sion-er
pro-vi-sion-al
pro-vi-sion-ary
prov-o-ca-tion
pro-voc-a-tive
pro-voc-a-tive-ly
pro-voc-a-tive-ness
pro-voke
pro-voked
pro-vok-ing
pro-vost
prow-ess
prowl
prowl-er
prox-i-mal
prox-i-mate
prox-i-mate-ly
prox-im-i-ty
proxy
prox-ies
prude
pru-dence
pru-dent
pru-den-tial
prud-ery
prud-er-ies

prud-ish
prune
pruned
prun-ing
pru-ri-ent
pru-ri-ence
pru-ri-en-cy
psalm-book
psalm-ist
pseu-do
pseud-onym
pseud-on-y-mous
pseu-do-preg-nan-cy
pseu-do-preg-nant
pseu-do-sci-ence
pseu-do-sci-en-tif-ic
pshaw
psil-o-cy-bin
pso-ri-a-sis
pso-ri-at-ic
psych
psyched
psych-ing
psy-che-del-ic
psy-chi-a-trist
psy-chi-a-try
psy-chi-at-ric
psy-chi-at-ri-cal-ly
psy-chic
psy-chi-cal
psy-chi-cal-ly
psy-cho
psy-cho-anal-y-sis
psy-cho-an-a-lyt-ic
psy-cho-an-a-lyt-i-cal
psy-cho-an-a-lyst
psy-cho-an-a-lyze
psy-cho-an-a-lyzed
psy-cho-an-a-lyz-ing
psy-cho-bi-ol-o-gy
psy-cho-bi-o-log-ic
psy-cho-bi-o-log-i-cal
psy-cho-dra-ma
psy-cho-dy-nam-ic
psy-cho-dy-nam-ics
psy-cho-gen-e-sis
psy-cho-ge-net-ic
psy-cho-gen-ic
psy-cho-gen-i-cal-ly
psy-cho-log-i-cal
psy-cho-log-ic
psy-cho-log-i-cal-ly
psy-chol-o-gist
psy-chol-o-gy
psy-cho-mo-tor
psy-cho-neu-ro-sis

psy-cho-neu-rot-ic
psy-cho-path
psy-cho-pa-thol-o-gy
  psy-cho-path-o-log-ic
psy-chop-a-thy
  psy-cho-path-ic
  psy-cho-path-i-cal-ly
psy-cho-sis
  psy-cho-ses
  psy-chot-ic
  psy-chot-i-cal-ly
psy-cho-ther-a-py
  psy-cho-ther-a-pist
pto-maine
pu-ber-ty
pu-bes-cence
  pu-bes-cen-cy
  pu-bes-cent
pu-bic
pub-lic
  pub-lic-ly
pub-li-ca-tion
pub-li-cist
pub-li-ci-ty
pub-li-cize
  pub-li-cized
  pub-li-ciz-ing
pub-lish
  pub-lish-a-ble
pub-lish-er
puce
puck-er
pud-ding
pud-dle
  pud-dled
  pud-dling
pudgy
  pudg-i-er
  pudg-i-est
pueb-lo
  pueb-los
pu-er-ile
  pu-er-il-i-ty
puff
  puffy
puff-er
pu-gi-lism
  pu-gi-list
  pu-gi-lis-tic
pug-na-cious
  pug-nac-i-ty
pulke
  puked
  puk-ing
pull-back
pul-let

pul-ley
pul-mo-nary
pulp
pul-pit
pulp-wood
pul-sate
  pul-sat-ed
  pul-sat-ing
pul-sa-tion
pul-sa-tor
  pul-sa-to-ry
pulse
  pulsed
  puls-ing
pul-ver-ize
pu-ma
  pu-mas
pum-ice
  pu-mi-ceous
pum-mel
pump
  pump-a-ble
  pump-er
pum-per-nick-el
pump-kin
pun
  punned
  pun-ning
punch
  punch-er
punch--drunk
punchy
  punch-i-er
  punch-i-est
punc-tu-al
punc-tu-ate
  punc-tu-at-ed
  punc-tu-at-ing
  punc-tu-a-tor
punc-tu-a-tion
punc-ture
  punc-tured
  punc-tur-ing
pun-dit
pun-gent
  pun-gen-cy
  pun-gent-ly
pun-ish
  pun-ish-able
  pun-ish-ment
pu-ni-tive
pun-ster
punt-er
pu-ny
  pu-ni-er
  pu-ni-est

pup
  pupped
  pup-ping
pu-pa
  pu-pae
  pu-pas
  pu-pal
pu-pate
  pu-pat-ed
  pu-pat-ing
  pu-pa-tion
pu-pil
pup-pet
pup-pe-teer
pep-pet-ry
  pup-pet-ries
pup-py
  pup-pies
  pup-py-ish
pur-chase
  pur-chased
  pur-chas-ing
pure
  pure-ly
pur-ga-tive
pur-ga-to-ry
  pur-ga-to-ries
  pur-ga-to-ri-al-
purge
  purged
pu-ri-fy
pur-ism
  pur-ist
  pu-ris-tic
pu-ri-tan
  pu-ri-tan-i-cal
  pu-ri-tan-i-cal-ly
pu-ri-ty
purl
pur-loin
  pur-loin-er
pur-port
  pur-port-ed
  pur-port-ed-ly
pur-pose
  pur-posed
  pur-pos-ing
  pur-pose-ly
  pur-pos-ive
purse
  pursed
  purs-ing
purs-er
pur-su-ant
pur-sue
  pur-sued

pur-su-ing
pur-suit
pur-sy
pu-ru-lent
  pu-ru-lence
  pu-ru-len-cy
pur-vey
  pur-vey-or
pur-vey-ance
pur-view
pushy
pu-sil-lan-i-mous
  pu-sil-la-nim-i-ty
  pu-sal-lan-i-mous-ly
pus-sy
pussy-foot
pussy-wil-low
pus-tule
  pus-tu-lar
  pus-tu-late
put
  put-ing
pu-ta-tive
  pu-ta-tive-ly
put--on
pu-tre-fac-tion
pu-tre-fy
  pu-tre-fied
  pu-tre-fy-ing
pu-trid
  pu-trid-i-try
putt
  putt-ed
  putt-ing
putt-er
  put-ter-er
put-ty
  put-tied
  put-ty-ing
put--up
puz-zle
puz-zle-ment
py-lon
pyr-a-mid
  py-ra-mi-dal
pyre
py-ric
py-ro-ma-nia
  py-ro-ma-ni-ac
  py-ro-ma-ni-a-cal
py-rom-e-ter
  py-rom-e-try
py-ro-tech-nics
  py-ro-tech-nic
  py-ro-tech-ni-cal
py-thon

quack-ery
  quack-er-ies
quad-ran-gle
  quad-ran-gu-lar
quad-rant
  quad-ran-tal
quad-ra-phon-ic
quad-rate
  quad-rat-ed
  quad-rat-ing
qua-drat-ic
  qua-drat-i-cal-ly
qua-drat-ics
quad-ra-ture
quad-ri-lat-er-al
qua-drille
qua-dril-lion
  qua-dril-lionth
qua-droon
quad-ru-ped
  quad-ru-pe-dal
qua-dru-ple
  qua-dru-pled
  qua-dru-pling
qua-dru-plet
qua-dru-pli-cate
  qua-dru-pli-cat-ed
  qua-dru-pli-cat-ing
quaff
  quaff-er
quag-mire
  quag-mired
  quag-miry
quail
quaint
quake
qual-i-fi-ca-tion
qual-i-fied
  qual-i-fied-ly
qual-i-fy
  qual-i-fy-ing
  qual-i-fi-a-ble
  qual-i-fier
qual-i-ta-tive
qual-i-ty
  qual-i-ties
qualm
  qualm-ish
quan-da-ry
  quan-dar-ies
quan-ti-fy
  quan-ti-fy-ing
  quan-ti-fi-ca-tion
quan-ti-ta-tive
quan-ti-ty
  quan-ti-ties

quan-tum
  quan-ta
quar-an-tine
  quar-an-tin-able
quar-rel
  quar-reled
  quar-rel-ing
  quar-rel-er
quar-rel-some
quar-ri-er
quar-ry
  quar-ries
  quar-ried
  quar-ry-ing
quart
quar-ter
  quar-ter-back
  quar-ter-ing
  quar-ter-ly
  quar-ter-lies
quar-ter-mas-ter
quar-tet
quartz
quash
qua-si
qua-ter-na-ry
qua-train
qua-ver
  quav-er-ing-ly
qua-very
quay
quea-sy
  quea-si-er
  quea-si-est
  quea-si-ly
queen
  queen-ly
queer
quell
  quell-er
quench
  quench-able
  quench-er
que-ry
  que-ries
  que-ried
  que-ry-ing
quest
ques-tion
  ques-tion-er
ques-tion-able
  ques-tion-ably
ques-tion-naire
queue
  queued
  queu-ing

quib-ble
quick
quick-en
 quick-en-er
quick--freeze
quick-sand
quick-sil-ver
quick-tem-pered
quick--wit-ted
 quick--wit-ted-ly
 quick--wit-ted-ness
qui-es-cent
 qui-es-cence
qui-et
 qui-et-ly
 qui-et-ter
qui-e-tude
quill
quilt
quilt-er
quilt-ing
quince
quin-til-lion
quin-tu-ple
 quin-tu-pled
 quin-tu-pling
quin-tu-plet
quip
 quipped
 quip-ping
quirk
 quirky
quis-ling
quit
 quit-ed
 quit-ing
quit-claim
quite
quits
quit-er
quiv-er
quix-ot-ic
quiz
quiz-zi-cal
 quiz-zi-cal-ly
quoin
quoit
quon-dam
quo-rum
quo-ta
quot-able
 quot-a-bil-i-ty
quo-ta-tion
quote
quo-tid-i-an
quo-tient

rab-bet
 rab-bet-ted
 rab-bet-ting
rab-bi
 rab-bis
ra-bin-ate
rab-bin-i-cal
 rab-bin-i-al-ly
rab-bit
rab-ble
 rab-bled
 rab-bling
ra-bid
 ra-bid-ly
ra-bies
rac-coon
race
 raced
 rac-er
 rac-ing
race-course
race-horse
ra-ceme
rac-er
ra-ce-ric
ra-ce-ri-za-tion
race-track
ra-chis
 ra-chis-es
 rach-i-des
ra-cial
 ra-cial-ism
 ra-cial-ly
rac-ism
 ra-cial-ism
 rac-ist
rack-et
rack-e-teer
ra-con-teur
racy
 rac-i-ly
 rac-i-ness
ra-dar
ra-di-al
 ra-di-al-ly
ra-di-ance
 ra-di-an-cy
ra-di-ant
ra-di-ate
 ra-di-at-ed
 ra-di-at-ing
ra-di-a-tion
ra-di-a-tor
rad-i-cal
 rad-i-cal-ly
 rad-i-cal-ism

ra-dio
ra-dio-ac-tive
ra-dio-ac-tive-i-ty
ra-di-o fre-quen-cy
ra-dio-gram
ra-dio-graph
 ra-diog-ra-phy
ra-di-ol-o-gy
 ra-di-ol-o-gist
rad-ish
ra-di-um
ra-di-us
 ra-dii
 ra-di-us-es
ra-don
raf-fia
raf-fi-nose
raff-ish
raf-fle
 raf-fled
 raf-fling
raft
raft-er
rag
rag-ged
rag-gle
rag-man
rag-time
rag-weed
raid-er
rail-ing
rail-lery
 rail-ler-ies
rail-road
 rail-road-er
 rail-road-ing
rail-way
rai-ment
rain-bow
rain-fall
rainy
raise
 raised
rai-sin
rake
 raked
 rak-ing
rake--off
rak-ish
 rak-ish-ly
ral-li-form
ral-ly
 ral-lied
ram
 rammed
ram-ble

ram-bled
ram-bling
ram-bler
ram-bunc-tious
ram-bu-tan
ram-i-fi-ca-tion
ram-i-fy
  ram-i-fied
  ram-i-fy-ing
ram-page
  ram-paged
  ram-pag-ing
ram-pan-cy
ram-pant
  ram-pant-ly
ram-part
ram-rod
ram-shack-le
ranch-er
ran-cid
  ran-cid-i-ty
ran-cor
  ran-cor-ous
ran-dom
  ran-dom-ly
range
  ranged
  rang-ing
rang-er
rangy
  rang-i-er
  rang-i-est
ran-kle
  ran-kling
ran-sack
rant-er
ran-u-la
rap
  rapped
  rap-ping
ra-pa-cious
  ra-pa-cious-ly
  ra-pac-i-ty
rape
  rap-ist
ra-phe
- raph-ide
rap-id
ra-pi-er
rap-ine
rap-pel
rap-port
rap-proche-ment
rap-scal-lion
rap-to-ri-al
rap-ture

rap-tur-ous
rare
  rar-er
  rar-est
rare-bit
rar-efy
  rar-efied
  rar-efy-ing
rare-ly
rar-i-ty
  rar-i-ties
ras-cal
  ras-cal-i-ty
  ras-cal-ly
rash
ra-so-ri-al
rasp
rasp-ber-ry
rat
  rat-ted
  rat-ting
rat-able
ratch-et
rate
  rat-ed
  rat-ing
rath-er
rat-icide
rat-i-fy
  rat-i-fi-ca-tion
ra-tio
  ra-tios
ra-ti-o-ci-na-tion
ra-tion
ra-tio-nal
  ra-tio-nal-i-ty
  ra-tio-nal-ly
ra-tion-able
  ra-tio-nal-ism
  ra-tio-nal-ize
  ra-tio-nal-iz-ing
  ra-tio-nal-i-za-tion
rat-line
rat-tan
rat-tle
  rat-tled
  rat-tling
rat-tle-snake
rat-ty
  rat-ti-er
  rat-ti-est
rau-cous
  rau-cous-ly
raun-chy
  raun-chi-er
  raun-chi-est

rav-age
  rav-aged
rave
rav-el
ra-ven
rav-en-ous
  rav-en-ous-ly
ra-vine
rav-i-o-li
rav-ish
  rav-ish-ment
rav-ish-ing
raw
raw-hide
ray-on
raze
  razed
  raz-ing
ra-zor
raz-zle--daz-zle
re-act
  re-ac-tive
re-ac-tion
re-ac-tion-ary
  re-ac-tion-ar-ies
re-ac-ti-vate
  re-ac-ti-vat-ed
  re-ac-ti-vat-ing
re-ac-tor
read-able
read-er
read-ing
re-ad-just
  re-ad-just-ment
ready
  read-i-er
  read-i-est
  read-ied
  read-y-ing
  read-i-ly
  read-i-ness
ready--made
re-agent
re-al
re-al-ism
  re-al-ist
  re-al-is-tic
  re-al-is-ti-cal-ly
re-al-ize
  re-al-ized
  re-al-iz-ing
  re-al-iz-a-ble
  re-al-i-za-tion
re-al-ly
realm
Re-al-tor

re-al-ty
ream-er
re-an-i-mate
  re-an-i-mat-ed
  re-an-i-mat-ing
  re-an-i-ma-tion
reap-er
re-ap-pear
  re-ap-pear-ance
re-ap-por-tion
re-ap-por-tion-ment
rear ad-mir-ral
re-arm
  re-ar-ma-ment
re-ar-range
  re-ar-ranged
  re-ar-rang-ing
  re-ar-range-ment
rear-ward
rea-son
  rea-son-er
rea-son-able
  rea-son-abil-i-ty
  rea-son-able-ness
  rea-son-ably
rea-son-ing
re-as-sem-ble
  re-as-sem-bled
  re-as-sem-bling
  re-as-sem-bly
re-as-sume
  re-as-sump-tion
re-as-sure
  re-as-sured
  re-as-sur-ing
  re-as-sur-ance
  re-as-sur-ing-ly
re-bate
  re-bat-ed
  re-bat-ing
  re-bat-er
reb-el
re-bel
  re-belled
  re-bel-ling
re-bel-lion
re-bel-lious
  re-bel-lious-ly
re-birth
re-born
re-bound
re-buff
re-build
  re-built
  re-build-ing
re-buke

re-bus
  re-bus-es
re-but
  re-but-tal
re-cal-ci-trant
  re-cal-ci-trance
  re-cal-ci-tran-cy
re-call
re-cant
  re-can-ta-tion
re-ca-pit-u-late
re-cap-ture
  re-cap-tured
re-cede
  re-ced-ed
  re-ced-ing
re-ceipt
re-ceiv-able
re-ceive
  re-ceiv-ed
  re-ceiv-ing
re-ceiv-er
re-ceiv-er-ship
re-cent
  re-cent-ly
  re-cen-cy
re-cep-ta-cle
re-cep-tion
re-cep-tion-ist
re-cep-tive
re-cess
re-ces-sion
  re-ces-sion-ary
re-ces-sion-al
re-ces-sive
re-charge
  re-charg-ed
  re-charg-ing
rec-i-pe
re-cip-i-ent
  re-cip-i-ence
  re-cip-i-en-cy
re-cip-ro-cal
  re-cip-ro-cal-ly
re-cip-ro-cate
rec-i-proc-i-ty
re-cit-al
rec-i-ta-tion
rec-i-ta-tive
re-cite
  re-cited
  re-cit-ing
reck-less
  reck-less-ly
reck-on
re-claim

rec-la-ma-tion
re-cline
  re-clined
rec-luse
rec-og-ni-tion
rec-og-ni-zance
rec-og-nize
  rec-og-nized
  rec-og-niz-ing
  rec-og-niz-a-ble
re-coil
  re-coil-less
re-col-lect
re-col-lect
  re-col-lec-tion
rec-om-mend
  rec-om-mend-able
  rec-om-mend-er
rec-om-men-da-tion
rec-om-pense
  rec-om-pensed
  rec-om-pens-ing
rec-on-cile
  rec-on-ciled
rec-on-dite
re-con-di-tion
re-con-firm
re-con-nais-sance
re-con-noi-ter
  re-con-noi-tered
  re-con-noi-ter-ing
re-con-sid-er
  re-con-sid-er-a-tion
re-con-struct
re-con-struc-tion
re-cord
re-cord-er
re-count
re-coup
re-course
re-cov-er
re-cov-ery
  re-cov-er-ies
rec-re-ant
re-cre-ate
  re-cre-at-ed
  re-cre-at-ing
  re-cre-a-tion
rec-re-ation
  rec-re-ation-al
re-crim-i-nate
  re-crim-i-nat-ed
  re-crim-i-nat-ing
re-cruit
  re-cruit-er
  re-cruit-ment

rec-tal
rect-an-gle
rect-an-gu-lar
rec-ti-fi-er
rec-ti-fy
  rec-ti-fied
  rec-ti-fy-ing
  rec-ti-fi-ca-tion
rec-ti-lin-ear
rec-ti-tude
rec-tor
rec-to-ry
  rec-to-ries
rec-tum
  rec-tums
  rec-ta
re-cum-bent
  re-cum-ben-cy
  re-cum-bent-ly
re-cu-per-ate
re-cur
  re-cur-ring
  re-cur-rence
re-cur-rent
red-bird
red--blood-ed
re-dec-o-rate
  re-dec-o-rat-ed
  re-dec-o-ra-tion
re-ded-i-cate
  re-ded-i-cat-ed
  re-ded-i-ca-tion
re-deem
  re-deem-able
re-deem-er
re-demp-tion
  re-demp-tive
red--hand-ed
red--hot
re-di-rect
  re-di-rec-tion
red--let-ter
red--neck
re-do
red-o-lence
red-o-len-cy
red-o-lent
re-dou-ble
  re-dou-bled
  re-dou-bling
re-doubt-able
  re-doubt-ably
re-dound
re-dress
red-start
re-duce

re-duc-tion
re-dun-dance
re-dun-dant
re-du-pli-cate
  re-du-pli-cat-ed
  re-du-pli-ca-tion
red-wood
re-echo
  re-ech-oed
reedy
  reed-i-er
reef-er
re-elect
  re-elec-tion
re-em-pha-sie
  re-em-pha-sized
  re-em-pha-siz-ing
re-en-force
  re-en-forced
  re-en-forc-ing
  re-en-force-ment
re-en-list
  re-en-list-ment
re-en-ter
  re-en-trance
re-en-try
  re-en-tries
re-es-tab-lish
  re-es-tab-lish-ment
re-ex-am-ine
  re-ex-am-i-na-tion
re-fec-to-ry
  re-fec-to-ries
re-fer
  re-fer-ral
ref-er-ee
ref-er-ence
  ref-er-enced
  ref-er-enc-ing
ref-er-en-dum
  ref-er-en-dums
  ref-er-en-da
ref-er-ent
re-fill
  re-fill-able
re-fine
  re-fined
  re-fin-ing
re-fine-ment
re-fin-ery
  re-fin-er-ies
re-fin-ish
re-fit
  re-fit-ted
  re-fit-ting
re-flect

re-flec-tion
re-flec-tive
  re-flec-tive-ly
  re-flec-tive-ness
re-flec-tor
re-flex
re-flex-ive
re-for-est
  re-for-est-a-tion
re-form
re-form-a-tory
re-fract
  re-frac-tive
re-frac-tion
re-frac-to-ry
  re-frac-to-ri-ly
re-frain
re-fresh
  re-fresh-ing
re-fresh-ment
re-frig-er-ant
  re-frig-er-ate
  re-frig-er-at-ed
re-frig-er-a-tor
re-fu-el
ref-uge
ref-u-gee
re-ful-gence
re-ful-gent
re-fund
re-fur-bish
re-fus-al
re-fuse
  re-fused
  re-fus-ing
ref-use
re-fute
re-gain
re-gal
  re-gal-ly
re-gale
  re-galed
  re-gal-ing
re-ga-lia
re-gard
re-gard-ful
re-gard-ing
re-gard-less
  re-gard-less-ly
re-gat-ta
re-gen-cy
  re-gen-cies
re-gen-er-ate
  re-gen-er-at-ed
  re-gen-er-at-ing
  re-gen-er-a-vy

re-gen-er-a-tion
re-gen-er-a-tive
re-gent
re-grime
reg-i-men
reg-i-ment
reg-i-men-tal
reg-i-men-ta-tion
re-gion
re-gion-al
re-gion-al-ly
reg-is-ter
reg-is-tered
reg-is-trant
reg-is-trar
reg-is-tra-tion
reg-is-try
reg-is-tries
re-gress
re-gres-sion
re-gres-sor
re-gret
re-gret-ted
re-gret-ting
re-gret-ta-ble
re-gret-ta-bly
re-gret-er
re-gret-ful
re-gret-ful-ly
reg-u-lar
reg-u-lar-i-ty
reg-u-late
reg-u-lat-ed
reg-u-lat-ing
reg-u-la-tive
reg-u-la-tor
reg-u-la-to-ry
reg-u-la-tion
re-gur-gi-tate
re-gur-gi-tat-ed
re-gur-gi-tat-ing
re-gur-gi-ta-tion
re-ha-bil-i-tate
re-ha-bil-i-tat-ed
re-ha-bil-i-tat-ing
re-ha-bil-i-ta-tion
re-ha-bil-i-ta-tive
re-hash
re-hears-al
re-hearse
re-hearsed
re-hears-ing
re-hears-er
reign
re-im-burse
re-im-bursed

re-im-burs-ing
re-im-burse-meny
rein
re-in-car-na-tion
rein-deer
re-in-force
re-in-forced
re-in-forc-ing
re-in-force-ment
re-in-state
re-in-stat-ed
re-in-stat-ing
re-in-state-ment
re-it-er-ate
re-it-er-at-ed
re-it-er-at-ing
re-it-er-a-tion
re-ject
re-jec-tion
re-joice
re-joiced
re-joic-ing
re-joic-er
re-joic-ing-ly
re-join
re-join-der
re-ju-ve-nate
re-ju-ve-nat-ed
re-ju-ve-nat-ing
re-ju-ve-na-tion
re-ju-ve-na-tor
re-kin-dle
re-kin-dled
re-kin-dling
re-lapse
re-lapsed
re-laps-ing
re-laps-er
re-late
re-lat-ed
re-lat-ing
re-lat-er
re-lat-or
re-la-tion
re-la-tion-al
re-la-tion-ship
rel-a-tive
rel-a-tive-ly
rel-a-tiv-ism
rel-a-tiv-ist
rel-a-tiv-is-tic
rel-a-tiv-i-ty
rel-a-tiv-ize
re-la-tor
re-lax
re-lax-er

re-lax-ation
re-lay
re-laid
re-lay-ing
re-lay
re-layed
re-lay-ing
re-lease
re-leas-ed
re-leas-ing
re-leas-a-ble
re-leas-er
rel-e-gate
rel-e-gat-ed
rel-e-ga-tion
re-lent
re-lent-less
rel-e-vant
rel-e-vance
rel-e-van-cy
rel-e-vant-ly
re-li-able
re-li-abil-i-ty
re-li-able-ness
re-li-ably
re-li-ance
re-li-ant
rel-ic
re-lief
re-leive
re-liev-ed
re-liev-ing
re-liev-able
re-liev-er
re-li-gion
re-li-gi-os-i-ty
re-li-gious
re-lin-quish
rel-ish
re-live
re-lived
re-liv-ing
re-lo-cate
re-lo-ct-ed
re-lo-cat-ing
re-lo-ca-tion
re-luc-tance
re-luc-tant
re-ly
re-lied
re-ly-ing
re-main
re-main-der
re-mand
re-mark
re-mark-able

re-mark-able-ness
re-mark-ably
re-me-di-a-ble
re-me-di-al
rem-e-dy
rem-e-dies
rem-e-died
rem-e-dy-ing
re-mem-ber
re-mem-brance
re-mind
re-mind-er
re-mind-ful
rem-i-nisce
rem-i-nisced
rem-i-nisc-ing
rem-i-nis-cence
rem-i-nis-cent
re-miss
re-mis-sion
re-mit
re-mit-ted
re-mit-ting
re-mit-tance
rem-nant
re-mod-el
re-mon-strance
re-mon-strate
re-mon-strat-ed
re-mon-strat-ing
re-morse
re-morse-ful
re-morse-ful-ly
re-morse-less
re-mote
re-mot-er
re-mot-est
re-mount
re-mov-able
re-mov-al
re-move
re-moved
re-mov-ing
re-mu-ner-ate
re-mu-ner-at-ed
re-mu-ner-at-ing
re-mu-ner-a-tion
re-nais-sance
re-na-scence
re-na-scent
rend
rend-er
ren-dez-vous
ren-dez-voused
ren-dez-vous-ing
ren-di-tion

ren-e-gade
re-nege
re-neged
re-neg-ing
re-new
re-new-al
ren-net
re-nounce
re-nounced
re-nounc-ing
ren-o-vate
ren-o-vat-ed
ren-o-vat-ing
ren-o-va-tion
re-nown
re-nowned
rent-al
re-nun-ci-a-tion
re-or-ga-ni-za-tion
re-or-ga-nize
re-or-ga-niz-ed
re-or-gan-iz-ing
re-pair
re-pair-man
re-pair-men
rep-a-ra-ble
rep-a-ra-tion
rep-ar-tee
re-pa-tri-ate
re-pa-tri-at-ed
re-pay
re-paid
re-pay-ing
re-pay-ment
re-peal
re-peat
re-peat-able
re-peat-ed
re-peat-er
re-pel
re-pelled
re-pel-ling
re-pel-lent
re-pent
re-pent-ance
re-pen-tant
re-per-cus-sion
rep-er-toire
rep-er-to-ry
rep-er-to-ries
rep-e-ti-tion
rep-e-ti-tious
re-pet-i-tive
re-place
re-placed
re-plac-ing

re-plac-able
re-place-ment
re-plen-ish
re-plete
re-ple-tion
rep-li-ca
re-ply
re-plied
re-ply-ing
re-plies
re-port
re-port-ed-ly
re-port-er
rep-or-to-ri-al
re-pose
re-posed
re-pos-ing
re-pose-ful
re-pos-i-to-ry
re-pos-i-tor-ies
re-pos-sess
re-pos-ses-sion
rep-re-hend
rep-re-hen-si-ble
rep-re-sent
rep-re-sen-ta-tion
rep-re-sen-ta-tive
re-press
re-pres-sion
re-prieve
re-prieved
re-priev-ing
rep-ri-mand
re-print
re-pris-al
re-proach
re-proach-ful
rep-ro-bate
rep-ro-ba-tion
re-pro-duce
re-pro-duced
re-pro-duc-ing
re-pro-duc-tion
re-pro-duc-tive
re-proof
re-prove
re-proved
re-prov-ing
rep-tile
rep-til-ian
re-pub-lic
re-pub-li-can
re-pub-li-can-ism
re-pu-di-ate
re-pu-di-at-ed
re-pu-di-at-ing

re-pu-di-a-tion
  re-pu-di-a-tion-ist
re-pugn
  re-pug-nan-cy
re-pug-nant
re-pulse
  re-pulsed
  re-puls-ing
re-pul-sion
re-pul-sive
rep-u-ta-ble
  rep-u-ta-bly
  rep-u-ta-bil-i-ty
rep-u-ta-tion
re-pute
  re-put-ed
  re-put-ing
  re-put-ed-ly
re-quest
re-qui-em
re-quire
  re-quired
  re-quir-ing
re-quire-ment
req-ui-site
re-quit-al
re-quite
  re-quit-ed
  re-quit-ing
re-run
  re-run-ning
re-sale
re-scind
res-cue
  res-cued
  res-cu-ing
  res-cu-er
re-search
  re-search-er
re-sem-blance
re-sem-ble
  re-sem-bled
  re-sem-bling
re-sent
re-sent-ful
re-sent-ment
re-ser-va-tion
re-serve
  re-served
  re-serv-ing
re-serv-ist
res-er-voir
re-set
  re-set-ting
re-side
  re-sid-ed

re-sid-ing
res-i-dence
res-i-den-cy
  res-i-den-cies
res-i-dent
res-i-den-tial
re-sid-u-al
res-i-due
re-sign
res-ig-na-tion
re-signed
re-sil-ient
  re-sil-ience
  re-sil-ien-cy
res-in
res-in-ous
re-sist
re-sist-er
  re-sist-ible
re-sist-ance
  re-sis-tant
re-sist-less
re-sis-tor
res-o-lute
  res-o-lu-tion
re-solve
  re-solved
  re-solv-ing
res-o-nance
res-o-nant
res-o-nate
  res-o-nat-ed
  res-o-nat-ing
  res-o-na-tor
re-sort
re-sound
  re-sound-ing
re-source
  re-source-ful
re-spect
  re-spect-ful
  re-spect-ful-ly
re-spect-able
  re-spect-a-bil-i-ty
re-spect-ing
re-spec-tive
re-spec-tive-ly
res-pi-ra-tion
  res-pi-ra-to-ry
res-pi-ra-tor
re-spire
  re-spired
  re-spir-ing
re-spite
re-splend-ant
  re-splend-ence

re-spond
re-spon-dent
re-sponse
re-spon-si-bil-i-ty
  re-spon-si-bil-i-ties
re-spon-si-ble
re-spon-sive
res-tau-rant
rest-ful
res-ti-tu-tion
res-tive
rest-less
res-to-ra-tion
re-stor-a-tive
re-store
  re-stored
  re-stor-ing
re-strain
re-straint
re-strict
  re-strict-ed
  re-strict-ed-ly
re-stric-tion
re-stric-tive
re-sult
re-sul-tant
re-sume
  re-sumed
  re-sum-ing
re-sump-tion
re-sur-gence
re-sur-gent
res-ur-rect
res-ur-rec-tion
re-sus-ci-tate
  re-sus-ci-tat-ed
  re-sus-ci-tat-ing
  re-sus-ci-ta-tion
  re-sus-ci-ta-tor
re-tail
  re-tail-er
re-tain
re-tainer
re-take
  re-took
  re-tak-en
  re-tak-ing
re-tal-i-ate
  re-tal-i-at-ed
  re-tal-i-at-ing
  re-tal-i-a-tion
re-tard
  re-tard-ant
re-tar-da-tion
re-tard-ed
re-ten-tion

re-ten-tive
ret-i-cence
ret-i-cent
ret-i-na
ret-i-nas
ret-i-nae
ret-i-nal
ret-i-nue
re-tire
re-tired
re-tir-ing
re-tire-ment
re-tool
re-tort
re-touch
re-trace
re-traced
re-trac-ing
re-tract
re-trac-tion
re-trac-tor
re-trac-tile
re-tread
re-treat
re-trench
re-trench-ment
re-tri-al
ret-ri-bu-tion
re-trieve
re-trieved
re-triev-ing
re-triev-er
ret-ro-ac-tive
ret-ro-grade
ret-ro-grad-ed
ret-ro-grad-ing
ret-ro-gress
ret-ro-gees-sion
ret-ro-ges-sive
ret-ro--rock-et
ret-ro-spect
ret-ro-spec-tion
ret-ro-spec-tive
re-turn
re-turn-able
re-turn-ee
re-union
re-unite
re-unit-ed
re-unit-ing
rev
rev-ved
rev-ving
re-vamp
re-veal
rev-eil-le

rev-el
rev-el-er
rev-e-la-tion
rev-el-ry
rev-el-ries
re-venge
re-venged
re-veng-ing
re-venge-ful
rev-e-nue
rev-e-nu-er
re-ver-ber-ate
re-ver-ber-at-ed
re-ver-ber-at-ing
re-ver-ber-a-tion
re-vere
re-vered
re-ver-ing
rev-er-ence
rev-er-enced
rev-er-enc-ing
rev-er-end
rev-er-ent
rev-er-en-tial
rev-er-ie
re-ver-sal
re-verse
re-versed
re-vers-ing
re-vers-i-ble
re-ver-sion
re-vert
re-view
re-view-er
re-vile
re-viled
re-vil-ing
re-vise
re-vised
re-vis-ing
re-vi-sion
re-vi-sion-ist
re-vi-sion-ism
re-viv-al
re-viv-al-ist
re-vive
re-vived
re-viv-ing
rev-o-ca-ble
rev-o-ca-tion
re-voke
re-voked
re-vok-ing
re-volt
rev-o-lu-tion
rev-o-lu-tion-ary

rev-o-lu-tion-ar-ies
rev-o-lu-tion-ist
rev-o-lu-tion-ize
rev-o-lu-tion-ized
rev-o-lu-tion-iz-ing
re-volve
re-volved
re-volv-ing
re-volv-er
re-vue
re-vul-sion
re-write
re-wrote
re-writ-ten
re-writ-ting
rhap-sod-ic
rhap-sod-i-cal
rhap-sod-i-cal-ly
rhap-so-dize
rhap-so-dized
rhap-so-diz-ing
rhap-so-dy
rhap-so-dies
rhap-so-dist
rhea
rhe-ni-um
rheo-stat
rhe-tor
rhet-o-ric
rhe-tor-i-cal
rhet-o-ri-cian
rheum
rheu-mat-ic
rheu-mat-i-cal-ly
rheu-ma-tism
rhine-stone
rhi-no
rhi-noc-er-os
rhi-noc-er-os-es
rhi-zome
rho-di-um
rho-do-den-dron
rhom-bic
rhom-boid
rhom-boi-dal
rhom-bus
rhom-bus-es
rhom-bi
rhu-barb
rhyme
rhymed
rhym-ing
rhyme-ster
rhythm
rhyth-mic
rhyth-mi-cal

rhyth-mi-cal-ly
rib
  ribbed
  rib-bing
rib-ald
  rib-ald-ry
  rib-ald-ries
rib-bon
ri-bo-fla-vin
rib-bo-nu-cle-ase
rice
  riced
  ric-ing
rich-es
rich-less
rick-ets
rick-ety
  rick-et-i-er
  rick-et-i-est
rick-shaw
ric-o-chet
rid
  rid-ded
  rid-ding
rid-dance
rid-dle
  rid-dled
  rid-dling
ride
  rid-den
  rid-ding
ride-er
ridge
  ridged
  ridg-ing
ridge-pole
rid-i-cule
  rid-i-culed
  rid-i-cul-ing
ri-dic-u-lous
rif-fle
  rif-fled
  rif-fling
riff-raff
rig
  rigged
  rig-ging
rig-ger
righ-teous
right-ful
right-hand
right-hand-ed
right-ism
rig-id
  ri-gid-i-ty
rig-ma-role

rig-or
rig-or-ous
rile
  riled
  ril-ing
rim
rime
ring-er
ring-lead-er
ring-let
ring-mas-ter
ring-worm
rinse
  rinsed
  rins-ing
ri-ot-ous
rip
ripped
  rip-ping
  rip-per
ri-par-i-an
rip-en
rip-off
rip-ple
  rip-pled
  rip-pling
rip-saw
rip-tide
rise
  rose
  ris-en
  ris-ing
ris-er
ris-i-ble
  ris-i-bil-i-ty
risky
  risk-i-er
  risk-i-est
rit-u-al
rit-u-al-ism
  rit-u-al-ist
  rit-u-al-is-tic
  rit-u-al-is-ti-cal-ly
ritzy
  ritz-i-er
  ritz-i-est
ri-val
ri-val-ry
  ri-val-ries
riv-er
riv-er-side
riv-et
  riv-et-er
riv-i-era
riv-u-let
roach

road-runner
road-ster
road-way
roast-er
rob
  robbed
  rob-bing
  rob-ber
rob-bery
  rob-ber-ies
robe
  robed
  rob-ing
rob-in
ro-bot
ro-bust
rock-er
rock-et
rock-et-ry
rocky
  rock-i-er
  rock-i-est
ro-co-co
ro-dent
ro-deo
  ro-de-os
roe-buck
roent-gen
rog-er
roque
  ro-guish
  ro-guish-ly
roqu-ery
  roqu-er-ies
roist-er
roll-er
  roll-er bear-ing
  roll-er coast-er
  roll-er skate
rol-lick
  rol-lick-ing
roll-ing pin
ro-ly-po-ly
  ro-ly-po-lies
ro-maine
ro-mance
  ro-manced
  ro-manc-ing
ro-man-tic
ro-man-ti-cism
ro-man-ti-cize
  ro-man-ti-ciz-ing
romp-er
roof-ing
rook-ery
  rook-er-ies

rook-ie
room-er
room-ful
room-mate
roomy
room-i-er
room-i-est
room-i-ly
room-i-ness
roos-ter
root-stock
rope
roped
rop-ing
ropy
rop-i-er
rop-i-est
ro-sa-ry
ro-sa-ries
ro-se-ate
rose-bud
rose--col-ored
rose-mary
rose-mar-ies
ro-sette
ros-in
ros-ter
ros-trum
ros-tra
ros-trums
rosy
ros-i-er
ros-i-est
rot
rot-ted
rot-ting
ro-ta-ry
ro-tar-ies
ro-tate
ro-tat-ed
ro-tat-ing
ro-ta-tion
ro-tis-ser-ie
ro-tor
rot-ten
ro-tund
ro-tun-di-ty
ro-tun-di-ties
ro-tun-da
rouge
rouged
roug-ing
rough-age
rough--and--tumble
rough-en
rough-house

rough-neck
rough-shod
rou-lette
round-ed
round-er
round-ish
round-up
rouse
roused
rous-ing
rous-er
roust
roust-a-bout
rout
route
rout-ed
rout-ing
rout-er
rou-tine
rou-tin-ize
rou-tin-ized
rou-tin-iz-ing
rove
roved
rov-ing
rov-er
row-boat
row-dy
row-dies
row-di-er
row-di-est
row-lock
roy-al
roy-al-ly
roy-al-ist
roy-al-ty
roy-al-ties
rub
rubbed
rub-bing
rub-ber
rub-bery
rub-ber-ize
rub-ber-ized
rub-ber-iz-ing
rub-ber-neck
rub-bish
rub-bish-ly
rub-ble
rub-bly
rub-bli-er
rub-bli-est
rub-down
ru-bel-la
ru-be-o-la
ru-bi-cund

ru-bid-i-um
ru-bric
ru-by
ru-bies
ruck-sack
ruck-us
rud-der
rud-dy
rud-di-er
rud-di-est
rud-di-ly
rude
ru-di-ment
ru-di-ment-al
ru-di-men-ta-ry
rue
rued
ru-ing
rue-ful
rue-ful-ly
ruff
ruffed
ruf-fi-an
ruf-fle
ruf-fled
ruf-fling
rug-ged
rug-ged-ly
rug-ged-ness
ru-in
ru-in-ation
ru-in-ous
rule
ruled
rul-ing
rul-er
rum-ba
rum-baed
rum-ba-ing
rum-ble
rum-bled
rum-bling
rum-bler
rum-bly
ru-mi-nant
ru-mi-nate
ru-mi-nat-ed
ru-mi-nat-ing
ru-mi-na-tion
ru-mi-na-tor
rum-mage
rum-maged
rum-mag-ing
rum-mag-er
rum-my
rum-mies

ru-mor
ru-mor-mon-ger
rum-ple
  rum-pled
  rum-pling
rum-pus
run
  run-ning
run-about
run-around
run-away
run-ner
run-ner--up
run-ny
  run-ni-er
  run-ni-est
run-off
run--on
runt
  runty
  runt-i-er
  runt-i-est
run--through
run-way
rup-ture
  rup-tured
  rup-tur-ing
ru-ral
  ru-ral-ly
  ru-ral-ize
  ru-ral-ized
  ru-ral-iz-ing
  ru-ral-i-za-tion
rus-set
rus-tic
rus-ti-cate
  rus-ti-cat-ed
  rus-ti-cat-ing
  rus-ti-ca-tion
rus-tle
  rus-tled
  rus-tling
rus-tler
rust-proof
rus-ty
  rust-i-er
  rust-i-est
rut
  rut-ted
  rut-ting
ru-ta-ba-ga
ru-the-ni-um
ruth-less
  ruth-less-ly
rut-ty

S

sa-ber
sa-ber-toothed ti-ger
sa-ble
sab-o-tage
  sab-o-taged
  sab-o-tag-ing
sab-o-teur
sa-bra
sac-cha-rin
sac-er-do-tal
sa-chet
sack-cloth
sack-ful
  sack-fuls
  sack-ing
sac-ra-ment
  sac-ra-men-tal
sa-cred
  sa-cred-ly
  sa-cred-ness
sac-ri-fice
  sac-ri-ficed
  sac-ri-fic-ing
  sac-ri-fic-er
  sac-ri-fi-cial
sac-ri-lege
sac-ri-le-gious
sc-ro-il-li-ac
sac-ro-sanct
  sac-ro-sanc-i-ty
sac-rum
  sac-rums
  sac-ra
sa-cral
sad
  sad-der
  sad-dest
  sad-ly
  sad-ness
sad-den
sad-dle
  sad-dled
  sad-dling
sad-dle-backed
sad-dle-bag
sad-ism
  sad-ist
sa-dis-tic
sad-o-mas-o-chism
  sad-o-mas-o-chist
sa-fa-ri
  sa-fa-ris
safe
  saf-er
  saf-est
safe--con-duct

safe-crack-er
  safe-crack-ing
safe--de-pos-it
safe-guard
safe-keep-ing
safe-ty
  safe-ties
safe-ty match
safe-ty pin
safe-ty valve
safe-ty zone
saf-flow-er
sag
  sagged
  sag-ging
sa-ga
sa-ga-cious
  sa-gac-i-ty
sage
  sag-er
  sag-est
sage-brush
sail-boat
sail-cloth
sail-er
sail-fish
sail-ing
sail-or
saint
  saint-hood
saint-ed
saint-ly
  saint-li-er
  saint-li-est
sa-ke
sal-a-ble
  sal-a-ble
  sal-a-bil-i-ty
  sal-a-bly
sa-la-cious
sal-ad
sal-a-man-der
sa-la-mi
sal-a-ry
  sal-a-ries
sales-man
  sales-men
sales-man-ship
sales-per-son
  sales-peo-ple
sales-room
sa-li-ent
  sa-li-ence
  sa-li-en-cy
  sa-li-ent-ly
sa-line

sa-lin-i-ty
sa-li-va
sal-i-vary
sal-i-vate
sal-i-vat-ed
sal-i-vat-ing
sal-i-va-tion
sal-low
sal-low-ish
sal-ly
sal-lies
sal-lied
sal-ly-ing
salm-on
sa-lon
sa-loon
salt-cel-lar
salt-ed
sal-tine
salt-shak-er
salt-wa-ter
salt-wort
salt-y
salt-i-er
salt-i-est
salt-i-ness
sa-lu-bri-ous
sal-u-tar-y
sal-u-ta-tion
sa-lu-ta-to-ry
sa-lu-ta-to-ries
sa-lute
sa-luted
sa-lut-ing
sa-lut-er
sal-vage
sal-vaged
sal-vag-ing
sal-vage-a-ble
sal-vag-er
sal-va-tion
salve
salved
salv-ing
salv-or
sal-vo
sal-vos
sal-voes
sam-ba
sam-baed
sam-ba-ing
same-ness
sam-o-var
sam-ple
sam-pled
sam-pling

sam-pler
san-a-to-ri-um
sanc-ti-fy
sanc-ti-fied
sanc-ti-fy-ing
sanc-ti-fi-ca-tion
sanc-ti-fi-er
sanc-ti-mo-ny
sanc-ti-mo-ni-ous
sanc-tion
sanc-tion-a-ble
sanc-tion-er
sanc-ti-ty
sanc-ti-ties
sanc-tu-ary
sanc-tu-ar-ies
sanc-tum
sanc-ta
san-dal
san-dal-wood
sand-bag
sand-bagged
sand-bank
sand-blast
sand-box
sand-cast
sand-cast-ed
sand-cast-ing
sand-lot
sand-man
sand-men
sand-pa-per
sand-pi-per
sand-stone
sand-wich
sandy
sand-i-er
sand-i-est
sane
san-er
san-est
sane-ly
sang-froid
san-gui-nary
san-quine
san-quine-ly
san-i-tar-i-um
san-i-tar-i-ums
san-i-tar-ia
san-i-tary
san-i-tar-i-ly
san-i-ta-tion
san-i-tize
san-i-tized
san-i-tiz-ing
san-i-ty

sap
sapped
sap-ping
sap-head
sap-head-ed
sa-pi-ent
sa-pi-ence
sa-pi-en-cy
sap-less
sap-ling
sa-pon-i-fy
sa-pon-i-fied
sa-pon-i-fy-ing
sap-per
sap-phire
sap-phism
sap-py
sap-pi-er
sap-pi-est
sap-suck-er
sap-wood
sa-ran
sar-casm
sar-cas-tic
sar-cas-ti-cal-ly
sar-co-ma
sar-co-mas
sar-co-ma-ta
sar-coph-a-gus
sar-coph-a-gus-es
sar-dine
sar-don-ic
sar-don-i-cal-ly
sar-gas-sum
sa-ri
sa-ris
sa-rong
sar-sa-pa-ril-la
sar-to-ri-al
sa-shay
sas-sa-fras
sas-sy
sas-si-er
sas-si-est
sa-tan-ic
sa-tan-i-cal
sa-tan-ism
sa-tan-ist
satch-el
sate
sat-ed
sat-ing
sa-teen
sat-el-lite
sa-ti-a-ble
sa-ti-a-bly

sa-ti-a-bil-i-ty
sa-ti-ate
  sa-ti-at-ed
  sa-ti-at-ing
  sa-ti-a-tion
sa-ti-e-ty
sat-in
  sat-iny
sat-ire
sa-tir-i-cal
  sa-tir-i-cal-ly
sat-i-rist
sat-i-rize
  sat-i-rized
  sat-i-riz-ing
  sat-i-riz-er
sat-is-fac-tion
sat-is-fac-to-ry
  sat-is-fa-to-ri-ly
sat-is-fy
  sat-is-fied
  sat-is-fy-ing
  sat-is-fi-a-ble
  sat-is-fi-er
  sat-is-fy-ing-ly
sat-u-rate
  sat-u-rat-ed
  sat-u-rat-ing
  sat-u-ra-tion
sat-ur-na-li-a
sat-ur-nine
sa-tyr
  sa-tyr-ic
sauce
  sauced
  sauc-ing
sau-cer
sau-cy
sau-er-bra-ten
sau-er-kraut
sau-na
saun-ter
  saun-ter-er
sau-sage
  sau-sage-like
sav-age
  sav-age-ry
  sav-age-ries
sa-van-na
sa-vant
save
  saved
  sav-ing
  sav-er
sav-ior
sa-voir-faire

sa-vor
  sa-vor-er
sa-vory
  sa-vor-i-er
  sa-vor-i-est
sav-vy
saw-buck
saw-dust
sawed--off
saw-horse
saw-mill
saw-toothed
saw-yer
sax-o-phone
  sax-o-phon-ist
say
  said
  say-ing
  say-a-ble
  say-er
say-s-o
scab
  scabbed
  scab-bing
  scab-bard
  scab-by
  scab-bi-er
  scab-bi-est
sca-bies
scaf-fold
  sac-fold-ing
sca-lar
scal-a-wag
scald
  scald-ing
scale
  scaled
  scal-ing
  scale-less
scamp
  scamp-er
scan
scan-dal
scan-dal-ize
  scan-dal-ized
  scan-dal-iz-ing
  scan-dal-mon-ger
  scan-dal-ous
scan-sion
scant
  scant-ness
scan-ties
scanty
  scant-i-er
  scant-i-est
scape-goat

scape-grace
scap-u-la
  scap-u-las
  scap-u-lae
scar
  scarred
  scar-ring
scarce
  scar-ci-ty
scare
  scared
  scar-ing
  scar-er
scare-crow
scare-mon-ger
scarf
  scarfs
scarf-skin
scar-i-fy
  scar-i-fied
  scar-i-fy-ing
scar-let
scarp
scary
  scar-i-er
  scar-i-est
scat
  scat-ted
  scat-ting
scathe
scat-o-log-i-cal
scat-ter
  scat-ter-a-ble
  scat-ter-er
scav-enge
  scav-enged
  scav-eng-ing
  scav-en-ger
sce-nar-i-o
  sce-nar-i-os
sce-nar-ist
scen-ery
  scen-er-ies
sce-nic
  sce-ni-cal
scent
  scent-ed
scep-ter
  scep-tered
  scep-ter-ing
sched-ule
  sched-ul-ed
  sched-ul-ing
sche-ma
  sche-ma-ta
  sche-mat-i-cal-ly

sche-ma-tize
  sche-ma-tized
  sche-ma-tiz-ing
scheme
  schem-er
  schem-ing
scher-zo
  scher-zos
  scher-zi
schism
schis-mat-ic
  schis-mat-i-cal
schist
schizo
  schiz-os
schiz-oid
schiz-o-phre-ni-a
  schiz-o-phren-ic
schle-miel
schmaltz
  schmaltzy
schmo
schnapps
schnau-zer
schnit-zel
schnook
schnor-kel
schnoz-zle
schol-ar
schol-ar-ly
  schol-ar-li-ness
schol-ar-ship
scho-las-tic
  scho-las-ti-cal
scho-las-ti-cism
school board
school bus
school-child
  school-chil-dern
school-ing
school-mas-ter
school-teach-er
  school-teach-ing
school-work
schoon-er
schuss
schwa
sci-at-ic
sci-ence
sci-en-tif-ic
  sci-en-tif-i-cal-ly
sci-en-tist
scim-i-tar
scin-tig-ra-phy
scin-til-la
scin-til-lant

scin-til-late
  scin-til-lat-ed
  scin-til-lat-ing
  scin-til-la-tion
sci-on
scis-sor
  scis-sors
scle-ra
  scle-rot-i-ca
scle-ro-sis
  scle-ro-ses
scle-rot-ic
scle-rous
scoff
  scoff-er
  scoff-ing-ly
scold
  scold-er
  scold-ing
scol-lop
sconce
scone
scoop
scoot-er
scope
scorch
  scorched
  scorch-ing
  scorch-er
score
  scored
  scor-ing
  score-less
  scor-er
score-board
score-keep-er
scorn
  scorn-er
  scorn-ful
scot-free
scot-tie
scoun-drel
  scoun-drel-ly
scour
  scour-er
scourge
  scourged
  scourg-ing
  scourg-er
  scour-ing
scout-ing
scout-mas-ter
scowl
  scowl-er
srab-ble
  scrab-bled

scrab-bling
scrab-bler
scrag
  scragged
  scrag-ging
scrag-gly
  scrag-gli-er
  scrag-gli-est
scrag-gy
  scrag-gi-er
  scrag-gi-est
scram
  scrammed
  scram-ming
scram-ble
  scram-bled
  scram-bling
  scram-bler
scrap
  scrapped
  scrap-ping
scrap-book
scrape
scrap-per
scrap-py
  scrap-pi-er
  scrap-pi-est
  scrap-pi-ly
scratch
  scratch-a-ble
  scratch-er
scratch-y
  scratch-i-er
  scratch-i-est
  scratch-i-ly
  scratch-i-ness
scrawl
scrawn-y
  scrawn-i-er
  scrawn-i-est
screamer
  scream-ing-ly
screech
  screech-er
screen
  scrren-a-ble
  screen-er
screen-play
screw
screw-driv-er
screw-y
  screw-i-er
  screw-i-est
scrib-ble
  scrib-bled
  scrib-bling

scrib-bler
scribe
 scribed
 scrib-ing
 scrib-al
scrim
 scrim-mage
 scrim-mag-ing
scrimp-y
 scrimp-i-er
 scrimp-i-est
script
 scrip-tur-al
 scrip-ture
 script-writ-er
scroll-work
scrooge
scro-tum
 scro-ta
scrounge
 scroung-er
scrub
 scrubbed
 scrub-bing
 scrub-ber
scrub-by
 scrub-bi-er
 scrub-bi-est
scrub-wom-an
 scrub-wom-en
scruffy
 scruff-i-er
 scruff-i-est
scrump-tious
scru-ple
 scru-bled
 scru-bling
scru-pu-lous
 scru-pu-los-i-ty
 scru-pu-lous-ly
scru-ta-ble
scru-ti-nize
 scru-ti-nized
scru-ti-ny
 scru-ti-nies
scu-ba
scud
 scud-ded
 scud-ding
scuf-fle
 scuf-fled
 scuf-fling
scul-ler-y
 scul-ler-ies
sculp-tor
sculp-ture

sculp-tur-ed
sculp-tur-ing
sculp-tur-al
scum
 scummed
 scum-ming
scur-ri-lous
 scur-ril-i-ty
 scur-ril-i-ties
scur-ry
 scur-ri-ed
 scur-ry-ing
scur-vy
scut-tle
 scut-tled
 scut-tling
 scut-tle-butt
scythe
 scythed
 scyth-ing
sea-bed
sea-coast
sea-drome
sea-far-ing
 sea-far-er
sea-food
sea gull
sea horse
seal
 seal-er
sea-lam-prey
sea legs
sea lev-el
seal-ing wax
sea li-on
seal-skin
seam
 seam-er
sea-maid
sea-man
 sea-men
sea-man-ship
seam-stree
seam-y
 seam-i-er
 seam-i-est
sea ot-ter
sea-plane
sea-port
search
 search-a-ble
 search-er
 search-ing
 search-light
 search war-rant
sea-scape

sea ser-pent
sea-shell
sea-shore
sea-sick
 sea-sick-ness
sea-side
sea-son
 sea-son-er
sea-son-a-ble
sea-son-al
 sea-son-al-ly
sea-son-ing
seat-ing
sea ur-chin
sea-ward
sea-weed
sea-wor-thy
 sea-wor-thi-ness
se-ba-ceous
se-cant
se-cede
 se-ced-ed
 se-ced-ing
 se-ced-er
se-ces-sion
 se-ces-sion-ist
se-clude
 se-clud-ed
 se-clud-ing
se-clu-sion
 se-clu-sive
sec-ond
sec-ond-ar-y
 sec-ond-ar-i-ly
sec-ond--best
sec-ond--class
sec-ond-quess
sec-ond-hand
sec-ond-rate
sec-ond--sto-ry man
se-cre-cy
 se-cre-cies
se-cret
sec-re-tar-i-at
sec-re-tary
 sec-re-tar-ies
 sec-re-tar-i-al
se-crete
 se-cret-ed
 se-cret-ing
se-cre-tion
se-cre-tive
se-cre-to-ry
 se-cre-to-ries
sec-tar-i-an
 sec-tar-i-an-ism

sec-tion
sec-tion-al
sec-tor
  sec-to-ri-al
sec-u-lar
sec-u-lar-ism
sec-u-lar-ize
  sec-u-lar-ized
  sec-u-lar-iz-ing
se-cure
  se-cured
  se-cur-ing
se-cu-ri-ty
  se-cu-ri-ties
se-dan
se-date
  se-dat-ed
  se-dat-ing
se-da-tion
sed-a-tive
sed-en-tary
  sed-en-tar-i-ness
sedge
sed-i-ment
  sed-i-men-tal
  sed-i-men-ta-ry
  sed-i-men-ta-tion
se-di-tion
  se-di-tion-ary
se-di-tious
se-duce
  se-duced
  se-duc-ing
  se-duc-er
se-duc-tive
  se-duc-tive-ness
sed-u-lous
  se-du-li-ty
  sed-u-lous-ness
seed-bed
seed-case
seed-ing
seed-pod
seedy
  seed-i-er
  seed-i-est
see-ing
seek
  sought
  seek-ing
seem-ing
  seem-ing-ness
seem-ly
seep
  seepy
  seep-i-er

seep-i-est
seep-age
se-er
seer-ess
seer-suck-er
see-saw
seethe
  seethed
  seeth-ing
seg-ment
  seg-men-tal
  seg-men-tary
  seg-men-ta-tion
seg-re-gate
  seg-re-gat-ed
  seg-re-gat-ing
  seg-re-ga-tion
  seg-re-ga-tion-sit
sei-gneur
seine
  seined
  sein-ing
seis-mic
  seis-mal
  seis-mi-cal
  seis-mi-cal-ly
seis-mo-graph
  seis-mog-ra-pher
  seis-mo-graph-ic
  seis-mog-ra-phy
seis-mol-o-gy
  seis-mo-log-ic
  seis-mo-log-i-cal
  seis-mol-o-gist
seize
  seized
  seiz-ing
  seiz-er
sei-zure
sel-dom
se-lect
  se-lect-ed
  se-lec-tor
  se-lec-tion
  se-lec-tive
  se-lec-tiv-i-ty
se-le-ni-um
self-a-base-ment
self-ab-ne-ga-tion
self-a-buse
self--ad-dressed
self-ag-gran-dize-ment
  self-ag-gran-diz-ing
self--as-sur-ance
  self--as-sured
self--cen-tered

self--cen-tered-ness
self--col-lect-ed
self--com-mand
self--com-posed
self--con-fessed
self--con-fi-dence
  self--con-fi-dent
self--con-scious
  self--con-scious-ness
self--con-tained
self--con-trol
  self--con-trolled
self--cor-rect-ing
self--crit-i-cal
self--crit-i-cism
self--de-cep-tion
  self--de-cep-tive
self--de-fense
self--de-ni-al
  self--de-ny-ing
self--de-ter-mi-na-tion
  self--de-ter-min-ing
self--dis-ci-pline
  self--dis-ci-plined
self--ed-u-cate-ed
  self--ed-u-ca-tion
self--ef-fac-ing
self--em-ployed
  self--em-ploy-ment
self--es-teem
self--ev-i-dent
  self--ev-i-dence
self--ex-plan-a-to-ry
self--ex-pres-sion
  self--ex-pres-sive
self--ful-fill-ing
self--ful-fill-ment
self--gov-ern-ment
  self--gov-erned
  self--gov-ern-ing
self--help
self--im-age
self--im-por-tance
  self--im-por-tant
self--im-posed
self--im-prove-ment
self--in-duced
self--in-dul-gence
  self--in-dul-gent
self--in-flict-ed
self--in-ter-est
  self--in-ter-est-ed
self-ish
  self--ish-ness
self--kow-ledge
self-less

self-less-ness
self--love
  self--lov-ing
self--made
self--per-pet-u-at-ing
  self-per-pet-u-a-tion
self--pity
  self--pit-y-ing
self--pol-li-na-tion
self--pos-sessed
  self--pos-sess-ed-ly
  self--pos-ses-sion
self--pres-er-va-tion
self--pro-pelled
  self--pro-pel-ling
self--re-al-i-za-tion
self--re-li-ance
  self--re-li-ant
self--re-spect
  self--re-spect-ing
self--re-straint
  self--re-strain-ing
self--right-eous
  self--right-eous-ness
self--sac-ri-fice
  self--sac-ri-fic-ing
self--same
self--sat-is-fied
  self--sat-is-fac-tion
  self--sat-is-fy-ing
self--ser-vice
self--serv-ing
self--start-er
  self--start-ing
self--styled
self--suf-fi-cient
  self--suf-fic-ing
  self--suf-fi-cien-cy
self--sup-port
  self--sup-port-ing
self--taught
self--will
  self--willed
sell
  sell-ing
sell-er
sell-out
sel-vage
  sel-vaged
se-man-tics
  se-man-tic
  se-man-ti-cal
  se-man-ti-cal-ly
sem-a-phore
  sem-a-phor-ed
  sem-a-phor-ing

sem-blance
se-men
se-mes-ter
sem-i-an-nu-al
  sem-i-an-nu-al-ly
sem-i-ar-id
sem-i-au-to-mat-ic
sem-i-cir-cle
  sem-i-cir-cu-lar
sem-i-clas-si-cal
  sem-i-clas-sic
sem-i-co-lon
sem-i-con-duc-tor
  sem-i-con-duct-ing
sem-i-con-scious
  sem-i-con-sious-ness
sem-i-de-tached
sem-i-fi-nal
  sem-i-fi-nal-ist
sem-i-flu-id
sem-i-for-mal
sem-i-gloss
sem-i-liq-uid
sem-i-month-ly
sem-i-nal
  sem-i-nal-ly
sem-i-nar-y
  sem-i-nar-ies
  sem-i-nar-ian
sem-i-of-fi-cial
  sem-i-of-fi-cial-ly
sem-i-per-ma-nent
sem-i-per-me-a-ble
sem-i-pre-cious
sem-i-pri-vate
sem-i-pro-fes-sion-al
sem-i-pro
sem-i-pub-lic
sem-i-skilled
sem-i-sol-id
sem-i-trail-er
sem-i-trop-ic
  sem-i-trop-i-cal
  sem-i-trop-ics
sem-i-vow-el
sem-i-week-ly
  sem-i-week-lies
sem-i-year-ly
sen-a-ry
sen-ate
sen-a-tor
  sen-a-tor-ship
sen-a-to-ri-al
  sen-a-to-ri-al-ly
send--off
se-nile

se-nil-i-ty
sen-ior
sen-ior-i-ty
sen-na
sen-sate
san-sa-tion
sen-sa-tion-al
  sen-sa-tion-al-ly
  sen-sa-tion-al-ism
sense
  sensed
  sens-ing
sense-less
  sense-less-ness
sen-si-bil-i-ty
  sen-si-ble-ness
sen-si-ble
  sen-si-ble-ness
  sen-si-bly
sen-si-tive
sen-si-tiv-i-ty
  sen-si-tiv-i-ties
sen-si-tize
  sen-si-tized
  sen-si-tiz-ing
  sen-si-ti-za-tion
  sen-si-tizer
sen-sor
sen-so-ry
sen-so-ri-al
sen-su-al
  sen-su-al-i-ty
  sen-su-al-ly
  sen-su-al-ism
  sen-su-al-ist
  sen-su-al-ize
  sen-su-al-ized
  sen-su-al-iz-ing
  sen-su-al-i-za-tion
sen-su-ous
sen-tence
  sen-tenced
  sen-tenc-ing
sen-tient
sen-ti-ment
sen-ti-men-tal
  sen-ti-men-tal-ly
sen-ti-men-til-i-ty
  sen-ti-men-tal-i-ties
  sen-ti-men-tal-ist
sen-ti-men-tal-ize
  sen-ti-men-tal-ized
  sen-ti-men-tal-iz-ing
sen-ti-nel
  sen-ti-neled
  sen-ti-nel-ing

sen-try
  sen-tries
se-pal
  se-paled
  se-palled
sep-a-ra-ble
  sep-a-ra-bil-i-ty
  sep-e-ra-bly
sep-a-rate
  sep-a-rat-ed
  sep-a-rat-ing
sep-a-ra-tion
sep-a-ra-tist
  sep-a-ra-tism
sep-a-ra-tive
sep-a-ra-tor
se-pi-a
sep-sis
  sep-ses
sep-ten-ni-al
sep-tet
sep-tic
  sep-ti-cal-ly
  sep-tic-i-ty
sep-tu-a-ge-nar-i-an
sep-tum
  sep-ta
sep-tu-ple
  sep-tu-pled
  sep-tu-pling
sep-ul-cher
  sep-u-chered
  sep-u-cher-ing
  se-pul-chral
se-quel
se-quence
se-quent
se-quen-tial
  se-quen-tial-ly
se-ques-ter
  se-ques-tered
  se-ques-tra-ble
se-ques-tra-tion
se-quin
  se-quined
se-quoi-a
se-ra-pe
ser-aph
  ser-aphs
  ser-a-phim
  se-raph-ic
ser-e-nade
  ser-e-nad-ed
  ser-e-nad-ing
  ser-e-nad-er
ser-en-dip-i-ty

ser-en-dip-i-tous
se-rene
  se-rene-ness
se-ren-i-ty
  se-ren-i-ties
serf
serge
ser-geant
ser-geant at arms
ser-geant ma-jor
se-ri-al
  se-ri-al-ly
  se-ri-al-ist
  se-ri-al-i-za-tion
  se-ri-al-ize
  se-ri-al-ized
  se-ri-a!-iz-ing
se-ries
se-ri-ous
  se-ri-ous-ly
  se-ri-ous-ness
  se-ri-ous--mind-ed
  se-ri-us--mind-ed-ly
ser-mon
  ser-mon-ize
  ser-mon-ized
  ser-mon-iz-ing
se-rol-o-gy
  se-ro-log-ic
  se-ro-log-i-cal
  se-rol-o-gist
se-rous
ser-pent
ser-pen-tine
ser-rate
  ser-rat-ing
ser-ra-tion
se-rum
  se-rums
  se-ra
serv-ant
serve
  served
  serv-ing
serv-er
serv-ice
  serv-iced
  serv-ic-ing
serv-ice-a-ble
  serv-ice-a-bil-i-ty
  serv-ice-a-ble-ness
  serv-ice-a-bly
serv-ice-man
ser-vile
  ser-vil-i-ty
  ser-vile-ness

ser-vi-tude
ser-vo-mech-an-ism
ses-a-me
ses-qui-cen-ten-ni-al
ses-sion
set-back
set-in
set-off
set-ter
set-ting
set-tle
  set-tled
  set-tling
set-tle-ment
set-tler
set-to
set-up
sev-en
sev-enth
sev-en-teen
  sev-en-teenth
sev-en-ty
  sev-en-ti-eth
sev-er
  sev-er-a-bil-i-ty
  sev-er-a-ble
sev-er-al
  sev-er-al-ly
  sev-er-al-fold
sev-er-ance
se-vere
  se-ver-er
  se-ver-est
  se-vere-ness
se-ver-i-ty
  se-ver-i-ties
sew
sew-age
sew-ing
sew-ing ma-chine
sex-less
sex-ol-o-gy
  sex-o-log-i-cal
  sex-ol-o-gist
sex-tant
sex-tet
sex-ton
sex-tu-ple
  sex-tu-pled
  sex-tu-pling
sex-tu-plet
sex-u-al
  sex-u-al-ly
  sex-u-al-i-ty
sex-y
  sex-i-er

sex-i-est
shab-by
shab-bi-er
shab-bi-est
shab-bi-ly
shack-le
shack-led
shack-ling
shack-ler
shade
shad-ed
shad-ing
shade-less
shad-ow
shad-ow-box
shad-owy
shad-y
shad-i-er
shad-i-est
shad-i-ly
shaft-ing
shag
shagged
shag-ging
shag-gi-ly
shake
shak-en
shak-ing
shake-down
shak-er
shake-up
shak-y
shak-i-er
shak-i-est
shak-i-ly
shal-lot
shal-low
shal-low-ness
sham
shammed
sham-ming
sha-man
sha-man-ism
sha-man-ist
sham-bles
shame
shamed
sham-ing
shame-faced
shame-fac-ed-ly
shame-ful
shame-ful-ly
shame-ful-ness
sham-mer
sham-my
sham-poo

sham-pooed
sham-poo-ing
sham-poo-er
sham-rock
shan-tey
shan-ties
shan-ty-town
shape
shaped
shap-ing
shap-a-ble
shap-er
shape-less
shape-ly
shape-li-ier
shape-li-est
share
shared
shar-ing
shar-er
share-crop-per
share-crop
share-cropped
share-crop-ping
share-hold-er
shark-skin
sharp-en
sharp-en-er
sharp-er
sharp-eyed
sharp-ie
sharp-shoot-er
sharp-shoot-ing
sharp-tongued
sharp-wit-ted
sharp-wit-ted-ly
sharp-wit-ted-ness
shat-ter
shat-ter-proof
shave
shaved
shav-ing
shav-er
shawl
sheaf
sheaves
shear
sheared
shear-ing
shear-er
sheath
sheath-less
sheathe
sheathed
sheath-ing
sheath-er

shed
shed-ding
sheen
sheeny
sheen-i-er
sheep-dog
sheep-herd-er
sheep-herd-ing
sheep-ish
sheep-skin
sheer
sheer-ly
sheet-ing
sheik
shelf
shelves
shell
shelled
shel-lac
shel-lacked
shel-lack-ing
shell-fire
shell-fish
shell shock
shel-ter
shel-ter-er
shelve
shelved
shelv-ing
she-nan-i-gan
shep-herd
shep-herd-ess
sher-bet
sher-iff
sher-ry
sher-ries
shib-bo-leth
shield
shield-er
shift
shift-er
shift-less
shift-y
shift-i-er
shift-i-est
shift-i-ly
shil-ly--shal-ly
shil-ly-shal-lied
shil-ly-shal-ly-ing
shim-mer
shim-mery
shim-mer-i-er
shim-mer-i-est
shim-my
shim-mies
shim-mied

183

shim-my-ing
shin
　shinned
　shin-ning
shin-bone
shin-dig
shine
　shined
　shone
　shin-ing
shin-er
shin-gle
　shin-gled
　shin-gling
　shin-gler
shin-gles
shin-ing
　shin-ing-ly
shin-ny
　shin-nied
　shin-ny-ing
shin-y
　shin-i-er
　shin-i-est
ship
　shipped
　ship-ping
ship-a-ble
ship-board
ship-build-er
　ship-build-ing
ship-mate
ship-ment
ship-per
ship-yard
shirk
　shirker
shirt-tail
shirt-waist
shish ke-bab
shiv-er
　shiv-ery
　shiv-er-i-er
　shiv-er-i-est
shoal
shock-er
shock-ing
shod-dy
　shod-di-er
　shod-di-ly
　shod-di-ness
shoe-horn
shoe-lace
shoe-mak-er
sho-er
shoe-string

shoo--in
shoot
　shot
　shoot-ing
　shoot-er
shop
　shopped
　shop-ping
shop-keep-er
shop-lift-er
　shop-lift-ing
shop-per
shop-talk
shop-worn
shore
　shore-line
short
　short-ly
　short-ness
short-age
short--change
　short--changed
　short--chang-ing
short-com-ing
short-cut
　short-cut-ting
short-en
　short-en-er
short-en-ing
short-hand
short--hand-ed
short--lived
short--sight-ed
　short--sight-ed-ly
　short--sight-ed-ness
short--tem-pered
short--term
short-wave
short--wind-ed
shot-gun
　shot-gunned
　shot-gun-ning
shoul-der
shoul-der blade
shout-er
shout-ing
shove
　shoved
　shov-ing
　shov-er
shov-el
　shov-eled
　shov-el-ing
shov-el-ful
show
　showed

shown
　show-ing
show-bill
show-boat
show-case
　show-cased
　show-cas-ing
show-down
show-er
　show-ery
show-man
　show-men
　show-man-ship
show-off
show-piece
show-place
show-room
show-y
　show-i-er
　show-i-est
　show-i-ly
shrap-nel
shred
　shred-ded
　shred-ding
　shred-der
shrew
shrewd
　shrewd-ly
　shrewd-ness
shrew-ish
shriek
shrill
　shirl-ly
shrimp
shrine
　shrined
　shrin-ing
shrink
　shrunk-ed
　shrink-a-ble
　shrink-er
shrink-age
shriv-el
　shriv-eled
　shriv-el-ing
shroud
shrub-bery
　shrub-ber-ies
shrub-by
　shrub-bi-er
　shrub-bi-est
shrug
　shrugged
　shrug-ging
shuck-er

shud-der
shud-dery
suf-fle
shuf-fled
shuf-fling
shuf-fler
shuf-fle-board
shun
shunned
shun-ning
shun-ner
shunt
shunt-er
shut-down
shut-eye
shut-in
shut-off
shut-out
shut-ter
shut-tle
shut-tled
shut-tling
shut-tle-like
shy
shi-er
shy-est
shy-ness
shy-ster
sib-i-lant
sib-i-lance
sib-ling
sick
sicked
sick-ing
sick-bed
sick-en
sick-en-ing
sick-ish
sick-le
sick-ly
sick-li-er
sick-li-est
sick-ness
sick-room
side-arm
side-board
sid-ed
side-kick
side-line
side-lined
side-lin-ing
side--long
side-show
side-split-ting
side-step
side-step-ped

side-step-ping
side-swipe
side-swiped
side-swip-ing
side-track
side-ways
sid-ing
si-dle
si-dled
si-dling
siege
si-en-na
si-er-ra
si-es-ta
sieve
sieved
siev-ing
sift-er
sift-ings
sigh-er
sight-ed
sight-less
sight-ly
sight-read
sight-read-ing
sight-see-ing
sight-see-er
sig-nal
sig-naled
sig-nal-ing
sig-nal-er
sig-nal-man
sig-nal-men
sig-na-to-ry
sig-na-to-ries
sig-na-ture
sign-board
sig-net
sig-nif-i-cance
sig-nif-i-cant
sig-ni-fi-ca-tion
sig-ni-fy
sig-ni-fied
sig-ni-fy-ing
sig-ni-fi-a-ble
sig-ni-fi-er
sign-post
si-lage
si-lence
si-lenced
si-lenc-ing
si-lenc-er
si-lent
si-lent part-ner
sil-hou-ette
sil-hou-et-ted

sil-hou-et-ting
sil-ic-a
sil-i-con
sil-i-cone
silk-en
silk-like
silk-weed
silk-worm
silk-y
silk-i-er
silk-i-est
silk-i-ly
sil-ly
sil-li-er
sil-li-est
sil-li-ness
si-lo
si-los
si-loed
si-lo-ing
silt
sil-ta-tion
silt-y
silt-i-er
silt-i-est
sil-ver
sil-ver-fish
sil-ver-fox
sil-ver-ware
sil-ver-y
sim-i-an
sim-i-lar
sim-i-lar-i-ty
sim-i-lar-i-ties
sim-i-le
si-mil-i-tude
sim-mer
si-mon-ize
si-mon-ized
si-mon-iz-ing
sim-pa-ti-co
sim-per
sim-per-er
sim-per-ing-ly
sim-ple
sim-pler
sim-plest
sim-ple-ness
sim-ple--mind-ed
sim-ple sen-tence
sim-ple-ton
sim-plex
sim-plic-i-ty
sim-plic-i-ties
sim-pli-fy
sim-pli-fied

sim-pli-fy-ing
sim-pli-fi-ca-tion
sim-pli-fi-er
sim-plism
sim-plis-tic
sim-plis-ti-cal-ly
sim-ply
sim-u-late
sim-u-lat-ed
sim-u-lat-ing
sim-u-la-tion
sim-u-la-tive
sim-u-la-tor
si-mul-cast
si-mul-cast-ing
si-mul-ta-ne-ous
si-mul-ta-ne-ous-ly
si-mul-ta-ne-i-ty
sin
sinned
sin-ning
sin-cere
sin-cer-i-ty
si-ne-cure
si-ne qua non
sin-ew
sin-ew-y
sin-ful
sin-ful-ly
sin-ful-ness
sing
sing-ing
sing-a-ble
singe
singed
singe-ing
sing-er
sin-gle
sin-gled
sin-gling
sin-gle-ness
sin-gle-brest-ed
sin-gle--hand-ed
sin-gle-hand-ed-ly
sin-gle--mind-ed
sin-gle--mind-ed-ly
sin-gle--space
sin-gle--spaced
sin-gle--spac-ing
sin-gle-ton
sin-gle--track
sin-gly
sing-song
sin-gu-lar
sin-gu-lar-i-ty
sin-gu-lar-i-ties

sin-is-ter
sin-is-ter-ness
sink-a-ble
sink-er
sink-hole
sin-less
sin-ner
sin-u-ate
sin-u-at-ed
sin-u-at-ing
sin-u-ous
sin-u-os-i-ty
sin-u-ous-ness
si-nus
si-nus-i-tis
sip
sipped
sip-ping
sip-per
si-phon
sire
sired
sir-ing
si-ren
sir-loin
sis-sy
sis-sies
sis-si-fied
sis-sy-ish
sis-ter
sis-ter-li-ness
sis-ter-ly
sis-ter-in-law
sis-ters-in-law
si-tar
sit-in
sit-ter
sit-ting
sit-u-ate
sit-u-at-ed
sit-u-at-ing
sit-u-a-tion
six--pack
six--shoot-er
six-teen
six-teenth
sixth
six-ty
six-ti-eth
siz-a-ble
siz-a-ble-ness
siz-a-bly
size
sized
siz-ing
siz-zle

siz-zled
siz-zling
siz-zler
skate
skat-ed
skat-ing
skat-er
ske-dad-dle
ske-dad-dled
ske-dad-dling
skein
skel-e-ton
skel-e-tal
skep-tic
skep-ti-cal
skep-ti-cism
sketch
sketch-er
sketch-book
sketch-y
sketch-i-er
sketch-i-est
sketch-i-ly
skew-er
skew-ness
ski
skied
ski-ing
ski-er
skid
skid-ded
skid-ding
skid-der
skilled
skil-let
skill-ful
skill-ful-ly
skill-ful-ness
skim
skimmed
skim-ming
skim-mer
skimp
skimp-i-ly
skimp-y
skimp-i-er
skimp-i-est
skin
skinned
skin-ning
skin--deep
skin dive
skin div-ing
skin div-er
skin-flint
skin-less

skin-ner
skin-ny
  skin-ni-er
  skin-ni-est
skin-tight
skip-per
skir-mish
  skir-mish-er
skirt-er
  skirt-ing
skit-ter
skit-tish
skiv-vy
  skiv-vies
skoal
skul-dug-ger-y
skulk-er
skull-cap
skunk
sky
  skies
  skied
  sky-ing
sky-blue
sky-cap
sky-div-ing
sky-rock-et
sky-svap-er
sky-ward
sky-way
sky-writ-ing
  sky-writ-er
slab
  slabbed
  slab-bing
slack
  slack-ness
slack-en
slack-er
slack-jawed
slake
  slaked
  slak-ing
sla-lom
slam
  slammeed
  slam-ming
slam-bang
slan-der
  slan-der-er
  slan-der-ous
slang
  slang-i-er
  slang-i-est
slant
  slant-ways

slant-wise
slap
  slapp-ed
  slap-ping
  slap-per
slap-dash
slap-hap-py
  slap-hap-pi-er
  slap-hap-pi-est
slap-stick
slash-er
slash-ing
slat
  slat-ted
  slat-ting
slate
  slat-ed
  slat-ing
slath-er
slat-tern
  slat-tern-ly
slaugh-ter
  slaugh-ter-er
slaugh-ter-house
slave
  slaved
  slav-ing
slav-er
slav-er-y
slav-ish
  sla-vish-ly
slay
  slain
  slay-ing
  slay-er
slea-zy
  slea-zi-er
  slea-zi-est
sled
  sled-ded
  sled-ding
  sled-der
sledge
  sledged
  sledg-ing
sleek
  sleek-er
  sleek-ness
sleep-er
sleep-less
  sleep-less-ness
sleep-walk
  sleep-walk-er
  sleep-walk-ing
sleep-y
  sleep-i-er

sleep-i-est
sleep-i-ly
sleep-y-head
sleet
  sleet-y
  sleet-i-ness
sleeve
  sleeved
  sleev-ing
  sleeve-less
sleigh
  sleigh-er
sleight
slen-der
  slen-der-ness
slen-der-ize
  slen-der-ized
  slen-der-iz-ing
sleuth
slice
  sliced
  slic-ing
  slic-er
slick-er
slick-ness
slide
slid
  slid-ing
  slid-er
slight
  slight-er
  slight-ing
slim
  slim-mer
  slim-mest
  slimmed
  slim-ming
  slim-ness
slime
  slimed
  slim-ing
slimy
  slim-i-er
  slim-i-est
  slim-i-ly
sling-er
sling-shoot
slink-y
  slink-i-er
  slink-i-est
slip
  slipped
  slip-ping
slip-cov-er
slip-knot
slip--on

187

slip-o-ver
slip-page
slip-per
slip-per-y
  slip-per-i-er
  slip-per-i-est
slip-py
slip-shod
slip-stick
slip-up
slit
  slit-ting
  slit-ter
slith-er
  slith-ery
sliv-er
  sliv-er-er
  sliv-er-like
slob-ber
  slob-ber-er
  slob-ber-ing-ly
sloe--eyed
slo-gan
  slo-gan-eer
slop
  slopped
  slop-ping
slope
  sloped
  slop-ing
  slop-er
slop-py
  slop-pi-er
  slop-pi-est
  slo-pi-ly
  slop-pi-ness
slosh-y
  slosh-i-er
  slosh-i-est
slot
  slot-ted
  slot-ting
sloth
  sloth-ful
  sloth-ful-ly
slouch
  slouch-er
  slouch-i-ly
  slouch-i-ness
  slouch-y
  slouch-i-er
  slouch-i-est
slough
  slough-y
  slough-i-er
  slough-i-est

slov-en
slov-en-ly
  slov-en-li-ness
slow-down
slow--mo-tion
slow-poke
slow--wit-ted
sludge
  slug-y
  sludg-i-er
  sludg-i-est
slug
  slugged
  slug-ging
  slug-ger
slug-gard
  slug-gard-li-ness
slug-gish
  slug-gish-ness
sluice
  sluiced
  sluic-ing
slum
  slummed
  slum-ming
slum-ber
  slum-ber-er
slum-ber-ous
slur
  slurred
  slur-ring
slush
  slush-i-ness
  slush-y
  slush-i-er
  slush-i-est
slut
  slut-tish
sly
smack
  smack-ing
small--mind-ed
  small—mind-ed-ness
small-pox
small--time
  small—tim-er
smart
  smart-ness
smart al-eck
  smart-al-eck-y
smart-en
smash
smash-ing
smash--up
smat-ter
  smat-ter-er

smat-ter-ing
smear
  smear-er
smear-y
  smear-i-er
  smear-i-est
smell
  smelled
  smel-ling
  smell-er
  smell-y
  smell-i-er
  smell-i-est
smelt
smelt-er
  smelt-ery
smid-gen
snile
  smil-er
  smil-ing-ly
smirch
smirk
  smirk-er
  smirk-ing-ly
smite
  smote
  smit-ten
  smit-ting
  smit-er
smith-er-eens
smit-ten
smock-ing
smog-gy
  smog-gi-er
  smog-gi-est
smoke
  smoked
  smok-ing
  smoke-less
smoke-house
  smok-er
smoke-stack
smok-ing jack-et
smok-y
  smok-i-er
  smok-i-est
  smok-i-ly
smol-der
smooth
  smooth-er
  smooth-ness
smooth-en
smooth-ie
smoth-er
  smoth-er-y
  smoth-er-i-er

smoth-er-i-est
smudge
  smudged
  smudg-ing
  smudg-i-ly
smug
  smug-ger
  smug-gest
  smug-ly
  smug-ness
smug-gle
  smug-gled
  smug-gling
  smug-gler
smut
  smut-ted
  smut-ting
smut-ty
  smut-ti-er
  smut-ti-est
  smut-ti-ly
sna-fu
  sna-fued
  sna-fu-ing
snag
  snagged
  snag-ging
  snag-gy
snag-gle-tooth
  snag-gle-teeth
  snag-gle-toothed
snail
  snail-like
  snail-paced
snake
snake-bite
snake-skin
snak-y
  snak-i-er
  snak-i-est
snap
  snapped
  snap-ping
snap-back
snap-drag-on
snap-per
snap-pish
  snap-pish-ness
snap-py
  snap-pi-er
  snap-pi-est
  snap-pi-ly
snap-shot
snare
  snared
  snar-ing

snar-er
snarl
  snarl-er
  snarl-y
  snarl-i-er
  snarl-i-est
snatch
  snatch-i-er
  snatch-i-est
  snatch-i-ly
snaz-zy
  snaz-zi-er
  snaz-zi-est
sneak-er
sneak-ing
sneak-y
  sneak-i-er
  sneak-i-est
  sneak-i-ly
sneer
  sneer-er
  sneer-ing-ly
sneeze
  sneezed
  sneez-ing
  sneez-er
  sneez-y
  sneez-i-er
  sneez-i-est
snick-er
snif-fle
  snif-fled
  snif-fling
  snif-fler
snif-fy
  snif-fi-er
  snif-fi-est
  snif-fi-ly
snif-ter
snip
  snipped
  snip-ping
  snip-per
snipe
  sniped
  snip-ing
  snip-er
snip-py
  snip-pi-er
  snip-pi-est
  snip-pi-ly
snitch-er
sniv-el
  sniv-eled
  sniv-el-ing
  sniv-el-er

snob
  snob-ber-y
  snob-bish
  snob-bish-ness
snoop
  snoop-y
  snoop-i-er
  snoop-i-est
  snoop-er
snoot-y
  snoot-i-er
  snoot-i-est
  snoot-i-ly
  snoot-i-ness
snooze
  snoozed
  snooz-ing
  snooz-er
snore
  snored
  snor-ing
  snor-er
snor-kel
snort
  snort-er
snot-ty
  snot-ti-er
  snot-ti-est
snout
  snout-ed
  snout-y
  snout-i-er
  snout-i-est
snow-ball
snow-blow-er
snow-bound
snow-cap
snow-drift
snow-fall
snow-flake
snow-man
  snow-men
snow-mo-bile
snow-plow
snow-shoe
  snow-shoed
  snow-shoe-ing
snow-suit
snow--white
snow-y
  snow-i-er
  snow-i-est
snub
  snubbed
  snub-bing
  snub-ber

snub-by
  snub-bi-er
  snub-bi-est
  snub-bi-ness
snub--nosed
snuf-fle
snuff-y
  snuff-i-er
  snuff-i-est
snug
snug-gle
  snug-gled
  snug-gling
soak
  soak-age
  soak-er
  soak-ing-ly
so--and--so
soap-box
soap-suds
soap-y
  soap-i-er
  soap-i-est
soap-i-ly
  soap-i-ness
soar-er
sob
  sobbed
  sob-bing
  sob-ber
so-ber
  so-ber-ing-ly
  so-ber-ness
so-bri-e-ty
so-bri-quet
so--called
soc-cer
so-cia-ble
  so-cia-bil-i-ty
  so-cia-bly
so-cial
  so-ci-al-i-ty
  so-cial-ly
  so-cial-ism
so-cial-ist
  so-cial-is-tic
  so-cial-is-ti-cal-ly
so-cial-ite
so-cial-ize
  so-cial-ized
  so-cial-iz-ing
  so-cial-i-za-tion
  so-cial-iz-er
so-ci-e-ty
  so-ci-e-ties
  so-ci-e-tal

so-ci-o-ec-o-nom-ic
so-ci-ol-o-gy
  so-ci-ol-o-log-i-cal
  so-ci-ol-o-gist
so-ci-o-po-lit-i-cal
sock-et
sod
  sod-ded
  sod-ding
so-da
so-dal-i-ty
  so-dal-i-ties
sod-den
  sod-den-ness
so-di-um
sod-om-y
so-ev-er
so-fa
soft
  soft-ness
soft-ball
soft--boiled
sof-ten
  sof-ten-er
soft--head-ed
soft--heart-ed
  soft--heart-ed-ness
soft ped-al
  soft-ped-aled
  soft-ped-al-ing
soft--shell
soft--shoe
soft--spok-en
soft-ware
soft-wood
soft-y
sof-ties
sog-gy
  sog-gi-er
  sog-gi-est
  sog-gi-ly
  sog-gi-ness
so-journ
  so-journ-er
sol-ace
  sol-aced
  sol-ac-ing
  sol-ac-er
so-lar
so-lar-i-um
  so-lar-i-ums
so-lar-ia
so-lar-ize
  so-lar-ized
  so-lar-iz-ing
so-lar-i-za-tion

sol-der
  sol-der-er
sol-dier
sol-dier-y
sol-e-cism
sole-ly
sol-emn
  sol-emn-ly
  sol-emn-less
so-lem-ni-ty
  so-lem-ni-ties
sol-em-nize
  sol-em-nized
  sol-em-niz-ing
  sol-em-ni-za-tion .
sole-ness
so-lic-it
  so-lic-i-ta-tion
so-lic-i-tor
so-lic-i-tous
  so-lic-i-tous-ness
so-lic-i-tude
sol-id
  so-lid-i-ty
  sol-id-ness
sol-i-dar-i-ty
  sol-i-dar-i-ties
so-lid-i-fy
  so-lid-i-fied
  so-lid-i-fy-ing
  so-lid-i-fi-ca-tion
so-lil-o-quize
  so-lil-o-quized
  so-lil-o-quiz-ing
  so-lil-o-quist
so-lil-o-quy
  so-lil-o-quies
sol-i-taire
sol-i-tar-y
  sol-i-tar-ies
  sol-i-tar-i-ly
  sol-i-tar-i-ness
sol-i-tude
so-lo
  so-loed
  so-lo-ing
  so-lo-ist
sol-stice
sol-u-ble
  sol-u-bil-i-ty
  sol-u-bly
sol-ute
so-lu-tion
solve
  solved
  solv-ing

190

solv-a-ble
solv-a-bil-i-ty
solv-er
sol-vent
sol-ven-cy
so-mat-ic
so-ma-to-type
som-ber
som-ber-ly
som-ber-ness
som-bre-ro
som-bre-ros
some-bod-y
some-bod-ies
some-day
some-how
some-place
som-er-sault
some-thing
some-time
some-times
some-way
some-what
some-where
sosm-nam-bu-late
som-no-lent
som-no-lence
som-no-len-cy
so-nar
so-na-ta
song-bird
song-fest
song-ster
song-stress
song-writ-er
son-ic
son--in--law
sons--in--law
son-net
son-ny
son-nies
so-no-rous
so-nor-i-ty
so-no-rous-ness
soon-er
soothe
soothed
sooth-ing
sooth-er
sooth-say-er
sooth-say-ing
soot-y
soot-i-er
soot-i-est
soot-i-ly
sop

sopped
sop-ping
soph-ist
soph-ism
so-phis-tic
so-phis-ti-cal
so-phis-ti-cate
so-phis-ti-cat-ed
so-phis-ti-cat-ing
so-phis-ti-ca-tion
so-phis-ti-ca-tor
soph-ist-ry
soph-ist-ries
soph-o-more
soph-o-mor-ic
soph-o-mor-i-cal
soph-o-mor-i-cal-ly
sop-o-rif-ic
sop-py
sop-pi-er
sop-pi-est
so-pran-o
so-pran-os
sor-cer-er
sor-cer-ess
sor-cer-y
sor-cer-ies
sor-cer-ous
sor-did
sor-did-ness
sore
sor-er
sor-est
sore-ly
sore-ness
sore-head
sore-head-ed
sor-ghum
so-ror-i-ty
so-ror-i-ties
sor-rel
sor-row
sor-row-er
sor-row-ful
sor-ry
sor-ri-er
sor-ri-est
sor-ri-ly
sort-a-ble
sort-er
sort-ie
so--so
sot
sot-ted
sot-tish
sot-tish-ness

sot-vo vo-ce
sought
soul-ful
soul-ful-ly
soul-ful-ness
soul-less
soul-searching
sound
sound-a-ble
sound-ly
sound-ness
sound-box
sound-er
sound-ing
sound-less
sound-less-ly
sound-proof
soup-y
soup-i-er
soup-i-est
sour
sour-ish
sour-ness
sour-ball
source
souse
soused
sous-ing
south-bound
south-east
south-east-er
south-east-er-ly
south-east-ern
south-east-ward
south-east-ward-ly
south-er
south-er-ly
south-ern
south-ern-most
south-ern-er
south-paw
south-ward
south-ward-ly
south-west
south-west-er
south-west-ern
south-west-ern-er
south-west-ward
south-west-ward-ly
sou-ve-nir
sov-er-eign
sov-er-eign-ty
sov-er-eign-ties
so-vi-et
sow-er
soy-bean

space
  spaced
  spac-ing
  space-less
  spac-er
space-craft
space-man
  space-men
space-ship
space-walk
spa-cious
  spa-cious-ness
spade
  spad-ed
  spad-ing
  spade-ful
  spad-er
spade-work
spa-ghet-ti
span
  spanned
  span-ning
span-gle
  span-gled
  span-gling
span-iel
spank-er
spank-ing
spar
  sparred
  spar-ring
spare
  spared
  spar-ing
  spar-er
  spar-est
  spar-a-ble
  spare-ness
spare-rib
spar-ing
  spar-ing-ness
spark-er
spar-kle
  spar-kled
  spar-kling
spar-kler
spar-row
spar-row-grass
sparse
  spars-er
  spars-est
spasm
spas-mod-ic
  spas-mod-i-cal
  spas-mod-i-cal-ly
spas-tic

spas-ti-cal-ly
spat
  spat-ted
  spat-ting
spa-tial
  spa-cial
  spa-ti-al-i-ty
  spa-tial-ly
spat-ter
spat-u-la
spawn
speak
  spok-en
  speak-ing
  speak-a-ble
speak-eas-y
  speak-eas-ies
speak-er
  speak-er-ship
spear-er
spear-head
spear-mint
spe-cial
  spe-cial-ly
spe-cial-ist
spe-cial-ize
  spe-cial-ized
  spe-cial-iz-ing
  spe-cial-i-za-tion
spe-cial-ty
  spe-cial-ties
spe-cie
spe-cies
spec-i-fia-ble
spe-cif-ic
  spe-cif-i-cal-ly
  spec-i-fic-i-ty
spec-i-fi-ca-tion
spec-i-fy
  spec-i-fied
  spec-i-fy-ing
  spec-i-fi-er
spec-i-men
spe-cious
  spe-ci-os-i-ty
  spe-ci-os-i-ties
  spe-cious-ness
speck-le
  speck-led
  speck-ling
spec-ta-cle
  spec-ta-cled
spec-tac-u-lar
  spec-tac-u-lar-ly
spec-ta-tor
spec-ter

spec-tral
spec-tro-scope
  spec-tro-scop-ic
  spec-tro-scop-i-cal
  spec-tros-co-py
spec-trum
  spec-tra
  spec-trums
spec-u-late
  spec-u-lat-ed
  spec-u-lat-ing
  spec-u-la-tion
  spec-u-la-tive
  spec-u-la-tor
speech-i-fy
  speech-i-fie
  speech-i-fy-ing
speech-less
  speech-less-ness
speed
  speed-ed
  speed-ing
  speed-er
  speed-ster
speed-boat
  speed-boat-ing
speed-om-e-ter
speed--up
speed-way
speed-y
  speed-i-er
  speed-i-est
  speed-i-ly
  speed-i-ness
spe-le-ol-o-gy
  spe-le-ol-o-gist
spell
  spelled
  spell-ing
spell-bind
  spell-bouns
  spell-bind-ing
  spell-bind-er
spell-er
spe-lun-ker
spend
  spent
  spend-ing
  spend-a-ble
  spend-er
spend-thrift
sper-ma-cet-i
sper-mat-ic
sper-ma-to-zo-on
  sper-ma-to-zo-a
  sper-ma-tozo-ic

spew-er
sphag-num
sphere
  sphered
  spher-ing
  spher-ic
  sphe-ric-i-ty
  sphe-roid
  sphe-roi-dal
sphinc-ter
  sphin-ter-al
  sphin-ter-ic
sphinx
  sphinxes
  sphin-ges
spice
  spiced
  spic-ing
spi-cule
  spic-u-lar
  spic-u-late
spic-y
  spic-i-er
  spic-i-esst
  spic-i-ly
spi-der
spi-der-y
spiel
  spiel-er
spi-er
spiff-y
  spiff-i-er
  spiff-i-est
spig-ot
spike
  spiked
  spik-ing
spik-y
  spik-i-er
  spik-i-est
spill
  spilled
  spill-ing
spil-lage
spill-way
spin
  spun
  spin-ning
spin-ach
spi-nal
  spi-nal-ly
spin-dle
  spin-dled
  spin-dling
spin-dle-legs
  spin-dle-leg-ged

spin-dly
  spin-dli-er
  spin-dli-est
spine-less
spin-et
spin-na-ker
spin-ner
spin-ning wheel
spin--off
spi-nose
spi-nous
spin-ster
spin-y
  spin-i-ness
spi-ra-cle
spi-ral
  spi-raled
  spi-ral-ing
  spi-ral-ly
spire
  spired
  spir-ing
spir-it
  spir-it-ed
  spir-it-ism
  spir-ir-ist
  spir-it-less
  spir-it-les-ness
  spir-i-tous
  spir-it-u-al
    spir-it-u-al-ly
    spir-it-u-al-ism
    spir-it-u-al-ist
    spir-it-u-al-is-tic
    spir-it-u-al-i-ty
    spir-it-u-al-i-ties
    spir-it-u-al-ize
    spir-it-u-al-ized
    spir-it-u-al-iz-ing
    spir-it-u-al-i-za-tion
  spir-it-u-ous
    spir-it-u-os-i-ty
spi-ro-chete
spit
  spat
  spit-ting
  spit-ter
spite
  spit-ed
  spit-ing
spite-ful
spit-fire
spit-tle
spit-toon
splash
  splash-er

splashy
  splash-i-er
  splash-i-est
  splash-i-ly
splash-board
splash-down
splat-ter
splay-foot
  splay-feet
  splay-foot-ed
spleen
  spleen-ful
splen-did
splen-dif-er-ous
sple-net-ic
splice
  spliced
  splic-ing
  splic-er
splin-ter
  splin-tery
split
  split-ting
  split-a-ble
  split-ter
  split--lev-el
  split--sec-ond
splotch
  spotch-y
  splotch-i-er
  splotch-i-est
splurge
  splurged
  splurg-ing
splut-ter
  splut-ter-er
spoil
  spoil-ed
  spoil-ing
spoil-age
spoil-er
spoil-sport
spoke
  spoked
  spok-ing
spo-ken
spokes-man
  spokes-men
  spokes-wom-an
  spokes-wom-en
sponge
  sponged
  spong-ing
spong-er
spon-gy
  spon-gi-er

spon-gi-est
spon-gi-ness
spon-sor
 spon-sor-ship
spon-ta-ne-i-ty
 spon-ta-ne-i-ties
spon-ta-ne-ous
 spon-ta-ne-ous-ly
 spon-ta-ne-ous-ness
spook
 spook-ish
spook-y
 spook-i-er
 spook-i-est
 spook-i-ly
spoon-er-ism
 spoon-er-is-tic
spoon--fed
spoon--feed
 spoon--feed-ing
spoon-ful
 spoon-fuls
spo-rad-ic
 spo-rad-i-cal
 spo-rad-i-cal-ly
spo-ran-gi-um
 spo-ran-gia
spore
 spored
 spor-ing
sport
sport-ing
 sport-ing-ly
spor-tive
sports-cast
 sports-cast-er
sports-man
sports-wear
sports-writ-er
sport-y
 sport-i-er
 sport-i-est
 sport-i-ly
spot
 spot-ted
 spot-ting
 spot-less
 spot-less-ly
spot-light
spot-ted
spot-ted fe-ver
spot-ter
spot-ty
 spot-ti-er
 spot-ti-est
 spot-ti-ly

spouse
spout
 spout-er
sprain
sprawl
spray
 spray-er
spread
 spread-ing
spread--ea-gle
 spread--ea-gled
 spread--ea-gling
spread-er
sprig
 sprigged
 sprig-ging
spright-ly
 spright-li-er
 spright-li-est
spring
 spring-ing
 spring-board
spring--clean-ing
spring-time
spring-y
 spring-i-er
 spring-i-est
 spring-i-ly
sprin-kle
 sprin-kled
 sprin-kling
 sprink-ler
sprint
 sprint-er
sprock-et
spruce
 spruc-er
 spruc-est
 spruced
 spruc-ing
spry
 spry-er
 spry-est
 spry-ly
spue
 spued
 spu-ing
spume
 spumed
 spum-ing
 spum-ous
spunk-y
 spunk-i-er
 spunk-i-est
 spunk-i-ly
 spunk-i-ness

spur
 spurred
 spur-ring
spu-ri-ous
 spu-ri-ous-ness
spurner
spurt
 spurt-er
 spur-tive
sput-nik
sput-ter
 sput-ter-er
spu-tum
 spu-ta
spy
 spies
 spied
 spy-ing
spy-glass
squad-ron
squal-id
 squal-id-ly
 squal-id-ness
squall
 squally
 squall-i-er
 squall-i-est
squal-or
squan-der
 squan-der-er
square
 squared
 squar-ing
 square-ly
 square-ness
square-dance
 square-danced
 square-danc-ing
squar-ish
 squar-ish-ly
squash
 squash-er
 squash-es
squash-y
 squash-i-er
 squash-i-est
squat
 squat-ted
 squat-ting
 squat-ly
squat-ter
squat-ty
 squat-ti-er
 squat-ti-est
squawk
 squawk-er

sqauwk-y
squawk-i-er
squawk-i-est
squeak
squeak-er
squeak-ing-ly
squeak-y
squeak-i-er
squeak-i-est
squeal
squeal-er
squeam-ish
squeam-ish-ly
squeam-ish-ness
squee-gee
squeeze
squeez-ed
squeez-ing
squeez-er
squelch
squelch-er
squib
squid
squig-gle
squig-gled
squig-gling
squint
squint-er
squint-ing-ly
squinty
squint-i-er
squint-i-est
squint--eyed
squire
squired
squir-ing
squirm
squirmy
squirm-i-er
squirm-i-est
squir-rel
squirt
squirt-er
squish
squish-y
squish-i-er
squish-i-est
stab
stabbed
stab-bing
stab-ber
sta-bil-i-ty
sta-bil-i-ties
sta-bi-lize
sta-bi-lized
sta-bi-liz-ing

sta-bi-li-za-tion
sta-bi-liz-er
sta-ble
sta-bled
sta-bling
stac-ca-to
stack-er
sta-di-um
staff-er
stag
stagged
stag-ging
stage-coach
stage-hand
stage--struck
stag-ger
stag-ger-er
stag-ger-ing
stag-nant
stag-nan-cy
stag-nate
stag-nat-ed
stag-nat-ing
stag-na-tion
stag-y
stag-i-er
stag-i-est
stag-i-ly
stag-i-ness
stain
stain-a-ble
stained
stain-er
stained glass
stain-less
stair-case
stair-way
stair-well
stake
staked
stak-ing
stake-hold-er
sta-lac-tite
sta-lag-mite
stale
stal-er
stal-est
staled
stal-ing
stale-ness
stale-mate
stale-mat-ed
stale-mat-ing
stalk
stalled
stal-lion

stal-wart
stal-wart-ness
sta-men
sta-mens
stam-i-na
stam-mer
stam-mer-ing-ly
stam-pede
stam-ped-ed
stam-ped-ing
stam-ped-er
stam-ped-ing-ly
stamp-er
stance
stand
stand-ing
stand-er
stand-ard
stand-ard-ize
stand-ard-ized
stand-ard-iz-ing
stand-ard-i-za-tion
stand-by
stnad-ee
stand--in
stand--off-ish
stand--off-ish-ness
stand-out
stand-pipe
stand-point
stand-still
sta-nine
stan-za
stan-za-ic
sta-pes
sta-pes
sta-ped-es
sta-pe-di-al
staph-y-lo-coc-cus
sta-ple
sta-pled
sta-pling
sta-pler
star
star-board
star-dom
stare
stared
star-ing
star-er
star-fish
star-gaze
star-gazed
star-gaz-ing
star-let
star-light

star-ling
star-ry
  star-ri-er
  star-ri-est
  star-ri-ly
star-ry--eyed
star-span-gled
start-er
star-tle
  star-tled
  star-tling
  star-tling-ly
star-va-tion
starve
  starved
  starv-ing
sta-sis
state
  stat-ed
  stat-ing
  stat-a-ble
state-craft
state-hood
state-less
  state-less-ness
state-ly
  state-li-er
  state-li-est
state-ment
state-room
state-side
states-man
  states-men
  states-man-like
  states-man-ship
stat-ic
stat-ics
sta-tion
sta-tion-ar-y
ssta-tion-er
sta-tion-er-y
stat-ism
  stat-ist
sta-tic-tic
  sta-tis-ti-cal
  sta-tic-ti-cal-ly
stat-is-ti-cian
sta-tis-tics
sta-tor
stat-u-ar-y
  stat-u-ar-ies
stat-ue
stat-u-esque
stat-u-ette
stat-ure
sta-tus

stat-ute
staunch
stave
  staved
  stav-ing
stay
  stay-ed
  stay-ing
  stay-er
stead-fast
  stead-fast-ly
stead-y
steal
  stol-en
  steal-ing
  steal-er
stealth
  stealth-y
  stealth-i-er
  stealth-i-est
steam-boat
steam-er
steam-fit-ter
  steam-fit-ting
steam-roll-er
steam-ship
steam-y
  steam-i-er
  steam-i-est
  steam-i-ly
ste-a-tite
sted-fast
steel-head
steel-works
  steel-work-er
steel-y
  steel-i-er
steel-yard
steep
  steep-ly
  steep-en
stee-ple
stee-ple-chase
  stee-ple-chas-er
stee-ple-jack
steer
  steer-a-ble
  steer-er
steer-age
stein
stel-lar
stem
  stemmed
stem-ware
stem-wind-er
  stem-wind-ing

stench
  stench-y
  stench-i-er
  stench-i-est
sten-cil
  sten-ciled
  sten-cil-ing
ste-nog-ra-pher
ste-nog-ra-phy
  sten-o-graph-ic
  sten-o-raph-i-cal-ly
sten-to-ri-an
step
  stepped
  step-ping
step-broth-er
step-child
  step-child-ren
step-daugh-ter
step-fa-ther
step-lad-der
step-moth-er
step-par-ent
stepped-up
step-sis-ter
step-son
ster-e-o
  ster-e-os
  ster-e-o-phon-ic
  ster-e-o-phon-i-cal-ly
  ster-e-o-scope
  ster-e-o-scop-ic
  ster-e-o-type
  ster-e-o-typed
  ster-e-o-typ-ing
ster-ile
  ste-ril-i-ty
ster-i-lize
  ster-i-lized
  ster-i-liz-ing
  ster-i-li-za-tion
  ster-i-li-zer
ster-ling
stern
  stern-ly
  stern-ness
ster-num
  ster-na
  ster-nums
stern-wheel-er
ster-oid
steth-o-scope
  steth-o-scop-ic
ste-ve-dore
  ste-ve-dored
  ste-ve-dor-ing

196

ste-ward
stew-ard-ness
stick-er
stick-ing
stick-le-back
stick-ler
stick-pin
stick-up
stick-y
  stick-i-er
  stick-i-est
stiff
  stiff-ly
  stiff-ness
stiff-en
  stiff-en-er
stiff--necked
sti-fle
  sti-fled
  sti-fling
  sti-fler
  sti-fling-ly
stig-ma
  stig-mas
  stig-ma-ta
  stig-ma-tic
  stig-mat-i-cal-ly
stig-ma-tize
  stig-ma-tized
  stig-ma-tiz-ing
  stig-ma-ti-za-tion
sti-let-to
  sti-let-tos
  sti-let-toes
still-birth
  still-born
still life
still-ness
stilt-ed
  stilt-ed-ly
stim-u-lant
stim-u-late
  stim-u-lat-ed
  stim-u-lat-ing
  stim-u-la-tion
  stim-u-la-tive
stim-u-lus
  stim-u-li
sting
  sting-ing
  sting-er
  sting-ing-ly
stin-gy
  stin-gi-er
  stin-gi-est
  stin-gi-ly

  stin-gi-ness
stink
  stink-ing
  stink-er
  stink-y
  stink-i-er
  stink-i-est
stint-er
sti-pend
stip-ple
  stip-pled
  stip-pling
stip-u-late
  stip-u-lat-ed
  stip-u-lat-ing
  stip-u-la-tion
  stip-u-la-to-ry
stir
  stirred
  stir-ring
  stri-ring-ly
stir-rup
stitch
  stitch-er
stock-ade
  stock-ad-ed
  stock-ad-ing
stock-brok-er
stock-hold-er
Stock-holm
stock-ing
stock-pile
  stock-piled
  stock-pil-ing
stock-y
  stock-i-er
  stock-i-est
  stock-i-ly
  stock-i-ness
stock-yard
stodg-y
  stodg-i-er
  stodg-i-est
  stodg-i-ly
sto-ic
sto-i-cal
stoke
  stoked
  stok-ing
  stok-er
stol-id
  sto-lid-i-ty
  stol-id-ly
sto-ma
  sto-ma-ta
  sto-mas

stom-ach
stom-ach-er
stone
  stoned
  ston-ing
stone-deaf
stone-ma-son
  stone-ma-son-ry
stone-wall
ston-y
  ston-i-er
  ston-i-est
  ston-i-ly
stop
  stopped
  stop-ping
stop-gap
stop-light
stop-o-ver
stop-page
stop-per
stop-watch
stor-age
store
  stored
  stor-ing
store-house
store-keep-er
store-room
sto-ried
storm-y
  storm-i-er
  storm-i-est
  storm-i-ly
  storm-i-ness
sto-ry
  sto-ries
  sto-ry-ing
sto-ry-book
sto-ry-tell-er
  stor-y-tell-ing
stout
  stout-ly
  stout-ness
stout--heart-ed
stove
  stoved
  stov-ing
stove-pipe
stow-age
stow-a-way
stra-bis-mus
strad-dle
  strad-dled
  strad-dling
  strad-dler

strafe
  strafed
  straf-ing
strag-gle
  strag-gled
  strag-gling
  strag-gler
strag-gly
  strag-gli-er
  strag-gli-est
straight-en
  straight-en-er
straight-for-ward
  straight-for-ward-ly
straight-way
strain-er
strait-en
strait-jack-et
strait-laced
strange
  strang-er
  strang-est
  strang-ly
  strange-ness
stran-ger
stran-gle
  stran-gled
  stran-gling
  stran-gler
stran-gu-la-tion
  stm-gu-late
  stran-gu-lat-ed
  stran-gu-lat-ing
strap
  srapped
  strap-ping
  strap-less
stra-te-gic
  str-te-gi-cal-ly
strat-e-gy
  strat-e-gies
  strat-e-gist
strat-i-fi-ca-tion
strat-i-fy
  strat-i-fied
  strat-i-fy-ing
stra-to-cu-mu-lus
strat-o-sphere
  strat-o-spher-ic
stra-tum
  stra-ta
  stra-tums
stra-tus
  stra-ti
straw-ber-ry
  straw-ber-ries

stray-er
stray-ing
streak
  streaky
  streak-i-er
  streak-i-est
stream-er
stream-line
  stream-lined
  stream-lin-ing
street-car
street-walk-er
  street-walk-ing
strength-en
  strength-en-er
stren-u-ous
  stren-u-os-i-ty
  stren-u-ous-ly
strep-to-coc-cus
  strep-to-coc-ci
  strep-to-coc-cal
  strep-to-coc-cic
strep-to-my-cin
stress
  stress-ful
  stress-ful-ly
  stress-ful-ness
stretch
  stretch-a-bil-i-ty
  stretch-a-ble
stretch-er
strew
  strewed
  strew-ing
stri-a
  stri-ae
stri-ate
  stri-at-ed
  stri-at-ing
strick-en
strict
  strict-ly
  strict-ness
stric-ture
stride
  strid-den
  strid-ding
stri-dent
strid-u-la-tion
strife
  strife-ful
  strife-less
strike
  strick-en
  strick-ing
string

strung
string-ing
strin-gent
  strin-gen-cy
  strin-gent-ly
string-y
  string-i-er
  string-i-est
strip
  stripped
  strip-ping
stripe
  striped
  strip-ing
  strip-ling
  strip-per
strip-tease
  strip-teas-er
strive
  strove
  striv-en
  striv-ing
stro-bo-scope
  stro-bo-scop-ic
  stro-bo-scop-i-cal-ly
stroke
  stroked
  strok-ing
stroll-er
strong
  strong-ish
  strong-ly
strong--arm
strong-box
strong-hold
strong-mind-ed
  strong-mind-ed-ly
  strong-mind-ed-ness
stron-ti-um
  stron-tic
strop
  stropped
  strop-ping
struc-tur-al
  struc-tur-al-ly
struc-ture
  struc-tured
  struc-tur-ing
  struc-ture-less
strug-gle
  strug-gled
  strug-gling
  strug-gler
strum
  strum-mer
  strum-pet

strut
  strut-ted
  strut-ting
strych-nine
  strych-nia
  strych-nic
stub
  stubbed
  stub-bing
  stub-by
  stub-bi-er
  stub-bi-est
stub-ble
  stub-bled
  stub-bling
  stub-by
  stub-bi-er
  stub-bi-est
stub-born
  stub-born-ly
  stub-born-ness
stuc-co
  stuc-coes
  stuc-cos
  stuc-coed
  stuc-co-ing
stuck--up
stud
  stud-ded
  stud-ding
stu-dent
stud-ied
  stud-ied-ly
  stud-ied-ness
stu-di-o
  stu-di-os
stu-di-ous
  stu-di-ous-ly
  stu-di-ous-ness
stud-y
  stud-ies
  stud-ied
  stud-y-ing
stuff-er
stuff-ing
stuff-y
stul-ti-fy
  stul-ti-fied
  stul-ti-fy-ing
  stul-ti-fi-ca-tion
  stul-ti-fi-er
stum-ble
  stum-bled
  stum-bling
  stum-bler
  stum-bling-ly

stump
  stump-er
  stumpy
  stump-i-er
  stump-i-est
stun-ning
stunt
  stunt-ed
  stunt-ed-ness
stu-pe-fy
  stu-pe-fied
  stu-pe-fy-ing
  stu-pe-fac-tion
  stu-pe-fi-er
  stu-pe-fy-ing-ly
stu-pen-dous
  stu-pen-dous-ly
  stu-pen-dous-ness
stu-pid
  stu-pid-i-ty
  stu-pid-ly
  stu-pid-ness
stu-por
  stu-por-ous
stur-dy
  stur-di-er
  stur-di-est
  stur-geon
stut-ter
  stut-ter-er
  stut-ter-ing-ly
style
  styled
  styl-ing
  styl-er
styl-ish
  styl-ish-ly
  styl-ish-ness
styl-ist
  sty-lis-tic
  sty-lis-ti-cal
  sty-lis-ti-cal-ly
styl-ize
  styl-ized
  styl-iz-ing
  styl-i-za-tion
  styl-iz-er
sty-lus
  sty-lus-es
  sty-li
sty-mie
  sty-mies
  sty-mied
  sty-mie-ing
styp-tic
  styp-ti-cal

styp-tic-i-ty
suave
  suave-ly
  suave-ness
  suav-i-ty
sub
  subbed
  sub-bing
sub-al-tern
sub-arc-tic
sub-as-sem-bly
  sub-as-sem-blies
  sub-as-sem-bler
sub-base-ment
sub-chas-er
sub-class
sub-com-mit-tee
sub-con-scious
  sub-con-scious-ly
  sub-con-scious-ness
sub-con-ti-nent
  sub-con-ti-nen-tal
sub-con-tract
  sub-con-trac-tor
sub-cul-ture
  sub-cul-tur-al
sub-cu-ta-ne-ous
  sub-cu-ta-ne-ous-ly
sub-ded-u-tante
sub-di-vide
  sub-di-vid-ed
  sub-di-vid-ing
  sub-di-vid-a-ble
  sub-di-vid-er
sub-di-vi-sion
  sub-di-vi-sion-al
sub-due
  sub-dued
  sub-du-ing
  sub-du-a-ble
  sub-du-al
  sub-du-er
sub-en-try
  sub-en-tries
sub-freez-ing
sub-group
sub-head
sub-hu-man
sub-ject
  sub-jec-tion
sub-jec-tive
  sub-jec-tive-ly
  sub-jec-tive-ness
  sub-jec-tiv-i-ty
sub-join
sub-ju-gate

sub-ju-gat-ed
sub-ju-gat-ing
sub-ju-ga-tion
sub-ju-ga-tor
sub-junc-tive
sub-lease
sub-leased
sub-leas-ing
sub-let
sub-let-ting
sub-li-mate
sub-li-mat-ed
sub-li-mat-ing
sub-li-ma-tion
sub-lime
sub-lim-i-nal
sub-lim-i-nal-ly
sub-lim-i-ty
sub-lim-i-ties
sub-ma-chine gun
sub-mar-gin-al
sub-ma-rine
sub-merge
sub-merged
sub-merg-ing
sub-mer-gence
sub-mer-gi-ble
sub-merse
sub-mersed
sub-mers-ing
sub-mer-sion
sub-mers-i-ble
sub-mi-cro-scop-ic
sub-mis-sion
sub-mis-sive
sub-mis-sive-ly
sub-mis-sive-ness
sub-mit
sub-mit-ted
sub-mit-ting
sub-nor-mal
sub-nor-mal-i-ty
sub-or-di-nate
sub-or-di-nat-ed
sub-or-di-nat-ing
sub-or-di-nate-ly
sub-or-di-nate-ness
sub-or-di-na-tion
sub-or-di-na-tive
sub-orn
sub-or-na-tion
sub-orn-er
sub-poe-na
sub-poe-naed
sub-poe-na-ing
sub-scribe

sub-scribed
sub-scrib-ing
sub-scrib-er
sub-scrip-tion
sub-se-quent
sub-se-quence
sub-se-quent-ly
sub-ser-vi-ent
sub-ser-vi-ence
sub-ser-vi-en-cy
sub-side
sub-sid-ed
sub-sid-ing
sub-sid-ence
sub-sid-i-ar-y
sub-sid-i-ar-ies
sub-si-dize
sub-si-dized
sub-si-diz-ing
sub-si-dy
sub-si-dies
sub-sist
sub-sist-ence
sub-soil
sub-son-ic
sub-stance
sub-stand-ard
sub-stan-tial
sub-stan-ti-al-i-ty
sub-stan-tial-ly
sub-stan-ti-ate
sub-stan-ti-at-ed
sub-stan-ti-at-ing
sub-stan-tive
sub-stan-ti-val
sub-stan-ti-val-ly
sub-stan-tive-ly
sub-sti-tute
sub-sti-tut-ed
sub-sti-tut-ing
sub-sti-tu-tion
sub-stra-tum
sub-stra-ta
sub-stra-tums
sub-struc-ture
sub-sume
sub-sumed
sub-sum-ing
sub-sum-a-ble
sub-sump-tive
sub-sump-tion
sub-teen
sub-tend
sub-ter-fuge
sub-ter-ra-ne-an
sub-ter-ra-ne-ous

sub-ter-ra-ne-an-ly
sub-ter-ra-ne-ous-ly
sub-ti-tle
sub-tle
sub-tle-ness
sub-tle-ty
sub-tle-ties
sub-tly
sub-tract
sub-tract-er
sub-trac-tion
sub-trac-tive
sub-tra-hend
sub-trop-i-cal
sub-trop-ic
sub-trop-ics
sub-urb
sub-ur-ban
sub-ur-ban-ite
sub-ur-bia
sub-ver-sion
sub-ver-sion-ary
sub-ver-sive
sub-ver-sive-ly
sub-ver-sive-ness
sub-vert
sub-vert-er
sub-way
suc-ceed
suc-ceed-er
suc-cess
suc-cess-ful-ly
suc-cess-ful-ness
suc-ces-sion
suc-ces-sion-al
suc-ces-sion-al-ly
suc-ces-sive
suc-ces-sive-ly
suc-ces-sive-ness
suc-ces-sor
suc-cinct
suc-cinct-ly
suc-cinct-ness
suc-cor
suc-cor-er
suc-co-tash
suc-co-bus
suc-cu-bi
suc-cu-lent
suc-cu-lence
suc-cu-len-cy
suc-cu-lent-ly
suc-cumb
suck-er
suck-le
suck-led

suck-ling
su-crose
suc-tion
sud-den-ly
  sud-den-less
suds-y
  suds-i-er
  suds-i-est
sue
  sued
  su-ing
  su-er
suede
su-et
  su-ety
suf-fer
  suf-fer-a-ble
  suf-fer-a-bly
  suf-fer-ing
suf-fer-ance
suf-fice
  suf-ficed
  suf-fic-ing
  suf-fic-er
suf-fi-cien-cy
  suf-fi-cien-cies
suf-fi-cient
  suf-fi-cient-ly
suf-fix
suf-fo-cate
  suf-fo-cat-ed
  suf-fo-cat-ing
suf-frage
suf-fra-gette
suf-fuse
  suf-fused
  suf-fus-ing
sug-ar
  sug-ary
  sug-ar-i-er
  sug-ar-i-est
sug-ar-coat
sug-gest
  sug-gest-er
  sug-gest-i-ble
sug-ges-tion
sug-ges-tive
  sug-ges-tive-ly
  sug-ges-tive-ness
su-i-cide
  su-i-cid-ed
  su-i-cid-ing
  su-i-cid-al
suit-a-ble
  suit-a-bil-i-ty
suit-case

suite
suit-ing
suit-or
sul-fa
sul-fa-nil-a-mide
sul-fate
sul-fide
sul-fur
sul-fu-ric
sul-fur-ous
  sul-fur-ous-ly
sulk-y
sul-ly
  sul-lied
  sul-ly-ing
sul-tan
  sul-tan-ic
sul-tan-a
  sul-tan-ess
  sul-tan-ate
sul-try
  sul-tri-er
  sul-tri-est
sum
su-mac
sum-ma-rize
  sum-ma-rized
  sum-ma-riz-ing
  sum-ma-ri-za-tion
sum-ma-ry
  sum-ma-ries
  sum-mar-i-ly
sum-ma-tion
  sum-ma-tion-al
sum-mer
  sum-mery
  sum-mer-house
sum-mit
sum-mon
  sum-mon-er
sum-mons
  sum-mons-es
sump-tu-ar-y
sump-tu-ous
  sump-tu-ous-ly
sun
  sunned
  sun-ning
sun-bathe
sun-beam
sun-bon-net
sun-burn
  sun-burned
  sun-burnt
sun-dae
sun-der

sun-der-ance
sun-di-al
sun-down
sun-dries
sun-dry
sun-dries
sun-fish
sun-flow-er
sun-glass-es
sunk-en
sun-light
sun-lit
sun-ny
sun-rise
sun-set
sun-shine
  sun-shiny
sun-spot
sun-stroke
sun-up
sup
  supped
su-per
su-per-a-bun-dant
  su-per-a-bun-dance
su-per-an-nu-ate
su-perb
  su-perb-ly
su-per-car-go
  su-per-car-goes
su-per-charge
  su-per-charg-er
su-per-cil-i-ous
  su-per-cil-i-ous-ly
su-per-e-go
su-per-e-rog-a-to-ry
su-per-fi-cial
  su-per-fi-ci-al-i-ty
  su-per-fi-ci-al-i-ties
su-per-high-way
su-per-hu-man
  su-per-hu-man-i-ty
  su-per-hu-man-ly
su-per-im-pose
  su-per-im-posed
  su-per-im-pos-ing
su-per-in-tend
  su-per-in-tend-en-cy
  su-per-in-tend-ent
su-pe-ri-or
  su-pe-ri-or-i-ty
  su-pe-ri-or-ly
su-per-la-tive
  su-per-la-tive-ly
su-per-man
su-per-mar-ket

su-per-nal
su-per-nal-ly
su-per-nat-u-ral
su-per-nu-mer-ar-y
su-per-nu-mer-ar-ies
su-per-pow-er
su-per-scribe
su-per-scib-ing
su-per-scrip-tion
su-per-script
su-per-sede
su-per-sed-ed
su-per-sed-ing
su-per-son-ic
su-per-son-i-cal-ly
su-per-star
su-per-sti-tion
su-per-sti-tious
su-per-sti-tious-ly
su-per-struc-ture
su-per-vene
su-per-vened
su-per-ven-ing
su-per-ven-tion
su-per-vise
su-per-vised
su-per-vis-ing
su-per-vi-sion
su-pine
su-pine-ly
sup-per
sup-plant
sup-plan-ta-tion
sup-plant-er
sup-ple
sup-pler
sup-plest
sup-ple-ment
sup-ple-men-tal
sup-pli-ant
sup-pli-ant-ly
sup-pli-cant
sup-ply
sup-port
sup-port-a-ble
sup-port-er
sup-por-tive
sup-pose
sup-po-si-tion
sup-po-si-tion-al
sup-pos-i-to-ry
sup-press
sup-pres-sion
sup-pres-sor
sup-pu-rate
sup-pu-rat-ed

sup-pu-ra-tion
sup-pu-ra-tive
su-pra-re-nal gland
su-prem-a-cy
su-prem-a-cies
su-prem-a-cist
su-preme
su-preme-ly
sur-cease
sur-charge
sur-charged
sur-charg-ing
sur-cin-gle
sure
sur-er
sur-est
sure-ly
sure--fire
sure--foot-ed
sure--foot-ed-ly
sure-ty
sure-ties
sure-ty-ship
surf
surfy
surf-i-er
sur-face
sur-faced
sur-fac-ing
surf-board
surf-board-er
sur-feit
sur-feit-er
surge
surged
surg-ing
sur-geon
sur-ger-y
sur-ger-ies
sur-gi-cal
sur-ly
sur-mise
sur-mised
sur-mis-ing
sur-mount
sur-mount-a-ble
sur-name
sur-pass
sur-pass-a-ble
sur-pass-ing
sur-plice
sur-plus
sur-plus-age
sur-prise
sur-prised
sur-pris-ing

sur-re-al-ism
sur-re-al-ist
sur-re-al-is-tic
sur-ren-der
sur-rep-ti-tious
sur-rep-ti-tious-ly
sur-rey
sur-reys
sur-ro-gate
sur-ro-gat-ed
sur-ro-gat-ing
sur-round
sur-round-er
sur-round-ing
sur-tax
sur-veil-lance
sur-veil-lant
sur-vey
sur-vey-ing
sur-vey-or
sur-viv-al
sur-vive
sur-vived
sur-viv-ing
sur-vi-vor
sus-cep-ti-ble
sus-cep-ti-bil-i-ty
sus-cep-ti-bly
sus-pect
sus-pend
sus-pend-er
sus-pense
sus-pense-ful
sus-pen-sion
sus-pi-cious
sus-pi-cious-ly
sus-tain
sus-tain-a-ble
sus-tain-er
sus-tain-ment
sus-te-nance
su-ture
su-ze-rain
su-ze-rain-ly
svelte
svelte-ly
swab
swabbed
swab-bing
swab-ber
swad-dle
swad-dled
swad-dling
swag-ger
swag-ger-er
swag-ger-ing

swain
  swain-ish
swal-low
  swal-low-er
swal-low-tail
swa-mi
  swa-mis
swamp
  swampy
swank
  swank-i-ly
swan's--down
swap
  swapped
  swap-ping
sward
swarth-y
  swarth-i-er
  swarth-i-est
swas-ti-ka
swat
swathe
  swathed
  swath-ing
swat
  sway-a-ble
  sway-er
sway-back
  sway-backed
swear
  swore
  swear-ing
  swear-er
swear-word
sweat
  sweat-er
  sweat-shop
sweep
  swept
  sweep-ing
  sweep-er
sweep-stakes
sweet
  sweet-ish
  sweet-ly
sweet-bread
  sweet-bri-er
sweet-en
  sweet-en-er
  sweet-en-ing
sweet-heart
sweet-meat
sweet-talk
swell
  swelled
  swoll-en

swell-ing
swell-head
swel-ter
  swel-ter-ing
swerve
  swerved
  swerv-ing
swift
  swift-ly
swim-ming
  swim-ming-ly
swin-dle
  swin-dled
  swin-dling
  swin-dler
swipe
  swiped
  swip-ing
swirl
swish
  swish-er
switch
  switch-er
switch-blade
switch-board
switch--hit-ter
swiv-el
  swiv-eled
  swiv-el-ing
swiz-zle
swoon
  swoon-er
  swoon-ing-ly
swoop-er
swop
  swopped
  swop-ping
sword
sword-fish
sword-play
  sword-play-er
swords-man
  swords-man
  swords-man-ship
syc-a-more
syc-o-phant
  syc-o-phan-cy
  syc-o-phan-tic
syl-lab-ic
syl-lab-i-cate
  syl-lab-i-cat-ed
  syl-lab-i-cat-ing
  syl-lab-i-ca-tion
syl-la-ble
  syl-la-bled
  syl-la-bling

syl-la-bus
  syl-la-bus-es
  syl-la-bi
syl-lo-gism
  sul-lo-gis-tic
sylph-like
syl-van
sym-bi-o-sis
  sym-bi-ot-ic
  sym-bi-ot-i-cal-ly
sym-bol
  sym-bol-ic
  sym-bol-i-cal
  sym-bol-ism
  sym-bol-ist
sym-bol-ize
  sym-bol-ized
  sym-bol-iz-ing
  sym-bol-i-za-tion
  sym-bol-iz-er
sym-me-try
  sym-me-tries
sym-pa-thize
  sym-pa-thized
  sym-pa-thiz-ing
  sym-pa-thiz-er
sym-pa-thy
  sym-pa-thies
sym-pho-ny
  sym-pho-nies
  sym-phon-ic
sym-po-si-um
  sym-po-sia
  sym-po-si-ums
symp-tom
symp-to-mat-ic
  symp-to-mat-i-cal
  symp-to-mat-i-cal-ly
syn-a-gogue
  syn-gog-al
  syn-gog-i-cal
syn-apse
sync
  synced
  sync-ing
syn-chro-nism
  syn-chro-nis-tic
  syn-chro-nis-ti-cal
  syn-chro-nis-ti-cal-ly
syn-chro-nize
  syn-chro-nized
  syn-chro-niz-ing
  syn-chro-ni-za-tion
syn-chro-nous
  syn-chro-nous-ly
syn-co-pate

T

syn-co-pat-ed
syn-co-pat-ing
syn-co-pa-tion
syn-co-pa-tor
syn-di-cate
syn-di-cat-ed
syn-di-cat-ing
syn-drome
syn-drom-ic
syn-od
syn-od-al
syn-o-nym
syn-no-nym-ic
syn-no-nym-i-cal
syn-no-nym-i-ty
syn-on-y-mous
syn-on-y-mous-ly
syn-on-y-my
syn-on-y-mies
syn-op-sis
syn-op-ses
syn-op-ti-cal
syn-tac-tic
syn-tac-ti-cal
syn-tac-ti-cal-ly
syn-tax
syn-the-sis
syn-the-ses
syn-the-sist
syn-the-size
syn-the-sized
syn-the-siz-ing
syn-the-ic
syn-thet-i-cal
syn-thet-i-cal-ly
syph-i-lis
syph-i-lit-ic
sy-ringe
sy-ringed
sy-ring-ing
syr-up
syr-upy
syr-up-i-er
syr-up-i-est
sys-tem
sys-tem-at-ic
sys-tem-at-i-cal
sys-tem-a-tize
sys-tem-a-tized
sys-tem-a-tiz-ing
sys-tem-a-ti-za-tion
sys-tem-a-tiz-er
sys-tem-ic
sys-tem-i-cal-ly
sys-to-le
sys-tol-ic

tap
tab-er-na-cle
ta-ble
ta-ble-spoon
tab-leau
tab-let
tab-loid
ta-boo
tab-u-lar
tab-u-lar-ly
ta-chom-e-ter
tac-it
tac-it-ly
tack
tack-er
tack claw
tacki-ness
tack-le
ta-co
tact
tact-ful
tact-less
tac-tic
tac-tic-al
tac-tic-ian
tad
tad-pole
taf-fe-ta
taf-fet-ized
taff-rail
tag
tag-ger
tail
tail-gate
tai-lor
taint
take
talc
tale
tal-ent
tal-ent-ed
tal-ent scout
talk
talk-er
talk-a-tive
tall
tall-ish
tal-low
tal-low
tal-ly
tal-on
tal-on-ed
tam-bou-rine
tame
tame-ly
tam-per

tan
tan-dem
tang
tangy
tan-gent
tan-gen-cy
tan-gen-tial
tan-ger-ine
tan-gi-ble
tan-gi-bil-ity
tan-gle
tanglement
tan-go
tank
tank-ful
tan-kard
tan-ta-lize
tan-ta-lizer
tan-ta-liz-ingly
tan-ta-lum
tan-trum
tap
tape
ta-per
tap-es-try
tap-i-o-ca
taps
tar-dy
tar-di-ness
tar-get
tar-iff
tar-nish
tar-nish-able
tar-ot
tar-pau-lin
tar-ry
tart
tart-ly
tart-ness
tar-tan
tar-tar
tar-tar-ic
task
tas-sel
taste
taste-ful
taste-less
tat-ter
tat-tle
tat-tler
tattle-tale
tat-too
tat-too
tat-too-er
taught
taut

taut-ly
taut-ness
tau-tol-o-gy
tav-ern
tav-ern-er
tax
tax-able
tax-a-tion
tax-ex-empt
tax shel-ter
tax-i
taxi-cab
tax-i-der-my
tax-i-derm-ist
tea
teach
teach-ing
teach-able
teach-er
team
team-ster
tear
teary
tease
teaser
tech-ne-tium
tech-ni-cal
tech-ni-cal-ly
tech-nique
tech-nol-o-gy
te-dious
te-dious-ly
tee
teem
teens
teeth
tele-cast
tele-graph
tele-graph-er
tele-graph-ic
te-lep-a-thy
te-lep-a-thic
te-lep-a-thist
tele-phone
tele-phoner
tele-pho-to
tele-pho-to-graph
tele-scope
tele-scopic
tele-thon
tele-vi-sion
tel-ex
tell
tell-able
tell-ing
tell-er

tel-lu-ri-um
tem-per
tem-per-able
tem-per-a-ment
tem-per-a-ment-al
tem-per-ance
tem-per-ate
tem-per-ate-ly
tem-per-a-ture
tem-pest
tem-ple
tem-po
tem-po-rary
tempt
tempt-er
ten
te-na-cious
te-na-cious-ly
ten-ant
tend
ten-den-cy
ten-der
ten-der-ly
ten-der-ness
ten-der-loin
ten-don
ten-dril
ten-dril-ed
ten-nis
ten-or
tense
ten-sion
ten-sion-al
tent
ten-ta-cle
ten-ta-tive
ten-ta-tive-ly
ten-ure
te-pee
tep-id
tep-id-ly
ter-bi-um
ter-cen-ten-a-ry
term
ter-mi-nal
ter-mi-nate
ter-mi-nation
ter-mite
ter-race
ter-rain
ter-ra-pin
ter-res-tri-al
ter-ri-ble
ter-ri-bly
ter-ri-er
ter-rif-ic

ter-rif-ical-ly
ter-ri-fy
ter-ri-fied
ter-ri-fying
ter-ri-to-ry
ter-ri-to-rial
ter-ri-to-rial-ly
ter-ror
ter-ror-ism
terse
test
test-er
tes-ta-ment
tes-ta-ment-ary
tes-tate
tes-ti-fy
tes-ti-fier
tes-ti-mo-ni-al
tes-ti-mo-ny
tes-tis
test tube
test-tube baby
tet-a-nus
teth-er
text
text-book
tex-tile
tex-ture
tex-tural
tex-tural-ly
thal-li-um
than
thank
thank-ful
thank-ful-ly
thank-ful-ness
thank-less
thanks
that
thatch
thaw
the
the-atre
the-at-ri-cal
the-at-ri-cals
theft
their
the-ism
them
theme
the-matic
them-selves
then
thence
thence-forth
thence-for-ward

the-oc-ra-cy
the-oc-rat
the-ol-o-gy
the-ol-o-gian
the-o-rize
the-o-re-ti-cian
the-o-ri-za-tion
the-o-rist
the-o-ry
ther-a-peu-tics
ther-a-peu-tist
ther-a-py
ther-a-pist
there
there-abouts
there-after
there-by
there-fore
there-from
there-in
ther-mal
ther-mom-e-ter
ther-mom-e-tric
ther-mo-plas-tic
ther-mo-stat
ther-mo-stat-ic
the-sau-rus
these
the-sis
they
they'd
they'll
they're
they've
thick
thick-ly
thick-ness
thick-en
thief
thieve
thigh
thim-ble
thim-ble-ful
thin
thin-ly
thin-ness
thing
think
think-able
think-er
third
thirst
thirst-y
thir-teen
this
this-tle

thith-er
thong
tho-rax
tho-racic
tho-ri-um
thorn
thorn-y
thor-ough
thor-ough-ness
thor-ough-ly
thor-ough-bred
thor-ough-fare
those
though
thought
thought-ful
thought-less
thou-sand
thrash
thrash-er
thread
thread-y
thread-bare
threat
threat-en
three
thresh
thresh-old
threw
thrice
thrift
thrift-i-ly
thrift-i-ness
thrift-y
thrill
thrill-ing
thrill-ing-ly
thrive
throat
throb
throm-bo-sis
throng
throt-tle
through
through-out
throw
thru
thrush
thrust
thru-way
thud
thug
thug-gish
thumb
thump
thun-der

thun-der-bolt
thun-der-cloud
thun-der-show-er
thus
thwack
thwart
thy
thyme
thy-roid
thy-rox-ine
ti-ara
tick
tick-et
tick-le
tick-ler
tidal wave
tid-bit
tide
tid-ings
ti-dy
ti-di-ly
ti-di-ness
tie
tier
tier-ed
ti-ger
tiger-eye
tight
tight-en
tight-en-er
tight-rope
tights
tile
till
till-er
tilt
tim-ber
time
time--shar-ing
time tri-al
tim-id
tin
tinc-ture
tin-der
tin-der-box
tine
tinge
tin-gle
tin-gly
tink-er
tin-kle
tin-ny
tin-sel
tint
ti-ny
tip

tip-ple
tip-sy
  tip-si-ness
ti-rade
tire
tire-less
  tire-less-ly
tis-sue
ti-ta-ni-um
tithe
  tither
tit-il-late
  tit-il-lat-ing
  tit-il-la-tive
  tit-il-lat-ing-ly
  tit-il-lat-ion
ti-tle
to
toad
  toad-stool
toast
  toast-y
toast-er
to-bac-co
to-bog-gan
  to-bog-gan-ist
to-day
tod-dle
  tod-dler
tod-dy
toe
tof-fee
to-geth-er
  to-geth-er-ness
toil
  toil-some
toi-let
toi-lette
to-ken
tol-er-ate
  tol-er-a-tion
  tol-er-ance
  tol-er-ant
toll
tom-a-hawk
to-ma-to
tomb
tom-boy
  tom-boy-ish
tomb-stone
tom-cat
to-mor-row
ton
tone
tongs
tongue

ton-ic
to-night
ton-sil
ton-sil-lec-to-my
too
tool
tooth
  tooth-ed
  tooth-less
top
to-paz
top-coat
top-ic
top-most
to-pog-ra-phy
top-ple
top-sy--tur-vy
torch
tor-ment
  tor-ment-ing-ly
  tor-ment-or
tor-na-do
tor-pe-do
tor-pid
  tor-pid-ity
  tor-pid-ly
tor-rent
  tor-rent-ial
tor-rid
  tor-rid-ly
tor-sion
  tor-sion-al
tor-so
tort
tor-toise
tor-tu-ous
  tor-tu-ous-ness
toss
tot
to-tal
  to-tal-ly
to-tal-i-tar-i-an
  to-tal-i-tar-i-an
tote
to-tem
tot-ter
tou-can
touch
  touch-able
tough
  tough-ly
  tough-ness
tou-pee
tour
  tour-ism
  tour-ist

tour-na-ment
tour-ni-quet
tou-sle
tout
  tout-er
tow
to-ward
tow-el
tow-er
  tow-er-ing
town
town-ship
tox-e-mi-a
tox-ic
tox-in
toy
trace
  trace-able
  trace-ably
  trac-er
track
  track-able
  track-er
tract
trac-tion
trac-tor
trade
  trade-able
  trade-mark
  trade--off
tra-di-tion
  tra-di-tion-al
  tra-di-tion-al-ly
tra-duce
  tra-duce-ment
  tra-ducer
traf-fic
trag-e-dy
trail
  trail-er
train
  train-able
  train-er
  train-ing
trait
trai-tor
tra-jec-to-ry
tram-mel
  tram-mel-er
tramp
tram-ple
  tram-pler
tram-po-line
  tram-po-lin-ist
trance
tran-quil

207

tran-quil-lity
tran-quil-ly
tran-quil-ize
trans-act
trans-action
trans-actor
tran-scend
tran-scend-ent
tran-scend-ence
tran-scribe
tran-script
tran-scrip-tion
trans-fer
trans-fer-able
trans-fer-ence
trans-fer-er
trans-fig-ure
trans-fig-ura-tion
trans-fix
trans-fix-ion
trans-form
trans-for-mable
trans-for-ma-tion
trans-for-mer
trans-fuse
trans-fus-ion
trans-fus-er
trans-gress
trans-gress-ion
trans-gress-or
trans-gres-sive
tran-sient
tran-sient-ly
tran-sit
trans-late
trans-la-tion
tran-sla-tor
trans-lu-cent
trans-mis-sion
trans-mit
trans-miss-ible,
trans-mitt-able
trans-mitt-er
trans-mute
trans-mu-ta-tion
tran-som
trans-par-ent
trans-par-ency
trans-par-ent-ly
tran-spire
trans-plant
trans-plant-able
trans-port
trans-port-able
trans-por-ta-tion
trans-port-er

trans-pose
trans-sex-u-al
trap
tra-peze
trap-shoot-ing
trau-ma
tra-vail
trav-el
trav-el-er
tra-verse
tra-vers-able
tra-ver-sal
tra-ver-ser
trawl
tray
treach-er-ous
treach-er-ous-ly
treach-ery
tread
trea-son
trea-son-able
trea-son-ous
treas-ure
treas-ur-er
treas-ur-y
treat
treat-able
treat-er
treat-ment
treb-le
tree
tree-less
tre-foil
trek
trel-lis
trem-ble
trem-bler
trem-bly
tre-men-dous
trem-or
trench
trench-er
trend
trend-set-ter
tres-pass
tres-tle
tri-al
tri-an-gle
tri-an-gu-lar-i-ty
tribe
trib-u-la-tion
trib-un-al
trib-ute
tri-ceps
trick
trick-y

trick-er-y
trick-le
tri-col-or
tri-col-or-ed
tri-cy-cle
tri-dent
tried
tri-en-ni-al
tri-en-ni-al-ly
tri-fle
trig-ger
trill
tril-lion
trim
tri-ni-tro-tol-u-ene
trin-ket
tri-o
trip
tripe
trip-le
trip-let
trip-li-cate
tri-pod
trite
tri-umph
tri-umph-ant
tri-umph-ant-ly
triv-i-al
Tro-jan
troll
trol-ley
trom-bone
troop
troop-er
tro-phy
trop-ic
trop-i-cal
trop-i-cal-ly
tro-pism
tro-po-sphere
trot
troth
trou-ble
trou-bler
trou-bling-ly
trough
trounce
troupe
trou-sers
trous-seau
trout
trow-el
trow-el-er
tru-ant
truce
truck

truck-er
trudge
true
  true-ness
trump
trum-pet
trunk
truss
trust
  trust-er
  trust-less
truth
  truth-ful
  truth-ful-ly
  truth-ful-ness
try
  try-ing
tryst
tsu-na-mi
tub
tu-ba
tube
tu-ber
tu-ber-cu-lo-sis
tuck
tuft
tug
tu-i-tion
tu-lip
tum-ble
  tum-bler
tum-ble-down
tum-brel
tu-mor
tu-mult
tu-mul-tu-ous
tu-na
tun-dra
tune
tune-ful
tung-sten
tu-nic
tun-nel
tur-ban
tur-bine
tur-bu-lent
  tur-bu-lent-ly
tu-reen
turf
tur-key
tur-moil
turn
  turn-er
turn-buck-le
turn-down
tur-nip

turn-key
turn-off
turn-over
tur-pen-tine
tur-quoise
tur-ret
tur-tle
tur-tle-neck
tusk
tus-sle
tu-tor
tut-ti--frut-ti
tu-tu
tux-e-do
twain
twang
tweak
tweed
twee-zers
twelve
twen-ty
twice
twid-dle
twig
twi-light
twill
twin
twine
twinge
  twing-ed
twin-kle
twirl
twist
  twist-er
twit
twitch
twit-ter
  twit-ter-y
two-fold
two--time
ty-coon
tyke
type
type-face
type-set-ter
type-writ-er
ty-phoid
ty-phoon
typ-i-cal
  typ-i-cal-ly
typ-i-fy
  typ-i-fy-ing
typ-ist
ty-po
ty-ran-no-sau-rus
tyr-an-ny

U

ubiq-ui-tous
  ubiq-ui-tary
  ubiq-ui-tous-ly
  ubiq-ui-ty
ud-der
ug-ly
  ug-li-er
  ug-li-est
ukase
uku-le-le
ul-cer
  ul-cer-ous
ul-cer-ate
  ul-cer-at-ed
  ul-cer-at-ing
  ul-cer-at-ion
ul-na
  ul-nae
ul-ster
ul-te-ri-or
  ul-te-ri-or-ly
ul-ti-mate
  ul-ti-mate-ly
ul-ti-ma-tum
  ul-ti-ma-tums
  ul-ti-ma-ta
ul-tra
ul-tra-con-serv-a-tive
ul-tra-high
ul-tra-ma-rine
ul-tra-son-ic
ul-tra-vi-o-let
ul-u-late
  ul-u-lat-ed
  ul-u-lat-ing
um-bel
  um-bel-lar
  um-bel-late
  um-bel-lat-ed
um-ber
um-bil-i-cal
um-bra
  um-bras
  um-brae
um-brage
  um-bra-geous
um-brel-la
umi-ak
um-laut
um-pire
  um-pired
  um-pir-ing
ump-teen
  ump-teenth
un-a-bashed
  un-a-bash-ed-ly

un-a-ble
un-a-bridged
un-ac-cep-t-able
un-ac-cept-ed
un-ac-com-pa-nied
un-ac-count-able
un-ac-count-a-bly
un-ac-cus-tomed
un-ac-quaint-ed
un-a-dorned
un-a-dul-ter-at-ed
. un-a-dul-ter-at-ed-ly
un-ad-vised
un-ad-vis-ed-ly
un-af-fect-ed
un-af-fect-ed-ly
un-a-fraid
un--Amer-i-can
unan-i-mous
una-nim-i-ty
unan-i-mous-ly
un-an-swer-able
un-an-swered
un-ap-pe-tiz-ing
un-ap-pre-ci-at-ed
un-ap-pre-ci-a-tive
un-ap-proach-able
un-ap-proach-ably
un-ap-proached
un-armed
un-a-shamed
un-asked
un-a-spir-ing
un-as-sail-able
un-as-sail-ably
un-as-sailed
un-at-tached
un-at-tain-able
un-at-tained
un-at-tend-ed
un-au-thor-ized
un-a-vail-a-ble
un-a-vail-a-bil-i-ty
un-a-vail-a-bly
un-a-void-a-ble
un-a-void-a-bil-i-ty
un-a-void-ably
un-a-ware
un-a-ware-ness
un-a-wares
un-backed
un-bal-anced
un-bar
un-barred
un-bar-ring
un-bear-able

un-bear-ably
un-beat-en
un-beat-able
un-be-com-ing
un-be-com-ing-ly
un-be-lief
un-be-liev-able
un-be-liev-ably
un-be-liev-er
un-be-liev-ing
un-be-liev-ing-ly
un-bend
un-bend-ed
un-bend-ing
un-bi-ased
un-bi-ased-ly
un-bid-den
un-bind
un-bound
un-bind-ing
un-blem-ished
un-bolt
un-bolt-ed
un-born
un-bos-om
un-bound
un-bound-ed-ly
un-bowed
un-bread-able
un-bri-dle
un-bri-dled
un-bri-dling
un-bro-ken
un-bro-ken-ly
un-buck-le
un-buck-led
un-buck-ling
un-bur-den
un-but-ton
un-but-toned
un--called--for
un-can-ny
un-can-ni-er
un-can-ni-est
un-can-ni-ly
un-cap
un-capped
un-cap-ping
un-ceas-ing
un-ceas-ing-ly
un-cer-e-mo-ni-ous
un-cer-e-mo-ni-ous-ly
un-cer-tain
un-cer-tain-ly
un-cer-tain-ty
un-cer-tain-ties

un-chal-lenged
un-change-able
un-change-ably
un-changed
un-chang-ing
un-char-i-ta-ble
un-char-i-ta-bly
un-chart-ed
un-chris-tian
un-cir-cum-cised
un-civ-il
un-civ-il-ly
un-civ-i-lized
un-class-i-fi-able
un-clas-si-fied
un-cle
un-clean
un-clean-ly
un-clear
un-cloak
un-clothe
un-clut-tered
un-coil
un-com-fort-able
un-com-fort-ably
un-com-mit-ted
un-com-mon
un-com-mon-ly
un-com-mu-ni-ca-tive
un-com-pre-hend-ing
un-com-pro-mis-ing
un-com-pro-mised
un-con-cern
un-con-cerned
un-con-di-tion-al
un-con-di-tion-al-ly
un-con-firmed
un-con-nect-ed
un-con-nect-ed-ly
un-con-quer-a-ble
un-con-quered
un-con-scion-able
un-con-scion-ably
un-con-scious
un-con-scious-ly
un-con-scious-ness
un-con-sti-tui-tion-al
un-con-strained
un-con-test-ed
un-con-trol-la-ble
un-con-trol-la-bly
un-con-trolled
un-con-ven-tion-al
un-con-ven-tion-al-ly
un-count-ed
un-cou-ple

un-cou-pled
un-cou-pling
un-couth
un-couth-ly
un-couth-ness
un-cov-er
un-cov-ered
unc-tion
unc-tu-ous
unc-tu-os-i-ty
unc-tu-ous-ly
un-curl
un-cut
un-daunt-ed
un-daunt-ed-ly
un-de-ceive
un-de-ceived
un-de-ceiv-ing
un-de-ceiv-a-ble
un-de-cid-ed
un-de-cid-ed-ly
un-de-cid-ed-ness
un-de-fined
un-de-fin-a-ble
un-de-mon-stra-tive
un-de-ni-a-ble
un-de-ni-a-bly
un-de-nied
un-de-pend-able
un-de-pend-a-bil-i-ty
un-der
un-der-a-chiev-er
un-der-a-chiev-ment
un-der-act
un-der-age
un-der-arm
un-der-bel-ly
un-der-car-riage
un-der-charge
un-der-charged
un-der-charg-ing
un-der-class-man
un-der-class-men
un-der-clothes
un-der-coast
un-der-cov-er
un-der-cur-rent
un-der-cut
un-der-cut-ting
un-der-de-vel-oped
un-der-de-vel-op-ing
un-der-dog
un-der-done
un-der-es-ti-mate
un-der-es-ti-mat-ed
un-der-es-ti-mat-ing

un-der-es-ti-ma-tion
un-der-foot
un-der-gar-ment
un-der-go
un-der-went
un-der-gone
un-der-grad-u-ate
un-der-ground
un-der-growth
un-der-hand
un-der-lie
un-der-lay
un-der-lain
un-der-ly-ing
un-der-line
un-der-lined
un-der-lin-ing
un-der-ling
un-der-mine
un-der-mined
un-der-min-ing
un-der-min-er
un-der-most
un-der-neath
un-der-pants
un-der-pass
un-der-pin-ning
un-der-priv-i-leged
un-der-rate
un-der-rat-ed
un-der-rat-ing
un-der-score
un-der-scored
un-der-scor-ing
un-der-sea
un-der-sec-re-tary
un-der-sec-re-tar-ies
un-der-sell
un-der-sold
un-der-ell-ing
un-der-sell-er
un-der-shirt
un-der-shot
un-der-side
un-der-signed
un-der-stand
un-der-stood
un-der-stand-ing
un-der-stand-a-ble
un-der-stand-a-bly
un-der-stand-ing-ly
un-der-state
un-der-stat-ed
un-der-stat-ing
un-der-state-ment
un-der-stood

un-der-study
un-der-stud-ied
un-der-stud-y-ing
un-der-stud-ies
un-der-take
un-der-took
un-der-tak-en
un-der-tak-ing
un-der-tak-er
un-der-the-coun-ter
un-der-tone
un-der-tow
un-der-wa-ter
un-der-wear
un-der-weight
un-der-world
un-der-write
un-der-wrote
un-der-writ-ten
un-der-writ-ing
un-der-writ-er
un-de-sir-a-ble
un-de-sir-a-bil-i-ty
un-de-sir-a-bly
un-de-ter-mined
un-dies
un-dip-lo-mat-ic
un-dip-lo-mat-i-cal-ly
un-dis-ci-plined
un-dis-closed
un-dis-posed
un-dis-tin-guished
un-di-vid-ed
un-do
un-did
un-done
un-do-ing
un-do-er
un-doubt-ed
un-doubt-ed-ly
un-doubt-ing
un-dress
un-dress-ed
un-dress-ing
un-due
un-du-lant
un-du-late
un-du-lat-ed
un-du-lat-ing
un-du-la-tion
un-du-ly
un-dy-ing
un-earth
un-earth-ly
un-easy
un-eas-i-er

un-eas-i-est
un-ease
un-eas-i-ly
un-eas-i-ness
un-em-ployed
un-em-ploy-ment
un-e-qual
un-e-qual-ly
un-e-qual-ed
un-e-quiv-o-cal
un-e-quiv-o-cal-ly
un-err-ing
un-err-ing-ly
un-eth-i-cal
un-eth-i-cal-ly
un-e-ven
un-e-ven-ly
un-e-ven-ness
un-ex-cep-tion-able
un-ex-pect-ed
un-ex-pect-ed-ly
un-fail-ing
un-fail-ing-ly
un-faith-ful
un-faith-ful-ly
un-faith-ful-ness
un-fa-mil-iar
un-fa-mil-i-ar-i-ty
un-fa-mil-iar-ly
un-fast-en
un-fas-ten-a-ble
un-fas-ten-er
un-fath-om-a-ble
un-fa-vor-a-ble
un-fa-vor-a-bly
un-feel-ing
un-feel-ing-ly
un-feigned
un-feign-ed-ly
un-fet-ter
un-fet-tered
un-fin-ished
un-fit
un-fit-ly
un-fit-ness
un-fit-ting
un-flat-ter-ing
un-flinch-ing
un-flinch-ing-ly
un-fold
un-for-get-ta-ble
un-for-get-ta-bly
un-for-giv-a-ble
un-for-tu-nate
un-for-tu-nate-ly
un-found-ed

un-found-ed-ness
un-friend-ly
un-friend-li-er
un-friend-li-est
un-friend-li-ness
un-frock
un-furl
un-gain-ly
un-gain-li-ness
un-gird
un-gird-ed
un-gird-ing
un-glazed
un-god-ly
un-god-li-er
un-god-li-est
un-god-li-ness
un-gov-ern-able
un-gov-ern-ably
un-gra-cious
un-gra-cious-ly
un-gra-cious-ness
un-gram-mat-i-cal
un-gram-mat-i-cal-ly
un-grate-ful
un-grate-ful-ly
un-grate-ful-ness
un-guard-ed
un-guard-ed-ly
un-guent
un-gu-late
un-ham-pered
un-hand
un-handy
un-hand-i-er
un-hand-i-est
un-hap-py
un-hap-pi-er
un-hap-pi-est
un-hap-pi-ly
un-hap-pi-ness
un-harmed
un-healthy
un-health-i-er
un-health-i-ly
un-heard
un-heed-ed
un-heed-ful
un-heed-ing
un-hinge
un-hinged
un-hing-ing
un-hitch
un-ho-ly
un-ho-li-er
un-ho-li-est

un-hol-li-ly
un-ho-li-ness
un-hook
un-horse
un-horsed
un-hors-ing
un-hur-ried
un-hurt
uni-cam-er-al
uni-cam-er-al-ly
uni-cel-lu-lar
uni-corn
uni-fi-ca-tion
uni-form
uni-formed
uni-form-i-ty
uni-form-ly
uni-fy
uni-fied
uni-fy-ing
uni-fi-er
uni-lat-er-al
uni-lat-er-al-ism
uni-lat-er-al-ly
un-imag-in-able
un-im-pair-ed
un-im-peach-able
un-im-peach-a-bly
un-im-por-tance
un-im-por-tant
un-im-proved
un-in-hib-it-ed
un-in-hib-it-ed-ly
un-in-ter-est-ed
un-in-ter-est-ing
un-ion
un-ion-ism
un-ion-ist
un-ion-ize
un-ion-ized
un-ion-iz-ing
un-ion-i-za-tion
unique
unique-ly
unique-ness
uni-son
unit
unite
unit-ed
unit-ing
unit-er
uni-ty
uni-ties
uni-valve
uni-valved
uni-val-vu-lar

212

uni-ver-sal
  uni-ver-sal-i-ty
  uni-ver-sal-ly
  uni-ver-sal-ness
uni-ver-sal-ize
  uni-ver-sal-ized
  uni-ver-sal-iz-ing
uni-verse
uni-ver-si-ty
  uni-ver-si-ties
un-just
  un-just-ly
un-kempt
un-kind
  un-kind-ness
  un-kind-ly
un-known
un-law-ful
  un-law-ful-ly
  un-law-ful-ness
un-learn
  un-learned
  un-learn-ing
  un-learn-ed
  un-learn-ed-ly
un-leash
un-less
un-let-ter-ed
un-like
  un-like-ness
un-like-ly
  un-like-li-er
  un-like-li-est
  un-like-li-ness
un-lim-ber
un-lim-it-ed
un-load
  un-load-er
un-lock
un-looked--for
un-loose
  un-loosed
  un-loos-ing
  un-loos-en
un-lucky
  un-luck-i-er
  un-luck-i-est
  un-luck-i-ly
un-make
  un-made
  un-mak-ing
  un-mak-er
un-man
  un-manned
  un-man-ning
un-mask

un-mean-ing
  un-mean-ing-ly
un-men-tion-able
un-mer-ci-ful
  un-mer-ci-ful-ly
un-mis-tak-able
  un-mis-tak-a-bly
un-mit-i-gat-ed
  un-mit-i-gat-ed-ly
un-nat-u-ral
  un-nat-u-ral-ly
  un-nat-u-ral-ness
un-nec-es-sary
  un-nec-es-sar-i-ly
un-nerve
  un-nerved
  un-nerv-ing
un-num-bered
un-ob-jec-tion-able
un-or-gan-ized
un-pack
un-par-al-leled
un-par-don-able
un-pleas-ant
  un-pleas-ant-ly
  un-pleas-ant-ness
un-plumbed
un-pop-u-lar
  un-pop-u-lar-i-ty
  un-pop-u-lar-ly
un-prec-e-dent-ed
  un-prec-e-dent-ed-ly
un-prin-ci-pled
un-print-able
un-pro-fes-sion-al
  un-pro-fes-sion-al-ly
un-qual-i-fied
  un-qual-i-fied-ly
un-ques-tion-able
  un-ques-tion-ably
  un-ques-tioned
un-quote
  un-quot-ed
  un-quot-ing
un-rav-el
  un-rav-eled
  un-rav-el-ing
  un-rav-el-ment
un-read
un-re-al
un-rea-son-able
  un-rea-son-ably
  un-rea-son-ing
un-re-fined
un-re-gen-er-ate
un-re-lat-ed

un-re-lent-ing
  un-re-lent-ing-ly
un-remit-ting
un-re-serve
  un-re-served
  un-re-serv-ed-ly
un-rest
un-ri-valed
un-roll
un-ruf-fled
un-ru-ly
  un-ruy-li-er
  un-ru-li-est
un-sad-dle
  un-sad-dled
  un-sad-dling
un-said
un-sa-vory
un-say
  un-say-ing
un-scathed
un-schooled
un-scram-ble
  un-scram-bled
  un-scram-bling
un-screw
un-scru-pu-lous
  un-scru-pu-lous-ly
un-seal
un-sea-son-able
  un-sea-son-ably
un-seat
un-seem-ly
un-set-tle
  un-set-tled
  un-set-tling
un-sheathe
  un-sheathed
  un-sheath-ing
un-shod
un-sight-ly
  un-sight-li-er
  un-sight-li-est
un-skilled
  un-skill-ful
  un-skill-ful-ly
un-snap
  un-snapped
  un-snap-ping
un-snarl
un-so-phis-ti-cat-ed
  un-so-phis-ti-cat-ed-ly
  un-so-phis-ti-ca-tion
un-sound
  un-sound-ly
un-spar-ing

un-spar-ing-ly
un-speak-a-ble
un-speak-a-bly
un-sta-ble
un-sta-bly
un-steady
un-stead-i-er
un-stead-i-est
un-stead-i-ly
un-stop
un-stopped
un-stop-ping
un-strung
un-stud-ied
un-sung
un-tan-gle
un-tan-gled
un-tan-gling
un-taught
un-think-able
un-think-ing
un-think-ing-ly
un-ti-dy
un-tie
un-tied
un-ty-ing
un-til
un-time-ly
un-time-li-ness
un-to
un-told
un-touch-a-ble
un-touch-a-bly
un-to-ward
un-to-ward-ly
un-truth
un-tu-tored
un-used
un-u-su-al
un-u-su-al-ly
un-u-su-al-ness
un-ut-ter-able
un-ut-ter-ably
un-var-nished
un-veil
un-wary
un-war-i-ly
un-well
un-whole-some
un-whole-some-ly
un-wieldy
un-wield-i-ness
un-will-ing
un-will-ing-ly
un-will-ing-ness
un-wind

un-wound
un-wind-ing
un-wise
un-wise-ly
un-wit-ting
un-wit-ting-ly
un-wont-ed
un-wont-ed-ly
un-wor-thy
un-wor-thi-ly
un-wor-thi-ness
un-wrap
un-wrapped
un-wrap-ping
un-yield-ing
up-beat
up-braid
up-braid-er
up-braid-ing
up-com-ing
up-coun-try
up-date
up-dat-ed
up-dat-ing
up-end
up-grade
up-grad-ed
up-grad-ing
up-heav-al
up-heave
up-heaved
up-heav-ing
up-hill
up-hold
up-held
up-hold-ing
up-hol-ster
up-hol-ster-er
up-hol-stery
up-keep
up-land
up-lift
up-most
up-on
up-per
up-per--class
up-per-cut
up-per-cut-ting
up-per-most
up-pish
up-pish-ly
up-pi-ty
up-raise
up-raised
up-rais-ing
up-rear

up-right
up-right-ly
up-right-ness
up-ris-ing
up-roar
up-roar-i-ous
up-root
up-root-er
up-set
up-set-ting
up-shot
up-side
up-stage
up-staged
up-stag-ing
up-stairs
up-stand-ing
up-start
up-state
up-stream
up-swing
up-take
up-to-date
up-town
up-trend
up-turn
up-ward
up-ward-ly
up-ward-ness
ura-ni-um
ur-ban
ur-bane
ur-bane-ly
ur-ban-i-ty
ur-ban-ize
ur-ban-ized
ur-ban-iz-ing
ur-ban-i-za-tion
ur-chin
urea
ure-al
ure-ter
ure-thra
ure-thrae
ure-thras
ure-thral
uge
urged
urg-ing
urg-er
urg-ing-ly
ur-gent
ur-gen-cy
ur-gen-cies
ur-gent-ly
uric

uri-nal
uri-nal-y-sis
  uri-nal-y-ses
uri-nary
  uri-nar-ies
uri-nate
urine
urol-o-gy
  uro-log-ic
  uro-log-i-cal
  urol-o-gist
us-able
  us-ably
  us-abil-i-ty
us-age
use
  used
  us-ing
  us-er
use-ful
  use-ful-ly
  use-ful-ness
use-less
  use-less-ly
  use-less-ness
ush-er
usu-al
  usu-al-ly
usurp
  usur-pa-tion
  usurp-er
usu-ry
  usu-ries
  usu-rer
  usu-ri-ous
uten-sil
uter-us
  ut-eri
util-i-tar-ian
util-i-ty
  util-i-ties
uti-lize
  uti-lized
  uti-liz-ing
  uti-li-za-tion
ut-most
ut-ter
  ut-ter-a-ble
  ut-ter-er
ut-ter-ance
ut-ter-most
uvu-la
  uvu-las
  uvu-lae
ux-o-ri-ous
  ux-o-ri-ous-ly

va-can-cy
  va-can-cies
va-cant
  va-cant-ly
va-cate
  va-cat-ed
  va-cat-ing
va-ca-tion
vac-ci-nate
  vac-ci-nat-ed
  vac-ci-nat-ing
  vac-ci-na-tion
vac-cine
vac-il-late
  vac-il-lat-ed
  vac-il-lat-ing
  vac-il-la-tion
  vac-il-la-tor
va-cu-i-ty
  va-cu-i-ties
vac-u-ous
  vac-u-ous-ly
vac-u-um
  vac-u-ums
  vac-ua
vac-u-um--packed
vag-a-bond
  vag-a-bond-age
  vag-a-bond-ish
  vag-a-bond-ism
  va-gary
  va-gar-ies
  va-gar-i-ous
  va-gar-i-ous-ly
va-gi-na
  va-gi-nas
  va-gi-nae
  vag-i-nal
va-grant
  va-gran-cy
  va-gran-cies
  va-grant-ly
vague
  vague-ly
  vague-ness
vain
  vain-ly
  vain-ness
vain-glo-ry
  vain-glo-ries
  vain-glo-ri-ous
val-ance
  val-anced
val-e-dic-tion
  val-e-dic-to-ri-an
val-e-dic-to-ry

  val-e-dic-to-ries
va-lence
  va-len-cy
val-en-tine
va-let
val-iant
  val-iant-ly
val-id
  val-id-ly
  val-id-ness
val-i-date
  val-i-dat-ed
  val-i-dat-ig
  val-i-da-tion
va-lid-i-ty
  va-lid-i-ties
va-lise
val-ley
  val-leys
val-or
  val-or-ous
  val-or-ous-ly
val-u-able
  val-u-ably
val-u-a-tion
  val-u-a-tion-al
val-ue
  val-ued
  val-u-ing
  val-ue-less
valve
  valve-less
  val-vu-lar
va-moose
vam-pire
  vam-pir-ic
  vam-pir-ism
va-na-di-um
van-dal
  van-dal-ism
  van-dal-ize
  van-dal-ized
  van-dal-iz-ing
vane
  vaned
  vane-less
van-guard
va-nil-la
van-ish
  van-ish-er
van-i-ty
  van-i-ties
van-quish
  van-quish-a-ble
  van-quish-er
van-tage

vap-id
va-pid-i-ty
vap-id-ly
va-por
va-por-er
va-por-ish
va-por-ize
va-por-ized
va-por-iz-ing
va-por-i-za-tion
va-por-iz-er
va-por-ous
va-por-opus-ly
va-que-ro
va-que-ros
var-i-able
var-i-abil-i-ty
var-i-ably
var-i-ance
var-i-ant
var-i-a-tion
var-i-a-tion-al
var-i-a-tion-al-ly
var-i-col-ored
var-i-cose
var-ied
var-ied-ness
var-ie-gate
var-ie-gat-ed
var-ie-gat-ing
var-ie-ga-tion
var-ie-ga-tor
va-ri-etal
va-ri-etal-ly
va-ri-ety
va-ri-e-ties
var-i-ous
var-i-ous-ly
var-nish
var-nish-er
var-si-ty
var-si-ties
vary
var-ied
vary-ing
var-i-er
vary-ing-ly
vas-cu-lar
vas-cu-lar-i-ty
va-sec-to-my
va-sec-to-mies
vas-o-mo-tor
vas-sal
vas-sal-age
vast-ness
vat

vat-ted
vat-ting
vaude-ville
vault
vault-ed
vault-er
vault-ing
vaunt
vaunt-er
vaunt-ing-ly
vec-tor
vec-to-ri-al
veer-ing
veg-e-ta-ble
veg-e-tal
veg-e-tar-i-an
veg-e-tar-i-an-ism
veg-e-tate
veg-e-tat-ed
veg-e-tat-ing
veg-e-ta-tion
veg-e-ta-tion-al
veg-e-ta-tive
ve-he-ment
ve-he-mence
ve-he-men-cy
ve-hi-cle
ve-hic-u-lar
veil
veiled
veil-ing
vein
veiny
vein-i-er
vein-i-est
vein-ing
vel-lum
ve-loc-i-ty
ve-loc-i-ties
vel-our
ve-lum
ve-la
vel-vet
vel-vet-ed
vel-ve-teen
vel-vety
vel-vet-i-er
vel-vet-i-est
ve-nal
ve-nal-i-ty
ve-nal-ly
ve-na-tion
ve-na-tion-al
vend-er
vend-or
ven-det-ta

vend-i-ble
vend-i-bil-i-ty
ve-neer
ve-neer-er
ve-neer-ig
ven-er-able
ven-er-abil-i-ty
ven-er-ably
ven-er-ate
ven-er-a-tion
ven-er-a-tor
ve-ne-re-al
venge-ance
venge-ful
venge-ful-ness
ve-ni-al
ve-ni-al-i-ty
ve-ni-al-ness
ve-ni-al-ly
ven-i-son
ven-om
ven-om-ous
ve-nous
ve-nous-ly
vent
vent-ed
vent-ing
ven-ti-late
ven-ti-lat-ed
ven-ti-lat-ing
ven-ti-la-tion
ven-ti-la-tor
ven-tral
ven-tral-ly
ven-tri-cle
ven-tril-o-quism
ven-tri-lo-qui-al
ven-tril-o-quist
ven-tril-o-quize
ven-tril-o-quized
ven-tril-o-quiz-ing
ven-ture
ven-ture-some
ven-tur-ous
ve-ra-cious
ve-rac-i-ty
ve-rac-i-ties
ve-ran-da
ver-bal
ver-bal-ly
ver-bal-ize
ver-bal-ized
ver-bal-iz-ing
ver-bal-i-za-tion
ver-bal-iz-er
ver-ba-tim

ver-bi-age
ver-bose
  ver-bose-ness
  ver-bos-i-ty
ver-bo-ten
ver-dant
  ver-dan-cy
ver-dict
ver-di-gris
ver-dure
  ver-dured
  ver-dur-ous
verge
  verged
  verg-ing
ver-i-fi-ca-tion
ver-i-fy
  ver-i-fied
  ver-i-fy-ing
  ver-i-fi-abil-i-ty
  ver-i-fi-able
  ver-i-fi-er
veri-si-mil-i-tude
  veri-ta-ble
  veri-ta-bly
ver-i-ty
  ver-i-ties
ver-meil
ver-mic-u-lar
  ver-mic-u-late
  ver-mic-u-lat-ed
ver-mi-fuge
ver-mil-ion
ver-min
  ver-min-ous
ver-mouth
ver-nac-u-lar
  ver-nac-u-lar-ism
ver-nal
  ver-nal-ly
ver-sa-tile
  ver-sa-til-i-ty
versed
ver-si-fy
  ver-si-fied
  ver-si-fy-ing
  ver-si-fi-er
  ver-si-fi-ca-tion
ver-sion
  ver-sion-al
ver-sus
ver-te-bra
  ver-te-brae
ver-te-bral
  ver-te-bral-ly
ver-te-brate

ver-tex
  ver-tex-es
  ver-ti-ces
ver-ti-cal
  ver-ti-cal-i-ty
  ver-ti-cal-ly
ver-ti-go
  ver-ti-goes
  ver-tig-i-nes
ves-i-cant
  ves-i-ca-to-ry
  ves-i-ca-to-ries
ves-i-cate
  ves-i-cat-ed
  ves-i-cat-ing
  ves-i-ca-tion
ves-i-cle
ve-sic-u-lar
ves-pers
ves-sel
ves-tal
vest-ed
ves-ti-bule
  ves-ti-buled
  ves-ti-bul-ing
  ves-tib-u-lar
ves-tige
  ves-tig-i-al
  ves-tig-i-al-ly
vest-ment
vest-pock-et
ves-try
  ves-tries
vet
  vet-ted
  vet-ting
vet-er-an
vet-er-i-nar-i-an
vet-er-i-nary
ve-to
vex
  vex-er
  vex-ing-ly
vex-a-tion
  vex-a-tious
vexed
via
vi-a-ble
  vi-a-bil-i-ty
vi-a-bly
vi-a-duct
vi-al
vi-and
vi-brant
  vi-bran-cy
vi-brate

vi-brat-ed
vi-brat-ing
vi-bra-tion
vi-bra-to
  vi-bra-tos
vi-bra-tor
vi-bra-to-ry
vi-bur-num
vic-ar
  vic-ar-ship
vic-ar-age
vi-car-i-ous
  vi-car-i-ous-ly
vice ad-mi-ral
vice--con-sul
vice--pres-i-dent
vice-roy
  vice-roy-al
vice ver-sa
vi-cin-i-ty
  vi-cin-i-ties
vi-cious
  vi-cious-ly
vi-cis-si-tude
vic-tim
  vic-tim-ize
  vic-tim-ized
  vic-tim-iz-ing
  vic-tim-iz-er
vic-tor
vic-to-ri-ous
  vic-to-ri-ous-ly
vic-to-ry
  vic-to-ries
vict-ual
vid-eo
vie
  vied
  vy-ing
  vi-er
view-er
  view-less
  view-point
vig-il
  vig-i-lance
  vig-i-lant
  vig-i-lan-te
vi-gnette
vig-or
  vig-or-ous
  vig-or-ous-ly
vi-king
vile
vil-i-fy
  vil-i-fied
  vil-i-fy-ing

vil-i-fi-ca-tion
vil-la
vil-lage
vil-lain
vil-lain-ous
vil-lainy
vil-lain-ies
vil-lein
vil-lous
vil-lus
vil-li
vin-ci-ble
vin-ci-bil-i-ty
vin-di-cate
vin-di-cat-ed
vin-di-cat-ing
vin-dic-tive
vin-dic-tive-ly
vin-dic-tive-ness
vin-e-gar
vin-e-gary
vine-yard
vi-nous
vin-tage
vint-ner
vi-nyl
vi-ol
vi-o-la
vi-o-list
vi-o-la-ble
vi-o-la-bil-i-ty
vi-o-late
vi-o-lat-ed
vi-o-lat-ing
vi-o-la-tor
vi-o-la-tion
vi-o-lence
vi-o-lent
vi-o-let
vi-o-lin
vi-o-lin-ist
vi-o-lon-cel-lo
vi-o-lon-cel-list
vi-per
vi-ra-go
vi-ral
vir-eo
vir-e-os
vir-gin
vir-gin-al
vir-gin-i-ty
vir-gule
vir-ile
vi-ril-i-ty
vi-rol-o-gy
vi-rol-o-gist

vir-tu-al
vir-tue
vir-tu-os-i-ty
vir-tu-os-i-ties
vir-tu-o-so
vir-tu-ous
vir-tu-ous-ly
vir-u-lence
vir-u-len-cy
vir-u-lent
vi-rus
vi-rus-es
vi-sa
vis-age
vis-cera
vis-cer-al
vis-cid
vis-cid-ly
vis-cos-i-ty
vis-cos-i-ties
vis-count
vis-count-cy
vis-count-ship
vis-count-ess
vis-cous
vis-i-bil-i-ty
vis-i-bil-i-ties
vis-i-ble
vi-sion
vi-sion-ary
vi-sion-ar-ies
vis-it
vis-i-tant
vis-it-a-tion
vis-it-ing
vis-i-tor
vi-sor
vis-ta
vis-u-al
vis-u-al-ly
vis-u-al-ize
vis-u-al-ized
vis-u-al-iz-ing
vis-u-al-i-za-tion
vi-tal
vi-tal-i-ty
vi-tal-i-ties
vi-tal-ize
vi-tal-ized
vi-tal-iz-ing
vi-tal-i-za-tion
vi-tals
vi-ta-min
vi-ti-ate
vit-re-ous
vit-re-os-i-ty

vit-ri-fy
vit-ri-fied
vit-ri-fy-ing
vit-ri-fi-a-ble
vit-ri-fi-ca-tion
vit-ri-ol
vit-ri-ol-ic
vi-tu-per-ate
vi-tu-per-at-ed
vi-tu-per-at-ing
vi-tu-per-a-tion
vi-va
vi-va-cious
vi-vac-i-ty
vi-vac-i-ties
viv-id
viv-i-fy
viv-i-fied
viv-i-fy-ing
vi-vip-ar-ous
vivi-sec-tion
vix-en
vi-zier
vi-zor
vo-cab-u-lar-y
vo-cab-u-lar-ies
vo-cal
vo-cal-ic
vo-cal-ist
vo-cal-ize
vo-cal-ized
vo-cal-iz-ing
vo-cal-i-za-tion
vo-ca-tion
vo-ca-tion-al
vo-cif-er-ous
vod-ka
voice
voiced
voic-ing
voice-less
voice-print
void-able
vol-a-tile
vol-a-til-i-ty
vol-can-ic
vol-can-i-cal-ly
vol-ca-no
vol-ca-noes
vol-ca-nos
vo-li-tion
vol-ley
vol-leys
vol-ley-ball
volt-age
vol-ta-ic

volt-me-ter
vol-u-ble
  vol-u-bly
  vol-u-bil-i-ty
vol-ume
vo-lu-mi-nous
  vo-lu-mi-nous-ly
vol-un-tary
  vol-un-tar-i-ly
vol-un-teer
vo-lup-tu-ary
  vo-lup-tu-ar-ies
vo-lup-tu-ous
vom-it
voo-doo
vo-ra-cious
vo-rac-i-ty
vor-tex
  vor-tex-es
  vor-ti-ces
vo-ta-ry
  vor-ta-ries
vote
  vot-ed
  vot-ing
vot-er
vo-tive
vouch-er
vouch-safe
  vouch-safed
  vouch-saf-ing
vow-el
voy-age
  voy-aged
  voy-ag-ing
  voy-ag-er
vo-ya-geur
vo-yeur
  vo-yeur-ism
  voy-eur-is-tic
vul-can-ite
vul-gar
  vul-gar-ism
vul-gar-i-ty
  vul-gar-i-ties
vul-gar-ize
  vul-gar-ized
  vul-gar-iz-ing
vul-gate
vul-ner-a-ble
  vul-ner-a-bly
vul-pine
vul-ture
vul-va
  vul-vae
  vul-vas

wab-ble
  wab-bled
  wab-bling
wacky
  wack-i-er
  wack-i-est
  wack-i-ly
wad
  wad-ded
  wad-ding
wad-dle
  wad-dled
  wad-dling
  wad-dler
  wad-dly
  wad-dli-er
  wad-dli-est
wade
  wad-ed
  wad-ing
wad-er
waf-er
waf-fle
wag
  wagged
  wag-ging
  wag-ger
  wag-gish
wage
  waged
  wag-ing
wa-ger
wag-gery
  wag-ger-ies
wag-gle
  wag-gled
  wag-gling
wag-on
  wag-on-er
wain-scot
  wain-scot-ing
wain-wright
waist-band
waist-coat
waist-line
wait-er
wait-ing
wait-ress
waive
  waived
  waiv-ing
  waiv-er
wake
  waked
  wok-en
  wak-ing

wake-ful
  wake-ful-ly
wak-en
wale
  waled
  wal-ing
walk-a-way
walk-er
walk-ie-talk-ie
walk-out
walk-o-ver
walk-up
walk-way
wal-al-by
  wal-la-bies
wall-board
wal-let
wall-eye
  wall-eyed
wall-flow-er
wal-lop
wall-pa-per
wall-to-wall
wal-nut
wal-rus
  wal-rus-es
wam-pum
wan
  wan-ner
  wan-nest
  wan-ness
wan-der
  wan-der-lust
wane
  waned
  wan-ing
wan-gle
  wan-gled
  wan-gling
  wan-gler
want-ing
wan-ton
wa-pi-ti
  wa-pi-ties
war
  warred
  war-ring
war-ble
  war-bled
  war-bling
war-bler
war-den
  war-den-ship
ward-er
ward-robe
ware-house

war-fare
war-head
war-horse
war-like
war-lock
warm
  warm-er
  warm-est
warm--blood-ed
warm-heart-ed
war-mon-ger
warmth
warn-ing
war-path
war-rant
  war-ran-ty
  war-ran-ties
war-ren
war-ri-or
war-ship
war-time
wary
  war-i-er
  war-i-est
  war-i-ly
wash-able
wash-ba-sin
wash-board
wash-bowl
wash-cloth
wash-er
wash-ing
wash-out
wash-room
wash-stand
wash-tub
wasn't
wasp
  wasp-ish
  wasp-ish-ly
was-sail
wast-age
waste
  wast-ed
  wast-ing
  waste-ful
  waste-ful-ly
  waste-ful-ness
waste-bas-ket
waste-land
waste-pa-per
wast-er
wast-rel
watch-dog
watch-ful
watch-man

watch-men
watch-tow-er
watch-word
wa-ter
wat-er-buck
wa-ter-col-or
wa-ter-course
wa-ter-cress
wa-ter-fall
wa-ter-foul
wa-ter-front
wa-ter-less
wa-ter lev-el
wa-ter lily
  wa-ter lil-ies
wa-ter line
wa-ter-llogged
Wa-ter-loo
wa-ter main
wa-ter-man
  wa-ter-men
wa-ter-mark
wa-ter-mel-on
wa-ter moc-ca-sin
wa-ter-proof
wa-ter-re-pel-lent
wa-ter-shed
wa-ter-side
wa-ter ski
  wa-ter-skied
  wa-ter-ski-ing
wa-ter-spout
wa-ter-tight
wa-ter-way
wa-ter-works
wa-tery
watt-age
watt-hour
wat-tle
  wat-tled
  wat-tling
wave
  waved
  wav-ing
wave-length
wave-let
wa-ver
wav-y
  wav-i-er
  wav-i-est
  wav-i-ly
wax
  waxed
  wax-ing
wax-en
wax-wing

wax-work
waxy
  wax-i-er
  wax-i-est
way-far-er
  way-far-ing
way-lay
  way-laid
  way-lay-ing
way-side
way-ward
weak-en
weak-kneed
weak-ling
weak-ly
  weak-li-er
  weak-li-est
weak-mind-ed
weak-ness
wealthy
  wealth-i-er
  wealth-i-est
  wealth-i-ly
wean
weap-on
  weap-on-ry
wear
  wear-ing
wea-ri-some
wea-ry
  wea-ri-er
  wea-ri-est
  wea-ried
  wea-ry-ing
  wea-ri-ly
wea-sel
weath-er
weath-er--beat-en
weath-er-cock
weath-er-glass
weath-er-ing
weath-er-man
  weath-er-men
weath-er-proof
weather vane
weave
  weaved
  wov-en
  weav-ing
weav-er
web
  webbed
  web-bing
web-foot
  web-foot-ed
wed-ding

wedge
  wedged
  wedg-ing
wed-lock
weedy
  weed-i-er
  weed-i-est
week-day
week-end
week-ly
weep-ing
wee-vil
weigh
weight
weighty
  weight-i-er
  weight-i-est
  weight-i-ly
weird
  weird-er
  weird-est
wel-come
  wel-comed
  wel-com-ing
wel-fare
well--be-ing
well-born
well--bred
well--dis-posed
well--done
well--found-ed
well--groomed
well--ground-ed
well--known
well--mean-ing
well--nigh
well--off
well--read
well--spo-ken
well-spring
well--thought--of
well--timed
well--to--do
well--wish-er
well--worn
wel-ter
  wel-ter-weight
were-wolf
  were-wolves
west-bound
west-er-ly
west-ern
  west-ern-er
west-ern-ize
  west-ern-ized
  west-ern-iz-ing

west-ern-i-za-tion
west-ern-most
west-ward
wet
  wet-ter
  wet-test
wet-back
whale
  whaled
  whal-ing
whale-boat
whale-bone
whal-er
wharf
  wharves
what-ev-er
what-not
what-so-ev-er
wheat
wheat-en
whee-dle
  whee-dled
  whee-dling
  whee-dler
wheel and ax-le
wheel-bar-row
wheel-chair
wheeled
wheel-house
wheel-wright
wheeze
  wheezed
  wheez-ing
wheezy
  wheez-i-er
  wheez-i-est
  wheez-i-ly
whelm
whelp
whence-so-ev-er
where-abouts
where-as
where-by
where-fore
where-in
where-on
where-so-ev-er
where-to
where-up-on
wher-ev-er
where-with
where-with-al
wher-ry
  wher-ries
whet
  whet-ted

whet-ting
wheth-er
whet-stone
whch-ev-er
whim-per
whim-si-cal
whim-sy
  whim-sies
whine
  whined
  whin-ing
whin-ny
  whin-nied
  whin-nying
  whin-nies
whip
  whipped
  whip-ping
whip-lash
whip-per-snap-per
whip-pet
whip-poor-will
whir
  whirred
  whir-ring
whirl-i-gig
whirl-pool
whirl-wind
whisk-er
whis-key
  whis-ky
  whis-keys
  whis-kies
whis-per
whist
whis-tle
  whis-tled
  whis-tling
  whis-tler
white
  whit-er
  whit-est
  whit-ish
white--col-lar
white-fish
whit-en
white-wash
white water
whith-er
whit-ing
whit-tle
  whit-tled
  whit-tling
  whit-tler
whiz
  whizzed

221

whiz-zing
whiz-zes
whoa
who-ev-er
whole-heart-ed
whole-sale
 whole-saled
 whole-sal-ing
 whole-sal-er
whole-some
whole-wheat
whol-ly
whom-ev-er
whom-so-ev-er
whoop-ing
whop-per
whop-ping
whorled
whose-so-ev-er
who-so-ev-er
wick-ed
wick-er
wick-er-work
wick-et
wide
 wid-er
 wid-est
wide--awake
wide--eyed
wid-en
wide-spread
wid-geon
wid-ow
wid-ow-er
wid-ow-hood
width
wield-er
wieldy
wie-ner
wig-gle
 wig-gled
 wig-gling
 wig-gly
 wig-gli-er
wig-gler
wig-wag
 wig-wagged
 wig-wag-ging
wig-wam
wild-cat
 wild-cat-ted
 wild-cat-ting
wild-cat strike
wil-der-ness
wild-fire
wild-fowl

wild--goose chase
wild-life
wild-wood
wile
 wiled
 wil-ing
 wil-i-ly
 wil-i-ness
 willed
 will-ful
wil-lies
will-ing
will--o'--the--wisp
wil-low
 wil-lowy
wil-ly--nil-ly
wim-ble
wim-ple
win
 win-ning
wince
 winced
 winc-ing
wind
 wound
 wind-ing
wind-bag
wind-break
wind-ed
wind-fall
wind-flow-er
wind-jam-mer
wind-lass
wind-mill
win-dow
wind-pipe
wind-row
wind-shield
wind-storm
wind-up
wind-ward
windy
 wind-i-er
 wind-i-est
wine
 wined
 win-ing
win-ery
 win-er-ies
wine-skin
winged
wing-span
wing-spread
win-ner
win-ning
win-some

win-ter
win-ter-gree
win-ter-ize
 win-ter-ized
 win-ter-iz-ing
 win-ter-i-za-tion
win-try
wipe
 wiped
 wip-ing
wire-haired
wire-les
wire-tap
wir-ing
wiry
 wir-i-er
 wir-i-est
wis-dom
wise
 wis-er
 wis-est
wise-acre
wise-crack
wish-bone
wish-ful
wishy-washy
wisp
 wispy
wis-ter-ia
wist-ful
witch-craft
witch-ery
 witch-er-ies
witch-ing
with-draw
with-er
 with-ered
 with-er-ing
with-hold
 with-held
 with-hold-ing
with-in
with-out
with-stand
 with-stood
 with-stand-ing
wit-less
wit-ness
wit-ted
wit-ti-cism
wit-ting
 wit-ting-ly
wit-ty
 wit-ti-er
 wit-ti-est
wiz-ard

wi-zard-ly
wi-zard-ry
wiz-en
  wiz-ened
wob-ble
woe-be-gone
woe-ful
wolf-hound
wolf-ram
wol-ver-ine
wom-an
  wom-en
  wom-an-ly
  wom-an-hood
womb
wom-bat
wom-en-folk
won-der
won-der-ful
won-der-land
won-der-ment
won-drous
wont-ed
wood-bine
wood-chuck
wood-cock
wood-craft
wood-cut
wood-cut-ter
wood-ed
wood-en
wood-land
wood-man
  wood-men
wood-peck-er
wood-pile
wood-shed
woods-man
  woods-men
woodsy
  woods-i-er
  woods-i-est
wood-wind
wood-work
woody
  wood-i-er
  wood-i-est
woof-er
wool-en
wool-gath-er-ing
wool-ly
  wool-li-er
  wool-li-est
wool-ly-head-ed
woozy
  wooz-i-er

wooz-i-est
word-book
word-ing
word-less
  word-less-ly
wordy
  word-i-er
  word-i-est
work-a-ble
  work-a-bil-i-ty
  work-a-day
work-bench
work-book
work-day
worked-up
work-er
work-horse
work-house
work-ing
work-ing-man
  work-ing-men
work-man
  work-men
work-man-like
work-man-ship
work-out
work-room
work-shop
work-ta-ble
world-ly
  world-li-er
  world-li-est
world-ly--wise
world-wide
worm--eat-en
worm-wood
wormy
  worm-i-er
  worm-i-est
worn--out
wor-ri-some
wor-ry
  wor-ried
  wor-ry-ing
  wor-ries
wor-ry-wart
wors-en
wor-ship
  wor-ship-ful
wor-sted
worth-less
worth-while
wor-thy
  wor-thi-er
  wor-thi-est
  wor-thi-ness

would--be
wouldn't
wound-ed
wraith
wran-gle
  wran-gled
  wran-gling
  wran-gler
wrap
  wrapped
  wrap-ping
  wrap-per
wrath-ful
wreak
wreath
wreathe
  wreathed
  wreath-ing
wreck-age
wreck-er
wrench
wres-tle
  wres-tled
  wres-tling
wretch-ed
wrig-gle
  wrig-gled
  wrig-gling
  wrig-gly
wring
  wrung
  wring-ing
  wring-er
wrin-kle
  wrin-kled
  wrin-kling
wrist-band
write
  wrote
  writ-ten
  writ-ing
write-in
writ-er
writhe
  writhed
  writh-ing
wrong-do-er
  wrong-do-ing
wronged
wrong-ful
wrong-head-ed
wrought
wry
  wri-er
  wri-est
  wry-ly

X

X chro-mo-some
xe-bec
xe-non
xen-o-pho-bia
X-ray
x-sec-tion
xy-lem
xy-lo-phone
xy-lose

Y

yacht
  yacht-ing
  yachts-man
  yachts-men
yak
yam
yank
Yan-kee
yap
  yapped
  yap-ping
yard-age
yard-arm
yard-mas-ter
yard-stick
yarn
yar-row
yawn
year
year-book
year-ling
year-long
year-ly
yearn
  yearn-ing
year--round
yeast
yeasty
  yeast-i-er
  yeast-i-est
yel-low
  yel-low-ish
yel-low-bird
yel-low fe-ver
yel-low-ham-mer
yel-low jack-et
yelp
yen
  yenned
  yen-ning
yeo-man
  yeo-men

ye-shi-va
  ye-shi-vas
yes-ter-day
yes-ter-year
ye-ti
yew
yield
yield-ing
yip
  yipped
  yip-ping
yo-del
  yo-deled
  yo-del-ing
  yo-del-er
yo-ga
  yo-gic
yo-gi
  yo-gis
yo-gurt
yoke
  yoked
  yok-ing
yo-kel
yolk
yon-der
yore
young
young-ling
young-ster
your-self
  your-selves
youth-ful
yowl
yt-ter-bi-um
yt-tri-um
yuc-ca
yule-tide
yum-my
  yum-mi-er
  yum-mi-est

Z

za-ny
  za-nies
  za-ni-er
  za-n-est
  za-ni-ly
  za-ni-ness
zeal-ot
zeal-ous
ze-bra
  ze-bras

ze-bu
ze-nith
zeph-yr
zep-pe-lin
ze-ro
  ze-ros
  ze-roes
zest
  zesty
  zest-i-er
  zest-i-est
zig-zag
  zig-zagged
  zig-zag-ging
zinc
zing
zin-nia
zip
  zipped
  zip-ping
zip-per
zip-py
  zip-pi-er
  zip-pi-est
zir-con
zir-con-ni-um
zith-er
zo-di-ac
  zo-di-a-cal
zom-bie
  zom-bi
zon-al
zone
  zoned
  zon-ing
zoo
  zoos
zo-ol-o-gy
  zo-o-log-i-cal
  zo-o-log-i-cal-ly
  zo-ol-o-gist
zuc-chi-ni
zwie-back
zy-gote